S0-AEO-414

Greenberg's®
AMERICAN FLYER®
FACTORY MANUAL

Edited by
Richard D. Smith
and
I. D. Smith

with the assistance of
Maureen Crum

Greenberg Publishing Company, Inc.
7566 Main Street
Sykesville, MD 21784
(301) 795-7447

Manufactured in the United States of America

ISBN: 0-89778-036-1

FOREWORD

Greenberg's American Flyer Factory Manual with Consumer Instruction Sheets, 1946 - 1966, provides the most comprehensive listing of repair and maintenance information, with parts listings, heretofore assembled. The Manual has been in the works for some time. Richard D. Smith is the American Flyer enthusiast who recognized the need for a manual of this scope. Over a number of years he gathered together a very large number of S Gauge Manual pages; it was a major accomplishment.

I. D. Smith reviewed the entire volume and made a number of very helpful suggestions as to the organization and placement of pages.

As editor, staff member Maureen Crum played an important role in completing this Manual. She reviewed the pages assembled by Darla Cooke, and removed duplicate pages, keeping those which differed in some way from other pages on a particular item. It was decided to preserve these pages as these subtle differences sometimes provide important information about American Flyer trains. Ms. Crum modified many drawings so that they would fit well to the 6 x 9 inch format. She cleaned up original pages that contained spots and tears; however, she retained the dealer hand-written corrections and the rubber-stamped "Void" markings on pages 349 and 350. Finally she indexed and paginated the entire 710 pages.

The Manual is a reproduction: most of the original pages were 8-1/2 x 11 inches, a few were 6 x 9 inches. Most of the original pages were printed on a mimeograph machine and often have light and/or broken type. We have done our best to reproduce the weak copy. All of the pages in the book were adjusted to accommodate the current format; larger pages were reduced or re-configured to fit. New headings were set for user convenience and all references to previous forms were maintained at the bottom of each page for future reference. Ms. Crum's ability to carefully review each and every page, while never losing sight of the total product, and her visual perspicacity have made this a complete and easy-to-use reference book.

The prices listed in this book are the original prices charged by American Flyer. Fortunately many parts are currently available from several dealers who specialize in American Flyer S Gauge. However their prices are quite appropriately many times higher than those charged 30 to 40 years ago. For a list of American Flyer parts dealers, please send a self-addressed stamped envelope to Greenberg Publishing Company.

Linda Greenberg

August 15, 1988

TABLE OF CONTENTS

DIESELS AND MOTORIZED UNITS

STEAM LOCOMOTIVES AND TENDERS

FREIGHT CARS

ACCESSORIES

TRANSFORMERS

TRACKS, SWITCHES, COUPLERS

DIESEL AND ELECTRIC LOCOMOTIVES
General Instructions

This locomotive is equipped with a remote controlled reversing unit which permits the direction of travel of the train to be controlled from a distant point.

The reversing unit is located at about the center of the locomotive and projects downward through a hole in the chassis. This unit is a two position sequence reverse which will allow the locomotive to run either forward or reverse.

If the train is moving forward and the current is turned off, then on again, it will travel in reverse. Therefore, in changing direction it is advisable to bring the train to a full stop then start up in the opposite direction.

LOCKING THE REVERSING UNIT

To make the reversing unit inoperative, that is, to allow the train to continue in the same direction irrespective of the number of times the circuit is broken, it has been equipped with a locking lever. If the reversing unit is to function the locking lever should be pulled down. If the reversing unit is to be locked in one direction, push the locking lever up.

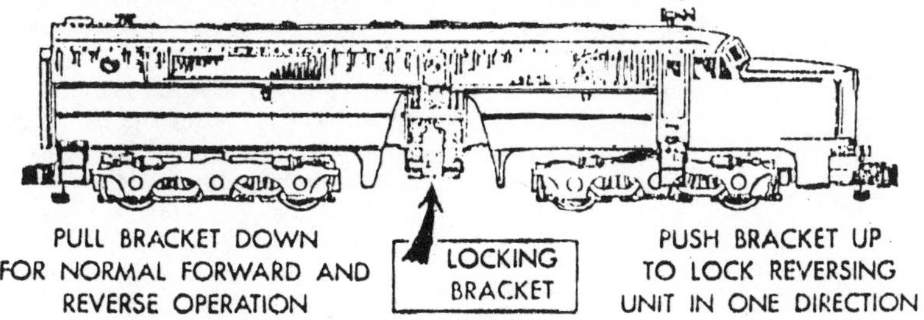

PULL BRACKET DOWN FOR NORMAL FORWARD AND REVERSE OPERATION

LOCKING BRACKET

PUSH BRACKET UP TO LOCK REVERSING UNIT IN ONE DIRECTION

To lock the reversing unit in desired direction, have the locomotive running in opposite direction. Remove from track, hold upright, and push the locking lever up. This will move the contacts to opposite side and the unit will be locked to run only in the direction opposite of what it had been going.

HEADLIGHT REPLACEMENT

To change lamps follow directions below:

DIESEL A UNITS: Lamp is attached to bracket at front of the locomotive. This bracket can be removed by taking out the one screw holding it in place. It is removed more easily if the truck sides are first taken off. These are held on by two small screws on the bottom motor plate.

GP7 LOCOMOTIVE: Remove the 4 body mounting screws and lift body off chassis.

BALDWIN SWITCHER: Remove one screw in back of locomotive then remove cab.

G E ELECTRIC: Remove one screw at the top of the locomotive then take chassis out of the cab.

CURRENT PICK-UP

The current for the locomotive is picked up by the front and rear trucks on the locomotive and the contact shoes mounted on the front and rear trucks.

Ref: Form No. 4071

AUTOMATIC COUPLING

In addition to the Remote Control, your train is also equipped with the new Automatic Knuckle Couplers in the front and back. It is possible for you to couple the cars together without having to handle them in any way. Place the cars on the tracks, run your locomotive forward or backward slowly up to the first car. When they hit, reverse the Locomotive and you will find the car is coupled to the Locomotive. Repeat the operation to pick up the rest of the cars. To uncouple the cars, raise the couplers apart using your No. 706 R.C. Uncoupler or the No. 704 Manual Uncoupler.

LUBRICATION OF MOTOR

This train, like its prototype, must be kept well lubricated at all times to insure perfect performance and long life. For most satisfactory performance we suggest a lubrication job at least once to every four hours of actual operation. Also BEFORE OPERATING when you first get the train and after it has been put away for any length of time.

Oil the car axles and the Locomotive at the following points: — See Figure 1 below:

1. Turn locomotive on its back and put about two drops of oil in each oil hole in bottom of power trucks. Do not place oil in the holes on the non-powered trucks but be sure axles are lubricated where they ride in the chassis. This applies to the powered and non-powered trucks.

2. On bottom of truck is a steel cover plate and truck side assembly that can be removed by unfastening two screws. This exposes the drive gears which should be lubricated with a small amount of vaseline. Place a drop of oil on the axle at the axle bearings. The cover plate should be replaced to keep dust and dirt out of gears.

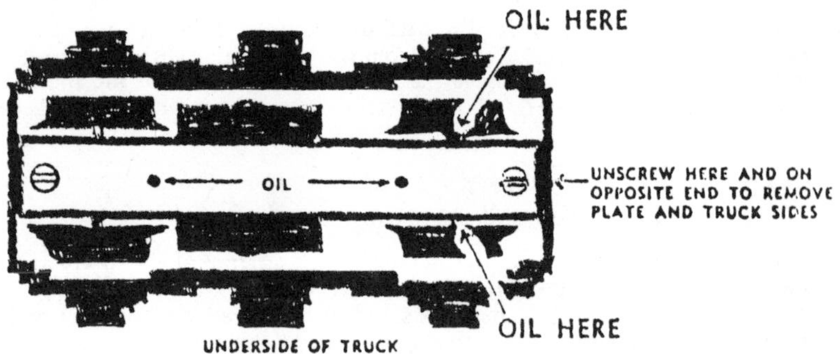

FIG. 1

A small drop of oil is all that is necessary. Apply oil with a toothpick or needle. After oiling, run train around track a few times and then wipe the rails to remove any oil that might have run down on them. This not only keeps the rails bright and shiny but provides a good electrical contact and prevents the drive wheels from skidding.

REPAIR PART SPECIFICATION CHANGE

DELETE FROM PARTS PRICE LIST

XA12523 Armature (Obsolete)

ADD TO PARTS PRICE LIST

XA14816 Armature Conversion consisting of:

1 - XA14816 Armature
1 - XA15A695 Brush Mounting Plate
2 - PA13128 Motor Brushes
2 - PA13129 Brush Tube Cover
2 - PA13130 Brush Springs
2 - PA13131 Brush Tubes
2 - PA15044 Brush Tube Cover Brace
2 - W57 Lock Washers
1 - S264 Screw
1 - S5A14 Screw
1 - S5A15 Screw

INSTRUCTIONS

1. Remove old Brush Bearing and Armature from motor.
2. Reassemble XA14816 Armature Conversion as shown in Exploded View. The wiring of the Locomotive has not been changed.

Locomotives requiring Conversion are:

Nos. 21115 - 21129 - 21130 and 21139.

PLEASE CORRECT YOUR PARTS LISTS.

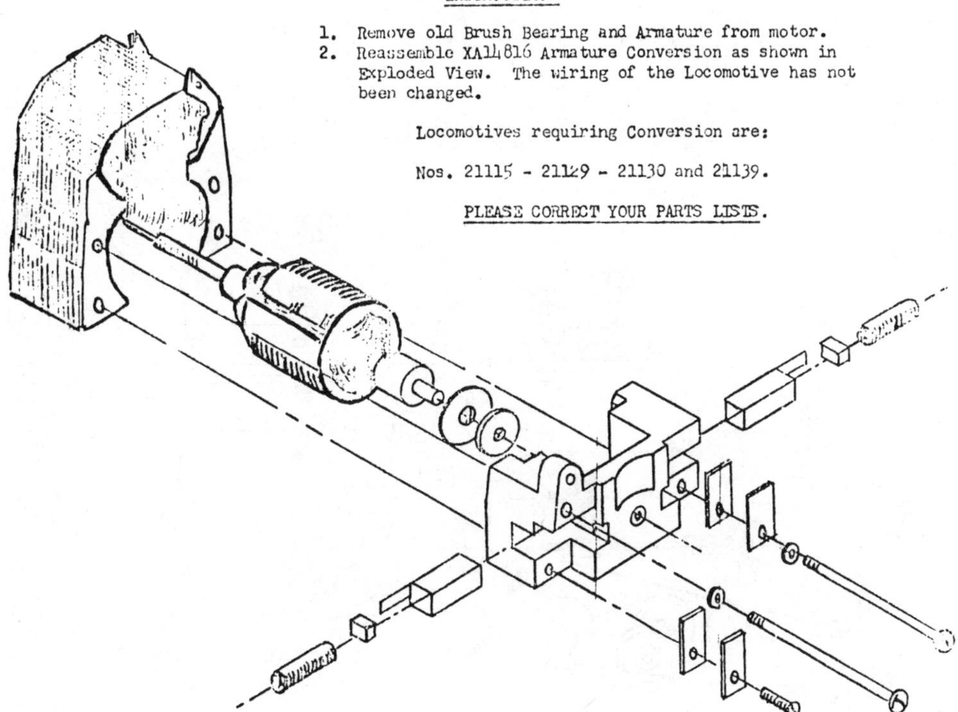

Ref: Nov. 20, 1963

BALDWIN DIESEL SWITCHER
Model Nos. 355, 21801, 21801-1, 21808, 21812, 21813, 21918, 21918-1

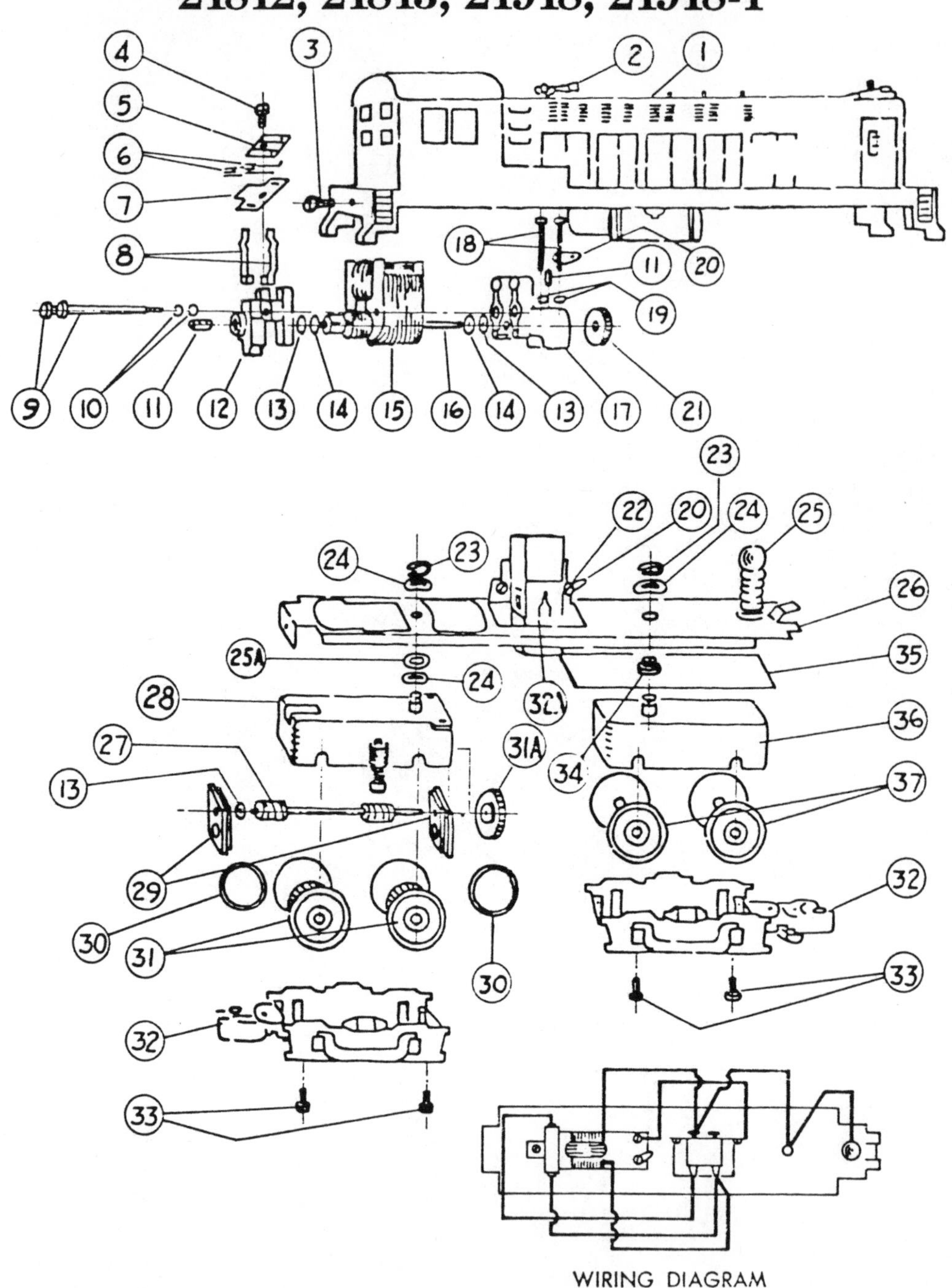

 Ref: Form No. 1993; June 1, 1960

PARTS LIST 21801 NORTH WESTERN DIESEL LOCO.

PART NO.	DESCRIPTION	PCS/ UNIT	COST
XA14B156-RP	CAB W/TRIM ASSY.	1	3.27
PA11409	AIR CHIME (DECORATION)	1	.08
PA14A168	HEADLIGHT LENS	1	.02
PA14A407-R	RIGHT MOTOR BRUSH SPRING	1	.08
PA14A407-L	LEFT MOTOR BRUSH SPRING	1	.08
PA14A169	MOTOR BRUSH MOUNT	1	.02
PA14A588	MOTOR BRUSH HOLDER	2	.03
PA14A414	MOTOR BRUSH	2	.18
S-1	#4-40 X 1/4" RD. HD. SCREW (MOTOR)	1	.01
W-57	POSITIVE LOCKWASHER .025 THICK	2	.01
S-4A82	#40-40 THD. SHOULDERED SCREW	2	.27
PA14B162-A	BRUSH & BEARING CAP	1	.42
XA14A969-A	MOTOR FIELD ASSY.	1	1.41
XA14B161-A	MOTOR MOUNT	1	.64
XA14B862	MOTOR ARMATURE ASSY.	1	3.64
S-4A81-A	#4-40 THD. X 25/32" FILLISTER HD. SCREW	2	.02
PA14A164-A	ARMATURE BEARING	2	.10
PA14A165	WORM SHAFT BEARING	2	.05
PA14-5-D	WASHER (1.31 - 1.41 DIA. HOLE)	2	.01
PA14A587	36 TOOTH GEAR (UPPER)	1	.10
PA11448	WORM	2	.18
PA14A636	SHAFT (WORM DRIVE)	1	.25
PA14A586	24 TOOTH GEAR (LOWER)	1	.12
PA10209	INSULATING BUSHING (TRUCK)	1	.02
PA14A171	COLLECTOR BUTTON (PICK UP SHOE)	2	.08
PA14A597	SPRING (FOR COLLECTOR BUTTON)	2	.02
P10118	SPRING HOLDER (FOR COLLECTOR BUTTON)	1	.04
P10434	RETAINING RING (FOR COLLECTOR BUTTON)	2	.01
P10800-B	RETAINING RING (FOR COLLECTOR BUTTON)	2	.02
PA9522	OIL WICK	2	.01
P325-D	FIBER WASHER (ARMATURE SHAFT) (.161 DIA.HOLE)	3	.01
PA14A100	INSULATING STRIP (CHASSIS)	1	.08
S-171	#2 X 3/16 TYPE "Z" P.K. SCREW BD.HD.	4	.01
W-7	STEEL WASHER (.210 - .202 DIA.HOLE)	1	.01
P1131-A	THRUST WASHER	1	.01
S-172	#4 X 3/16" BD.HD. TYPE "Z" P.K.SCREW	2	.02
W-114	SPRING WASHER (MOTOR PIVOT .190 DIA.HOLE)	3	.07
W-46	LOCKWASHER (CLASS M)	2	.01
PA6173	TERMINAL (SOLDER)	2	.01
LW-1B1	BLACK LEAD WIRE	-	.02
XA15A147	LOCOMOTIVE CHASSIS & LAMP SOCKET ASSY.	1	.48
PA8999	14 VOLT BULB	1	.36
S-230-B	#4 X 1/4" TYPE "Z" P.K.SCREW BD.HD.	1	.01
XA14A729	REAR CHASSIS & STUD ASSY. (TRUCK ASSY)	1	.67
XA15A706	FRONT CHASSIS & STUD ASSY. (TRUCK ASSY)	1	.51

PARTS LIST

21801 NORTH WESTERN DIESEL LOCO. CONT'D.

XA14A148	TRUCK SIDE & COUPLER ASSY.	2	1.05
PA13A791	TUBULAR RIVET	2	.02
PA14A890	PUL-MOR (TIRE)	2	.05
XA12A047	KNUCKLE COUPLER ASSY.	2	.29
PA12A355-A	LEAF SPRING (FOR COUPLER)	2	.02
XA14A932	WHEEL & AXLE ASSY. (FRONT TRUCK)	2	.36
PA14B888	SOLID WHEEL (FRONT)	2	.08
PA15A226	FRONT TRUCK AXLE	2	.05
XA14A870	INSULATED WHEEL ASSY.	2	.18
XA14A933	PUL-MOR WHEEL GEAR & AXLE ASSY. (REAR TRUCK)	2	.58
PA14B888	SOLID WHEEL (REAR)	2	.08
PA15A218	20 TOOTH GEAR (REAR)	2	.09
PA15A225	REAR TRUCK AXLE	2	.06
XA14A891	REAR TRUCK INSULATED PUL-MOR WHEEL ASSY.	2	.28
XA14C429	REMOTE CONTROL UNIT	-	---

21812 T & P DIESEL SWITCHER LOCO.

SAME AS 21801 -
EXCEPT USE:

XA14B156-CRP	CAB W/TRIM ASSY.	1	2.93

21918 SEABOARD SWITCHER

SAME AS 21801-
EXCEPT USE:

XA14B156-ARP	CAB W/TRIM ASSY.	1	3.30

NOTE: PRICES SUBJECT TO CHANGE WITHOUT NOTICE.

PARTS LIST

21801-1 NORTH WESTERN DIESEL SWITCHER LOCO. (NON-MOTORIZED)

PART NO.	DESCRIPTION	PCS/ UNIT	COST
XA14B156-DRP	CAB ASSEMBLY	1	3.29
PA11409	AIR CHIME (DECORATION)	1	.08
PA14A168	HEADLIGHT LENS	1	.02
S-230-B	#4 X $\frac{1}{4}$" P.K. BD. HD. TYPE "Z" SCREW	1	.01
W-7	STEEL WASHER (.210 - .202 DIA.HOLE)	1	.01
S-171	#2 X 3/16 BD.HD. TYPE "Z" P.K. SCREW	4	.01
W-114	SPRING WASHER (PIVOT) (.190 DIA.HOLE)	3	.07
PA14B159-C	LOCOMOTIVE CHASSIS	1	.34
PA14A100	INSULATING STRIP (CHASSIS)	1	.08
PA10209	INSULATING BUSHING (FRONT TRUCK)	1	.02
P1131-A	THRUST WASHER (FRONT TRUCK)	1	.01
XA15A706	CHASSIS & STUD ASSY. (FRONT & REAR TRUCK ASSY)	2	.51
XA14A932	WHEEL & AXLE ASSY. (FRONT & REAR TRUCK ASSY)	4	.36
PA14B888	SOLID WHEEL	4	.08
PA15A226	TRUCK AXLE	4	.05
XA14A870	INSULATED WHEEL ASSY.	4	.18
XA14A148	TRUCK SIDE & COUPLER ASSY.	2	1.04
PA12A355-A	LEAF SPRING (FOR COUPLER)	2	.02
PA13A791	TUBULAR RIVET	2	.02
XA12A047	KNUCKLE COUPLER ASSY.	2	.29
P10800-B	RETAINING RING (PIVOT)	2	.02

21918-1 SEABOARD DIESEL SWITCHER (NON-MOTORIZED)

SAME AS 21801-1 (NON-MOTORIZED)
EXCEPT ELIMINATE:

XA14B156-DRP	CAB ASSY. W/TRIM	1	
PA14B159-C	LOCOMOTIVE CHASSIS	1	

ADD THE FOLLOWING:

XA14B156-BRP	CAB ASSY. W/TRIM	1	3.30
XA15A147	LOCOMOTIVE CHASSIS & LAMP SOCKET ASSY.	1	.48
PA8999	14 VOLT BULB	1	.36

NOTE: PRICES SUBJECT TO CHANGE WITHOUT NOTICE.

PARTS LIST

21808 NORTH WESTERN DIESEL SWITCHER LOCO.

SAME AS 21801 LOCO.
EXCEPT ELIMINATE THE FOLLOWING PARTS:

XA14B156-RP	CAB W/TRIM ASSY.	1
XA14C429	REMOTE CONTROL UNIT	1
S-4A81-A	#4-40 THD. X 25/32" FILLISTER HD SCREW	2
PA14A587	36 TOOTH GEAR (UPPER)	1
S-172	#4 X 3/16" BD.HD. TYPE "Z" P.K. SCREW	2
W-46	LOCKWASHER (CLASS M)	2
PA6173	SOLDER TERMINAL	1
XA15A147	LOCOMOTIVE CHASSIS & LAMP SOCKET ASSY.	1
PA8999	14 VOLT BULB	1

ADD THE FOLLOWING PARTS:

XA15B331-RP	CAB ASSY. W/TRIM	1	3.27
S-4A81	#4-40 THD. FILLISTER HD. SCREW (MOTOR)	2	.02
P14N305	RIVET (SWITCH)	2	.01
PA15A200	SWITCH	1	.46
PA15A330	SWITCH SLIDE	1	.02
PA14B159-B	LOCOMOTIVE CHASSIS	1	.40

21813 M & SL DIESEL SWITCHER LOCO.

SAME AS 21808 LOCO.
EXCEPT USE:

XA15B653-RP	CAB W/TRIM ASSY.	1	2.58

NOTE: PRICES SUBJECT TO CHANGE WITHOUT NOTICE.

DIA. NO.	PART NO.	DESCRIPTION	PRICE
1	XA14B156-RP	Cab Assembly	3.27 ea.
	PA14A168	Headlight Lens (NOT SHOWN)	.02 ea.
2	PA11409	Air Chime	.08 ea.
3	S230B	#4 x¼" Type Z P.K. B.H. Screw	.01 ea.
4	S1	4 - 40 x ¼" Screw	.01 ea.
5	P10118	Spring Holder	.04 ea.
6	PA14A407 R	Brush Spring (Right)	.08 ea.
	PA14A407 L	Brush Spring (Left)	.08 ea.
7	PA14A169	Brush Mount	.02 ea.
8	PA14A588	Brush Holder (NOT SOLD ASSEMBLED)	.03 ea.
	PA14A414	Brush	.18 ea.
9	S4A82	4 - 40 Shoulder Screw	.27 ea.
10	W57	Lock Washer	.01 ea.
11	PA9522	Oil Wick	.01 ea.
12	XA14B162-ARP	Brush & Bearing Cap	.62 ea.
13	PA1405 D	Washer	.06 doz.
14	P325D	Fibre Washer	.01 ea.
15	XA14A969-A	Field Assembly	1.41 ea.
16	XA14B862	Armature Assembly	3.64 ea.
17	XA15A777	Bearing & Mount Assembly	.81 ea.
18	S4A81A	4 - 40 Fil Hd. Screw	.02 ea.
19	W46	Lock Washer	.01 ea.
20	PA6173	Terminal	.01 ea.
21	PA14A586	24 Tooth Gear	.12 ea.
22	S172	#4 x 3/16" Type Z B.H. P.K. Screw	.02 ea.
23	P10800B	Retaining Ring	.02 ea.
24	W114	Spring Washer	.07 ea.
25	PA8999	14 Volt Bulb	.30 ea.
25A	W7	Steel Washer	.01 ea.
26	XA14A730	Chassis & Lamp Socket Assembly	.37 ea.
27	XA14A638	Worm Shaft & Gear Assembly	.48 ea.
28	XA14A729	Chassis & Stud Assembly (Powered Only)	.67 ea.
	PA14A171	Collector Button	.08 ea.
	PA14A597	Collector Spring	.02 ea.
	P10434	Retaining Ring	.01 ea.
29	PA14A165	Worm Shaft Bearing	.05 ea.
30	PA14A890	Pul-Mor Tire	.05 ea.
31	XA14A933	Pul-Mor Wheel Axle & Gear	.58 ea.
	XA14A891	Pul-Mor Wheel Assembly (Insulated)	.28 ea.
	PA15A225	Axle	.06 ea.
	PA15A218	20 Tooth Gear	.09 ea.
32	XA14A148	Truckside & Coupler Assembly	1.04 ea.
	PA12A355-A	Leaf Spring	.02 ea.
	PA13A791	Rivet	.02 ea.
	XA12A047	Knuckle Coupler	.29 ea.
32A	XA10587-E	Remote Control Assembly	4.04 ea.
	XA9612BRP	Bottom Finger Unit	.33 ea.
	XA9612CRP	Top Finger Unit	.33 ea.
	XA8716	Drum	.95 ea.

Cont'd

DIA. NO.	PART NO.	DESCRIPTION	PRICE
33	S171	#2 x 3/16" Type Z B.H. P.K. Screw	.01 ea.
34	PA10209	Insulating Bushing	.02 ea.
35	PA14A100	Insulating Strip	.08 ea.
36	XA15A706	Chassis & Stud Assembly (Not Powered)	.51 ea.
37	XA14A932	Wheel & Axle Assembly (Front Truck)	.36 ea.
	PA14B888	Solid Wheel	.08 ea.
	PA15A226	Truck Axle	.05 ea.
	XA14A870	Insulated Wheel Assembly	.18 ea.

Prices subject to change without notice.

#21801 NORTHWESTERN DIESEL W/R. C.

#21812 T. & P. DIESEL

#21918 SEABOARD DIESEL

DIA. NO.	PART NO.	DESCRIPTION	PRICE
1	XA14B156RP	Cab Assembly (#21801)	3.27
	XA14B156ARP	Cab Assembly (#21918)	3.30
	XA14B156-CRP	Cab Assembly (#21812)	2.93
	PA14A168	Headlight Lens (NOT SHOWN)	.02
2	PA1409	Air Chime	.08
3	S230B	#4 x 1/4" Type Z. P. K. B. H. Screw	.01
4	S1	4 - 40 x 1/4" Screw	.01
5	P10118	Spring Holder	.04
6	PA14A407 R	Brush Spring (Right)	.08
	PA14A407 L	Brush Spring (Left)	.08
7	PA14A169	Brush Mount	.02
8	PA14A588	Brush Holder (NOT SOLD ASSEMBLED)	.03
	PA14A414	Brush	.18
9	S4A82	4 - 40 Shoulder Screw	.27
10	W57	Lock Washer	.01
11	PA9522	Oil Wick	.01
12	XA14B162ARP	Brush & Bearing Cap	.62
13	PA1405 D	Washer	.06
14	P325 D	Fiber Washer	.01
15	XA14A969-A	Field Assembly	1.41
16	XA14B862	Armature Assembly	3.64
17	XA15A777	Bearing & Mount Assembly	.81
18	S4A81A	4 -40 Fil Hd. Screw	.02
19	W46	Lock Washer	.01
20	PA6173	Terminal	.01
21	PA14A586	24 Tooth Gear	.12
22	S172	#4 x 3/16" Type Z, B. H.P.K. Screw	.02
23	P10800 B	Retaining Ring	.02
24	W114	Spring Washer	.07
25	PA8999	14 Volt Bulb	.30
25A	W7	Steel Washer	.01
26	XA15A147	Chassis & Lamp Socket Assy.	.48
27	XA14A638	Worm Shaft & Gear Assembly	.48
28	XA14A729	Chassis & Stud Assy. (Powered Only)	.67
	PA14A171	Collector Button	.08
	PA14A597	Collector Spring	.02
	P10434	Retaining Ring	.01

Con't

DIA. NO.	PART NO.	DESCRIPTION	PRICE
29	PA14A165	Worm Shaft Bearing	.05
30	PA14A890	Pul-Mor Tire	.05
31	XA14A933	Pul-Mor Wheel Axle & Gear	.58
	XA14A891	Pul-Mor Wheel Assy. (Insulated)	.28
	PA15A225	Axle	.06
	PA15A218	20 Tooth Gear	.09
32	XA14A148	Truckside & Coupler Assembly	1.04
	PA12A355-A	Leaf Spring	.02
	PA13A791	Rivet	.02
	XA12A047	Knuckle Coupler	.29
32A	XA14C429	2 pos. Remote Control	2.76
	PA14C432	Coil Support	.04
	PA14A444	Housing	.05
	XA14B433	Coil Assembly	.69
	XA14A435	Plunger	.14
	XA14A994	Contact	.77
33	S171	#2 x 3/16" Type Z B. H. P. K. Screw	.01
34	PA10209	Insulating Bushing	.02
35	PA14A100	Insulating Strip	.08
36	XA15A706	Chassis & Stud Assembly (Not Powered)	.51
37	XA14A932	Wheel & Axle Assembly (Front Truck)	.36
	PA14B888	Solid Wheel	.08
	PA15A226	Truck Axle	.05
	XA14A870	Insulated Wheel Assembly	.18

Prices subject to change without notice

BALDWIN SWITCHER DIESEL (NON MOTORIZED)

#21801-1 NORTHWESTERN & #21918-1 SEABOARD

DIA. NO.	PART NO.	DESCRIPTION	PRICE
1	XA14B156-DRP	Cab Assembly (21801-1)	3.29
	XA14B156-BRP	Cab Assembly (21918-1)	3.30
	PA14A168	Headlight Lens (NOT SHOWN)	.02
2	PA11409	Air Chime	.08
3	S230-B	#4 x ¼" Type Z P.K. B. H. Screw	.01
		DIAGRAM NO'S. 4 THRU 22 NOT USED ON ABOVE	
23	P10800 B	Retaining Ring	.02
24	W114	Spring Washer	.07
25	PA8999	14 Volt Bulb (USED ON 21918-1 ONLY)	.30
25A	W7	Steel Washer	.01
26	PA14B159 C	Locomotive Chassis (used on 21801-1)	.34
	XA15A147	Locomotive Chassis (used on 21918-1)	.48
27		NOT USED	
28		NOT USED	
29		NOT USED	
30		NOT USED	
31		NOT USED	
32	XA14A148	Truckside & Coupler Assembly	1.04
32A		NOT USED	
33	S171	Screw	.01
34	PA10209	Insulating Bushing	.02
35	PA14A100	Insulating Strip	.08
36	XA15A706	Chassis and Stud Assy. (21801-1)	.51
	XA14A729	Chassis and Stud Assy. (21918-1)	.67
37	XA14A932	Wheel and Axle Assembly	.36
	PA14B888	Solid Wheel	.08
	PA15A226	Truck Axle	.05
	XA14A870	Insulated Wheel Assembly	.18

Prices subject to change without notice

#21808 NORTHWESTERN DIESEL
&
#21813 M & ST. L DIESEL

DIA. NO.	PART NO.	DESCRIPTION	PRICE
1	XA15B331-RP	Cab Assy. (21808)	3.27 ea.
	XA15B653-RP	Cab Assy. (21813)	2.58 ea.
	PA14A168	Headlight Lens (NOT SHOWN)	.02 ea.
2	PA11409	Air Chime	.08 ea.
3	S230B	#4 x ¼" Type Z P.K. B.H. Screw	.01 ea.
4	S1	4-40 x ¼" Screw	.01 ea.
5	P10118	Spring Holder	.04 ea.
6	PA14A407 R	Brush Spring (Right)	.08 ea.
	PA14A407 L	Brush Spring (Left)	.08 ea.
7	PA14A169	Brush Mount	.02 ea.
8	PA14A588	Brush Holder (NOT SOLD ASSEMBLED)	.03 ea.
	PA14A414	Brush	.18 ea.
9	S4A82	4 -40 Shoulder Screw	.27 ea.
10	W57	Lock Washer	.01 ea.
11	PA9522	Oil Wick	.01 ea.
12	XA14B162ARP	Brush & Bearing Cap	.62 ea.
13	PA1405 D	Washer	.06 dz.
14	P325D	Fiber Washer	.01 ea.
15	XA14A969-A	Field Assembly	1.41 ea.
16	XA14B862	Armature Assembly	3.64 ea.
17	XA15A777	Bearing & Mount Assembly	.81 ea.
18	S4A81A	4 - 40 Fil Hd. Screw	.02 ea.
19	W46	Lock Washer	.01 ea.
20	PA6173	Terminal (Used on #XA15A777, Not used with R. C. Unit)	.01 ea.
21	PA14A586	24 Tooth Gear	.12 ea.
22		NOT USED	
23	P10800B	Retaining Ring	.02 ea.
24	W114	Spring Washer	.07 ea.
25		NOT USED	
25A	W7	Steel Washer	.01 ea.
26	PA14B159B	Chassis	.40 ea.
27	XA14A638	Worm Shaft & Gear Assembly	.48 ea.
28	XA14A729	Chassis & Stud Assembly (Powered Only)	.67 ea.
	PA14A171	Collector Button	.08 ea.
	PA14A597	Collector Spring	.02 ea.
	P1034	Retaining Ring	.01 ea.
29	PA14A165	Worm Shaft Bearing	.05 ea.
30	PA14A890	Pul-Mor Tire	.05 ea.
31	XA14A933	Pul-Mor Wheel Axle & Gear	.58 ea.
	XA14A891	Pul-Mor Wheel Assembly (Insulated)	.28 ea.
	PA15A225	Axle	.06 ea.
	PA15A218	20 Tooth Gear	.09 ea.

Con't

DIA. NO.	PART NO.	DESCRIPTION	PRICE
32	XA14A148	Truckside & Coupler Assembly	1.04 ea.
	PA12A355-A	Leaf Spring	.02 ea.
	PA13A791	Rivet	.02 ea.
	XA12A047	Knuckle Coupler	.29 ea.
32A	PA15A200	Switch	.46 ea.
	PA15A330	Switch Slide (NOT SHOWN)	.02 ea.
	P14N305	Switch Rivet (NOT SHOWN)	.01 ea.
33	S171	#2 x 3/16" Type Z B. H. P. K. Screw	.01 ea.
34	PA10209	Insulating Bushing	.02 ea.
35	PA14A100	Insulating Strip	.08 ea.
36	XA15A706	Chassis & Stud Assembly (Not Powered)	.51 ea.
37	XA14A932	Wheel & Axle Assembly (Front Truck)	.36 ea.
	PA14B888	Solid Wheel	.08 ea.
	PA15A226	Truck Axle	.05 ea.
	XA14A870	Insulated Wheel Assembly	.18 ea.

Prices subject to change without notice

#21801 NORTHWESTERN DIESEL W/R.C.
#21812 T & P DIESEL
#21918 SEABOARD DIESEL

DIA NO.	PART NO.	DESCRIPTION	PRICE
1	XA14B156-RP	Cab Assembly (21801)	3.43 ea.
	XA14B156-ARP	Cab Assembly (21918)	3.47 ea.
	XA14B156-CRP	Cab Assembly (21812)	3.08 ea.
	PA14A168	Headlight Lens (NOT SHOWN)	.02 ea.
2	PA11409	Air Chime	.08 ea.
3	S230-B	#4 x 1/4" Type "Z" P.K. B.H. Screw	.01 ea.
4	S1	4-40 x 1/4" Screw	.01 ea.
5	P10118	Spring Holder	.04 ea.
6	PA14A407-L&R	Brush Spring	.08 ea.
7	PA14A169	Brush Mount	.02 ea.
8	PA14A588	Brush Holder	.03 ea.
	PA14A414	Brush (Not Sold Assembled)	.19 ea.
9	S4A82	4 - 40 Shoulder Screw	.28 ea.
10	W57	Lock Washer	.01 ea.
11	PA9522	Oil Wick	.01 ea.
12	XA14B162-ARP	Brush and Bearing Cap	.65 ea.
13	PA1405-D	Washer	.06 dz.
14	P325-D	Fibre Washer	.01 ea.
15	XA14A969-A	Field Assembly	1.48 ea.
16	XA14B862	Armature Assembly	3.82 ea.
17	XA15A777	Bearing and Mount Assembly	.85 ea.
18	S4A81-A	4 - 40 Fil Hd. Screw	.02 ea.
19	W46	Lock Washer	.01 ea.
20	PA6173	Terminal	.01 ea.
21	PA14A586	24 Tooth Gear	.13 ea.
22	S172	#4 x 3/16" Type "Z" B.H. P.K Screw	.02 ea.
23	P10800-B	Retaining Ring	.02 ea.
24	W114	Spring Washer	.07 ea.
25	PA8999	14 Volt Bulb	.32 ea.
25A	W7	Steel Washer	.01 ea.
26	XA15A147	Chassis and Lamp Socket Assembly	.50 ea.
27	XA14A638	Worm Shaft and Gear Assembly	.50 ea.
28	XA14A729	Chassis and Stud Assembly (Powered Only)	.70 ea.
	PA14A171	Collector Button	.08 ea.
	PA14A597	Collector Spring	.02 ea.
	P10434	Retaining Ring	.01 ea.
29	PA14A165	Worm Shaft Bearing	.05 ea.
30	PA14A890	Pul-Mor Tire	.05 ea.
31	XA14A933	Pul-Mor Wheel Axle and Gear	.61 ea.
	XA14A891	Pul-Mor Wheel Assembly (Insulated)	.29 ea.
	PA15A225	Axle	.06 ea.
	PA15A218	20 Tooth Gear	.09 ea.

(Cont'd)

DIA. NO.	PART NO.	DESCRIPTION	PRICE
32	XA14A148	Truckside and Coupler Assembly	1.09 ea.
	PA12A355-A	Leaf Spring	.02 ea.
	PA13A791	Rivet	.02 ea.
	XA12A047	Knuckle Coupler	.30 ea.
32A	XA14C429	2 Pos. Remote Control	2.90 ea.
	PA14C432	Coil Housing	.04 ea.
	PA14A444	Coil Support	.05 ea.
	XA14B433	Coil Assembly	.72 ea.
	XA14A435	Plunger	.15 ea.
	XA14A994	Contact	.81 ea.
33	S171	#2 x 3/16" Type "Z" B.H. P.K. Screw	.01 ea.
34	PA10209	Insulating Bushing	.02 ea.
35	PA14A100	Insulating Strip	.08 ea.
36	XA15A706	Chassis and Stud Assembly (Not Powered)	.54 ea.
37	XA14A932	Wheel and Axle Assembly (Front Truck)	.38 ea.
	PA14B888	Solid Wheel	.08 ea.
	PA15A226	Truck Axle	.05 ea.
	XA14A870	Insulated Wheel Assembly	.19 ea.

Prices subject to change without notice.

BALDWIN SWITCHER DIESEL (NON MOTORIZED)

#21801-1 NORTHWESTERN & 21918-1 SEABOARD

DIA. NO.	PART NO.	DESCRIPTION	PRICE
1	XA14B156-DRP	Cab Assembly (21801-1)	3.45
	XA14B156-BRP	Cab Assembly (21918-1)	3.47
	PA14A168	Headlight Lens (NOT SHOWN)	.02
2	PA11409	Air Chime	.08
3	S230-B	#4x¼" Type "Z" P.K.B.H. Screw	.01
4-22		NOT USED	
23	P10800-B	Retaining Ring	.02
24	W114	Spring Washer	.07
25	PA8999	14 Volt Bulb (Used on 21918-1 only)	.32
25A	W7	Steel Washer	.01
26	PA14B159-C	Locomotive Chassis (used on 21801-1)	.36
	XA15A147	Locomotive Chassis (used on 21918-1)	.50
27-31		NOT USED	
32	XA14A148	Truckside & Coupler Assembly	1.09
32A		NOT USED	
33	S171	Screw	.01
34	PA10209	Insulating Bushing	.02
35	PA14A100	Insulating Strip	.08
36	XA15A706	Chassis & Stud Assy. (used on 21801-1)	.54
	XA14A729	Chassis & Stud Assy. (used on 21918-1)	.70
37	XA14A932	Wheel and Axle Assembly	.38
	PA14B888	Solid Wheel	.08
	PA15A226	Truck Axle	.05
	XA14A870	Insulated Wheel Assembly	.19

Prices subject to change without notice.

#21808 NORTHWESTERN DIESEL

AND

#21813 M & ST. L. DIESEL

DIA. NO.	PART NO.	DESCRIPTION	PRICE
1	XA15B331-RP	Cab Assembly (21808)	3.43
	XA15B653-RP	Cab Assembly (21813)	2.71
	PA14A168	Headlight Lens (NOT SHOWN)	.02
2	PA11409	Air Chime	.08
3	S230-B	#4 x ¼" Type "Z" P.K. B.H. Screw	.01
4	S1	4-40 x ¼" Screw	.01
5	P10118	Spring Holder	.04
6	PA14A407-R	Brush Spring (Right)	.08
	PA14A407-L	Brush Spring (Left)	.08
7	PA14A169	Brush Mount	.02
8	PA14A588	Brush Holder	.03
	PA14A414	Brush (Not Sold Assembled)	.19
9	S4A82	4-40 Shoulder Screw	.28
10	W57	Lock Washer	.01
11	PA9522	Oil Wick	.01
12	XA14B162-ARP	Brush and Bearing Cap	.65
13	PA1405-D	Washer	.06
14	P325-D	Fibre Washer	.01
15	XA14A969-A	Field Assembly	1.48
16	XA14B862	Armature Assembly	3.82
17	XA15A777	Bearing and Mount Assembly	.85
18	S4A81-A	4-40 Fil Hd. Screw	.02
19	W46	Lock Washer	.01
20	PA6173	Terminal	.01
21	PA14A586	24 Tooth Gear	.13
22		NOT USED	
23	P10800-B	Retaining Ring	.02
24	W114	Spring Washer	.07
25		NOT USED	
25A	W7	Steel Washer	.01
26	PA14B159-B	Chassis	.42
27	XA14A638	Worm Shaft and Gear Assembly	.50
28	XA14A729	Chassis & Stud Assembly (Powered Only)	.70
	PA14A171	Collector Button	.08
	PA14A597	Collector Spring	.02
	P10434	Retaining Ring	.01
29	PA14A165	Worm Shaft Bearing	.05
30	PA14A890	Pul-Mor Tire	.05
31	XA14A933	Pul-Mor Wheel Axle and Gear	.61
	XA14A891	Pul-Mor Wheel Assembly (Insulated)	.29
	PA15A225	Axle	.06
	PA15A218	20 Tooth Gear	.09

DIA. NO.	PART NO.	DESCRIPTION	PRICE
32	XA14A148	Truckside and Coupler Assembly	1.09
	PA12A355-A	Leaf Spring	.02
	PA13A791	Rivet	.02
	XA12A047	Knuckle Coupler	.30
32A	PA15A200	Switch	.48
	PA15A330	Switch Slide (NOT SHOWN)	.02
	P14N305	Switch Rivet (NOT SHOWN)	.01
33	S171	#2 x 3/16" Type "Z" P.K. B.H. Screw	.01
34	PA10209	Insulating Bushing	.02
35	PA14A100	Insulating Strip	.08
36	XA15A706	Chassis and Stud Assembly (Not Powered)	.54
37	XA14A932	Wheel and Axle Assembly (Front Truck)	.38
	PA14B888	Solid Wheel	.08
	PA15A226	Truck Axle	.05
	XA14A870	Insulated Wheel Assembly	.19

Prices subject to change without notice.

#355 BALDWIN DIESEL SWITCHER LOCO

DIA. NO.	PART NO.	DESCRIPTION	PRICE
33	S171	#2 x 3/16" Type Z B.H. P.K. Screw	.01
34	PA10209	Insulating Bushing	.02
35	PA14A100	Insulating Strip	.08
36	XA15A706	Chassis & Stud Assy. (Not Powered)	.54
37	XA14A932	Wheel & Axle Assembly (Front Truck)	.38
	PA14B888	Solid Wheel	.08
	PA15A226	Truck Axle	.05
	XA14A870	Insulated Wheel Assembly	.19

****

#21801 NORTHWESTERN DIESEL W/R.C.
#21812 T & P DIESEL
#21918 SEABOARD DIESEL

SAME AS #355 BALDWIN DIESEL SWITCHER LOCO WITH THESE EXCEPTIONS:

DIA. NO.	PART NO.	DESCRIPTION	PRICE
#1	XA14B156RP	Cab Assembly (21801)	3.43
#26	XA15A147	Chassis & Lamp Socket Assy	.50
#32A	XA14C429	2 Pos Remote Control	2.90
	PA14C432	Coil Housing	.04
	PA14A444	Coil Support	.05
	XA14B433	Coil Assy	.72
	XA14A435	Plunger	.15
	XA14A994	Contact	.81

****

#21808 NW DIESEL & #21813 M & ST.L. DIESEL

SAME AS ABOVE BUT WITH THESE EXCEPTIONS:

DIA. NO.	PART NO.	DESCRIPTION	PRICE
#1	XA15B331RP	Cab Assy (21808)	3.43
#22 & #25		NOT USED	
#26	PA14B159B	Chassis	.42
#32A	PA15A200	Switch	.48
	PA15A330	Switch Slide (NOT SHOWN)	.02
	P14N305	Switch Rivet (NOT SHOWN)	.01

****

#21801-1 NORTHWESTERN & 21818-1 SEABORD BALDWIN SWITCHER DIESEL (NON MOTORIZED)

SAME AS ABOVE BUT WITH THESE EXCEPTIONS:

DIA. NO.	PART NO.	DESCRIPTION	PRICE
#1	XA14B156-DRP	Cab Assy (21801-1)	3.45
	XA14B156-BRP	Cab Assy (21918-1)	3.47
	PA14A168	Headlight Lens (NOT SHOWN)	.02
#4-22		NOT USED	
#25	PA8999	14 Volt Bulb &Used on 21918-1 only	.32
#25A	W7	Steel Washer	.01
#26	PA14B159C	Loco Chassis 'Used on 21801-1)	.36
	XA15A147	Loco Chassis 'Used on 21918-1)	.50
#32	XA14A148	Truckside & CouplerAssy	1.09
#32A		NOT USED	

DIESEL LOCOMOTIVE WITH BUILT-IN AIR CHIME ELECTRONIC HORN

Model Nos. 360 and 361

(This pair was called 362 by Gilbert.)

SPECIFICATIONS

Tested at: 12 Volts A.C. .... using 180" oval of track.

(A) Locomotive to run a minimum of 9½ RPM or 9½ times forward and reverse, around 180" oval of track.

Load: Not to draw more than 3.25 Amps while pulling 3 Passenger Cars.

Motor: Universal A.C. or D.C.

 Ref: Form No. M2899; Dec. 1950

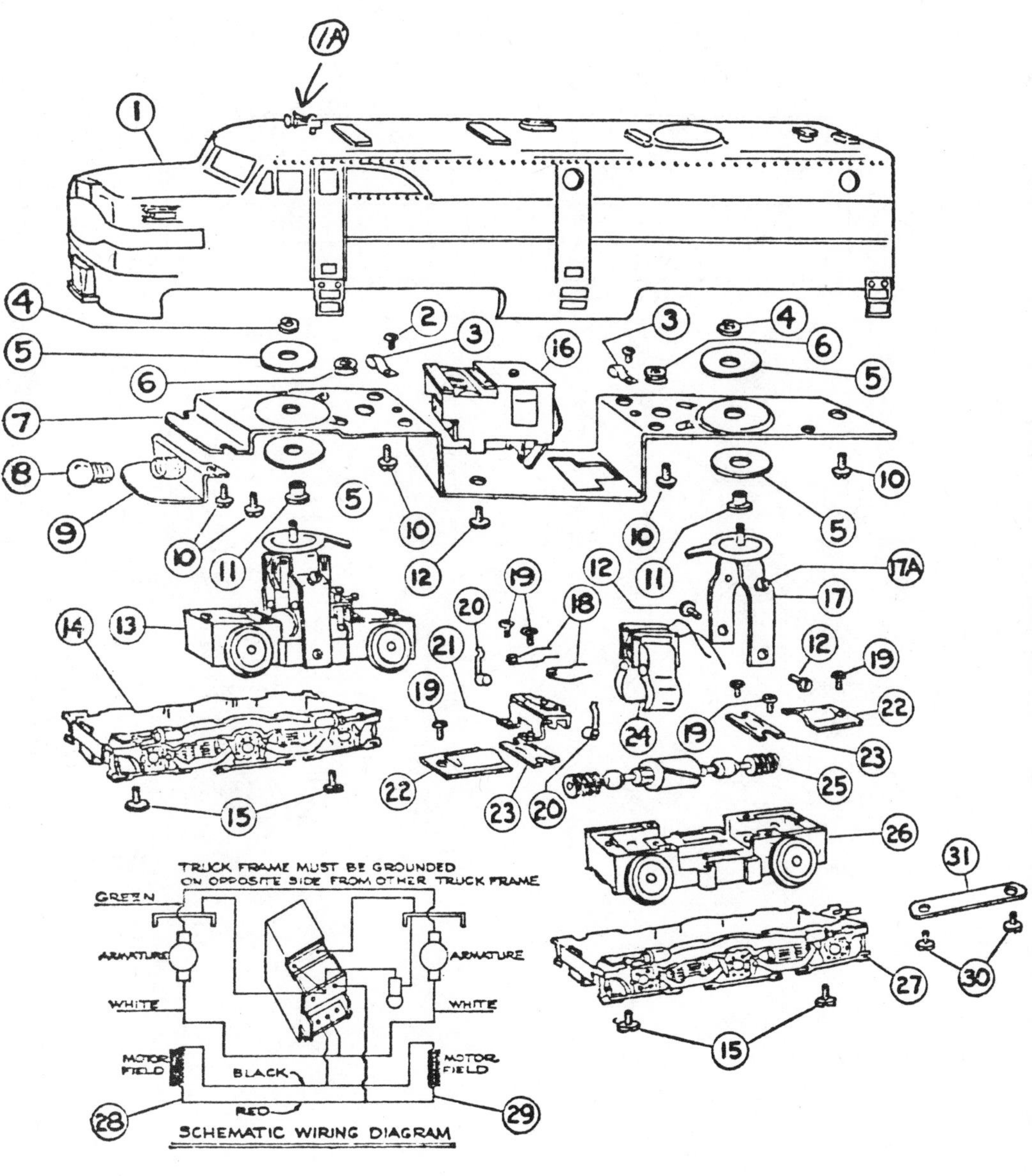

Ref: Form No. M2899; Dec. 1950

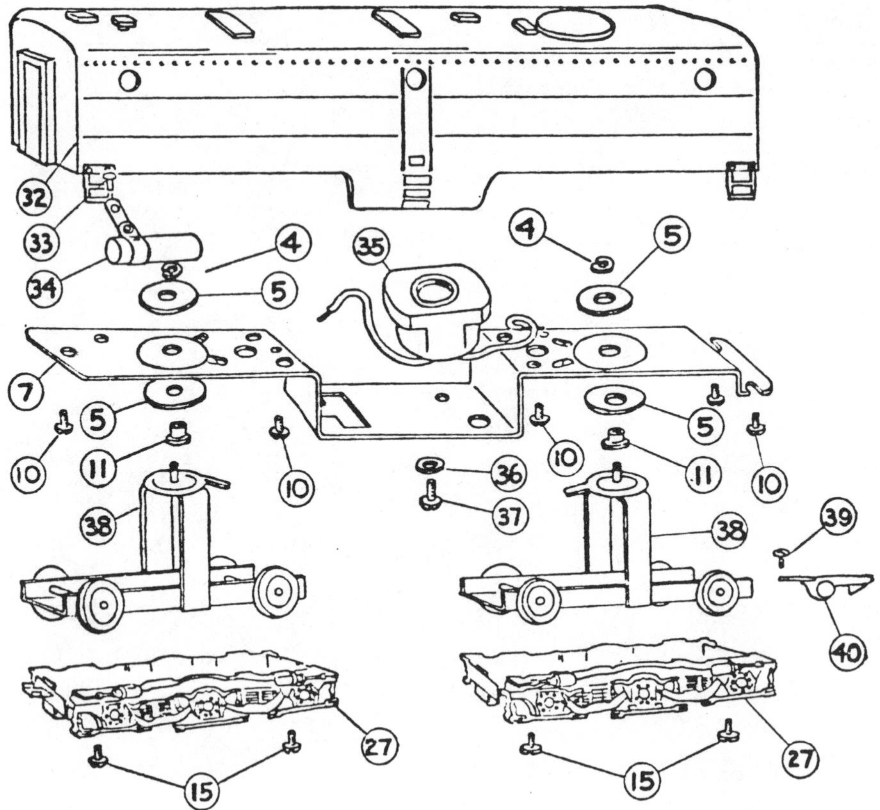

 Ref: Form No. M2899; Dec. 1950

Diagram Number	Part No.	Description	Price
1 A	PA 11409	PLASTIC HORN	.05 ea.
1	XA11378-RP	A Unit Cabin	$6.07 ea.
2	S147	Screw	.01 "
3	PA11048	Wire Clip	.02 "
4	P10800-A	Retaining Ring	.04 "
5	PA8715	Fibre Washer	.05 dz.
6	PA4356	Rubber Grommet	.02 ea.
7	PA11452	Chassis	.48 "
8	PA8999	Bulb	.25 "
9	XA11477	Lamp Bracket Assembly	.09 "
10	S319	Screw	.01 "
11	PA1312	Insulating Bushing	.10 dz.
12	S230	Screw	.01 ea.
13	XA11412	Motor Assembly (not sold as a complete assembly)	
14	XA11456-A	Truck Side & Bottom Plate Assembly	.98 "
15	S249	Screw	.01 "
16	XA10587-E	Remote Control Unit	2.50 "
	XA8716	Drum only	.60 "
	PA9612-C	Top Finger	.50 "
	PA9612-B	Bottom Finger	.50 "
17	XA11457	Field Clamp Assembly	.37 "
17A	S-0	Screw	.05 dz.
18	P11000-R	Brush Spring (right)	.03 ea.
	P11000-L	Brush Spring (left)	.03 "
19	S171	Screw	.10 dz.

Diagram Number	Part No.	Description	Price
20	XA11654	Brush Holder Assembly	$ .25 ea.
21	XA11421-RP	Brush Bracket Assembly	.20 "
22	PA11441	Worm Cover	.01 "
23	PA11453	Bearing Strap	.01 "
24	XA11461	Field Assembly	.71 "
25	XA11445	Armature Assembly	3.39 "
26	XA11463-RP	Truck Chassis & Wheel Assembly	2.50 "
	PA11343	Solid Wheel	10. "
	XA11473	Insul. Wheel Assembly	.34 "
27	XA11485-B	Truck Side and Bottom Plate Assembly (coupler end)	1.66 "
28	PA11500	Long 4 Conductor cable	.21 "
29	PA11500-A	Short 4 Conductor cable	.12 "
30	S326	Screw	.01 "
31	PA11505	Draw Bar	.01 "
32	XA11379-RP	B Unit Cabin	5.71 "
33	PA4362	Rivet	.01 "
34	PA11365	Condenser	.68 "
35	PA11364	Speaker	2.18 "
36	W84	Washer	.01 "
37	S-50-A	Screw	.01 "
38	XA11596-A	Wheel and Chassis Assembly	1.25 "
39	S334	Screw	.01 "
40	XA11484	Coupler Arm Assembly	.12 "
	PA11589	Coupler Spring	.02 "
	PA11361	Rectifier Tube for Whistle Controller	4.14 "

 Ref: Form No. M2899; Dec. 1950

SERVICE INSTRUCTIONS FOR No. 362 SANTA FE DIESEL LOCOMOTIVE

The first thing to do is to place Locomotive on Track, connect Transformer and Whistle Control Unit and test for operation.

1. **If the trouble is in the motors in the "A" unit we suggest that you check as follows:**
   a. Check Brushes (※20) for wear or poor contact.
   b. Check Brush Springs (※18) for position and proper tension.
   c. Check wires and solder joints for loose connections.
   d. Commutator on Armature Assembly (※25) may be dirty.
   e. Check operation of Remote Control Unit (※16).
   f. See if motor is properly lubricated.
   g. Wheels and track must be kept clean to insure proper electrical contact.

2. **To Check Whistle in "B" Unit and Control Box turn the Control Lever Down. If it does not blow properly check as follows:**
   a. Check hook-up and operating instructions.
   b. See if filament in tube is burning alright.
   c. Check sound adjustment on Whistle Controller as per instruction sheet which comes with the unit.
   d. Check for shorted Condenser (※34).
   e. Check Speaker (※35) operation.

3. **To Check Whistle Control Box Only.**
   a. Take a spare Speaker (※35) and connect to Track Terminal with red wire to base post clip and black wire to other clip.
   b. If Whistle blows, Control Box is O.K., but Speaker in "B" Unit will have to be replaced.
   c. When Whistle Control Box is found to be defective, it should be returned to the A. C. Gilbert Company for service unless a new tube will correct the trouble.

4. **To Check Whistle Without Control Box.**
   a. With Locomotive on the Track and handle of Transformer turned on, raise and lower the rear truck of the "B" Unit just enough to break the electrical circuit. You will hear a noticeable click from the Speaker if everything is O.K. If this sound is not heard the Speaker (※35 or Condenser (※34) should be replaced.

5. **To Disassemble and Replace Parts on "A" Unit.**
   a. The first step is to remove the S319 Screws (※10) and take off Cabin (※1).
   b. Motor is exposed and you can check wiring and other points of the unit.
   c. Brush Holder Assembly (※20) and Brush Springs (※18) can be replaced without taking Motor Unit (※13) from Chassis (※7).
   d. When replacing Brush Holder Assembly (※20), unsolder lead wire and remove tension from Brush Spring (※18).
   e. To replace Brush Springs (※18), remove Brush Holder Assembly (※20) first so spring can be pulled forward and slipped out.
   f. When replacing Armature (※25) or Magnet (※24) we recommend removing Motor Unit (※13) from Chassis (※7) as follows:
      1. Unsolder lead wire to stud on Field Clamp Assembly (※17).
      2. Take off Retaining Ring (※4) and Fibre Washers (※5).
   g. Remove S249 Screws (※15) and take off Truck Side and Bottom Plate Assembly (※27).
   h. Loosen the two S-0 Screws (※17A).
   i. Take out S230 Screws and remove Field Clamp Assembly (※17).
   j. Remove S171 Screws and take off Worm Cover (※22) and Bearing Strap (※23).

NOTE: When reassembling motor it is necessary to adjust the two S-0 Screws (※17A) on the Field Clamp Assembly (※17) which centralizes the Magnet Assembly (※24). The reason is to prevent the Armature Assembly (※25) from striking the plates on the Magnet Assembly (※24).

When placing Motor Unit (※13) back in Chassis (※9), the stop on the Field Clamp Assembly (※17) must be facing inward so that the stop will always be parallel with the Commutator on the Armature Assembly (※25).

DIESEL LOCOMOTIVE WITH AIR CHIME WHISTLE

Model Nos. 360 and 364

(This pair was called 365 by Gilbert.)

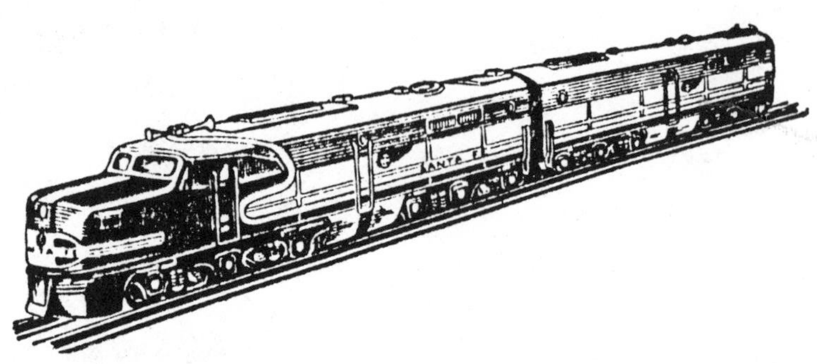

SPECIFICATIONS

Tested at: 12 Volts A.C. .... Using 180" oval of track.

(A) Locomotive to run a minimum of 9½ RPM or 9½ times forward and reverse, around 180" oval of track.

Load: Not to draw more than 3.25 Amps while pulling 3 Passenger Cars.

Motor: Universal A.C. or D.C.

 Ref: Form No. M3151; Nov. 1, 1952

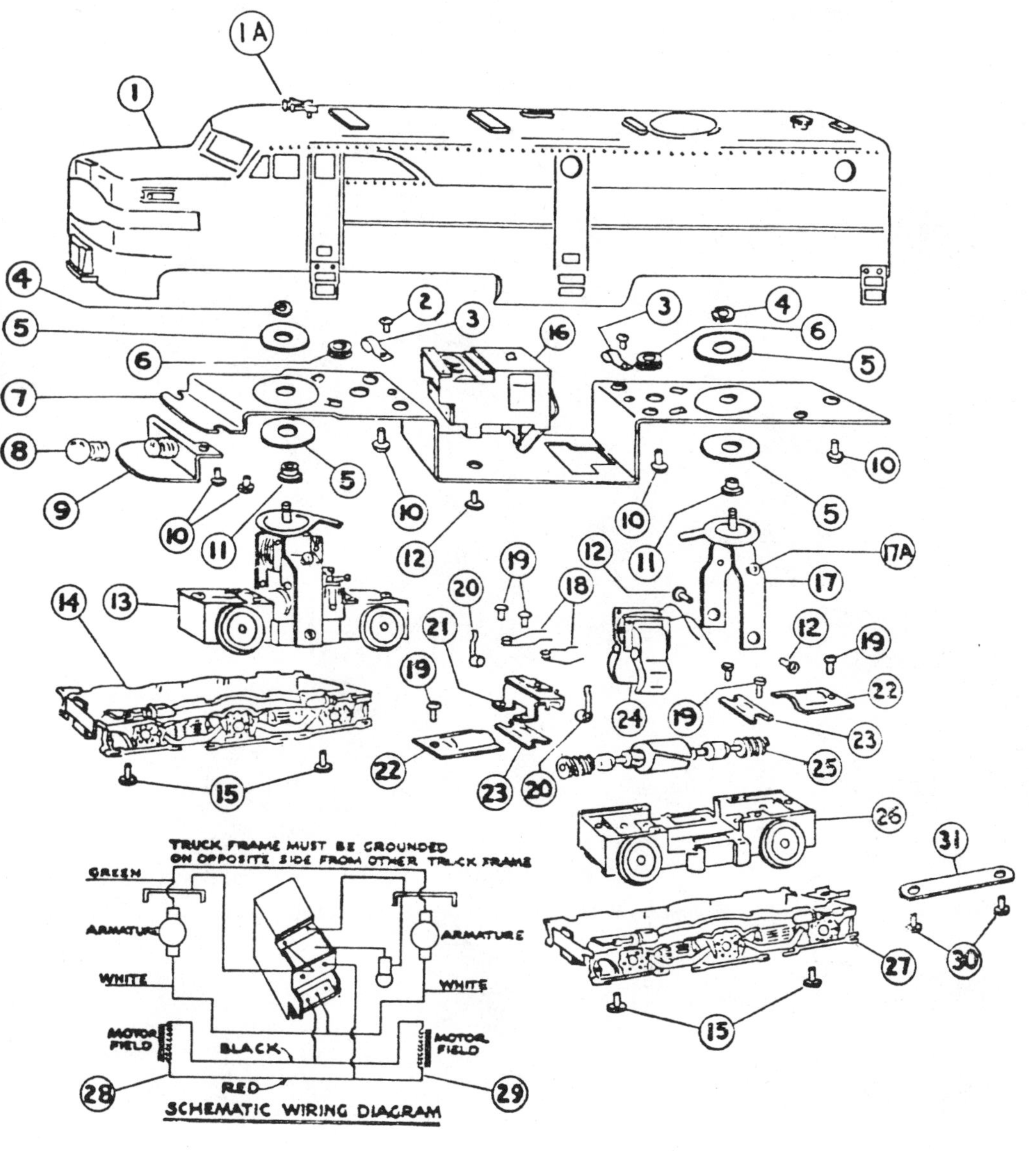
1A
1
2
3
4
5
6
7
8
9
10
11
12
13
14
15
16
17
17A
18
19
20
21
22
23
24
25
26
27
28
29
30
31
TRUCK FRAME MUST BE GROUNDED
ON OPPOSITE SIDE FROM OTHER TRUCK FRAME
GREEN
ARMATURE
ARMATURE
WHITE
WHITE
MOTOR FIELD
MOTOR FIELD
BLACK
RED
SCHEMATIC WIRING DIAGRAM

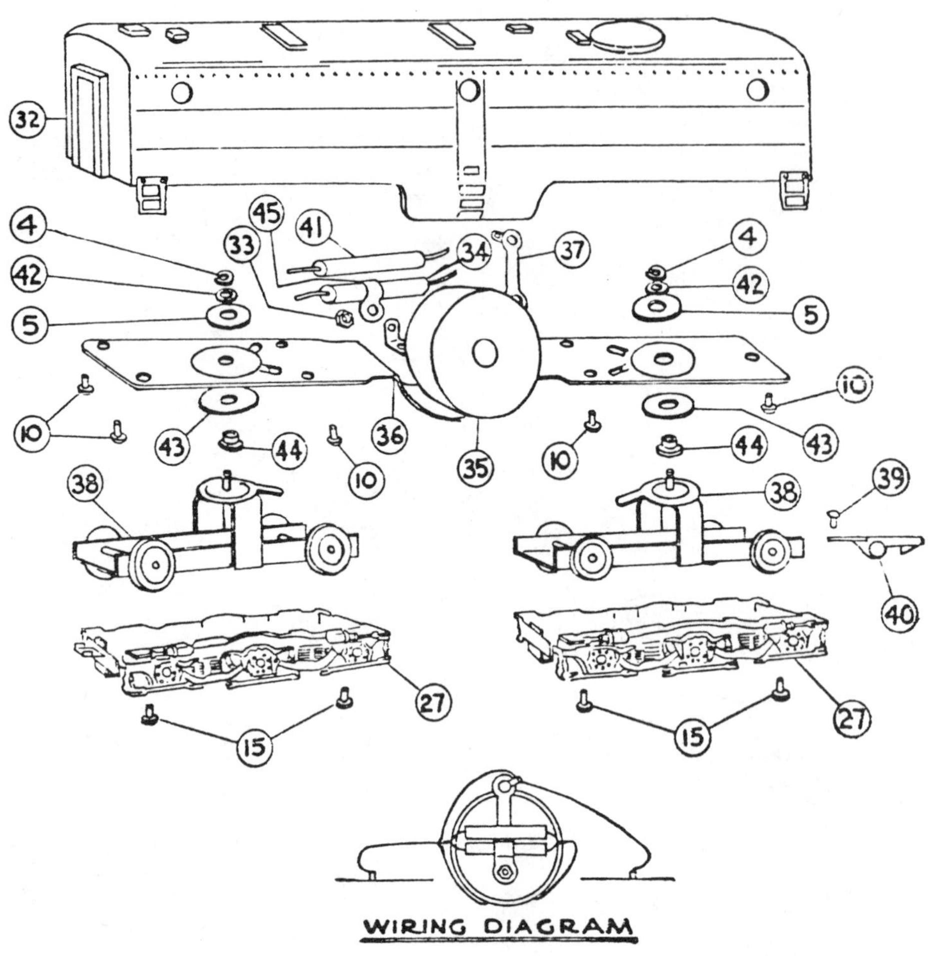

WIRING DIAGRAM

 Ref: Form No. M3151; Nov. 1, 1952

Diagram Number	Part No.	Description	Price
1	XA11378-RP	A Unit Cabin with trimmings........	$3.81 ea.
1A	PA11409	Plastic Horn	.05 "
2	S147	Screw	.01 "
3	PA11048	Wire Clip	.02 "
4	P10800-A	Retaining Ring	.04 "
5	PA8715	Fibre Washer	.09 dz.
6	PA4356	Rubber Grommet	.02 ea.
7	PA11452	Chassis	.53 "
8	PA8999	Bulb	.25 "
9	XA11477	Lamp Bracket Assembly...........	.21 "
10	S319	Screw	.01 "
11	PA1312	Insulating Bushing	.11 dz.
12	S230	Screw	.10 "
13	XA11412	Motor Assembly (not sold as a complete assembly)	
14	XA11456-A	Truck Side & Bottom Plate Assembly.	1.09 ea.
15	S249	Screw	.01 "
16	XA10587-E	Remote Control Unit..............	1.32 "
	XA8716	Drum only	.59 "
	XA9612-CRP	Top Finger Unit.................	.30 "
	XA9612-BRP	Bottom Finger Unit...............	.30 "
17	XA11457	Field Clamp Assembly............	.41 "
17A	S-0	Screw	.05 dz.
18	P11000-R	Brush Spring (right)...............	.03 ea.
	P11000-L	Brush Spring (left)...............	.03 "
19	S171	Screw	.01 "
20	XA11684	Brush Holder Assembly...........	.25 "

All prices subject to change without notice.

Diagram Number	Part No.	Description	Price
21	XA11454-RP	Brush Bracket Assembly	.13 "
22	PA11441	Worm Cover	.01 "
23	PA11453	Bearing Strap	.01 "
24	XA11461	Field Assembly	.79 "
25	XA11445	Armature Assembly	3.76 "
26	XA12B065-RP	Truck Chassis & Wheel Assembly	2.21 "
27	XA11485-B	Truck Side and Bottom Plate Assembly (coupler end)	1.84 "
28	PA11652	4 Conductor Cable	.18 ft.
30	S326	Screw	.01 ea.
31	PA11505	Draw Bar	.01 "
32	XA11688-RP	"B" Unit Cabin with trimmings	5.71 "
33	N-1	Nut	.01 "
34	PA11685	Resistor	.26 "
35	XA11710	Speaker	3.06 "
36	XA11687-RP	Chassis and Bracket Assembly	.54 "
37	XA10818-F	Insulator & Terminal Assembly	.03 "
38	XA11598-A	Wheel & Chassis Assembly	1.25 "
39	S334	Screw	.01 "
40	XA11484	Coupler Arm Assembly	.20 "
	PA11589	Coupler Spring	.02 "
41	PA11A991	Condenser	1.04 "
42	W83	Washer	.03 "
43	W124	Washer	.01 "
44	PA11455	Insulating Bushing	.06 "
45	PA10818	Bus Bar	.01 "

 Ref: Form No. M3151; Nov. 1, 1952

SERVICE INSTRUCTIONS FOR No. 365 SANTA FE DIESEL LOCOMOTIVE

The first thing to do is to place Locomotive on Track, connect Transformer and Whistle Control Unit and test for operation.

1. **If the trouble is in the motors in the "A" unit we suggest that you check as follows:**
   a. Check Brushes (※20) for wear or poor contact.
   b. Check Brush Springs (※18) for position and proper tension.
   c. Check wires and solder joints for loose connections.
   d. Commutator on Armature Assembly (※25) may be dirty.
   e. Check operation of Remote Control Unit (※16).
   f. See if motor is properly lubricated.
   g. Wheels and track must be kept clean to insure proper electrical contact.

2. **To Disassemble and Replace Parts on "A" Unit.**
   a. The first step is to remove the S319 Screws (※10) and take off Cabin (※1).
   b. Motor is exposed and you can check wiring and other points of the unit.
   c. Brush Holder Assembly (※20) and Brush Springs (※18) can be replaced without taking Motor Unit (※13) from Chassis (※7).
   d. When replacing Brush Holder Assembly (※20), unsolder lead wire and remove tension from Brush Spring (※18).
   e. To replace Brush Springs (※18), remove Brush Holder Assembly (※20) first so spring can be pulled forward and slipped out.
   f. When replacing Armature (※25) or Magnet (※24) we recommend removing Motor Unit (※13) from Chassis (※7) as follows:
      1. Unsolder lead wire to stud on Field Clamp Assembly (※17).
      2. Take off Retaining Ring (※4) and Fibre Washers (※5).
   g. Remove S249 Screws (※15) and take off Truck Side and Bottom Plate Assembly (※27).
   h. Loosen the two S-0 Screws (※17A).
   i. Take out S230 Screws and remove Field Clamp Assembly (※17).
   j. Remove S171 Screws and take off Worm Cover (※22) and Bearing Strap (※23).

NOTE: When reassembling motor it is necessary to adjust the two S-0 Screws (※17A) on the Field Clamp Assembly (※17) which centralizes the Magnet Assembly (※24). The reason is to prevent the Armature Assembly (※25) from striking the plates on the Magnet Assembly (※24).

When placing Motor Unit (※13) back in Chassis (※7), the stop on the Field Clamp Assembly (※17) must be facing inward so that the stop will always be parallel with the Commutator on the Armature Assembly (※25).

3. **Instructions for correcting Whistle failure in the ※364 B Unit as follows:**
   a. Recheck the instruction sheet in order to make sure hook-up is correct. If both the Transformer instructions and the Air Chime Whistle Instructions are followed, this will cause a duplication of wiring. The result will be that you will only have a faint buzz while the train is running or in a neutral position. Follow the Air Chime Whistle wiring instructions only and be sure to have only two wires going to the ※690 Track Terminal.
   b. The Generator Tube ※PA11665 on the control box may be weak and need replacing.
   c. If the trouble still persists it will be necessary to remove the "B" unit cab from the chassis by unscrewing the five screws (※10).
   d. The unit is exposed and you can check all wires and solder joints for loose connections. Be sure the lead wires on the resistor and condenser are covered with an insulating sleeve.
   e. Check the condenser (※41) by adding another condenser in series with temporary connections. If this corrects the trouble the defective condenser can be removed and a new one connected in its place.
   f. To check resistor (※34) use another resistor and follow same procedure.
   g. The speaker seldom has to be replaced unless the wire or covering is broken.

DIA. NO.	PART NO.		DESCRIPTION	PRICE
1	XA11378-RP		"A" UNIT CABIN W/TRIM NOT AVAILABLE	
		SUB.	W/ XA12D075-ARP CABIN	4.20 EA.
1A	PA11409		PLASTIC HORN	.08 EA.
2	S147		SCREW	.01 EA.
3	PA11048		WIRE CLIP NOT AVAILABLE	
4	P10800-A		RETAINING RING	.25 DZ.
5	PA8715		FIBRE WASHER	.10 DZ.
6	PA4356		RUBBER GROMMET	.02 EA.
7	PA11452		CHASSIS NOT AVAILABLE	
		SUB.	W/ PA11452-B CHASSIS	.59 EA.
8	PA8999		BULB	.30 EA.
9	XA11477		LAMP BRACKET ASSY.	.24 EA.
10	S319		SCREW	.02 EA.
11	PA1312		INSULATING BUSHING NOT USED	
		USE	PA11455 BUSHING	.14 EA.
12	S230-B		SCREW	.01 EA.
	S4A06		SCREW (SECURES YOKE & FIELD CLAMP TO CHASSIS)	.03 EA.
13	XA11412		MOTOR ASSY. NOT AVAILABLE	
		SUB.	W/XA13B038-B MOTOR	12.16 EA.
14	XA11456-A		TRUCK SIDE & BOTTOM PLATE ASSY. NOT AVAILABLE	
		SUB.	W/XA13A802 TRUCK SIDE & PLATE ASSY.	1.06 EA.
15	S249		SCREW	.15 DZ.
16	XA10587-E		REMOTE CONTROL UNIT	4.04 EA.
	XA8716		DRUM ONLY	.93 EA.
	XA9612-CRP		TOP FINGER UNIT	.33 EA.
	XA9612-BRP		BOTTOM FINGER UNIT	.33 EA.
17	XA11457		FIELD CLAMP ASSY. (OLD STYLE) NOT USED W/XA13B083-B MOTOR	.45 EA.
	PA13A034		FIELD CLAMP (NEW STYLE)	.34 EA.
	XA13A037		YOKE ASSY.	.26 EA.
17A	S-0		SCREW (OLD STYLE)	.01 EA.
	S165		SCREW USED W/NEW STYLE FIELD CLAMP	.03 EA.
18	P11000-R		BRUSH SPRING (RIGHT)	.03 EA.
	P11000-L		BRUSH SPRING (LEFT)	.03 EA.
19	S171		SCREW	.01 EA.
20	PA11684		BRUSH (NOT SOLD ASSEMBLED)	.32 EA.
	P10132		BRUSH HOLDER	.01 EA.
21	XA11454-RP		BRUSH BRACKET ASSY.	.14 EA.
22	PA11441		WORM COVER	.01 EA.
23	PA11453		BEARING STRAP	.02 EA.
24	XA11461		FIELD ASSY. NOT AVAILABLE	
		SUB.	W/XA13A036 FIELD ASSY.	1.34 EA.
25	XA11445		ARMATURE ASSY. NOT AVAILABLE	
		SUB.	W/XA14B873-RP ARMATURE	3.94 EA.
26	XA12B065-RP		TRUCK CHASSIS & WHEEL ASSY. NOT AVAILABLE	
		SUB.	W/XA12A074-RP TRUCK CHASSIS & W.ASSY	2.37 EA.
	PA11343		SOLID WHEEL (OLD STYLE)	.06 EA.
	PA14A888		SOLID WHEEL (NEW STYLE)	.08 EA.
	XA11473		INSULATED WHEEL (OLD STYLE)	.25 EA.

CON'T

DIA. NO.	PART NO.		DESCRIPTION	PRICE
	XA12A249		PUL-MOR WHEEL (OLD STYLE)	.72 EA.
	XA14A891		PUL-MOR WHEEL (NEW STYLE)	.28 EA.
	PA14A890		PUL-MOR	.05 EA.
	PA10005		AXLE NOT AVAILABLE	
		SUB.	W/PA15A226 AXLE	.05 EA.
	PA10006		AXLE NOT AVAILABLE	
		SUB.	W/PA15A281 AXLE	.07 EA.
	PA11447		WORM GEAR NOT AVAILABLE	
		SUB.	W/PA15A218 GEAR	.09 EA.
	PA11463		THRUST PLATE	.08 DZ.
27	XA11485-B		TRUCK SIDE & BOTTOM PLATE ASSY. NOT AVAILABLE (COUPLER END)	
		SUB.	W/XA13A804 T. S. & B. P. ASSY.	1.54 EA.
28	PA11652		4 CONDUCTOR CABLE NOT AVAILABLE	
		SUB.	W/PA13A208-A CABLE (PLASTIC)	.04 FT.
30	S326		SCREW NOT AVAILABLE	
31	PA11505		DRAW BAR NOT AVAILABLE	
32	XA11688-RP		"B" UNIT CABIN W/TRIM	6.28 EA.
33	N-1		NUT NOT USED W/ NEW STYLE SPEAKER	
34	PA11685		RESISTOR	.29 EA.
35	XA11710		SPEAKER NOT AVAILABLE	
		SUB.	W/XA14A127 SPEAKER	4.57 EA.
			PA14A216 BRACKET	.08 EA.
			S171 SCREW	.01 EA.
			S172 SCREW	.02 EA.
36	XA11687-RP		CHASSIS & BRACKET ASSY.	.59 EA.
37	XA10818-F		INSULATOR & TERMINAL ASSY. NOT USED W/ NEW STYLE SPEAKER	
38	XA11598-A		WHEEL & CHASSIS ASSY. NOT AVAILABLE	
		SUB.	W/XA14A930-B ASSY.	1.52 EA.
39	S334		SCREW NOT AVAILABLE	
40	XA11484		COUPLER ARM ASSY. NOT AVAILABLE	
41	PA11A991		CONDENSER NOT AVAILABLE	
		SUB.	W/PA14A914 CONDENSER	1.40 EA.
42	W83		WASHER	.04 EA.
43	W124		WASHER	.25 DZ.
44	PA11455		INSULATING BUSHING	.14 EA.
45	PA10818		BUS BAR NOT AVAILABLE	

LINK COUPLERS & TRUCKS NOT AVAILABLE, CONVERT TO KNUCKLE COUPLERS BY USING THE SUBSTITUTES.

PRICES SUBJECT TO CHANGE WITHOUT NOTICE.

GP-7 GM DIESEL ROAD SWITCHER
Model No. 370

SPECIFICATIONS

Tested at:	12 Volts A.C. .... using 160″ oval of track.
	Entire Train to run at a minimum of 8⅓ R.P.M. or 8⅓ times around 160″ oval of track in forward and reverse direction at 12 volts A.C.
Load:	Not to draw more than 2 amps while pulling 4 Box or Cattle Cars.
Motor:	Universal A.C. or D.C.

 Ref: Form No. M2900; Dec. 1, 1950

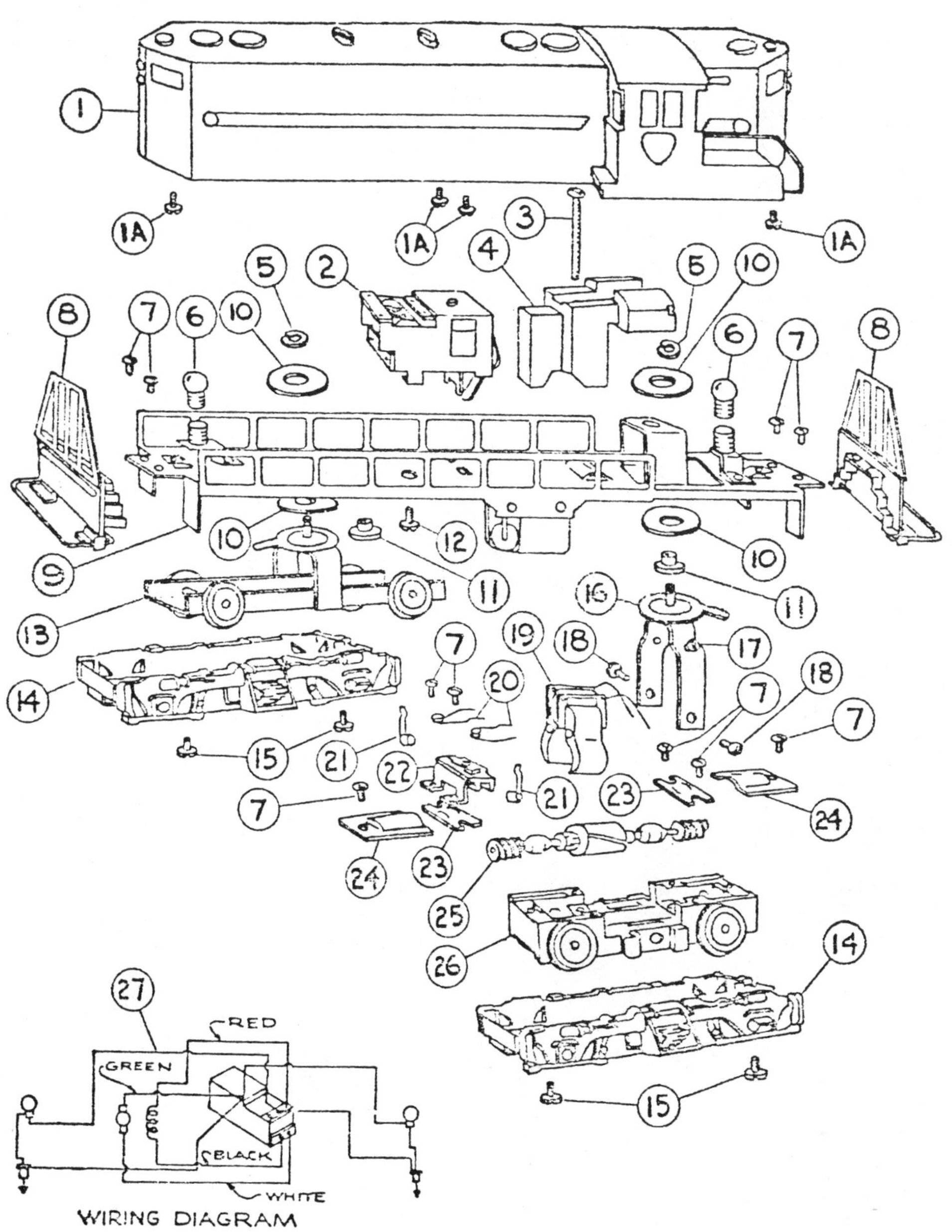
1
1A
1A
3
1A
4
5
2
5
10
8
7
6
10
6
7
8
10
12
10
9
11
11
16
13
19
18
17
7
14
20
18
7
7
15
21
22
21
23
24
7
24
23
25
26
14
27
RED
GREEN
BLACK
WHITE
15
WIRING DIAGRAM

Diagram Number	Part No.	Description	Price
1	*XA11384-BRP	Body Assembly with trimmings.......	$2.55 ea.
1A	S-183	Screw	.10 dz.
2	XA10587-E	Remote Control Unit..............	1.32 ea.
3	S-33	Screw	.01 "
4	PA11526	Weight	1.04 "
5	P10800-A	Retaining Ring	.04 "
6	PA8999	Bulb	.25 "
7	S171	Screw	.01 "
8	XA11511-RP	End Rail Assembly................	.68 "
9	XA11508-RP	Chassis Assembly with trimmings.....	1.29 "
10	PA8715	Washer	.09 dz.
11	PA11455	Fibre Bushing	.06 ea.
12	S230-B	Screw	.10 dz.
13	XA11598-A	Wheel and Chassis Assembly........	1.25 ea.
14	XA11422	Truck Side and Bottom Plate Assembly	.87 "
15	S249	Screw	.01 "
16	XA11457	Field Clamp Assembly.............	.41 "

All prices subject to change without notice.

 Ref: Form No. M2900; Dec. 1, 1950

Diagram Number	Part No.	Description	Price
17	S-0	Screw	$ .05 dz.
18	S230	Screw	.10 "
19	XA11461	Field Assembly	.79 ea.
20	P11000-R	Brush Spring (right)...............	.03 "
	P11000-L	Brush Spring (left)................	.03 "
21	XA11684	Brush Holder Assembly............	.25 "
22	XA11454	Brush Bracket Assembly............	.13 "
23	PA11453	Bearing Strap	.01 "
24	PA11441	Worm Cover	.01 "
25	XA11445	Armature Assembly	3.76 "
26	XA12B065-RP	Truck Chassis and Wheel Assembly..	2.21 "
	PA11448	Worm Gear	.15 "
	PA11447	Drive Gear	.20 "
	PA11343	Solid Wheel	.05 "
	XA11473	Insulated Wheel Assembly..........	.23 "
27	PA11652	4 Wire Conductor Cable...........	.18 ft.

*Note: XA11384-RP Body Assembly in aluminum finish not available.
Cabin listed above will be same as cabin on #372 Diesel Switcher.

SERVICE INSTRUCTIONS FOR No. 370 DIESEL SWITCHER

The first thing to do is to place Locomotive on track, connect transformer and test for operation.

1. **If the trouble is in the motor, we suggest that you check as follows:**

   a. Check brushes (※21) for wear or poor contact.

   b. Check brush springs (※20) for position and proper tension.

   c. Check wires and solder joints for loose connections.

   d. Commutator on Armature assembly (※25) may be dirty.

   e. Check operation of remote control unit (※2).

   f. See if motor is properly lubricated.

   g. Wheels and track must be kept clean to insure proper electrical contact.

2. **To Disassemble and Replace Parts on Motor Unit:**

   a. The first step is to remove the S183 Screws (※1A) and take off Cabin (※1).

   b. Motor is exposed and you can check wiring and other points of the unit.

   c. Brush holder assembly (※21) and brush springs (※20) can be replaced without taking motor unit from chassis (※9).

   d. When replacing brush holder assembly (※21), unsolder lead wire and remove tension from brush spring (※20).

   e. To replace brush springs (※20), remove brush holder assembly (※21) first so spring can be pulled forward and slipped out.

   f. When replacing armature (※25) or Magnet (※19) we recommend removing motor unit from chassis (※9) as follows:

      1. Unsolder lead wire to stud on field clamp assembly (※16).

      2. Take off retaining ring (※5) and fibre washers (※10).

   g. Remove S249 screws (※15) and take off truck side and bottom plate assembly (※14).

   h. Back off on the two S-0 screws (※17).

   i. Take out S230 screws and remove field clamp assembly (※16).

   j. Remove S171 screws and take off worm cover (※24) and bearing strap (※23).

NOTE: When reassembling motor it is necessary to adjust the two S-0 Screws (※17) on the field clamp assembly (※16) which centralizes the magnet assembly (※19). The reason is to prevent the armature assembly (※25) from striking the plates on the magnet assembly (※19).

When placing motor unit back in chassis (※9), the stop on the field clamp assembly (※16) must be facing outward so that the stop will always be parallel with the commutator on the armature assembly ※25).

 Ref: Form No. M2900; Dec. 1, 1950

Diagram Number	Part No.	Description	Price
1	XA11384-RP	Body Assembly with Trimmings	$2.85 ea.
1A	S183	Screw	.10 dz.
2	XA10587-E	Remote Control Unit	2.50 ea.
3	S-33	Screw	.01 "
4	PA11526	Weight	.94 "
5	P10800-A	Retaining Ring	.04 "
6	PA8999	Bulb	.25 "
7	S171	Screw	.10 dz.
8	XA11511-RP	End Rail Assembly	.61 ea.
9	XA11508-RP	Chassis Assembly with Trimmings	1.16 "
10	PA8715	Washer	.05 dz.
11	PA11455	Fibre Bushing	.05 ea.
12	S230-B	Screw	.10 dz.
13	XA11598-A	Wheel and Chassis Assembly	1.25 ea.
14	XA11422	Truck Side and Bottom Plate Assembly	.78 "

Diagram Number	Part No.	Description	Price
15	S249	Screw	$ .01 ea.
16	XA11457	Field Clamp Assembly	.37 "
17	S-0	Screw	.05 dz.
18	S230	Screw	.01 ea.
19	XA11461	Field Assembly	.71 "
20	P11000-R	Brush Spring (Right)	.03 "
	P11000-L	Brush Spring (Left)	.03 "
21	X10132	Brush Holder Assembly	.25 "
22	XA11421-RP	Brush Bracket Assembly	.20 "
23	PA11453	Bearing Strap	.01 "
24	PA11441	Worm Cover	.01 "
25	XA11445	Armature Assembly	3.39 "
26	XA11463-RP	Truck Chassis and Wheel Assembly	2.50 "
	PA11343	Solid Wheel	.10 "
	XA11473	Insulated Wheel Assembly	.34 "
27	PA11500	4 wire conductor cable	.21 "

DIAGRAM	PART NUMBER	DESCRIPTION	PRICE
1	XA11384-RP	Body Assembly with Trimmings	$ 2.85 ea.
1A	S183	Screw	.10 doz.
2	XA10587-E	Remote Control Unit	2.50 ea.
3	S-33	Screw	.01 "
4	PA11526	Weight	.94 "
5	P10800-A	Retaining Ring	.04 "
6	PA8999	Bulb	.25 "
7	S171	Screw	.10 doz.
8	XA11511-RP	End Rail Assembly	.61 ea.
9	XA11508-RP	Chassis Assembly with Trimmings	1.16 "
10	PA8715	Washer	.05 doz.
11	PA11455	Fibre Bushing	.05 ea.
12	S230-B	Screw	.10 doz.
13	XA11598-A	Wheel and Chassis Assembly	1.25 ea.
14	XA11422	Truck Side and Bottom Plate Assembly	.78 "
15	S249	Screw	.01 "
16	XA11457	Field Clamp Assembly	.37 "
17	S-0	Screw	.05 doz.
18	S230	Screw	.01 ea.
19	XA11461	Field Assembly	.71 "
20	P11000-R	Brush Spring (Right)	.03 "
	P11000-L	Brush Spring (Left)	.03 "
21	X10132	Brush Holder Assembly	.25 "
22	XA11421-RP	Brush Bracket Assembly	.20 "
23	PA11453	Bearing Strap	.01 "
24	PA11441	Worm Cover	.01 "
25	XA11445	Armature Assembly	3.39 "
26	XA11463-RP	Truck Chassis and Wheel Assembly	2.50 "
27	PA11500	4 wire conductor cable	.21 "

The Service Instructions for the #370 Diesel Switcher are the same as those for the #362 Santa Fe Diesel in respect to the Motor Unit Assembly.

* * * SPECIAL NOTICE * * *

The Service Instructions and Parts Price List on the #362 Santa Fe and the #370 Switcher are issued at this time as a temporary expedient and will be replaced at a later date with Illustrated Parts Lists and Diagrams.

GP-7 DIESEL ROAD SWITCHER
Model No. 371

SPECIFICATIONS

Tested at: 12 Volts A.C. .... using 160″ oval of track.
Entire Train to run at a minimum of 8⅓ R.P.M. or 8⅓ times around 160″ oval of track in forward and reverse directions at 12 volts A.C.

Load: Not to draw more than 2 amps while pulling 4 Box or Cattle Cars.

Motor: Universal A.C. or D.C.

 Ref: Form No. 1560; July 1, 1954

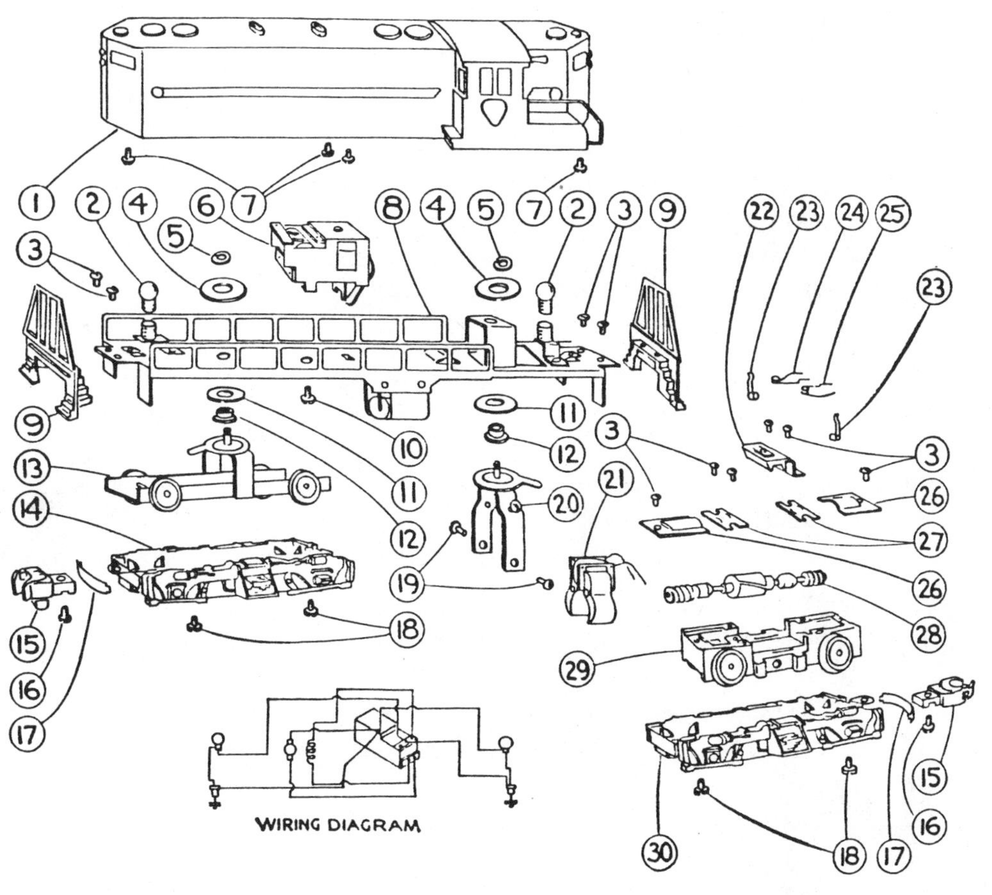
WIRING DIAGRAM

Diagram Number	Part No.	Description	Price
1	XA11384 RP	Cabin	$2.85 ea.
2	PA8999	Bulb	.25 "
3	S171	Screw	.01 "
4	W124	Washer	.01 "
5	P10800-A	Retaining Ring	.04 "
6	XA10587-E	Remote Control Unit	2.50 "
	XA9612-C	Top Finger Unit	.50 "
	XA9612-B	Bottom Finger Unit	.50 "
	XA8716	Drum Only	.60 "
7	S183	Screw	.10 dz.
8	XA11598-A	Chassis Assy	1.25 ea.
9	XA11B913 RP	End Rail Assy	.60 "
10	S230-B	Screw	.10 dz.
11	PA8715	Washer	.05 "
12	PA11455	Insulating Bushing	.05 ea.
13	XA11598-A	Wheel & Chassis Assy	1.25 "
14	XA11A901	Truck Plate & Collector Assy	.94 "
15	XA12A047	Knuckle Coupler	.22 ea.
16	S3A71	Coupler Screw	.01 "
17	PA12A355-A	Leaf Spring	.01 "
18	S249	Screws	.01 "
19	S230	Screw	.10 dz.
20	XA11457	Field Clamp Assy	.37 ea.
21	XA12A064	Magnet Assy	1.25 "
22	XA11421 RP	Brush Bracket Assy	.20 "
23	XA11684	Brush Holder Assy	.25 "
24	P11000-L	Brush Spring (left)	.03 "
25	P11000-R	Brush Spring (right)	.03 "
26	PA11441	Worm Cover	.01 "
27	PA11453	Bearing Strap	.01 "
28	XA12A062	Armature Assy	3.50 "
29	XA12C065 RP	Truck and Chassis Assy	1.94 "
30	XA12A668	Truck Plate & Collector Assy	.99 "

 Ref: Form No. 1560; July 1, 1954

Diagram Number	Part No.	Description	Price
1	XA11384 RP	Cabin	$2.85 ea.
2	PA8999	Bulb	.25 "
3	S171	Screw	.01 "
4	W124	Washer	.01 "
5	P10800-A	Retaining Ring	.04 "
6	XA10587-E	Remote Control Unit	2.50 "
	XA9612-C	Top Finger Unit	.50 "
	XA9612-B	Bottom Finger Unit	.50 "
	XA8716	Drum Only	.60 "
7	S183	Screw	.10 dz.
8	~~XA11598-A~~	Chassis Assy XA11508-RP	~~1.25~~ ea. 1.16
9	XA11B913 RP	End Rail Assy	.60 "
10	S230-B	Screw	.10 dz.
11	PA8715	Washer	.05 "
12	PA11455	Insulating Bushing	.05 ea.
13	XA11598-A	Wheel & Chassis Assy	1.25 "
14	XA11A901	Truck Plate & Collector Assy	.94 "
15	XA12A047	Knuckle Coupler	.22 ea.
16	S3A71	Coupler Screw	.01 "
17	PA12A355-A	Leaf Spring	.01 "
18	S249	Screws	.01 "
19	S230	Screw	.10 dz.
20	XA11457	Field Clamp Assy	.37 ea.
21	XA12A064	Magnet Assy	1.25 "
22	~~XA11421~~ RP	Brush Bracket Assy XA11454RP	~~.80~~ " 10
23	XA11684	Brush Holder Assy	.25 "
24	P11000-L	Brush Spring (left)	.03 "
25	P11000-R	Brush Spring (right)	.03 "
26	PA11441	Worm Cover	.01 "
27	PA11453	Bearing Strap	.01 "
28	XA12A062	Armature Assy	3.50 "
29	XA12C065 RP	Truck and Chassis Assy	1.94 "
30	~~XA12A668~~ XA13A041	Truck Plate & Collector Assy	~~.39~~ " 59

SERVICE INSTRUCTIONS FOR NO. 371 DIESEL SWITCHER

The first thing to do is to place Locomotive on track, connect transformer and test for operation.

1. If the trouble is in the Motor, we suggest that you check as follows:

a. Check Brushes (※23) for wear or poor contact.

b. Check Brush Springs, (※24) and (※25) for position and proper tension.

c. Check Wires and solder joints for loose connections.

d. Commutator on Armature assembly (※28) may be dirty.

e. Check operation of Remote Control Unit (※6).

f. See if motor is properly lubricated.

g. Wheels and Track must be kept clean to insure proper electrical contact.

2. To disassemble and replace parts on Motor Unit:

a. The first step is to remove the S183 Screws (※7) and take off Cabin (※1).

b. Motor is exposed and you can check wiring and other points of the unit.

c. Brush Holder assembly (※22) and Brush Springs (※24) and (※25) can be replaced without taking motor unit from Chassis, (※8).

d. When replacing Brush Holder assembly (※22) unsolder lead wire and remove tension from Brush Spring, (※24) and (※25).

e. To replace Brush Springs (※24) and (※25) remove Brush Holder Assembly (※22) first so Spring can be pulled forward and slipped out.

f. When replacing armature (※28) or Magnet (※21) we recommend removing motor unit from Chassis (※8) as follows:

1. Unsolder Lead Wire to Stud on Field Clamp assembly (※20).
2. Take off Retaining Ring (※5) and Fibre Washers (※11).

g. Remove ※S249 Screws (※18) and take off Truck Side and Bottom Plate assembly (※30).

h. Back off on the two S-0 Screws on the Clamp assembly.

i. Take out S230 Screws (※19) and remove Field Clamp Assembly (※20).

j. Remove S171 Screws (※3) and take off Worm Cover (※26) and Bearing Strap (※27).

NOTE: When reassembling Motor it is necessary to adjust the two S-0 Screws on the Field Clamp Assembly (※20) which centralizes the Magnet Assembly (※21). The reason is to prevent the Armature Assembly (※28) from striking the plates on the Magnet Assembly, (※21).

When placing motor unit back in Chassis (※8), the stop on the Field Clamp assembly (※20) must be facing outward so that the stop will always be parallel with the commutator on the armature assembly (※28).

GP-7 DIESEL ROAD SWITCHER
Model Nos. 371, 372, 21234, 21831, 21851

Although Model No. 21851 is included on Gilbert's specification sheets, this model does not appear in *Greenberg's Guide To American Flyer S Gauge*. It is not known what 21851 is.

SPECIFICATIONS

Tested at: 12 Volts A.C. .... using 160" oval of track.

(A) Diesel to pull 4 cars and run a minimum of 9 R.P.M. or 9 times forward or reverse around 160" oval of track.

Load: Not to draw more than 1.8 amps. while pulling 4 cars.

Motor: Universal A.C. or D.C.

Ref: Form No. 1768; Oct. 1, 1956

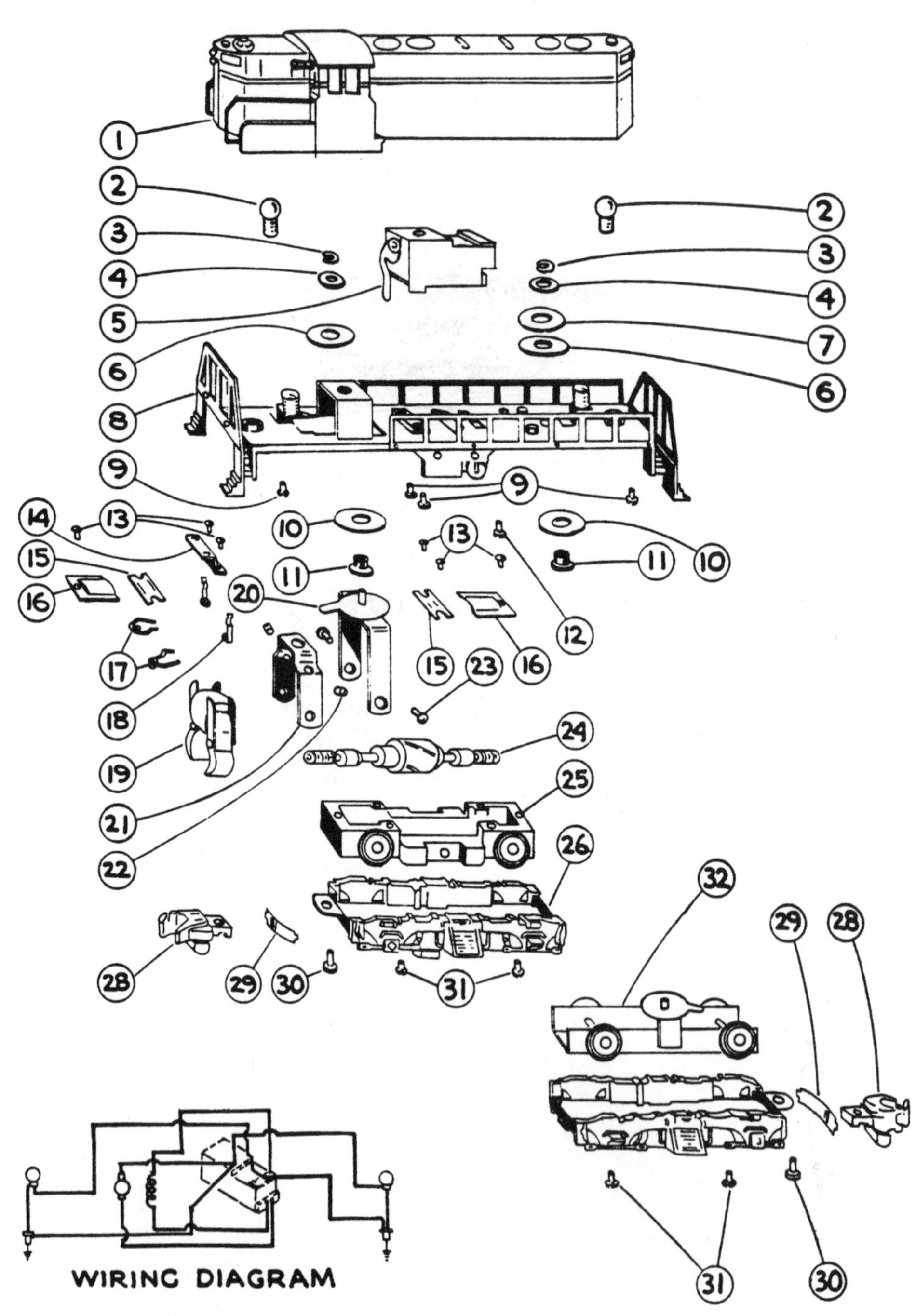

 Ref: Form No. 1768; Oct. 1, 1956

SERVICE INSTRUCTIONS FOR No. 372 UNION PACIFIC GP-7 DIESEL

The first thing to do is place unit on track, connect transformer and test for operation.

1. **If the trouble is in the motor, we suggest that you remove cabin and check as follows:**
   a. Check brushes (#18) for wear or poor contact.
   b. Check brush springs (#17) for position and proper tension.
   c. Check wires and solder joints for loose connections.
   d. Commutator on Armature assembly (#24) may be dirty.
   e. Check operation of remote control unit (#5).
   f. See if motor is properly lubricated.
   g. Wheels must be kept clean to insure proper electrical contact.

2. **To Disassemble and Replace Parts on Motor Unit:**
   a. Turn unit upside down; remove screws (#9) and take off cabin (#1).
   b. The next step is to take off Truck Assemblies (#26) by removing Screws (#31). To replace Knuckler Coupler (#28) remove Rivet (#30). Adjust the new coupler by placing diesel on the track, close the knuckle, so that the weight is all the way down; then either bend the coupler up or down, whichever is necessary to bring the bottom of the weight about 1/32" above the top of rails.
   c. Motor is exposed and you can check wiring and other points of the unit.
   d. Unsolder lead wire to Yoke Assembly (#20).
   e. Remove Tru-Arc ring (#3) along with washers (#4 & 6) and you can lift up Chassis then motor assembly will be free.
   f. When replacing mounting bracket (#14) unsolder lead wires and remove tension from brush springs (#17) taking out Brushes (#18) and remove two Screws (#13).
   g. To replace Armature (#24) or magnet (#19) it is necessary to back off on the two S-0 set Screws (#22) and remove two screws (#23). You can now take off Yoke Assy. (#20) and Field Clamp (#21). Remove Screws (#13) and take off bearing straps (#15) and Worm Covers (#16). Lift up Armature (#24) from chassis and take off magnet (#19).

3. **To Replace Remote Control Unit:**
   a. Unsolder lead wires.
   b. Remove Screw (#12).
   c. Lift up and slip unit out of slots in Chassis (#8).
   d. To change just fingers only, straighten out lugs on frame of Remote Control Unit. After wires have been unsoldered, replace defective part.

4. **To Replace Wheel & Chassis Assembly (#32):**
   a. Unsolder lead wire to truck.
   b. Remove tru-Arc Ring (#3) along with washers (#4, 6 & 7).

NOTE: When reassembling motor it isnecessary to adjust the two S. O. Set Screws on the Field Clamp (#21), which centralizes the Magnet Assy., (#19). The reason is to prevent the Armature Assy. (#24) from striking the plates on the magnet.

When placing motor unit back in chassis (#8), the stop on the Yoke Assy (#20) must be facing outward so that the stop will always be parallel with the commutator on the Armature Assy. (#24).

PARTS AND PRICE LIST

Diagram Number	Part No.	Description	Price
1.	XA11384-BRP	Body	2.64 ea.
2.	PA8999	Bulb	.25 ea.
3.	P10800-A	Tru-arc Ring	.04 ea.
4.	W83	Washer	.03 ea.
5.	XA10587-E	Remote Control Unit	1.32 ea.
6.	W124	Washer	.01 ea.
7.	W126	Steel Washer	.05 dz.
8.	XA14A094-A	Chassis & Lamp Bracket Assy.	2.38 ea.
9.	S4N30	Screw	.01 ea.
10.	PA8715	Fibre Washer	.09 dz.
11.	PA11455	Fibre Bushing	.06 ea.
12.	S230B	Screw	.10 dz.
13.	S171	Screw	.01 ea.
14.	XA11454-RP	Mounting Bracket	.13 ea.
15.	PA11453	Bearing Strap	.01 ea.
16.	PA11441	Worm Cover	.01 ea.
17.	P11000-R & L	Brush Springs (left & right)	.03 ea.
18.	XA11684	Brush	.25 ea.
19.	XA13A036	Field Assy.	.85 ea.
20.	XA13A037	Yoke Assy.	.24 ea.
21.	PA13A034	Field Clamp	.24 ea.
22.	S165	Set Screw	.02 ea.
23.	S4A06	Screw	.01 ea.
24.	XA12A062	Armature	3.67 ea.
25.	XA12A074-RP	Truck Chassis	2.15 ea.
26.	XA13A809-B	Truck	.74 ea.
27.	XA13A810-B	Truck & Coupler Assy. (parts 26, 28-30)	1.07 ea.
28.	XA12A047	Coupler Assy.	~~.22 ea.~~ $.29
29.	PA12A355-A	Leaf Spring	.01 ea.
30.	PA13A791	Tubular Rivet	.01 ea.
31.	S249	Screw	.01 ea.
32.	XA11598-A	Wheel & Chassis Assy.	1.25 ea.

All prices subject to change without notice.

PARTS LIST

21851 GP-7 DIESEL LOCOMOTIVE WITH BELL

PART NO.	DESCRIPTION	PCS/ UNIT	COST
XA-13B038-B	PUL-MOR MOTOR ASSEMBLY	1	12.16 EA.
XA-15B157-JRP	BODY ASSY W/TRIM	1	4.45 EA.
PA-11518	HEADLIGHT LENS	4	.02 EA.
PA-8999	14V. CLEAR LAMP	2	.36 EA.
PA-11512	HORN (DECORATION)	2	.04 EA.
XA-15A154-C	CHASSIS & LAMP SOCKET ASSY	1	3.31 EA.
S-4N30	#2 x ½" TYPE "Z" P.K. SCREW (SECURES BODY TO CHASSIS)	4	.12 DOZ.
PA-15A447	TENSION SPRING	1	.07 EA.
XA-15A441	SPRING & BRACKET ASSY	1	.37 EA.
XA-15A445	YOKE & STRUCK-UP CHASSIS ASSY	1	.85 EA.
PA-15A449	PIN (SECURES XA15A441 SPRING & BRKT. ASSY)	1	.03 EA.
PA-10190-0	2-½" LONG SLEEVING	1	.15 FT.
LW-1B1	BLACK LEAD WIRE		.02 FT.
PA-15A226	AXLE SHAFT (REAR TRUCK)	2	.05 EA.
PA-15A446	CAM (REAR TRUCK)	1	.04 EA.
PA-14B888	SOLID WHEEL (REAR TRUCK LEFT SIDE)	2	.10 EA.
XA-13A810	TRUCK & COUPLER ASSY	2	1.65 EA.
PA-13A791	TUBULAR RIVET (TRUCK)	2	.02 EA.
PA-12A355-A	LEAF SPRING (FOR COUPLER)	2	.01 EA.
XA-12A047	KNUCKLE COUPLER ASSY	2	.31 EA.
XA-13A809	TRUCK ASSY	2	1.17 EA.
PA-11533	COLLECTOR SPRING (PICK UP)	2	.02 EA.
PA-11677-A	SHOE (TRACK)	2	.07 EA.
-249	#2 x 5/16 TYPE "Z" C'SINK F.H.P.K. SCREW (SECURES REAR TRUCK SIDE)	2	.15 DOZ.
P-10800-A	TRU-ARC RETAINING RING	2	.25 DOZ.
W-2A28	.191 DIA.HOLE COPPER PLATED SPRING WASHER (REAR PIVOT)	1	.25 DOZ.
PA-11455	FIBER BUSHING (PIVOT)	2	.14 EA.
W-124-B	¼" DIA.HOLE 1/32 THK.STEEL WASHER (REAR PIVOT)	1	.25 DOZ.
XA-14A870	INSULATED WHEEL ASSY (REAR TRUCK RIGHT SIDE)	2	.19 EA.
W-124-A	¼" DIA. HOLE 1/16 THK.STEEL WASHER (REAR PIVOT)	1	.35 DOZ.
S-5N40	#2-56 x ¼" LG.TYPE "F" SELF TAPPING FLAT HD. SCREW (SECURES FRONT TRUCK SIDE)	2	.12 DOZ
XA-15A444	BELL & BRACKET ASSY	1	.18 EA.
PA-5602	TUBULAR RIVET (SECURES BELL & BRKT. TO CHASSIS)	1	.01 EA.
XA-14C429	2 POSITION REMOTE CONTROL UNIT	1	2.69 EA.
S-172	#4 x 3/16 TYPE "Z" BD.HD.P.K. SCREW (SECURES R/C UNIT TO CHASSIS)	2	.15 DOZ.
W-124-C	¼" DIA.HOLE 1/32 THK.BLACK FIBER WASHER (FRONT PIVOT)	1	.12 DOZ.
W-124	¼" DIA.HOLE 1/16 THK.BLACK FIBER WASHER (FRONT PIVOT)	1	.25 DOZ.
W-83	.161 DIA.HOLE STEEL WASHER (FRONT PIVOT)	1	.50 DOZ.

21234 C & O DIESEL LOCOMOTIVE WITH BELL

SAME AS 21851 DIESEL LOCOMOTIVE-
EXCEPT ELIMINATE THE FOLLOWING:

PART NO.	DESCRIPTION	PCS/ UNIT
PA-10190-0	2-½" LG. SLEEVING	1
XA-15A154-C	CHASSIS & LAMP SOCKET ASSY	1

Ref: Feb. 1959

PARTS LIST

21234 C & O DIESEL LOCO W/BELL - (CONT'D.)

-15B157-JRP	BODY ASSEMBLY	1	
PA-11512	HORN (DECORATION)	2	

ADD THE FOLLOWING PARTS:

XA-15A154-D	CHASSIS & LAMP SOCKET ASSY	1	3.47 EA.
XA-11B384-KRP	BODY WITH TRIM	1	3.25 EA.
PA-11512-A	HORN (DECORATION)	2	.04 EA.

21831 T & P DIESEL SWITCHER

SAME AS 21851 DIESEL -
EXCEPT ELIMINATE THE FOLLOWING:

PA-10190-0	SLEEVING - 2-½" LONG	1	
XA-15A444	BELL & BRACKET ASSY	1	
PA-5602	TUBULAR RIVET	1	
XA-15A445	YOKE & STRUCK UP CHASSIS ASSY	1	
XA-15A441	SPRING & BRACKET ASSY	1	
PA-15A449	PIN	1	
PA-15A446	CAM	1	
XA-15B157-JRP	CABIN W/TRIM	1	
PA-15A447	TENSION SPRING	1	
XA-15A154-C	CHASSIS & LAMP SOCKET ASSY	1	

ADD THE FOLLOWING PARTS:

XA-14A930-A	WHEEL & STRUCK UP CHASSIS ASSY	1	1.60 EA.
XA-15A154-A	CHASSIS & LAMP SOCKET ASSY	1	3.49 EA.
XA-15B157-RP	CABIN W/TRIM	1	4.45 EA.

21821 U.P. DIESEL SWITCHER

SAME AS 21831 -
EXCEPT ELIMINATE THE FOLLOWING:

XA-15B157-RP	BODY ASSY	1	
XA-13A810	TRUCK & COUPLER ASSY	1	
XA-13A809	TRUCK ASSY	1	
XA-15A154-A	CHASSIS & LAMP BRACKET ASSY	1	

ADD THE FOLLOWING PARTS:

XA-11C384-HRP	BODY WITH TRIM	1	4.59 EA.
XA-13A810-B	TRUCK & COUPLER ASSY	1	1.58 EA.
XA-13A809-B	TRUCK ASSY	1	1.12 EA.
XA-15A154	CHASSIS & LAMP BRKT. ASSY	1	3.49 EA.

NOTE: PRICES SUBJECT TO CHANGE WITHOUT NOTICE.

#372 U.P. DIESEL PARTS LIST

DIA. NO.	PART NO.	DESCRIPTION	PRICE
1	XA11384-BRP	Body	2.90 ea.
2	PA8999	Bulb	.30 ea.
3	P10800-A	Tru-arc Ring	.25 dz.
4	W83	Washer	.04 ea.
5	XA10587-E	Remote Control Unit	4.04 ea.
	XA8716	Drum	.95 ea.
	XA9612-BRP	Bottom Finger Unit	.33 ea.
	XA9612-CRP	Top Finger Unit	.33 ea.
6	W124	Washer	.25 dz.
7	W126	Steel Washer	.06 dz.
8	XA14A094-A	Chassis & Lamp Bracket Assembly	2.62 ea.
	XA11B913-RP	End Rail	.74 ea.
9	S4N30	Screw	.01 ea.
10	PA8715	Fibre Washer	.10 dz.
11	PA11455	Fibre Bushing	.14 ea.
12	S230B	Screw	.01 ea.
13	S171	Screw	.01 ea.
14	XA11454-RP	Mounting Bracket	.14 ea.
15	PA11453	Bearing Strap	.02 ea.
16	PA11441	Worm Cover	.01 ea.
17	P11000-R & L	Brush Springs (left & right)	.03 ea.
18	PA11684	Brush (not sold assembled)	.32 ea.
	P10132	Brush Holder	.01 ea.
19	XA13A036	Field Assembly	1.34 ea.
20	XA13A037	Yoke Assembly	.26 ea.
21	PA13A034	Field Clamp	.34 ea.
22	S165	Set Screw	.03 ea.
23	S4A06	Screw	.03 ea.
24	XA14B873-RP	Armature	3.94 ea.
25	XA12A074-RP	Truck Chassis	2.37 ea.
	XA14A891	Pul-Mor Wheel Assembly	.28 ea.
	PA14A890	Pul-Mor	.05 ea.
	PA14B888	Solid Wheel	.08 ea.
	PA15A281	Axle	.07 ea.
	PA15A218	Worm Gear	.09 ea.
	PA11463	Thrust Plate	.08 dz.
26	XA13A809-B	Truck	1.12 ea.
	XA13A810-B	Truck & Coupler Assy. (parts 26,28,29,30)	1.58 ea.
28	XA12A047	Coupler Assembly	.29 ea.
29	PA12A355-A	Leaf Spring	.02 ea.
30	PA13A791	Tubular Rivet	.02 ea.
31	S249	Screw	.15 dz.
32	XA11598-A	Wheel & Chassis Assembly NOT AVAILABLE	
		Sub. with XA14A930-A Assembly	1.60 ea.
		NOT SHOWN	
	XA13B038-B	Motor Assembly	12.16 ea.
	PA13A208-A	4 Conductor Cable (plastic)	.04 ft.

Prices subject to change without notice

Ref: Form No. 1768, June 1, 1960

#21234 C & O DIESEL

DIA. NO.	PART NO.	DESCRIPTION	PRICE
1	XA11384-KRP	Body	3.25 ea.
2	PA8999	Bulb	.30 ea.
3	P10800-A	Tru-arc Ring	.25 dz.
4	W83	Washer (motor end)	.04 ea.
	W2A28	Spring Washer	.25 dz.
5	XA14C429	Remote Control Unit	2.76 ea.
	XA14A994	Contact Assembly	.77 ea.
	XA14A435	Plunger Assembly	.14 ea.
	XA14B433	Coil Assembly	.69 ea.
	PA14A444	Coil Support	.05 ea.
	PA14C432	Coil Housing	.04 ea.
6	W124	Washer (motor end)	.25 dz.
	W124A	Steel Washer	.35 dz.
7		NOT USED	
8	XA15A154-D	Chassis & Lamp Bracket Assembly	3.47 ea.
9	S4N30	Screw	.01 ea.
10	W124C	Fibre Washer (motor end)	.12 dz.
	W124B	Steel Washer	.35 dz.
11	PA11455	Fibre Bushing	.14 ea.
12	S172	Screw	.02 ea.
13	S171	Screw	.01 ea.
14	XA11454-RP	Mounting Bracket	.14 ea.
15	PA11453	Bearing Strap	.02 ea.
16	PA11441	Worm Cover	.01 ea.
17	P11000-R & L	Brush Springs (left & right)	.03 ea.
18	PA11684	Brush (not sold assembled)	.32 ea.
	P10132	Brush Holder (not sold assembled)	.01 ea.
19	XA13A036	Field Assembly	1.34 ea.
20	XA13A037	Yoke Assembly	.26 ea.
21	PA13A034	Field Clamp	.34 ea.
22	S165	Set Screw	.03 ea.
23	S4A06	Screw	.03 ea.
24	XA14B873-RP	Armature	3.94 ea.
25	XA12A074-RP	Truck Chassis	2.37 ea.
	XA14A891	Pul-Mor Wheel Assembly	.28 ea.
	PA14A890	Pul-Mor	.05 ea.
	PA14B888	Solid Wheel	.08 ea.
	PA15A281	Axle	.07 ea.
	PA15A218	Worm Gear	.09 ea.
	PA11463	Thrust Plate	.08 dz.
26	XA13A809-A	Truck	1.13 ea.
	XA13A810-A	Truck & Coupler Assy. (parts 26,28,29,30)	1.60 ea.
28	XA12A047	Coupler Assembly	.29 ea.
29	PA12A355-A	Leaf Spring	.02 ea.
30	PA13A791	Tubular Rivet	.02 ea.
31	S249	Screw	.15 dz.
32	XA15A445	Yoke, Wheel & Chassis Assembly	.85 ea.
	PA15A446	Cam (not shown)	.04 ea.
	XA14A870	Insulated Wheel	.18 ea.
	PA14B888	Solid Wheel	.08 ea.
	PA15A225	Axle (worm)	.06 ea.
	PA15A226	Axle (plain)	.05 ea.

 Ref: Form No. 1768; June 1, 1960

DIA. NO.	PART NO.	DESCRIPTION	PRICE
		NOT SHOWN	
	XA13B038-B	Motor Complete	12.16 ea.
	XA15A441	Spring & Bracket Assembly	.37 ea.
	XA15A444	Bell & Bracket	.18 ea.
	PA15A447	Tension Spring	.07 ea.
	PA15A449	Pin (secures XA15A441 Spring & Brkt. Assembly)	.03 ea.

Prices subject to change without notice.

#21831 T & P DIESEL

DIA. NO.	PART NO.	DESCRIPTION	PRICE
1	XA15B157-RP	Body	4.45 ea.
2	PA8999	Bulb	.30 ea.
3	P10800-A	Tru-arc Ring	.25 dz.
4	W83	Washer (motor end)	.04 ea.
	W2A28	Spring Washer	.25 dz.
5	XA14C429	Remote Control Unit	2.76 ea.
	XA14A994	Contact Assembly	.77 ea.
	XA14A435	Plunger Assembly	.14 ea.
	XA14B433	Coil Assembly	.69 ea.
	PA14A444	Coil Support	.05 ea.
	PA14C432	Coil Housing	.04 ea.
6	W124	Washer (motor end)	.25 dz.
	W124A	Steel Washer	.35 dz.
7		NOT USED	
8	XA15A154-A	Chassis & Lamp Bracket Assembly	3.49 ea.
9	S4N30	Screw	.01 ea.
10	W124C	Fibre Washer (motor end)	.12 dz.
	W124B	Steel Washer	.35 dz.
11	PA11455	Fibre Bushing	.14 ea.
12	S172	Screw (used on R. Control)	.02 ea.
13	S171	Screw	.01 ea.
14	XA11454-RP	Mounting Bracket	.14 ea.
15	PA11453	Bearing Strap	.02 ea.
16	PA11441	Worm Cover	.01 ea.
17	P11000-R & L	Brush Springs (left & right)	.03 ea.
18	PA11684	Brush (not sold assembled)	.32 ea.
	P10132	Brush Holder (not sold assembled)	.01 ea.
19	XA13A036	Field Assembly	1.34 ea.
20	XA13A037	Yoke Assembly	.26 ea.
21	PA13A034	Field Clamp	.34 ea.
22	S165	Set Screw	.03 ea.
23	S4A06	Screw	.03 ea.
24	XA14B873-RP	Armature	3.94 ea.
25	XA12A074-RP	Truck Chassis	2.37 ea.
	XA14A891	Pul-Mor Wheel Assembly	.28 ea.
	PA14A890	Pul-Mor	.05 ea.
	PA14B888	Solid Wheel	.08 ea.
	PA15A281	Axle	.07 ea.
	PA15A218	Worm Gear	.09 ea.
	PA11463	Thrust Plate	.08 dz.
26	XA13A809	Truck	1.17 ea.
	XA13A810	Truck & Coupler Assy. (parts 26,28,29,30)	1.65 ea.
28	XA12A047	Coupler Assembly	.29 ea.
29	PA12A355-A	Leaf Spring	.02 ea.
30	PA13A791	Tubular Rivet	.02 ea.
31	S249	Screw	.15 dz.
32	XA14A930-A	Wheel & Chassis Assembly	1.60 ea.
		NOT SHOWN	
	XA13B038-B	Motor Complete	12.16 ea.
	LW-1B1	Black Lead Wire	.02 ft.

Prices subject to change without notice

 Ref: Form No. 1768; June 1, 1960

#371 & 372 U. P. DIESEL PARTS LIST

#370 - PARTS OBSOIETE

DIA. NO.	PART NO.	DESCRIPTION	PRICE
1	XA11384-BRP	Body	3.05 ea.
2	PA8999	Bulb	.32 ea.
3	P10800-A	Tru-arc Ring	.26 dz.
4	W83	Washer	.04 ea.
5	XA10587-E	Remote Control Unit	4.24 ea.
	XA8716	Drum	1.00 ea.
	XA9612-BRP	Bottom Finger Unit	.35 ea.
	XA9612-CRP	Top Finger Unit	.35 ea.
6	W124	Washer	.26 dz.
7	W126	Steel Washer	.06 dz.
8	XA14A094-A	Chassis & Lamp Bracket Assembly	2.75 ea.
	XA11B913-RP	End Rail	.78 ea.
9	S4N30	Screw	.01 ea.
10	PA8715	Fibre Washer	.11 dz.
11	PA11455	Fibre Bushing	.15 ea.
12	S230B	Screw	.01 ea.
13	S171	Screw	.01 ea.
14	XA11454-RP	Mounting Bracket	.15 ea.
15	PA11453	Bearing Strap	.02 ea.
16	PA11441	Worm Cover	.01 ea.
17	P11000 R & L	Brush Springs (Left & Right)	.03 ea.
18	PA11684	Brush	.34 ea.
	P10132	Brush Holder	.01 ea.
19	XA13A036	Field Assembly	1.41 ea.
20	XA13A037	Yoke Assembly	.27 ea.
21	PA13A034	Field Clamp	.36 ea.
22	S165	Set Screw	.03 ea.
23	S4A06	Screw	.03 ea.
24	XA14B873-RP	Armature	4.14 ea.
25	XA12A074-RP	Truck Chassis	2.49 ea.
	XA14A891	Pul-Mor Wheel Assembly	.29 ea.
	PA14A890	Pul-Mor	.05 ea.
	PA14B888	Solid Wheel	.08 ea.
	PA15A281	Axle	.07 ea.
	PA15A218	Worm Gear	.09 ea.
	PA11463	Thrust Plate	.08 dz.
26	XA13A809-B	Truck	1.18 ea.
	XA13A810-B	Truck & Coupler Assy. (Parts 26-28-29-30)	1.66 ea.
28	XA12A047	Coupler Assembly	.30 ea.
29	PA12A355-A	Leaf Spring	.02 ea.
30	PA13A791	Tubular Rivet	.02 ea.
31	S249	Screw	.16 dz.
32	XA14A930-A	Wheel & Chassis Assembly	1.68 ea.
		NOT SHOWN	
	XA13B038-B	Motor Assembly	12.77 ea.
	PA13A208-A	4 Conductor Cable (Plastic)	.04 ft.

Prices subject to change without notice.

Ref: Form No. 1768; Oct. 1, 1962

#21234 C & O AND #21831 T & P DIESELS

DIA. NO.	PART NO.	DESCRIPTION	PRICE
1	XA11334-KRP	Body (21234)	3.41 ea.
	XA15B157-RP	Body (21831)	4.67 ea.
2	PA8999	Bulb	.32 ea.
3	P10800-A	Tru-Arc Ring	.26 dz.
4	W83	Washer (Motor End)	.04 ea.
	W2A28	Spring Washer	.26 dz.
5		NOT USED	
	XA14C429	Remote Control Unit(in loco NOT SHOWN)	2.90 ea.
	XA14A994	Contact Assembly	.81 ea.
	XA14A435	Plunger Assembly	.15 ea.
	XA14B433	Coil Assembly	.72 ea.
	PA14A444	Coil Support	.05 ea.
	PA14C432	Coil Housing	.04 ea.
6	W124	Washer (Motor End)	.26 dz.
	W124A	Steel Washer	.37 dz.
7		NOT USED	
8	XA15A154-D	Chassis & Lamp Brkt. Assy. (21234)	3.64 ea.
	XA15A154-A	Chassis & Lamp Brkt. Assy. (21831)	3.66 ea.
9	S4N30	Screw	.01 ea.
10	W124C	Fibre Washer (Motor End)	.13 dz.
	W124B	Steel Washer	.37 dz.
11	PA11455	Fibre Bushing	.15 ea.
12	S172	Screw	.02 ea.
13	S171	Screw	.01 ea.
14	XA11454-RP	Mounting Bracket	.15 ea.
15	PA11453	Bearing Strap	.02 ea.
16	PA11441	Worm Cover	.01 ea.
17	P11000 R & L	Brush Springs (Left & Right)	.03 ea.
18	PA11684	Brush	.34 ea.
	P10132	Brush Holder	.01 ea.
19	XA13A036	Field Assembly	1.41 ea.
20	XA13A037	Yoke Assembly	.27 ea.
21	PA13A034	Field Clamp	.36 ea.
22	S165	Set Screw	.03 ea.
23	S4A06	Screw	.03 ea.
24	XA14B873-RP	Armature	4.14 ea.
25	XA12A074-RP	Truck Chassis	2.49 ea.
	XA14A891	Pul-Mor Wheel Assembly	.29 ea.
	PA14A890	Pul-Mor	.05 ea.
	PA14B888	Solid Wheel	.08 ea.
	PA15A281	Axle	.07 ea.
	PA15A218	Worm Gear	.09 ea.
	PA11463	Thrust Plate	.08 dz.
26	XA13A809-A	Truck (21234)	1.19 ea.
	XA13A809	Truck (21831)	1.23 ea.
	XA13A810-A	Truck & Coupler Assy. (21234) (parts 26-28-29-30)	1.68 ea.
	XA13A810	Truck & Coupler Assy. (21831) (parts 26-28-29-30)	1.73 ea.

Cont'd

Ref: Form No. 1768; Oct. 1, 1962

DIA.NO.	PART NO.	DESCRIPTION	PRICE
28	XA12A047	Coupler Assembly	.30 ea.
29	PA12A355-A	Leaf Spring	.02 ea.
30	PA13A791	Tubular Rivet	.02 ea.
31	S249	Screw	.16 dz.
32	XA15A445	Yoke, Wheel & Chassis Assy. (21234)	.89 ea.
	PA15A446	Cam (NOT SHOWN)	.04 ea.
	XA14A870	Insulated Wheel	.19 ea.
	PA14B888	Solid Wheel	.08 ea.
	PA15A225	Axle (Worm)	.06 ea.
	PA15A226	Axle (Plain	.05 ea.
	XA14A930-A	Wheel & Chassis Assy. (21831)	1.68 ea.

NOT SHOWN

PART NO.	DESCRIPTION	PRICE
XA13B038-B	Motor Complete	12.77 ea.
XA15A441	Spring & Bracket Assy. (21234)	.39 ea.
XA15A444	Bell & Bracket (21234)	.19 ea.
PA15A447	Tension Spring (21234)	.07 ea.
PA15A449	Pin (Secures XA15A441 Spring & Bracket Assembly 21234)	.03 ea.

Prices subject to change without notice

GP-7 TWIN UNIT DIESEL WITH AIR CHIME HORN

Model Nos. 374/375, 377/378

SPECIFICATIONS

Tested at: 12 Volts A.C. .... using 160" oval of track.
(A) Locomotive to run a minimum of 9 R.P.M. or 9 Times forward and reverse, around 160" oval of track.

Load: Not to draw more than 2.5 amps. while pulling 4 Box Cars.

Motor: Universal A.C. or D.C.

 Ref: Form No. 1600; Feb. 15, 1955

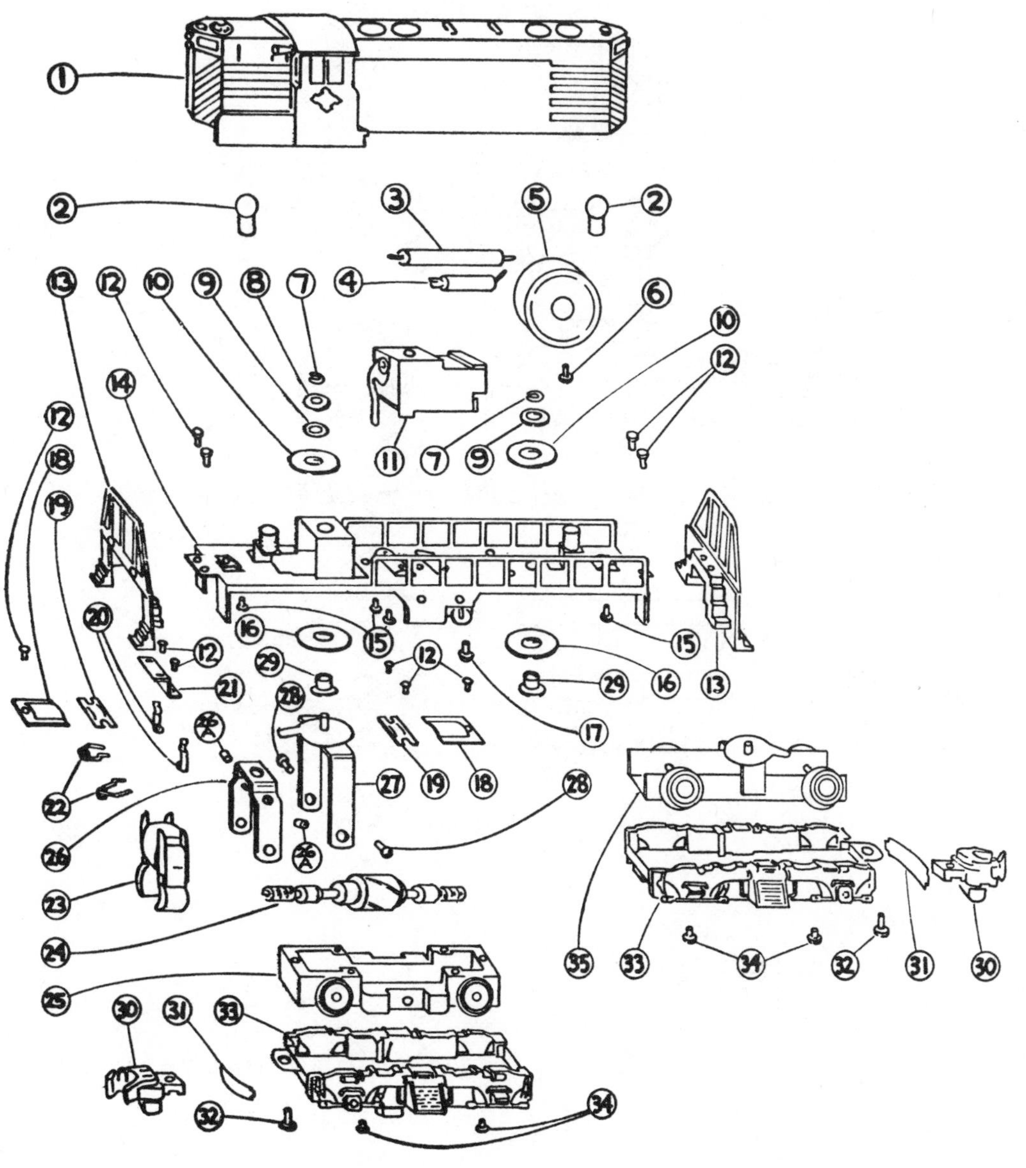
1
2
3
5
2
13
12
10
9
8
7
4
6
10
12
14
11
7
9
12
18
19
16
15
15
20
12
29
12
16
13
21
28
26A
17
22
27
19
18
28
26
26A
23
24
35
33
34
32
31
30
25
30
31
33
32
34

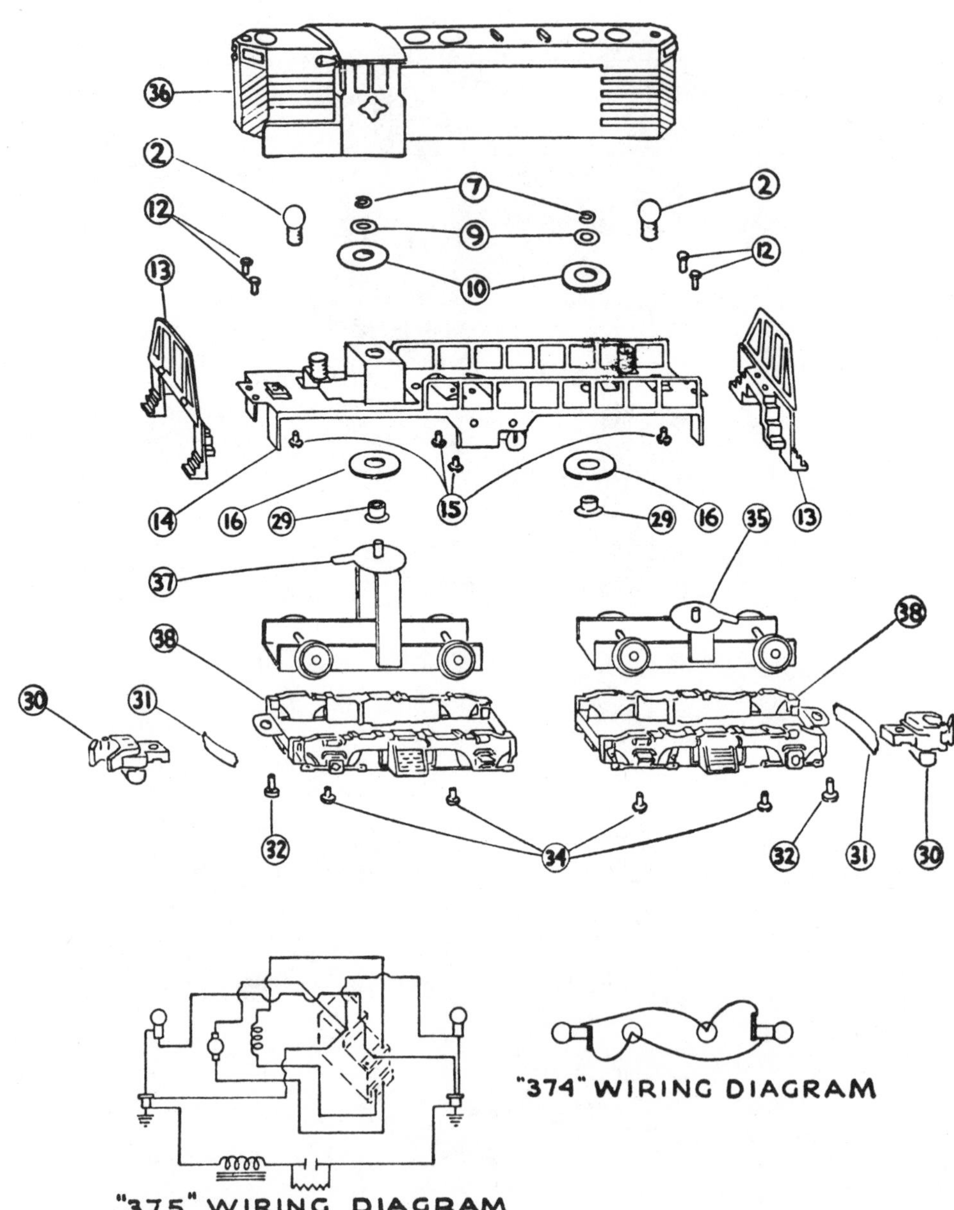

 Ref: Form No. 1600; Feb. 15, 1955

Diagram Number	Part No.	Description	Price
1	*XA11384 ARP	Cabin (375)	$2.85 ea.
2	PA8999	Bulb	.25 "
3	PA11685	Resistor	.26 "
4	PA11A991	Condenser	1.00 "
5	XA12B144	Whistle Ass'y.	6.18 "
6	S322	Screw	.02 "
7	P10800-A	Retaining Ring	.04 "
8	W83	Washer	.30 dz.
9	W143	Washer	.05 "
10	W124	Washer	.01 "
11	XA10587-E	Remote Control Unit	2.50 ea.
	XA9612-C	Top Finger Unit	.50 "
	XA9612-B	Bottom Finger Unit	.50 "
	XA8716	Drum only	.60 "
12	S171	Screw	.01 "
13	XA11B913 RP	End Rail Assy.	.60 "
14	XA12B418	Chassis Assy.	3.05
15	S183	Screw	.10 dz.
16	PA8715	Washer	.05 "
17	S230-B	Screw	.10 "
		Motor Assy (not sold as a complete assy)	
18	PA11441	Worm Cover	.01 ea.
19	PA11453	Bearing Strap	.01 "
20	XA11684	Brush Holder Assy.	.25 "

*Note: When ordering cabins specify either #375 or #374, whichever is needed.

Diagram Number	Part No.	Description	Price
21	XA11421 RP	Brush Bracket Assy.	.20 ea.
22	P11000-L or R	Brush Spring (left or right)	.03 "
23	XA13A036	Magnet Assy.	.77 "
24	XA12A062	Armature Assy.	3.50 "
25	XA12C065 RP	Wheel & Chassis Assy.	1.94 "
	XA12A249	Pull-Mor Wheel Assy.	.65 "
	PA11343	Solid Wheel	.10 "
	XA11473	Insulated Wheel	.34 "
	PA10006	Gear Axle	.10 "
26	PA13A034	Field Clamp	.22 "
26A	S165	Set Screw	.02 "
27	XA13A037	Yoke Ass'y.	.18 "
28	S4A06	Screw	.01 "
29	PA11445	Fibre Bushing	.05 "
30	XA12A047	Knuckle Coupler	.22 "
31	PA12A355-A	Leaf Spring	.01 "
32	S3A71	Coupler Screw	.01 "
33	XA13A041	Truck & Collector Assy.	1.22 "
34	S249	Screw	.01 "
35	XA11598-A	Wheel & Chassis Assy.	1.25 "
36	*XA11384-ARP	Cabin (374)	2.85 "
37	XA11596-A	Wheel & Chassis Assy.	1.25 "
38	XA11A901-A	Truck Assy.	.94 "

SERVICE INSTRUCTIONS FOR NO. 3745 GP-7 TWIN UNIT DIESEL

The first thing to do is to place Locomotive on Track, connect Transformer and Whistle Control Unit, and test for operation.

1. **If the trouble is in the motor in the "375" Unit, we suggest that you check as follows:**
   a. Check Brushes (※20) for wear or poor contact.
   b. Check Brush Springs (※22) for position and proper tension.
   c. Check wires and soldered joints for loose connections.
   d. Commutator on Armature Assembly (※24) may be dirty.
   e. Check operation of Remote Control Unit (※11).
   f. See if motor is properly lubricated.
   g. Wheels and Track must be kept clean to insure proper electrical contact.

2. **To disassemble and replace parts on "375" Motor Unit.**
   a. The first step is to remove the S319 Screws (※15) and take off Cabin (※1).
   b. Motor is exposed and you can check wiring and other points of the unit.
   c. Brush Holder Assembly (※20) and Brush Springs (※22) can be replaced without taking Motor Unit from Chassis (※14).
   d. When replacing Brush Holder Assembly (※20) unsolder lead wire and remove tension from Brush Springs (※22).
   e. To replace Brush Springs (※22) remove Brush Holder Assembly (※20) first so spring can be pulled forward and slipped out.
   f. When replacing Armature (※24) or Magnet (※23) we recommend removing Motor Unit from Chassis (※14) as follows:
      1. Unsolder lead wire to stud on Yoke Assembly (※27).
      2. Take off Retaining Ring (※7) and Washers (※8-9 and 10) along with Washers (※16) and Fibre Bushing (※29).
   g. Remove S249 Screws (※34) and take off Truck Side and Bottom Plate Assembly (※33).
   h. Remove (※27) Yoke Assembly by spreading open slightly and lift up.
   i. Loosen the two S165 Set Screws (※26A) on the Field Clamp (※26).
   j. Take out two S4A06 Screws (※28) and remove Field Clamp (※26).
   k. Remove S171 Screws (※12) and take off Worm Cover (※18) and Bearing Strap (※19).

NOTE: When reassembling motor it is necessary to adjust the two S165 Set Screws (※26A) on the Field Clamp (※26) to centralize the Magnet Assembly (※23). The reason is to prevent the Armature Assembly (※24) from striking the plates on the Magnet Assembly (※23). When placing the Motor Unit back in the Chassis (※14) the stop on top of the Yoke Assembly (※27) must be facing outward so that the stop will always be parallel with the Commutator on the Armature Assembly (※24).

3. **Instructions for correcting Whistle failure.**
   a. Recheck the instruction sheet in order to make sure hook-up is correct. If both the Transformer instructions and the Air Chime Whistle Instructions are followed, this will cause a duplication of wiring. The result will be that you will only have a faint buzz while the train is running or in a neutral position. Follow the Air Chime Whistle wiring instructions only and be sure to have only two wires going to the ※690 Track Terminal.
   b. The Generator Tube (※PA11665-A) on the control box may be weak and need replacing.
   c. If the trouble still persists it will be necessary to remove the Cabin (※1) from the Chassis by unscrewing the five S183 Screws (※15).
   d. The Unit is exposed and you can check all wires and soldered joints for loose connections. Be sure the lead wires on the condenser are covered with an insulating sleeve.
   e. Check the condenser (※4) by adding another condenser in series with temporary connections. If this corrects the trouble, defective condenser can be removed and a new one connected in its place. The Resistor (※3) can be checked in the same manner.
   f. The Speaker (※5) seldom has to be replaced unless the covering is broken.

GP-7 Twin Unit Diesel — Nos. 374/375

Diagram No.	Part No.	Description	Price
1	*XA11384 ARP	Cabin (375)	$ 2.55 ea.
2	PA8999	Bulb	.25 "
3	PA11685	Resistor	.26 "
4	PA11A991	Condenser	1.04 "
5	XA12B144	Whistle Ass'y	6.18 "
6	S322	Screw	.02 "
7	P10800 A	Retaining Ring	.04 "
8	W83	Washer	.03 "
9	W143	Washer	.01 "
10	W124	Washer	.01 "
11	XA10587 E	Remote Control Unit	1.32 "
	XA9612 CRP	Top Finger Unit	.30 "
	XA9612 BRP	Bottom Finger Unit	.30 "
	XA8716	Drum only	.59 "
12	S171	Screw	.01 "
13	XA11B913 RP	End Rail Ass'y	.67 "
14	XA12B418	Chassis Ass'y	3.39 "
15	S183	Screw	.10 dz.
16	PA8715	Washer	.05 "
17	S230-B	Screw	.10 "
		Motor Ass'y (not sold as a complete ass'y)	
18	PA11441	Worm Cover	. ea.
19	PA11453	Bearing Strap	.01 "
20	XA11684	Brush Holder Ass'y	.25 "
21	XA11454 RP	Brush Bracket Ass'y	.13 "
22	P11000 L or R	Brush Spring (left or right)	.03 "
23	XA13A036	Magnet Ass'y	.85 "
24	XA12A062	Armature Ass'y	3.67 "
25	XA12C065 RP	Wheel & Chassis Ass'y	2.21 "
	XA12A249	Pull-Mor Wheel Ass'y	.65 "
	PA11343	Solid Wheel	.05 "
	XA11473	Insulated Wheel	.23 "
	PA10006	Gear Axle	.10 "
26	PA13A034	Field Clamp	.24 "
26A	S165	Set Screw	.02 "
27	XA13A037	Yoke Ass'y	.24 "
28	S4A06	Screw	.01 "
29	PA11455	Fibre Bushing	.05 "
30	XA12A047	Knuckle Coupler	.22 "
31	PA12A355 A	Leaf Spring	.01 "
32	S3A71	Coupler Screw	.01 "
33	XA13A041	Truck & Collector Ass'y	.65 "
34	S249	Screw	.01 "
35	XA11598 A	Wheel & Chassis Ass'y	1.25 "
36	*XA11384 ARP	Cabin (374)	2.55 "
37	XA11596 A	Wheel & Chassis Ass'y	1.25 "
38	XA11A901	Truck Ass'y	.94

*Note: When ordering cabins specify either #375 or #374.

DIA. NO.	PART NO.	DESCRIPTION	PRICE
1	#XA11384-ARP	CABIN (375)	2.81 EA.
2	PA8999	BULB	.30 EA.
3	PA11685	RESISTOR (OLD STYLE)	.29 EA.
		RESISTOR NOT USED ON NEW STYLE	
4	PA11A991	CONDENSER NOT AVAILABLE	
		SUB. WITH PA14A914 CONDENSER	1.40 EA.
5	XA12B144	SPEAKER NOT AVAILABLE	
		SUB. WITH XA14A127 SPEAKER	4.57 EA.
	PA14A216	BRACKET	.08 EA.
	S171	SCREW	.01 EA.
6	S172	SCREW	.02 EA.
7	P10800-A	RETAINING RING	.25 DZ.
8	W83	WASHER	.04 EA.
9	W143	WASHER (MOTOR END ONLY)	.01 EA.
	W126	WASHER	.06 DZ.
10	PA8715	WASHER (USED ON MOTOR END IN 375 & IN 374 ALSO)	.10 DZ.
	W124	WASHER (375)	.25 DZ.
11	XA10587-E	REMOTE CONTROL UNIT	4.04 EA.
	XA9612-CRP	TOP FINGER UNIT	.33 EA.
	XA9612-BRP	BOTTOM FINGER UNIT	.33 EA.
	XA8716	DRUM ONLY	.95 EA.
12	S171	SCREW	.01 EA.
13	XA11B913-RP	END RAIL ASSEMBLY	.74 EA.
14	XA12B418	CHASSIS ASSEMBLY (OLD STYLE)	3.73 EA.
	XA14A094-B	CHASSIS (NEW STYLE, USED WITH NEW SPEAKER)	2.60 EA.
15	S4N30	SCREW	.01 EA.
16	PA8715	WASHER	.10 DZ.
17	S230-B	SCREW	.01 EA.
18	PA11441	WORM COVER	.01 EA.
19	PA11453	BEARING STRAP	.02 EA.
20	P10132	BRUSH HOLDER (NOT SOLD ASSEMBLED)	.01 EA.
	PA11684	BRUSH (NOT SOLD ASSEMBLED)	.32 EA.
21	XA11454-RP	BRUSH BRACKET ASSEMBLY	.14 EA.
22	P11000-L OR R	BRUSH SPRING (LEFT OR RIGHT)	.03 EA.
23	XA13A036	MAGNET ASSEMBLY	1.34 EA.
24	XA14B873-RP	ARMATURE ASSEMBLY	3.94 EA.
25	XA12A074-RP	WHEEL & CHASSIS ASSEMBLY	2.37 EA.
	XA12A249	PUL-MOR WHEEL ASSY. (OLD STYLE)	.72 EA.
	XA14A891	PUL-MOR WHEEL ASSY. (NEW STYLE)	.28 EA.
	PA14A890	PUL-MOR	.05 EA.
	PA11343	SOLID WHEEL (OLD STYLE)	.06 EA.
	PA14A888	SOLID WHEEL (NEW STYLE)	.08 EA.
	XA11473	INSULATED WHEEL (OLD STYLE)	.25 EA.
	PA10006	GEAR AXLE NOT AVAILABLE	
		SUB. WITH PA15A281 WORM AXLE	.07 EA.
	PA15A218	WORM GEAR	.09 EA.
	PA11463	THRUST PLATE	.08 DZ.

CON'T

NO.	PART NO.	DESCRIPTION	PRICE
26	PA13A034	FIELD CLAMP	.34 EA.
26A	S165	SET SCREW	.03 EA.
27	XA13A037	YOKE ASSEMBLY	.26 EA.
28	S4A06	SCREW	.03 EA.
29	PA11455	FIBRE BUSHING	.14 EA.
30	XA12A047	KNUCKLE COUPLER	.29 EA.
31	PA12A355-A	LEAF SPRING	.02 EA.
32	S3A71	COUPLER SCREW (OLD STYLE)	.03 EA.
	PA13A791	LONG COUPLER STUD (NEW STYLE, USED WITH XA13A809 TRUCK)	.02 EA.
33	XA13A041	TRUCK & COLLECTOR ASSY. NOT AVAILABLE	
		SUB. WITH XA13A809 TRUCK & COIL ASSY. (USE PA13A791 STUD)	1.17 EA.
	XA13A810	TRUCK W/COUPLER (CONSISTS OF PARTS 30-31-32-33)	1.65 EA.
34	S249	SCREW	.15 DZ.
35	XA11598-A	WHEEL & CHASSIS ASSY. NOT AVAILABLE	
		SUB. WITH XA11598-B WHEEL & CHASSIS (OLD STYLE WHEELS)	1.12 EA.
		XA14A930-A WHEEL & CHASSIS ASSY. (NEW STYLE WHEELS)	1.60 EA.
36 *	XA11384-ARP	CABIN (374)	2.81 EA.
37	XA11596-A	WHEEL & CHASSIS ASSEMBLY	1.38 EA.
38	XA11A901	TRUCK ASSEMBLY NOT AVAILABLE	
		SUB. WITH XA13A809 TRUCK ASSY.	1.17 EA.

NOT SHOWN

PART NO.	DESCRIPTION	PRICE
XA13B038-B	MOTOR ASSEMBLY	12.16 EA.
LW-181	BLACK LEAD WIRE	.02 FT.
PA13A208-A	4 CONDUCTOR CABLE (PLASTIC)	.04 FT.

* NOTE: WHEN ORDERING CABINS SPECIFY EITHER #375 OR #374 WHICHEVER IS NEEDED.

PRICES SUBJECT TO CHANGE WITHOUT NOTICE.

 Ref: Form No. 1600; June 1, 1960

NO.	PART NO.	DESCRIPTION	PRICE
1	XA11384-ERP	CABIN (377)	2.94 EA.
2	PA8999	BULB	.30 EA.
3	PA14A275	RESISTOR (LOCATED IN #378)	.21 EA.
4	PA14A914	CONDENSER (LOCATED IN #378)	1.40 EA.
5	XA14A127	SPEAKER (LOCATED IN #378)	4.57 EA.
	PA14A216	BRACKET	.08 EA.
	S171	SCREW	.01 EA.
6	S172	SCREW (LOCATED IN #378)	.02 EA.
7	P10800-A	RETAINING RING	.25 DZ.
8	W83	WASHER	.04 EA.
9	W126	WASHER	.06 DZ.
10	PA8715	WASHER	.10 DZ.
11	XA10587-E	REMOTE CONTROL UNIT	4.04 EA.
	XA9612-CRP	TOP FINGER UNIT	.33 EA.
	XA9612-BRP	BOTTOM FINGER UNIT	.33 EA.
	XA8716	DRUM	.95 EA.
12	S171	SCREW	.01 EA.
13	XA11B913-RP	END RAIL ASSY. NOT SOLD SEPARATELY (PART OF CHASSIS #14)	
14	XA13B166-A	CHASSIS ASSY.	2.35 EA.
15	S4N30	SCREW	.01 EA.
16	PA8715	WASHER	.10 DZ.
17	S230-B	SCREW	.01 EA.
18	PA11441	WORM COVER	.01 EA.
19	PA11453	BEARING STRAP	.02 EA.
20	P10132	BRUSH HOLDER	.01 EA.
	PA11684	BRUSH (NOT SOLD ASSEMBLED)	.32 EA.
21	XA11454-RP	BRUSH BRACKET ASSY.	.14 EA.
22	P11000-L OR R	BRUSH SPRING (LEFT OR RIGHT)	.03 EA.
23	XA13A036	MAGNET ASSY.	1.34 EA.
24	XA14B873-RP	ARMATURE ASSY.	3.94 EA.
25	XA12A074-RP	WHEEL & CHASSIS ASSY.	2.37 EA.
	XA14A891	PUL-MOR WHEEL ASSY.	.28 EA.
	PA14A890	PUL-MOR	.05 EA.
	PA14A888	SOLID WHEEL	.08 EA.
	PA15A281	WORM GEAR AXLE	.07 EA.
	PA15A218	WORM GEAR	.09 EA.
	PA11463	THRUST PLATE	.08 DZ.
26	PA13A034	FIELD CLAMP	.34 EA.
26A	S165	SET SCREW	.03 EA.
27	XA13A037	YOKE ASSY.	.26 EA.
28	S4A06	SCREW	.03 EA.
29	PA11455	FIBRE BUSHING	.14 EA.
30	XA12A047	KNUCKLE COUPLER	.29 EA.
31	PA12A355-A	LEAF SPRING	.02 EA.
32	PA13A791	COUPLER SCREW	.02 EA.
33	XA13A809	TRUCK & COLLECTOR ASSY.	1.17 EA.
	XA13A810	TRUCK & COLLECTOR W/COUPLER	1.65 EA.
34	S249	SCREW	.15 DZ.
35	XA14A930-A	WHEEL & CHASSIS ASSY.	1.60 EA.
36	XA11A384-FRP	CABIN (377)	2.67 EA.
37	XA14A931	WHEEL & CHASSIS ASSY.	1.38 EA.

CON'T.

NO.	PART NO.	DESCRIPTION	PRICE
38	XA13A809	TRUCK ASSEMBLY	1.17 EA.
	XA13A810	TRUCK & COLLECTOR W/COUPLER	1.65 EA.
		NOT SHOWN	
	XA13B038-B	MOTOR ASSEMBLY (LOCATED IN #378)	12.16 EA.
	PA13A870	DIESEL SOUND GENERATOR(LOCATED IN #378)	4.52 EA.
	W55	FIBRE WASHER (LOCATED IN #378)	.09 DZ.
	PA10209	BUSHING (LOCATED IN #378)	.02 EA.
	N25	NUT 8-32 HEX (LOCATED IN #378)	.02 EA.
	LW-1B1	BLACK LEAD WIRE	.02 FT.

PRICES SUBJECT TO CHANGE WITHOUT NOTICE.

NO.	PART NO.	DESCRIPTION	PRICE
1	*XA11384-ARP	Cabin (375)	2.95 ea.
2	PA8999	Bulb	.32 ea.
3	PA11685	Resistor (Old Style)	.30 ea.
		Resistor not used on New Style	
4	PA14A914	Condenser (Sub. for PA11A991 obsolete)	1.47 ea.
5	XA14A127-Conv.	Speaker (Sub. for XA12B144 obsolete)	4.91 ea.
6	S172	Screw	.02 ea.
7	P10800-A	Retaining Ring	.26 dz.
8	W83	Washer	.04 ea.
9	W143	Washer (Motor End Only)	.01 ea.
	W126	Washer	.06 dz.
10	PA8715	Washer (Motor End 374-375)	.11 dz.
	W124	Washer (375)	.26 dz.
11	XA10587-E	Remote Control Unit	4.24 ea.
	XA9612-CRP	Top Finger Unit	.35 ea.
	XA9612-BRP	Bottom Finger Unit	.35 ea.
	XA8716	Drum Only	1.00 ea.
12	S171	Screw	.01 ea.
13	XA11B913-RP	End Rail Assembly	.78 ea.
14		Chassis Assembly OBSOLETE	
15	S4N30	Screw	.01 ea.
16	PA8715	Washer	.11 dz.
17	S230-B	Screw	.01 ea.
18	PA11441	Worm Cover	.01 ea.
19	PA11453	Bearing Strap	.02 ea.
20	P10132	Brush Holder	.01 ea.
	PA11684	Brush	.34 ea.
21	XA11454-RP	Brush Bracket Assembly	.15 ea.
22	P11000-L or R	Brush Spring (Left or Right)	.03 ea.
23	XA13A036	Magnet Assembly	1.41 ea.
24	XA14B873-RP	Armature Assembly	4.14 ea.
25	XA12A074-RP	Wheel & Chassis Assembly	2.49 ea.
	XA14A891	Pul-Mor Wheel Assy. (New Style)	.29 ea.
	PA14A890	Pul-Mor	.05 ea.
	PA14A888	Solid Wheel (New Style)	.08 ea.
	PA15A281	Gear Axle	.07 ea.
	PA15A218	Worm Gear	.09 ea.
	PA11463	Thrust Plate	.08 dz.
26	PA13A034	Field Clamp	.36 ea.
26A	S165	Set Screw	.03 ea.
27	XA13A037	Yoke Assembly	.27 ea.
28	S4A06	Screw	.03 ea.
29	PA11455	Fibre Bushing	.15 ea.
30	XA12A047	Knuckle Coupler	.30 ea.
31	PA12A355-A	Leaf Spring	.02 ea.
32	PA13A791	Long Coupler Stud	.02 ea.
33	XA13A809	Truck & Collector Assy.	1.23 ea.
	XA13A810	Truck w/ coupler (Parts 30-31-32-33)	1.73 ea.
34	S249	Screw	.16 dz.

Continued

NO.	PART NO.	DESCRIPTION	PRICE
35	XA14A930-A	Wheel & Chassis Assy.	1.68 ea.
36	*XA11384-ARP	Cabin (374)	2.95 ea.
37	XA11596-A	Wheel & Chassis Assembly	1.45 ea.
38	XA13A809	Truck Assembly	1.23 ea.

NOT SHOWN

PART NO.	DESCRIPTION	PRICE
XA13B038-B	Motor Assy.	12.77 ea.
LW1B1	Black Lead Wire	.02 ft.
PA13A208-A	4 Conductor Cable (Plastic)	.04 ft.

* NOTE: When ordering cabins specify either #374 or #375 whichever is needed.

Prices subject to change without notice.

NO.	PART NO.	DESCRIPTION	PRICE
1	XA11384-ERP	Cabin (377)	3.09 ea.
2	PA8999	Bulb	.32 ea.
3	PA14A275	Resistor (Located in #378)	.22 ea.
4	PA14A914	Condenser (Located in #378)	1.47 ea.
5	XA14A127	Speaker (Located in #378)	4.80 ea.
	PA14A216	Bracket	.08 ea.
	S171	Screw	.01 ea.
6	S172	Screw (Located in #378)	.02 ea.
7	P10800-A	Retaining Ring	.26 dz.
8	W83	Washer	.04 ea.
9	W126	Washer	.06 dz.
10	PA8715	Washer	.11 dz.
11	XA10587-E	Remote Control Unit	4.24 ea.
	XA9612-CRP	Top Finger Unit	.35 ea.
	XA9612-BRP	Bottom Finger Unit	.35 ea.
	XA8716	Drum	1.00 ea.
12	S171	Screw	.01 ea.
13	XA11B913-RP	End Rail Assembly	.78 ea.
14	XA13B166-A	Chassis Assembly	2.47 ea.
15	S4N30	Screw	.01 ea.
16	PA8715	Washer	.11 dz.
17	S230-B	Screw	.01 ea.
18	PA11441	Worm Cover	.01 ea.
19	PA11453	Bearing Strap	.02 ea.
20	P10132	Brush Holder	.01 ea.
	PA11684	Brush	.34 ea.
21	XA11454-RP	Brush Bracket Assembly	.15 ea.
22	P11000-L or R	Brush Spring (Left or Right)	.03 ea.
23	XA13A036	Magnet Assembly	1.41 ea.
24	XA14B873-RP	Armature Assembly	4.14 ea.
25	XA12A074-RP	Wheel and Chassis Assembly	2.49 ea.
	XA14A891	Pul-Mor Wheel Assembly	.29 ea.
	PA14A890	Pul-Mor	.05 ea.
	PA14A888	Solid Wheel	.08 ea.
	PA15A281	Worm Gear Axle	.07 ea.
	PA15A218	Worm Gear	.09 ea.
	PA11463	Thrust Plate	.08 dz.
26	PA13A034	Field Clamp	.36 ea.
26A	S165	Set Screw	.03 ea.
27	XA13A037	Yoke Assembly	.27 ea.
28	S4A06	Screw	.03 ea.
29	PA11455	Fibre Bushing	.15 ea.
30	XA12A047	Knuckle Coupler	.30 ea.
31	PA12A355-A	Leaf Spring	.02 ea.
32	PA13A791	Coupler Screw	.02 ea.
33	XA13A809	Truck and Collector Assembly	1.23 ea.
	XA13A810	Truck and Collector Assembly w/coupler	1.73 ea.
34	S249	Screw	.16 dz.
35	XA14A930-A	Wheel and Chassis Assembly	1.68 ea.
36	XA11A384-FRP	Cabin (377)	2.80 ea.
37	XA14A931	Wheel and Chassis Assembly	1.45 ea.

Cont'd

NO.	PART NO.	DESCRIPTION	PRICE
38	XA13A809	Truck Assembly	1.23 ea.
	XA13A810	Truck and Collector Assembly w/coupler	1.73 ea.
		NOT SHOWN	
	XA13B038-B	Motor Assembly (Located in #378)	12.77 ea.
	PA13A870	Diesel Sound Generator (Located in #378)	4.75 ea.
	W55	Fibre Washer (Located in #378)	.09 dz.
	PA10209	Bushing (Located in #378)	.02 ea.
	N25	Nut 8-32 Hex (Located in #378)	.02 ea.
	LW-1B1	Black Lead Wire	.02 ft.

Prices subject to change without notice.

SILVER STREAK DIESEL WITH AIR CHIME WHISTLE

Model No. 405

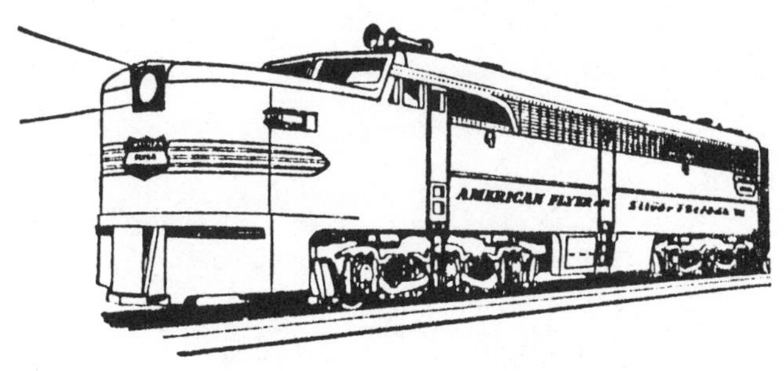

SPECIFICATIONS

Tested at: 12 Volts A.C. .... using 180" oval of track.

(A) Locomotive to run a minimum of 9 R.P.M. or 9 times forward and reverse, around 180" oval of track.

Load: Not to draw more than 2 amps. while pulling 4 Passenger Cars.

Motor: Universal A.C. or D.C.

Ref: Form No. 1822; Feb. 1, 1957

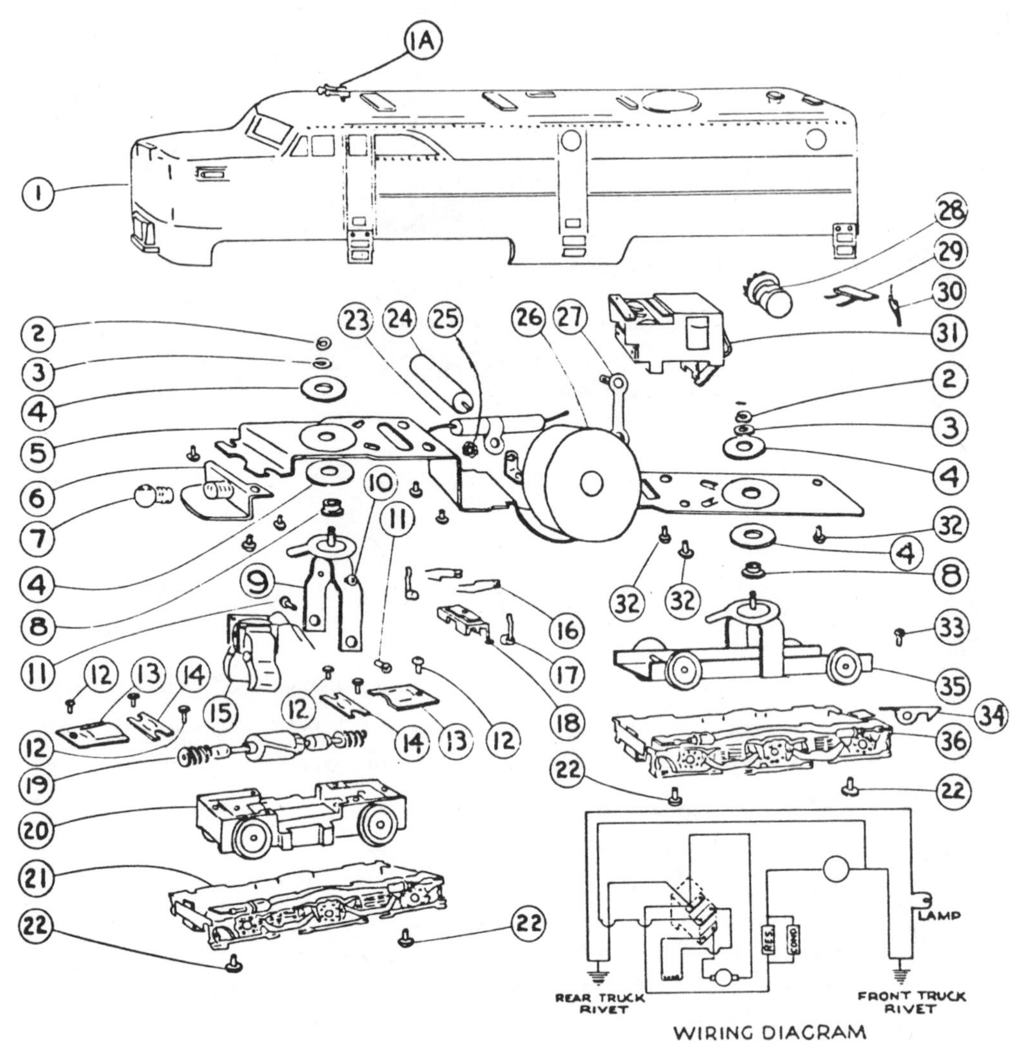

 Ref: Form No. 1822; Feb. 1, 1957

Diagram Number	Part No.	Description	Price
1	XA12D075-RP	A Unit Cabin w/trimmings	$4.40 ea.
2	P10800-A	Retaining Ring	.04 "
3	W83	Washer	.30 dz.
4	W124	Fibre Washer	.01 ea.
5	XA12B059-RP	Chassis & Bracket Assem.	.35 "
6	XA11477	Lamp Bracket Assem.	.09 "
7	PA8999	Bulb	.25 "
8	PA11455	Fibre Bushing	.05 "
9	XA11457	Field Clamp Assem.	.37 "
10	S-0	Screw	.05 dz.
11	S-230	Screw	.10 "
12	S-171	Screw	.01 ea.
13	PA11441	Worm cover	.01 "
14	PA11453	Bearing Strap	.01 "
15	XA12A064	Field Assem.	1.25 "
16	P11000-L	Brush Spring (left)	.03 "
	P11000-R	Brush Spring (right)	.03 "
17	XA11684	Brush Holder Assem.	.25 "
18	XA11421-RP	Brush Bracket Assem.	.20 "
19	XA12A062	Armature Assem.	3.50 "
20	XA11463-RP	Truck Chassis & Wheel Ass'y.	2.50 "
	PA11343	Solid Wheel	.10 "
	XA11473	Insulated Wheel Ass'y.	.34 ea.
	XA12A249	Pull-Mor Wheel Ass'y	.65 "
	PA10005	Plain Axle	.10 "
	PA10006	Gear Axle	.10 "
	PA11447	20-T Worm gear	.30 "
21	XA11456-A	Truck Side & Bottom Plate Ass'y.	.98 "
22	S249	Screw	.01 "
23	PA11685	Resistor	.26 "
24	PA11A991	Condenser	1.00 "
25	N-1	Nut	.01 "
26	XA11710	Speaker	2.76 "
27	XA10818-F	Insulator & Terminal Ass'y.	.03 "
28	XA8716	Drum	.60 "
29	XA9612-C	Top Finger Unit	.50 "
30	XA9612-B	Bottom Finger Unit	.50 "
31	XA10587-E	Remote Control Unit	2.50 "
32	S319	Screw	.01 "
33	S334	Screw	.01 "
34	XA11484	Coupler Arm Ass'y.	.20 "
	PA11589	Coupler Spring	.02 "
35	XA11598-A	Wheel & Chassis Ass'y.	1.25 "
36	XA11485-B	Truck Side & Bottom Plate Ass'y.	1.66 "

Diagram Number	Part No.	Description	Price
*1	XA12D075-DRP	A Unit Cabin w/Trimmings.	$3.17 ea.
1A	PA11409	Plastic Horn	.05 "
2	P10800-A	Retaining Ring	.04 "
3	W83	Washer	.03 "
4	W124	Fibre Washer	.01 "
5	XA12B059-RP	Chassis & Bracket Assy.	.39 "
6	XA11477	Lamp Bracket Assy.	.21 "
7	PA8999	Bulb	.25 "
8	PA11455	Fibre Bushing	.06 "
9	XA11457	Field Clamp Assy.	.41 "
10	S-0	Screw	.05 dz.
11	S-230	Screw	.10 "
12	S171	Screw	.01 ea.
13	PA11441	Worm Cover	.01 "
14	PA11453	Bearing Strap	.01 "
15	XA13A036	Field Assy.	.85 "
16	P11000-L	Brush Spring (left).	.03 "
	P11000-R	Brush Spring (right).	.03 "
17	XA11684	Brush Holder Assy.	.25 "
18	XA11454-RP	Brush Bracket Assy.	.13 "
19	XA12A062	Armature Assy.	3.67 "
20	XA12B065-RP	Truck Chassis & Wheel Assy.	2.21 "
	PA11343	Solid Wheel	.05 "
	XA11473	Insulated Wheel Assy.	.23 "

All prices subject to change without notice.

Diagram Number	Part No.	Description	Price
	XA12A249	Pull-Mor Wheel Assy.	$ .65 ea.
	PA10005	Plain Axle	.10 "
	PA10006	Gear Axle	.10 "
	PA11447	20-T Worm Gear	.20 "
21	XA11456-A	Truck Side & Bottom Plate Assy.	1.09 "
22	S249	Screw	.01 "
23	PA11685	Resistor	.26 "
24	PA11A991	Condenser	1.04 "
25	N-1	Nut	.01 "
26	XA11710	Speaker	3.06 "
27	XA10818-F	Insulator & Terminal Assy.	.03 "
28	XA8716	Drum	.59 "
29	XA9612-CRP	Top Finger Unit	.30 "
30	XA9612-BRP	Bottom Finger Unit	.30 "
31	XA10587-E	Remote Control Unit	1.32 "
32	S319	Screw	.01 "
33	S334	Screw	.01 "
34	XA11484	Coupler Arm Assy.	.20 "
	PA11589	Coupler Spring	.02 "
35	XA11598-A	Wheel & Chassis Assy.	1.25 "
36	XA11485-B	Truck Side & Bottom Plate Assy.	1.84 "

*Note: XA12D075-DRP Cabin in metalized finish is not available. Cabin listed above will be same as cabin on #466 Comet.

SERVICE INSTRUCTIONS FOR No. 405 SILVER STREAK DIESEL LOCOMOTIVE

The first thing to do is to place Locomotive on Track, connect Transformer and Whistle Control Unit and test for operation.

1. **If the trouble is in the motor, we suggest that you check as follows:**
   a. Check Brushes (#17) for wear or poor contact.
   b. Check Brush Spring (#16) for position and proper tension.
   c. Check wires and solder joints for loose connections.
   d. Commutator on Armature Assembly (#19) may be dirty.
   e. Check operation of Remote Control Unit (#31).
   f. See if motor is properly lubricated.
   g. Wheels and track must be kept clean to insure proper electrical contact.

2. **To Disassemble and Replace Parts on Motor Unit.**
   a. The first step is to remove the S319 Screws (#32), and take off Cabin (1).
   b. Motor is exposed and you can check wiring and other points of the unit.
   c. Brush Holder Assembly (#18) and Brush Springs (#16) can be replaced without taking Motor Unit from Chassis (#5).
   d. When replacing Brush Holder Assembly (#18) unsolder lead wire and remove tension from Brush Spring, (#16).
   e. To replace Brush Springs (#16) remove Brush Holder Assembly, (#18) first, so spring can be pulled forward and slipped out.
   f. When replacing Armature (#19) or Magnet (#15) we recommend removing Motor Unit from Chassis (#5) as follows:
      1. Unsolder lead wire to stud on Field Clamp Assembly (#9).
      2. Take off Retaining Rings (#2) & (#3) and Fibre Washers (#4).
   g. Remove S249 Screws (#22) and take off Truck Side and Bottom Plate Assembly (#21).
   h. Loosen the two S-O Screws (#9A).
   i. Take out S230 Screws and remove Field Clamp Assembly (#9).
   j. Remove S171 Screws and take off worm cover, (#13) and Bearing Strap (#14).

NOTE: When reassembling motor it is necessary to adjust the two S-O Screws (#9A) on the Field Clamp Assembly, (#9) which centralizes the Magnet Assembly (#15). The reason is to prevent the Armature Assembly (#19) from striking the plates on the Magnet Assembly (#15).

When placing the Motor Unit back in Chassis, (#5) the stop on the Field Clamp Assembly (#19) must be facing inward so that the stop will always be parallel with the Commutator on the Armature Assembly (#19).

3. **Instructions for correcting Whistle failure as follows:**
   a. Recheck the instructions in order to make sure hook-up is correct. If both the Transformer instructions and the Air Chime Whistle instructions are followed, this will cause a duplication of wiring. The result will be that you will only have a faint buzz while the train is running or in a neutral position. Follow the Air Chime Whistle wiring instructions only, and be sure to have only two wires going to the #690 Track Terminal.
   b. The Generator Tube #PA11665 on the control box may be weak and need replacing.
   c. If the trouble still persists it will be necessary to remove the Cabin (#1) from the chassis by unscrewing the screws (#32).
   d. The unit is exposed and you can check all wires and solder joints for loose connections. Be sure the lead wires on the resistor and condenser are covered with an insulating sleeve.
   e. Check the condenser (#24) by adding another condenser in series with temporary connections. If this corrects the trouble the defective condenser can be removed and a new one connected in its place.
   f. To check resistor (23) use another resistor and follow same procedure.
   g. The speaker seldom has to be replaced unless the wire or covering is broken.

DIA. NO.	PART NO.	DESCRIPTION	PRICE
1	XA12D075-RP	A Unit Cabin w/trimmings NOT AVAILABLE	
		Substitute with XA12D075DRP Cabin (Comet Cabin)	3.49 ea.
1A	PA11409	Plastic Horn	.08 ea.
2	P10800-A	Retaining Ring	.25 doz.
3	W83	Washer	.04 ea.
4	W124	Fibre Washer	.25 doz.
5	XA12B059-RP	Chassis & Bracket Assembly	.43 ea.
6	XA11477	Lamp Bracket Assembly	.24 ea.
7	PA8999	Bulb	.30 ea.
8	PA11455	Fibre Bushing	.14 ea.
9	XA11457	Field Clamp Assembly	.45 ea.
10	S-0	Screw	.01 ea.
11	S230-B	Screw	.01 ea.
12	S171	Screw	.01 ea.
13	PA11441	Worm Cover	.01 ea.
14	PA11453	Bearing Strap	.02 ea.
15	XA13A036	Field Assembly	1.34 ea.
16	P11000-L	Brush Spring (Left)	.03 ea.
	P11000-R	Brush Spring (Right)	.03 ea.
17	PA11684	Brush (Not Sold Assembled)	.32 ea.
	P10132	Brush Holder	.01 ea.
18	XA11454-RP	Brush Bracket Assembly	.14 ea.
19	XA14B873-RP	Armature Assembly	3.94 ea.
20	XA12A074-RP	Truck Chassis & Wheel Assembly	2.37 ea.
	PA11343	Solid Wheel (OLD STYLE)	.06 ea.
	PA14A888	Solid Wheel (NEW STYLE)	.08 ea.
	XA11473	Insulated Wheel Assembly (OLD STYLE)	.25 ea.
	XA12A249	Pul-Mor Wheel Assembly (OLD STYLE)	.72 ea.
	XA14A891	Pul-Mor Wheel Assembly (NEW STYLE)	.28 ea.
	PA14A890	Pul-Mor	.05 ea.
	PA10005	Plain Axle NOT AVAILABLE	
		Substitute with PA15A226 Axle	.05 ea.
	PA10006	Gear Axle NOT AVAILABLE	
		Substitute with PA15A281 Axle	.07 ea.
	PA11447	20-T Worm Gear NOT AVAILABLE	
		Substitute with PA15A218 Gear	.09 ea.
	PA11463	Thrust Plate	.08 doz.
21	XA11456-A	Truck Side & Bottom Plate Assy. NOT AVAILABLE	
		Substitute with XA13A802 Knuckle Coupler Truck	1.06 ea.
22	S249	Screw	.15 doz.
23	PA11685	Resistor	.29 ea.
24	PA11A991	Condenser NOT AVAILABLE	
		Substitute with PA14A914 Condenser	1.40 ea.
25		NOT USED	
26	XA11710	Speaker NOT AVAILABLE	
		Substitute with XA14A127 Speaker	4.57 ea.
		PA14A216 Bracket	.08 ea.
		S171 Screw	.01 ea.
		S172 Screw	.02 ea.
27		NOT USED	
28	XA8716	Drum	.95 ea.

Cont'd

NO.	PART NO.	DESCRIPTION	PRICE
29	XA9612-CRP	Top Finger Unit	.33 ea.
30	XA9612-BRP	Bottom Finger Unit	.33 ea.
31	XA10587-E	Remote Control Unit	4.04 ea.
32	S319	Screw	.02 ea.
33	S334	Screw NOT AVAILABLE	
		Substitute with PA13A791 Long Stud	.02 ea.
34	XA11484	Coupler Arm Assembly NOT AVAILABLE	
		Substitute with XA12A047 Knuckle Coupler	.29 ea.
35	XA11598-A	Wheel & Chassis Assembly NOT AVAILABLE	
		Substitute with XA14A930-B Assembly	1.52 ea.
36	XA11485-B	Truck Side & Bottom Plate Assy. NOT AVAILABLE	
		Substitute with XA13A802 Assembly	1.06 ea.

Link Couplers & Trucks not available, convert to Knuckle Couplers.

NOT SHOWN

PART NO.	DESCRIPTION	PRICE
XA13B038-B	Motor	12.16 ea.
PA13A208-A	4 Conductor Cable (Plastic)	.04 ft.

Prices subject to change without notice.

DIESEL LOCOMOTIVE

Model No. 466 Comet

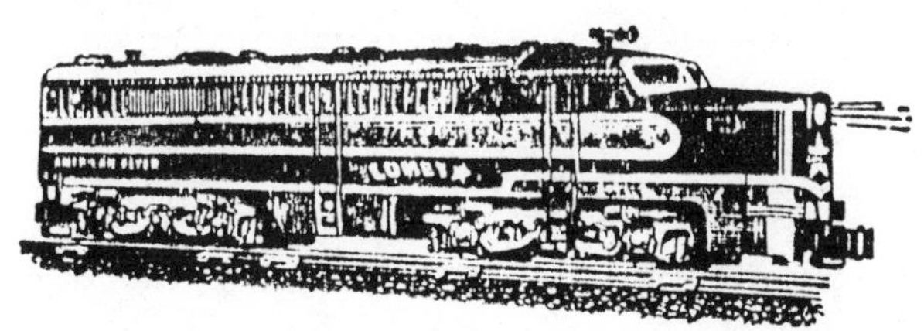

SPECIFICATIONS

Tested at: 12 Volts A.C. ....using 180" oval of track.

(A) Locomotive to run a minimum of 9 R.P.M. or 9 times forward and reverse, around 180" oval of track.

Load: Not to draw more than 2 amps. while pulling 4 Passenger Cars.

Motor: Universal A.C. or D.C.

Ref: Form No. 1500; Dec. 15, 1953

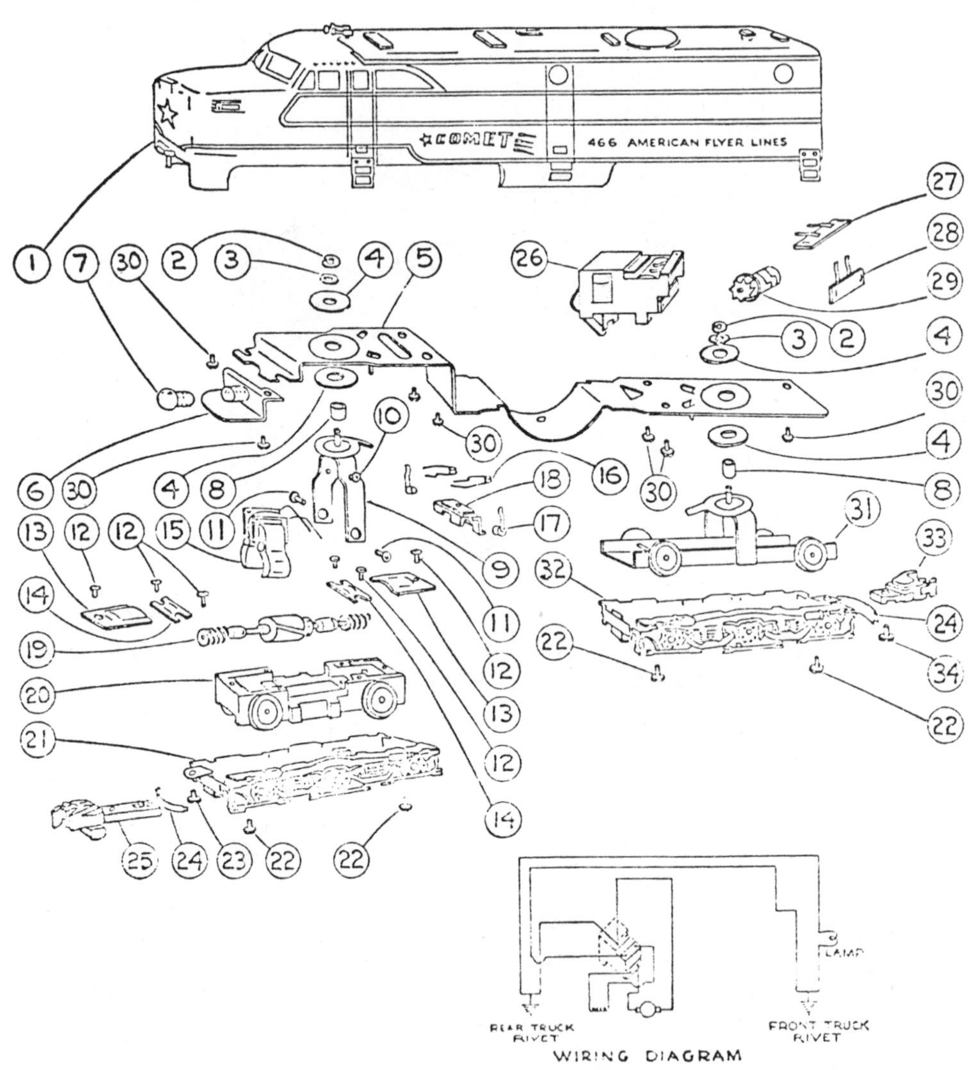
466 AMERICAN FLYER LINES
COMET
REAR TRUCK RIVET
FRONT TRUCK RIVET
LAMP
WIRING DIAGRAM

Diagram Number	Part No.	Description	Price
1	XA12D075-DRP	A Unit Cabin w/Trimmings.........	$3.17 ea.
1A	PA11409	Plastic Horn	.05 "
2	P10800-A	Retaining Ring	.04 "
3	W83	Washer	.03 "
4	W124	Washer	.01 "
5	PA12B059	Chassis	.34 "
6	XA11477	Lamp Bracket Assy................	.21 "
7	PA8999	Bulb	.25 "
8	PA11455	Fibre Bushing	.06 "
9	XA11457	Field Clamp Assy.................	.41 "
10	S-0	Set Screw	.05 dz.
11	S-230	Screw	.10 "
12	S-171	Screw	.01 ea.
13	PA11441	Worm Cover	.01 "
14	PA11453	Bearing Strap	.01 "
15	XA13A036	Field Assy.	.85 "
16	P11000-R	Brush Spring (right)..............	.03 "
	P11000-L	Brush Spring (left)...............	.03 "
17	XA11684	Brush Holder Assy................	.25 "
18	XA11454-RP	Brush Bracket Assy...............	.13 "
19	XA12A062	Armature Assy.	3.67 "

All prices subject to change without notice.

Diagram Number	Part No.	Description	Price
20	XA12A074-RP	Truck Chassis Assy.	$2.15 ea.
	PA11343	Solid Wheel	.05 "
	XA11473	Insuated Wheel Assy.	.23 "
	XA12A249	Pull-Mor Wheel Assy.	.65 "
	PA10005	Plain Axle	.10 "
	PA10006	Gear Axle	.10 "
	PA11447	Worm Gear	.20 "
21	XA13A802	Truck & Collector Assy.	.70 "
	XA13A803	Truck & Coupler Arm Assy. (consists of parts 21-23-24-25)	1.11 "
22	S249	Screw	.01 "
23	PA13A790	Rivet	.02 "
24	PA12A355	Leaf Spring	.01 "
25	XA12A358	Coupler & Arm Assy.	.31 "
26	XA10587-E	Remote Control Unit	1.32 "
27	XA9612-CRP	Top Finger Unit	.30 "
28	XA9612-BRP	Bottom Finger Unit	.30 "
29	XA8716	Drum	.59 "
30	S319	Screw	.01 "
31	XA11598-A	Wheel & Chassis Assembly	1.25 "
32	XA13A802	Truck & Collector Assy.	.70 "
	XA13A804	Truck & Coupler Assy. (consists of parts 24-32-33-34)	1.02 "
33	XA12A047	Knuckle Coupler	.22 "
34	PA13A791	Rivet	.01 "

SERVICE INSTRUCTIONS FOR No. 466 COMET DIESEL LOCOMOTIVE

The first thing to do is to place Locomotive on Track, connect Transformer and test for operation.

1. **If the trouble is in the motor, we suggest that you check as follows:**
   a. Check Brushes (※17) for wear or poor contact.
   b. Check Brush Spring (※16) for position and proper tension.
   c. Check wires and solder joints for loose connections.
   d. Commutator on Armature Assembly (※19) may be dirty.
   e. Check operation of Remote Control Unit (※26).
   f. See if motor is properly lubricated.
   g. Wheels and Track must be kept clean to insure proper electrical contact.

2. **To Disassemble and Replace Parts on Motor Unit.**
   a. The first step is to remove the S319 Screws (※30) and take off Cabin (※1).
   b. Motor is exposed and you can check wiring and other points of the unit.
   c. Brush Holder Assembly (※18) and Brush Springs (16) can be replaced without taking motor unit from Chassis (※5).
   d. When replacing Brush Holder Assembly (※18) unsolder lead wire and remove tension from Brush Springs (※16).
   e. To replace Brush Springs (※16) remove Brush Holder Assembly, (※18) first, so spring can be pulled forward and slipped out.
   f. When replacing Armature (※19) or Magnet (※15) we recommend removing Motor Unit from Chassis (※5) as follows:
      1. Unsolder lead wire to stud on Field Clamp Assembly (※9).
      2. Take Off Retaining Rings (※2) and (3) and Fibre Washers (※4).
   g. Remove S249 Screws (※22) and take off truck side and bottom plate assembly (※21).
   h. Loosen the two S-O Screws (※10).
   i. Take out (※230) Screws and Remove Field Clamp Assembly (※9).
   j. Remove S171 Screws and take off Worm Cover (※13) and bearing strap (※14).

NOTE: When reassembling motor it is necessary to adjust the two S-O Screws (※10) on the Field Clamp Assembly (※9) which centralizes the Magnet Assembly (※15). The reason is to prevent the Armature Assembly (※19) from striking the plates on the Magnet Assembly (※15).

When placing the Motor Unit back in Chassis (※5) the stop on the Field Clamp Assembly (※9) must be facing inward so that the stop will always be parallel with the Commutator on the Armature Assembly (※19).

DIESEL LOCOMOTIVE

Model Nos. 466 Comet, 479 Silver Flash

SPECIFICATIONS

Tested at: 12 Volts A.C. .... using 180″ oval of track.

(A) Locomotive to run a minimum of 9 R.P.M. or 9 times forward and reverse, around 180″ oval of track.

Load: Not to draw more than 2 amps. while pulling 4 Passenger Cars.

Motor: Universal A.C. or D.C.

 Ref: Form No. 1821; Feb. 1, 1957

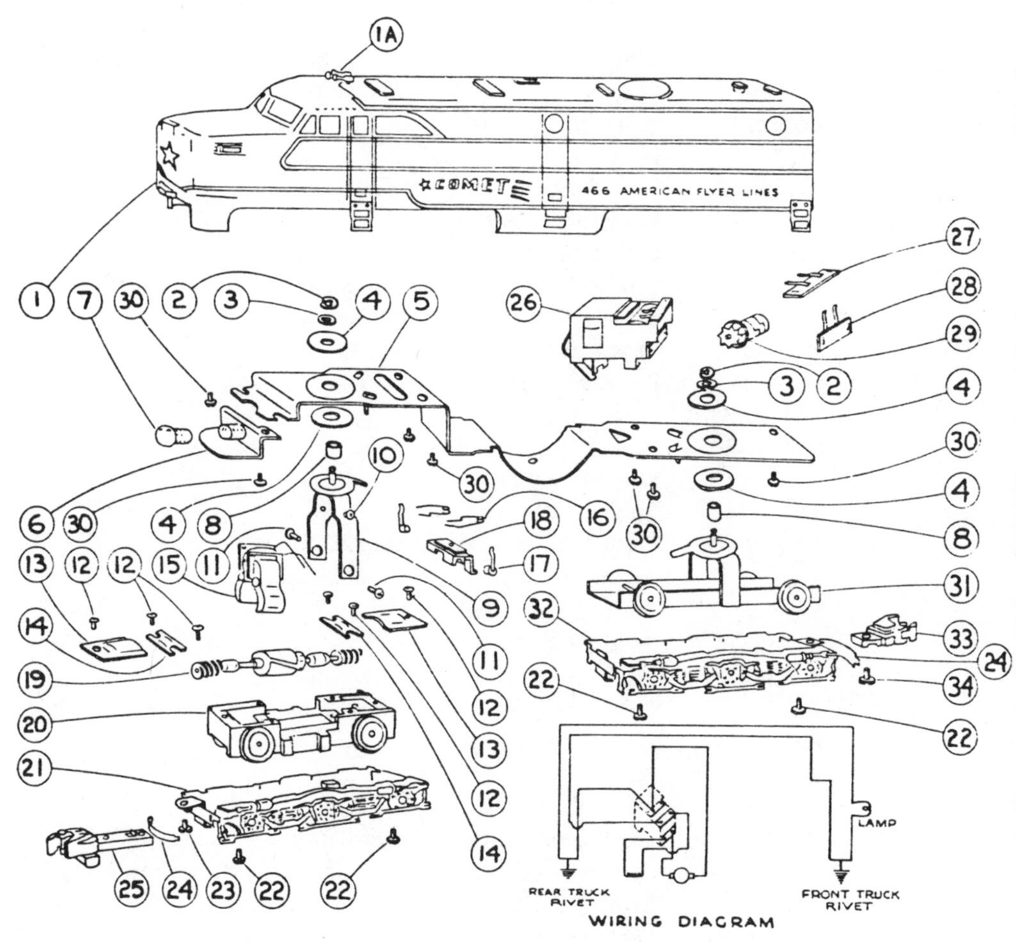
1A
466 AMERICAN FLYER LINES
COMET
1
7
30
2
3
4
5
26
27
28
29
6
8
9
10
11
12
13
14
15
16
17
18
19
20
21
22
23
24
25
31
32
33
34
LAMP
REAR TRUCK RIVET
FRONT TRUCK RIVET
WIRING DIAGRAM

Diagram Number	Part No.	Description	Price
1		A Unit Cabin w/trimmings	$6.07 ea.
2	P10800-A	Retaining ring	.04 "
3	W83	Washer	.30 dz.
4	W124	Washer	.01 ea.
5	PA12B059	Chassis	.31 "
6	XA11477	Lamp Bracket Ass'y.	.09 "
7	PA8999	Bulb	.25 "
8	PA11455	Fibre Bushing	.05 "
9	XA11457	Field Clamp Ass'y.	.37 "
10	S-0	Set Screw	.05 dz.
11	S-230	Screw	.10 dz.
12	S-171	Screw	.01 ea.
13	PA11441	Worm cover	.01 "
14	PA11453	Bearing Strap	.01 "
15	XA12A064	Field Ass'y.	1.25 "
16	P11000-R	Brush Spring (right)	.03 "
	P11000-L	Brush Spring (left)	.03 "
17	XA11684	Brush Holder Ass'y.	.25 "
18	XA11421-RP	Brush Bracket Ass'y.	.20 "
19	XA12A062	Armature Ass'y.	3.50 "
20	XA12A074	Truck Chassis Ass'y.	.77 ea.
	PA11343	Solid Wheel	.10 "
	XA11473	Insulated Wheel Ass'y.	.34 "
	XA12A249	Pull-Mor Wheel Ass'y.	.65 "
	PA10005	Plain Axle	.10 "
	PA10006	Gear Axle	.10 "
	PA11447	Worm Gear	.30 "
21	XA12A468	Truck Side Plate & Collector Ass'y	1.22 "
22	S249	Screw	.01 "
23	S3A70	Screw	.02 "
24	PA12A355	Leaf Spring	.01 "
25	XA12A358	Coupler & Arm Ass'y.	.31 "
26	XA10587-E	Remote Control Unit	2.50 "
27	XA9612-C	Top Finger Unit	.50 "
28	XA9612-B	Bottom Finger Unit	.50 "
29	XA8716	Drum	.60 "
30	S319	Screw	.01 "
31	XA11598-A	Wheel & Axle Ass'y.	1.25 "
32	XA12A356	Truck Side & Bottom Plate Ass'y.	1.02 "
33	XA12A047	Knuckle Coupler	.22 ea.
34	S3A71	Screw	.01 ea.

DIA. NO.	PART NO.	DESCRIPTION	PRICE
1	XA12D075-DRP	A Unit Cabin w/trimmings (466)	3.49 ea.
	XA12D075-FRP	A Unit Cabin w/trimmings (479)	4.84 ea.
1-A	PA11409	Plastic Horn	.08 ea.
2	P10800-A	Retaining Ring	.25 dz.
3	W83	Washer	.04 ea.
4	W124	Washer	.25 dz.
5	PA12B059	Chassis	.37 ea.
6	XA11477	Lamp Bracket Assembly	.24 ea.
7	PA8999	Bulb	.30 ea.
8	PA11455	Fibre Bushing	.14 ea.
9	XA11457	Field Clamp Assembly (466)	.45 ea.
	PA13A034	Field Clamp (479)	.34 ea.
	XA13A037	Yoke Assembly (479)	.26 ea.
10	S-0	Set Screw (466)	.01 ea.
	S165	Screw (479)	.03 ea.
11	S-230-B	Screw (466)	.01 ea.
	S4A06	Screw (479)	.03 ea.
12	S171	Screw	.01 ea.
13	PA11441	Worm Cover	.01 ea.
14	PA11453	Bearing Strap	.02 ea.
15	XA13A036	Field Assembly	1.34 ea.
16	P11000-R	Brush Spring (right)	.03 ea.
	P11000-L	Brush Spring (left)	.03 ea.
17	PA11684	Brush	.32 ea.
	P10132	Brush Holder (not sold assembled)	.01 ea.
18	XA11454-RP	Brush Bracket Assembly	.14 ea.
19	XA14B873-RP	Armature Assembly	3.94 ea.
20	XA12A074-RP	Truck Chassis Assembly	2.37 ea.
	PA11343	Solid Wheel (old style)	.06 ea.
	PA14A888	Solid Wheel (new style)	.08 ea.
	XA11473	Insulated Wheel Assembly (old style)	.25 ea.
	XA12A249	Pul-Mor Wheel Assembly (old style)	.72 ea.
	XA14A891	Pul-Mor Wheel Assembly (new style)	.28 ea.
	PA14A890	Pul-Mor	.05 ea.
	PA10005	Plain Axle NOT AVAILABLE	
		Sub. with PA15A226 Axle	.05 ea.
	PA10006	Gear Axle NOT AVAILABLE	
		Sub. with PA15A281 Axle	.07 ea.
	PA11447	Worm Gear NOT AVAILABLE	
		Sub. with PA15A218 Worm Gear	.09 ea.
	PA11463	Thrust Plate	.08 dz.
21	XA13A802	Truck & Collector Assembly	1.06 ea.
	XA13A803	Truck & Coupler Arm Assembly (consists of parts 21-23-24-25)	1.69 ea.
22	S249	Screw	.15 dz.
23	PA13A790	Rivet	.03 ea.
24	PA12A355-A	Leaf Spring	.02 ea.
25	XA12A358	Coupler & Arm Assembly	.34 ea.
26	XA10587-E	Remote Control Unit	4.04 ea.
27	XA9612-CRP	Top Finger Unit	.33 ea.
28	XA9612-BRP	Bottom Finger Unit	.33 ea.

con't

DIA. NO.	PART NO.	DESCRIPTION	PRICE
29	XA8716	Drum	.95 ea.
30	S319	Screw	.02 ea.
31	XA11598-B	Wheel & Chassis Assembly	1.12 ea.
32	XA13A802	Truck & Collector Assembly	1.06 ea.
	XA13A804	Truck & Coupler Assembly (consists of parts 24-32-33-34)	1.54 ea.
33	XA12A047	Knuckle Coupler	.29 ea.
34	PA13A791	Rivet	.02 ea.
		NOT SHOWN	
	XA13B038-B	Motor	12.16 ea.
	PA13A208-A	4 Conductor Cable (plastic)	.04 ft.

Prices subject to change without notice

DIA. NO.	PART NO.	DESCRIPTION	PRICE
1	XA12D075-DRP	A Unit Cabin w/ trimmings (466)	3.66 ea
	XA12D075-FRP	A Unit Cabin w/ trimmings (479)	5.08 ea
1-A	PA11409	Plastic Horn	.08 ea
2	P10800-A	Retaining Ring	.26 dz
3	W83	Washer	.04 ea
4	W124	Washer	.26 dz
5	PA12B059	Chassis	.39 ea
6	XA11477	Lamp Bracket Assembly	.25 ea
7	PA8999	Bulb	.32 ea
8	PA11455	Fibre Bushing	.15 ea
9	XA11457	Field Clamp Assembly (466)	.47 ea
	PA13A034	Field Clamp (479)	.36 ea
	XA13A037	Yoke Assembly (479)	.27 ea
10	S-0	Set Screw (466)	.01 ea
	S165	Screw (479)	.03 ea
11	S230-B	Screw (466)	.01 ea
	S4A06	Screw (479)	.03 ea
12	S171	Screw	.01 ea
13	PA11441	Worm Cover	.01 ea
14	PA11453	Bearing Strap	.02 ea
15	XA13A036	Field Assembly	1.41 ea
16	P11000-R	Brush Spring (Right)	.03 ea
	P11000-L	Brush Spring (Left)	.03 ea
17	PA11684	Brush	.34 ea
	P10132	Brush Holder	.01 ea
18	XA11454-RP	Brush Bracket Assembly	.15 ea
19	XA14B873-RP	Armature Assembly	4.14 ea
20	XA12A074-RP	Truck Chassis Assembly	2.49 ea
	PA14A888	Solid Wheel (NEW STYLE)	.08 ea
	XA14A891	Pul-Mor Wheel Assembly (NEW STYLE)	.29 ea
	PA14A890	Pul-Mor	.05 ea
	PA15A226	Plain Axle	.05 ea
	PA15A281	Gear Axle	.07 ea
	PA15A218	Worm Gear	.09 ea
	PA11463	Thrust Plate	.08 dz
21	XA13A802	Truck and Collector Assembly	1.11 ea
	XA13A803	Truck and Coupler Arm Assembly (Consists of Parts 21-23-24-25)	1.77 ea
22	S249	Screw	.16 dz
23	PA13A790	Rivet	.03 ea
24	PA12A355-A	Leaf Spring	.02 ea
25	XA12A358	Coupler and Arm Assembly	.36 ea
26	XA10587-E	Remote Control Unit	4.24 ea
27	XA9612-CRP	Top Finger Unit	.35 ea
28	XA9612-BRP	Bottom Finger Unit	.35 ea
29	XA8716	Drum	1.00 ea
30	S319	Screw	.02 ea
31	XA14A930-A	Wheel and Chassis Assembly	1.68 ea
32	XA13A802	Truck and Collector Assembly	1.11 ea
	XA13A804	Truck and Coupler Assembly (Consists of Parts 24-32-33-34)	1.62 ea

Cont'd

DIA. NO.	PART NO.	DESCRIPTION	PRICE
33	XA12A047	Knuckle Coupler	.30 ea.
34	PA13A791	Rivet	.02 ea.
		NOT SHOWN	
	XA13B038-B	Motor	12.77 ea.
	PA13A208-A	4 Conductor Cable (Plastic)	.04 ft.

Prices subject to change without notice.

ALCO B-UNIT DIESEL WITH ROAR
Model Nos. 467, 471, 476, 480

SPECIFICATIONS

Tested at: 12 Volts A.C. .... using 180" oval of track.

Load: Not to draw more than 1.4 amps. at 12 volts.
Roar noise is to start when transformer is turned on and increase in intensity as voltage is raised.

Ref: Form No. 1760; Aug. 1, 1956

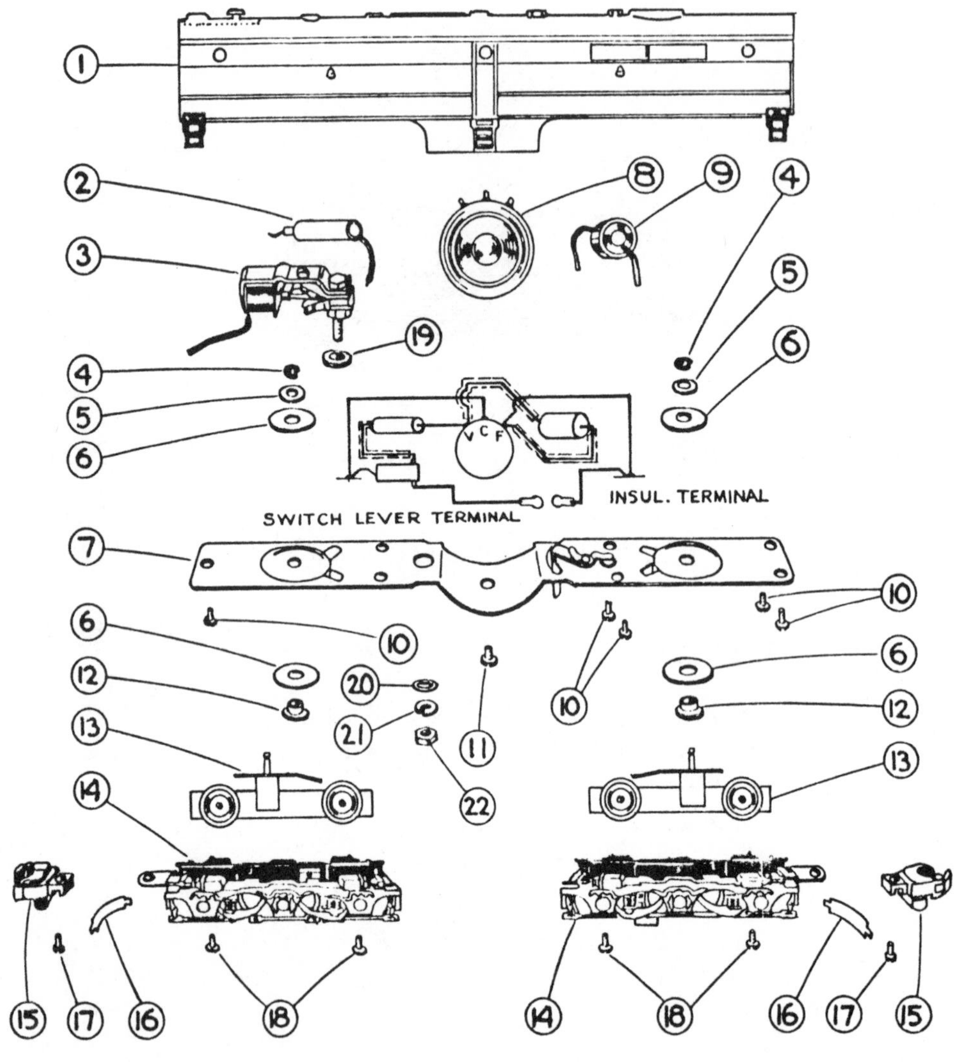

 Ref: Form No. 1760; Aug. 1, 1956

Diagram Number	Part No.	Description	Price
1	XA13B872RP	Cabin (467 Comet)	$2.53 ea.
	XA13B873RP	Cabin (476 Rocket)	2.58 ea.
	XA13B874RP	Cabin (480 Silver Flash) ..	2.58 ea.
	XA13B875RP	Cabin (471 Chief)	2.60 ea.
2	PA13A869	Capacitor	.98 ea.
3	PA13A870	Diesel Sound Generator ..	3.12 ea.
4	PA10800-A	Truax Ring	.04 ea.
5	W83	Washer	.03 ea.
6	W124	Washer	.01 ea.
7	XA11B687-BRP	Chassis	.42 ea.
8	XA11B831	Dynamic Speaker	3.87 ea.
9	PA12N820	Capacitor	2.10 ea.
10	S319	Screw	.01 ea.
11	S172	Screw	.10 dz.
12	PA11455	Bushing	.06 ea.
13	XA11598-A	Wheel & Chassis Assy.	1.25 ea.
14	XA13A802	Truck Assy.	.70 ea.
15	XA12A047	Coupler Assy.	.22 ea.
16	PA12A355-A	Leaf Spring	.01 ea.
17	PA13A791	Rivet	.01 ea.
18	S249	Screw	.01 ea.
19	PA10209	Bushing	.02 ea.
20	P4136-C	Washer	.05 dz.
21	P4654	Lockwasher	.05 dz.
22	N25	Nut	.01 ea.

Ref: Form No. 1760; Aug. 1, 1956

DIESEL LOCOMOTIVE UNITS PA, PB, PA

Model Nos. 470/471/473; 484/485/486; 490/491/493; 21902/21902-1/21902-2; 21910/21910-1/21910-2

SPECIFICATIONS

Tested at: 12 Volts A.C. .... using 180″ oval of track.

(A) Locomotive to run a minimum of 9 R.P.M. or 9 times forward and reverse, around 180″ oval of track.

Load: Not to draw more than 3.25 amps. while pulling 4 Passenger Cars.

Motor: Universal A.C. or D.C.

 Ref: Form No. 1818; Feb. 1, 1957

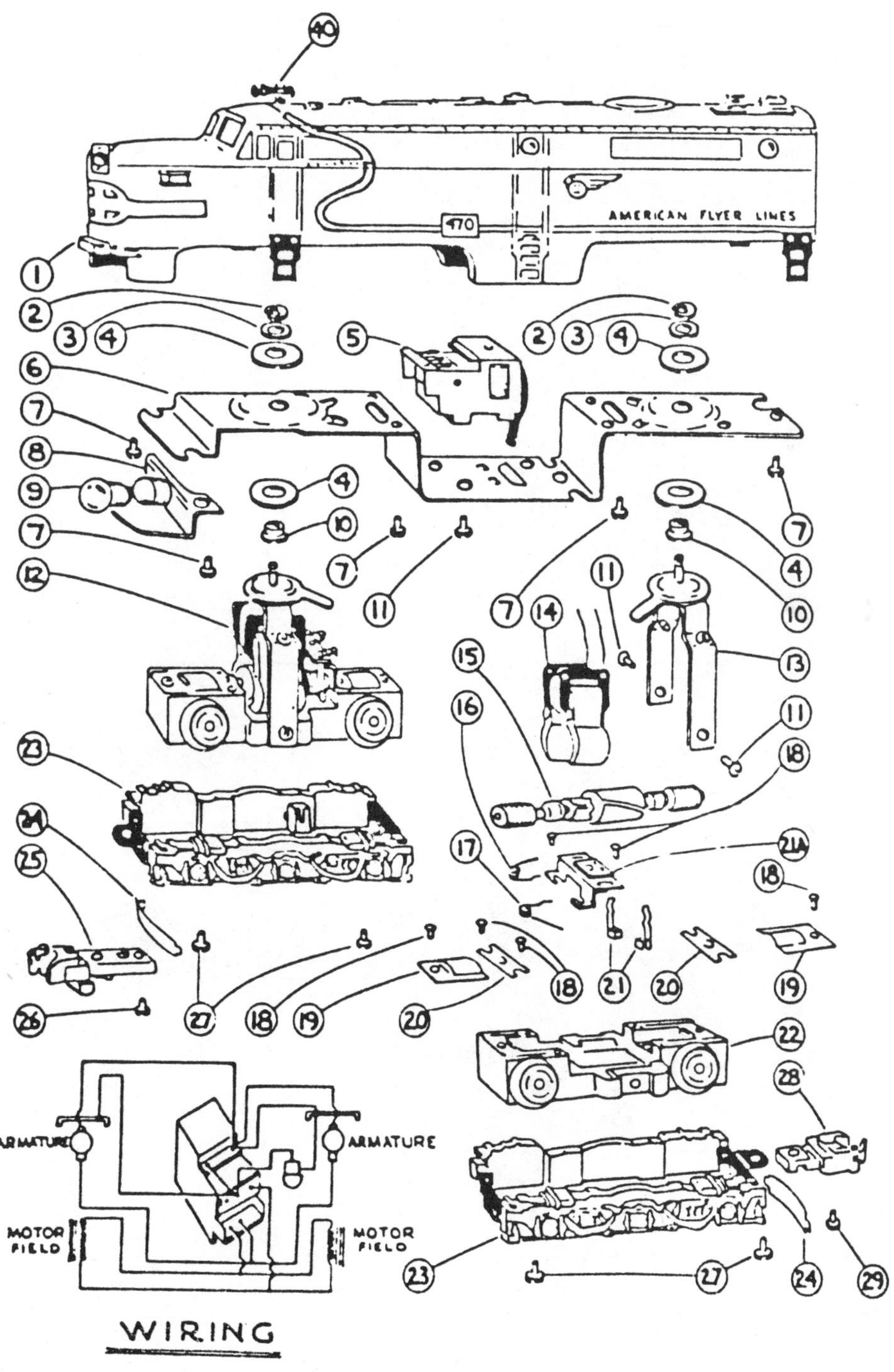

AMERICAN FLYER LINES
470
ARMATURE
ARMATURE
MOTOR FIELD
MOTOR FIELD
WIRING

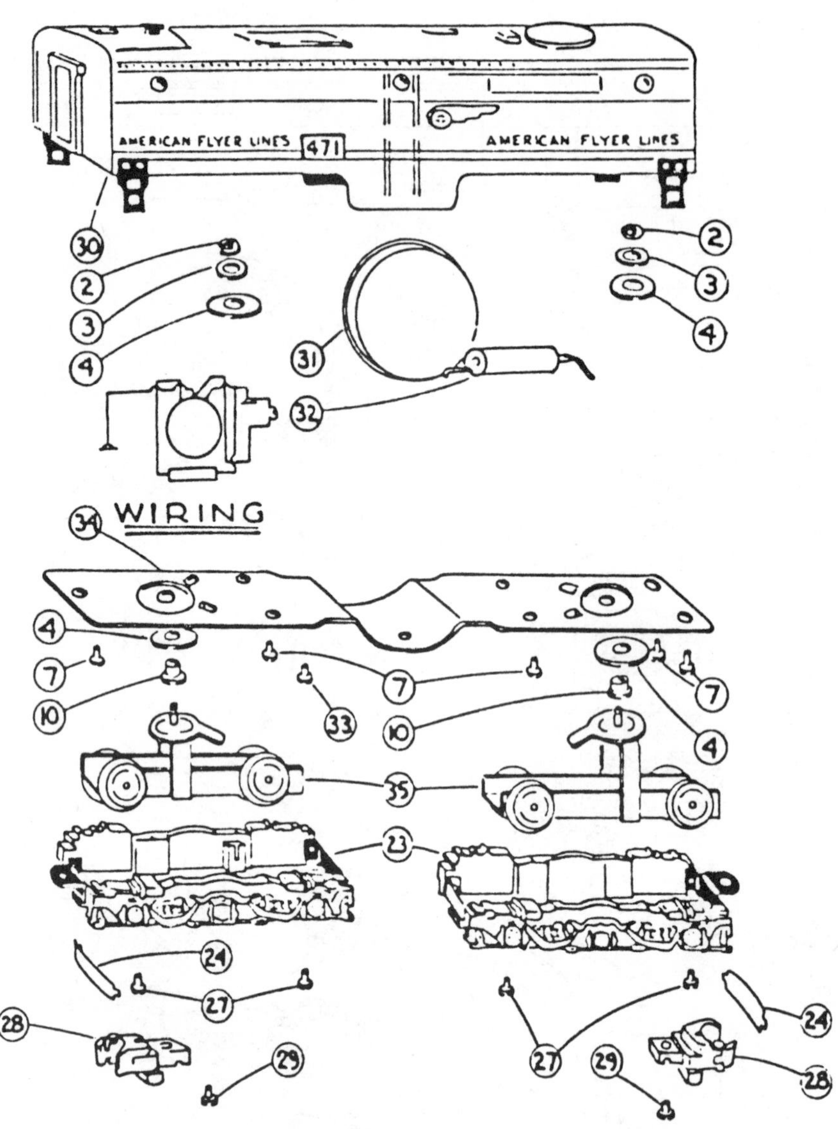

 Ref: Form No. 1818; Feb. 1, 1957

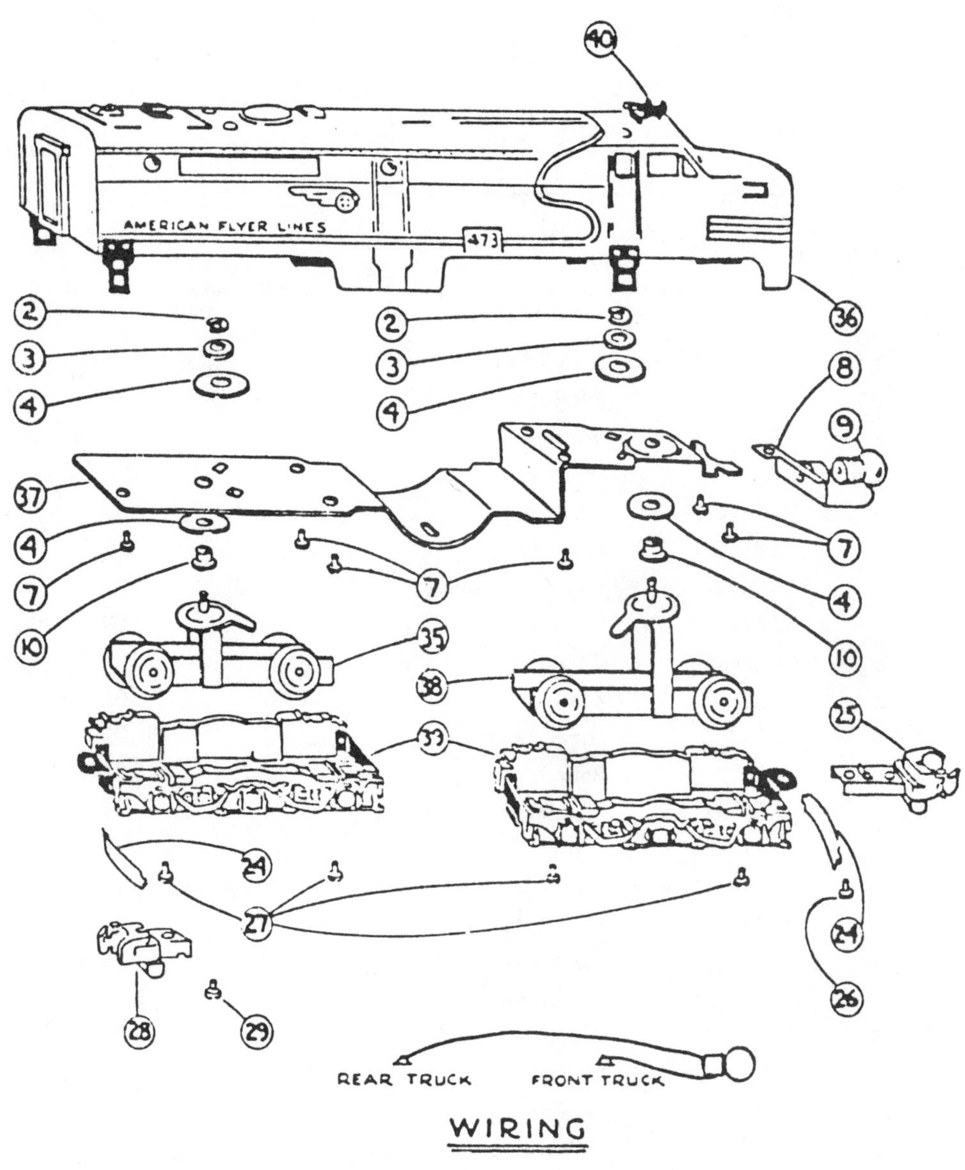
40
AMERICAN FLYER LINES
473
36
2
3
4
2
3
4
8
9
37
4
7
10
7
7
4
10
35
38
33
25
24
27
24
26
28
29
REAR TRUCK
FRONT TRUCK
WIRING

Diagram Number	Part No.	Description	Price
		A UNIT	
1	XA12D075 ARP	A Unit Cabin w/Trimmings	$3.43 ea.
2	P10800-A	Retaining Ring	.04 "
3	W83	Washer	.30 dz.
4	W124	Washer	.01 ea.
5	XA10587-E	R.C. Unit	2.50 "
	XA9612-B	Bottom Finger Unit	.50 "
	XA9612-C	Top Finger Unit	.50 "
	XA8716	Drum	.60 "
6	PA11452-B	Chassis	.54 "
7	S319	Screw	.01 "
8	XA11477	Lamp Bracket	.09 "
9	PA8999	Bulb	.25 "
10	PA11455	Fibre Bushing	.05 "
11	S230	Screw	.10 dz.
12	XA12B583-A	Motor Assy (not sold as a complete Assy)	
13	XA11457	Field Clamp Assy	.37 ea.
14	XA12A064	Field Assy	1.25 "
15	XA12A062	Armature Assy	3.50 "
16	P11000-L	Brush Spring (left)	.03 "
17	P11000-R	Brush Spring (right)	.03 "
18	S171	Screw	.01 "
19	PA11441	Worm Cover	.01 "
20	PA11453	Bearing Strap	.01 "

Diagram Number	Part No.	Description	Price
21	XA11684	Brush Holder Assy	$ .25 ea.
21A	XA11421 RP	Brush Bracket Assy	.20 "
22	XA12C065 RP	Truck Chassis Assy	1.94 "
23	XA12A468	Truck Side Plate & Collector Assy	1.22 "
24	PA12A355	Leaf Spring	.01 "
25	XA12A358	Coupler & Arm Assy	.31 "
26	S3A70	Coupler Screw	.02 "
27	S249	Screw	.01 "
28	XA12A047	Knuckle Coupler	.22 "
29	S3A70	Screw	.02 "
		B UNIT	
30	XA11688B RP	B Unit Cabin	3.38 ea.
31	XA11B831	Speaker	3.87 "
32	PA12N820	Capacitor	1.89 "
33	S172	Screw	.10 dz.
34	PA11687	Chassis	.27 ea.
35	XA11598-A	Wheel & Chassis Assy	1.25 "
		A UNIT DUMMY	
36	XA12D075 ERP	A Unit Cabin	3.58 ea.
37	PA12B059	Chassis	.31 "
38	XA11596-A	Wheel and Chassis Assy	1.25 "
39	XA12A356	Truck Side & Plate Assy	1.02 "
4)	PA11409	Air Chime (horn)	.05 "

SERVICE INSTRUCTIONS FOR NO. 4713 SANTA FE DIESEL LOCOMOTIVE

The first thing to do is to place Locomotive on track, connect Transformer and Whistle Control Unit and test for operation.

1. If the trouble is in the motors in the "A" Unit we suggest that you check as follows:

a. Check Brushes (※21) for wear or poor contact.

b. Check Brush Springs (※16 & ※17) for position and proper tension.

c. Check wires and solder joints for loose connections.

d. Commutator on Armature Assembly (※15) may be dirty.

e. Check operation of Remote Control Unit (※5).

f. See if motor is properly lubricated.

g. Wheels and track must be kept clean to insure proper electrical contact.

2. To disassemble and replace parts on "A" Unit

a. The first step is to remove the S319 Screws (※7) and take off Cabin (※1).

b. Motor is exposed and you can check wiring and other points of the unit.

c. Brush Holder Assembly (※21A) and Brush Springs (※16 & ※17) can be replaced without taking Motor Unit (※12) from Chassis (※6).

d. When replacing Brush Holder Assembly (※21A) unsolder lead wire and remove tension from Brush Spring (※16 & ※17).

e. To replace Brush Springs (※16 & ※17) remove Brush Holder Assembly (※21A) first so spring can be pulled forward and slipped out.

f. When replacing Armature (※15) or Magnet (※14) we recommend removing Motor Unit (※12) from Chassis (※6) as follows:

1. Unsolder lead wire to stud on Field Clamp Assembly (※13).
2. Take off Retaining Ring (※2) and Fibre Washers (※4).

g. Remove S249 Screws (※27) and take off Truck Side and Bottom Plate Assembly (※23).

h. Loosen the two S-0 Screws on the Field Clamp Assembly (※13).

i. Take out S230 Screws and remove Field Clamp Assembly (※13).

j. Remove S171 Screws and take off Worm Cover (※19) and Bearing Strap (※20).

NOTE: When reassembling Motor it is necessary to adjust the two S-0 Screws on the Field Clamp Assembly (※13) which centralizes the Magnet Assembly (※14). The reason is to prevent the Armature Assembly (※15) from striking the plates on the Magnet Assembly (※14).

When placing the Motor Unit (※12) back in Chassis (※6) the stop on the Field Clamp Assembly (※13) must be facing inward so that the stop will always be parallel with the Commutator on the Armature Assembly (※15).

3. Instructions for correcting Whistle failure in the "B" Unit as follows:

a. Recheck the instruction sheet in order to make sure hook-up is correct. If both the Transformer instructions and the Air Chime Whistle Instructions are followed, this will cause a duplication of wiring. The result will be that you will only have a faint buzz while the train is running or in a neutral position. Follow the Air Chime Whistle wiring instructions only and be sure to have only two wires going to the ※690 Track Terminal.

b. The Generator Tube ※PA11665 on the control box may be weak and need replacing.

c. If the trouble still persists it will be necessary to remove the "B" Unit cab from the Chassis by unscrewing the five screws (※7).

d. The Unit is exposed and you can check all wires and solder joints for loose connections. Be sure the lead wires on the condenser are covered with an insulating sleeve.

e. Check the condenser (※32) by adding another condenser in series with temporary connections. If this corrects the trouble the defective condenser can be removed and a new one connected in its place.

f. The speaker seldom has to be replaced unless the wire or covering is broken.

SERVICE INSTRUCTIONS FOR No. 471 DIESEL ROAR "B" UNIT

The first thing to do is to place the "B" Unit on track, connect Transformer and Whistle Control Unit and test for operation.

1. **If you are having trouble with the Whistle in your "B" Unit check as follows:**
   a. Recheck the instruction sheet in order to make sure hook-up is correct. If both the Transformer instructions and the Air Chime Whistle Instructions are followed, this will cause a duplication of wiring. The result will be that you will only have a faint buzz while the train is running or in a neutral position. Follow the Air Chime Whistle wiring instructions only and be sure to have only two wires going to the ※690 Track Terminal.
   b. The Generator Tube ※PA11665-A on the control box may be weak and need replacing.
   c. If the trouble still persists it will be necessary to remove the "B" unit Cab from the Chassis (※7) by unscrewing the five screws (※10).
   d. The Unit is exposed and you can check all wires and soldered joints for loose connections. Be sure the lead wires on the capacitor are covered with an insulating sleeve.
   e. Check the capacitor (※9) by adding another capacitor in series with temporary connections. If this corrects the trouble the defective capacitor can be removed and a new one connected in its place.
   f. The Speaker (※8) seldom has to be replaced unless the wire or covering is broken.
2. **If you are having some difficulty with the Roar, check as follows:**
   a. Remove five screws (※10) and pull Cabin (※3) off Chassis (※7).
   b. The unit is exposed and you can check all wires and soldered joints for loose connections. Be sure the lead wires on the capacitors are covered with an insulating sleeve.
   c. Check the capacitor (※2) by adding another capacitor in series with temporary connections. If this corrects the trouble the defective part can be removed and a new one connected in its place.
   d. The action of the switch lever on the chassis (※7) should be checked to insure proper contact.
   e. Inspect coil for burn out and also pitted points on Sound Generator Unit (※3).
3. **To disassemble and replace parts on "B" Unit.**
   a. The first step is to remove the five S319 Screws (※10) and take Cabin (※1) off of Chassis (※7).
   b. Unsolder the wires on capacitor (※2) and capacitor (※9) to replace defective part.
   c. Remove Nut (※22), Lockwasher (※21) and washer (※20) from Chassis (※7) and then remove bushing (※19) and generator (※3).
   d. To replace Speaker (※8), unsolder wires on speaker (※8) and remove screw (※11) underneath Chassis (※7).
   e. Unsolder wire on truck stud and remove Truax Ring (※4), Washer (※5), Washer (※6) and pull out wheel and Chassis Assembly (※13) from Chassis (※7).
   f. To remove Truck Side unscrew two screws (※18) at bottom of Truck Assembly (※14).
   g. To replace Leaf Spring (※16) or Knuckle Coupler (※15) from Truck Assembly (※14) remove Rivet (※17).

PARTS LIST 21902 THE CHIEF DIESEL POWERED "A" UNIT

NO.	DESCRIPTION	PCS/ UNIT	COST	
XA-15B140-RP	CABIN W/TRIM	1	5.03	EA.
PA-11409	AIR CHIME (DECORATION)	1	.08	EA.
PA-11488	HEADLIGHT LENS	1	.04	EA.
XA-13B038-B	PUL-MOR MOTOR ASSY	2	12.16	EA.
XA-15A383	LAMP BRACKET ASSY	1	.29	EA.
XA-13A803	FRONT TRUCK & COUPLER ASSY	1	1.69	EA.
PA-12A357	COUPLER ARM (FRONT TRUCK)	1	.07	EA.
PA-13A790	TUBULAR RIVET (FRONT TRUCK)	1	.36	DOZ
PA-12A355-A	LEAF SPRING (COUPLER)	2	.01	EA.
XA-12A057	KNUCKLE COUPLER ASSY	2	.98	EA.
XA-13A804	REAR TRUCK & COUPLER ASSY	1	1.54	EA.
XA-13A802	REAR & FRONT TRUCK ASSY	2	1.06	EA.
PA-13A791	TUBULAR RIVET (REAR TRUCK)	1	.25	DOZ
PA-11B452-C	LOCOMOTIVE CHASSIS	1	1.13	EA.
PA-11493	AIR INTAKE	1	.04	EA.
PA-8999	14V CLEAR BULB	1	.36	EA.
W-83	.161 DIA.HOLE STEEL WASHER (FRONT PIVOT)	1	.50	DOZ.
W-124	.161 DIA. HOLE 1/16 THK FIBER WASHER (FRONT PIVOT)	2	.25	DOZ.
P-10800-A	TRU-ARC RETAINING RING (PIVOT)	2	.25	DOZ.
PA-11455	FIBER BUSHING (USE ONE ON EACH PIVOT)	2	.14	EA.
S-172	#4 x 3/16 TYPE "Z" B.H.P.K. SCREW (SECURE R/C UNIT)	2	.01	EA.
W-	¼" DIA.HOLE 1/16 THK.STEEL WASHER (REAR PIVOT)	2	.35	DOZ.
-14C429	2 PCS. REMOTE CONTROL UNIT	1	2.69	EA.
2A28	.191 DIA.HOLE COPPER PLATED SPRING WASHER (REAR PIVOT)	1	.02	EA.
S-319	#6 x 5/16" TYPE "Z" R.H.P.K. SCREW (CHASSIS TO CABIN)	5	.12	DOZ
S-5N40	#2-56 x ¼" LONG TYPE "F" SELF TAPPING FLAT HEAD SCREWS (USE 2 SC.TO ASSEM. TRUCKSIDE & BOTTC PLATE ASSY TO MOTOR ASSY)	4	.15	DOZ.
LW-1B1	BLACK LEAD WIRE		.02	FT.
P-11N017	#20 BARE COPPER WIRE ½" LONG	1	3.50	LB.

21910 S.F. FREIGHT DIESEL POWERED "A" UNIT

SAME AS 21902 DIESEL LOCOMOTIVE -
EXCEPT USE:

XA-14B125-RP	CABIN W/TRIM	1	4.15	EA.

21920 M.P. DIESEL POWERED "A" UNIT

SAME AS 21902 DIESEL LOCOMOTIVE-
EXCEPT USE:

XA-15B082-RP	CABIN W/TRIM	1	4.15	EA.

21922 M.P. DIESEL POWERED "A" UNIT

SAME AS 21902 DIESEL LOCOMOTIVE -
EXCEPT USE:

XA-15B594-RP	CABIN W/TRIM	1	4.15	EA.

NOTE: PRICES SUBJECT TO CHANGE WITHOUT NOTICE.

PARTS LIST

(NON-MOTORIZED UNITS)

21902-2 "THE CHIEF" DIESEL "A" UNIT W/O WHISTLE - CONT'D

ELIMINATE:

PA-15A589	SPRING FOR BELL HAMMER	1	
XA-15A445	TRUCK YOKE & CHASSIS ASSY	1	

ADD THE FOLLOWING:

XA-15B140-ARP	CABIN WITH TRIM	1	5.03 EA.
XA-13B422	CHASSIS & TRUCK SUPPORT BRACKET ASSY	1	.96 EA.
W-124-A	¼" DIA. HOLE 1/16 THK. STEEL WASHER	1	.03 EA.
W-2A28	.191 DIA. HOLE COPPER PLATED SPRING WASHER	1	.02 EA.

21910-2 S.F. DIESEL "A" UNIT W/O WHISTLE

SAME AS 21902-2 DIESEL -
EXCEPT USE:

XA-14B125-ARP	CABIN W/TRIM	1	4.15 EA.

NOTE: PRICES SUBJECT TO CHANGE WITHOUT NOTICE.

PARTS LIST (NON-MOTORIZED UNITS)

21910-1 S.F. FREIGHT "B" UNIT DIESEL W/HORN & ROAR

PART NO.	DESCRIPTION	PCS/ UNIT	COST
XA-14A930-A	YOKE, WHEEL & STRUCK UP CHASSIS ASSY	2	1.60 EA.
PA-14B888	SOLID WHEEL	4	.10 EA.
PA-15A226	AXLE SHAFT	4	.05 EA.
XA-14A870	INSULATED WHEEL ASSY	4	.19 EA.
XA-13A804	TRUCK & COUPLER ASSY	2	1.54 EA.
PA-13A791	TUBULAR RIVET (TRUCK)	2	.02 EA.
PA-12A355-A	LEAF SPRING (COUPLER)	2	.01 EA.
XA-12A047	KNUCKLE COUPLER ASSY	2	.31 EA.
XA-13A802	TRUCK ASSY	2	1.06 EA.
XA-14A127	PERMANENT MAGNETIC SPEAKER	1	4.48 EA.
XA-11B687-DRP	LOCOMOTIVE CHASSIS & SWITCH ASSY	1	.60 EA.
PA-14A914	CAPACITOR	1	1.40 EA.
PA-13A870	DIESEL SOUND GENERATOR	1	4.52 EA.
XA-11688-GRP	"B" UNIT CAB W/TRIM	1	3.69 EA.
PA-11493	AIR INTAKE	1	.04 EA.
PA-14A216	BRACKET (SPEAKER)	1	.08 EA.
PA-11455	FIBER BUSHING (PIVOT)	2	.14 EA.
PA-10209	BUSHING (SOUND GENERATOR)	1	.02 EA.
P-10800-A	TRU-ARC RETAINING RING	2	.02 EA.
[illegible]-181	BLACK LEAD WIRE		.02 FT.
S-249	#2 x 5/16 TYPE "Z" P.K. SCREW FLAT CT'SINK HEAD (SECURE SIDE PLATE)	4	.01 EA.
S-319	#6 x 5/16 TYPE "Z" P.K. SCREW ROUND HEAD (SECURE CHASSIS TO BODY)	5	.01 EA.
N-25	#8-32 HEX NUT (SOUND TO CHASSIS)	1	.02 EA.
W-83	.161 DIA.HOLE STEEL WASHER (FRONT PIVOT)	1	.04 EA.
W-124	¼" DIA.HOLE 1/16 THK.BLACK WASHER (FRONT PIVOT)	2	.02 EA.
P-4126-C	.158-.160 DIA.HOLE FIBER WASHER	1	.05 DOZ.
P-1131-C	.3205-.3185 DIA.HOLE VELLUMOID WASHER	1	.01 EA.
P-4654	.200 I.D. LOCKWASHER (FOR N25 NUT)	1	.01 EA.
S-316	#6 x ¼" TYPE "A" P.K. SCREW BIND.HEAD (SECURE SPEAKER TO CHASSIS)	1	.01 EA.
S-183	#2 x ¼" P.K. BD.HD.TYPE "Z" SCREW (SECURE SPEAKER BRACKET)	1	.01 EA.
W-124-A	¼" DIA.HOLE 1/16" THK STEEL WASHER (REAR PIVOT)	2	.03 EA.
W-2A28	.191 DIA.HOLE SPRING WASHER COPPER PLATED (REAR PIVOT)	1	.02 EA.

21902-1 "THE CHIEF" DIESEL "B" UNIT WITH ROAR

SAME AS 21910-1 DIESEL-
EXCEPT ELIMINATE THE FOLLOWING PART:

XA-11688-GRP	"B" UNIT CAB	1	

ADD THE FOLLOWING PART:

XA-13B875-RP	"B" CAB W/TRIM	1	4.15 EA.

NOTE: PRICES SUBJECT TO CHANGE WITHOUT NOTICE.

NO.	PART NO.	DESCRIPTION	PRICE
1	XA12D075-ARP	CABIN W/TRIMMINGS (470)	4.20 EA.
	XA14B125-RP	CABIN W/TRIMMINGS (484)	4.15 EA.
	XA14B122-RP	CABIN W/TRIMMINGS (490)	3.25 EA.
	XA15B140-RP	CABIN W/TRIMMINGS (21902)	5.03 EA.
	XA14B125-RP	CABIN W/TRIMMINGS (21910)	4.15 EA.
2	P10800-A	RETAINING RING	.25 DZ.
3	W83	WASHER	.04 EA.
	W2A28	SPRING WASHER (NOT USED ON OLD STYLE 4713)	.25 DZ.
4	W124	WASHER	.25 DZ.
	W124A	STEEL WASHER (NOT USED ON O.S.4173)	.35 DZ.
5	XA10587-E	REMOTE CONTROL UNIT (USED ON #470-484-490)	4.04 EA.
	XA9612-BRP	BOTTOM FINGER UNIT	.33 EA.
	XA9612-CRP	TOP FINGER UNIT	.33 EA.
	XA8716	DRUM	.95 EA.
	XA14C429	REMOTE CONTROL UNIT (USED ON 21902 & 21910)	2.76 EA.
	XA14A994	CONTACT ASSY.	.77 EA.
	XA14A435	PLUNGER ASSY.	.14 EA.
	XA14B433	COIL ASSY.	.69 EA.
	PA14A444	COIL SUPPORT	.05 EA.
	PA14C432	COIL HOUSING	.04 EA.
6	PA11452-B	CHASSIS (USED ON #470,484 & 490)	.59 EA.
	PA11452-C	CHASSIS (USED ON 21902 & 21910)	1.13 EA.
7	S319	SCREW	.02 EA.
8	XA11477	LAMP BRACKET (USED ON 470,473, 484,486,490 & 493)	.24 EA.
	XA15A383	LAMP BRACKET (USED ON 21902, 21902-2, 21910, 21910-2)	.29 EA.
9	PA8999	BULB	.30 EA.
10	PA11455	FIBRE BUSHING	.14 EA.
11	S172	SCREW (SECURES REMOTE CONTROL UNIT)	.02 EA.
	S4A06	SCREW (SECURES YOKE & FIELD CLAMP TO CHASSIS)	.03 EA.
12	XA13B038-B	MOTOR ASSY.	12.16 EA.
13	XA11457	FIELD CLAMP ASSY. (4713 ONLY) (NOT USED W/ABOVE MOTOR)	.45 EA.
	XA13A037	YOKE ASSY.	.26 EA.
	PA13A034	FIELD CLAMP	.34 EA.
	S165	SCREW	.03 EA.
14	XA13A036	FIELD ASSY.	1.34 EA.
15	XA14B873-RP	ARMATURE ASSY.	3.94 EA.
16	P11000-L	BRUSH SPRING (LEFT)	.03 EA.
17	P11000-R	BRUSH SPRING (RIGHT)	.03 EA.
18	S171	SCREW	.01 EA.
19	PA11441	WORM COVER	.01 EA.
20	PA11453	BEARING STRAP	.02 EA.
21	PA11684	BRUSH (NOT SOLD ASSEMBLED)	.32 EA.
	P10132	BRUSH HOLDER	.01 EA.
22	XA12B065-RP	TRUCK CHASSIS ASSY. NOT AVAILABLE USE XA12A074-RP TRUCK CHASSIS ASSY.	2.37 EA.

CON'T

NO.	PART NO.	DESCRIPTION	PRICE
	PA11343	SOLID WHEEL (OLD STYLE)	.06 EA.
	PA14A888	SOLID WHEEL (NEW STYLE)	.08 EA.
	XA11473	INSULATED WHEEL (OLD STYLE)	.25 EA.
	XA12A249	PUL-MOR WHEEL ASSY. (OLD STYLE)	.72 EA.
	XA14A891	PUL-MOR WHEEL ASSY. (NEW STYLE)	.28 EA.
	PA14A890	PUL-MOR	.05 EA.
	PA15A281	AXLE	.07 EA.
	PA15A218	WORM GEAR	.09 EA.
	PA11463	THRUST PLATE	.08 DZ.
	XA13A803	TRUCK W/COLLECTOR & COUPLER ARM ASSY. (PARTS 23,24,25,26)	1.69 EA.
	XA13A804	TRUCK W/COLLECTOR & COUPLER ASSY. (PARTS 23,24,28,29)	1.54 EA.
23	XA13A802	TRUCK AND COLLECTOR ASSY.	1.06 EA.
24	PA12A355-A	LEAF SPRING	.02 EA.
25	XA12A358	COUPLER AND ARM ASSY.	.34 EA.
26	PA13A790	RIVET	.36 DZ.
27	S249	SCREW	.15 DZ.
	S5N40	SCREW (USED ON #21902 & 21910)	.15 DZ.
28	XA12A047	KNUCKLE COUPLER	.29 EA.
29	PA13A791	RIVET	.02 EA.
30	XA11688-BRP	"B" UNIT CABIN (471)	3.06 EA.
	XA11688-GRP	"B" UNIT CABIN (485)	2.93 EA.
	XA14B121-RP	"B" UNIT CABIN (491)	3.08 EA.
	XA13B875-RP	"B" UNIT CABIN (21902-1)	4.15 EA.
	XA11688-GRP	"B" UNIT CABIN (21910-1)	2.93 EA.
31	XA11B831	SPEAKER NOT AVAILABLE	
		USE XA14A127 SPEAKER (NEW STYLE)	4.57 EA.
		PA14A216 BRACKET	.08 EA.
		S171 SCREW	.01 EA.
32	PA14A914	CAPACITOR	1.40 EA.
33	S172	SCREW (HOLDS SPEAKER BRACKET)	.02 EA.
34	PA11687	CHASSIS	.33 EA.
	PA11687-D	CHASSIS (USED ON 21902-1 & 21910-1)	.70 EA.
35	XA14A930-A	YOKE, WHEEL & CHASSIS ASSY.	1.60 EA.
36	XA12D075-ERP	"A" UNIT DUMMY CABIN (473)	4.37 EA.
	XA14B125-ARP	"A" UNIT DUMMY CABIN (486)	4.03 EA.
	XA14B122-ARP	"A" UNIT DUMMY CABIN (493)	3.75 EA.
	XA15B140-ARP	"A" UNIT DUMMY CABIN (21902-2)	5.03 EA.
	XA14B125-ARP	"A" UNIT DUMMY CABIN (21910-2)	4.03 EA.
37	PA12B059	CHASSIS	.37 EA.
	XA13B422	CHASSIS (USED ON 21902-2 & 21910-2)	.96 EA.
38	XA11596-A	WHEEL & CHASSIS ASSY. (4173 ONLY)	1.38 EA.
	XA14A930-A	WHEEL & CHASSIS ASSY	1.60 EA.
	XA13A801	TRUCK W/COUPLER ASSY. (PARTS 24,28,29,39)	1.33 EA.
	XA13A800	TRUCK W/COUPLER ARM ASSY. (PARTS 24,25,26,39)	1.47 EA.
39	XA13A799	TRUCK ASSY.	.62 EA.
40	PA11409	AIR CHIME (HORN)	.08 EA.

CON'T

NO.	PART NO.	DESCRIPTION	PRICE
		PARTS NOT SHOWN	
	PA13A870	Diesel Sound Generator	4.52 EA.
	PA10209	Insulating Bushing	.02 EA.
	P1131-C	Washer	.01 EA.
	N25	8-32 Hex Nut	.02 EA.
	P4654	Lockwasher	.01 EA
	W55-B	Washer	.06 DZ
	PA13A208-A	4 Conductor Cable (plastic) (470-484-490)	.04 FT
	LW-181	Lead Wire (21902-21910)	.02 FT

PRICES SUBJECT TO CHANGE WITHOUT NOTICE.

Diesel Units — Nos. 470/474/473, 484/485/486, 490/491/493, 21902/21902-1/21902-2, 21910/21910-1/21910-2

NO.	PART NO.	DESCRIPTION	PRICE
1	XA12D075-ARP	Cabin w/trimmings (470)	4.41 ea.
	XA14B125-RP	Cabin w/ trimmings (484)	4.36 ea.
	XA14B122-RP	Cabin w/trimmings (490)	3.41 ea.
	XA15B140-RP	Cabin w/trimmings (21902)	5.28 ea.
	XA14B125-RP	Cabin w/trimmings (21910)	4.36 ea.
2	P10800-A	Retaining Ring	.26 dz.
3	W83	Washer	.04 ea.
	W2A28	Spring Washer (Not Used on Old Style 470)	.26 dz.
4	W124	Washer	.26 dz.
	W124A	Steel Washer (Not Used on O.S. 470)	.37 dz.
5	XA10587-E	Remote Control Unit (Used On 470-484-490)	4.24 ea.
	XA9612-BRP	Bottom Finger Unit	.35 ea.
	XA9612-CRP	Top Finger Unit	.35 ea.
	XA8716	Drum	1.00 ea.
	XA14C429	Remote Control Unit (Used On 21902-21910)	2.90 ea.
	XA14A994	Contact Assembly	.81 ea.
	XA14A435	Plunger Assembly	.15 ea.
	XA14B433	Coil Assembly	.72 ea.
	PA14A444	Coil Support	.05 ea.
	PA14C432	Coil Housing	.04 ea.
6		Chassis (Used on 470-484-490) OBSOLETE	
	PA11452-C	Chassis (Used On 21902-21910)	1.19 ea.
7	S319	Screw	.02 ea.
8	XA11477	Lamp Bracket (Used on 470-473-484-486-490-493)	.25 ea.
	XA15A383	Lamp Bracket (Used on 21902-21902-2-21910-21910-2)	.30 ea.
9	PA8999	Bulb	.32 ea.
10	PA11455	Fibre Bushing	.15 ea.
11	S172	Screw (Secures Remote Control Unit)	.02 ea.
	S4A06	Screw (Secures Yoke & Field Clamp to Chassis)	.03 ea.
12	XA13B038-B	Motor Assembly	12.77 ea.
13	XA11457	Field Clamp Assembly (470 Only) (Not used w/above Motor)	.47 ea.
	XA13A037	Yoke Assembly	.27 ea.
	PA13A034	Field Clamp	.36 ea.
	S165	Screw	.03 ea.
14	XA13A036	Field Assembly	1.41 ea.
15	XA14B873-RP	Armature Assembly	4.14 ea.
16	P11000-L	Brush Spring (Left)	.03 ea.
17	P11000-R	Brush Spring (Right)	.03 ea.
18	S171	Screw	.01 ea.
19	PA11441	Worm Cover	.01 ea.
20	PA11453	Bearing Strap	.02 ea.
21	PA11684	Brush	.34 ea.
	P10132	Brush Holder	.01 ea.
22	XA12A074-RP	Truck Chassis Assembly	2.49 ea.
	PA14A888	Solid Wheel (New Style)	.08 ea.
	XA14A891	Pul-Mor Wheel Assembly (New Style)	.29 ea.
	PA14A890	Pul-Mor	.05 ea.
	PA15A281	Axle	.07 ea.
	PA15A218	Worm Gear	.09 ea.
	PA11463	Thrust Plate	.08 dz.
	XA13A803	Truck w/Collector & Coupler Arm Assembly (Parts 23-24-25-26)	1.77 ea.
	XA13A804	Truck w/Collector & Coupler Assembly (Parts 23-24-28-29)	1.62 ea.

Cont'd

 Ref: Form No. 1818; Oct. 1, 1962

NO.	PART NO.	DESCRIPTION	PRICE
23	XA13A802	Truck and Collector Assembly	1.11 ea.
24	PA12A355-A	Leaf Spring	.02 ea.
25	XA12A358	Coupler and Arm Assembly	.36 ea.
26	PA13A790	Rivet	.38 dz.
27	S249	Screw	.16 dz.
	S5N40	Screw (Used on #21902 and 21910)	.16 dz.
28	XA12A047	Knuckle Coupler	.30 ea.
29	PA13A791	Rivet	.02 ea.
30	XA11688-BRP	"B" Unit Cabin (471)	3.21 ea.
	XA11688-GRP	"B" Unit Cabin (485)	3.08 ea.
	XA14B121-RP	"B" Unit Cabin (491)	3.23 ea.
	XA13B875-RP	"B" Unit Cabin (21902-1)	4.36 ea.
	XA11688-GRP	"B" Unit Cabin (21910-1) (Marked 485)	3.08 ea.
31	XA14A127 Conv.	Speaker Substitute for XA11B831 Obsolete	4.91 ea.
32	PA14A914	Capacitor	1.47 ea.
33	S172	Screw (Holds Speaker Bracket)	.02 ea.
34	PA11687	Chassis	.35 ea.
	PA11687-D	Chassis (Used On 21902-1 & 21910-1)	.74 ea.
35	XA14A930-A	Yoke, Wheel and Chassis Assembly	1.68 ea.
36	XA12D075-ERP	"A" Unit Dummy Cabin (473)	4.59 ea.
	XA14B125-ARP	"A" Unit Dummy Cabin (486)	4.23 ea.
	XA14B122-ARP	"A" Unit Dummy Cabin (493)	3.94 ea.
	XA15B140-ARP	"A" Unit Dummy Cabin (21902-2)	5.28 ea.
	XA14B125-ARP	"A" Unit Dummy Cabin (21910-2) (Marked 486)	4.23 ea.
37	PA12B059	Chassis	.39 ea.
	XA13B422	Chassis (Used on 21902-2-21910-2)	1.01 ea.
38	XA11596-A	Wheel & Chassis Assembly (473)	1.45 ea.
	XA14A930-A	Wheel and Chassis Assembly	1.68 ea.
	XA13A801	Truck w/coupler Assembly (Parts 24-28-29-39)	1.40 ea.
	XA13A800	Truck w/coupler Arm Assembly (Parts 24-25-26-39)	1.54 ea.
39	XA13A799	Truck Assembly	.65 ea.
40	PA11409	Air Chime (Horn)	.08 ea.

PARTS NOT SHOWN

PART NO.	DESCRIPTION	PRICE
PA13A870	Diesel Sound Generator	4.75 ea.
PA10209	Insulating Bushing	.02 ea.
P1131-C	Washer	.01 ea.
N25	8-32 Hex Nut	.02 ea.
P4654	Lockwasher	.01 ea.
W55-B	Washer	.06 dz.
PA13A208-A	4 Conductor Cable (Plastic) (470-484-490)	.04 ft.
LW-1B1	Lead Wire (21902-21910)	.02 ft.

Prices subject to change without notice.

Ref: Form No. 1818; Oct. 1, 1962

DIESEL LOCOMOTIVES
Model Nos. 472, 481, 497, 21551, 21927
ELECTRIC LOCOMOTIVES
Model Nos. 499, 21573

Model numbers 499 and 21573 refer to the New Haven EP-5 GE Electric locomotive. These models are included here because of the similarity of construction. Gilbert has even included some sheets just on the electrics.

SPECIFICATIONS

Tested at: 12 Volts A.C. .... using 160" oval of track.

(A) Locomotive to run a minimum of 9 R.P.M. or 9 times forward and reverse, around 160" oval of track.

Load: Not to draw more than 1.8 amps. while pulling 4 Passenger Cars.

Motor: Universal A.C. or D.C.

 Ref: Form No. 1771; Oct. 1, 1956

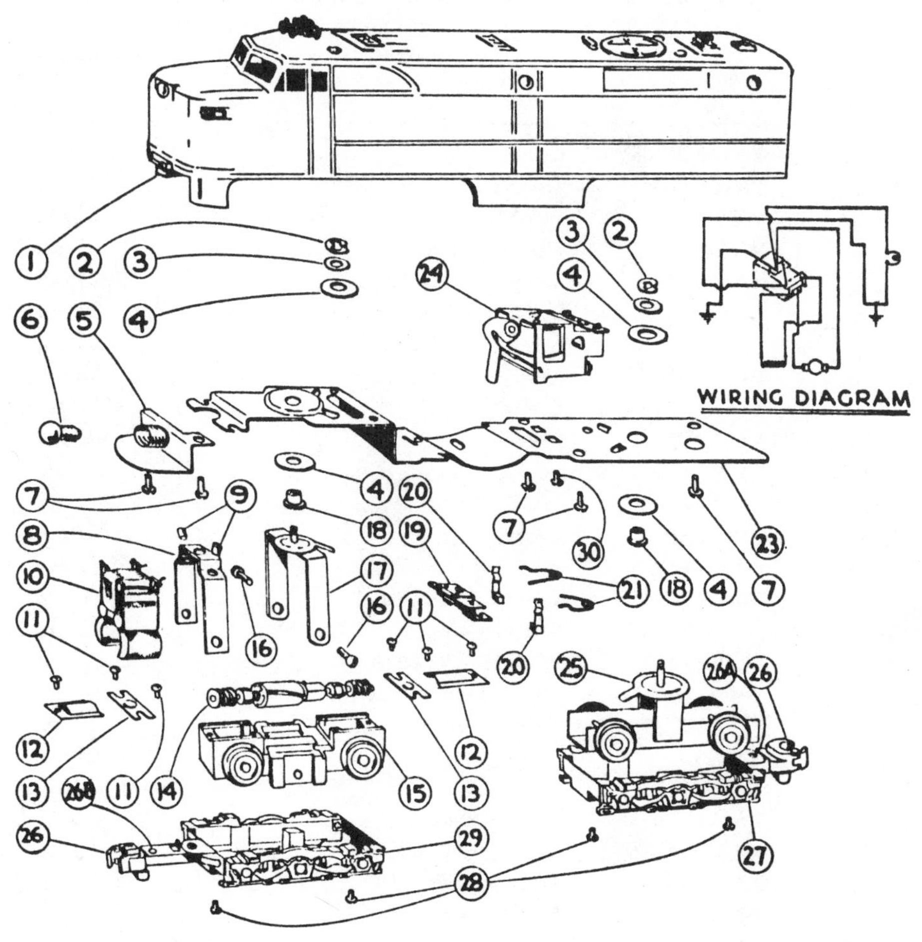
WIRING DIAGRAM

PARTS AND PRICE LIST

Diagram Number	Part No.	Description	Price
1.	XA14B221-RP	Cabin	3.43 ea.
2.	PA10800-A	Tru-arc Retaining Ring	.04 ea.
3.	W83	Washer	.03 ea.
4.	W124	Fibre Washer	.01 ea.
5.	XA11477	Lamp Bracket Assy.	.21 ea.
6.	PA8999	Bulb	.25 ea.
7.	S319	Screw	.01 ea.
8.	PA13A034	Field Clasp	.24 ea.
9.	S165	Screw	.02 ea.
10.	XA13A036	Field Assy.	.85 ea.
11.	S171	Screw	.01 ea.
12.	PA11441	Worm Cover	.01 ea.
13.	PA11453	Bearing Strap	.01 ea.
14.	XA12A062	Armature	3.67 ea.
15.	XA12A074-RP	Truck Chassis Assy.	2.12 ea.
	XA12A249	Wheel Assy.	.65 ea.
	XA11473	Insulated Wheel Assy.	.23 ea.
	PA11343	Solid Wheel	.05 ea.
	PA10006	Axle	.10 ea.
16.	S4A06	Screw	.01 ea.
17.	XA13A037	Yoke Assy.	.24 ea.
18.	PA11455	Fibre Bushing	.06 ea.
19.	XA11454-RP	Mounting Bracket	.13 ea.
20.	XA11684	Brush Holder Assy.	.25 ea.
21.	P11000-R & L	Brush Spring	.03 ea.
23.	PA12B059	Chassis	.34 ea.
24.	XA10587-E	Remote Control	1.32 ea.
25.	XA11598-A	Wheel & Chassis Assy.	1.25 ea.
26.	XA12A047	Coupler	.22 ea.
26-A.	PA13A791	Tubular Rivet	.01 ea.
26-B.	PA13A790	Tubular Rivet	.02 ea.
27.	XA13A804	Rear Truck & Coupler Assy.	1.02 ea.
28.	S249	Screw	.01 ea.
29.	XA13A803	Front Truck & Coupler Assy.	1.11 ea.
30.	S230-B	Screw	.10 dz.

All prices subject to change without notice.

SERVICE INSTRUCTIONS FOR No. 472 DIESEL

The first thing to do is place unit on track, connect transformer and test for operation.

1. **If the trouble is in the motor, we suggest that you remove cabin and check as follows:**
   a. Check Brushes (#20) for wear or poor contact.
   b. Check Brush Springs (#21) for position and proper tension.
   c. Check wires and solder joints for loose connections.
   d. Commutator on Armature Assembly (#14) may be dirty.
   e. Check operation of Remote Control Unit (#24).
   f. See if Motor is properly lubricated.
   g. Wheels must be kept clean to insure proper electrical contact.

2. **To Disassemble and Replace Parts on Motor Unit:**
   a. Turn unit upside down and remove screws (#7) to take off Cabin (#1).
   b. The next step is to take off Truck Assemblies (#27 & 29) by removing Screws (#28). To replace knuckle Coupler (#26) remove Rivets (#26A & 26B). Adjust the new coupler by placing diesel on the track so that the weight is all the way down, then either bend the coupler up or down, whichever is necessary to bring the bottom of the weight about 1/32" above the top of rails.
   c. Motor is exposed and you can check wiring and other points of the unit.
   d. Unsolder lead wire to Yoke Assembly (#17).
   e. Remove Tru-Arc Ring (#2) along with Washers (#3 4) and you can lift up chassis and motor assy. will be free.
   f. When replacing mounting Bracket (#19) unsolder lead wires and remove tension of Brush Springs (#21) taking out Brushes (#20). Remove two Screws (#11).
   g. To replace Armature (#14) or magnet (#10) it is necessary to back off on the two S165 screws (#9) and remove two Screws (#16). You can now take off Yoke Assy. (#17) and Field Clamp (#8). Remove screws (#11) and take off Bearing Straps (#13) and Worm Covers (#12). Lift up Armature (#14) from chassis and take off Magnet (#10).

3. **To Replace Remote Control Unit:**
   a. Unsolder lead wires.
   b. Remove screw (#30).
   c. Lift up and slip unit out of slots in Chassis (#23).
   d. To change just fingers only, straighten out lugs on frame of Remote Control Unit, after wires have been unsoldered, and replace defective part.

4. **To Replace Wheel and Chassis Assembly #25:**
   a. Unsolder lead wire to truck.
   b. Remove Tru-Arc Ring (#2) along with Washers (#3 & 4).

NOTE: When reassembling motor it is necessary to adjust the two S165 Screws (#9) on the Field Clamp (#8), which centralizes the Magnet Assy. (#10). The reason is to prevent the Armature Assy. (#14) from striking the plates on the Magnet.

When placing motor unit back in Chassis (#23), the stop on the Yoke Assy. (#17) must be faced outward so that the stop will always be parallel with the commutator on the Armature Assy. (#14).

NO.	PART NO.	DESCRIPTION	PRICE
1	XA14B221-RP	CABIN (#472)	3.77 EA.
	XA14B128-BRP	CABIN (#497)	3.95 EA.
	PA11409	PLASTIC HORN	.08 EA.
2	P10800-A	TRU-ARC RETAINING RING	.25 DZ.
3	W83	WASHER	.04 EA.
4	W124	FIBRE WASHER	.25 DZ.
5	XA11477	LAMP BRACKET ASSY.	.24 EA.
6	PA8999	BULB	.30 EA.
7	S319	SCREW	.02 EA.
8	PA13A034	FIELD CLAMP	.34 EA.
9	S165	SCREW	.03 EA.
10	XA13A036	FIELD ASSY.	1.34 EA.
11	S171	SCREW	.01 EA.
12	PA11441	WORM COVER	.01 EA.
13	PA11453	BEARING STRAP	.02 EA.
14	XA14B873-RP	ARMATURE	3.94 EA.
15	XA12A074-RP	TRUCK CHASSIS ASSY.	2.37 EA.
	XA12A249	WHEEL ASSY. (OLD STYLE)	.72 EA.
	XA14A891	PUL-MOR WHEEL (NEW STYLE)	.28 EA.
	PA14A890	PUL-MOR	.05 EA.
	XA11473	INSULATED WHEEL ASSY. (OLD STYLE)	.25 EA.
	PA11343	SOLID WHEEL (OLD STYLE)	.06 EA.
	PA14B888	SOLID WHEEL (NEW STYLE)	.08 EA.
	PA10006	AXLE NOT AVAILABLE	
		SUB. WITH PA15A281 AXLE	.07 EA.
	PA15A218	WORM GEAR	.09 EA.
	PA11463	THRUST PLATE	.08 DZ.
16	S4A06	SCREW	.03 EA.
17	XA13A037	YOKE ASSY.	.26 EA.
18	PA11455	FIBRE BUSHING	.14 EA.
19	XA11454-RP	MOUNTING BRACKET	.14 EA.
20	PA11684	BRUSH (NOT SOLD ASSEMBLED)	.32 EA.
	P10132	BRUSH HOLDER	.01 EA.
21	P11000-R & L	BRUSH SPRING	.03 EA.
23	PA12B059	CHASSIS	.37 EA.
24	XA10587-E	REMOTE CONTROL	4.04 EA.
	XA8716	DRUM	.95 EA.
	XA9612-BRP	BOTTOM FINGER UNIT	.33 EA.
	XA9612-CRP	TOP FINGER UNIT	.33 EA.
25	XA11598-B	WHEEL & CHASSIS ASSY.	1.12 EA.
26	XA12A047	COUPLER	.29 EA.
26-A	PA13A791	TUBULAR RIVET	.02 EA.
26-B	PA13A790	TUBULAR RIVET	.03 EA.
27	XA13A804	REAR TRUCK & COUPLER ASSY.	1.54 EA.
	PA12A355A	LEAF SPRING	.02 EA.
28	S249	SCREW	.15 DZ.
29	XA13A803	FRONT TRUCK & COUPLER ASSY.	1.69 EA.
	XA12A358	ARM & COUPLER ASSY.	.34 EA.
30	S230-B	SCREW	.01 EA.
		NOT SHOWN	
	XA13B038-B	MOTOR	12.16 EA.
	PA13A208-A	4 CONDUCTOR CABLE (PLASTIC)	.04 FT.

PRICES SUBJECT TO CHANGE WITHOUT NOTICE.

 Ref: Form No. 1771; June 1, 1960

NO.	PART NO.	DESCRIPTION	PRICE
1	XA14B224-RP	CABIN	3.26 EA.
	PA11409	PLASTIC HORN	.08 EA.
2	P10800-A	TRU-ARC RETAINING RING	.25 DZ.
3	W83	WASHER	.04 EA.
4	W124	FIBRE WASHER	.25 DZ.
5	XA11477	LAMP BRACKET ASSY.	.24 EA.
6	PA8999	BULB	.30 EA.
7	S319	SCREW	.02 EA.
8	PA13A034	FIELD CLAMP	.34 EA.
9	S165	SCREW	.03 EA.
10	XA13A036	FIELD ASSY.	1.34 EA.
11	S171	SCREW	.01 EA.
12	PA11441	WORM COVER	.01 EA.
13	PA11453	BEARING STRAP	.02 EA.
14	XA14B873-RP	ARMATURE	3.94 EA.
15	XA12A074-RP	TRUCK CHASSIS ASSY.	2.37 EA.
	XA12A249	WHEEL ASSY. (OLD STYLE)	.72 EA.
	XA14A891	PUL-MOR WHEEL (NEW STYLE)	.28 EA.
	PA14A890	PUL-MOR	.05 EA.
	XA11473	INSULATED WHEEL ASSY. (OLD STYLE)	.25 EA.
	PA11343	SOLID WHEEL (OLD STYLE)	.06 EA.
	PA14B888	SOLID WHEEL (NEW STYLE)	.08 EA.
	PA10006	AXLE NOT AVAILABLE	
		SUB. WITH PA15A281 AXLE	.07 EA.
	PA15A218	WORM GEAR	.09 EA.
	PA11463	THRUST PLATE	.08 DZ.
16	S4A06	SCREW	.03 EA.
17	XA13A037	YOKE ASSY.	.26 EA.
18	PA11455	FIBRE BUSHING	.14 EA.
19	XA11454-RP	MOUNTING BRACKET	.14 EA.
20	PA11684	BRUSH (NOT SOLD ASSEMBLED)	.32 EA.
	P10132	BRUSH HOLDER	.01 EA.
21	P11000-R & L	BRUSH SPRING	.03 EA.
23	PA12B059-B	CHASSIS	.44 EA.
24	XA10587-E	REMOTE CONTROL	4.04 EA.
	XA8716	DRUM	.95 EA.
	XA9612-BRP	BOTTOM FINGER UNIT	.33 EA.
	XA9612-CRP	TOP FINGER UNIT	.33 EA.
25	XA11598-B	WHEEL & CHASSIS ASSY.	1.12 EA.
26	XA12A047	COUPLER	.29 EA.
26-A	PA13A791	TUBULAR RIVET	.02 EA.
26-B	PA13A790	TUBULAR RIVET	.03 EA.
27	XA13A804	REAR TRUCK & COUPLER ASSY.	1.54 EA.
	PA12A355A	LEAF SPRING	.02 EA.
28	S249	SCREW	.15 DZ.
29	XA13A803	FRONT TRUCK & COUPLER ASSY.	1.69 EA.
	XA12A358	ARM & COUPLER ASSY.	.34 EA.
30	S230-B	SCREW	.01 EA.

CON'T

PART NO.	DESCRIPTION	PRICE
	NOT SHOWN	
XA13B038-B	Motor	12.16 EA.
XA14B127	Speaker	4.57 EA.
PA14A275	Resistor	.21 EA.
PA14A914	Condenser	1.40 EA.
PA13A870	Diesel Sound Generator	4.52 EA.
PA13A208-A	4 Conductor Cable (plastic)	.04 FT.
PA14A216	Speaker Bracket	.08 EA.
S172	Screw	.02 EA.
S171	Screw	.01 EA.

Prices subject to change without notice.

NO.	PART NO.	DESCRIPTION	PRICE
1	XA14B321-RP	CABIN	3.01 EA.
	PA11409	PLASTIC HORN	.08 EA.
	XA14B188	PANTOGRAPH ASSY. (NOT SHOWN)	2.85 EA.
2	P10800-A	TRU-ARC RETAINING RING	.25 DZ.
3	W83	WASHER	.04 EA.
4	W124	FIBRE WASHER	.25 DZ.
5		NOT USED	
6	PA8999	BULB	.30 EA.
7	S4N90	SCREW (SECURES CABIN)	.03 EA.
8	PA13A034	FIELD CLAMP	.34 EA.
9	S165	SCREW	.03 EA.
10	XA13A036	FIELD ASSY.	1.34 EA.
11	S171	SCREW	.01 EA.
12	PA11441	WORM COVER	.01 EA.
13	PA11453	BEARING STRAP	.02 EA.
14	XA14B873-RP	ARMATURE	3.94 EA.
15	XA12A074-RP	TRUCK CHASSIS ASSY.	2.37 EA.
	XA12A249	WHEEL ASSY. (OLD STYLE)	.72 EA.
	XA14A891	PUL-MOR WHEEL ASSY. (NEW STYLE)	.28 EA.
	PA14A890	PUL-MOR	.05 EA.
	XA11473	INSULATED WHEEL ASSY. (OLD STYLE)	.25 EA.
	PA11343	SOLID WHEEL (OLD STYLE)	.06 EA.
	PA14B888	SOLID WHEEL (NEW STYLE)	.08 EA.
	PA10006	AXLE NOT AVAILABLE	
	SUB.	WITH PA15A281 AXLE	.07 EA.
	PA15A218	WORM GEAR	.09 EA.
	PA11463	THRUST PLATE	.08 DZ.
6	S4A06	SCREW	.03 EA.
17	XA13A037	YOKE ASSY.	.26 EA.
18	PA11455	FIBRE BUSHING	.14 EA.
19	XA11454-RP	MOUNTING BRACKET	.14 EA.
20	PA11584	BRUSH (NOT SOLD ASSEMBLED)	.32 EA.
	P10132	BRUSH HOLDER	.01 EA.
21	P1100-R & L	BRUSH SPRING	.03 EA.
23	XA14C340	CHASSIS & LAMP SOCKET	1.22 EA.
24	XA10587-E	REMOTE CONTROL	4.04 EA.
	XA8716	DRUM	.95 EA.
	XA9612-BRP	BOTTOM FINGER UNIT	.33 EA.
	XA9612-CRP	TOP FINGER UNIT	.33 EA.
25	XA11598-B	WHEEL & CHASSIS ASSY.	1.12 EA.
26	XA12A047	COUPLER	.29 EA.
26-A	PA13A791	TUBULAR RIVET	.02 EA.
26-B	PA13A790	TUBULAR RIVET	.03 EA.
27	XA13A804	REAR TRUCK & COUPLER ASSY.	1.54 EA.
28	S249	SCREW	.15 DZ.
29	XA14A351	FRONT TRUCK & COUPLER ASSY.	1.64 EA.
	PA12A355-A	LEAF SPRING	.02 EA.
	XA14A352	ARM & COUPLER ASSY.	.32 EA.
30	S230-B	SCREW	.01 EA.
		NOT SHOWN	
	XA14A127	SPEAKER (ONLY TYPE AVAILABLE)	4.57 EA.
	PA14A914	CONDENSER	1.40 EA.
	PA14A216	BRACKET	.08 EA.
	S171	SCREW (SCREWS USED WITH ABOVE BRACKET)	.01 EA.
	S172	SCREW	.02 EA.
	PA13A208-A	4 CONDUCTOR CABLE (PLASTIC)	.04 FT.
	XA13B038-B	MOTOR	12.16 EA.

Ref: Form No. 1771; June 1, 1960

Diesel — No. 21551, 21927

DIA. NO.	PART NO.	DESCRIPTION	PRICE
1	XA15B076-RP	Cabin (21551)	4.15 ea.
	XA15B140-BRP	Cabin (21927)	5.03 ea.
	PA11409	Plastic Horn	.08 ea.
2	P10800-A	Tru-arc Retaining Ring	.25 dz.
3	W83	Washer	.04 ea.
4	W124	Fibre Washer (motor end)	.25 dz.
	W124-A	Steel Washer	.35 dz.
5	XA15A383	Lamp Bracket Assembly	.29 ea.
6	PA8999	Bulb	.30 ea.
7	S319	Screw	.02 ea.
8	PA13A034	Field Clamp	.34 ea.
9	S165	Screw	.03 ea.
10	XA13A036	Field Assembly	1.34 ea.
11	S171	Screw	.01 ea.
12	PA11441	Worm Cover	.01 ea.
13	PA11453	Bearing Strap	.02 ea.
14	XA14B873-RP	Armature	3.94 ea.
15	XA12A074-RP	Truck Chassis Assembly	2.37 ea.
	PA15A218	Worm Gear	.09 ea.
	XA14A891	Pul-Mor Wheel Assembly	.28 ea.
	PA14A890	Pul-Mor	.05 ea.
	PA14B888	Solid Wheel	.08 ea.
	PA15A281	Axle	.07 ea.
	PA11463	Thrust Plate	.08 dz.
16	S4A06	Screw	.03 ea.
17	XA13A037	Yoke Assembly	.26 ea.
18	PA11455	Fibre Bushing	.14 ea.
19	XA11454-RP	Mounting Bracket	.14 ea.
20	PA11684	Brush	.32 ea.
	P10132	Brush Holder (not sold assembled)	.01 ea.
21	P11000-R & L	Brush Spring	.03 ea.
23	XA15B145	Chassis	1.41 ea.
24	XA14C429	Remote Control	2.76 ea.
	XA14A994	Contact Assembly	.77 ea.
	XA14A435	Plunger Assembly	.14 ea.
	XA14B433	Coil Assembly	.69 ea.
	PA14A444	Coil Support	.05 ea.
	PA14C432	Coil Housing	.04 ea.
25	XA14A930-A	Wheel & Chassis Assembly	1.60 ea.
	PA15A226	Axle	.05 ea.
	PA14B888	Solid Wheel	.08 ea.
	XA14A870	Insulated Wheel	.18 ea.
26	XA12A047	Coupler	.29 ea.
26-A	PA13A791	Tubular Rivet	.02 ea.
26-B	PA13A790	Tubular Rivet	.03 ea.
27	XA13A804	Rear Truck & Coupler Assembly	1.54 ea.
	PA12A355A	Leaf Spring	.02 ea.
28	S249	Screw (motor end)	.15 dz.
	S5N40	Screw	.15 dz.
29	XA13A803	Front Truck & Coupler Assembly	1.69 ea.
	XA12A358	Arm & Coupler Assy.	.34 ea.
30	S172	Screw (for R.C. Unit)	.02 ea.
		NOT SHOWN	
	XA13B038-B	Motor Assy.	12.16 ea.
	LW-1B1	Black Lead Wire	.02 ft.

 Ref: Form No. 1771; June 1, 1960

DIA. NO.	PART NO.	DESCRIPTION	PRICE
1	XA14B321-ARP	Cabin	10.52 ea.
	PA11409	Plastic Horn	.08 ea.
	XA14B188	Pantograph	2.85 ea.
2	P10800-A	Tru-arc Retaining Ring	.25 dz.
3	W83	Washer (motor end)	.04 ea.
	W2A28	Spring Washer	.25 dz.
4	W124	Fibre Washer (motor end)	.25 dz.
	W124A	Steel Washer	.35 dz.
5		NOT USED	
6	PA8999	Bulb	.30 ea.
7	S4N90	Screw (secures Cabin)	.03 ea.
8	PA13A034	Field Clamp	.34 ea.
9	S165	Screw	.03 ea.
10	XA13A036	Field Assembly	1.34 ea.
11	S171	Screw	.01 ea.
12	PA11441	Worm Cover	.01 ea.
13	PA11453	Bearing Strap	.02 ea.
14	XA14B873-RP	Armature	3.94 ea.
15	XA12A074-RP	Truck Chassis Assembly	2.37 ea.
	XA14A891	Pul-Mor Wheel Assembly	.28 ea.
	PA14A890	Pul-Mor	.05 ea.
	PA14B888	Solid Wheel	.08 ea.
	PA15A281	Axle	.07 ea.
	PA15A218	Worm Gear	.09 ea.
	PA11463	Thrust Plate	.08 dz.
16	S4A06	Screw	.03 ea.
17	XA13A037	Yoke Assembly	.26 ea.
18	PA11455	Fibre Bushing	.14 ea.
19	XA11454-RP	Mounting Bracket	.14 ea.
20	PA11684	Brush	.32 ea.
	P10132	Brush Holder (not sold assembled)	.01 ea.
21	P11000-R & L	Brush Spring	.03 ea.
23	XA14C340-A	Chassis	.99 ea.
24	XA14C429	Remote Control	2.76 ea.
	XA14A994	Contact Assembly	.77 ea.
	XA14A435	Plunger Assembly	.14 ea.
	XA14B433	Coil Assembly	.69 ea.
	PA14A444	Coil Support	.05 ea.
	PA14C432	Coil Housing	.04 ea.
25	XA14A930-A	Wheel & Chassis Assembly	1.60 ea.
	PA14B888	Solid Wheel	.08 ea.
	PA15A226	Axle	.05 ea.
	XA14A870	Insulated Wheel	.18 ea.
26	XA12A047	Coupler	.29 ea.
26-A	PA13A791	Tubular Rivet	.02 ea.
26-B	PA13A790	Tubular Rivet	.03 ea.
27	XA13A804	Rear Truck & Coupler Assembly	1.54 ea.
28	S249	Screw	.15 dz.
29	XA14A351	Front Truck & Coupler Assembly	1.64 ea.
	PA12A355-A	Leaf Spring	.02 ea.
	XA14A352	Coupler & Arm Assembly	.32 ea.
30	S172	Screw (secures R.C. Unit)	.02 ea.

NOT SHOWN

PART NO.	DESCRIPTION	PRICE
XA13B038-B	Motor	12.16 ea.
LW-1B1	Black Lead Wire	.02 ft.

DIA. NO.	PART NO.	DESCRIPTION	PRICE
1	XA14B221-RP	Cabin (472)	3.96 ea.
	XA14B128-BRP	Cabin (497)	4.15 ea.
	PA11409	Plastic Horn	.08 ea.
2	P10800-A	Tru-Arc Retaining Ring	.26 dz.
3	W83	Washer	.04 ea.
4	W124	Fibre Washer	.26 dz.
5	XA11477	Lamp Bracket Assy.	.25 ea.
6	PA8999	Bulb	.32 ea.
7	S319	Screw	.02 ea.
8	PA13A034	Field Clamp	.36 ea.
9	S165	Screw	.03 ea.
10	XA13A036	Field Assy.	1.41 ea.
11	S171	Screw	.01 ea.
12	PA11441	Worm Cover	.01 ea.
13	PA11453	Bearing Strap	.02 ea.
14	XA14B873-RP	Armature	4.14 ea.
15	XA12A074-RP	Truck Chassis Assy.	2.49 ea.
	XA14A891	Pul-Mor Wheel (NEW STYLE)	.29 ea.
	PA14A890	Pul-Mor	.05 ea.
	PA14B888	Solid Wheel (NEW STYLE)	.08 ea.
	PA15A281	Axle	.07 ea.
	PA15A218	Worm Gear	.09 ea.
	PA11463	Thrust Plate	.08 dz.
16	S4A06	Screw	.03 ea.
17	XA13A037	Yoke Assy.	.27 ea.
18	PA11455	Fibre Bushing	.15 ea.
19	XA11454-RP	Mounting Bracket	.15 ea.
20	PA11684	Brush	.34 ea.
	P10132	Brush Holder	.01 ea.
21	P11000-R & L	Brush Spring	.03 ea.
23	PA12B059	Chassis	.39 ea.
24	XA10587-E	Remote Control Unit	4.24 ea.
	XA8716	Drum	1.00 ea.
	XA9612-BRP	Bottom Finger Unit	.35 ea.
	XA9612-CRP	Top Finger Unit	.35 ea.
25	XA14A930-A	Wheel & Chassis Assy.	1.68 ea.
26	XA12A047	Coupler	.30 ea.
26-A	PA13A791	Tubular Rivet	.02 ea.
26-B	PA13A790	Tubular Rivet	.03 ea.
27	XA13A804	Rear Truck & Coupler Assy.	1.62 ea.
	PA12A355A	Leaf Spring	.02 ea.
28	S249	Screw	.16 dz.
29	XA13A803	Front Truck & Coupler Assy.	1.77 ea.
	XA12A358	Arm & Coupler Assy.	.36 ea.
30	S230-B	Screw	.01 ea.

NOT SHOWN

PART NO.	DESCRIPTION	PRICE
XA13B038-B	Motor	12.77 ea.
PA13A208-A	4 Conductor Cable (Plastic)	.04 ft.

Prices subject to change without notice

 Ref: Form No. 1771; Oct. 1, 1962

DIA NO.	PART NO.	DESCRIPTION	PRICE
1	XA14B224-RP	Cabin	3.42 ea.
	PA11409	Plastic Horn	.08 ea.
2	P10800-A	Tru-Arc Retaining Ring	.26 dz.
3	W83	Washer	.04 ea.
4	W124	Fibre Washer	.26 dz.
5	XA11477	Lamp Bracket Assembly	.25 ea.
6	PA8999	Bulb	.32 ea.
7	S319	Screw	.02 ea.
8	PA13A034	Field Clamp	.36 ea.
9	S165	Screw	.03 ea.
10	XA13A036	Field Assembly	1.41 ea.
11	S171	Screw	.01 ea.
12	PA11441	Worm Cover	.01 ea.
13	PA11453	Bearing Strap	.02 ea.
14	XA14B873-RP	Armature	4.14 ea.
15	XA12A074-RP	Truck Chassis Assembly	2.49 ea.
	XA14A891	Pul-Mor Wheel (NEW STYLE)	.29 ea.
	PA14A890	Pul-Mor	.05 ea.
	PA14B888	Solid Wheel (NEW STYLE)	.08 ea.
	PA15A281	Axle	.07 ea.
	PA15A218	Worm Gear	.09 ea.
	PA11463	Thrust Plate	.08 dz.
16	S4A06	Screw	.03 ea.
17	XA13A037	Yoke Assembly	.27 ea.
18	PA11455	Fibre Bushing	.15 ea.
19	XA11454-RP	Mounting Bracket	.15 ea.
20	PA11684	Brush	.34 ea.
	P10132	Brush Holder	.01 ea.
21	P11000 R & L	Brush Spring	.03 ea.
23	PA12B059-B	Chassis	.46 ea.
24	XA10587-E	Remote Control Unit	4.24 ea.
	XA8716	Drum	1.00 ea.
	XA9612-BRP	Bottom Finger Unit	.35 ea.
	XA9612-CRP	Top Finger Unit	.35 ea.
25	XA14A930-A	Wheel & Chassis Assembly	1.68 ea.
26	XA12A047	Coupler	.30 ea.
26-A	PA13A791	Tubular Rivet	.02 ea.
26-B	PA13A790	Tubular Rivet	.03 ea.
27	XA13A804	Rear Truck & Coupler Assembly	1.62 ea.
	PA12A355A	Leaf Spring	.02 ea.
28	S249	Screw	.16 dz.
29	XA13A803	Front Truck & Coupler Assembly	1.77 ea.
	XA12A358	Arm & Coupler Assembly	.36 ea.
30	S230-B	Screw	.01 ea.
		NOT SHOWN	
	XA13B038-B	Motor	12.77 ea.
	XA14B127	Speaker	4.80 ea.
	PA14A275	Resistor	.22 ea.
	PA14A914	Condenser	1.47 ea.
	PA13A870	Diesel Sound Generator	4.75 ea.
	PA13A208-A	4 Conductor Cable (Plastic)	.04 ft.
	PA14A216	Speaker Bracket	.08 ea.
	S172	Screw	.02 ea.
	S171	Screw	.01 ea.

Ref: Form No. 1771; Oct. 1, 1962

DIA NO.	PART NO.	DESCRIPTION	PRICE
1		Cabin (OBSOLETE)	
	PA11409	Plastic Horn	.08 ea.
	XA14B188	Pantograph Assembly (NOT SHOWN)	2.99 ea.
2	P10800-A	Tru-Arc Retaining Ring	.26 dz.
3	W83	Washer	.04 ea.
4	W124	Fibre Washer	.26 dz.
5		NOT USED	
6	PA8999	Bulb	.32 ea.
7	S4N90	Screw (Secures Cabin)	.03 ea.
8	PA13A034	Field Clamp	.36 ea.
9	S165	Screw	.03 ea.
10	XA13A036	Field Assembly	1.41 ea.
11	S171	Screw	.01 ea.
12	PA11441	Worm Cover	.01 ea.
13	PA11453	Bearing Strap	.02 ea.
14	XA14B873-RP	Armature	4.14 ea.
15	XA12A074-RP	Truck Chassis Assembly	2.49 ea.
	XA14A891	Pul-Mor Wheel Assembly (New Style)	.29 ea.
	PA14A890	Pul-Mor	.05 ea.
	PA14B888	Solid Wheel (New Style)	.08 ea.
	PA15A281	Axle	.07 ea.
	PA15A218	Worm Gear	.09 ea.
	PA11463	Thrust Plate	.08 dz.
16	S4A06	Screw	.03 ea.
17	XA13A037	Yoke Assembly	.27 ea.
18	PA11455	Fibre Bushing	.15 ea.
19	XA11454-RP	Mounting Bracket	.15 ea.
20	PA11684	Brush	.34 ea.
	P10132	Brush Holder	.01 ea.
21	P11000-R & L	Brush Spring	.03 ea.
23	XA14C340	Chassis and Lamp Socket	1.28 ea.
24	XA10587-E	Remote Control Unit	4.24 ea.
	XA8716	Drum	1.00 ea.
	XA9612-BRP	Bottom Finger Unit	.35 ea.
	XA9612-CRP	Top Finger Unit	.35 ea.
25	XA11598-B	Wheel and Chassis Assembly	1.18 ea.
26	XA12A047	Coupler	.30 ea.
26-A	PA13A791	Tubular Rivet	.02 ea.
26-B	PA13A790	Tubular Rivet	.03 ea.
27	XA13A804	Rear Truck and Coupler Assembly	1.62 ea.
28	S249	Screw	.16 dz.
29	XA14A351	Front Truck and Coupler Assembly	1.72 ea.
	PA12A355-A	Leaf Spring	.02 ea.
	XA14A352	Arm and Coupler Assembly	.34 ea.
30	S230-B	Screw	.01 ea.
		NOT SHOWN	
	XA14A127	Speaker (Only Type Available)	4.80 ea.
	PA14A914	Condenser	1.47 ea.
	PA14A216	Bracket	.08 ea.
	S171	Screw (Screws used with	.01 ea.
	S172	Screw above Bracket)	.02 ea.
	PA13A208-A	4 Conductor Cable (Plastic)	.04 ft.
	XA13B038-B	Motor	12.77 ea.

 Ref: Form No. 1771; Oct. 1, 1962

NO.	PART NO.	DESCRIPTION	PRICE
1	XA15B076-RP	Cabin (21551)	4.36 ea.
	XA15B140-BRP	Cabin (21927)	5.28 ea.
	PA11409	Plastic Horn	.08 ea.
2	P10800-A	Tru-Arc Retaining Ring	.26 dz.
3	W83	Washer	.04 ea.
4	W124	Fibre Washer (Motor End)	.26 dz.
	W124-A	Steel Washer	.37 dz.
5	XA15A383	Lamp Bracket Assembly	.30 ea.
6	PA8999	Bulb	.32 ea.
7	S319	Screw	.02 ea.
8	PA13A034	Field Clamp	.36 ea.
9	S165	Screw	.03 ea.
10	XA13A036	Field Assembly	1.41 ea.
11	S171	Screw	.01 ea.
12	PA11441	Worm Cover	.01 ea.
13	PA11453	Bearing Strap	.02 ea.
14	XA14B873-RP	Armature	4.14 ea.
15	XA12A074-RP	Truck Chassis Assembly	2.49 ea.
	PA15A218	Worm Gear	.09 ea.
	XA14A891	Pul-Mor Wheel Assembly	.29 ea.
	PA14A890	Pul-Mor	.05 ea.
	PA14B888	Solid Wheel	.08 ea.
	PA15A281	Axle	.07 ea.
	PA11463	Thrust Plate	.08 dz.
16	S4A06	Screw	.03 ea.
17	XA13A037	Yoke Assembly	.27 ea.
18	PA11455	Fibre Bushing	.15 ea.
19	XA11454-RP	Mounting Bracket	.15 ea.
20	PA11684	Brush	.34 ea.
	P10132	Brush Holder	.01 ea.
21	P11000-R & L	Brush Spring	.03 ea.
23	XA15B145	Chassis	1.48 ea.
24	XA14C429	Remote Control Unit	2.90 ea.
	XA14A994	Contact Assembly	.81 ea.
	XA14A435	Plunger Assembly	.15 ea.
	XA14B433	Coil Assembly	.72 ea.
	PA14A444	Coil Support	.05 ea.
	PA14C432	Coil Housing	.04 ea.
25	XA14A930-A	Wheel & Chassis Assembly	1.68 ea.
	PA15A226	Axle	.05 ea.
	PA14B888	Solid Wheel	.08 ea.
	XA14A870	Insulated Wheel	.19 ea.
26	XA12A047	Knuckle Coupler	.30 ea.
26-A	PA13A791	Tubular Rivet	.02 ea.
26-B	PA13A790	Tubular Rivet	.03 ea.
27	XA13A804	Rear Truck & Coupler Assy.	1.62 ea.
	PA12A355-A	Leaf Spring	.02 ea.
28	S249	Screw (Motor End)	.16 dz.
	S5N40	Screw	.16 dz.
29	XA13A803	Front Truck & Coupler Assembly	1.77 ea.
	XA12A358	Arm & Coupler Assy.	.36 ea.
30	S172	Screw (For R.C. Unit)	.02 ea.
		NOT SHOWN	
	XA13B038-B	Motor Assembly	12.77 ea.
	LW-1B1	Black Lead Wire	.02 ft.

GE Electric No. 21573

NO.	PART NO.	DESCRIPTION	PRICE
1		OBSOLETE	
	PA11409	Plastic Horn	.08 ea.
	XA14B188	Pantograph	2.99 ea.
2	P10800-A	Tru-Arc Retaining Ring	.26 dz.
3	W83	Washer (Motor End)	.04 ea.
	W2A28	Spring Washer	.26 dz.
4	W124	Fibre Washer (Motor End)	.26 dz.
	W124-A	Steel Washer	.37 dz.
5		NOT USED	
6	PA8999	Bulb	.32 ea.
7	S4N90	Screw (Secures Cabin)	.03 ea.
8	PA13A034	Field Clamp	.36 ea.
9	S165	Screw	.03 ea.
10	XA13A036	Field Assembly	1.41 ea.
11	S171	Screw	.01 ea.
12	PA11441	Worm Cover	.01 ea.
13	PA11453	Bearing Strap	.02 ea.
14	XA14B873-RP	Armature	4.14 ea.
15	XA12A074-RP	Truck Chassis Assembly	2.49 ea.
	XA14A891	Pul-Mor Wheel Assembly	.29 ea.
	PA14A890	Pul-Mor	.05 ea.
	PA14B888	Solid Wheel	.08 ea.
	PA15A281	Axle	.07 ea.
	PA15A218	Worm Gear	.09 ea.
	PA11463	Thrust Plate	.08 dz.
16	S4A06	Screw	.03 ea.
17	XA13A037	Yoke Assembly	.27 ea.
18	PA11455	Fibre Bushing	.15 ea.
19	XA11454-RP	Mounting Bracket	.15 ea.
20	PA11684	Brush	.34 ea.
	P10132	Brush Holder	.01 ea.
21	P11000-R & L	Brush Spring	.03 ea.
23	XA14C340-A	Chassis	1.04 ea.
24	XA14C429	Remote Control Unit	2.90 ea.
	XA14A994	Contact Assembly	.81 ea.
	XA14A435	Plunger Assembly	.15 ea.
	XA14B433	Coil Assembly	.72 ea.
	PA14A444	Coil Support	.05 ea.
	PA14C432	Coil Housing	.04 ea.
25	XA14A930-A	Wheel & Chassis Assembly	1.68 ea.
	PA14B888	Solid Wheel	.08 ea.
	PA15A226	Axle	.05 ea.
	XA14A870	Insulated Wheel	.19 ea.
26	XA12A047	Coupler	.30 ea.
26-A	PA13A791	Tubular Rivet	.02 ea.
26-B	PA13A790	Tubular Rivet	.03 ea.
27	XA13A804	Rear Truck & Coupler Assembly	1.62 ea.
28	S249	Screw	.16 dz.
29	XA14A351	Front Truck & Coupler Assy.	1.72 ea.
	PA12A355-A	Leaf Spring	.02 ea.
	XA14A352	Coupler & Arm Assembly	.34 ea.
30	S172	Screw (Secures R.C. Unit)	.02 ea.

NOT SHOWN

PART NO.	DESCRIPTION	PRICE
XA13B038-B	Motor	12.77 ea.
LW-1B1	Black Lead Wire	.02 ft.

 Ref: Form No. 1771; Oct. 1, 1962

DIESEL LOCOMOTIVE

Model Nos. 474/475, 490/492, 494/495, 21551, 21561 21920/21920-1, 21922/21922-1, 21925/21925-1

SPECIFICATIONS

Tested at: 12 Volts A.C. .... using 180" oval of track.

(A) Locomotive to run a minimum of 9 R.P.M. or 9 times forward and reverse, around 180" oval of track.

Load: Not to draw more than 3.25 amps. while pulling 4 Passenger Cars.

Motor: Universal A.C. or D.C.

Ref: Form No. 1817; Feb. 1, 1957

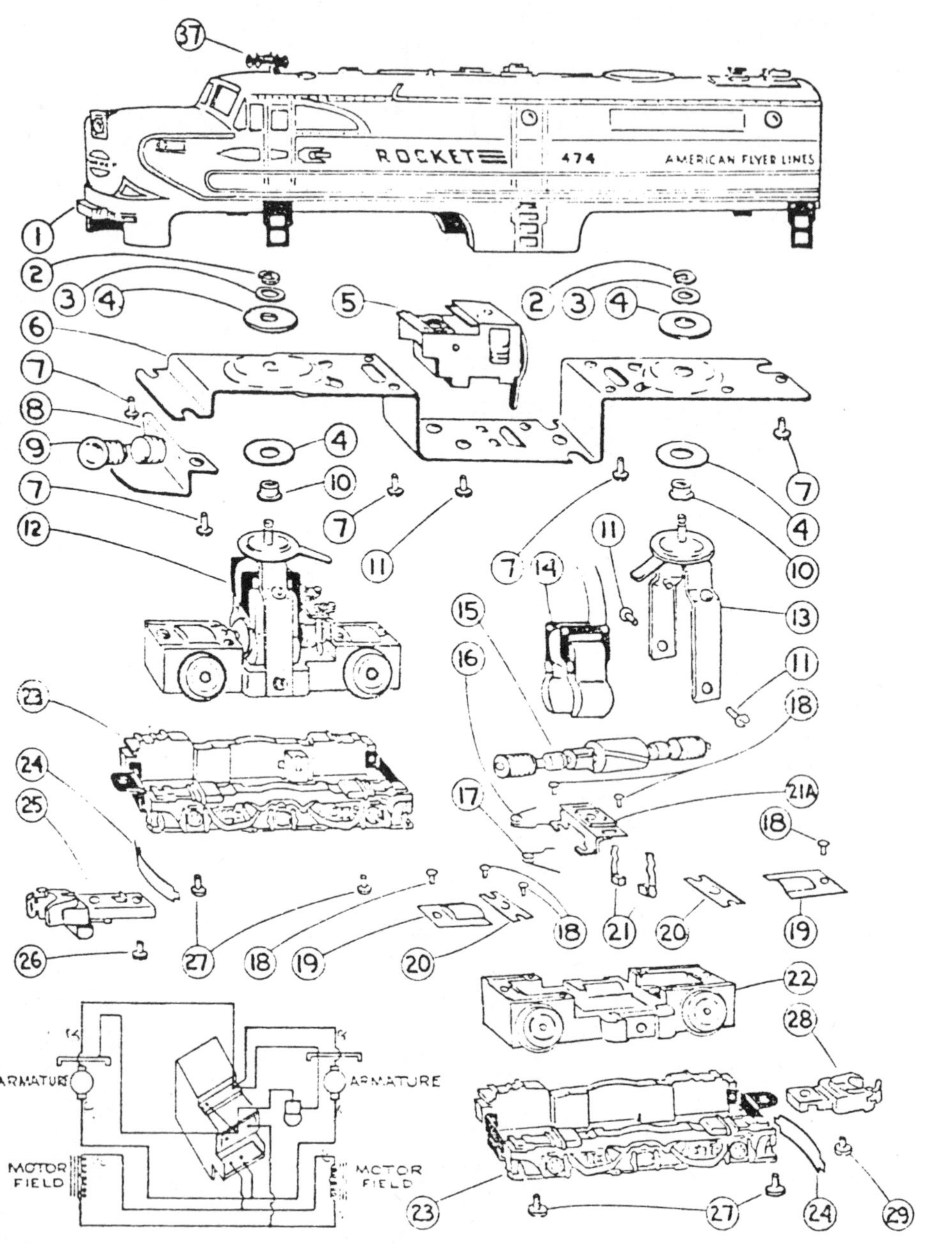

 Ref: Form No. 1817; Feb. 1, 1957

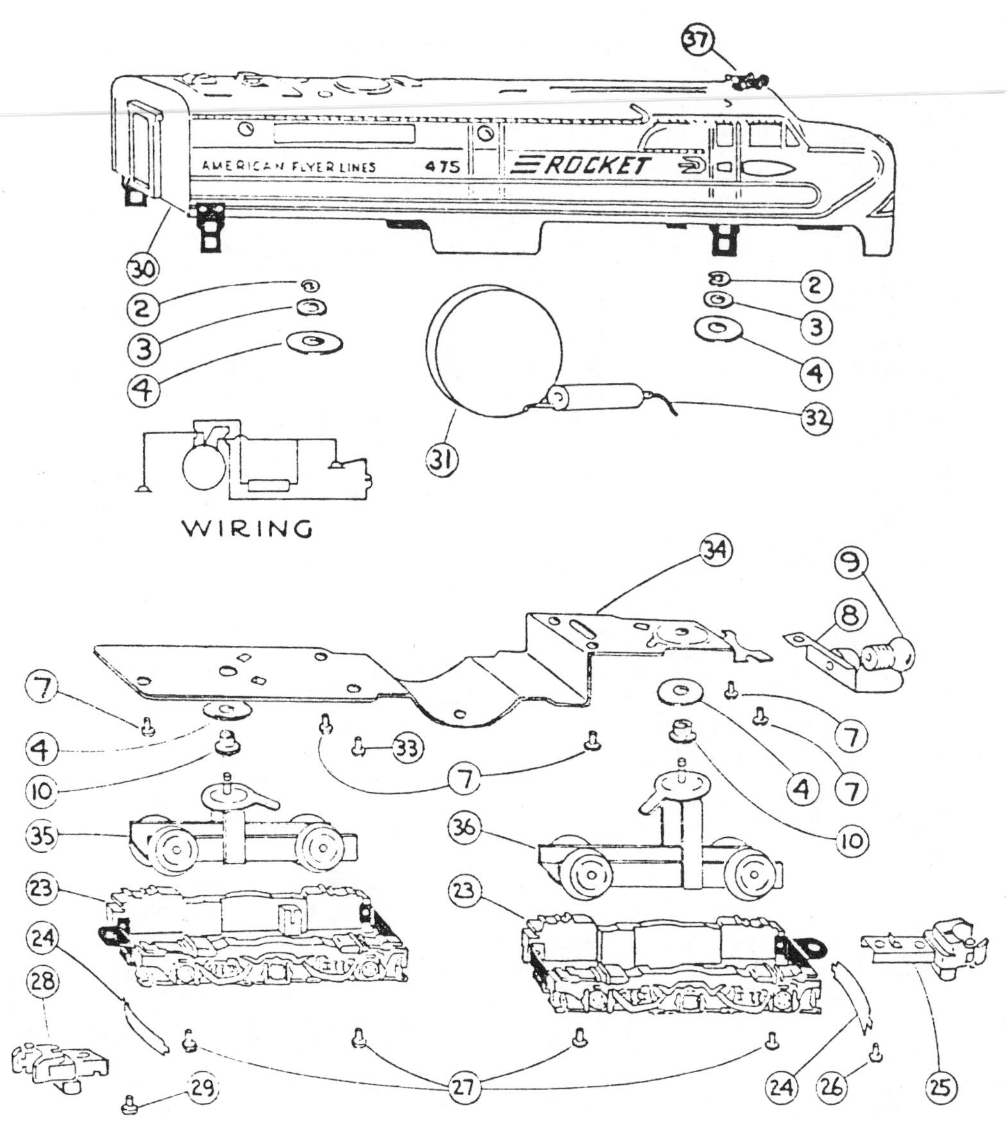

Ref: Form No. 1817; Feb. 1, 1957

PARTS LIST

21925 U.P. DIESEL POWERED "A" UNIT

SAME AS 21902 DIESEL LOCOMOTIVE -
EXCEPT ELIMINATE THE FOLLOWING PARTS:

XA-15B140-RP	CABIN W/TRIM	1	
XA-13A803	FRONT TRUCK & COUPLER ASSY	1	
XA-13A804	REAR TRUCK & COUPLER ASSY	1	
XA-13A802	FRONT & REAR TRUCK ASSY	2	

ADD THE FOLLOWING PARTS:

XA-15B549-RP	CABIN W/TRIM	1	3.91 EA.
XA-13A803-B	FRONT TRUCK & COUPLER ASSY	1	1.69 EA.
XA-13A804-B	REAR TRUCK & COUPLER ASSY	1	1.54 EA.
XA-13A802-B	FRONT & REAR TRUCK ASSY	2	1.06 EA.

21551 N.P. DIESEL LOCOMOTIVE "A" UNIT (1 MOTOR)

SAME AS 21902 DIESEL LOCO. (2 MOTOR)-
EXCEPT ELIMINATE THE FOLLOWING PARTS:

XA-15B140-RP	CABIN W/TRIM	1	
XA-13B038-B	PUL-MOR MOTOR ASSY	1	
PA-11B452-C	LOCOMOTIVE CHASSIS	1	
S 40	#2-56 x $\frac{1}{4}$" LG. TYPE "F" SELF TAPPING FLAT HD. SCREWS	2	
-11017	#20 BARE COPPER WIRE $\frac{1}{2}$" LONG	1	

ADD THE FOLLOWING PARTS:

XA-15B076-RP	CABIN W/TRIM	1	4.15 EA.
XA-15B145	CHASSIS ASSY W/TRUCK SUPPORT BRACKET	1	1.41 EA.
S-249	#2 x 5/16 FLAT C'SINK HD. TYPE "Z" P.K. SCREW (SECURES XA-14A930-A ASSY)	2	.12 DOZ
XA-14A930-A	YOKE, WHEEL & STRUCK-UP CHASSIS ASSY (FRONT)	1	1.60 EA.
XA-14A870	INSULATED WHEEL ASSY (FRONT TRUCK)	2	.19 EA.
PA-14B888	SOLID WHEEL	2	.10 EA.
PA-15A226	AXLE SHAFT	2	.05 EA.

21561 N.H. DIESEL LOCOMOTIVE "A" UNIT (1 MOTOR)

SAME AS 21551 N.P. DIESEL -
EXCEPT USE:

XA-14B128 - CRP	CABIN W/TRIM	1	3.95 EA.

NOTE: PRICES SUBJECT TO CHANGE WITHOUT NOTICE.

(NON-MOTORIZED UNITS)

21920-1 M.P. "A" UNIT WITH HORN

SAME AS 21910-1 DIESEL

EXCEPT ELIMINATE THE FOLLOWING PARTS:

XA-11688-GRP	CABIN W/TRIM	1
XA-11B687-DRP	LOCO CHASSIS & SWITCH ASSY	1
XA-13A804	FRONT TRUCK & COUPLER ASSY	1
PA-13A870	DIESEL SOUND GENERATOR	1
PA-10209	BUSHING	1
N-25	8-32 HEX NUT	1
P-4126-C	.158-.160 DIA.HOLE FIBER WASHER	1
P-1131-C	.3205-.3185 DIA.HOLE VELLUMOID WASHER	1
P-4654	LOCKWASHER	1
S-316	#6 x ¼" TYPE "A" BD.HD. P.K. SCREW	1

ADD THE FOLLOWING PARTS:

XA-15B082-ARP	CABIN W/TRIM	1	4.15 EA.
XA-13B422-A	CHASSIS & TRUCK SUPPORT ASSY	1	.96 EA.
XA-13A803	FRONT TRUCK & COUPLER ASSY	1	1.69 EA.
A-12A357	FRONT COUPLER ARM	1	.07 EA.
A-8999	14V. CLEAR BULB	1	.36 EA.
-11409	AIR CHIME (DECORATION)	1	.08 EA.
W-77	.104-.102 DIA.HOLE STEEL WASHER (USE W/ PA5601)	1	.05 DOZ.
PA-5601	TUBULAR RIVET (SECURES SPEAKER BRKT.TO CHASSIS)	1	.01 EA.
PA-11488	HEADLIGHT LENS	1	.04 EA.
PA-15A383	LAMP BRACKET ASSY	1	.29 EA.

21922-1 M.P. "A" UNIT DIESEL W/BELL

XA-15B594-ARP	CABIN W/TRIM	1	4.15 EA.
PA-11409	AIR CHIME (DECORATION)	1	.08 EA.
PA-11488	HEADLIGHT LENS	1	.04 EA.
PA-8999	14V CLEAR LAMP BULB	1	.36 EA.
PA-11493	AIR INTAKE	1	.04 EA.
XA-14A930	YOKE WHEEL & CHASSIS ASSY	1	1.53 EA.
PA-14B888	SOLID WHEEL	4	.10 EA.
PA-15A226	AXLE SHAFT	4	.05 EA.
XA-14A870	INSULATED WHEEL ASSY	4	.19 EA.
XA-13A801	REAR TRUCK & COUPLER ASSY	1	1.33 EA.
PA-13A791	TUBULAR RIVET (REAR TRUCK)	1	.02 EA.
PA-12A355-A	LEAF SPRING (COUPLER)	2	.01 EA.
XA-12A047	KNUCKLE COUPLER ASSY	2	.31 EA.
XA-13A799	TRUCK ASSY	2	.84 EA.
XA-13A800	FRONT TRUCK & COUPLER ASSY	1	1.47 EA.
PA-13A790	TUBULAR RIVET (FRONT TRUCK)	1	.03 EA.
-12A357	FRONT COUPLER ARM	1	.07 EA.
-13B422-B	CHASSIS & TRUCK SUPPORT ASSY	1	1.03 EA.
XA-15A383	LAMP BRACKET ASSY	1	.29 EA.
XA-15A593	BELL & BRACKET ASSY	1	.20 EA.
XA-15A591-RP	SPRING & BRACKET ASSY	1	.38 EA.
PA-15A589	SPRING FOR BELL HAMMER	1	.04 EA.
XA-15A445	TRUCK YOKE & CHASSIS ASSY	1	.85 EA.
PA-11455	BUSHING	2	.14 EA.

(NON-MOTORIZED UNITS)

21922-1 M.P. "A" UNIT DIESEL W/BELL - CONT'D.

PA-15A447	TENSION SPRING	1	.07	EA
PA-15A446	CAM	1	.04	EA
LW-181	BLACK LEAD WIRE		.02	FT
P-10800-A	TRU-ARC RETAINING RING	2	.02	EA
PA-15A449	PIN (TO HOLD SPRING & BRKT. ASSY)	1	.03	EA
PA-5602	TUBULAR RIVET (SECURE BELL & BRKT ASSY)	1	.01	EA
W-124	¼" DIA.HOLE 1/16 THK.FIBER WASHER (FRONT PIVOT)	2	.02	EA
W-83	.161 DIA.HOLE STEEL WASHER (REAR PIVOT)	2	.04	EA
W-124-A	¼" DIA.HOLE 1/16 THK.STEEL WASHER (REAR PIVOT)	1	.03	EA
W-131-A	¼" DIA.HOLE .062 THK.STEEL WASHER (REAR PIVOT)	1	.02	EA
S-249	#2 x 5/16 FLAT CT'SINK HD. TYPE "Z" P.K. SCREW SECURE TRUCK PLATE)	4	.01	EA
S-319	#6 x 5/16 TYPE "Z" P.K. SCREW RD.HD. (SECURE CHASSIS TO BODY)	5	.01	EA

21925-1 U.P. "A" UNIT DIESEL W/BELL

SAME AS 21922-1 -
EXCEPT ELIMINATE THE FOLLOWING PARTS:

XA-15B594-ARP	CABIN W/TRIM ASSY	1
A-13A801	REAR TRUCK & COUPLER ASSY	1
XA-13A800	FRONT TRUCK & COUPLER ASSY	1
XA-13A799	TRUCK ASSY	2

ADD THE FOLLOWING PARTS:

XA-15B549-ARP	CABIN W/TRIM	1	4.15	EA
XA-13A801-A	REAR TRUCK & COUPLER ASSY	1	1.54	EA
XA-13A800-A	FRONT TRUCK & COUPLER ASSY	1	1.69	EA
XA-13A799-A	TRUCK ASSY	2	.84	EA

21902-2 "THE CHIEF" DIESEL "A" UNIT W/O WHISTLE

SAME AS 21922-1 LOCO -
EXCEPT ELIMINATE THE FOLLOWING PARTS:

XA-15B594-ARP	CABIN W/TRIM	1
PA-14A888	SOLID WHEEL	2
PA-15A226	AXLE SHAFT	2
XA-14A870	INSULATED WHEEL ASSY	2
XA-13B422-B	CHASSIS & TRUCK SUPPORT BRACKET	1
XA-15A593	BELL & BRACKET ASSY	1
XA-15A591	SPRING & BRACKET ASSY	1
W-131-A	¼" DIA.HOLE .062 THK.STEEL WASHER	1
W-83	.161 DIA.HOLE STEEL WASHER	1
A-5602	TUBULAR RIVET	1
PA-15A449	PIN	1
PA-15A446	CAM	1
PA-15A447	TENSION SPRING	1

NOTE: PRICES SUBJECT TO CHANGE WITHOUT NOTICE.

NO.	PART NO.	DESCRIPTION	PRICE
1	XA12D075-BRP	A Unit Cabin w/trimmings (474)	3.73 ea.
	PA11488	Headlight Lens	.04 ea.
2	P10800-A	Retaining Ring	.25 dz.
3	W83	Washer	.04 ea.
4	W124	Washer	.25 dz.
5	XA10587-E	Remote Control Unit	4.04 ea.
	XA9612-BRP	Bottom Finger Unit	.33 ea.
	XA9612-CRP	Top Finger Unit	.33 ea.
	XA8716	Drum	.95 ea.
6	PA11452-B	Chassis	.59 ea.
7	S319	Screw	.02 ea.
8	XA11477	Lamp Bracket	.24 ea.
9	PA8999	Bulb	.30 ea.
10	PA11455	Fibre Bushing	.14 ea.
11	S230-B	Screw (secures R.C. Unit)	.01 ea.
	S4A06	Screw (secures yoke & field clamp to chassis)	.03 ea.
12	XA13B038-B	Motor Assembly	12.16 ea.
13	XA11457	Field Clamp Assembly (old style)	.45 ea.
	XA13A037	Yoke Assembly (new style)	.26 ea.
	PA13A034	Field Clamp (new style)	.34 ea.
	S165	Set Screw (new style)	.03 ea.
14	XA13A036	Field Assembly	1.34 ea.
15	XA14B873-RP	Armature Assembly	3.94 ea.
16	P11000-L	Brush Spring (left)	.03 ea.
17	P11000-R	Brush Spring (right)	.03 ea.
18	S171	Screw	.01 ea.
19	PA11441	Worm Cover	.01 ea.
20	PA11453	Bearing Strap	.02 ea.
21	PA11684	Brush (not sold assembled)	.32 ea.
	P10132	Brush Holder	.01 ea.
21A	XA11454-RP	Brush Bracket Assembly	.14 ea.
22	XA12B065-RP	Truck Chassis Assy. NOT AVAILABLE	
		Sub. with XA12A074-RP Truck Chassis Assembly	2.37 ea.
	PA11343	Solid Wheel (old style)	.06 ea.
	PA14A888	Solid Wheel (new style)	.08 ea.
	XA11473	Insulated Wheel Assy. (old style)	.25 ea.
	XA12A249	Pul-Mor Wheel Assembly (old style)	.72 ea.
	XA14A391	Pul-Mor Wheel Assembly (new style)	.28 ea.
	PA14A890	Pul-Mor	.05 ea.
	PA10006	Gear Axle NOT AVAILABLE	
		Sub. with PA15A281 Axle	.07 ea.
	PA11447	20-T Worm Gear NOT AVAILABLE	
		Sub. with PA15A218 Gear	.09 ea.
	PA11463	Thrust Plate	.08 dz.
	XA13A803	Truck & Collector w/coupler arm assy. (consists of parts 23,24,25,26)	1.69 ea.
	XA13A804	Truck & Collector w/coupler assy. (consists of parts 23,24,28, 29)	1.54 ea.

cont'd

NO.	PART NO.	DESCRIPTION	PRICE
23	XA13A802	Truck & Collector Assembly	1.06 ea.
24	PA12A355-A	Leaf Spring	.02 ea.
25	XA12A358	Coupler & Arm Assembly	.34 ea.
26	PA13A790	Rivet	.03 ea.
27	S249	Screw	.15 dz.
28	XA12A047	Knuckle Coupler	.29 ea.
29	PA13A791	Rivet	.02 ea.
30	XA12D075-BRP	A Unit Cabin (dummy #475)	3.73 ea.
31	XA11B831	Speaker NOT AVAILABLE	
		Sub. with XA14A127 Speaker	4.57 ea.
		PA14A216 Bracket	.08 ea.
		S171 Screw	.01 ea.
32	PA12N820	Capacitor NOT AVAILABLE	
		Sub. with PA14A914 Capacitor	1.40 ea.
33	S172	Screw (holds speaker bracket)	.02 ea.
34	PA12B059	Chassis (old style)	.37 ea.
	XA13B422-A	Chassis (new style)	.96 ea.
35	XA11598-A	Wheel & Chassis Assembly NOT AVAILABLE	
		Sub. with XA14A930-B Wheel & Chassis Assy.	1.52 ea.
	PA11343	Solid Wheel (old style)	.06 ea.
	PA14A888	Solid Wheel (new style)	.08 ea.
	XA11473	Insulated Wheel (old style)	.25 ea.
	XA14A870	Insulated Wheel (new style)	.18 ea.
	PA15A226	Axle (new style)	.05 ea.
36	XA11596-A	Wheel & Chassis Assembly (old style)	1.38 ea.
	XA14A930-B	Wheel & Chassis Assembly (new style)	1.60 ea.
37	PA11409	Air Chime	.08 ea.

Prices subject to change without notice.

NO.	PART NO.	DESCRIPTION	PRICE
1	XA14B122-RP	CABIN (490)	3.25 EA.
	XA14B128-RP	CABIN (494)	3.92 EA.
2	P10800-A	RETAINING RING	.25 DZ.
3	W83	WASHER	.04 EA.
4	W124	WASHER	.25 DZ.
5	XA10587-E	REMOTE CONTROL UNIT	4.04 EA.
	XA9612-BRP	BOTTOM FINGER UNIT	.33 EA.
	XA9612-CRP	TOP FINGER UNIT	.33 EA.
	XA8716	DRUM	.95 EA.
6	PA11452-B	CHASSIS	.59 EA.
7	S319	SCREW	.02 EA.
8	XA11477	LAMP BRACKET	.24 EA.
9	PA8999	BULB	.30 EA.
10	PA11455	FIBRE BUSHING	.14 EA.
11	S230-B	SCREW (SECURES R. C. UNIT)	.01 EA.
	S4A06	SCREW (SECURES YOKE & FIELD CLAMP TO CHASSIS)	.03 EA.
12	XA13B038-B	MOTOR ASSY.	12.16 EA.
13	XA13A037	YOKE ASSY.	.26 EA.
	PA13A034	FIELD CLAMP	.34 EA.
	S165	SCREW	.03 EA.
14	XA13A036	FIELD ASSY.	1.34 EA.
15	XA14B873-RP	ARMATURE ASSY.	3.94 EA.
16	P11000-L	BRUSH SPRING (LEFT)	.03 EA.
17	P11000-R	BRUSH SPRING (RIGHT)	.03 EA.
18	S171	SCREW	.01 EA.
19	PA11441	WORM COVER	.01 EA.
20	PA11453	BEARING STRAP	.02 EA.
21	PA11684	BRUSH (NOT SOLD ASSEMBLED)	.32 EA.
	P10132	BRUSH HOLDER	.01 EA.
21A	XA11454-RP	BRUSH BRACKET ASSY.	.14 EA.
22	XA12A074-RP	TRUCK CHASSIS ASSY.	2.37 EA.
	PA14B888	SOLID WHEEL	.08 EA.
	PA15A281	AXLE	.07 EA.
	XA14A891	PUL-MOR WHEEL ASSY.	.28 EA.
	PA14A890	PUL-MOR	.05 EA.
	PA15A218	WORM GEAR	.09 EA.
	PA11463	THRUST PLATE	.08 DZ.
	XA13A803	TRUCK & COLLECTOR W/COUPLER ARM ASSY. (PARTS 23,24,25,26)	1.69 EA.
	XA13A804	TRUCK & COLLECTOR W/COUPLER ASSY. (PARTS 23,24,28,29)	1.54 EA.
23	XA13A802	TRUCK & COLLECTOR ASSY.	1.06 EA.
24	PA12A355-A	LEAF SPRING	.02 EA.
25	XA12A358	COUPLER & ARM ASSY.	.34 EA.
26	PA13A790	RIVET	.03 EA.
27	S249	SCREW	.15 DZ.
28	XA12A047	KNUCKLE COUPLER	.29 EA.
29	PA13A791	RIVET	.02 EA.

CON'T

NO.	PART NO.	DESCRIPTION	PRICE
30	XA14B122-BRP	CABIN (492)	4.30 EA.
	XA14B128-ARP	CABIN (495)	3.08 EA.
31	XA14A127	SPEAKER	4.57 EA.
	PA14A216	BRACKET	.08 EA.
	S171	SCREW	.01 EA.
32	PA14A914	CAPACITOR	1.40 EA.
33	S172	SCREW (HOLDS SPEAKER BRACKET)	.02 EA.
34	XA13B422-A	CHASSIS	.96 EA.
35	XA14A930-B	WHEEL & CHASSIS ASSY.	1.52 EA.
	PA14A888	SOLID WHEEL	.08 EA.
	XA14A870	INSULATED WHEEL	.18 EA.
	PA15A226	AXLE	.05 EA.
36	XA14A930-B	WHEEL & CHASSIS ASSY.	1.52 EA.
37	PA11409	AIR CHIME	.08 EA.

PARTS NOT SHOWN

PART NO.	DESCRIPTION	PRICE
PA13A870	DIESEL SOUND GENERATOR	4.52 EA.
PA10209	INSULATING BUSHING	.02 EA.
P1131-C	WASHER	.01 EA.
N25	8-32 HEX NUT	.02 EA.
P4654	LOCKWASHER	.01 EA.
W55-B	WASHER	.06 DZ.
PA14A215	SPACER	.12 EA.
	(ABOVE USED TO SECURE DIESEL SOUND GENERATOR TO CHASSIS)	

PRICES SUBJECT TO CHANGE WITHOUT NOTICE.

NO.	PART NO.	DESCRIPTION	PRICE
1	XA15B082-RP	Cabin w/trim (21920)	3.47 ea.
	PA11488	Headlight Lens	.04 ea.
2	P10800-A	Retaining Ring	.25 dz.
3	W83	Washer	.04 ea.
	W2A28	Spring Washer	.25 dz.
4	W124	Washer	.35 dz.
	W124-A	Steel Washer (underneath chassis)	.35 dz.
5	XA14C429	Remote Control Unit	2.76 ea.
	XA14A994	Contact Assembly	.77 ea.
	XA14A435	Plunger Assembly	.14 ea.
	XA14B433	Coil Assembly	.69 ea.
	PA14A444	Coil Support	.05 ea.
	PA14C432	Coil Housing	.04 ea.
6	PA11B452-C	Chassis	1.13 ea.
7	S319	Screw	.02 ea.
8	XA15A383	Lamp Bracket	.29 ea.
9	PA8999	Bulb	.30 ea.
10	PA11455	Fibre Bushing	.14 ea.
11	S172	Screw (secures R.C. Unit)	.02 ea.
	S4A06	Screw (secures yoke & field Clamp to chassis)	.03 ea.
12	XA13B038-B	Motor Assembly	12.16 ea.
13	XA13A037	Yoke Assembly	.26 ea.
	PA13A034	Field Clamp	.34 ea.
	S165	Screw	.03 ea.
14	XA13A036	Field Assembly	1.34 ea.
15	XA14B873-RP	Armature Assembly	3.94 ea.
16	P11000-L	Brush Spring (left)	.03 ea.
17	P11000-R	Brush Spring (right)	.03 ea.
18	S171	Screw	.01 ea.
19	PA11441	Worm Cover	.01 ea.
20	PA11453	Bearing Strap	.02 ea.
21	PA11684	Brush (not sold assembled)	.32 ea.
	P10132	Brush Holder (not sold assembled)	.01 ea.
21-A	XA11454-RP	Brush Bracket Assembly	.14 ea.
22	XA12A074-RP	Truck Chassis Assembly	2.37 ea.
	PA14B888	Solid Wheel	.08 ea.
	PA15A281	Axle	.07 ea.
	XA14A891	Pul-Mor Wheel Assembly	.28 ea.
	PA14A890	Pul-Mor	.05 ea.
	PA15A218	Worm Gear	.09 ea.
	PA11463	Thrust Plate	.08 dz.
	XA13A803	Truck & Collector w/coupler Arm Assy. (consists of parts 23,24,25,26)	1.69 ea.
	XA13A804	Truck & Collector w/coupler Assy. (consists of parts 23,24,28,29)	1.54 ea.
23	XA13A802	Truck & Collector Assembly	1.06 ea.
24	PA12A355-A	Leaf Spring	.02 ea.
25	XA12A358	Coupler & Arm Assembly	.34 ea.

cont'd

NO.	PART NO.	DESCRIPTION	PRICE
26	PA13A790	Rivet	.03 ea.
27	S5N40	Screw	.15 dz.
28	XA12A047	Knuckle Coupler	.29 ea.
29	PA13A791	Rivet	.02 ea.
30	XA15B082-ARP	A Unit Cabin (dummy)	4.15 ea.
31	XA14A127	Speaker	4.57 ea.
	PA14A216	Bracket	.08 ea.
	S171	Screw	.01 ea.
32	PA14A914	Capacitor	1.40 ea.
33	S172	Screw (for speaker bracket)	.02 ea.
34	XA13B422-A	Chassis	.96 ea.
35	XA14A930-B	Wheel & Chassis Assembly	1.60 ea.
	PA14B888	Solid Wheel	.08 ea.
	PA15A226	Axle	.05 ea.
	XA14A870	Insulated Wheel	.18 ea.
36	XA14A930-B	Wheel & Chassis Assembly	1.60 ea.
37	PA11409	Air Chime	.08 ea.

Prices subject to change without notice.

NO.	PART NO.	DESCRIPTION	PRICE
1	XA15B594-RP	Cabin w/trim (21922)	4.15 ea.
	XA15B549-RP	Cabin w/trim (21925)	3.91 ea.
	PA11488	Headlight Lens	.04 ea.
2	P10800-A	Retaining Ring	.25 dz.
3	W83	Washer	.04 ea.
	W2A28	Spring Washer	.25 dz.
4	W124	Washer	.35 dz.
	W124A	Steel Washer	.35 dz.
	W131	Steel Washer (dummy A Front)	.06 dz.
5	XA14C429	Remote Control Unit	2.76 ea.
	XA14A994	Contact Assembly	.77 ea.
	XA14A435	Plunger Assembly	.14 ea.
	XA14B433	Coil Assembly	.69 ea.
	PA14A444	Coil Support	.05 ea.
	PA14C432	Coil Housing	.04 ea.
6	PA11B452-C	Chassis	1.13 ea.
7	S319	Screw	.02 ea.
8	XA15A383	Lamp Bracket Assembly	.29 ea.
9	PA8999	Bulb	.30 ea.
10	PA11455	Fibre Bushing	.14 ea.
11	S172	Screw (secures R.C. Unit)	.02 ea.
	S4A06	Screw (secures yoke & field clamp to chassis)	.03 ea.
12	XA13B038-B	Motor Assembly	12.16 ea.
13	XA13A037	Field Clamp Assembly	.26 ea.
	PA13A034	Field Clamp	.34 ea.
	S165	Screw	.03 ea.
14	XA13A036	Field Assembly	1.34 ea.
15	XA14B873-RP	Armature Assembly	3.94 ea.
16	P11000-L	Brush Spring (left)	.03 ea.
17	P11000-R	Brush Spring (right)	.03 ea.
18	S171	Screw	.01 ea.
19	PA11441	Worm Cover	.01 ea.
20	PA11453	Bearing Strap	.02 ea.
21	PA11684	Brush (not sold assembled)	.32 ea.
	P10132	Brush Holder	.01 ea.
21-A	XA11454-RP	Brush Bracket Assembly	.14 ea.
22	XA12A074-RP	Truck Chassis Assembly	2.37 ea.
	PA14B888	Solid Wheel	.08 ea.
	PA15A281	Axle	.07 ea.
	XA14A891	Pul-Mor Wheel Assembly	.28 ea.
	PA14A890	Pul-Mor	.05 ea.
	PA15A218	Worm Gear	.09 ea.
	PA11463	Thrust Plate	.08 dz.
	XA13A803	Truck & Collector w/coupler Assy. (21922) (consists of parts 23,24,25,26)	1.69 ea.
	XA13A803-B	Truck & Collector w/coupler Assy. (21925)	1.69 ea.
	XA13A804	Truck & Collector w/coupler Assy. (21922) (consists of parts 23,24,28,29)	1.54 ea.
	XA13A804-B	Truck & Collector w/coupler Assy. (21925)	1.54 ea.

cont't

NO.	PART NO.	DESCRIPTION		PRICE
23	XA13A802	Truck & Collector Assy.	(21922)	1.06 ea.
	XA13A801	Rear Truck & Coupler	(21922-1)	1.33 ea.
	XA13A800	Front Truck & Coupler	(21922-1)	1.47 ea.
	XA13A802-B	Truck & Collector Assy.	(21925)	1.06 ea.
	XA13A801-A	Rear Truck & Coupler	(21925-1)	1.54 ea.
	XA13A800-A	Front Truck & Coupler	(21925-1)	1.69 ea.
24	PA12A355-A	Leaf Spring		.02 ea.
25	XA12A358	Coupler & Arm Assembly		.34 ea.
26	PA13A790	Rivet		.03 ea.
27	S5N40	Screw		.15 dz.
28	XA12A047	Knuckle Coupler		.29 ea.
29	PA13A791	Rivet		.02 ea.
30	XA15B594-ARP	Cabin (dummy)	(21922-1)	4.15 ea.
	XA15B549-ARP	Cabin (dummy)	(21925-1)	4.15 ea.
31		NOT USED		
32		NOT USED		
33		NOT USED		
34	XA13B422-B	Chassis		1.03 ea.
35	XA14A930	Wheel & Chassis Assembly		1.53 ea.
36	XA15A445-A	Wheel & Chassis Assembly	(used w/bell)	1.70 ea.
37	PA11409	Air Chime		.08 ea.

PARTS NOT SHOWN

PART NO.	DESCRIPTION	PRICE
XA15A593	Bell & Bracket Assembly	.20 ea.
XA15A591-RP	Spring & Bracket Assembly	.38 ea.
PA15A447	Tension Spring	.07 ea.
PA15A449	Pin	.03 ea.

Prices subject to change without notice.

NO.	PART NO.	DESCRIPTION	PRICE
1	XA12D075-BRP	A Unit Cabin w/trimmings (474)	3.92 ea.
	PA11488	Headlight Lens	.04 ea.
2	P10800-A	Retaining Ring	.26 dz.
3	W83	Washer	.04 ea.
4	W124	Washer	.26 dz.
5	XA10587-E	Remote Control Unit	4.24 ea.
	XA9612-BRP	Bottom Finger Unit	.35 ea.
	XA9612-CRP	Top Finger Unit	.35 ea.
	XA8716	Drum	1.00 ea.
6		Chassis (Obsolete)	
7	S319	Screw	.02 ea.
8	XA11477	Lamp Bracket	.25 ea.
9	PA8999	Bulb	.32 ea.
10	PA11455	Fibre Bushing	.15 ea.
11	S230-B	Screw (Secures R. C. Unit)	.01 ea.
	S4A06	Screw (Secures Yoke & Field Clamp to Chassis	.03 ea.
12	XA13B038-B	Motor Assembly	12.77 ea.
13	XA11457	Field Clamp Assembly (Old Style)	.47 ea.
	XA13A037	Yoke Assembly (New Style)	.27 ea.
	PA13A034	Field Clamp (New Style)	.36 ea.
	S165	Set Screw (New Style)	.03 ea.
14	XA13A036	Field Assembly	1.41 ea.
15	XA14B873-RP	Armature Assembly	4.14 ea.
16	P11000-L	Brush Spring (left)	.03 ea.
17	P11000-R	Brush Spring (right)	.03 ea.
18	S171	Screw	.01 ea.
19	PA11441	Worm Cover	.01 ea.
20	PA11453	Bearing Strap	.02 ea.
21	PA11684	Brush	.34 ea.
	P10132	Brush Holder	.01 ea.
21A	XA11454-RP	Brush Bracket Assembly	.15 ea.
22	XA12A074-RP	Truck Chassis Assembly	2.49 ea.
	PA14A888	Solid Wheel (New Style)	.08 ea.
	XA14A891	Pul-Mor Wheel Assembly (New Style)	.29 ea.
	PA14A890	Pul-Mor	.05 ea.
	PA15A281	Gear Axle	.07 ea.
	PA15A218	20-T Worm Gear	.09 ea.
	PA11463	Thrust Plate	.08 dz.
	XA13A803	Truck & Collector w/coupler Arm. Assy. (Consists of Parts 23-24-25-26)	1.77 ea.
	XA13A804	Truck & Collector w/coupler Assy. (Consists of Parts 23-24-28-29)	1.62 ea.
23	XA13A802	Truck & Collector Assembly	1.11 ea.
24	PA12A355-A	Leaf Spring	.02 ea.
25	XA12A358	Coupler & Arm Assembly	.36 ea.
26	PA13A790	Rivet	.03 ea.
27	S249	Screw	.16 dz.
28	XA12A047	Knuckle Coupler	.30 ea.
29	PA13A791	Rivet	.02 ea.
30	XA12D075-BRP	A Unit Cabin (Dummy #475)	3.92 ea.
31	XA14A127 Conv.	Speaker—Sub. for XA11B831—Obsolete	4.91 ea.
32	PA14A914	Capacitor	1.47 ea.
33	S172	Screw (Holds Speaker Bracket)	.02 ea.
34	XA13B422-A	Chassis (New Style)	1.01 ea.
35	XA14A930-B	Wheel and Chassis Assembly	1.60 ea.
	PA14A888	Solid Wheel (New Style)	.08 ea.
	XA14A870	Insulated Wheel (New Style)	.19 ea.
	PA15A226	Axle (New Style)	.05 ea.
36	XA14A930-B	Wheel and Chassis Assembly (New Style)	1.60 ea.
37	PA11409	Air Chime	.08 ea.

Ref: Form No. 1817; Oct. 1, 1962

NO.	PART NO.	DESCRIPTION	PRICE
1	XA14B122-RP	Cabin (490)	3.41 ea.
	XA14B128-RP	Cabin (494)	4.12 ea.
2	P10800-A	Retaining Ring	.26 dz.
3	W83	Washer	.04 ea.
4	W124	Washer	.26 dz.
5	XA10587-E	Remote Control Unit	4.24 ea.
	XA9612-BRP	Bottom Finger Unit	.35 ea.
	XA9612-CRP	Top Finger Unit	.35 ea.
	XA8716	Drum	1.00 ea.
6	PA11452-B	Chassis	.62 ea.
7	S319	Screw	.02 ea.
8	XA11477	Lamp Bracket	.25 ea.
9	PA8999	Bulb	.32 ea.
10	PA11455	Fibre Bushing	.15 ea.
11	S230-B	Screw (Secures R. C. Unit)	.01 ea.
	S4A06	Screw (Secures Yoke & Field Clamp to Chassis)	.03 ea.
12	XA13B038-B	Motor Assembly	12.77 ea.
13	XA13A037	Yoke Assembly	.27 ea.
	PA13A034	Field Clamp	.36 ea.
	S165	Screw	.03 ea.
14	XA13A036	Field Assembly	1.41 ea.
15	XA14B873-RP	Armature Assembly	4.14 ea.
16	P11000-L	Brush Spring (Left)	.03 ea.
17	P11000-R	Brush Spring (Right)	.03 ea.
18	S171	Screw	.01 ea.
19	PA11441	Worm Cover	.01 ea.
20	PA11453	Bearing Strap	.02 ea.
21	PA11684	Brush	.34 ea.
	P10132	Brush Holder	.01 ea.
21-A	XA11454-RP	Brush Bracket Assembly	.15 ea.
22	XA12A074-RP	Truck Chassis Assembly	2.49 ea.
	PA14B888	Solid Wheel	.08 ea.
	PA15A281	Axle	.07 ea.
	XA14A891	Pul-Mor Wheel Assembly	.29 ea.
	PA14A890	Pul-Mor	.05 ea.
	PA15A218	Worm Gear	.09 ea.
	PA11463	Thrust Plate	.08 dz.
	XA13A803	Truck & Collector w/coupler arm assembly (Parts 23-24-25-26)	1.77 ea.
	XA13A804	Truck & Collector w/coupler Assembly (Parts 23-24-28-29)	1.62 ea.
23	XA13A802	Truck & Collector Assembly	1.11 ea.
24	PA12A355-A	Leaf Spring	.02 ea.
25	XA12A358	Coupler & Arm Assembly	.36 ea.
26	PA13A790	Rivet	.03 ea.
27	S249	Screw	.16 dz.
28	XA12A047	Knuckle Coupler	.30 ea.
29	PA13A791	Rivet	.02 ea.
30	XA14B122-BRP	Cabin (492)	4.52 ea.

Cont'd

NO.	PART NO.	DESCRIPTION	PRICE
	XA14B128-ARP	Cabin (495)	3.23 ea.
31	XA14A127	Speaker	4.80 ea.
	PA14A216	Bracket	.08 ea.
	S171	Screw	.01 ea.
32	PA14A914	Capacitor	1.47 ea.
33	S172	Screw (Holds Speaker Bracket)	.02 ea.
34	XA13B422-A	Chassis	1.01 ea.
35	XA14A930-B	Wheel & Chassis Assembly	1.60 ea.
	PA14A888	Solid Wheel	.08 ea.
	XA14A870	Insulated Wheel	.19 ea.
	PA15A226	Axle	.05 ea.
36	XA14A930-B	Wheel & Chassis Assembly	1.60 ea.
37	PA11409	Air Chime	.08 ea.

PARTS NOT SHOWN

PART NO.	DESCRIPTION	PRICE
PA13A870	Diesel Sound Generator	4.75 ea.
PA10209	Insulating Bushing	.02 ea.
P1131-C	Washer	.01 ea.
N25	8-32 Hex Nut	.02 ea.
P4654	Lockwasher	.01 ea.
W55-B	Washer	.06 dz.
PA14A215	Spacer	.13 ea.

(Above used to secure Diesel Sound Generator to Chassis)

Prices subject to change without notice.

Ref: Form No. 1817; Oct. 1, 1962

NO.	PART NO.	DESCRIPTION	PRICE
1	XA15B082-RP	Cabin w/trim (21920)	3.64 ea.
	PA11488	Headlight Lens	.04 ea.
2	P10800-A	Retaining Ring	.26 dz.
3	W83	Washer	.04 ea.
	W2A28	Spring Washer	.26 dz.
4	W124	Washer	.26 dz.
	W124-A	Steel Washer (Underneath Chassis)	.37 dz.
5	XA14C429	Remote Control Unit	2.90 ea.
	XA14A994	Contact Assembly	.81 ea.
	XA14A435	Plunger Assembly	.15 ea.
	XA14B433	Coil Assembly	.72 ea.
	PA14A444	Coil Support	.05 ea.
	PA14C432	Coil Housing	.04 ea.
6	PA11B452-C	Chassis	1.19 ea.
7	S319	Screw	.02 ea.
8	XA15A383	Lamp Bracket	.30 ea.
9	PA8999	Bulb	.32 ea.
10	PA11455	Fibre Bushing	.15 ea.
11	S172	Screw (Secures R. C. Unit)	.02 ea.
	S4A06	Screw (Secures Yoke & Field Clamp to Chassis)	.03 ea.
12	XA13B038-B	Motor Assembly	12.77 ea.
13	XA13A037	Yoke Assembly	.27 ea.
	PA13A034	Field Clamp	.36 ea.
	S165	Screw	.03 ea.
14	XA13A036	Field Assembly	1.41 ea.
15	XA14B873-RP	Armature Assembly	4.14 ea.
16	P11000-L	Brush Spring (Left)	.03 ea.
17	P11000-R	Brush Spring (Right)	.03 ea.
18	S171	Screw	.01 ea.
19	PA11441	Worm Cover	.01 ea.
20	PA11453	Bearing Strap	.02 ea.
21	PA11684	Brush	.34 ea.
	P10132	Brush Holder	.01 ea.
21-	XA11454-RP	Brush Bracket Assembly	.15 ea.
22	XA12A074-RP	Truck Chassis Assembly	2.49 ea.
	PA14B888	Solid Wheel	.08 ea.
	PA15A281	Axle	.07 ea.
	XA14A891	Pul-Mor Wheel Assembly	.29 ea.
	PA14A890	Pul-Mor	.05 ea.
	PA15A218	Worm Gear	.09 ea.
	PA11463	Thrust Plate	.08 dz.
	XA13A803	Truck & Collector w/coupler Arm Assy. (Consists of Parts 23-24-25-26)	1.77 ea.
	XA13A804	Truck & Collector w/coupler Assy. (Consists of Parts 23-24-28-29)	1.62 ea.
23	XA13A802	Truck & Collector Assembly	1.11 ea.
24	PA12A355-A	Leaf Spring	.02 ea.
25	XA12A358	Coupler and Arm Assembly	.36 ea.
26	PA13A790	Rivet	.03 ea.
27	S5N40	Screw	.16 dz.
28	XA12A047	Knuckle Coupler	.30 ea.
29	PA13A791	Rivet	.02 ea.
30	XA15B082-ARP	"A" Unit Cabin (Dummy)	4.36 ea.

(Cont'd

NO.	PART NO.	DESCRIPTION	PRICE
31	XA14A127	Speaker	4.80 ea.
	PA14A216	Bracket	.08 ea.
	S171	Screw	.01 ea.
32	PA14A914	Capacitor	1.47 ea.
33	S172	Screw (For Speaker Bracket)	.02 ea.
34	XA13B422-A	Chassis	1.01 ea.
35	XA14A930-B	Wheel and Chassis Assembly	1.60 ea.
	PA14B888	Solid Wheel	.08 ea.
	PA15A226	Axle	.05 ea.
	XA14A870	Insulated Wheel	.19 ea.
36	XA14A930-B	Wheel and Chassis Assembly	1.60 ea.
37	PA11409	Air Chime	.08 ea.

Prices subject to change without notice.

NO.	PART NO.	DESCRIPTION	PRICE
1	XA15B594-RP	Cabin w/ trim (21922)	4.36 ea.
	XA15B549-RP	Cabin w/ trim (21925)	4.11 ea.
	PA11488	Headlight Lens	.04 ea.
2	P10800-A	Retaining Ring	.26 dz.
3	W83	Washer	.04 ea.
	W2A28	Spring Washer	.26 dz.
4	W124	Washer	.26 dz.
	W124A	Steel Washer	.37 dz.
	W131	Steel Washer (Dummy A Front)	.06 dz.
5	XA14C429	Remote Control Unit	2.90 ea.
	XA14A994	Contact Assembly	.81 ea.
	XA14A435	Plunger Assembly	.15 ea.
	XA14B433	Coil Assembly	.72 ea.
	PA14A444	Coil Support	.05 ea.
	PA14C432	Coil Housing	.04 ea.
6	PA11B452-C	Chassis	1.19 ea.
7	S319	Screw	.02 ea.
8	XA15A383	Lamp Bracket Assembly	.30 ea.
9	PA8999	Bulb	.32 ea.
10	PA11455	Fibre Bushing	.15 ea.
11	S172	Screw (Secures R.C. Unit)	.02 ea.
	S4A06	Screw (Secures Yoke & Field Clamp to Chassis)	.03 ea.
12	XA13B038-B	Motor Assembly	12.77 ea.
13	XA13A037	Yoke Assembly	.27 ea.
	PA13A034	Field Clamp	.36 ea.
	S165	Screw	.03 ea.
14	XA13A036	Field Assembly	1.41 ea.
15	XA14B873-RP	Armature Assembly	4.14 ea.
16	P11000-L	Brush Spring (Left)	.03 ea.
17	P11000-R	Brush Spring (Right)	.03 ea.
18	S171	Screw	.01 ea.
19	PA11441	Worm Cover	.01 ea.
20	PA11453	Bearing Strap	.02 ea.
21	PA11684	Brush	.34 ea.
	P10132	Brush Holder	.01 ea.
21A	XA11454-RP	Brush Bracket Assembly	.15 ea.
22	XA12A074-RP	Truck Chassis Assembly	2.49 ea.
	PA14B888	Solid Wheel	.08 ea.
	PA15A281	Axle	.07 ea.
	XA14A891	Pul-Mor Wheel Assembly	.29 ea.
	PA14A890	Pul-Mor	.05 ea.
	PA15A218	Worm Gear	.09 ea.
	PA11463	Thrust Plate	.08 dz.
	XA13A803	Truck & Collector w/ coupler (21922) (Consists of Parts 23,24,25,26)	1.77 ea.
	XA13A803-B	Truck & Collector w/ coupler (21925)	1.77 ea.
	XA13A804	Truck & Collector w/ coupler (21922) (Consists of Parts 23,24,28,29)	1.62 ea.
	XA13A804-B	Truck & Collector w/ coupler (21925)	1.62 ea.

Continued

NO.	PART NO.	DESCRIPTION	PRICE
23	XA13A802	Truck & Collector Assy. (21922)	1.11 ea.
	XA13A801	Rear Truck & Coupler (21922-1)	1.40 ea.
	XA13A800	Front Truck & Coupler (21922-1)	1.54 ea.
	XA13A802-B	Truck & Collector Assy (21925)	1.11 ea.
	XA13A801-A	Rear Truck & Coupler (21925-1)	1.62 ea.
	XA13A800-A	Front Truck & Coupler (21925-1)	1.77 ea.
24	PA12A355-A	Leaf Spring	.02 ea.
25	XA12A358	Coupler & Arm Assembly	.36 ea.
26	PA13A790	Rivet	.03 ea.
27	S5N40	Screw	.16 dz.
28	XA12A047	Knuckle Coupler	.30 ea.
29	PA13A791	Rivet	.02 ea.
30	XA15B594-ARP	Cabin (Dummy) (21922-1)	4.36 ea.
	XA15B549-ARP	Cabin (Dummy) (21925-1)	4.36 ea.
31		NOT USED	
32		NOT USED	
33		NOT USED	
34	XA13B422-B	Chassis	1.08 ea.
35	XA14A930	Wheel & Chassis Assembly	1.61 ea.
36	XA15A445-A	Wheel & Chassis Assembly (used w/Bell)	1.79 ea.
37	PA11409	Air Chime	.08 ea.

PARTS NOT SHOWN

PART NO.	DESCRIPTION	PRICE
XA15A593	Bell & Bracket Assembly	.21 ea.
XA15A591-RP	Spring & Bracket Assembly	.40 ea.
PA15A447	Tension Spring	.07 ea.
PA15A449	Pin	.03 ea.

Prices subject to change without notice

ALCO DIESEL LOCOMOTIVE
Model Nos. 477/478 Silver Flash

SPECIFICATIONS

Tested at: 12 Volts A.C. .... using 180" oval of track.

(A) Locomotive to run a minimum of 9 R.P.M. or 9 Times forward and reverse, around 180" oval of track.

Load: Not to draw more than 3.25 amps. while pulling 4 Passenger Cars.

Motor: Universal A.C. or D.C.

 Ref: Form No. 1816; Feb. 1, 1957

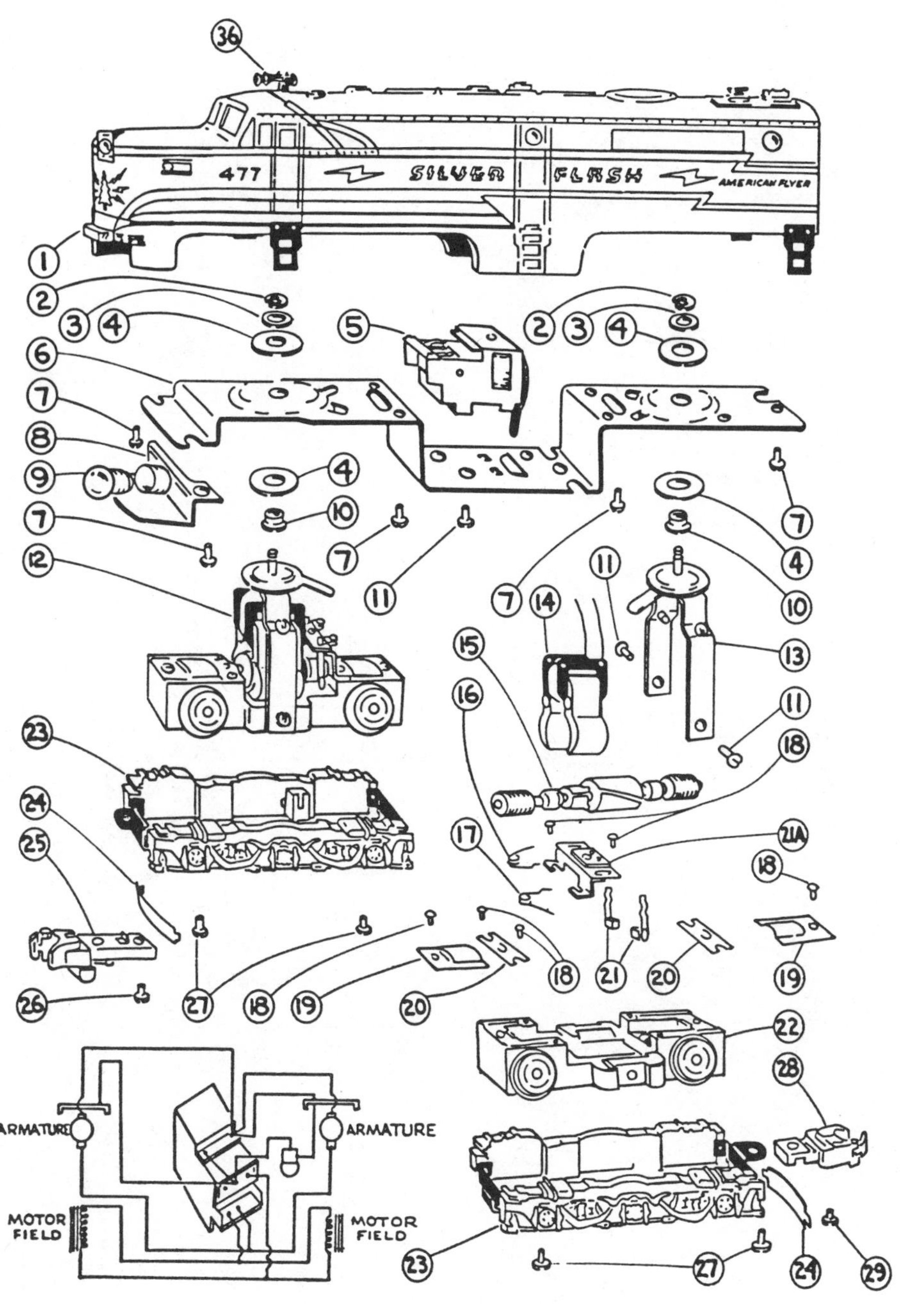

Ref: Form No. 1816; Feb. 1, 1957

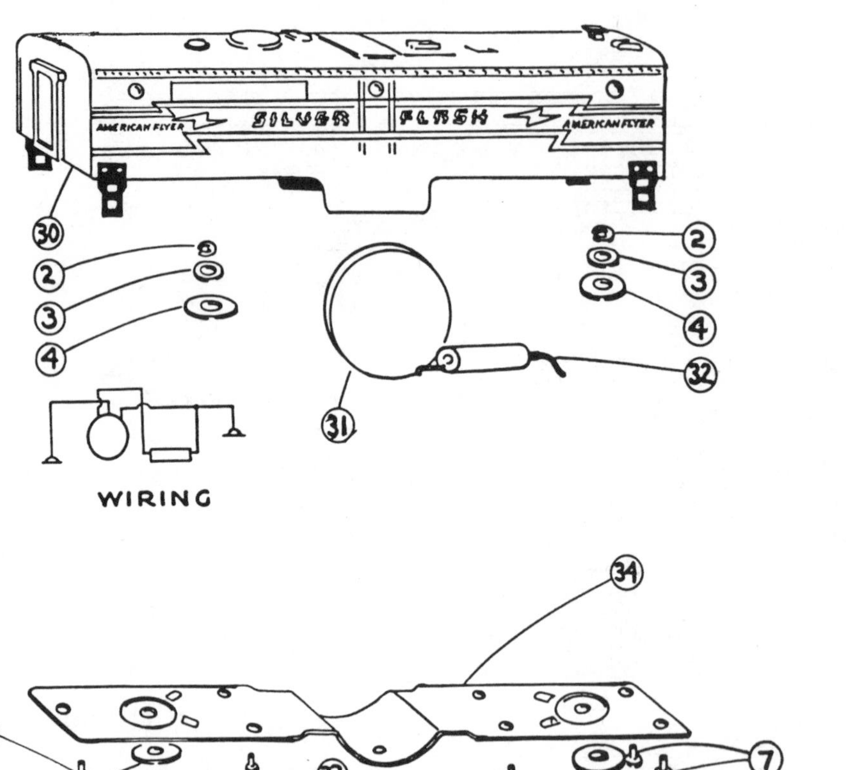

 Ref: Form No. 1816; Feb. 1, 1957

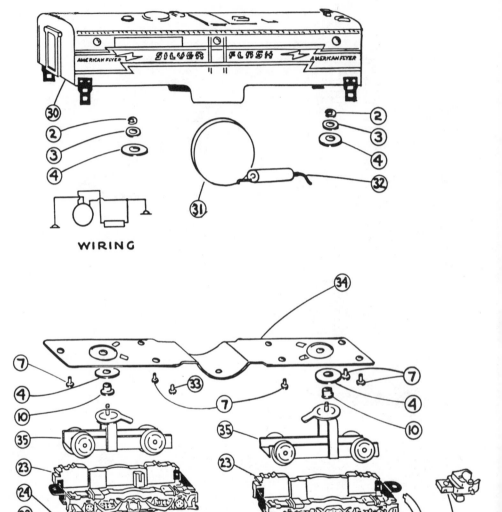

NO.	PART NO.	DESCRIPTION	PRICE
1	XA12D075-CRP	"A" UNIT CABIN W/TRIMMINGS (477)	4.25 EA.
2	P10800-A	RETAINING RING	.25 DZ.
3	W83	WASHER	.04 EA.
4	W124	WASHER	.25 DZ.
5	XA10587-E	REMOTE CONTROL UNIT	4.04 EA.
	XA9612-BRP	BOTTOM FINGER UNIT	.33 EA.
	XA9612-CRP	TOP FINGER UNIT	.33 EA.
	XA8716	DRUM	.95 EA.
6	PA11452-B	CHASSIS	.59 EA.
7	S319	SCREW	.02 EA.
8	XA11477	LAMP BRACKET	.24 EA.
9	PA8999	BULB	.30 EA.
10	PA11455	FIBRE BUSHING	.14 EA.
11	S230-B	SCREW (SECURES R.C. UNIT)	.01 EA.
	S4A06	SCREW (SECURES YOKE & FIELD CLAMP TO CHASSIS)	.03 EA.
12	XA13B038-B	MOTOR ASSY.	12.16 EA.
13	XA11457	FIELD CLAMP ASSY. (OLD STYLE)	.45 EA.
	PA13A034	FIELD CLAMP ASSY. (NEW STYLE)	.34 EA.
	XA13A307	YOKE ASSY.	.26 EA.
	S165	SCREW (SET) (USED W/FIELD CLAMP)	.03 EA.
14	XA13A036	FIELD ASSY.	1.34 EA.
15	XA14B873-RP	ARMATURE ASSY.	3.94 EA.
16	P11000-L	BRUSH SPRING (LEFT)	.03 EA.
17	P11000-R	BRUSH SPRING (RIGHT)	.03 EA.
18	S171	SCREW	.01 EA.
19	PA11441	WORM COVER	.01 EA.
20	PA11453	BEARING STRAP	.02 EA.
21	PA11684	BRUSH (NOT SOLD ASSEMBLED)	.32 EA.
	P10132	BRUSH HOLDER (NOT SOLD ASSEMBLED)	.01 EA.
21A	XA11454-RP	BRUSH BRACKET ASSY.	.14 EA.
22	XA12B065-RP	TRUCK CHASSIS ASSY. NOT AVAILABLE	
	SUB.	W/ XA12A074-RP TRUCK CHASSIS ASSY.	2.37 EA.
	PA11343	SOLID WHEEL (OLD STYLE)	.06 EA.
	PA14A888	SOLID WHEEL (NEW STYLE)	.08 EA.
	XA11473	INSULATED WHEEL ASSY. (OLD STYLE)	.25 EA.
	XA12A249	PUL-MOR WHEEL ASSY. (OLD STYLE)	.72 EA.
	XA14A891	PUL-MOR WHEEL ASSY. (NEW STYLE)	.28 EA.
	PA14A890	PUL-MOR	.05 EA.
	PA10006	GEAR AXLE NOT AVAILABLE	
	SUB.	W/ PA15A281 AXLE	.07 EA.
	PA11447	20 - T WORM GEAR NOT AVAILABLE	
	SUB.	W/ PA15A218 GEAR	.09 EA.
	PA11463	THRUST PLATE	.08 DZ.
	XA13A803	TRUCK & COLLECTOR W/COUPLER ARM ASSY. (PARTS 23,24,25,26)	1.69 EA.
	XA13A804	TRUCK & COLLECTOR W/COUPLER ASSY. (PARTS 23,24,28,29)	1.54 EA.
23	XA13A802	TRUCK & COLLECTOR ASSY.	1.06 EA.
24	PA12A355-A	LEAF SPRING	.02 EA.
25	XA12A358	COUPLER & ARM ASSY.	.34 EA.

CON'T

NO.	PART NO.	DESCRIPTION	PRICE
26	PA13A790	RIVET	.36 DZ.
27	S249	SCREW	.15 DZ.
28	XA12A047	KNUCKLE COUPLER	.29 EA.
29	PA13A791	RIVET	.02 EA.
30	XA11688-ARP	"B" UNIT CABIN (478)	3.62 EA.
31	XA11B831	SPEAKER NOT AVAILABLE	
	SUB. W/	XA14A127 SPEAKER	4.57 EA.
		PA14A216 BRACKET	.08 EA.
		S171 SCREW	.01 EA.
32	PA12N820	CAPACITOR NOT AVAILABLE	
	SUB. W/	PA14A914 CAPACITOR	1.40 EA.
33	S172	SCREW (HOLDS SPEAKER BRACKET)	.02 EA.
34	PA11687	CHASSIS	.33 EA.
35	XA11598-A	WHEEL & CHASSIS ASSY. NOT AVAILABLE	
	SUB. W/	XA14A930-B WHEEL & CHASSIS ASSY.	1.52 EA.
	PA11343	SOLID WHEEL (OLD STYLE)	.06 EA.
	PA14A888	SOLID WHEEL (NEW STYLE)	.08 EA.
	XA11473	INSULATED WHEEL (OLD STYLE)	.25 EA.
	XA14A870	INSULATED WHEEL (NEW STYLE)	.18 EA.
	PA15A226	AXLE (NEW STYLE)	.05 EA.
36	PA11409	AIR CHIME	.08 EA.

PRICES SUBJECT TO CHANGE WITHOUT NOTICE.

 Ref: Form No. 1816; June 1, 1960

DIA. NO.	PART NO.		DESCRIPTION	PRICE
1	XA12D075-CRP		"A" Unit Cabin w/ Trimmings (477)	4.46 ea.
2	P10800-A		Retaining Ring	.26 dz.
3	W83		Washer	.04 ea.
4	W124		Washer	.26 dz.
5	XA10587-E		Remote Control Unit	4.24 ea.
	XA9612-BRP		Bottom Finger Unit	.35 ea.
	XA9612-CRP		Top Finger Unit	.35 ea.
	XA8716		Drum	1.00 ea.
6			Chassis Obsolete	
7	S319		Screw	.02 ea.
8	XA11477		Lamp Bracket	.25 ea.
9	PA8999		Bulb	.32 ea.
10	PA11455		Fibre Bushing	.15 ea.
11	S230-B		Screw (Secures R. C. Unit)	.01 ea.
	S4A06		Screw (Secures Yoke & Field Clamp to Chassis)	.03 ea.
12	XA13B038-B		Motor Assy.	12.77 ea.
13	PA13A034		Field Clamp Assy. (New Style)	.36 ea.
	XA13A037		Yoke Assy.	.27 ea.
	S165		Screw (Set) (Used w/ Field Clamp)	.03 ea.
14	XA13A036		Field Assy.	1.41 ea.
15	XA14B873-RP		Armature Assy.	4.14 ea.
16	P11000-L		Brush Spring (Left)	.03 ea.
17	P11000-R		Brush Spring (Right)	.03 ea.
18	S171		Screw	.01 ea.
19	PA11441		Worm Cover	.01 ea.
20	PA11453		Bearing Strap	.02 ea.
21	PA11684		Brush	.34 ea.
	P10132		Brush Holder	.01 ea.
21A	XA11454-RP		Brush Bracket Assy.	.15 ea.
22	XA12A074-RP		Truck Chassis Assy.	2.49 ea.
	PA14A888		Solid Wheel (New Style)	.08 ea.
	XA14A891		Pul-Mor Wheel Assy. (New Style)	.29 ea.
	PA14A890		Pul-Mor	.05 ea.
	PA15A281		Gear Axle	.07 ea.
	PA15A218		20-T Worm Gear	.09 ea.
	PA11463		Thrust Plate	.08 dz.
	XA13A803		Truck & Collector w/ coupler arm assy. (Parts 23,24,25,26)	1.77 ea.
	XA13A804		Truck & Collector w/ Coupler Assy. (Parts 23,24,28,29)	1.62 ea.
23	XA13A802		Truck & Collector Assy.	1.11 ea.
24	PA12A355-A		Leaf Spring	.02 ea.
25	XA12A358		Coupler & Arm Assy.	.36 ea.
26	PA13A790		Rivet	.38 dz.
27	S249		Screw	.16 dz.
28	XA12A047		Knuckle Coupler	.30 ea.
29	PA13A791		Rivet	.02 ea.
30	XA11688-ARP		"B" Unit Cabin (478)	3.80 ea.
31	XA14A127	Conv.	Speaker (sub. for XA11B831)	4.91 ea.
32	PA14A914		Condenser (sub. for PA12N820)	1.47 ea.
33	S172		Screw (Holds Speaker Bracket)	.02 ea.
34	PA11687-B		Chassis	.50 ea.
35	XA14A930-B		Wheel & Chassis Assy.	1.60 ea.
	PA14A888		Solid Wheel (New Style)	.08 ea.
	XA14A870		Insulated Wheel (New Style)	.19 ea.
	PA15A226		Axle (New Style)	.05 ea.
36	PA11409		Air Chime	.08 ea.

Ref: Form No. 1816; Oct. 1, 1962

EMD F-9 DIESEL LOCOMOTIVE

Model Nos. 21205/21205-1, 21206/21206-1, 21210, 21215/21215-1, L2004/L2004-1

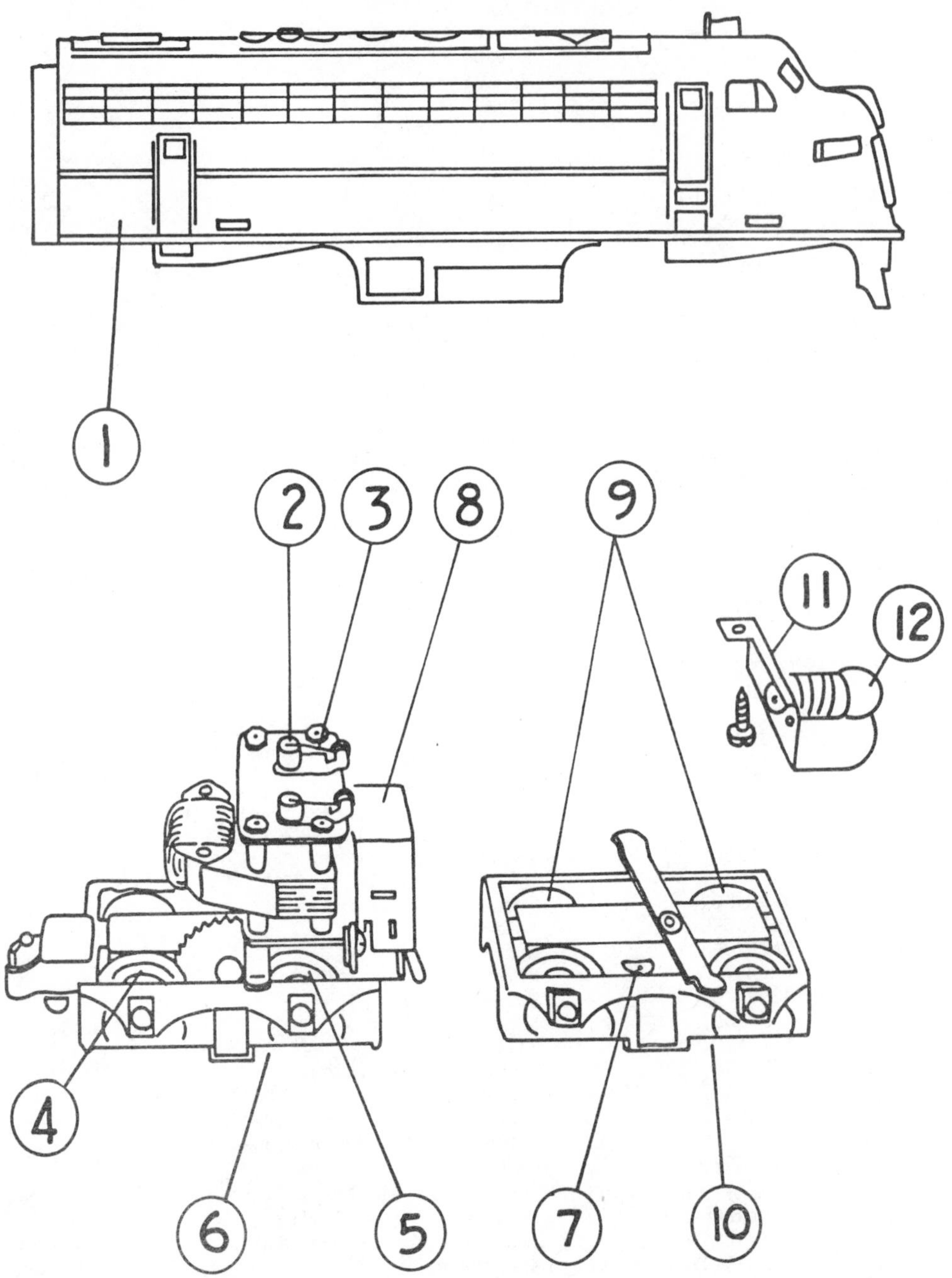

 Ref: Form No. 2041; May 1962

NO.	PART NO.	DESCRIPTION	PRICE
1	XA30N071-ARP	Cabin (Boston & Maine) 21205	1.78 ea.
	XA30N071-HRP	Cabin (Burlington) 21210	2.73 ea.
	XA30N071-BRP	Cabin (Union Pacific) 21215	2.71 ea.
	XA30B071-ABRP	Cabin (Santa Fe) 21206	1.98 ea.
	XA30B071-ACRP	Cabin (Rio Grande) L2004	2.73 ea.
2	PA30A032	Brush	.10 ea.
3	PA16A380	Brush Spring	.02 ea.
4	XA30A091	Wheel, Axle, Gear & Bearing Assy.	.58 ea.
	PA15A034	Pul-Mor	.06 ea.
5	XA30A095	Wheel, Axle & Bearing Assy.	.53 ea.
6	XA30A089	Bottom Plate Assy. (Motor End)	.51 ea.
7	XA30A078	Collector Assembly	.08 ea.
8	XA14C429	Remote Control Assembly	2.90 ea.
	XA14A994	Contact Assembly	.81 ea.
	XA14A435	Plunger Assembly	.15 ea.
	XA14B433	Coil Assembly	.72 ea.
	PA14A444	Coil Support	.05 ea.
	PA14C432	Coil Housing	.04 ea.
9	XA30A073	Wheel and Axle Assembly	.36 ea.
10	XA30A076	Bottom Plate Assy. w/coupler (21210 - 21215)	.36 ea.
	PA30B077	Bottom Plate (no coupler) (L2004 - 21205 - 21206)	.04 ea.
11	XA15158-A	Lamp Bracket Assy. (Used on 21210 & 21215)	.25 ea.
12	PA8999	Bulb (Used on 21210 & 21215)	.32 ea.
		NOT SHOWN	
	XA30102	Truck Body Assy. w/gear (Motor End)	1.68 ea.
	PA30D072-A	Plastic Truck Frame (Motor End)	.17 ea.
	XA9547-E	Field Assembly	1.30 ea.
	XA30083	Armature	2.60 ea.
	XA30A033	Brush Plate Assembly	.33 ea.
	XA30103	Truck Body Assy. (Front)	.63 ea.
	PA30D072	Plastic Truck Frame (Front)	.17 ea.
	S319	6 x 5/16 Type "Z" P.K. Screw for Lamp Bracket	.02 ea.

Dummy A Unit (Not Motorized)

NO.	PART NO.	DESCRIPTION	PRICE
1	XA30N071CDRP	Cabin for L2004-1	2.73 ea.
	XA30B071CCRP	Cabin for 21205-1	1.66 ea.
	XA30B071CBRP	Cabin for 21206-1	1.98 ea.
	XA30B071CARP	Cabin for 21215-1	3.05 ea.
2 and 3		NOT USED	
4 and 5	XA30A073	Wheel and Axle Assembly	.36 ea.
6	XA30A076	Metal Bottom Plate Assy. w/coupler	.36 ea.
	XA12A047	Knuckle Coupler	.30 ea.
7 and 8		NOT USED	
9	XA30A073	Wheel and Axle Assembly	.36 ea.
10	XA30A076	Metal Bottom Plate Assy. w/knuckle coupler	.36 ea.
	XA12A047	Knuckle Coupler	.30 ea.
11 and 12		NOT USED	

MAINTENANCE CAR

Model No. 23743

XA15A986 Motor & Chassis Assembly 4.98 ea.

STEAM SWITCHER LOCOMOTIVE AND TENDER WITH SMOKE AND CHOO-CHOO UNIT, PULL-MOR WHEELS, AND KNUCKLE COUPLER

Model Nos. 263, 343, 21004, 21005, 21145

Although the 263, the 21004, and the 21005 locomotives have six drivers, Gilbert included them with the eight-drivered locomotives on this page. On some of the following pages, Gilbert has separated the six-driver and eight-driver locomotives to clarify parts use.

SPECIFICATIONS

Tested at: 12 Volts A.C. .... using 140″ oval of track.

(A) Motor to be tested with Remote Control Unit at 12 Volts and not to draw more than 1.55 amps.

(B) Locomotive to run at a minimum of 9 R.P.M. or 9 times forward around 140″ oval of track per minute.

(C) Locomotive to run at a minimum of 8.5 R.P.M. or 8½ times reverse around 140″ oval of track per minute.

Load: Not to draw more than 2.1 amps. while pulling 4 box cars.

Motor: Universal A.C. or D.C.

Ref: Form No. 1825; Feb. 1, 1957

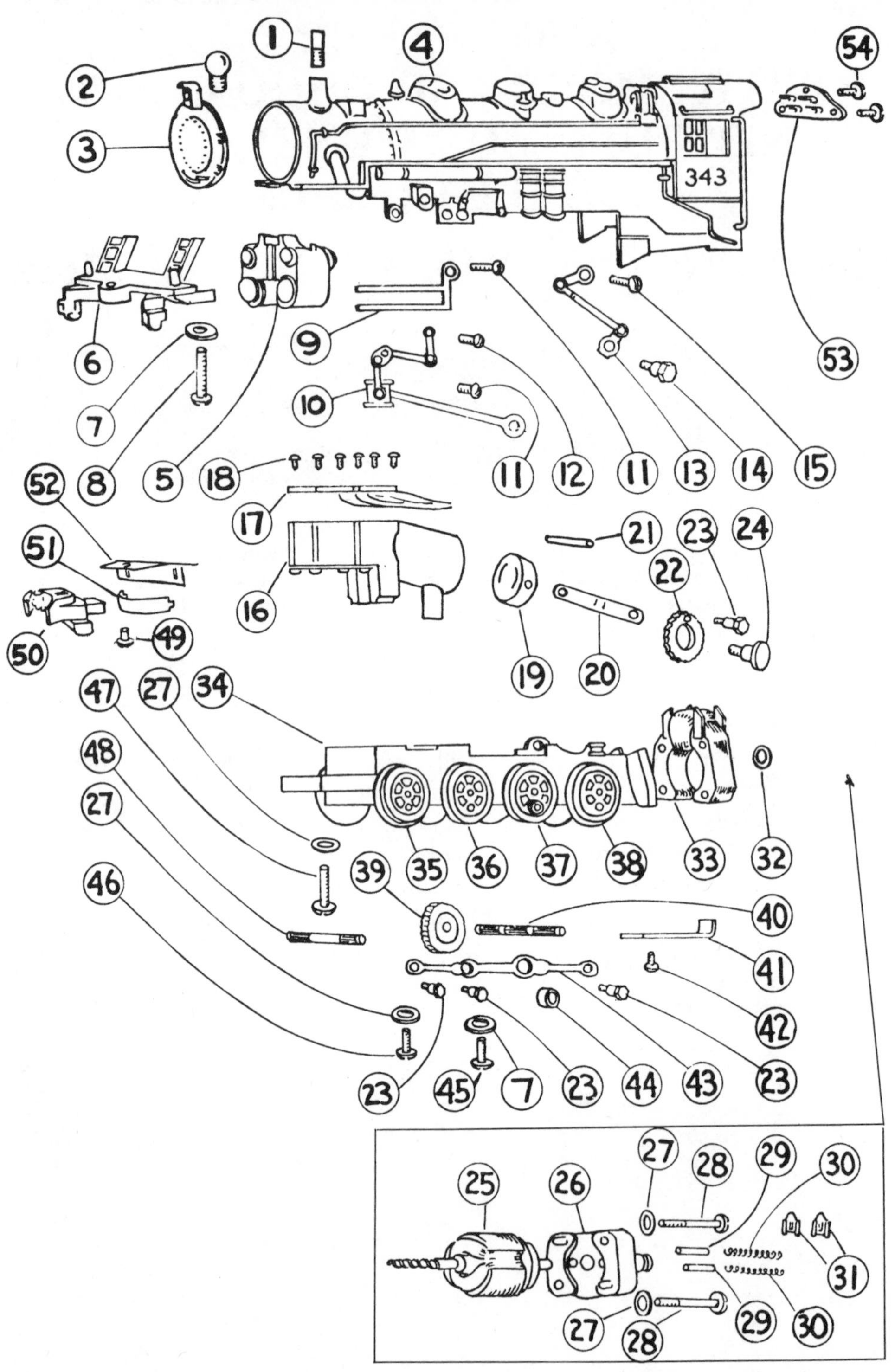

 Ref: Form No. 1825; Feb. 1, 1957

56
57
58
61
60
59
62
63
2
55
62
63
66
66
67
64
65
66
68
69
50
67
70
71
72
73
74

TO BOTTOM CONN.
BRUSH
TO TOP CONN.

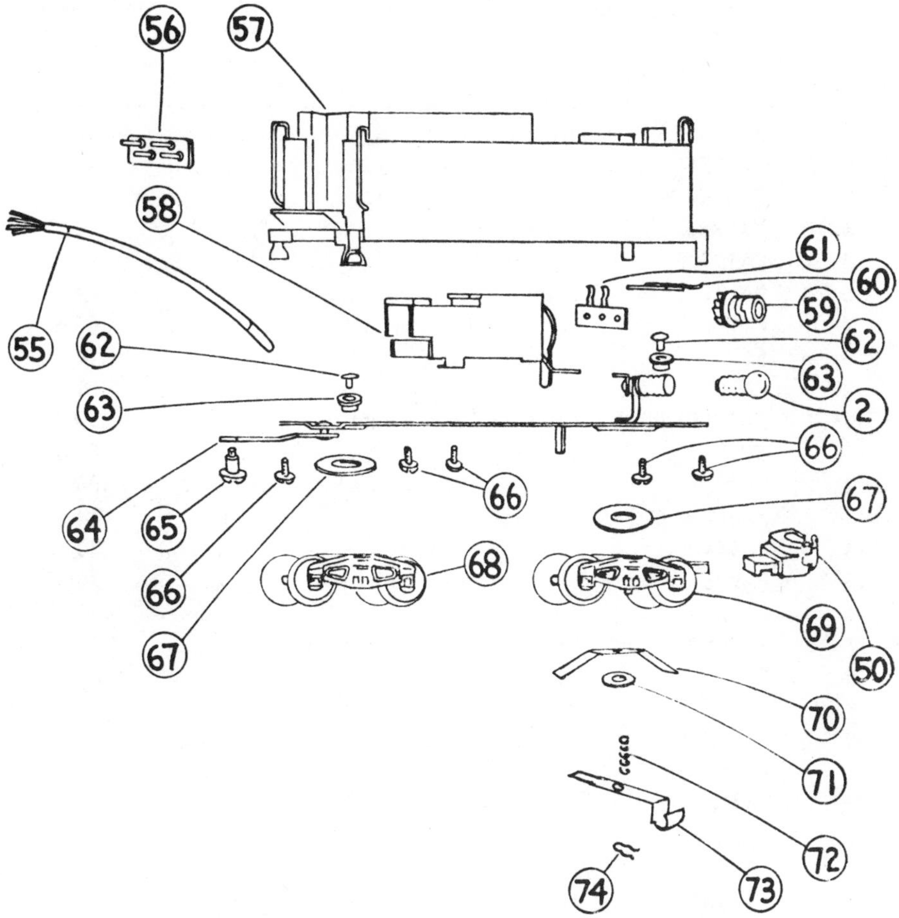

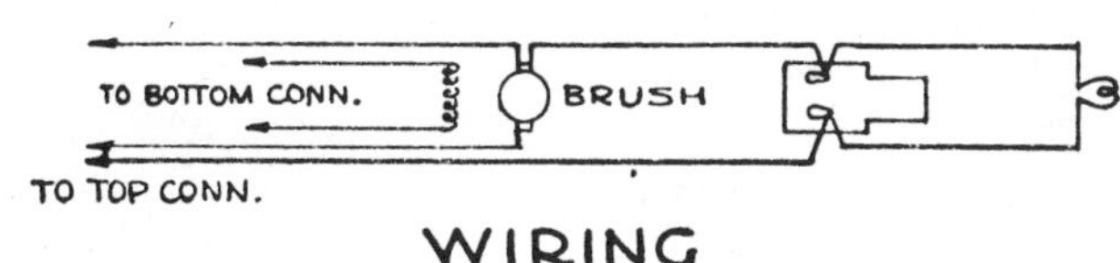

WIRING

Diagram Number	Part No.	Description	Price
1	PA12A190	Smoke Stack	$ .02 ea.
2	PA8999	14 Volt Lamp	.25 "
3	XA9467-B	Boiler Front	.60 "
4	XA9466-C RP	Boiler Assy	4.26 "
5	PA10109	Cylinder	.70 "
6	PA12C478-A	Pilot	.71 "
7	P4654	Lock Washer	.05 dz.
8	S55	Screw	.10 "
9	PA10595-R & L	Crosshead Guide (right or left)	.10 ea.
10	XA10596-R & L	Crosshead Assy (right or left)	.50 "
11	S-1	Screw	.05 dz.
12	PA10598	Link Stud	.30 "
13	XA10447-B	Eccentric Crank	.30 ea.
14	PA5447	Eccentric Crank Screw	.30 dz.
15	PA9288	Shouldered Screw	.30 "
16	PA10513	Smoke Box	1.00 ea.
17	XA10523	Heating Element and Plate Assy	1.00 "
18	S183	Screw	.10 dz.
19	PA10518-A	Piston	.20 ea.
20	PA10516	Piston Lever	.05 "
21	PA10520	Piston Pin	.05 "
22	PA10671	Worm Gear	.40 "
23	PA7421	Screw	.30 dz.
24	PA10162	Worm Gear Stud	.10 ea.
25	XA11077	Armature	2.50 "
26	XA9565-A	Brush Bracket	.50 "
27	PA3769	Lock Washer	.05 dz.
28	S295	Screw	.10 ea.
29	PA9603	Brush	.15 "
30	PA10757-A	Brush Spring	.05 "
31	PA10754	Brush Cap	.02 "
32	PA10766	Armature Spacer	.05 dz.
33	XA9547	Field Assy	1.00 ea.
34	XA10504	Chassis	1.10 "
35	XA12A472	Flanged Wheel	.40 "
36	XA10104-B	Flangeless Wheel	.40 "
37	XA10104-A2	Flangeless Wheel w/Stud	.40 "

 Ref: Form No. 1825; Feb. 1, 1957

Diagram Number	Part No.	Description	Price
38	XA12A473	Pull-Mor Wheel	$ .53 ea.
39	PA9473	Worm Gear	.40 "
40	PA10006	Worm Gear Axle	.10 "
41	PA10017	Grease Pan	.02 "
42	S271	Screw	.10 dz.
43	PA9476	Side Rod	.20 ea.
44	PA7237	Piston Rod Spacer	.05 "
45	S16C	Screw	.10 dz.
46	S24	Screw	.02 ea.
47	S52	Screw	.10 dz.
48	PA10005	Axle	.10 ea.
49	S3A71	Screw	.01 "
50	XA12A047	Knuckle Coupler	.22 "
51	PA12A355	Leaf Spring	.01 "
52	PA12A479	Coupler Rachet	.03 "
53	XA10662-A	Jack Panel	.20 "
54	S222	Screw	.01 "
55	PA10511-C	4 Conductor Cable	.12 "
56	XA10663	Male Plug Assy	.20 "
57	PA9778-B	Tender Body	2.00 "
58	XA10587-E	R. Control	2.50 "
59	XA8716	Drum	.60 "
60	XA9612-C	Finger Top	.50 "
61	XA9612-B	Finger Bottom	.50 "
62	PA10235-A	Coupler Rivet	.03 "
63	PA10209	Insulating Bushing	.02 "
64	XA10592	Chassis	.33 "
65	PA4938	Stud	.30 dz.
66	S-0	Screw	.05 "
67	PA8715-B	Fiber Washer	.05 "
68	XA12A516	Front Truck Assy	.60 ea.
69	XA12A350	Rear Truck Assy	.87 "
70	PA10207	Contact Spring	.02 "
71	PA1405	Tin Washer	.05 dz.
72	PA11A956	Spring	.01 ea.
73	PA11A936	Tender Pickup	.02 "
74	PA11A944	Hair Pin Cotter	.01 "

Ref: Form No. 1825; Feb. 1, 1957

SERVICE INSTRUCTIONS FOR NO. 343 SWITCHER LOCOMOTIVE AND TENDER WITH SMOKE, CHOO-CHOO, PULL-MOR AND KNUCKLE COUPLER

The first thing to do is to place Locomotive and Tender on track, connect transformer and test for operation. Make sure all rods, linkage and other parts are not bent or broken. It is also important that the wheels on the Tender be clean to insure a good electrical contact.

1. If the Locomotive and Tender does not operate properly proceed as follows:

a. Remove male plug (※56) from the Jack Panel (※53).

b. Now take another similar tender with a Remote Control Unit in it which is in good working order and connect it to the Locomotive. In this way, you will be able to determine whether the Locomotive or Tender is defective.

2. If the trouble is in the Locomotive you can make the following checks:

a. Inspect Brushes for wear or poor contact and Brush Springs for position and proper tension.

b. Check wires and solder joints on Male Plug (※56) and Jack Panel (※53) for broken or loose connections.

c. Clean or polish commutator if dirty or worn.

3. If these initial steps do not correct the trouble it will be necessary to disassemble the Locomotive as follows:

a. Unscrew smoke stack (※1).

b. Remove screws (※14) on each side and take off Rods (※10), and (※13) and spacer (※44) from center drive wheel.

c. Pull out Boiler Front (※3) from Boiler Assembly (※4) and unsolder the two wires at the lamp bracket.

d. Turn Locomotive upside down and remove two screws (※47) and you can now remove motor assembly from Boiler (※4).

e. To remove motor, push forward approximately a ¼" to clear clamp on Boiler (※4) and then lift the rear of motor up and pull motor out.

f. The motor is now exposed and you can inspect the wiring and other points of the unit, making any necessary replacements.

4. When the trouble appears to be in the Tender proceed as follows:

a. Remove four S-0 Screws (※66) and take off Tender Body (※57).

b. Inspect wiring and solder joints for loose or broken connections.

c. Check Finger Units (※60) and (※61) on Remote Control Unit (※58) to see if they are burnt or not making proper contact.

d. The drum (※59) should be checked to see if it is pitted or worn.

e. The pawl on the Remote Control Unit may be broken or need adjusting.

f. It is generally not necessary to replace the complete Remote Control Unit, but sometimes the Finger Units, the drum, or both need adjusting or replacing.

NO.	PART NO.	DESCRIPTION	PRICE
1	P10174-A	Smoke Stack	.08
2	P13N922	Bulb (located in Loco.)	.57
	PA8999	Bulb (located in Tender)	.30
3	PA14C369	Boiler Front	.24
	PA10543	Headlight Lens	.02
4	XA14D368-RP	Boiler	2.74
	PA14A381	Motor Mount	.02
5 & 6	PA14C651	Pilot and Cylinder	.32
7		NOT USED	
8	S-222	#4 x 5/16 type Z B. H. P. K. Screw	.01
9		NOT USED	
10	XA14A382-L & R	Crosshead Assembly	.73
11	S-171	#2 x 3/16 type Z B. H. P. K. Screw	.01
12		NOT USED	
13		NOT USED	
14	PA5447	Eccentric Crank Screw	.04
15		NOT USED	
16	XA13B894-RP	Smoke Box	2.13
17	XA14A208-A	Heating Element	.91
18	S-183	2 x 1/4 type Z R. H. P. K. Screw	.01
19	PA10518-A	Piston	.29
20	PA14A380	Piston Lever	.03
21	PA10520	Piston Pin	.03
22	PA10671	Worm Gear	.32
23	PA7421	Piston Rod Screw	.03
24	PA10162	Worm Gear Stud	.08
25	XA14B719	Armature Assembly	3.56
26	XA15A695	Brush Mounting Plate and Bearing Assembly (Bearing not supplied separately)	.55
	PA13A131	Motor Brush Tube (not shown)	.03
27	PA3769	Lock Washer	.01
28	S-33	6-32x1 1/4 R. H. Screw (for Brush Bracket)	.01
	S-29	6-32x1 3/8 R. H. Screw (for Brush Bracket & R. C. Unit)	.01
	S-240	4x1/4 type "F" P.K. Screw (for R. C. Unit & Motor Cover Brace) (not shown)	.02
29	PA13A128	Brush	.12
30	PA13A130	Brush Spring	.03
31	PA13A129	Motor Brush Tube Cover	.01
	PA15A044	Motor Brush Tube Cover Brace	.05
32	W-83	Armature Spacer	.04
33	XA9547	Field Assembly	1.22
34	PA14D392	Boiler Chassis	2.01
	PA13A187	Bearing	.04
35	XA12A472	Flanged Wheel Assembly	.40
36		NOT USED	
37	XA10104-C2	Flangeless Wheel w/stud	.66
38	XA12A473	Pul-Mor Wheel Assembly	.73
39	PA9473	Worm Gear	.36
40	PA15A281	Rear Axle	.07
41	PA10017	Grease Pan	.07
42	S-271	#4 x 1/4 type "F" F. H. P. K. Screw	.02
43	PA14A377	Side Rod	.11
44	PA7237	Piston Rod Spacer	.02

DIA. NO.	PART NO.	DESCRIPTION	PRICE
1	PA12A190	Smoke Stack	.03
2	PA8999	14 Volt Lamp	.30
3	XA9467-B	Boiler Front	.89
	PA10543	Headlight Lens	.02
4	XA9466-CRP	Boiler Assembly	5.20
	PA9286-A	Motor Mount	.05
5	PA10109	Cylinder	.82
6	PA12C478	Pilot	1.42
7	P4654	Lock Washer	.01
8	S55	Screw	.01
9	PA10595 R & L	Crosshead Guide (right or left)	.12
10	XA10596 R & L	Crosshead Assembly (right or left)	.46
11	S-1	Screw	.01
12	PA10598	Link Stud	.05
13	XA10447-B	Eccentric Crank	.26
14	PA5447	Eccentric Crank Screw	.04
15	PA9288	Shouldered Screw	.03
16	XA10513	Smoke Box Assy. NOT AVAILABLE	
		Sub. with XA13B894-RP Smoke Box Assy.	2.13
	PA10513	Smoke Box NOT AVAILABLE	
		Sub. with PA13B894 Smoke Box	.76
	PA14A209	Separator	.02
17	XA10523	Heating Elem. & Plate Assy. NOT AVAILABLE	
		Sub. with XA14A208-A Assembly	.91
18	S183	Screw	.01
19	PA10518-A	Piston	.29
20	PA10516	Piston Lever	.14
21	PA10520	Piston Pin	.03
22	PA10671	Worm Gear	.32
23	PA7421	Screw	.03
24	PA10162	Worm Gear Stud	.08
25	XA11077	Armature	3.39
26	XA9565-A	Brush Bracket	1.00
27	PA3769	Lock Washer	.01
28	S295	Screw	.02
29	PA9603	Brush	.13
30	PA10757-A	Brush Spring	.02
31	PA10754	Brush Cap	.02
32	PA10766	Armature Spacer	.01
33	XA9547	Field Assembly	1.22
34	XA10504	Chassis w/bushing	1.34
35	XA12A472	Flanged Wheel	.40
36	XA10104-B	Flangeless Wheel	.45
37	XA10104-A2	Flangeless Wheel w/stud	.66
38	XA12A473	Pul-Mor Wheel	.73
39	PA9473	Worm Gear	.36
40	PA10006	Worm Gear Axle NOT AVAILABLE	
		Sub. with PA15A281 Axle	.07
41	PA10017	Grease Pan	.07
42	S271	Screw	.02
43	PA9476	Side Rod	.17
44	PA7237	Piston Rod Spacer	.02

Con't

 Ref: Form No. 1825; June 1, 1960

DIA. NO.	PART NO.	DESCRIPTION	PRICE
45	S16-C	Screw	.12 dz.
46	S24	Screw	.01 ea.
47	S52	Screw	.01 ea.
48	PA10005	Axle NOT AVAILABLE Sub. with PA15A226 Axle	.05 ea.
49	S3A71	Screw	.03 ea.
50	XA12A047	Knuckle Coupler	.29 ea.
51	PA12A355-A	Leaf Spring	.02 ea.
52	PA12A479-A	Coupler Ratchet	.07 ea.
53	XA10662-A	Jack Panel	.24 ea.
54	S230-B	Screw	.01 ea.
55	PA10511	4 Conductor Cable	.13 ea.
56	XA10663	Male Plug Assembly	.24 ea.
57	XA9778-BRP	Tender Body	2.42 ea.
58	XA10587-E	Remote Control	4.04 ea.
59	XA8716	Drum	.95 ea.
60	XA9612-CRP	Top Finger Unit	.33 ea.
61	XA9612-BRP	Bottom Finger Unit	.33 ea.
62	PA10235-A	Coupler Rivet	.07 ea.
63	PA10209	Insulating Bushing	.02 ea.
64	XA10592	Chassis	.41 ea.
65	PA4938	Stud	.04 ea.
66	S-0	Screw	.01 ea.
67	PA8715-B	Fibre Washer	.02 ea.
68	XA12A516	Front Truck Assembly	.44 ea.
69	XA12A350	Rear Truck Assembly	.80 ea.
	XA10238	Wheel & Axle Assembly	.09 ea.
	PA9990	Wheel	.03 ea.
	PA10238	Axle	.01 ea.
	PA10140	Wheel	.06 ea.
70	PA10207	Contact Spring	.02 ea.
71	PA1405	Tin Washer	.01 ea.
72	PA11A956	Spring	.02 ea.
73	PA11A936	Tender Pickup	.04 ea.
74	PA11A944	Hair Pin Cotter	.01 ea.
		NOT SHOWN	
	LW-1B1	Black Lead Wire	.02 ft.
	WLA92	Armature Washer (front)	.02 ea.

Prices subject to change without notice

DIA. NO.	PART NO.	DESCRIPTION	PRICE
1	P10174-A	Smoke Stack	.08 ea.
2	P13N922	Bulb (located in loco.)	.60 ea.
	PA8999	Bulb (located in tender)	.32 ea.
3	PA14C369	Boiler Front	.25 ea.
	PA10543	Headlight Lens	.02 ea.
4	XA14D368-RP	Boiler	2.88 ea.
	PA14A381	Motor Mount	.02 ea.
5 & 6	PA14C651	Pilot and Cylinder	.34 ea.
7		NOT USED	
8	S-222	#4 x 5/16 type Z B. H. P. K. Screw	.01 ea.
9		NOT USED	
10	XA14A382-L & R	Crosshead Assembly	.77 ea.
11	S-171	#2 x 3/16 type Z B. H. P. K. Screw	.01 ea.
12 & 13		NOT USED	
14	PA5447	Eccentric Crank Screw	.04 ea.
15		NOT USED	
16	XA13B894-RP	Smoke Box	2.24 ea.
17	XA14A208-A	Heating Element	.96 ea.
18	S-183	2 x 1/4 type Z R. H. P. K. Screw	.01 ea.
19	PA10518-A	Piston	.30 ea.
20	PA14A380	Piston Lever	.03 ea.
21	PA10520	Piston Pin	.03 ea.
22	PA10671	Worm Gear	.34 ea.
23	PA7421	Piston Rod Screw	.03 ea.
24	PA10162	Worm Gear Stud	.08 ea.
25	XA14B719	Armature Assembly	3.74 ea.
26	XA15A695	Brush Mounting Plate & Bearing Assy.	.58 ea.
	PA13A131	Motor Brush Tube (Not Shown)	.03 ea.
27	PA3769	Lock Washer	.01 ea.
28	S-33	6-32x 1 1/4 R.H. Screw (for brush bracket)	.01 ea.
	S-29	6-32x 1 3/8 R. H. Screw (for Brush Bracket & R.C. Unit)	.01 ea.
	S-240	4x 1/4 type "F" P.K. Screw (for R.C. Unit & Motor Cover Brace) (NOT SHOWN)	.02 ea.
29	PA13A128	Brush	.13 ea.
30	PA13A130	Brush Spring	.03 ea.
31	PA13A129	Motor Brush Tube Cover	.01 ea.
	PA15A044	Motor Brush Tube Cover Brace	.05 ea.
32	W-83	Armature Spacer	.04 ea.
33	XA9547	Field Assembly	1.28 ea.
34	PA14D392	Boiler Chassis	2.11 ea.
	PA13A187	Bearing	.04 ea.
35	XA12A472	Flanged Wheel Assembly	.42 ea.
36		NOT USED	
37	XA10104-C2	Flangeless Wheel w/stud	.69 ea.
38	XA12A473	Pul-Mor Wheel Assembly	.77 ea.
39	PA9473	Worm Gear	.38 ea.
40	PA15A281	Rear Axle	.07 ea.
41	PA10017	Grease Pan	.07 ea.
42	S-271	#4 x 1/4 type "F" F.H.P. K. Screw	.02 ea.
43	PA14A377	Side Rod	.12 ea.
44	PA7237	Piston Rod Spacer	.02 ea.

Cont'd

DIA. NO.	PART NO.	DESCRIPTION	PRICE
45		NOT USED	
46	S-24	#6-32 x 7 1/8 R. H. Screw	.01 ea.
47	S-91	#6-x 3/8 type Z R. H. P. K. Screw	.02 ea.
48	PA15A226	Axle	.05 ea.
49	S3A71	Coupler Screw	.03 ea.
50	XA12A047	Knuckle Coupler	.30 ea.
51	PA12A355-A	Leaf Spring	.02 ea.
52,53, & 54		NOT USED	
55 & 56	XA14A513	Plug Assembly	.34 ea.
57	XA14N394-RP	Tender Body	1.93 ea.
58		NOT USED	
	XA14C429 (NOT SHOWN)	Remote Control Unit (rear of Loco)	2.90 ea.
	XA14A994	Contact Assembly	.81 ea.
	XA14A435	Plunger Assembly	.15 ea.
	XA14B433	Coil Assembly	.72 ea.
	PA14A444	Coil Support	.05 ea.
	PA14C432	Coil Housing	.04 ea.
59,60 & 61		NOT USED	
62	PA10235-A	Rivet for Tender Truck	.07 ea.
63	PA10209	Insulating Bushing	.02 ea.
64	PA14B385	Chassis	.22 ea.
65	S5A12	Shoulder Screw	.05 ea.
66	S230-B	Screw (used on front of Tender & bottom of Tender to hold weight)	.01 ea.
67	PA8715-B	Insulating Washer	.02 ea.
68	XA14B811	Front Truck (263)	.58 ea.
	XA15B800	Front Truck (21004)	.45 ea.
69	XA12A350	Rear Truck (263)	.84 ea.
	XA12A050-B	Rear Truck (21004)	.83 ea.
70	PA10207	Contact Spring	.02 ea.
71		NOT USED	
72	PA15A965	Coil Spring (263)	.13 ea.
73	PA11A936	Tender Pick-Up (263)	.04 ea.
74	PA11A944	Hair Pin Cotter (263	.01 ea.

PARTS NOT SHOWN

PART NO.	DESCRIPTION	PRICE
PA14A391	Coupler (connects Loco and Tender)	.03 ea.
PA15A382	Weight (in Tender)	.62 ea.
P11A132	Rivet (in Tender	.02 ea.
XA14A968	Light Socket (located in Tender)	.16 ea.
PA4361	Rivet (located in Tender)	.01 ea.
X13A832	Bulb Clip Assy. (screws into Boiler Front)	.17 ea.

Prices subject to change without notice.

DIA. NO	PART NO.	DESCRIPTION	PRICE
1	PA12A190	Smoke Stack	.03 ea.
2	PA8999	14 Volt Lamp	.32 ea.
3	XA9467-B	Boiler Front	.93 ea.
	PA10543	Headlight Lens	.02 ea.
4	XA9466-CRP	Boiler Assembly	5.46 ea.
	PA9286-A	Motor Mount	.05 ea.
5	PA10109	Cylinder	.86 ea.
6	PA12C478	Pilot	1.49 ea.
7	P4654	Lock Washer	.01 ea.
8	S55	Screw	.01 ea.
9	PA10595-R & L	Crosshead Guide (Right or Left)	.13 ea.
10	XA10596 R & L	Crosshead Assy. (Right or Left)	.48 ea.
11	S-1	Screw	.01 ea.
12	PA10598	Link Stud	.05 ea.
13	XA10447-B	Eccentric Crank	.27 ea.
14	PA 5447	Eccentric Crank Screw	.04 ea.
15	PA9288	Shouldered Screw	.03 ea.
16	* XA13B894RP	Smoke Box	2.24 ea.
17	XA14A208-A	Heating Element & Plate Assy.	.96 ea.
18	S183	Screw	.01 ea.
19	PA10518-A	Piston	.30 ea.
20	PA10516	Piston Lever	.15 ea.
21	PA10520	Piston Pin	.03 ea.
22	PA10671	Worm Gear	.34 ea.
23	PA7421	Screw	.03 ea.
24	PA10162	Worm Gear Stud	.08 ea.
25	XA11077	Armature	3.56 ea.
26	XA9565-A	Brush Bracket	1.05 ea.
27	PA3769	Lock Washer	.01 ea.
28	S295	Screw	.02 ea.
29	PA9603	Brush	.14 ea.
30	PA10757-A	Brush Spring	.02 ea.
31	PA10754	Brush Cap	.02 ea.
32	PA10766	Armature Spacer	.01 ea.
33	XA9547	Field Assembly	1.28 ea.
34	XA10504	Chassis w/bushings	1.41 ea.
35	XA12A472	Flanged Wheel	.42 ea.
36	XA10104-B	Flangeless Wheel	.47 ea.
37	XA10104-A2	Flangeless Wheel w/stud	.69 ea.
38	XA12A473	Pul-Mor Wheel	.77 ea.
39	PA9473	Worm Gear	.38 ea.
40	PA15A281	Worm Gear Axle	.07 ea.
41	PA10017	Grease Pan	.07 ea.
42	S271	Screw	.02 ea.
43	PA9476	Side Rod	.18 ea.
44	PA7237	Piston Rod Spacer	.02 ea.
45	S16-C	Screw	.13 dz.
46	S24	Screw	.01 ea.
47	S52	Screw	.01 ea.

Cont'd

DIA. NO.	PART NO.	DESCRIPTION	PRICE
48	PA15A226	Plain Axle	.05 ea.
49	S3A71	Screw	.03 ea.
50	XA12A047	Knuckle Coupler	.30 ea.
51	PA12A355-A	Leaf Spring	.02 ea.
52	PA12A479-A	Coupler Ratchet	.07 ea.
53	XA10662-A	Jack Panel	.25 ea.
54	S230-B	Screw	.01 ea.
55	PA13A208A	4 Conductor Cable (Plastic)	.04 ft.
56	XA10663	Male Plug Assembly	.25 ea.
57	XA9778-BRP	Tender Body	2.54 ea.
58	XA10587-E	Remote Control Unit	4.24 ea.
59	XA8716	Drum	1.00 ea.
60	XA9612-CRP	Top Finger Unit	.35 ea.
61	XA9612-BRP	Bottom Finger Unit	.35 ea.
62	PA10235-A	Coupler Rivet	.07 ea.
63	PA10209	Insulating Bushing	.02 ea.
64	XA10592	Chassis	.43 ea.
65	PA4938	Stud	.04 ea.
66	S-0	Screw	.01 ea.
67	PA8715-B	Fibre Washer	.02 ea.
68	XA12A516	Front Truck Assembly	.46 ea.
69	XA12A350	Rear Truck Assembly	.84 ea.
	XA10238	Wheel & Axle Assembly	.09 ea.
	PA9990	Wheel	.03 ea.
	PA10238	Axle	.01 ea.
	PA10140	Wheel	.06 ea.
70	PA10207	Contact Spring	.02 ea.
71	PA1405	Tin Washer	.01 ea.
72	PA11A956	Spring	.02 ea.
73	PA11A936	Tender Pickup	.04 ea.
74	PA11A944	Hair Pin Cotter	.01 ea.

* #16 When using XA13B894RP remove screw on solder terminal.

NOT SHOWN

LW-1B1	Black Lead Wire	.02 ft.
W1A92	Armature Washer (Front)	.02 ea.

Prices subject to change without notice.

STEAM LOCOMOTIVE AND TENDER WITH PISTON-TYPE SMOKE AND CHOO-CHOO UNIT

Model No. 282

SPECIFICATIONS

Tested at: 12 Volts A.C. .... using 140" oval of track.

(A) Motor to be tested with Remote Control Unit at 12 Volts, and not to draw more than 1.7 amps.

(B) Locomotive to run a minimum of 9 R.P.M. or 9 times forward, around 140" oval of track per minute.

(C) Locomotive to run a minimum of 8.5 R.P.M. or 8½ times reverse, around 140" oval of track per minute.

Load: Not to draw more than 2.1 amps. while pulling 4 Box Cars.

Motor: Universal A.C. or D.C.

 Ref: Form No. 1815; Feb. 1, 1957

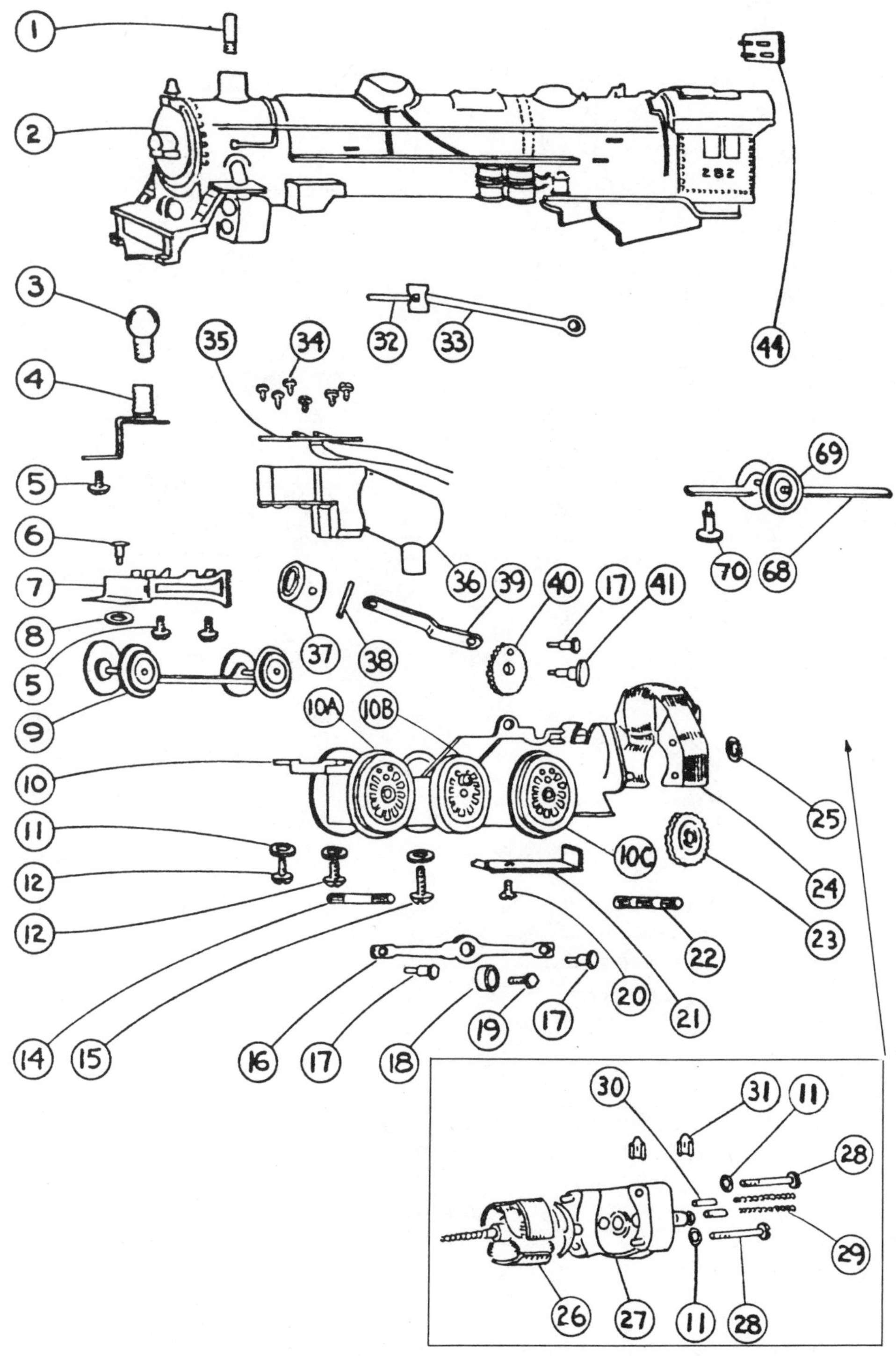

Ref: Form No. 1815; Feb. 1, 1957

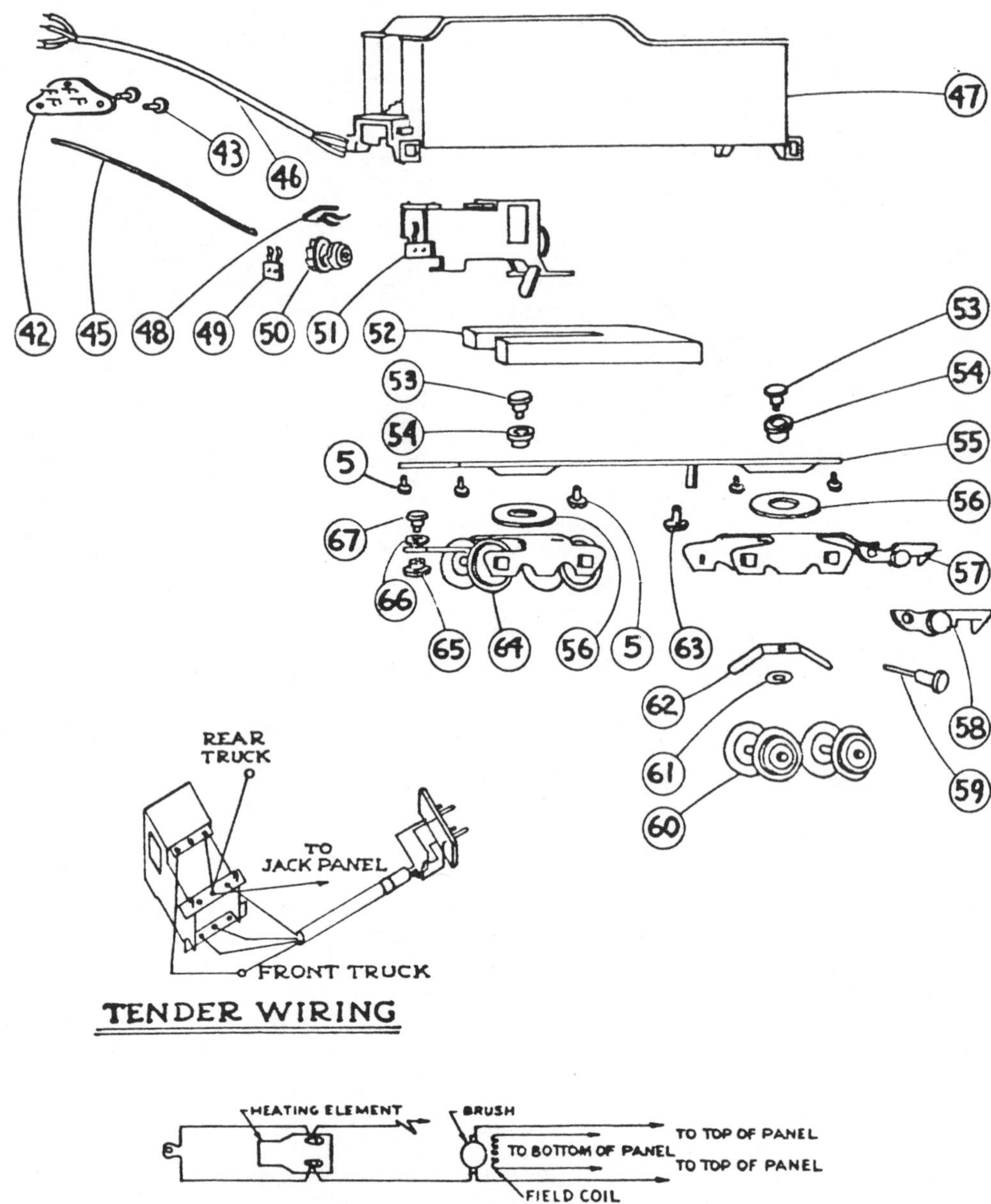

TENDER WIRING

HEATING ELEMENT
BRUSH
TO TOP OF PANEL
TO BOTTOM OF PANEL
TO TOP OF PANEL
FIELD COIL

LOCOMOTIVE WIRING

 Ref: Form No. 1815; Feb. 1, 1957

Diagram Number	Part No.	Description	Price
1	PA12A190	Smoke Stack	$ .03 ea.
2	XA11736-RP	Boiler Assembly	2.00 "
3	PA8999	Bulb	.25 "
4	XA10890	Lamp Bracket Assembly	.25 "
5	S230-B	Screw	.10 dz.
	XA10887	Crosshead Guide & Pilot Truck Assembly (consists of parts 6 to 9 inclusive)	.60 ea.
6	PA10707	Stud	.05 "
7	PA10887	Crosshead	.15 "
8	PA5035-A	Washer	.10 dz.
9	XA10012	Front Truck Assembly	.40 ea.
	PA9990-A	Front Truck Wheel only	.10 "
10	PA10506	Chassis	1.20 "
10-A	XA10009	Flanged Drive Wheel w/Tapped Hole	.40 "
10-B	XA10009-C1	Flangeless Drive Wheel w/Stud	.40 "
11	PA3769	Washer	.05 dz.
12	S319	Screw	.01 ea.
13	S46	Screw	.05 dz.
14	PA10005	Plain Axle	.10 ea.
15	S16-C	Screw	.10 dz.
16	PA9280-A	Side Rod	.20 ea.
17	PA7421	Side Rod screw	.30 dz.
18	PA7237	Spacer	.05 ea.
19	PA5447	Screw	.30 dz.
20	S271	Screw	.10 "
21	PA10017	Grease Pan	.02 ea.
22	PA10006	Gear Axle	.10 "
23	PA10672	Worm gear (motor)	.30 "
24	XA9547	Magnet Assembly	1.00 "
25	PA10766	Washer	.05 dz.
26	XA11077	Armature Assembly	2.50 ea.
27	XA9565-A	Brush Bracket Assembly	.50 "
28	S295	Screw	.10 "
29	PA10757-A	Brush Spring	.05 "
30	PA9603	Brush	.15 "
31	PA10754	Brush Cap	.02 "
32	PA10888	Crosshead	.05 "
33	PA10889	Connecting Rod	.10 "
	XA10513	Chassis Smoke Box Assembly (consists of parts 34-35-36)	2.00 "
34	S183	Screw	.10 dz.

Diagram Number	Part No.	Description	Price
35	XA10523	Heating Element & Plate Assembly	1.00 ea.
36	PA10513	Chassis Smoke Box	1.00 "
	XA10514	Piston-Lever Assembly (consists of parts 37-38-39)	.40 "
37	PA10518	Piston	.20 "
38	PA10520	Piston Pin	.05 "
39	PA10514	Piston Lever	.05 "
40	PA10671	Worm Gear (smoke)	.40 "
41	PA10162	Worm Gear Stud	.10 "
42	XA10662-A	Jack Panel	.20 "
43	S222	Screw	.01 "
44	XA10669	Male Plug Assembly	.20 "
45	PA9273-A	6" Lead Wire	.02 "
46	PA10511-C	4 Conductor Cable	.12 "
47	PA12D078-A	Tender Body	.63 "
48	XA9612-C	Top Finger Unit	.50 "
49	XA9612-B	Bottom Finger Unit	.50 "
50	XA8716	Drum	.60 "
51	XA10587-E	Remote Control Unit	2.50 "
52	PA11A926	Tender Weight	.18 "
53	PA10235-A	Truck Rivet	.03 "
54	PA10209	Insulating Bushing	.02 "
55	PA12B080	Tender Chassis	.22 "
56	PA8715-B	Insulating Washer	.05 dz.
57	XA11582	Rear Truck Frame Assembly	.12 ea.
58	XA10469	Coupler & Weight Assembly	.15 "
59	PA10467	Coupler Pin	.10 "
60	XA10238	Wheel & Axle Assembly	.25 set
	PA10140	Metal Wheel	.15 ea.
	PA9990	Plastic Wheel	.10 "
	PA10238	Axle	.02 "
61	PA1405	Tin Washer	.05 dz.
62	PA10207	Contact Spring	.02 ea.
63	S184	Screw	.10 dz.
64	XA11582-A	Front Truck Frame Assembly	.21 ea.
65	PA1312	Bushing	.10 dz.
66	PA1067-A	Washer	.05 dz.
67	PA10751	Stud	.02 ea.
68	XA10891	Coupler & Yoke Assembly	.30 "
69	PA10019-A	Rear Truck Wheel only	.10 "
70	PA4939	Truck Stud	.05 "

 Ref: Form No. 1815; Feb. 1, 1957

Diagram Number	Part No.	Description	Price
1	PA12A190	Smoke Stack	$ .02 ea.
2	XA11736-RP	Boiler Assembly	1.02 "
3	PA8999	Bulb	.25 "
4	XA10890	Lamp Bracket Assembly	.28 "
5	S230-B	Screw	.10 dz.
	XA10887	Crosshead Guide & Pilot Truck Assembly (consists of parts 6 to 9 inclusive)	.60 ea.
6	PA10707	Stud	.05 "
7	PA10887	Crosshead	.15 "
8	PA5035-A	Washer	.11 dz.
9	XA10012	Front Truck Assembly	.40 ea.
	PA9990-A	Front Truck Wheel only	.11 "
10	XA10506	Chassis	1.33 "
10A	XA13A865	Flanged Drive Wheel Assembly	.29 "
10B	XA10009-C1	Flangeless Drive Wheel w/stud	.32 "
10C	XA13A864	Pull-Mor Wheel Assembly	.51 "
11	PA3769	Washer	.05 dz.
12	S319	Screw	.01 ea.
14	PA10005	Plain Axle	.10 "
15	S16-C	Screw	.11 dz.
16	PA9280-A	Side Rod	.10 ea.
17	PA7421	Side Rod Screw	.30 dz.
18	PA7237	Spacer	.05 ea.
19	PA5447	Screw	.30 dz.
20	S271	Screw	.10 "
21	PA10017	Grease Pan	.04 ea.
22	PA10006	Gear Axle	.10 "
23	PA10672	Worm Gear (motor)	.20 "
24	XA9547	Magnet Assembly	1.11 "
25	PA10766	Washer	.05 dz.
26	XA11077	Armature Assembly	2.19 ea.
27	XA9565-A	Brush Bracket Assembly	.71 "
28	S295	Screw	.02 "
29	PA10757-A	Brush Spring	.05 "
30	PA9603	Brush	.15 "
31	PA10754	Brush Cap	.02 "
32	PA10888	Crosshead	.05 "
33	PA10889	Connecting Rod	.11 "
	*XA10513	Chassis Smoke Box Assembly (consists of parts 34-35-36) NOT AVAILABLE	
34	S183	Screw	.10 dz.

All prices subject to change without notice.

*Parts so marked NOT AVAILABLE, substitute with:

Dia. 36	XA13B894RP	Smoke Box Assy. (new style)	$1.55 ea.
	PA13B894	Smoke Box (new style)	.59 "
	PA14A209	Separator (new style)	.01 "

Ref: Form No. 1815; Feb. 1, 1957

Diagram Number	Part No.	Description	Price
35	**XA10523	Heating Element & Plate Assembly . . .	.66 ea.
36	*PA10513	Chassis Smoke Box . . . . NOT AVAILABLE	
37	PA10518-A	Piston	.17 "
38	PA10520	Piston Pin	.05 "
39	PA10514	Piston Lever	.08 "
40	PA10671	Worm Gear (Smoke)	.27 "
41	PA10162	Worm Gear Stud	.05 "
42	XA10662-A	Jack Panel	.22 "
43	S230-B	Screw	.10 dz.
44	XA10663	Male Plug Assembly	.22 "
45	PA9273-A	6" lead Wire	.02 "
46	PA10511-C	4 Conductor Cable	.12 "
47	PA12D078-A	Tender Body	.64 "
48	XA9612-CRP	Top Finger Unit	.30 "
49	XA9612-BRP	Bottom Finger Unit	.30 "
50	XA8716	Drum	.59 "
51	XA10587-E	Remote Control Unit	1.32 "
52	PA11A926	Tender Weight	.32 "
53	PA10235-A	Truck Rivet	.03 "
54	PA10209	Insulating Bushing	.02 "
55	PA12B080	Tender Chassis	.20 "
56	PA8715-B	Insulating Washer	.05 dz.
57	XA11582	Rear Truck Frame Assembly	.24 ea.
58	XA10469	Coupler & Weight Assembly	.17 "
59	PA10467	Coupler Pin	.11 "
60	XA10238	Wheel & Axle Assembly	.17 set
	PA10140	Metal Wheel	.15 ea.
	PA9990	Plastic Wheel	.05 "
	PA10238	Axle	.02 "
61	PA1405	Tin Washer	.05 dz.
62	PA10207	Contact Spring	.02 ea.
63	S184	Screw	.10 dz.
64	XA11582-A	Front Truck Frame Assembly w/o Wheels	.24 ea.
65	PA1312	Bushing	.11 dz.
66	PA1067-A	Washer	.05 "
67	PA10751	Stud	.02 ea.
68	XA10891	Coupler & Yoke Assembly	.33 "
69	PA10019-A	Rear Truck Wheel Only	.05 "
70	PA4939	Truck Stud	.05 "

**The XA10523 Heating Element and Plate Assy. is still available, and interchangeable with the new style PA13B894 Smoke Box. The new style XA14A208 Heating Element and Plate Assembly, priced at $.66 each, is used only on the new style PA13B894 Smoke Box.

 Ref: Form No. 1815; Feb. 1, 1957

NO.	PART NO.	DESCRIPTION	PRICE
1	PA12A190	Smoke Stack	.03 ea.
2	XA11736-RP	Boiler Assembly	1.99 ea.
3	PA8999	Bulb	.30 ea.
4	XA10890	Lamp Bracket Assembly	.22 ea.
5	S230-B	Screw	.01 ea.
	XA10887	Crosshead Guide & Pilot Truck Assy. (Consists of parts 6 to 9 inclusive)	.84 ea.
6	PA10707	Stud	.07 ea.
7	PA10887	Crosshead	.21 ea.
8	PA5035-A	Washer	.06 dz.
9	XA10012	Front Truck Assembly	.44 ea.
	PA9990-A	Front Truck Wheel Only	.12 ea.
10	XA10506	Chassis	1.46 ea.
10A	XA13A865	Flanged Drive Wheel Assy.	.37 ea.
10B	XA10009-C1	Flangeless Drive Wheel w/stud	.35 ea.
10C	XA13A864	Pul-Mor Wheel Assembly	.80 ea.
11	PA3769	Washer	.01 ea.
12	S319	Screw	.02 ea.
14	PA10005	Plain Axle NOT AVAILABLE	
		Substitute with PA15A226 Axle	.05 ea.
15	S16-C	Screw	.12 dz.
16	PA9280-A	Side Rod	.16 ea.
17	PA7421	Side Rod Screw	.03 ea.
18	PA7237	Spacer	.02 ea.
19	PA5447	Screw	.04 ea.
20	S271	Screw	.02 ea.
21	PA10017	Grease Pan	.07 ea.
22	PA10006	Gear Axle NOT AVAILABLE	
		Substitute with PA15A281 Axle	.07 ea.
23	PA10672	Worm Gear (Motor)	.06 ea.
24	XA9547	Magnet Assembly	1.22 ea.
25	PA10766	Washer	.01 ea.
26	XA11077	Armature Assembly	2.41 ea.
27	XA9565-A	Brush Bracket Assembly	1.00 ea.
28	S295	Screw	.02 ea.
29	PA10757-A	Brush Spring	.02 ea.
30	PA9603	Brush	.13 ea.
31	PA10754	Brush Cap	.02 ea.
32	PA10888	Crosshead	.08 ea.
33	PA10889	Connecting Rod	.09 ea.
34	S183	Screw	.01 ea.
35	XA10523	Heating Element & Plate Assy. NOT AVAILABLE	
		Substitute with XA14A208-A	.91 ea.
36	PA10513	Chassis Smoke Box NOT AVAILABLE	
	XA10513	Chassis Smoke Box Assy. NOT AVAILABLE	
		Substitute with XA13B894RP Smoke Box Assy.	2.13 ea.
	PA13B894	Smoke Box	.76 ea.
	PA14A209	Separator	.02 ea.
37	PA15018-A	Piston	.29 ea.

DIA. NO.	PART NO.	DESCRIPTION	PRICE
1	PA12A190	Smoke Stack	.03 ea.
2	XA11736ERP	Boiler Assembly (Marked 21085)	2.09 ea.
3	PA8999	Bulb	.32 ea.
4	XA10890	Lamp Bracket Assembly	.23 ea.
5	S230-B	Screw	.01 ea.
	XA10887	Crosshead Guide & Pilot Truck Assy. (Consists of Parts 6 to 9 inclusive)	.88 ea.
6	PA10707	Stud	.07 ea.
7	PA10887	Crosshead	.22 ea.
8	PA5035-A	Washer	.13 dz.
9	XA10012	Front Truck Assembly	.46 ea.
	PA9990-A	Front Truck Wheel Only	.13 ea.
10	PA10506-A	Chassis	1.87 ea.
10A	XA13A865	Flanged Drive Wheel Assembly	.39 ea.
10B	XA10009-C1	Flangeless Drive Wheel w/stud	.37 ea.
10C	XA13A864	Pul-Mor Wheel Assembly	.84 ea.
11	PA3789	Washer	.01 ea.
12	S319	Screw	.02 ea.
14	PA15A226	Plain Axle	.05 ea.
15	S16-C	Screw	.13 dz.
16	PA9280-A	Side Rod	.17 ea.
17	PA7421	Side Rod Screw	.03 ea.
18	PA7237	Spacer	.02 ea.
19	PA5447	Screw	.04 ea.
20	S271	Screw	.02 ea.
21	PA10017	Grease Pan	.07 ea.
22	PA15A281	Gear Axle	.07 ea.
23	PA10672	Worm Gear (Motor)	.06 ea.
24	XA9547	Magnet Assembly	1.28 ea.
25	PA10766	Washer	.01 ea.
26	XA11077	Armature Assembly	3.56 ea.
27	XA9565-A	Brush Bracket Assembly	1.05 ea.
28	S295	Screw	.02 ea.
29	PA10757-A	Brush Spring	.02 ea.
30	PA9603	Brush	.14 ea.
31	PA10754	Brush Cap	.02 ea.
32	PA10888	Crosshead	.08 ea.
33	PA10889	Connecting Rod	.09 ea.
34	S183	Screw	.01 ea.
35	XA14A208A	Heating Element & Plate Assy.	.96 ea.
36	XA13B894-RP	Smoke Box Assembly	2.24 ea.
37	PA10518-A	Piston	.30 ea.
38	PA10520	Piston Pin	.03 ea.
39	PA10514	Piston Lever	.15 ea.
40	PA10671	Worm Gear (Smoke)	.34 ea.
41	PA10162	Worm Gear Stud	.08 ea.
42	XA10662-A	Jack Panel	.25 ea.
43	S230-B	Screw	.01 ea.
44	XA10663	Male Plug Assembly	.25 ea.
45	PA9273-A	Lead Wire	.03 ft.

Cont'd

 Ref: Form No. 1815; Oct. 1, 1962

DIA. NO.	PART NO.	DESCRIPTION	PRICE
46	PA13A208A	4 Conductor Cable (Plastic)	.04 ft.
47		Tender Body - Obsolete - No Longer Available - No Substitution	
48	XA9612-CRP	Top Finger Unit	.35 ea.
49	XA9612-BRP	Bottom Finger Unit	.35 ea.
50	XA8716	Drum	1.00 ea.
51	XA10587-E	Remote Control Unit	4.24 ea.
52	PA10593	Tender Weight	.27 ea.
53	PA10235-A	Truck Rivet	.07 ea.
54	PA10209	Insulating Bushing	.02 ea.
55		Tender Chassis - Obsolete - No Longer Available - No Substitution	
56	PA8715-B	Insulating Washer	.02 ea.
57	XA12A050-B	Rear Truck Assembly w/Knuckle Coupler Substitute for XA11582 Obsolete	.83 ea.
58		Coupler & Weight Assy. Obsolete	
59		Coupler Pin Obsolete	
60	XA10238	Wheel & Axle Assy.	.09 ea.
	PA10140	Metal Wheel	.06 ea.
	PA9990	Plastic Wheel	.03 ea.
	PA10238	Axle	.01 ea.
61	PA1405	Tin Washer	.01 ea.
62	PA10207	Contact Spring	.02 ea.
63	S184	Screw	.02 ea.
64	XA15B800	Front Truck Assy. Substitute for XA11582-A Obsolete	.45 ea.
65	PA1312	Bushing	.13 dz.
66	PA1067-A	Washer	.06 dz.
67	PA10751	Stud	.02 ea.
68	XA15A784	Draw Bar Assy. Used w/XA15B800 Truck Assy.	.23 ea.
	XA10891	Coupler & Yoke Assy. Used Only w/XA11582A Frt. Truck Assy.	.38 ea.
69	PA10019-A	Rear Truck Wheel Only	.06 ea.
70	PA4939	Truck Stud	.06 ea.

Prices subject to change without notice

STEAM LOCOMOTIVE AND TENDER WITH PISTON-TYPE SMOKE AND CHOO-CHOO UNIT

Model Nos. 283, 287, 21085

SPECIFICATIONS

Tested at: 12 Volts A.C. ....using 140″ oval of track.

(A) Motor to be tested with Remote Control Unit at 12 Volts, and not to draw more than 1.7 amps.

(B) Locomotive to run a minimum of 9 R.P.M. or 9 times forward, around 140″ oval of track per minute.

(C) Locomotive to run a minimum of 8.5 R.P.M. or 8½ times reverse, around 140″ oval of track per minute.

Load: Not to draw more than 2.1 amps. while pulling 4 Box Cars.

Motor: Universal A.C. or D.C.

 Ref: Form No. 1646; July 15, 1955

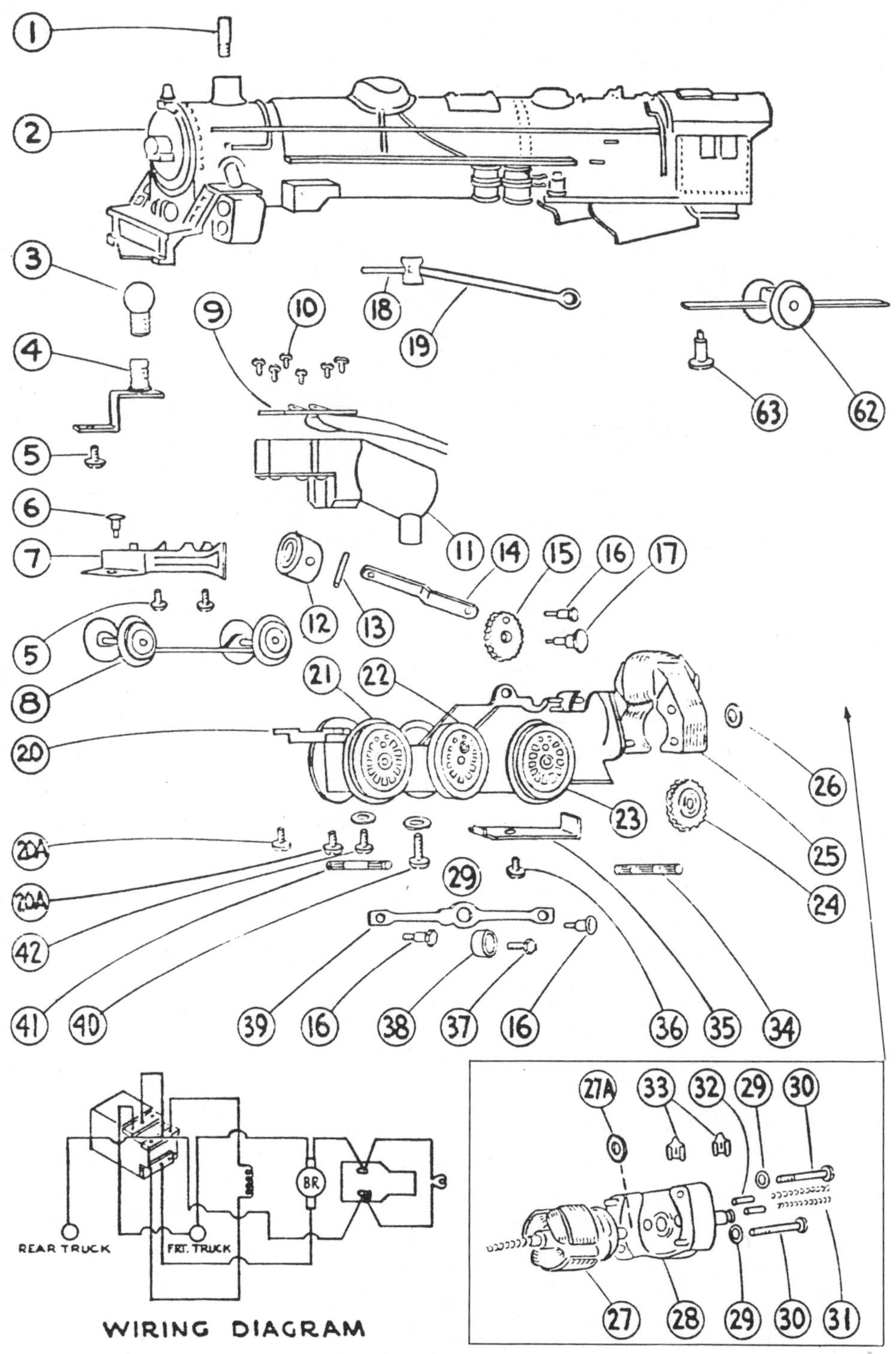
1
2
3
4
5
6
7
5
8
9
10
18
19
11
14
15
16
17
12
13
62
63
21
22
20
26
23
25
24
20A
20A
42
41
40
29
39
16
38
37
16
36
35
34
REAR TRUCK
FRT. TRUCK
BR
WIRING DIAGRAM
27A
33
32
29
30
27
28
29
30
31

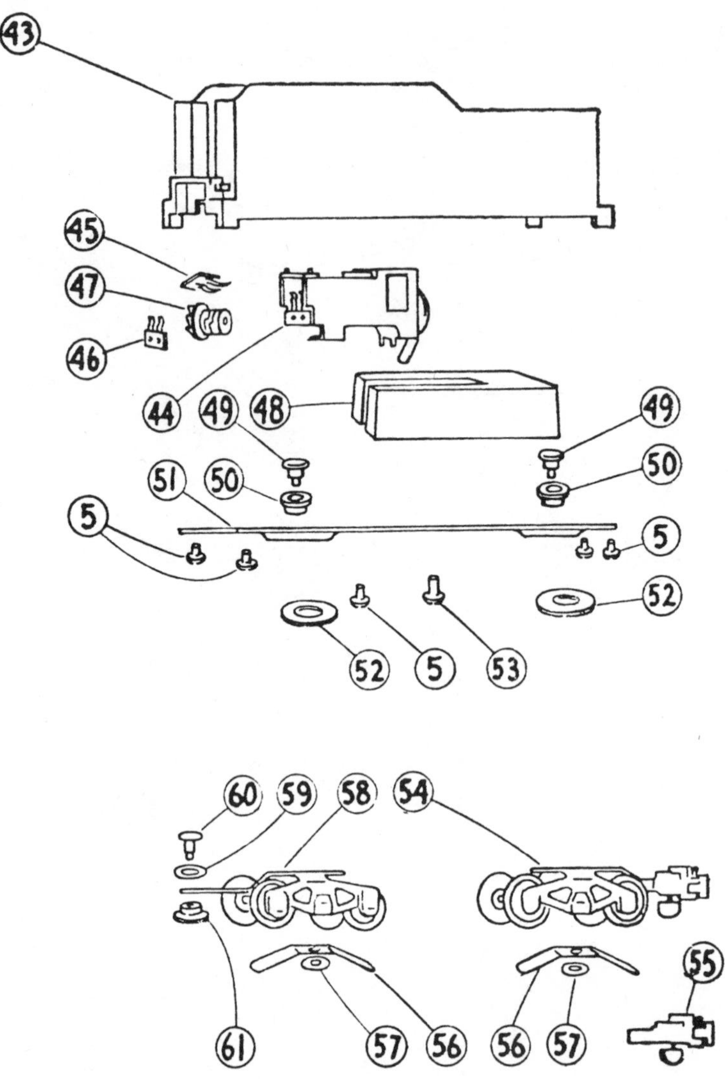

 Ref: Form No. 1646; July 15, 1955

Diagram Number	Part No.	Description	Price
* 1	PA12A190	Smoke Stack	$ .02 ea.
2	XA11736BRP	Boiler (for 283)	.92 "
	XA11736ARP	Boiler (for 287)	.96 "
3	PA8999	Bulb	.25 "
4	XA10890	Lamp Bracket Assembly	.25 "
5	S230B	Screw	.10 dz.
	XA10887	Crosshead Guide & Pilot Truck	.60 ea.
6	PA10707	Stud	.05 "
7	PA10887	Crosshead	.15 "
8	XA10012	Front Truck Assy.	.40 "
	PA9990-A	Front Truck Wheel	.10 "
* 9	XA10523	Heating Element & Plate Assy.	1.00 "
*10	S183	Screw	.10 dz.
*11	PA10513	Smoke Box	1.00 ea.
	*XA10513	Chassis Smoke Box Assy. (consists of Parts 9-10-11)	2.00 ea.
*12	PA10518-A	Piston	.14 "
*13	PA10520	Piston Pin	.05 "
*14	PA10514	Piston Lever	.05 "
*15	PA10671	Worm Drive Gear	.40 "
*16	PA7421	Piston Rod Screw	.30 dz.
*17	PA10162	Worm Gear Stud	.10 ea.
18	PA10888	Crosshead	.05 ea.
19	PA10889	Connecting Rod	.10 ea.
20	PA10506	Chassis	1.20 ea.
20-A	S319	Screw	.01 ea.
21	XA12A449	Flanged Wheel Assembly	.40 ea.
22	XA10009C1	Flangeless Wheel & Stud	.40 ea.
23	XA12A447	Pull-Mor Wheel	.52 ea.
24	PA10672	Worm Gear	.30 ea.
25	XA9547-B	Field Assembly	1.00 ea.
26	PA10766	Armature Spacer	.05 dz.
27	XA11077	Armature	2.50 ea.
27-A	W1A92	Washer	.01 ea.
28	XA9565-A	Brush Bracket Assy.	.50 ea.
29	PA3769	Lock Washer	.05 dz.
30	S295	Shouldered Screw	.10 ea.

NOTE: Parts marked with an asterisk, are not used in the #287 Locomotive, as it does not include the Smoke or Choo-Choo Unit and when repairing it, disregard the service instructions covering this portion.

Diagram Number	Part No.	Description	Price
31	PA10757-A	Brush Spring	.05 ea.
32	PA9603	Brush	.15 ea.
33	PA10754	Brush Cap	.02 ea.
34	PA10006	Worm Gear Axle	.10 ea.
35	PA10017	Grease Pan	.02 ea.
36	S271	Screw	.10 dz.
37	PA5447	Eccentric Crank Screw	.30 dz.
38	PA7237	Piston Rod Spacer	.05 ea.
39	PA9280-A	Side Rod	.20 ea.
40	S16C	Screw	.10 dz.
41	PA10005	Axle	.10 ea.
42	S46	Screw	.05 dz.
43	PA12D078-A	Tender Body	.63 ea.
44	XA10587-E	Remote Control Unit	2.50 ea.
45	XA9612-C	Top Finger Unit	.50 ea.
46	XA9612-B	Bottom Finger Unit	.50 ea.
47	XA8716	Drum	.60 ea.
48	PA11A926	Tender Weight	.18 ea.
49	PA10235-A	Truck Rivet	.03 ea.
50	PA10209	Insulating Bushing	.02 ea.
51	PA12B080	Tender Chassis	.30 ea.
52	PA8715-B	Fibre Washer	.05 dz.
53	S184	Screw	.10 dz.
54	XA12A050-A	Rear Truck Assembly	.56 ea.
	XA10238	Wheel and Axle Assembly	.25 set
	PA10140	Metal Wheel	.15 ea.
	PA9990	Plastic Wheel	.10 ea.
	PA10238	Axle	.02 ea.
55	XA12A047	Knuckle Coupler	.22 ea.
56	PA10207	Contact Spring	.02 ea.
57	PA1405	Tin Washer	.05 dz.
58	XA12A921	Front Truck Assembly	.46 ea.
59	PA1067-A	Washer	.05 dz.
60	PA10751	Stud	.02 ea.
61	PA1312	Bushing	.10 dz.
62	XA10749	Coupler and Yoke Assembly	.30 ea.
63	PA4939	Stud	.05 ea.

 Ref: Form No. 1646; July 15, 1955

SERVICE INSTRUCTIONS FOR No. 283 AND No. 287 LOCOMOTIVE AND TENDER WITH SMOKE AND CHOO-CHOO

The first thing to do is to place locomotive and tender on track, connect transformer and test for operation. Make sure all rods, linkage and other parts are not bent or broken. It is also important that the wheels on the tender be clean to insure a good electrical contact.

1. To check bulb (#3), proceed as follows:

a. Move truck to one side and remove S230-B Screw (#5), holding Lamp Bracket Assembly (#4).

b. Tighten Bulb (#3) in Lamp Bracket (#4), as it is sometimes loose and does not make good contact. If burned out, unscrew bulb and replace.

2. If the trouble is in the locomotive, you can make the following checks:

a. Inspect brushes for wear or poor contact and brush springs for proper tension.

b. Clean or polish commutator on Armature Assembly (#27). If locomotive is still running slow, the armature may need replacing.

c. Make sure wheel and axle assemblies are placed correctly in the truck assembly. Clean metal wheels on tender to insure a good electrical contact.

3. If these initial steps do not correct the trouble, it will be necessary to disassemble the locomotive as follows:

a. Unscrew Smoke Stack (#1).

b. Remove Screw (#63) to take off Coupler and Yoke Assembly (#62) from Locomotive.

c. Remove Screws (#37) on each side and take off Rods (#18 and #19) and Spacer (#38) from center drive wheel.

d. Turn locomotive upside down and remove two Screws (#20-A) and you can now remove motor assembly from Boiler (#2).

e. Take out Lamp Bracket Assembly (#4), by removing Screws (#5).

f. To remove motor, push forward approximately ¼" to clear clamp on Boiler (#2) and then lift the rear of motor up and pull motor out.

g. The motor is now exposed and you can inspect the wiring and other points of the unit, making any necessary replacement.

h. When smoke does not emit from the Smoke Box Assembly (#11), put in some smoke fluid and if it still does not function, the Heating Element (#9) may have a broken wire, and need replacing.

i. To check or replace Heating Element (#9), just remove six Screws (#10). When replacing element assembly, it will be necessary to take off the bottom cover and gasket, so that the wick of the new unit can be pulled through and properly inserted in the Smoke Box Assembly.

4. When the trouble appears to be in the tender, proceed as follows:

a. Remove Screws (#5) holding the tender body to the chassis and take off Body Assembly (#43).

b. Inspect wiring and soldered joints for loose or broken connections.

c. Check Finger Units (#45 and #46) on Remote Control Unit (#44) to see if they are burnt or not making proper contact.

d. The Drum (#47) should be checked to see if it is pitted or worn.

e. The pawl on the Remote Control Unit may be broken or need adjusting.

f. It is generally not necessary to replace the complete Remote Control Unit but sometimes the finger units, the drum, or both need adjusting or replacing.

5. To replace knuckle coupler (#55), proceed as follows:

a. Use a long nosed plier or similar instrument and pry back the two lugs on the rear truck of the tender to remove broken coupler.

b. Insert new part and bend back lugs.

c. Adjust new coupler by placing locomotive and tender on the track, close the knuckle, so that the weight is all the way down; then, either bend the coupler up or down, whichever is necessary to bring the bottom of the weight about 1/32" above the top of the rails.

No.	Part No.	Description	Price
*1	PA12A190	Smoke Stack	.02 ea.
2	XA11736 BRP	Boiler (for 283)	1.02 "
	XA11736 ARP	Boiler (for 287)	1.07 "
3	PA8999	Bulb	.25 "
4	XA10890	Lamp Bracket Assembly	.28 "
5	S230B	Screw	.10 dz.
	XA10887	Crosshead Guide & Pilot Truck	.60 ea.
6	PA10707	Stud	.05 "
7	PA10887	Crosshead	.15 "
8	XA10012	Front Truck Assembly	.40 "
	PA9990-A	Front Truck Wheel	.11 "
*9	XA10523	Heating Element & Plate Assembly	1.11 "
*10	S183	Screw	.10 dz.
*11	PA10513	Smoke Box	1.11 ea.
	*XA10513	Chassis Smoke Box Assembly (consists of Parts 9-10-11)	2.22 "
*12	PA10518-A	Piston	.17 "
*13	PA10520	Piston Pin	.05 "
*14	PA10514	Piston Lever	.08 "
*15	PA10671	Worm Drive Gear	.27 "
*16	PA7421	Piston Rod Screw	.30 dz.
*17	PA10162	Worm Gear Stud	.05 ea.
18	PA10888	Crosshead	.05 "
19	PA10889	Connecting Rod	.11 "
20	PA10506	Chassis	1.37 "
20 A	S319	Screw	.01 "
21	XA13A865	Flanged Wheel Assembly	.29 "
22	XA10009C1	Flangeless Wheel & Stud	.32 "
23	XA13A864	Pull-Mor Wheel	.51 "
24	PA10672	Worm Gear	.20 "
25	XA9547 B	Field Assembly	1.11 "
26	PA10766	Armature Spacer	.05 dz.
27	XA11077	Armature	2.19 ea.
27 A	W1A92	Washer	.01 "
28	XA9565-A	Brush Bracket Assembly	.71 "
29	PA3769	Lock Washer	.05 dz.
30	S295	Shouldered Screw	.02 ea.
31	PA10757-A	Brush Spring	.05 "
32	PA9603	Brush	.15 "
33	PA10754	Brush Cap	.02 "
34	PA10006	Worm Gear Axle	.10 "
35	PA10017	Grease Pan	.04 "
36	S271	Screw	.10 dz.
37	PA5447	Eccentric Crank Screw	.30 "
38	PA7237	Piston Rod Spacer	.05 ea.
39	PA9280-A	Side Rod	.10 "
40	S16C	Screw	.11 dz.

(cont'd)

No.	Part No.	Description	Price
41	PA10005	Axle	.10 ea.
42	S46	Screw	.05 dz.
43	PA12D078 A	Tender Body	.64 ea.
44	XA10587 E	Remote Control Unit	1.32 "
45	XA9612 CRP	Top Finger	.30 "
46	XA9612 BRP	Bottom Finger Unit	.30 "
47	XA8716	Drum	.59 "
48	PA11A926	Tender Weight	.32 "
49	PA10235 A	Truck Rivet	.03 "
50	PA10209	Insulating Bushing	.02 "
51	PA12B080	Tender Chassis	.20 "
52	PA8715 B	Fibre Washer	.05 dz.
53	S184	Screw	.10 "
54	XA12A050 A	Rear Truck Assembly	.65 ea.
	XA10238	Wheel and Axle Assembly	.17 set
	PA10140	Metal Wheel	.15 ea.
	PA9990	Plastic Wheel	.05 "
	PA10238	Axle	.02 "
55	XA12A047	Knuckle Coupler	.22 "
56	PA10207	Contact Spring	.02 "
57	PA1405	Tin Washer	.05 dz.
58	XA12A921	Front Truck Assembly	.46 ea.
59	PA1067 A	Washer	.05 dz.
60	PA10751	Stud	.02 ea.
61	PA1512	Bushing	.11 dz.
62	XA10749	Coupler and Yoke Assembly	.30 ea.
63	PA4939	Stud	.05 "

NOTE:

Parts marked with an asterisk are not used in the #287 Locomotive, as it does not include the Smoke or Choo Choo Unit and when repairing it, disregard the service instructions covering this portion.

DIA. NO.	PART NO.	DESCRIPTION	PRICE
1	PA12A190	Smoke Stack	.03 ea.
2	XA11736BRP	Boiler	1.12 ea.
3	PA8999	Bulb	.30 ea.
4	XA10890	Lamp Bracket Assembly	.22 ea.
5	S230B	Screw	.01 ea.
	XA10887	Crosshead Guide & Pilot Truck	.84 ea.
6	PA10707	Stud	.07 ea.
7	PA10887	Crosshead	.21 ea.
8	XA10012	Front Truck Assembly	.44 ea.
	PA9990-A	Front Truck Wheel	.12 ea.
9	XA10523	Heating Element & Plate Assy. NOT AVAILABLE	
		Substitute with XA14A208-A	.91 ea.
10	S183	Screw	.01 ea.
11	PA10513	Smoke Box NOT AVAILABLE	
	XA10513	Chassis Smoke Box Assy. (Consists of Parts 9-10-11) NOT AVAILABLE	
		Substitute with XA13B894-RP Smoke Box Assy.	2.13 ea.
12	PA10518-A	Piston	.29 ea.
13	PA10520	Piston Pin	.03 ea.
14	PA10514	Piston Lever	.14 ea.
15	PA10671	Worm Drive Gear	.32 ea.
16	PA7421	Piston Rod Screw	.03 ea.
17	PA10162	Worm Gear Stud	.08 ea.
18	PA10888	Crosshead	.08 ea.
19	PA10889	Connecting Rod	.09 ea.
20	PA10506	Chassis	1.51 ea.
20-A	S319	Screw	.02 ea.
21	XA13A865	Flanged Wheel Assy.	.37 ea.
22	XA10009-C1	Flangeless Wheel & Stud	.35 ea.
23	XA13A864	Pul-Mor Wheel	.80 ea.
24	PA10672	Worm Gear	.06 ea.
25	XA9547-B	Field Assembly	1.22 ea.
26	PA10766	Armature Spacer	.01 ea.
27	XA11077	Armature	2.41 ea.
27-A	W1A92	Washer	.02 ea.
28	XA9565-A	Brush Bracket Assembly	1.00 ea.
29	PA3769	Lock Washer	.01 ea.
30	S295	Shouldered Screw	.02 ea.
31	PA10757-A	Brush Spring	.02 ea.
32	PA9603	Brush	.13 ea.
33	PA10754	Brush Cap	.02 ea.
34	PA10006	Worm Gear Axle NOT AVAILABLE	
		Substitute with PA15A281	.07 ea.
35	PA10017	Grease Pan	.07 ea.
36	S271	Screw	.02 ea.
37	PA5447	Eccentric Crank Screw	.04 ea.
38	PA7237	Piston Rod Spacer	.02 ea.
39	PA9280-A	Side Rod	.16 ea.
40	S16-C	Screw	.12 dz.
41	PA10005	Axle NOT AVAILABLE	
		Substitute with PA15A226	.05 ea.

Cont'd

DIA. NO.	PART NO.	DESCRIPTION	PRICE
42	S46	Screw	.01 ea.
43	PA12D078-A	Tender Body OLD STYLE NOT AVAILABLE	
		Substitute with XA12D078-CRP NEW STYLE	1.09 ea.
44	XA10587-E	Remote Control Unit	4.04 ea.
45	XA9612-CRP	Top Finger	.33 ea.
46	XA9612-BRP	Bottom Finger Unit	.33 ea.
47	XA8716	Drum	.95 ea.
48	PA11A926	Tender Weight NOT AVAILABLE	
		Substitute with PA10593	.26 ea.
49	PA10235-A	Truck Rivet	.07 ea.
50	PA10209	Insulating Bushing	.02 ea.
51	PA12B080	Tender Chassis OLD STYLE NOT AVAILABLE	
		Substitute with PA12B080 NEW STYLE	.17 ea.
52	PA8715-B	Fibre Washer	.02 ea.
53	S184	Screw	.02 ea.
54	XA12A050-B	Rear Truck Assembly	.79 ea.
	XA10238	Wheel & Axle Assembly	.09 ea.
	PA10140	Metal Wheel	.06 ea.
	PA9990	Plastic Wheel	.03 ea.
	PA10238	Axle	.01 ea.
55	XA12A047	Knuckle Coupler	.29 ea.
56	PA10207	Contact Spring	.02 ea.
57	PA1405	Tin Washer	.01 ea.
58	XA12A921	Front Truck Assy. NOT AVAILABLE	
		Substitute with XA15A800	.43 ea.
59	PA1067 -A	Washer	.06 ea.
60	PA10751	Stud	.02 ea.
61	PA1312	Bushing	.12 dz.
62	XA10749	Coupler and Yoke Assy. NOT AVAILABLE	
		Substitute with XA15A784	.22 ea.
63	PA4939	Stud	.06 ea.

Prices subject to change without notice

IA. NO.	PART NO.	DESCRIPTION	PRICE
1		NOT USED	
2	XA11736-ART	Boiler	1.12 ea.
3	PA8999	Bulb	.30 ea.
4	XA10890	Lamp Bracket Assembly	.22 ea.
5	S230B	Screw	.01 ea.
	XA10887	Crosshead Guide & Pilot Truck	.84 ea.
6	PA10707	Stud	.07 ea.
7	PA10887	Crosshead	.21 ea.
8	XA10012	Front Truck Assembly	.44 ea.
	PA9990-A	Front Truck Wheel	.12 ea.
9		NOT USED	
10		NOT USED	
11		NOT USED	
12		NOT USED	
13		NOT USED	
14		NOT USED	
15		NOT USED	
16		NOT USED	
17		NOT USED	
18	PA10888	Crosshead	.08 ea.
19	PA10889	Connecting Rod	.09 ea.
20	PA10506	Chassis	1.51 ea.
20-A	S319	Screw	.02 ea.
21	XA13A865	Flanged Wheel Assembly	.37 ea.
22	XA10009-C1	Flangeless Wheel & Stud	.35 ea.
23	XA13A864	Pul-Mor Wheel	.80 ea.
24	PA10672	Worm Gear	.06 ea.
25	XA9547-B	Field Assembly	1.22 ea.
26	PA10766	Armature Spacer	.01 ea.
27	XA11077	Armature	2.41 ea.
27-A	W1A92	Washer	.02 ea.
28	XA9565-A	Brush Bracket Assembly	1.00 ea.
29	PA3769	Lock Washer	.01 ea.
30	S295	Shouldered Screw	.02 ea.
31	PA10757-A	Brush Spring	.02 ea.
32	PA9603	Brush	.13 ea.
33	PA10754	Brush Cap	.02 ea.
34	PA10006	Worm Gear Axle NOT AVAILABLE	
		Substitute with PA15A281	.07 ea.
35	PA10017	Grease Pan	.07 ea.
36	S271	Screw	.02 ea.
37	PA5447	Eccentric Crank Screw	.04 ea.
38	PA7237	Piston Rod Spacer	.02 ea.
39	PA9280-A	Side Rod	.16 ea.
40	S16C	Screw	.12 dz.
41	PA10005	Axle NOT AVAILABLE	
		Substitute with PA15A226	.05 ea.

Cont'd

 Ref: Form No. 1646, June 1, 1960

DIA. NO.	PART NO.	DESCRIPTION	PRICE
42	S46	Screw	.01 ea.
43	PA12D078-A	Tender Body OLD STYLE NOT AVAILABLE	
		Substitute with XA12D078-CRP NEW STYLE	1.09 ea.
44	XA10587-E	Remote Control Unit	4.04 ea.
45	XA9612CRP	Top Finger	.33 ea.
46	XA9612-BRP	Bottom Finger Unit	.33 ea.
47	XA8716	Drum	.95 ea.
48	PA11A926	Tender Weight NOT AVAILABLE	
		Substitute with PA10593	.26 ea.
49	PA10235-A	Truck Rivet	.07 ea.
50	PA10209	Insulating Bushing	.02 ea.
51	PA12B080	Tender Chassis OLD STYLE NOT AVAILABLE	
		Substitute with PA12B080 NEW STYLE	.17 ea.
52	PA8715-B	Fibre Washer	.02 ea.
53	S184	Screw	.02 ea.
54	XA12A050	Rear Truck Assembly	.79 ea.
	XA10238	Wheel and Axle Assembly	.09 ea.
	PA10140	Metal Wheel	.06 ea.
	PA9990	Plastic Wheel	.03 ea.
	PA10238	Axle	.01 ea.
55	XA12A047	Knuckle Coupler	.29 ea.
56	PA10207	Contact Spring	.02 ea.
57	PA1405	Tin Washer	.01 ea.
58	XA12A921	Front Truck Assy. NOT AVAILABLE	
		Substitute with XA15A800	.43 ea.
59	PA1067-A	Washer	.06 ea.
60	PA10751	Stud	.02 ea.
61	PA1312	Bushing	.12 dz.
62	XA10749	Coupler and Yoke Assy. NOT AVAILABLE	
		Substitute with XA15A784	.22 ea.
63	PA4939	Stud	.06 ea.

Prices subject to change without notice

NO.	PART NO.	DESCRIPTION	PRICE
1	PA12A190	Smoke Stack	.03 ea.
2	XA11736ERP	Boiler Marked 21085	2.09 ea.
3	PA8999	Bulb	.32 ea.
4	XA10890	Lamp Bracket Assembly	.23 ea.
5	S230B	Screw	.01 ea.
	XA10887	Crosshead Guide & Pilot Truck	.88 ea.
6	PA10707	Stud	.07 ea.
7	PA10887	Crosshead	.22 ea.
8	XA10012	Front Truck Assembly	.46 ea.
	PA9990-A	Front Truck Wheel	.13 ea.
9	XA14A208-A	Heating Element & Plate Assy.	.96 ea.
10	S183	Screw	.01 ea.
11	XA13B894RP	Smoke Box Assembly	2.24 ea.
12	PA10518-A	Piston	.30 ea.
13	PA10520	Piston Pin	.03 ea.
14	PA10514	Piston Lever	.15 ea.
15	PA10671	Worm Drive Gear	.34 ea.
16	PA7421	Piston Rod Screw	.03 ea.
17	PA10162	Worm Gear Stud	.08 ea.
18	PA10888	Crosshead	.08 ea.
19	PA10889	Connecting Rod	.09 ea.
20	PA10506-A	Chassis	1.87 ea.
20-	S319	Screw	.02 ea.
21	XA13A865	Flanged Wheel Assembly	.39 ea.
22	XA10009-C1	Flangeless Wheel & Stud	.37 ea.
23	XA13A864	Pul-Mor Wheel	.84 ea.
24	PA10672	Worm Gear	.06 ea.
25	XA9547-B	Field Assembly	1.28 ea.
26	PA10766	Armature Spacer	.01 ea.
27	XA11077	Armature	3.56 ea.
27-	W1A92	Washer	.02 ea.
28	XA9565-A	Brush Bracket Assembly	1.05 ea.
29	PA3769	Lock Washer	.01 ea.
30	S295	Shouldered Screw	.02 ea.
31	PA10757-A	Brush Spring	.02 ea.
32	PA9603	Brush	.14 ea.
33	PA10754	Brush Cap	.02 ea.
34	PA15A281	Worm Gear Axle	.07 ea.
35	PA10017	Grease Pan	.07 ea.
36	S271	Screw	.02 ea.
37	PA5447	Eccentric Crank Screw	.04 ea.
38	PA7237	Piston Rod Spacer	.02 ea.
39	PA9280-A	Side Rod	.17 ea.
40	S16-C	Screw	.13 dz.
41	PA15A226	Plain Axle	.05 ea.
42	S46	Screw	.01 ea.
43		Tender Body - Obsolete - No Longer Available No Substitute	
44	XA10587-E	Remote Control Unit	4.24 ea.
45	XA9612-CRP	Top Finger	.35 ea.
46	XA9612-BRP	Bottom Finger Unit	.35 ea.

Cond't

NO.	PART NO.	DESCRIPTION	PRICE
47	XA8716	Drum	1.00 ea.
48	PA10593	Tender Weight	.27 ea.
49	PA10235-A	Truck Rivet	.07 e
50	PA10209	Insulating Bushing	.02 ea.
51		Tender Chassis - Obsolete No Longer Available - No Substitute	
52	PA8715-B	Fibre Washer	.02 ea.
53	S184	Screw	.02
54	XA12A050-B	Rear Truck Assembly	.83 ea.
	XA10238	Wheel & Axle Assembly	.09 ea.
	PA10140	Metal Wheel	.06 ea.
	PA9990	Plastic Wheel	.03 ea.
	PA10238	Axle	.01 ea.
55	XA12A047	Knuckle Coupler	.30 ea.
56	PA10207	Contact Spring	.02 ea.
57	PA1405	Tin Washer	.01 ea.
58	XA15B800	Front Truck Assembly Substitute for XA12A921 OBSOLETE	.45 ea.
59	PA1067-A	Washer	.06 dz.
60	PA10751	Stud	.02 ea.
61	PA1312	Bushing	.13 dz.
62	XA15A784	Draw Bar Used w/XA15B800 Truck	.23 ea.
	XA10891	Coupler & Yoke Assy. Substitute for XA10749 OBSOLETE	.38 ea.
63	PA4939	Stud	.06 ea.

Prices subject to change without notice

****

#287 LOCOMOTIVE & TENDER

#287 Loco & Tender same as #283 with these exceptions:

DIA NO.	PART NO.	DESCRIPTION
1		NOT USED
9 thru 17		NOT USED

NO.	PART NO.	DESCRIPTION	PRICE
1		NOT USED	
2	XA11736ERP	Boiler (Marked 21085)	2.09 ea.
3	PA8999	Bulb	.32 ea.
4	XA10890	Lamp Bracket Assembly	.23 ea.
5	S230B	Screw	.01 ea.
	XA10887	Crosshead Guide & Pilot Truck	.88 ea.
6	PA10707	Stud	.07 ea.
7	PA10887	Crosshead	.22 ea.
8	XA10012	Front Truck Assembly	.46 ea.
	PA9990-A	Front Truck Wheel	.13 ea.
9		NOT USED	
10		NOT USED	
11		NOT USED	
12		NOT USED	
13		NOT USED	
14		NOT USED	
15		NOT USED	
16		NOT USED	
17		NOT USED	
18	PA10888	Crosshead	.08 ea.
19	PA10889	Connecting Rod	.09 ea.
20	PA10506-A	Chassis	1.87 ea.
20-A	S319	Screw	.02 ea.
21	XA13A865	Flanged Wheel Assembly	.39 ea.
22	XA10009-C1	Flangeless Wheel & Stud	.37 ea.
23	XA13A864	Pul-Mor Wheel	.84 ea.
24	PA10672	Worm Gear	.06 ea.
25	XA9547-B	Field Assembly	1.28 ea.
26	PA10766	Armature Spacer	.01 ea.
27	XA11077	Armature	3.56 ea.
27-A	W1A92	Washer	.02 ea.
28	XA9565-A	Brush Bracket Assembly	1.05 ea.
29	PA3769	Lock Washer	.01 ea.
30	S295	Shouldered Screw	.02 ea.
31	PA10757-A	Brush Spring	.02 ea.
32	PA9603	Brush	.14 ea.
33	PA10754	Brush Cap	.02 ea.
34	PA15A281	Worm Gear Axle	.07 ea.
35	PA10017	Grease Pan	.07 ea.
36	S271	Screw	.02 ea.
37	PA5447	Eccentric Crank Screw	.04 ea.
38	PA7237	Piston Rod Spacer	.02 ea.
39	PA9280-A	Side Rod	.17 ea.
40	S16C	Screw	.13 dz.
41	PA15A226	Plain Axle	.05 ea.
42	S46	Screw	.01 ea.
43		Tender Body - Obsolete - No Longer Available - No Substitute	

Cont'd

NO.	PART NO.	DESCRIPTION	PRICE
44	XA10587-E	Remote Control Unit	4.24 ea.
45	XA9612CRP	Top Finger	.35 ea.
46	XA9612BRP	Bottom Finger Unit	.35 ea.
47	XA8716	Drum	1.00 ea.
48	PA10593	Tender Weight	.27 ea.
49	PA10235-A	Truck Rivet	.07 ea.
50	PA10209	Insulating Bushing	.02 ea.
51		Tender Chassis - Obsolete - No Longer Available - No Substitute	
52	PA8715-B	Fibre Washer	.02 ea.
53	S184	Screw	.02 ea.
54	XA12A050-B	Rear Truck Assembly	.83 ea.
	XA10238	Wheel & Axle Assembly	.09 ea.
	PA10140	Metal Wheel	.06 ea.
	PA9990	Plastic Wheel	.03 ea.
	PA10238	Axle	.01 ea.
55	XA12A047	Knuckle Coupler	.30 ea.
56	PA10207	Contact Spring	.02 ea.
57	PA1405	Tin Washer	.01 ea.
58	XA15B800	Front Truck Assembly	.45 ea.
		Substitute for XA12A921 Frt. Truck Assembly - OBSOLETE	
59	PA1067-A	Washer	.06 dz.
60	PA10751	Stud	.02 ea.
61	PA1312	Bushing	.13 dz.
62	XA15A784	Draw Bar Used w/XA15B800 Truck	.23 ea.
	XA10891	Coupler & Yoke	.38 ea.
		Substitute for XA10749 - OBSOLETE	
63	PA4939	Stud	.06 ea.

PRICES SUBJECT TO CHANGE WITHOUT NOTICE.

PACIFIC LOCOMOTIVE AND TENDER WITH SMOKE, CHOO-CHOO, AND AIR CHIME WHISTLE

Model Nos. 285, 295

SPECIFICATIONS

Tested at: 12 Volts A.C. .... using 140" oval track.

(A) Motor to be tested with Remote Control Unit at 12 Volts, and not to draw more than 1.7 amps.

(B) Locomotive to run a minimum of 9 R.P.M. or 9 times forward, around 140" oval of track per minute pulling 4 cars.

(C) Locomotive to run a minimum of 8.5 R.P.M. or 8½ times reverse, around 140" oval of track per minute pulling 4 cars.

Load: Not to draw more than 2.1 amps. while pulling 4 Box Cars.

Motor: Universal A.C. or D.C.

 Ref: Form No. M3146; Nov. 1, 1952

PACIFIC LOCOMOTIVE AND TENDER WITH SMOKE, CHOO-CHOO AND AIR CHIME WHISTLE

Model Nos. 285, 295

SPECIFICATIONS

Tested at: 12 Volts A.C. .... using 140″ oval track.

(A) Motor to be tested with Remote Control Unit at 12 Volts, and not to draw more than 1.7 amps.

(B) Locomotive to run a minimum of 9 R.P.M. or 9 times forward, around 140″ oval of track per minute pulling 4 cars.

(C) Locomotive to run a minimum of 8.5 R.P.M. or 8½ times reverse, around 140″ oval of track per minute pulling 4 cars.

Load: Not to draw more than 2.1 amps. while pulling 4 Box Cars.

Motor: Universal A.C. or D.C.

Ref: Form No. 1813; Feb. 1, 1957

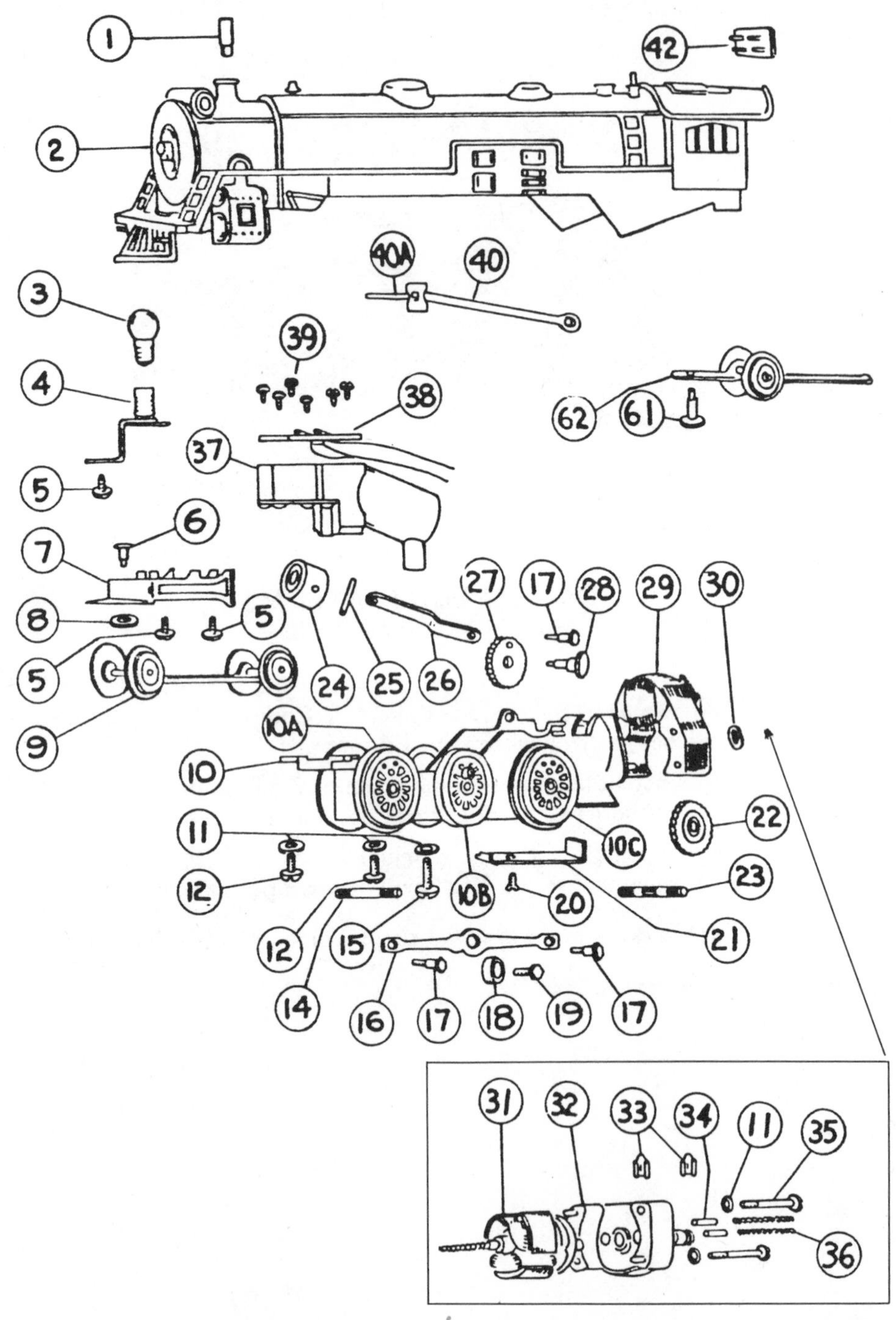

 Ref: Form No. 1813; Feb. 1, 1957

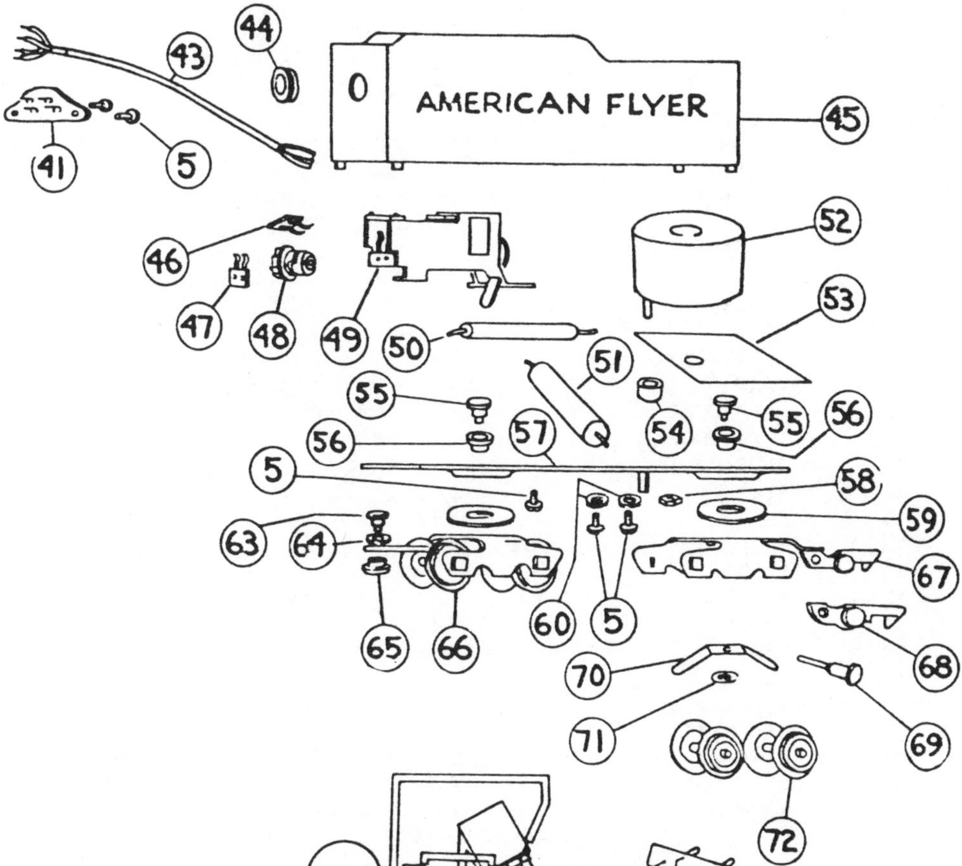

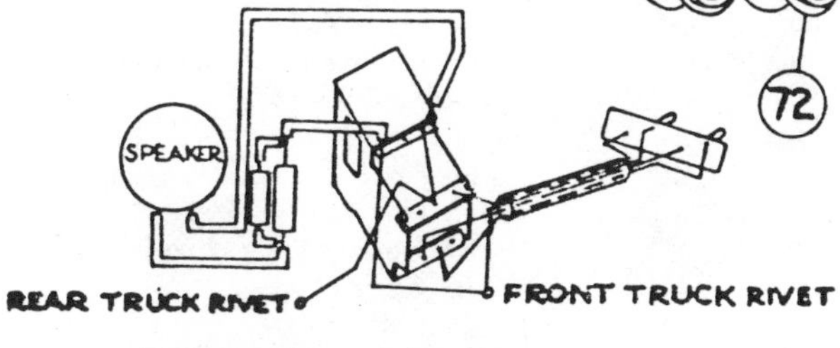

AMERICAN FLYER

SPEAKER

REAR TRUCK RIVET

FRONT TRUCK RIVET

TENDER WIRING

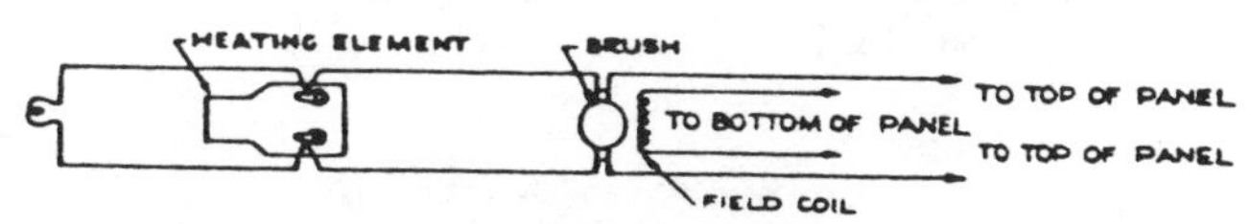

LOCOMOTIVE WIRING

Diagram Number	Part No.	Description	Price
1	PA10536	Smoke Stack	$ .03 ea.
2	XA11736-RP	Boiler Assembly with Trimmings (No. 285 Loco & Tender) Plastic	2.00 ea.
	XA10886-RP	Boiler Assembly with Trimmings (No. 295 Loco & Tender) Die Cast	2.00 ea.
3	PA8999	14 Volt Lamp	.25 "
4	XA10890	Lamp Bracket Assembly	.25 "
5	S230-B	Screw	.10 dz.
	XA10887	Crosshead Guide and Pilot Truck Assembly (consists of parts 6-7-8-9)	.60 ea.
6	PA10707	Stud	.05 "
7	PA10887	Crosshead	.15 "
8	PA5035-A	Washer	.10 dz.
9	XA10012	Front Truck Assembly	.40 ea.
	PA9990-A	Front Truck Wheel only	.10 "
10	*XA10506	Chassis Assembly with bushings only	1.20 "
10A	XA10009	Flanged wheel with tapped hole	.40 "
10B	XA10009-C1	Flangeless wheel and stud	.40 "
11	PA3769	Washer	.05 dz.
12	S14	Screw	.05 "
13	S46	Screw	.05 "
14	PA10005	Plain axle	.10 ea.
15	S16-C	Screw	.10 dz.
16	PA9280-A	Side Rod	.20 ea.
17	PA7421	Screw	.30 dz.
18	PA7237	Piston Rod Spacer	.05 ea.
19	PA5447	Screw	.30 dz.
20	S271	Screw	.10 "
21	PA10017	Grease Pan	.02 ea.
22	PA10672	Worm Gear (motor)	.30 "
23	PA10006	Worm Gear Axle	.10 "
	XA10514	Piston and Lever Assembly (consists of parts 24-25-26)	.40 "
24	PA10518	Piston	.20 "
25	PA10520	Piston Pin	.05 "
26	PA10514	Piston Lever	.05 "
27	PA10671	Worm Gear (smoke drive)	.40 "
28	PA10162	Worm Gear Stud	.10 "
29	XA9547	Magnet Assembly	1.00 "
30	PA10766	Washer	.05 dz.
31	XA11077	Armature Assembly	2.50 ea.
32	XA9565-A	Brush Bracket Assembly	.50 "
33	PA10754	Brush Cap	.02 "
34	PA9603	Carbon Brush	.15 "
35	S295	Screw	.10 "
36	PA10757	Brush Spring	.05 "
	XA10513	Chassis Smoke Box Assembly (consists of parts 37-38-39)	2.00 ea.

 Ref: Form No. M3146; Nov. 1, 1952

Diagram Number	Part No.	Description	Price
37	PA10513	Chassis Smoke Box	$1.00 ea.
38	XA10523	Heating Element & Plate Assembly	1.00 "
39	S183	Screw	.10 dz.
40	PA10889	Connecting Rod	.10 ea.
40A	PA10888	Crosshead	.05 "
41	XA10662	Jack Panel	.20 "
42	XA10663	Male Plug	.20 "
43	PA10511-C	4 Conductor Cable	.12 "
44	PA4356	Rubber Grommet	.02 "
45	XA9461-B	Tender Body Assembly	1.00 "
46	XA9612-C	Top Finger Unit	.50 ea.
47	XA9612-B	Bottom Finger Unit	.50 "
48	XA8716	Drum Only	.60 "
49	XA10587-E	Remote Control Unit	2.50 "
50	PA11685	Resistor	.26 "
51	PA11A991	Condenser	1.00 "
52	XA11710	Speaker	2.76 "
53	PA11664	Receiver Insulation	.02 "
54	W37	Rubber Washer	.03 "
55	PA10235-A	Truck Rivet	.03 "
56	PA10209	Insulating Bushing	.02 "
57	PA10590	Tender Chassis	.30 "
58	N-1A	Nut	.01 "
59	PA8715-B	Washer	.05 dz.
60	W46	Lockwasher	.05 "
61	PA4939	Truck Stud	.05 ea.
	XA11718	Truck & Coupler Assembly (consists of parts 62-63-64-65-66)	.80 "
62	XA10891	Coupler & Yoke Assembly	.30 "
	PA10019-A	Rear Truck Wheel Only	.10 "
63	PA10751	Stud	.02 "
64	PA1067-A	Washer	.05 dz.
65	PA1312	Insulating Bushing	.10 "
66	XA11712	Front Truck Assembly with Wheels	.50 ea.
67	XA11714	Rear Truck Assembly with Wheels	.75 "
68	XA10469	Coupler & Weight	.15 "
	PA10692	Coupler Weight Only	.05 "
69	PA10467	Coupler Pin	.10 "
70	PA10207	Contact Spring	.02 "
71	PA1405	Washer	.05 dz.
72	XA10238	Wheel & Axle Assembly (metal & plastic wheels)	.25 set
	PA10140	Metal Wheel	.15 ea.
	PA9990	Plastic Wheel	.10 "
	PA10238	Axle	.02 "

* XA10506 Chassis Assembly is not sold as a complete assembly with wheels.

All prices subject to change without notice.

Diagram Number	Part No.	Description	Price
1	PA12A190	Smoke Stack	$ .02 ea.
2	XA11736-BRP	Boiler Assembly with Trimmings (No. 285 Loco & Tender) Plastic...	1.02 "
	XA10886-RP	Boiler Assembly with Trimmings (No. 295 Loco & Tender) Die Cast.	2.22 "
3	PA8999	14 Volt Lamp	.25 "
4	XA10890	Lamp Bracket Assembly	.28 "
5	S230-B	Screw	.10 dz.
	XA10887	Crosshead Guide and Pilot Truck Assembly (consists of parts 6-7-8-9)	.60 ea.
6	PA10707	Stud	.05 "
7	PA10887	Crosshead	.15 "
8	PA5035-A	Washer	.11 dz.
9	XA10012	Front Truck Assembly	.40 ea.
	PA9990-A	Front Truck Wheel only	.11 "
10	*XA10506	Chassis Assembly with bushings only..	1.33 ea.
10A	XA13A865	Flanged Wheel	.29 "
10B	XA10009-C1	Flangeless Wheel and Stud	.32 "
10C	XA13A864	Pull-Mor Wheel Assembly	.51 "
11	PA3769	Washer	.05 dz.
12	S14	Screw	.05 "
14	PA10005	Plain Axle	.10 ea.
15	S16-C	Screw	.11 dz.
16	PA9280-A	Side Rod	.10 ea.
17	PA7421	Screw	.30 dz.
18	PA7237	Piston Rod Spacer	.05 ea.
19	PA5447	Screw	.30 dz.
20	S271	Screw	.10 "
21	PA10017	Grease Pan	.04 ea.
22	PA10672	Worm Gear (motor)	.20 "
23	PA10006	Worm Gear Axle	.10 "
24	PA10518-A	Piston	.17 "
25	PA10520	Piston Pin	.05 "
26	PA10514	Piston Lever	.08 "
27	PA10671	Worm Gear (smoke drive)	.27 "
28	PA10162	Worm Gear Stud	.05 "
29	XA9547	Magnet Assembly	1.11 "
30	PA10766	Washer	.05 dz.
31	XA11077	Armature Assembly	2.19 ea.
32	XA9565-A	Brush Bracket Assembly	.71 "
33	PA10754	Brush Cap	.02 "
34	PA9603	Carbon Brush	.15 "
35	S295	Screw	.02 "
36	PA10757-A	Brush Spring	.05 "
	***XA10513	Chassis Smoke Box Assembly (consists of parts 37-38-39)..	NOT AVAILABLE
37	***PA10513	Chassis Smoke Box	NOT AVAILABLE
38	****XA10523	Heating Element & Plate Assembly...	.66 ea.

*** Parts so marked NOT AVAILABLE, substitute with:

Dia. 37	XA13B894RP	Smoke Box Assy. (new style)	$1.55 ea.
	PA13B894	Smoke Box (new style)	.59 "
	PA14A209	Separator (new style)	.01 "

 Ref: Form No. 1813; Feb. 1, 1957

Diagram Number	Part No.	Description	Price
39	S183	Screw	.10 dz.
40	PA10889	Connecting Rod	.11 ea.
40A	PA10888	Crosshead	.05 "
41	XA10662-A	Jack Panel	.22 "
42	XA10663	Male Plug	.22 "
43	PA10511-C	4 Conductor Cable	.12 "
44	PA4356	Rubber Grommet	.02 "
45	**	Tender Body Assembly (NOT AVAILABLE)	
46	XA9612-CRP	Top Finger Unit	.30 "
47	XA9612-BRP	Bottom Finger Unit	.30 "
48	XA8716	Drum Only	.59 "
49	XA10587-E	Remote Control Unit	1.32 "
50	PA11685	Resistor	.26 "
51	PA11A991	Condenser	1.04 "
52	XA11710	Speaker	3.06 "
53	PA11654	Receiver Insulation	.02 "
54	W37	Rubber Washer	.03 "
55	PA10235-A	Truck Rivet	.03 "
56	PA10209	Insulating Bushing	.02 "
57	**	Tender Chassis (NOT AVAILABLE	
58	N-1A	Nut	.01 "
59	PA8715-B	Washer	.05 dz.
60	W46	Lockwasher	.05 "
61	PA4939	Truck Stud	.05 ea.
	XA11718	Truck & Coupler Assembly (consists of parts 62-63-64-65-66).	.89 "
62	XA10891	Coupler & Yoke Assembly	.33 "
	PA10019-A	Rear Truck Wheel Only	.05 "
63	PA10751	Stud	.02 "
64	PA1067-A	Washer	.05 dz.
65	PA1312	Insulating Bushing	.11 "
66	XA11712	Front Truck Assy. (NOT AVAILABLE)	
67	XA11714	Rear Truck Assy. (NOT AVAILABLE)	
68	XA10469	Coupler & Weight	.17 ea.
	PA10692	Coupler Weight only	.05 "
69	PA10467	Coupler Pin	.11 "
70	PA10207	Contact Spring	.02 "
71	PA1405	Washer	.05 dz.
72	XA10238	Wheel and Axle Assembly (Metal & Plastic Wheels)	.17 set
	PA10140	Metal Wheel	.15 ea.
	PA9990	Plastic Wheel	.05 "
	PA10238	Axle	.02 "

*XA10506 Chassis Assembly is not sold as a complete assembly with wheels.

**Parts so marked NOT AVAILABLE, substitute with:

Dia. 45	PA12D078-A	Tender Body	.64 ea.
Dia. 57	PA12B080	Tender Chassis	.20 "

****The XA10523 Heating Element and Plate Assy. is still available, and interchangeable with the new style PA13B894 Smoke Box. The new style XA14A208 Heating Element and Plate Assembly, priced at $.66 each, is used only on the new style PA13B894 Smoke Box.

SERVICE INSTRUCTIONS FOR #285 & #295 LOCOMOTIVE AND TENDER WITH SMOKE, CHOO-CHOO AND WHISTLE.

The first thing to do is to place Locomotive and Tender on track, connect transformer and whistle control unit, and test for operation. Make sure all rods, linkage and other parts are not bent or broken. It is also important that the wheels on the Tender be clean to insure a good electrical contact.

1. **If the whistle is satisfactory, but the Locomotive and Tender does not operate properly proceed as follows:**
   a. Remove screw (#61) and also male plug (#42) from the Jack Panel (#41).
   b. Now take another similar tender with a remote control unit in it which is in good working order and connect it to the Locomotive. In this way you will be able to determine whether the Locomotive or Tender is defective.
2. **If the trouble is in the Locomotive you can make the following checks:**
   a. Inspect brushes for wear or poor contact and brush springs for position and proper tension.
   b. Check wires and solder joints on male plug (#42) and Jack Panel (#41) for broken or loose connections.
   c. Clean or polish commutator if dirty or worn.
3. **If these initial steps do not correct the trouble it will be necessary to disassemble the locomotive as follows:**
   a. Unscrew smoke stack (#1).
   b. Remove screws (#19) on each side and take off Rods (#40 and #40A) and spacer (#18) from center drive wheel.
   c. Turn Locomotive upside down and remove two screws (#12) and you can now remove motor assembly from Boiler (#2).
   d. To remove motor, push forward approximately a ¼" to clear clamp on boiler (#2) and then lift rear of motor up and pull motor out.
   e. The motor is now exposed and you can inspect the wiring and other points of the unit, making any necessary replacements.
4. **When the trouble appears to be in the Tender, proceed as follows:**
   a. Straighten out four prongs holding body to chassis, and take off Tender body (#45).
   b. Inspect wiring and solder joints for loose or broken connections.
   c. Check finger units (#46 and #47) on Remote Control Unit (#49) to see if they are burnt or not making proper contact.
   d. The drum (#48) should be checked to see if it is pitted or worn.
   e. The pawl on the Remote Control Unit may be broken or need adjusting.
   f. It is generally not necessary to replace the complete Remote Control Unit, but sometimes the finger units, the drum, or both need adjusting or replacing.
5. **If Locomotive and Tender operates satisfactorily, but the whistle does not function correctly check as follows:**
   a. Recheck the instruction sheet in order to make sure hook-up is correct. If both the transformer instructions and the Air Chime Whistle Instructions are followed, this will cause a duplication of wiring. The result will be that you will only have a faint buzz while the train is running or in a neutral position.

      Follow the Air Chime Whistle wiring instructions only and be sure to have only two wires going to the #690 track terminal.
   b. The Generator Tube #PA11665 on the control box may be weak and need replacing.
   c. If the trouble still persists it will be necessary to remove the Tender Body (#45) from the chassis by straightening out the four prongs.
   d. The unit is exposed and you can check all wires and solder joints for loose connections. Be sure the lead wires on the resistor and condenser are covered with an insulating sleeve.
   e. Check the condenser (#51) by adding another condenser in series with temporary connections. If this corrects the trouble the defective condenser can be removed and a new one connected in its place.
   f. To check resistor (#50) use another resistor and follow same procedure.

INSTRUCTIONS FOR HOOKING UP AND OPERATING THE AIR CHIME WHISTLE CONTROL

To install the air chime whistle control unit . . .

FIRST remove all wires which are now supplying current to the track for train operation. Disregard any other wiring instructions which may be received with the transformer or track terminal.

NEXT, study the following diagram and proceed as per instructions below. Only one track terminal is to be used and the *wires must be connected as shown* in the diagram.

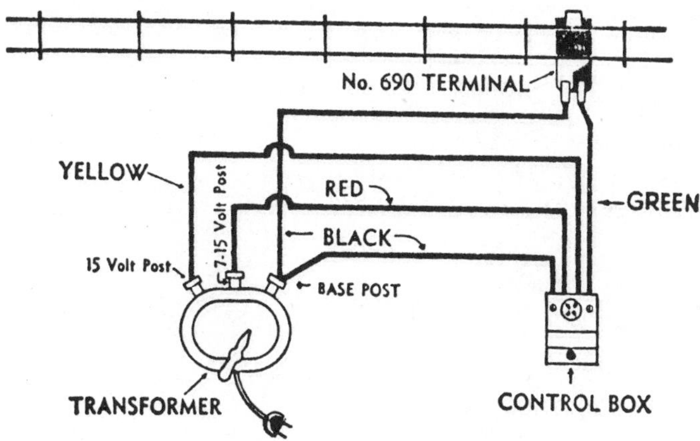

WIRING INSTRUCTIONS

Connect the **BLACK wire** from the Control Box to the **BASE POST** on the transformer.

Connect the **RED wire** from the Control Box to the **7-15 VOLT POST** on the transformer.

Connect the **YELLOW wire** from the Control Box to the **15 VOLT POST** on the transformer.

Connect the separate **BLACK WIRE** packed with the track terminal from the **BASE POST** on the transformer to the **BASE POST CLIP** on the 690 Track Terminal.

Connect the **GREEN wire** from the Control Box to the other clip on the 690 Track Terminal.

NOTE: Be sure no other wires run direct from the transformer to the track. If jumper or booster wires are to be used on large layouts to give an even flow of current, be sure wires are run from the No. 690 track terminal shown in the diagram to another track terminal. Do not run wires direct from the transformer to the track.

OPERATION

Next, place the generator on the Control Box, inserting the 4 prongs into the holes. This can only be installed one way. There are two large and two small prongs which fit into their respective holes.

The whistle is now ready to operate; place the locomotive on the track, then turn power on, press the Control Box button and whistle should blow.

If whistle is to be blown while locomotive is standing still, the power should be on and locomotive reverse control should be in neutral position.

DIA. NO.	PART NO.	DESCRIPTION	PRICE
1	PA12A190	Smoke Stack	.03 ea.
2	XA11736-BRP	Boiler Assy. w/trimmings	1.12 ea.
3	PA8999	14 Volt Lamp	.30 ea.
4	XA10890	Lamp Bracket Assy.	.22 ea.
5	S230-B	Screw	.01 ea.
	XA10887	Crosshead Guide & Pilot Truck (Consists of Part 6-7-8-9)	.84 ea.
6	PA10707	Stud	.07 ea.
7	PA10887	Crosshead	.21 ea.
8	PA5035-A	Washer	.06 dz.
9	XA10012	Front Truck Assy.	.44 ea.
	PA9990-A	Front Truck Wheel Only	.12 ea.
10	XA10506-A	Chassis Assy. w/bushings only	1.78 ea.
10A	XA13A865	Flanged Wheel	.37 ea.
10B	XA10009-C1	Flangeless Wheel & Stud	.35 ea.
10C	XA13A864	Pul-Mor Wheel Assy.	.80 ea.
11	PA3769	Washer	.01 ea.
12	S14	Screw	.01 ea.
14	PA10005	Plain Axle NOT AVAILABLE	
		Substitute with PA15A226 Axle	.05 ea.
15	S16-C	Screw	.12 dz.
16	PA9280-A	Side Rod	.16 ea.
17	PA7421	Screw	.03 ea.
18	PA7237	Piston Rod Spacer	.02 ea.
19	PA5447	Screw	.04 ea.
20	S271	Screw	.02 ea.
21	PA10017	Grease Pan	.07 ea.
22	PA10672	Worm Gear (motor)	.06 ea.
23	PA10006	Worm Gear Axle NOT AVAILABLE	
		Substitute with PA15A281 Axle	.07 ea.
24	PA10518-A	Piston	.29 ea.
25	PA10520	Piston Pin	.03 ea.
26	PA10514	Piston Lever	.14 ea.
27	PA10671	Worm Gear (smoke drive)	.32 ea.
28	PA10162	Worm Gear Stud	.08 ea.
29	XA9547	Magnet Assy.	1.22 ea.
30	PA10766	Washer	.01 ea.
31	XA11077	Armature Assy.	3.39 ea.
32	XA9565-A	Brush Bracket Assy.	1.00 ea.
33	PA10754	Brush Cap	.02 ea.
34	PA9603	Carbon Brush	.13 ea.
35	S295	Screw	.02 ea.
36	PA10757-A	Brush Spring	.02 ea.
	XA10513	Chassis Smoke Box Assy. NOT AVAILABLE	
		Substitute with XA13B894-RP Smoke Box	2.13 ea.
37	PA10513	Chassis Smoke Box NOT AVAILABLE	
		Substitute with PA13B894 Smoke Box	.76 ea.
		PA14A209 Separator	.02 ea.
38	XA10523	Heating Element & Plate Assy. NOT AVAILABLE	
		Substitute with XA14A208A Element & Plate Assy.	.91 ea.
39	S183	Screw	.01 ea.

Cont'd

DIA. NO.	PART NO.	DESCRIPTION	PRICE
40	PA10889	Connecting Rod	.09 ea.
40A	PA10888	Crosshead	.08 ea.
41	XA10662-A	Jack Panel	.24 ea.
42	XA10663	Male Plug	.24 ea.
43	PA10511-C	4 Conductor Cable	.13 ea.
44	PA4356	Rubber Grommet	.02 ea.
45	XA9461-B	Tender Body Assy. NOT AVAILABLE	
		Substitute with PA12D078A Tender Body	.70 ea.
46	XA9612-CRP	Top Finger Unit	.33 ea.
47	XA9612-BRP	Bottom Finger Unit	.33 ea.
48	XA8716	Drum Only	.95 ea.
49	XA10587-E	Remote Control Unit	4.04 ea.
50	PA11685	Resistor	.29 ea.
51	PA11A991	Condenser NOT AVAILABLE	
		Substitute with PA14A914 Condenser	1.40 ea.
52	XA11710	Speaker NOT AVAILABLE	
		Substitute with XA14A127 Speaker	4.57 ea.
53	PA11664	Receiver Insulation NOT AVAILABLE	
54	W37	Rubber Washer	.03 dz.
55	PA10235-A	Truck Rivet	.07 ea.
56	PA10209	Insulating Bushing	.02 ea.
57	PA10590	Tender Chassis NOT AVAILABLE	
		Substitute with PA12B080 Tender Chassis	.17 ea.
58	N1-A	Nut	.01 ea.
59	PA8715-B	Washer	.02 ea.
60	W46	Lockwasher	.01 ~~.06~~ ea.
61	PA4939	Truck Stud	.06 ~~[illegible]~~ ea.
	XA11718	Truck & Coupler Assy. NOT AVAILABLE	
62	XA10891	Coupler & Yoke Assy.	.36 ea.
	PA10019-A	Rear Truck Wheel Only	.06 ea.
63	PA10751	Stud	.02 ea.
64	PA1067-A	Washer	.06 dz.
65	PA1312	Insulating Bushing	.12 dz.
66	XA11712	Front Truck Assy. NOT AVAILABLE	
67	XA11714	Rear Truck Assy. NOT AVAILABLE	
68	XA10469	Coupler & Weight NOT AVAILABLE	
	PA10692	Coupler Weight Only NOT AVAILABLE	
69	PA10467	Coupler Pin NOT AVAILABLE	
70	PA10207	Contact Spring	.02 ea.
71	PA1405	Washer	.01 ea.
72	XA10238	Wheel & Axle Assy. (Metal & Plastic Wheels)	.09 ea.
	PA10140	Metal Wheel	.06 ea.
	PA9990	Plastic Wheel	.03 ea.
	PA10238	Axle	.01 ea.

Link Couplers and Trucks no longer available,
Convert to knuckle couplers.

Price subject to change without notice.

DIA. NO.	PART NO.	DESCRIPTION	PRICE
1	PA12A190	Smoke Stack	.03 ea.
2	XA10886-RP	Boiler Assy. w/trimmings NOT AVAILABLE	
		Substitute with XA10886-GRP	4.41 ea.
3	PA8999	14 Volt Lamp	.30 ea.
4	XA10890	Lamp Bracket Assy.	.22 ea.
5	S230-B	Screw	.01 ea.
	XA10887	Crosshead Guide & Pilot Truck (Consists of Parts 6-7-8-9)	.84 ea.
6	PA10707	Stud	.07 ea.
7	PA10887	Crosshead	.21 ea.
8	PA5035-A	Washer	.06 dz.
9	XA10012	Front Truck Assy.	.44 ea.
	PA9990-A	Front Truck Wheel Only	.12 ea.
10	XA10506	Chassis Assy. w/bushings only	1.46 ea.
10A	XA13A865	Flanged Wheel	.37 ea.
10B	XA10009-C1	Flangeless Wheel & Stud	.35 ea.
10C	XA13A864	Pul-Mor Wheel Assy.	.80 ea.
11	PA3769	Washer	.01 ea.
12	S14	Screw	.01 ea.
14	PA10005	Plain Axle NOT AVAILABLE	
		Substitute with PA15A226 Axle	.05 ea.
15	S16-C	Screw	.12 dz.
16	PA9280-A	Side Rod	.16 ea.
17	PA7421	Screw	.03 ea.
18	PA7237	Piston Rod Spacer	.02 ea.
19	PA5447	Screw	.04 ea.
20	S271	Screw	.02 ea.
21	PA10017	Grease Pan	.07 ea.
22	PA10672	Worm Gear (Motor)	.06 ea.
23	PA10006	Worm Gear Axle NOT AVAILABLE	
		Substitute with PA15A281 Axle	.07 ea.
24	PA10518-A	Piston	.29 ea.
25	PA10520	Piston Pin	.03 ea.
26	PA10514	Piston Lever	.14 ea.
27	PA10671	Worm Gear (Smoke Drive)	.32 ea.
28	PA10162	Worm Gear Stud	.08 ea.
29	XA9547	Magnet Assy.	1.22 ea.
30	PA10766	Washer	.01 ea.
31	XA11077	Armature Assy.	2.41 ea.
32	XA9565-A	Brush Bracket Assy.	1.00 ea.
33	PA10754	Brush Cap	.02 ea.
34	PA9603	Carbon Brush	.13 ea.
35	S295	Screw	.02 ea.
36	PA10757-A	Brush Spring	.02 ea.
	XA10513	Chassis Smoke Box Assy. NOT AVAILABLE	
		Substitute with XA13B894RP Smoke Box	2.13 ea.

Cont'd

DIA. NO.	PART NO.	DESCRIPTION	PRICE
37	PA10513	Chassis Smoke Box NOT AVAILABLE	
		Substitute with PA13B894 Smoke Box	.76 ea.
		PA14A209 Separator	.02 ea.
38	XA10523	Heating Element & Plate Assy. NOT AVAILABLE	
		Substitute with XA14A208 Element & Plate Assy.	.91 ea.
39	S183	Screw	.01 ea.
40	PA10889	Connecting Rod	.09 ea.
40A	PA10888	Crosshead	.08 ea.
41	XA10662-A	Jack Panel	.24 ea.
42	XA10663	Male Plug	.24 ea.
43	PA10511-C	4 Conductor Cable	.13 ea.
44	PA4356	Rubber Grommet	.02 ea.
45	XA9461-B	Tender Body Assy. NOT AVAILABLE	
		Substitute with PA12D078A Tender Body	.70 ea.
46	XA9612-CRP	Top Finger Unit	.33 ea.
47	XA9612-BRP	Bottom Finger Unit	.33 ea.
48	XA8716	Drum Only	.95 ea.
49	XA10587-E	Remote Control Unit	4.04 ea.
50	PA11685	Resistor	.29 ea.
51	PA11A991	Condenser NOT AVAILABLE	
		Substitute with PA14A914 Condenser	1.40 ea.
52	XA11710	Speaker NOT AVAILABLE	
		Substitute with XA14A127 Speaker	4.48 ea.
53	PA11664	Receiver Insulation NOT AVAILABLE	
54	W37	Rubber Washer	.03 dz.
55	PA10235-A	Truck Rivet	.07 ea.
56	PA10209	Insulating Bushing	.02 ea.
57	PA10590	Tender Chassis NOT AVAILABLE	
		Substitute with PA12B080 Tender Chassis	.17 ea.
58	N1A	Nut	.01 ea.
59	PA8715-B	Washer	.02 ea.
60	W46	Lockwasher	.06 ea.
61	PA4939	Truck Stud	.05 ea.
	XA11718	Truck & Coupler Assy. NOT AVAILABLE	
62	XA10891	Coupler & Yoke Assy.	.36 ea.
	PA10019-A	Rear Truck Wheel Only	.06 ea.
63	PA10751	Stud	.02 ea.
64	PA1067-A	Washer	.06 dz.
65	PA1312	Insulating Bushing	.12 dz.
66	XA11712	Front Truck Assy. NOT AVAILABLE	
67	XA11714	Rear Truck Assy. NOT AVAILABLE	
68	XA10469	Coupler & Weight NOT AVAILABLE	
	PA10692	Coupler & Weight Only NOT AVAILABLE	
69	PA10467	Coupler Pin NOT AVAILABLE	
70	PA10207	Contact Spring	.02 ea.
71	PA1405	Washer	.01 ea.
72	XA10238	Wheel & Axle Assy. (metal & plastic wheels)	.09 ea.
	PA10140	Metal Wheel	.06 ea.
	PA9990	Plastic Wheel	.03 ea.
	PA10238	Axle	.01 ea.

Link Couplers & Trucks no longer available,
Convert to knuckle Couplers

Prices subject to change without notice

NO.	PART NO.	DESCRIPTION	PRICE
1	PA12A190	Smoke Stack	.03 ea.
2	XA11736ERP	Boiler Assy. Marked 21085	2.09 ea.
3	PA8999	14 Volt Lamp	.32 ea.
4	XA10890	Lamp Bracket Assembly	.23 ea.
5	S230-B	Screw	.01 ea.
	XA10887	Crosshead Guide & Pilot Truck (Consists of Parts 6-7-8-9)	.88 ea.
6	PA10707	Stud	.07 ea.
7	PA10887	Crosshead	.22 ea.
8	PA5035-A	Washer	.06 dz.
9	XA10012	Front Truck Assembly	.46 ea.
	PA9990-A	Front Truck Wheel Only	.13 ea.
10	PA10506-A	Chassis Assy. w/bushings only	1.87 ea.
10A	XA13A865	Flanged Wheel	.39 ea.
10B	XA10009-C1	Flangeless Wheel & Stud	.37 ea.
10C	XA13A864	Pul-Mor Wheel Assembly	.84 ea.
11	PA3769	Washer	.01 ea.
12	S14	Screw	.01 ea.
14	PA15A226	Plain Axle	.05 ea.
15	S16-C	Screw	.13 dz.
16	PA9280-A	Side Rod	.17 ea.
17	PA7421	Screw	.03 ea.
18	PA7237	Piston Rod Spacer	.02 ea.
19	PA5447	Screw	.04 ea.
20	S271	Screw	.02 ea.
21	PA10017	Grease Pan	.07 ea.
22	PA10672	Worm Gear (Motor)	.06 ea.
23	PA15A281	Worm Gear Axle	.07 ea.
24	PA10518-A	Piston	.30 ea.
25	PA10520	Piston Pin	.03 ea.
26	PA10514	Piston Lever	.15 ea.
27	PA10671	Worm Gear (Smoke Drive)	.34 ea.
28	PA10162	Worm Gear Stud	.08 ea.
29	XA9547	Magnet Assembly	1.28 ea.
30	PA10766	Washer	.01 ea.
31	XA11077	Armature Assembly	3.56 ea.
32	XA9565-A	Brush Bracket Assembly	1.05 ea.
33	PA10754	Brush Cap	.02 ea.
34	PA9603	Carbon Brush	.14 ea.
35	S295	Screw	.02 ea.
36	PA10757-A	Brush Spring	.02 ea.
37	XA13B894-RP	Smoke Box	2.24 ea.
38	XA14A208A	Heating Element & Plate Assy.	.96 ea.
39	S183	Screw	.01 ea.
40	PA10889	Connecting Rod	.09 ea.
40A	PA10888	Crosshead	.08 ea.
41	XA10662-A	Jack Panel	.25 ea.
42	XA10663	Male Plug	.25 ea.

Cond't

 Ref: Form No. 1813; Oct. 1, 1962

NO.	PART NO.	DESCRIPTION	PRICE
43	XA13A208-A	4 Conductor Cable (Plastic)	.04 ft.
44	PA4356	Rubber Grommet	.02 ea.
45		Tender Body - Obsolete No Longer Available - No Substitute	
46	XA9612-CRP	Top Finger Unit	.35 ea.
47	XA9612-BRP	Bottom Finger Unit	.35 ea.
48	XA8716	Drum Only	1.00 ea.
49	XA10587-E	Remote Control Unit	4.24 ea.
50	PA11685	Resistor	.30 ea.
51	PA14A914	Condenser Substitute for PA11A991 OBSOLETE	1.47 ea.
52	XA14A127	Conversion Speaker Substitute for XA11710 Speaker OBSOLETE	4.91 ea.
53		Receiver Insulation- OBSOLETE	
54	W37	Rubber Washer	.03 dz.
55	PA10235-A	Truck Rivet	.07 ea.
56	PA10209	Insulating Bushing	.02 ea.
57		Tender Chassis - Obsolete - No Longer Available - No Substitute	
58		Nut - NOT USED	
59	PA8715-B	Washer	.02 ea.
60	W46	Lock Washer	.01 ea.
61	PA4939	Truck Stud	.06 ea.
62	XA10891	Coupler & Yoke Assembly	.38 ea.
	PA10019-A	Rear Truck Wheel Only	.06 ea.
63	PA10751	Stud	.02 ea.
64	PA1067-A	Washer	.06 dz.
65	PA1312	Insulating Bushing	.13 dz.
66		Front Truck Assy. OBSOLETE	
67		Rear Truck Assy. OBSOLETE	
68		Coupler & Weight OBSOLETE	
69		Coupler Pin OBSOLETE	
70	PA10207	Contact Spring	.02 ea.
71	PA1405	Washer	.01 ea.
72	XA10238	Wheel & Axle Assy. (Metal & Plastic Wheels)	.09 ea.
	PA10140	Metal Wheel	.06 ea.
	PA9990	Plastic Wheel	.03 ea.
	PA10238	Axle	.01 ea.

Prices subject to change without notice.

NO.	PART NO.	DESCRIPTION	PRICE
1	PA12A190	Smoke Stack	.03 ea.
2	XA10886-DRP	Boiler Assy. Marked w/293	3.71 ea.
3	PA8999	14 Volt Lamp	.32 ea.
4	XA10890	Lamp Bracket Assembly	.23 ea.
5	S230-B	Screw	.01 ea.
	XA10887	Crosshead Guide & Pilot Truck (Consists of Parts 6-7-8-9)	.88 ea.
6	PA10707	Stud	.07 ea.
7	PA10887	Crosshead	.22 ea.
8	PA5035-A	Washer	.13 dz.
9	XA10012	Front Truck Assembly	.46 ea.
	PA9990-A	Front Truck Wheel Only	.13 ea.
10	PA10506-A	Chassis Assy.	1.87 ea.
10A	XA13A865	Flanged Wheel	.39 ea.
10B	XA10009-C1	Flangeless Wheel & Stud	.37 ea.
10C	XA13A864	Pul-Mor Wheel Assembly	.84 ea.
11	PA3769	Washer	.01 ea.
12	S14	Screw	.01 ea.
14	PA15A226	Plain Axle	.05 ea.
15	S16-C	Screw	.13 dz.
16	PA9280-A	Side Rod	.17 ea.
17	PA7421	Screw	.03 ea.
18	PA7237	Piston Rod Spacer	.02 ea.
19	PA5447	Screw	.04 ea.
20	S271	Screw	.02 ea.
21	PA10017	Grease Pan	.07 ea.
22	PA10672	Worm Gear (Motor)	.06 ea.
23	PA15A281	Worm Gear Axle	.07 ea.
24	PA10518-A	Piston	.30 ea.
25	PA10520	Piston Pin	.03 ea.
26	PA10514	Piston Lever	.15 ea.
27	PA10671	Worm Gear (Smoke Drive)	.34 ea.
28	PA10162	Worm Gear Stud	.08 ea.
29	XA9547	Magnet Assembly	1.28 ea.
30	PA10766	Washer	.01 ea.
31	XA11077	Armature Assembly	3.56 ea.
32	XA9565-A	Brush Bracket Assembly	1.05 ea.
33	PA10754	Brush Cap	.02 ea.
34	PA9603	Carbon Brush	.14 ea.
35	S295	Screw	.02 ea.
36	PA10757-A	Brush Spring	.02 ea.
*37	XA13B894RP	Smoke Box Assembly	2.24 ea.
38	XA14A208A	Heating Element & Plate Assy.	.96 ea.
39	S183	Screw	.01 ea.
40	PA10889	Connecting Rod	.09 ea.
40A	PA10888	Crosshead	.08 ea.
41	XA10662-A	Jack Panel	.25 ea.
42	XA10663	Male Plug	.25 ea.

Cont'd

NO.	PART NO.	DESCRIPTION	PRICE
43	PA13A208A	4 Conductor Cable (Plastic)	.04 ft.
44	PA4356	Rubber Grommet	.02 ea.
45		Tender Body - Obsolete - No Longer Available - No Substitute	
46	XA9612-CRP	Top Finger Unit	.35 ea.
47	XA9612-BRP	Bottom Finger Unit	.35 ea.
48	XA8716	Drum Only	1.00 ea.
49	XA10587-E	Remote Control Unit	4.24 ea.
50	PA11685	Resistor	.30 ea.
51	PA14A914	Condenser Substitute for PA11A991 Condenser Obsolete	1.47 ea.
52	XA14A127	Conv. Speaker Substitute for XA11710 Speaker - OBSOLETE	4.91 ea.
53		Receiver Insulation - OBSOLETE	
54	W37	Rubber Washer	.03 dz.
55	PA10235-A	Truck Rivet	.07 ea.
56	PA10209	Insulating Bushing	.02 ea.
57		Tender Chassis - OBSOLETE - No Longer Available - No Substitute	
58	N1A	Nut	.01 ea.
59	PA8715-B	Washer	.02 ea.
60	W46	Lock Washer	.01 ea.
61	PA4939	Truck Stud	.06 ea.
62	XA10891	Coupler & Yoke Assembly	.38 ea.
	PA10019-A	Rear Truck Wheel Only	.06 ea.
63	PA10751	Stud	.02 ea.
64	PA1067-A	Washer	.06 dz.
65	PA1312	Insulating Bushing	.13 dz.
66		Front Truck Assembly - OBSOLETE	
67		Rear Truck Assembly - OBSOLETE	
68		Coupler and Weight - OBSOLETE Coupler and Weight Only - OBSOLETE	
69		Coupler Pin - OBSOLETE	
70	PA10207	Contact Spring	.02 ea.
71	PA1405	Washer	.01 ea.
72	XA10238	Wheel & Axle Assy. (Metal and Plastic Wheels)	.09 ea.
	PA10140	Metal Wheel	.06 ea.
	PA9990	Plastic Wheel	.03 ea.
	PA10238	Axle	.01 ea.

* #37 When using XA13B894RP Smoke Box Assembly remove screw on Solder Terminal.

Prices subject to change without notice.

LOCOMOTIVE AND TENDER WITH PISTON-TYPE SMOKE AND CHOO-CHOO UNIT

Model No. 290, 21085 (1959-60)(1961-62)

SPECIFICATIONS

Tested at: 12 Volts A.C. .... using 140" oval of track.

(A) Motor to be tested with Remote Control Unit at 12 Volts, and not to draw more than 1.7 amps.

(B) Locomotive to run a minimum of 9 R.P.M. or 9 times forward, around 140" oval of track per minute.

(C) Locomotive to run a minimum of 8.5 R.P.M. or 8½ times reverse, around 140" oval of track per minute.

Load: Not to draw more than 2.1 amps. while pulling 4 Box Cars.

Motor: Universal A.C. or D.C.

 Ref: Form No. M2819; June 1, 1950

LOCOMOTIVE AND TENDER WITH PISTON-TYPE SMOKE AND CHOO-CHOO UNIT

Model No. 290

SPECIFICATIONS

Tested at: 12 Volts A.C. .... using 140" oval of track.

(A) Motor to be tested with Remote Control Unit at 12 Volts, and not to draw more than 1.7 amps.

(B) Locomotive to run a minimum of 9 R.P.M. or 9 times forward, around 140" oval of track per minute.

(C) Locomotive to run a minimum of 8.5 R.P.M. or 8½ times reverse, around 140" oval of track per minute.

Load: Not to draw more than 2.1 amps. while pulling 4 Box Cars.

Motor: Universal A.C. or D.C.

Ref: Form No. 1814; Feb. 1, 1957

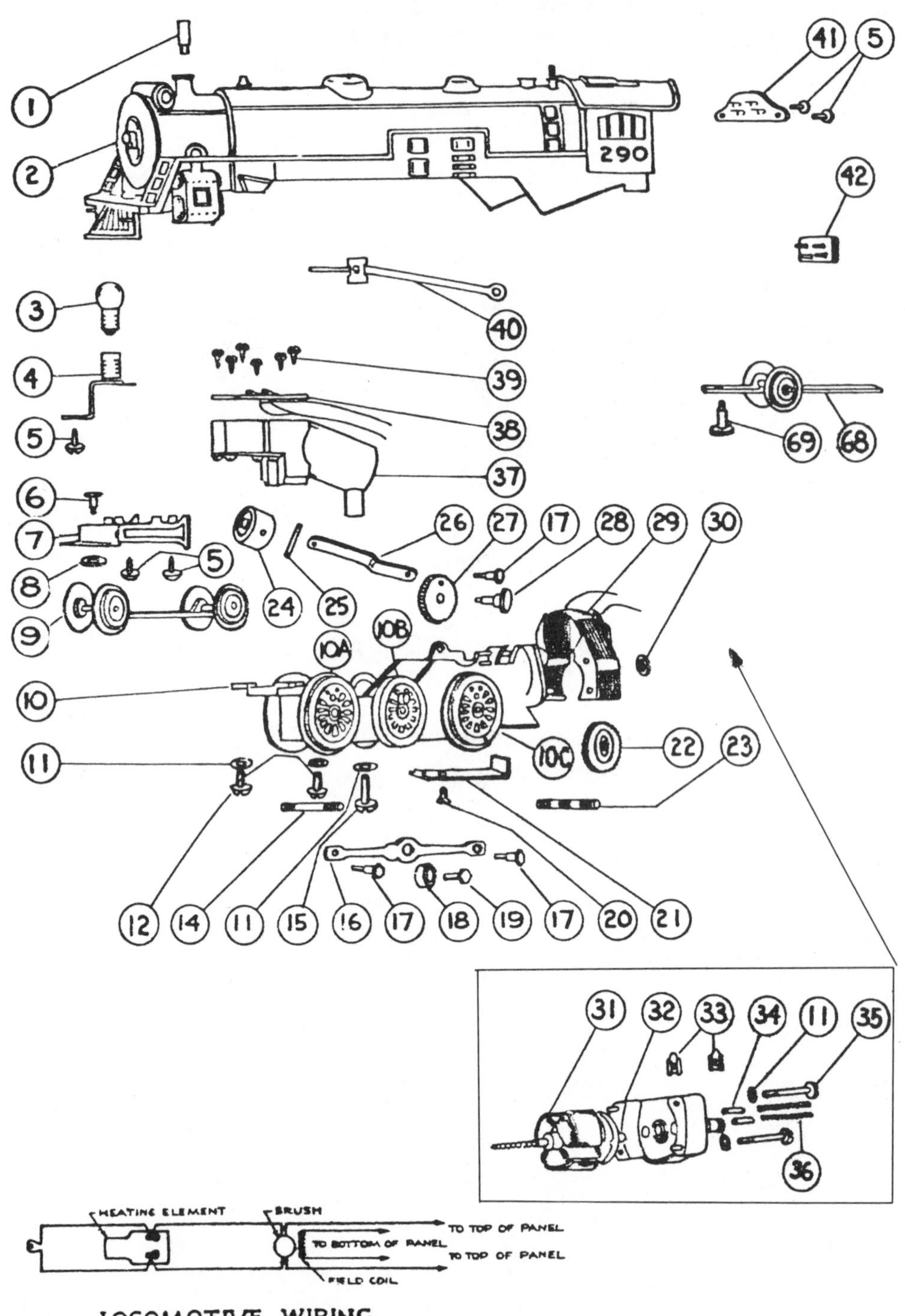

LOCOMOTIVE WIRING

 Ref: Form No. M2819, June 1, 1950

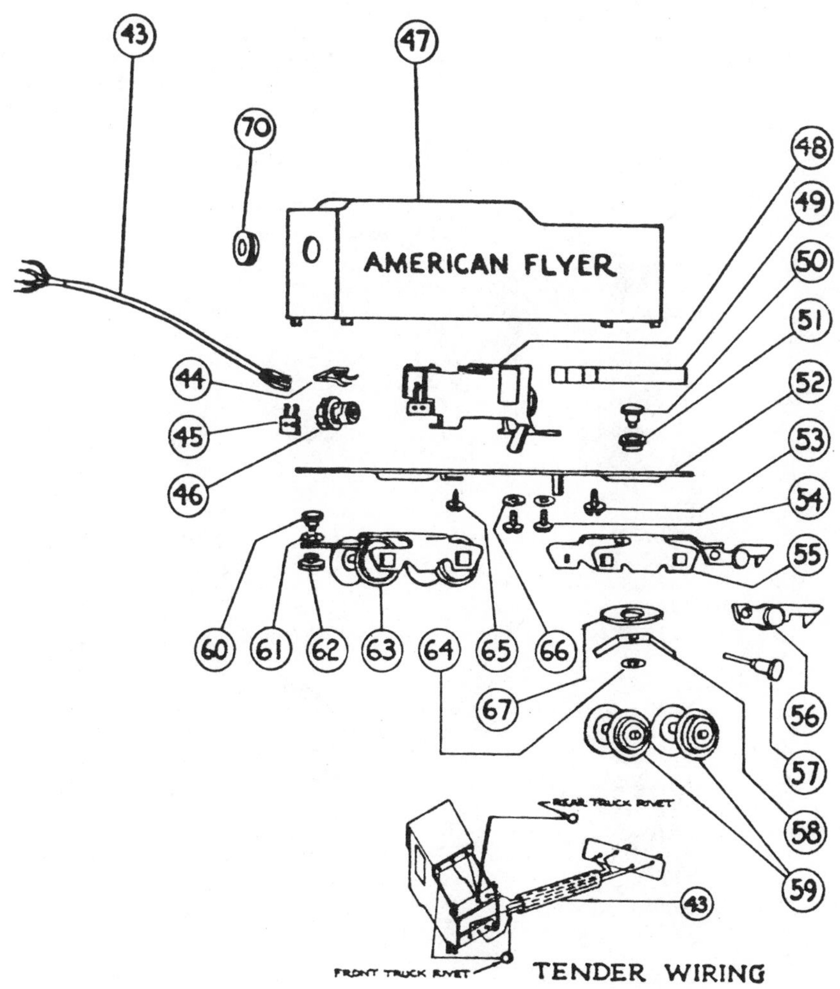

TENDER WIRING

Ref: Form No. M2819, June 1, 1950

Diagram Number	Part No.	Description	Price
1	PA12A190	Smoke Stack	$ .02 ea.
2	XA10886-A	Boiler Assembly	2.22 "
3	PA8999	14 Volt Lamp....................	.25 "
4	XA10890	Lamp Bracket Assembly............	.28 "
5	S230-B	Screw	.10 dz.
	XA10887	Crosshead Guide and Pilot Truck Assembly (consists of parts 6-7-8-9)	.60 ea.
6	PA10707	Stud	.05 "
7	PA10887	Crosshead	.15 "
8	PA5035-A	Washer	.11 dz.
9	XA10012	Front Truck Assembly.	.40 ea.
	PA9990-A	Front Truck Wheel only...........	.11 "
10	*XA10506	Chassis Assembly with bushings only.	1.37 "
10A	XA13A865	Flanged Wheel	.29 "
10B	XA10009-C1	Flangeless Wheel and Stud.........	.32 "
10C	XA13A864	Pull-Mor Wheel	.51 "
11	PA3769	Washer	.05 dz.
12	S14	Screw	.05 "
14	PA10005	Plain Axle	.10 ea.
15	S16-C	Screw	.11 dz.
16	PA9280-A	Side Rod	.10 ea.
17	PA7421	Screw	.30 dz.
18	PA7237	Piston Rod Spacer...............	.05 ea.
19	PA5447	Screw	.30 dz.
20	S271	Screw	.10 "
21	PA10017	Grease Pan	.04 ea.
22	PA10672	Worm Gear (motor)...............	.20 "
23	PA10006	Worm Gear Axle..................	.10 "
24	PA10518-A	Piston	.17 "
25	PA10520	Piston Pin	.05 "
26	PA10514	Piston Lever	.08 "
27	PA10671	Worm Gear (smoke drive)..........	.27 "
28	PA10162	Worm Gear Stud..................	.05 "
29	XA9547	Magnet Assembly A.C.............	1.11 "
30	PA10766	Washer	.05 dz.
31	XA11077	Armature Assembly A.C............	2.19 ea.
	XA9569	Armature Assembly A.C.......NOT AVAILABLE	
32	XA9565-A	Brush Bracket Assembly...........	.71 "
33	PA10754	Brush Cap	.02 "
34	PA9603	Carbon Brush A.C................	.15 "
35	S295	Screw	.02 "
36	PA10757-A	Brush Spring	.05 "
	**XA10513	Chassis Smoke Box Assembly (consists of parts 37-38-39). NOT AVAILABLE	
37	**PA10513	Chassis Smoke Box........ NOT AVAILABLE	
38	***XA10523	Heating Element & Plate Assembly..	.66 ea.
39	S183	Screw	.10 dz.
40	PA10889	Connecting Rod	.11 ea.
41	XA10662-A	Jack Panel	.22 ea.

All prices subject to change without notice.

Diagram Number	Part No.	Description	Price
42	XA10663	Male Plug	$ .22 ea.
43	PA10511-C	4 Conductor Cable	.12 "
44	XA9612-CRP	Top Finger Unit (Remote Control)	.30 "
45	XA9612-BRP	Bottom Finger Unit (Remote Control)	.30 "
46	XA8716	Drum (Remote Control)	.59 "
47	****	Tender Body Assembly (NOT AVAILABLE)	
48	XA10587	Remote Control Unit	1.32 "
49	PA10593	Tender Weight	.24 "
50	PA10235-A	Truck Rivet	.03 "
51	PA10209	Insulating Bushing	.02 "
52	****	Tender Chassis (NOT AVAILABLE)	
53	S184	Screw	.10 dz.
54	S-O	Screw	.05 "
55	XA11582	Rear Truck Assembly w/o wheels	.24 ea.
56	XA10469	Coupler and weight	.17 "
	PA10692	Coupler weight only	.05 "
57	PA10467	Coupler Pin	.11 "
58	PA10207	Contact Spring	.02 "
59	XA10238	Wheel and Axle Assembly	.17 set
	PA10140	Metal Wheel	.15 ea.
	PA9990	Plastic Wheel	.05 "
	PA10238	Axle	.02 "
	XA10891-A	Truck & Coupler Assembly (consists of parts 60-61-62-63-68)	.89 "
60	PA10751	Stud	.02 "
61	PA1067-A	Washer	.05 dz.
62	PA1312	Insulating Bushing	.11 "
63	XA11582-A	Front Truck Assembly w/o wheels	.24 ea.
64	PA1405	Washer	.05 dz.
65	S230-B	Screw	.10 "
66	W46	Lockwasher	.05 "
67	PA8715-B	Washer	.05 "
68	XA10891	Coupler & Yoke Assembly	.33 ea.
	PA10019-A	Rear Truck wheel only	.05 "
69	PA4939	Truck Stud	.05 "
70	PA4356	Rubber Grommet	.02 "

*XA10506 Chassis Assembly is not sold as a complete assembly with wheels.

**Parts so marked NOT AVAILABLE, substitute with:

Dia. 37	XA13B894RP	Smoke Box Assy. (new style)	$1.55 ea.
	PA13B894	Smoke Box (new style)	.59 "
	PA14A209	Separator (new style)	.01 "

***The XA10523 Heating Element and Plate Assy. is still available, and interchangeable with the new style PA13B894 Smoke Box. The new style XA14A208 Heating Element and Plate Assembly, priced at $.66 each, is used only on the new style PA13B894 Smoke Box.

****Parts so marked NOT AVAILABLE substitute with:

Dia. 47	PA12D078-A	Tender Body	$ .64 ea.
Dia. 52	PA12B080	Tender Chassis	.20 "

Ref: Form No. M2819, June 1, 1950

DIA. NO.	PART NO.	DESCRIPTION
1	PA10536	SMOKE STACK
2	XA10886-A	BOILER ASSEMBLY
3	PA8999	14 VOLT BULB
4	XA10890	LAMP BRACKET ASSEMBLY
5	S230-B	SCREW
	XA10887	CROSSHEAD GUIDE AND PILOT TRUCK ASSEMBLY (PARTS 6-7-8-9)
6	PA10707	STUD
7	PA10887	CROSSHEAD GUIDE
8	PA5035-A	WASHER
9	XA10012	FRONT TRUCK ASSEMBLY
	PA9990-A	FRONT TRUCK WHEEL
10	XA10506	CHASSIS ASSEMBLY WITH BUSHINGS
10A	XA10009	FLANGED WHEEL WITH TAPPED HOLE
10B	XA10009-C1	FLANGELESS WHEEL AND STUD
11	PA3769	WASHER
12	S14	SCREW
13	S46	SCREW
14	PA10005	PLAIN AXLE
15	S16-C	SCREW
16	PA9280-A	SIDE ROD
17	PA7421	SCREW
18	PA7237	PISTON ROD SPACER
19	PA5447	SCREW
20	S271	SCREW
21	PA10017	GREASE PAN
22	PA10672	WORM GEAR (MOTOR)
23	PA10006	WORM GEAR AXLE
	XA10514	PISTON AND LEVER ASSEMBLY (PARTS 24-25-26)
24	PA10518	PISTON
25	PA10520	PISTON PIN
26	PA10514	PISTON LEVER
27	PA10671	WORM GEAR (SMOKE DRIVE)
28	PA10162	WORM GEAR STUD
29	XA9547	MAGNET ASSEMBLY A.C.
30	PA10766	WASHER
31	XA11077	ARMATURE ASSEMBLY A.C.
	XA9569	ARMATURE ASSEMBLY A.C.
32	XA9565-A	BRUSH BRACKET ASSEMBLY
33	PA10754	BRUSH CAP
34	PA9603	CARBON BRUSH A.C.
35	S295	SCREW
36	PA10757	BRUSH SPRING
	XA10513	CHASSIS SMOKE BOX ASSEMBLY (PARTS 37-38-39)
37	PA10513	CHASSIS SMOKE BOX
38	XA10523	HEATING ELEMENT AND PLATE ASSEMBLY
39	S183	SCREW
40	PA10889	CONNECTING ROD
40A	PA10888	CROSSHEAD
41	XA10662	JACK PANEL
42	XA10663	MALE PLUG
43	PA10511-C	4 CONDUCTOR CABLE
44	XA9612-CRP	TOP FINGER UNIT

 Ref: New, June 1, 1950

DIA. NO.	PART NO.	DESCRIPTION
45	XA9612-BRP	BOTTOM FINGER UNIT
46	XA8716	DRUM
47	XA9461-B	TENDER BODY ASSEMBLY
48	XA10587	REMOTE CONTROL UNIT
49	PA10593	TENDER WEIGHT
50	PA10235-A	TRUCK RIVET
51	PA10209	INSULATING BUSHING
52	PA10590	TENDER CHASSIS
53	S184	SCREW
54	S0	SCREW
55	XA9987-C	REAR TRUCK ASSEMBLY
56	XA10469	COUPLER AND WEIGHT
	PA10692	COUPLER WEIGHT
57	PA10467	COUPLER PIN
58	PA10207	CONTACT SPRING
59	XA10140	WHEEL AND AXLE ASSEMBLY
	PA10140	BRASS WHEEL
	PA9990	PLASTIC WHEEL
	PA9989	AXLE
	XA10891-A	TRUCK AND COUPLER ASSEMBLY (PARTS 60-61-62-63-68)
60	PA10751	STUD
61	PA1067-A	WASHER
62	PA1312	INSULATING BUSHING
63	XA9987-G	FRONT TRUCK ASSEMBLY
64	PA1405	WASHER
65	S230-B	SCREW
66	W46	LOCK WASHER
67	PA8715-B	WASHER
68	XA10891	COUPLER AND YOKE ASSEMBLY
	PA10019-A	REAR TRUCK WHEEL
69	PA4939	TRUCK STUD
70	PA4356	RUBBER GROMMET

* *

NOTES

NOTE 1: PART NUMBER XA10506, CHASSIS ASSEMBLY, DIA. NO. 10, IS NOT SOLD AS A COMPLETE ASSEMBLY WITH WHEELS.

NOTE 2: PART NUMBER XA11077, ARMATURE ASSEMBLY, DIA. NO. 31, WITH 1/16" OIL SLINGER CANNOT BE USED WITH XA9565-A BRUSH BRACKET ASSEMBLY MANUFACTURE BEFORE OCTOBER 1949, UNLESS YOU GRIND 1/16" OFF THE BOSS WHICH THE BEARING SETS INTO ON THE BRUSH BRACKET ASSEMBLY.

NOTE 3: PART NUMBER XA9569, ARMATURE ASSEMBLY, DIA. NO. 31, CAN BE USED WITH XA9565-A BRUSH BRACKET ASSEMBLY MANUFACTURED AFTER OCTOBER 1949 PROVIDING THAT YOU USE 1/16" WASHER TO TAKE UP END PLAY.

DIA. NO.	PART NO.	DESCRIPTION	PRICE
1	PA12A190	Smoke Stack	.03 ea.
2	XA10886-A	Boiler Assy. NOT AVAILABLE	
		Substitute with XA10886-FRP	4.41 ea.
3	PA8999	14 Volt Lamp	.30 ea.
4	XA10890	Lamp Bracket Assembly	.22 ea.
5	S230-B	Screw	.01 ea.
	XA10887	Crosshead Guide and Pilot Truck Assy. (Consists of Parts 6-7-8-9)	.84 ea.
6	PA10707	Stud	.07 ea.
7	PA10887	Crosshead	.21 ea.
8	PA5035-A	Washer	.12 dz.
9	XA10012	Front Truck Assembly	.44 ea.
	PA9990-A	Front Truck Wheel Only	.12 ea.
10	XA10506-A	Chassis Assembly with Bushings Only	1.78 ea.
10A	XA13A865	Flanged Wheel	.37 ea.
10B	XA10009-C1	Flangeless Wheel and Stud	.35 ea.
10C	XA13A864	Pul-Mor Wheel	.80 ea.
11	PA3769	Washer	.01 ea.
12	S14	Screw	.01 ea.
14	PA10005	Plain Axle NOT AVAILABLE	
		Substitute with PA15A226	.05 ea.
15	S16-C	Screw	.12 dz.
16	PA9280-A	Side Rod	.16 ea.
17	PA7421	Screw	.03 ea.
18	PA7237	Piston Rod Spacer	.02 ea.
19	PA5447	Screw	.04 ea.
20	S271	Screw	.02 ea.
21	PA10017	Grease Pan	.07 ea.
22	PA10672	Worm Gear (Motor)	.06 ea.
23	PA10006	Worm Gear Axle NOT AVAILABLE	
		Substitute with PA15A821 Axle	.07 ea.
24	PA10518-A	Piston	.29 ea.
25	PA10520	Piston Pin	.03 ea.
26	PA10514	Piston Lever	.14 ea.
27	PA10671	Worm Gear (Smoke Drive)	.32 ea.
28	PA10162	Worm Gear Stud	.08 ea.
29	XA9547	Magnet Assembly A. C.	1.22 ea.
30	PA10766	Washer	.01 ea.
31	XA11077	Armature Assembly A. C.	3.39 ea.
	XA9569	Armature Assembly A. C. NOT AVAILABLE	
32	XA9565-A	Brush Bracket Assembly	1.00 ea.
33	PA10754	Brush Cap	.02 ea.
34	PA9603	Carbon Brush A. C.	.13 ea.
35	S295	Screw	.02 ea.
36	PA10757-A	Brush Spring	.02 ea.
	XA10513	Chassis Smoke Box Assembly NOT AVAILABLE	
		Substitute with XA13B894RP Smoke Box Assy. (New Style)	2.13 ea.
37	PA10513	Chassis Smoke Box NOT AVAILABLE	
		Substitute with PA13B894 Smoke Box (New Style)	.76 ea.
		PA14A209 Separator (New Style)	.02 ea.
38	XA10523	Heating Element & Plate Assy. NOT AVAILABLE	
		Substitute with XA14A208A H. element & Plate	.91 ea.
39	S183	Screw	.01 ea.
40	PA10889	Connecting Rod	.09 ea.

Cont'd

DIA. NO.	PART NO.	DESCRIPTION	PRICE
41	XA10662-A	Jack Panel	.24 ea.
42	XA10663	Male Plug	.24 ea.
43	PA10511-C	4 Conductor Cable	.13 ea.
44	XA9612-CRP	Top Finger Unit (Remote Control)	.33 ea.
45	XA9612-BRP	Bottom Finger Unit (Remote Control)	.33 ea.
46	XA8716	Drum (Remote Control)	.95 ea.
47	XA9461-B	Tender Body Assy. NOT AVAILABLE	
		Substitute with PA12D078-A Tender Body	.70 ea.
48	XA10587	Remote Control Unit	4.04 ea.
49	PA10593	Tender Weight	.26 ea.
50	PA10235-A	Truck Rivet	.07 ea.
51	PA10209	Insulating Bushing	.02 ea.
52	PA10590	Tender Chassis NOT AVAILABLE	
		Substitute with PA12B080 Tender Chassis	.17 ea.
53	S184	Screw	.02 ea.
54	S-0	Screw	.01 ea.
55	XA11582	Rear Truck Assy. w/o wheels NOT AVAILABLE	
56	XA10469	Coupler & Weight NOT AVAILABLE	
	PA10692	Coupler Weight Only NOT AVAILABLE	
57	PA10467	Coupler Pin NOT AVAILABLE	
58	PA10207	Contact Spring	.02 ea.
59	XA10238	Wheel & Axle Assy.	.09 ea.
	PA10140	Metal Wheel	.06 ea.
	PA9990	Plastic Wheel	.03 ea.
	PA10238	Axle	.01 ea.
	XA10891-A	Truck & Coupler Assy. NOT AVAILABLE (Consists of Parts 60-61-62-63-68)	
60	PA10751	Stud	.02 ea.
61	PA1067-A	Washer	.06 dz.
62	PA1312	Insulating Bushing	.12 dz.
63	XA11582-A	Front Truck Assy. w/o wheels NOT AVAILABLE	
64	PA1405	Washer	.01 ea.
65	S230-B	Screw	.01 ea.
66	W46	Lockwasher	.01 ea.
67	PA8715-B	Washer	.02 ea.
68	XA10891	Coupler & Yoke Assy.	.36 ea.
	PA10019-A	Rear Truck Wheel Only	.06 ea.
69	PA4939	Truck Stud	.06 ea.
70	PA4356	Rubber Grommet	.02 ea.

Link Couplers & trucks no longer available
Convert to Knuckle Couplers.

Prices subject to change without notice

NO.	PART NO.	DESCRIPTION	PRICE
1	PA12A190	Smoke Stack	.03 ea.
2	XA10886-DRP	Boiler Assy. (Marked w/293)	3.71 ea.
3	PA8999	14 Volt Lamp	.32 ea.
4	XA10890	Lamp Bracket Assembly	.23 ea.
5	S230-B	Screw	.01 ea.
	XA10887	Crosshead Guide & Pilot Truck Assy (Consists of Parts 6-7-8-9)	.88 ea.
6	PA10707	Stud	.07 ea.
7	PA10887	Crosshead	.22 ea.
8	PA5035-A	Washer	.13 dz.
9	XA10012	Front Truck Assembly	.46 ea.
	PA9990-A	Front Truck Wheel Only	.13 ea.
10	PA10506-A	Chassis Assy.	1.87 ea.
10A	XA13A865	Flanged Wheel	.39 ea.
10B	XA10009-C1	Flangeless Wheel and Stud	.37 ea.
10C	XA13A864	Pul-Mor Wheel	.84 ea.
11	PA3769	Washer	.01 ea.
12	S14	Screw	.01 ea.
14	PA15A226	Plain Axle	.05 ea.
15	S16-C	Screw	.13 dz.
16	PA9280-A	Side Rod	.17 ea.
17	PA7421	Screw	.03 ea.
18	PA7237	Piston Rod Spacer	.02 ea.
19	PA5447	Screw	.04 ea.
20	S271	Screw	.02 ea.
21	PA10017	Grease Pan	.07 ea.
22	PA10672	Worm Gear (Motor)	.06 ea.
23	PA15A281	Worm Gear Axle	.07 ea.
24	PA10518-A	Piston	.30 ea.
25	PA10520	Piston Pin	.03 ea.
26	PA10514	Piston Lever	.15 ea.
27	PA10671	Worm Gear (Smoke Drive)	.34 ea.
28	PA10162	Worm Gear Stud	.08 ea.
29	XA9547	Magnet Assembly A.C.	1.28 ea.
30	PA10766	Washer	.01 ea.
31	XA11077	Armature Assembly A.C.	3.56 ea.
	XA9569	Armature Assembly A.C. NOT AVAILABLE	
32	XA9565-A	Brush Bracket Assembly	1.05 ea.
33	PA10754	Brush Cap	.02 ea.
34	PA9603	Carbon Brush A.C.	.14 ea.
35	S295	Screw	.02 ea.
36	PA10757-A	Brush Spring	.02 ea.
#37	XA13B894RP	Smoke Box Assembly	2.24 ea.
38	XA14A208-A	Heating Element & Plate	.96 ea.
39	S183	Screw	.01 ea.
40	PA10889	Connecting Rod	.09 ea.

Cont'd

 Ref: Form No. 1814; Oct. 1, 1962

NO.	PART NO.	DESCRIPTION	PRICE
41	XA10662-A	Jack Panel	.25 ea.
42	XA10663	Male Plug	.25 ea.
43	PA13A208-A	4 Conductor Cable (Plastic)	.04 ft.
44	XA9612-CRP	Top Finger Unit (Remote Control)	.35 ea.
45	XA9612-BRP	Bottom Finger Unit (Remote Control)	.35 ea.
46	XA8716	Drum (Remote Control)	1.00 ea.
47		Tender Body - Obsolete - No Longer Available - No Substitute	
48	XA10587	Remote Control Unit	4.24 ea.
49	PA10593	Tender Weight	.27 ea.
50	PA10235-A	Truck Rivet	.07 ea.
51	PA10209	Insulating Bushing	.02 ea.
52		Tender Chassis - Obsolete No Longer Available - No Substitute	
53	S184	Screw	.02 ea.
54	S-0	Screw	.01 ea.
55	XA12A050-B	Rear Truck w/Knuckle Coupler Substitute for XA11A582 OBSOLETE	.83 ea.
56		Coupler & Weight OBSOLETE	
57		Coupler Pin OBSOLETE	
58	PA10207	Contact Spring	.02 ea.
59	XA10238	Wheel & Axle Assembly	.09 ea.
	PA10140	Metal Wheel	.06 ea.
	PA9990	Plastic Wheel	.03 ea.
	PA10238	Axle	.01 ea.
60	PA10751	Stud	.02 ea.
61	PA1067-A	Washer	.06 dz.
62	PA1312	Insulating Bushing	.13 dz.
63	XA15B800	Front Truck Substitute for XA11582-A Front Truck - OBSOLETE	.45 ea.
64	PA1405	Washer	.01 ea.
65	S230-B	Screw	.01 ea.
66	W46	Lock Washer	.01 ea.
67	PA8715-B	Washer	.02 ea.
68	XA15A784	Draw Bar Assy. Used w/XA15B800 Truck Assembly	.23 ea.
	XA10891	Coupler & Yoke Assy. Used w/XA11A582 Truck - OBSOLETE	.38 ea.
	PA10019-A	Rear Truck Wheel Only	.06 ea.
69	PA4939	Truck Stud	.06 ea.
70	PA4356	Rubber Grommet	.02 ea.

*Dia. 37 - When using XA13B894RP Smoke Box Assembly remove screw on Solder Terminal.

Prices subject to change without notice

LOCOMOTIVE AND TENDER WITH PISTON-TYPE SMOKE, CHOO-CHOO UNIT, AND PULL-MOR

Model No. 293

SPECIFICATIONS

Tested at: 12 Volts A.C. .... using 140″ oval of track.

(A) Motor to be tested with Remote Control Unit at 12 Volts, and not to draw more than 1.7 amps.

(B) Locomotive to run a minimum of 9 R.P.M. or 9 times forward, around 140″ oval of track per minute.

(C) Locomotive to run a minimum of 8.5 R.P.M. or 8½ times reverse, around 140″ oval of track per minute.

Load: Not to draw more than 2.1 amps. while pulling 4 Box Cars.

Motor: Universal A.C. or D.C.

 Ref: Form No. 1494; Dec. 15, 1953

LOCOMOTIVE AND TENDER WITH PISTON-TYPE SMOKE, CHOO-CHOO UNIT, AND PULL-MOR

Model Nos. 293, 21095, 21099

SPECIFICATIONS

Tested at: 12 Volts A.C. .... using 140″ oval of track.

(A) Motor to be tested with Remote Control Unit at 12 Volts, and not to draw more than 1.7 amps.

(B) Locomotive to run a minimum of 9 R.P.M. or 9 times forward, around 140″ oval of track per minute.

(C) Locomotive to run a minimum of 8.5 R.P.M. or 8½ times reverse, around 140″ oval of track per minute.

Load: Not to draw more than 2.1 amps. while pulling 4 Box Cars.

Motor: Universal A.C. or D.C.

Ref: Form No. 1812; Feb. 1, 1957

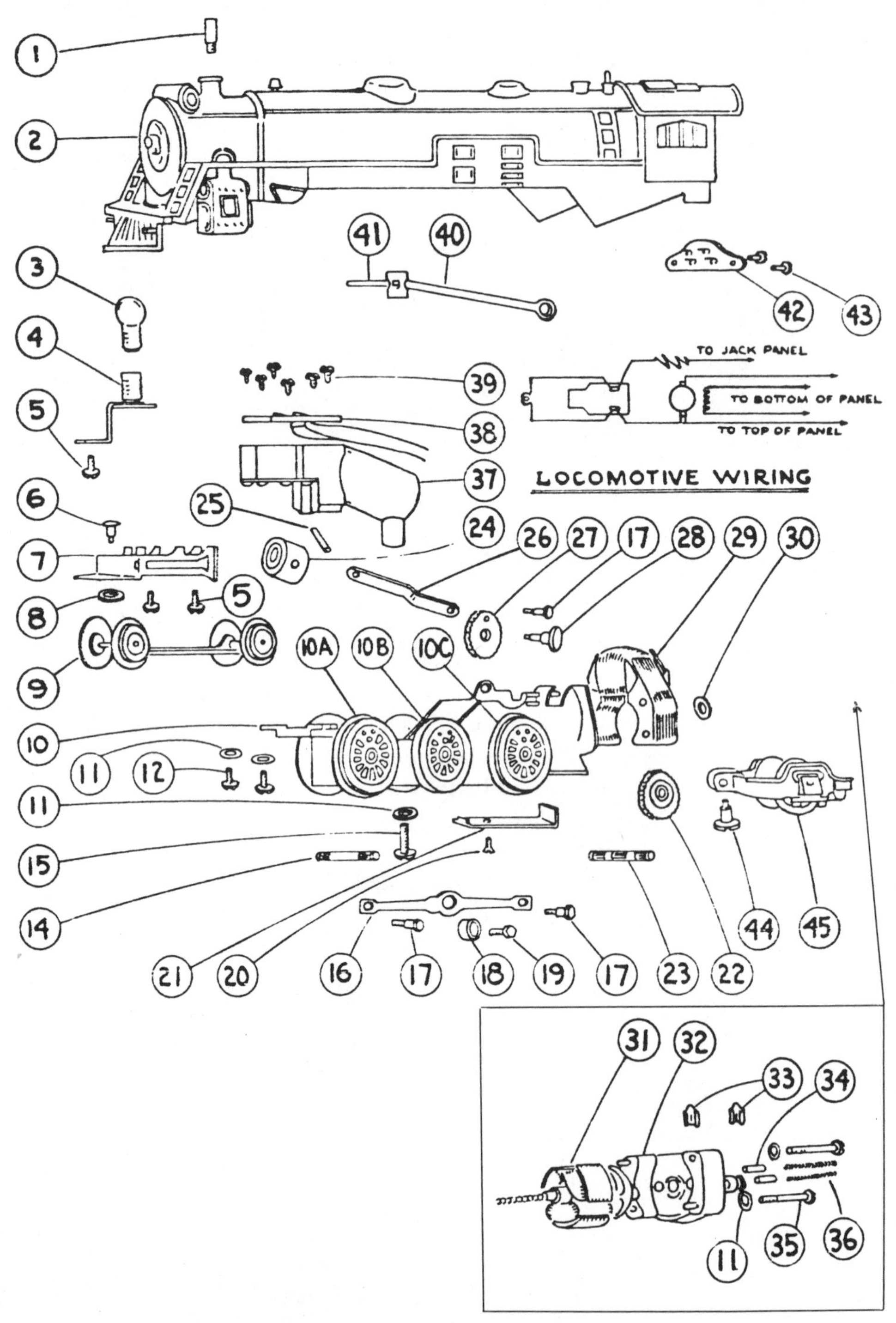

 Ref: Form No. 1494; Dec. 15, 1953

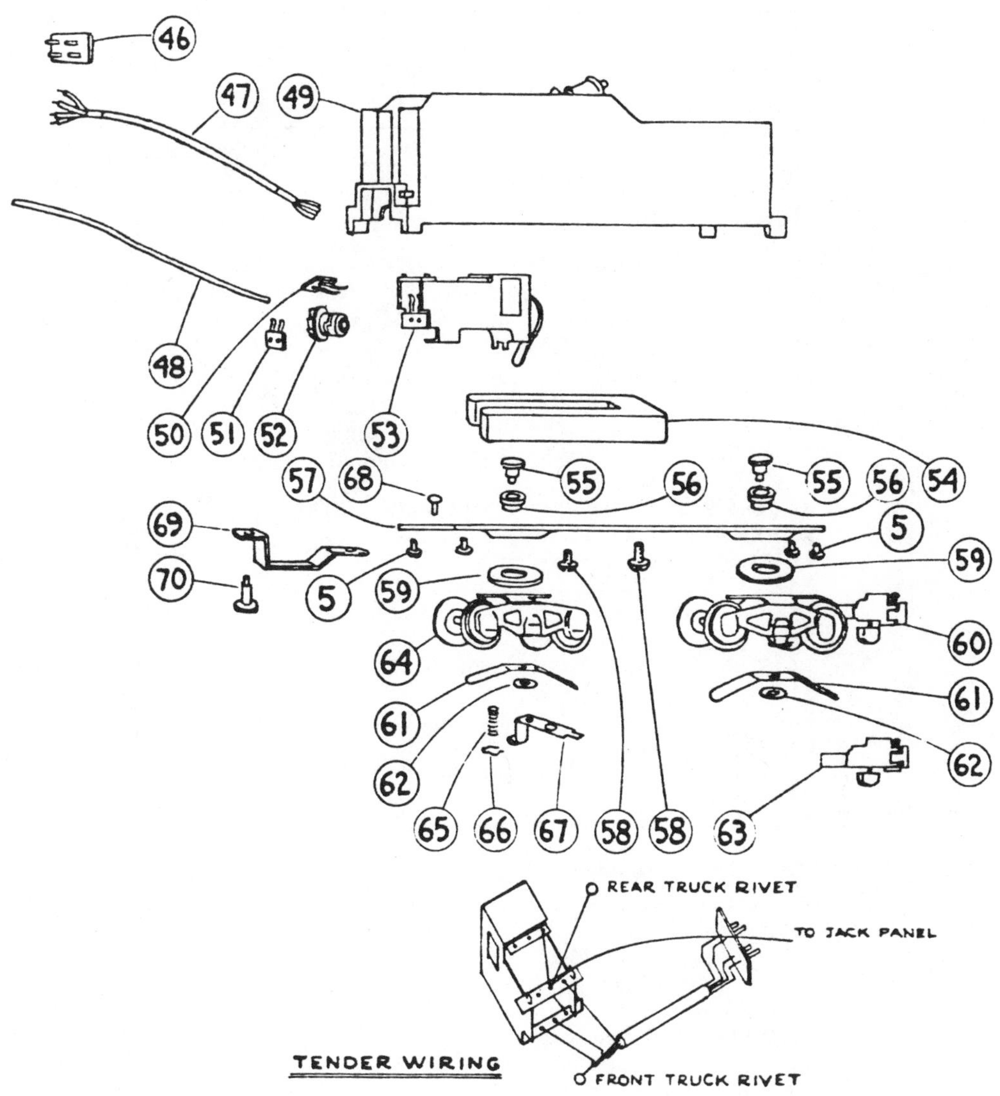
46
47
49
48
50
51
52
53
54
57
68
55
56
55
56
54
69
5
59
70
5
59
64
60
61
61
62
62
65
66
67
58
58
63
REAR TRUCK RIVET
TO JACK PANEL
TENDER WIRING
FRONT TRUCK RIVET

Diagram Number	Part No.	Description	Price
1	PA12A190	Smoke Stack	$ .02 ea.
2	XA10A886-D	Boiler Assembly	2.00 "
3	PA8999	Bulb	.25 "
4	XA10890	Lamp Bracket	.25 "
5	S230-B	Screw	.10 dz.
	XA10887	Crosshead Guide & Pilot Truck Assembly (consists of parts 6-7-8-9)	.60 ea.
6	PA10707	Stud	.05 "
7	PA10887	Crosshead	.15 "
8	PA5035-A	Washer	.10 dz.
9	XA10012	Front Truck Assembly	.40 ea.
	PA9990-A	Front Truck wheel only	.10 "
10	PA10506	Chassis	1.20 "
10A	XA12A449	Flanged Wheel with tapped hole	.40 "
10B	XA10009-C1	Flangless Wheel and Stud	.40 "
10C	XA12A447	Pull-Mor Wheel	.52 "
11	PA3769	Washer	.05 dz.
12	S14	Screw	.05 "
13	S46	Screw	.05 "
14	PA10005	Plain Axle	.10 ea.
15	S16-C	Screw	.10 dz.
16	PA9280-A	Side Rod	.20 ea.
17	PA7421	Screw	.30 dz.
18	PA7237	Piston Rod Spacer	.05 ea.
19	PA5447	Screw	.30 dz.
20	S271	Screw	.10 "
21	PA10017	Grease Pan	.02 ea.
22	PA10672	Worm Gear (motor)	.30 "
23	PA10006	Worm Gear Axle	.10 "
	XA10514	Piston & Lever Assembly (consists of parts 24-25-26)	.40 "
24	PA10518-A	Piston	.20 "
25	PA10520	Piston Pin	.05 "
26	PA10514	Piston Lever	.05 "
27	PA10671	Worm Gear (smoke drive)	.40 "
28	PA10162	Worm Gear Stud	.10 "
29	XA9547	Magnet Assembly A.C.	1.00 "
30	PA10766	Washer	.05 dz.
31	XA11077	Armature Assembly A.C.	2.50 ea.
32	XA9565-A	Brush Bracket Assembly	.50 "

Diagram Number	Part No.	Description	Price
33	PA10754	Brush Cap	.02 ea.
34	PA9603	Carbon Brush AC	.15 ″
35	S295	Screw	.10 ″
36	PA10757-A	Brush Spring	.05 ″
	XA10513	Chassis Smoke Box Assembly (consists of parts 37-38-39)	2.00 ″
37	PA10513	Chassis Smoke Box	1.00 ″
38	XA10523	Heating Element & Plate Assembly	1.00 ″
39	S183	Screw	.10 dz.
40	PA10889	Connecting Pod	.15 ea.
41	PA10888	Crosshead	.05 ″
42	XA10662-A	Jack Panel	.20 ″
43	S222	Screw	.01 ″
44	PA4939	Truck Stud	.05 ″
45	XA10020	Rear Truck Assembly	.70 ″
46	XA10663	Male Plug	.20 ″
47	PA10511-C	4 Conductor Cable	.12 ″
48	PA10249-T	9″ Lead Wire	.02 ″
49	XA12A081RP	Tender Body Assembly w/trimmings	1.00 ″
50	XA9612-C	Top Finger Unit (Remote Control)	.50 ″
51	XA9612-B	Bottom Finger Unit (Remote Control)	.50 ″
52	XA8716	Drum (Remote Control)	.60 ″
53	XA10587-E	Remote Control Unit	2.50 ″
54	PA11A926	Tender Weight	.18 ″
55	PA10235-A	Truck Rivet	.03 ″
56	PA10209	Insulating Bushing	.02 ″
57	PA12B080	Tender Chassis	.30 ″
58	S184	Screw	.10 dz.
59	PA8715-B	Washer	.05 ″
60	XA12A350	Rear Truck Assembly	.87 ea.
61	PA10207	Contact Spring	.02 ″
62	PA1405	Washer	.05 dz.
63	XA12A047	Knuckle Coupler	.22 ea.
64	XA12A516	Front Truck Assembly	.60 ea.
65	PA11A956	Spring	.01 ″
66	PA11A944	Hair Pin Cotter	.01 ″
67	PA11A936	Tender Pick-up	.02 ″
68	PA4366	Rivet	.24 dz.
69	PA12A520	Coupler Strap	.02 ea.
70	PA4938	Screw	.30 dz.

NO.	PART NO.	DESCRIPTION	PRICE
1	PA12A190	Smoke Stack	.03 ea.
2	XA10A886-DRP	Boiler Assembly	3.71 ea.
3	PA8999	Bulb	.32 ea.
4	XA10890	Lamp Bracket	.23 ea.
5	S230-B	Screw	.01 ea.
	XA10887	Crosshead Guide & Pilot Truck Assy. (Consists of Parts 6-7-8-9)	.88 ea.
	PA8887	Cone Spring	.02 ea.
6	PA10707	Stud	.07 ea.
7	PA10887	Crosshead Guide	.22 ea.
8	PA5035-A	Washer	.06 dz.
9	XA10012	Front Truck Assembly	.46 ea.
	PA9990-A	Front Truck Wheel Only	.13 ea.
10	PA10506-A	Chassis	1.87 ea.
10A	XA13A865	Flanged Wheel	.39 ea.
10B	XA10009-C1	Flangeless Wheel and Stud	.37 ea.
10C	XA13A864	Pul-Mor Wheel	.84 ea.
11	PA3769	Washer	.01 ea.
12	S14	Screw - 6-32 R.H.	.01 ea.
14	PA15A226	Plain Axle	.05 ea.
15	S16-C	Screw	.13 dz.
16	PA9280-A	Side Rod	.17 ea.
17	PA7421	Screw	.03 ea.
18	PA7237	Piston Rod Spacer	.02 ea.
19	PA5147	Screw	.04 ea.
20	S271	Screw	.02 ea.
21	PA10017	Grease Pan	.07 ea.
22	PA10672	Worm Gear (Motor)	.06 ea.
23	PA15A281	Worm Gear Axle	.07 ea.
24	PA10518-A	Piston	.30 ea.
25	PA10520	Piston Pin	.03 ea.
26	PA10514	Piston Lever	.15 ea.
27	PA10671	Worm Gear (Smoke Drive)	.34 ea.
28	PA10162	Worm Gear Stud	.08 ea.
29	XA9547	Magnet Assembly A.C.	1.28 ea.
30	PA10766	Washer	.01 ea.
31	XA11077	Armature Assembly A.C.	3.56 ea.
32	XA9565-A	Brush Bracket Assembly	1.05 ea.
33	PA10754	Brush Cap	.02 ea.
34	PA9603	Carbon Brush A.C.	.14 ea.
35	S295	Screw	.02 ea.
36	PA10757-A	Brush Spring	.02 ea.
*37	XA13B894RP	Smoke Box Assembly	2.24 ea.
38	XA14A208-A	Heating Element & Plate Assy.	.96 ea.
39	S183	Screw	.01 ea.
40	PA10889	Connecting Rod	.09 ea.
41	PA10888	Crosshead	.08 ea.
42	XA10662-A	Jack Panel	.25 ea.

Cont'd

NO.	PART NO.	DESCRIPTION	PRICE
43	S230-B	Screw	.01 ea.
44	PA4939	Truck Stud	.06 ea.
45	XA15A261	Truck Assembly	.72 ea.
		Substitute for XA10020 Truck Assy.	OBSOLETE
46	XA10663	Male Plug	.25 ea.
47	PA13A208-A	4 Conductor Cable (Plastic)	.04 ft.
48	PA10249	Lead Wire	.02 ea.
49		Tender Body - Obsolete - No Longer Available - No Substitute	
50	XA9612-CRP	Top Finger Unit (Remote Control)	.35 ea.
51	XA9612-BRP	Bottom Finger Unit (Remote Control)	.35 ea.
52	XA8716	Drum (Remote Control)	1.00 ea.
53	XA10587-E	Remote Control Unit	4.24 ea.
54	PA10593	Tender Weight	.27 ea.
55	PA10235-A	Truck Rivet	.07 ea.
56	PA10209	Insulating Bushing	.02 ea.
57		Tender Chassis - Obsolete - No Longer Available - No Substitute	
58	S184	Screw	.02 ea.
59	PA8715-B	Washer	.02 ea.
60	XA12A350	Rear Truck Assembly	.84 ea.
61	PA10207	Contact Spring	.02 ea.
62	PA1405	Washer	.01 ea.
63	XA12A047	Knuckle Coupler	.30 ea.
64	XA12A516	Front Truck Assembly	.46 ea.
65	PA11A956	Spring	.02 ea.
66	PA11A944	Hair Pin Cotter	.01 ea.
67	PA11A936	Tender Pick-Up	.04 ea.
68	PA4366	Rivet	.01 ea.
69	PA12A520	Coupler Strap	.04 ea.
70	PA4938	Screw	.04 ea.

* #37 When using XA13B894RP Smoke Box Assembly remove screw on Solder Terminal.

Prices subject to change without notice.

LOCOMOTIVE AND TENDER WITHOUT SMOKE AND CHOO-CHOO UNIT

Model No. 300

SPECIFICATIONS

Tested at: 12 Volts A.C. .... using 140" oval of track.

(A) Motor to be tested with Remote Control Unit at 12 Volts and not to draw more than 1.5 amps.

(B) Locomotive to run a minimum of 9 R.P.M. or 9 times forward, around 140" oval of track per minute.

(C) Locomotive to run a minimum of 8.5 R.P.M. or 8½ times reverse, around 140" oval of track per minute.

Load: Not to draw more than 1.75 amps. while pulling 4 Box Cars.

Motor: Universal A.C. or D.C.

 Ref: Form No. M2820; June 1, 1950

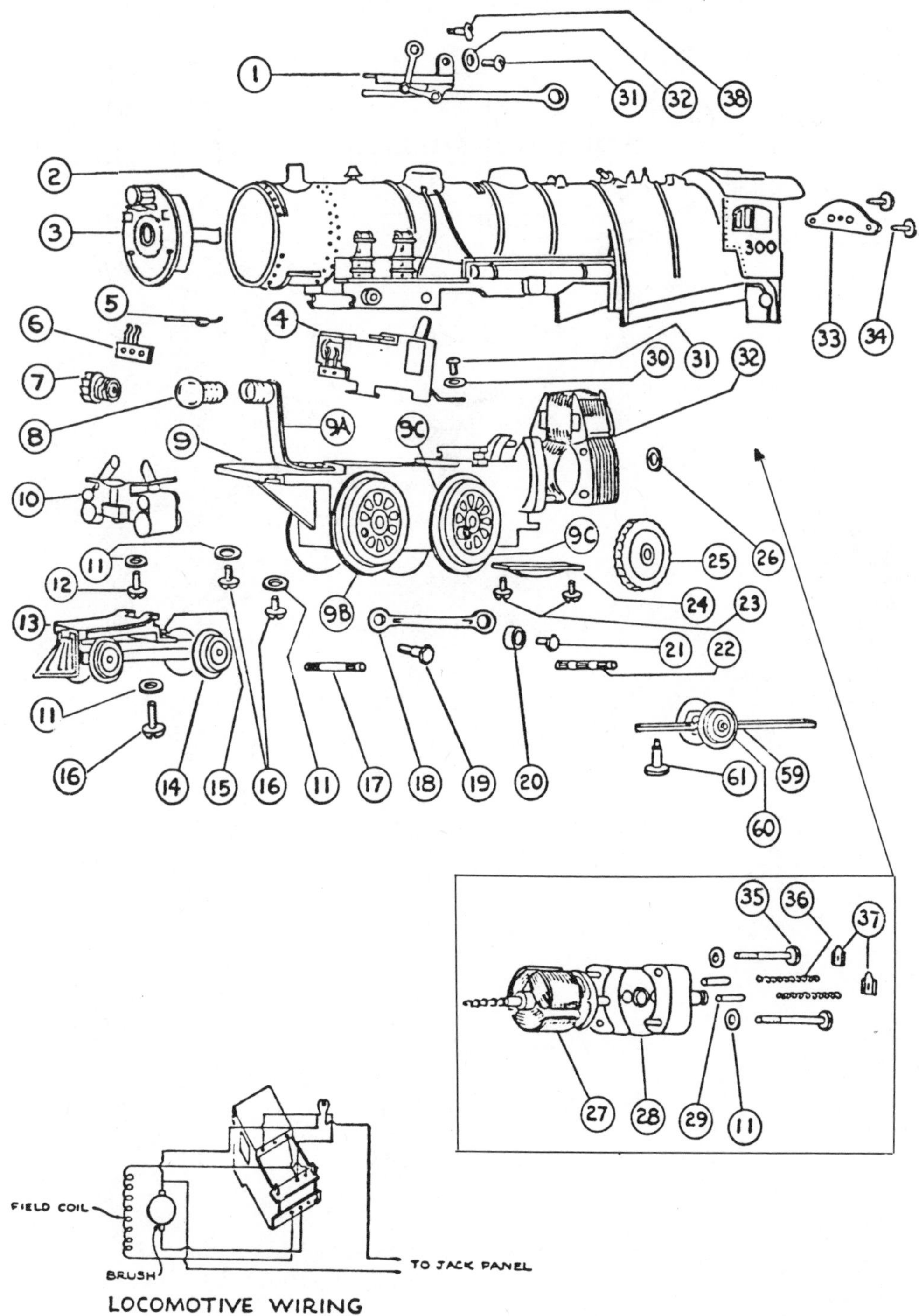

Ref: Form No. M2820; June 1, 1950

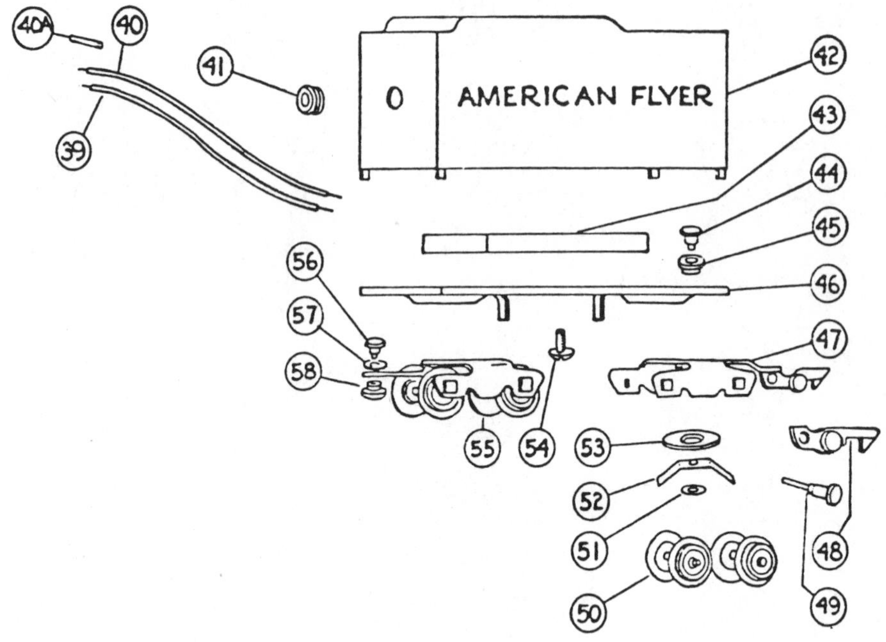
40A
40
39
41
0
AMERICAN FLYER
42
43
44
45
46
47
56
57
58
55
54
53
52
51
50
48
49

Diagram Number	Part No.	Description	Price
1	XA10669 R or L	Crosshead Assembly (Right or Left)	$ .50 ea.
2	XA9443-B	Boiler Assembly	2.00 "
3	XA9444-C	Boiler Front Assembly	.30 "
4	XA10587-B	Remote Control Unit	2.50 "
5	XA9612-C	Top Finger Unit (Remote Control)	.50 "
6	XA9612-B	Bottom Finger Unit (Remote Control)	.50 "
7	XA8716	Drum (Remote Control)	.60 "
8	PA8999	14 Volt Lamp	.25 "
9	*XA10075	Chassis Assembly with bushings only	.90 "
9A	XA9592	Lamp Bracket Assembly only	.25 "
9B	XA10009-1	Flanged Wheel with tapped hole	.40 "
9C	.XA10009-A1	Flanged Wheel and Stud	.40 "
10	PA10076	Cylinder & Steamchest	.70 "
11	PA3769	Lockwasher	.05 dz.
12	S16	Screw	.05 "
	XA10081-A	Front Truck & Pilot Assembly (consists of parts 13-14-15)	1.10 ea.
13	PA9446	Pilot	.70 "
14	XA10081	Front Truck Assembly	.40 "
	PA9990-A	Front Truck wheel only	.10 ea.
15	PA4360	Rivet	.05 dz.
16	S14	Screw	.05 "
17	PA10005	Plain Axle	.10 ea.
18	PA9452	Side Rod	.20 "
19	PA7421	Screw	.30 dz.
20	PA7237	Piston Rod Spacer	.05 ea.
21	PA5447	Screw	.30 dz.
22	PA10006	Worm Gear Axle	.10 ea.
23	S230-B	Screw	.10 dz.
24	PA10080	Motor Cover Plate	.02 ea.
25	PA10672	Worm Gear (motor)	.30 "
26	PA10766	Washer	.05 dz.
27	**XA11077	Armature Assembly A.C.	2.50 ea.
	*** XA9569	Armature Assembly A.C.	2.50 "
28	XA9565-A	Brush Bracket Assembly	.50 "
29	PA9603	Carbon Brush A.C.	.15 "
30	W46	Washer	.03 dz.
31	S-1	Screw	.05 "
32	XA9547	Magnet Assembly A.C.	1.00 ea.
33	XA10287	Jack Panel	.20 "
34	S230-B	Screw	.10 dz.
35	S295	Screw	.10 ea.
36	PA10757	Brush Spring	.05 "

Ref: Form No. M2820; June 1, 1950

Diagram Number	Part No.	Description	Price
37	PA10754	Brush Cap	.02 ea.
38	PA9288	Screw	.30 dz.
39	P9273-K	5" Wire Lead	.02 ea.
40	P9273-J	9" Wire Lead	.02 ea.
40A	PA10291	Male Plug	.02 ea.
41	PA4356	Rubber Grommet	.02 "
42	XA9461	Tender Body	1.00 "
43	PA10058	Tender Weight	.35 "
44	PA10235-A	Truck Rivet	.03 "
45	PA10209	Insulating Bushing	.02 "
46	PA10590	Tender Chassis	.30 "
47	XA9987-C	Rear Truck Assembly with wheels	.75 "
48	XA10469	Coupler and Weight	.15 "
	PA10692	Weight only	.05 "
49	PA10467	Coupler Pin	.10 "
50	XA10140	Wheel & axle Assembly (brass & plastic wheels)	.25 set
	PA10140	Brass wheel	.15 ea.
	PA9990	Plastic wheel	.10 "
	PA9989	Axle	.02 "
51	PA1405	Washer	.05 dz.
52	PA10207	Contact Spring	.02 ea.
53	PA8715-B	Washer	.05 dz.
54	S184	Screw	.10 "
	XA10749-A	Truck & Coupler Assembly (consists of parts 55-56-57-58-59)	.80 ea.
55	XA9987-G	Front Truck Assembly with wheels	.50 "
56	PA10751	Stud	.02 "
57	PA1067A	Washer	.05 dz.
58	PA1312	Insulating Bushing	.10 "
59	XA10749	Coupler & Yoke Assembly	.30 ea.
60	PA10019-A	Rear Truck Wheel only	.10 "
61	PA4939	Truck Stud	.05 "

*XA10506 Chassis Assembly is not sold as a complete assembly with wheels.

**XA11077 Armature Assembly with 1/16" oil slinger cannot be used with XA9565-A Brush Bracket Assembly manufactured before Oct. 1949, unless you grind 1/16" off the boss which the bearing sets into on the Brush Bracket Assembly.

***XA9569 Armature Assembly can be used with XA9565-A Brush Bracket Assembly manufactured after Oct. 1949 providing that you use 1/16" washer to take up end play.

LOCOMOTIVE AND TENDER WITH CHOO-CHOO UNIT

Model No. 301

SPECIFICATIONS

Tested at: 12 Volts A.C. .... using 140″ oval of track.

(A) Motor to be tested with Remote Control Unit at 12 Volts and not to draw more than 1.5 amps.

(B) Locomotive to run a minimum of 9 R.P.M. or 9 times forward, around 140″ oval of track per minute.

(C) Locomotive to run a minimum of 8.5 R.P.M. or 8½ times reverse, around 140″ oval of track per minute.

Load: Not to draw more than 1.75 amps. while pulling 4 Box Cars.

Motor: Universal A.C. or D.C.

Ref: Form No. 1811; Feb 1, 1957

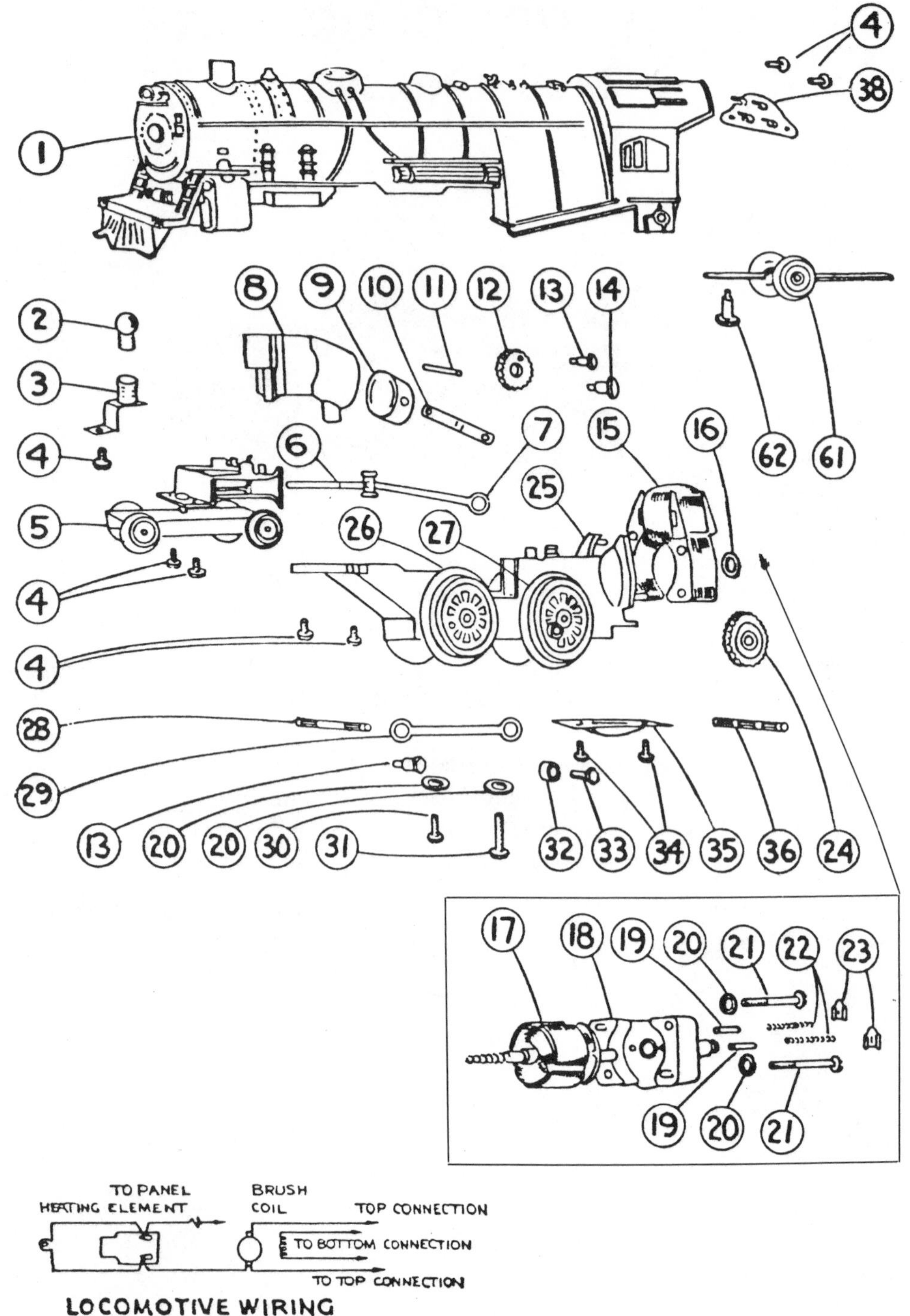

 Ref: Form No. 1811; Feb. 1, 1957

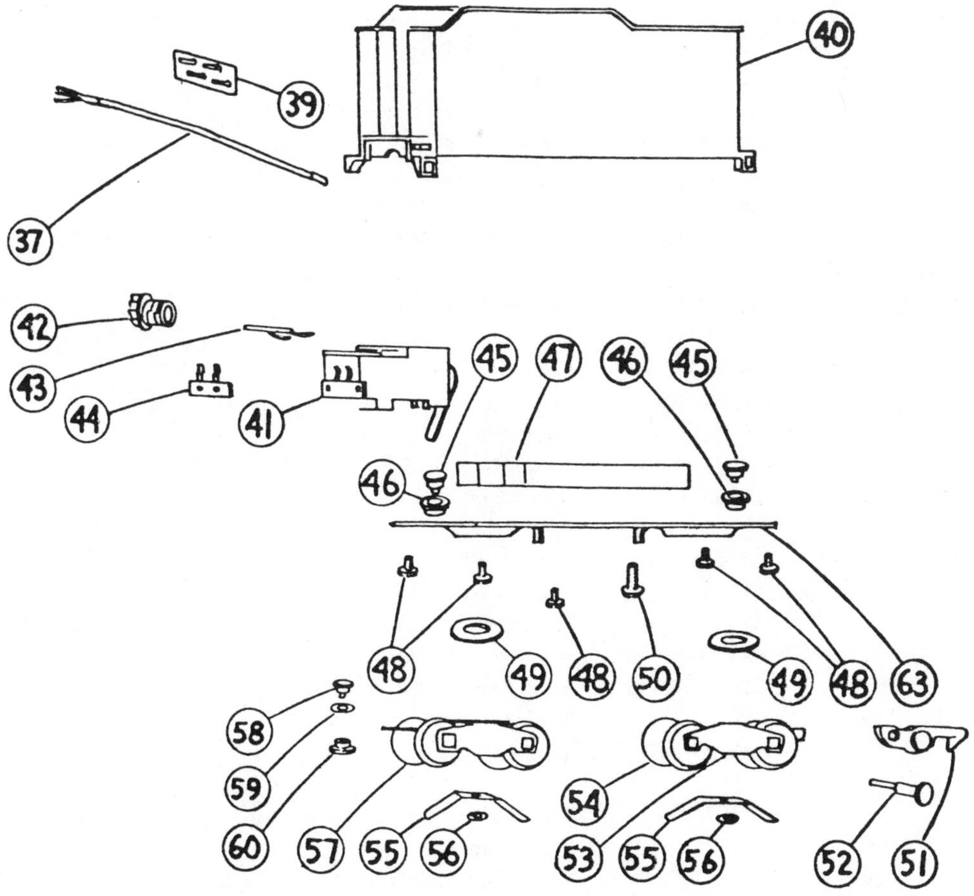

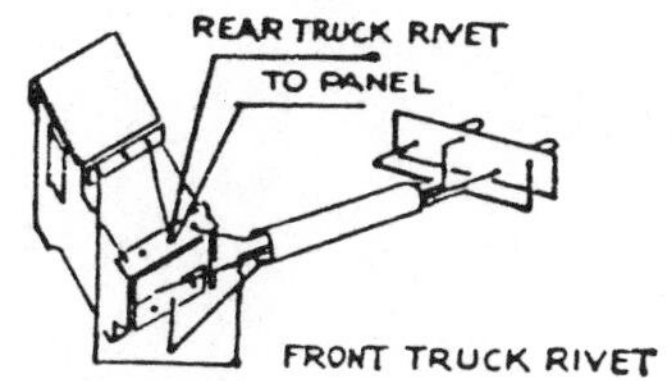

TENDER WIRING

Diagram Number	Part No.	Description	Price
1	XA11A975-RP	Boiler Assembly	$1.75 ea.
2	PA8999	Bulb	.25 "
3	XA10890	Lamp Bracket Assembly	.28 "
4	S230-B	Screw	.10 dz.
5	XA13A085	Guide & Truck Assy.	.44 ea.
	PA10887	Crosshead Guide	.15 "
	XA13A084	Pilot Truck	.21 "
	PA4367	Rivet	.01 "
6	PA11099	Crosshead	.05 "
7	PA10889	Connecting Rod	.11 "
8	XA12B438-RP	Choo-Choo Unit	.75 "
9	PA10518-A	Piston	.17 "
10	PA10517	Piston Lever	.08 "
11	PA10520	Piston Pin	.05 "
12	PA10671	Worm Gear	.27 "
13	PA7421	Screw	.30 dz.
14	PA10162	Worm Gear Stud	.05 ea.
15	XA9547	Magnet Assembly	1.11 "
16	PA10766	Armature Spacer	.05 dz.
17	XA11077	Armature Assembly	2.19 ea.
18	XA9565-A	Brush Bracket Assembly	.71 "
19	PA9603	Brush	.15 "
20	PA3769	Washer	.05 dz.
21	S295	Screw	.02 ea.
22	PA10757-A	Brush Spring	.05 "
23	PA10754	Brush Cap	.02 "
24	PA10672	Worm Gear (motor)	.20 "
25	PA10512	Chassis	1.23 "
26	XA13A865	Flanged Wheel Assembly	.29 "
27	XA13A866	Pull-Mor Wheel & Stud Assembly	.57 "
28	PA10005	Plain Axle	.10 "
29	PA9452	Side Rod	.10 "
30	S18	Screw	.05 dz.
31	S16-C	Screw	.11 "
32	PA7237	Piston Rod Spacer	.05 ea.
33	PA5447	Screw	.30 dz.

All prices subject to change without notice.

 Ref: Form No. 1811; Feb. 1, 1957

Diagram Number	Part No.	Description	Price
34	S230	Screw	$ .10 dz.
35	PA10080	Motor Cover Plate................	.02 ea.
36	PA10006	Gear Axle	.10 "
37	PA10511-C	4 Conductor Cable................	.12 "
38	XA10662-A	Jack Panel	.22 "
39	XA10663	Male Plug	.22 "
40	PA12D078	Tender Body	.73 "
41	XA10587-E	Remote Control Unit.............	1.32 "
42	XA8716	Drum only	.59 "
43	XA9612-CRP	Top Finger Unit.................	.30 "
44	XA9612-BRP	Bottom Finger Unit...............	.30 "
45	PA10235-A	Truck Rivet	.03 "
46	PA10209	Insulating Bushing	.02 "
47	PA11A926	Tender Weight	.32 "
48	S230-B	Screw	.10 dz.
49	PA8715-B	Washer	.05 "
50	S184	Screw	.10 "
51	XA10469	Coupler & Weight Assembly........	.17 ea.
52	PA10467	Coupler Pin	.11 "
53	XA11582	Rear Truck Frame Assy............	.24 "
54	XA10238	Wheel & Axle Assembly..........	.17 set
	PA9990	Plastic Wheel	.05 ea.
	PA10140	Metal Wheel	.15 "
	PA10238	Axle	.02 "
55	PA10207	Contact Spring	.02 "
56	PA1405	Tin Washer	.05 dz.
	XA11715	Front Truck & Yoke Assembly (consists of parts 57 to 61).......	.89 ea.
57	XA11582-A	Front Truck Frame Assy. w/o Wheels.	.24 "
58	PA10751	Stud	.02 "
59	PA1067-A	Washer	.05 dz.
60	PA1312	Insulating Bushing	.11 "
61	XA10749	Coupler & Yoke Assembly..........	.30 ea.
62	PA4939	Screw	.05 "
63	PA12B080	Tender Chassis	.20 "

SERVICE INSTRUCTIONS FOR NO. 301 LOCOMOTIVE AND TENDER WITH CHOO-CHOO

The first thing to do is to place Locomotive and Tender on track, connect Transformer and test for operation. Make sure all rods, linkage and other parts are not bent or broken. It is also important that the wheels on the Tender be clean to insure a good electrical contact.

1. If the Locomotive and Tender does not operate properly proceed as follows:

a. Remove screw (※62) and also Male Plug (※39) from the Jack Panel (※38).

b. Now take another similar tender with a Remote Control Unit in it which is in good working order and connect it to the Locomotive. In this way, you will be able to determine whether the Locomotive or Tender is defective.

2. If the trouble is in the Locomotive you can make the following checks:

a. Inspect Brushes for wear or poor contact and Brush Springs for position and proper tension.

b. Check wires and solder joints on Male Plug (※39) and Jack Panel (※38) for broken or loose connections.

c. Clean or polish commutator on Armature (※17) if dirty or worn.

3. If these initial steps do not correct the trouble it will be necessary to disassemble the Locomotive as follows:

a. Remove screws (※33) on each side and take off Rods (※7) and spacer (※32) from drive wheel (※27).

b. Take off Rear Truck (※61) by removing screw (※62).

c. Turn Locomotive upside down and remove two screws (※4) and you can now remove Motor Assembly from Boiler (※1).

d. Take off Lamp Bracket (※3) by removing Screw (※4).

e. To remove motor, push forward approximately a ¼" to clear clamp on Boiler (※1) and then lift rear of motor up and pull motor out.

f. The motor is now exposed and you can inspect the wiring and other points of the unit, making any necessary replacements.

4. When the trouble appears to be in the Tender proceed as follows:

a. Remove four S-0 Screws (※48) and take off Tender Body (※40).

b. Inspect wiring and solder joints for loose or broken connections.

c. Check Finger Units (※43) and (※44) on Remote Control Unit (※51) to see if they are burnt out or not making proper contact.

d. The drum (※42) should be checked to see if it is pitted or worn.

e. The pawl on the Remote Control Unit (※41) may be broken or need adjusting.

f. It is generally not necessary to replace the complete Remote Control Unit, but sometimes the Finger Units, the drum, or both need adjusting or replacing.

 Ref: Form No. 1811; Feb. 1, 1957

DIA. NO.	PART NO.	DESCRIPTION	PRICE
1	XA11A975-RP	Boiler Assy.	1.36 ea.
	PA10542	Headlight lens	.02 ea.
	PA9286	Motor Mount	.02 ea.
2	PA8999	Bulb	.30 ea.
3	XA10890	Lamp Bracket Assy.	.22 ea.
4	S230-B	Screw #4 x 1/4" Type "Z" P.K.	.01 ea.
5	XA13A085	Guide & Truck Assy.	.52 ea.
	PA10887	Crosshead Guide	.21 ea.
	XA13A084	Pilot Truck	.23 ea.
	PA4367	Rivet	.01 ea.
6	PA11099	Crosshead	.08 ea.
7	PA10889	Connecting Rod	.09 ea.
8	XA12B438-RP	Choo-Choo Unit	.83 ea.
9	PA10518-A	Piston	.29 ea.
10	PA10517	Piston Lever	.02 ea.
11	PA10520	Piston Pin	.03 ea.
12	PA10671	Worm Gear	.32 ea.
13	PA7421	Screw	.03 ea.
14	PA10162	Worm Gear Stud	.08 ea.
15	XA9547	Magnet Assy.	1.22 ea.
16	PA10766	Armature Spacer	.01 ea.
17	XA11077	Armature Assembly	3.39 ea.
18	XA9565-A	Brush Bracket Assembly	1.00 ea.
19	PA9603	Brush	.13 ea.
20	PA3769	Washer	.01 ea.
21	S295	Screw #6-32 x 1-7/32" Shouldered	.02 ea.
22	PA10757-A	Brush Spring	.02 ea.
23	PA10754	Brush Cap	.02 ea.
24	PA10672	Worm Gear (motor)	.06 ea.
25	PA10512	Chassis	1.35 ea.
26	XA13A865	Flanged Wheel Assembly	.37 ea.
27	XA13A866	Pul-Mor Wheel & Stud Assembly	.63 ea.
	PA14A869	Pul-Mor	.05 ea.
28	PA10005	Axle NOT AVAILABLE	
		Substitute with PA15A226 Axle	.05 ea.
29	PA9452	Side Rod	.02 ea.
30	S18	Screw #6-32 x 3/4 R.H.	.01 ea.
31	S16-C	Screw	.12 dz.
32	PA7237	Piston Rod Spacer	.02 ea.
33	PA5447	Screw	.04 ea.
34	S230-B	Screw #4 x ¼" Type "Z" P.K.	.01 ea.
35	PA10080	Motor Cover Plate	.02 ea.
36	PA10006	Gear Axle NOT AVAILABLE	
		Substitute with PA15A281 Axle	.07 ea.
37	PA10511-C	4 Conductor Cable	.13 ea.
38	XA10662-A	Jack Panel	.24 ea.
39	XA10663	Male Plug	.24 ea.
40	PA12D078	Tender Body NOT AVAILABLE	
		Substitute with PA12D078 New Style	.80 ea.

Con't

DIA. NO.	PART NO.	DESCRIPTION	PRICE
41	XA10587-E	Remote Control Unit	4.04 ea.
42	XA8716	Drum only	.95 ea.
43	XA9612-CRP	Top Finger Unit	.33 ea.
44	XA9612-BRP	Bottom Finger Unit	.33 ea.
45	PA10235-A	Truck Rivet	.07 ea.
46	PA10209	Insulating Bushing	.02 ea.
47	PA11A926	Tender Weight NOT AVAILABLE	
		Substitute with PA10593 Weight	.26 ea.
48	S230-B	Screw #4 x $\frac{1}{4}$" Type "Z" P.K.	.01 ea.
49	PA8715-B	Washer	.02 ea.
50	S184	Screw	.02 ea.
51	XA10469	Coupler & Weight Assembly NOT AVAILABLE	
52	PA10467	Coupler Pin NOT AVAILABLE	
53	XA11582	Rear Truck Frame Assembly NOT AVAILABLE	
54	XA10238	Wheel & Axle Assembly	.09 ea.
	PA9990	Plastic Wheel	.03 ea.
	PA10140	Metal Wheel	.06 ea.
	PA10238	Axle	.01 ea.
55	PA10207	Contact Spring	.02 ea.
56	PA1405	Tin Washer	.01 ea.
	XA11715	Front Truck & Yoke Assy. (consists of parts 57 to 61) NOT AVAILABLE	
57	XA11582-A	Front Truck Frame Assy. w/o wheels NOT AVAILABLE	
58	PA10751	Stud	.02 ea.
59	PA1067-A	Washer	.06 dz.
60	PA1312	Insulating Bushing	.12 dz.
61	XA10749	Coupler & Yoke Assy.	.33 ea.
62	PA4939	Screw	.06 ea.
63	PA12B080	Tender Chassis NOT AVAILABLE	
		Substitute with PA12B080 NEW STYLE	.17 ea.

LINK COUPLER & TRUCKS NOT AVAILABLE.
CONVERT TO KNUCKLE COUPLERS BY USING FOLLOWING PARTS:

Bubble #53	XA12A050-B	Rear Truck Assy.	.72 ea.
Bubble #57	XA15B800	Front Truck Assy.	.43 ea.
Bubble #61	XA15A784	Draw Bar Assembly	.22 ea.

Prices subject to change without notice.

NO.	PART NO.	DESCRIPTION	PRICE
1	XA11A975ERP	Boiler Assy. Marked 21105	2.06 ea.
	PA10542	Headlight Lens	.02 ea.
	PA16A052	Left Motor Mount	.04 ea.
	PA16A053	Right Motor Mount	.04 ea.
2	PA8999	Bulb	.32 ea.
3	XA10890	Lamp Bracket Assembly	.23 ea.
4	S230-B	#4 x 1/4" Type "Z" P.K. Screw	.01 ea.
5	XA13A085	Guide & Truck Assembly	.55 ea.
	PA10887	Crosshead Guide	.22 ea.
	XA13A084	Pilot Truck	.24 ea.
	PA4367	Rivet	.01 ea.
6	PA11099	Crosshead	.08 ea.
7	PA10889	Connecting Rod	.09 ea.
8	XA12B438-RP	Choo-Choo Unit	.87 ea.
9	PA10518-A	Piston	.30 ea.
10	PA10517	Piston Lever	.02 ea.
11	PA10520	Piston Pin	.03 ea.
12	PA10671	Worm Gear	.34 ea.
13	PA7421	Screw	.03 ea.
14	PA10162	Worm Gear Stud	.08 ea.
15	XA9547	Magnet Assembly	1.28 ea.
16	PA10766	Armature Spacer	.01 ea.
17	XA11077	Armature Assembly	3.56 ea.
18	XA9565-A	Brush Bracket Assembly	1.05 ea.
19	PA9603	Brush	.14 ea.
20	PA3769	Washer	.01 ea.
21	S295	#6-32 x 1-7/32" Shouldered Screw	.02 ea.
22	PA10757-A	Brush Spring	.02 ea.
23	PA10754	Brush Cap	.02 ea.
24	PA10672	Worm Gear (Motor)	.06 ea.
25	PA10512	Chassis	1.42 ea.
26	XA13A865	Flanged Wheel Assembly	.39 ea.
27	XA13A866	Pul-Mor Wheel & Stud Assembly	.66 ea.
	PA14A869	Pul-Mor	.05 ea.
28	PA15A226	Plain Axle	.05 ea.
29	PA9452	Side Rod	.02 ea.
30	S18	#6-32 x 3/4 R.H. Screw	.01 ea.
31	S16-C	Screw	.13 dz.
32	PA7237	Piston Rod Spacer	.02 ea.
33	PA5447	Screw	.04 ea.
34	S230-B	#4 x ¼" Type "Z" P.K. Screw	.01 ea.
35	PA10080	Motor Cover Plate	.02 ea.
36	PA15A281	Gear Axle	.07 ea.
37	PA13A208-A	4 Conductor Cable (Plastic)	.04 ft.
38	XA10662-A	Jack Panel	.25 ea.
39	XA10663	Male Plug	.25 ea.
40		Tender Body - OBSOLETE - No Longer Available - No Substitute	

Cont'd

NO.	PART NO.	DESCRIPTION	PRICE
41	XA10587-E	Remote Control Unit	4.24 ea.
42	XA8716	Drum Only	1.00 ea.
43	XA9612-CRP	Top Finger Unit	.35 ea.
44	XA9612-BRP	Bottom Finger Unit	.35 ea.
45	PA10235-A	Truck Rivet	.07 ea.
46	PA10209	Insulating Bushing	.02 ea.
47	PA10593	Tender Weight	.27 ea.
48	S230-B	#4 x ¼" Type "Z" P.K. Screw	.01 ea.
49	PA8715-B	Washer	.02 ea.
50	S184	Screw	.02 ea.
51		Coupler & Weight Assy. - OBSOLETE	
52		Coupler Pin - OBSOLETE	
53	XA12A050-B	Rear Truck Assy. w/Knuckle Coupler. Substitute for XA11A582 Rear Truck - OBSOLETE	.83 ea.
54	XA10238	Wheel & Axle Assembly	.09 ea.
	PA9990	Plastic Wheel	.03 ea.
	PA10140	Metal Wheel	.06 ea.
	PA10238	Axle	.01 ea.
55	PA10207	Contact Spring	.02 ea.
56	PA1405	Tin Washer	.01 ea.
	XA11715	Front Truck & Yoke Assy. (Consists of Parts 57 to 61) OBSOLETE	
57	XA15B800	Front Truck Assy. - Substitute for XA11582-A Frt. Truck - OBSOLETE	.45 ea.
58	PA10751	Stud	.02 ea.
59	PA1067-A	Washer	.06 dz.
60	PA1312	Insulating Bushing	.13 dz.
61	XA15A784	Draw Bar Assy. Used Only with XA15B800 Truck Assy.	.23 ea.
	XA10891	Coupler & Yoke Assy. Substitute for XA10749 - OBSOLETE	.38 ea.
62	PA4939	Screw	.06 ea.
63		Tender Chassis - OBSOLETE - No Longer Available - No Substitute	

Prices subject to change without notice

 Ref: Form No. 1811; Oct. 1, 1962

LOCOMOTIVE AND TENDER WITH PISTON-TYPE SMOKE AND CHOO-CHOO UNIT

Model No. 302

SPECIFICATIONS

Tested at: 12 Volts A.C. .... Using 140" oval of track.

(A) Motor to be tested with Remote Control Unit at 12 Volts, and not to draw more than 1.75 amps.

(B) Locomotive to run a minimum of 8 R.P.M. or 8 times forward, around 140" oval track per minute.

(C) Locomotive to run a minimum of 7.5 R.P.M. or 7½ times reverse, around 140" oval of track per minute.

Load: Not to draw more than 2.1 amps. while pulling 4 Box Cars.

Motor: Universal A.C. or D.C.

Ref: Form No. M2821; June 1, 1950

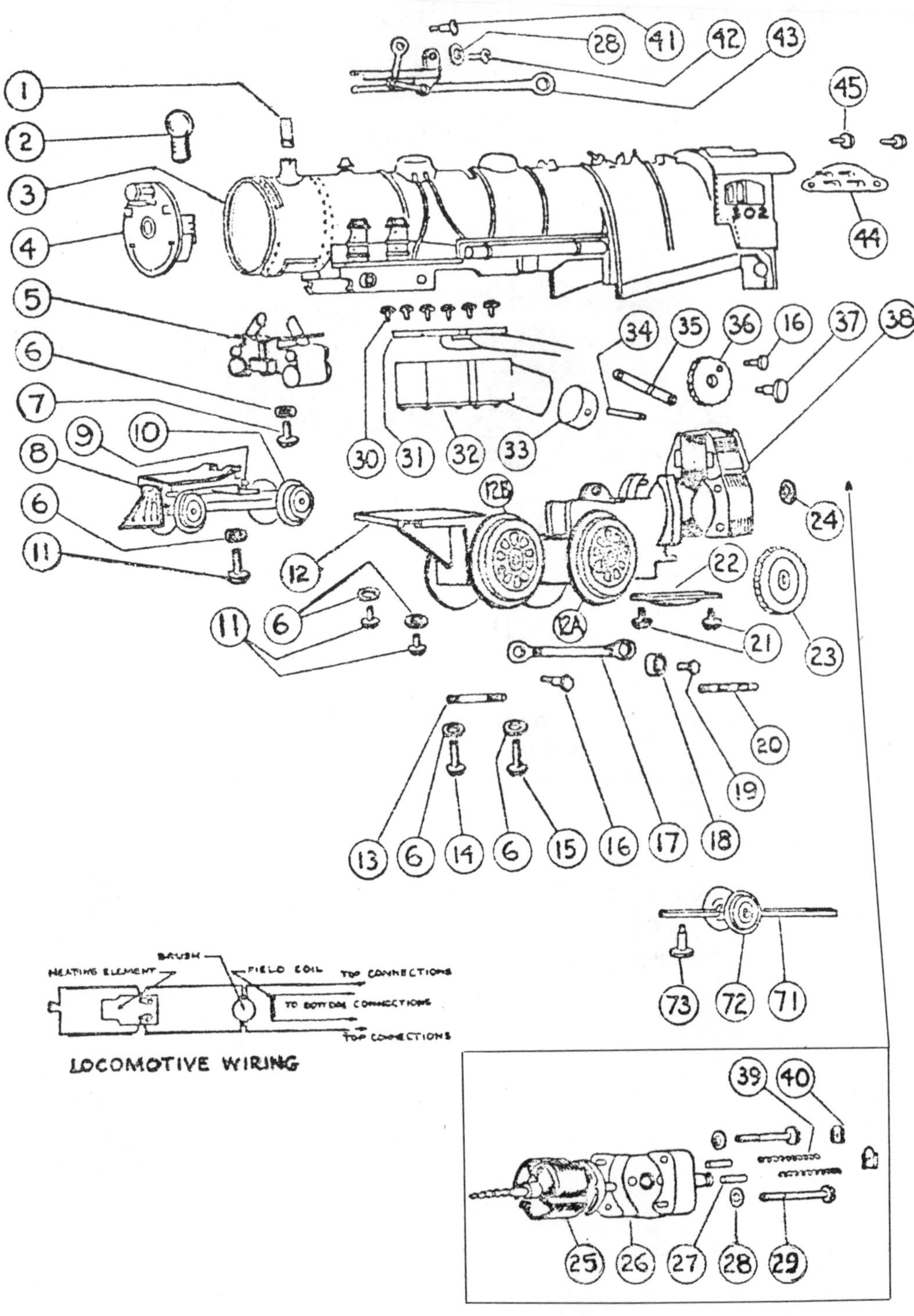

 Ref: Form No. M2821; June 1, 1950

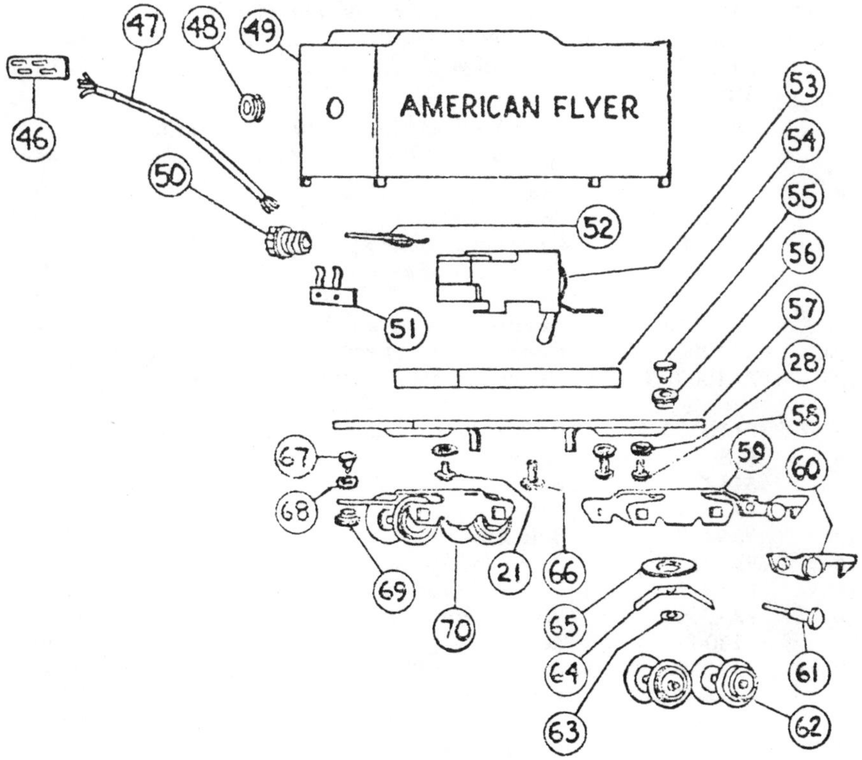

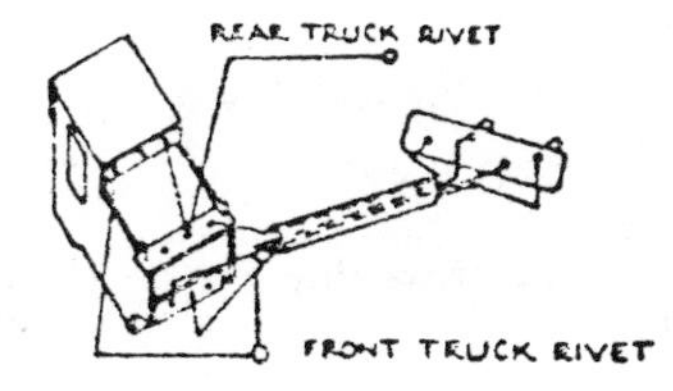

TENDER WIRING

Diagram Number	Part No.	Description	Price
1	PA10536	Smoke Stack	$ .03 ea.
2	PA8999	14 Volt Lamp	.25 "
3	XA9443-A	Boiler Assembly	2.00 "
4	XA9444-A	Boiler Front Assembly with lamp bracket	.60 "
5	PA10076	Cylinder & Steamchest	.70 "
6	PA3769	Lockwasher	.05 dz.
7	S16	Screw	.05 "
	XA10081-A	Front Truck & Pilot Assembly (consists of parts 8-9-10)	1.10 ea.
8	PA9446	Pilot	.70 "
9	PA4360	Rivet	.05 dz.
10	XA10081	Front Truck Assembly	.40 ea.
	PA9990-A	Front Truck wheel only	.10 "
11	S14	Screw	.05 dz.
12	*XA10512	Chassis Assembly with bushings only	.90 ea.
12A	XA10009-A1	Flanged wheel assembly with stud	.40 "
12B	XA10009-1	Flanged wheel assembly with tapped hole	.40 "
13	PA10005	Plain Axle	.10 "
14	S18	Screw	.05 dz.
15	S16-C	Screw	.10 "
16	PA7421	Screw	.30 "
17	PA9452	Side Rod	.20 ea.
18	PA7237	Piston Rod Spacer	.05 "
19	PA5447	Eccentric Crank Screw	.30 dz.
20	PA10006	Worm Gear Axle	.10 ea.
21	S230-B	Screw	.10 dz.
22	PA10080	Motor Cover Plate	.02 ea.
23	PA10672	Worm Gear (motor)	.30 "
24	PA10766	Washer	.05 dz.
25	**XA11077	Armature Assembly A.C.	2.50 ea.
	*** XA9569	Armature Assembly A.C.	2.50 "
26	XA9565-A	Brush Bracket Assembly	.50 "
27	PA9603	Carbon Brush A.C.	.15 "
28	W46	Washer	.03 dz.
29	S295	Screw	.10 ea.
	XA10513	Chassis Smoke Box Assembly (consists of parts 30-31-32)	2.00 "
30	S183	Screw	.10 dz.
31	XA10523	Heating Element & Plate Assembly	1.00 ea.
32	PA10513	Chassis Smoke Box	1.00 "
	XA10517	Piston & Piston Lever Assembly (consists of parts 33-34-35)	.40 "
33	PA10518	Piston	.20 "
34	PA10520	Piston Pin	.05 "
35	PA10517	Piston Lever	.05 "
36	PA10671	Worm Gear (smoke drive)	.40 "
37	PA10162	Worm Gear Stud	.10 ea.
38	XA9547	Magnet Assembly A.C.	1.00 "

 Ref: Form No. M2821; June 1, 1950

Diagram Number	Part No.	Description	Price
39	PA10757	Brush Spring	.05 ea.
40	PA10754	Brush Cap	.02 "
41	PA9288	Screw	.30 dz.
42	S1	Screw	.05 "
43	XA10669 R or L	Crosshead Assembly (Right or Left)	.50 ea.
44	XA10662	Jack Panel	.20 "
45	S230-B	Screw	.10 dz.
46	XA10663	Male Plug	.20 ea.
47	PA10511-C	4 Conductor Cable	.12 "
48	PA4356	Rubber Grommet	.02 "
49	XA9461	Tender Body	1.00 "
50	XA8716	Drum only (Remote Control)	.60 "
51	XA9612-B	Bottom Finger Unit (Remote Control)	.50 "
52	XA9612-C	Top Finger Unit (Remote Control)	.50 "
53	XA10587	Remote Control Unit	2.50 "
54	PA10593	Tender Weight	.22 "
55	PA10235-A	Truck Rivet	.03 "
56	PA10209	Insulating Bushing	.02 "
57	PA10590	Tender Chassis	.30 "
58	S-0	Screw	.05 dz.
59	XA9987-C	Rear Truck Assembly with wheels	.75 ea.
60	XA10469	Coupler & Weight Assembly	.15 "
	PA10692	Weight only	.05 "
61	PA10467	Coupler Pin	.10 "
62	XA10140	Wheel & Axle Assembly (Brass & Plastic)	.25 set
	PA10140	Brass wheel	.15 ea.
	PA9990	Plastic wheel	.10 "
	PA9989	Axle	.02 "
63	PA1405	Washer	.05 dz.
64	PA10207	Contact Spring	.02 ea.
65	PA8715-B	Washer	.05 dz.
66	S184	Screw	.10 "
	XA10749-A	Truck & Coupler Assembly (consists of parts 67-68-69-70-71)	.80 ea.
67	PA10751	Stud	.02 "
68	PA1067-A	Washer	.05 dz.
69	PA1312	Insulating Bushing	.10 "
70	XA9987-G	Front Truck Assembly with wheels	.50 ea.
71	XA10749	Coupler & Yoke Assembly	.30 "
72	PA10019-A	Rear Truck Wheel only	.10 "
73	PA4939	Truck Stud	.05 "

*XA10512 Chassis Assembly is not sold as a complete assembly with wheels.

**XA11077 Armature Assembly with 1/16" oil slinger cannot be used with XA9565-A Brush Bracket Assembly manufactured before Oct. 1949, unless you grind 1/16" off the boss which the bearing sets into on the Brush Bracket Assembly.

***XA9569 Armature Assembly can be used with XA9565-A Brush Bracket Assembly manufactured after Oct. 1949 providing that you use 1/16" washer to take up end play.

Ref: Form No. M2821; June 1, 1950

LOCOMOTIVE AND TENDER WITH PISTON-TYPE SMOKE AND CHOO-CHOO UNIT

Model No. 302

SPECIFICATIONS

Tested at: 12 Volts A.C. .... using 140″ oval of track.

(A) Motor to be tested with Remote Control Unit at 12 Volts, and not to draw more than .175 amps.

(B) Locomotive to run a minimum of 9 R.P.M. or 9 times forward, around 140″ oval of track per minute.

(C) Locomotive to run a minimum of 8.5 R.P.M. or 8½ times reverse, around 140″ oval of track per minute.

Load: Not to draw more than 2 amps. while pulling 4 Box Cars.

Motor: Universal A.C. or D.C.

 Ref: Form No. 1495; Dec. 15, 1953

LOCOMOTIVE AND TENDER WITH PISTON-TYPE SMOKE AND CHOO-CHOO UNIT

Model No. 302

SPECIFICATIONS

Tested at: 12 Volts A.C. .... using 140" oval of track.

(A) Motor to be tested with Remote Control Unit at 12 Volts, and not to draw more than .175 amps.

(B) Locomotive to run a minimum of 9 R.P.M. or 9 times forward, around 140" oval of track per minute.

(C) Locomotive to run a minimum of 8.5 R.P.M. or 8½ times reverse, around 140" oval of track per minute.

Load: Not to draw more than 2 amps. while pulling 4 Box Cars.

Motor: Universal A.C. or D.C.

Ref: Form No. 1810; Feb. 1, 1957

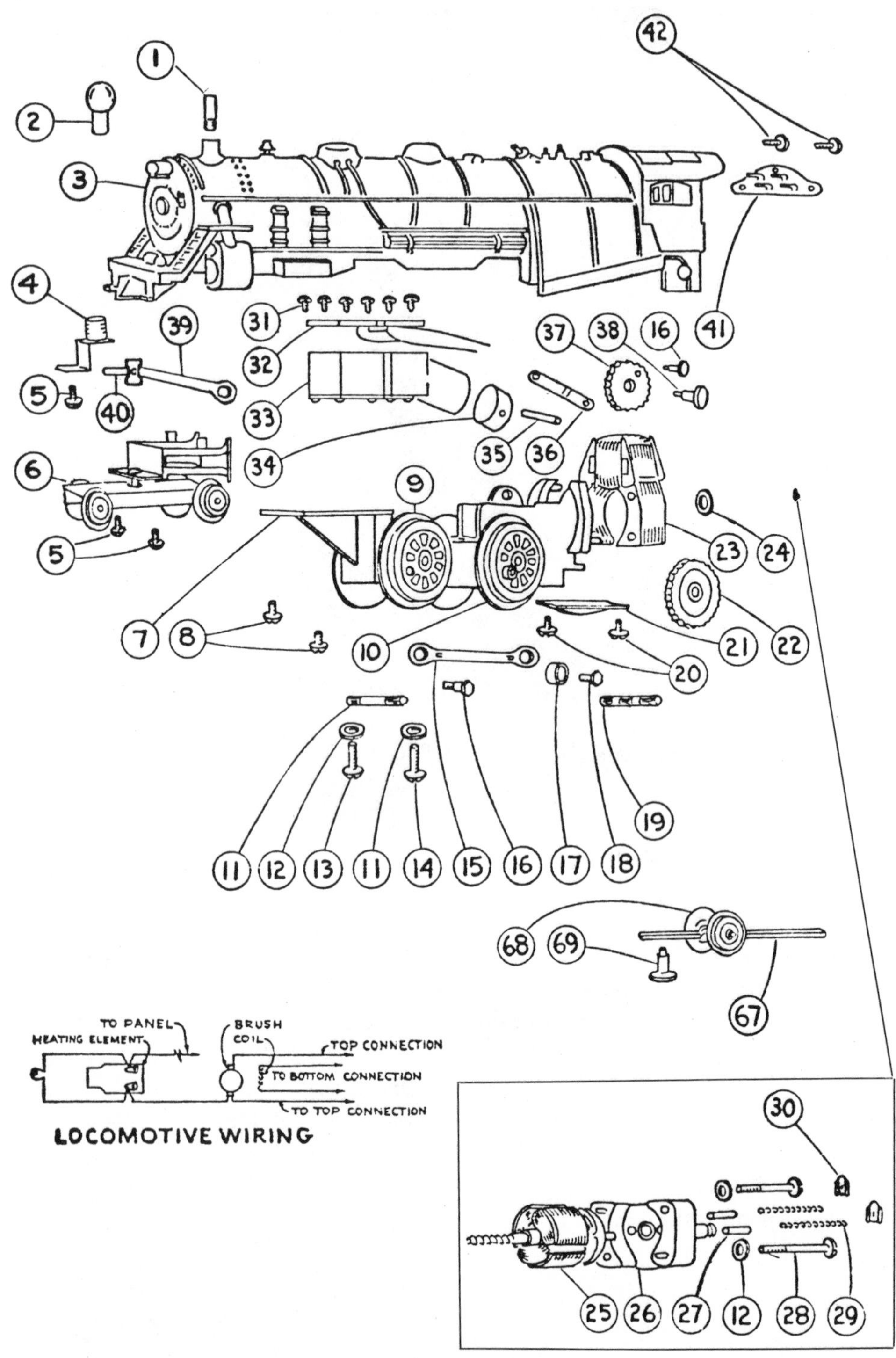

 Ref: Form No. 1810; Feb. 1, 1957

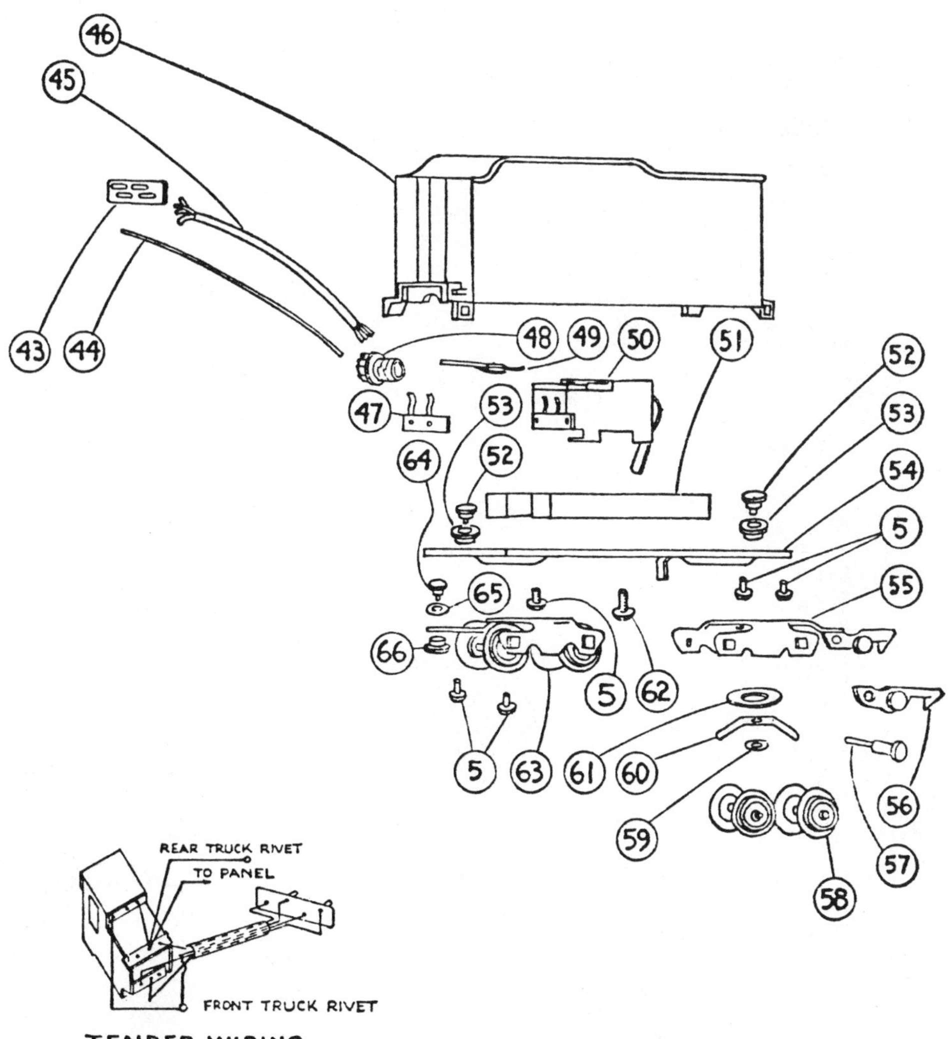

TENDER WIRING

DIA. NO.	PART NO.	DESCRIPTION	PRICE
1	PA12A190	Smoke Stack	.03 ea.
2	PA8999	Bulb	.30 ea.
3	XA11A975-RP	Boiler Assembly	1.36 ea.
	PA10542	Headlight Lens	.02 ea.
	PA9286	Motor Mount	.02 ea.
4	XA10890	Lamp Bracket Assembly	.22 ea.
5	S230-B	Screw #4 x 1/4" Type "Z" P.K.	.01 ea.
6	XA13A085	Guide & Truck Assembly	.52 ea.
	PA10887	Crosshead Guide	.21 ea.
	XA13A084	Pilot Truck	.23 ea.
	PA4367	Rivet	.01 ea.
7	PA10512	Chassis	1.35 ea.
8	S319	Screw #6 x 5/16 Type "Z" P.K.	.02 ea.
9	XA13A865	Flanged Wheel	.37 ea.
10	XA13A866	Pul-Mor Wheel and Stud	.63 ea.
	PA14A869	Pul-Mor	.05 ea.
11	PA10005	Plain Axle NOT AVAILABLE	
		Substitute with PA15A226 Axle	.05 ea.
12	PA3769	Washer	.01 ea.
13	S18	Screw #6-32 x 3/4 R.H.	.01 ea.
14	S16-C	Screw	.12 dz.
15	PA9452	Side Rod	.02 ea.
16	PA7421	Side Rod Screw	.03 ea.
17	PA7237	Piston Rod Spacer	.02 ea.
18	PA5447	Screw	.04 ea.
19	PA10006	Gear Axle NOT AVAILABLE	
		Substitute with PA15A281 Axle	.07 ea.
20	S-230-B	Screw #4 x 1/4" Type "Z" P.K.	.01 ea.
21	PA10080	Motor Cover Plate	.02 ea.
22	PA10672	Worm Gear (motor)	.06 ea.
23	XA9547	Magnet Assembly	1.22 ea.
24	PA10766	Washer	.01 ea.
25	XA11077	Armature Assembly	3.39 ea.
26	XA9565-A	Brush Bracket Assembly	1.00 ea.
27	PA9603	Brush	.13 ea.
28	S295	Screw #6-32 x 1-7/32" Shouldered	.02 ea.
29	PA10757-A	Brush Spring	.02 ea.
30	PA10754	Brush Cap	.02 ea.
31	S183	Screw #2 x ¼ Type "Z" P.K.	.01 ea.
32	XA10523	Heating Element & Plate Assy. NOT AVAILABLE	
		Substitute with XA14A208-A Assy.	.91 ea.
33	PA10513	Chassis Smoke Box NOT AVAILABLE	
		Substitute with PA13B894 Smoke Box	.76 ea.
	PA14A209	Separator	.02 ea.
	XA10513	Chassis Smoke Box Assy. (consists of parts 31-32-33) NOT AVAILABLE	
		Substitute with XA13B894-RP Smoke Box	2.13 ea.
34	PA10518-A	Piston	.29 ea.
35	PA10520	Piston Pin	.03 ea.

Con't

DIA. NO.	PART NO.	DESCRIPTION	PRICE
36	PA10517	Piston Lever	.02 ea.
37	PA10671	Worm Gear (smoke drive)	.32 ea.
38	PA10162	Worm Gear Stud	.08 ea.
39	PA10889	Connecting Rod	.09 ea.
40	PA11099	Crosshead	.08 ea.
41	XA10662-A	Jack Panel	.24 ea.
42	S230-B	Screw #4 x 1/4" Type "Z" P.K.	.01 ea.
43	XA10663	Male Plug	.24 ea.
44	PA9273-A	6" lead wire	.02 ea.
45	PA10511-C	4 Conductor Cable	.13 ea.
46	PA12D078	Tender Body Assy. NOT AVAILABLE	
		Substitute with PA12D078 NEW STYLE	.80 ea.
47	XA9612-BRP	Bottom Finger Unit	.33 ea.
48	XA8716	Drum	.95 ea.
49	XA9612-CRP	Top Finger Unit	.33 ea.
50	XA10587-E	Remote Control Unit	4.04 ea.
51	PA11A926	Tender Weight NOT AVAILABLE	
		Substitute with PA10593 Weight	.26 ea.
52	PA10235-A	Truck Rivet	.07 ea.
53	PA10209	Insulating Bushing	.02 ea.
54	PA12B080	Tender Chassis NOT AVAILABLE	
		Substitute with PA12B080 NEW STYLE	.17 ea.
55	XA11582	Rear Truck Frame Assy. NOT AVAILABLE	
56	XA10469	Coupler & Weight Assy. NOT AVAILABLE	
	PA10692	Coupler Weight only NOT AVAILABLE	
57	PA10467	Coupler Pin NOT AVAILABLE	
58	XA10238	Wheel & Axle Assy.	.09 ea.
	PA10140	Metal Wheel	.06 ea.
	PA9990	Plastic Wheel	.03 ea.
	PA10238	Axle	.01 ea.
59	PA1405	Tin Washer	.01 ea.
60	PA10207	Contact Spring	.02 ea.
61	PA8715-B	Washer	.02 ea.
62	S184	Screw	.02 ea.
63	XA11582-A	Front Truck Frame Assy. NOT AVAILABLE	
64	PA10751	Stud	.02 ea.
65	PA1067-A	Washer	.06 dz.
66	PA1312	Insulating Bushing	.12 dz.
67	XA10749	Coupler & Yoke Assy.	.33 ea.
68	PA10019-A	Wheel only	.06 ea.
69	PA4939	Truck Stud	.06 ea.

LINK COUPLER & TRUCKS NOT AVAILABLE
CONVERT TO KNUCKLE COUPLERS BY USING FOLLOWING PARTS:

Bubble #55	XA12A050-B	Rear Truck Assy.	.72 ea.
Bubble #63	XA15B800	Front Truck Assy.	.43 ea.
Bubble #67	XA15A784	Draw Bar Assy.	.22 ea.

Prices subject to change without notice.

Ref: Form No. 1810; June 1, 1960

NO.	PART NO.	DESCRIPTION	PRICE
1	PA12A190	Smoke Stack	.03 ea.
2	PA8999	Bulb	.32 ea.
3	XA11A975ERP	Boiler Assembly Marked 21105	2.06 ea.
	PA10542	Headlight Lens	.02 ea.
	PA16052	Left Motor Mount	.04 ea.
	PA16053	Right Motor Mount	.04 ea.
4	XA10890	Lamp Bracket Assembly	.23 ea.
5	S230-B	#4 x 1/4" Type "Z" P.K. Screw	.01 ea.
6	XA13A085	Guide & Truck Assembly	.55 ea.
	PA10887	Crosshead Guide	.22 ea.
	XA13A084	Pilot Truck	.24 ea.
	PA4367	Rivet	.01 ea.
7	PA10512	Chassis	1.42 ea.
8	S319	#6 x 5/16 Type "Z" P.K. Screw	.02 ea.
9	XA13A865	Flanged Wheel	.39 ea.
10	XA13A866	Pul-Mor Wheel and Stud	.66 ea.
	PA14A869	Pul-Mor	.05 ea.
11	PA15A226	Plain Axle	.05 ea.
12	PA3769	Washer	.01 ea.
13	S18	#6-32 x 3/4 R.H. Screw	.01 ea.
14	S16-C	Screw	.13 dz.
15	PA9452	Side Rod	.02 ea.
16	PA7421	Side Rod Screw	.03 ea.
17	PA7237	Piston Rod Spacer	.02 ea.
18	PA5447	Screw	.04 ea.
19	PA15A281	Worm Gear Axle	.07 ea.
20	S-230-B	#4 x 1/4" Type "Z" P.K. Screw	.01 ea.
21	PA10080	Motor Cover Plate	.02 ea.
22	PA10672	Worm Gear (Motor)	.06 ea.
23	XA9547	Magnet Assembly	1.28 ea.
24	PA10766	Washer	.01 ea.
25	XA11077	Armature Assembly	3.56 ea.
26	XA9565-A	Brush Bracket Assembly	1.05 ea.
27	PA9603	Brush	.14 ea.
28	S295	#6-32 x 1-7/32" Shouldered Screw	.02 ea.
29	PA10757-A	Brush Spring	.02 ea.
30	PA10754	Brush Cap	.02 ea.
31	S183	#2 x ¼ Type "Z" **P.K.** Screw	.01 ea.
32	XA14A208-A	Heating Element & Plate Assy.	.96 ea.
33	XA13B894-RP	Smoke Box	2.24 ea.
34	PA10518-A	Piston	.30 ea.
35	PA10520	Piston Pin	.03 ea.
36	PA10517	Piston Lever	.02 ea.
37	PA10671	Worm Gear (Smoke Drive)	.34 ea.
38	PA10162	Worm Gear Stud	.08 ea.
39	PA10889	Connecting Rod	.09 ea.
40	PA11099	Crosshead	.08 ea.

Cont'd

NO.	PART NO.	DESCRIPTION	PRICE
41	XA10662-A	Jack Panel	.25 ea.
42	S230-B	#4 x ¼" Type "Z" P.K. Screw	.01 ea.
43	XA10663	Male Plug	.25 ea.
44	PA9273-A	Lead Wire	.02 ea.
45	PA13A208A	4 Conductor Cable (Plastic)	.04 ft.
46		Tender Body - OBSOLETE - No Longer Available - No Substitute	
47	XA9612-BRP	Bottom Finger Unit	.35 ea.
48	XA8716	Drum	1.00 ea.
49	XA9612-CRP	Top Finger Unit	.35 ea.
50	XA10587-E	Remote Control Unit	4.24 ea.
51	PA10593	Tender Weight	.27 ea.
52	PA10235-A	Truck Rivet	.07 ea.
53	PA10209	Insulating Bushing	.02 ea.
54		Tender Chassis - OBSOLETE - No Longer Available - No Substitute	
55	XA12A050-B	Rear Truck Assy. - Substitute for XA11582 Rear Truck Assy. - OBSOLETE	.83 ea.
56		Coupler and Weight Assy. - OBSOLETE	
		Coupler Weight Only - OBSOLETE	
57		Coupler Pin - OBSOLETE	
58	XA10238	Wheel & Axle Assy.	.09 ea.
	PA10140	Metal Wheel	.06 ea.
	PA9990	Plastic Wheel	.03 ea.
	PA10238	Axle	.01 ea.
59	PA1405	Tin Washer	.01 ea.
60	PA10207	Contact Spring	.02 ea.
61	PA8715-B	Washer	.02 ea.
62	S184	Screw	.02 ea.
63	XA15B800	Frt. Truck Assy. Substitute for XA11582-A Frt. Truck Assy. - OBSOLETE	.45 ea.
64	PA10751	Stud	.02 ea.
65	PA1067-A	Washer	.06 dz.
66	PA1312	Insulating Bushing	.13 dz.
67	XA15A784	Draw Bar Assy. Used only with XA15B800 Truck Assy.	.23 ea.
	XA10891	Coupler & Yoke Assy. Substitute for XA10749 - OBSOLETE	.38 ea.
68	PA10019-A	Wheel Only	.06 ea.
69	PA4939	Truck Stud	.06 ea.

Prices subject to change without notice.

LOCOMOTIVE AND TENDER WITH PISTON-TYPE SMOKE AND CHOO-CHOO UNIT, PULL-MOR WHEELS, AND KNUCKLE COUPLER

Model No. 303

SPECIFICATIONS

Tested at: 12 Volts A.C. .... using 140" oval of track.

(A) Motor to be tested with Remote Control Unit at 12 Volts, and not to draw more than .175 amps.

(B) Locomotive to run a minimum of 9 R.P.M. or 9 times forward, around 140" oval of track per minute.

(C) Locomotive to run a minimum of 8.5 R.P.M. or 8½ times reverse, around 140" oval of track per minute.

Load: Not to draw more than 2 amps. while pulling 4 Box Cars.

Motor: Universal A.C. or D.C.

 Ref: Form No. 1557, July 1, 1954

LOCOMOTIVE AND TENDER WITH PISTON-TYPE SMOKE AND CHOO-CHOO UNIT, PULL-MOR WHEELS, AND KNUCKLE COUPLER

Model Nos. 303, 308, 21105

SPECIFICATIONS

Tested at: 12 Volts A.C. .... using 140″ oval of track.

(A) Motor to be tested with Remote Control Unit at 12 Volts, and not to draw more than .175 amps.

(B) Locomotive to run a minimum of 9 R.P.M. or 9 times forward, around 140″ oval of track per minute.

(C) Locomotive to run a minimum of 8.5 R.P.M. or 8½ times reverse, around 140″ oval of track per minute.

Load: Not to draw more than 2 amps. while pulling 4 Box Cars.

Motor: Universal A.C. or D.C.

Ref: Form No. 1809; Feb. 1, 1957

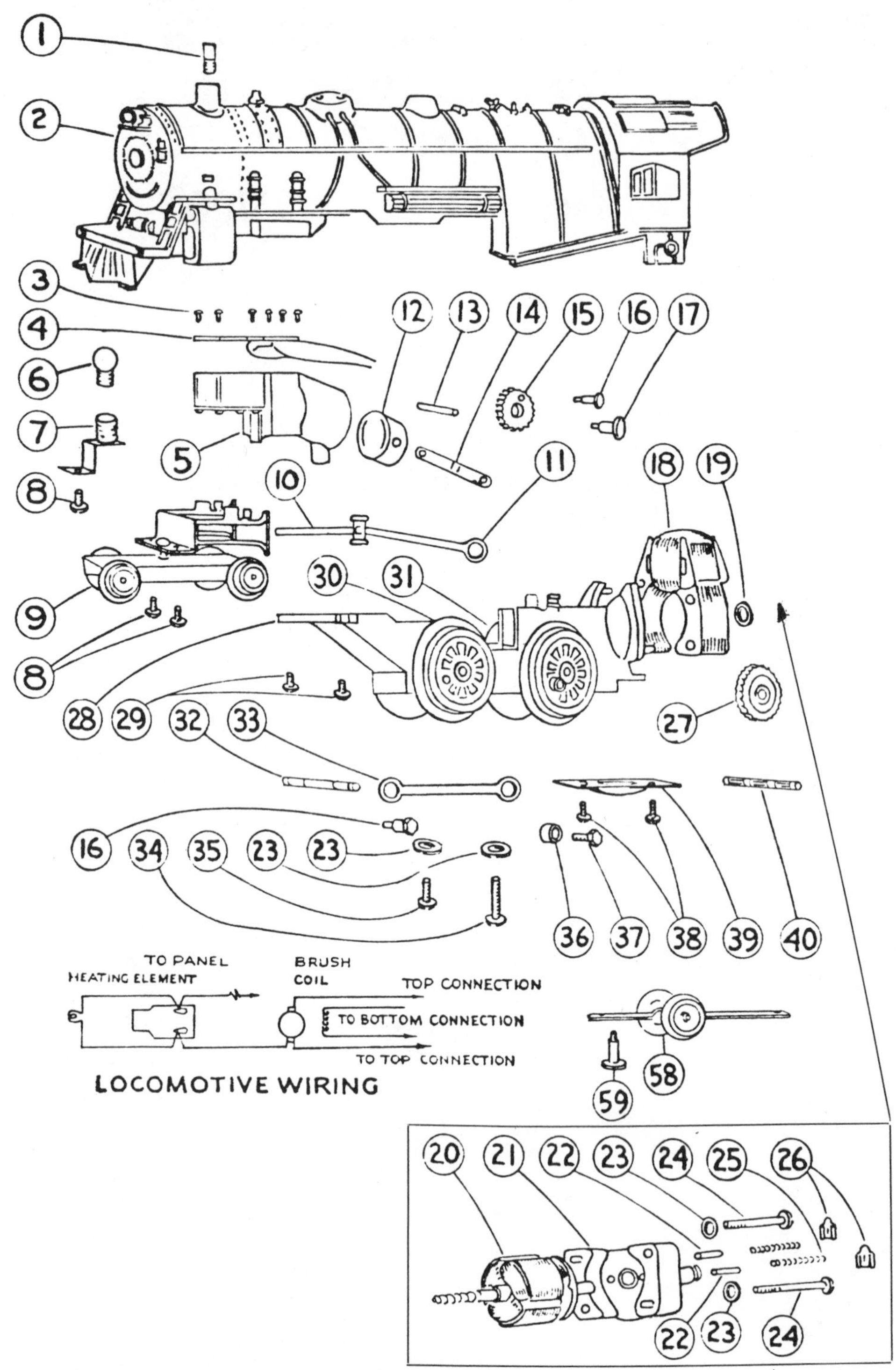

 Ref: Form No. 1809; Feb. 1, 1957

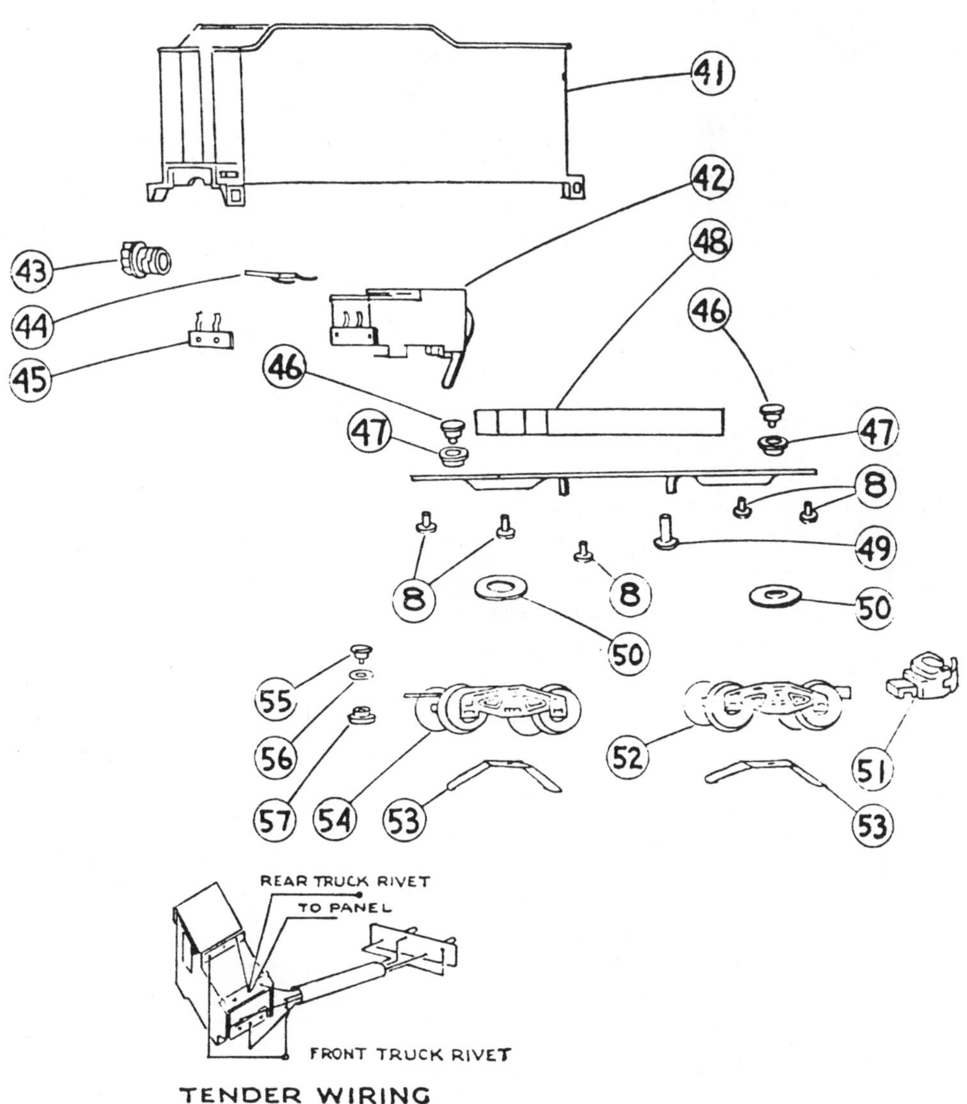

TENDER WIRING

Ref: Form No. 1809; Feb. 1, 1957

Diagram Number	Part No.	Description	Price
1	PA12A190	Smoke Stack	$ .02 ea.
2	XA11A975-B RP	Boiler Assy	1.44 "
3	S183	Screw	.10 dz.
	XA10513	Smoke Box Assy	2.00 ea.
4	XA10523	Heating Eelement & Plate Assy	1.00 "
5	PA10513	Smoke Box	1.00 "
6	PA8999	Bulb	.25 "
7	XA10890	Lamp Bracket Assy	.25 "
8	S230-B	Screw	.10 dz.
9	XA10887-A	Guide & Truck Assy	.60 ea.
10	PA11099	Crosshead	.05 "
11	PA10889	Connecting Rod	.10 "
12	PA10518-A	Piston	.20 "
13	PA10520	Piston Pin	.05 "
14	PA10517	Piston Lever	.40 "
15	PA10671	Worm Gear	.40 "
16	PA7421	Screw	.30 dz.
17	PA10162	Worm Gear Stud	.10 ea.
18	XA9547-B	Magnet Assy	1.00 "
19	PA10766	Armature Spacer	.05 dz.
20	XA11077	Armature Assy	2.50 ea.
21	XA9565-A	Brush Bracket Assy	.50 "
22	PA9603	Brush	.15 "
23	PA3769	Washer	.05 dz.
24	S295	Screw	.10 ea.
25	PA10757-A	Brush Spring	.05 "
26	PA10754	Brush Cap	.02 "
27	PA10672	Worm Gear (Motor)	.30 "
28	PA10512	Chassis	.91 "
29	S319	Screw	.01 "
30	XA12A449	Flanged Wheel Assy	.40 "

 Ref: Form No. 1557; July 1, 1954

Diagram Number	Part No.	Description	Price
31	XA12A987	Pull Mor Wheel & Stud Assy	$ .64 ea.
32	PA10005	Plain Axle	.10 "
33	PA9452	Side Rod	.20 "
34	S18	Screw	.05 dz.
35	S16C	Screw	.10 "
36	PA7237	Piston Rod Spacer	.05 ea.
37	PA5447	Screw	.30 dz.
38	S230	Screw	.10 "
39	PA10080	Motor Cover Plate	.02 ea.
40	PA10006	Worm Gear Axle	.10 "
41	PA12D078	Tender Body	.63 "
42	XA10587-E	Remote Control Unit	2.50 "
43	XA8716	Drum Only	.60 "
44	XA9612-C	Top Finger Unit	.50 "
45	XA9612-B	Bottom Finger Unit	.50 "
46	PA10235-A	Truck Rivet	.03 "
47	PA10209	Insulating Bushing	.02 "
48	PA11A926	Tender Weight	.18 "
49	S184	Screw	.10 dz.
50	PA8715-B	Washer	.05 "
51	XA12A047	Knuckle Coupler	.22 ea.
52	XA12A050-A	Rear Truck Assy	.56 "
53	PA10207	Contact Spring	.02 "
	XA12B907	Front Truck & Yoke Assy (consists of parts 54-58)	.77 "
54	XA12A921	Front Truck Assy	.46 "
55	PA10751	Stud	.02 "
56	PA1067-A	Washer	.05 dz.
57	PA1312	Insulating Bushing	.10 "
58	XA10749	Coupler & Yoke Assy	.30 ea.
59	PA4939	Screw	.05 "

Diagram Number	Part No.	Description	Price
1	PA12A190	Smoke Stack	$ .02 ea.
2	XA11A975-BRP	Boiler Assy.	1.60 "
3	S183	Screw	.10 dz.
	*XA10513	Smoke Box Assy.	NOT AVAILABLE
4	**XA10523	Heating Element & Plate Assy.	.66 ea.
5	*PA10513	Smoke Box	NOT AVAILABLE
6	PA8999	Bulb	.25 "
7	XA10890	Lamp Bracket Assy.	.28 "
8	S230-B	Screw	.10 dz.
9	XA13A085	Guide & Truck Assy.	.44 ea.
	PA10887	Crosshead Guide	.15 "
	XA13A084	Pilot Truck	.21 "
	PA4367	Rivet	.01 "
10	PA11099	Crosshead	.05 "
11	PA10889	Connecting Rod	.11 "
12	PA10518-A	Piston	.17 "
13	PA10520	Piston Pin	.05 "
14	PA10517	Piston Lever	.08 "
15	PA10671	Worm Gear	.27 "
16	PA7421	Screw	.30 dz.
17	PA10162	Worm Gear Stud	.05 ea.
18	XA9547-B	Magnet Assy.	1.11 "
19	PA10766	Armature Spacer	.05 dz.
20	XA11077	Armature Assy.	2.19 ea.
21	XA9565-A	Brush Bracket Assy.	.71 "
22	PA9603	Brush	.15 "
23	PA3769	Washer	.05 dz.
24	S295	Screw	.02 ea.
25	PA10757-A	Brush Spring	.05 "
26	PA10754	Brush Cap	.02 "
27	PA10672	Worm Gear (motor)	.20 "
28	PA10512	Chassis	1.23 "
29	S319	Screw	.01 "

All prices subject to change without notice.

*Parts so marked NOT AVAILABLE, substitute with:

Dia. 5	XA13B894RP	Smoke Box Assy. (new style)	$1.55 ea.
	PA13B894	Smoke Box (new style)	.59 "
	PA14A209	Separator (new style)	.01 "

 Ref: Form No. 1809; Feb. 1, 1957

Diagram Number	Part No.	Description	Price
30	XA13A865	Flanged Wheel Assy.	$ .29 ea.
31	XA13A866	Pull-Mor Wheel & Stud Assy.	.57 "
32	PA10005	Plain Axle	.10 "
33	PA9452	Side Rod	.10 "
34	S18	Screw	.05 dz.
35	S16C	Screw	.11 "
36	PA7237	Piston Rod Spacer	.05 ea.
37	PA5447	Screw	.30 dz.
38	S230-B	Screw	.10 "
39	PA10080	Motor Cover Plate	.02 ea.
40	PA10006	Worm Gear Axle	.10 "
41	PA12D078	Tender Body	.73 "
42	XA10587-E	Remote Control Unit	1.32 "
43	XA8716	Drum Only	.59 "
44	XA9612-CRP	Top Finger Unit	.30 "
45	XA9612-BRP	Bottom Finger Unit	.30 "
46	PA10235-A	Truck Rivet	.03 "
47	PA10209	Insulating Bushing	.02 ea.
48	PA11A926	Tender Weight	.32 "
49	S184	Screw	.10 dz.
50	PA8715-B	Washer	.05 "
51	XA12A047	Knuckle Coupler	.22 ea.
52	XA12A050-A	Rear Truck Assy.	.65 "
53	PA10207	Contact Spring	.02 "
	XA14B348	Front Truck & Yoke Assy.	.65 "
54	XA14A349	Front Truck Assy.	.30 "
55	PA14A346	Stud	.02 "
56	PA1067-A	Washer	.05 dz.
57	PA14A347	Insulating Bushing	.02 ea.
58	XA10749	Coupler & Yoke Assy.	.30 ea.
59	PA4939	Screw	.05 "
60	XA12B080	Tender Chassis	.20 "

**The XA10523 Heating Element and Plate Assy. is still available, and interchangeable with the new style PA13B894 Smoke Box. The new style XA14A208 Heating Element and Plate Assembly, priced at $.66 each, is used only on the new style PA13B894 Smoke Box.

SERVICE INSTRUCTIONS FOR NO. 303 LOCOMOTIVE AND TENDER WITH SMOKE, CHOO-CHOO, PULL-MOR WHEELS AND KNUCKLE COUPLER

The first thing to do is to place Locomotive and Tender on track, connect Transformer and test for operation. Make sure all rods, linkage and other parts are not bent or broken. It is also important that the wheels on the tender be clean to insure a good electrical contact.

1. **If the trouble is in the Locomotive you can make the following checks:**
   a. Inspect Brushes for wear or poor contact and Brush Springs for position and proper tension.
   b. Check wires and solder joints for broken or loose connections.
   c. Clean or polish commutator on Armature (※20) if dirty or worn.

2. **If these initial steps do not correct the trouble it will be necessary to disassemble the Locomotive as follows:**
   a. Unscrew smoke stack (※1).
   b. Remove Screws (※37) on each side and take off Rods (※11) and spacer (※36) from drive wheel (※31).
   c. Take off Rear Truck (※58) by removing Screw (※59).
   d. Take off Lamp Bracket (※7) by removing Screw (※8).
   e. Turn Locomotive upside down and remove two Screws (※29) and you can now remove motor assembly from Boiler (※2).
   f. To remove motor, push forward approximately a ¼" to clear clamp on Boiler (※2) and then lift rear of motor up and pull motor out.
   g. The motor is now exposed and you can inspect the wiring and other points of the unit, making any necessary replacements.

3. **When the trouble appears to be in the Tender proceed as follows:**
   a. Remove four S-0 Screws (※8) and take off Tender Body (※41).
   b. Inspect wiring and solder joints for loose or broken connections.
   c. Check Finger Units (※44) and (※45) on Remote Control Unit (※42), to see if they are burnt or not making proper contact.
   d. The drum (※43) should be checked to see if it is pitted or worn.
   e. The pawl on the Remote Control Unit may be broken or need adjusting.
   f. It is generally not necessary to replace the complete Remote Control Unit, but some times the Finger Units, the drum, or both need adjusting or replacing.

DIA. NO.	PART NO.	DESCRIPTION	PRICE
1	PA12A190	Smoke Stack	.03 ea.
2	XA11A975-BRP	Boiler Assembly	1.36 ea.
	PA10542	Headlight Lens	.02 ea.
	PA9286	Motor Mount	.02 ea.
3	S183	Screw #2 x 1/4"Type "Z" P.K.	.01 ea.
	XA10513	Smoke Box Assembly NOT AVAILABLE Substitute with XA13B894RP Smoke Box	2.13 ea.
4	XA10523	Heating Element & Plate Assembly NOT AVAILABL Substitute with XA14A208-A H.E. & Plate Assy.	.91 ea.
5	PA10513	Smoke Box NOT AVAILABLE Substitute with PA13B894 Smoke Box	.76 ea.
	PA14A209	Separator	.02 ea.
6	PA8999	Bulb	.30 ea.
7	XA10890	Lamp Bracket Assembly	.22 ea.
8	S230-B	Screw #4 x 1/4"Type "Z" P.K.	.01 ea.
9	XA13A085	Guide & Truck Assembly	.52 ea.
	PA10887	Crosshead Guide	.21 ea.
	XA13A084	Pilot Truck	.23 ea.
	PA4367	Rivet	.01 ea.
10	PA11099	Crosshead	.08 ea.
11	PA10889	Connecting Rod	.09 ea.
12	PA10518-A	Piston	.29 ea.
13	PA10520	Piston Pin	.03 ea.
14	PA10517	Piston Lever	.02 ea.
15	PA10671	Worm Gear	.32 ea.
16	PA7421	Screw	.03 ea.
17	PA10162	Worm Gear Stud	.08 ea.
18	XA9547	Magnet Assembly	1.22 ea.
19	PA10766	Armature Spacer	.01 ea.
20	XA11077	Armature Assembly	2.41 ea.
21	XA9565-A	Brush Bracket Assembly	1.00 ea.
22	PA9603	Brush	.13 ea.
23	PA3769	Washer	.01 ea.
24	S295	Screw #6-32 x 1-7/32" Shouldered	.02 ea.
25	PA10757-A	Brush Spring	.02 ea.
26	PA10754	Brush Cap	.02 ea.
27	PA10672	Worm Gear (motor)	.06 ea.
28	PA10512	Chassis	1.35 ea.
29	S319	Screw #6 x 5/16 Type "Z" P.K.	.02 ea.
30	XA13A865	Flanged Wheel Assembly	.37 ea.
31	XA13A866	Pul-Mor Wheel & Stud Assembly	.63 ea.
32	PA10005	Plain Axle NOT AVAILABLE Substitute with PA15A226 Axle	.05 ea.
33	PA9452	Side Rod	.02 ea.
34	S18	Screw 6-32 x 3/4 R.H.	.01 ea.
35	S16C	Screw	.12 dz.
36	PA7237	Piston Rod Spacer	.02 ea.
37	PA5447	Screw	.04 ea.
38	S230-B	Screw #4 x 1/4 " Type "Z" P.K.	.01 ea.
39	PA10080	Motor Cover Plate	.02 ea.
40	PA10006	Worm Gear Axle NOT AVAILABLE Substitute with PA15A281 Axle	.07 ea.

con't

DIA. NO.	PART NO.	DESCRIPTION	PRICE
41	PA12D078	Tender Body NOT AVAILABLE	
		Substitute with PA12D078 NEW STYLE	.80 ea.
42	XA10587-E	Remote Control Unit	4.04 ea.
43	XA8716	Drum Only	.95 ea.
44	XA9612-CRP	Top Finger Unit	.33 ea.
45	XA9612-BRP	Bottom Finger Unit	.33 ea.
46	PA10235-A	Truck Rivet	.07 ea.
47	PA10209	Insulating Bushing	.02 ea.
48	PA11A926	Tender Weight NOT AVAILABLE	
		Substitute with PA10593 Weight	.26 ea.
49	S184	Screw	.02 ea.
50	PA8715-B	Washer	.02 ea.
51	XA12A047	Knuckle Coupler	.29 ea.
52	XA12A050-B	Rear Truck Assembly	.79 ea.
	XA10238	Wheel & Axle Assembly	.09 ea.
	PA10140	Brass Wheel	.06 ea.
	PA9990	Plastic Wheel	.03 ea.
	PA10238	Axle	.01 ea.
53	PA10207	Contact Spring	.02 ea.
54	XA14A349	Front Truck Assembly NOT AVAILABLE	
		Substitute with XA15A800 Truck	.43 ea.
55	* PA14A346	Stud	.01 ea.
56	* PA1067-A	Washer	.06 dz.
57	* PA14A347	Insulating Bushing	.09 ea.
58	XA10749	Coupler & Yoke Assembly NOT AVAILABLE	
		Substitute with XA15A784 Draw Bar Assembly	.22 ea.
59	PA4939	Screw	.06 ea.
60	XA12B080	Tender Chassis NOT AVAILABLE	
		Substitute with XA12B080 NEW STYLE	.22 ea.

* Part # 55-56-57 not used with # 54 - XA15A800 Truck, or # 58 - XA15A784 Draw Bar Assembly.

Prices subject to change without notice.

 Ref: Form No. 1809; June 1, 1960

DIA. NO.	PART NO.	DESCRIPTION	PRICE
1		Not Used	
2	XA11A975-CRP	Boiler Assy.	1.57 ea.
	PA10542	Headlight Lens	.02 ea.
	PA9286	Motor Mount	.02 ea.
3		Not Used	
4		Not Used	
5	XA12B438-RP	Choo Choo	.83 ea.
6	PA8999	Bulb	.30 ea.
7	XA10890	Lamp Bracket Assy.	.22 ea.
8	S230-B	Screw #4 X 1/4 Type "Z" P.K.	.01 ea.
9	XA13A085	Guide & Truck Assy.	.52 ea.
	PA10887	Crosshead Guide	.21 ea.
	XA13A084	Pilot Truck	.23 ea.
	PA4367	Rivet	.01 ea.
10	PA11099	Crosshead	.08 ea.
11	PA10889	Connecting Rod	.09 ea.
12	PA10518-A	Piston	.29 ea.
13	PA10520	Piston Pin	.03 ea.
14	PA10517	Piston Lever	.02 ea.
15	PA10671	Worm Gear	.32 ea.
16	PA7421	Screw	.03 ea.
17	PA10162	Worm Gear Stud	.08 ea.
18	XA9547	Magnet Assy.	1.22 ea.
19	PA10766	Armature Spacer	.01 ea.
20	XA11077	Armature Assy.	3.39 ea.
	W1A92	Washer	.02 ea.
21	XA9565-A	Brush Bracket Assy.	1.00 ea.
22	PA9603	Brush	.13 ea.
23	PA3769	Washer	.01 ea.
24	S295	Screw	.02 ea.
25	PA10757-A	Brush Spring	.02 ea.
26	PA10754	Brush Cap	.02 ea.
27	PA10672	Worm Gear (motor)	.06 ea.
28	PA10512	Chassis	1.35 ea.
	PA13A187	Motor Bearing	.04 ea.
29	S319	Screw #6 X 5/16 Type "Z" P.K.	.02 ea.
30	XA13A865	Flanged Wheel Assy.	.37 ea.
31	XA13A866	Pull-Mor Wheel & Stud Assy.	.63 ea.
32	PA10005	Plain Axle Not Available sub. with PA15A226 Axle	.05 ea.
33	PA9452	Side Rod	.02 ea.
34		Not Used	
35	S18	Screw	.01 ea.
36	PA7237	Piston Rod Spacer	.02 ea.
37	PA5447	Screw	.04 ea.
38	S230-B	Screw 4 X 1/4 type "Z" P.K.	.01 ea.
39	PA10080	Motor Cover Plate	.02 ea.
40	PA10006	Worm Gear Axle Not Available sub. with PA15A281 Axle	.07 ea.
41	PA12D078	Tender Body Not Available sub. with PA12D078 New Style	.80 ea.

Cont.

NO.	PART NO.	DESCRIPTION	PRICE
2	XA10587-E	Remote Control Unit	4.04 ea.
43	XA8716	Drum Only	.95 ea.
44	XA9612-CRP	Top Finger Unit	.33 ea.
45	XA9612-BRP	Bottom Finger Unit	.33 ea.
46	PA10235-A	Truck Rivet	.07 ea.
47	PA10209	Insulating Bushing	.02 ea.
48	PA11A926	Tender Weight Not Available sub. with PA10593 Weight	.26 ea.
49	S184	Screw	.02 ea.
50	PA8715-B	Washer	.02 ea.
51	XA12A047	Knuckle Coupler	.29 ea.
52	XA12A050-B	Rear Truck Assembly	.72 ea.
	XA10238	Wheel & Axle Assy.	.09 ea.
	PA9990	Plastic Wheel	.03 ea.
	PA10238	Axle	.01 ea.
	PA10140	Brass Wheel	.06 ea.
53	PA10207	Contact Spring	.02 ea.
54	XA14A349	Front Truck Assy. Not Available sub. with XA15B800	.43 ea.
55	* PA14A346	Stud	.01 ea.
56	* PA1067-A	Washer	.06 dz.
57	* PA14A347	Insulating Bushing	.09 dz.
58	XA10749	Coupler & Yoke Assy. Not available sub. with XA15A784 draw bar assy.	.22 ea.
59	PA4939	Screw	.06 ea.
60	XA12B080	Tender Chassis Not Available sub. with #PA12B080 New Style	.17 ea.

* Bubbles # 55- 56- 57- not used with #54 XA15B800 Truck or #58, Coupler & Yoke Assy.

Prices subject to change without notice.

 Ref: Form No. 1809; June 1, 1960

NO.	PART NO.	DESCRIPTION	PRICE
1	PA12A190	Smoke Stack	.03 ea.
2	XA11A975ERP	Boiler Assembly Marked 21105	2.06 ea.
	PA10542	Headlight Lens	.02 ea.
	PA16052	Left Motor Mount	.04 ea.
	PA16053	Right Motor Mount	.04 ea.
3	S183	#2 x ¼" Type "Z" P.K. Screw	.01 ea.
4	XA14A208-A	Heating Element & Plate Assy.	.96 ea.
5	XA13B894RP	Smoke Box	2.24 ea.
6	PA8999	Bulb	.32 ea.
7	XA10890	Lamp Bracket Assembly	.23 ea.
8	S230-B	#4 x ¼" Type "Z" P.K. Screw	.01 ea.
9	XA13A085	Guide and Truck Assembly	.55 ea.
	PA10887	Crosshead Guide	.22 ea.
	XA13A084	Pilot Truck	.24 ea.
	PA4367	Rivet	.01 ea.
10	PA11099	Crosshead	.08 ea.
11	PA10889	Connecting Rod	.09 ea.
12	PA10518-A	Piston	.30 ea.
13	PA10520	Piston Pin	.03 ea.
14	PA10517	Piston Lever	.02 ea.
15	PA10671	Worm Gear	.34 ea.
16	PA7421	Screw	.03 ea.
17	PA10162	Worm Gear Stud	.08 ea.
18	XA9547	Magnet Assembly	1.28 ea.
19	PA10766	Armature Spacer	.01 ea.
20	XA11077	Armature Assembly	3.56 ea.
21	XA9565-A	Brush Bracket Assembly	1.05 ea.
22	PA9603	Brush	.14 ea.
23	PA3769	Washer	.01 ea.
24	S295	#6-32 x 1-7/32" Shouldered Screw	.02 ea.
25	PA10757-A	Brush Spring	.02 ea.
26	PA10754	Brush Cap	.02 ea.
27	PA10672	Worm Gear (Motor)	.06 ea.
28	PA10512	Chassis	1.42 ea.
29	S319	#6 x 5/16" Type "Z" P.K. Screw	.02 ea.
30	XA13A865	Flanged Wheel Assembly	.39 ea.
31	XA13A866	Pul-Mor Wheel & Stud Assy.	.66 ea.
32	PA15A226	Plain Axle	.05 ea.
33	PA9452	Side Rod	.02 ea.
34	S18	6-32 x 3/4 R.H. Screw	.01 ea.
35	S16C	Screw	.13 dz.
36	PA7237	Piston Rod Spacer	.02 ea.
37	PA5447	Screw	.04 ea.
38	S230-B	#4 x ¼" Type "Z" P.K. Screw	.01 ea.
39	PA10080	Motor Cover Plate	.02 ea.
40	PA15A281	Worm Gear Axle	.07 ea.
41		Tender Body - Obsolete - No Longer Available - No Substitute	

Cont'd

NO.	PART NO.	DESCRIPTION	PRICE
42	XA10587-E	Remote Control Unit	4.24 ea.
43	XA8716	Drum Only	1.00 ea.
44	XA9612-CRP	Top Finger Unit	.35 ea.
45	XA9612-BRP	Bottom Finger Unit	.35 ea.
46	PA10235-A	Truck Rivet	.07 ea.
47	PA10209	Insulating Bushing	.02 ea.
48	PA10593	Tender Weight	.27 ea.
49	S184	Screw	.02 ea.
50	PA8715-B	Washer	.02 ea.
51	XA12A047	Knuckle Coupler	.30 ea.
52	XA12A050-B	Rear Truck Assembly	.83 ea.
	XA10238	Wheel & Axle Assembly	.09 ea.
	PA10140	Brass Wheel	.06 ea.
	PA9990	Plastic Wheel	.03 ea.
	PA10238	Axle	.01 ea.
53	PA10207	Contact Spring	.02 ea.
54	XA15A800	Front Truck Assy. Substitute for XA14A349 Frt. Truck - OBSOLETE	.45 ea.
55	PA14A346	Stud	.02 ea.
56	PA1067-A	Washer	.06 dz.
57	PA14A347	Insulating Bushing	.01 ea.
58	XA15A784	Draw Bar Assy. Used Only on XA15B800 Truck Assy.	.23 ea.
	XA10891	Coupler & Yoke Assy. Substitute for XA10749 - OBSOLETE	.38 ea.
59	PA4939	Screw	.06 ea.
60		Tender Chassis - Obsolete - No Longer Available - No Substitute	

#308 LOCO & TENDER

(SAME AS #303 LOCO & TENDER WITH THESE EXCEPTIONS)

NO.	PART NO.	DESCRIPTION	PRICE
1	NOT USED		
2	XA11A975CRP	Boiler Assembly	1.65 ea
3		NOT USED	
4		NOT USED	
5	XA12B438RP	Choo-Choo	.87 ea
20	XA11077	Armature Assy	3.56 ea
	W1A92	Washer	.02 ea
28	PA10512	Chassis	1.42 ea
	PA13A187	Motor Bearing	.04 ea
34		NOT USED	
35	S18	Screw	.01 ea
52	Add to list on #303..PA10140	Brass Wheel	.06 ea
54	XA15B800	Front Truck Assy-Sub for XA14A349 - OBSOLETE	

NO.	PART NO.	DESCRIPTION	PRICE
1		Not Used	
2	XA11A975-CRP	Boiler Assembly	1.65 ea.
	PA10542	Headlight Lens	.02 ea.
	PA16052	Left Motor Mount	.04 ea.
	PA16053	Right Motor Mount	.04 ea.
3		Not Used	
4		Not Used	
5	XA12B438-RP	Choo-Choo	.87 ea.
6	PA3999	Bulb	.32 ea.
7	XA10890	Lamp Bracket Assembly	.23 ea.
8	S230-B	#4 x ¼ Type "Z" P.K. Screw	.01 ea.
9	XA13A085	Guide and Truck Assembly	.55 ea.
	PA10887	Crosshead Guide	.22 ea.
	XA13A084	Pilot Truck	.24 ea.
	PA4367	Rivet	.01 ea.
10	PA11099	Crosshead	.08 ea.
11	PA10839	Connecting Rod	.09 ea.
12	PA10518-A	Piston	.30 ea.
13	PA10520	Piston Pin	.03 ea.
14	PA10517	Piston Lever	.02 ea.
15	PA10671	Worm Gear	.34 ea.
16	PA7421	Screw	.03 ea.
17	PA10162	Worm Gear Stud	.08 ea.
18	XA9547	Magnet Assembly	1.28 ea.
19	PA10766	Armature Spacer	.01 ea.
20	XA11077	Armature Assembly	3.56 ea.
	W1A92	Washer	.02 ea.
21	XA9565-A	Brush Bracket Assembly	1.05 ea.
22	PA9603	Brush	.14 ea.
23	PA3769	Washer	.01 ea.
24	S295	Screw	.02 ea.
25	PA10757-A	Brush Spring	.02 ea.
26	PA10754	Brush Cap	.02 ea.
27	PA10672	Worm Gear (Motor)	.06 ea.
28	PA10512	Chassis	1.42 ea.
	PA13A187	Motor Bearing	.04 ea.
29	S319	#6 x 5/16 Type "Z" P.K. Screw	.02 ea.
30	XA13A865	Flanged Wheel Assembly	.39 ea.
31	XA13A866	Pul-Mor Wheel & Stud Assembly	.66 ea.
32	PA15A226	Plain Axle	.05 ea.
33	PA9452	Side Rod	.02 ea.
34		Not Used	
35	S18	Screw	.01 ea.
36	PA7237	Piston Rod Spacer	.02 ea.
37	PA5447	Screw	.04 ea.
38	S230-B	4 x ¼ Type "Z" P.K. Screw	.01 ea.
39	PA10080	Motor Cover Plate	.02 ea.
40	PA15A281	Worm Gear Axle	.07 ea.

Cont'd

NO.	PART NO.	DESCRIPTION	PRICE
41		Tender Body - OBSOLETE - No Longer Available - No Substitute	
42	XA10587-E	Remote Control Unit	4.24 ea.
43	XA8716	Drum Only	1.00 ea.
44	XA9612-CRP	Top Finger Unit	.35 ea.
45	XA9612-BRP	Bottom Finger Unit	.35 ea.
46	PA10235-A	Truck Rivet	.07 ea.
47	PA10209	Insulating Bushing	.02 ea.
48	PA10593	Tender Weight	.27 ea.
49	S184	Screw	.02 ea.
50	PA8715-B	Washer	.02 ea.
51	XA12A047	Knuckle Coupler	.30 ea.
52	XA12A050-B	Rear Truck Assembly	.83 ea.
	XA10238	Wheel & Axle Assembly	.09 ea.
	PA9990	Plastic Wheel	.03 ea.
	PA10238	Axle	.01 ea.
	PA10140	Brass Wheel	.06 ea.
53	PA10207	Contact Spring	.02 ea.
54	XA15B800	Front Truck Assy. Substitute for XA14A349 - OBSOLETE	.45 ea.
55	PA14A346	Stud	.02 ea.
56	PA1067-A	Washer	.06 dz.
57	PA14A347	Insulating Bushing	.01 ea.
58	XA15A784	Draw Bar Assy. Used only with XA15B800 Truck Assembly	.23 ea.
	XA10891	Coupler & Yoke Assy. Substitute for XA10749 - OBSOLETE	.38 ea.
59	PA4939	Screw	.06 ea.
60	XA12B080	Tender Chassis NOT AVAILABLE Substitute with PA12B080 NEW STYLE	.18 ea.

Prices subject to change without notice.

 Ref: Form No. 1809; Oct. 1, 1962

LOCOMOTIVE AND TENDER

Model Nos. 307, 21100, 21106, 21160, 21161

SPECIFICATIONS

Tested at: 12 Volts A.C. .... using 140" oval of track.

(A) Motor to be tested with Remote Control Unit at 12 Volts and not to draw more than 1.7 amps.

(B) Locomotive to run a minimum of 9 R.P.M. or 9 times forward, around 140" oval of track per minute.

(C) Locomotive to run a minimum of 8.5 R.P.M. or 8½ times reverse, around 140" oval of track per minute.

Load: Not to draw more than 2.1 amps. while pulling 4 Box Cars.

Motor: Universal A.C. or D.C.

Ref: Form No. 1599; Feb. 15, 1955

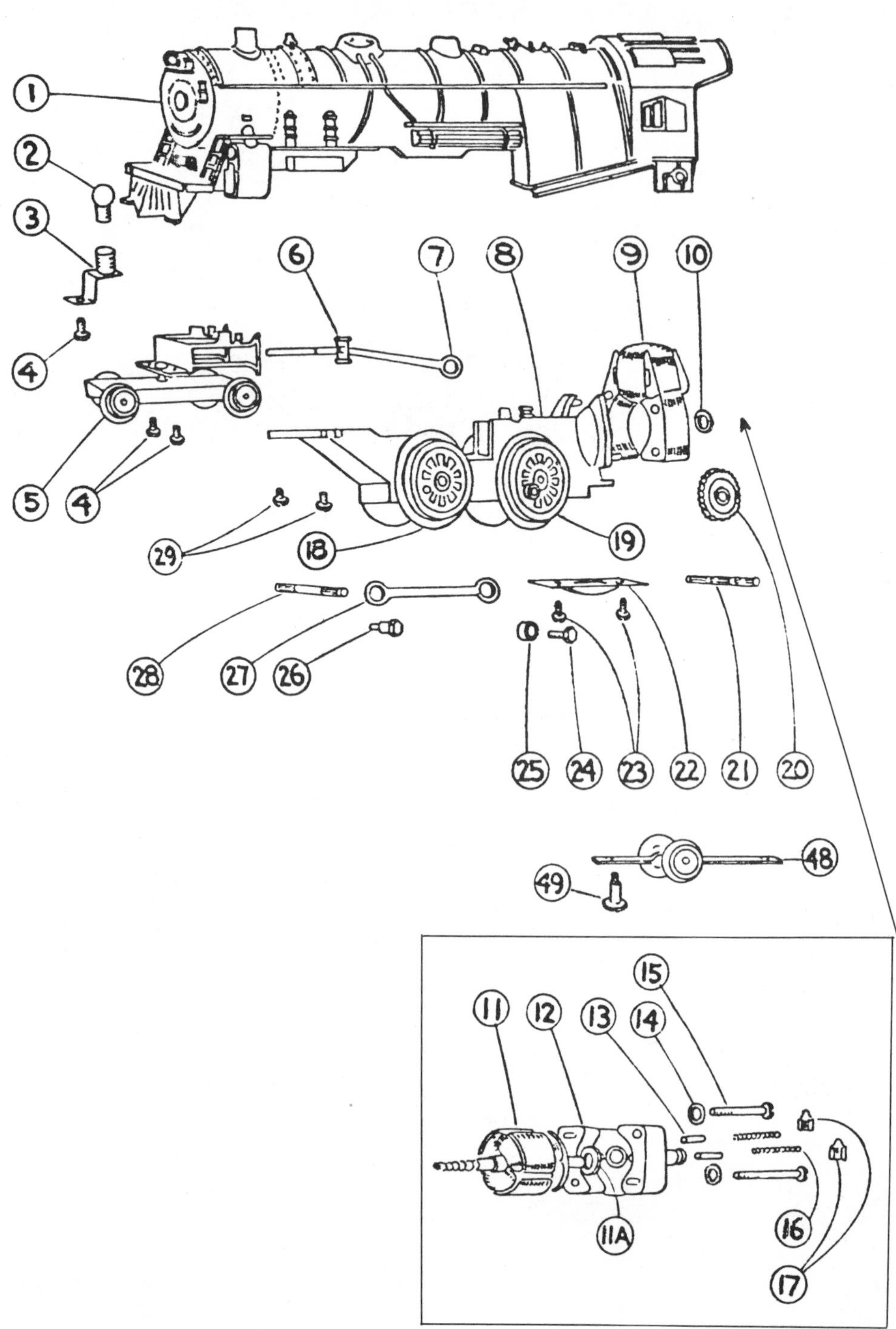

 Ref: Form No. 1599; Feb. 15, 1955

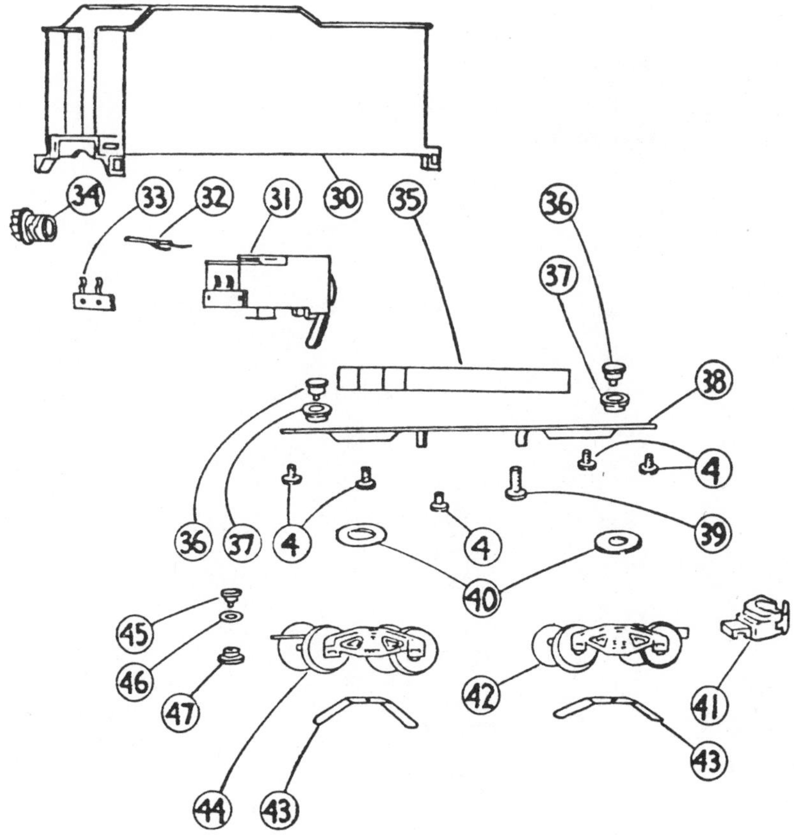

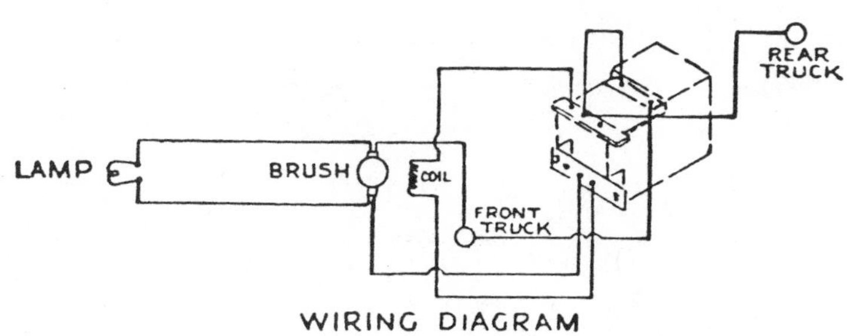

WIRING DIAGRAM

Ref: Form No. 1599; Feb. 15, 1955

Diagram Number	Part No.	Description	Price
1	XA11A975 ARP	Boiler Assy.	$1.12 ea.
2	PA8999	Bulb	.25 "
3	XA10890	Lamp Bracket Assy.	.25 "
4	S230-B	Screw	.10 dz.
5	~~XA10887-A~~	Guide & Truck Assy. XA13A085	.60 ea.
6	PA11099	Crosshead	.05 "
7	PA10889	Connecting Rod	.10 "
8	PA10512	Chassis	.91 "
9	XA9547-B	Magnet Assy.	1.00 "
10	PA10766	Armature Spacer	.05 dz.
11	XA11077	Armature Assy.	2.50 ea.
11A	W1A92	Washer	.01 "
12	XA9565-A	Brush Bracket Assy.	.50 ea.
13	PA9603	Brush	.15 "
14	PA3769	Washer	.05 dz.
15	S295	Screw	.10 ea.
16	PA10757-A	Brush Spring	.05 "
17	PA10754	Brush Cap	.02 "
18	XA12A447	Pull-Mor Wheel	.52 "
19	XA12A449-A	Flanged Wheel & Stud Assy.	.40 "
20	PA10672	Worm Gear (Motor)	.30 "
21	PA10006	Worm Gear Axle	.10 "
22	PA10080	Motor Cover Plate	.02 "
23	S230	Screw	.10 dz.
24	PA5447	Screw	.30 "

 Ref: Form No. 1599; Feb. 15, 1955

Diagram Number	Part No.	Description	Price
25	PA7237	Piston Rod Spacer	.05 ea.
26	PA7421	Screw	.30 dz.
27	PA9452	Side Rod	.20 ea.
28	PA10005	Plain Axle	.10 "
29	S319	Screw	.01 "
30	PA12D078	Tender Body	.63 "
31	XA10587-E	Remote Control Unit	2.50 "
32	XA9612-C R P	Top Finger Unit	~~.50~~ " .30
33	XA9612-B R P	Bottom Finger Unit	~~.50~~ " .30
34	XA8716	Drum Only	~~.60~~ " .50
35	PA11A926	Tender Weight	.18 "
36	PA10235-A	Truck Rivet	.03 "
37	PA10209	Insulating Bushing	.02 "
38	XA12B080	Tender Chassis	.30 "
39	S184	Screw	.10 dz.
40	PA8715-B	Washer	.05 "
41	XA12A047	Knuckle Coupler	.22 ea.
42	XA12A050-A	Rear Truck Assy.	.56 "
43	PA10207	Contact Spring	.02 "
44	XA12A921	Front Truck Assy.	.46 "
45	PA10751	Stud	.02 "
46	PA1067-A	Washer	.05 dz.
47	PA1312	Insulating Bushing	.10 "
48	XA10749	Coupler & Yoke Assy.	.30 ea.
49	PA4939	Screw	.05 "

SERVICE INSTRUCTIONS FOR 307 LOCOMOTIVE AND TENDER

The first thing to do is to place Locomotive and Tender on Track, connect Transformer and test for operation. Make sure all rods, linkage and other parts are not bent or broken. It is also important that the wheels on the Tender be clean to insure a good electrical contact.

1. **If the Locomotive and Tender does not operate properly, you can make the following checks:**
   a. Inspect Brushes (※13) for wear or poor contact.
   b. Clean or polish commutator on Armature (※11) if dirty or worn. Be sure slots are clean.
   c. Check wires and soldered joints for loose connections.
   d. Check operation of Remote Control Unit (※31).
   e. See if motor is properly lubricated.
   f. Wheels and track must be kept clean to insure proper electrical contact.

2. **If these initial steps do not correct the trouble, it will be necessary to change parts as follows:**

   BULB:
   a. Remove S230-B Screw (※4).
   b. Turn Truck Assembly (※5) so that it is parallel with steamchest on Cab (※1).
   c. Pull out Lamp Bracket Assembly (※3).

   BRUSHES OR SPRINGS:
   a. Remove PA4939 Screw (※49) to separate Locomotive and Tender.
   b. Slip off Brush Caps (※17) and take out Brush Springs (※16) and Brushes (※13).

   ARMATURE OR MAGNET:
   a. Follow steps to replace Brushes and Springs.
   b. Take off Brush Bracket Assembly (※12) by removing two Screws (※15).
   c. Armature and Magnet can now be replaced.

   DRIVE WHEELS OR BOILER ASSEMBLY:
   a. Remove PA4939 Screw (※49) to separate Locomotive and Tender.
   b. Remove PA5447 screws on each side, and lift off Connecting Rod (※7) and Spacers (※25) from stud on Drive Wheel (※19).
   c. Turn locomotive upside down and take off Guide and Truck Assembly (※5) by removing two Screws (※4).
   d. To take out motor assembly, remove two S319 Screws (※29), push forward approximately a ¼" to clear clamp on Boiler Assembly (※1) and then lift rear of motor up and pull out.
   e. The motor is now exposed and you can inspect the wiring and other points of the unit, making any necessary adjustments or replacements.

3. **When trouble appears to be in the Tender, proceed as follows:**
   a. Remove four S230B Screws (※4) and take off Tender Body (※30).
   b. Inspect wiring and soldered joints for loose or broken connections.
   c. Check Finger Units (※32) and (※33) on Remote Control Unit (※31) to see if they are burnt or not making proper contact.
   d. The drum (※34) should be checked to see if it is pitted or worn.
   e. The pawl on the Remote Control Unit (※31) may be broken or need adjusting.
   f. It is generally not necessary to replace the complete Remote Control Unit, but sometimes the Finger Units, the Drum, or both need adjusting or replacing.

NO.	PART NO.	DESCRIPTION	PRICE
1	XA11A975-ARP	Boiler Assembly	1.36 ea.
	PA10542	Headlight Lens	.02 ea.
	PA9286	Motor Mount	.02 ea.
2	PA8999	Bulb	.30 ea.
3	XA10890	Lamp Bracket Assembly	.22 ea.
4	S230-B	Screw 4 x ¼ Type "Z" P. K.	.01 ea.
5	XA13A085	Guide & Truck Assembly	.52 ea.
	PA10887	Crosshead Guide	.21 ea.
	XA13A084	Pilot Truck	.23 ea.
	PA4367	Rivet	.01 ea.
6	PA11099	Crosshead	.08 ea.
7	PA10889	Connecting Rod	.09 ea.
8	PA10512	Chassis	1.35 ea.
9	XA9547	Magnet Assembly	1.22 ea.
10	PA10766	Armature Spacer	.01 ea.
11	XA11077	Armature Assembly	3.39 ea.
11A	W1A92	Washer	.02 ea.
12	XA9565-A	Brush Bracket Assembly	1.00 ea.
13	PA9603	Brush	.13 ea.
14	PA3769	Washer	.01 ea.
15	S295	Screw	.02 ea.
16	PA10757-A	Brush Spring	.02 ea.
17	PA10754	Brush Cap	.02 ea.
18	XA12A447	Pul-Mor Wheel NOT AVAILABLE	
		Substitute with XA13A864	.80 ea.
19	XA12A449-A	Flanged Wheel & Stud Assy. NOT AVAILABLE	
		Substitute with XA13A866-A	.39 ea.
20	PA10672	Worm Gear (motor)	.06 ea.
21	PA10006	Worm Gear Axle NOT AVAILABLE	
		Substitute with PA15A281	.07 ea.
22	PA10080	Motor Cover Plate	.02 ea.
23	S230-B	Screw #4 x ¼ Type "Z" P.K.	.01 ea.
24	PA5447	Screw	.04 ea.
25	PA7237	Piston Rod Spacer	.02 ea.
26	PA7421	Screw	.03 ea.
27	PA9452	Side Rod	.02 ea.
28	PA10005	Plain Axle NOT AVAILABLE	
		Substitute with PA15A226	.05 ea.
29	S319	Screw #6 x 5/16 Type "Z" P. K.	.02 ea.
30	PA12D078	Tender Body NOT AVAILABLE	
		Substitute with PA12D078 Body NEW STYLE	.80 ea.
31	XA10587-E	Remote Control Unit	4.04 ea.
32	XA9612-CRP	Top Finger Unit	.33 ea.
33	XA9612-BRP	Bottom Finger Unit	.33 ea.
34	XA8716	Drum Only	.95 ea.
35	PA11A926	Tender Weight NOT AVAILABLE	
		Substitute with PA10593 Weight	.26 ea.

Cont'd

NO.	PART NO.	DESCRIPTION	PRICE
36	PA10235-A	Truck Rivet	.07 ea.
37	PA10209	Insulating Bushing	.02 ea.
38	XA12B080	Tender Chassis NOT AVAILABLE	
		Substitute with PA12B080 Chassis NEW STYLE	.17 ea.
39	S184	Screw	.02 ea.
40	PA8715-B	Washer	.02 ea.
41	XA12A047	Knuckle Coupler	.29 ea.
42	XA12A050-B	Rear Truck Assembly	.72 ea.
	XA10238	Wheel & Axle Assembly	.09 ea.
	PA9990	Plastic Wheel	.03 ea.
	PA10238	Axle	.01 ea.
	PA10140	Brass Wheel	.06 ea.
43	PA10207	Contact Spring	.02 ea.
44	XA12A921	Front Truck Assembly NOT AVAILABLE	
		Substitute with XA15B800	.43 ea.
45	*PA10751	Stud	.02 ea.
46	*PA1067-A	Washer	.06 doz.
47	*PA1312	Insulating Bushing	.12 doz.
48	XA10749	Coupler & Yoke Assy. NOT AVAILABLE	
		Substitute with XA15A784 Draw Bar Assembly	.22 ea.
49	PA4939	Screw	.06 ea.

* Bubbles # 45-46-47 not used with #44 XA15B800 truck or #48, XA15A784 Coupler & Yoke.

Prices subject to change without notice.

 Ref: Form No. 1599; June 1, 1960; Corr. Mar. 23, 1961

NO.	PART NO.	DESCRIPTION	PRICE
1	XA11A975ERP	Boiler Assembly Marked 21105	2.06 ea.
	PA10542	Headlight Lens	.02 ea.
	PA16052	Left Motor Mount	.04 ea.
	PA16053	Right Motor Mount	.04 ea.
2	PA8999	Bulb	.32 ea.
3	XA10890	Lamp Bracket Assembly	.23 ea.
4	S230-B	4 x ¼ Type "Z" P.K. Screw	.01 ea.
5	XA13A085	Guide and Truck Assembly	.55 ea.
	PA10887	Crosshead Guide	.22 ea.
	XA13A084	Pilot Truck	.24 ea.
	PA4367	Rivet	.01 ea.
6	PA11099	Crosshead	.08 ea.
7	PA10889	Connecting Rod	.09 ea.
8	PA10512	Chassis	1.42 ea.
9	XA9547	Magnet Assembly	1.28 ea.
10	PA10766	Armature Spacer	.01 ea.
11	XA11077	Armature Assembly	3.56 ea.
11A	W1A92	Washer	.02 ea.
12	XA9565-A	Brush Bracket Assembly	1.05 ea.
13	PA9603	Brush	.14 ea.
14	PA3769	Washer	.01 ea.
15	S295	Screw	.02 ea.
16	PA10757-A	Brush Spring	.02 ea.
17	PA10754	Brush Cap	.02 ea.
18	XA13A864	Pul-Mor Wheel	.84 ea.
19	XA13A866-A	Flanged Wheel & Stud Assy.	.41 ea.
20	PA10672	Worm Gear (Motor)	.06 ea.
21	PA15A281	Worm Gear Axle	.07 ea.
22	PA10080	Motor Cover Plate	.02 ea.
23	S230-B	#4 x ¼ Type "Z" P.K. Screw	.01 ea.
24	PA5447	Screw	.04 ea.
25	PA7237	Piston Rod Spacer	.02 ea.
26	PA7421	Screw	.03 ea.
27	PA9452	Side Rod	.02 ea.
28	PA15A226	Plain Axle	.05 ea.
29	S319	#6 x 5/16 Type "Z" P.K. Screw	.02 ea.
30		Tender Body - OBSOLETE - No Longer Available - No Substitute	
31	XA10587-E	Remote Control Unit	4.24 ea.
32	XA9612-CRP	Top Finger Unit	.35 ea.
33	XA9612-BRP	Bottom Finger Unit	.35 ea.
34	XA8716	Drum Only	1.00 ea.
35	PA10593	Tender Weight	.27 ea.
36	PA10235-A	Truck Rivet	.07 ea.
37	PA10209	Insulating Bushing	.02 ea.

Cont'd

NO.	PART NO.	DESCRIPTION	PRICE
38		Tender Chassis - OBSOLETE - No Longer Available - No Substitute	
39	S184	Screw	.02 ea.
40	PA8715-B	Washer	.02 ea.
41	XA12A047	Knuckle Coupler	.30 ea.
42	XA12A050-B	Rear Truck Assembly	.83 ea.
	XA10238	Wheel & Axle Assembly	.09 ea.
	PA9990	Plastic Wheel	.03 ea.
	PA10238	Axle	.01 ea.
	PA10140	Brass Wheel	.06 ea.
43	PA10207	Contact Spring	.02 ea.
44	XA15B800	Front Truck Assy. Substitute for XA12A921 Frt. Truck Assy. OBSOLETE	.45 ea.
45	PA10751	Stud	.02 ea.
46	PA1067-A	Washer	.06 dz.
47	PA1312	Insulating Bushing	.13 dz.
48	XA15A784	Draw Bar Assy. Used only with XA15B800	.23 ea.
	XA10891	Coupler & Yoke Assy. Substitute for XA10749 OBSOLETE	.38 ea.
49	PA4939	Screw	.06 ea.

Prices subject to change without notice

LOCOMOTIVE AND TENDER WITH PISTON-TYPE SMOKE AND CHOO-CHOO UNIT

Model No. 312

SPECIFICATIONS

Tested at: 12 Volts A.C. .... Using 140" oval of track.

(A) Motor to be tested with Remote Control Unit at 12 Volts, and not to draw more than .175 amps.

(B) Locomotive to run a minimum of 8 R.P.M. or 8 times forward, around 140" oval of track per minute.

(C) Locomotive to run a minimum of 7.5 R.P.M. or 7½ times reverse, around 140" oval of track per minute.

Load: Not to draw more than 2.1 amps. while pulling 4 Box Cars.

Motor: Universal A.C. or D.C.

Ref: Form No. M2822; June 1, 1950

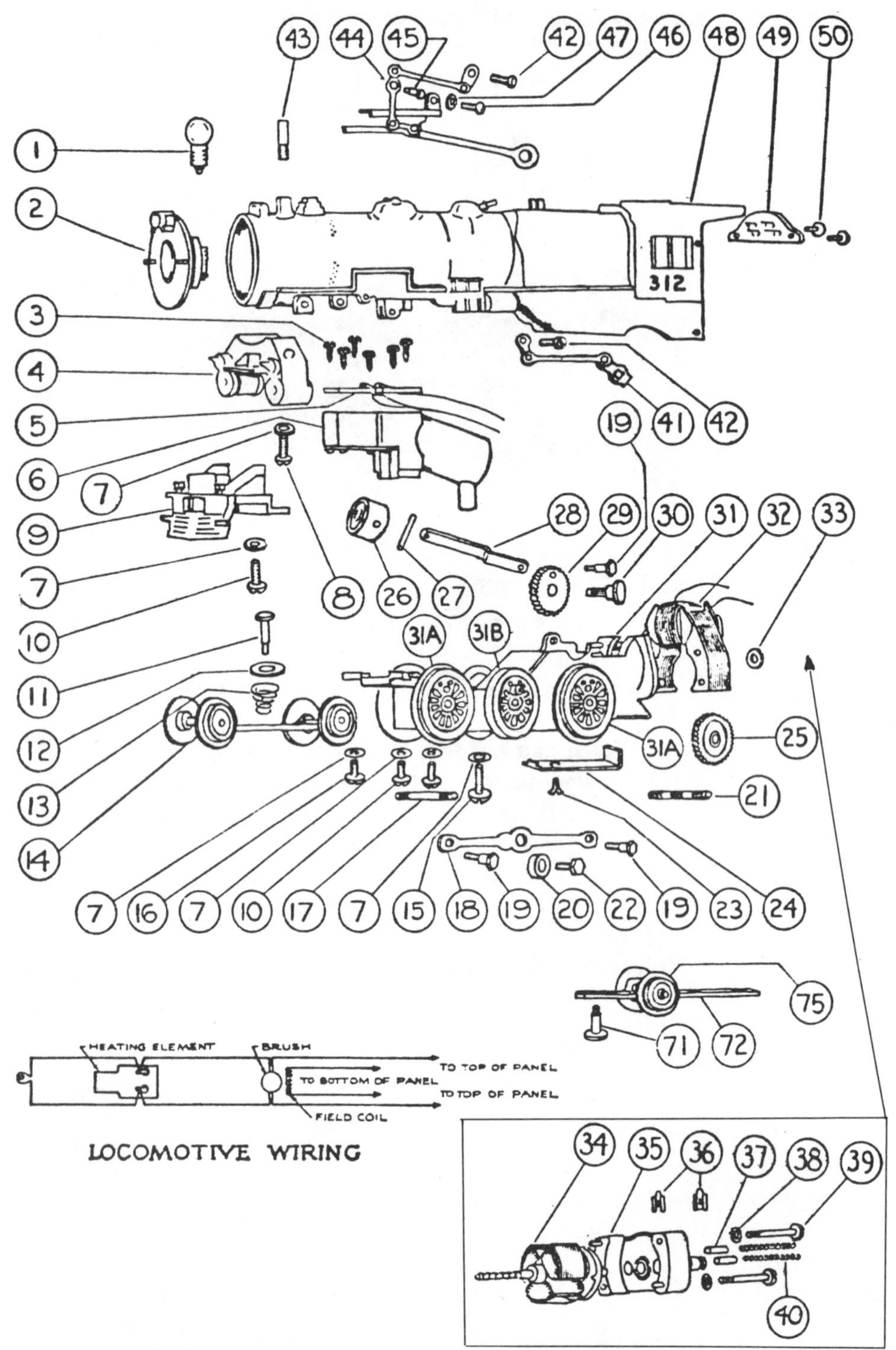

 Ref: Form No. M2822; June 1, 1950

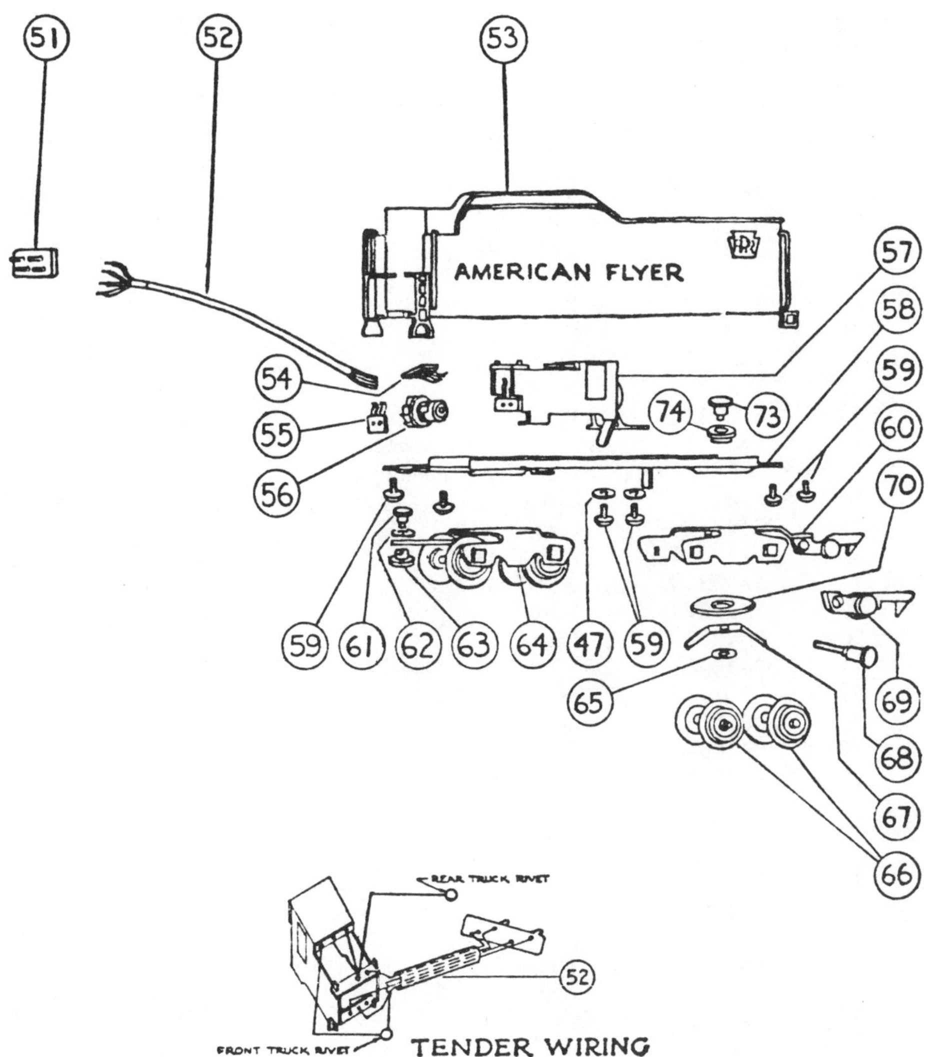
51
52
53
AMERICAN FLYER
57
58
59
60
70
54
55
56
74
73
59
61
62
63
64
47
59
65
69
68
67
66
REAR TRUCK RIVET
52
FRONT TRUCK RIVET
TENDER WIRING

	Part No.	Description	Price
1	PA8999	14 Volt Lamp	$ .25 ea.
2	XA9504-D	Boiler Front Assembly with lamp bracket	.60 "
3	S183	Screw	.10 dz.
4	PA10018	Cylinder and Steamchest	.70 ea.
5	XA10523	Heating Element and Plate Assembly	1.00 "
6	PA10513	Chassis Smoke Box	1.00 "
	XA10513	Chassis Smoke Box Assembly (consists of parts 3-5-6)	2.00 "
7	PA3769	Lockwasher	.05 dz.
8	S16	Screw	.05 "
9	PA9502	Pilot	.70 ea.
10	S46	Screw	.05 dz.
11	PA10707	Stud	.05 ea.
12	W6	Washer	.03 dz.
13	PA8887	Spring	.05 ea.
14	XA10012	Front Truck Assembly	.40 "
	PA9990-A	Front Truck wheel only	.10 "
15	S16-C	Screw	.10 dz.
16	S14	Screw	.05 "
17	PA10005	Plain Axle	.10 ea.
18	PA9280-A	Side Rod	.20 "
19	PA7421	Screw	.30 dz.
20	PA7237	Spacer	.05 ea.
21	PA10006	Worm Gear Axle	.10 "
22	PA5447	Screw	.30 dz.
23	S271	Screw	.10 "
24	PA10017	Grease Pan	.02 ea.
25	PA10672	Worm Gear (motor)	.30 "
	XA10514	Piston & Lever Assembly (consists of parts 26-27-28)	.40 "
26	PA10518	Piston	.20 "
27	PA10520	Piston Pin	.05 "
28	PA10514	Piston Lever	.05 "
29	PA10671	Worm Gear (smoke drive)	.40 "
30	PA10162	Worm Gear Stud	.10 "
31	*XA10506	Chassis Assembly with bushings only	1.20 "
31A	XA10009	Flanged wheel with tapped hole assembly	.40 "
31B	XA10009-B1	Flangeless wheel & stud assembly	.40 "
32	XA9547	Magnet Assembly A.C.	1.00 "
33	PA10766	Washer	.05 dz.
34	**XA11077	Armature Assembly A.C.	2.50 ea.
	***XA9569	Armature Assembly A.C.	2.50 "
35	XA9565-A	Brush Bracket Assembly	.50 "
36	PA10754	Brush Cap	.02 "
37	PA9603	Carbon Brush A.C.	.15 "
38	PA3769	Lockwasher	.05 dz.
39	S295	Screw	.10 ea.
40	PA10757	Brush Spring	.05 "
41	XA10447	Left or Right Eccentric Crank	.30 "

 Ref: Form No. M2822; June 1, 1950

42	PA10598	Screw	.30 dz.
43	PA10536	Smoke Stack	.03 ea.
44	XA10668 R or L	Crosshead Assembly (Right or Left)	.50 "
45	PA9288	Screw	.30 dz.
46	S1	Screw	.05 "
47	W46	Lockwasher	.05 "
48	XA9423-F	Boiler Assembly	2.25 ea.
49	XA10662	Jack Panel	.20 "
50	S230-B	Screw	.10 dz.
51	XA10663	Male Plug	.20 ea.
52	PA10511-A	4 Conductor Cable	.12 "
53	PA9667-B	Tender Body without Smoke Hole	2.50 "
54	XA9612-C	Top Finger Unit (Remote Control)	.50 "
55	XA9612-B	Bottom Finger Unit (Remote Control)	.50 "
56	XA8716	Drum (Remote Control)	.60 "
57	XA10587	Remote Control Unit	2.50 "
58	PA10588	Tender Chassis	.52 "
59	S-0	Screw	.05 dz.
60	XA9987-B	Rear Truck Assembly (complete with wheels)	.75 ea.
61	PA10751	Stud	.02 "
62	PA1067-A	Washer	.05 dz.
63	PA1312	Insulating Bushing	.10 "
64	XA9987-G	Front truck Assembly (complete with wheels)	.50 ea.
65	PA1405	Washer	.05 dz.
66	XA10140	Wheel & Axle Assembly	.25 set
	PA10140	Brass wheel	.15 ea.
	PA9990	Plastic wheel	.10 "
	PA9989	Axle	.02 "
67	PA10207	Contact Spring	.02 "
68	PA10467	Coupler Pin	.10 "
69	XA10469	Coupler and Weight	.15 "
	PA10692	Coupler weight only	.05 "
70	PA8715-BX	Washer	.05 dz.
71	PA4939	Truck Stud	.05 ea.
72	XA10749	Coupler & Yoke Assembly	.30 "
	XA10749-A	Truck and Coupler Assembly (consists of parts 61-62-63-64-72)	.80 "
73	PA10235-A	Truck Rivet	.03 "
74	PA10209	Insulating Bushing	.02 "
75	PA10019-A	Rear Truck Wheel only	.10 "

*XA10506 Chassis Assembly is not sold as a complete assembly with wheels.

**XA11077 Armature Assembly with 1/16" oil slinger cannot be used with XA9565-A Brush Bracket Assembly manufactured before Oct. 1949, unless you grind 1/16" off the boss which the bearing sets into on the Brush Bracket Assembly.

***XA9569 Armature Assembly can be used with XA9565-A Brush Bracket Assembly manfactured after Oct. 1949 providing that you use 1/16" washer to take up end play.

K5 LOCOMOTIVE AND TENDER WITH SMOKE, CHOO-CHOO, AIR CHIME WHISTLE, PULL-MOR WHEELS, AND KNUCKLE COUPLER

Model Nos. 313, 316, 21045, 21115

SPECIFICATIONS

Tested at: 12 Volts A.C. .... using 140" oval of track.

(A) Motor to be tested with Remote Control at 12 Volts and not to draw more than 1.7 Amps.

(B) Locomotive and tender to run a minimum of 9 R.P.M. or 9 times forward around 140" oval of track per minute pulling 4 cars.

(C) Locomotive and tender to run a minimum of 8.5 R.P.M. or 8½ times reverse around 140" oval of track per minute pulling 4 cars.

Load: Not to draw more than 2.1 Amps while pulling 4 Box Cars.

Motor: Universal A.C. or D.C.

Ref: Form No. 1558; July 1, 1954

K5 LOCOMOTIVE AND TENDER WITH SMOKE, CHOO-CHOO, AIR CHIME WHISTLE, PULL-MOR WHEELS, AND KNUCKLE COUPLER

Model Nos. 313, 316, 21045, 21115

SPECIFICATIONS

Tested at: 12 Volts A.C. .... using 140″ oval of track.

(A) Motor to be tested with Remote Control at 12 Volts and not to draw more than 1.7 Amps.

(B) Locomotive and tender to run a minimum of 9 R.P.M. or 9 times forward around 140″ oval of track per minute pulling 4 cars.

(C) Locomotive and tender to run a minimum of 8.5 R.P.M. or 8½ times reverse around 140″ oval of track per minute pulling 4 cars.

Load: Not to draw more than 2.1 Amps while pulling 4 Box Cars.

Motor: Universal A.C. or D.C.

Ref: Form 1807; Feb. 1, 1957

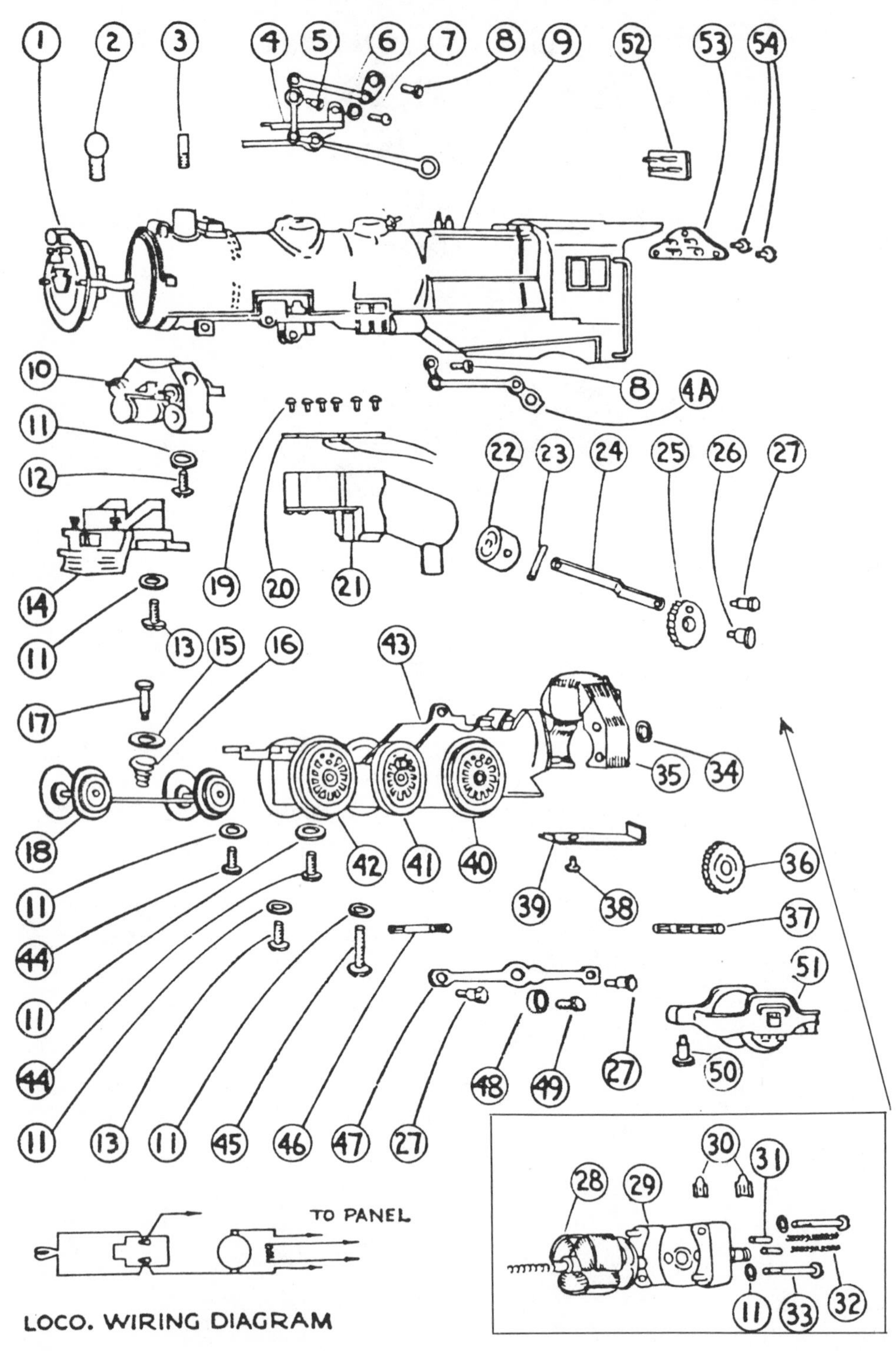

 Ref: Form No. 1807; Feb. 1, 1957

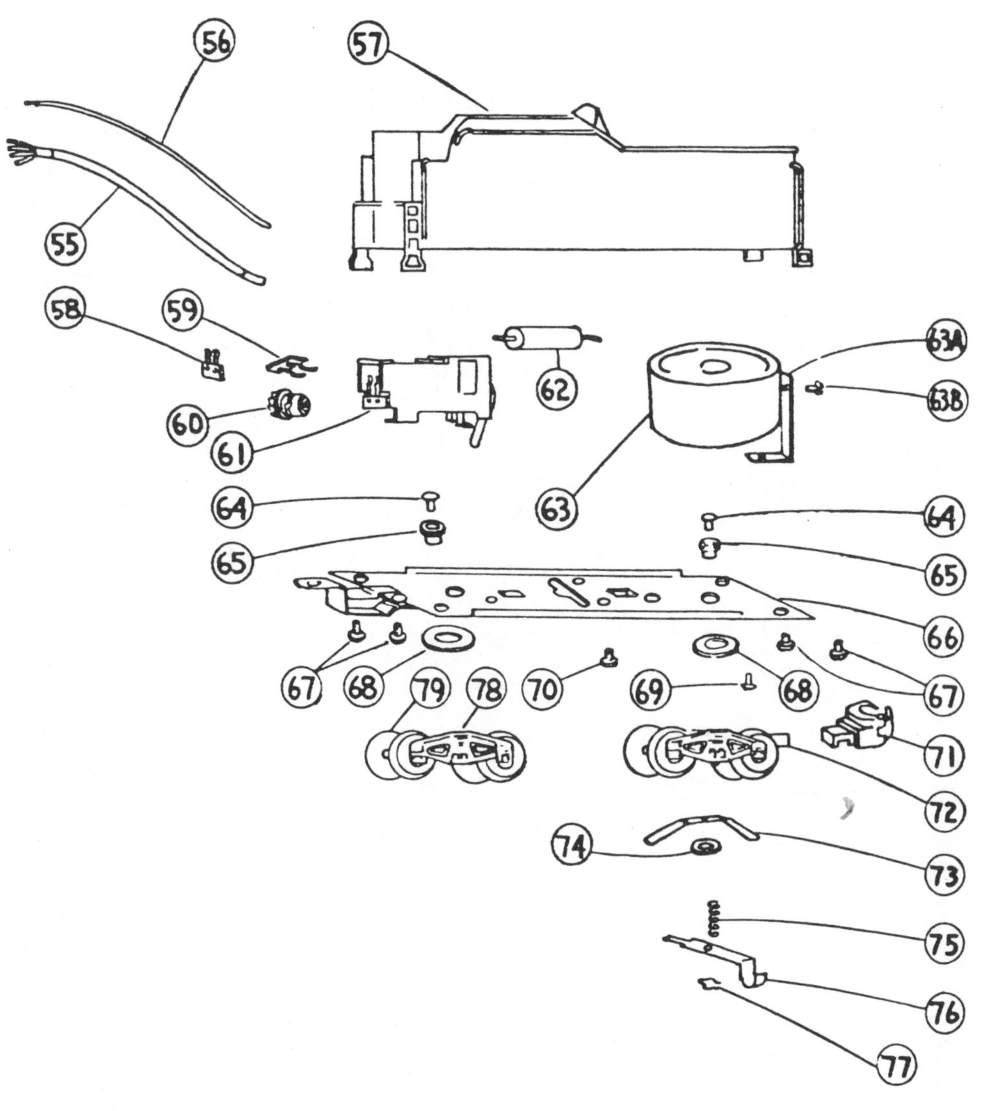

Ref: Form No. 1807; Feb. 1, 1957

INSTRUCTIONS FOR WIRING AND OPERATING AMERICAN FLYER'S WHISTLING LOCOMOTIVE AND TENDER

This locomotive is the standard Penn. K5 locomotive with a built in choo-choo and smoke unit, but the tender has a built in whistle unit which allows the operator to blow long or short blasts or any number of blasts as the train is running or standing still.

The whistle is designed to be used with A.C. current only and if your train system is to be operated on Direct current using either a No. 14 Rectiformer or No. 15 Rectifier and transformer, it cannot be used.

The Control Box for the whistle is very simple to hook up. Study the following diagram and proceed as follows:

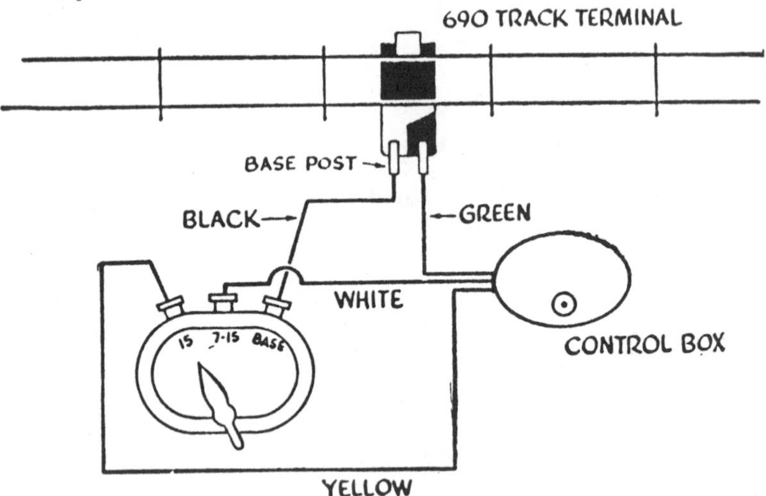

Connect the **YELLOW WIRE** from the Control Box to the **15 VOLT POST** on the transformer.

Connect the **WHITE WIRE** from the Control Box to the **7-15 VOLT POST** on the transformer.

Connect the **GREEN WIRE** from the Control Box to the **RIGHT HAND CLIP** on the No. 690 Track Terminal.

Connect the separate **BLACK WIRE** between the **BASE POST** on the transformer and the **BASE POST CLIP** on the No. 690 Track Terminal.

NOTE: Be sure that no wire runs direct from the 7 to 15 volt post on the transformer to the track terminal.

If the control box is to be hooked into a layout which has already been wired, be sure any wires from the 7-15 volt post to the track are removed. Then proceed with the hook up as shown on the instruction sheet.

In the case of extra feed or jumper wires to distant points on the track, be sure they are not hooked direct to transformer but to the No. 690 track terminal.

The train should now be ready to operate. Place the locomotive and tender on the track and turn on the transformer. While the train is running, flip on the switch projecting from the top of the whistle control box, as long as the switch is held in contact the whistle will blow.

The transformer handle should be turned on while blowing the whistle. If transformer is turned off and whistle is blown, the locomotive will be getting power causing it to run, therefore, stop it in a neutral position with transformer handle on to blow the whistle while train is standing.

OILING THE WHISTLE UNIT

To oil the whistle unit remove the 4 corner screws on the underneath side of the tender and remove the tender body, place a small amount of fine oil on the oil wick at each end of the armature shaft. One wick is located on the top plate in front of the brush holder and the other wick is located in the cross frame at the rear of the armature.

 Ref: Form No. M2758

SERVICE INSTRUCTIONS FOR NO. 316 LOCO AND TENDER – SMOKE AND CHOO-CHOO – AIR CHIME WHISTLE – PULL-MOR – KNUCKLE COUPLER

The first thing to do is to place Locomotive and Tender on track, connect transformer and whistle control unit, and test for operation. Make sure all rods, linkage, and other parts are not bent or broken. It is also important that the wheels on the Tender be clean to insure a good electrical contact.

1. **If the Whistle is satisfactory, but the Locotive and Tender does not operate properly, proceed as follows:**
   a. Remove screw (※50) and also male plug (※52) from the Jack Panel (※53).
   b. Now take another similar tender with a remote control unit in it which is in good working order and connect it to the locomotive. In this way, you will be able to determine whether the Locomotive or Tender is defective.
2. **If the trouble is in the Locomotive you can make the following checks:**
   a. Inspect brushes for wear or poor contact and brush springs for position and proper tension.
   b. Check wires and solder joints on male plug (※52) and Jack Panel (※53) for broken or loose connections.
   c. Clean or polish commutator if dirty or worn.
3. **If these initial steps do not correct the trouble it will be necessary to disassemble the Locomotive as follows:**
   a. Unscrew smoke stack (※3).
   b. Remove screws (※49) on each side and take off Rods (※4) and (※4A) and spacer (※48) from center drive wheel.
   c. Pull out Boiler Front (※1) and Boiler Assembly (※9) and unsolder the two wires at the lamp bracket.
   d. Turn Locomotive upside down and remove two screws (※44) and you can now remove motor assembly from Boiler (※9).
   e. To remove motor, push forward approximately a ¼" to clear clamp on Boiler (※9) and then lift rear of motor up and pull motor out.
   f. The motor is now exposed and you can inspect the wiring and other points of the unit, making any necessary replacements.
4. **When the trouble appears to be in the Tender, proceed as follows:**
   a. Remove four S-0 screws (※67) and take off Tender body (※57).
   b. Inspect wiring and solder joints for loose or broken connections.
   c. Check finger units (※58) and (※59) on remote control unit (※61) to see if they are burnt or not making proper contact.
   d. The drum (※60) should be checked to see if it is pitted or worn.
   e. The pawl on the remote control unit may be broken or need adjusting.
   f. It is generally not necessary to replace the complete Remote Control Unit, but sometimes the Finger Units, the drum or both need adjusting or replacing.
5. **If Locomotive and Tender operates satisfactorily, but the Whistle does not function correctly check as follows:**
   a. Recheck the instruction sheet in order to make sure hook-up is correct. If both the Transformer instructions and the Air Chime Whistle Instructions are followed, this will cause a duplication of wiring. The result will be that you will only have a faint buzz while the train is running or in a neutral position. Follow the Air Chime Whistle wiring instructions only and be sure to have only two wires going to the ※690 track terminal.
   b. The Generator Tube ※PA11665 on the control box may be weak and need replacing.
   c. If the trouble still persists it will be necessary to remove the Tender Body (※57) from the chassis by unscrewing the four S-0 screws (※67).
   d. The unit is exposed and you can check all wires and solder joints for loose connections. Be sure the lead wires on the condenser are covered with an insulating sleeve.
   e. Check the condenser (※62) by adding another condenser in series with temporary connections. If this corrects the trouble the defective condenser can be removed and a new one connected in its place.

Diagram Number	Part No.	Description	Price
1	XA9504-D RP	Boiler Front Assy	$ .60 ea.
2	PA8999	Bulb	.25 "
3	PA12A190	Smoke Stack	.03 "
4	XA10668-R	Crosshead Assy Right	.50 "
	XA10668-L	Crosshead Assy Left	.50 "
4A	XA10447	Eccentric Crank	.30 "
5	PA9288	Screw	.30 dz.
6	W46	Lockwasher	.05 "
7	S-1	Screw	.05 "
8	PA10598	Screw	.30 "
9	XA9423-H RP	Boiler Assy	4.71 ea.
10	PA10018	Cylinder	.70 "
11	PA3769	Washer	.05 dz.
12	S16	Screw	.05 "
13	S46	Screw	.05 "
	XA9502-D	Front Truck & Pilot Assy (consists of parts 14 to 18)	1.30 ea.
14	PA9502	Pilot Assy	.70 "
15	W6	Washer	.03 dz.
16	PA8887	Cone Spring	.05 ea.
17	PA10707	Stud	.05 "
18	XA10012	Front Truck Assy	.40 "
	XA10513	Smoke Box Assy (consists of parts 19-21)	2.00 "
19	S183	Screws	.10 dz.
20	XA10523	Heating Element & Plate Assy	1.00 ea.
21	PA10513	Smoke Box	1.00 "
22	PA10518-A	Piston	.20 "
23	PA10520	Pin	.05 "
24	PA10514	Piston Lever	.05 "
25	PA10671	Worm Gear	.40 "
26	PA10162	Stud	.10 "
27	PA7421	Screw	.30 dz.
28	XA11077	Armature Assy	2.50 ea.
29	XA9565-A	Brush Bracket Assy	.50 "
30	PA10754	Brush Cap	.02 "
31	PA9603	Brush	.15 "
32	PA10757-A	Brush Spring	.05 "
33	S295	Screw	"
34	PA10766	Armature Spacer	.05 dz.
35	XA9547	Magnet Assy	1.00 ea.
36	PA10672	Worm Gear (motor)	.30 "
37	PA10006	Worm Gear Axle	.10 "
38	S271	Screw	.10 dz.
39	PA10017-0A	Motor Cover Plate	.02 ea.
40	XA12A447	Pull Mor Wheel Assy	.52 "

 Ref: Form No. 1558; July 1, 1954

Diagram Number	Part No.	Description	Price
41	XA10009-B1	Flangeless Wheel & Stud Assy	$ .40 ea.
42	XA12A449	Flanged Wheel Assy	.40 "
43	PA10506	Chassis	1.34 "
44	S14	Screw	.05 dz.
45	S16C	Screw	.10 "
46	PA10005	Plain Axle	.10 ea.
47	PA9280-A	Side Rod	.20 "
48	PA7237	Side Rod Spacer	.05 "
49	PA5447	Screw	.30 dz.
50	PA4939	Screw	.05 ea.
51	XA10020	Rear Truck Assy	.70 "
	PA10019-A	Rear Truck Wheel Only	.10 "
52	XA10663	Male Plug	.20 "
53	XA10662-A	Jack Panel	.20 "
54	S222	Screw	.01 "
55	PA10511-A	4 Conductor Cable	.12 "
56	P9273-P	Wire Lead	.02 "
57	PA9667-B	Tender Body	2.50 "
58	XA9612-C	Top Finger Unit	.50 "
59	XA9612-B	Bottom Finger Unit	.50 "
60	XA8716	Drum Only	.60 "
61	XA10587-E	Remote Control Unit	2.50 "
62	PA12N820	Capacitor	1.89 "
63	XA11B831	Speaker	3.87 "
63A	PA12A901	Bracket	.01 "
63B	S172	Screw	.10 dz.
64	PA10235	Truck Rivet	.03 ea.
65	PA10209	Insulating Bushing	.02 "
66	XA10588	Chassis & Wire Retaining Assy	.30 "
67	S-0	Screw	.05 dz.
68	PA8715-B	Washer	.05 "
69	(PA5601)	Rivet	.10 "
70	S230-B	Screw	.10 "
71	XA12A047	Knuckle Coupler	.22 ea.
72	XA12A350	Rear Truck Assy	.87 "
73	PA10207	Contact Spring	.02 "
74	PA1405	Tin Washer	.05 dz.
75	PA11A956	Spring	.01 ea.
76	PA11A936	Tender Pick-up	.02 "
77	PA11A944	Hair Pin Cotter	.01 "
78	XA12A516	Front Truck Assy	.60 "
79	XA10238	Wheel and Axle Assy	.25 set
	PA9990	Plastic Wheel	.10 ea.
	PA10140	Metal Wheel	.15 "
	PA10238	Axle	.02 "

Ref: Form No. 1558; July 1, 1954

Diagram Number	Part No.	Description	Price
1	XA9504-DRP	Boiler Front Assy.	$ .71 ea.
2	PA8999	Bulb	.25 "
3	PA12A190	Smoke Stack	.02 "
4	XA10668-R	Crosshead Assy. Right	.55 "
	XA10668-L	Crosshead Assy. Left	.55 "
4A	XA10447	Eccentric Crank	.30 "
5	PA9288	Screw	.30 dz.
6	W46	Lockwasher	.05 "
7	S-1	Screw	.05 "
8	PA10598	Screw	.30 "
9	XA9423-HRP	Boiler Assy.	5.22 ea.
10	PA10018	Cylinder	.53 "
11	PA3769	Washer	.05 dz.
12	S16	Screw	.05 "
13	S46	Screw	.05 "
14	PA9502	Pilot Assy.	.78 ea.
15	W6	Washer	.03 dz.
16	PA8887	Cone Spring	.02 ea.
17	PA10707	Stud	.05 "
18	XA10012	Front Truck Assy.	.40 "
	*XA10513	Smoke Box Assembly (consists of parts 19-21)	NOT AVAILABLE
19	S183	Screw	.10 dz.
20	**XA10523	Heating Element & Plate Assy.	.66 ea.
21	*PA10513	Smoke Box	NOT AVAILABLE
22	PA10518-A	Piston	.17 "
23	PA10520	Pin	.05 "
24	PA10514	Piston Lever	.08 "
25	PA10671	Worm Gear	.27 "
26	PA10162	Stud	.05 "
27	PA7421	Screw	.30 dz.
28	XA11077	Armature Assy.	2.19 ea.
29	XA9565-A	Brush Bracket Assy.	.71 "
30	PA10754	Brush Cap	.02 "
31	PA9603	Brush	.15 "
32	PA10757-A	Brush Spring	.05 "
33	S295	Screw	.02 "
34	PA10766	Armature Spacer	.05 dz.
35	XA9547	Magnet Assy.	1.11 ea.
36	PA10672	Worm Gear (motor)	.20 "
37	PA10006	Worm Gear Axle	.10 "
38	S271	Screw	.10 dz.
39	PA10017	Motor Cover Plate	.04 ea.
40	XA13A864	Pull-Mor Wheel Assy.	.51 "

All prices subject to change without notice.

*Parts so marked NOT AVAILABLE, substitute with:

Dia. 21	XA13B894RP	Smoke Box Assy. (new style)	$1.55 ea.
	PA13B894	Smoke Box (new style)	.59 "
	PA14A209	Separator (new style)	.01 "

 Ref: Form No. 1807; Feb. 1, 1957

Diagram Number	Part No.	Description	Price
41	XA10009-B1	Flangeless Wheel & Stud Assy.	.45 "
42	XA13A865	Flanged Wheel Assy.	.29 "
43	XA10506	Chassis	1.33 "
44	S14	Screw	.05 dz.
45	S16C	Screw	.11 "
46	PA10005	Plain Axle	.10 ea.
47	PA9280-A	Side Rod	.10 "
48	PA7237	Side Rod Spacer	.05 "
49	PA5447	Screw	.30 dz.
50	PA4939	Screw	.05 ea.
51	XA10020	Rear Truck Assy.	.70 "
	PA10019-A	Rear Truck Wheel only	.05 "
52	XA10663	Male Plug	.22 "
53	XA10662-A	Jack Panel	.22 "
54	S222	Screw	.01 "
55	PA10511-A	4 Conductor Cable	.12 "
56	P9273-P	Wire Lead	.02 "
57	PA9667-B	Tender Body	2.58 "
58	XA9612-CRP	Top Finger Unit	.30 "
59	XA9612-BRP	Bottom Finger Unit	.30 "
60	XA8716	Drum only	.59 "
61	XA10587-E	Remote Control Unit	1.32 "
62	PA12N820	Capacitor	2.10 "
63	XA11B831	Speaker	2.95 "
63A	PA12A901	Bracket	.01 "
63B	S172	Screw	.10 dz.
64	PA10235-A	Truck Rivet	.03 ea.
65	PA10209	Insulating Bushing	.02 "
66	XA10588	Chassis & Wire Retaining Assy.	.32 "
67	S-0	Screw	.05 dz.
68	PA8715-B	Washer	.05 "
69	PA5601	Rivet	.24 "
70	S230-B	Screw	.10 "
71	XA12A047	Knuckle Coupler	.22 ea.
72	XA12A350	Rear Truck Assy.	.87 "
73	PA10207	Contact Spring	.02 "
74	PA1405	Tin Washer	.05 dz.
75	PA11A956	Spring	.02 ea.
76	PA11A936	Tender Pick-up	.02 "
77	PA11A944	Hair Pin Cotter	.01 "
78	XA12A516	Front Truck Assy.	.40 "
79	XA10238	Wheel and Axle Assy.	.17 set
	PA9990	Plastic Wheel	.05 ea.
	PA10140	Metal Wheel	.15 "
	PA10238	Axle	.02 "

**The XA10523 Heating Element and Plate Assy. is still available, and interchangeable with the new style PA13B894 Smoke Box. The new style XA14A208 Heating Element and Plate Assembly, priced at $.66 each, is used only on the new style PA13B894 Smoke Box.

#313 & #21045 LOCOMOTIVE AND TENDER
(SAME AS #316 WITH THE FOLLOWING EXCEPTIONS:)

DIA NO	PART NO	DESCRIPTION	PRICE
14	PA9502	Pilot	$ .90 ea
28	XA12B523	Armature Assembly	4.04 ea
33	S3A78	Screw	.02 ea
35	XA12A526	Magnet Assembly	1.80 ea
52-54		NOT USED	
62-63B		NOT USED	
69		NOT USED	

****

#21115 PENN K5 LOCO & TENDER (1958 STYLE)
(SAME AS #316 & #313 & #21045 WITH THE FOLLOWING EXCEPTIONS:)

DIA NO	PART NO	DESCRIPTION	PRICE
9	XA9423	Boiler w/trim	7.44 ea
	PA9579	Rear Mounting Bracket	.01 ea
	XA9578	Coupler Strap	.08 ea
28	XA14B816	Armature Assembly	4.15 ea
29	XA15A695	Motor BRUSH MOUNTING PLATE ASSY	.58 ea
	PA13A131	Motor Brush Tube	.03 ea
30	PA13A128	Motor Brush Tube Cover	.01 ea
	PA15A044	Motor Brush Tube Cover Brace	.05 ea
31	PA13A128	Motor Brush	.13 ea
32	PA13A130	Motor Brush Spring	.03 ea
33	S33	Screw	.01 ea
55	XA14A513	Plug Assembly	.34 ea
56	LW-1B1	Black Lead Wire	.02 ft
57	XA14D94orp	Tender Body w/trim assembly	3.30 ea
58-60		NOT USED	
61		NOT USED	
66	PA14A948	Tender Chassis	.41 ea
67		NOT USED	
74		NOT USED	
78	XA14B811	Front Truck Assy	.58 ea

PARTS NOT SHOWN:

PART NO	DESCRIPTION	PRICE
S230B	Screw (used w/tender body & chassis)	.01 ea
PA14A839	Coupler Strap (connectloco to tender)	.03 ea
PA15A382	Weight (For Tender)	.62 ea
PA11A132	Rivet (For Weight)	.02 ea

PRICES SUBJECT TO CHANGE WITHOUT NOTICE

NO.	PART NO.	DESCRIPTION	PRICE
1	XA9504-DRP	Boiler Front Assembly	.78 ea.
	PA10542	Headlight Lens	.02 ea.
2	PA8999	Bulb	.30 ea.
3	PA12A190	Smoke Stack	.03 ea.
4	XA10668-R	Crosshead Assembly (Right)	.92 ea.
	XA10668-L	Crosshead Assembly (Left)	.92 ea.
4A	XA10447	Eccentric Crank	.23 ea.
5	PA9288	Screw	.03 ea.
6	W46	Lockwasher	.01 ea.
7	S-1	Screw	.01 ea.
8	PA10598	Screw	.02 ea.
9	XA9423-JRP	Boiler Assembly	6.20 ea.
	PA9579	Rear Mounting Bracket	.01 ea.
	XA9578	Coupler Strap	.08 ea.
10	PA10018	Cylinder	.51 ea.
11	PA3769	Washer	.01 ea.
12	S16	Screw	.01 ea.
13	S46	Screw	.01 ea.
14	PA9502	Pilot	.86 ea.
15	W6	Washer	.01 ea.
16	PA8887	Cone Spring	.02 ea.
17	PA10707	Stud	.07 ea.
18	XA10012	Front Truck Assy.	.44 ea.
	PA13A082	Axle	.01 ea.
	PA9990	Plastic Wheel	.03 ea.
19	S183	Screw	.01 ea.
20	XA14A208-A	Heating Element & Plate Assy.	.91 ea.
21	XA13B894-RP	Smoke Box Assy. (Consists of parts 19-21)	2.13 ea.
	PA13B894	Smoke Box	.76 ea.
	PA14A209	Separator (Not Shown)	.02 ea.
22	PA10518-A	Piston	.29 ea.
23	PA10520	Pin	.03 ea.
24	PA10514	Piston Lever	.14 ea.
25	PA10671	Worm Gear	.32 ea.
26	PA10162	Stud	.08 ea.
27	PA7421	Screw	.03 ea.
28	XA12B523	Armature Assembly	3.85 ea.
29	XA9565-A	Brush Bracket Assembly	1.00 ea.
30	PA10754	Brush Cap	.02 ea.
31	PA9603	Brush	.13 ea.
32	PA10757-A	Brush Spring	.02 ea.
33	S3A78	Screw	.02 ea.
34	PA10766	Armature Spacer	.01 ea.
35	XA12A526	Magnet Assembly	1.71 ea.
36	PA10672	Worm Gear (Motor)	.06 ea.
37	PA15A281	Worm Gear Axle	.07 ea.
38	S271	Screw	.02 ea.
39	PA10017	Motor Cover Plate	.07 ea.
40	XA13A864	Pul-Mor Wheel Assembly	.80 ea.
41	XA10009-B1	Flangeless Wheel & Stud Assy.	.63 ea.
42	XA13A865	Flanged Wheel Assembly	.37 ea.
43	XA10506	Chassis w/bearing	1.46 ea.
	PA13A187	Bearing	.04 ea.

Cont'd

NO.	PART NO.	DESCRIPTION	PRICE
44	S14	Screw	.01 ea.
45		NOT USED	
46	PA15A226	Plain Axle	.05 ea.
47	PA9280-A	Side Rod	.16 ea.
48	PA7237	Side Rod Spacer	.02 ea.
49	PA5447	Screw	.04 ea.
50	PA4939	Screw	.06 ea.
51	XA10020	Rear Truck Assembly	.91 ea.
	PA10019-A	Rear Truck Wheel Only	.06 ea.
52		NOT USED	
53		NOT USED	
54		NOT USED	
55	PA13A208	Cable	.04 ft.
56	PA10249	Wire Lead	.03 ft.
57	PA9667-B	Tender Body	2.84 ea.
58	XA9612-CRP	Top Finger Unit	.33 ea.
59	XA9612-BRP	Bottom Finger Unit	.33 ea.
60	XA8716	Drum Only	.95 ea.
61	XA10587-E	Remote Control Unit	4.04 ea.
62		NOT USED	
63		NOT USED	
63A		NOT USED	
63B		NOT USED	
64	PA10235-A	Truck Rivet	.07 ea.
65	PA10209	Insulating Bushing	.02 ea.
66	XA10588	Chassis & Wire Retaining Assy.	.35 ea.
	PA12A520	Coupler Strap (Not Shown)	.04 ea.
	PA4362	Rivet (Not Shown)	.01 ea.
67	S-0	Screw	.01 ea.
68	PA8715-B	Washer	.02 ea.
69		NOT USED	
70	S230-B	Screw	.01 ea.
71	XA12A047	Knuckle Coupler	.29 ea.
72	XA12A350	Rear Truck Assembly	.80 ea.
73	PA10207	Contact Spring	.02 ea.
74	PA1405	Tin Washer	.01 ea.
75	PA11A956	Spring	.02 ea.
76	PA11A936	Tender Pick Up	.04 ea.
77	PA11A944	Hair Pin Cotter	.01 ea.
78	XA12A516	Front Truck Assembly	.44 ea.
79	XA10238	Wheel and Axle Assembly	.09 ea.
	PA9990	Plastic Wheel	.03 ea.
	PA10140	Metal Wheel	.06 ea.
	PA10238	Axle	.01 ea.

Prices subject to change without notice.

 Ref: Form No. 1807; June 1, 1960; Corr. Mar. 23, 1961

DIA. NO.	PART NO.	DESCRIPTION	PRICE
1	XA9504-DRP	Boiler Front Assembly	.78 ea.
	PA10542	Headlight Lens	.02 ea.
2	PA8999	Bulb	.30 ea.
3	PA12A190	Smoke Stack	.03 ea.
4	XA10668-R	Crosshead Assembly (Right)	.92 ea.
	XA10668-L	Crosshead Assembly (Left)	.92 ea.
4A	XA10447	Eccentric Crank	.23 ea.
5	PA9288	Screw	.03 ea.
6	W46	Lockwasher	.01 ea.
7	S-1	Screw	.01 ea.
8	PA10598	Screw	.02 ea.
9	XA9423-HRP	Boiler Assembly	5.74 ea.
	PA9579	Rear Mounting Bracket	.01 ea.
	XA9578	Coupler Strap	.08 ea.
10	PA10018	Cylinder	.51 ea.
11	PA3769	Washer	.01 ea.
12	S16	Screw	.01 ea.
13	S46	Screw	.01 ea.
14	PA9502	Pilot	.86 ea.
15	W6	Washer	.01 ea.
16	PA8887	Cone Spring	.02 ea.
17	PA10707	Stud	.07 ea.
18	XA10012	Front Truck Assembly	.44 ea.
	PA13A082	Axle	.01 ea.
	PA9990	Plastic Wheel	.03 ea.
19	S183	Screw	.01 ea.
20	XA10523	Heating Element & Plate Assy. NOT AVAILABLE	
		Substitute with XA14A208AH. E. & P. Assy.	.91 ea.
21	XA10513	Smoke Box Assy. NOT AVAILABLE	
		Substitute with XA13B894-RP Smoke Box Assy.	2.13 ea.
	PA10513	Smoke Box NOT AVAILABLE	
		Substitute with PA13B894 Smoke Box	.76 ea.
	PA14A209	Separator (NOT SHOWN)	.02 ea.
22	PA10518-A	Piston	.29 ea.
23	PA10520	Pin	.03 ea.
24	PA10514	Piston Lever	.14 ea.
25	PA10671	Worm Gear	.32 ea.
26	PA10162	Stud	.08 ea.
27	PA7421	Screw	.03 ea.
28	XA11077	Armature Assembly	3.39 ea.
29	XA9565-A	Brush Bracket Assembly	1.00 ea.
30	PA10754	Brush Cap	.02 ea.
31	PA9603	Brush	.13 ea.
32	PA10757-A	Brush Spring	.02 ea.
33	S295	Screw	.02 ea.
34	PA10766	Armature Spacer	.01 ea.
35	XA9547	Magnet Assembly	1.22 ea.
36	PA10672	Worm Gear (Motor)	.06 ea.
37	PA10006	Worm Gear Axle NOT AVAILABLE	
		Substitute with PA15A281 Axle	.07 ea.
38	S271	Screw	.02 ea.
39	PA10017	Motor Cover Plate	.07 ea.

Cont'd

DIA. NO.	PART NO.	DESCRIPTION	PRICE
40	XA13A864	Pul-Mor Wheel Assembly	.80 ea.
41	XA10009-B1	Flangeless Wheel & Stud Assembly	.63 ea.
42	XA13A865	Flanged Wheel Assembly	.37 ea.
43	PA10506-A	Chassis w/bearing	1.78 ea.
	PA13A187	Bearing	.04 ea.
44	S14	Screw	.01 ea.
45		NOT USED	
46	PA10005	Plain Axle NOT AVAILABLE	
		Substitute with PA15A226 Axle	.05 ea.
47	PA9280-A	Side Rod	.16 ea.
48	PA7237	Side Rod Spacer	.02 ea.
49	PA5447	Screw	.04 ea.
50	PA4939	Screw	.06 ea.
51	XA10020	Rear Truck Assembly	.91 ea.
	PA10019-A	Rear Truck Wheel Only	.06 ea.
52	XA10663	Male Plug	.24 ea.
53	XA10662-A	Jack Panel	.24 ea.
54	S230-B	Screw	.01 ea.
55	PA10511	4 Conductor Cable	.13 ea.
56	P9273	Wire Lead	.02 ea.
57	PA9667-B	Tender Body	2.84 ea.
58	XA9612-CRP	Top Finger Unit	.33 ea.
59	XA9612-BRP	Bottom Finger Unit	.33 ea.
60	XA8716	Drum Only	.95 ea.
61	XA10587-E	Remote Control Unit	4.04 ea.
62	PA12N820	Capacitor NOT AVAILABLE	
		Substitute with PA14A914 Capacitor	1.40 ea.
63	XA11B831	Speaker NOT AVAILABLE	
		Substitute with XA14A127 Speaker	4.57 ea.
63A	PA14A216	Bracket	.08 ea.
63B	S171	Screw	.01 ea.
64	PA10235-A	Truck Rivet	.07 ea.
65	PA10209	Insulating Bushing	.02 ea.
66	XA10588	Chassis & Wire Retaining Assy.	.35 ea.
	PA12A520	Coupler Strap (NOT SHOWN)	.04 ea.
	PA4362	Rivet (NOT SHOWN)	.01 ea.
67	S-0	Screw	.01 ea.
68	PA8715-B	Washer	.02 ea.
69	PA5601	Rivet NOT AVAILABLE	
		Substitute with S172 Screw	.02 ea.
70	S230-B	Screw	.01 ea.
71	XA12A047	Knuckle Coupler	.29 ea.
72	XA12A350	Rear Truck Assembly	.80 ea.
73	PA10207	Contact Spring	.02 ea.
74	PA1405	Tin Washer	.01 ea.
75	PA11A956	Spring	.02 ea.
76	PA11A936	Tender Pick-Up	.04 ea.
77	PA11A944	Hair Pin Cotter	.01 ea.
78	XA12A516	Front Truck Assembly	.44 ea.
79	XA10238	Wheel & Axle Assembly	.09 ea.
	PA9990	Plastic Wheel	.03 ea.
	PA10140	Metal Wheel	.06 ea.
	PA10238	Axle	.01 ea.

Prices subject to change without notice.

Ref: Form No. 1807; June 1, 1960; Corr. Mar. 23, 1961

NO.	PART NO.	DESCRIPTION	PRICE
1	XA9504-DRP	Boiler Front Assembly	.82 ea.
	PA10542	Headlight Lens	.02 ea.
2	PA8999	Bulb	.32 ea.
3	PA12A190	Smoke Stack	.03 ea.
4	XA10668-R	Crosshead Assembly (Right)	.97 ea.
	XA10668-L	Crosshead Assembly (Left)	.97 ea.
4A	XA10447	Eccentric Crank	.24 ea.
5	PA9288	Screw	.03 ea.
6	W46	Lock Washer	.11 dz.
7	S-1	Screw	.01 ea.
8	PA10598	Screw	.02 ea.
9	XA9423-JRP	Boiler Assembly	6.51 ea.
	PA9579	Rear Mounting Bracket	.01 ea.
	XA9578	Coupler Strap	.08 ea.
10	PA10018	Cylinder	.54 ea.
11	PA3769	Washer	.01 ea.
12	S16	Screw	.01 ea.
13	S46	Screw	.01 ea.
14	PA9502	Pilot	.90 ea.
15	W6	Washer	.01 ea.
16	PA8887	Cone Spring	.02 ea.
17	PA10707	Stud	.07 ea.
18	XA10012	Front Truck Assembly	.46 ea.
	PA13A082	Axle	.01 ea.
	PA9990	Plastic Wheel	.03 ea.
19	S183	Screw	.01 ea.
20	XA14A208-A	Heating Element & Plate Assy.	.96 ea.
* 21	XA13B894-RP	Smoke Box Assy. (Consists of parts 19-21)	2.24 ea.
22	PA10518-A	Piston	.30 ea.
23	PA10520	Pin	.03 ea.
24	PA10514	Piston Lever	.15 ea.
25	PA10671	Worm Gear	.34 ea.
26	PA10162	Stud	.08 ea.
27	PA7421	Screw	.03 ea.
28	XA12B523	Armature Assembly	4.04 ea.
29	XA9565-A	Brush Bracket Assembly	1.05 ea.
30	PA10754	Brush Cap	.02 ea.
31	PA9603	Brush	.14 ea.
32	PA10757-A	Brush Spring	.02 ea.
33	S3A78	Screw	.02 ea.
34	PA10766	Armature Spacer	.01 ea.
35	XA12A526	Magnet Assembly	1.80 ea.
36	PA10672	Worm Gear (Motor)	.06 ea.
37	PA15A281	Worm Gear Axle	.07 ea.
38	S271	Screw	.02 ea.
39	PA10017	Motor Cover Plate	.07 ea.
40	XA13A864	Pul-Mor Wheel Assembly	.84 ea.
41	XA10009-B1	Flangeless Wheel & Stud Assy.	.66 ea.

Cont'd

NO.	PART NO.	DESCRIPTION	PRICE
42	XA13A865	Flanged Wheel Assembly	.39 ea.
43	PA10506-A	Chassis	1.87 ea.
	PA13A187	Bearing	.04 ea.
44	S14	Screw	.01 ea.
45		NOT USED	
46	PA15A226	Plain Axle	.05 ea.
47	PA9280-A	Side Rod	.17 ea.
48	PA7237	Side Rod Spacer	.02 ea.
49	PA5447	Screw	.04 ea.
50	PA4939	Screw	.06 ea.
51	XA15A261	Rear Truck Assy. Substitute for XA10020 Truck Assy. - OBSOLETE	.72 ea.
	PA10019-A	Rear Truck Wheel Only	.06 ea.
52		NOT USED	
53		NOT USED	
54		NOT USED	
55	PA13A208-A	Cable	.04 ft.
56	PA10249	Wire Lead	.03 ft.
57	PA9667-B	Tender Body	2.98 ea.
58	XA9612-CRP	Top Finger Unit	.35 ea.
59	XA9612-BRP	Bottom Finger Unit	.35 ea.
60	XA8716	Drum Only	1.00 ea.
61	XA10587-E	Remote Control Unit	4.24 ea.
62		NOT USED	
63		NOT USED	
63A		NOT USED	
63E		NOT USED	
64	PA10235-A	Truck Rivet	.07 ea.
65	PA10209	Insulating Bushing	.02 ea.
66	XA10588	Chassis & Wire Retaining Assy.	.37 ea.
	PA12A520	Coupler Strap (Not Shown)	.04 ea.
	PA4362	Rivet (Not Shown)	.01 ea.
67	S-0	Screw	.01 ea.
68	PA8715-B	Washer	.02 ea.
69		NOT USED	
70	S230-B	Screw	.01 ea.
71	XA12A047	Knuckle Coupler	.30 ea.
72	XA12A350	Rear Truck Assembly	.84 ea.
73	PA10207	Contact Spring	.02 ea.
74	PA1405	Tin Washer	.05 dz.
75	PA11A956	Spring	.02 ea.
76	PA11A936	Tender Pick Up	.04 ea.
77	PA11A944	Hair Pin Cotter	.01 ea.
78	XA12A516	Front Truck Assy.	.46 ea.
79	XA10238	Wheel and Axle Assembly	.09 ea.
	PA9990	Plastic Wheel	.03 ea.
	PA10140	Metal Wheel	.06 ea.
	PA10238	Axle	.01 ea.

* #21 When Using XA13B894RP on #313 Remove Screw on Solder Terminal

Prices subject to change without notice

 Ref: Form. No. 1807; Oct. 1, 1962

DIA. NO.	PART NO.	DESCRIPTION	PRICE
1	XA9504-DRP	Boiler Front Assembly	.82 ea.
	PA10542	Headlight Lens	.02 ea.
2	PA8999	Bulb	.32 ea.
3	PA12A190	Smoke Stack	.03 ea.
4	XA10668-R	Crosshead Assembly (Right)	.97 ea.
	XA10668-L	Crosshead Assembly (Left)	.97 ea.
4A	XA10447	Eccentric Crank	.24 ea.
5	PA9288	Screw	.03 ea.
6	W46	Lockwasher	.01 ea.
7	S-1	Screw	.01 ea.
8	PA10598	Screw	.02 ea.
9	XA9423-JRP	Boiler Assembly	6.51 ea.
	PA9579	Rear Mounting Bracket	.01 ea.
	XA9578	Coupler Strap	.08 ea.
10	PA10018	Cylinder	.54 ea.
11	PA3769	Washer	.01 ea.
12	S16	Screw	.01 ea.
13	S46	Screw	.01 ea.
14	XA9502-D	Pilot w/ truck	1.47 ea.
15	W6	Washer	.01 ea.
16	PA8887	Cone Spring	.02 ea.
17	PA10707	Stud	.07 ea.
18	XA10012	Front Truck Assembly	.46 ea.
	PA13A082	Axle	.01 ea.
	PA9990	Plastic Wheel	.03 ea.
19	S183	Screw	.01 ea.
20	XA14A208-A	Heating Element & Plate Assy.	.96 ea.
* 21	XA13B894-RP	Smoke Box Assembly	2.24 ea.
22	PA10518-A	Piston	.30 ea.
23	PA10520	Pin	.03 ea.
24	PA10514	Piston Lever	.15 ea.
25	PA10671	Worm Gear	.34 ea.
26	PA10162	Stud	.08 ea.
27	PA7421	Screw	.03 ea.
28	XA11077	Armature Assembly	3.56 ea.
29	XA9565-A	Brush Bracket Assembly	1.05 ea.
30	PA10754	Brush Cap	.02 ea.
31	PA9603	Brush	.14 ea.
32	PA10757-A	Brush Spring	.02 ea.
33	S295	Screw	.02 ea.
34	PA10766	Armature Spacer	.01 ea.
35	XA9547	Magnet Assembly	1.28 ea.
36	PA10672	Worm Gear (Motor)	.06 ea.
37	PA15A281	Worm Gear Axle	.07 ea.
38	S271	Screw	.02 ea.
39	PA10017	Motor Cover Plate	.07 ea.
40	XA13A864	Pul-Mor Wheel Assembly	.84 ea.
41	XA10009-B1	Flangeless Wheel & Stud Assembly	.66 ea.
42	XA13A865	Flanged Wheel Assembly	.39 ea.
43	PA10506-A	Chassis w/ bearing	1.87 ea.
	PA13A187	Bearing	.04 ea.

Cont'd On The Other Side

DIA. NO.	PART NO.	DESCRIPTION	PRICE
44	S14	Screw	.01 ea.
45		NOT USED	
46	PA15A226	Plain Axle	.05 ea.
47	PA9280-A	Side Rod	.17 ea.
48	PA7237	Side Rod Spacer	.02 ea.
49	PA5447	Screw	.04 ea.
50	PA4939	Screw	.06 ea.
51	XA15A261	Rear Truck Assem. (sub. for XA10020 obsolete)	.72 ea.
	PA10019-A	Rear Truck Wheel Only	.06 ea.
52	XA10663	Male Plug	.25 ea.
53	XA10662-A	Jack Panel	.25 ea.
54	S230-B	Screw	.01 ea.
55	PA13208-A	4 Conductor Cable (Plastic)	.04 ft.
56	P9273	Wire Lead	.02 ea.
57	PA9667-B	Tender Body	2.98 ea.
58	XA9612-CRP	Top Finger Unit	.35 ea.
59	XA9612-BRP	Bottom Finger Unit	.35 ea.
60	XA8716	Drum Only	1.00 ea.
61	XA10587-E	Remote Control Unit	4.24 ea.
62	PA14A914	Capacitor	1.47 ea.
63	XA14A127	Speaker (sub. for XA11B831 obsolete)	4.80 ea.
64	PA10235-A	Truck Rivet	.07 ea.
65	PA10209	Insulating Bushing	.02 ea.
66		Chassis & Wire Retaining Assy. obsolete	
	PA12A520	Coupler Strap (NOT SHOWN)	.04 ea.
	PA4362	Rivet (NOT SHOWN)	.01 ea.
67	S-0	Screw	.01 ea.
68	PA8715-B	Washer	.02 ea.
69	S172	Screw	.02 ea.
70	S230-B	Screw	.01 ea.
71	XA12A047	Knuckle Coupler	.30 ea.
72	XA12A350	Rear Truck Assembly	.84 ea.
73	PA10207	Contact Spring	.02 ea.
74	PA1405	Tin Washer	.01 ea.
75	PA11A956	Spring	.02 ea.
76	PA11A936	Tender Pick-Up	.04 ea.
77	PA11A944	Hair Pin Cotter	.01 ea.
78	XA12A516	Front Truck Assembly	.46 ea.
79	XA10238	Wheel & Axle Assembly	.09 ea.
	PA9990	Plastic Wheel	.03 ea.
	PA10140	Metal Wheel	.06 ea.
	PA10238	Axle	.01 ea.

*21 - When using XA13B894-RP, remove screw on solder terminal.

Prices subject to change without notice.

LOCOMOTIVE AND TENDER WITH WHISTLE, SMOKE, AND CHOO-CHOO UNIT
Model No. 314AW

SPECIFICATIONS

Tested at: 12 Volts A. C. .... Using 140" oval of track.

(A) Motor to be tested with Remote Control at 12 Volts and not to draw more than 1.75 Amps. Train and whistle unit are not to draw more than 2.8 Amps at 12 Volts.

(B) Locomotive and tender to run a minimum of 9 R.P.M. or 9 times forward around 140" oval of track per minute.

(C) Locomotive and tender to run a minimum of 8.5 R.P.M. or 8½ times reverse around 140" oval of track per minute.

Load: Not to draw more than 2.1 Amps while pulling 4 Box Cars.

Motor: Universal A.C. or D.C. -- Whistle will operate on A.C. only.

Ref: Form No. M2876; Oct. 1, 1950

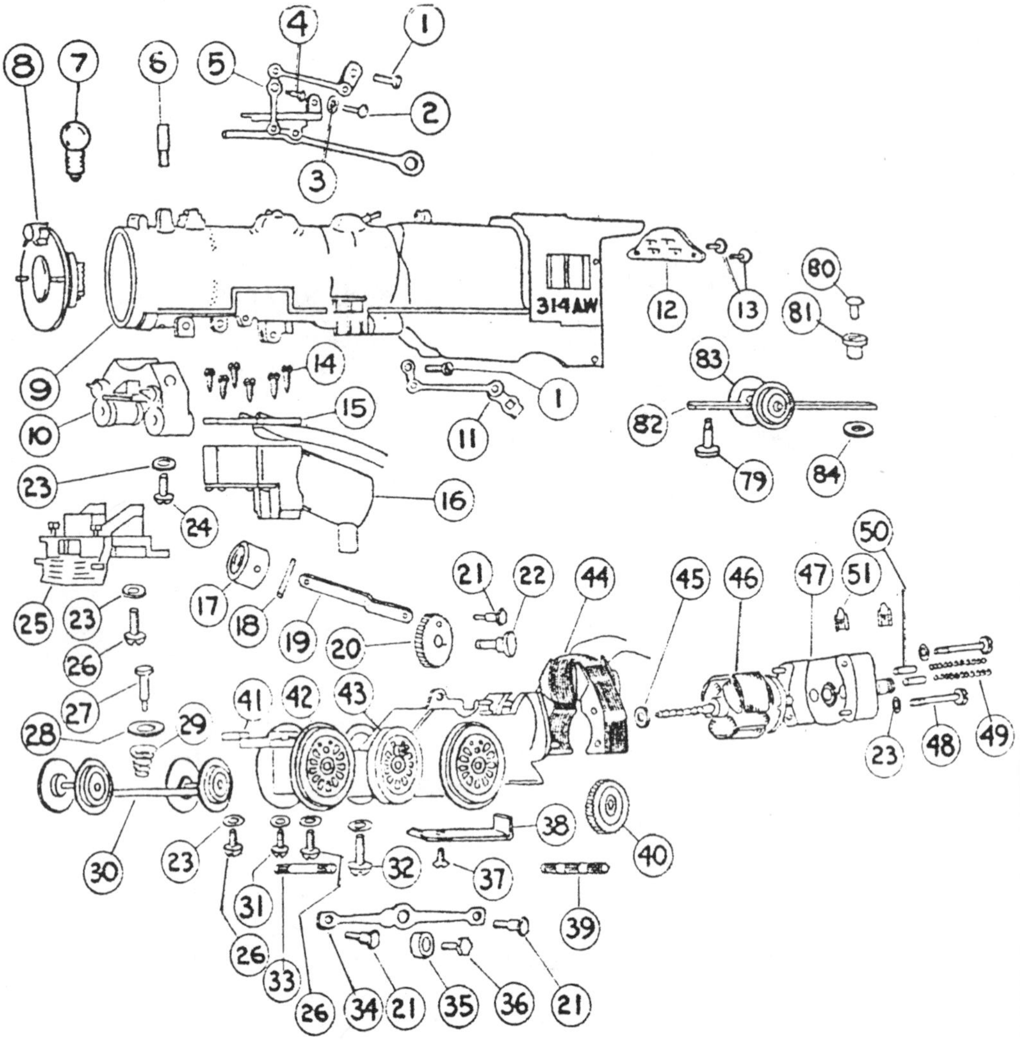

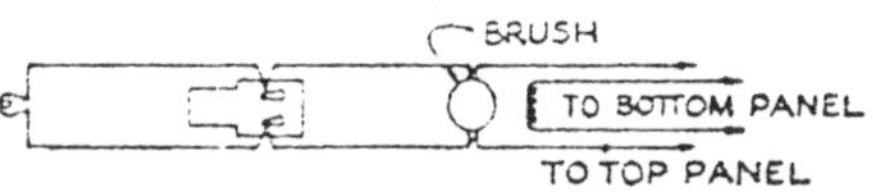

Ref: Form No. M2876; Oct. 1, 1950

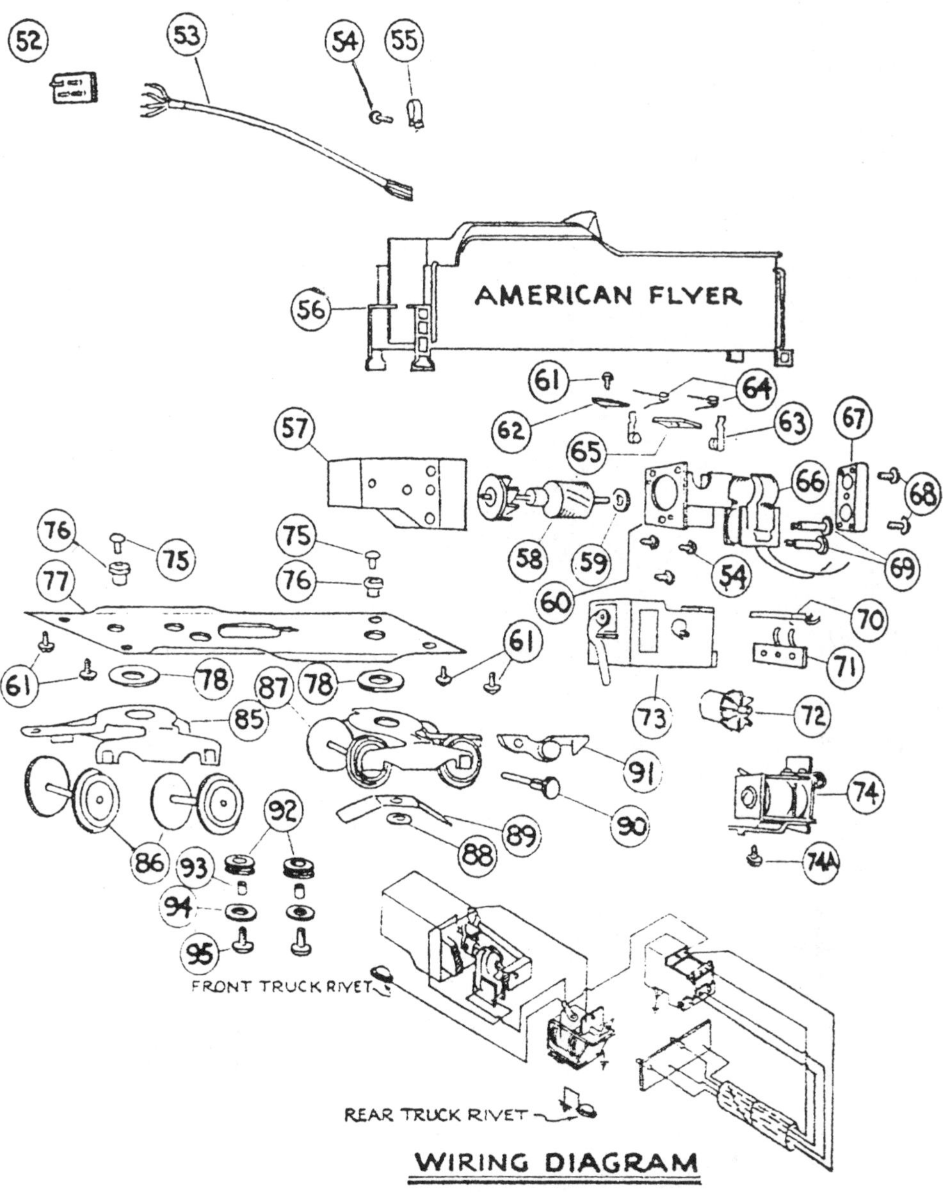
52
53
54
55
AMERICAN FLYER
56
61
64
57
62
63
67
65
66
68
76
75
75
58
59
60
54
69
77
76
70
61
61
71
78
87
78
61
85
73
72
91
74
92
90
89
86
93
88
74A
94
95
FRONT TRUCK RIVET
REAR TRUCK RIVET
WIRING DIAGRAM

Diagram Number	Part No.	Description	Price
1	PA10598	Link Stud	$ .30 dz.
2	S-1	Screw	.05 "
3	W-46	Washer	.05 "
4	PA9288	Shouldered Screw	.30 "
5	XA10668-R	Crosshead Assembly Right	.50 ea.
	XA10668-L	Crosshead Assembly Left	.50 "
6	PA10536	Smoke Stack	.03 "
7	PA8999	14 Volt Lamp	.25 "
8	XA9504-D	Boiler Front Assembly	.60 "
9	XA9423-F	Boiler Assembly	2.25 "
10	PA10018	Cylinder	.70 "
11	XA10447	Eccentric Crank Assembly	.30 "
12	XA10662	Jack Panel	.20 "
13	S230-B	Screw	.10 dz.
14	S-183	Screw	.10 "
	XA10513	Chassis Smoke Box Assembly (consists of parts 15-16)	2.00 ea.
15	XA10523	Heating Element and Plate Assembly	1.00 "
16	PA10513	Chassis Smoke Box	1.00 "
	XA10514	Piston and Piston Lever Assembly (consists of parts 17-18-19)	.40 "
17	PA10518	Piston	.20 "
18	PA10520	Piston Pin	.05 "
19	PA10514	Piston Lever	.05 "
20	PA10671	Worm Gear (Smoke Drive)	.40 "
21	PA7421	Screw	.30 dz.
22	PA10162	Worm Gear Stud	.10 ea.
23	PA3769	Washer	.05 dz.
24	S-16	Screw	.05 "
25	PA9502	Pilot	.70 ea.
26	S-46	Screw	.05 dz.
27	PA10707	Front Truck Stud	.05 ea.
28	W6	Front Truck Washer	.03 dz.
29	PA8887	Front Truck Spring	.05 ea.
30	XA10012	Front Truck	.40 "
	XA9502-C	Front Truck & Pilot Assembly (consists of parts 25-27-28-29-30)	1.30 "
31	S-14	Screw	.05 dz.
32	S-16C	Screw	.10 "
33	PA10005	Plain Axle	.10 ea.
34	PA9280-A	Side Rod	.20 "
35	PA7237	Piston Rod Spacer	.05 "
36	PA5447	Screw	.30 dz.
37	S271	Screw	.10 "
38	PA10017	Grease Pan	.02 ea.
39	PA10006	Worm Gear Axle	.10 "
40	PA10672	Worm Gear (motor)	.30 "
41	*XA10506	Chassis Assembly with bearings only	1.20 "
42	XA10009	Drive Wheel with Flanges	.40 "
43	XA10009-B1	Drive Wheel with wheel and stud	.40 "
44	XA9547	Field Assembly (motor	1.00 "
45	PA10766	Armature Spacer	.05 dz.
46	**XA9569	Armature Assembly A.C.	2.50 ea.
	***XA11077	Armature Assembly A.C.	2.50 "
47	XA9565-A	Brush Bracket Assembly	.50 "
48	S295	Screw	.10 "
49	PA10757	Brush Spring	.05 "
50	PA9603	Brush A.C.	.15 "
51	PA10754	Brush Cap	.02 "
52	XA10663	Male Plug	.20 "
53	PA10511-E	4 Conductor Cable	.12 "

 Ref: Form No. M2876; Oct. 1, 1950

Diagram Number	Part No.	Description	Price
54	S243	Screw	.10 dz.
55	PA11048	Wire Clip	.02 ea.
56	PA9667-C	Tender Body Assembly with whistle holes	2.50 "
57	XA10982-RP	Whistle Housing Assembly	1.10 "
58	XA10985	Armature and Fan Assembly	2.95 "
59	PA329-A	Armature Spacer	.10 dz.
60	PA11083	Mounting Plate	.30 ea.
61	S-0	Screw	.05 dz.
62	P10118	Spring Holder	.08 ea.
63	X10132-A	Brush Holder Assembly	.25 "
64	P10128-R	Spring	.02 "
	P10128-L	Spring	.02 "
65	P10119	Fibre Strip	.05 dz.
66	XA11042	Field Assembly A.C. (whistle)	.75 ea.
67	PA11000	Front End Bearing	.30 "
68	S284	Screw	.10 dz.
69	PA11050	Shouldered Screw	.04 ea.
70	PA9612-C	Top Finger Unit (Remote Control)	.50 "
71	PA9612-B	Bottom Finger Unit (Remote Control)	.50 "
72	XA8716	Drum Only (Remote Control)	.60 "
73	XA10587-E	Remote Control Unit	2.50 "
74	XA11011	Whistle Relay Assembly	1.80 "
75	PA10235-A	Truck Rivet	.03 "
76	PA10209	Insulating Bushing	.02 "
77	PA11003	Tender Chassis	.30 "
78	PA8715-BX	Washer	.05 dz.
79	PA4938	Stud	.30 "
80	PA10751	Stud	.02 ea.
81	PA1312	Fibre Bushing	.10 dz.
82	XA10749	Coupler and Yoke Assembly	.30 ea.
83	PA10019-A	Rear Truck Wheel only	.10 "
84	PA1067-A	Washer	.05 dz.
85	XA9987-G	Front Truck Assembly (complete with wheels)	.50 ea.
	XA10749-A	Truck and Coupler Assembly (consists of parts 80-81-82-83-84-85)	.80 "
86.	XA10140	Wheel & Axle Assembly (one brass & one plastic wheel to a set)	.25 set
	PA10140	Brass Wheel only	.15 ea.
	PA9990	Plastic Wheel only	.10 "
	PA9989	Axle only	.02 "
87	XA9987-C	Rear Truck Assembly	.75 "
88	PA1405	Washer	.05 dz.
89	PA10207	Contact Spring	.02 ea.
90	PA10467	Coupler Pin	.10 "
91	XA10469	Coupler & Weight Assembly	.15 "
	PA10692	Coupler Weight only	.05 "
92	PA4356	Grommet	.02 "
93	PA11049	Grommet Bushing	.02 "
94	W67	Washer	.10 dz.
95	S266	Screw	.10 "

*XA10506 Chassis Assembly is not sold as a complete assembly with wheels.

**XA9569 Armature Assembly can be used with XA9565-A Brush Bracket Assembly manufactured after Oct. 1949 providing that you use 1/16" washer to take up end play.

***XA11077 Armature Assembly with 1/16" oil slinger cannot be used with XA9565-A Brush Bracket Assembly manufactured before Oct. 1949, unless you grind 1/16" off the boss which the bearing sets into on the Brush Bracket Assembly.

SERVICE INSTRUCTIONS FOR TENDER OF NO. 314 PENNSYLVANIA K5 WHISTLING LOCOMOTIVE AND TENDER

The No. 314 Pennsylvania K5 Whistling Locomotive and tender is a standard Pennsylvania Locomotive with the addition of a motor driven whistling unit and a contact making relay built into the tender.

The coil on the relay is energized by throwing on the switch in the whistle control box. This in turn causes the relay points to close, giving current to the motor in the whistle unit.

When the control box lever is thrown on, it superimposes a small amount of direct current into the tracks along with the alternating current which operates the train. This direct current is what causes the relay coil to actuate. The D.C. operates the relay and the A.C. runs the whistle motor.

Therefore, it is very important that the adjustment and spacing of the relay points be correct.

In case a No. 314 Locomotive and tender is returned to you for repair, place it on your own test track, connect a whistle control box to the track, be sure the box is attached according to the instructions in the accompanying sheet. Test for operation first, if the whistle will not blow, remove the body from the tender by first removing the 4 corner screws on the underneath side of the tender.

Next, with the locomotive and tender on the track, with tender body removed, throw the control box lever and observe the action of the mechanism.

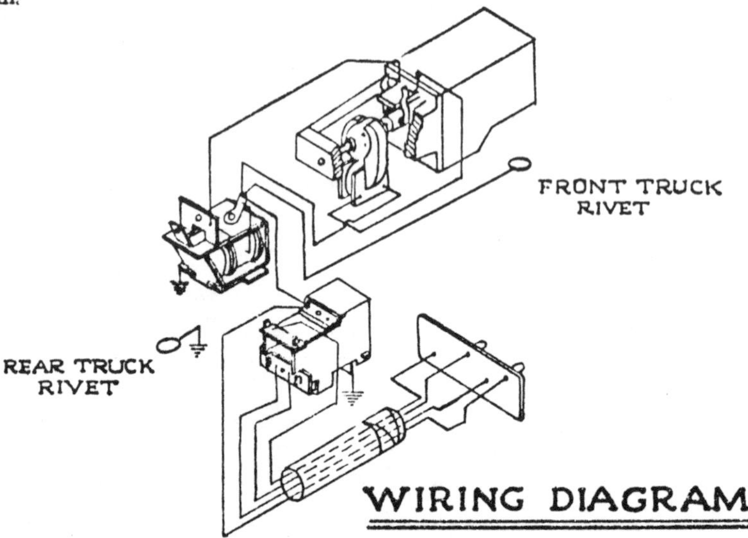

1. If the relay points close and the motor does not run:

a. Check to see if the armature (no. 1) is free to revolve.

b. See that brushes (no. 2) are making contact on the commutator (no. 7).

c. See that brush springs (no. 3) are in position on the brush holders.

d. Check all wires and solder joints to see that there are no loose connections.

e. Check relay points (no. 4) to see that they are not pitted or corroded.

2. If the relay points are making contact and the motor runs:

a. Fan (no. 5) may be loose on armature shaft.

b. Air wicks (no. 6) for armature shaft may need oil.

c. Brush springs (no. 3) may have lost tension.

d. Commutator (no. 7) may be dirty.

3. When control box lever is thrown and relay points do not close, or just flutter:

a. Points may be too far apart and brass stop (no. 8) must be adjusted to close gap. It should be adjusted so contacts are nearly closed, open only 1/64″. When relay points are closed, there still should be approximately 1/64″ movement on the end of the iron armature (no. 9) on which the contact is fastened.

b. Relay armature (no. 9) may be bound up with dirt or dust, it should be very free to move.

4. If whistle operates and remote control unit does not function:

a. Check wire (no. 10) soldered to rear truck rivet as it may be curled up underneath Remote Control armature or pawl not allowing it to operate.

5. If trouble occurs in the whistle control box, we advise returning box to the factory where we have necessary facilities to check the units.

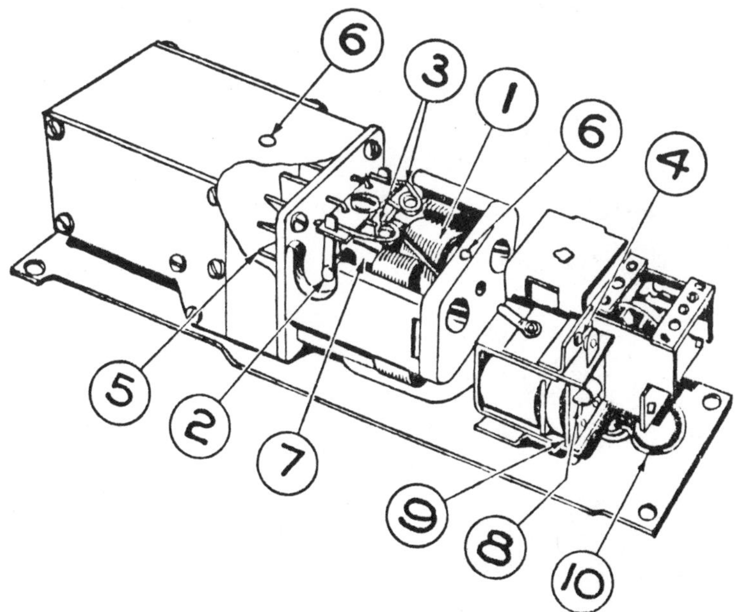

K5 LOCOMOTIVE AND TENDER WITH SMOKE, CHOO-CHOO, AND AIR CHIME WHISTLE

Model No. 315

SPECIFICATIONS

Tested at: 12 Volts A. C. .... Using 140" oval track.

(A) Motor to be tested with Remote Control at 12 Volts and not to draw more than 1.7 Amps.

(B) Locomotive and tender to run a minimum of 9 R.P.M. or 9 times forward around 140" oval of track per minute pulling 4 cars.

(C) Locomotive and tender to run a minimum of 8.5 R.P.M. or 8½ times reverse around 140" oval of track per minute pulling 4 cars.

Load: Not to draw more than 2.1 Amps while pulling 4 Box Cars.

Motor: Universal A.C. or D.C.

 Ref: Form No. M3147; Nov. 1, 1952

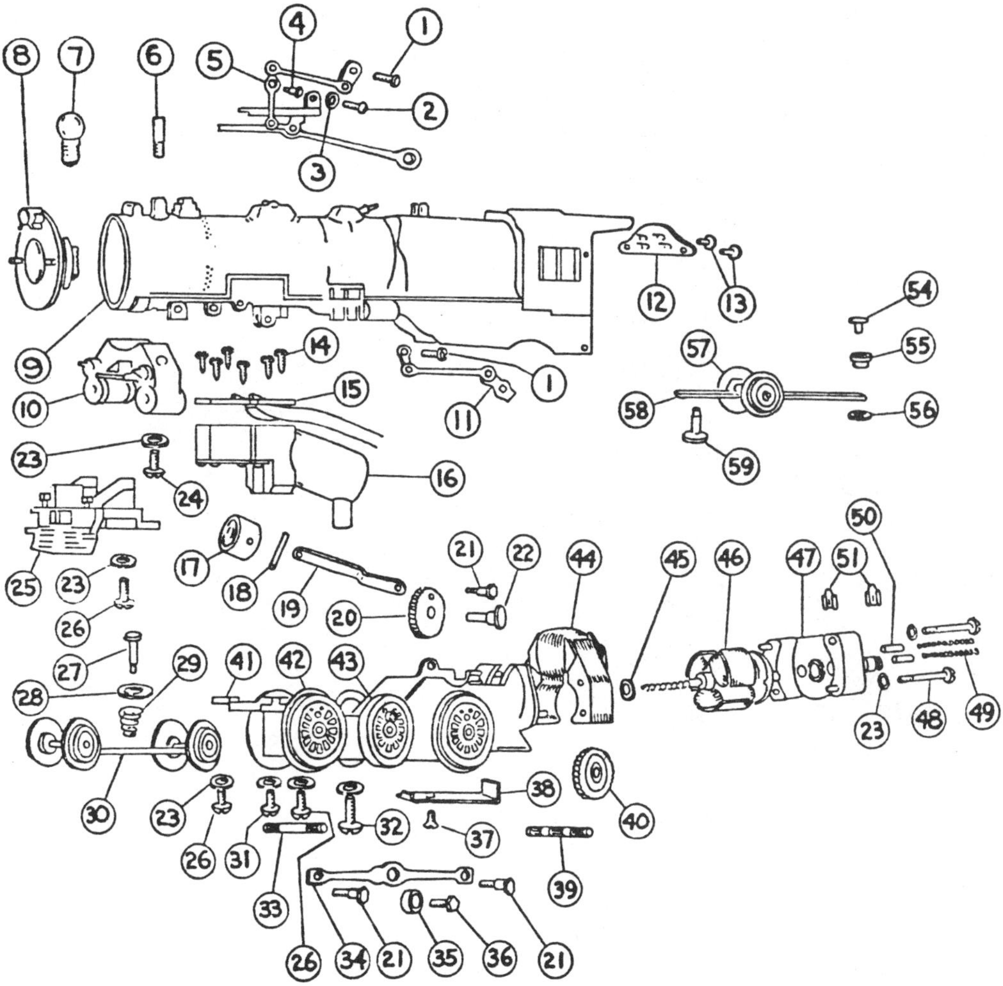

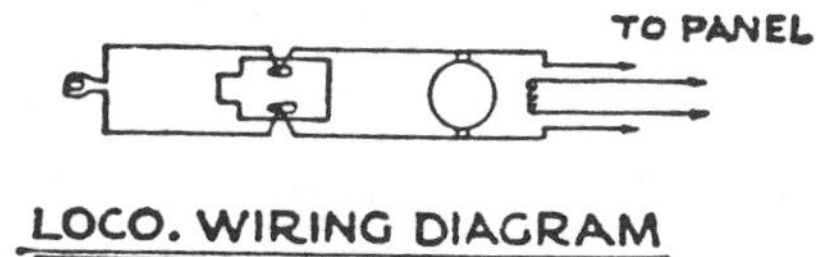

LOCO. WIRING DIAGRAM

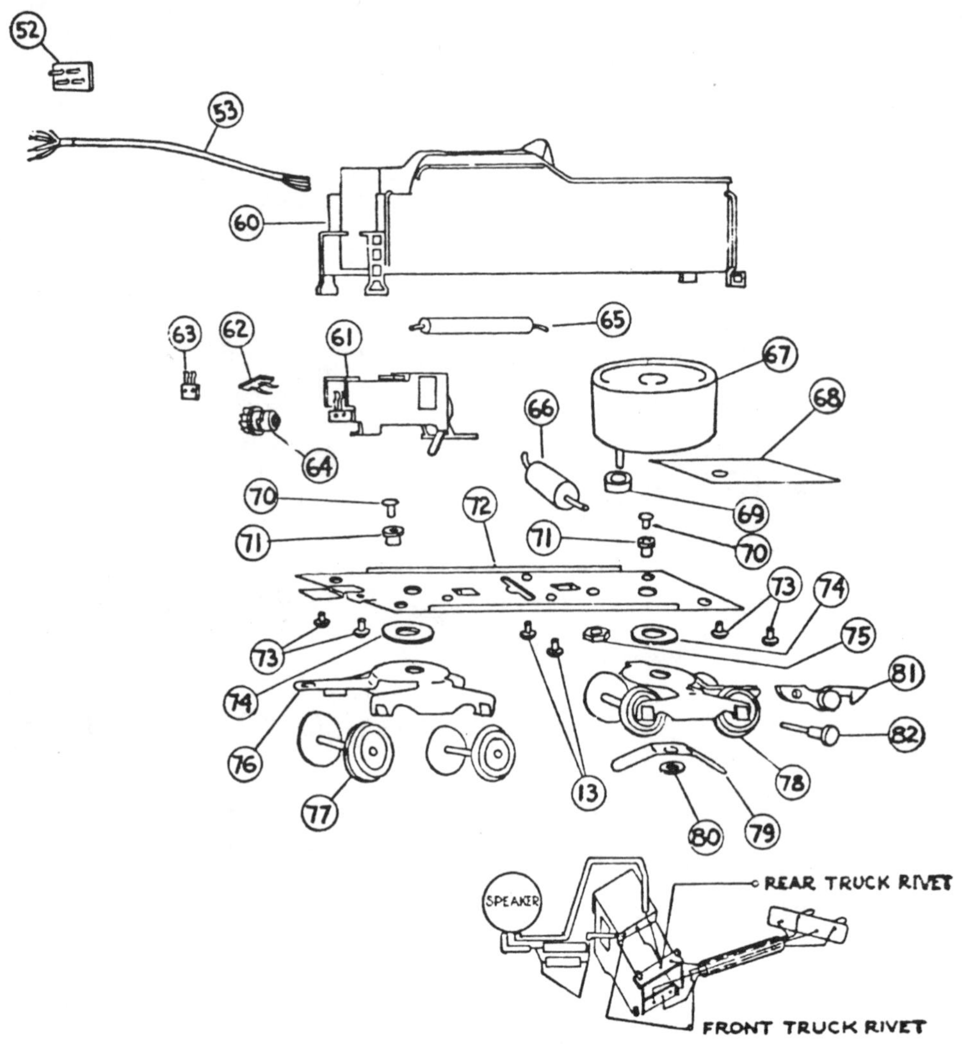

TENDER WIRING DIAGRAM

 Ref: Form No. M3147; Nov. 1, 1952

K5 LOCOMOTIVE AND TENDER WITH SMOKE, CHOO-CHOO, AND AIR CHIME WHISTLE

Model No. 315

SPECIFICATIONS

Tested at: 12 Volts A. C. .... Using 140″ oval track.

(A) Motor to be tested with Remote Control at 12 Volts and not to draw more than 1.7 Amps.

(B) Locomotive and tender to run a minimum of 9 R.P.M. or 9 times forward around 140″ oval of track per minute pulling 4 cars.

(C) Locomotive and tender to run a minimum of 8.5 R.P.M. or 8½ times reverse around 140″ oval of track per minute pulling 4 cars.

Load: Not to draw more than 2.1 Amps while pulling 4 Box Cars.

Motor: Universal A.C. or D.C.

Ref: Form No. 1808; Feb. 1, 1957

Diagram Number	Part No.	Description	Price
1	PA10598	Link Stud	$ .30 dz.
2	S-1	Screw	.05 "
3	W-46	Washer	.05 "
4	PA9288	Shouldered Screw	.30 "
5	XA10668-R	Crosshead Assembly Right	.50 ea.
	XA10668-L	Crosshead Assembly Left	.50 "
6	PA10536	Smoke Stack	.03 "
7	PA8999	14 Volt Lamp	.25 "
8	XA9504-D	Boiler Front Assembly	.60 "
9	XA9423-F	Boiler Assembly	2.25 "
10	PA10018	Cylinder	.70 "
11	XA10447	Eccentric Crank Assembly	.30 "
12	XA10662	Jack Panel	.20 "
13	S230-B	Screw	.10 dz.
	XA10513	Chassis Smoke Box Assembly (consists of parts 14-15-16)	2.00 ea.
14	S183	Screw	.10 dz.
15	XA10523	Heating Element and Plate Assembly	1.00 ea.
16	PA10513	Chassis Smoke Box	1.00 "
	XA10514	Piston and Piston Lever Assembly (consists of parts 17-18-19)	.40 "
17	PA10518	Piston	.20 "
18	PA10520	Piston Pin	.05 "
19	PA10514	Piston Lever	.05 "
20	PA10671	Worm Gear (Smoke Drive)	.40 "
21	PA7421	Screw	.30 dz.
22	PA10162	Worm Gear Stud	.10 ea.
23	PA3769	Washer	.05 dz.
24	S-16	Screw	.05 "
25	PA9502	Pilot	.70 ea.
26	S-46	Screw	.05 dz.
27	PA10707	Front Truck Stud	.05 ea.
28	W6	Front Truck Washer	.03 dz.
29	PA8887	Front Truck Spring	.05 ea.
30	XA10012	Front Truck	.40 "
	XA9502-C	Front Truck & Pilot Assembly (consists of parts 25-27-28-29-30)	1.30 "
31	S-14	Screw	.05 dz.
32	S-16C	Screw	.10 "
33	PA10005	Plain Axle	.10 ea.
34	PA9280-A	Side Rod	.20 "
35	PA7237	Piston Rod Spacer	.05 "
36	PA5447	Screw	.30 dz.
37	S271	Screw	.10 "
38	PA10017	Grease Pan	.02 ea.
39	PA10006	Worm Gear Axle	.10 "
40	PA10672	Worm Gear (motor)	.30 "
41	*XA10506	Chassis Assembly with bearings only	1.20 "
42	XA10009	Flanged Drive Wheel	.40 "
43	XA10009-B1	Flangeless Drive Wheel with stud	.40 "

 Ref: Form No. 1808; Feb. 1, 1957

Diagram Number	Part No.	Description	Price
44	XA9547	Field Assembly	$1.00 ea.
45	PA10766	Armature Spacer	.05 dz.
46	XA11077	Armature Assembly	2.50 ea.
47	XA9565-A	Brush Bracket Assembly	.50 "
48	S295	Screw	.10 "
49	PA10757	Brush Spring	.05 "
50	PA9603	Brush	.15 "
51	PA10754	Brush Cap	.02 "
52	XA10663	Male Plug	.20 "
53	PA10511-E	4 Conductor Cable	.12 "
54	PA10751	Stud	.02 "
55	PA1312	Fibre Bushing	.10 dz.
56	PA1067-A	Washer	.05 "
57	PA10019-A	Rear Truck Wheel Only	.10 ea.
58	XA10749	Coupler and Yoke Assembly	.30 ea.
59	PA4938	Stud	.30 dz.
60	XA9667-RP	Tender Body Assembly with Trimmings	2.86 ea.
61	XA10587-E	Remote Control Unit	2.50 "
62	XA9612-C	Top Finger Unit	.50 "
63	XA9612-B	Bottom Finger Unit	.50 "
64	XA8716	Drum	.60 "
65	PA11685	Resistor	.26 "
66	PA11A991	Condenser	1.00 "
67	XA11710	Speaker	2.76 "
68	PA11664	Receiver Insulation	.02 "
69	W99	Rubber Washer	.03 "
70	PA10235-A	Truck Rivet	.03 "
71	PA10209	Insulating Bushing	.02 "
72	XA10588	Chassis & Wire Retainer Assembly	.30 "
73	S-0	Screw	.05 dz.
74	PA8715-BX	Insulating Washer	.05 "
75	N-1A	Nut	.01 ea.
76	XA9987-G	Front Truck Assembly (complete with wheels)	.50 "
	XA10749-A	Truck & Coupler Assembly (consists of parts 54-55-56-57-58-76)	.80 "
77	XA10238	Wheel & Axle Assembly (metal & plastic wheels)	.25 set
	PA10140	Metal Wheel only	.15 ea.
	PA9990	Plastic Wheel only	.10 "
	PA9989	Axle only	.02 "
78	XA9987-C	Rear Truck Assembly (complete with wheels)	.75 "
79	PA10207	Contact Spring	.02 "
80	PA1405	Washer	.05 dz.
81	XA10469	Coupler & Weight Assembly	.15 ea.
	PA10692	Coupler Weight only	.05 "
82	PA10467	Coupler Pin	.10 "

* XA10506 Chassis Assembly is not sold as a complete assembly with wheels.

Ref: Form No. 1808; Feb. 1, 1957

SERVICE INSTRUCTIONS FOR No. 315 LOCOMOTIVE AND TENDER WITH SMOKE, CHOO-CHOO AND WHISTLE.

The first thing to do is to place Locomotive and Tender on track, connect transformer and whistle control unit, and test for operation. Make sure all rods, linkage and other parts are not bent or broken. It is also important that the wheels on the Tender be clean to insure a good electrical contact.

1. **If the whistle is satisfactory, but the Locomotive and Tender does not operate properly proceed as follows:**
   a. Remove screw (※59) and also male plug (※52) from the Jack Panel (※12).
   b. Now take another similar tender with a Remote Control Unit in it which is in good working order and connect it to the Locomotive. In this way, you will be able to determine whether the Locomotive or Tender is defective.
2. **If the trouble is in the Locomotive you can make the following checks:**
   a. Inspect brushes for wear or poor contact and brush springs for position and proper tension.
   b. Check wires and solder joints on male plug (※52) and Jack Panel (※12) for broken or loose connections.
   c. Clean or polish commutator if dirty or worn.
3. **If these initial steps do not correct the trouble it will be necessary to disassemble the locomotive as follows:**
   a. Unscrew smoke stack (※6).
   b. Remove screws (※36) on each side and take off Rods (※5 and ※11) and spacer (※35) from center drive wheel.
   c. Pull out Boiler Front (※8) from Boiler Assembly (※9) and unsolder the two wires at the lamp bracket.
   d. Turn Locomotive upside down and remove two screws (※26) and you can now remove motor assembly from Boiler (※9).
   e. To remove motor, push forward approximately a ¼" to clear clamp on Boiler (※9) and then lift rear of motor up and pull motor out.
   f. The motor is now exposed and you can inspect the wiring and other points of the unit, making any necessary replacements.
4. **When the trouble appears to be in the Tender, proceed as follows:**
   a. Remove four S-0 screws (※73) and take off Tender body (※60).
   b. Inspect wiring and solder joints for loose or broken connections.
   c. Check finger units (※62 and ※63) on remote Control Unit (※61) to see if they are burnt or not making proper contact.
   d. The drum (※64) should be checked to see if it is pitted or worn.
   e. The pawl on the Remote Control Unit may be broken or need adjusting.
   f. It is generally not necessary to replace the complete Remote Control Unit, but sometimes the Finger Units, the drum, or both need adjusting or replacing.
5. **If Locomotive and Tender operates satisfactorily, but the whistle does not function correctly check as follows:**
   a. Recheck the instruction sheet in order to make sure hook-up is correct. If both the Transformer instructions and the Air Chime Whistle Instructions are followed, this will cause a duplication of wiring. The result will be that you will only have a faint buzz while the train is running or in a neutral position. Follow the Air Chime Whistle wiring instructions only and be sure to have only two wires going to the ※690 track terminal.
   b. The Generator Tube ※PA11665 on the control box may be weak and need replacing.
   c. If the trouble still persists it will be necessary to remove the Tender Body (※60) from the chassis by unscrewing the four S-0 screws (※73).
   d. The unit is exposed and you can check all wires and solder joints for loose connections. Be sure the lead wires on the resistor and condenser are covered with an insulating sleeve.
   e. Check the condenser (※66) by adding another condenser in series with temporary connections. If this corrects the trouble the defective condenser can be removed and a new one connected in its place.
   f. To check resistor (※65) use another resistor and follow same procedure.

 Ref: Form No. 1808; Feb. 1, 1957

NO.	PART NO.	DESCRIPTION	PRICE
1	PA10598	Link Stud	.02 ea.
2	S-1	Screw	.01 ea.
3	W-46	Washer	.01 ea.
4	PA9288	Shouldered Screw	.03 ea.
5	XA10668-R	Crosshead Assembly (Right)	.92 ea.
	XA10668-L	Crosshead Assembly (Left)	.92 ea.
6	PA12A190	Smoke Stack	.03 ea.
7	PA8999	14 Volt Lamp	.30 ea.
8	XA9504-DRP	Boiler Front Assembly	.78 ea.
	PA10542	Headlight Lens	.02 ea.
9	XA9423-F	Boiler Assembly	2.75 ea.
	PA9579	Mounting Bracket (Rear)	.01 ea.
	XA9578	Coupler Strap	.08 ea.
10	PA10018	Cylinder	.51 ea.
11	XA10447	Eccentric Crank Assembly	.23 ea.
12	XA10662	Jack Panel	.24 ea.
13	S230-B	Screw	.01 ea.
14	S183	Screw	.01 ea.
15	XA10523	Heating Element & Plate Assy. NOT AVAILABLE	
		Sub. with XA14A208-A H.E. & P. Assy.	.91 ea.
16	XA10513	Smoke Box Assembly NOT AVAILABLE	
		Sub. with XA13B894-RP Smoke Box	2.13 ea.
	PA10513	Smoke Box NOT AVAILABLE	
		Sub. with PA13B894 Smoke Box	.76 ea.
	PA14A209	Separator (NOT SHOWN)	.02 ea.
17	PA10518-A	Piston	.29 ea.
18	PA10520	Piston Pin	.03 ea.
19	PA10514	Piston Lever	.14 ea.
20	PA10671	Worm Gear (Smoke Drive)	.32 ea.
21	PA7421	Screw	.03 ea.
22	PA10162	Worm Gear Stud	.08 ea.
23	PA3769	Washer	.01 ea.
24	S-16	Screw	.01 ea.
25	PA9502	Pilot	.86 ea.
26	S-46	Screw	.01 ea.
27	PA10707	Front Truck Stud	.07 ea.
28	W-6	Front Truck Washer	.01 ea.
29	PA8887	Front Truck Spring	.02 ea.
30	XA10012	Front Truck	.44 ea.
	PA13A082	Axle	.01 ea.
	PA9990	Plastic Wheel	.03 ea.
	XA9502-C	Front Truck & Pilot Assy.(Consists of Parts 25-27-28-29-30)	2.14 ea.
31	S-14	Screw	.01 ea.
32		NOT USED	
33	PA10005	Plain Axle NOT AVAILABLE	
		Sub. with PA15A226 Axle	.05 ea.
34	PA9280-A	Side Rod	.16 ea.
35	PA7237	Piston Rod Spacer	.02 ea.
36	PA5447	Screw	.04 ea.
37	S271	Screw	.02 ea.
38	PA10017	Grease Pan	.07 ea.
39	PA10006	Worm Gear Axle NOT AVAILABLE	
		Substitute with PA15A281 Axle	.07 ea.
40	PA10672	Worm Gear (Motor)	.06 ea.
41	XA10506	Chassis Assy. with Bearings only	1.46 ea.
	PA13A187	Bearing	.04 ea.
42	XA13A865	Flanged Drive Wheel	.37 ea.

Ref: Form No. 1808; June 1, 1960

DIA. NO.	PART NO.	DESCRIPTION	PRICE
43	XA10009-B1	Flangeless Drive Wheel w/Stud	.63 ea.
43-A	XA13A864	Pul-Mor Wheel Assembly	.80 ea.
44	XA9547	Field Assembly	1.22 ea.
45	PA10766	Armature Spacer	.01 ea.
46	XA11077	Armature Assembly	3.39 ea.
47	XA9565-A	Brush Bracket Assembly	1.00 ea.
48	S295	Screw	.02 ea.
49	PA10757-A	Brush Spring	.02 ea.
50	PA9603	Brush	.13 ea.
51	PA10754	Brush Cap	.02 ea.
52	XA10663	Male Plug	.24 ea.
53	PA10511	4 Conductor Cable	.13 ea.
54	PA10751	Stud	.02 ea.
55	PA1312	Fibre Bushing	.12 doz.
56	PA1067-A	Washer	.06 doz.
57	PA10019-A	Rear Truck Wheel Only	.06 ea.
58	*XA10749	Coupler & Yoke Assy. NOT AVAILABLE	
59	PA4938	Screw	.04 ea.
60	XA9667-RP	Tender Body Assy. w/trimmings	3.49 ea.
61	XA10587-E	Remote Control Unit	4.04 ea.
62	XA9612-CRP	Top Finger Unit	.33 ea.
63	XA9612-BRP	Bottom Finger Unit	.33 ea.
64	XA8716	Drum	.95 ea.
65	PA11685	Resistor	.29 ea.
66	PA11A991	Condenser NOT AVAILABLE	
		Substitute with PA14A914 Condenser	1.40 ea.
67	XA11710	Speaker NOT AVAILABLE	
		Substitute with XA14A127 Speaker	4.57 ea.
	PA14A216	Speaker Bracket	.08 ea.
	S230-B	Screw	.01 ea.
	S171	Screw	.01 ea.
68		NOT USED	
69		NOT USED	
70	PA10235-A	Truck Rivet	.07 ea.
71	PA10209	Insulating Bushing	.02 ea.
72	XA10588	Chassis & Wire Retainer Assy.	.35 ea.
73	S-0	Screw	.01 ea.
74	PA8715-B	Insulating Washer	.02 ea.
75		NOT USED	
76	* XA11712	Front Truck Assy. NOT AVAILABLE	
77	XA10238	Wheel & Axle Assembly	.09 ea.
	PA10140	Metal Wheel Only	.06 ea.
	PA9990	Plastic Wheel Only	.03 ea.
	PA10238	Axle Only	.01 ea.
78	* XA11714	Rear Truck Assy. NOT AVAILABLE	
79	PA10207	Contact Spring	.02 ea.
80	PA1405	Washer	.01 ea.
81	XA10469	Coupler & Weight Assy. NOT AVAILABLE	
	PA10692	Coupler Weight Only NOT AVAILABLE	
82	PA10467	Coupler Pin NOT AVAILABLE	

LINK COUPLERS & TRUCK NOT AVAILABLE, CONVERT TO KNUCKLE COUPLERS BY USING:

DIA. NO.	PART NO.	DESCRIPTION	PRICE
* #58	XA15A784	Coupler & Yoke Assembly	.22 ea.
#76	XA14B811	Front Truck Assembly	.55 ea.
	PA11A944	Hair Pin Cotter	.01 ea.
	PA11A956	Spring	.02 ea.
	PA11A936	Tender Pick Up	.04 ea.
#78	XA12A350	Rear Truck Assembly Plus parts listed under #76	.80 ea.
	PA14A839	Coupler Strap (Connect Loco & Tender)	.03 ea.

 Ref: Form No. 1808; June 1, 1960

DIA NO.	PART NO.	DESCRIPTION	PRICE
1	PA10598	Link Stud	.02 ea.
2	S-1	Screw	.01 ea.
3	W-46	Washer	.01 ea.
4	PA9288	Shouldered Screw	.03 ea.
5	XA10668-R	Crosshead Assembly (Right)	.97 ea.
	XA10668-L	Crosshead Assembly (Left)	.97 ea.
6	PA12A190	Smoke Stack	.03 ea.
7	PA8999	14 Volt Lamp	.32 ea.
8	XA9504-DRP	Boiler Front Assembly	.82 ea.
	PA10542	Headlight Lens	.02 ea.
9	XA9423-JRP	Boiler Assembly	6.51 ea.
	PA9579	Mounting Bracket (Rear)	.01 ea.
	XA9578	Coupler Strap	.08 ea.
10	PA10018	Cylinder	.54 ea.
11	XA10447	Eccentric Crank Assembly	.24 ea.
12	XA10662	Jack Panel	.25 ea.
13	S230-B	Screw	.01 ea.
14	S183	Screw	.01 ea.
15	XA14A208-A	Heating Element & Plate Assembly	.96 ea.
** 16	XA13B894-RP	Smoke Box Assembly	2.24 ea.
17	PA10518-A	Piston	.30 ea.
18	PA10520	Piston Pin	.03 ea.
19	PA10514	Piston Lever	.15 ea.
20	PA10671	Worm Gear (Smoke Drive)	.34 ea.
21	PA7421	Screw	.03 ea.
22	PA10162	Worm Gear Stud	.08 ea.
23	PA3769	Washer	.01 ea.
24	S-16	Screw	.01 ea.
25	XA9502P	Pilot w/Truck	1.47 ea.
26	S-46	Screw	.01 ea.
27	PA10707	Front Truck Stud	.07 ea.
28	W-6	Front Truck Washer	.01 ea.
29	PA8887	Front Truck Spring	.02 ea.
30	XA10012	Front Truck	.46 ea.
	PA13A082	Axle	.01 ea.
	PA9990	Plastic Wheel	.03 ea.
31	S-14	Screw	.01 ea.
32		NOT USED	
33	PA15A226	Plain Axle	.05 ea.
34	PA9280-A	Side Rod	.17 ea.
35	PA7237	Piston Rod Spacer	.02 ea.
36	PA5447	Screw	.04 ea.
37	S271	Screw	.02 ea.
38	PA10017	Grease Pan	.07 ea.
39	PA15A281	Worm Gear Axle	.07 ea.
40	PA10672	Worm Gear (Motor)	.06 ea.
41	PA10506-A	Chassis Assembly with Bearings only	1.87 ea.
	PA13A187	Bearing	.04 ea.
42	XA13A865	Flanged Drive Wheel	.39 ea.
43	XA10009-BI	Flangeless Drive Wheel w/ stud	.66 ea.

Cont'd

NO.	PART NO.	DESCRIPTION	PRICE
43-A	XA13A864	Pul-Mor Wheel Assembly	.84 ea.
44	XA9547	Field Assembly	1.28 ea.
45	PA10766	Armature Spacer	.01 ea.
46	XA11077	Armature Assembly	3.56 ea.
47	XA9565-A	Brush Bracket Assembly	1.05 ea.
48	S295	Screw	.02 ea.
49	PA10757-A	Brush Spring	.02 ea.
50	PA9603	Brush	.14 ea.
51	PA10754	Brush Cap	.02 ea.
52	XA10663	Male Plug	.25 ea.
53	PA13208-A	4 Conductor Cable—Plastic	.04 ft.
54	PA10751	Stud	.02 ea.
55	PA1312	Fibre Bushing	.13 dz.
56	PA1067-A	Washer	.06 dz.
57	PA10019-A	Rear Truck Wheel Only	.06 ea.
58	XA15A784	Draw Bar Assy. (Used w/ XA14B811 Front Truck Assy)	.23 ea.
	XA10891	Coupler & Yoke Assy. (Sub. for XA10749-Obsolete)	.38 ea.
59	PA4938	Screw	.04 ea.
60	XA9667-RP	Tender Body Assembly w/ trimmings	3.66 ea.
61	XA10587-E	Remote Control Unit	4.24 ea.
62	XA9612-CRP	Top Finger Unit	.35 ea.
63	XA9612-BRP	Bottom Finger Unit	.35 ea.
64	XA8716	Drum	1.00 ea.
65	PA11685	Resistor	.30 ea.
66	PA14A914	Condenser—Sub. for PA11A991-Obsolete	1.47 ea.
67	XA14A127 Conv.	Speaker—Sub. for XA11710—Obsolete	4.91 ea.
68		NOT USED	
69		NOT USED	
70	PA10235-A	Truck Rivet	.07 ea.
71	PA10209	Insulating Bushing	.02 ea.
72		Chassis & Wire Retainer Assembly—Obsolete	
73	S-0	Screw	.01 ea.
74	PA8715-B	Insulating Washer	.02 ea.
75		NOT USED	
76	XA14B811	Front Truck Assy.—Sub. for XA11712—Obsolete	.58 ea.
	PA11A944	Hair Pin Cotter	.01 ea.
	PA11A956	Spring	.02 ea.
	PA11A936	Tender Pick Up	.04 ea.
77	XA10238	Wheel and Axle Assembly	.09 ea.
	PA10140	Metal Wheel Only	.06 ea.
	PA9990	Plastic Wheel Only	.03 ea.
	PA10238	Axle Only	.01 ea.
78	XA12A350	Rear Truck Assy. -Sub. for XA11714-Obsolete (Plus Parts listed under Dia. # 76)	.84 ea.
79	PA10207	Contact Spring	.02 ea.
80	PA1405	Washer	.01 ea.
81		Coupler & Weight Assembly—Obsolete	
82		Coupler Pin—Obsolete	

* #16 When using XA13B894-RP remove
Screw on Solder Terminal

Prices subject to change without notice.

 Ref: Form No. 1808; Oct. 1, 1962

LOCOMOTIVE AND TENDER WITH PISTON-TYPE SMOKE AND CHOO-CHOO UNIT

Model No. 322

SPECIFICATIONS

Tested at: 12 Volts A.C. .... Using 140" oval of track.

(A) Motor to be tested with Remote Control Unit at 12 Volts, and not to draw more than .175 amps.

(B) Locomotive to run a minimum of 8 R.P.M. or 8 times forward, around 140" oval track per minute.

(C) Locomotive to run a minimum of 7.5 R.P.M. or 7½ times reverse, around 140" oval of track per minute.

Load: Not to draw more than 2.1 amps. while pulling 4 Box Cars.

Motor: Universal A.C. or D.C.

Ref: Form No. M2823; June 1, 1950

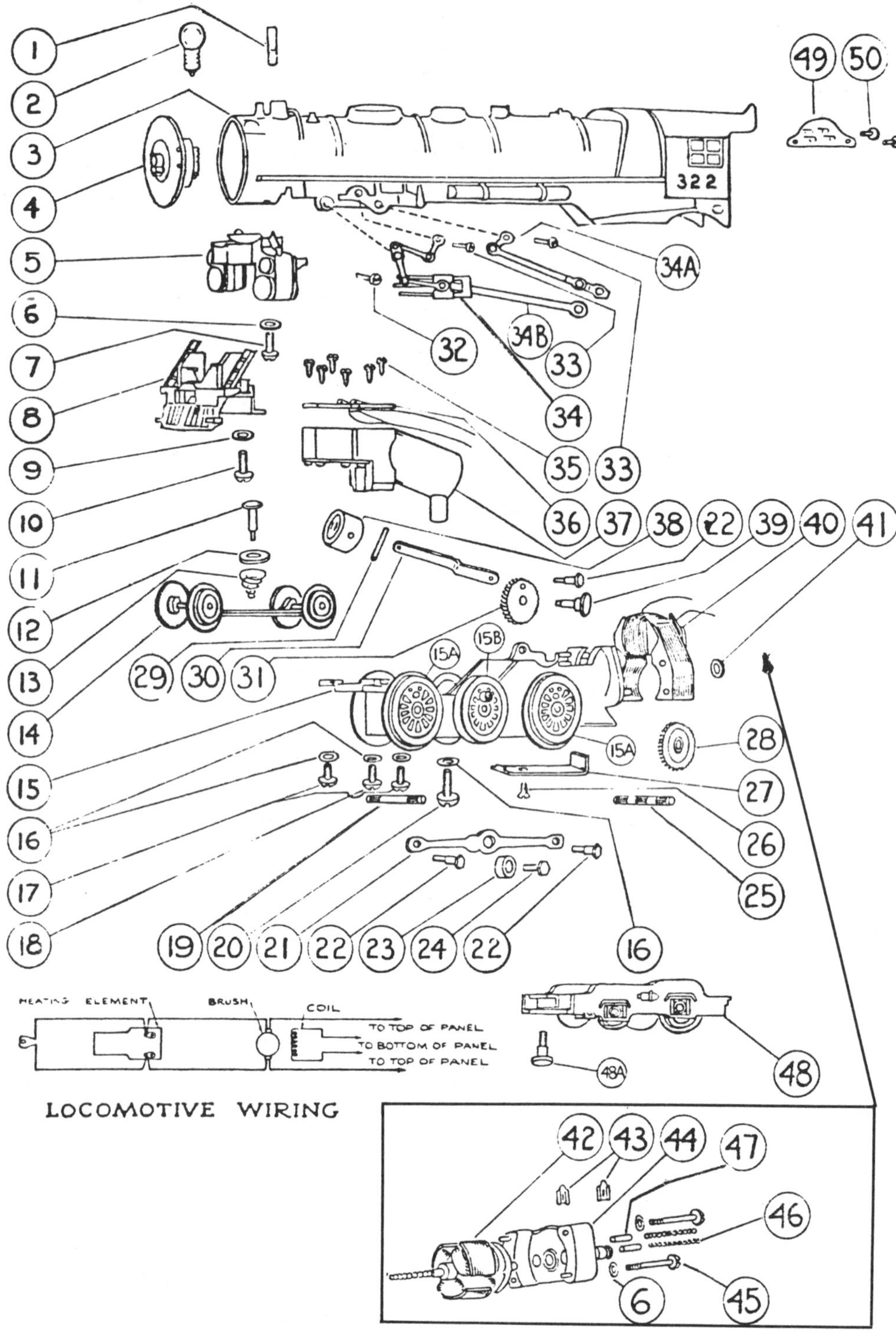

 Ref: Form No. M2823; June 1, 1950

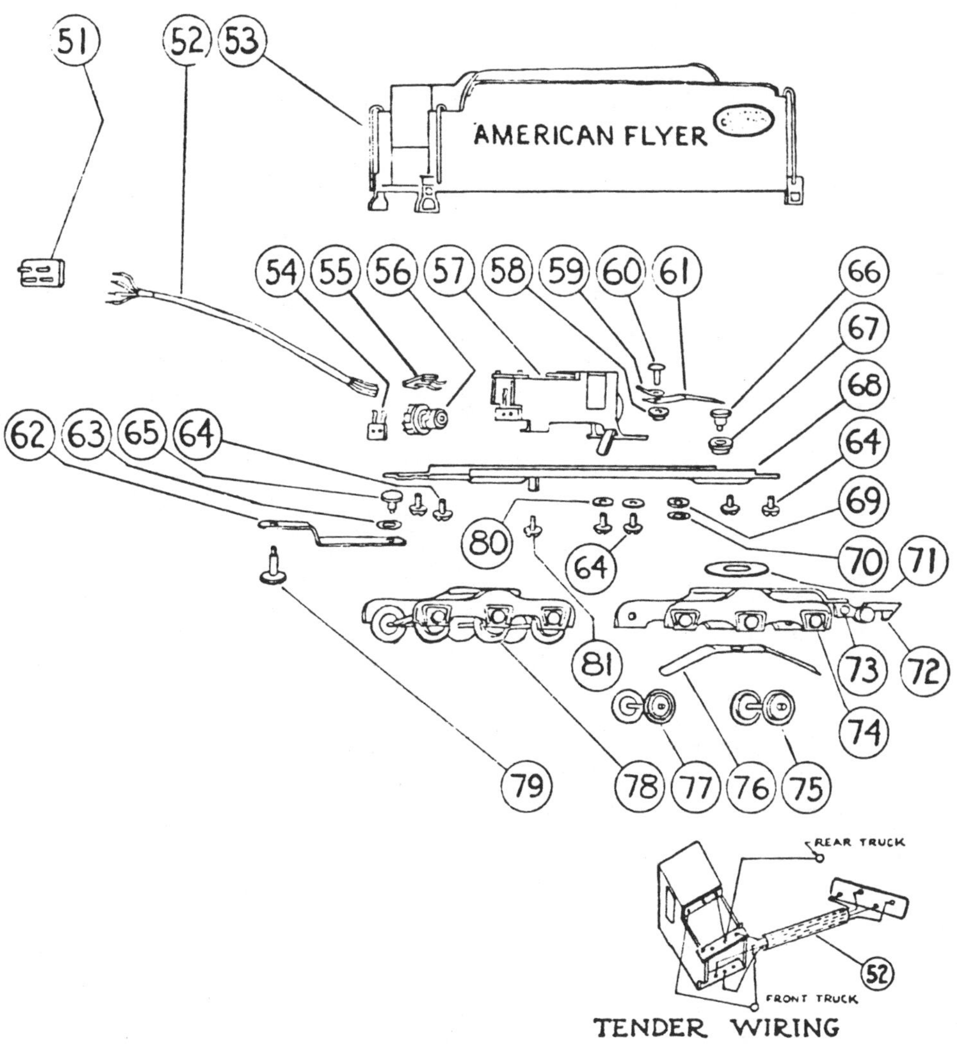
51
52
53
AMERICAN FLYER
54
55
56
57
58
59
60
61
66
67
68
64
69
62
63
65
64
80
64
70
71
81
73
72
74
79
78
77
76
75
REAR TRUCK
52
FRONT TRUCK
TENDER WIRING

Diagram Number	Part No.	Description	Price
1	PA10536	Smoke Stack	.03 ea.
2	PA8999	14 Volt Lamp	.25 "
3	XA9210-A	Boiler Assembly	2.25 "
4	XA9216-B	Boiler Front Assembly with lamp bracket	.60 "
5	PA10056	Cylinder and Steamchest	.70 "
6	PA3769	Lockwasher	.05 dz.
7	S47	Screw	.05 "
8	PA9245	Pilot	.70 ea.
9	PA3769	Lockwasher	.05 dz.
10	S16	Screw	.05 "
11	PA10707	Front Truck Stud	.05 ea.
12	W6	Washer	.03 "
13	PA8887	Front Truck Spring	.05 ea.
14	XA10012	Front Truck	.40 "
	PA9990-A	Front Truck Wheel only	.10 ea.
15	*XA10506	Chassis Assembly with bushings only	1.20 "
15A	XA10009	Flanged wheel with tapped hole	.40 "
15B	XA10009-81	Flangeless wheel and stud	.40 "
16	PA3769	Lockwasher	.05 dz.
17	S14	Screw	.05 "
18	S46	Screw	.05 "
19	PA10005	Plain Axle	.10 ea.
20	S16-C	Screw	.10 dz.
21	PA9280-A	Side Rod	.20 ea.
22	PA7421	Screw	.30 dz.
23	PA7237	Spacer for Piston Rod	.05 ea.
24	PA5447	Screw	.30 dz.
25	PA10006	Worm Gear Axle	.10 ea.
26	S271	Screw	.10 dz.
27	PA10017	Grease Pan	.02 ea.
28	PA10672	Worm Gear (motor)	.30 "
29	PA10520	Piston Pin	.05 "
30	PA10514	Piston Lever	.05 "
	~~XA10514~~	~~Piston & Lever Assembly (consists of parts 29-30-38)~~	.40 "
31	PA10671	Worm Gear (smoke drive)	.40 "
32	PA9283	Screw	.30 dz.
33	PA10598	Link Stud	.30 "
34	PA10595 R or L	Crosshead Guide (Right or Left)	.05 ea.
34A	XA10447-A	Eccentric Crank Assembly	.30 ea.
34B	XA10597 R or L	Crosshead Assembly (Right or Left)	.50 "
	XA10513	Chassis Smoke Box Assembly (consists of parts 35-36-37)	2.00 "
35	S183	Screw	.10 dz.
36	XA10523	Heating Element and Plate Assembly	1.00 ea.
37	PA10513	Chassis Smoke Box	1.00 "
38	PA10518 A	Piston	.20 "
39	PA10162	Worm Gear Stud	.10 "
40	XA9547	Magnet Assembly A.C.	1.00 "
41	PA10766	Washer	.05 dz.
42	**XA11077	Armature Assembly A.C.	2.50 ea.
	**XA9569	Armature Assembly A.C.	2.50 "
43	[illegible]10754	Brush Cap	.05 "

 Ref: Form No. M2823; June 1, 1950

Diagram Number	Part No.	Description	Price
44	XA9565-A	Brush Bracket Assembly	.50 ea.
45	S295	Screw	.10 "
46	PA10757-A	Brush Spring	.05 "
47	PA9603	Carbon Brush A.C.	.15 "
48	XA10002	Rear Truck Assembly	.70 "
48A	PA4938	Rear Truck Stud	.30 dz.
49	XA10662	Jack Panel	.20 ea.
50	S230-B	Screw	.10 dz.
51	XA10663	Male Plug	.20 ea.
52	PA10511-A	4 Conductor Cable	.12 "
53	PA9312-B	Tender Body	3.00 "
54	XA9612-B	Bottom Finger Unit (Remote Control)	.50 "
55	XA9612-C	Top Finger Unit (Remote Control)	.50 "
56	XA8716	Drum (Remote Control Unit)	.60 "
57	XA10587	Remote Control Unit	2.50 "
58	PA1312	Insulating Bushing	.10 dz.
59	PA6173	Soldering Terminal	.02 ea.
60	PA4408	Tubular Rivet	.24 dz.
61	PA10138	Contact Strip	.02 ea.
62	PA10244	Coupler	.10 "
63	W79	Washer	.10 dz.
64	S-0	Screw	.05 "
65	PA4366	Tubular Rivet	.24 "
66	PA10235-A	Truck Rivet	.03 ea.
67	PA10209	Insulating Bushing	.02 "
68	PA10582	Tender Chassis	.52 "
69	PA1310	Washer	.05 dz.
70	PA1405	Washer	.05 "
71	PA8715-B	Washer	.05 "
72	XA10469	Coupler and Weight	.15 ea.
	PA10692	Coupler weight only	.05 "
73	PA10467	Coupler Pin	.10 "
74	XA10139-A	Rear Truck Assembly with wheels	1.00 "
75	XA10238-A	Wheel and Axle Assembly (plastic wheels)	.25 set
76	PA10241	Contact Spring	.05 ea.
77	XA10238	Wheel & Axle Assembly (Brass & plastic wheels)	.25 set
	PA9990	Plastic Wheel	.10 ea.
	PA10140	Brass wheel	.15 "
	PA10238	Axle	.02 "
78	XA10139-RP	Front Truck Assembly with wheels	1.00 "
79	PA4939	Truck Stud	.05 "
80	W46	Washer	.05 dz.
81	S230-B	Screw	.10 "

*XA10506 Chassis Assembly is not sold as a complete assembly with wheels.

**XA11077 Armature Assembly with 1/16" oil slinger cannot be used with XA9565-A Brush Bracket Assembly manufactured before Oct. 1949 unless you grind 1/16" off the boss which the bearing sets into on the Brush Bracket Assembly.

***XA9569 Armature Assembly can be used with XA9565-A Brush Bracket Assembly manufactured after Oct. 1949 providing that you use 1/[illegible] washer [illegible]

LOCOMOTIVE AND TENDER WITH SMOKE AND CHOO-CHOO UNIT

Model No. 324AC

SPECIFICATIONS

Tested at: 12 Volt .... Using 140" oval of track.

(A) Motor to be tested with remote control unit at 12 volts and not to draw more than .175 amps.

(B) Locomotive to run a minimum of 8 RPM or 8 times forward, around 140" oval of track per minute.

(C) Locomotive to run a minimum of 7.5 RPM or 7½ times reverse, around 140" oval of track per minute.

Load: Not to draw more than 2.1 amps while pulling 4 Box Cars at 12 Volts.

Motor: Universal A.C. or D.C.

 Ref: Form No. M2901; Dec. 1, 1950

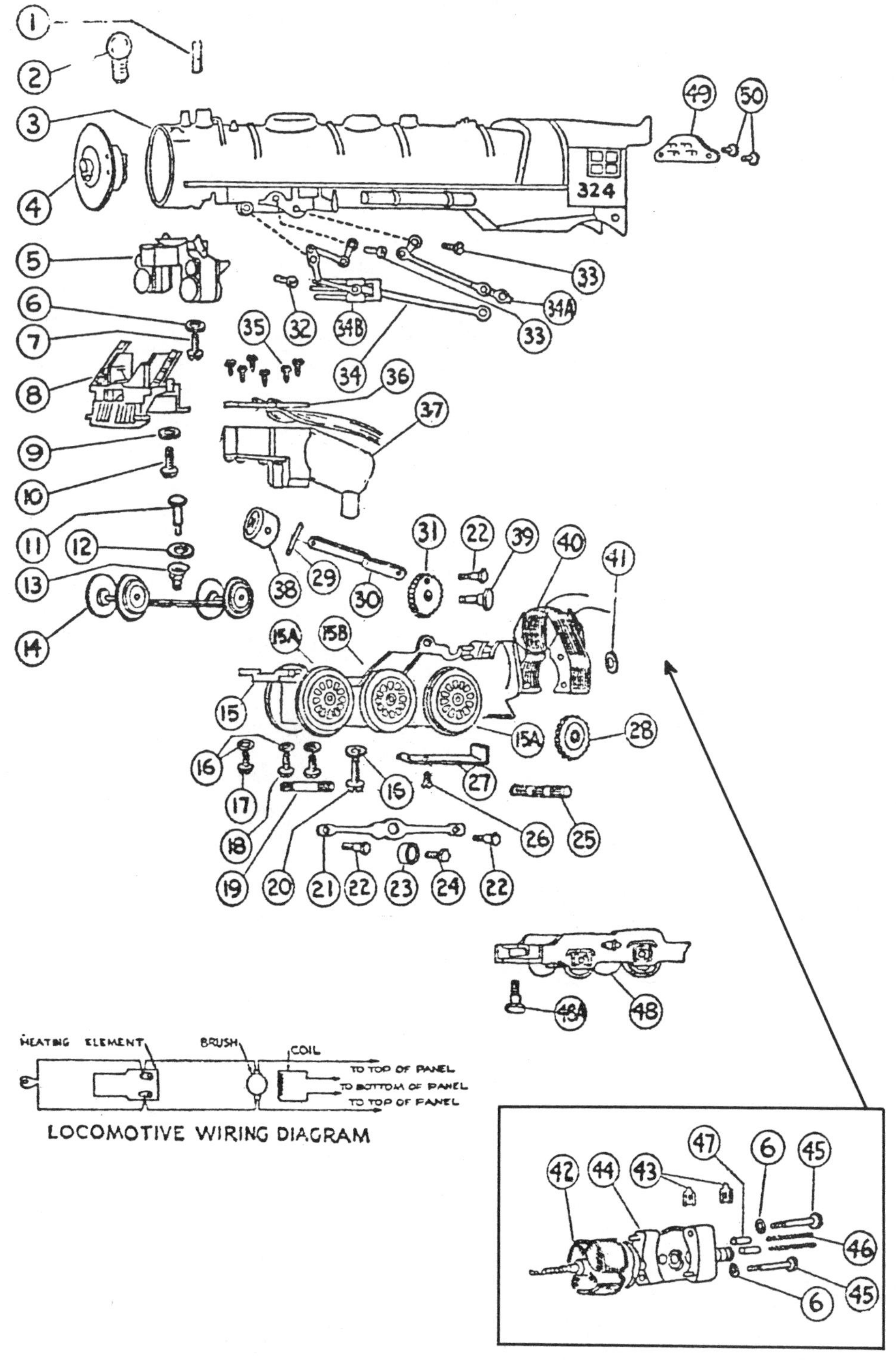

Ref: Form No. M2901; Dec. 1, 1950

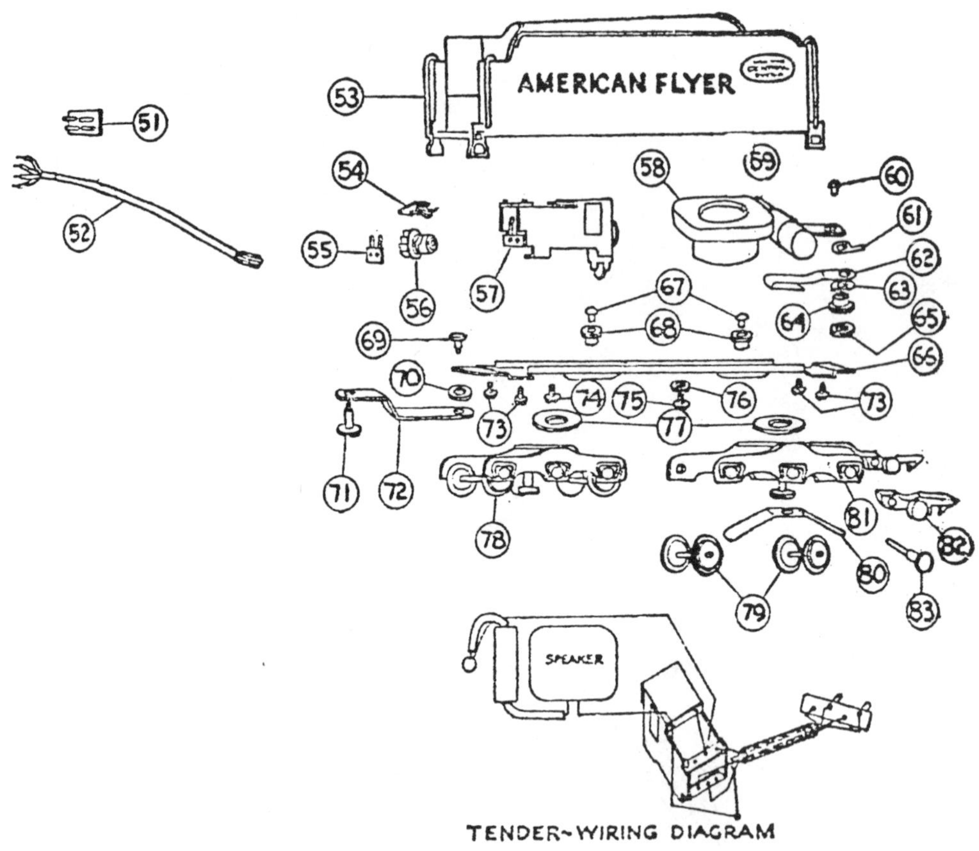

 Ref: Form No. M2901; Dec. 1, 1950

Diagram Number	Part No.	Description	Price
1	PA10536	Smoke stack	$ .03 ea.
2	PA8999	14 Volt Lamp	.25 "
3	XA9210-A	Boiler Assembly	2.25 "
4	XA9216-B	Boiler Front Assembly with lamp bracket	.60 "
5	PA10056	Cylinder and Steamchest	.70 "
6	PA3769	Lockwasher	.05 dz.
7	S47	Screw	.05 "
8	PA9245	Pilot	.70 ea.
9	PA3769	Lockwasher	.05 dz.
10	S16	Screw	.05 dz.
11	PA10707	Front Truck Stud	.05 ea.
12	W6	Washer	.03 "
13	PA8887	Front Truck Spring	.05 "
14	XA10012	Front Truck	.40 "
	PA9990-A	Front Truck Wheel only	.10 "
15	*XA10506	Chassis Assembly with bushings only	1.20 "
15A	XA10009	Flanged wheel with tapped hole	.40 "
15B	XA10009-B1	Flangeless wheel and stud	.40 "
16	PA3769	Lockwasher	.05 dz.
17	S14	Screw	.05 "
18	S46	Screw	.05 "
19	PA10005	Plain Axle	.10 ea.
20	S16-C	Screw	.10 dz.
21	PA9280-A	Side Rod	.20 ea.
22	PA7421	Screw	.30 dz.
23	PA7237	Spacer for Piston Rod	.05 ea.
24	PA5447	Screw	.30 dz.
25	PA10006	Worm gear axle	.10 ea.
26	S271	Screw	.10 dz.
27	PA10017	Grease Pan	.02 ea.
28	PA10672	Worm Gear (motor)	.30 "
29	PA10520	Piston Pin	.05 "
30	PA10514	Piston Lever	.05 "
	XA10514	Piston & Lever Assembly (consists of parts 29-30-38)	.40 "
31	PA10671	Worm Gear (smoke drive)	.40 "
32	PA9288	Screw	.30 dz.
33	PA10598	Link Stud	.30 "
34	XA10597 R	Crosshead Assembly (Right)	.50 ea.
	XA10597 L	Crosshead Assembly (Left)	.50 "
34A	XA10447-A	Eccentric Crank Assembly	.30 "
34B	PA10595 R	Crosshead Guide (Right)	.05 "
	PA10595 L	Crosshead Guide (Left)	.05 "
	XA10513	Chassis Smoke Box Assembly (consists of parts 35-36-37)	2.00 "
35	S183	Screw	.10 dz.
36	XA10523	Heating Element and Plate Assembly	1.00 ea.
37	PA10513	Chassis Smoke Box	1.00 ea.
38	PA10518	Piston	.20 "
39	PA10162	Worm Gear Stud	.10 "
40	XA9547	Magnet Assembly A.C.	1.00 "
41	PA10766	Washer	.05 dz.
42	**XA11077	Armature Assembly A.C.	2.50 ea.
	***XA9569	Armature Assembly A.C.	2.50 "
43	PA10754	Brush Cap	.02 "

Ref: Form No. M2901; Dec. 1, 1950

Diagram Number	Part No.	Description	Price
44	XA9565-A	Brush Bracket Assembly	$ .50 ea.
45	S295	Screw	.10 "
46	PA10757	Brush Spring	.05 "
47	PA9603	Carbon Brush A.C.	.15 "
48	XA10002	Rear Truck Assembly	.70 "
48A	PA4938	Rear Truck Stud	.30 dz.
49	XA10662	Jack Panel	.20 ea.
50	S230-B	Screw	.10 dz.
51	XA10663	Male Plug	.20 ea.
52	PA10511-A	4 Conductor Cable	.12 "
53	PA9312-B	Tender Body with trimmings	3.00 "
54	XA9612-C	Top Finger Unit (Remote Control) Ch	.50 "
55	XA9612-B	Bottom Finger Unit (Remote Control)	.50 "
56	XA8716	Drum (Remote Control Unit)	.60 "
57	XA10587	Remote Control Unit	2.50 "
58	PA11364	Speaker	2.18 "
59	PA11365	Condenser	.68 "
60	PA4408	Tubular Rivet	.24 dz.
61	PA6173	Soldering Terminal	.02 ea.
62	PA10138	Contact Strip	.02 "
63	PA1310	Washer	.05 dz.
64	PA1312	Insulating Bushing	.10 "
65	PA1405	Washer	.05 "
66	XA10582-A	Chassis & Wire Retainer Assembly	.27 ea.
67	PA10235-A	Truck Rivet	.03 "
68	PA10209	Insulating Bushing	.02 "
69	PA4366	Tubular Rivet	.24 "
70	W79	Washer	.10 dz.
71	PA4939	Stud	.05 "
72	PA10244	Coupler	[illegible] "
73	S-O	Screw	.05 "
74	S230	Screw	.10 "
75	S-50-A	Screw	[illegible]
76	W29	Washer	[illegible] "
77	PA8715-B	Washer	.05 "
78	XA11504-A	Front Truck Assembly with wheels	[illegible]
79	XA10238	Wheel & axle Assembly (Brass & Plastic wheels)	.25
	PA9990	Plastic Wheel	.10
	PA10140	Brass Wheel	.18 "
	PA10238	Axle	.02 "
80	PA10241	Contact Spring	.05
81	XA11504	Rear Truck Assembly with wheels	[illegible]
82	XA10469	Coupler and Weight	.15
	PA10692	Coupler weight only	.05
83	PA10467	Coupler Pin	.10 "

*XA10506 Chasis Assembly is not sold as a complete assembly with wheels.

**XA11077 Armature Assembly with 1/16" oil slinger ca. ot be used with XA9565-A Brush Bracket Assembly manufactured before Oct. 1949, unless you grind 1/16" off the boss which the bearing sets into on the Brush Bracket Assembly.

***XA9569 Armature Assembly can be used with XA9565-A Brush Bracket Assembly manufactured after Oct. 1949 providing that you use 1/16" washer to take up end play.

SERVICE INSTRUCTIONS FOR THE ELECTRONIC WHISTLE ON THE No. 324AC LOCOMOTIVE AND TENDER

1. To Check Whistle in "B" Unit and Control Box turn the Control Lever Down. If it does not blow properly check as follows:

a. Check hook-up and operating instructions.

b. See if filament in tube is burning alright.

c. Check sound adjustment on Whistle Controller as per instruction sheet which comes with the unit.

d. Check for shorted condenser (#59).

e. Check Speaker (#58) operation.

2. To Check Whistle Control Box Only.

a. Take a spare speaker (#58) and connect to Track Terminal with red wire to base post clip and black wire to other clip.

b. If Whistle blows, Control Box is O.K., but Speaker in "B" Unit will have to be replaced.

c. When Whistle Control Box is found to be defective, it should be returned to the A. C. Gilbert Company for service unless a new tube will correct the trouble.

3. To Check Whistle Without Control Box.

a. With Locomotive on the Track and handle of Transformer turned on, raise or lower the rear truck of the "B" unit just enough to break the electrical circuit. You will hear a noticeable click from the speaker if everything is O.K. If this sound is not heard, the Speaker (#58) or Condenser (#59) should be replaced.

LOCOMOTIVE AND TENDER WITH SMOKE, CHOO-CHOO, AND AIR CHIME WHISTLE

Model Nos. 325, K325

SPECIFICATIONS

Tested at: 12 Volt...Using 140" oval track.

(A) Motor to be tested with remote control unit at 12 volts and not to draw more than .175 amps.

(B) Locomotive to run a minimum of 9 RPM or 9 times forward, around 140" oval of track per minute.

(C) Locomotive to run a minimum of 8.5 RPM or 8½ times reverse, around 140" oval of track per minute.

Load: Not to draw more than 2.1 amps while pulling 4 Box Cars at 12 Volts.

Motor: Universal A.C. or D.C.

 Ref: Form 1806; Feb. 1, 1957

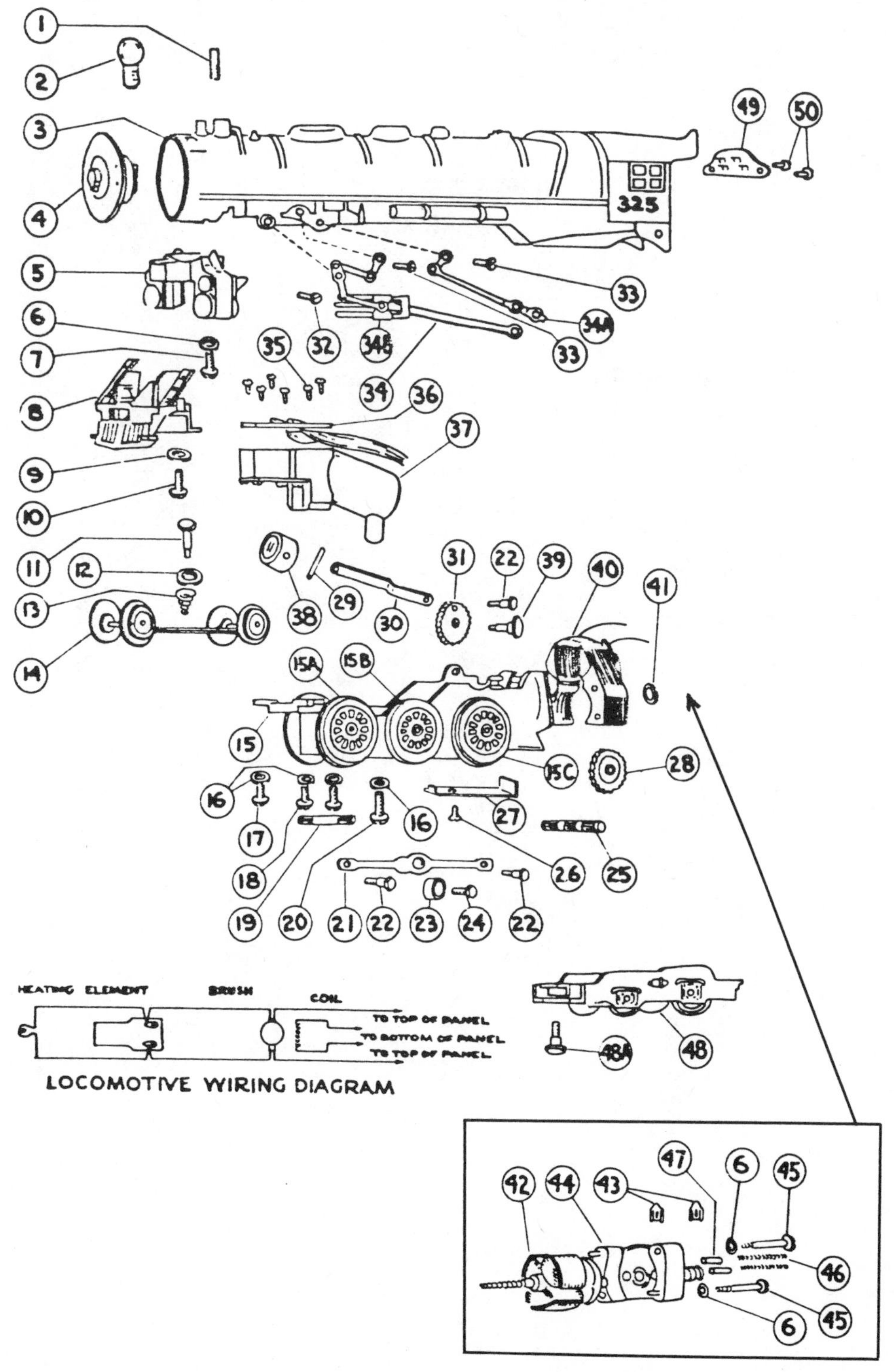

1
2
3
4
5
6
7
8
9
10
11
12
13
14
15
15A
15B
15C
16
17
18
19
20
21
22
23
24
25
26
27
28
29
30
31
32
33
34
34A
34B
35
36
37
38
39
40
41
42
43
44
45
46
47
48
48A
49
50
325
HEATING ELEMENT
BRUSH
COIL
TO TOP OF PANEL
TO BOTTOM OF PANEL
TO TOP OF PANEL
LOCOMOTIVE WIRING DIAGRAM

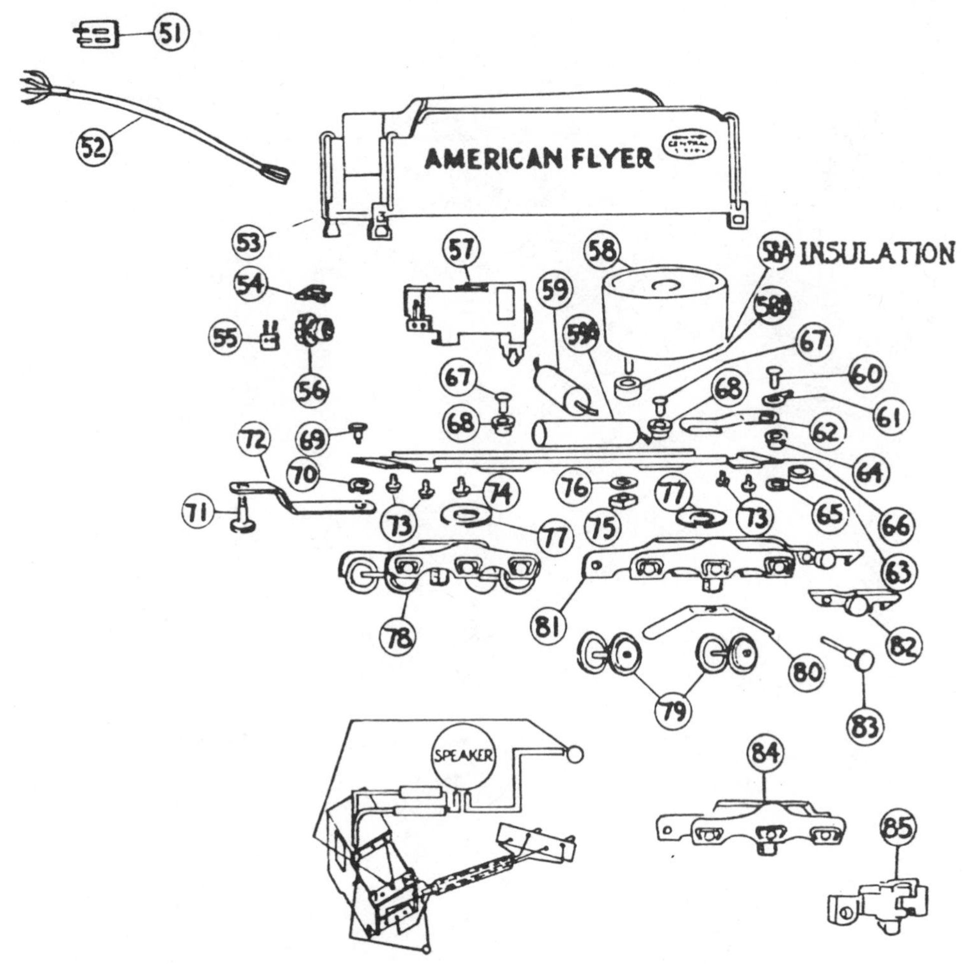

 Ref: Form 1806; Feb. 1, 1957

Diagram Number	Part No.	Description	Price
1	PA12A190	Smoke Stack	$ .02 ea.
2	PA8999	14 Volt Lamp....................	.25 "
3	XA9210-A	Boiler Assembly	2.50 "
4	XA9216-B	Boiler front Assembly with lamp bracket..............	.85 "
5	PA10056	Cylinder and Steamchest...........	.54 "
6	PA3769	Lockwasher	.05 dz.
7	S47	Screw	.05 "
8	PA9245	Pilot	.71 ea.
9	PA3769	Lockerwasher	.05 dz.
10	S16	Screw	.05 "
11	PA10707	Front Truck Stud................	.05 ea.
12	W6	Washer	.03 dz.
13	PA8887	Front Truck Spring..............	.02 ea.
14	XA10012	Front Truck	.40 "
	PA9990-A	Front Truck Wheel only...........	.11 "
15	*XA10506	Chassis Assembly with bushings only..	1.33 "
15A	XA13A865	Flanged wheel	.29 "
15B	XA10009-B1	Flangeless wheel and stud..........	.45 "
15C	XA13A864	Pull-Mor Wheel Assy..............	.51 "
16	PA3769	Lockwasher	.05 dz.
17	S14	Screw	.05 "
18	S46	Screw	.05 "
19	PA10005	Plain Axle	.10 ea.
20	S16-C	Screw	.11 dz.
21	PA9280-A	Side Rod	.10 ea.
22	PA7421	Screw	.30 dz.
23	PA7237	Spacer for piston Rod.............	.05 ea.
24	PA5447	Screw	.30 dz.
25	PA10006	Worm gear axle..................	.10 ea.
26	S271	Screw	.10 dz.
27	PA10017	Grease Pan	.04 ea.
28	PA10672	Worm Gear (motor)..............	.20 ea.
29	PA10520	Piston Pin	.05 "
30	PA10514	Piston Lever	.08 "
31	PA10671	Worm Gear (smoke drive)..........	.27 "
32	PA9288	Screw	.30 dz.
33	PA10598	Link Stud	.30 "
34	XA10597 R	Crosshead Assembly (right).........	.32 ea.
	XA10597 L	Crosshead Assembly (left)..........	.32 "
34A	XA10447-A	Eccentric Crank Assembly..........	.30 "
34B	PA10595 R	Crosshead Guide (right)............	.07 "
	PA10595L	Crosshead Guide (left).............	.07 "
	** XA10513	Chassis Smoke Box Assembly (consists of parts 35-36-37). NOT AVAILABLE	
35	S183	Screw	.10 dz.
36	*** XA10523	Heating Element and Plate Assembly.	.66 ea.
37	** PA10513	Chassis Smoke Box .... NOT AVAILABLE	
38	PA10518-A	Piston	.17 "
39	PA10162	Worm Gear Stud................	.05 "
40	XA12A526	Magnet Assembly	1.55 ea.
41	PA10766	Washer	.05 dz.
42	XA12A523	Armature Assembly	3.50 "
43	PA10754	Brush Cap	.02 "

All prices subject to change without notice.

**Parts so marked NOT AVAILABLE, substitute with:

Dia. 37	XA13B894RP	Smoke Box Assy. (new style)	$1.55 ea.
	PA13B894	Smoke Box (new style)	.59 "
	PA14A209	Separator (new style)	.01 "

Ref: Form 1806; Feb. 1, 1957

Item Number	Part No.	Description	Price
44	XA9565-A	Brush Bracket Assembly	.71
45	S-3A73	Screw	.02
46	PA10757-A	Brush Spring	.05 "
47	PA9603	Carbon Brush	.15 "
48	XA10002	Rear Truck Assembly	.73 "
48A	PA4938	Rear Truck Stud	.03 "
49	XA10662 A	Jack Panel	.22 "
50	S230-B	Screw	.10 dz.
51	XA10663	Male plug	.22 ea.
52	PA10511-A	4 Conductor Cable	.12 "
53	XA9312-RP	Tender Body with trimmings	3.33 "
54	XA9612-CRP	Top Finger Unit (Remote Control)	.30 "
55	XA9612-BRP	Bottom Finger Unit (Remote Control)	.30 "
56	XA8716	Drum (Remote Control Unit)	.59 "
57	XA10587-E	Remote Control Unit	1.32 "
58	XA11710	Speaker	3.06 "
58A	PA11664	Receiver Insulation	.02 "
58B	W99	Rubber Washer	.03 "
59	PA11A991	Condenser	1.04 "
59A	PA11685	Resistor	.26 "
60	PA4408	Tubular Rivet	.01 "
61	PA6173	Soldering Terminal	.02 "
62	PA10138	Contact Strip	.02 "
63	PA1310	Washer	.05 dz.
64	PA1312	Insulating Bushing	.11 "
65	PA1405	Washer	.05 "
66	XA10582-A	Chassis & Wire Retainer Assembly	.30 ea.
67	PA10235-A	Truck Rivet	.03 "
68	PA10209	Insulating Bushing	.02 "
69	PA4366	Tubular Rivet	.01 "
70	W79	Washer	.10 dz.
71	PA4939	Stud	.05 ea.
72	PA10244	Coupler	.05 "
73	S-O	Screw	.05 dz.
74	S230	Screw	.10 ea.
75	N-1A	Nut	.01 ea.
76	PA3769	Washer	.05 dz.
77	PA8715-B	Washer	.05 "
78	XA11A909	Front Truck Assembly with wheels	.68 ea.
79	XA10238	Wheel & Axle Assembly (Metal & Plastic Wheels)	.17 set
	PA9990	Plastic Wheel	.05 ea.
	PA10140	Metal Wheel	.15 "
	PA10238	Axle	.02 "
80	PA10241	Contact Spring	.07 "
81	XA11504-E	Rear Truck Assembly with wheels No. 325	1.39 "
82	XA10469	Coupler and Weight	.17 "
	PA10692	Coupler weight only	.05 "
83	PA10467	Coupler Pin	.11 "
84	XA12A053	Rear Truck Assembly with Wheels (K325)	1.00 "
85	XA12A047	Knuckle Coupler (K325)	.22 "

*XA10506 Chassis Assembly is not sold as a complete assembly with wheels.

***The XA10523 Heating Element and Plate Assy. is still available, and interchangeable with the new style PA13B894 Smoke Box. The new style XA14A208 Heating Element and Plate Assembly, priced at $.66 each, is used only on the new style PA13B894 Smoke Box.

SERVICE INSTRUCTIONS FOR Nos. 325 & K325 LOCOMOTIVE AND TENDER WITH SMOKE, CHOO-CHOO AND WHISTLE.

The first thing to do is to place Locomotive and Tender on track, connect transformer and whistle control unit, and test for operation. Make sure all rods, linkage and other parts are not bent or broken. It is also important that the wheels on the Tender be clean to insure a good electrical contact.

1. **If the whistle is satisfactory, but the Locomotive and Tender does not operate properly proceed as follows:**
   a. Remove screw (※71) and also male plug (※51) from the Jack Panel (※49).
   b. Now take another similar tender with a Remote Control Unit in it which is in good working order and connect it to the Locomotive. In this way, you will be able to determine whether the Locomotive or Tender is defective.

2. **If the trouble is in the Locomotive you can make the following checks:**
   a. Inspect brushes for wear or poor contact and brush springs for position and proper tension.
   b. Check wires and solder joints on male plug (※51) and Jack Panel (※49) for broken or loose connections.
   c. Clean or polish commutator if dirty or worn.

3. **If these initial steps do not correct the trouble it will be necessary to disassemble the locomotive as follows:**
   a. Unscrew smoke stack (※1).
   b. Remove screws (※24) on each side and take off Rods (※34 and 34A) and spacer (※23) from center drive wheel.
   c. Take off Rear Truck (※48) by removing screw (※48A).
   d. Pull out Boiler Front (※4) from Boiler Assembly (※3) and unsolder the two wires at the lamp bracket.
   e. Turn Locomotive upside down and remove two screws (※18) and you can now remove motor assembly from Boiler (※3).
   f. To remove motor, push forward approximately a ¼" to clear clamp on Boiler (※3) and then lift rear of motor up and pull motor out.
   g. The motor is now exposed and you can inspect the wiring and other points of the unit, making any necessary replacements.

4. **When the trouble appears to be in the Tender, proceed as follows:**
   a. Remove four S-0 screws (※73) and take off Tender body (※53).
   b. Inspect wiring and solder joints for loose or broken connections.
   c. Check finger units (※54 and ※55) on Remote Control Unit (※57) to see if they are burnt or not making proper contact.
   d. The drum (※56) should be checked to see if it is pitted or worn.
   e. The pawl on the Remote Control Unit may be broken or need adjusting.
   f. It is generally not necessary to replace the complete Remote Control Unit, but sometimes the Finger Units, the drum, or both need adjusting or replacing.

5. **If Locomotive and Tender operates satisfactorily, but the whistle does not function correctly check as follows:**
   a. Recheck the instruction sheet in order to make sure hook-up is correct. If both the Transformer instructions and the Air Chime Whistle Instructions are followed, this will cause a duplication of wiring. The result will be that you will only have a faint buzz while the train is running or in a neutral position. Follow the Air Chime Whistle wiring instructions only and be sure to have only two wires going to the ※690 track terminal.
   b. The Generator Tube ※PA11665 on the control box may be weak and need replacing.
   c. If the trouble still persists it will be necessary to remove the Tender Body (※53) from the chassis by unscrewing the four S-0 screws (※73).
   d. The unit is exposed and you can check all wires and solder joints for loose connections. Be sure the lead wires on the resistor and condenser are covered with an insulating sleeve.
   e. Check the condenser (※59) by adding another condenser in series with temporary connections. If this corrects the trouble the defective condenser can be removed and a new one connected in its place.
   f. To check resistor (※59A) use another resistor and follow same procedure.

DIA. NO.	PART NO.	DESCRIPTION	PRICE
1	PA12A190	Smoke Stack	.03 ea.
2	PA8999	14 Volt Lamp	.30 ea.
3	XA9210-A	Boiler Assy. NOT AVAILABLE	
		Substitute with XA11A939-RP Boiler Assy.	2.75 ea.
4	XA9216-B	Boiler Front Assy. w/Lamp Bracket	.94 ea.
	PA10542	Headlight Lens	.02 ea.
5	PA10056	Cylinder and Steamchest	.47 ea.
6	PA3769	Lockwasher	.01 ea.
7	S47	Screw	.01 ea.
8	PA9245	Pilot	1.34 ea.
9	PA3769	Lockwasher	.01 ea.
10	S16	Screw	.01 ea.
11	PA10707	Front Truck Stud	.07 ea.
12	W6	Washer	.01 ea.
13	PA8887	Front Truck Spring	.02 ea.
14	XA10012	Front Truck	.44 ea.
	PA9990-A	Front Truck Wheel Only	.12 ea.
15	PA10506-A	Chassis Assy. w/bushings only	1.78 ea.
15A	XA13A865	Flanged Wheel	.37 ea.
15B	XA10009-B1	Flangeless Wheel & Stud	.63 ea.
15C	XA13A864	Pul-Mor Wheel Assembly	.80 ea.
16	PA3769	Lockwasher	.01 ea.
17	S14	Screw	.01 ea.
18	S46	Screw	.01 ea.
19	PA10005	Plain Axle NOT AVAILABLE	
		Substitute with PA15A226 Axle	.05 ea.
20		NOT USED	
21	PA9280-A	Side Rod	.16 ea.
22	PA7421	Screw	.03 ea.
23	PA7237	Spacer for Piston Rod	.02 ea.
24	PA5447	Screw	.04 ea.
25	PA10006	Worm Gear Axle NOT AVAILABLE	
		Substitute with PA15A281 Axle	.07 ea.
26	S271	Screw	.02 ea.
27	PA10017	Grease Pan	.07 ea.
28	PA10672	Worm Gear (Motor)	.06 ea.
29	PA10520	Piston Pin	.03 ea.
30	PA10514	Piston Lever	.14 ea.
31	PA10671	Worm Gear (Smoke Drive)	.32 ea.
32	PA9288	Screw	.03 ea.
33	PA10598	Link Stud	.02 ea.
34	XA10597-R	Crosshead Assy. (Right)	.46 ea.
	XA10597-L	Crosshead Assy. (Left)	.46 ea.
34A	XA10447-A	Eccentric Crank Assembly	.27 ea.
34B	PA10595-R	Crosshead Guide (Right)	.12 ea.
	PA10595-L	Crosshead Guide (Left)	.12 ea.
35	S183	Screw	.01 ea.
36	XA10523	Heating Element & Plate Assy. NOT AVAILAB[illegible]	
		Substitute with XA14A208-A Assembly	.91 ea.
37	XA10513	Chassis Smoke Box Assy. NOT AVAILABLE	
		Substitute with XA13B894-RP Assembly	2.13 ea.
	PA10513	Smoke Box NOT AVAILABLE	
		Substitute with PA13B894 Smoke Box	.76 ea.
	PA14A209	Separator	.02 ea.
38	PA10518-A	Piston	.29 ea.
39	PA10162	Worm Gear Stud	.08 ea.
40	XA12A526	Magnet Assembly	1.71 ea.

 Ref: Form 1806; June 1, 1960; Corr. Mar. 23, 1961

DIA. NO.	PART NO.		DESCRIPTION	PRICE
41	PA10766		Washer	.01 ea.
42	XA12A523		Armature Assembly	3.85 ea.
43	PA10754		Brush Cap	.02 ea.
44	XA9565-A		Brush Bracket Assembly	1.00 ea.
45	S3A78		Screw NOT AVAILABLE	
		Sub.	with S29 Screw	.01 ea.
46	PA10757-A		Brush Spring	.02 ea.
47	PA9603		Carbon Brush	.13 ea.
48	XA10002		Rear Truck Assembly NOT AVAILABLE	
		Sub.	with XA14B837 Truck	.99 ea.
48A	PA4938		Rear Truck Stud	.04 ea.
49	XA10662-A		Jack Panel	.24 ea.
50	S230-B		Screw	.01 ea.
51	XA10663		Male Plug	.24 ea.
52	PA10511		4 Conductor Cable	.13 ea.
53	XA9312-RP		Tender Body w/trimmings	3.66 ea.
54	XA9612-CRP		Top Finger Unit	.33 ea.
55	XA9612-BRP		Bottom Finger Unit	.33 ea.
56	XA8716		Drum	.95 ea.
57	XA10587-E		Remote Control Unit	4.04 ea.
58	XA11710		Speaker NOT AVAILABLE	
		Sub.	with XA14A127 Speaker	4.57 ea.
58A			NOT USED	
58B			NOT USED	
59	PA11A991		Condenser NOT AVAILABLE	
		Sub.	with PA14A914 Condenser	1.40 ea.
59A	PA11685		Resistor	.29 ea.
60			NOT USED	
61			NOT USED	
62			NOT USED	
63			NOT USED	
64			NOT USED	
65			NOT USED	
66	XA10582-A		Chassis & Wire Retainer Assembly	.33 ea.
67	PA10235-A		Truck Rivet	.07 ea.
68	PA10209		Insulating Bushing	.02 ea.
69	PA4366		Tubular Rivet	.01 ea.
70	W79		Washer	.11 dz.
71	PA4939		Stud	.06 ea.
72	PA10244		Coupler	.06 ea.
73	S-0		Screw	.01 ea.
74	S230B		Screw	.01 ea.
75			NOT USED	
76			NOT USED	
77	PA8715-B		Washer	.02 ea.
78	XA11A909		Front Truck Assembly w/wheels	.75 ea.
79	XA10238		Wheel & Axle Assembly (metal & plastic wheel:	.09 ea.
	PA9990		Plastic Wheel	.03 ea.
	PA10140		Metal Wheel	.06 ea.
	PA10238		Axle	.01 ea.
80	PA10241		Contact Spring	.13 ea.
81	XA11504-E		Rear Truck Assembly w/wheels (325 only)	1.42 ea.
82	XA10469		NOT AVAILABLE	
	PA10692		Coupler Weight NOT AVAILABLE	
83	PA10467		Coupler Pin NOT AVAILABLE	
84	XA12A053		Rear Truck Assembly w/wheels (K325)	1.30 ea.
85	XA12A047		Knuckle Coupler (K325)	.29 ea.

Ref: Form 1806; June 1, 1960; Corr. Mar. 23, 1961

NO.	PART NO.	DESCRIPTION	PRICE
1	PA12A190	Smoke Stack	.03 ea.
2	PA8999	14 volt lamp	.32 ea.
3	XA11A939-CRP	Boiler Assembly (Marked 21130)	7.01 ea.
4	XA9216-B	Boiler Front Assy. w/Lamp Bracket	.99 ea.
	PA10542	Headlight Lens	.02 ea.
5	PA10056	Cylinder and Steamchest	.49 ea.
6	PA3769	Lockwasher	.01 ea.
7	S47	Screw	.01 ea.
8	PA9245	Pilot	1.41 ea.
9	PA3769	Lockwasher	.01 ea.
10	S16	Screw	.01 ea.
11	PA10707	Front Truck Stud	.07 ea.
12	W6	Washer	.01 ea.
13	PA8887	Front Truck Spring	.02 ea.
14	XA10012	Front Truck	.46 ea.
	PA9990-A	Front Truck Wheel Only	.13 ea.
15	PA10506-A	Chassis Assy. w/ Bushings Only	1.87 ea.
15A	XA13A865	Flanged Wheel	.39 ea.
15B	XA10009-B1	Flangeless Wheel & Stud	.66 ea.
15C	XA13A864	Pul-Mor Wheel Assembly	.84 ea.
16	PA3769	Lockwasher	.01 ea.
17	S14	Screw	.01 ea.
18	S46	Screw	.01 ea.
19	PA15A226	Plain Axle	.05 ea.
20		NOT USED	
21	PA9280-A	Side Rod	.17 ea.
22	PA7421	Screw	.03 ea.
23	PA7237	Spacer For Piston Rod	.02 ea.
24	PA5447	Screw	.04 ea.
25	PA15A281	Worm Gear Axle	.07 ea.
26	S271	Screw	.02 ea.
27	PA10017	Grease Pan	.07 ea.
28	PA10672	Worm Gear (Motor)	.06 ea.
29	PA10520	Piston Pin	.03 ea.
30	PA10514	Piston Lever	.15 ea.
31	PA10671	Worm Gear (Smoke Drive)	.34 ea.
32	PA9288	Screw	.03 ea.
33	PA10598	Link Stud	.02 ea.
34	XA10597-R	Crosshead Assy. (Right)	.48 ea.
	XA10597-L	Crosshead Assy. (Left)	.48 ea.
34A	XA10447-A	Eccentric Crank Assembly	.28 ea.
34B	PA10595-R	Crosshead Guide (Right)	.13 ea.
	PA10595-L	Crosshead Guide (Left)	.13 ea.
35	S183	Screw	.01 ea.
36	XA14A208A	Heating Element & Plate Assy.	.96 ea.
* 37	XA13B894-RP	Smoke Box	2.24 ea.
38	PA10518-A	Piston	.30 ea.
39	PA10162	Worm Gear Stud	.08 ea.
40	XA12A526	Magnet Assembly	1.80 ea.
41	PA10766	Washer	.01 ea.
42	XA12A523	Armature Assembly	4.04 ea.
43	PA10754	Brush Cap	.02 ea.
44	XA9565-A	Brush Bracket Assembly	1.05 ea.
45	S29	Screw	.01 ea.

Cont'd

DIA. NO.	PART NO.		DESCRIPTION	PRICE
46	PA10757-A		Brush Spring	.02 ea.
47	PA9603		Carbon Brush	.14 ea.
48	XA14B837		Rear Truck Assembly	1.04 ea.
48A	PA4938		Rear Truck Stud	.04 ea.
49	XA10662-A		Jack Panel	.25 ea.
50	S230-B		Screw	.01 ea.
51	XA10663		Male Plug	.25 ea.
52	PA13208-A		4 Conductor Cable (Plastic)	.04 ft.
53	XA9312-RP		Tender Body w/Trimmings	3.84 ea.
54	XA9612-CRP		Top Finger Unit	.35 ea.
55	XA9612-BRP		Bottom Finger Unit	.35 ea.
56	XA8716		Drum	1.00 ea.
57	XA10587-E		Remote Control Unit	4.24 ea.
58	XA14A127	Conv.	Speaker (sub. for XA11710 obsolete)	4.91 ea.
58A-58B			NOT USED	
59	PA14A914		Condenser (sub. for Pa11A991)	1.47 ea.
59A	PA11685		Resistor	.30 ea.
60-65			NOT USED	
66	XA10582-A		Chassis & Wire Retainer Assy.	.35 ea.
67	PA10235-A		Truck Rivet	.07 ea.
68	PA10209		Insulating Bushing	.02 ea.
69	PA4366		Tubular Rivet	.01 ea.
70	W79		Washer	.01 ea.
71	PA4939		Stud	.06 ea.
72	PA10244		Coupler	.06 ea.
73	S-O		Screw	.01 ea.
74	S230-B		Screw	.01 ea.
75-76			NOT USED	
77	PA8715-B		Washer	.02 ea.
78	XA11A909		Front Truck Assembly w/Wheels	.79 ea.
79	XA10238		Wheel & Axle Assy. (Metal& Plastic Wheels)	.09 ea.
	PA9990		Plastic Wheel	.03 ea.
	PA10140		Metal Wheel	.06 ea.
	PA10238		Axle	.01 ea.
80	PA10241		Contact Spring	.14 ea.
81			Rear Truck Assy. w/ wheels (325 only obsolete)	
82			OBSOLETE	
83			Coupler Pin obsolete	
84	XA12A053		Rear Truck Assy. w/wheels (K325& 325)	1.37 ea.
85	XA12A047		Knuckle Coupler (K325)	.30 ea.

*37 When using XA13B894-RP remove screw on solder terminal

Prices subject to change without notice

HUDSON LOCOMOTIVE AND TENDER WITH SMOKE, CHOO-CHOO, AIR CHIME WHISTLE, AND PULL-MOR

Model No. 326

SPECIFICATIONS

Tested at: 12 Volts A.C. .... using 140″ oval of track.

(A) Motor to be tested with Remote Control Unit at 12 Volts, and not to draw more than .175 amps.

(B) Locomotive to run a minimum of 9 R.P.M. or 9 times forward, around 140″ oval of track per minute.

(C) Locomotive to run a minimum of 8.5 R.P.M. or 8½ times reverse, around 140″ oval of track per minute.

Load: Not to draw more than 2.1 amps. while pulling 4 Box Cars.

Motor: Universal A.C. or D.C.

 Ref: Form No. 1496; Dec. 15, 1953

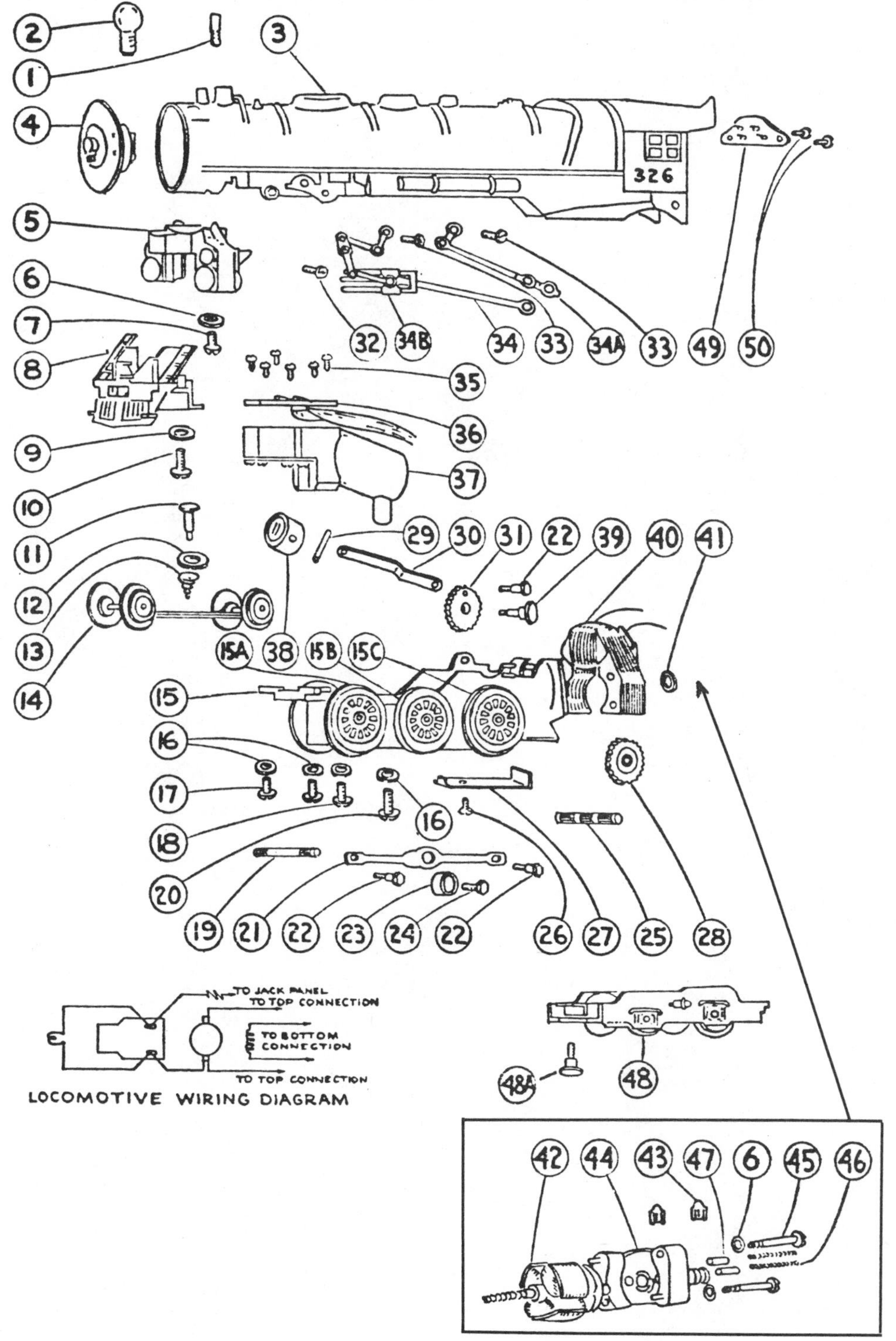

Ref: Form No. 1496; Dec. 15, 1953

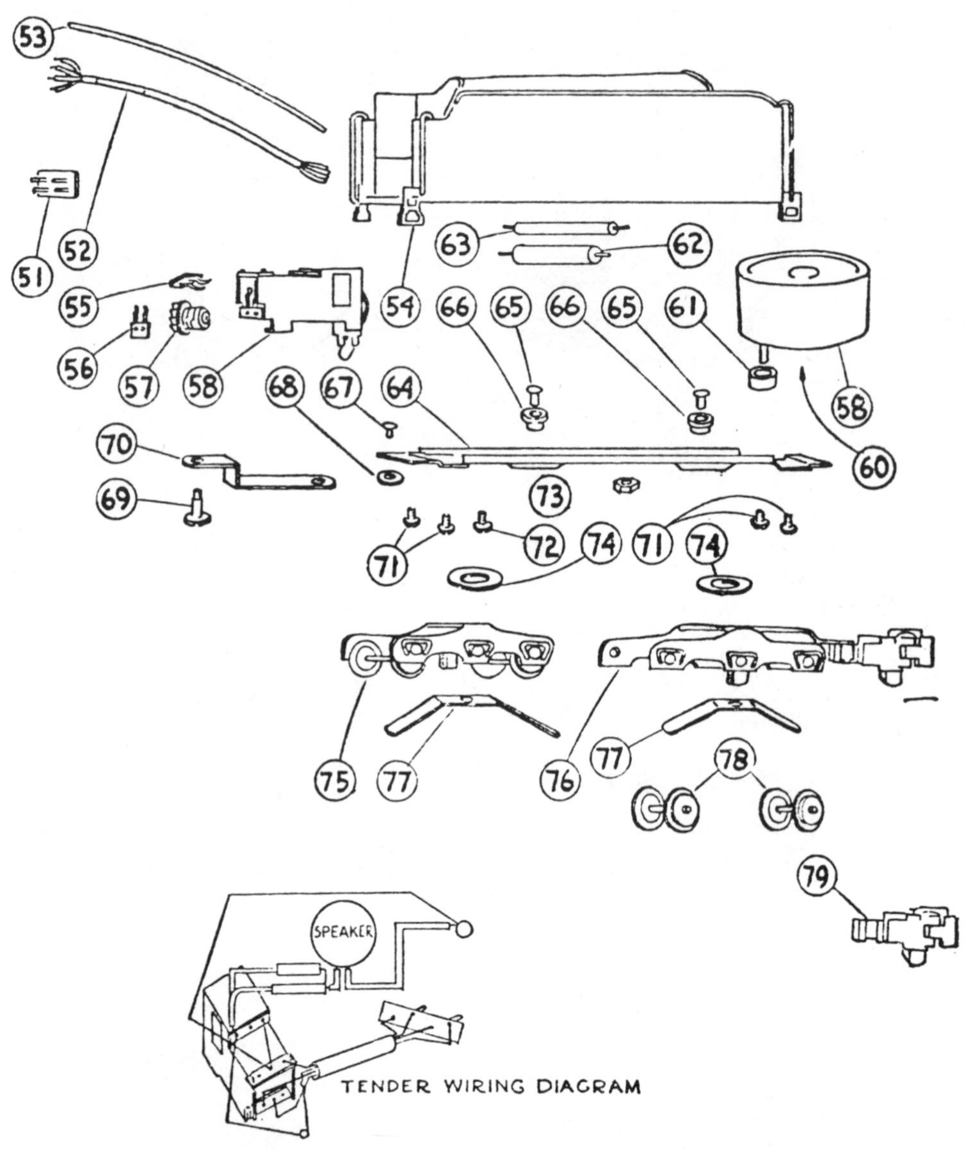

 Ref: Form No. 1496; Dec. 15, 1953

Diagram Number	Part No.	Description	Price
1	PA12A190	Smoke Stack	$ .02 ea.
2	PA8999	14 Volt Lamp	.25 "
3	XA11A939RP	Boiler Assembly	2.50 "
4	XA9216-B	Boiler Front Assembly with lamp bracket	.85 "
5	PA10056	Cylinder and Steamchest	.54 "
6	PA3769	Lockwasher	.05 dz.
7	S47	Screw	.05 "
8	PA9245	Pilot	.71 ea.
9	PA3769	Lockwasher	.05 dz.
10	S16	Screw	.05 "
11	PA10707	Front Truck Stud	.05 ea.
12	W6	Washer	.03 dz.
13	PA8887	Front Truck Spring	.02 ea.
14	XA10012	Front Truck	.40 "
	PA9990-A	Front Truck Wheel Only	.11 "
15	XA10506	Chassis Assembly	1.33 "
15A	XA13A865	Flanged Wheel	.29 "
15B	XA10009-B1	Flangeless Wheel and Stud	.45 "
15C	XA13A864	Pull-Mor Wheel	.51 "
16	PA3769	Lockwasher	.05 dz.
17	S14	Screw	.05 "
18	S46	Screw	.05 "
19	PA10005	Plain Axle	.10 ea.
20	S16-C	Screw	.11 dz.
21	PA9280-A	Side Rod	.10 ea.
22	PA7421	Screw	.30 dz.
23	PA7237	Spacer for Piston Rod	.05 ea.
24	PA5447	Screw	.30 dz.
25	PA10006	Worm Gear Axle	.10 ea.
26	S271	Screw	.10 dz.
27	PA10017	Grease Pan	.04 ea.
28	PA10672	Worm Gear (motor)	.20 "
29	PA10520	Piston Pin	.05 "
30	PA10514	Piston Lever	.08 "
31	PA10671	Worm Gear (smoke drive)	.27 "
32	PA9288	Screw	.30 dz.
33	PA10598	Link Stud	.30 "
34	XA10597-R	Crosshead Assembly (Right)	.32 ea.
34A	XA10447-A	Eccentric Crank Assembly	.30 "
34B	PA10595-R	Crosshead Guide (Right)	.07 "
	PA10595-L	Crosshead Guide (Left)	.07 "
	* XA10513	Chassis Smoke Box Assembly (consists of parts 35-36-37).	NOT AVAILABLE
35	S183	Screw	.10 dz.
36	** XA10523	Heating Element and Plate Assembly	.66 ea.
37	* PA10513	Chassis Smoke Box	NOT AVAILABLE

All prices subject to change without notice.

*Parts so marked NOT AVAILABLE, substitute with:

	Part No.	Description	Price
Dia. 37	XA13B894RP	Smoke Box Assy. (new style)	$1.55 ea.
	PA13B894	Smoke Box (new style)	.59 "
	PA14A209	Separator (new style)	.01 "

Ref: Form No. 1496; Dec. 15, 1953

Diagram Number	Part No.	Description	Price
38	PA10518-A	Piston	$ .17 ea.
39	PA10162	Worm Gear Stud	.05 "
40	XA12A526	Magnet Assembly	1.55 "
41	PA10766	Washer	.05 dz.
42	XA12A523	Armature Assembly	3.50 ea.
43	PA10754	Brush Cap	.02 "
44	XA9565-A	Brush Bracket Assembly	.71 "
45	S3A78	Screw	.02 "
46	PA10757-A	Brush Spring	.05 "
47	PA9603	Carbon Brush	.15 "
48	XA10002	Rear Truck Assembly	.73 "
48A	PA4938	Rear Truck Stud	.03 "
49	XA10662-A	Jack Panel	.22 "
50	S222	Screw	.01 "
51	XA10663	Male Plug	.22 "
52	PA10511-A	4 Conductor Cable	.12 "
53	P9273-Z	7½" Lead Wire	.02 "
54	XA9312RP	Tender Body with Trimmings	3.00 "
55	XA9612-CRP	Top Finger Unit (Remote Control)	.30 "
56	XA9612-BRP	Bottom Finger Unit (Remote Control)	.30 "
57	XA8716	Drum (Remote Control Unit)	.59 "
58	XA10587-E	Remote Control Unit	1.32 "
59	XA11710	Speaker	3.06 "
60	PA11664	Receiver Insulation	.02 "
61	W99	Rubber Washer	.03 "
62	PA11A991	Condenser	1.04 "
63	PA11685	Resistor	.26 "
64	XA10582-A	Chassis & Wire Retainer Assembly	.30 "
65	PA10235-A	Truck Rivet	.03 "
66	PA10209	Insulating Bushing	.02 "
67	PA4366	Tubular Rivet	.01 "
68	W79	Washer	.10 dz.
69	PA4939	Stud	.05 ea.
70	PA10244	Coupler	.05 "
71	S-O	Screw	.05 dz.
72	S230	Screw	.10 "
73	N-1A	Nut	.01 ea.
74	PA8715-B	Washer	.05 dz.
75	XA11A909	Front Truck Assembly with Wheels	.68 ea.
76	XA12A053	Rear Truck Assembly with Wheels	1.00 "
77	PA10241	Contact Spring	.07 "
78	XA10238	Wheel and Axle Assembly (Metal & Plastic Wheels)	.17 set
	PA9990	Plastic Wheel	.05 ea.
	PA10140	Metal Wheel	.15 "
	PA10238	Axle	.02 "
79	XA12A047	Knuckle Coupler	.22 "

**The XA10523 Heating Element and Plate Assy. is still available, and interchangeable with the new style PA13B894 Smoke Box. The new style XA14A208 Heating Element and Plate Assembly, priced at $.66 each, is used only on the new style PA13B894 Smoke Box.

SERVICE INSTRUCTIONS FOR No. 326 LOCOMOTIVE AND TENDER WITH SMOKE AND CHOO-CHOO, WHISTLE, AND KNUCKLE COUPLER

The first thing to do is to place Locomotive and Tender on track, connect transformers and whistle control unit, and test for operation: Make sure all rods, linkage, and other parts are not bent or broken. It is also important that the wheels on the tender be clean to insure a good electrical contact.

1. If the whistle is satisfactory, but the Locomotive and Tender does not operate properly, proceed as follows:

a. Remove screw (#48A), and also male plug (#51) from the Jack Panel (#49).

b. Now take another similar tender with a Remote Control Unit in it which is in good working order and connect it to the Locomotive. In this way, you will be able to determine whether the locomotive or tender is defective.

2. If the trouble is in the Locomotive you can make the following checks:

a. Inspect brushes for wear or poor contact, and brush springs for position and proper tension.

b. Check wires and solder joints on male plug (#51) and Jack Panel (#49) for broken or loose connections.

c. Clean or polish commutator if dirty or worn.

3. If these initial steps do not correct the trouble, it will be necessary to disassemble the locomotive, as follows:

a. Unscrew smoke stack (#1).

b. Remove screws (#24) on each side, and take off Rods (#34) and (#34A) and spacer (#23) from center drive wheel.

c. Take off rear truck (#48) by removing screw (48A).

d. Pull out Boiler Front (#4) from Boiler Assembly (#3) and unsolder the two wires at the lamp bracket.

e. Turn Locomotive upside down, and remove two screws (#17) and you can now remove motor assembly from Boiler (#3).

f. To remove motor, push forward approximately a ¼" to clear clamp on Boiler (#3) and then lift rear of motor up, and pull motor out.

g. The motor is now exposed, and you can inspect the wiring and other points of the unit making any necessary replacements.

4. When the trouble appears to be in the Tender, proceed as follows:

a. Remove four S-O Screws (#71) and take off Tender Body (#54).

b. Inspect wiring and solder joints for loose or broken connections.

c. Check Finger Units (#56) and (#57) on Remote Control Unit (#58) and see if they are burnt or not making proper contact.

d. The drum (#57) should be checked to see if it is pitted or worn.

e. The pawl on the Remote Control Unit may be broken or need adjusting.

f. It is generally not necessary to replace the complete Remote Control Unit, but sometimes the finger units, the drum, or both need adjusting or replacing.

5. If the Locomotive and Tender operates satisfactorily, but the whistle does not function correctly, check as follows:

a. Recheck the instructions sheet in order to make sure hook-up is correct. If both the Transformer instructions, and the Air Chime Whistle Instructions are followed, this will cause a duplication of wiring. The result will be that you will only have a faint buzz while the train is running or in a neutral position. Follow the Air Chime Whistle wiring instructions only, and be sure that you have only two wires going to the #690 track terminal.

b. The Generator Tube #PA11665 on the control box may be weak and need replacement.

c. If the trouble still persists it will be necessary to remove the Tender Body (#54) from the chassis, by unscrewing the four S-O screws (#71).

d. The unit is exposed and you can check all wires and solder joints for loose connections. Be sure the lead wires on the resistor and condenser are covered with an insulating sleeve.

e. Check the condenser (#62) by adding another condenser in series with temporary connections. If this corrects the trouble, the defective condenser can be removed and a new one connected in its place.

f. To check resistor (#63) use another resistor, and follow same procedure.

Hudson Locomotive/Tender — No. 326

DIA. NO.	PART NO.	DESCRIPTION	PRICE
1	PA12A190	Smoke Stack	.03 ea.
2	PA8999	14 Volt Lamp	.30 ea.
3	XA11A939-RP	Boiler Assembly	2.75 ea.
	XA9578	Crossbar	.08 ea.
	PA9579	Motor Mount	.01 ea.
4	XA9216-B	Boiler Front Assembly w/lamp bracket	.94 ea.
	PA10542	Headlight Lens	.02 ea.
5	PA10056	Cylinder and Steamchest	.47 ea.
6	PA3769	Lockwasher	.01 ea.
7	S47	Screw	.01 ea.
8	PA9245	Pilot	1.34 ea.
9	PA3769	Lockwasher	.01 ea.
10	S16	Screw	.01 ea.
11	PA10707	Front Truck Stud	.07 ea.
12	W6	Washer	.01 ea.
13	PA8887	Front Truck Spring	.02 ea.
14	XA10012	Front Truck	.44 ea.
	PA9900-A	Front Truck Wheel Only	.12 ea.
15	PA10506-A	Chassis Assembly	1.78 ea.
15A	XA13A865	Flanged Wheel	.37 ea.
15B	XA10009-B1	Flangeless Wheel & Stud	.63 ea.
15C	XA13A864	Pul-Mor Wheel	.80 ea.
16	PA3769	Lockwasher	.01 ea.
17	S14	Screw	.01 ea.
18	S46	Screw	.01 ea.
19	PA10005	Plain Axle NOT AVAILABLE	
	Sub.	with PA15A226 Axle	.05 ea.
20		NOT USED	
21	PA9280-A	Side Rod	.16 ea.
22	PA7421	Screw	.03 ea.
23	PA7237	Spacer for Piston Rod	.02 ea.
24	PA5447	Screw	.04 ea.
25	PA10006	Worm Gear Axle NOT AVAILABLE	
	Sub.	with PA15A281 Axle	.07 ea.
26	S271	Screw	.02 ea.
27	PA10017	Grease Pan	.07 ea.
28	PA10672	Worm Gear (Motor)	.06 ea.
29	PA10520	Piston Pin	.03 ea.
30	PA10514	Piston Lever	.14 ea.
31	PA10671	Worm Gear (smoke drive)	.32 ea.
32	PA9288	Screw	.03 ea.
33	PA10598	Link Stud	.02 ea.
34	XA10597-R	Crosshead Assembly (right)	.46 ea.
	XA10597-L	Crosshead Assembly (left)	.46 ea.
34A	XA10447-A	Eccentric Crank Assembly	.27 ea.
34B	PA10595-R	Crosshead Guide (right)	.12 ea.
	PA10595-L	Crosshead Guide (left)	.12 ea.
35	S183	Screw	.01 ea.
36	XA10523	Heating Element & Plate Assembly NOT AVAILABLE	
	Sub.	with XA14A208A Assembly	.91 ea.
37	XA10513	Smoke Box Assembly NOT AVAILABLE	
	Sub.	with XA13B894-RP Smoke Box Assembly	2.13 ea.
	PA10513	Smoke Box NOT AVAILABLE	
	Sub.	with PA13B894 Smoke Box	.76 ea.
	PA14A209	Separator	.02 ea.

 Ref: Form No. 1805; June 1, 1960; Corr. Mar. 23, 1961

DIA. NO.	PART NO.	DESCRIPTION	PRICE
38	PA10518-A	Piston	.29 ea.
39	PA10162	Worm Gear Stud	.08 ea.
40	XA12A526	Magnet Assembly	1.71 ea.
41	PA10766	Washer	.01 ea.
42	XA12A523	Armature Assembly	3.85 ea.
43	PA10754	Brush Cap	.02 ea.
44	XA9565-A	Brush Bracket Assembly	1.00 ea.
45	S3A78	Screw NOT AVAILABLE	
	Sub.	with S29 Screw	.01 ea.
46	PA10757-A	Brush Spring	.02 ea.
47	PA9603	Carbon Brush	.13 ea.
48	XA10002	Rear Truck Assembly NOT AVAILABLE	
	Sub.	with XA14B837 Rear Truck	.99 ea.
48A	PA4938	Rear Truck Stud	.04 ea.
49	XA10662-A	Jack Panel	.24 ea.
50	S222	Screw	.01 ea.
51	XA10663	Male Plug	.24 ea.
52	PA10511	4 Conductor Cable	.13 ea.
53	P9273	$7\frac{1}{2}$" Lead Wire	.02 ea.
54	XA9312-RP	Tender Body w/trimmings	3.66 ea.
55	XA9612-CRP	Top Finger Unit	.33 ea.
56	XA9612-BRP	Bottom Finger Unit	.33 ea.
57	XA8716	Drum	.95 ea.
58	XA10587-E	Remote Control Unit	4.04 ea.
59	XA11710	Speaker NOT AVAILABLE	
	XA11B831	Speaker NOT AVAILABLE	
	Sub.	with XA14A127 Speaker	4.57 ea.
	PA14A216	Speaker Bracket (used w/XA14A127 Speaker)	.08 ea.
	S171	Screw " " "	.01 ea.
	S172	4.3/16 B.D.H.D. Type Z P.K. Screw "	.02 ea.
60		NOT USED	
61		NOT USED	
62	PA11A991	Condenser NOT AVAILABLE	
	Sub.	with PA14A914 Condenser	1.40 ea.
63	PA11685	Resistor	.29 ea.
64	XA10582-A	Chassis & Wire Retainer Assembly	.33 ea.
65	PA10235-A	Truck Rivet	.07 ea.
66	PA10209	Insulating Bushing	.02 ea.
67	PA4366	Tubular Rivet	.01 ea.
68	W79	Washer	.11 dz.
69	PA4939	Stud	.06 ea.
70	PA10244	Coupler	.06 ea.
71	S-0	Screw	.01 ea.
72	S230B	Screw	.01 ea.
73		NOT USED	
74	PA8715-B	Washer	.02 ea.
75	XA11A909	Front Truck Assembly w/wheels	.75 ea.
76	XA12A053	Rear Truck Assembly w/wheels	1.30 ea.
77	PA10241	Contact Spring	.13 ea.
78	XA10238	Wheel & Axle Assembly (metal & plastic wheel:	.09 ea.
	PA9990	Plastic Wheel	.03 ea.
	PA10140	Metal Wheel	.06 ea.
	PA10238	Axle	.01 ea.
79	XA12A047	Knuckle Coupler	.29 ea.

Prices subject to change without notice.

Ref: Form No. 1805; June 1, 1960; Corr. Mar. 23, 1961

Hudson Locomotive/Tender — No. 326

NO.	PART NO.	DESCRIPTION	PRICE
1	PA12A190	Smoke Stack	.03 ea.
2	PA8999	14 Volt Lamp	.32 ea.
3	XA11A939-CRP	Boiler Assembly (Marked 21130)	7.01 ea.
	XA9578	Crossbar	.08 ea.
	PA9579	Motor Mount	.01 ea.
4	XA9216-B	Boiler Front Assembly w/lamp bracket	.99 ea.
	PA10542	Headlight Lens	.02 ea.
5	PA10056	Cylinder and Steamchest	.49 ea.
6	PA3769	Lockwasher	.01 ea.
7	S47	Screw	.01 ea.
8	PA9245	Pilot	1.41 ea.
9	PA3769	Lockwasher	.01 ea.
10	S16	Screw	.01 ea.
11	PA10707	Front Truck Stud	.07 ea.
12	W6	Washer	.01 ea.
13	PA8887	Front Truck Spring	.02 ea.
14	XA10012	Front Truck	.46 ea.
	PA9900-A	Front Truck Wheel Only	.13 ea.
15	PA10506-A	Chassis Assembly	1.87 ea.
15A	XA13A865	Flanged Wheel	.39 ea.
15B	XA10009-B1	Flangeless Wheel & Stud	.66 ea.
15C	XA13A864	Pul-Mor Wheel	.84 ea.
16	PA3769	Lockwasher	.01 ea.
17	S14	Screw	.01 ea.
18	S46	Screw	.01 ea.
19	PA15A226	Plain Axle	.05 ea.
20		NOT USED	
21	PA9280-A	Side Rod	.17 ea.
22	PA7421	Screw	.03 ea.
23	PA7237	Spacer for Piston Rod	.02 ea.
24	PA5447	Screw	.04 ea.
25	PA15A281	Worm Gear Axle	.07 ea.
26	S271	Screw	.02 ea.
27	PA10017	Grease Pan	.07 ea.
28	PA10672	Worm Gear (Motor)	.06 ea.
29	PA10520	Piston Pin	.03 ea.
30	PA10514	Piston Lever	.15 ea.
31	PA10671	Worm Gear (Smoke Drive)	.34 ea.
32	PA9288	Screw	.03 ea.
33	PA10598	Link Stud	.02 ea.
34	XA10597-R & L	Crosshead Assembly	.48 ea.
34A	XA10447-A	Eccentric Crank Assembly	.28 ea.
34B	PA10595-R & L	Crosshead Guide	.13 ea.
35	S183	Screw	.01 ea.
36	XA14A208-A	Heating Element & Plate Assembly	.96 ea.
* 37	XA13B894-RP	Smoke Box Assembly	2.24 ea.
38	PA10518-A	Piston	.30 ea.
39	PA10162	Worm Gear Stud	.08 ea.
40	XA12A526	Magnet Assembly	1.80 ea.
41	PA10766	Washer	.01 ea.
42	XA12A523	Armature Assembly	4.04 ea.

(Cont'd

 Ref: Form No. 1805; Oct. 1, 1962

NO.	PART NO.	DESCRIPTION	PRICE
43	PA10754	Brush Cap	.02 ea.
44	XA9565-A	Brush Bracket Assembly	1.05 ea.
45	S29	Screw	.01 ea.
46	PA10757-A	Brush Spring	.02 ea.
47	PA9603	Carbon Brush	.14 ea.
48	XA14B837	Rear Truck Assembly	1.04 ea.
48A	PA4938	Rear Truck Stud	.04 ea.
49	XA10662-A	Jack Panel	.25 ea.
50	S222	Screw	.01 ea.
51	XA10663	Male Plug	.25 ea.
52	PA13208-A	4 Conductor Cable (Plastic)	.04 ft.
53	P9273	Lead Wire	.03 ft.
54	XA9312-RP	Tender Body w/ trimmings	3.84 ea.
55	XA9612-CRP	Top Finger Unit	.35 ea.
56	XA9612-BRP	Bottom Finger Unit	.35 ea.
57	XA8716	Drum	1.00 ea.
58	XA10587-E	Remote Control Unit	4.24 ea.
59	XA14A127-Conv.	Speaker--Sub. for XA11710 & XA11B831-Obsolete	4.91 ea.
60		NOT USED	
61		NOT USED	
62	PA14A914	Condenser--Sub. for PA11A991	1.47 ea.
63	PA11685	Resistor	.30 ea.
64	XA10582-A	Chassis & Wire Retainer Assembly	.35 ea.
65	PA10235-A	Truck Rivet	.07 ea.
66	PA10209	Insulating Bushing	.02 ea.
67	PA4366	Tubular Rivet	.01 ea.
68	W79	Washer	.01 ea.
69	PA4939	Stud	.06 ea.
70	PA10244	Coupler	.06 ea.
71	S-0	Screw	.01 ea.
72	S230-B	Screw	.01 ea.
73		NOT USED	
74	PA8715-B	Washer	.02 ea.
75	XA11A909	Front Truck Assembly w/wheels	.79 ea.
76	XA12A053	Rear Truck Assembly w/wheels	1.37 ea.
77	PA10241	Contact Spring	.14 ea.
78	XA10238	Wheel & Axle Assy. (Metal & Plastic Wheels)	.09 ea.
	PA9990	Plastic Wheel	.03 ea.
	PA10140	Metal Wheel	.06 ea.
	PA10238	Axle	.01 ea.
79	XA12A047	Knuckle Coupler	.30 ea.

* #37 When using XA13B894-RP remove Screw on Solder Terminal.

Prices subject to change without notice.

Ref: Form No. 1805; Oct. 1, 1962

LOCOMOTIVE AND TENDER WITH PISTON-TYPE SMOKE AND CHOO-CHOO UNIT

Model No. 332

SPECIFICATIONS

Tested at: 12 Volts D.C. .... Using 140″ oval of track. Not to draw more than 1.3 amps.

(A) Locomotive to run a minimum of 9.5 R.P.M. or 9½ times forward, around 140″ oval of track per minute.

(B) Locomotive to run a minimum of 9 R.P.M. or 9 times in reverse, around 140″ oval of track per minute.

Load: Not to draw more than 2 amps. while pulling 4 Box or Cattle Cars.

Motor: D.C.

 Ref: Form No. M2824; June 1, 1950

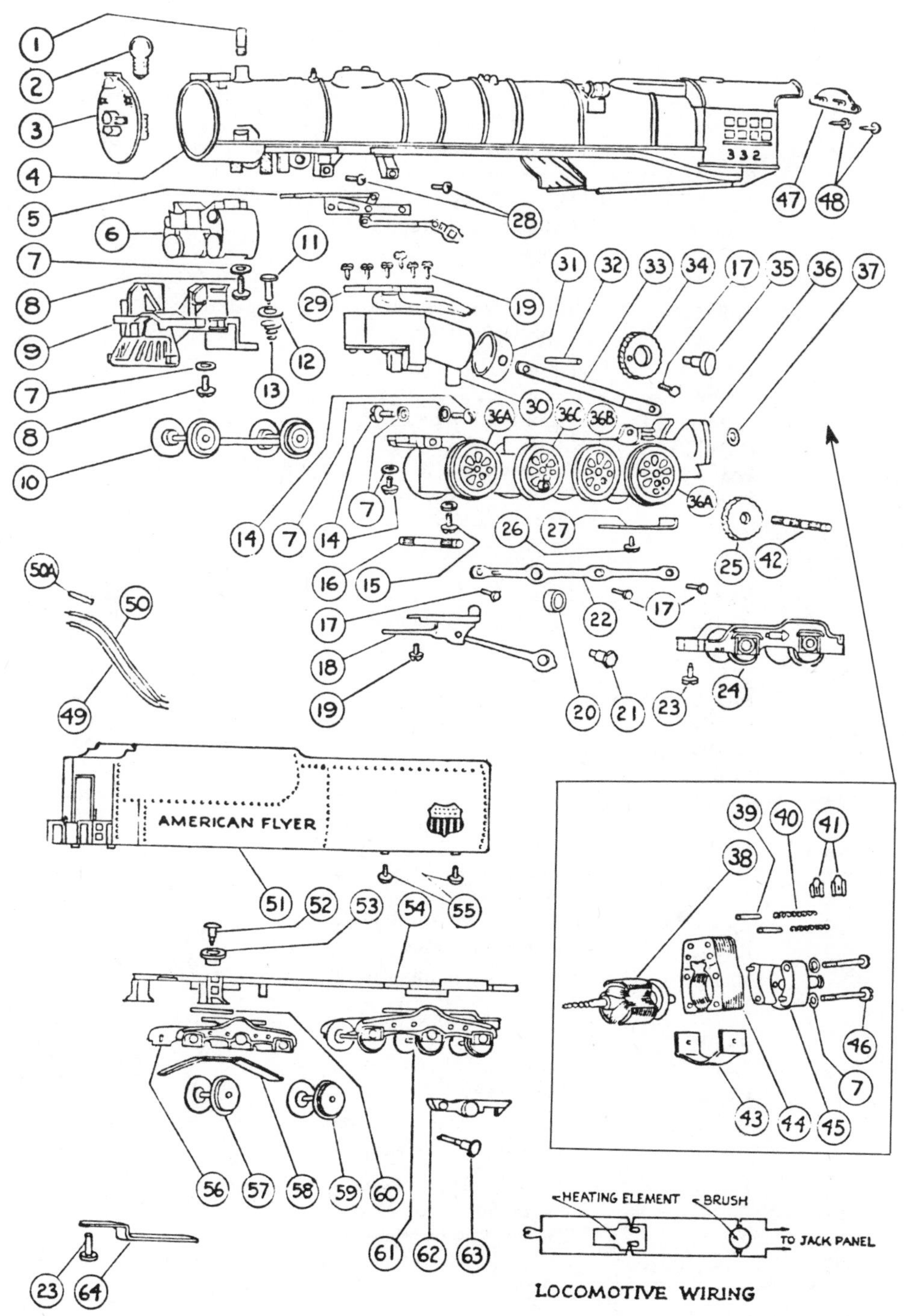

Ref: Form No. M2824; June 1, 1950

Diagram Number	Part No.	Description	Price
1	PA10536	Smoke Stack	$ .03 ea.
2	PA8999	14 Volt Lamp	.25 "
3	XA8960-C	Boiler Front Assembly with lamp socket	.60 "
4	XA8956-C	Boiler Assembly	2.50 "
5	XA10057 R or L	Valve Link Assembly (Right or Left)	.50 "
6	PA10030	Cylinder and Steamchest	.70 "
7	PA3769	Lockwasher	.05 dz.
8	S16	Screw	.05 "
9	XA8959-A	Pilot & Front Truck Assembly (consists of parts 9-10-11-12-13)	1.10 ea.
9	PA8959	Pilot	.70 "
10	XA10012-A	Front Truck	.40 "
	PA9990-D	Front Truck Wheel only	.10 "
11	PA10707	Stud	.05 "
12	W6	Washer	.03 dz.
13	PA8887	Front Truck Spring	.05 ea.
14	S46	Screw	.05 dz.
15	S18	Screw	.05 "
16	PA10005	Plain Axle	.10 ea.
17	PA7421	Screw	.30 dz.
18	XA10669RA	Crosshead Assembly	.30 ea.
	XA10669LA	Crosshead Assembly	.30 "
19	S183	Screw	.10 dz.
20	PA7237	Piston Rod Spacer	.05 ea.
21	PA5447	Screw	.30 dz.
22	PA8994-A	Side Rod	.20 ea.
23	PA4938	Stud	.30 dz.
24	XA10002-A	Rear Truck Assembly	.70 ea.
25	PA10672	Worm Gear (motor)	.30 "
26	S271	Screw	.10 dz.
27	PA10017	Grease Pan	.02 ea.
28	S171	Screw	.10 dz.
29	XA10523	Heating Element & Plate Assembly	1.00 ea.
30	PA10513	Chassis Smoke Box	1.00 "
	XA10513	Chassis Smoke Box Assembly (consists of parts 19-29-30)	2.00 "
31	PA10518	Piston	.20 "
32	PA10520	Piston Pin	.05 "
33	PA10515	Piston Lever	.05 "
	XA10515	Piston & Piston Lever Assembly (consists of parts 31-32-33)	.40 "
34	PA10671	Worm Gear (smoke drive)	.40 "
35	PA10162	Worm Gear Stud	.10 "
36	*XA10505	Chassis Assembly with bushings	1.50 "
36A	XA10010	Flanged Wheel Assembly with tapped hole	.40 "

 Ref: Form No. M2824; June 1, 1950

Diagram Number	Part No.	Description	Price
36B	XA10010-A	Flangeless Wheel Assembly with tapped hole	.40 ea.
36C	XA10010-A3	Flangeless Wheel Assembly with stud	.40 "
37	PA10766	Washer	.05 dz.
38	**XA11001	Armature Assembly D.C.	2.50 ea.
	***XA10476	Armature Assembly D.C.	2.50 ea.
39	PA10778	Carbon Brush D.C.	.15 "
40	PA10757	Brush Spring	.05 "
41	PA10754	Brush Cap	.02 "
42	PA10006	Worm Gear Axle	.10 "
43	PA10549	Magnet Cover	.06 "
44	XA10355	Magnet Assembly D.C.	1.50 "
45	.XA9565-A	Brush Bracket Assembly	.50 "
46	S295	Screw	.10 "
47	XA10287	Jack Panel	.20 "
48	S230-B	Screw	.10 dz.
49	P9273-N	5½" Lead wire	.02 ea.
50	P9273-H	10" Lead wire	.02 "
50A	PA10291	Male Plug	.02 "
51	XA8914	Tender Tank & End Cap Assembly	2.50 "
52	PA9988	Stud	.03 "
53	PA10240	Insulating Bushing	.02 "
54	PA10591	Tender Chassis	.94 "
55	S-1	Screw	.05 dz.
56	XA10139-RP	Front Truck Assembly	1.00 ea.
57	XA10238	Wheel & axle assembly (brass & plastic wheels)	.25 set
	PA10140	Brass wheel	.15 ea.
	PA9990	Plastic wheel	.10 "
	PA10238	Axle	.02 "
58	PA10241	Contact Spring	.05 "
59	XA10238-A	Wheel & Axle Assembly (plastic wheels)	.25 set
60	PA8715-B	Washer	.05 dz.
61	XA10139-A	Rear Truck Assembly	1.00 ea.
62	XA10469	Coupler & Weight Assembly	.15 "
	PA10692	Weight only	.05 "
63	PA10467	Coupler Pin	.10 "
64	PA10239	Coupler	.10 "

*XA10505 Chassis Assembly is not sold as a complete assembly with wheels.

**XA11001 Armature Assembly with 1/16" oil slinger cannot be used with XA9565-A Brush Bracket Assembly manufactured before Oct. 1949, unless you grind 1/16" off the boss which the bearing sets into on the Brush Bracket Assembly.

***XA10476 Armature Assembly can be used with XA9565-A Brush Bracket Assembly manufactured after Oct. 1949 providing that you use 1/16" washer to take up end play.

LOCOMOTIVE AND TENDER WITH SMOKE AND CHOO-CHOO UNIT

Model No. 332AC

SPECIFICATIONS

Tested at: 12 Volts A.C. .... Using 140" oval track.
Not to draw more than 1.3 amps.

(A) Locomotive to run a minimum of 9 R.P.M. or 9 times forward, around 140" oval of track per minute pulling 4 cars.

(B) Locomotive to run a minimum of 8.5 R.P.M. or 8½ times in reverse, around 140" oval of track per minute pulling 4 cars.

Load: Not to draw more than 2.1 amps. while pulling 4 Box or Cattle Cars.

Motor: Universal A.C. or D.C.

 Ref: Form No. M3149; Nov. 1, 1952

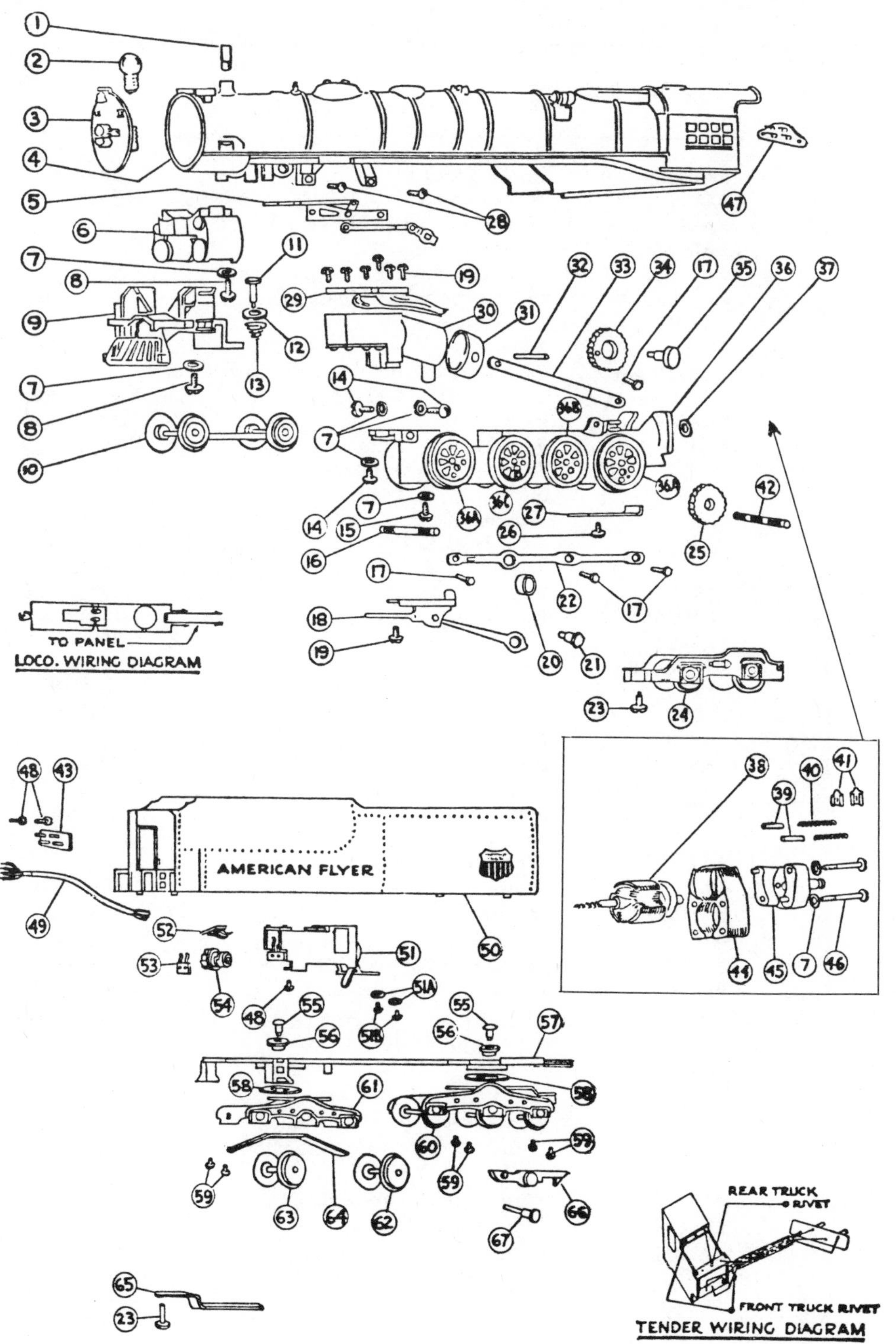

Ref: Form No. M3149; Nov. 1, 1952

Diagram Number	Part No.		Description	Price
1	PA10536		Smoke Stack	$ .03 ea.
2	PA8999		14 Volt Lamp	.25 "
3	XA8960-C		Boiler Front Assembly with lamp socket	.60 "
4	XA8956-C		Boiler Assembly	2.50 "
5	XA10057	R or L	Valve Link Assembly (Right or Left)	.50 "
6	PA10030		Cylinder and Steamchest	.70 "
7	PA3769		Lockwasher	.05 dz.
8	S16		Screw	.05 "
	XA8959-A		Pilot & Front Truck Assembly (consists of parts 9-10-11-12-13)	1.10 ea.
9	PA8959		Pilot	.70 "
10	XA10012-A		Front Truck	.40 "
	PA9990-D		Front Truck Wheel only	.10 "
11	PA10707		Stud	.05 "
12	W6		Washer	.03 dz.
13	PA8887		Front Truck Spring	.05 ea.
14	S46		Screw	.05 dz.
15	S18		Screw	.05 "
16	PA10005		Plain Axle	.10 ea.
17	PA7421		Screw	.30 dz.
18	XA10669RA		Crosshead Assembly	.30 ea.
	XA10669LA		Crosshead Assembly	.30 "
19	S183		Screw	.10 dz.
20	PA7237		Piston Rod Spacer	.05 ea.
21	PA5447		Screw	.30 dz.
22	PA8994-A		Side Rod	.20 ea.
23	PA4938		Stud	.30 dz.
24	XA10002-A		Rear Truck Assembly	.70 ea.
25	PA10672		Worm Gear (motor)	.30 "
26	S271		Screw	.10 dz.
27	PA10017		Grease Pan	.02 ea.
28	S171		Screw	.10 dz.
29	XA10523		Heating Element & Plate Assembly	1.00 ea.
30	PA10513		Chassis Smoke Box	1.00 "
	XA10513		Chassis Smoke Box Assembly (consists of parts 19-29-30)	2.00 "
31	PA10518		Piston	.20 "
32	PA10520		Piston Pin	.05 "
33	PA10515		Piston Lever	.05 "
	XA10515		Piston & Piston Lever Assembly (consists of parts 31-32-33)	.40 "
34	PA10671		Worm Gear (smoke drive)	.40 "
35	PA10162		Worm Gear Stud	.10 "
36	XA10505		Chassis Assembly with bushings	1.50 "

 Ref: Form No. M3149; Nov. 1, 1952

Diagram Number	Part No.	Description	Price
36A	XA10010	Flanged Wheel Assembly with tapped hole	$ .40 ea.
36B	XA10010-A	Flangeless Wheel Assembly with tapped hole	.40 "
36C	XA10010-A3	Flangeless Wheel Assembly with stud	.40 "
37	PA10766	Washer	.05 dz.
38	XA11077	Armature Assembly A.C.	2.50 ea.
39	PA9603	Carbon Brush A.C.	.15 "
40	PA10757	Brush Spring	.05 "
41	PA10754	Brush Cap	.02 "
42	PA10006	Worm Gear Axle	.10 "
43	XA10663	Male Plug	.20 "
44	XA9547	Magnet Assembly A.C.	1.00 "
45	XA9565-A	Brush Bracket Assembly	.50 "
46	S-295	Screw	.10 "
47	XA10662	Jack Panel	.20 "
48	S230-B	Screw	.10 dz.
49	PA10511-A	4 Conductor Cable	.12 ea.
50	XA8914	Tender Tank & End Cap Assembly	2.50 "
51	XA10587	Remote Control Unit	2.50 "
51A	W46	Lockwasher	.05 dz.
51B	S-0	Screw	.05 "
52	XA9612 C	Top Finger Unit	.50 ea.
53	XA9612 B	Bottom Finger Unit	.50 "
54	XA8716	Drum only	.60 "
55	PA9988	Truck Rivet	.03 "
56	PA10240	Fibre Bushing	.02 "
57	PA10591-A	Chassis	.94 "
58	PA8715-B	Washer	.05 dz.
59	S-1	Screw	.05 "
60	XA10139-A	Rear Truck Assembly of Wheels	1.00 ea.
61	XA10139-RP	Front Truck Assembly with Wheels	1.00 "
62	XA10238	Wheel & Axle Assembly (metal & plastic wheels)	.25 set
	PA10140	Metal Wheel	.15 ea.
	PA9990	Plastic Wheel	.10 "
	PA10238	Axle	.02 "
63	XA10238-A	Wheel & Axle Assembly (plastic wheels)	.25 set
64	PA10241	Contact Spring	.05 ea.
65	PA10239	Coupler	.10 "
66	XA10469	Coupler & Weight Assembly	.15 "
	PA10692	Weight only	.05 "
67	PA10467	Coupler Pin	.10 "

* XA10505 Chassis Assembly is not sold as a complete assembly with wheels.

Ref: Form No. M3149; Nov. 1, 1952

SERVICE INSTRUCTIONS FOR 332 A.C. PACIFIC LOCOMOTIVE AND TENDER WITH SMOKE, CHOO-CHOO.

The first thing to do is to place Locomotive and Tender on track, connect transformer and whistle control unit, and test for operation. Make sure all rods, linkage and other parts are not bent or broken. It is also important that the wheels on the Tender be clean to insure a good electrical contact.

1. **If the whistle is satisfactory, but the Locomotive and Tender does not operate properly proceed as follows:**
   a. Remove screw (#23) and also male plug (#43) from the Jack Panel (#47).
   b. Now take another similar tender with a Remote Control Unit in it which is in good working order and connect it to the Locomotive. In this way, you will be able to determine whether the Locomotive or Tender is defective.

2. **If the trouble is in the Locomotive you can make the following checks:**
   a. Inspect brushes for wear or poor contact and brush springs for position and proper tension.
   b. Check wires and solder joints on male plug (#43) and Jack Panel (#47) for broken or loose connections.
   c. Clean or polish commutator if dirty or worn.

3. **If these initial steps do not correct the trouble it will be necessary to disassemble the locomotive as follows:**
   a. Unscrew smoke stack (#1).
   b. Remove screws (#21) on each side and take off Rods (#5 and #18) and spacer (#20) from center drive wheel.
   c. Take off Rear Truck (#24) by removing screw (#23).
   d. Pull out Boiler Front (#3) from Boiler Assembly (#4) and unsolder the two wires at the lamp bracket.
   e. Turn Locomotive upside down and remove two screws (#14) and you can now remove motor assembly from Boiler (#4).
   f. To remove motor, push forward approximately a ¼" to clear clamp on Boiler (#4) and then lift rear of motor up and pull motor out.
   g. The motor is now exposed and you can inspect the wiring and other points of the unit, making any necessary replacements.

4. **When the trouble appears to be in the Tender, proceed as follows:**
   a. Remove four S-0 screws (#59) and take off Tender body (#50).
   b. Inspect wiring and solder joints for loose or broken connections.
   c. Check finger units (#52 and #53) on Remote Control Unit (#51) to see if they are burnt or not making proper contact.
   d. The drum (#54) should be checked to see if it is pitted or worn.
   e. The pawl on the Remote Control Unit may be broken or need adjusting.
   f. It is generally not necessary to replace the complete Remote Control Unit, but sometimes the Finger Units, the drum, or both need adjusting or replacing.

 Ref: Form No. M3149; Nov. 1, 1952

LOCOMOTIVE AND TENDER WITH SMOKE AND CHOO-CHOO UNIT

Model No. 332AC

SPECIFICATIONS

Tested at: 12 Volts A.C. .... Using 140" oval track.
Not to draw more than 1.3 amps.

(A) Locomotive to run a minimum of 9 R.P.M. or 9 times forward, around 140" oval of track per minute pulling 4 cars.

(B) Locomotive to run a minimum of 8.5 R.P.M. or 8½ times in reverse, around 140" oval of track per minute pulling 4 cars.

Load: Not to draw more than 2.1 amps. while pulling 4 Box or Cattle Cars.

Motor: Universal A.C. or D.C.

Ref: Form No. 1827; Feb. 1, 1957

Diagram Number	Part No.	Description	Price
1	PA12A190	Smoke Stack	$ .02 ea.
2	PA8999	14 Volt Lamp..................	.25 "
3	XA8960-C	Boiler Front Assembly with Lamp Socket	.80 "
4	XA8956-C	Boiler Assembly	2.78 "
5	XA10057 R or L	Valve Link Assembly (right or left)....	.50 "
6	PA10030	Cylinder and Steamchest...........	.54 "
7	PA3769	Lockwasher	.05 dz.
8	S16	Screw	.05 "
	XA8959-A	Pilot & Front Truck Assembly (consists of parts 9-10-11-12-13)...	1.41 ea.
9	PA8959	Pilot	.86 "
10	XA10012-A	Front Truck	.44 "
	PA9990-D	Front Truck Wheel only............	.11 "
11	PA13A404	Stud	.03 "
12	W6	Washer	.03 dz.
13	PA8887	Front Truck Spring................	.02 ea.
14	S46	Screw	.05 dz.
15	S18	Screw	.05 "
16	PA10005	Plain Axle	.10 ea.
17	PA7421	Screw	.30 dz.
18	XA10669RA	Crosshead Assembly	.30 ea.
	XA10669LA	Crosshead Assembly	.30 "
19	S183	Screw	.10 dz.
20	PA7237	Piston Rod Spacer................	.05 ea.
21	PA5447	Screw	.30 dz.
22	PA8994-A	Side Rod	.11 ea.
23	PA4938	Stud	.03 "
24	XA10002	Rear Truck Assembly.............	.73 "
25	PA10672	Worm Gear (motor)...............	.20 "
26	S271	Screw	.10 dz.
27	PA10017	Grease Pan	.04 ea.
28	S171	Screw	.01 "
29	***XA10523	Heating Element & Plate Assembly...	.66 ea.
30	**PA10513	Chassis Smoke Box..........	NOT AVAILABLE
	**XA10513	Chassis Smoke Box Assembly (consists of parts 19-29-30)	NOT AVAILABLE
31	PA10518-A	Piston	.17 "
32	PA10520	Piston Pin	.05 "
33	PA10515	Piston Lever	.08 "
34	PA10671	Worm Gear (smoke drive)..........	.27 "
35	PA10162	Worm Gear Stud.................	.05 "
36	*XA10505	Chassis Assembly with bushings.....	1.67 "
36A	XA13A861	Flanged Wheel Assembly..........	.30 "

All prices subject to change without notice.

**Parts so marked NOT AVAILABLE, substitute with:

Dia. 30	XA13B894RP	Smoke Box Assy. (new style)	$1.55 ea.
	PA13B894	Smoke Box (new style)	.59 "
	PA14A209	Separator (new style)	.01 "

 Ref: Form No. 1827; Feb. 1, 1957

Diagram Number	Part No.	Description	Price
36B	XA10010-A	Flangeless Wheel Assembly with tapped hole.	.30 "
36C	XA10010-A3	Flangeless Wheel Assembly with stud.	.46 "
36D	XA13A863	Pull-Mor Wheel	.52 "
37	PA10766	Washer	.05 dz.
38	XA12A523	Armature Assembly A.C.	3.50 ea.
39	PA9603	Carbon Brush A.C.	.15 "
40	PA10757-A	Brush Spring	.05 "
41	PA10754	Brush Cap	.02 "
42	PA10006	Worm Gear Axle	.10 "
43	XA10663	Male Plug	.22 "
44	XA12A526	Magnet Assembly A.C.	1.55 "
45	XA9565-A	Brush Bracket Assembly.	.71 "
46	S3A78	Screw	.03 "
47	XA10662-A	Jack Panel	.22 "
48	S230-B	Screw	.10 dz.
49	PA10511-A	4 Conductor Cable.	.12 ea.
50	XA8914	Tender Tank & End Cap Assembly. . .	3.62 "
51	XA10587	Remote Control Unit.	1.32 "
51A	W46	Lockwasher	.05 dz.
51B	S-0	Screw	.05 "
52	XA9612-CRP	Top Finger Unit.	.30 ea.
53	XA9612-BRP	Bottom Finger Unit.	.30 "
54	XA8716	Drum only	.59 "
55	PA9988	Truck Rivet	.03 "
56	PA10240	Fibre Bushing	.04 "
57	PA10591-A	Chassis	1.41 "
58	PA8715-B	Washer	.05 dz.
59	S-1	Screw	.05 "
60	XA11504-E	Rear Truck Assembly with wheels.	1.39 ea.
61	XA11909	Front Truck Assembly with wheels. . . .	.68 "
62	XA10238	Wheel & Axle Assembly (metal & plastic wheels).	.17 set
	PA10140	Metal Wheel	.15 ea.
	PA9990	Plastic Wheel	.05 "
	PA10238	Axle	.02 "
63	XA10238-A	Wheel & Axle. . (plastic wheels)	.17 set
64	PA10241	Contact Spring	.07 ea.
65	PA10239	Coupler	.05 "
66	XA10469	Coupler & Weight Assembly.	.17 "
	PA10692	Weight only	.05 "
67	PA10467	Coupler Pin	.11 "

*XA10505 Chassis assembly is not sold as a complete assembly with wheels.

***The XA10523 Heating Element and Plate Assy. is still available, and interchangeable with the new style PA13B894 Smoke Box. The new style XA14A208 Heating Element and Plate Assembly, priced at $.66 each, is used only on the new style PA13B894 Smoke Box.

U.P. LOCOMOTIVE AND TENDER WITH SMOKE, CHOO-CHOO, AND AIR CHIME WHISTLE

Model Nos. 335, K335

SPECIFICATIONS

Tested at: 12 Volts A.C. .... Using 140" oval of track.
Not to draw more than 1.3 amps.

(A) Locomotive to run a minimum of 9.5 R.P.M. or 9½ times forward, around 140" oval of track per minute.

(B) Locomotive to run a minimum of 9 R.P.M. or 9 times in reverse, around 140" oval of track per minute.

Load: Not to draw more than 2 amps. while pulling 4 Box or Cattle Cars.

Motor: Universal A.C. or D.C.

 Ref: Form No. 1826; Feb. 1, 1957

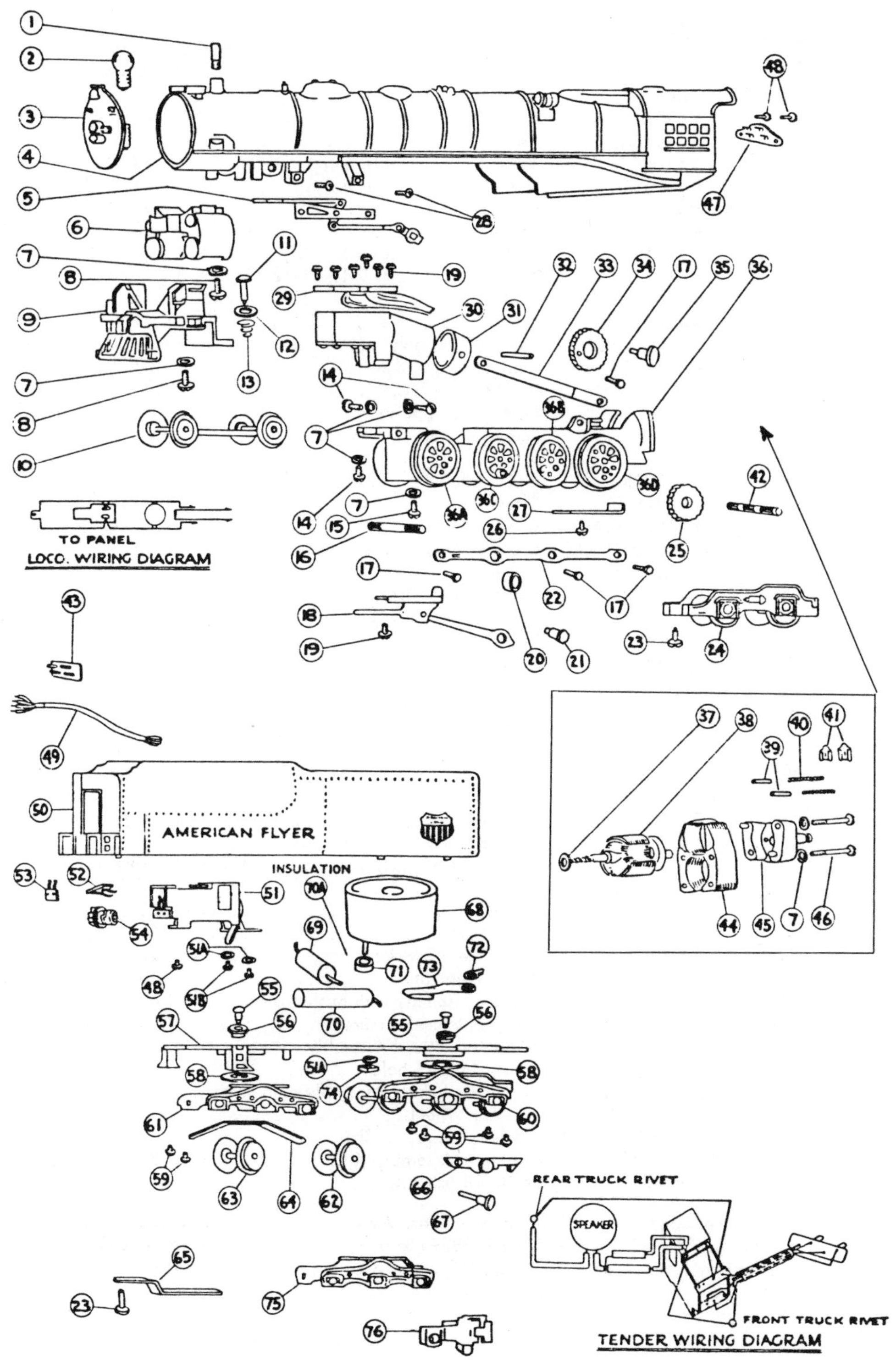

Ref: Form No. 1826; Feb. 1, 1957

Diagram Number	Part No.	Description	Price
1	PA12A190	Smoke Stack	$ .02 ea.
2	PA8999	14 Volt Lamp	.25 "
3	XA8960-C	Boiler Front Assembly with Lamp Socket	.80 "
4	XA8956-C	Boiler Assembly	2.78 "
5	XA10057 R or L	Valve Link Assembly (Right or Left)	.50 "
6	PA10030	Cylinder and Steamchest	.54 "
7	PA3769	Lockwasher	.05 dz.
8	S16	Screw	.05 "
	XA8959-A	Pilot & Front Truck Assembly (consists of parts 9-10-11-12-13)	1.41 ea.
9	PA8959	Pilot	.86 "
10	XA10012-A	Front Truck	.44 "
	PA9990-D	Front Wheel only	.11 "
11	PA13A404	Stud	.03 "
12	W6	Washer	.03 dz.
13	PA8887	Front Truck Spring	.02 ea.
14	S46	Screw	.05 dz.
15	S18	Screw	.05 "
16	PA10005	Plain Axle	.10 ea.
17	PA7421	Screw	.30 dz.
18	XA10669-RA	Crosshead Assembly	.30 ea.
	XA10669-LA	Crosshead Assembly	.30 "
19	S183	Screw	.10 dz.
20	PA7237	Piston Rod Spacer	.05 ea.
21	PA5447	Screw	.30 dz.
22	PA8994-A	Side Rod	.11 ea.
23	PA4938	Stud	.03 "
24	XA10002	Rear Truck Assembly	.73 "
25	PA10672	Worm Gear (motor)	.20 "
26	S271	Screw	.10 dz.
27	PA10017	Grease Pan	.04 ea.
28	S171	Screw	.10 dz.
29	*** XA10523	Heating Element & Plate Assembly	.66 ea.
30	** PA10513	Chassis Smoke Box	NOT AVAILABLE
	** XA10513	Chassis Smoke Box Assembly (consists of parts 19-29-30)	NOT AVAILABLE
31	PA10518-A	Piston	.17 "
32	PA10520	Piston Pins	.05 "
33	PA10515	Piston Lever	.08 "
34	PA10671	Worm Gear (smoke drive)	.27 "
35	PA10162	Worm Gear Stud	.05 "
36	*XA10505	Chassis Assembly with bushings	1.67 "
36A	XA13A861	Flanged Wheel Assembly	.30 "
36B	XA10010-A	Flangeless Wheel Assembly with tapped hole	.30 "
36C	XA10010-A3	Flangeless Wheel Assembly with stud	.46 "
36D	XA13A863	Pull-Mor Wheel	.52 "
37	PA10766	Washer	.05 dz.
38	XA12A523	Armature Assembly A.C.	3.50 ea.
39	PA9603	Carbon Brush A.C.	.15 "

***The XA10523 Heating Element and Plate Assy. is still available, and interchangeable with the new style PA13B894 Smoke Box. The new style XA14A208 Heating Element and Plate Assembly, priced at $.66 each, is used only on the new style PA13B894 Smoke Box.

 Ref: Form No. 1826; Feb. 1, 1957

Diagram Number	Part No.	Description	Price
40	PA10757-A	Brush Spring	.05 "
41	PA10754	Brush Cap	.02 "
42	PA10006	Worm Gear Axle................	.10 "
43	XA10663	Male Plug	.22 "
44	XA12A526	Magnet Assembly A.C............	1.55 "
45	XA9565-A	Brush Bracket Assembly...........	.71 "
46	S3A78	Screw	.03 "
47	XA10662-A	Jack Panel	.22 "
48	S230-B	Screw	.10 dz.
49	PA10511-A	4 Conductor Cable................	.12 ea.
50	XA8914	Tender Tank & End Cap Assembly....	3.62 "
51	XA10587	Remote Control Unit.............	1.32 "
51A	W46	Lockwasher	.05 dz.
51B	S-0	Screw	.05 "
52	XA9612-CRP	Top Finger Unit.................	.30 ea.
53	XA9612-BRP	Bottom Finger Unit...............	.30 "
54	XA8716	Drum	.59 "
55	PA9988	Truck Rivet	.03 "
56	PA10240	Fibre Bushing	.04 "
57	PA10591-A	Chassis	1.41 "
58	PA8715-B	Washer	.05 dz.
59	S-1	Screw	.05 "
60	XA11504-E	Rear Truck Assembly with Wheels (335)	1.39 ea.
61	XA11A909	Front Truck Assembly with Wheels (335)	.68 "
62	XA10238	Wheel & Axle Assembly (metal & plastic wheels)..........	.17 set
	PA10140	Metal Wheel	.15 ea.
	PA9990	Plastic Wheel	.05 "
	PA10238	Axle	.02 "
63	XA10238-A	Wheel & Axle Assembly (plastic wheels)	.17 set
64	PA10241	Contact Spring	.07 ea.
65	PA10239	Coupler Bar	.05 "
66	XA10469	Coupler & Weight Assembly........	.17 "
	PA10692	Weight only	.05 "
67	PA10467	Coupler Pin	.11 "
68	XA11710	Speaker	3.06 "
69	PA11A991	Condenser	1.04 "
70	PA11685	Resistor	.26 "
70A	PA11664	Receiver Insulation	.02 "
71	W99	Rubber Washer	.03 "
72	PA6173	Soldering Terminal	.02 "
73	PA10138	Contact Strip	.02 "
74	N-1	Nut	.01 "
75	XA12A053	Rear Truck Assembly with wheels (K335)	1.00 "
76	XA12A047	Knuckle Coupler (K335)...........	.22 "

*XA10505 Chassis Assembly is not sold as a complete assembly with wheels.

**Parts so marked NOT AVAILABLE, substitute with:

Dia. 30	XA13B894RP	Smoke Box Assy. (new style)	$1.55 ea.
	PA13B894	Smoke Box (new style)	.59 "
	PA14A209	Separator (new style)	.01 "

All prices subject to change without notice.

SERVICE INSTRUCTIONS FOR Nos. 335 & K335 LOCOMOTIVE AND TENDER WITH SMOKE, CHOO-CHOO AND WHISTLE.

The first thing to do is to place Locomotive and Tender on track, connect transformer and whistle control unit, and test for operation. Make sure all rods, linkage and other parts are not bent or broken. It is also important that the wheels on the Tender be clean to insure a good electrical contact.

1. **If the whistle is satisfactory, but the Locomotive and Tender does not operate properly proceed as follows:**
   a. Remove screw (※23) and also male plug (※43) from the Jack Panel (※47).
   b. Now take another similar tender with a Remote Control Unit in it which is in good working order and connect it to the Locomotive. In this way, you will be able to determine whether the Locomotive or Tender is defective.

2. **If the trouble is in the Locomotive you can make the following checks:**
   a. Inspect brushes for wear or poor contact and brush springs for position and proper tension.
   b. Check wires and solder joints on male plug (※43) and Jack Panel (※47) for broken or loose connections.
   c. Clean or polish commutator if dirty or worn.

3. **If these initial steps do not correct the trouble it will be necessary to disassemble the locomotive as follows:**
   a. Unscrew smoke stack (※1).
   b. Remove screws (※21) on each side and take off Rods (※5 and ※18) and spacer (※20) from center drive wheel.
   c. Take off rear truck (※24) by removing screw (※23).
   d. Pull out Boiler Front (※3) from Boiler Assembly (※4) and unsolder the two wires at the lamp bracket.
   e. Turn Locomotive upside down and remove two screws (※14) and you can now remove motor assembly from Boiler (※4).
   f. To remove motor, push forward approximately a ¼" to clear clamp on Boiler (※4) and then lift rear of motor up and pull motor out.
   g. The motor is now exposed and you can inspect the wiring and other points of the unit, making any necessary replacements.

4. **When the trouble appears to be in the Tender, proceed as follows:**
   a. Remove four S-0 Screws (※59) and take off Tender body (※50).
   b. Inspect wiring and solder joints for loose or broken connections.
   c. Check finger units (※52 and ※53) on Remote Control Unit (※51) to see if they are burnt or not making proper contact.
   d. The drum (※54) should be checked to see if it is pitted or worn.
   e. The pawl on the Remote Control Unit may be broken or need adjusting.
   f. It is generally not necessary to replace the complete Remote Control Unit, but sometimes the finger units, the drum, or both need adjusting or replacing.

5. **If Locomotive and Tender operates satisfactorily, but the whistle does not function correctly check as follows:**
   a. Recheck the instruction sheet in order to make sure hook-up is correct. If both the Transformer instructions and the Air Chime Whistle Instructions are followed, this will cause a duplication of wiring. The result will be that you will only have a faint buzz while the train is running or in a neutral position. Follow the Air Chime Whistle wiring instructions only and be sure to have only two wires going to the ※690 track terminal.
   b. The Generator Tube ※PA11665 on the control box may be weak and need replacing.
   c. If the trouble still persists it will be necessary to remove the Tender Body (※50) from the chassis by unscrewing the four S-0 screws (※59).
   d. The unit is exposed and you can check all wires and solder joints for loose connections. Be sure the lead wires on the resistor and condenser are covered with an insulating sleeve.
   e. Check the condenser (※69) by adding another condenser in series with temporary connections. If this corrects the trouble the defective condenser can be removed and a new one connected in its place.
   f. To check resistor (※70) use another resistor and follow same procedure.

NO.	PART NO.	DESCRIPTION	PRICE
1	PA12A190	SMOKE STACK	.03 EA.
2	PA8999	14 VOLT LAMP	.30 EA.
3	XA8960-C	BOILER FRONT ASSY. W/LAMP SOCKET	.88 EA.
	PA10542	HEADLIGHT LENS	.02 EA.
4	XA8956-C	BOILER ASSEMBLY	3.06 EA.
	PA9579	MOUNTING BRACKET	.01 EA.
	XA8887	COUPLER STRAP ASSEMBLY	.02 EA.
5	XA10057-R OR L	VALVE LINK ASSEMBLY (RIGHT OR LEFT)	.57 EA.
6	PA10030	CYLINDER AND STEAMCHEST	.66 EA.
7	PA3769	LOCKWASHER	.01 EA.
8	S16	SCREW	.01 EA.
	XA8959-A	PILOT & FRONT TRUCK ASSEMBLY (CONSISTS OF PARTS 9-10-11-12-13)	1.98 EA.
9	PA8959	PILOT	.95 EA.
10	XA10012	FRONT TRUCK	.44 EA.
	PA9990	FRONT WHEEL ONLY	.03 EA.
11	PA13A404	STUD	.08 EA.
12	W6	WASHER	.01 EA.
13	PA8887	FRONT TRUCK SPRING	.02 EA.
14	S46	SCREW	.01 EA.
15	S18	SCREW	.01 EA.
16	PA10005	PLAIN AXLE NOT AVAILABLE	
		SUB. WITH PA15A226 AXLE	.05 EA.
17	PA7421	SCREW	.03 EA.
18	XA10669-RA	CROSSHEAD ASSEMBLY	.45 EA.
	XA10669-LA	CROSSHEAD ASSEMBLY	.45 EA.
19	S183	SCREW	.01 EA.
20	PA7237	PISTON ROD SPACER	.02 EA.
21	PA5447	SCREW	.04 EA.
22	PA8994-A	SIDE ROD	.20 EA.
23	PA4938	STUD	.04 EA.
24	XA10002	REAR TRUCK ASSY. NOT AVAILABLE	
		SUB. WITH XA14B837 REAR TRUCK ASSY.	.99 EA.
25	PA10672	WORM GEAR (MOTOR)	.06 EA.
26	S271	SCREW	.02 EA.
27	PA10017-A	GREASE PAN	.07 EA.
28	S171	SCREW	.01 EA.
29	XA10523	HEATING ELEM. & PLATE ASSY. NOT AVAILABLE	
		SUB. WITH XA14A208-A ASSEMBLY	.91 EA.
30	XA10513	CHASSIS SMOKE BOX ASSY. NOT AVAILABLE	
		SUB. WITH XA13B894RP SMOKE BOX ASSY.	2.13 EA.
	PA10513	SMOKE BOX NOT AVAILABLE	
		SUB. WITH PA13B894 SMOKE BOX	.76 EA.
	PA14A209	SEPARATOR	.02 EA.
31	PA10518-A	PISTON	.29 EA.
32	PA10520	PISTON PINS	.03 EA.
33	PA10515	PISTON LEVER	.14 EA.
34	PA10671	WORM GEAR (SMOKE DRIVE)	.32 EA.
35	PA10162	WORM GEAR STUD	.08 EA.
36	XA10505	CHASSIS WITH BUSHINGS	1.84 EA.
36A	XA13A861	FLANGED WHEEL ASSEMBLY	.39 EA.
36B	XA10010-A	FLANGELESS WHEEL ASSEMBLY	.36 EA.
36C	XA10010-A3	FLANGELESS WHEEL ASSEMBLY W/STUD	.64 EA.
36D	XA13A863	PUL-MOR WHEEL	.82 EA.
37	PA10766	WASHER	.01 EA.
38	XA12A523	ARMATURE ASSEMBLY	3.85 EA.
39	PA9603	CARBON BRUSH	.13 EA.
40	PA10757-A	BRUSH SPRING	.02 EA.

NO.	PART NO.	DESCRIPTION	PRICE
41	PA10754	BRUSH CAP	.01 EA.
42	PA10006	WORM GEAR AXLE NOT AVAILABLE	
		SUB. WITH PA15A281 AXLE	.07 EA.
43	XA10663	MALE PLUG	.24 EA.
44	XA12A526	MAGNET ASSEMBLY	1.71 EA.
45	XA9565-A	BRUSH BRACKET ASSEMBLY	1.00 EA.
46	S3A78	SCREW NOT AVAILABLE	
		SUB. WITH S29 SCREW	.01 EA.
47	XA10662	JACK PANEL	.24 EA.
48	S230-B	SCREW	.01 EA.
49	PA10511	4 CONDUCTOR CABLE	.13 EA.
50	XA8914	TENDER TANK & END CAP ASSEMBLY	3.98 EA.
51	XA10587	REMOTE CONTROL UNIT	4.04 EA.
51A	W46	LOCKWASHER	.06 DZ.
51B	S-0	SCREW	.01 EA.
52	XA9612-CRP	TOP FINGER UNIT	.33 EA.
53	XA9612-BRP	BOTTOM FINGER UNIT	.33 EA.
54	XA8716	DRUM	.95 EA.
55	PA9988	TRUCK RIVET	.04 EA.
56	PA10240	FIBRE BUSHING	.06 EA.
57	PA10591-A	CHASSIS	1.55 EA.
58	PA8715-B	WASHER	.02 EA.
59	S-1	SCREW	.01 EA.
60	XA11504-E	REAR TRUCK ASSEMBLY W/PICK UP (335)	1.42 EA.
61	XA11A909	FRONT TRUCK ASSEMBLY W/PICKUP (335)	.75 EA.
62	XA10238	WHEEL & AXLE ASSY. (METAL & PLASTIC WHEELS)	.09 EA.
	PA10140	METAL WHEEL	.06 EA.
	PA9990	PLASTIC WHEEL	.03 EA.
	PA10238	AXLE	.01 EA.
63		SAME AS #62	
64	PA10241	CONTACT SPRING	.13 EA.
65	PA10239	COUPLER BAR	.06 EA.
66		NOT AVAILABLE	
67		NOT AVAILABLE	
68	XA11710	SPEAKER NOT AVAILABLE	
		SUB. WITH XA14A127	4.57 EA.
	PA14A216	SPEAKER BRACKET	.08 EA.
	S171	SCREW	.01 EA.
	S230-B	SCREW	.01 EA.
69	PA11A991	CONDENSER NOT AVAILABLE	
		SUB. WITH PA14A914 CONDENSER	1.40 EA.
70	PA11685	RESISTOR	.29 EA.
70A		NOT USED	
71		NOT USED	
72		NOT USED	
73		NOT USED	
74		NOT USED	
75	XA12A053	REAR TRUCK ASSY. W/WHEELS (K335)	1.30 EA.
76	XA12A047	KNUCKLE COUPLER (K335)	.29 EA.

PRICES SUBJECT TO CHANGE WITHOUT NOTICE.

 Ref: Form No. 1826; June 1, 1960

NO.	PART NO.	DESCRIPTION	PRICE
1	PA12A190	Smoke Stack	.03 ea.
2	PA8999	14 Volt Lamp	.32 ea.
3	XA8960-C	Boiler Front Assy. w/Lamp Socket	.92 ea.
	PA10542	Headlight Lens	.02 ea.
4		Boiler Assembly- OBSOLETE	
	PA9579	Mounting Bracket	.01 ea.
	XA8887	Coupler Strap Assembly	.02 ea.
5	XA10057 R or L	Valve Link Assy. (Right or Left)	.60 ea.
6	PA10030	Cylinder and Steamchest	.69 ea.
7	PA3769	Lock Washer	.01 ea.
8	S16	Screw	.01 ea.
9	PA8959	Pilot	1.00 ea.
10	XA10012	Front Truck	.46 ea.
	PA9990	Front Wheel Only	.03 ea.
11	PA13A404	Stud	.08 ea.
12	W6	Washer	.01 ea.
13	PA8887	Front Truck Spring	.02 ea.
14	S46	Screw	.01 ea.
15	S18	Screw	.01 ea.
16	PA15A226	Plain Axle	.05 ea.
17	PA7421	Screw	.03 ea.
18	XA10669-RA	Crosshead Assembly	.47 ea.
	XA10669-LA	Crosshead Assembly	.47 ea.
19	S183	Screw	.01 ea.
20	PA7237	Piston Rod Spacer	.02 ea.
21	PA5447	Screw	.04 ea.
22	PA8994-A	Side Rod	.21 ea.
23	PA4938	Stud	.04 ea.
24	XA14B837	Rear Truck Assembly	1.04 ea.
25	PA10672	Worm Gear (Motor)	.06 ea.
26	S271	Screw	.02 ea.
27	PA10017-A	Grease Pan	.07 ea.
28	S171	Screw	.01 ea.
29	XA14A208-A	Heating Element & Plate Assy.	.96 ea.
30*	XA13B894RP	Smoke Box	2.24 ea.
31	PA10518-A	Piston	.30 ea.
32	PA10520	Piston Pin	.03 ea.
33	PA10515	Piston Lever	.15 ea.
34	PA10671	Worm Gear (smoke Drive)	.34 ea.
35	PA10162	Worm Gear Stud	.08 ea.
36	PA10505	Chassis	2.39 ea.
36A	XA13A861	Flanged Wheel Assembly	.41 ea.
36B	XA10010-A	Flangeless Wheel Assembly	.38 ea.
36C	XA10010-A3	Flangeless Wheel Assy. w/stud	.67 ea.
36D	XA13A863	Pul-Mor Wheel	.86 ea.
37	PA10766	Washer	.01 ea.
38	XA12A523	Armature Assembly	4.04 ea.
39	PA9603	Carbon Brush	.14 ea.
40	PA10757-A	Brush Spring	.02 ea.

Cont'd

DIA. NO.	PART NO.	DESCRIPTION	PRICE
41	PA10754	Brush Cap	.01 ea.
42	PA15A281	Worm Gear Axle	.07 ea.
43	XA10663	Male Plug	.25 ea.
44	XA12A526	Magnet Assembly	1.80 ea.
45	XA9565-A	Brush Bracket Assembly	1.05 ea.
46	S29	Screw	.01 ea.
47	XA10662	Jack Panel	.25 ea.
48	S230-B	Screw	.01 ea.
49	PA13A208-A	4 Conductor Cable (Plastic)	.04 ft.
50	XA8914	Tender Tank & End Cap Assy.	4.18 ea.
51	XA10587	Remote Control Unit	4.24 ea.
51A	W46	Lock Washer	.06 dz.
51B	S-0	Screw	.01 ea.
52	XA9612-CRP	Top Finger Unit	.35 ea.
53	XA9612-BRP	Bottom Finger Unit	.35 ea.
54	XA8716	Drum	1.00 ea.
55	PA9988	Truck Rivet	.04 ea.
56	PA10240	Fibre Bushing	.06 ea.
57	PA10591-A	Chassis	1.63 ea.
58	PA8715-B	Washer	.02 ea.
59	S-1	Screw	.01 ea.
60		Rear Truck Assy.w/Pick Up (335)	OBSOLETE
61	XA11A909	Front Truck Assy. w/Pick Up (335)	.79 ea.
62	XA10238	Wheel & Axle Assy. (Metal & Plastic Wheels)	.09 ea.
	PA10140	Metal Wheel	.06 ea.
	PA9990	Plastic Wheel	.03 ea.
	PA10238	Axle	.01 ea.
63		SAME AS #62	
64	PA10241	Contact Spring	.14 ea.
65	PA10239	Coupler Bar	.06 ea.
66		NOT AVAILABLE	
67		NOT AVAILABLE	
68	XA14A127	Conv. Speaker Substitute for XA11710 OBSOLETE	4.91 ea.
69	PA14A914	Condenser Substitute for PA11A991	1.47ea.
70	PA11685	Resistor	.30 ea.
70A Thru 74		NOT USED	
75	XA12A053	Rear Truck Assy. w/wheels (K335 & 335)	1.37 ea.
76	XA12A047	Knuckle Coupler (K335)	.30 ea.

* When using XA13B894RP remove screw on solder terminal.

Prices subject to change without notice.

U.P. LOCOMOTIVE AND TENDER WITH SMOKE, CHOO-CHOO, AIR CHIME WHISTLE, AND PULL-MOR

Model Nos. 336, 21139

SPECIFICATIONS

Tested at: 12 Volts A.C. .... using 140" oval of track.

Not to draw more than 1.3 amps.

(A) Locomotive to run a minimum of 11 R.P.M. or 11 times forward, around 140" oval of track per minute.

(B) Locomotive to run a minimum of 10 R.P.M. or 10 times in reverse, around 140" oval of track per minute.

Load: Not to draw more than 2 amps. while pulling 4 Box or Cattle Cars.

Motor: Universal A.C. or D.C.

Ref: Form No. 1824; Feb. 1, 1957

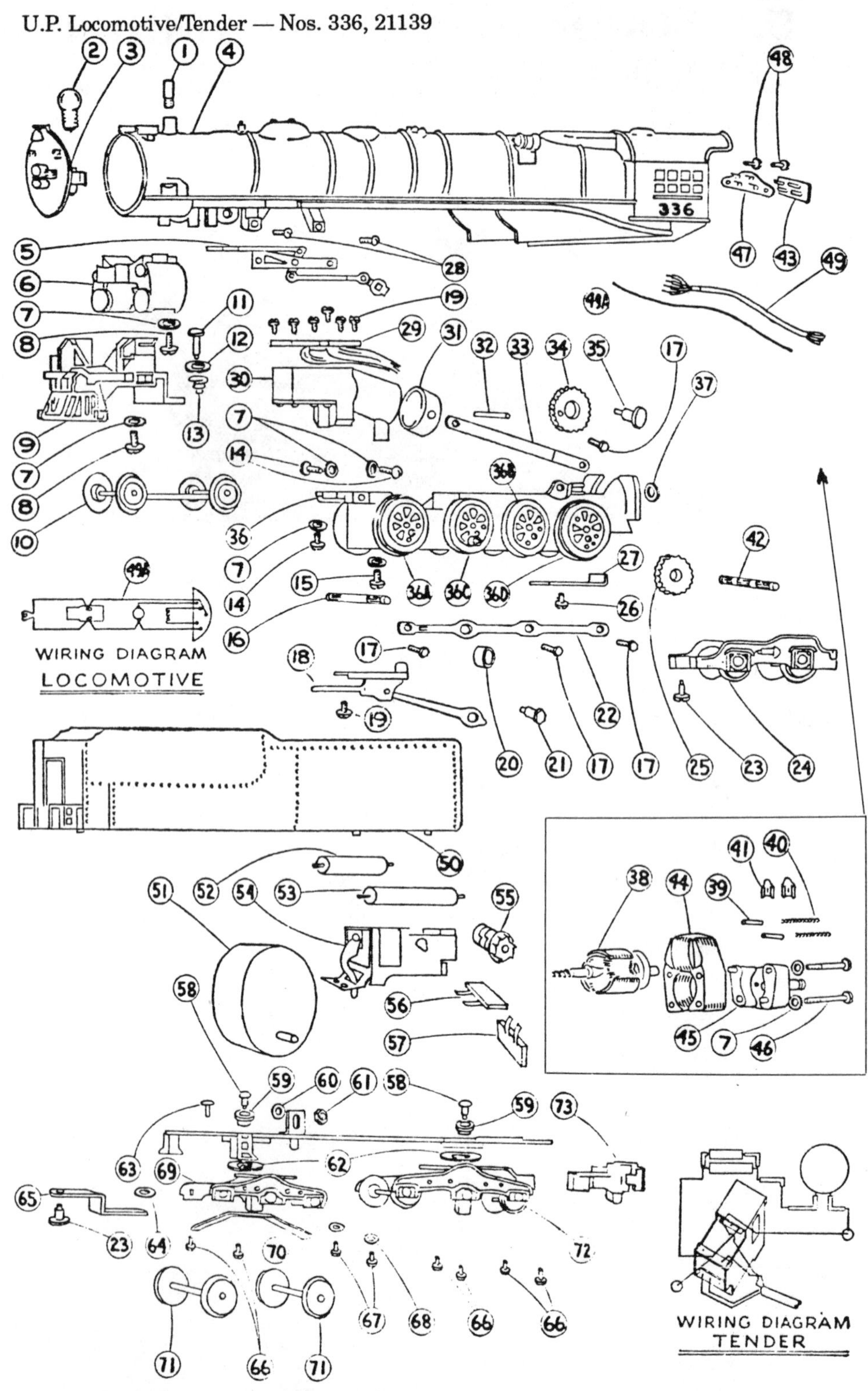

 Ref: Form No. 1824; Feb. 1, 1957

Diagram Number	Part No.	Description	Price
1	PA12A190	Smoke Stack	$ .02 ea.
2	PA8999	14 Volt Lamp	.25 "
3	XA8960-C	Boiler Front Assembly with Lamp Socket	.80 "
4	XA8956-L	Boiler Assembly	5.21 "
5	XA10057 R or L	Valve Link Assembly (right or left)	.50 "
6	PA10030	Cylinder and Steamchest	.54 "
7	PA3769	Lockwasher	.05 dz.
8	S-16	Screw	.05 "
	XA8959-A	Pilot & Front Truck Assembly (consists of parts 9-10-11-12-13)	1.41 ea.
9	PA8959	Pilot	.86 "
10	XA10012-A	Front Truck	.44 "
	PA9990-D	Front Truck Wheel only	.11 "
11	PA13A404	Stud	.03 "
12	W-6	Washer	.03 dz.
13	PA8887	Front Truck Spring	.02 ea.
14	S46	Screw	.05 dz.
15	S18	Screw	.05 "
16	PA10005	Plain Axle	.10 ea.
17	PA7421	Screw	.30 dz.
18	XA10669RA	Crosshead Assembly	.30 ea.
	XA10669LA	Crosshead Assembly	.30 "
19	S183	Screw	.10 dz.
20	PA7237	Piston Rod Spacer	.05 ea.
21	PA5447	Screw	.30 dz.
22	PA8994-A	Side Rod	.11 ea.
23	PA4938	Stud	.03 "
24	XA10002	Rear Truck Assembly	.73 "
25	PA10672	Worm Gear (motor)	.20 "
26	S271	Screw	.10 dz.
27	PA10017	Grease Pan	.04 ea.
28	S171	Screw	.10 dz.
29	** XA10523	Heating Element & Plate Assembly	.66 ea.
30	* PA10513	Chassis Smoke Box	NOT AVAILABLE
	* XA10513	Chassis Smoke Box Assembly (consists of parts 19-29-30)	NOT AVAILABLE
31	PA10518-A	Piston	.17 "
32	PA10520	Piston Pin	.05 "
33	PA10515	Piston Lever	.08 "
34	PA10671	Worm Gear (smoke drive)	.27 "
35	PA10162	Worm Gear Stud	.05 "
36	XA10505	Chassis Assembly with Bushings	1.67 "
36A	XA13A861	Flanged Wheel Assembly	.30 "
36B	XA10010-A	Flangeless Wheel Assembly with Tapped Hole	.30 "

All prices subject to change without notice.

*Parts so marked NOT AVAILABLE, substitute with:

Dia. 30	XA13B894RP	Smoke Box Assy. (new style)	$1.55 ea.
	PA13B894	Smoke Box (new style)	.59 "
	PA14A209	Separator (new style)	.01 "

Ref: Form No. 1824; Feb. 1, 1957

Diagram Number	Part No.	Description	Price
36C	XA10010-A3	Flangeless Wheel Assembly with Stud.	$ .46 ea.
36D	XA13A863	Pull-Mor Wheel	.52 "
37	PA10766	Washer	.05 dz.
38	XA12A523	Armature Assembly, A.C.	3.50 ea.
39	PA9603	Carbon Brush, A.C.	.15 "
40	PA10757-A	Brush Spring	.05 "
41	PA10754	Brush Cap	.02 "
42	PA10006	Worm Gear Axle	.10 "
43	XA10663	Male Plug	.22 "
44	XA12A526	Magnet Assembly, A.C.	1.55 "
45	XA9565-A	Brush Bracket Assembly	.71 "
46	S3A78	Screw	.03 "
47	XA10662-A	Jack Panel	.22 "
48	S230-B	Screw	.10 dz.
49	PA10511-E	4 Conductor Cable	.12 ea.
49A	PA10249-Y	10½" Lead Wire	.02 "
50	XA8914-RP	Tender Body Assembly with Trimgs.	4.51 "
51	XA11710	Speaker	3.06 "
52	PA11A991	Condenser	1.04 "
53	PA11685	Resistor	.26 "
54	XA10587-E	Remote Control Unit	1.32 "
55	XA8716	Drum	.59 "
56	XA9612-CRP	Top Finger Unit	.30 "
57	XA9612-BRP	Bottom Finger Unit	.30 "
58	PA9988	Rivet	.03 "
59	PA10240	Fibre Bushing	.04 "
60	P1034	Washer	.10 dz.
61	N-1	Nut	.01 ea.
62	PA8715-B	Washer	.05 dz.
63	P4652	Rivet	.01 ea.
64	W79	Washer	.10 dz.
65	PA10239	Coupler Bar	.05 ea.
66	S-1	Screw	.05 dz.
67	W-46	Washer	.05 "
68	S-0	Screw	.05 "
69	XA11A909	Front Truck with Wheels	.68 ea.
70	PA10241	Contact Spring	.07 "
71	XA10238	Wheel & Axle Assembly	.17 set
	PA10140	Metal Wheel	.15 ea.
	PA9990	Plastic Wheel	.05 "
	PA10238	Axle	.02 "
72	XA12A053	Rear Truck with Wheels	1.00 "
73	XA12A047	Knuckle Coupler	.22 "

NOTE: If new style drive wheels are used on old style chassis, remove .025-.030 from front edge of motor mount to clear new wheels.

**The XA10523 Heating Element and Plate Assy. is still available, and interchangeable with the new style PA13B894 Smoke Box. The new style XA14A208 Heating Element and Plate Assembly, priced at $.66 each, is used only on the new style PA13B894 Smoke Box.

SERVICE INSTRUCTIONS FOR No. 336 U.P. LOCOMOTIVE AND TENDER WITH SMOKE AND CHOO-CHOO WHISTLE, AND KNUCKLE COUPLER

The first thing to do is to place Locomotive and Tender on track, connect Transformer and whistle control unit, and test for operation: Make sure all rods, linkage, and other parts are not bent or broken. It is also important that the wheels on the tender be clean to insure a good electrical contact.

1. **If the whistle is satisfactory, but the Locomotive and Tender does not operate properly proceed as follows:**
   a. Remove screw (#23) and also male plug (#43) from the Jack Panel (#47).
   b. Now take another similar tender with a Remote Control Unit in it which is in good working order and connect it to the Locomotive. In this way, you will be able to determine whether the Locomotive or Tender is defective.
2. **If the trouble is in the Locomotive you can make the following checks:**
   a. Inspect brushes for wear or poor contact, and brush springs for position and proper tension.
   b. Check wires and solder joints on male plug (#43) and Jack Panel (#47) for broken or loose connections.
   c. Clean or polish commutator if dirty or worn.
3. **If these initial steps do not correct the trouble, it will be necessary to disassemble the Locomotive, as follows:**
   a. Unscrew smoke stack (#1).
   b. Remove screws (#21) on each side, and take off Rods (#5) and (#18) and spacer (#20) from center drive wheel.
   c. Take off rear truck (#24) by removing screw (23).
   d. Pull out Boiler Front (#3) from Boiler Assembly (#4) and unsolder the two wires at the lamp bracket.
   e. Turn Locomotive upside down, and remove two screws (#14) and you can now remove motor assembly from Boiler (#4).
   f. To remove motor, push forward approximately a ¼" to clear clamp on Boiler (#4) and then lift rear of motor up, and pull motor out.
   g. The motor is now exposed, and you can inspect the wiring and other points of the unit making any necessary replacements.
4. **When the trouble appears to be in the Tender, proceed as follows:**
   a. Remove four S-O Screws (#66) and take off Tender Body (#50).
   b. Inspect wiring and solder joints for loose or broken connections.
   c. Check Finger Units (#56) and (#57) on Remote Control Unit (#54) to see if they are burnt or not making proper contact.
   d. The drum (#55) should be checked to see if it is pitted or worn.
   e. The pawl on the Remote Control Unit may be broken or need adjusting.
   f. It is generally not necessary to replace the complete Remote Control Unit, but sometimes the finger units, the drum, or both need adjusting, or replacing.
5. **If the Locomotive and Tender operates satisfactorily, but the whistle does not function correctly, check as follows:**
   a. Recheck the instruction sheet in order to make sure hook-up is correct. If both the Transformer instructions, and the Air Chime Whistle Instructions are followed, this will cause a duplication of wiring. The result will be that you will only have a faint buzz while the train is running or in a neutral position. Follow the Air Chime Whistle wiring instructions only, and be sure to have only two wires going to the (#690) Track Terminal.
   b. The Generator Tube (#PA11665 on the control box may be weak and need replacement.
   c. If the trouble still persists it will be necessary to remove the Tender Body (#50) from the chassis, by unscrewing the four S-O screws (#66).
   d. The unit is exposed and you can check all wires and solder joints for loose connections. Be sure the lead wires on the resistor and condenser are covered with an insulating sleeve.
   e. Check the condenser (#52) by adding another condenser in series with temporary connections. If this corrects the trouble the defective condenser can be removed and a new one connected in its place.
   f. To check resistor (#53) use another resistor, and follow same procedure.

NO.	PART NO.	DESCRIPTION	PRICE
1	PA12A190	SMOKE STACK	.03 EA.
2	PA8999	14 VOLT LAMP	.30 EA.
3	XA8960-C	BOILER FRONT ASSY. W/LAMP SOCKET	.88 EA.
	PA10542	HEADLIGHT LENS	.02 EA.
4	XA8956-L	BOILER ASSEMBLY	5.73 EA.
	PA9579	MOUNTING BRACKET	.01 EA.
	XA9578	COUPLER STRAP ASSEMBLY	.08 EA.
5	XA10057 R OR L	VALVE LINK ASSEMBLY (RIGHT OR LEFT)	.57 EA.
6	PA10030	CYLINDER & STEAMCHEST	.66 EA.
7	PA3769	LOCKWASHER	.01 EA.
8	S-16	SCREW	.01 EA.
	XA8959-A	PILOT & FRONT TRUCK ASSEMBLY (CONSISTS OF PARTS 9-10-11-12-13)	1.98 EA.
9	PA8959	PILOT	.95 EA.
10	XA10012	FRONT TRUCK	.48 EA.
	PA9990	FRONT TRUCK WHEEL ONLY	.03 EA.
11	PA13A404	STUD	.08 EA.
12	W-6	WASHER	.01 EA.
13	PA8887	FRONT TRUCK SPRING	.02 EA.
14	S46	SCREW	.01 EA.
15	S18	SCREW	.01 EA.
16	PA10005	PLAIN AXLE NOT AVAILABLE	
		SUB. WITH PA15A226 AXLE	.05 EA.
17	PA7421	SCREW	.03 EA.
18	XA10669RA	CROSSHEAD ASSEMBLY	.45 EA.
	XA10669LA	CROSSHEAD ASSEMBLY	.45 EA.
19	S183	SCREW	.01 EA.
20	PA7237	PISTON ROD SPACER	.02 EA.
21	PA5447	SCREW	.04 EA.
22	PA8994-A	SIDE ROD	.20 EA.
23	PA4938	STUD	.04 EA.
24	XA10002	REAR TRUCK ASSEMBLY NOT AVAILABLE	
		SUB. WITH XA14B837 TRUCK	.99 EA.
25	PA10672	WORM GEAR (MOTOR)	.06 EA.
26	S271	SCREW	.02 EA.
27	PA10017A	GREASE PAN	.07 EA.
28	S171	SCREW	.01 EA.
29	XA10523	HEATING ELEM. & PLATE ASSY. NOT AVAILABLE	
		SUB. WITH XA14A208A ASSEMBLY	.91 EA.
30	XA10513	CHASSIS SMOKE BOX ASSEMBLY NOT AVAILABLE	
		SUB. WITH XA13B894RP SMOKE BOX ASSY.	2.13 EA.
	PA10513	SMOKE BOX NOT AVAILABLE	
		SUB. WITH PA13B894 SMOKE BOX	.76 EA.
	PA14A209	SEPARATOR	.02 EA.
31	PA10518-A	PISTON	.29 EA.
32	PA10520	PISTON PIN	.03 EA.
33	PA10515	PISTON LEVER	.14 EA.
34	PA10671	WORM GEAR (SMOKE DRIVE)	.32 EA.
35	PA10162	WORM GEAR STUD	.08 EA.
36	XA10505	CHASSIS WITH BUSHINGS	1.84 EA.
36A	XA13A861	FLANGED WHEEL ASSEMBLY	.39 EA.
36B	XA10010-A	FLANGELESS WHEEL ASSY. W/TAPPED HOLE	.36 EA.
36C	XA10010-A3	FLANGELESS WHEEL ASSY. W/STUD	.64 EA.
36D	XA13A863	PUL-MOR WHEEL	.82 EA.
37	PA10766	WASHER	.01 EA.
38	XA12A523	ARMATURE ASSEMBLY	3.85 EA.
39	PA9603	CARBON BRUSH	.13 EA.
40	PA10757-A	BRUSH SPRING	.02 EA.

CON'T

NO.	PART NO.	DESCRIPTION	PRICE
41	PA10754	BRUSH CAP	.01 EA.
42	PA10006	WORM GEAR AXLE NOT AVAILABLE	
		SUB. WITH PA15A281 AXLE	.07 EA.
43	XA10663	MALE PLUG	.24 EA.
44	XA12A526	MAGNET ASSEMBLY	1.71 EA.
45	XA9565-A	BRUSH BRACKET ASSEMBLY	1.00 EA.
46	S3A78	SCREW NOT AVAILABLE	
		SUB. WITH S29 SCREW	.01 EA.
47	XA10662	JACK PANEL	.24 EA.
48	S230-B	SCREW	.01 EA.
49	PA10511	4 CONDUCTOR CABLE	.13 EA.
49A	PA10249	10½" LEAD WIRE	.02 EA.
50	XA8914RP	TENDER BODY ASSY. W/TRIMMINGS	4.96 EA.
	PA10591-A	TENDER CHASSIS	1.55 EA.
51	XA11710	SPEAKER NOT AVAILABLE	
	XA11B831	SPEAKER NOT AVAILABLE	
		SUB. WITH XA14A127 SPEAKER	4.57 EA.
	PA14A216	MOUNTING BRACKET	.08 EA.
	S171	SCREW	.01 EA.
	S230B	SCREW	.01 EA.
52	PA11A991	CONDENSER NOT AVAILABLE	
		SUB. WITH PA14A914 CONDENSER	1.40 EA.
53	PA11685	RESISTOR	.29 EA.
54	XA10587-E	REMOTE CONTROL UNIT	4.04 EA.
	S230B	SCREW (R.C. UNIT)	.01 EA.
55	XA8716	DRUM	.95 EA.
56	XA9612-CRP	TOP FINGER UNIT	.33 EA.
57	XA9612-BRP	BOTTOM FINGER UNIT	.33 EA.
58	PA9988	RIVET	.04 EA.
59	PA10240	FIBRE BUSHING	.06 EA.
60		NOT USED	
61		NOT USED	
62	PA8715-B	WASHER	.02 EA.
63	P4652	RIVET	.01 EA.
64	W79	WASHER	.11 DZ.
65	PA10239	COUPLER BAR	.06 EA.
66	S-1	SCREW	.01 EA.
67		NOT USED	
68		NOT USED	
69	XA11A909	FRONT TRUCK W/WHEELS	.75 EA.
70	PA10241	CONTACT SPRING	.13 EA.
71	XA10238	WHEEL AND AXLE ASSEMBLY	.09 EA.
	PA10140	METAL WHEEL	.06 EA.
	PA9990	PLASTIC WHEEL	.03 EA.
	PA10238	AXLE	.01 EA.
72	XA12A053	REAR TRUCK W/WHEELS	1.30 EA.
	PA11677-A	SHOE	.08 EA.
	PA11533	SPRING	.02 EA.
73	XA12A047	KNUCKLE COUPLER	.29 EA.

PRICES SUBJECT TO CHANGE WITHOUT NOTICE.

NO.	PART NO.	DESCRIPTION	PRICE
1	PA12A190	Smoke Stack	.03 ea.
2	PA8999	14 Volt Lamp	.32 ea.
3	XA8960-C	Boiler Front Assy. w/Lamp Socket	.92 ea.
	PA10542	Headlight Lens	.02 ea.
4	XA8956-L	Boiler Assembly	6.02 ea.
	PA9579	Mounting Bracket	.01 ea.
	XA9578	Coupler Strap Assembly	.08 ea.
5	XA10057-R or L	Valve Link Assembly (right or Left)	.60 ea.
6	PA10030	Cylinder & Steamchest	.69 ea.
7	PA3769	Lock Washer	.01 ea.
8	S-16	Screw	.01 ea.
9	PA8959	Pilot	1.00 ea.
10	XA10012	Front Truck	.46 ea.
	PA9990	Front Truck Wheel Only	.03 ea.
11	PA13A404	Stud	.08 ea.
12	W-6	Washer	.01 ea.
13	PA8887	Front Truck Spring	.02 ea.
14	S46	Screw	.01 ea.
15	S18	Screw	.01 ea.
16	PA15A226	Plain Axle	.05 ea.
17	PA7421	Screw	.03 ea.
18	XA10669RA	Crosshead Assembly	.47 ea.
	XA10669LA	Crosshead Assembly	.47 ea.
19	S183	Screw	.01 ea.
20	PA7237	Piston Rod Spacer	.02 ea.
21	PA5447	Screw	.04 ea.
22	PA8994-A	Side Rod	.21 ea.
23	PA4938	Stud	.04 ea.
24	XA14B837	Rear Truck Assembly	1.04 ea.
25	PA10672	Worm Gear (Motor)	.06 ea.
26	S271	Screw	.02 ea.
27	PA10017A	Grease Pan	.07 ea.
28	S171	Screw	.01 ea.
29	XA14A208A	Heating Element & Plate Assy.	.96 ea.
30 *	XA13B894RP	Smoke Box Assembly	2.24 ea.
31	PA10518-A	Piston	.30 ea.
32	PA10520	Piston Pin	.03 ea.
33	PA10515	Piston Lever	.15 ea.
34	PA10671	Worm Gear (smoke drive)	.34 ea.
35	PA10162	Worm Gear Stud	.08 ea.
36	PA10505	Chassis	2.39 ea.
36A	XA13A861	Flanged Wheel Assembly	.41 ea.
36B	XA10010-A	Flangeless Wheel Assy. w/tapped hole	.38 ea.
36C	XA10010-A3	Flangeless Wheel Assy. w/stud	.67 ea.
36D	XA13A863	Pul-Mor Wheel	.86 ea.
37	PA10766	Washer	.01 ea.
38	XA12A523	Armature Assembly	4.04 ea.
39	PA9603	Carbon Brush	.14 ea.
40	PA10757-A	Brush Spring	.02 ea.
41	PA10754	Brush Cap	.01 ea.
42	PA15A281	Worm Gear Axle	.07 ea.

Cont'd

NO.	PART NO.	DESCRIPTION	PRICE
43	XA10663	Male Plug	.25 ea.
44	XA12A526	Magnet Assembly	1.80 ea.
45	XA9565-A	Brush Bracket Assembly	1.05 ea.
46	S29	Screw	.01 ea.
47	XA10662-A	Jack Panel	.25 ea.
48	S230-B	Screw	.01 ea.
49	PA13A208A	4 Conductor Cable (Plastic)	.04 ft.
49A	PA10249	Lead Wire	.02 ea.
50	XA8914RP	Tender Body Assy.	5.21 ea.
	PA10591-A	Tender Chassis	1.63 ea.
51	XA14A127	Conv. Speaker Substitute for XA11710 & XA11B831 OBSOLETE	4.91 ea.
52	PA14A914	Condenser Substitute for PA11A991	1.47 ea.
53	PA11685	Resistor	.30 ea.
54	XA10587-E	Remote Control Unit	4.24 ea.
	S230B	Screw (R.C. Unit)	.01 ea.
55	XA8716	Drum	1.00 ea.
56	XA9612-CRP	Top Finger Unit	.35 ea.
57	XA9612-BRP	Bottom Finger Unit	.35 ea.
58	PA9988	Rivet	.04 ea.
59	PA10240	Fibre Bushing	.06 ea.
60		NOT USED	
61		NOT USED	
62	PA8715-B	Washer	.02 ea.
63	P4652	Rivet	.01 ea.
64	W79	Washer	.01 ea.
65	PA10239	Coupler Bar	.06 ea.
66	S-1	Screw	.01 ea.
67		NOT USED	
68		NOT USED	
69	XA11A909	Front Truck w/wheels	.79 ea.
70	PA10241	Contact Spring	.14 ea.
71	XA10238	Wheel and Axle Assembly	.09 ea.
	PA10140	Metal Wheel	.06 ea.
	PA9990	Plastic Wheel	.03 ea.
	PA10238	Axle	.01 ea.
72	XA12A053	Rear Truck w/wheels	1.37 ea.
	PA11677A	Shoe	.08 ea.
	PA11533	Spring	.02 ea.
73	XA12A047	Knuckle Coupler	.30 ea.

* #30 When using XA13B894RP remove screw on solder terminal

Prices subject to change without notice.

LOCOMOTIVE AND TENDER WITH SMOKE AND CHOO-CHOO UNIT

Model No. 342AC

SPECIFICATIONS

Tested at: 12 Volts A.C. .... using 140" oval of track.

(A) Motor to be tested with Remote Control Unit at 12 Volts and not to draw more than 1.55 amps.

(B) Locomotive to run at a minimum of 9 RPM or 9 times forward around 140" oval of track per minute.

(C) Locomotive to run at a minimum of 8.5 RPM or 8½ times reverse around 140" oval of track per minute.

Load: Not to draw more than 2.1 amps while pulling 4 box cars.

Motor: Universal A.C. or D.C.

Ref: Form No. M2877; Oct. 1, 1950

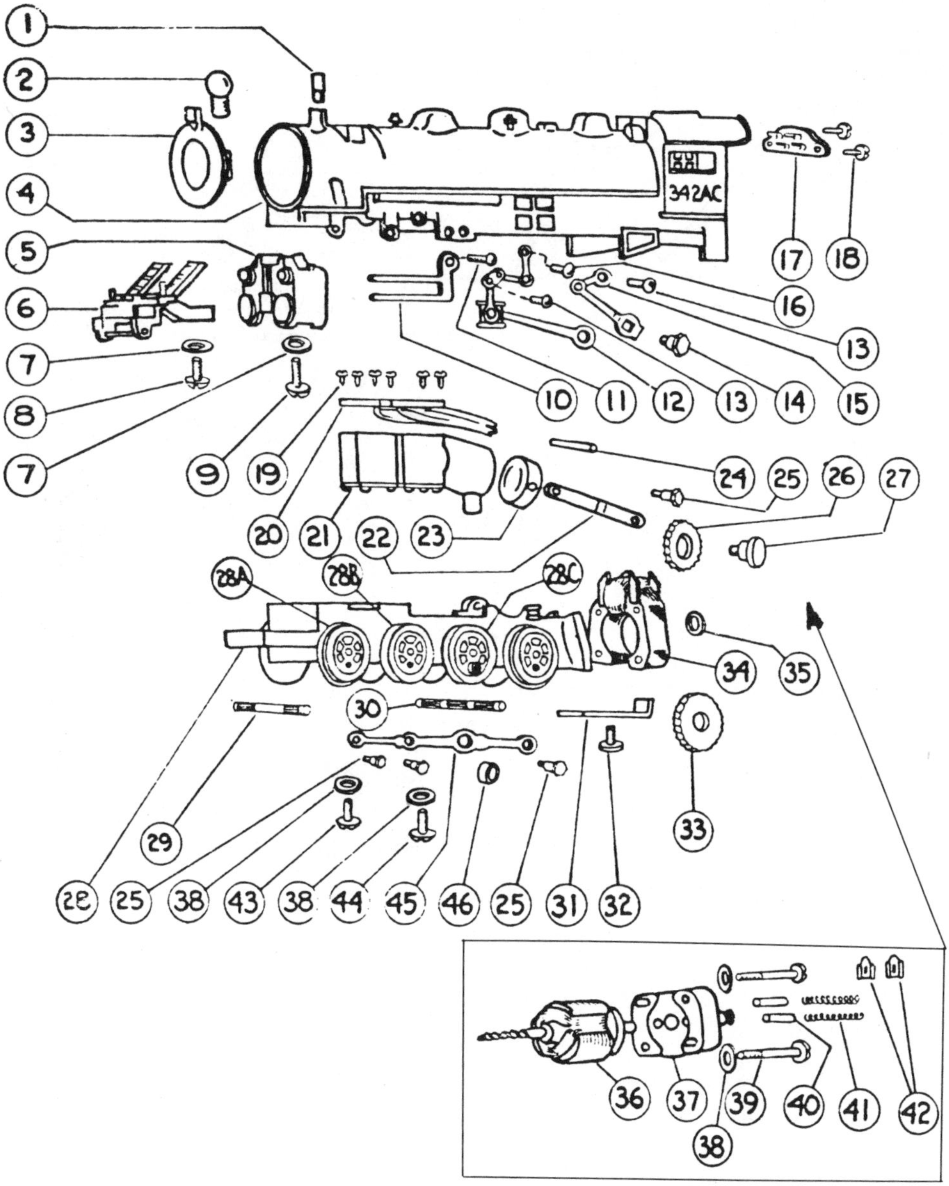

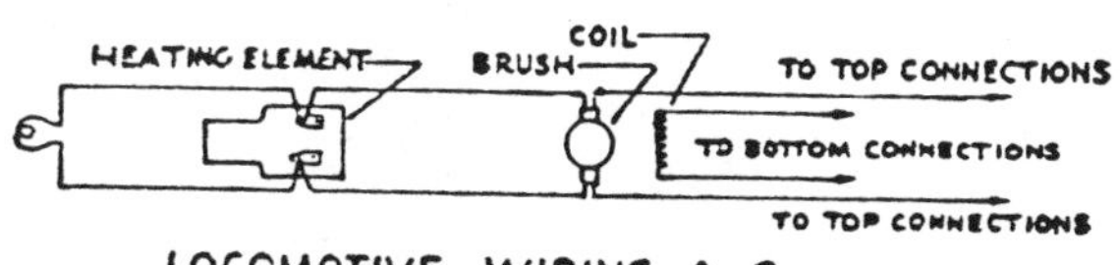

LOCOMOTIVE WIRING A.C.

Locomotive/Tender — No. 342AC

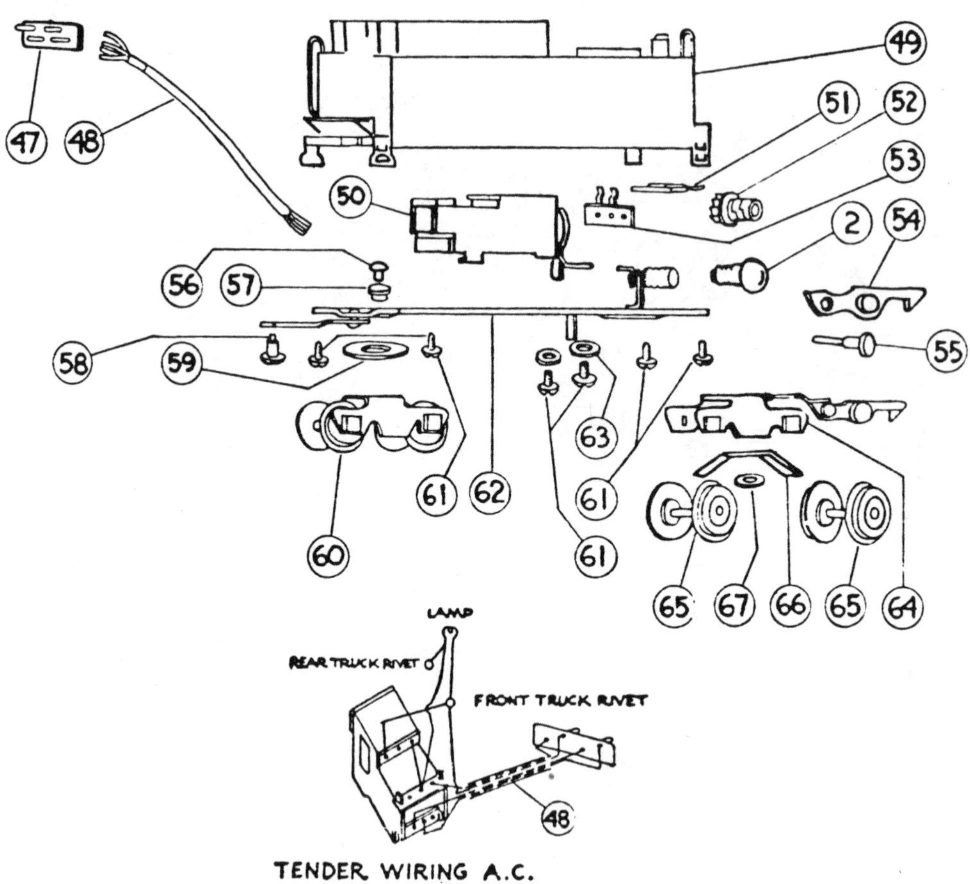

TENDER WIRING A.C.

Ref: Form No. M2877; Oct. 1, 1950

Diagram Number	Part No.	Description	Price
1	PA10536	Smoke Stack	$ .03 ea.
2	PA8999	14 Volt Lamp	.25 ea.
3	XA9467-B	Boiler Front Ass'y with lamp bracket	.60 ea.
4	XA9466-AC	Boiler Ass'y	2.50 ea.
5	PA10109	Cylinder and Steam Chest	.70 ea.
6	PA9460	Pilot	.70 ea.
7	PA4654	Lockwasher	.05 dz.
8	S55	Screw	.10 dz.
9	S52	Screw	.10 dz.
10	PA10595-R	Guide Bar (Right)	.05 ea.
	PA10595-L	Guide Bar (Left)	.05 ea.
11	S1	Screw	.05 dz.
12	XA10596-R	Crosshead Ass'y (Right)	.50 ea.
	XA10596-L	Crosshead Ass'y (Left)	.50 ea.
13	PA9288	Screw	.30 dz.
14	PA5447	Screw	.30 dz.
15	XA10447-B	Eccentric Crank	.30 ea.
16	PA10598	Link Stud	.30 dz.
17	XA10662	Jack Panel	.20 ea.
18	S230-B	Screw	.10 dz.
	XA10513	Chassis Smoke Box Ass'y (consists of parts 10-20-21)	2.00 ea.
19	S183	Screw	.10 dz.
20	XA10523	Heating Element and Plate Ass'y	1.00 ea.
21	PA10513	Chassis Smoke Box	1.00 ea.
	XA10516	Piston and Piston Lever Ass'y (consists of parts 22-23-24)	.40 ea.
22	PA10516	Piston Lever	.05 ea.
23	PA10518	Piston	.20 ea.
24	PA10520	Piston Pin	.05 ea.
25	PA7421	Screw	.30 dz.
26	PA10671	Worm Gear (smoke drive)	.30 ea.
27	PA10162	Worm Gear Stud	.10 ea.
28	*XA10504	Chassis with bushings only	1.10 ea.
28A	XA10104	Flanged wheel with tapped hole	.40 ea.
28B	XA10104-B	Flangeless wheel with tapped hole	.40 ea.
28C	XA10104-A2	Flangeless wheel with stud	.40 ea.
29	PA10005	Plain Axle	.10 ea.
30	PA10006	Worm gear axle	.10 ea.
31	PA10017	Grease Pan	.02 ea.
32	S271	Screw	.10 dz.
33	PA9473	Worm Gear (motor)	.40 ea.
34	XA9547	Magnet Ass'y A.C.	1.00 ea.
35	PA10766	Washer	.05 dz.
36	**XA11077	Armature Assy. A.C. (Used after Oct. 1949)	2.50 ea.

Diagram Number	Part No.	Description	Price
	***XA9569	Armature Ass'y A.C. (Used before Oct. 1949)	$2.50 ea.
37	XA9565-A	Brush Bracket Ass'y	.50 ea.
38	PA3769	Washer	.05 dz.
39	S295	Screw	.10 ea.
40	PA9603	Carbon Brush A.C.	.15 ea.
41	PA10757	Brush Spring	.05 ea.
42	PA10754	Brush Cap	.02 ea.
43	S24	Screw	.02 ea.
44	S16C	Screw	.10 dz.
45	PA9476	Side Rod	.20 ea.
46	PA7237	Piston Rod Spacer	.05 ea.
47	XA10663	Male Plug	.20 ea.
48	PA10511-C	4 conductor cable	.12 ea.
49	PA9778-B	Tender Body	2.00 ea.
50	XA10587	Remote Control Unit (complete)	2.50 ea.
51	XA9612-C	Top finger unit (remote control)	.50 ea.
52	XA8716-A	Drum Only (remote control)	.60 ea.
53	XA9612-B	Bottom finger unit (remote control)	.50 ea.
54	XA10469	Coupler and weight ass'y	.15 ea.
	PA10692	Coupler weight only	.05 ea.
55	PA10467	Coupler Pin	.10 ea.
56	PA10235-A	Truck Stud	.03 ea.
57	PA10209	Insulating Bushing	.02 ea.
58	PA4938	Stud	.30 dz.
59	PA8715-B	Washer	.05 dz.
60	XA9987-D	Front truck ass'y	.75 ea.
61	S-O	Screw	.05 dz.
62	XA10592-A	Tender Chassis with lamp bracket and draw bar	.35 ea.
63	W-46	Washer	.05 dz.
64	XA9987-C	Rear truck ass'y	.75 ea.
65	XA10140	Wheel and Axle ass'y	.25 set
	PA10140	Brass Wheel	.15 ea.
	PA9990	Plastic Wheel	.10 ea.
	PA9989	Axle	.02 ea.
66	PA10207	Contact Spring	.02 ea.
67	PA1405	Washer	.05 dz.

*XA10504 Chassis Assembly is not sold as a complete assembly with wheels.

**XA11077 Armature Assembly with 1/16" oil slinger cannot be used with XA9565-A Brush Bracket Assembly manufactured before Oct. 1949, unless you grind 1/16" off the boss which the bearing sets into on the Brush Bracket Assembly.

***XA9569 Armature Assembly can be used with XA9565-A Brush Bracket Assembly manufactured after Oct. 1949 providing that you use 1/16" washer to take up end play.

LOCOMOTIVE AND TENDER WITH SMOKE AND CHOO-CHOO UNIT

Model No. 342DC

SPECIFICATIONS

Tested at: 12 Volts D.C. .... Using 140" oval of track.
Not to draw more than 1.3 Amps.

(A) Locomotive to run a minimum of 9.5 R.P.M. or 9½ times forward around 140" oval of track per minute.

(B) Locomotive to run a minimum of 9 R.P.M. or 9 times in reverse, around 140" oval of track per minute.

Load: Not to draw more than 2 Amps. while pulling 4 Box or Cattle Cars.

Motor: D.C.

Ref: Form No. M2878; Oct. 1, 1950

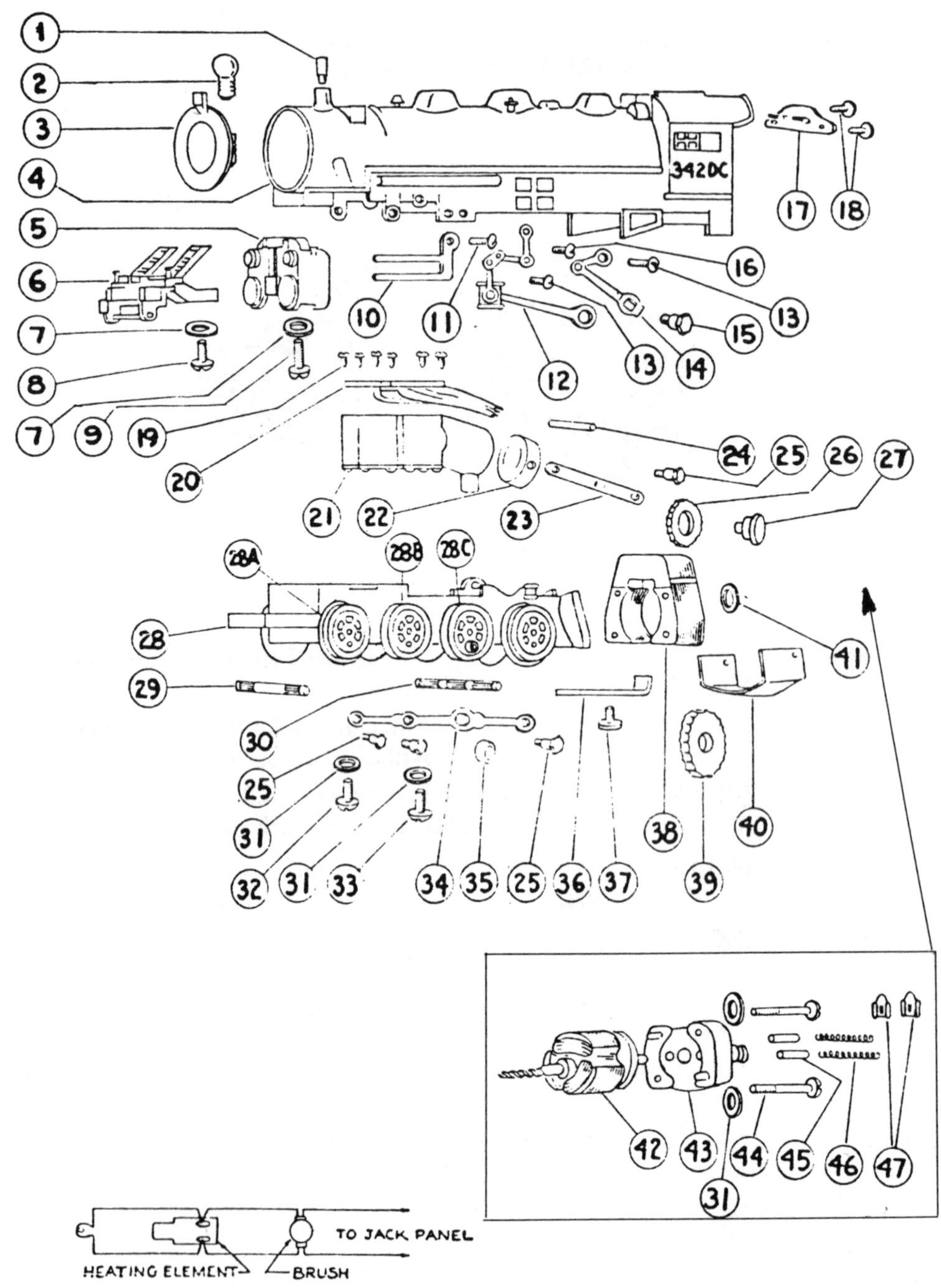

WIRING DIAGRAM D.C.

 Ref: Form No. M2878; Oct. 1, 1950

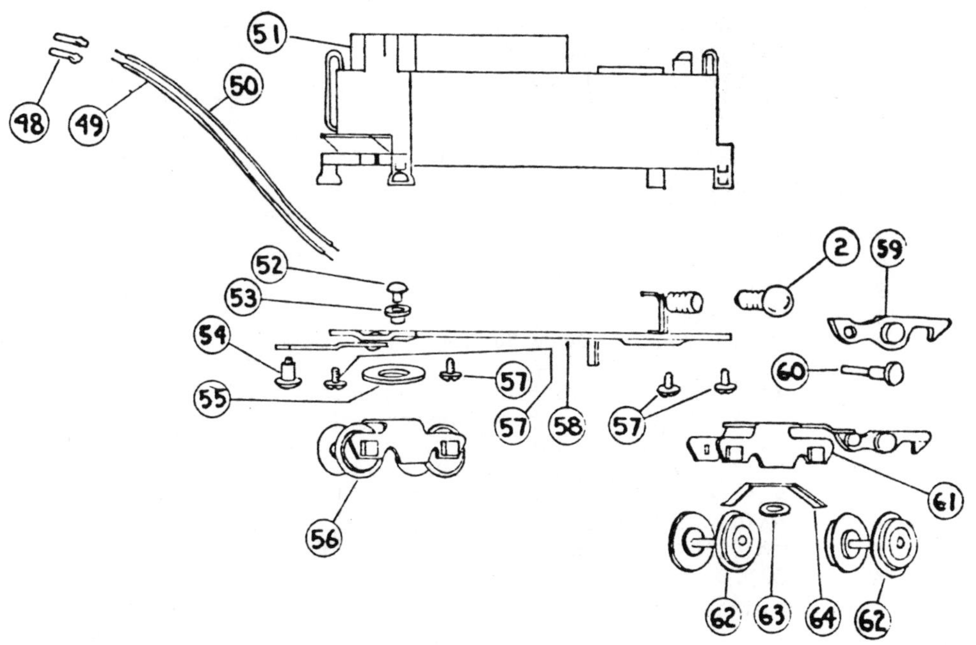
51
50
48
49
52
53
54
55
57
57
58
57
2
59
60
61
56
62
63
64
62

Diagram Number	Part No.	Description	Price
1	PA10536	Smoke Stack	$ .03 ea.
2	PA8999	14 Volt Lamp	.25 "
3	XA9467-B	Boiler Front Assembly with Lamp Bracket	.60 "
4	XA9466-DC	Boiler Assembly	2.50 "
5	PA10109	Cylinder & Steamchest	.70 "
6	PA9460	Pilot	.70 "
7	PA4654	Lockwasher	.05 dz.
8	S55	Screw	.10 "
9	S52	Screw	.10 "
10	PA10595-R	Guide Bar (Right)	.05 ea.
	PA10595-L	Guide Bar (Left)	.05 "
11	S1	Screw	.05 dz.
12	XA10596-R	Crosshead Assembly (Right)	.50 ea.
	XA10596-L	Crosshead Assembly (Left)	.50 "
13	PA9288	Screw	.30 dz.
14	XA10447-B	Eccentric Crank	.30 ea.
15	PA5447	Screw	.30 dz.
16	PA10598	Link Stud	.30 "
17	XA10287	Jack Panel	.20 ea.
18	S230-B	Screw	.10 dz.
	XA10513	Chassis Smoke Box Assembly (consists of parts 19-20-21)	2.00 ea.
19	S183	Screw	.10 dz.
20	XA10523	Heating Element & Plate Assembly	1.00 ea.
21	PA10513	Chassis Smoke Box	1.00 "
	XA10516	Piston & Piston Lever Assembly (consists of parts 22-23-24)	.40 "
22	PA10518	Piston	.20 "
23	PA10516	Piston Lever	.05 "
24	PA10520	Piston Pin	.05 "
25	PA7421	Screw	.30 dz.
26	PA10671	Worm Gear (Smoke Drive)	.30 ea.
27	PA10162	Worm Gear Stud	.10 "
28	*XA10504	Chassis with bushings only	1.10 "
28A	XA10104	Flanged Wheel with tapped hole	.40 "
28B	XA10104-B	Flangeless Wheel with tapped hole	.40 "
28C	XA10104-A2	Flangeless Wheel with stud	.40 "
29	PA10005	Plain Axle	.10 "
30	PA10006	Worm Gear Axle	.10 "
31	PA3769	Washer	.05 dz.
32	S24	Screw	.02 ea.
33	S16-C	Screw	.10 dz.
34	PA9476	Side Rod	.20 ea.
35	PA7237	Piston Rod Spacer	.05 "

Diagram Number	Part No.	Description	Price
36	PA10017	Grease Pan	.02 ea.
37	S271	Screw	.10 dz.
38	XA10355	Magnet Assembly D.C.	1.50 ea.
39	PA9473	Worm Gear (motor)	.40 "
40	PA10549	Magnet Cover	.06 "
41	PA10766	Washer	.05 dz.
42	**XA10476	Armature Assembly D.C.	2.50 ea.
	***XA11001	Armature Assembly D.C.	2.50 "
43	XA9565-A	Brush Bracket Assembly	.50 "
44	S295	Screw	.10 "
45	PA10778	Carbon Brush D.C.	.15 "
46	PA10757	Brush Spring	.05 "
47	PA10754	Brush Cap	.02 "
48	PA10291	Male Plug	.02 "
49	P-9273-N	5½" Wire Lead	.02 "
50	P-9273-I	8½" Wire Lead	.02 "
51	PA9778-B	Tender Body	2.00 "
52	PA10235-A	Truck Stud	.03 "
53	PA10209	Insulating Bushing	.02 "
54	PA4938	Stud	.30 dz.
55	PA8715-B	Washer	.05 "
56	XA9987-D	Front Truck Assembly	.75 ea.
57	S-0	Screw	.05 dz.
58	XA10592-A	Tender Chassis with lamp bracket and draw bar	.35 ea.
59	XA10469	Coupler and Weight Assembly	.15 "
	PA10692	Coupler Weight only	.05 "
60	PA10467	Coupler Pin	.10 "
61	XA9987-C	Rear Truck Assembly	.75 "
62	XA10140	Wheel & Axle Assembly	.25 set
	PA10140	Brass Wheel only	.15 ea.
	PA9990	Plastic Wheel only	.10 "
	PA9989	Axle only	.02 "
63	PA1405	Washer	.05 dz.
64	PA10207	Contact Spring	.02 ea.

*XA10504 Chassis Assembly is not sold as a complete assembly with wheels.

**XA10476 Armature Assembly with 1/16" oil slinger cannot be used with XA9565-A Brush Bracket Assembly manufactured before Oct. 1949, unless you grind 1/16" off the boss which the bearing sets into on the Brush Bracket Assembly.

***XA11001 Armature Assembly can be used with XA9565-A Brush Bracket Assembly manufactured after Oct. 1949 providing that you use 1/16" washer to take up end play.

LOCOMOTIVE AND TENDER WITH SMOKE, CHOO-CHOO UNIT, PULL-MOR, AND WHISTLE

Model No. 346

SPECIFICATIONS

Tested at: 12 Volts A.C. .... using 140" oval of track.

(A) Motor to be tested with Remote Control Unit at 12 Volts and not to draw more than 1.55 amps.

(B) Locomotive to run at a minimum of 9 R.P.M. or 9 times forward around 140" oval of track per minute.

(C) Locomotive to run at a minimum of 8.5 R.P.M. or 8½ times reverse around 140" oval of track per minute.

Load: Not to draw more than 2.3 amps. while pulling 4 box cars.

Motor: Universal A.C. or D.C.

 Ref: Form No. 1659; July 15, 1955

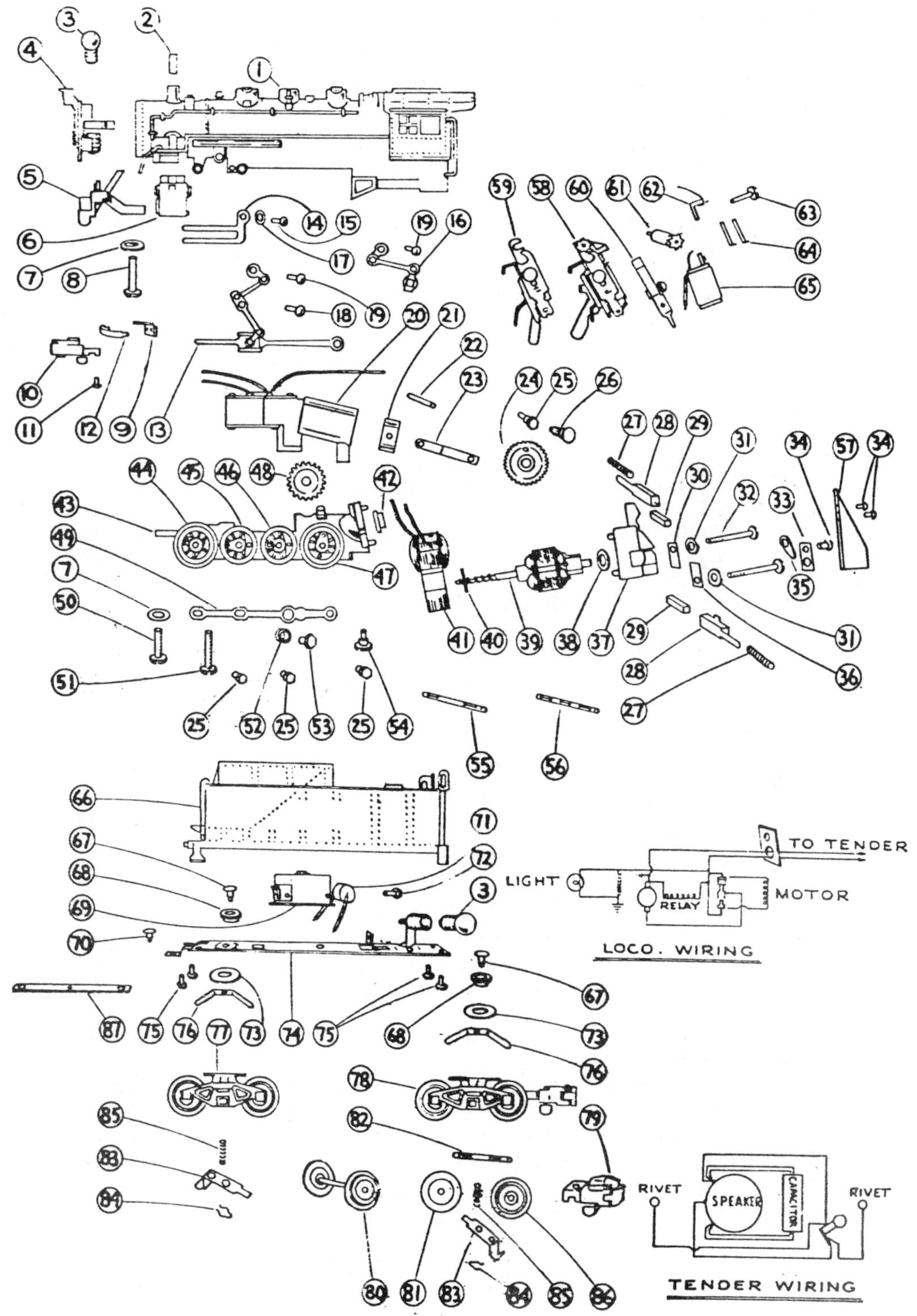

Ref: Form No. 1659; July 15, 1955

Diagram Number	Part No.	Description	Price
1	XA9466-DRP	Boiler Assy	$3.42 ea.
2	PA12A190	Smoke Stack	.02 "
3	PA8999	Lamp	.25 "
4	XA9467-BRP	Boiler Front Assy	1.07 "
5	PA12C478	Pilot Assy	.69 "
	PA8895	Front Rail	.04 "
6	PA10109	Cylinder	.70 "
7	P4654	Lockwasher	.05 dz.
8	S55	Screw	.10 "
9	PA12A479	Coupler Ratchet	.03 ea.
10	XA12A047	Coupler	.22 "
11	S3A71	Upper Screw	.02 "
12	PA12A355-A	Leaf Spring	.01 "
13	XA10596 R & L	Crosshead Assy	.50 "
14	PA10595 R & L	Crosshead Guide	.10 "
15	S-1	Screw	.05 dz.
16	XA10447-B	Eccentric Crank Assy	.30 ea.
17	W46	Lockwasher	.05 dz.
18	PA10598	Link Stud	.30 "
19	PA9288	Shouldered Screw	.30 "
20	XA10513	Smoke Box (complete)	2.00 ea.
	PA10513	Smoke Box	1.00 "
	XA10523	Heating Element	1.00 "
21	PA10518-A	Piston	.14 "
22	PA10520	Piston Pin	.05 "
23	PA10516	Piston Lever	.05 "
24	PA10671	Drive Gear	.40 "
25	PA7421	Piston Rod Screw	.30 dz.
26	PA10162	Worm Gear Stud	.10 ea.
27	PA13A130	Brush Spring	.02 "
28	PA13A131	Brush Tube	.03 "
29	PA13A128	Brush	.20 "
30	PA13A129	Brush Tube Cover	.01 "
31	PA3769	Lockwasher	.05 dz.
32	S295	Shouldered Screw	.10 ea.
33	PA13A838	Lead Wire Holder	.05 dz.
34	S183	Screw	.10 "
35	P10817	Solder Terminal	.01 ea.
36	PA13A129-A	Brush Tube Cover	.01 "
37	XA13C121-RP	Brush Mounting Plate with Bearing	.20 "
38	P325-A	Fibre Washer	.15 dz.
39	XA13B926	Armature Assembly	1.62 ea.
40	W83	Steel Washer	.30 dz.
41	XA13A927	Field Assy	1.00 ea.
42	PA13A187	Rear Bearing	.03 "

 Ref: Form No. 1659; July 15, 1955

Diagram Number	Part No.	Description	Price
43	*XA10504ARP	Complete Chassis Assy.	
	XA10504A	Chassis Assy	1.10 ea.
44	XA12A472	Flanged Wheel	.40 "
45	XA10104-B	Flangeless Wheel	.40 "
46	XA10104-A2	Flangeless Wheel	.40 "
47	XA12A473	Pull-Mor Wheel	.53 "
48	PA9473	Worm Gear	.40 "
49	PA9476	Side Rod	.20 "
50	S52	Screw	.10 dz.
51	S24	Screw	.02 ea.
52	PA7237	Piston Rod Spacer	.05 "
53	PA5447	Eccentric Crank Screw	.30 dz.
54	PA4938	Stud	.30 "
55	PA10005	Plain Axle	.10 ea.
56	PA10006	Gear Axle	.10 "
57	PA13B204	Cover	.12 "
58	XA13B102	Remote Control Assy	1.45 "
59	XA13A198	Frame Assy	.31 "
60	PA13A107	Field Core	.07 "
61	XA13A114	Rotor Insert and Ratchet	.25 "
62	XA13A199	Contact Insulator Assy	.15 "
63	S4A05	Screw	.02 "
64	PA13A110	Contact	.01 "
65	XA13A132	Coil Assy	.25 "
66	XA9998-BRP	Tender Body	1.97 "
67	PA10235-A	Truck Rivet	.03 "
68	PA10209	Bushing	.02 "
69	XA11B831	Speaker	3.87 "
70	PA4362	Rivet	.01 "
71	PA12A820	Capacitor	1.15 "
72	S172	Screw	.10 dz.
73	PA8715-B	Fiber Washer	.05 "
74	XA13B364	Chassis and Lamp Assy	.45 ea.
75	S0	Screw	.05 dz.
76	PA10207	Contact Spring	.02 ea.
77	XA12A516	Front Truck Assy	.60 "
78	XA12A350	Rear Truck Assy	.87 "
79	XA12A047	Knuckle Coupler	.22 "
80	XA10238	Wheel and Axle Assy	.25 set
81	PA10140	Metal Wheel	.15 ea.
82	PA10238	Axle	.02 "
83	PA11A936	Tender Pick Up	.02 "
84	PA11A944	Hair Pin Cotter	.01 "
85	PA11A956	Spring	.01 "
86	PA9990	Plastic Wheel	.10 "
87	PA13A209	Coupler	.01 "

***XA10504ARP is not sold as a complete assembly with wheels.**

Ref: Form No. 1659; July 15, 1955

SERVICE INSTRUCTIONS FOR NO. 346 LOCOMOTIVE AND TENDER WITH SMOKE, CHOO-CHOO, PULL-MOR AND WHISTLE

The first thing to do is to place locomotive and tender on track, connect transformer and test for operation. Make sure all rods, linkage and other parts are not bent or broken. It is also important that the wheels on the tender be clean, to insure a good electrical contact.

1. To replace Boiler Front (#4) or Bulb (#3).
- a. Pull out Boiler Front (#4) from Boiler Assembly (#1).
- b. Unscrew Bulb (#3) from lamp bracket and replace.
- c. To replace Boiler Front (#4), unsolder two lead wires.

2. To replace Knuckle Coupler (#10) or Pilot (#5).
- a. Take off Screw (#11) and you can replace the Knuckle Coupler (#10) or the Leaf Spring (#12).
- b. Next step to replace Pilot (#5) is to remove Screw (#8).

3. To replace Tender Pick Up (#83), Spring (#85) or Wheel and Axle Assembly (#80).
- a. Remove Hair Pin cotter (#84) and parts #83 and #85 can be replaced.
- b. To take out Wheel and Axle Assembly (#80) it is important that the side frames on truck be bent back properly so that it will not become loose from truck frame. Use pliers to hold the frame and truck side and bend back slightly until wheel and axle is free.

4. To replace Knuckle Coupler (#79) on Tender proceed as follows:
- a. Use a long nosed pliers or similar tool and pry back the two lugs on the rear truck of the Tender to remove broken coupler.
- b. Insert new part and bend back lugs.
- c. Adjust new coupler by placing Locomotive and Tender on the track, close the knuckle so that the weight is all the way down; then, either bend the coupler up or down, whichever is necessary to bring the bottom of the weight about 1/32" above the top of the rails.

5. To disassemble and replace Locomotive parts, proceed as follows:
- a. Unscrew Smoke Stack (#2).
- b. Take off Screw (#54) to remove coupler (#87) from locomotive.
- c. Cover (#57) can be taken off by removing two Screws (#34).
- d. Remove Screws (#53) on each side and take off Rods (#16 and #13) and Spacer (#52) from drive wheel with stud.
- e. Remove (#15-18-19) to take off Crosshead Assembly and Crosshead Guide (#14).
- f. Pull out Boiler Front (#4) and unsolder lead wires.
- g. Take off Pilot #5) by removing Screw (#8).
- h. Remove Screw (#50) and take off Cylinder (#8) by pulling back motor assembly and push forward on cylinder and lift out.
- i. To remove motor assembly from Boiler (#1) push assembly forward approximately a ¼" to clear Clamp on Boiler Assembly (#1) and then lift rear of motor up and pull out.
- j. To replace Piston (#21) or Piston Lever (#23).
  1. Remove Screw (#25) holding Piston Lever (#23) to Drive Gear (#24).
  2. Pull out Piston (#21) from Smoke Box Assembly (#20).
  3. Push out Piston Pin (#22).
- k. When smoke does not emit from the Smoke Box Assembly (#20), put in some smoke fluid and if it still does not function, the heating element assembly may have a broken wire and need replacing. To replace element assembly, take out Screw (#5) to release Smoke Box Assembly (#20) and unsolder lead wires and remove six P.K. screws from top and four screws holding bottom cover. It is necessary to remove bottom cover so that the wick of the new unit can be pulled through and properly inserted in the Smoke Box Assembly (#20).
- l. To change Brush Springs (#27) and Brushes (#29) unsolder lead wire from coil on Remote Control unit and bend back brass strip on Brush Tubes (#28) and these parts will come out quite easily.
- m. To remove Remote Control Unit (#58).
  1. Unsolder lead wire.
  2. Remove Screw (#34) holding parts (#33 and #35) to Brush Mounting Plate (#37).
  3. Lift off unit from Mounting Plate.
- n. Remove Screw (#63) to disassemble and replace parts on Remote Control Unit (#58).
- o. To replace Brush Mounting Plate (#37).
  1. Follow steps L and M.
  2. Remove two Screws (32), Lockwashers (#31), Brush Tube covers (#30 and #36).
  3. Slip out Brush Tubes (#28).
  4. Pull out Brush Mounting Plate.
- p. To change Armature (#39) or Field Assembly (#41)
  1. Follow steps L, M and O.
  2. Parts now can be replaced.

6. To disassemble and replace Tender parts, proceed as follows:
- a. Remove four Screws (#75) holding Tender Body (#66) to Tender Chassis (#74).
- b. To replace Capacitor (#71), unsolder two lead wires going to Speaker (#69) and then lift up and pull out part.
- c. To replace Speaker (#69).
  1. Unsolder all lead wires.
  2. Lift up Capacitor (#71) which will enable Screw (#72) to be removed.
- d. To replace Front or Rear Trucks (#77 and #78).
  1. Unsolder two lead wires which are attached to the Truck Rivet (#67).
  2. Take off parts (#83, 84 and 85).
  3. Remove Truck Rivet (#67) and Contact Spring (#76).

Diagram No.	Part No.	Description	Price
1	XA9466 DRP	Boiler Assy	$ 3.80 ea.
2	PA12A190	Smoke Stack	.02 "
3	PA8999	Lamp	.25 "
4	XA9467 BRP	Boiler Front Assy	1.19 "
5	PA12C478	Pilot Assy	.96 "
	PA8895	Front Rail	.05 "
6	PA10109	Cylinder	.70 "
7	P4654	Lockwasher	.05 dz.
8	S55	Screw	.10 "
9	PA12A479	Coupler Ratchet	.04 ea.
10	XA12A047	Coupler	.22 "
11	S3A71	Upper Screw	.01 "
12	PA12A355 A	Leaf Spring	.01 "
13	XA10596 R & L	Crosshead Assy	.32 "
14	PA10595 R & L	Crosshead Guide	.07 "
15	S-1	Screw	.05 dz.
16	XA10447 B	Eccentric Crank Assy	.30 ea.
17	W46	Lockwasher	.05 dz.
18	PA10598	Link Stud	.30 "
19	PA9288	Shouldered Screw	.30 "
20	XA10513	Smoke Box (complete)	2.22 ea.
	PA10513	Smoke Box	1.11 "
	XA10523	Heating Element	1.11 "
21	PA10518 A	Piston	.17 "
22	PA10520	Piston Pin	.05 "
23	PA10516	Piston Lever	.08 "
24	PA10671	Drive Gear	.27 "
25	PA742[illegible]	Piston Rod Screw	.30 dz.
26	PA10162	Worm Gear Stud	.05 ea.
27	PA13A130	Brush Spring	.02 "
28	PA13A131	Brush Tube	.04 "
29	PA13A128	Brush	.22 "
30	PA13A129	Brush Tube Cover	.01 "
31	PA3769	Lockwasher	.05 dz.
32	S295	Shouldered Screw	.02 ea.
33	PA13A838	Lead Wire Holder	.08 dz.
34	S183	Screw	.10 "
35	P10817	Solder Terminal	.01 ea.
36	PA13A129-A	Brush Tube Cover	.02 "
37	XA13C121 RP	Brush Mounting Plate with Bearing	.44 "
38	P325 A	Fibre Washer	.15 dz.
39	XA13B926	Armature Assembly	1.80 ea.
40	W83	Steel Washer	.03 "
41	XA13A927	Field Assy	1.11 "
42	PA13A187	Rear Bearing	.03 "
43	*XA10504 ARP	Complete Chassis Assembly	
	XA10504 A	Chassis Assembly	1.22 "
44	XA12A472	Flanged Wheel	.30 "
45	XA10104 B	Flangeless Wheel	.30 "
46	XA10104 A2	Flangeless Wheel	.44 "

(cont'd)

Diagram No.	Part No.	Description	Price
47	XA12A473	Pull-Mor Wheel	.53 ea.
48	PA9473	Worm Gear	.30 "
49	PA9476	Side Rod	.20 "
50	S52	Screw	.10 dz.
51	S24	Screw	.02 ea.
52	PA7237	Piston Rod Spacer	.05 "
53	PA5447	Eccentric Crank Screw	.30 dz.
54	PA4938	Stud	.03 ea.
55	PA10005	Plain Axle	.10 "
56	PA10006	Gear Axle	.10 "
57	PA13B204	Cover	.12 "
58	XA13B102	Remote Control Assy	1.45 "
59	XA13A198	Frame Assembly	.48 "
60	XA13A107 RP	Field Core Assembly	.29 "
61	XA13A114	Rotor Insert and Ratchet	.46 "
62	XA13A199	Contact Insulator Assy	.15 "
63	S4A05	Screw	.02 "
64	PA13A110	Contact	.05 "
65	XA13A132	Coil Assembly	.76 "
66	XA9778 BRP	Tender Body	1.97 "
67	PA10235 A	Truck Rivet	.03 "
68	PA10209	Bushing	.02 "
69	XA11B831	Speaker	2.95 "
70	PA4362	Rivet	.01 "
71	PA12A820	Capacitor	1.15 "
72	S172	Screw	.10 dz.
73	PA8715 B	Fibre Washer	.05 "
74	XA13B364	Chassis and Lamp Assy	.50 ea.
75	SO	Screw	.05 dz.
76	PA10207	Contact Spring	.02 ea.
77	XA12A516	Front Truck Assy	.40 "
78	XA12A350	Rear Truck Assy	.87 "
79	XA12A047	Knuckle Coupler	.22 "
80	XA10238	Wheel and Axle Assy	.17 set
81	PA10140	Metal Wheel	.15 ea.
82	PA10238	Axle	.02 "
83	PA11A936	Tender Pick Up	.02 "
84	PA11A944	Hair Pin Cotter	.01 "
85	PA11A956	Spring	.02 "
86	PA9990	Plastic Wheel	.05 "
87	PA13A209	Coupler	.01 "

*XA10504-ARP is not sold as a complete assembly with wheels.

 Ref: Form No. 1659; July 6, 1956

NO.	PART NO.	DESCRIPTION	PRICE
1	XA9466-DRP	Boiler Assembly	4.18 ea.
	PA9286-A	Motor Mount	.02 ea.
2	PA12A190	Smoke Stack	.03 ea.
3	PA8999	Lamp	.30 ea.
4	XA9467-BRP	Boiler Front Assembly	1.31 ea.
	PA10543	Headlight Lens	.05 ea.
5	PA12C478	Pilot Assembly	1.42 ea.
	PA8895	Front Rail	.08 ea.
6	PA10109	Cylinder	.82 ea.
7	P4654	Lockwasher	.01 ea.
8	S55	Screw	.01 ea.
9	PA12A479	Coupler Ratchet	.04 ea.
10	XA12A047	Coupler	.29 ea.
11	S3A71	Upper Screw	.05 ea.
12	PA12A355-A	Leaf Spring	.02 ea.
13	XA10596 R & L	Crosshead Assembly	.46 ea.
14	PA10595 R & L	Crosshead Guide	.12 ea.
15	S-1	Screw	.01 ea.
16	XA10447-B	Eccentric Crank Assembly	.26 ea.
17	W46	Lockwasher	.01 ea.
18	PA10598	Link Stud	.02 ea.
19	PA9288	Shouldered Screw	.03 ea.
20	XA10513	Smoke Box Assy. NOT AVAILABLE	
		Sub. with XA13B894-RP Smoke Box Assembly	2.13 ea.
	PA10513	Smoke Box NOT AVAILABLE	
		Sub. with PA13B894 Smoke Box	.76 ea.
	PA14A209	Separator	.02 ea.
	XA10523	Heating Element NOT AVAILABLE	
		Sub. with XA14A208-A Heating Element	.91 ea.
21	PA10518-A	Piston	.29 ea.
22	PA10520	Piston Pin	.03 ea.
23	PA10516	Piston Lever	.14 ea.
24	PA10671	Drive Gear	.32 ea.
25	PA7421	Piston Rod Screw	.03 ea.
26	PA10162	Worm Gear Stud	.08 ea.
27	PA13A130	Brush Spring	.03 ea.
28	[illegible]	Brush Tube	.03 ea.
29	PA13A128	Brush	.12 ea.
30	PA13A129	Brush Tube Cover	.01 ea.
31	PA3769	Lockwasher	.01 ea.
32	S-33	Screw	.01 ea.
	S-240	4 x ¼ Type "F" P.K. Screw (R.C. Unit)	.02 ea.
	S-264	4 x 5/16 Type "F" P.K. Screw (R.C. Unit)	.02 ea.
	S-29	6-32 x 1 3/8 R.H. Screw (Brush Bracket)	.01 ea.
		(above not shown)	
33		NOT USED	
34		NOT USED	
35	PA6173	Solder Terminal	.01 ea.
36	PA15A044	Brush Tube Cover Brace	.05 ea.
37	XA13C121-RP	Brush Mounting Plate NOT AVAILABLE	
		(must convert "to new" Remote Control Unit & Brush Mounting Plate. See Remote Control Conversion Sheet)	
38	W1A92	Fibre Washer	.02 ea.
39	XA13B926	Armature Assembly	3.73 ea.
40	PA10766	Steel Washer	.01 ea.
41	XA13A927	Field Assembly	1.42 ea.

Locomotive/Tender — No. 346

NO.	PART NO.	DESCRIPTION	PRICE
42	PA13A187	Rear Bearing	.04 ea.
43	XA10504-A	Chassis Assembly	1.34 ea.
44	XA12A472	Flanged Wheel	.40 ea.
45	XA10104-B	Flangeless Wheel	.45 ea.
46	XA10104-A2	Flangeless Wheel	.66 ea.
47	XA12A473	Pul-Mor Wheel	.73 ea.
48	PA9473	Worm Gear	.36 ea.
49	PA9476	Side Rod	.17 ea.
50	S52	Screw	.01 ea.
51	S24	Screw	.01 ea.
52	PA7237	Piston Rod Spacer	.02 ea.
53	PA5447	Eccentric Crank Screw	.04 ea.
54	PA4038	Stud	.04 ea.
55	PA15A226	Plain Axle	.05 ea.
56	PA15A281	Gear Axle	.07 ea.
57	PA13B204-A	Cover	.22 ea.
58	XA13B102	Remote Control Assy. NOT AVAILABLE	
		See Remote Control Conversion Sheet	
59	XA13A198	Frame Assembly NOT AVAILABLE	
60	XA13A107-RP	Field Core Assembly NOT AVAILABLE	
61	XA13A114	Rotor Insert & Ratchet NOT AVAILABLE	
62	XA13A199	Contact Insulator Assembly NOT AVAILABLE	
63	S4A05	Screw NOT AVAILABLE	
64	PA13A110	Contact NOT AVAILABLE	
65	XA13A132	Coil Assembly NOT AVAILABLE	
66	XA9778-BRP	Tender Body	2.42 ea.
67	PA10235-A	Truck Rivet	.07 ea.
68	PA10209	Bushing	.02 ea.
69	XA11B831	Speaker NOT AVAILABLE	
		Sub. with XA14A127 Speaker	4.57 ea.
	PA14A216	Speaker Bracket	.08 ea.
	S172	Screw	.02 ea.
	S171	Screw (for speaker bracket)	.01 ea.
70	PA4362	Rivet	.01 ea.
71	PA12A820	Capacitor NOT AVAILABLE	
		Sub. with PA14A914 Capacitor	1.40 ea.
72		NOT USED	
73	PA8715-B	Fibre Washer	.02 ea.
74	XA13B364	Chassis and Lamp Assembly	.55 ea.
75	SO	Screw	.01 ea.
76	PA10207	Contact Spring	.02 ea.
77	XA12A516	Front Truck Assembly	.44 ea.
78	XA12A350	Rear Truck Assembly	.80 ea.
79	XA12A047	Knuckle Coupler	.29 ea.
80	XA10238	Wheel and Axle Assembly	.09 ea.
81	PA10140	Metal Wheel	.06 ea.
82	PA10238	Axle	.01 ea.
83	PA11A936	Tender Pick Up	.04 ea.
84	PA11A944	Hair Pin Cotter	.01 ea.
85	PA11A956	Spring	.02 ea.
86	PA9990	Plastic Wheel	.03 ea.
87	PA13A209	Coupler	.01 ea.
		NOT SHOWN	
	LW-1B1	Black Lead Wire	.02 ft.

Ref: Form No. 1659; June 1, 1960

NO.	PART NO.	DESCRIPTION	PRICE
1	XA9466-DRP	Boiler Assembly	4.39 ea.
	PA9286-A	Motor Mount	.05 ea.
2	PA12A190	Smoke Stack	.03 ea.
3	PA8999	Lamp	.32 ea.
4	XA9467-BRP	Boiler Front Assembly	1.38 ea.
	PA10543	Headlight Lens	.02 ea.
5	PA12C478	Pilot Assembly	1.49 ea.
	PA8895	Front Rail	.08 ea.
6	PA10109	Cylinder	.86 ea.
7	P4654	Lock Washer	.01 ea.
8	S55	Screw	.01 ea.
9	PA12A479	Coupler Ratchet	.04 ea.
10	XA12A047	Coupler	.30 ea.
11	S3A71	Upper Screw	.03 ea.
12	PA12A355-A	Leaf Spring	.02 ea.
13	XA10596 R & L	Crosshead Assembly	.48 ea.
14	PA10595 R. & L	Crosshead Guide	.13 ea.
15	S-1	Screw	.01 ea.
16	XA10447-B	Eccentric Crank Assembly	.27 ea.
17	W46	Lock Washer	.11 dz.
18	PA10598	Link Stud	.02 ea.
19	PA9288	Shouldered Screw	.03 ea.
20 *	XA13B894RP	Smoke Box	2.24 ea.
	XA14A208A	Heating Element	.96 ea.
21	PA10518-A	Piston	.30 ea.
22	PA10520	Piston Pin	.03 ea.
23	PA10516	Piston Lever	.15 ea.
24	PA10671	Drive Gear	.34 ea.
25	PA7421	Piston Rod Screw	.03 ea.
26	PA10162	Worm Gear Stud	.08 ea.
27	PA13A130	Brush Spring	.03 ea.
28	PA13A131	Brush Tube	.03 ea.
29	PA13A128	Brush	.13 ea.
30	PA13A129	Brush Tube Cover	.01 ea.
31	PA3769	Lock Washer	.01 ea.
32	S-33	Screw	.01 ea.
	S-240	4 x ¼ Type "F" P.K. Screw (R. C. Unit)	.02 ea.
	S264	4 x 5/16 Type "F" P.K. Screw (R. C. Unit)	.02 ea.
	S-29	6-32 x 1 3/8 R.H. Screw (Brush Bracket) (Above not shown)	.01 ea.
33		NOT USED	
34		NOT USED	
35	PA6173	Solder Terminal	.01 ea.
36	PA15A044	Brush Tube Cover Brace	.05 ea.
37	XA15A695	Brush Mtg. Plate Substitute for XA13C121RP - OBSOLETE - (See R. C. Conv. Sheet)	.58 ea.
38	W1A92	Fibre Washer	.02 ea.
39	XA13B926	Armature Assembly	3.92 ea.
40	PA10766	Steel Washer	.01 ea.
41	XA13A927	Field Assembly	1.49 ea.
42	PA13A187	Rear Bearing	.04 ea.
43	XA10504-A	Chassis Assembly	1.41 ea.

Ref: Form No. 1659; Oct. 1, 1962

NO.	PART NO.	DESCRIPTION	PRICE
44	XA12A472	Flanged Wheel	.42 ea.
45	XA10104-B	Flangeless Wheel	.47 ea.
46	XA10104-A2	Flangeless Wheel	.69 ea.
47	XA12A473	Pul-Mor Wheel	.77 ea.
48	PA9473	Worm Gear	.38 ea.
49	PA9476	Side Rod	.18 ea.
50	S52	Screw	.01 ea.
51	S24	Screw	.01 ea.
52	PA7237	Piston Rod Spacer	.02 ea.
53	PA5447	Eccentric Crank Screw	.04 ea.
54	PA4938	Stud	.04 ea.
55	PA15A226	Plain Axle	.05 ea.
56	PA15A281	Gear Axle	.07 ea.
57	PA13B204-A	Cover	.23 ea.
58	XA14C429-Conv.	R.C. Assy. Substitute for XA13B102 - OBSOLETE (See R. C. Conv. Sheet)	3.17 ea.
59		Frame Assembly - OBSOLETE	
60		Field Core Assembly - OBSOLETE	
61		Rotor Insert & Ratchet - OBSOLETE	
62		Contact Insulator Assy. - OBSOLETE	
63		Screw - OBSOLETE	
64		Contact - OBSOLETE	
65		Coil Assy. - OBSOLETE	
66	XA9778-BRP	Tender Body	2.54 ea.
67	PA10235-A	Truck Rivet	.07 ea.
68	PA10209	Bushing	.02 ea.
69	XA14A127-Conv.	Speaker Substitute for XA11B831 - OBSOLETE	4.91 ea.
70	PA4362	Rivet	.01 ea.
71	PA14A914	Capacitor	1.47 ea.
72		NOT USED	
73	PA8715-B	Fibre Washer	.02 ea.
74	XA13B364	Chassis and Lamp Assembly	.58 ea.
75	SO	Screw	.01 ea.
76	PA10207	Contact Spring	.02 ea.
77	XA12A516	Front Truck Assembly	.46 ea.
78	XA12A350	Rear Truck Assembly	.84 ea.
79	XA12A047	Knuckle Coupler	.30 ea.
80	XA10238	Wheel and Axle Assembly	.09 ea.
81	PA10140	Metal Wheel	.06 ea.
82	PA10238	Axle	.01 ea.
83	PA11A936	Tender Pick Up	.04 ea.
84	PA11A944	Hair Pin Cotter	.01 ea.
85	PA11A956	Spring	.02 ea.
86	PA9990	Plastic Wheel	.03 ea.
87	PA13A209	Coupler	.01 ea.

* #20 When using XA13B894RP remove screw on solder terminal.

NOT SHOWN

LW-1B1	Black Lead Wire	.02 ft.

Prices subject to change without notice.

 Ref: Form No. 1659; Oct. 1, 1962

INSTRUCTIONS FOR CONVERSION OF XA13A102 R.C. Unit
TO
XA14C429 R.C. UNIT ON 343 AND 346
LOCOMOTIVE AND TENDER

Refer to exploded view of XA14C429 R. C. Unit along with #346 Parts Price Sheet when converting locomotive with new style remote control unit and use the following method:

REMOVING XA13A102 R.C. UNIT

1.) Disassemble locomotive as covered by #5 in Service Instructions on back of price sheet.

2.) Bend back end of Brush Tube (#28) and remove Brush Spring (#27) and Brushes (#29).

3.) Unsolder all wires from R. C. Unit and Motor Unit.

4.) Remove Screws (#32 & #34) and take off R.C. Unit (#58).

5.) Slip out Brush Tubes (#28) after Brush Mounting Plate has been removed from motor.

INSTALLING XA14C429 R. C. UNIT

1.) Assemble new XA14C423-RP Brush Mounting Plate (#12) using an S33 (#4) Screw inserting it through the hole in Magnet Assembly, attaching it to Motor Assembly.

2.) Attach new XA14C429 R.C. Unit to Brush Mounting Plate using S29 Screw (#16).

3.) Insert Brush Tube (#11) in place. The next step is to put on new PA15A044 Fibre Brush Tube Cover Brace, (#2) along with PA13A129 Brush Tube Cover (#1), replacing (#30) PA13A129 Brush Tube Cover on #346 Parts Price List, and these parts will be held in place by S264 Screw (#8).

4.) The other Brush Tube (#11) can be inserted and held in place by the other PA13A129-A Brush Tube Cover, Brush Tube Cover Brace and an S33 Screw (#4).

5.) Use another S-264 Screw (#8) along with solder terminal (#7) and assemble to other side of Brush Mounting Plate holding R. C. Unit.

6.) Rewire motor unit as follows:

1. On the lower left and right finger units, solder two magnet lead wires.

2. Solder one lead wire from Coil along with one Tender lead wire to solder terminal on right hand side.

3. The other wire from coil with a covering of spaghetti, along with other tender lead wire, and wire from Smoke Unit are soldered to left hand Brush Tube.

4. Use jumper wire from upper or third terminal on R.C. Unit to Brush Tube (#11) on right hand side of motor.

7.) Put back brushes (#10) and Spring (#9) and bend in place the end of Brush Tubes.

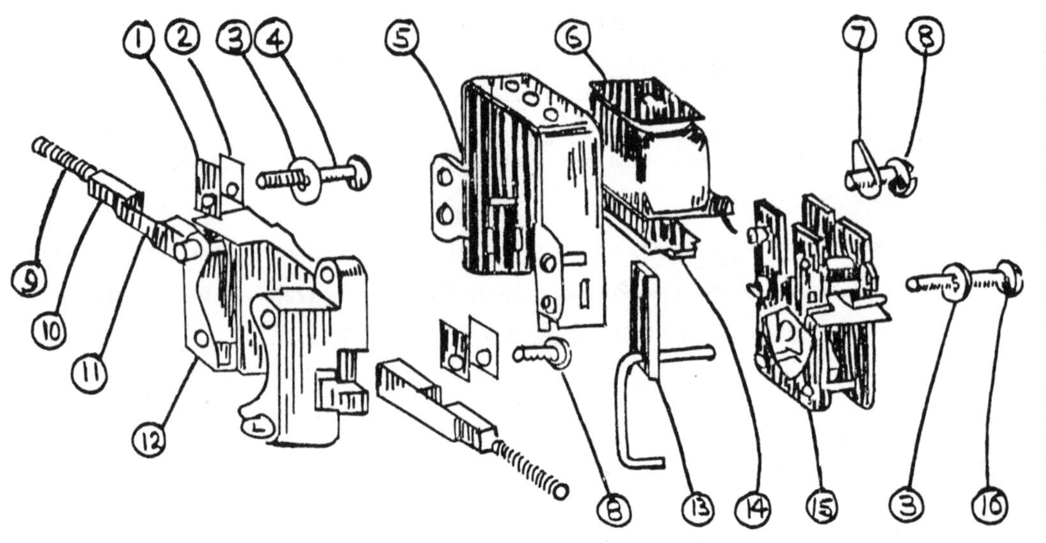

EXPLODED VIEW OF XA14C429 REMOTE CONTROL UNIT and
XA14C423-RP BRUSH MOUNTING PLATE ASSEMBLIES

DIA. NO.	PART NO.	DESCRIPTION	PRICE
1	PA13A129	Brush Tube Cover	.01 ea.
2	PA15A044	*Brush Tube Cover Brace	.05 ea.
3	PA3769	Lockwasher	.01 ea.
4	*S-33	Screw	.01 ea.
5	PA714A444	Coil Housing	.05 ea.
6	XA14B433	Coil Assy.	.69 ea.
7	PA6173	Solder Terminal	.01 ea.
8	*S-264	Screw	.02 ea.
9	PA13A130	Brush Spring	.03 ea.
10	PA13A128	Brush	.12 ea.
11	PA13A131	Brush Tube	.03 ea.
12	~~XA14C423-RP~~	Brush Mounting Plate XA15A695	~~.14 ea.~~ .55
13	XA14A435	Plunger Assy.	.14 ea.
14	PA14C432	Coil Support	.04 ea.
15	XA14A994	Contact Assy.	.77 ea.
16	*S-29	Screw	.01 ea.
	*XA14C429	R.C. Unit Complete	2.76 ea.

NOTE: * Parts so marked are used in the conversion only. Other parts listed are for identification of the conponent parts of new R.C. Unit to be used until a new exploded parts price sheet is issued. When ordering parts for #343 or #346 Locomotive and Tender with an XA13A102 R.C. Unit, use a #346 Price List along with this sheet for remote control unit.

Price subject to change without notice

LOCOMOTIVE AND TENDER WITHOUT SMOKE AND CHOO-CHOO UNIT

Model No. 350

SPECIFICATIONS

Tested at: 12 Volts A.C. .... using 140" oval of track.

(A) Motor to be tested with Remote Control Unit at 12 Volts and not to draw more than 1.75 amps.

(B) Locomotive to run a minimum of 9 RPM or 9 times forward around 140" oval of track per minute.

(C) Locomotive to run a minimum of 8.5 RPM or 8½ times reverse around 140" oval of track per minute.

Load: Not to draw more than 1.75 amps while pulling 4 box cars.

Motor: Universal A.C. or D.C.

Ref: Form No. M2879; Oct. 1, 1950

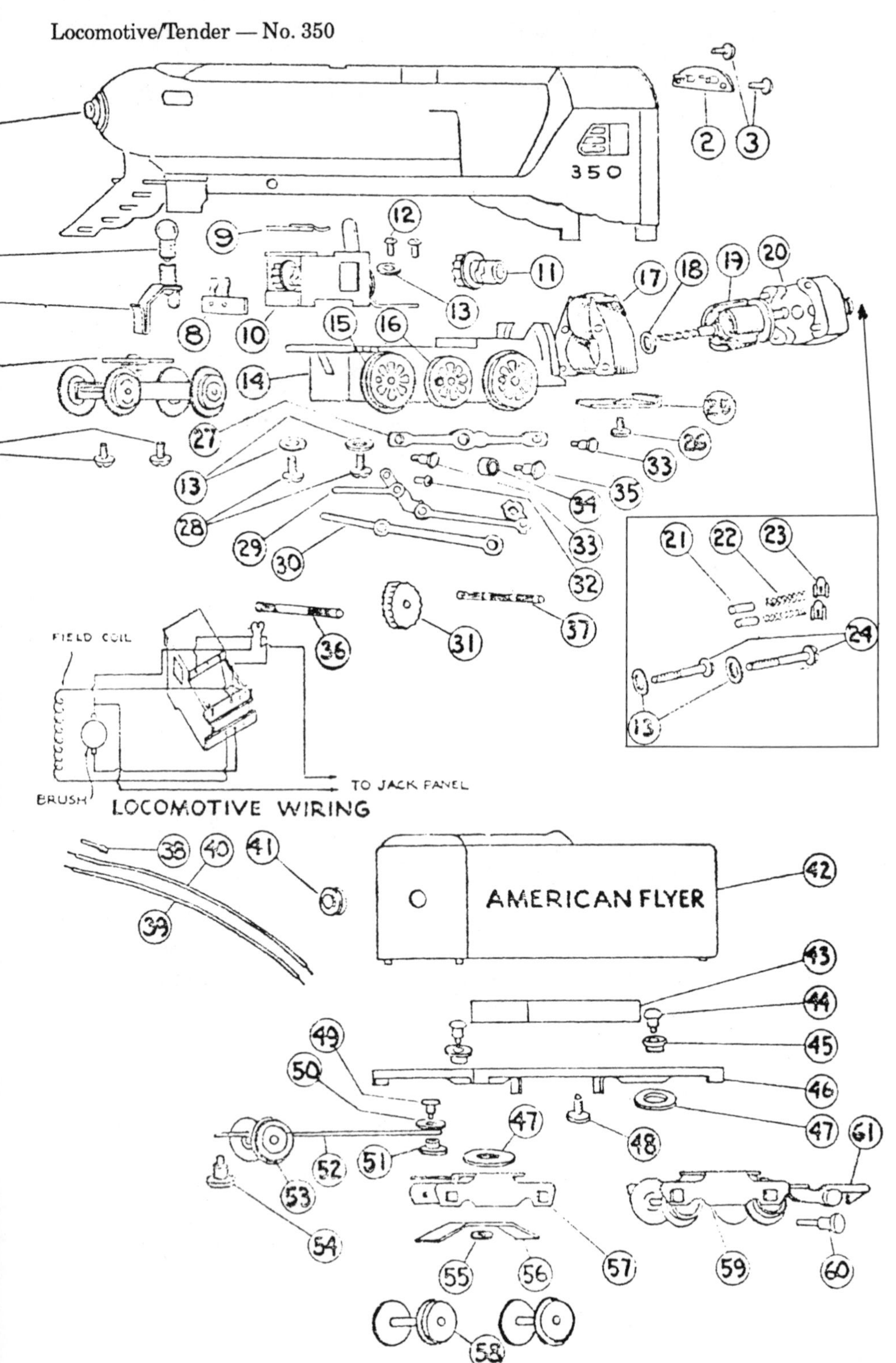

 Ref: Form No. M2879; Oct. 1, 1950

Diagram Number	Part No.	Description	Price
1	XA9512-B	Boiler Ass'y	$2.50 ea.
2	XA10335	Jack Panel	.20 "
3	S230-B	Screw	.10 dz.
4	PA8999	14 Volt Lamp	.25 ea.
5	XA9593	Light Bracket Ass'y	.25 "
6	XA10490	Truck and Strap Ass'y	.40 "
7	S172	Screw	.10 dz.
8	XA9612-B	Bottom Finger Unit (Remote Control)	.50 ea.
9	XA9612-C	Top Finger Unit (Remote Control)	.50 "
10	XA10587-B	Remote Control Unit	2.50 "
11	XA8716	Drum only (Remote Control)	.60 "
12	S202	Screw	.05 dz.
13	PA3769	Washer	.05 "
14	*XA10000	Chassis Ass'y with bushings only	1.20 ea.
15	XA10009	Flanged Wheel with tapped hole	.40 "
16	XA10009-B1	Flangeless Wheel and Stud	.40 "
17	XA9547	Magnet Ass'y	1.00 "
18	PA10766	Washer	.05 dz.
19	**XA11077	Armature Ass'y A.C. (used after Oct. 1949)	2.50 ea.
	***XA9569	Armature Ass'y A.C. (used before Oct. 1949)	2.50 ea.
20	XA9565-A	Brush Bracket Ass'y	.50 "
21	PA9603	Carbon Brush A.C.	.15 "
22	PA10757	Brush Spring	.05 "
23	PA10754	Brush Cap	.02 "
24	S295	Screw	.10 "
25	PA10017	Grease Pan	.02 "
26	S233	Screw	.10 dz.
27	PA9280-A	Side Rod	.20 ea.
28	S14	Screw	.05 dz.
29	XA8996 R	Valve Link Ass'y (Right)	.50 ea.
	XA8996 L	Valve Link Ass'y (Left)	.50 "
30	XA8567-A	Connecting Rod Ass'y	.30 "
31	PA10672	Worm Gear	.30 "
32	PA5602	Tubular Rivet	.24 dz.
33	PA7421	Piston Rod Screw	.30 "
34	PA7237	Piston Rod Spacer	.05 ea.
35	PA5447	Eccentric Crank Screw	.30 dz.
36	PA10005	Plain Axle	.10 ea.
37	PA10006	Worm Gear Axle	.10 "

Diagram Number	Part No.	Description	Price
38	PA10291	Male Plug	$ .02 ea.
39	PA10249Q	7½" Black Lead Wire	.02 "
40	PA10249T	9" Black Lead Wire	.02 "
41	PA4356	Rubber Grommet	.02 "
42	XA9376	Tender Body	1.00 "
43	PA10058	Weight	.35 "
44	PA10235-A	Truck Rivet	.03 "
45	PA10209	Insulating Bushing	.02 "
46	PA9375	Tender Chassis	.30 "
47	PA8715-B	Washer	.05 dz.
48	S184	Screw	.10 "
49	PA10751	Stud	.02 ea.
50	PA1067-A	Washer	.05 dz.
51	PA1312	Fibre Bushing	.10 "
52	XA10749	Coupler & Yoke Assembly	.30 ea.
53	PA10019-A	Rear Truck Wheel only	.10 "
54	PA4939	Screw	.05 "
55	PA1405	Washer	.05 dz.
56	PA10207	Contact Spring	.02 ea.
57	XA9987-G	Front Truck Assembly	.50 "
	XA10749-A	Truck & Coupler Assembly (consists of parts 49-50-51-52-53-57)	.80 "
58	XA10140	Wheel & Axle Assembly	.25 set
	PA10140	Brass Wheel only	.15 ea.
	PA9990	Plastic Wheel only	.10 "
	PA9989	Axle only	.02 "
59	XA9987-C	Rear Truck Assembly	.75 "
60	PA10467	Coupler Pin	.10 "
61	XA10469	Coupler & Weight Assembly	.15 "
	PA10692	Weight only	.05 "

*XA10000 Chassis Assembly is not sold as a complete assembly with wheels.

**XA11077 Armature Assembly with 1/16" oil slinger cannot be used with XA9565-A Brush Bracket Assembly manufactured before Oct. 1949, unless you grind 1/16" off the boss which the bearing sets into on the Brush Bracket Assembly.

***XA9569 Armature Assembly can be used with XA9565-A Brush Bracket Assembly manufactured after Oct. 1949 providing that you use 1/16" washer to take up end play.

 Ref: Form No. M2879; Oct. 1, 1950

LOCOMOTIVE AND TENDER WITH SMOKE AND CHOO-CHOO

Model No. 354

SPECIFICATIONS

Tested at: 12 Volts A.C. .... using 140" oval of track.

(A) Motor to be tested with Remote Control Unit at 12 Volts, and not to draw more than 1.7 amps.

(B) Locomotive to run a minimum of 9 R.P.M. or 9 times forward, around 140" oval of track per minute.

(C) Locomotive to run a minimum of 8.5 R.P.M. or 8½ times reverse, around 140" oval of track per minute.

Load: Not to draw more than 2.1 amps. while pulling 4 Box Cars.

Motor: Universal A.C. or D.C.

Ref: Form No. 1647; July 15, 1955

Locomotive/Tender — No. 354

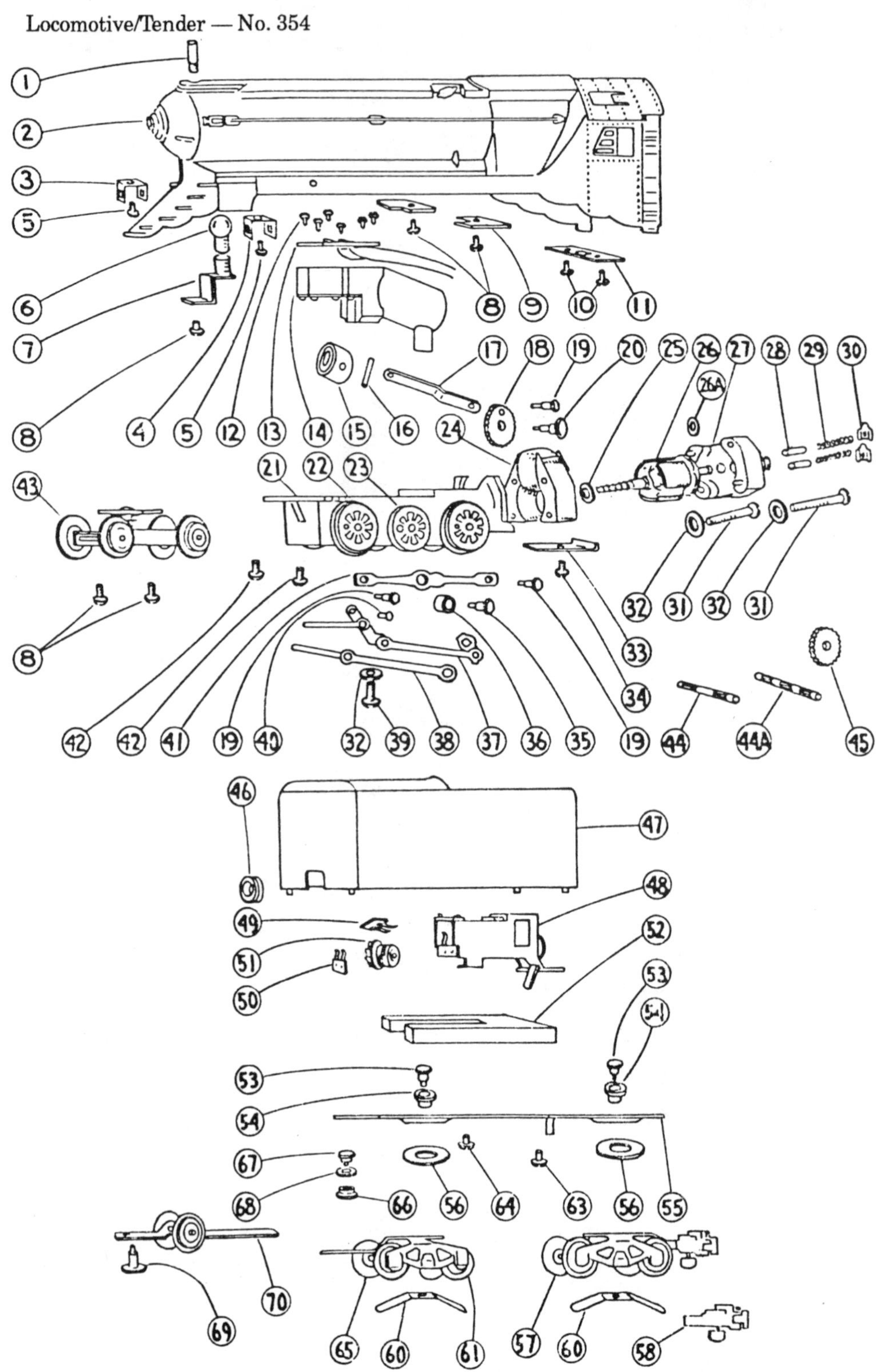

 Ref: Form No. 1647; July 15, 1955

Diagram Number	Part No.	Description	Price
1	PA12A190	Smoke Stack	$ .02 ea.
2	XA9512-ARP	Boiler Assembly	.98 "
3	PA9595-AR	Piston Rod Guide	.03 "
4	PA9595-AL	Piston Rod Guide	.03 "
5	S281	Screw	.01 "
6	PA8999	Bulb	.25 "
7	XA10890	Lamp Bracket Assembly	.25 "
8	S172	Screw	.10 dz.
9	PA9579-A	Rear Mounting Bracket	.01 ea.
10	S171	Screw	.01 "
11	PA9578-A	Coupler Strap	.01 "
12	S183	Screw	.10 dz.
13	XA10523	Heating Element and Plate Assembly	1.00 ea.
14	PA10513	Chassis Smoke Box	1.00 "
	XA10513	Chassis Smoke Box (Consists of parts 12-13-14)	2.00 "
15	PA10518-A	Piston	.14 "
16	PA10520	Piston Pin	.05 "
17	PA10514	Piston Lever	.05 "
18	PA10671	Worm Gear (Smoke Drive)	.40 "
19	PA7421	Side Rod Screw	.30 dz.
20	PA10162	Worm Gear Stud	.10 ea.
21	PA10506	Chassis	1.20 "
22	XA10009	Flanged Wheel w/tapped hole	.40 "
23	XA10009-B1	Flangeless wheel w/stud	.40 "
24	XA9547	Magnet Assembly	1.C0 "
25	PA10766	Armature Spacer	.05 dz.
26	XA11077	Armature Assembly	2.50 ea.
26-A	W1A92	Washer	.01 "
27	XA9565-A	Brush Bracket Assembly	.50 "
28	PA9603	Brush	.15 "
29	PA10757-A	Brush Spring	.05 "
30	PA10754	Brush Cap	.02 "
31	S295	Screw	.10 "
32	PA3769	Washer	.05 dz.
33	PA10017	Grease Pan	.02 ea.
34	S233	Screw	.10 dz.
35	PA5447	Screw	.30 "
36	PA7237	Spacer	.05 ea.

Diagram Number	Part No.	Description	Price
37	XA8996-R	Valve Link Assembly Right	.50 ea.
	XA8996-L	Valve Link Assembly Left	.50 "
38	XA8567-A	Connecting Rod Assembly	.30 "
39	S16-C	Screw	.10 dz.
40	PA5603	Rivet	.01 ea.
41	PA9280-A	Side Rod	.20 ea.
42	S14	Screw	.05 dz.
43	XA10490	Truck and Strap Assembly	.40 ea.
44	PA10005	Plain Axle	.10 "
44-A	PA10006	Worm Gear Axle	.10 "
45	PA10672	Gear	.30 "
46	PA4356	Rubber Grommet	.02 "
47	XA9376-RP	Tender Body Assembly w/trim	1.00 "
48	XA10587-E	Remote Control Unit	2.50 "
49	XA9612-C	Top Finger Unit	.50 "
50	XA9612-B	Bottom Finger Unit	.50 "
51	XA8716	Drum	.60 "
52	PA11A926	Tender Weight	.18 "
53	PA10235-A	Truck Rivet	.03 "
54	PA10209	Insulating Bushing	.02 "
55	PA9375-H	Tender Chassis	.21 "
56	PA8715-B	Washer	.05 dz.
57	XA12A050-A	Rear Truck Assembly	.56 ea.
58	XA12A047	Knuckle Coupler	.22 "
60	PA10207	Contact Spring	.02 ea.
61	XA10238	Wheel and Axle Assembly	.25 set
	PA10140	Metal Wheel	.15 ea.
	PA9990	Plastic Wheel	.10 "
	PA10238	Axle	.02 "
63	S184	Screw	.10 dz.
64	S230-B	Screw	.10 dz.
65	XA12A907	Front Truck Assembly	.70 ea.
66	PA1312	Bushing	.10 dz.
67	PA10751	Stud	.02 ea.
68	PA1067-A	Washer	.05 dz.
69	PA4939	Truck Stud	.05 ea.
70	XA10749	Coupler and Yoke Assembly	.30 "
	PA10019-A	Rear Truck Wheel only	.10 "

 Ref: Form No. 1647; July 15, 1955

SERVICE INSTRUCTIONS FOR No. 354 LOCOMOTIVE AND TENDER WITH SMOKE AND CHOO-CHOO

The first thing to do is to place locomotive and tender on track, connect transformer and test for operation. Make sure all rods, linkage and other parts are not bent or broken. It is also important that the wheels on the tender be clean to insure a good electrical contact.

1. **To check bulb (#6), proceed as follows:**
   a. Move Truck and Strap Assembly (#43), to one side and remove S172 Screw (#8) holding Lamp Bracket Assembly (#7).
   b. Tighten Bulb (#6) in Lamp Bracket (#7), as it is sometimes loose and does not make good contact. If burned out, unscrew bulb and replace.
2. **If the trouble is in the locomotive, you can make the following checks:**
   a. Inspect brushes for wear or poor contact and brush springs for proper tension.
   b. Clean or polish Commutator on Armature Assembly (#26). If Locomotive is still running slow, the armature may need replacing.
   c. Make sure wheel and axle assemblies are placed correctly in the truck assembly. Clean metal wheels on tender to insure a good electrical contact.
3. **If these initial steps do not correct the trouble, it will be necessary to disassemble the locomotive as follows:**
   a. Unscrew Smoke Stack (#1).
   b. Remove Screw (#69) to take off Coupler and Yoke Assembly (#70) from locomotive.
   c. Remove Screws (#35) on each side and take off Rods (#37), and (#38) and Spacer (#36) from center drive wheel.
   d. Turn locomotive upside down and remove two Screws (#42) and you can now remove motor assembly from Boiler (#2).
   e. Take out Lamp Bracket Assembly (#7) by removing Screws (#8).
   f. To remove motor, push forward approximately ¼" to clear clamp on Boiler (#2) and then lift the rear of motor up and pull motor out.
   g. The motor is now exposed and you can inspect the wiring and other points of the unit, making any necessary replacements.
   h. When smoke does not emit from the Smoke Box Assembly (#14), put in some smoke fluid and if it still does not function, the Heating Element (#13) may have a broken wire, and need replacing.
   i. To check or replace Heating Element (#13), just remove six Screws (#12). When replacing element assembly, it will be necessary to take off the bottom cover gasket, so that the wick of the new unit can be pulled through and properly inserted in the Smoke Box Assembly.
4. **When the trouble appears to be in the tender, proceed as follows:**
   a. Straighten lips holding Tender Body (#47) to Chassis (#55).
   b. Inspect wiring and soldered joints for loose or broken connections.
   c. Check Finger Units (#49) and (#50) on Remote Control Unit (#48) to see if they are burnt or not making proper contact.
   d. The Drum (#51), should be checked to see if it is pitted or worn.
   e. The Pawl on the Remote Control Unit may be broken or need adjusting.
   f. It is generally not necessary to replace the complete Remote Control Unit, but sometimes the Finger Units, the drum, or both need adjusting or replacing.
5. **To replace knuckle coupler (#58), proceed as follows:**
   a. Use a long nosed plier or similar instrument and pry back the two lugs on the rear truck of the tender to remove broken coupler.
   b. Insert new part and bend back lugs.
   c. Adjust new coupler by placing locomotive and tender on the track, close the knuckle, so that the weight is all the way down; then, either bend the coupler up or down, whichever is necessary to bring the bottom of the weight about 1/32" above the top of the rails.

Locomotive/Tender — No. 354

Diagram No.	Part No.	Description	Price
1	PA12A190	Smoke Stack	$ .02 Ea.
2	XA9512-ARP	Boiler Assembly	1.09 "
3	PA9595-AR	Piston Rod Guide	.03 "
4	PA9595 AL	Piston Rod Guide	.03 "
5	S281	Screw	.01 "
6	PA8999	Bulb	.25 "
7	XA10890	Lamp Bracket Assembly	.28 "
8	S172	Screw	.10 dz.
9	PA9579 A	Rear Mounting Bracket	.01 ea.
10	S171	Screw	.01 "
11	PA9578 A	Coupler Strap	.01 "
12	S183	Screw	.10 dz.
13	XA10523	Heating Element and Plate Assy	1.11 ea.
14	PA10513	Chassis Smoke Box	1.11 "
	XA10513	Chassis Smoke Box (consists of Parts 12-13-14)	2.22 "
15	PA10518 A	Piston	.17 "
16	PA10520	Piston Pin	.05 "
17	PA10514	Piston Lever	.08 "
18	PA10671	Worm Gear (Smoke Drive)	.27 "
19	PA7421	Side Rod Screw	.30 dz.
20	PA10162	Worm Gear Stud	.05 ea.
21	PA10506	Chassis	1.37 "
22	XA10009	Flanged Wheel w/tapped hole	.44 "
23	XA10009-B1	Flangeless wheel w/stud	.45 "
24	XA9547	Magnet Assembly	1.11 "
25	PA10766	Armature Spacer	.05 dz.
26	XA11077	Armature Assembly	2.19 ea.
26-A	W1A92	Washer	.01 "
27	XA9565-A	Brush Bracket Assy	.71 "
28	PA9603	Brush	.15 "
29	PA10757-A	Brush Spring	.05 "
30	PA10754	Brush Cap	.02 "
31	S295	Screw	.02 "
32	PA3769	Washer	.05 dz.
33	PA10017	Grease Pan	.04 ea.
34	S233	Screw	.11 dz.
35	PA5447	Screw	.30 "
36	PA7237	Spacer	.05 ea.
37	XA8996-R	Valve Link Assembly Right	.55 "
	XA8996-L	Valve Link Assembly Left	.55 "
38	XA8567-A	Connecting Rod Assembly	.33 "
39	S16-C	Screw	.11 dz.
40	PA5603	Rivet	.01 ea.
41	PA9280-A	Side Rod	.10 "
42	S14	Screw	.05 dz.
43	XA10490	Truck and Strap Assy	.44 ea.
44	PA10005	Plain Axle	.10 "
44-A	PA10006	Worm Gear Axle	.10 "
45	PA10672	Gear	.20 "

(cont'd)

Diagram No.	Part No.	Description	Price
46	PA4356	Rubber Grommet	.02 ea.
47	XA9376-RP	Tender Body Assembly w/trim	1.11 "
48	XA10587-E	Remote Control Unit	1.32 "
49	XA9612-CRP	Top Finger Unit	.30 "
50	XA9612-BRP	Bottom Finger Unit	.30 "
51	XA8716	Drum	.59 "
52	PA11A926	Tender Weight	.32 "
53	PA10235-A	Truck Rivet	.03 "
54	PA10209	Insulating Bushing	.02 "
55	PA9375-H	Tender Chassis	.23 "
56	PA8715-B	Washer	.05 dz.
57	XA12A050-A	Rear Truck Assembly	.65 ea.
58	XA12A047	Knuckle Coupler	.22 "
60	PA10207	Contact Spring	.02 ea.
61	XA10238	Wheel and Axle Assembly	.17 set
	PA10140	Metal Wheel	.15 ea.
	PA9990	Plastic Wheel	.05 "
	PA10238	Axle	.02 "
63	S184	Screw	.10 dz.
64	S230-B	Screw	.10 "
65	XA12A907	Front truck Assembly	.78 ea.
66	PA1312	Bushing	.11 dz.
67	PA10751	Stud	.02 ea.
68	PA1067-A	Washer	.05 dz.
69	PA4939	Truck Stud	.05 ea.
70	XA10749	Coupler and Yoke Assembly	.30 "
	PA10019-A	Rear Truck Wheel only	.05 "

NO.	PART NO.	DESCRIPTION	PRICE
1	PA12A190	Smoke Stack	.03 ea.
2	XA9512-ARP	Boiler Assembly	1.20 ea.
	PA10542	Headlight Lens	.02 ea.
3	PA9595-AR	Piston Rod Guide	.03 ea.
4	PA9595-AL	Piston Rod Guide	.03 ea.
5	S281	Screw	.01 ea.
6	PA8999	Bulb	.30 ea.
7	XA10890	Lamp Bracket Assembly	.22 ea.
8	S172	Screw (mfgd. to use either screw)	.02 ea.
	S230B	Screw	.01 ea.
9	PA9579-A	Rear Mounting Bracket	.01 ea.
10	S171	Screw	.01 ea.
11	PA9578-A	Coupler Strap	.01 ea.
12	S183	Screw	.01 ea.
13	XA10523	Heating Element & Plate Assy. NOT AVAILABLE	
		Sub. with XA14A208-A Assembly	.91 ea.
14	XA10513	Smoke Box Assembly NOT AVAILABLE	
		Sub. with XA13B894-RP Smoke Box	2.13 ea.
	PA10513	Smoke Box NOT AVAILABLE	
		Sub. with PA13B894 Smoke Box	.76 ea.
	PA14A209	Separator	.02 ea.
15	PA10518-A	Piston	.29 ea.
16	PA10520	Piston Pin	.03 ea.
17	PA10514	Piston Lever	.14 ea.
18	PA10671	Worm Gear (Smoke Drive)	.32 ea.
19	PA7421	Side Rod Screw	.03 ea.
20	PA10162	Worm Gear Stud	.08 ea.
21	PA10506	Chassis w/bearing NOT AVAILABLE	
		Sub. with PA10506-A Chassis w/bearing	1.78 ea.
	PA13A187	Bearing	.04 ea.
22	XA10009	Flanged Wheel w/tapped hole NOT AVAILABLE	
		Sub. with XA13A865 Flanged Wheel (front)	.37 ea.
		XA13A864 Pul-Mor Wheel (rear)	.80 ea.
23	XA10009-B1	Flangeless Wheel w/stud	.63 ea.
24	XA9547	Magnet Assembly	1.22 ea.
25	PA10766	Armature Spacer	.01 ea.
26	XA11077	Armature Assembly	3.39 ea.
26-A	W1A92	Washer	.02 ea.
27	XA9565-A	Brush Bracket Assembly	1.00 ea.
28	PA9603	Brush	.13 ea.
29	PA10757-A	Brush Spring	.02 ea.
30	PA10754	Brush Cap	.02 ea.
31	S295	Screw	.02 ea.
32	PA3769	Washer	.01 ea.
33	PA10017	Grease Pan	.07 ea.
34	S233	Screw	.12 dz.
35	PA5447	Screw	.04 ea.
36	PA7237	Spacer	.02 ea.
37	XA8996-R	Valve Link Assembly (right)	.61 ea.
	XA8996-L	Valve Link Assembly (left)	.61 ea.

con't

NO.	PART NO.	DESCRIPTION	PRICE
38	XA8567-A	Connecting Rod Assembly	.36 ea.
39	S16-C	Screw	.12 dz.
40	PA5603	Rivet	.02 ea.
41	PA9280-A	Side Rod	.16 ea.
42	S14	Screw	.01 ea.
43	XA10490	Truck and Strap Assembly	.48 ea.
44	PA10005	Plain Axle NOT AVAILABLE	
		Sub. with PA15A226 Axle	.05 ea.
44-A	PA10006	Worm Gear Axle NOT AVAILABLE	
		Sub. with PA15A281 Axle	.07 ea.
45	PA10672	Gear	.06 ea.
46	PA4356	Rubber Grommet	.02 ea.
47	XA9376-RP	Tender Body Assy. w/trim	1.22 ea.
48	XA10587-E	Remote Control Unit	4.04 ea.
49	XA9612-CRP	Top Finger Unit	.33 ea.
50	XA9612-BRP	Bottom Finger Unit	.33 ea.
51	XA8716	Drum	.95 ea.
52	PA11A926	Tender Weight NOT AVAILABLE	
		Sub. with PA10593 Weight	.26 ea.
53	PA10235-A	Truck Rivet	.07 ea.
54	PA10209	Insulating Bushing	.02 ea.
55	PA9375-H	Tender Chassis	.25 ea.
56	PA8715-B	Washer	.02 ea.
57	XA12A050-B	Rear Truck Assembly	.72 ea.
58	XA12A047	Knuckle Coupler	.29 ea.
60	PA10207	Contact Spring	.02 ea.
61	XA10238	Wheel & Axle Assembly	.09 ea.
	PA10140	Metal Wheel	.06 ea.
	PA9990	Plastic Wheel	.03 ea.
	PA10238	Axle	.01 ea.
63	S184	Screw	.02 ea.
64	S230-B	Screw	.01 ea.
65	XA12A907	Front Truck Assembly NOT AVAILABLE	
		Sub. with XA15A800 Truck	.43 ea.
66	* PA1312	Bushing	.12 dz.
67	* PA10751	Stud	.02 ea.
68	* PA1067-A	Washer	.06 dz.
69	PA4939	Truck Stud	.06 ea.
70	XA10749	Coupler & Yoke Assy. NOT AVAILABLE	
		Sub. with XA15A784 Draw Bar Assembly	.22 ea.

* NOTE: Bubbles #66, 67, 68, not used with #65-XA15A800 Truck or #70 Draw Bar Assembly/

When using substitute flanged wheel, or pul-mor, on old style PA10506, you must file off .025 on motor mounts above wheels.

NOT SHOWN

PART NO.	DESCRIPTION	PRICE
PA13A208-A	4 Conductor Cable (plastic)	.04 ft.
LW-1B1	Black Lead Wire	.02 ft.

Prices subject to change without notice.

Ref: Form No. 1647; June 1, 1960

NO.	PART NO.	DESCRIPTION	PRICE
1	PA12A190	Smoke Stack	.03 ea.
2	XA9512-ARP	Boiler Assembly	1.26 ea.
	PA10542	Headlight Lens	.02 ea.
3	PA9595-AR	Piston Rod Guide	.03 ea.
4	PA9595-AL	Piston Rod Guide	.03 ea.
5	S281	Screw	.01 ea.
6	PA8999	Bulb	.32 ea.
7	XA10890	Lamp Bracket Assembly	.23 ea.
8	S172	Screw	.02 ea.
	S230B	Screw	.01 ea
9	PA9579-A	Rear Mounting Bracket	.01 ea.
10	S171	Screw	.01 ea.
11	PA9578-A	Coupler Strap	.01 ea.
12	S183	Screw	.01 ea.
13	XA14A208-A	Heating Element & Plate Assy.	.96 ea.
14	XA13B894-RP	Smoke Box Assembly	2.24 ea.
15	PA10518-A	Piston	.30 ea.
16	PA10520	Piston Pin	.03 ea.
17	PA10514	Piston Lever	.15 ea.
18	PA10671	Worm Gear (smoke drive)	.34 ea.
19	PA7421	Side Rod Screw	.03 ea.
20	PA10162	Worm Gear Stud	.08 ea.
21	PA10506-A	Chassis	1.87 ea.
	PA13A187	Bearing	.04 ea.
22*	XA13A865	Flanged Wheel (Front)	.39 ea.
	XA13A864	Pul-Mor Wheel (Rear)	.84 ea.
		Substitute for XA10009 - OBSOLETE	
23	XA10009-B1	Flangeless Wheel w/stud	.66 ea.
24	XA9547	Magnet Assembly	1.28 ea.
25	PA10766	Armature Spacer	.01 ea.
26	XA11077	Armature Assembly	3.56 ea.
26-A	W1A92	Washer	.02 ea.
27	XA9565-A	Brush Bracket Assembly	1.05 ea.
28	PA9603	Brush	.14 ea.
29	PA10757-A	Brush Spring	.02 ea.
30	PA10754	Brush Cap	.02 ea.
31	S295	Screw	.02 ea.
32	PA3769	Washer	.01 ea.
33	PA10017	Grease Pan	.07 ea.
34	S233	Screw	.13 dz.
35	PA5447	Screw	.04 ea.
36	PA7237	Spacer	.02 ea.
37	XA8996-R	Valve Link Assy. (Right)	.64 ea.
	XA8996-L	Valve Link Assy. (Left)	.64 ea.
38	XA8567-A	Connecting Rod Assembly	.38 ea.
39	S16-C	Screw	.13 dz.
40	PA5603	Rivet	.02 ea.
41	PA9280-A	Side Rod	.17 ea.
42	S14	Screw	.01 ea.
43	XA10490	Truck and Strap Assembly	.50 ea.

Cont'd

NO.	PART NO.	DESCRIPTION	PRICE
44	PA15A226	Plain Axle	.05 ea.
44-A	PA15A281	Worm Gear Axle	.07 ea.
45	PA10672	Gear	.06 ea.
46	PA4356	Rubber Grommet	.02 ea.
47	XA9376-RP	Tender Body w/trim	1.28 ea.
48	XA10587-E	Remote Control Unit	4.24 ea.
49	XA9612-CRP	Top Finger Unit	.35 ea.
50	XA9612-BRP	Bottom Finger Unit	.35 ea.
51	XA8716	Drum	1.00 ea.
52	PA10593	Tender Weight	.27 ea.
53	PA10235-A	Truck Rivet	.07 ea.
54	PA10209	Insulating Bushing	.02 ea.
55	PA9375-H	Tender Chassis	.26 ea.
56	PA8715-B	Washer	.02 ea.
57	XA12A050-B	Rear Truck Assembly	.83 ea.
58	XA12A047	Knuckle Coupler	.30 ea.
60	PA10207	Contact Spring	.02 ea.
61	XA10238	Wheel & Axle Assembly	.09 ea.
	PA10140	Metal Wheel	.06 ea.
	PA9990	Plastic Wheel	.03 ea.
	PA10238	Axle	.01 ea.
63	S184	Screw	.02 ea.
64	S230-B	Screw	.01 ea.
65	XA15B800	Front Truck Assy. Substitute for XA12A907 OBSOLETE	.45 ea.
66	PA1312	Bushing	.13 dz.
67	PA10751	Stud	.02 ea.
68	PA1067-A	Washer	.06 dz.
69	PA4939	Truck Stud	.06 ea.
70	XA15A784	Draw Bar Used w/XA15B800 Truck	.23 ea.
	XA10891	Coupler and Yoke Assembly Substitute for XA10749 - OBSOLETE	.38 ea.

* #22 When using these wheels with Chassis PA10506 file off .025 from mounts above the front and rear wheels.

NOT SHOWN

PART NO.	DESCRIPTION	PRICE
PA13A208-A	4 Conductor Cable (plastic)	.04 ft.
LW-1B1	Black Lead Wire	.02 ft.

Prices subject to change without notice.

LOCOMOTIVE AND TENDER WITH SMOKE AND CHOO-CHOO UNIT

Model No. 356

SPECIFICATIONS

Tested at: 12 Volts A.C. ....using 140″ oval of track.

(A) Motor to be tested with Remote Control Unit at 12 Volts, and not to draw more than 1.7 amps.

(B) Locomotive to run a minimum of 9 R.P.M. or 9 times forward, around 140″ oval of track per minute.

(C) Locomotive to run a minimum of 8.5 R.P.M. or 8½ times reverse, around 140″ oval of track per minute.

Load: Not to draw more than 2.1 amps. while pulling 4 Box Cars.

Motor: Universal A.C. or D.C.

 Ref: Form No. 1823; Feb. 1, 1957

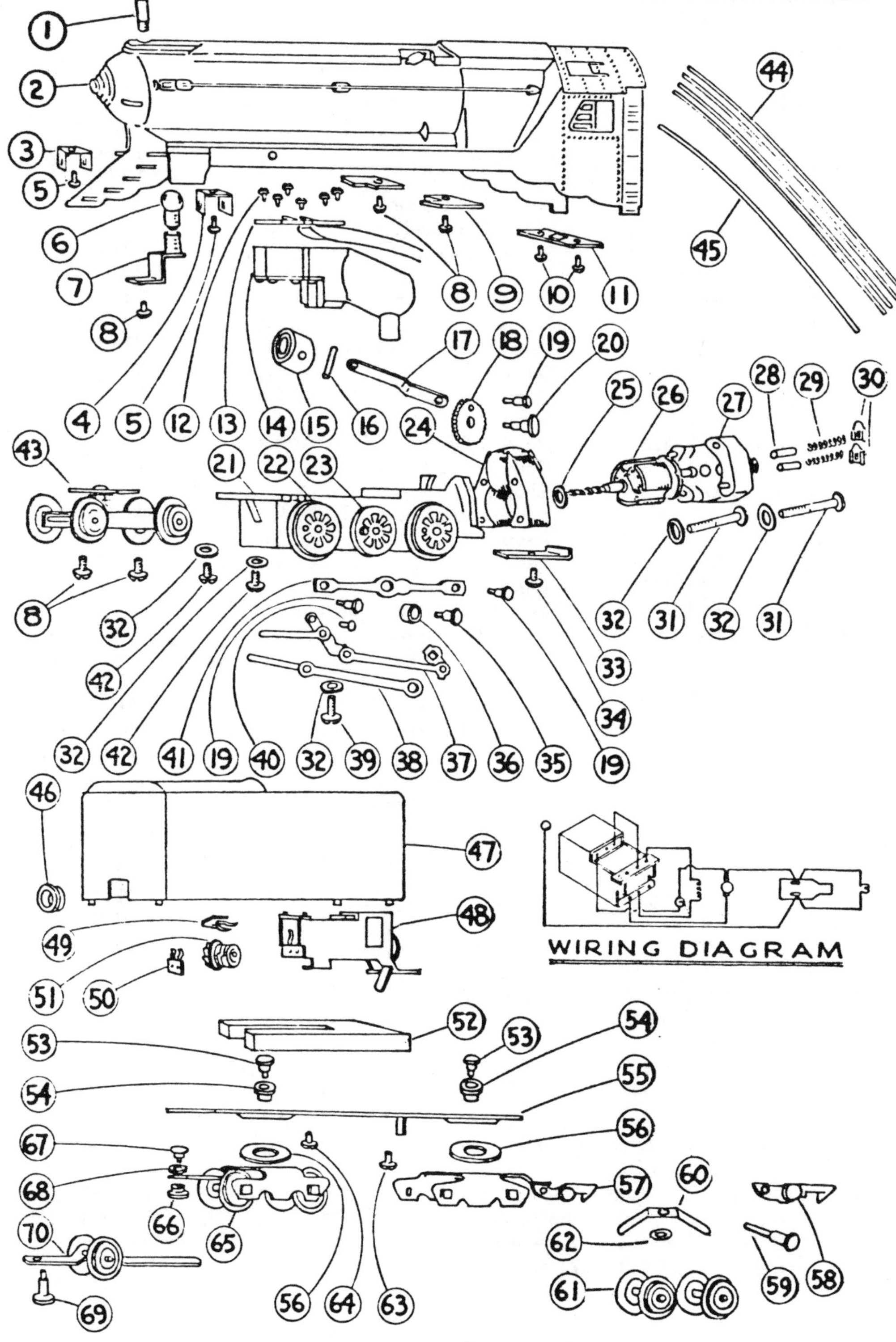

Ref: Form No. 1823; Feb. 1, 1957

Diagram Number	Part No.	Description	Price
1	PA12A190	Smoke Stack	$ .02 ea.
2	*XA9512-RP	Boiler Assembly	2.22 "
3	PA9595-AR	Piston Rod Guide................	.03 "
4	PA9595-AL	Piston Rod Guide................	.03 "
5	S230-B	Screw	.10 dz.
6	PA8999	Bulb	.25 "
7	XA10890	Lamp Bracket Assembly............	.28 "
8	S172	Screw	.10 dz.
9	PA9579-A	Rear Mounting Bracket............	.01 ea.
10	S171	Screw	.01 "
11	PA9578-A	Coupler Strap	.01 "
12	S183	Screw	.10 dz.
13	***XA10523	Heating Element & Plate Assembly...	.66 ea.
14	**PA10513	Chassis Smoke Box.......... NOT AVAILABLE	
	**XA10513	Chassis Smoke Box (consists of parts 12-13-14).. NOT AVAILABLE	
15	PA10518-A	Piston	.17 "
16	PA10520	Piston Pin	.05 "
17	PA10514	Piston Lever	.08 "
18	PA10671	Worm Gear (smoke drive)..........	.27 "
19	PA7421	Side Rod Screw.................	.30 dz.
20	PA10162	Worm Gear Stud.................	.05 ea.
21	XA10506	Chassis	1.33 ea.
22	XA10009	Flanged Wheel w/tapped hole......	.44 "
23	XA10009-B1	Flangeless Wheel w/stud..........	.45 "
24	XA9547	Magnet Assembly	1.11 "
25	PA10766	Armature Spacer	.05 dz.
26	XA11077	Armature Assembly	2.19 ea.
27	XA9565-A	Brush Bracket Assembly...........	.71 "
28	PA9603	Brush	.15 "
29	PA10757-A	Brush Spring	.05 "
30	PA10754	Brush Cap	.02 "
31	S295	Screw	.02 "
32	PA3769	Washer	.05 dz.
33	PA10017	Grease Pan	.04 ea.
34	S271	Screw	.10 dz.
35	PA5447	Screw	.30 "
36	PA7237	Spacer	.05 ea.
37	XA8996-R	Valve Link Assembly, right.........	.55 "
	XA8996-L	Valve Link Assembly, left..........	.55 "

All prices subject to change without notice.

***The XA10523 Heating Element and Plate Assy. is still available, and interchangeable with the new style PA13B894 Smoke Box. The new style XA14A208 Heating Element and Plate Assembly, priced at $.66 each, is used only on the new style PA13B894 Smoke Box.

 Ref: Form No. 1823; Feb. 1, 1957

Diagram Number	Part No.	Description	Price
38	XA8567-A	Connecting Rod Assembly..........	.33 "
39	S16-C	Screw	.11 dz.
40	PA5603	Rivet	.01 ea.
41	PA9280-C	Side Rod	.10 "
42	S14	Screw	.05 dz.
43	XA10490	Truck and Strap Assembly..........	.44 ea.
44	PA11652-D	4 Conductor Cable................	.17 "
45	PA10249-B	12" black lead wire..............	.02 "
46	PA4356	Rubber Grommet	.02 "
47	*XA9376-RP	Tender Body Assy. w/trimmings......	1.11 "
48	X10587-E	Remote Control Unit...............	1.32 "
49	XA9612-CRP	Top Finger Unit...................	.30 "
50	XA9612-BRP	Bottom Finger Unit................	.30 "
51	XA8716	Drum	.59 "
52	PA11A926	Tender Weight	.32 "
53	PA10235-A	Truck Rivet	.03 "
54	PA10209	Insulating Bushing	.02 "
55	PA9375-H	Tender Chassis	.23 "
56	PA8715-B	Washer	.05 dz.
57	XA11582	Rear Truck Assembly..............	.24 ea.
58	XA10469	Coupler & Weight Assem...........	.17 "
	PA10692	Coupler weight only..............	.05 "
59	PA10467	Coupler Pin	.10 "
60	PA10207	Contact Spring	.02 "
61	XA10238	Wheel and Axle Assem.............	.17 set
	PA10140	Metal Wheel	.15 ea.
	PA9990	Plastic Wheel	.05 "
	PA10238	Axle	.02 "
62	PA1405	Tin Washer	.05 dz.
63	S184	Screw	.10 "
64	S230-B	Screw	.10 "
65	XA11582-A	Front Truck Frame Assy. w/o wheels.	.24 ea.
66	PA1312	Bushing	.11 dz.
67	PA10751	Stud	.02 ea.
68	PA1067-A	Washer	.05 dz.
69	PA4939	Truck Stud	.05 ea.
70	XA10749	Coupler & Yoke Assy..............	.30 "
	PA10019-A	Rear Truck Wheel only............	.05 "

*Note: Parts so marked no longer metalized. ONLY AVAILABLE IN ALUMINUM FINISH, AS USED ON #354 LOCOMOTIVE AND TENDER.

**Parts so marked NOT AVAILABLE, substitute with:

Dia. 14	XA13B894RP	Smoke Box Assy. (new style)	$1.55 ea.
	PA13B894	Smoke Box (new style)	.59 "
	PA14A209	Separator (new style)	.01 "

Ref: Form No. 1823; Feb. 1, 1957

NO.	PART NO.	DESCRIPTION	PRICE
1	PA12A190	Smoke Stack	.03 ea.
2	XA9512-RP	Boiler Assembly NOT AVAILABLE	
		Substitute with XA9512-ARP Boiler (Aluminum Finish)	1.20 ea.
	PA10542	Headlight Lens	.02 ea.
3	PA9595-AR	Piston Rod Guide	.03 ea.
4	PA9595-AL	Piston Rod Guide	.03 ea.
5	S230-B	Screw	.01 ea.
6	PA8999	Bulb	.30 ea.
7	XA10890	Lamp Bracket Assembly	.22 ea.
8	S172	Screw	.02 ea.
9	PA9579-A	Rear Mounting Bracket	.01 ea.
10	S171	Screw	.01 ea.
11	PA9578-A	Coupler Strap	.01 ea.
12	S183	Screw	.01 ea.
13	XA10523	Heating Element & Plate Assy. NOT AVAILABLE	
		Substitute with XA14A208A Heating Elem. & P.Assy.	.91 ea.
14	XA10513	Smoke Box Assembly NOT AVAILABLE	
		Substitute with XA13B894-RP Smoke Box Assy.	2.13 ea.
	PA10513	Smoke Box NOT AVAILABLE	
		Substitute with PA13B894 Smoke Box	.76 ea.
	PA14A209	Separator	.02 ea.
15	PA10518-A	Piston	.24 ea.
16	PA10520	Piston Pin	.03 ea.
17	PA10514	Piston Lever	.14 ea.
18	PA10671	Worm Gear (Smoke Drive)	.32 ea.
19	PA7421	Side Rod Screw	.03 ea.
20	PA10162	Worm Gear Stud	.08 ea.
21	XA10506	Chassis NOT AVAILABLE	
		Substitute with PA10506-A Chassis w/bearing	1.78 ea.
	PA13A187	Bearing	.04 ea.
	PA15A226	Plain Axle	.05 ea.
	PA15A281	Worm Axle	.07 ea.
	PA10672	Worm Gear	.06 ea.
22	XA10009	Flanged Wheel w/tapped hole NOT AVAILABLE	
		Substitute with XA13A865 Flanged Wheel (Front)	.37 ea.
		XA13A864 Pul-Mor Wheel (Rear)	.80 ea.
23	XA10009-B1	Flangeless Wheel w/stud	.63 ea.
24	XA9547	Magnet Assembly	1.22 ea.
25	PA10766	Armature Spacer	.01 ea.
26	XA11077	Armature Assembly	3.39 ea.
27	XA9565-A	Brush Bracket Assembly	1.00 ea.
28	PA9603	Brush	.13 ea.
29	PA10757-A	Brush Spring	.06 ea.
30	PA10754	Brush Cap	.02 ea.
31	S295	Screw	.02 ea.
32	PA3769	Washer	.01 ea.
33	PA10017	Grease Pan	.07 ea.
34	S271	Screw	.02 ea.
35	PA5447	Screw	.04 ea.
36	PA7237	Spacer	.02 ea.
37	XA8996-R	Valve Link Assembly (Right)	.61 ea.
	XA8996-L	Valve Link Assembly (Left)	.61 ea.
38	XA8567-A	Connecting Rod Assembly	.36 ea.

Cont'd

NO.	PART NO.	DESCRIPTION	PRICE
39	S16-C	Screw	.12 doz.
40	PA5603	Rivet	.02 ea.
41	PA9280-A	Side Rod	.16 ea.
42	S14	Screw	.01 ea.
43	XA10490	Truck & Strap Assembly	.48 ea.
44	PA13A208-A	4 Conductor Cable	.04 ft.
45	LW-1B1	Black Lead Wire	.02 ft.
46	PA4356	Rubber Grommet	.02 ea.
47	XA9376-RP	Tender Body Assy.w/trimmings NOT AVAILABLE	
		Substitute with XA9376RP Tender Body (Aluminum Finish)	1.22 ea.
48	XA10587-E	Remote Control Unit	4.04 ea.
49	XA9612-CRP	Top Finger Unit	.33 ea.
50	XA9612-BRP	Bottom Finger Unit	.33 ea.
51	XA8716	Drum	.95 ea.
52	PA11A926	Tender Weight NOT AVAILABLE	
		Substitute with PA10593 Weight	.26 ea.
53	PA10235-A	Truck Rivet	.07 ea.
54	PA10209	Insulating Bushing	.02 ea.
55	PA9375-H	Tender Chassis	.25 ea.
56	PA8715-B	Washer	.02 ea.
57	XA11582	Rear Truck Assembly NOT AVAILABLE	
58	XA10469	Coupler & Weight Assembly NOT AVAILABLE	
	PA10692	Coupler Weight Only NOT AVAILABLE	
59	PA10467	Coupler Pin NOT AVAILABLE	
60	PA10207	Contact Spring	.02 ea.
61	XA10238	Wheel & Axle Assembly	.09 ea.
	PA10140	Metal Wheel	.06 ea.
	PA9990	Plastic Wheel	.03 ea.
	PA10238	Axle	.01 ea.
62		NOT USED	
63	S184	Screw	.02 ea.
64	S230-B	Screw	.01 ea.
65	XA11582-A	Front Truck Frame Assembly NOT AVAILABLE	
66 *	PA1312	Bushing	.12 doz.
67 *	PA10751	Stud	.02 ea.
68 *	PA1067-A	Washer	.06 doz.
69	PA4939	Truck Stud	.06 ea.
70 *	XA10749	Coupler & Yoke Assembly NOT AVAILABLE	

Link couplers and trucks not available, convert to Knuckle Couplers.

* Bubbles #66, 67, 68, & 70, not used when conversion to knuckle couplers is made.

Prices subject to change without notice.

NO.	PART NO.	DESCRIPTION	PRICE
1	PA12A190	Smoke Stack	.03 ea.
2	XA9512ARP	Boiler Assembly (Aluminum Finish) Substitute for XA9512RP	1.26 ea.
	PA10542	Headlight Lens	.02 ea.
3	PA9595-AR	Piston Rod Guide	.03 ea.
4	PA9595-AL	Piston Rod Guide	.03 ea.
5	S230-B	Screw	.01 ea.
6	PA8999	Bulb	.32 ea.
7	XA10890	Lamp Bracket Assembly	.23 ea.
8	S172	Screw	.02 ea.
9	PA9579-A	Rear Mounting Bracket	.01 ea.
10	S171	Screw	.01 ea.
11	PA9578-A	Coupler Strap	.01 ea.
12	S183	Screw	.01 ea.
13	XA14A208A	Heating Element & Plate Assy.	.96 ea.
14	XA13B894-RP	Smoke Box Assembly	2.24 ea.
15	PA10518-A	Piston	.30 ea.
16	PA10520	Piston Pin	.03 ea.
17	PA10514	Piston Lever	.15 ea.
18	PA10671	Worm Gear (Smoke Drive)	.34 ea.
19	PA7421	Side Rod Screw	.03 ea.
20	PA10162	Worm Gear Stud	.08 ea.
21	PA10506-A	Chassis	1.87 ea.
	PA13A187	Bearing	.04 ea.
	PA15A226	Plain Axle	.05 ea.
	PA15A281	Worm Axle	.07 ea.
	PA10672	Worm Gear	.06 ea.
22*	XA13A865	Flanged Wheel (Front) } Sub. for XA10009- OBSOLETE	.39 ea.
	XA13A864	Pul-Mor Wheel (Rear) }	.84 ea.
23	XA10009-B1	Flangeless Wheel w/stud	.66 ea.
24	XA9547	Magnet Assembly	1.28 ea.
25	PA10766	Armature Spacer	.01 ea.
26	XA11077	Armature Assembly	3.56 ea.
27	XA9565-A	Brush Bracket Assembly	1.05 ea.
28	PA9603	Brush	.14 ea.
29	PA10757-A	Brush Spring	.06 ea.
30	PA10754	Brush Cap	.02 ea.
31	S295	Screw	.02 ea.
32	PA3769	Washer	.01 ea.
33	PA10017	Grease Pan	.07 ea.
34	S271	Screw	.02 ea.
35	PA5447	Screw	.04 ea.
36	PA7237	Spacer	.02 ea.
37	XA8996 R & L	Valve Link Assy.(Right & Left)	.64 ea.
38	XA8567-A	Connecting Rod Assembly	.38 ea.
39	S16-C	Screw	.13 dz.
40	PA5603	Rivet	.02 ea.
41	PA9280-A	Side Rod	.17 ea.
42	S14	Screw	.01 ea.
43	XA10490	Truck & Strap Assembly	.50 ea.
44	PA13A208-A	4 Conductor Cable	.04 ft.
45	LW-1B1	Black Lead Wire	.02 ft.

Cont'd

 Ref: Form No. 1823; Oct. 1, 1962

NO.	PART NO.	DESCRIPTION	PRICE
46	PA4356	Rubber Grommet	.02 ea.
47	XA9276RP	Tender Body (Aluminum Finish) Substitute for Metalized Finish	1.28 ea.
48	XA10587-E	Remote Control Unit	4.24 ea.
49	XA9612-CRP	Top Finger Unit	.35 ea.
50	XA9612-BRP	Bottom Finger Unit	.35 ea.
51	XA8716	Drum	1.00 ea.
52	PA10593	Tender Weight	.27 ea.
53	PA10235-A	Truck Rivet	.07 ea.
54	PA10209	Insulating Bushing	.02 ea.
55	PA9375-H	Tender Chassis	.26 ea.
56	PA8715-B	Washer	.02 ea.
57	XA12A050-B	Rear Truck Assy. w/Knuckle Coupler Substitute for XA11582 - OBSOLETE	.83 ea.
58		Coupler & Weight Assembly - OBSOLETE Coupler Weight Only - OBSOLETE	
59		Coupler Pin - OBSOLETE	
60	PA10207	Contact Spring	.02 ea.
61	XA10238	Wheel & Axle Assembly	.09 ea.
	PA10140	Metal Wheel	.06 ea.
	PA9990	Plastic Wheel	.03 ea.
	PA10238	Axle	.01 ea.
62		NOT USED	
63	S184	Screw	.02 ea.
64	S230-B	Screw	.01 ea.
65	XA15B800	Front Truck Assembly Substitute for XA11582-A - OBSOLETE	.45 ea.
66	PA1312	Bushing	.13 dz.
67	PA10751	Stud	.02 ea.
68	PA1067-A	Washer	.06 dz.
69	PA4939	Truck Stud	.06 ea.
70	XA15A784	Draw Bar Used w/XA15B800 Truck Assy.	.23 ea.
	XA10891	Coupler & Yoke Assembly Used w/XA11582A Front Truck Assy.	.38 ea.

* #22 When using these wheels with Chassis PA10506 file off .025 from mounts above the front and rear wheels.

Prices subject to change without notice.

CIRCUS CARS AND WAGONS
Model No. 643

ASSEMBLY OF CIRCUS CARS AND WAGONS

Place the wooden block on the Circus Flat Car. Then insert the headed pins into the two holes in the block and through the holes in the chassis. The heads of the pins will act as stops to keep the cars from rolling off.

Next, place one of the Circus Wagons over the center of the wood block so the axles are between the heads of the two pins. Then place the remaining Circus Wagon and tractor on the car so the coupler pins are inserted in the coupler holes.

 Ref: Form No. M2833

TRACK CLEANING CAR
Model Nos. 648, 24533A/B

INSTRUCTIONS FOR USE OF TRACK CLEANING CAR

To obtain the best possible operation from your train set it is important that the track be clean and kept free from oil. The track cleaning or service car was designed to allow you to keep the tracks clean and bright with the least possible effort.

When the track is very dirty, best results will be obtained if the two front felt wipers are saturated with American Flyer No. 27 Track Cleaning Fluid, a safety fluid made expressly for cleaning all dirt, grime and oil from model railroad tracks. By wetting the front set of wipers they will tend to loosen the heavy dirt film on the track and allow the rear wipers to clean it off.

If the track has only an oil film no cleaning fluid is necessary as the wipers alone will clean the track.

When wipers become dirty or worn on one side, turn them slightly on their axle so a new surface will be in contact with the track.

24533 OPERATING TRACK CLEANING CAR

PART NO.	DESCRIPTION
	1961-62
XA16C084	TRUCK ASSEMBLY
P10A984-14	EYELET (FOR TRUCK ASSEMBLY)
XA10238-A	WHEEL AND AXLE ASSEMBLY
XA11573	SPRING AND CROSSBAR
PA11572	CLEANER (PAD)

* * * * * * * * * * * *

PART NO.	DESCRIPTION
	1960
XA12A051	TRUCK ASSEMBLY
XA12A047	KNUCKLE COUPLER
PA9988	RIVET
XA10238-A	WHEEL AND AXLE ASSEMBLY
XA11573	SPRING AND CROSSBAR
PA11572	CLEANER (PAD)

Ref: Form No. M2874

UNLOADING CARS
Model Nos. 714, 719

HOW TO HOOK UP AND OPERATE NO. 714 AND 719 UNLOADING CARS

First determine the location in your layout where you wish to unload the car. This should be along a straight section of track.

Then attach the No. 712 Special Rail Section as follows:

With the Locking Lever "A" facing left as shown by the dotted line in Fig. 1 insert the fiber base of the special rail section between the first and second ties on the desired section of straight track. See that the bottom portion of the outside rail rests underneath the raised part of the metal strip "B," then turn the Locking Lever "A" to the right as far as it will go, so it clamps over the bottom part of the inside rail. As shown in Fig. 1 there must be at least one section of straight track in front of the special rail section so that any rolling stock coming out of a curve will not overhang enough to cause interference.

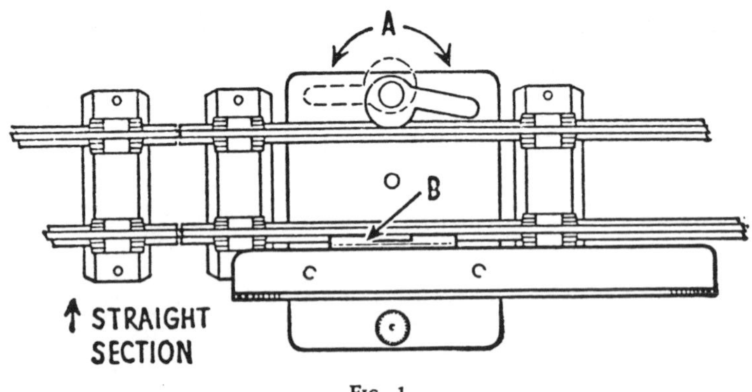

FIG. 1

Be sure BASE POST clip on track terminal supplying current to the track is hooked on to the OUTSIDE rail.

The No. 712 Special Pick-up Section should be fastened to the rail so the contact strip is running along side the rail which has the BASE POST current.

IF YOUR LAYOUT REQUIRES THE NO. 712 SPECIAL TRACK PICKUP SECTION TO BE LOCATED ON THE OPPOSITE SIDE OF THE TRACK, BE SURE YOU CHANGE THE WHEEL AND AXLE ASSEMBLIES IN THE ONE TRUCK SO THAT THE METAL WHEELS ARE ON THE RAIL WHICH HAS THE BASE POST CURRENT.

The car should be placed on the track so the small metal contact shoe which protrudes from one of the trucks, is on the same side as the special contact rail on the No. 712.

 Ref: Form No. 2847

DIRECTIONS FOR WIRING TO A TRANSFORMER:

Connect the transformer to the track terminal as described on the No. 690 Track Terminal envelope.

Connect the **TWO YELLOW** wires from the Control Box to the 15 Volt Post on the transformer.

Connect the **TWO BLACK** wires from the Control Box to the Terminal Post on the No. 712 Special Track Section. See Fig. 2.

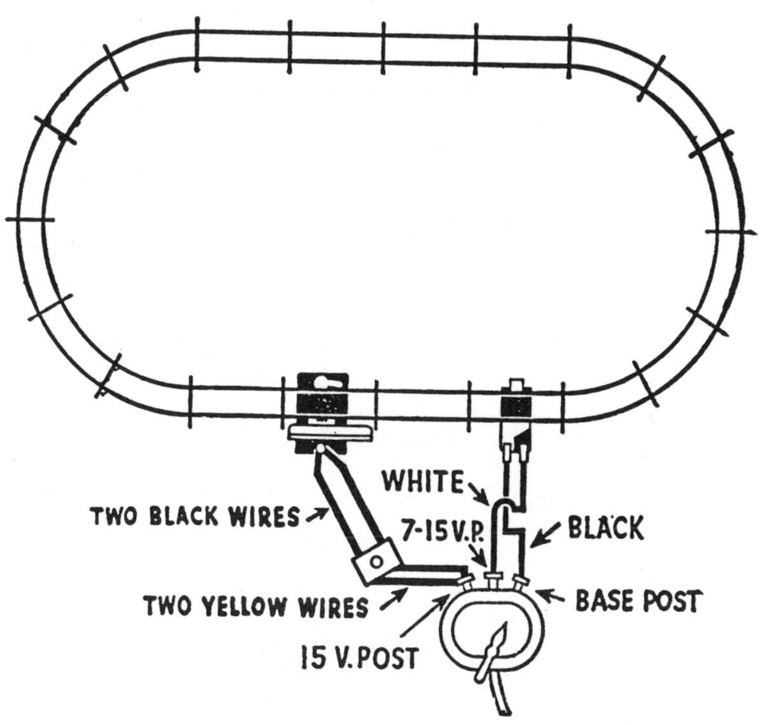

Fig. 2

DIRECTIONS FOR WIRING TO A NO. 14 ELECTRONIC RECTIFORMER:

Connect the two wires from the track terminal to the two posts on the Rectiformer marked "Direct Current for Trains."

Connect one of the **BLACK** wires from the Control Box to the Terminal Post on the No. 712 Special Track Section.

Connect the other **BLACK** wire to the Base Post clip on the track terminal.

Connect the two **YELLOW** wires to the two posts on the Rectiformer marked "Alternating Current for Accessories." See Fig. 3.

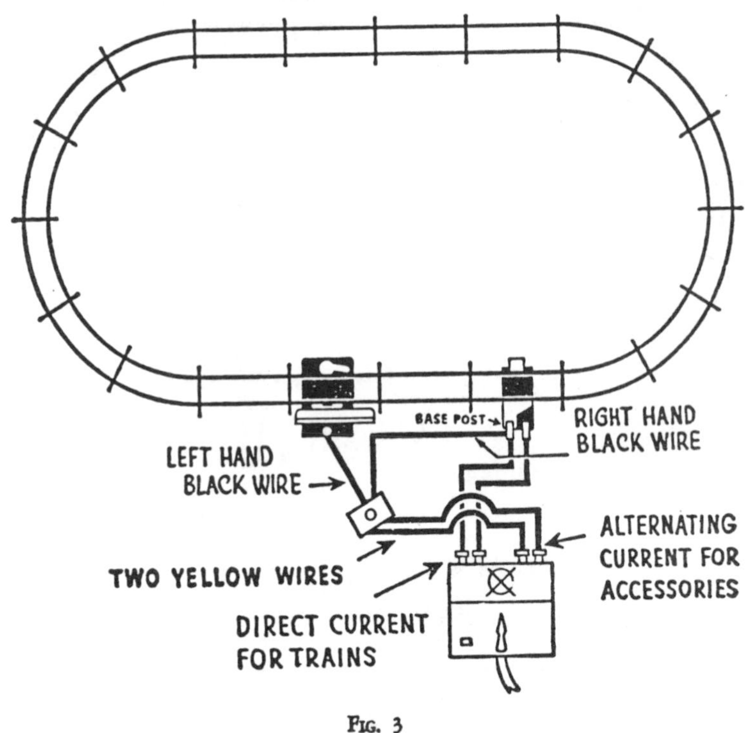

FIG. 3

DIRECTIONS FOR WIRING TO A NO. 15 RECTIFIER AND TRANSFORMER:

Study diagram 4 and proceed as follows:

Fasten the **RIGHT HAND BLACK** wire from the control box to the **BASE POST** clip on the **TRACK TERMINAL.**

Fasten the **RIGHT HAND YELLOW** wire to the **BASE POST** on the transformer.

Fasten the **LEFT HAND BLACK** wire to the terminal post on the special pick-up track section.

Fasten the **LEFT HAND YELLOW** wire to the **15 VOLT POST** on the transformer.

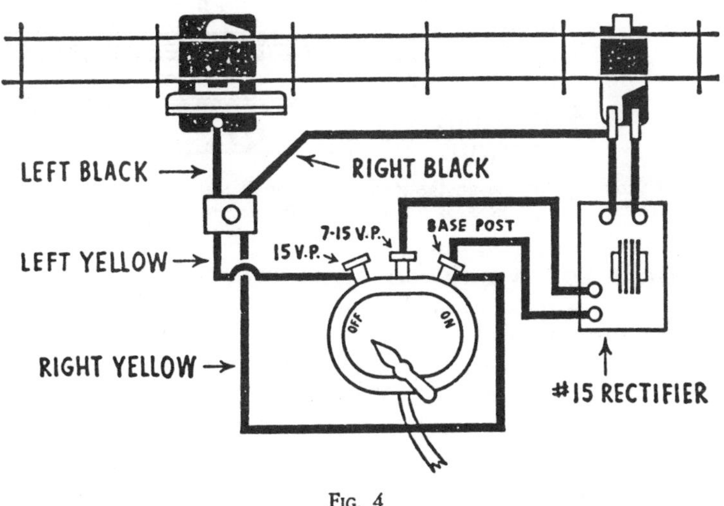

FIG. 4

When the train is operated and the automatic unloading car is to be used, stop the train so the small pick-up shoe protruding from one truck is resting on the metal strip on the special pick-up track section. Then by pushing the button on the control box the car will unload.

WHEN STOPPING THE TRAIN IT SHOULD BE DONE BY SHUTTING OFF THE CURRENT WITH THE TRANSFORMER HANDLE AND HANDLE SHOULD REMAIN TURNED OFF WHILE AUTOMATIC UNLOADING CAR IS DUMPING.

ARMY UNLOADING CAR
Model No. 715

HOW TO HOOK UP AND OPERATE

First determine the location in your layout where you wish to unload the car. This should be along a straight section of track.

Then attach the No. 712 Special Rail Section as follows:

With the Locking Lever "A" facing left as shown by the dotted line in Fig. 1, insert the fiber base of the special rail section between the first and second ties on the desired section of straight track. See that the bottom portion of the outside rail rests underneath the raised part of the metal strip "B," then turn the Locking Lever "A" to the right as far as it will go, so it clamps over the bottom part of the inside rail. As shown in Fig. 1 there must be at least one section of straight track in front of the special rail section so that any rolling stock coming out of a curve will not overhang enough to cause interference.

FIG. 1

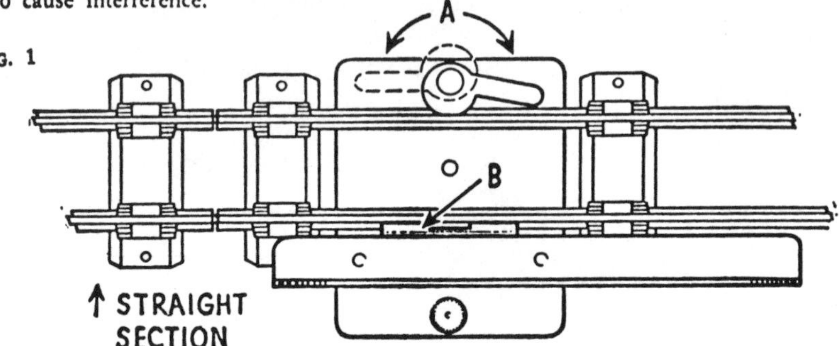

The car should be placed on the track so the small metal contact shoe which protrudes from one of the trucks, is on the same side as the special contact rail on the No. 712.

DIRECTIONS FOR WIRING TO A TRANSFORMER

Connect the wires from the transformer to the track terminal as described on the No. 690 Track Terminal envelope.

FIG. 2

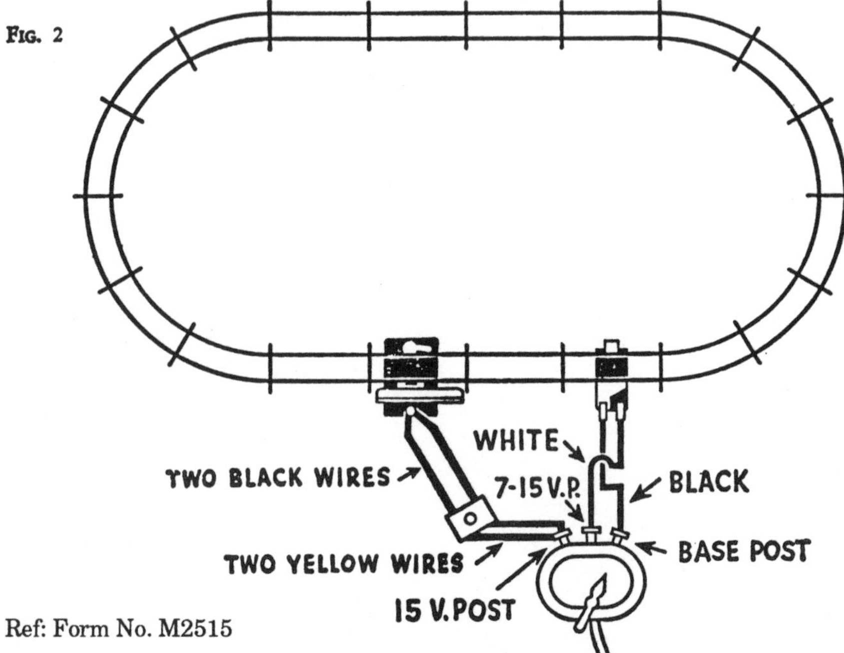

 Ref: Form No. M2515

Connect the **TWO YELLOW** wires from the Control Box to the 15 Volt Post on the transformer.

Connect the **TWO BLACK** wires from the Control Box to the Terminal Post on the No. 712 Special Track Section. See Fig. 2.

DIRECTIONS FOR WIRING TO A NO. 14 ELECTRONIC RECTIFORMER

Connect the two wires from the track terminal to the two posts on the Rectiformer marked "Direct Current for Trains."

Connect one of the **BLACK** wires from the Control Box to the Terminal Post on the No. 712 Special Track Section.

Connect the other **BLACK** wire to the Base Post clip on the track terminal.

Connect the two **YELLOW** wires to the two posts on the Rectiformer marked "Alternating Current for Accessories." See Fig. 3.

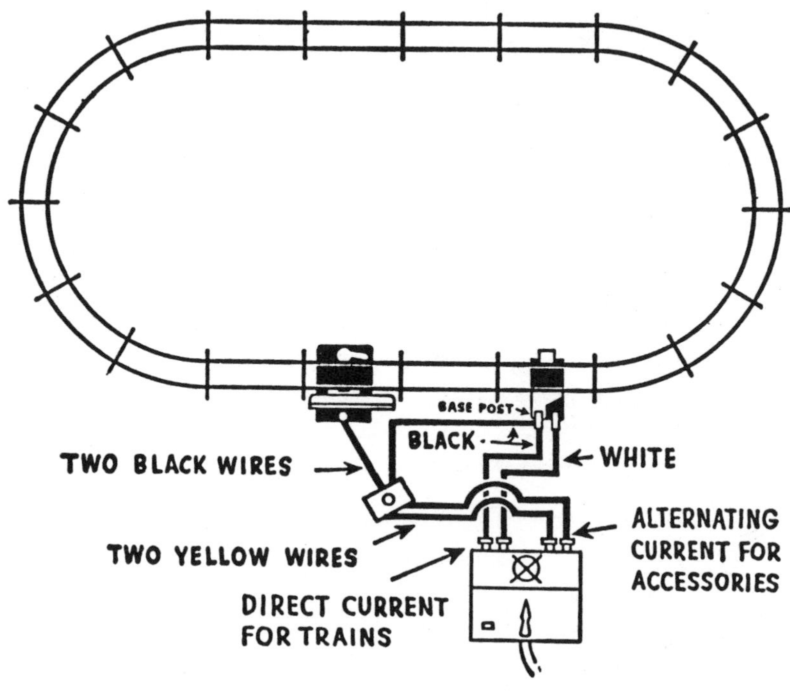

FIG. 3

Place the car on the track; place the tank on the car so that the rear axle fits into the two slots in the upright piece and the front wheels are over the long slot in the platform.

Run the train around the track, and stop it so that the contact shoe, which protrudes from the truck, is resting on the special contact rail. Press the Control Button until the platform swings out and the tank rolls off the car. Then release it and the platform will swing back into place automatically.

COAL DUMP CAR
Model No. 716

HOW TO HOOK UP AND OPERATE

First determine the location in your layout where you wish to dump the coal. This should be along a straight section of track.

Then attach the No. 712 Special Rail Section as follows:

With the Locking Lever "A" facing left as shown by the dotted line in Fig. 1, insert the fiber base of the special rail section between the first and second ties on the desired section of straight track. See that the bottom portion of the outside rail rests underneath the raised part of the metal strip "B," then turn the Locking Lever "A" to the right as far as it will go, so it clamps over the bottom part of the inside rail. As shown in Fig. 1 there must be at least one section of straight track in front of the special rail section so that any rolling stock coming out of a curve will not overhang enough to cause interference.

FIG. 1

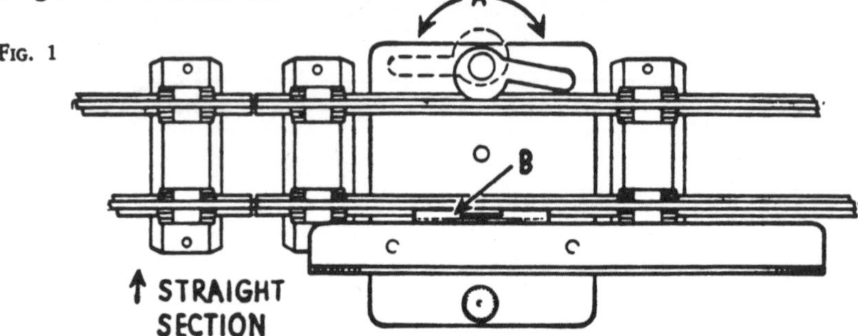

The car should be placed on the track so the small metal contact shoe which protrudes from one of the trucks, is on the same side as the special contact rail on the No. 712.

DIRECTIONS FOR WIRING TO A TRANSFORMER

Connect the transformer to the track terminal as described on the No. 690 Track Terminal envelope.

FIG. 2

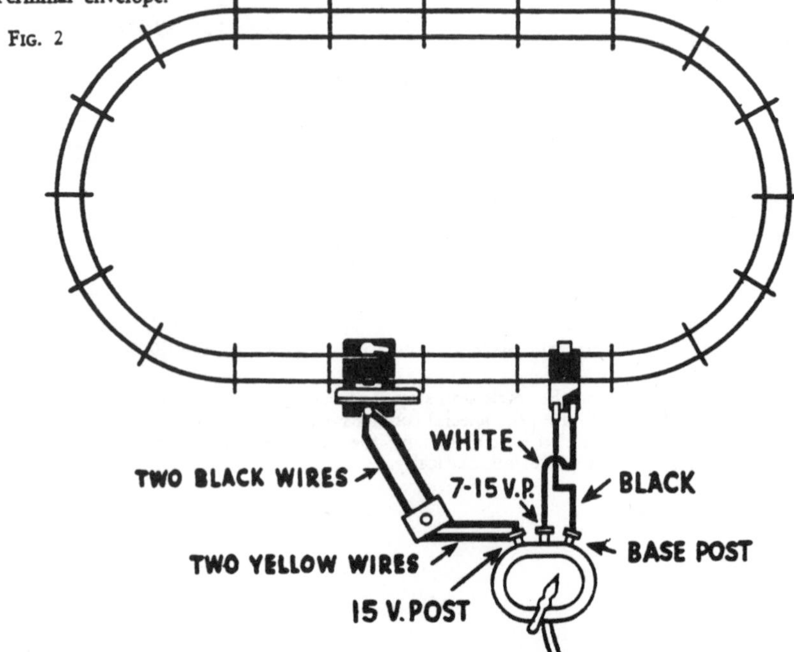

 Ref: Form No. M2516

Connect the **TWO YELLOW** wires from the Control Box to the 15 Volt Post on the transformer.

Connect the **TWO BLACK** wires from the Control Box to the Terminal Post on the No. 712 Special Track Section. See Fig. 2.

DIRECTIONS FOR WIRING TO A NO. 14 ELECTRONIC RECTIFORMER

Connect the two wires from the track terminal to the two posts on the Rectiformer marked "Direct Current for Trains."

Connect one of the **BLACK** wires from the Control Box to the Terminal Post on the No. 712 Special Track Section.

Connect the other **BLACK** wire to the Base Post clip on the track terminal.

Connect the two **YELLOW** wires to the two posts on the Rectiformer marked "Alternating Current for Accessories." See Fig. 3.

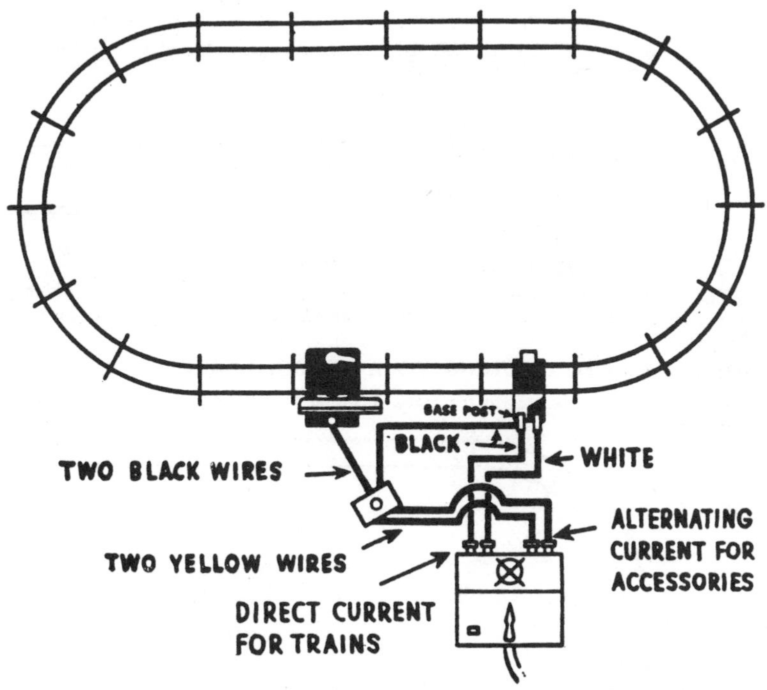

Fig. 3

Place the car on the track and place the tray opposite the special rail so it will be underneath the door of the car when it is stopped and making contact, and the coal will not spill out on the floor when the door is opened.

Place a small amount of coal in the car, run the train around the track stopping it so that the contact is on the special contact rail. Press the button and the door will open, allowing the coal to drop into the tray. Release the button and the door will close.

To add much more fun and realism to the train, the cars can be loaded by Remote Control by using the No. 732 Seaboard Coaler.

LOG UNLOADING CAR
Model No. 717

HOW TO HOOK UP AND OPERATE

First determine the location in your layout where you wish to unload the logs. This should be along a straight section of track.

Then attach the No. 712 Special Rail Section as follows:

With the Locking Lever "A" facing left as shown by the dotted line in Fig. 1, insert the fiber base of the special rail section between the first and second ties on the desired section of straight track. See that the bottom portion of the outside rail rests underneath the raised part of the metal strip "B," then turn the Locking Lever "A" to the right as far as it will go, so it clamps over the bottom part of the inside rail. As shown in Fig. 1 there must be at least one section of straight track in front of the special rail section so that any rolling stock coming out of a curve will not overhang enough to cause interference.

Fig. 1

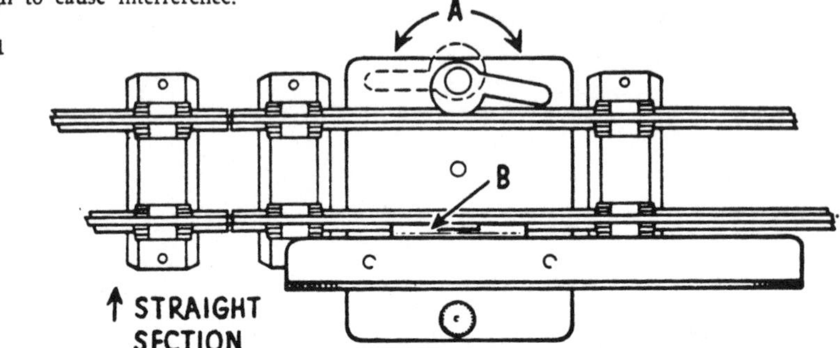

The car should be placed on the track so the small metal contact shoe which protrudes from one of the trucks, is on the same side as the special contact rail on the No. 712.

DIRECTIONS FOR WIRING TO A TRANSFORMER

Connect the transformer to the track terminal as described on the No. 690 Track Terminal envelope.

Fig. 2

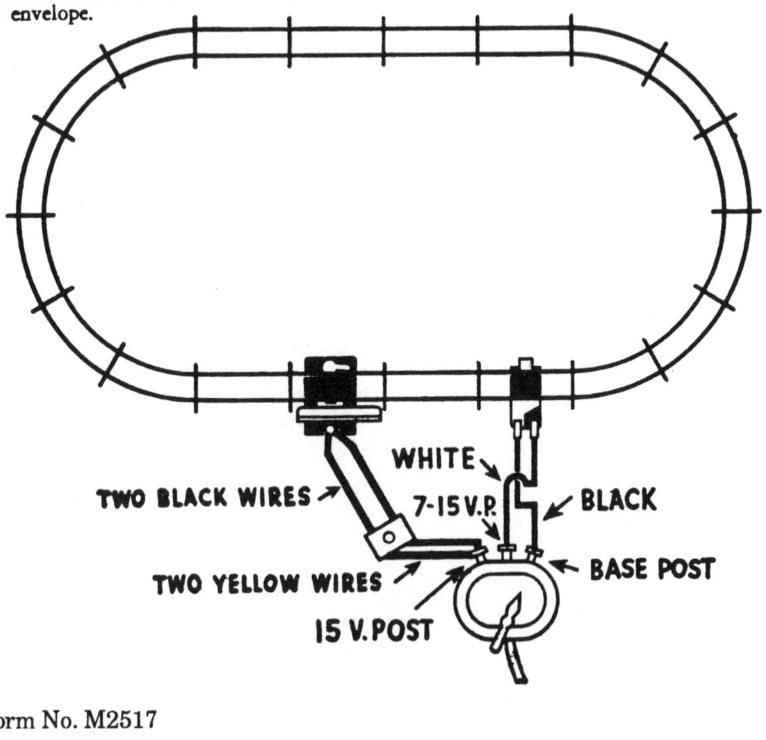

WHITE
TWO BLACK WIRES
7-15 V.P.
BLACK
BASE POST
TWO YELLOW WIRES
15 V. POST

Connect the **TWO YELLOW** wires from the Control Box to the 15 Volt Post on the transformer.

Connect the **TWO BLACK** wires from the Control Box to the Terminal Post on the No. 712 Special Track Section. See Fig. 2.

DIRECTIONS FOR WIRING TO A NO. 14 ELECTRONIC RECTIFORMER

Connect the two wires from the track terminal to the two posts on the Rectiformer marked "Direct Current for Trains."

Connect one of the **BLACK** wires from the Control Box to the Terminal Post on the No. 712 Special Track Section.

Connect the other **BLACK** wire to the Base Post clip on the track terminal.

Connect the two **YELLOW** wires to the two posts on the Rectiformer marked "Alternating Current for Accessories." See Fig. 3.

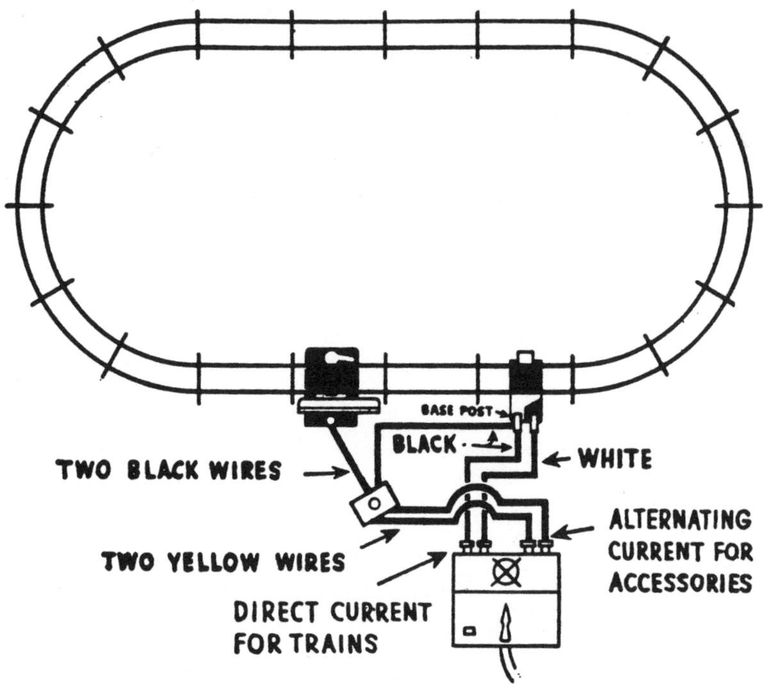

FIG. 3

Place the car on the track, place the three logs on top of it, then run the train around the track, stopping it so the contact shoe is resting on the special rail. Press the Control Button and the platform will tip, unloading the logs. Release the button and the platform will drop back in place.

One of the greatest play value pieces of train equipment is the No. 751 Log Loader which will load logs onto the above car by remote control, and the log car can also be used to dump the logs onto the log loader for reloading.

MAIL PICKUP CAR
Model No. 718

HOW TO HOOK UP AND OPERATE

First determine the location in your layout where you wish to pick up and unload the mail bags. This should be along a straight section.

Then attach the No. 713 Special Rail Section as follows:

With the Locking Lever "A" facing left as shown by the dotted line in Fig. 1, insert the fiber base of the special rail section between the first and second ties on the desired section of straight track. See that the bottom portion of the outside rail rests underneath the raised part of the metal strip "B," then turn the Locking Lever "A" to the right as far as it will go, so it clamps over the bottom part of the inside rail. As shown in Fig. 1 there must be at least one section of straight track in front of the special rail section so that any rolling stock coming out of a curve will not overhang enough to cause interference.

FIG. 1

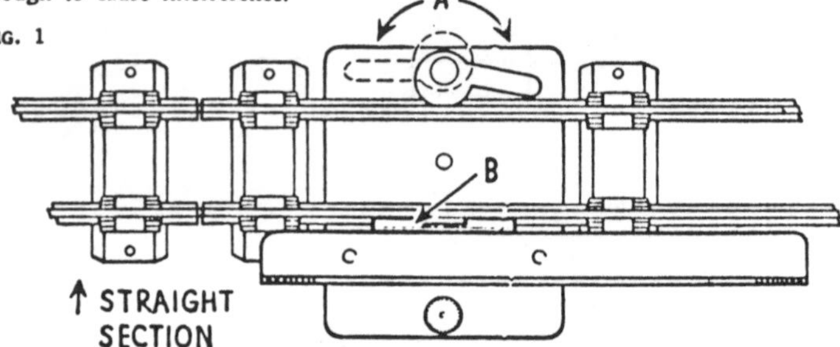

The car should be placed on the track so the small metal contact shoe which protrudes from one of the trucks, is on the same side as the special contact rail on the No. 713.

DIRECTIONS FOR WIRING TO A TRANSFORMER

Connect the transformer to the track terminal as described on the No. 690 Track Terminal envelope.

Connect the **LONG YELLOW** wire from the terminal post on the No. 713 Special Rail Section to a clip underneath the control box.

Connect the **SHORT YELLOW** wire from the other control box clip to the **15 VOLT POST** on the transformer.

DIRECTIONS FOR WIRING TO A NO. 14 RECTIFORMER

Follow above instructions, only hook the **SHORT YELLOW** wire to the "Alternating Current" post nearest the center of the Rectiformer.

Place the car on the track so that the opening and hook on the car are toward the front of the train, on the same side of the track as the special contact rail No. 713, and the train should be run in a forward direction. See Fig. 2.

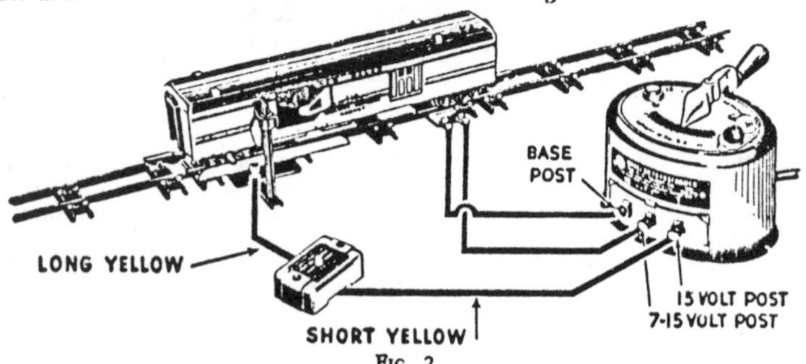

FIG. 2

Hang one of the mail bags on the standard, start the train and as it approaches the special track section, press the button and hold it down. When the mail car passes over the special track, the hook will swing out and pick up the mail bag.

After the car has passed, release the button. Hang the other mail bag on the standard and repeat the operation just mentioned, and the car will automatically pick up the mail bag and deliver the one it picked up on the first trip.

 Ref: Form No. M2518

OPERATING FREIGHT CARS

Model Nos. 732, 734

INSTRUCTIONS FOR OPERATING NO. 732 & NO. 734 CARS

The No. 732 and No. 734 operating cars are designed to be loaded either manually or by the No. 770 automatic loading platform, and the car will then be unloaded in a very realistic manner by just pushing a control button.

Current is supplied to the mechanism in the unit through the metal wheels on one truck and through the pick up finger on the other truck. The metal wheels pick up current from one of the rails and the finger picks up current fom the No. 712 special rail section.

To install, first determine the location in your layout where you wish the car to operate. This should be along a straight section of track.

Then attach the No. 712 Special Rail Section as follows:

With the Locking Lever "A" facing left as shown by the dotted line in Fig. 1, insert the fiber base of the special rail section between the first and second ties on the desired section of straight track. See that the bottom portion of the outside rail rests underneath the raised part of the metal strip "B", then turn the Locking Lever "A" to the right as far as it will go, so it clamps over the bottom part of the inside rail. As shown in Fig. 1 there must be at least one section of straight track in front of the special rail section so that any rolling stock coming out of a curve will not overhang enough to cause interference.

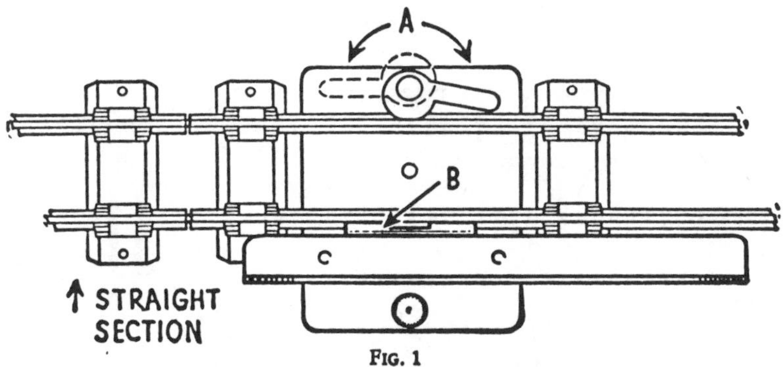

FIG. 1

The car should be placed on the track so the small metal contact shoe which protrudes from one of the trucks, is on the same side as the special contact rail on the No. 712.

IF YOUR LAYOUT REQUIRES THE NO. 712 SPECIAL TRACK PICKUP SECTION TO BE LOCATED ON THE OPPOSITE SIDE OF THE TRACK, BE SURE YOU CHANGE THE WHEEL AND AXLE ASSEMBLIES IN THE ONE TRUCK SO THAT THE METAL WHEELS ARE ON THE RAIL WHICH HAS THE BASE POST CURRENT.

DIRECTIONS FOR WIRING TO A TRANSFORMER

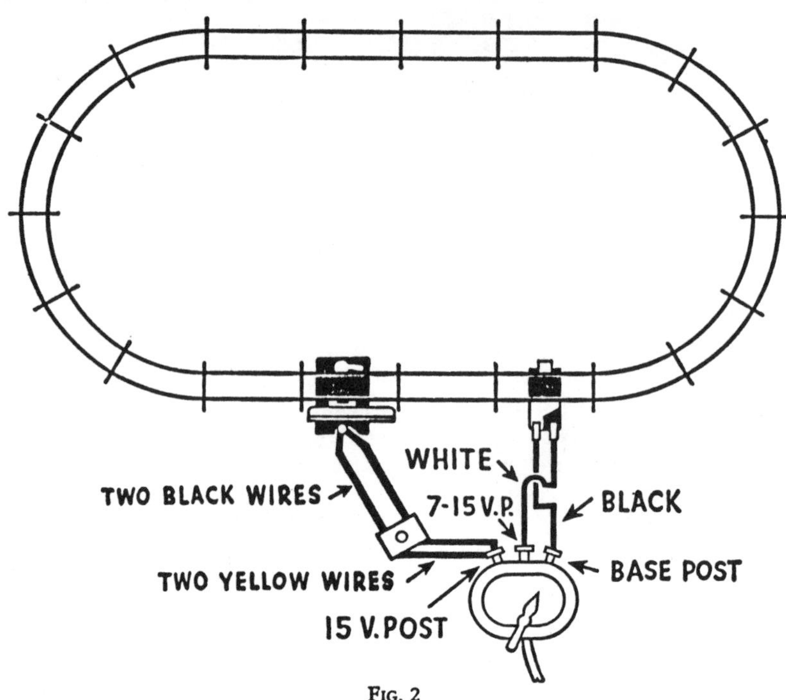

FIG. 2

Connect the **TWO YELLOW** wires from the Control Box to the 15 Volt Post on the transformer.

Connect the **TWO BLACK** wires from the Control Box to the Terminal Post on the No. 712 Special Track Section. See Fig. 2.

DIRECTIONS FOR WIRING TO A NO. 15 RECTIFIER AND TRANSFORMER

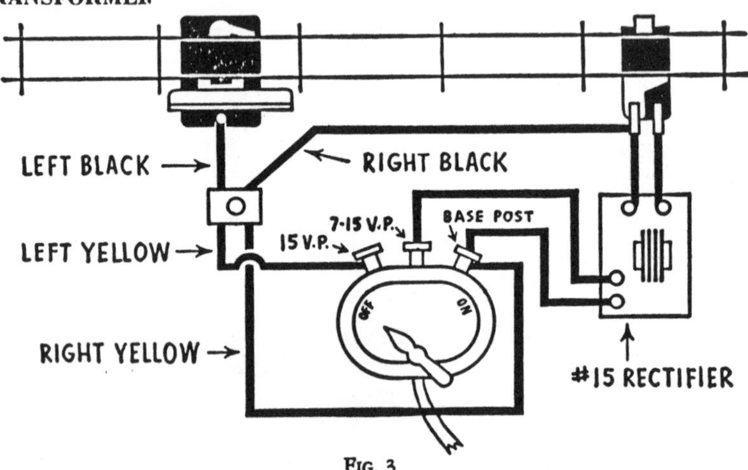

FIG. 3

Study the above diagram and proceed as follows:

Then fasten the **RIGHT HAND BLACK** wire from the control box to the **BASE POST** clip on the **TRACK TERMINAL.**

Fasten the **RIGHT HAND YELLOW** wire to the **BASE POST** on the transformer.

Fasten the **LEFT HAND BLACK** wire to the terminal post on the special pick-up track section.

Fasten the **LEFT HAND YELLOW** wire to the **15 VOLT POST** on the transformer.

DIRECTIONS FOR WIRING TO A NO. 14 OR NO. 16 ELECTRONIC RECTIFORMER

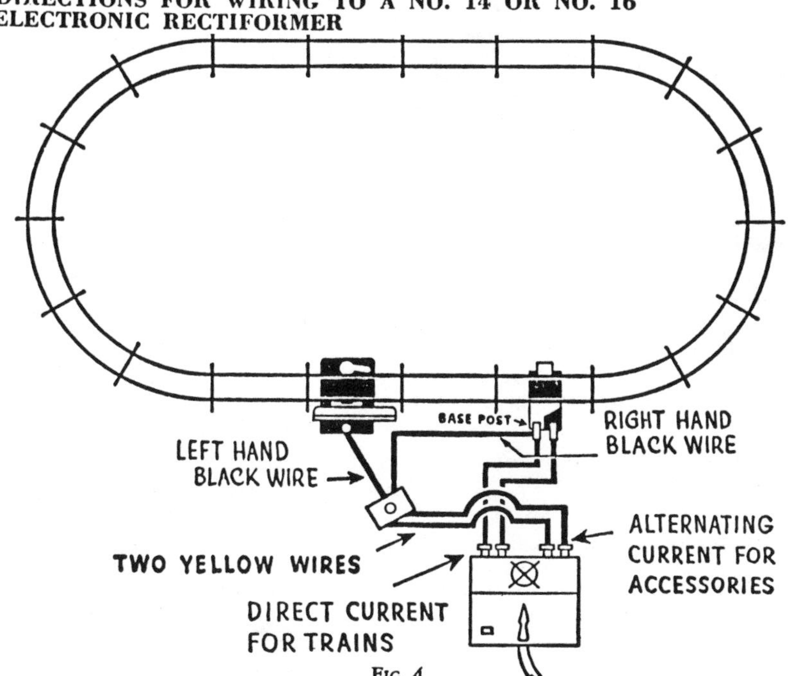

FIG. 4

Study the above diagram and proceed as follows:

Connect the two wires from the track terminal to the two posts on the Rectiformer marked "Direct Current for Trains".

Connect one of the **BLACK** wires from the Control Box to the Terminal Post on the No. 712 Special Track Section.

Connect the other **BLACK** wire to the Base Post clip on the track terminal.

Connect the two **YELLOW** wires to the two posts on the Rectiformer marked "Alternating Current for Accessories". See Fig. 4.

When the train is operated and the automatic unloading car is to be used, stop the train so the small pick-up shoe protruding from one truck is resting on the metal strip on the special pick-up track section. Then by pushing the button on the control box the car will unload.

WHEN STOPPING THE TRAIN IT SHOULD BE DONE BY SHUTTING OFF THE CURRENT WITH THE TRANSFORMER HANDLE AND HANDLES SHOULD REMAIN TURNED OFF WHILE AUTOMATIC UNLOADING CAR IS DUMPING.

The car can now be placed on the track and the small boxes of freight should be loaded onto the roller conveyor through the left hand door. They will then roll down the conveyor and be in position so the man in the car will throw them out of the right hand door when the car is stopped with the metal pick-up from the truck resting on the contact strip of the No. 712 special track section and the button is pushed.

To get the maximum amount of play value out of the unit, it should be loaded automatically using the No. 770 loading platform.

HAND CAR
Model No. 740

SERVICE INSTRUCTIONS

The first thing to do is to place car on track and test for operation.

1. To take off body assembly:

Remove the two S181 Screws (※25) and pry back lever on Link & Gear Assembly so that the Body Assembly (※1) can be taken off. To replace Figures (※2), remove S230 Screws (※4) and pry open slots holding the arms.

2. If trouble is in the motor we suggest that you check as follows:

a. Brushes (※9) for wear or poor contact.

b. Brush Springs (※7) for correct position and proper tension.

c. Check wires and solder joints for loose connections.

d. Make sure Contact Assembly (※13) does not have too much spring tension, as this will slow up operation.

e. See if wheels and other parts are properly lubricated and not binding in any way.

f. Wheels and track must be kept clean to insure proper electrical contact.

3. To disassemble and replace motor parts:

a. Brush Bracket Assembly (※10) and Brush Springs (※7) can be replaced without taking motor apart.

b. To change Contact Assembly (※13), unsolder lead wire and remove S183 Screw (※8).

c. When replacing Armature Assembly (※6) or Field Assembly (※5), the first step is to unsolder the lead wire of the field to the Brush Holder Assembly (※9). Take off tension on brush springs. Remove two S183 Screws (※8) and take off Brush Bracket Assembly (※10). Take off Link & Gear Assembly (※12) by removing S172 Screw (※11). Unscrew S165 Set Screw (※14).

d. To replace worn gear on motor, use a punch and drive out axle from the insulated wheel end and the gears will come right out.

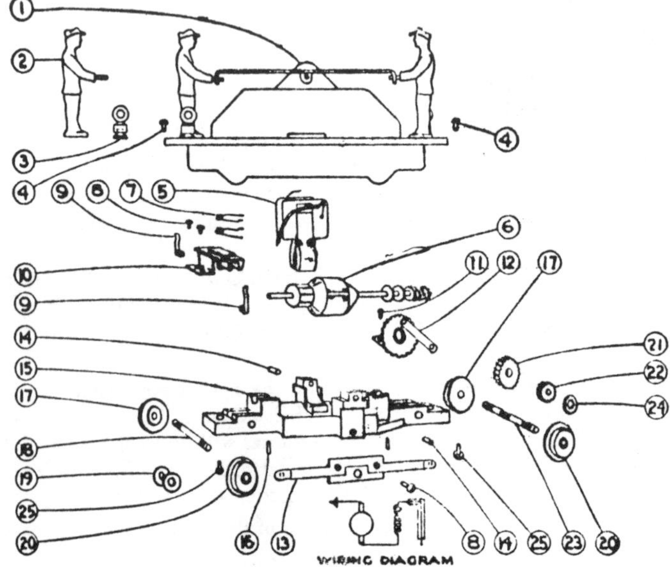

 Ref: Form No. 1453; Dec. 15, 1953

Diagram Number	Part No.	Description	Price
1	XA12N196-RP	Body Assembly Complete	$2.07 ea.
2	PA11610	Man	.25 "
3	PA12A217	Lantern	.06 "
4	S-230	Screw	.10 dz.
5	XA12A218	Field Assembly	1.00 ea.
6	XA12A213	Armature Assembly	2.50 "
7	P11000-L	Brush Spring (left)	.03 "
	P11000-R	Brush Spring (right)	.03 "
8	S-183	Screw	.10 dz.
9	XA11684	Brush Holder Assembly	.25 ea.
10	XA12A206-RP	Brush Bracket Assembly	.25 "
11	S-172	Screw	.10 dz.
12	XA12A202	Link & Gear Assembly	.20 ea.
13	XA12A200	Contact Assembly	.08 "
	XA12N197-RP	Chassis & Wheel Assembly (consists of parts 14 to 24 inclusive)	
14	S165	Set Screw	.02 "
15	PA12C197-A	Chassis	.84 "
16	PA11464	Oil Wick	.01 "
17	PA10140	Solid Wheel	.10 "
18	PA12A215	Plain Axle	.11 "
19	W67	Washer	.10 dz.
20	XA11656	Insulated Wheel	.10 ea.
21	PA12A212	Worm Gear	.40 "
22	PA12A208	Pinion	.03 "
23	PA12A209	Drive Axle	.12 "
24	P325-A	Fibre Lac Washer	.15 dz.
	XA12A211	Drive Wheel & Axle Assembly	
25	S-181	Screw	.01 ea.

Ref: Form No. 1453; Dec. 15, 1953

INSTRUCTIONS FOR OPERATING AND MAINTAINING THE NO. 740 HAND CAR

This No. 740 Hand Car is designed to be operated with 7 to 15 volts, AC or DC. The special-built motor will give many hours of trouble-free pleasure if lubricated properly and treated with ordinary care. To lubricate, study diagram below:

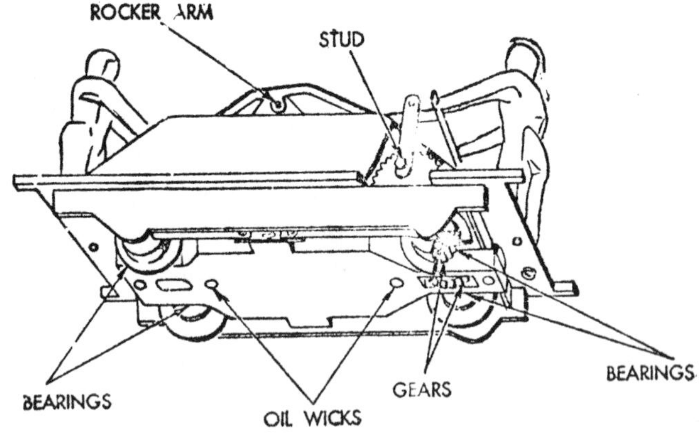

Proceed as follows.

Place a drop of oil at bearings where axles ride in the chassis.

One drop of oil on each oil wick, which lubricates the armature bearings.

A small amount of oil where rocker arm pivots on pin. (Both sides)

A drop of oil or some thin gear grease on both exposed gears.

With a tooth pick or small applicator, apply a little oil to the stud which holds the operating arm to the drive gear.

Care should be taken to keep wheels clear and free from oil at all times.

HAND CAR
Model No. 742

SERVICE INSTRUCTIONS

The first thing to do is to place car on track and test for operation.

1. **To take off Body Assembly (#1), Man (#2) and Rod and Plate Assembly (#23).**
   a. Remove two Screws (#4 and #27) and pry back lever on Link and Gear Assembly (#13) so that the body assembly can be taken off.
   b. To replace Man (#2) remove Screws (#4) and pry open slots holding the arms.
   c. To remove Rod and Plate Assembly (#23), it is necessary to pull Rod until the other end is free and keep plate with open side up and then lift up other end that is free and push from opposite end to remove.

2. **If trouble is in the motor we suggest that you check the following:**
   a. Brushes (#10) for wear or poor contact.
   b. Brush Springs (#8) for correct position and proper tension.
   c. Check wires and solder joints for loose connections.
   d. Make sure Contact Assembly (#21) does not have too much spring tension, as this will slow up operation.
   e. See if wheels and other parts are properly lubricated and not binding in any way.
   f. Wheels and track must be kept clean to insure proper electrical contact.

3. **To disassemble and replace motor parts as follows:**
   a. To change Contact Assembly (#21)
      1. Unsolder lead wire.
      2. Remove Screw (#30).
   b. To remove Brush Holder Assembly (#10) and Brush Springs (#8).
      1. Unsolder lead wire to Brush Holder.
      2. Take off tension on Brush Springs and replace.
   c. To replace Brush Bracket Assembly (#11)
      1. Remove two Screws (#9).
   d. To take off Link and Gear Assembly (#13).
      1. Remove Screw (#14) and take off part.
   e. To replace Switch (#16)
      1. Unsolder three lead wires.
      2. Take off Screw (#15).
   f. To change Field Assembly (#5) or Armature Assembly (#7).
      1. Follow steps A to E.
      2. Loosen Set Screws (#18) on each side of chassis holding Field In place.
   g. To replace Drive Gear (#29)
      1. Remove Screw (#30) holding Contact Assembly (#21) to chassis.
      2. Take off Insulated Wheel (#25).
      3. Drive out axle from the Insulated Wheel end and gears will come right off.

Ref: Form No. 1656; July 15, 1955

Hand Car — No. 742

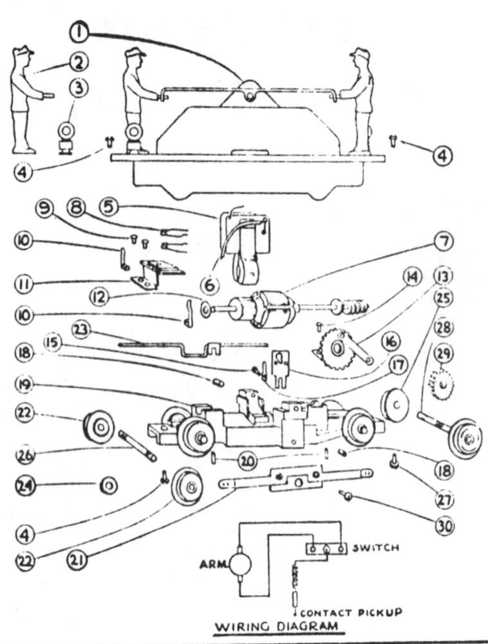

Diagram Number	Part No.	Description	Price
1	XA12C196ARP	Body Assembly	$1.40 ea.
2	PA11610	Man	.25 "
3	PA12A217	Lantern	.06 "
4	S230	Screw	.10 dz.
5	XA12A218	Field Assembly	1.00 ea.
6	PA10190-B	Yellow Sleeving	.10 dz.
7	XA12B213	Armature Assembly	2.45 ea.
8	P11000-R&L	Brush Spring	.03 "
9	S171	Screw	.01 "
10	XA11684	Brush Holder Assembly	.25 "
11	XA12A206 RP	Brush Bracket Support	.25 "
12	PA1067-A	Fibre Washer	.05 dz.
13	XA12A202	Link & Gear Assembly	.20 ea.
14	S172	Screw	.10 dz.
15	S98	Screw	.05 "
16	XA13A359	Switch Assembly	.33 ea.
17	PA13A352	Short Contact	.10 dz.
18	S165	Screw	.02 ea.
19	XA12C197BRP	Chassis & Wheel Assembly	1.86 "
20	PA11464	Oil Wick	.01 "
21	XA12A200	Contact Assembly	.08 "
22	PA10140	Solid Wheel	.15 "
23	XA13A356	Rod & Plate Assembly	.08 "
24	W79	Washer	.10 dz.
25	XA11656	Insulated Wheel Assembly	.10 ea.
26	PA12A215	Plain Axle	.11 "
27	S3A61	Screw	.01 "
28	XA12A211 RP	Drive Wheel & Axle Assembly	.43 "
29	PA12A212	Drive Gear	.40 "
30	S183	Screw	.10 dz.

 Ref: Form No. 1656; July 15, 1955

LOG UNLOADING CAR
Model Nos. 914, 25003

DUMP CAR
Model Nos. 919, 25025, 25060

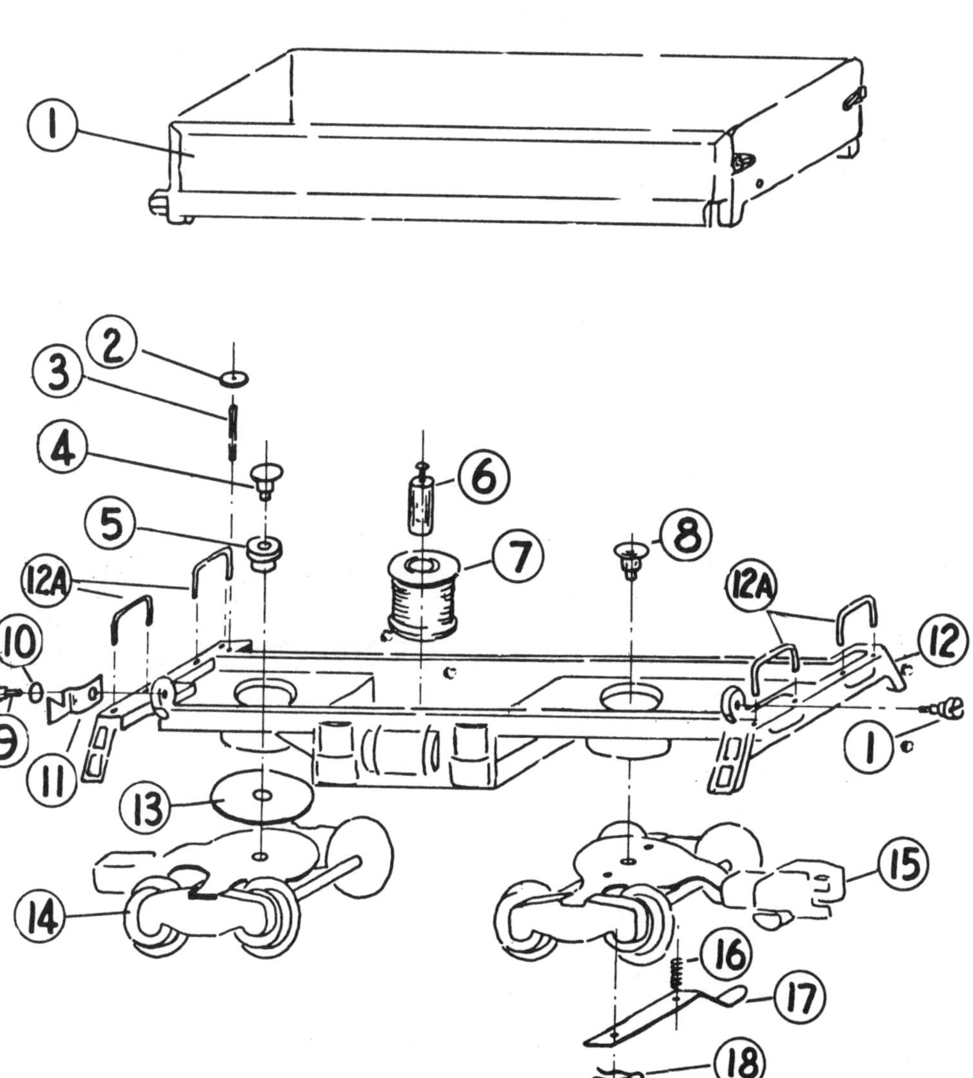

#914 AND #25003 LOG UNLOADING CAR

NO	PART NO	DESCRIPTION	PRICE
1		Body Not Available	
2	PA8963	Hand Wheel	.07 ea
3	PA10066	Hand Wheel Rod	.02 ea
4	PA9988	Tub.Rivet	.04 ea
5	PA10240	Bushing	.06 ea
6	XA11470	Plunger Assy	.09 ea
7	XA11465	Coil Assy	1.04 ea
8	PA10235	Tub Rivet	.03 ea
9	PA11431	Gear Support	.02 ea
10		NOT USED	
11		NOT USED	
12		CHASSIS NOT AVAILABLE	
13	PA8715B	Washer	.02 ea
14	XA12A050	Truck Assy	.74 ea
	XA12A047	Coupler Assembly	.30 ea
	XA10238A	Wheel & Axle Assy	.09 ea
	PA10238	Axle	.01 ea
	PA9991	Metal Wheel	.13 ea
	PA9990	Plastic Wheel	.03 ea
15	XA12A057	Truck Assembly	1.03 ea
	XA10238A	Wheel & Axle Assy	.09 ea
	PA9990	Plastic Wheel	.03 ea
	PA10238	Axle	.01 ea
16	P9275	Coil Spring	.02 ea
17	PA11A980	Contact Arm	.03 ea
18	PA11A944	Hair Pin Cotter	.01 ea
19		NOT USED	
20	XA14A964L	Single Control Box	.67 ea
21	XA12A038	Contact Rail Assy for std track	.54 ea
	XA30A158	Contact Rail Assy for Pikemaster truck	.45 ea
22	LW1B2	Yellow Wire	.02 ft
	PA13A777	Log (not shown)	.03 ea

#919 AND 25025 & 25060 DUMP CAR

SAME AS #914 & #25003 Log Unloading Car with these exceptions;

NO	PART NO	DESCRIPTION	PRICE
1	XA15A426RP	Body & door assembly	2.53 ea
10	W57	Washer	.01 ea
11	PA15A417	Catch	.04 ea
14	XA10238B	Wheel & Axle Assembly	.07 ea
19	PA15B390	Tray	.43 ea
20	XA14A964K	Single Control box	.67 ea
22	PA13A777	NOT LISTED	

PRICES SUBJECT TO CHANGE WITHOUT NOTICE

NO.	PART NO.	DESCRIPTION	PRICE
1	PA11425-B	Body (Aluminum only)	.49 ea.
2	PA8963	Hand Wheel	.07 ea.
3	PA10066	Hand Wheel Rod	.02 ea.
4	PA9988	Tub. Rivet	.04 ea.
5	PA10240	Bushing	.06 ea.
6	XA11470	Plunger Assembly	.09 ea.
7	XA11465	Coil Assembly	.99 ea.
8	PA10235	Tub. Rivet	.03 ea.
9	PA11431	Gear Support	.02 ea.
10		NOT USED	
11		NOT USED	
12	PA11436	Chassis	1.78 ea.
13	PA8715-B	Washer	.02 ea.
14	XA12A050	Truck Assembly	1.65 pr.
	XA12A047	Coupler Assembly	.29 ea.
	XA10238-A	Wheel & Axle Assembly	.08 ea.
	PA10238	Axle	.01 ea.
	PA9991	Metal Wheel	.12 ea.
	PA9990	Plastic Wheel	.03 ea.
15	XA12A057	Truck Assembly	.98 ea.
	XA10238-A	Wheel & Axle Assembly	.08 ea.
	PA9990	Plastic Wheel	.03 ea.
	PA10238	Axle	.01 ea.
16	P9275	Coil Spring	.02 ea.
17	PA11A980	Contact Arm	.03 ea.
18	PA11A944	Hair Pin Cotter	.01 ea.
19		NOT USED	
20	XA14A964-L	Single Control Box	.64 ea.
21	XA12A038	Contact Rail Assembly	.51 ea.
22	LW-1B2	Yellow Wire	.02 ft.
	PA13A777	Logs (not shown)	.03 ea.

Prices subject to change without notice.

NO.	PART NO.	DESCRIPTION	PRICE
1		Body Not Available	
2	PA8963	Hand Wheel	.07 ea.
3	PA10066	Hand Wheel Rod	.02 ea.
4	PA9988	Tub. Rivet	.04 ea.
5	PA10240	Bushing	.06 ea.
6	XA11470	Plunger Assembly	.09 ea.
7	XA11465	Coil Assembly	1.04 ea.
8	PA10235	Tub. Rivet	.03 ea.
9	PA11431	Gear Support	.02 ea.
10		NOT USED	
11		NOT USED	
12		Chassis Not Available	
13	PA8715-B	Washer	.02 ea.
14	XA12A050	Truck Assembly	.74 ea.
	XA12A047	Coupler Assembly	.30 ea.
	XA10238-A	Wheel & Axle Assembly	.09 ea.
	PA10238	Axle	.01 ea.
	PA9991	Metal Wheel	.13 ea.
	PA9990	Plastic Wheel	.03 ea.
15	XA12A057	Truck Assembly	1.03 ea.
	XA10238-A	Wheel & Axle Assembly	.09 ea.
	PA9990	Plastic Wheel	.03 ea.
	PA10238	Axle	.01 ea.
16	P9275	Coil Spring	.02 ea.
17	PA11A980	Contact Arm	.03 ea.
18	PA11A944	Hair Pin Cotter	.01 ea.
19		NOT USED	
20	XA14A964-L	Single Control Box	.67 ea.
21	XA12A038	Contact Rail Assembly For Standard Track	.54 ea.
	XA30A158	Contact Rail Assembly For Pike Master Track	.45 ea.
22	LW-1B2	Yellow Wire	.02 ft.
	PA13A777	Log (Not Shown)	.03 ea.

Prices subject to change without notice.

 Ref: Form No. M5232; Oct. 1, 1962

NO.	PART NO.	DESCRIPTION	PRICE
1	XA11437	Body (919) **NOT AVAILABLE** SUBSTITUTE WITH	
	XA15A426-RP	Body and Door Assembly (25025)	2.41 ea.
2	PA8963	Hand Wheel	.07 ea.
3	PA10066	Hand Wheel Rod	.02 ea.
4	PA9988	Tub. Rivet	.04 ea.
5	PA10240	Bushing	.06 ea.
6	XA11470	Plunger Assembly	.09 ea.
7	XA11465	Coil Assembly	.99 ea.
8	PA10235	Tub. Rivet	.03 ea.
9	PA11431	Gear Support	.02 ea.
10	W57	Washer	.01 ea.
11	PA15A417	Catch	.04 ea.
		Gear for #919 NOT AVAILABLE Sub. w/PA15A417	
12	PA11436	Chassis	1.78 ea.
13	PA8715B	Washer	.02 ea.
14	XA12A050	Truck Assembly	1.65 pr.
	XA12A047	Coupler Assembly	.29 ea.
	XA10238-B	Wheel & Axle Assembly	.07 ea.
	PA10238	Axle	.01 ea.
	PA9991	Metal Wheel	.12 ea.
	PA9990	Plastic Wheel	.03 ea.
15	XA12A057	Truck Assembly	.98 ea.
	XA10238-A	Wheel & Axle Assembly	.08 ea.
	PA9990	Plastic Wheel	.03 ea.
	PA10238	Axle	.01 ea.
16	P9275	Coil Spring	.02 ea.
17	PA11A980	Contact Arm	.03 ea.
18	PA11A944	Hair Pin Cotter	.01 ea.
19	PA15B390	Tray	.41 ea.
20	XA14A964-K	Single Control Box	.64 ea.
21	XA12A038	Contact Rail Assembly	.51 ea.
22	LW-1B2	Wire Yellow	.02 ft.

Prices subject to change without notice.

NO.	PART NO.	DESCRIPTION	PRICE
1	XA15A426-RP	Body and Door Assembly	2.53 ea.
2	PA8963	Hand Wheel	.07 ea.
3	PA10066	Hand Wheel Rod	.02 ea.
4	PA9988	Tub. Rivet	.04 ea.
5	PA10240	Bushing	.06 ea.
6	XA11470	Plunger Assembly	.09 ea.
7	XA11465	Coil Assembly	1.04 ea.
8	PA10235	Tub. Rivet	.03 ea.
9	PA11431	Gear Support	.02 ea.
10	W57	Washer	.01 ea.
11	PA15A417	Catch	.04 ea.
		Gear for #919 NOT AVAILABLE sub. w/PA15A417	
12		Chassis Not Available	
13	PA8715B	Washer	.02 ea.
14	XA12A050	Truck Assembly	.74 ea.
	XA12A047	Coupler Assembly	.30 ea.
	XA10238-B	Wheel & Axle Assembly	.07 ea.
	PA10238	Axle	.01 ea.
	PA9991	Metal Wheel	.13 ea.
	PA9990	Plastic Wheel	.03 ea.
15	XA12A057	Truck Assembly	1.03 ea.
	XA10238-A	Wheel & Axle Assembly	.09 ea.
	PA9990	Plastic Wheel	.03 ea.
	PA10238	Axle	.01 ea.
16	P9275	Coil Spring	.02 ea.
17	PA11A980	Contact Arm	.03 ea.
18	PA11A944	Hair Pin Cotter	.01 ea.
19	PA15B390	Tray	.43 ea.
20	XA14A964-K	Single Control Box	.67 ea.
21	XA12A038	Contact Rail Assembly For Standard S Gauge Track	.54 ea.
	XA30A158	Contact Rail Assembly For Pike Master Track	.45 ea.
22	LW-1B2	Wire Yellow	.02 ft.

Prices subject to change without notice.

 Ref: Form No. M5232; Oct. 1, 1962

BRAKEMAN CAR

Model Nos. 970, 25013, 25049

SERVICE INSTRUCTIONS

The first thing to do is to place locomotive on track, connect transformer and test for operation.

When the Car does not operate properly proceed as follows:

a. Make sure Wheel and Axle Assemblies are placed correctly in the truck ass'y and clean metal wheels to insure a good electrical contact.

b. Check position of Man to make sure it is not binding in any way.

TO CHECK AND REPLACE THE FOLLOWING PARTS:

1. **Body (#2) and Platform (#5)**
   a Slip the Man (#1) off pin.
   b. Remove four Pins (#15) separating chassis ass'y from Car Body (#2).
   c. Take off Platform (#5) by straightening lugs from bottom of chassis separating parts.
   The Vibrating Mat (#3) can be replaced at this point by straightening lugs and removing part from Platform (#5).

2. **Magnet Coil Ass'y (#7)**
   a. Follow steps a to c of #1.
   b. Take off Rod (#10) and Adjusting Screw (#9); unsoldering lead wires.

3. **Truck Ass'y (#17)**
   a. Follow steps a to c of #1.
   b. Remove Rivet (#13) separating parts.

4. **Knuckle Coupler (#17)**
   a. Use a long nosed plier or similar instrument and pry back the two lugs on the bracket of the truck to remove broken or defective coupler.
   b. Insert new part and bend lugs back into position holding new part secure.
   c. Adjust new coupler by placing car on the track, close the knuckle, so that the weight is all the way down, whichever is necessary to bring the bottom surface of the weight about 1/32" above the top of the rails.

Brakeman Car — Nos. 970, 25013, 25049

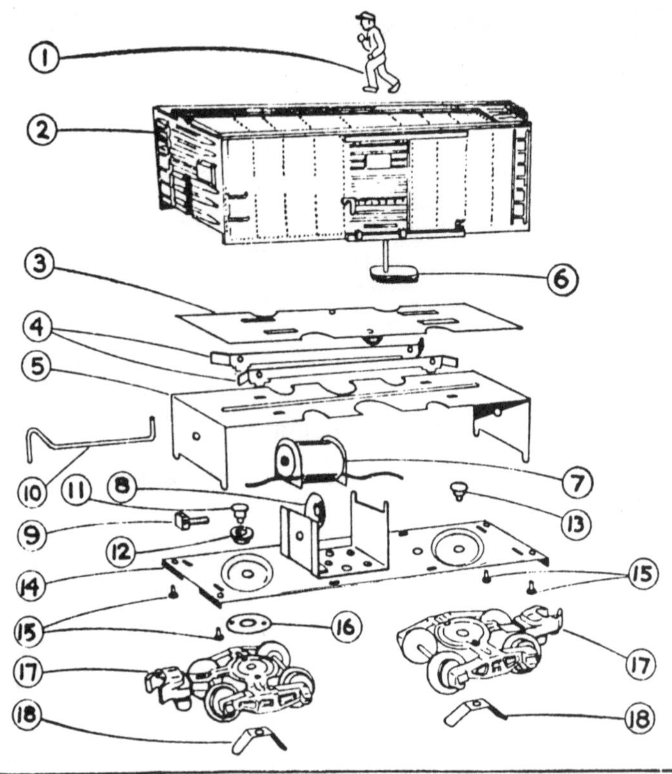

Diagram Number	Part No.	Description	Price
1.	PA13A445	Walking Brakeman	.88 ea.
2.	XA10C877-CRP	Box Car Body	1.78 ea.
3.	XA13A443-RP	Vibrating Mat	.37 ea.
4.	PA13A444	Guide Rail	.02 ea.
5.	PA13B442	Platform	.10 ea.
6.	XA13A446-RP	Nap Base	.25 ea.
7.	XA13A436	Magnet Coil Assy.	1.54 ea.
8.	W153	Spring Washer	.04 ea.
9.	S3A62	Adjusting Screw	.17 ea.
10.	PA13A736	Adjusting Rod	.01 ea.
11.	PA10235	Rivet	.03 ea.
12.	PA10209	Bushing	.02 ea.
13.	PA9381	Rivet	.02 ea.
14.	XA13B439-RP	Chassis	.38 ea.
15.	PA10456	Chassis Pin	.24 dz.
16.	PA8715-BX	Fibre Washer	.01 ea.
17.	XA12A050-A	Truck Assy.	.65 ea.
18.	PA10207	Contact Spring	.02 ea.

PRICES--VOID

All prices subject to change without notice.

 Ref: Form No. 1769; Oct. 1, 1956

NO.	PART NO.	DESCRIPTION	PRICE
1	PA13A445	Walking Brakeman	.48 ea.
2	XA9A966-ACB-RP	Box Car Body (White Only)	2.31 ea.
3	XA13A443-RP	Vibrating Mat	.41 ea.
4	PA13A444	Guide Rail	.02 ea.
5	PA13B442	Platform	.11 ea.
6	XA13A446-RP	Nap Base	.28 ea.
7	XA13A436	Magnet Coil Assembly	1.69 ea.
8	W153	Spring Washer	.04 ea.
9	S3A62	Adjusting Screw	.19 ea.
10	PA13A736	Adjusting Rod	.01 ea.
11	PA10235	Rivet	.03 ea.
12	PA10209	Bushing	.02 ea.
13	PA9381	Rivet	.02 ea.
14	XA13B439-RP	Chassis	.42 ea.
15	PA10456	Chassis Pin	.26 dz.
16	PA8715-BX	Fibre Washer	.01 ea.
17	XA12A050-A	Truck Assembly	.79 ea.
	XA10238-A	Wheel and Axle Assembly	.08 ea.
18	PA10207	Contact Spring	.02 ea.

Ref: Form No. 1769; June 1, 1960

1	PA13A445	Walking Brakeman	.50 ea.
2		Box Car Body Not Available	
3	XA13A443-RP	Vibrating Mat	.43 ea.
4		Guide Rail Not Available	
5		Platform Not Available	
6	XA13A446-RP	Nap Base	.29 ea.
7	XA13A436	Magnet Coil Assembly	1.77 ea.
8	W153	Spring Washer	.04 ea.
9	S3A62	Adjusting Screw	.20 ea.
10	PA13A736	Adjusting Rod	.01 ea.
11	PA10235	Rivet	.03 ea.
12	PA10209	Bushing	.02 ea.
13	PA9381	Rivet	.02 ea.
14		Chassis Not Available	
15	PA10456	Chassis Pin	.27 dz.
16	PA8715-BX	Fibre Washer	.01 ea.
17	XA12A050-A	Truck Assembly	.83 ea.
	XA10238-A	Wheel and Axle Assembly	.08 ea.
18	PA10207	Contact Spring	.02 ea.

Prices subject to change without notice.

Ref: Form No. 1769; Oct. 1962

LUMBER UNLOADING CAR

Model Nos. 971, 25016, 25058

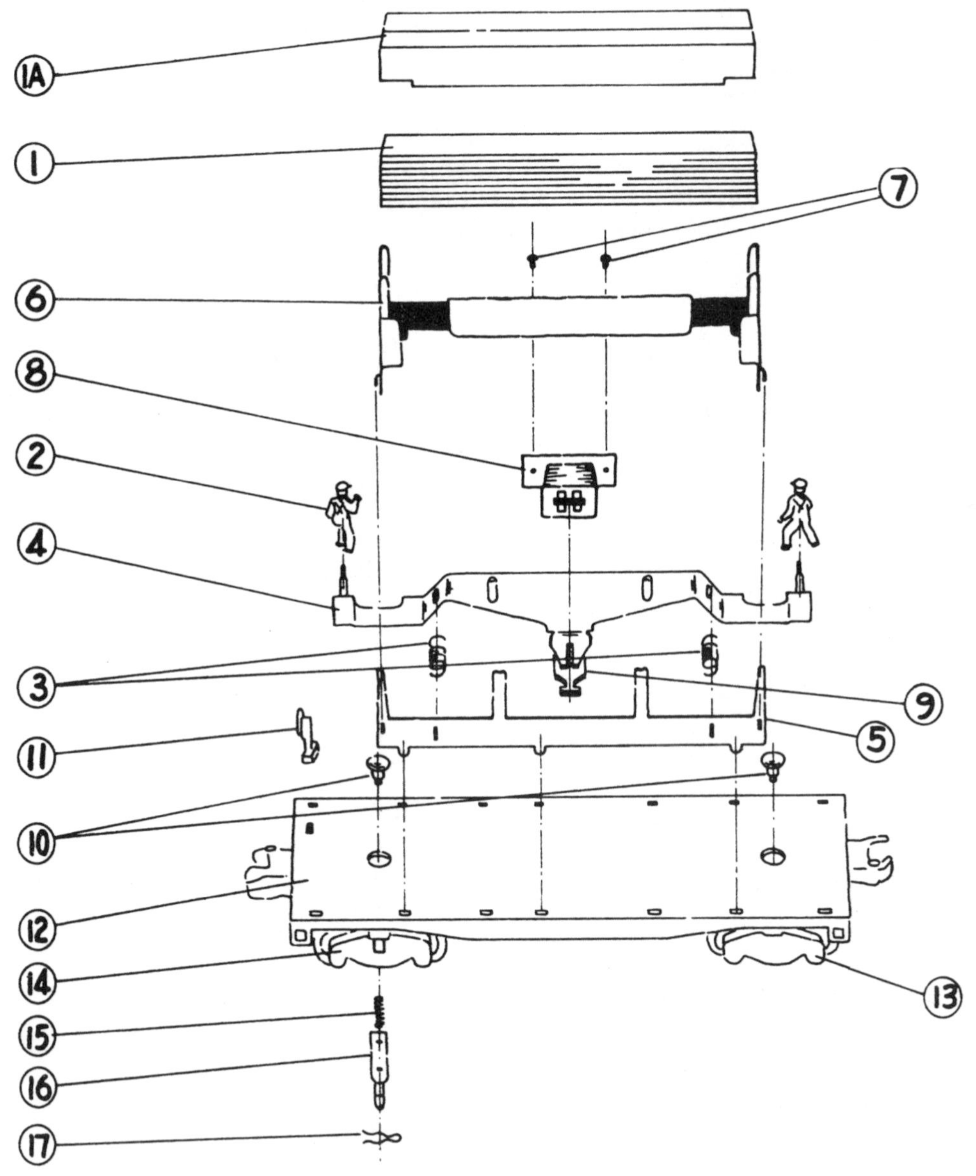

 Ref: Form No. M5233; June 1, 1960

NO.	PART NO.	DESCRIPTION	PRICE
1	PA13A849	Lumber	.07 ea.
1A	PA13A928	Lumber Pile	.29 ea.
2	PA13A445	Walking Brakeman	.48 ea.
3	PA13A845	Extension Spring	.14 ea.
4	PA13B844	Slide	.22 ea.
5	PA13A848	Platform Side	.20 ea.
6	PA13B847	Platform	.42 ea.
7	PA14N779	Eyelet	.02 dz.
8	XA13B840	Coil Assembly	.80 ea.
9	PA13A843	Core	.05 ea.
10	PA9988	Rivet	.04 ea.
11	PA14A408	Brake Wheel	.02 ea.
12	PA15A275-CBA	Flat Car Body	.65 ea.
13	XA12A050-A	Truck Assembly	.79 ea.
	XA12A047	Coupler Assembly	.29 ea.
	XA10238	Wheel and Axle Assembly	.09 ea.
	PA10140	Brass Wheel	.06 ea.
	PA9990	Plastic Wheel	.03 ea.
14	XA12A057	Truck Assembly	.98 ea.
	XA10238-A	Wheel & Axle Assembly	.08 ea.
	PA9990	Plastic Wheel	.03 ea.
	PA10238	Axle	.01 ea.
15	P9275	Coil Spring	.02 ea.
16	PA11A980	Contact Arm	.03 ea.
17	PA11A944	Hair Pin Cotter	.01 ea.
18	XA14A964-C	Single Control Box	.64 ea.
19	XA12A038	Contact Rail Assembly	.51 ea.
20	LW-1B2	Wire Yellow	.02 ft.

Prices subject to change without notice.

NO.	PART NO.	DESCRIPTION	PRICE
1	PA13A849	Lumber	.07 ea.
1A	PA13A928	Lumber Pile	.30 ea.
2	PA13A445	Walking Brakeman	.50 ea.
3	PA13A845	Extension Spring	.15 ea.
4	PA13B844	Slide	.23 ea.
5	PA13A848	Platform Side	.01 ea.
6	PA13B847	Platform	.44 ea.
7	PA14N779	Eyelet	.02 dz.
8	XA13B840	Coil Assembly	.84 ea.
9	PA13A843	Core	.05 ea.
10	PA9988	Rivet - 971, 25016 Trucks	.04 ea.
11	PA14A408	Brake Wheel	.02 ea.
12	PA15A275-CBA	Flat Car Body	.68 ea.
13	XA12A050	Truck Assembly (971 and 25016 ONLY)	.74 ea.
	* XA16A384	Truck Assembly (25058)	.84 ea.
	XA12A047	Coupler Assembly for XA12A050 ONLY	.30 ea.
	XA10238-B	Wheel and Axle Assembly	.07 ea.
	PA9991	Metal Wheel	.13 ea.
	PA9990	Plastic Wheel	.03 ea.
14	XA12A057	Truck & Wheel Assy. (971 & 25016 ONLY)	1.03 ea.
	* XA16B383	Truck Assembly (25058)	1.09 ea.
	PA16A387	Contact Spring (25058)	.05 ea.
	XA10238-A	Wheel & Axle Assembly	.08 ea.
	PA9990	Plastic Wheel	.03 ea.
	PA10238	Axle	.01 ea.
15	P9275	Coil Spring (971 & 25016 ONLY)	.02 ea.
	PA16A388	Contact Spring (25058)	.03 ea.
16	PA11A980	Contact Arm. (971 & 25016 ONLY)	.03 ea.
	PA16A385	Contact Arm. (25058 ONLY)	.09 ea.
17	PA11A944	Hair Pin Cotter (971 & 25016)	.01 ea.
18	XA14A964-C	Single Control Box	.67 ea.
19	XA12A038	Contact Rail Assy. for Standard S Gauge	.54 ea.
	XA30A158	Contact Rail Assy. for Pike Master	.45 ea.
20	LW-1B2	Wire Yellow	.02 ft.

* Snap on Truck No Rivets Used.

Prices subject to change without notice.

MILK CAR AND PLATFORM
Model Nos. 973, 25019

ACTION BOX CAR
Model No. 25042

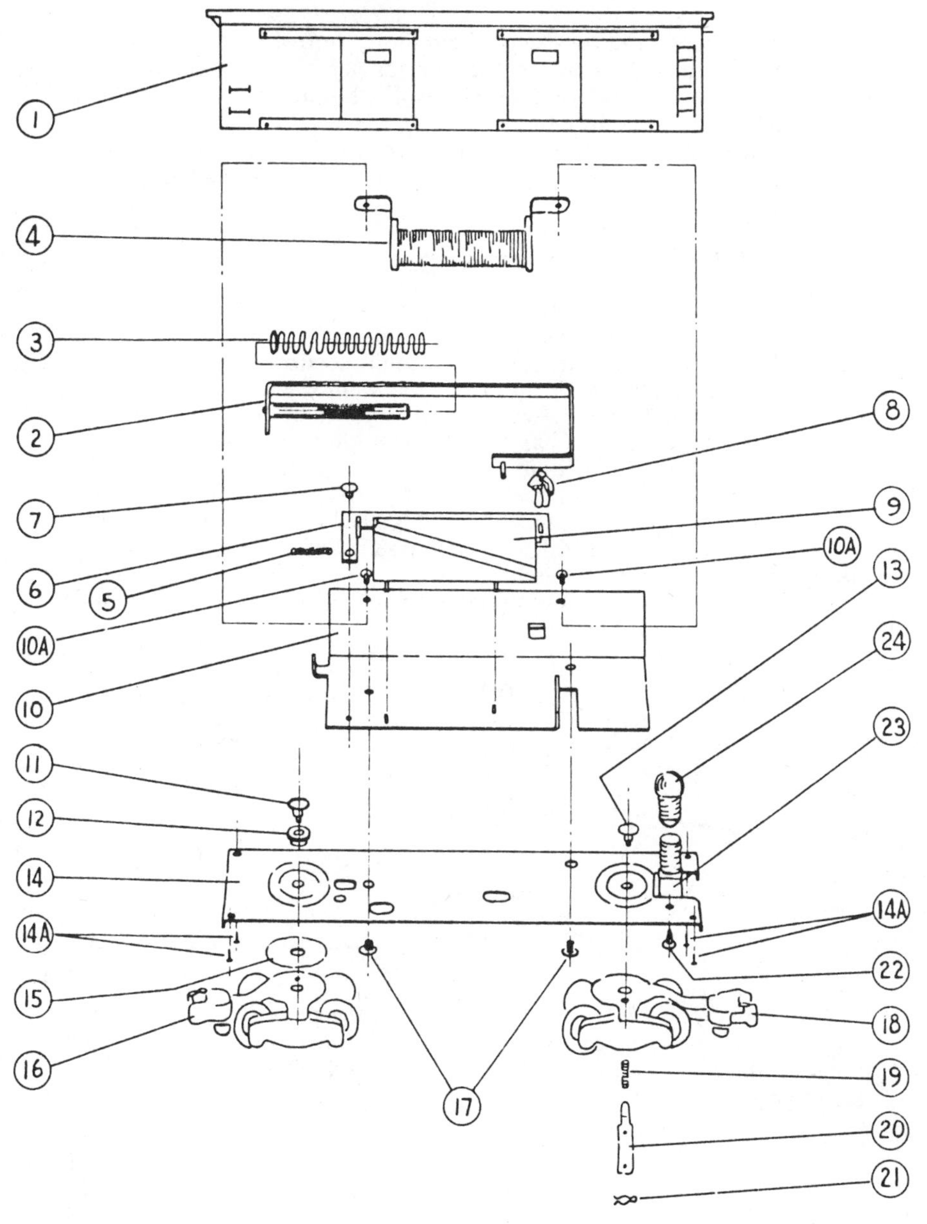

Ref: Form No. M5230; June 1, 1960

ACTION MILK CAR
HOOK-UP AND OPERATING INSTRUCTIONS

Your action milk car is one more of the American Flyer remote control action cars designed and constructed to offer you maximum enjoyment from its operation and realism. It is another complement to your layout scene.

At each press and release of the remote control button, automatically the unloading door opens, the interior lights, the milkman within tosses out a milk can and the door closes. Each time another milk can is fed by conveyor to the milkman.

The car is packed complete with a track pick-up segment, a remote control box, an unloading platform, (4) milk cans and (2) lengths of wire.

ATTACHING AND WIRING THE PICK-UP SEGMENT

Normally the base post terminal of your transformer is connected to the outer rail and the pick-up segment would be located on the outside of the track. However, select a straight section of track location and decide on which side of the track you want the car to dump.

If your layout necessitates the pick-up on the inside of track, this can be accommodated by changing the position of the metal wheels on the car truck to the opposite side of that truck. This is done by carefully spreading the truck sides only sufficiently to remove and reverse the wheels and axles. Press the truck sides together as they were originally.

In summary, the metal wheels must always run on the rail connected to the transformer base post.

See Fig. 1. Place pick-up segment in position under sleepers and snap the end type fasteners.

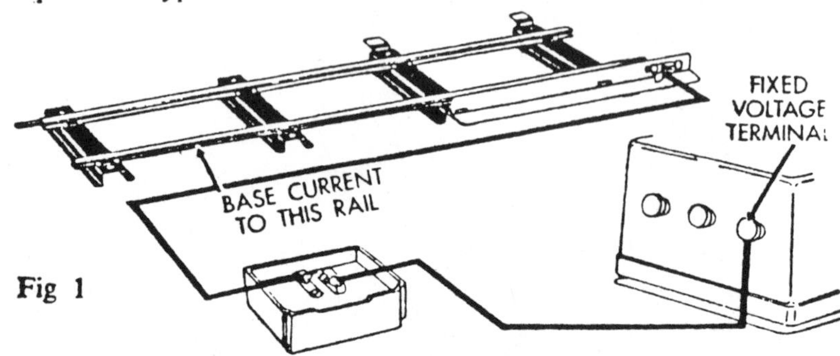

Fig 1

Connect one wire between the clip on the pick-up and one of the clips on the underside of the control box. Connect the remaining wire between the other control box clip and the FIXED VOLTAGE terminal at your transformer.

OPERATION

Check wiring and plug in transformer.

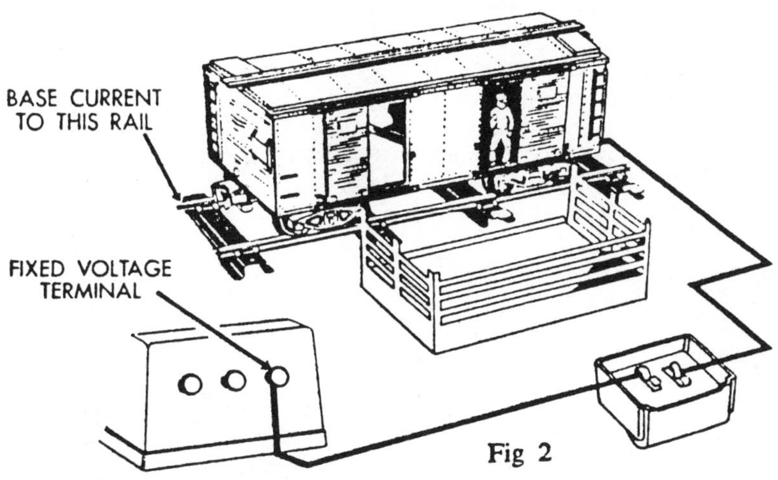

Fig 2

The left hand door of car slides manually. Open it, place the milk cans inside on the conveyor and close door. Place unloading platform in position to receive the milk cans.

Place loaded car on track, couple to train and run.

Stop train so that the car pick-up finger is in contact with the track pick-up segment.

Press remote control button and milkman inside the car will toss a milk can from the car onto the platform. Release the button and continue to press and release until the car is empty.

Do not hold button for much longer than necessary to actuate the unloading.

NO.	PART NO.	DESCRIPTION	PRICE
1	XA9966-RP	Box Car Body & Door Assy. for 25019 & 973	2.26 ea.
	XA15A437-RP	Box Car Body & Door Assy. for 25042 O.S.&N.S.	2.32 ea.
	PA9969	Door Guide w/8 S185 Screws (O.S. Body)	.02 ea.
	PA15A471	Door Guide (No Screws - N.S. Body)	.01 ea.
	PA9967-AR	Door for #25019	.13 ea.
	PA9967-A	Door for #25042	.16 ea.
	PA9967-AC	Door for #25019	.14 ea.
	PA9967-R	Door for #25042	.13 ea.
	PA12B666	Brake Handle	.01 ea.
2	XA11171-A	Solenoid Plunger Assembly	.42 ea.
3	PA11347	Spring	.04 ea.
4	XA1168	Solenoid Assembly	1.64 ea.
5	PA11196	Spring	.12 ea.
6	PA11170	Operating Arm	.14 ea.
7	PA11178	Shoulder Rivet	.03 ea.
8	PA11192	Man (White #25019)	.19 ea.
	PA11192	Man (Blue #25042)	.19 ea.
9	PA13B906	Chute	.22 ea.
10	PA11176	Base Plate	.32 ea.
11	PA10235	Truck Rivet	.03 ea.
12	PA10209	Insulating Bushing	.02 ea.
13	PA9381	Truck Rivet	.02 ea.
14	PA11183-A	Chassis	.46 ea.
14A	PA10456	Chassis Pin	.26 dz.
15	PA8715-BX	Washer	.01 ea.
16	XA12A050	Truck Assembly	1.65 pr.
	XA12A047	Coupler Assembly	.29 ea.
	XA10238-B	Wheel & Axle Assembly	.07 ea.
	PA10238	Axle	.01 ea.
	PA9991	Metal Wheel	.12 ea.
	PA9990	Plastic Wheel	.03 ea.
17	S268	P.K. Screw	.03 ea.
18	XA12A057	Truck Assembly	.98 ea.
	XA10238-A	Wheel & Axle Assembly	.08 ea.
	PA9990	Plastic Wheel	.03 ea.
	PA10238	Axle	.01 ea.
19	P9275	Coil Spring	.02 ea.
20	PA11A980	Contact Arm	.03 ea.
21	PA11A944	Hair Pin Cotter	.01 ea.
22	S322	#4 x $\frac{1}{4}$ P.K. Type A R.H. Screw	.02 ea.
23	XA13A433	Lamp Bracket Assembly	.22 ea.
24	PA9723	Lamp	.30 ea.
25	XA14A124	Platform Assembly #25019	.79 ea.
26	XA13A913	Milk Can Assembly (4) #25019	.14 ea.
	PA14A617	Drums for #25042	.05 ea.
27	XA14A964-M	Single Control Box #25019	.64 ea.
	XA14A964-D	Single Control Box #25042	.64 ea.
28	XA12A038	Contact Rail Assembly	.51 ea.
29	LW-1B2	Wire Yellow	.02 ft.

Prices subject to change without notice.

NO.	PART NO.	DESCRIPTION	PRICE
1 thru 10		NOT AVAILABLE	
11	PA10235	Truck Rivet	.03 ea
12	PA10209	Insulating Bushing	.02 ea.
13	PA9381	Truck Rivet	.02 ea.
14		Chassis Not Available	
14A	PA10456	Chassis Pin	.27 dz.
15	PA8715-BX	Washer	.01 ea.
16	XA12A050	Truck Assembly	.74 ea.
	XA12A047	Coupler Assembly	.30 ea.
	XA10238-B	Wheel & Axle Assembly	.07 ea.
17		NOT AVAILABLE	
18	XA12A057	Truck Assembly	1.03 ea.
	XA10238-A	Wheel & Axle Assembly	.08 ea.
19	P9275	Coil Spring	.02 ea.
20	PA11A980	Contact Arm	.03 ea.
21	PA11A944	Hair Pin Cotter	.01 ea.
22		#4 x $\frac{1}{4}$ P.K. Type A R.H. Screw Not Available	
23		Lamp Bracket Assembly Not Available	
24	PA9723	Lamp	.32 ea.
25		Platform Assy. #25019 Not Available	
26	XA13A913	Milk Can Assy. (4) #25019 & 973	.15 ea.
	PA14A617	Drums for 25042 & 25019	.05 ea.
27	XA14A964-M	Single Control Box #25019 & 973	.67 ea.
	XA14A964-D	Single Control Box #25042	.67 ea.
28	XA12A038	Contact Rail Assy. for Standard S Gauge	.54 ea.
29	LW-1B2	Wire Yellow	.02 ft.

Prices subject to change without notice.

ACTION CABOOSE

Model Nos. 977, 979, 25031, 25036, 25052

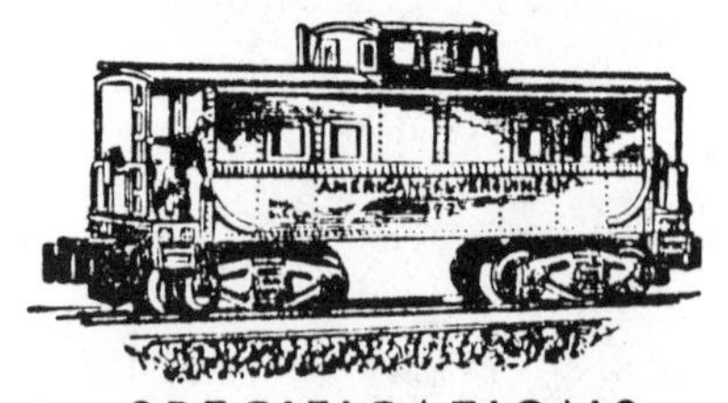

SPECIFICATIONS

Tested at: 10 Volts A.C. ...... Use Level Straight Track

A. When current is applied, man should snap back on platform and completely clear the outside of car. When current is broken, man should step to the edge of the platform so he appears to be hanging out of the rear platform looking down the side of the train.

B. The correct coupler adjustment should be 1/32" from the bottom of the weight to the top of the rails on the track.

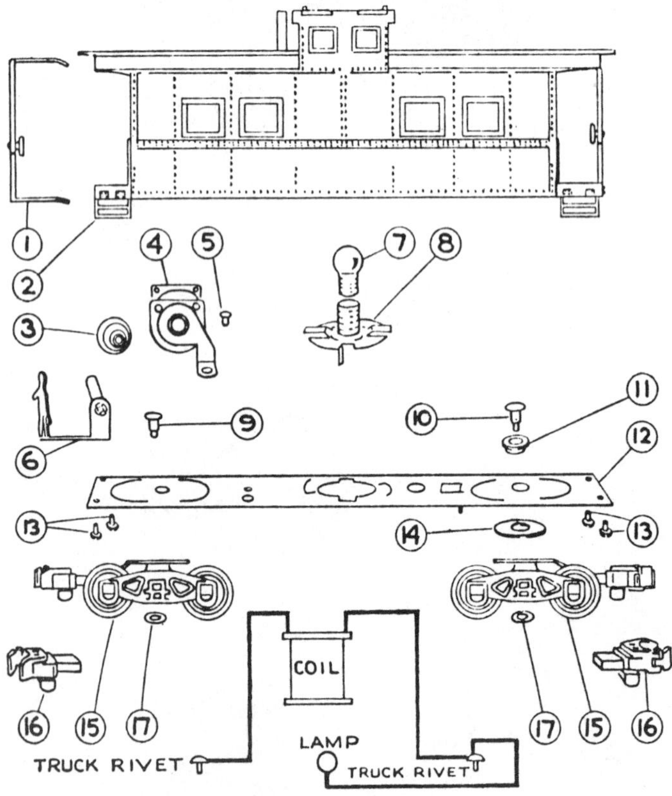

 Ref: Form No. 1648; July 15, 1955

Diagram Number	Part No.	Description	Price
1	XA10013RP	Caboose End	.11 ea.
2	XA9985-DRP	Caboose Body	1.11 "
3	PA13A243	Spring	.02 "
4	XA13A245	Solenoid Assy.	.82 "
5	PA5601	Rivet	.24 dz.
6	XA13A242	Plunger & Arm Assy.	.18 ea.
7	PA10665	Lamp	.25 "
8	XA9403-A	Lamp Bracket Assy.	.25 "
9	PA9381	Rivet	.02 "
10	PA10235A	Rivet	.03 "
11	PA10209	Bushing	.02 "
12	PA10833-B	Chassis	.16 "
13	PA10456	Chassis Pin	.24 dz.
14	PA8715-B	Washer	.05 "
15	XA12A050-A	Truck Assy.	.56 ea.
16	XA12A047	Knuckle Coupler	.22 "
17	PA1405	Washer	.05 dz.

SERVICE INSTRUCTIONS

The first thing to do is to place Caboose on track, connect transformer and test for operation.

TO CHECK OR REPLACE THE FOLLOWING PARTS:

1. Bulb (#7)

a. Remove Lamp Bracket Assembly (#8) by turning until lugs match the slots on Chassis and pull out.

b. Tighten Bulb (#7) in Lamp Bracket (#8), as it is sometimes loose and does not make good contact. If burned out, unscrew bulb and replace.

2. Knuckle Coupler (#16)

a. Use a long nosed plier or similar instrument and pry back the two lugs on the rear truck to remove broken coupler.

b. Insert new part and bend back lugs.

c. Adjust new coupler by placing caboose on the track, close the Knuckle, so that the weight is all the way down; then, either bend the coupler up or down, whichever is necessary to bring the bottom of the weight about 1/32" above the top of the rails.

3. Caboose body (#2)

a. Remove four pins (#13) to separate Chassis Assembly from Caboose Body (#2).

b. Take off Caboose End (#1), on man side, by bending back lug and pull out.

c. Bend back man slightly, until coil assembly has been cleared of body assembly, taking plunger and Arm Assembly (#6) out of Solenoid Assembly (#4), separating body and chassis.

4. Solenoid assembly (#4)

Follow steps a.-b.-c. of #3

d. The unit is now exposed and you can inspect the wiring and other points of the unit, such as spring and solenoid.

e. If Solenoid Assembly (#4) is burned out, remove rivet (#5).

Ref: Form No. 1648; July 15, 1955

Action Caboose — Nos. 977, 25031

NO.	PART NO.	DESCRIPTION	PRICE
1	XA10013RP	Caboose End	.12 ea.
2	XA9985-DRP	Caboose Body	1.22 ea.
3	PA13A243	Spring	.02 ea.
4	XA13A245	Solenoid Assembly	.90 ea.
5	PA5601	Rivet	.01 ea.
6	XA13A242	Plunger & Arm. Assy. NOT AVAILABLE	
		Sub. with X13A887 Plunger Assembly	.13 ea.
		P13A880 Man	.31 ea.
7	PA10665	Lamp	.27 ea.
8	XA9403-A	Lamp Bracket Assembly	.27 ea.
9	PA9381	Rivet	.02 ea.
10	PA10235-A	Rivet	.07 ea.
11	PA10209	Bushing	.02 ea.
12	PA10833-B	Chassis	.18 ea.
13	PA10456	Chassis Pin	.26 dz.
14	PA8715-B	Washer	.02 ea.
15	XA12A050-A	Truck Assembly	.79 ea.
	XA10238	Wheel & Axle Assembly	.09 ea.
16	XA12A047	Knuckle Coupler	.29 ea.
17		NOT USED	

Ref: Form No. 1648; June 1, 1960

NO.	PART NO.	DESCRIPTION	PRICE
1		Caboose End Not Available	
2		Caboose Body Not Available	
3	PA13A243	Spring	.02 ea.
4	XA13A245	Solenoid Assembly	.95 ea.
5	PA5601	Rivet	.01 ea.
6	X13A887	Plunger Assembly	.14 ea.
	P13A880	Man	.33 ea.
7	PA10665	Lamp	.32 ea.
8	XA9403-A	Lamp Bracket Assembly	.28 ea.
9	PA9381	Rivet	.02 ea.
10	PA10235-A	Rivet	.07 ea.
11	PA10209	Bushing	.02 ea.
12		Chassis Not Available	
13	PA10456	Chassis Pin	.27 dz.
14	PA8715-B	Washer	.02 ea.
15	XA12A050-A	Truck Assembly	.83 ea.
	XA10238	Wheel & Axle Assembly	.09 ea.
16	XA12A047	Knuckle Coupler	.30 ea.
17		NOT USED	

Prices subject to change without notice

 Ref: Form No. 1648; Oct. 1, 1962

NO.	PART NO.	DESCRIPTION	PRICE
1	XA14B593-RP	Caboose End Assembly	.27 ea.
2	XA14D596-RP	Caboose Body - 979 - 25036	2.36 ea.
	XA14D596-BRP	Caboose Body - 25052	2.36 ea.
3	PA13A243	Spring	.02 ea.
4	XA13A245	Solenoid Assembly	.90 ea.
5	PA5601	Rivet	.01 ea.
6	XA13A242	Plunger & Arm Assy. NOT AVAILABLE	
		Sub. with XA14A591 Plunger & Arm Assy.	.19 ea.
		PA13A880 Man	.31 ea.
7	PA10665	Lamp	.27 ea.
8	XA9403-A	Lamp Bracket Assembly	.27 ea.
9	PA9381	Rivet	.02 ea.
10	PA10235-A	Rivet	.07 ea.
11	PA10209	Bushing	.02 ea.
12	PA14C595	Chassis	.20 ea.
13		NOT USED	
14	PA8715-B	Washer	.02 ea.
15	XA12A050-A	Truck Assembly	.79 ea.
	XA10238	Wheel & Axle Assembly	.09 ea.
16	XA12A047	Knuckle Coupler	.29 ea.
17		NOT USED	

Ref: Form No. 1648; June 1, 1960

NO.	PART NO.	DESCRIPTION	PRICE
1		Caboose End Assembly Not Available	
2		Caboose Body-979-25036 Not Available	
		Caboose Body - 25052 Not Available	
3	PA13A243	Spring	.02 ea.
4	XA13A245	Solenoid Assembly	.95 ea.
5	PA5601	Rivet	.01 ea.
6		Plunger & Arm Assy. Not Available	
	PA13A880	Man	.33 ea.
7	PA10665	Lamp	.32 ea.
8	XA9403-A	Lamp Bracket Assembly	.28 ea.
9	PA9381	Rivet	.02 ea.
10	PA10235-A	Rivet	.07 ea.
11	PA10209	Bushing	.02 ea.
12		Chassis Not Available	
13		NOT USED	
14	PA8715-B	Washer	.02 ea.
15	XA12A050-A	Truck Assembly	.83 ea.
	XA10238	Wheel and Axle Assembly	.09 ea.
16	XA12A047	Knuckle Coupler	.30 ea.
17		NOT USED	

Prices subject to change without notice.

Ref: Form No. 1648; Oct. 1, 1962

WORK AND BOOM CAR
Model No. 24546

1960

PART NO.	DESCRIPTION
XA14A054	TRUCK ASSEMBLY
XA12A047	KNUCKLE COUPLER
PA14A040-B	EYELET
XA12038-A	WHEEL AND AXLE ASSEMBLY
PA11198-A	SIDING

* * * * *

1961-62

PART NO.	DESCRIPTION
XA16C084	TRUCK ASSEMBLY (SNAP ON)
XA10238-A	WHEEL AND AXLE ASSEMBLY
PA11198-A	SIDING

	#24546 Work & Boom Car (1960) & 1961-62	
XA14A054	Truck Assembly (1960)	.58 ea.
XA12A047	Knuckle Coupler "	.30 ea.
PA14A040-B	Eyelet "	.01 ea.
XA10238-A	Wheel & Axle Assembly (1960-61-62)	.08 ea.
*XA16C084	Truck Assembly	.32 ea.
PA11198-A	Siding	.34 ea.

* Snap on truck -- no eyelet used

Rev: Oct. 1, 1962

FLOODLIGHT CAR
Model No. 24549

1960

PART NO.	DESCRIPTION
XA12A050	TRUCK ASSEMBLY
XA12A047	KNUCKLE COUPLER
PA9988	RIVET
XA10238-B	WHEEL AND AXLE ASSEMBLY
PA16A387	CONTACT SPRING
XA8862-RP	SEARCHLIGHT BODY ASSEMBLY
PA8861	YOKE
PA8863	LENS
PA8864	SNAP RING
PA10665	BULB

1961-62

PART NO.	DESCRIPTION
XA16A384	TRUCK ASSEMBLY WITH CONTACT SPRING Snap on truck -- no eyelet used
XA10238-B	WHEEL AND AXLE ASSEMBLY
PA16A387	CONTACT SPRING
XA8862-RP	SEARCHLIGHT BODY ASSEMBLY
PA8861	YOKE
PA8863	LENS
PA8864	SNAP RING
PA10665	BULB

OPERATING CRANE CAR
Model No. 24561

PART NO.	DESCRIPTION
XA14A054	TRUCK ASSEMBLY
XA12A047	KNUCKLE COUPLER
XA10238-A	WHEEL AND AXLE ASSEMBLY
PA14A040	EYELET
XA9219	BLOCK ASSEMBLY

PART NO.	DESCRIPTION	PRICE
XA14A054	Truck Assembly #24561	.58
XA12A047	Knuckle Coupler #24561	.30
XA10238-A	Wheel & Axle Assembly #24561 & 24569	.08
PA14A040	Eyelet #24561	.01
*XA16C084	Truck Assembly for #24569	.32
XA9219	Block Assembly	.32

* Snap on truck -- no eyelet used

Rev: Oct. 1, 1962

OPERATING CRANE CAR
Model No. 24569

PART NO.	DESCRIPTION
XA16C084	TRUCK ASSEMBLY (SNAP ON)
XA10238-A	WHEEL AND AXLE ASSEMBLY
XA9219	BLOCK ASSEMBLY

PART NO.	DESCRIPTION	PRICE
XA14A054	Truck Assembly #24561	.58
XA12A047	Knuckle Coupler #24561	.30
XA10238-A	Wheel & Axle Assembly #24561 & 24569	.08
PA14A040	Eyelet #24561	.01
*XA16C084	Truck Assembly for #24569	.32
XA9219	Block Assembly	.32

* Snap on truck -- no eyelet used

Rev: Oct. 1, 1962

ROCKET LAUNCHER

Model No. 25045

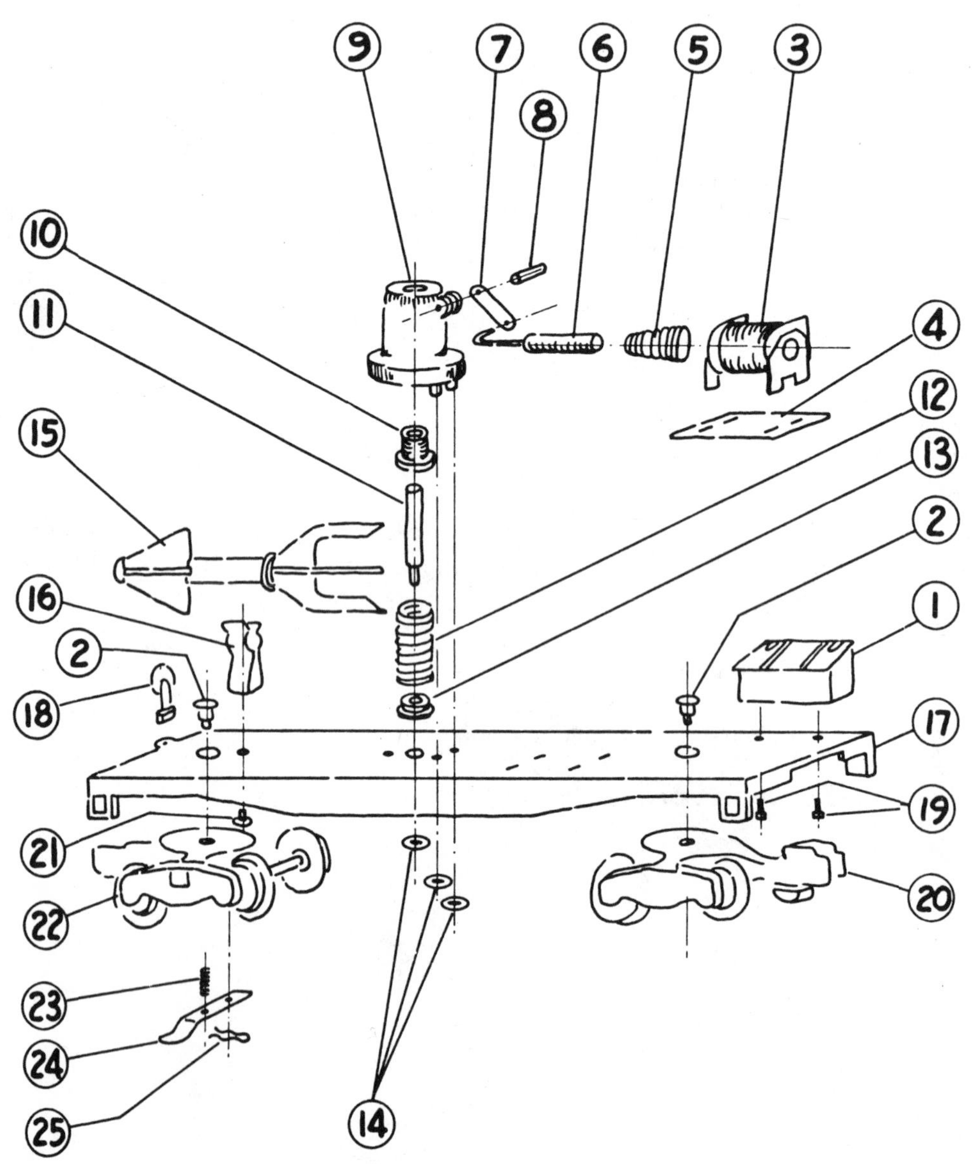

 Ref: Form No. M5234; June 1, 1960

NO.	PART NO.	DESCRIPTION	PRICE
1	PA13B304-B	Tool Box	.19 ea.
2	PA9988	Truck Rivet	.04 ea.
3	XA15B379	Coil Assembly	1.15 ea.
4	PA14A800	Bottom Plate	.01 ea.
5	PA14A618	Compression Spring	.02 ea.
6	XA14A620	Plunger & Rod Assembly	.13 ea.
7	PA14A621	Pawl	.02 ea.
8	PA14A625	Pin	.02 ea.
9	PA14B626	Housing	.45 ea.
10	PA14A623	Bushing	.09 ea.
11	PA15A391	Shaft	.04 ea.
12	PA14A622	Compression Spring	.04 ea.
13	PA14A929	Shouldered Washer	.06 ea.
14	W123	Washer	.06 dz.
15	P14A686	Rocket	.37 ea.
16	PA14A631	Rocket Clip	.09 dz.
17	PA15A275-EAA	Flat Car Body	.58 ea.
18	PA14A408	Brake Wheel	.02 ea.
19	PA10456	Chassis Pin	.26 dz.
20	XA12A050	Truck Assembly	1.65 pr.
	XA12A047	Coupler Assembly	.29 ea.
	XA10238-B	Wheel & Axle Assembly	.07 ea.
	PA10238	Axle	.01 ea.
	PA9990	Plastic Wheel	.03 ea.
	PA9991	Diecast Wheel	.12 ea.
21	PA4362	Tubular Rivet	.01 ea.
22	XA12A057	Truck Assembly	.98 ea.
	XA10238-A	Wheel & Axle Assembly	.08 ea.
	PA9990	Plastic Wheel	.03 ea.
	PA10238	Axle	.01 ea.
23	P9275	Coil Spring	.02 ea.
24	PA11A980	Contact Arm	.03 ea.
25	PA11A944	Hair Pin Cotter	.01 ea.
26	XA14A964-G	Single Control Box	.64 ea.
27	XA12A038	Contact Rail Assembly	.51 ea.

Prices subject to change without notice.

Ref: Form No. 5234; June 1, 1960

NO.	PART NO.	DESCRIPTION	PRICE
1	PA13B304-B	Tool Box	.20 ea.
2	PA9988	Truck Rivet	.04 ea.
3	XA15B379	Coil Assembly	1.21 ea.
4		Bottom Plate Not Available	
5	PA14A618	Compression Spring	.02 ea.
6	XA14A620	Plunger & Rod Assembly	.14 ea.
7	PA14A621	Cam	.02 ea.
8	PA14A625	Pin	.02 ea.
9		Housing Not Available	
10	PA14A623	Bushing	.09 ea.
11		Shaft Not Available	
12	PA14A622	Compression Spring	.04 ea.
13	PA14A929	Shouldered Washer	.06 ea.
14	W123	Washer	.06 dz.
15	P14A686	Rocket	.39 ea.
16	PA14A631	Rocket Clip	.09 dz.
17		Flat Car Body Not Available	
18	PA14A408	Brake Wheel	.02 ea.
19	PA10456	Chassis Pin	.27 dz.
20	XA12A050	Truck Assembly	.74 ea.
	XA12A047	Coupler Assembly	.30 ea.
	XA10238-B	Wheel & Axle Assembly	.07 ea.
	PA10238	Axle	.01 ea.
	PA9990	Plastic Wheel	.03 ea.
	PA9991	Diecast Wheel	.13 ea.
21	PA4362	Tubular Rivet	.01 ea.
22	XA12A057	Truck Assembly	1.03 ea.
	XA10238-A	Wheel & Axle Assembly	.08 ea.
	PA9990	Plastic Wheel	.03 ea.
	PA10238	Axle	.01 ea.
23	P9275	Coil Spring	.02 ea.
24	PA11A980	Contact Arm	.03 ea.
25	PA11A944	Hair Pin Cotter	.01 ea.
26	XA14A964-G	Single Control Box	.67 ea.
27	XA12A038	Contact Rail Assembly	.54 ea.

Prices subject to change without notice.

TNT CAR
Model No. 25057

PART NO.	DESCRIPTION
XA12A038	CONTACT RAIL ASSEMBLY (STANDARD TRACK)
XA30A158	CONTACT RAIL ASSEMBLY (PIKEMASTER TRACK)
XA14A964-X	CONTROL BOX ASSEMBLY
XA12A050	TRUCK ASSEMBLY
XA12A057	TRUCK ASSEMBLY
PA11A980	CONTACT ARM
PA11A944	HAIR PIN COTTER
P9275	SPRING
PA8715-B	INSULATING WASHER
PA10240	BUSHING
XA12A047	KNUCKLE COUPLER
PA9381	RIVET (USED ON XA12A050 TRUCK)
PA9988-T	RIVET (USED ON XA12A057 TRUCK)

ROCKET LAUNCHER CAR

Model No. 25059

PART NO.	DESCRIPTION
XA16A384	TRUCK ASSEMBLY (SNAP ON)
XA10238-B	WHEEL AND AXLE ASSEMBLY
XA16B383	TRUCK ASSEMBLY (SNAP ON)
XA10238-A	WHEEL AND AXLE ASSEMBLY
P14A686	ROCKET
PA16A057	PLUG
XA14A964-AC	CONTROL BOX

TNT CAR
Model No. 25061

PART NO.	DESCRIPTION
XA12A038	CONTACT RAIL ASSEMBLY (STANDARD TRACK)
XA30A158	CONTACT RAIL ASSEMBLY (PIKEMASTER TRACK)
XA14A964-X	CONTROL BOX ASSEMBLY
XA12A050	TRUCK ASSEMBLY
XA12A057	TRUCK ASSEMBLY
PA11A980	CONTACT ARM
PA11A944	HAIR PIN COTTER
P9275	SPRING
PA8715-B	INSULATING WASHER
PA10240	BUSHING
XA12A047	KNUCKLE COUPLER
PA9381	RIVET (USED ON XA12A050 TRUCK)
PA9988-T	RIVET (USED ON XA12A057 TRUCK)

MINE CARRIER CAR
Model No. 25062

PART NO.	DESCRIPTION
XA12A038	CONTACT RAIL ASSEMBLY (STANDARD TRACK)
XA30A158	CONTACT RAIL ASSEMBLY (BIKEMASTER TRACK)
XA16B717-A	CONTROL BOX ASSEMBLY
XA12A050	TRUCK ASSEMBLY
XA12A057	TRUCK ASSEMBLY
PA11A980	CONTACT ARM
PA11A944	HAIR PIN COTTER
P9275	SPRING
PA8715-B	INSULATING WASHER
PA10240	BUSHING
XA12A047	KNUCKLE COUPLER
PA9381	RIVET (USED ON XA12A050 TRUCK)
PA9988-T	RIVET (USED ON XA12A057 TRUCK)

TIE-JECTOR CAR
Model No. 25071

PART NO.	DESCRIPTION
PA16A285	RAIL TIE
XA16A551	TRACK TRIP (PIKEMASTER TRACK)
XA16A554	TRACK TRIP (STANDARD TRACK)
XA16C084	TRUCK ASSEMBLY
P10A984-10	EYELET

HAY-JECTOR CAR
Model No. 25082

PART NO.	DESCRIPTION
P16A983-A	BALES OF HAY
XA16A551	TRACK TRIP (PIKEMASTER TRACK)
XA16A554	TRACK TRIP (STANDARD TRACK)
XA16C084	TRUCK ASSEMBLY
P10A984-10	EYELET

ROCKET SLED
Model No. 25515

PART NO.	DESCRIPTION
XA15A986	MOTOR AND CHASSIS ASSEMBLY
PA15A971	PILOT
PA15B968	RELEASE
PA15A972	SPRING

S GAUGE — MECHANICAL CARS

This car is designed to be used on both Gilbert Pike Master track and Standard "S" Ga Track. When packed in an American Flyer Train Set, the activating trip designed for Pike Master track is included. When you purchase this car separately, you will find two activating trips — one to fit Pike Master track, and one to fit Standard "S" track. Select the trip which fits the type of track you have in your layout.

ATTACHING THE TRIP TO THE TRACK

The trip for use on the Pike Master track is snapped into position as shown in Fig. 1.

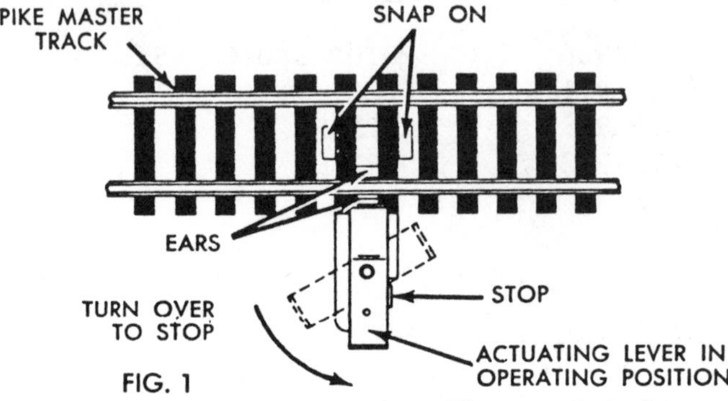

FIG. 1

The trip for use on standard American Flyer track is fastened into position by slipping the edge of one rail under the rail retainer and lock the cam against the other rail. (See Fig. 2.) These trips are designed for use on straight track sections only.

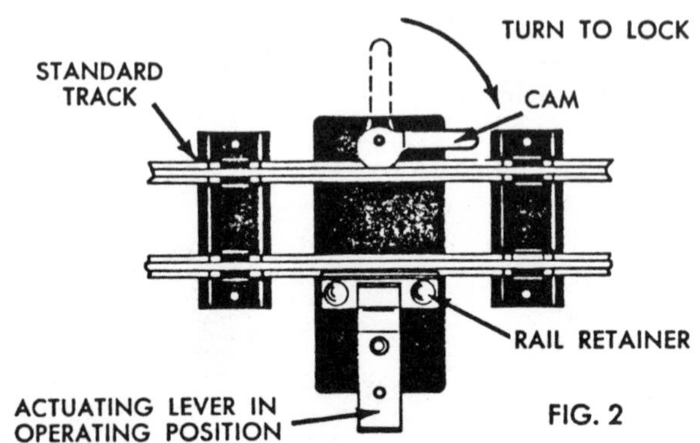

FIG. 2

OPERATION OF THE CAR

Place the Action Car on the track so that the operating arm is on the same side of the track as the actuating lever on the trip. Place the bales or ties into the top of the chute on the car. When the activating lever on the trip is in operating position and the car passes it in the direction indicated in Fig. 3 or 3A, a bale or tie will be automatically ejected.

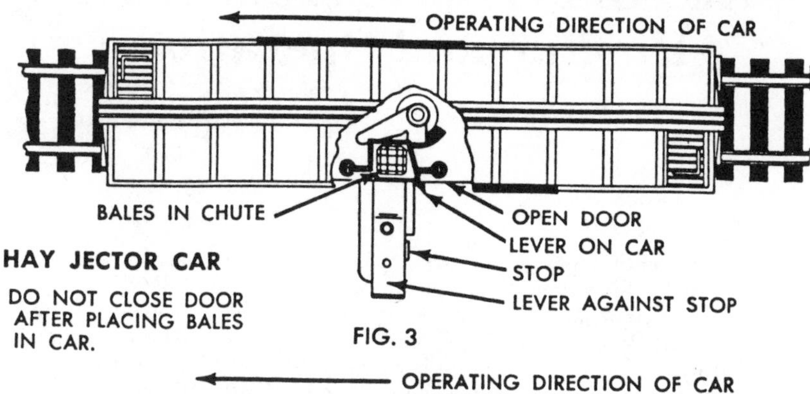

FIG. 3

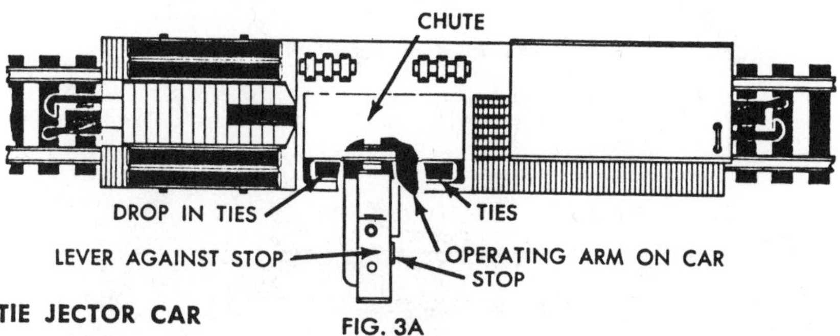

FIG. 3A

If you do not want the car to operate, swing the actuating lever on the trip out of the operating position.

Each action lever on cars and the cam portion of track trips are factory adjusted.

If these adjustments should change in shipping, either or both can be corrected by bending slightly to the sketch as shown.

Make sure action lever on car is free from binds after adjusting. M-5463

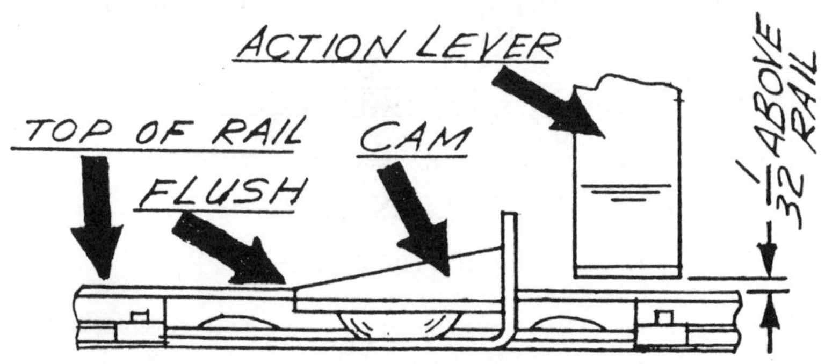

AUTOMATIC ACTION CARS
Hookup and Operation

The current to operate the cars is picked up by two metal wheels on one car truck which should run on the rail which has the BASE POST side of the current, and by a finger type pickup which protrudes from one of the truck sides and makes contact with the special rail section supplied with the car. This section is connected to the 15 Volt side of the current and only energized when the control box button is pressed.

ATTACHING THE SPECIAL PICKUP SECTION

There are two types of pickup sections used; one is a snap-on type and the other, a clamp-on type. The snap-on type fastens to the track as shown below in Figure 1.

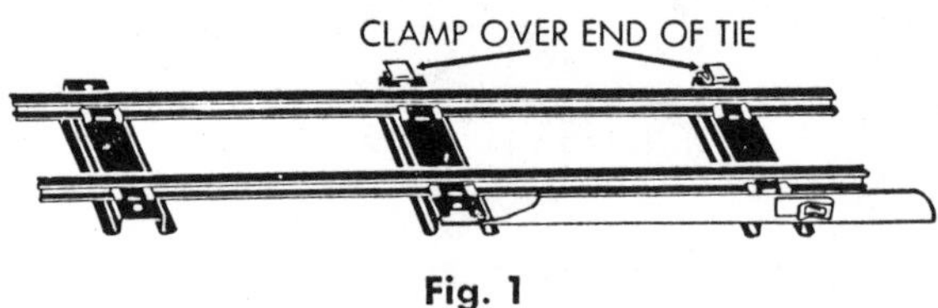

Fig. 1

It is used to operate such cars as the Automobile Unloading Car, Log Dump Car, Coal Dump Car, and Operating Box Car.

The clamp-on type is shown in Figure 2. For best operation there should be straight track both sides of the pickup section.

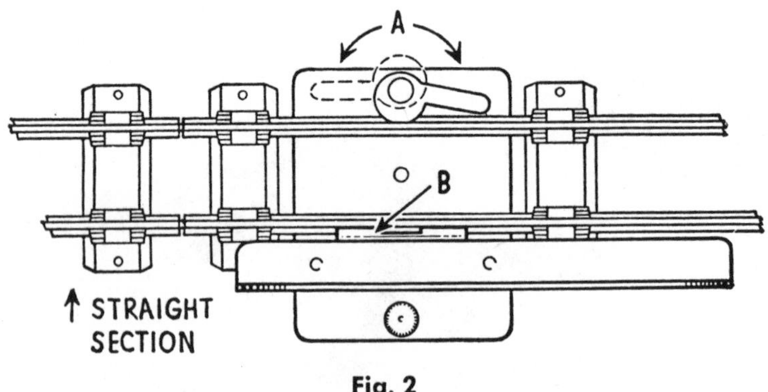

Fig. 2

Nest bottom of rail under metal part "B". Then close locking lever "A" on the other rail, as shown above.

WIRING THE SPECIAL PICKUP SECTION

Each automatic action car is packed with a control box and two pieces of wire for its operation. The only connections necessary are shown in the wiring diagram in Figure 3.

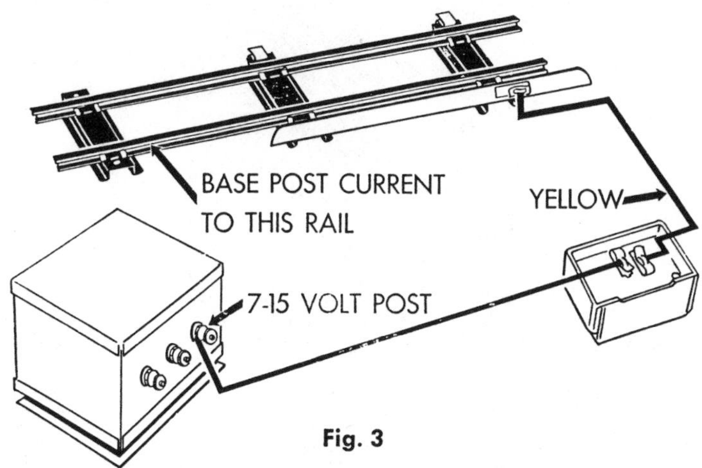

Fig. 3

You will note that the long YELLOW wire runs from the terminal on the track section to one of the clips underneath the control box, and the other wire runs from the other clip on the control box to the 15 VOLT POST on the transformer.

When the control box button is pressed, it closes the circuit and the 15 volt current is supplied to the pickup section. When the car is stopped, so the pickup finger on the truck makes contact with this special rail and the button is pressed, the operating coil in the car is energized, causing the car to perform its job.

NOTE: As was stated before, the other side or BASE POST side of the current is picked up by the two metal wheels on one side of the car trucks; if they should be riding on the rail which has the 7-15-VOLT side of the current they would not get enough power to operate the car properly.

You will note in Figure 3 that the pickup section is on the outside of the track and the base post current is in the outer rail. If your layout is set up so the pickup section is on the inside of the track, it would be necessary to change the position of the metal wheels on the truck. This can be done by very carefully spreading the truck so the wheels and axles can be removed and their position reversed; snap them back in place and press the truck sides back together again.

AUTOMOBILE UNLOADING CAR

Place the car on the track so the pickup finger on the truck is contacting the special pickup section on the track. Place the automobile on the car so the rear axle rests into the two slots in the metal part which is on the top of the car platform, and the front wheels are over the long slot in the platform. Note Figure 4.

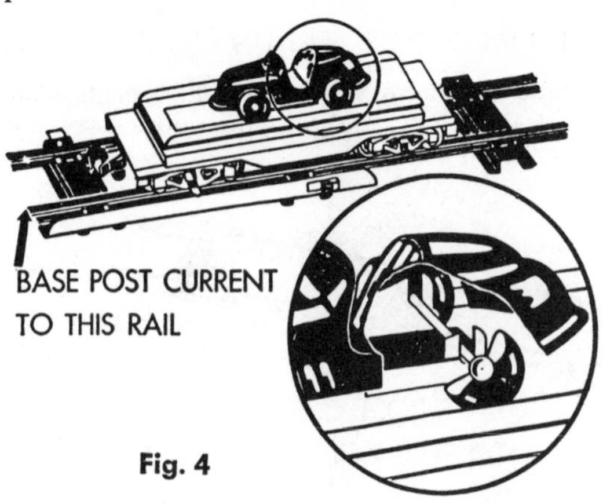

Fig. 4

When the car is in this position and the control box button is pressed, the platform swings out, the auto rolls down the ramp. Release the button and the platform swings back in place automatically, and is ready for reloading.

LOG DUMP CAR

Notice Figure No. 5. Have the car on the track with the logs loaded onto it; run train around and stop it so the pickup finger contacts the special pickup section; press the control button and the logs will automatically be unloaded and the platform will drop back in place.

To get the maximum amount of enjoyment from the Log Unloading Car, the car should be loaded with a Log Loader. With it, logs can be loaded and unloaded automatically by remote control and a real logging scene can be made on your layout.

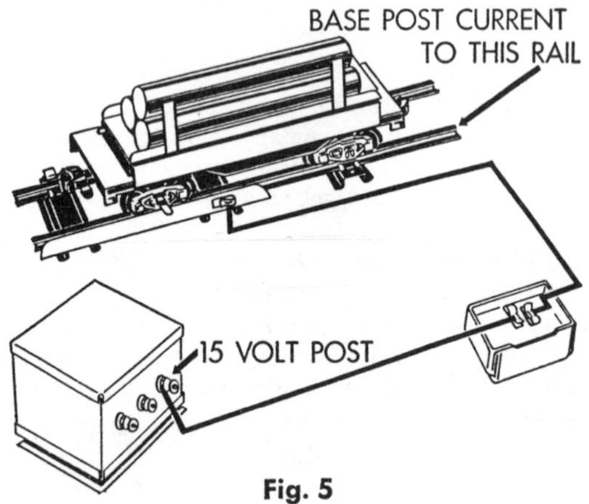

Fig. 5

LUMBER UNLOADING CAR

Hook up and operation of the Lumber Unloading Car is the same as for all other operating cars.

Have car on track so pick-up finger on truck contacts special rail section. Then press control button. Each time button is pressed, men will unload one plank from car.

COAL DUMP CAR

This type car is used to deliver coal to the coal yards, to haul the ballast along the track and to transport stones from a quarry. It is packed with a bag of coal and a metal coal bin which can be used to dump the coal into.

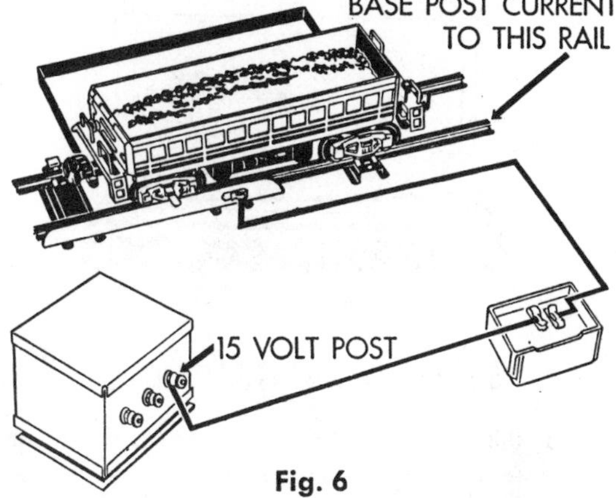

Fig. 6

Follow Figure 6. Place the coal bin where coal is to be dumped and hook up the special pickup section. When the car is stopped so the pickup finger makes contact on this section, it can be unloaded by pressing the control button.

OPERATING MILK OR BOX CAR

These operating cars have a conveyor ramp inside. The small metal boxes or cans supplied with the cars can be loaded onto the ramp by hand.

When the car is run around the track and stopped so the pickup finger has made contact with the special pickup section, press the control button and you will see the little man in the car open the door and push out one box. Each time the button is pushed, he goes through this procedure, then closes the door. See Figure 7.

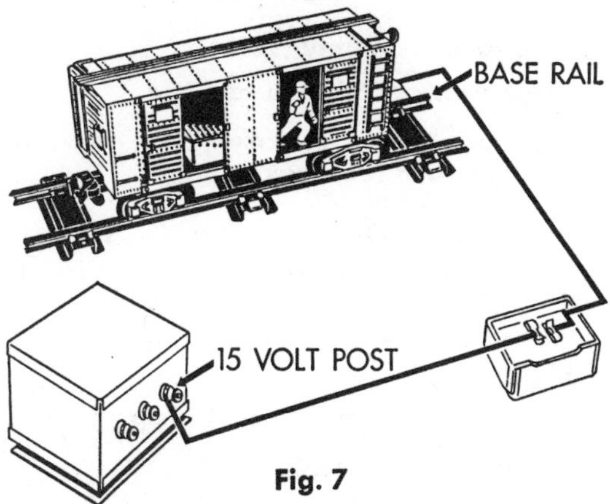

Fig. 7

BILLBOARD HORN
Model Nos. 561, 23561

SERVICE INSTRUCTIONS

The first thing to do is to connect wires from unit and control box to the transformer and test for operation. Before disassembling or replacing parts, adjust volume and tone by loosening S165 Screw (#6) and push adjustment in and out and then tighten the set screw.

TO CHECK OR REPLACE THE FOLLOWING PARTS:

1. **Sign and sign panel assembly (#1) and base (#17)**
   - a. Drill out two PA5601 Rivets (#3) and remove panel.
   - b. Straighten out lugs on Whistle Cover Assembly (#2) and separate from Base (#17)
2. **Whistle cover assembly (#2)**

   Follow steps a. and b. of #1
   - c. Remove two S293 Screws (#5) and Complete Whistle Unit is exposed.
3. **Coil assembly (#8)**

   Follow step c. of #2
   - a. Take off Tube (#13)
   - b. Remove three Screws (#12), separating Front Housing (#7), and Rear Housing (#10)
   - c. The Diaphragm (#9) will drop out.
   - d. Loosen Set Screw (#6) and pull out Coil Assembly (#8)

 Ref: Form No. 1644; July 15, 1955

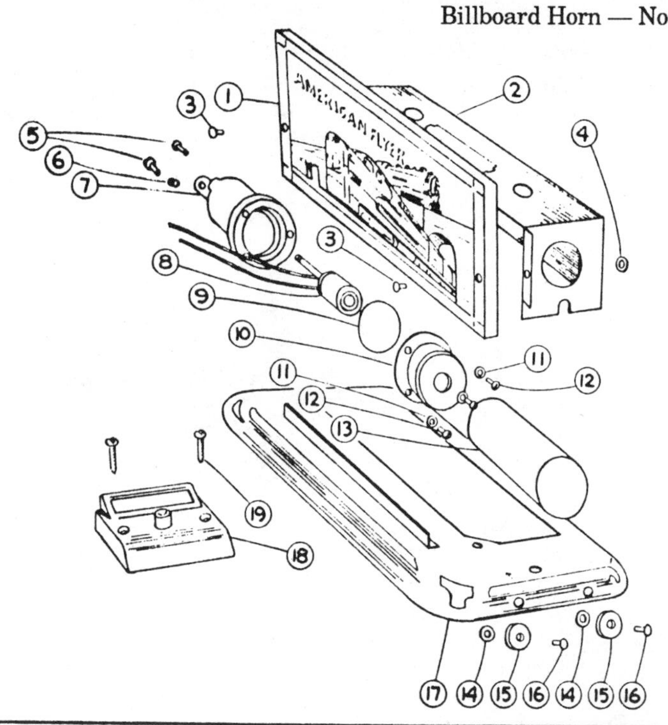

PRICES--VOID

Diagram Number	Part No.	Description	Price
1	XA13A295	Sign & Sign Panel Assy.	.37 ea.
2	XA9188-B	Whistle Cover Assy.	.48 "
3	PA5601	Rivet	.04 dz.
4	W77	Washer	.02 "
5	S293	Screw	.10 "
6	S165	Screw	.02 ea.
7	PA13C298	Front Housing	.32 "
8	XA13A292	Coil Assembly	.89 "
9	PA13A300	Diaphragm	.02 "
10	PA13B299	Rear Housing	.16 "
11	W57	Lockwasher	.04 dz.
12	S222	Screw	.01 ea
13	PA13A296	Tube	.06 "
14	W79	Washer	.10 dz.
15	PA11032	Rubber Washer	.02 ea.
16	PA4408	Tubular Rivet	.24 dz.
17	PA9193	Base	.35 ea.
18	XA10961-T	Control Box	.35 "
19	PA5556	Wood Screws	.01 "

OPERATING INSTRUCTIONS

You can blow either long or short blasts and reproduce any and all railroad signals used by the railroads with this realistic-sounding Diesel Billboard Horn.

To hook up, study the diagram below and proceed as follows:

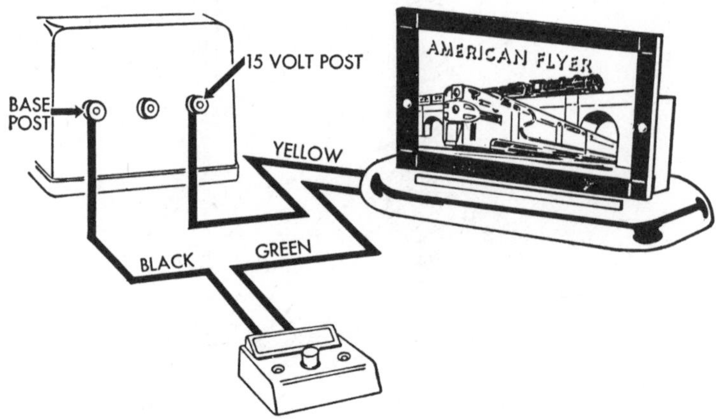

Connect YELLOW WIRE from horn to 15 VOLT POST on transformer. Connect GREEN WIRE from horn to one of the clips underneath the Control Box. Connect the BLACK WIRE from the other Control Box clip to the BASE POST on the transformer.

The horn is now ready to operate. Press the Control Box button and the horn will blow.

ADJUSTMENT: If the horn should get out of adjustment and not blow or sound right, it can very easily be readjusted.

Loosen the adjusting screw in the collar protruding from the side of the housing. Next, apply current and slowly pull the shaft out from the collar. You will note that this changes the sound. Move it slowly back and forth until the desired tone is reached; then tighten the set screw while holding the shaft in position.

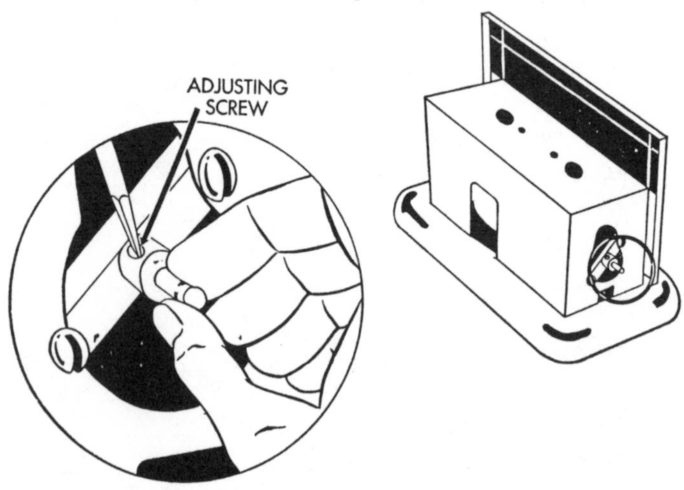

NO.	PART NO.	DESCRIPTION	PRICE
1	XA13A295	Sign & Sign Panel Assy.	(Not Available)
		Sub. with PA13C410 Sign Panel	.36 ea.
		PA13A420-A Sign	.18 ea.
2	XA9188-B	Whistle Cover Assembly	(Not Available)
		Sub. with PA13D407 Molded Housing	1.58 ea.
3		NOT USED	
4		NOT USED	
5	S323	#6 x 3/8 Rd. Hd. Screw	.02 ea.
6	S165	#6-32 x 1/8 Screw	.03 ea.
7	PA13C298	Front Housing	.51 ea.
8	XA13A292	Coil Assembly	1.69 ea.
9	PA13A300	Diaphragm	.09 ea.
10	PA13B299	Rear Housing	.29 ea.
11	W57	Lockwasher	.01 ea.
12	S222	#4 x 5/16 P.K. Screw	.01 ea.
13	PA13A296	Tube	.08 ea.
14		NOT USED	
15		NOT USED	
16		NOT USED	
17		NOT USED	
18	XA14A964-P	Control Box	.64 ea.
19		NOT USED	

Diagram Numbers 3-4-14-15-16-17 Not Available
Not needed when using substitution.

Prices subject to change without notice

NO.	PART NO.	DESCRIPTION	PRICE
1	PA13C410	Sign Panel	.36 ea.
	PA13A420-A	Sign	.18 ea.
2	PA13D407	Molded Housing	1.58 ea.
3		NOT USED	
4		NOT USED	
5	S323	#6 x 3/8 Rd. Hd. Screw	.02 ea.
6	S165	#6-32 x 1/8 Screw	.03 ea.
7	PA13C298	Front Housing	.51 ea.
8	XA13A292	Coil Assembly	1.69 ea.
9	PA13A300	Diaphragm	.09 ea.
10	PA13B299	Rear Housing	.29 ea.
11	W57	Lockwasher	.01 ea.
12	S222	#4 x 5/16 P.K. Screw	.01 ea.
13	PA13A296	Tube	.08 ea.
14		NOT USED	
15		NOT USED	
16		NOT USED	
17		NOT USED	
18	XA14A964-P	Control Box	.64 ea.
19		NOT USED	

NO.	PART NO.	DESCRIPTION	PRICE
1	PA13C410	Sign Panel	.38 ea.
	PA13A420-A	Sign	.19 ea.
2	PA13D407	Molded Housing	1.66 ea.
3		NOT USED	
4		NOT USED	
5	S323	#6 x 3/8 Rd. Hd. Screw	.02 ea.
6	S165	#6-32 x 1/8 Screw	.03 ea.
7	PA13C298	Front Housing	.54 ea.
8	XA13A292	Coil Assembly	1.77 ea.
9		Diaphragm Not Available	
10	PA13B299	Rear Housing	.30 ea.
11	W57	Lockwasher	.01 ea.
12	S222	#4 x 5/16 P.K. Screw	.01 ea.
13	PA13A296	Tube	.08 ea.
14 Thru 17		NOT USED	
18	XA14A964-P	Control Box	.67 ea.
19		NOT USED	

Dia. No. 5 Thru 13 , except No. 9, can be used for replacement parts on No. 561 Horn. All other parts not available (OBSOLETE).

 Ref: Form No. 1644; June 1, 1960 and Oct. 1, 1962

WHISTLING BILLBOARD
Model No. 566

SERVICE INSTRUCTIONS

The first thing to do is to connect wires from unit and control box, to the transformer and test for operation.

TO CHECK OR REPLACE THE FOLLOWING:

1. SIGN AND SIGN PANEL ASSEMBLY (#24) AND WHISTLE COVER (#26)

a. Drill out two PA5601 Rivets (#22) and remove PA10670 Sign Panel (#24)

b. Straighten out lugs on Whistle Cover Assembly (#26) and separate from base (#13)

2. BASE (#13)

a. Remove two S45 Screws (#14) and take off PA-9791 Spacer (#18), and N14 Nuts (#23) Follow step b. of #1

IF TROUBLE IS IN THE MOTOR, YOU CAN MAKE THE FOLLOWING CHECKS:

a. Inspect brushes for wear or poor contact and brush springs for proper tension.

b. Clean or polish commutator on Armature Assembly (#4). If motor is still running slow, the armature may need replacing.

c. Check to see if motor is oiled and not binding.

IF THESE INITIAL STEPS DO NOT CORRECT THE TROUBLE, IT WILL BE NECESSARY TO DISASSEMBLE THE MOTOR UNIT AS FOLLOWS:

a. Take off two Brush Caps (#10) and remove Brush Springs (#9) and Brushes (#8)

b. Remove seven S279 Screws (#1) and take off top Cover Plate (#2) with Bushing (#2-A) and Gasket (#3)

c. Pull out Armature Assembly (#4)

d. Remove two Screws (#12), Washers (#11) and Terminal (#19) to take off Brush Bracket Assembly (#7)

e. Take off Magnet Assembly (#6)

f. Remove five S279 Screws (#1) and take off Bottom Plate (#17) and Gasket (#16) to replace Whistle Housing (#5)

Ref: Form No. 1645; July 15, 1955

Whistling Billboard No. 566

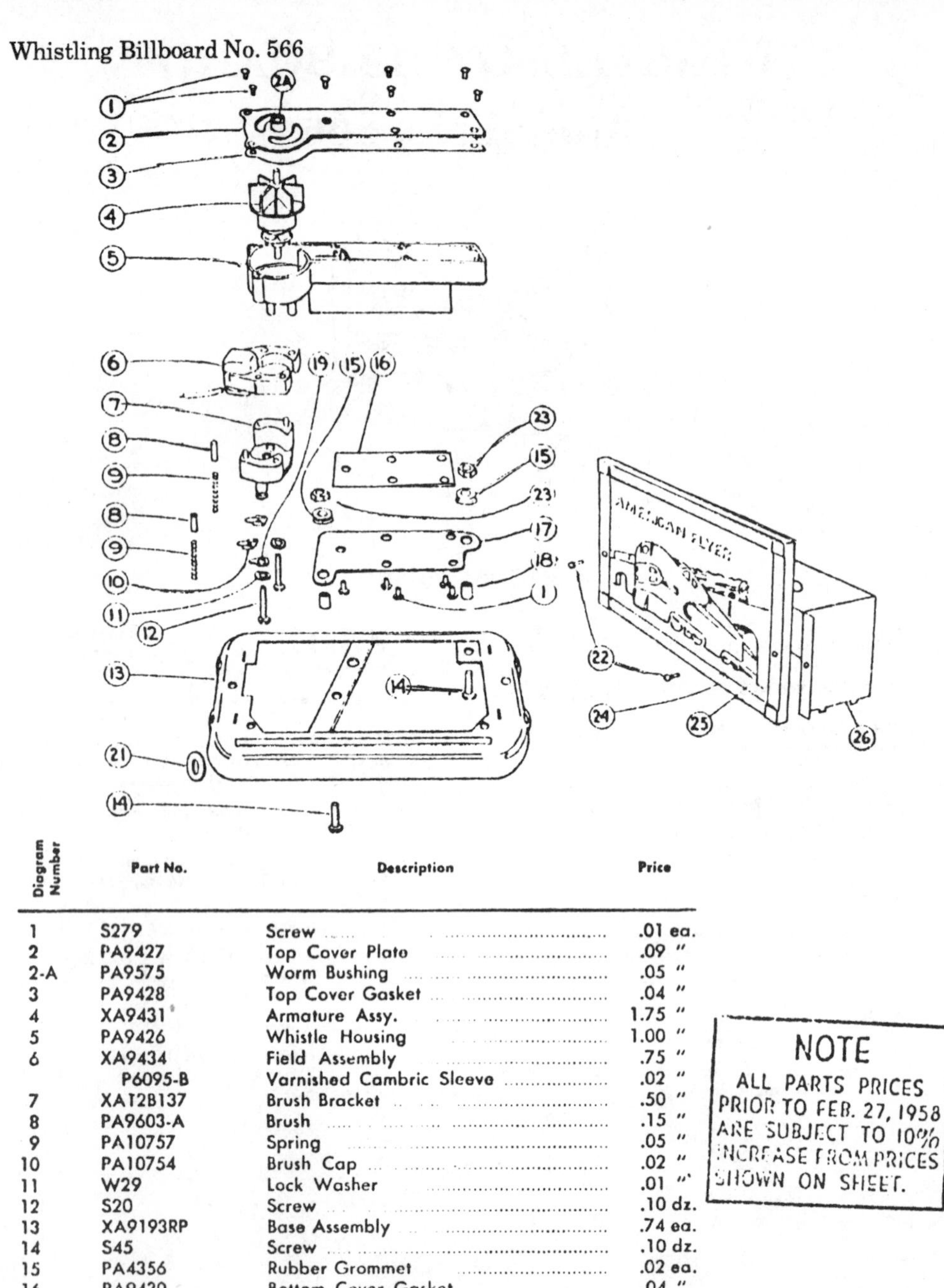

Diagram Number	Part No.	Description	Price
1	S279	Screw	.01 ea.
2	PA9427	Top Cover Plate	.09 "
2-A	PA9575	Worm Bushing	.05 "
3	PA9428	Top Cover Gasket	.04 "
4	XA9431	Armature Assy.	1.75 "
5	PA9426	Whistle Housing	1.00 "
6	XA9434	Field Assembly	.75 "
	P6095-B	Varnished Cambric Sleeve	.02 "
7	XA12B137	Brush Bracket	.50 "
8	PA9603-A	Brush	.15 "
9	PA10757	Spring	.05 "
10	PA10754	Brush Cap	.02 "
11	W29	Lock Washer	.01 "
12	S20	Screw	.10 dz.
13	XA9193RP	Base Assembly	.74 ea.
14	S45	Screw	.10 dz.
15	PA4356	Rubber Grommet	.02 ea.
16	PA9430	Bottom Cover Gasket	.04 "
17	PA9429	Bottom Cover Plate	.04 "
18	PA9791	Spacer	.02 "
19	PA6173	Terminal	.02 "
20	XA10961-B	Control Box	.50 "
21	P-558-E	Fiber Washer	.10 dz.
22	PA5601	Rivet	.04 "
23	N14	Nut	.01 ea.
24	PA10670	Sign Panel	.21 "
25	M3314	Sign	.03 "
26	XA9188-A	Whistle Cover Assembly	.47 "

NOTE

ALL PARTS PRICES PRIOR TO FEB. 27, 1958 ARE SUBJECT TO 10% INCREASE FROM PRICES SHOWN ON SHEET.

OPERATING INSTRUCTIONS

You can blow either long or short blasts and reproduce any and all Railroad whistle signals used by the Railroads with this simulated Billboard whistle unit.

To hook up study the diagram below and hook up as follows.

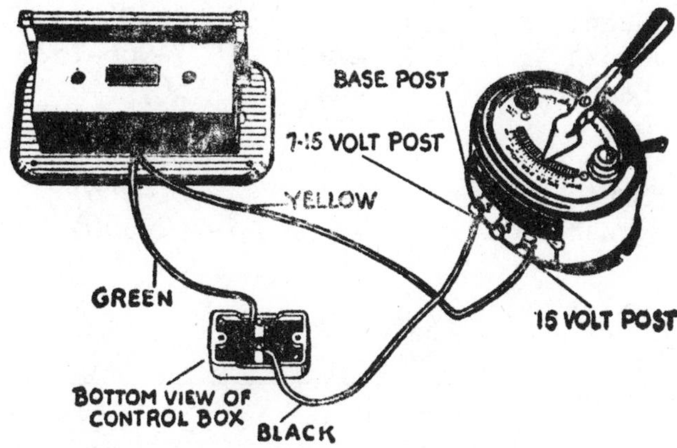

HOOK UP WHEN USING A TRANSFORMER

Connect **YELLOW WIRE** to **15 VOLT POST** on transformer.

Connect **GREEN WIRE** to one of the clips underneath the control box.

Connect **BLACK WIRE** from other control box clip to the **BASE POST** on the transformer.

HOOK UP WHEN USING A NO. 15 RECTIFORMER AND TRANSFORMER

Connect wires direct to transformer as shown above.

HOOK UP WHEN USING NO. 14 OR NO. 16 RECTIFORMER

Connect the **YELLOW AND BLACK WIRES** to the two posts on the Rectiformer marked "Alternating Current for Accessories".

The whistle is now ready to operate. Press the button on the Control Box and the whistle will blow.

OILING. To lubricate the motor, place a few drops of oil on the shaft bearings. Top bearing can be reached through a hole in the top of the housing and bottom bearing is covered with a felt wick which can be saturated with oil. Do not get oil on the motor brushes as this will cause the commutator to get dirty and gummed up and slow down the motor.

WHISTLING BILLBOARDS

PA9426	Whistle Housing	(577-566)	1.00 "
PA9428	Top Gasket	(577-566)	.04 "
PA9430	Bottom Gasket	(577-566)	.04 "
XA9431	Armature Assembly	(577-566)	1.75 "
XA9431-A	Armature Assembly	(762)	1.75 "
PA9432	Blower Fan	(577-762-566)	.25 "
XA9434	Magnet Assembly	(577-566-762)	.75 "
XA9565-A	Brush Bracket Assembly	(577-566-762)	.50 "
PA9575	Bearing	(577-566)	.05 "
PA9603-A	Brush	(566-577-762)	.15 "
XA10674	Sign & Sign	(577-762-566)	.40 "
PA10754	Brush Cap	(577-762-566)	.02 "
PA10757	Brush Spring	(577-762-566)	.05 "

Control Boxes

XA10961-B	Control Box for #566-577 Whistle	.50 ea.
XA10961-AB	Control Box for #751 Log Loader	.50 "
XA10961-AE	Control Box for #762 Whistle	.50 "
XA10961-AF	Control Box for #583-A Crane	.50 "
XA10961-AC	Control Box for #752 Coaler	.50 "
XA10961-3	Control Box for #752-A Coaler	.75 "
XA10961-D	Control Box for #596 Water Tank	.50 "
XA10961-E	Control Box for #706 Uncoupler	.50 "
XA10961-F	Control Box for #755 Talking Station	.50 "
XA10961-G	Control Box for #758 Sam	.50 "
XA10961-H	Control Box for #718 Mail Pick Up	.50 "
XA10961-J	Control Box for #715 Car	.80 "
XA10961-K	Control Box for #716 Car	.80 "
XA10961-L	Control Box for #714 and #717 Car	.80 "
XA10961-P	Control Box for #770 Platform	.50 "
XA10961-CA	Control Box for #771 Stockyard	1.20 "
XA10961-AG	Control Box for #758-A Sam	.50 "
XA10961-CP	Control Box for #766 Station	1.20 "

REMOTE CONTROL WHISTLE
Model No. 577

OPERATING INSTRUCTIONS

With this **remote control** unit you can operate the whistle at any time you desire by simply pressing a button switch.

You can blow either long or short blasts and reproduce any signals used in real railroading. To obtain satisfactory performance, you must follow the instructions shown on this sheet.

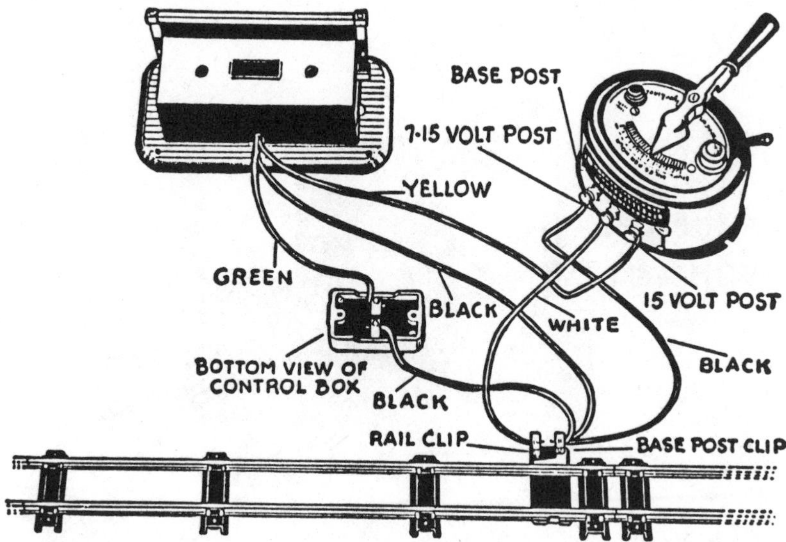

1. Connect the **base post** of the transformer to the **base post clip** of the track terminal. Connect the 7-15 Volt Post of the transformer to the other **rail clip** of the track terminal.

2. Connect the **yellow** wire from the whistle to the 15 Volt Post of the transformer.

3. Connect the **black** wire from the whistle to the **base post** of the transformer.

4. Connect the **green** wire from the whistle to one of the wire clips underneath the Control Button.

5. Connect the short **black** wire from the other wire clip underneath the Control Button to the **base post** of the transformer. **Note:** (Both **black** wires can be connected to the **base post clip** of the track terminal if so desired).

The whistle is now ready to operate and both lights should be lit. Press the button and the whistle will blow.

If either lamp should burn out, replace with a 14 Volt 3½G lamp.

Oiling: To lubricate the motor, place a few drops of oil or a small amount of Vasoline on the shaft bearings. Do this frequently as this motor operates at high speed. Lubricate motor on top and bottom of the whistle. Excess lubricant will gum up the commutator and will slow up the motor. Do not get any oil in the brushes of the motor.

Ref: Form No. M2444

ELECTROMATIC CRANE
Model Nos. 583, 583A

INSTRUCTIONS FOR CONNECTING AND OPERATING No. 583 ELECTROMATIC CRANE

Place Crane in position in your layout. See illustration below which shows the best arrangement of Crane in relation to track and hook up as follows:

1. Connect the YELLOW wire from the Crane to the **15 VOLT POST** of the transformer.
2. Connect the BLACK wire from the Crane to one of the clips underneath the Control Button.
3. Connect the short BLACK wire from the other Control Box clip to the BASE POST on the transformer.
4. The illustration shows the standard method of wiring the transformer to a track layout.

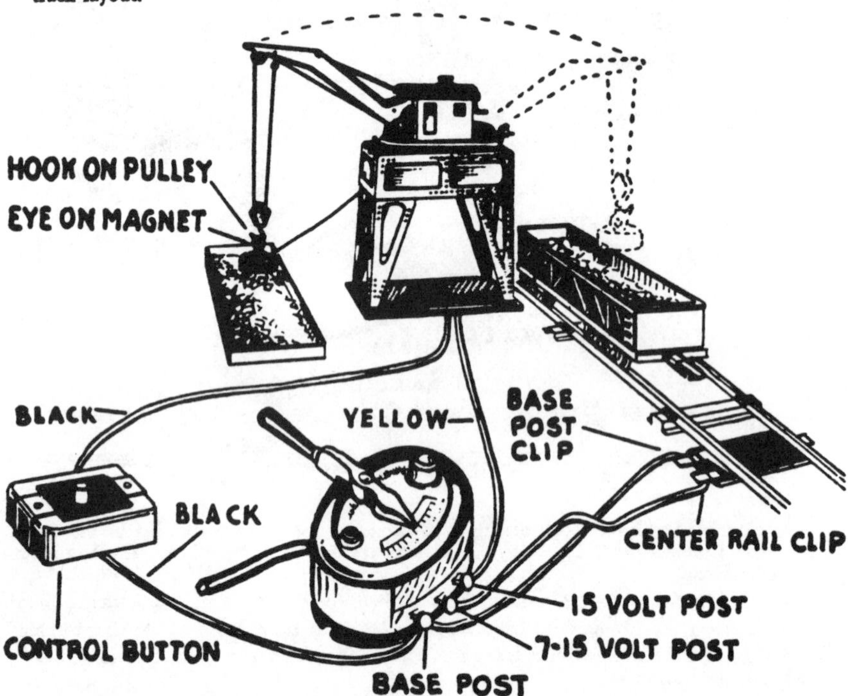

The Crane is equipped with a sequence reversing switch which performs a cycle of 4 steps, namely, Right — Neutral — Left — Neutral, so push the button, if Crane does not move, release and push again. The Crane will now move in one direction until pressure on button is released. To make Crane move in opposite direction, push the button twice and hold down. In operating, do not allow Crane to move more than one-half revolution.

After you operate the Crane once you can place it the proper distance from the rail to obtain the best position for picking the load up from the tray and dropping it into the car.

The hand wheel at rear of cab raises and lowers the boom for placing magnet at proper height over load of scrap iron in tray.

 Ref: Form No. M2448

INSTRUCTION FOR CONNECTING AND OPERATING NO. 583-A ELECTROMATIC CRANE

Place crane in position in your layout. See illustration below which shows the best arrangement of crane in relation to track and hook up as follows:

Diagram shows hook up to a transformer.

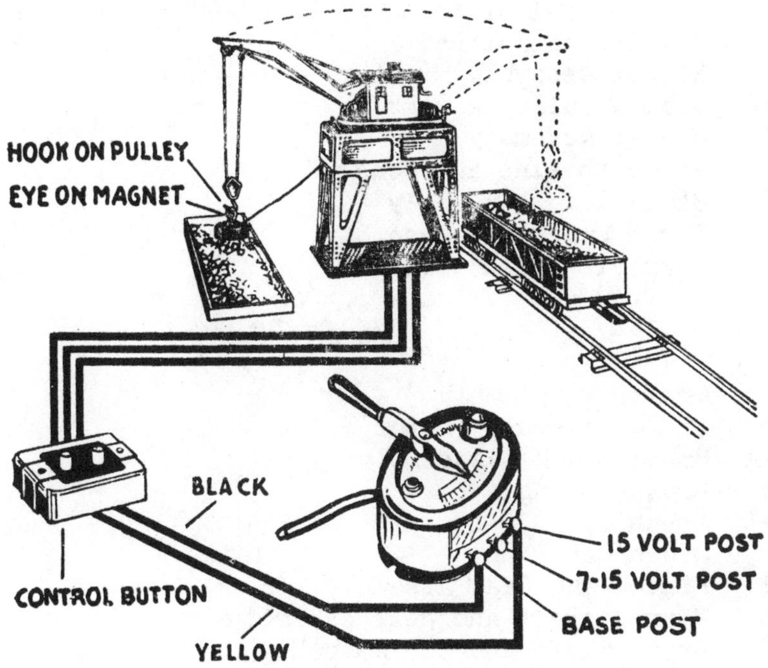

WHEN USING A TRANSFORMER

Connect **YELLOW** wire from control box to **15 VOLT POST** on transformer.

Connect **BLACK** wire from control box to **BASE POST** on transformer.

WHEN USING A TRANSFORMER AND NO. 15 RECTIFORMER

Connect wires from the control box direct to the transformer as described in the above paragraphs.

WHEN USING A NO. 14 OR 16 ELECTRONIC RECTIFORMER

Connect the **BLACK** and **YELLOW** wires from the control box to the two **ALTERNATING CURRENT POSTS** on the rectiformers.

The crane is equipped with a two button control box and a double wound motor.

Pushing the red button will cause the cab and boom to rotate in one direction, pushing the green button causes the motor to run in the opposite direction. Pushing either button will cause the electro magnet to be energized to pick up steel scrap. When button is released the motor will stop and steel scrap will be released.

In operating do not allow crane to revolve more than one half revolution.

After you operate the crane once you can place it the proper distance from the rail to obtain the best position for picking the load up from the tray and dropping it into the car.

The hand wheel at the rear of the cab raises and lowers the boom for placing magnet at the proper heights over the load of scrap iron in the tray.

#583 MAGNETIC CRANE

X9337-A	Armature Assembly	2.50 ea.
P9212	Brush springs	.05 "
P313-A	Brush	.15 "
XA8731	Remote Control Unit 1946-47-48	2.50 "
XA10587-D	Remote Control Unit 1949	2.50 "
XA9338	Magnet Assembly (motor)	1.00 "
XA9220-A	Boom & Pulley Assembly	1.00 "
XA9233	Magnet Assembly	1.25 "
P289-A	#50 Fish Line 24" long	.15 "
XA9219	Block & Pulley Ass'y	.25 "
X9378	Brush End Plate Assembly	.57 "
XA9230-R	Complete gearhousing	1.05 "

#583A CRANE

XA9569	Armature Assembly	2.50ea.
XA10266	Field Assembly (motor)	.85 "
XA9565-A	Brush Bracket Assembly	.50 "
PA10757	Brush Spring	.05 "
PA9603-A	Brush	.15 "
PA10754	Brush Cap	.02 "
XA11101	Pinion and Gear Assembly	.30 "
XA11100	Wormed shaft and gear assembly	.86 "
XA11105	Drive Shaft and Sq. Assembly	.06 "
XA9220-A	Boom and Pulley Assembly	1.00 "
XA9233	Magnet Assembly	1.25 "
P289-A	#50 Fish Line 24" long	.15 "
XA9219	Block and Pulley Assembly	.25 "

#583-A CRANE

PA402B	Tray	.40 ea.
XA9219	Block and Pulley Assembly	.25 ea.
XA9220-A	Boom and Pulley Assembly	1.00 "
PA9231	Roof and Chimney	.14 "
XA9233	Magnet Assembly	1.25 "
XA9565-A	Brush Bracket Assembly	.50 "
XA9569	Armature Assembly	2.50 "
PA9603-A	Brush	.15 "
XA10266	Field Assembly (Motor)	.85 "
PA10754	Brush Cap	.02 "
PA10757	Brush Spring	.05 "

 Ref: Sept. 22, 1950/Nov. 13, 1952

CROSSING GATE
Model No. 591

INSTRUCTIONS FOR SETTING UP AND OPERATING NO. 591 CROSSING GATE

To operate this gate, the first step is to determine its approximate location in your track layout. Then insulate the outside rail for about two sections of track in front of the gate and three sections after it, depending on the length of the train because as long as the tender of your train is in this insulated block, the gate will function.

To insulate the outside rail, remove the two pins in the outside rail at the ends of the dead block and replace them with the the fiber pins which are packed with this unit.

Now place the gate in front of the track in the desired location in your layout, so the gate will go down when the train is passing.

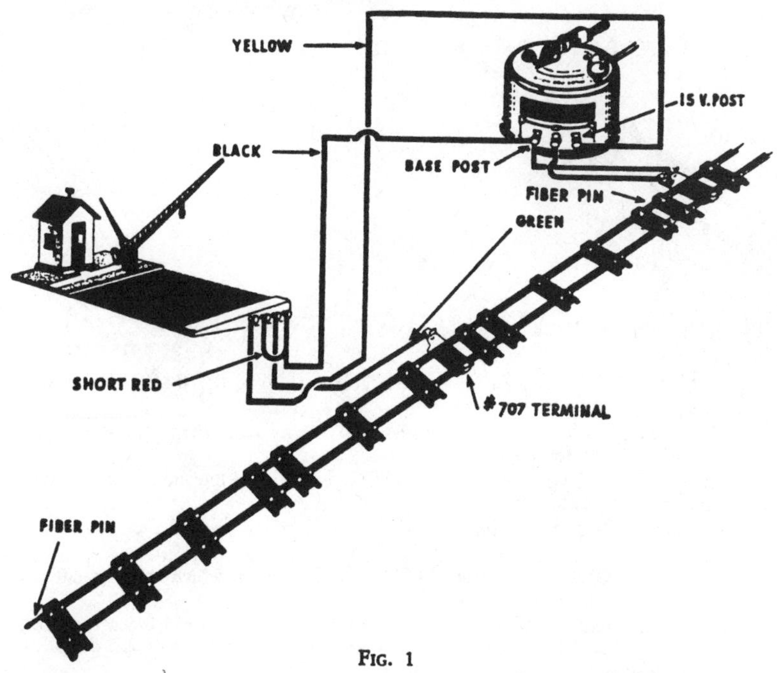

FIG. 1

TO HOOK UP TO A TRANSFORMER

Study Figure 1 and proceed as follows:

Fasten the No. 707 Track Terminal in the insulated section so the **BASE POST** clip is clamped on the insulated rail.

Connect the **YELLOW** wire from the **YELLOW** terminal to the **15 VOLT POST** on the transformer.

Connect the **BLACK** wire from the **BLACK** terminal to the **BASE POST** on the transformer.

Connect the **GREEN** wire from the **GREEN** terminal to the No. 707 Track Terminal located in the insulated section.

Connect the **RED** and **BLACK** terminals together with the short **RED** wire.

Ref: Form No. M2569

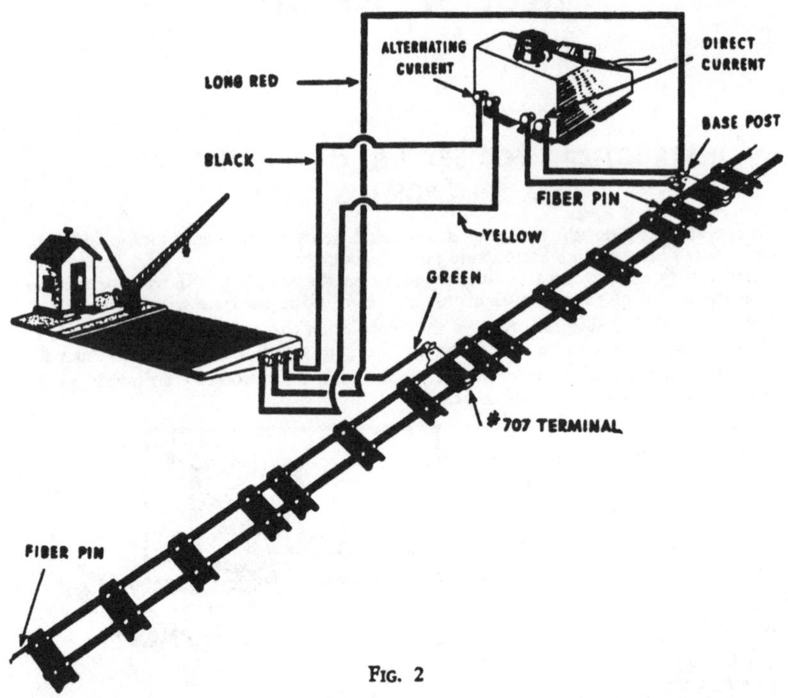

FIG. 2

TO HOOK UP TO A #14 ELECTRONIC RECTIFORMER

Study Figure 2 and proceed as follows:

Fasten No. 707 Track Terminal in the insulated section so the **BASE POST** clip is clamped on the insulated rail.

Connect the **YELLOW** wire from the **YELLOW** terminal to the inside alternating current post on the Rectiformer.

Connect the **BLACK** wire from the **BLACK** terminal to the outside alternating current post on the Rectiformer.

Connect the **GREEN** wire from the **GREEN** terminal to the No. 707 Track Terminal.

Connect the long **RED** wire to the **BASE POST** terminal which supplies current to the track.

The gate is now ready to operate. When the train enters the dead block the gates will go down and the lantern will light. After the train has passed through the block the gates will raise and the light in the lantern will go out.

CROSSING GATE
Model No. 592

XA9363	Guard Arm Assembly	.18 "
XA9365RP	Crossing Arm Assembly	.25 "
XA9371	Roof and Chimney Assembly	.22 "
XA10967	Coil Assembly	.80 "
XA10968	Solenoid Plunger Assembly	.28 "

WATER TANK
Model No. 596

INSTRUCTIONS FOR NO. 596 WATER TANK

1. Connect the **BLACK** wire to the **BASE POST** on the transformer.
2. Connect the **YELLOW** wire to the **15 VOLT POST** on the transformer.
3. Connect the **GREEN** wire to one of the clips underneath the Control Box.
4. Connect the **SHORT YELLOW** wire between the other clip on the Control Box and the **15 VOLT POST** on the transformer.

If these instructions have been followed the Air Beacon Light should be lit and the Water Spout should lower when the Control Button is pressed.

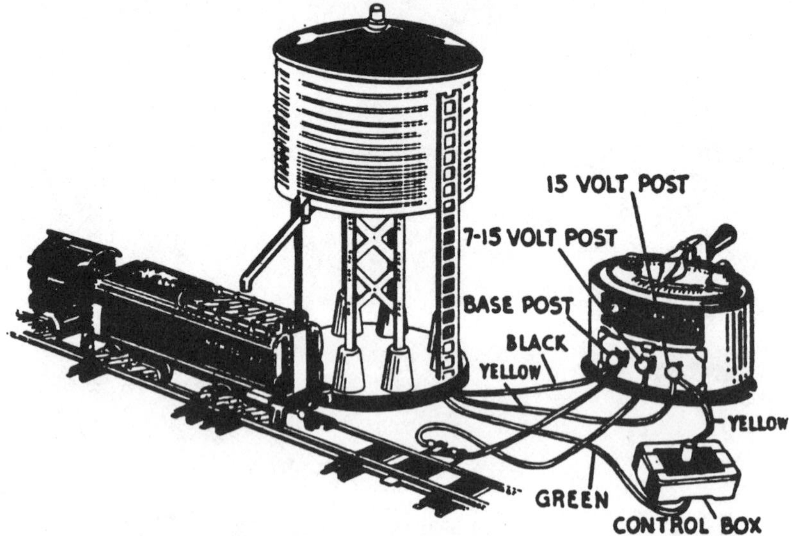

The illustration shows the Water Tank wiring in conjunction with standard wiring of transformer to track.

The Water Tank should be placed so that the spout can be lowered over the center of the track. The tender of your train can then be brought into position for filling.

 Ref: Form No. M2447

CROSSING GATE
Model No. 600

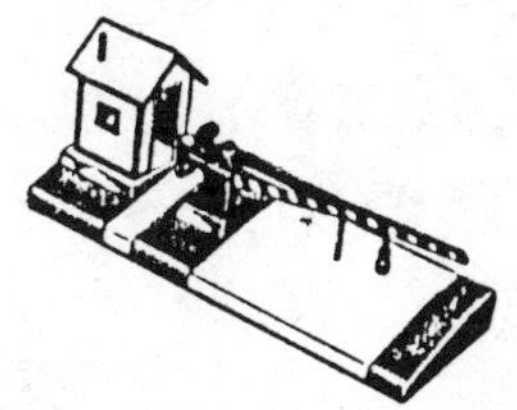

SERVICE INSTRUCTIONS

TO DISASSEMBLE AND REPLACE PARTS:

1. To remove Guard Arm (#3):

Spread open ends and lift Guard Arm (#3) off pins of Housing (#9).

2. To replace Bulb (#23) or Lamp Bracket (#18):

a. Take off Chimney and Roof (#1).

b. Unscrew Bulb (#23) from Lamp Bracket (#18).

c. Remove Screw (#22).

3. To remove Gate (#5):

Tap out Pin (#4) holding Gate Assembly to Housing (#9) just enough to release one half of weight on Gate Assembly.

4. To replace Solenoid Assembly (#19):

a. Remove Two Screws (#20).

b. Bend back lugs of Solenoid Housing (#17) and pry off Solenoid Assembly (#19).

c. Unsolder lead wires to solder terminal and Lamp Bracket Assembly (#18).

5. To replace Solenoid Plunger (#21) and Operating Link (#18):

a. Follow steps 3 and 4.

b. Lift off plunger from bottom of Operating Link.

6. To replace Housing (#9) or Solenoid Housing (#17):

a. Follow steps 4 and 5.

b. Push down on Solenoid Housing to separate from Base (#11).

7. To remove House (2):

a. Unscrew Binding Post Nuts (#15) and N-1 Nuts (#14).

b. Lift up House (#2) from Base (#11) and Plunger Assembly (#16) and Rubber Bumper (#10) will fall free.

c. Separate Coil, Bell and Bracket Assembly (#12) from House (#2).

8. To replace Base (#11):

Follow steps 2, 4, 5, 6, and 7.

Ref: Form No. 1759; Aug. 1, 1956

Crossing Gate — No. 600

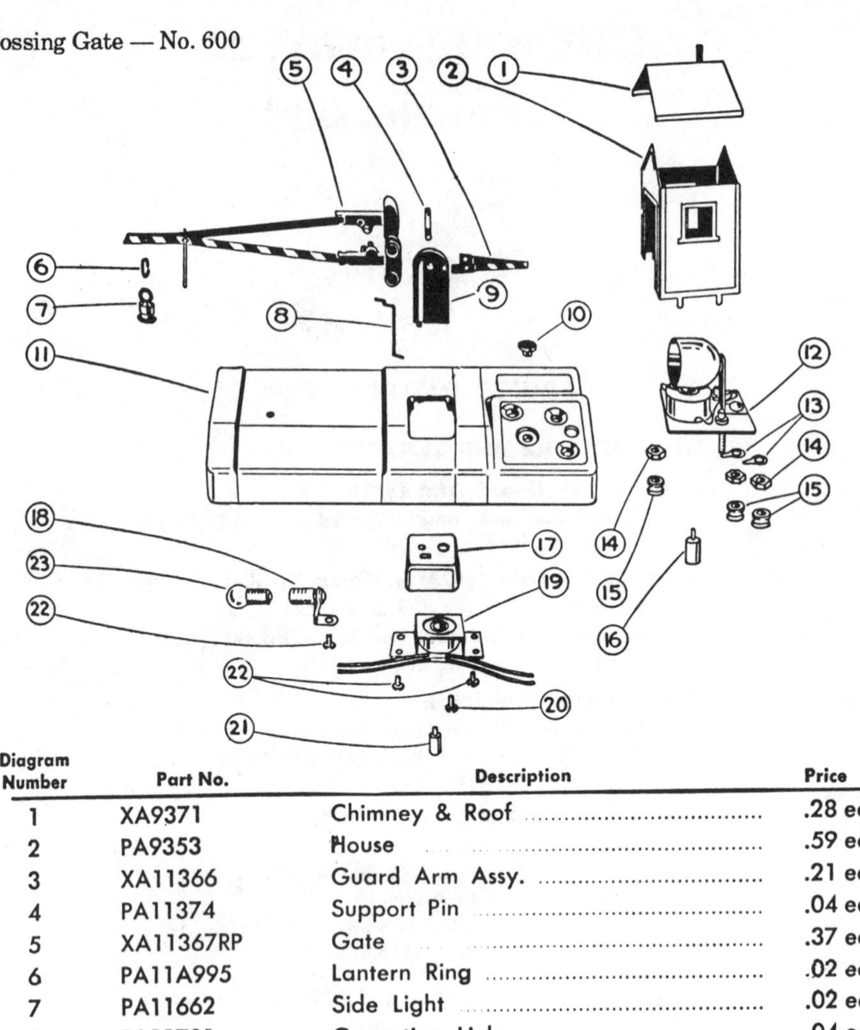

Diagram Number	Part No.	Description	Price
1	XA9371	Chimney & Roof	.28 ea.
2	PA9353	House	.59 ea.
3	XA11366	Guard Arm Assy.	.21 ea.
4	PA11374	Support Pin	.04 ea.
5	XA11367RP	Gate	.37 ea.
6	PA11A995	Lantern Ring	.02 ea.
7	PA11662	Side Light	.02 ea.
8	PA11701	Operating Link	.04 ea.
9	PA11371	Housing	.23 ea.
10	PA12A603	Rubber Bumper	.04 ea.
11	PA11689-A	Base	2.10 ea.
12	XA12A874	Coil, Bell, & Bracket Assy.	1.04 ea.
13	PA6173	Solder Terminal	.02 ea.
14	N1	Nut	.01 ea.
15	PA10037	Binding Post Nut	.02 ea.
16	XA12A601RP	Plunger Assy.	.05 ea.
17	PA11702	Solenoid Housing	.13 ea.
18	XA11704RP	Lamp Bracket	.11 ea.
19	XA11703	Solenoid Assy.	1.21 ea.
20	S282	Screw	.08 dz.
21	PA11705	Solenoid Plunger	.17 ea.
22	S183	Screw	.10 dz.
23	PA8999	Bulb	.25 ea.

 Ref: Form No. 1759; Aug. 1, 1956

TRACK TRIP
Model No. 697

USE OF #697 TRACK TRIP FOR THROWING TRACK SWITCHES AUTOMATICALLY

Switches can be thrown automatically by the Locomotive so that there is no chance of running into a switch which has been thrown against the oncoming train and causing a derailment.

This is accomplished by hooking the trip as shown in Figure 6.

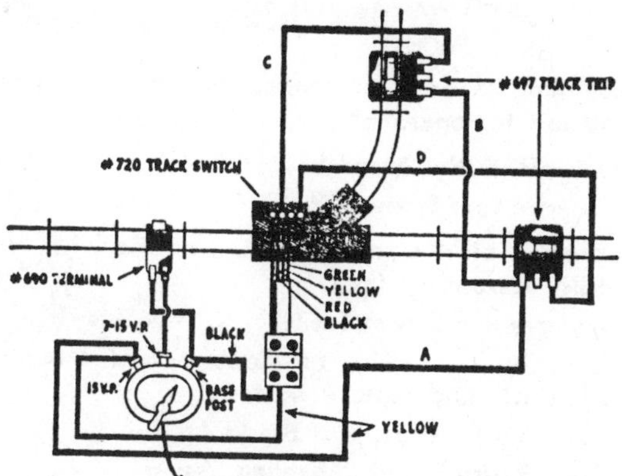

Figure 6.

Place a No. 697 trip ahead of the switch on both the curved and straight sections. Keep the trip about 2 sections of track from the switch. Hook the control box to the switches as instructed. Adjust trip so only the Locomotive will actuate it, then, when the train approaches the switch and the switch is set against it, the trip will automatically cause the frog to throw open so the train could pass thru without derailing.

Next hook wire "A" from Clip No. 1 on the one track trip to the **15 VOLT POST** on the transformer.

Connect the **TWO NO. 1 CLIPS** on track trips with wire "B".

Connect wire "C" from **No. #3 CLIP** on track trip which is on the curved rail to the **RED POST** on the track switch.

Connect wire "D" from the **No. 3 CLIP** on track trip which is on the straight rail to the **GREEN POST** on the track switch.

WHEN USING #14 ELECTRONIC RECTIFORMER.

Hook wire "A" to the **SAME ALTERNATING CURRENT POST** to which you have the **YELLOW WIRE** from the switch control box connected.

WHEN USING #15 DIRECTRONIC RECTIFIER.

Hook up direct to the transformer as shown in Figure 6.

HOOK UP No. 577 WHISTLES TO BLOW AUTOMATICALLY

Connect the green wire from the whistle to the No. 3 clip on a No. 697 track trip.

Connect a wire from the No. 1 Clip on the trip to the base post on the transformer.

In other words the No. 697 track trip acts the same as the control button and should be wired the same.

In addition to operating the above mentioned accessories the No. 697 track trip can be used in many ways to actuate lights, circuits, etc., which your ingenuity may suggest.

STEAM WHISTLE CONTROL
Model No. 710

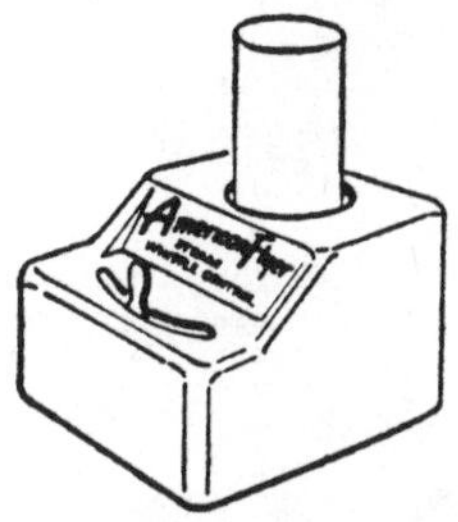

SERVICE INSTRUCTIONS

The first thing to do is to connect to track and transformer and test for operation.

1. To take off Body Assembly (#11)

a. Remove four Screws (#19).

2. To replace Coil Assembly (#4A) or Resistor and Mounting Assembly (#2)

a. Remove two Screws (#1).

b. Unsolder lead wire on Resistor and Mounting Assembly and replace part.

c. Take out Core Support Blocks (#3).

d. Push Resistor and Mounting Assembly (#2) to one side.

e. Unsolder Coil lead wires from Switch (#8), Socket (#13) and Solder Terminal (#14).

3. To replace Socket (#13)

a. Remove two Screws (#12) and take out two Sleeves (#7).

b. Unsolder all lead wires.

4. To replace Switch Arm (#6) or Spring (#15)

a. Take off Socket (#13).

b. Use Allen Wrench, size 1/32nd to unloosen Screw (#5), and Switch Arm can be removed.

c. To change Spring (#15), use needle-nosed pliers to open slightly the "U" bend on spring so that it can be removed from Switch Arm.

5. To replace Switch (#8)

a. Follow steps 1 to 4 removing necessary parts.

b. Remove Lock Nut holding Switch to Bracket.

c. Turn Post on Switch, either to full on or off position, so that Switch can be removed from Bracket.

d. Take off Washers (#17 and #18).

e. Unsolder lead wires from Switch.

 Ref: Form No. 1655; July 15, 1955

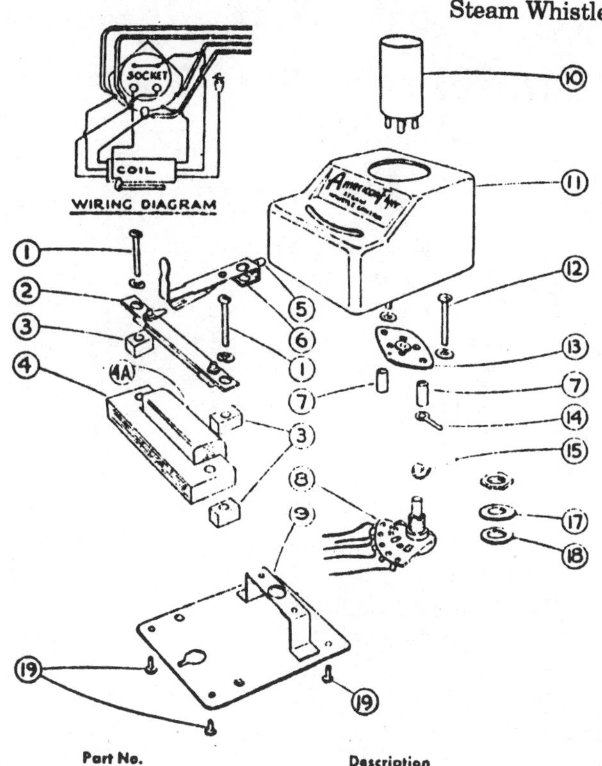

Diagram Number	Part No.	Description	Price
1	S4A11	Screw w/lockwasher	$ .03 ea.
2	XA13A225	Resistor and mounting assembly	.25 "
3	PA13A221	Core support block	.04 "
4	PA13A191	Lamination	.02 "
4A	XA13B237	Coil assembly	1.42 "
5	S273	Set screw	.14 "
6	XA13A233	Switch arm	.20 "
7	PA13A228	Sleeve	.07 "
8	XA13B215	Switch w/nut	.77 "
9	XA13A234	Base	.16 "
10	XA12A750	Vibrator	4.61 "
11	PA13C232	Case	.45 "
12	S4A09	Screw w/lockwasher	.03 "
13	PA11668-A	Socket	.13 "
14	PA10913	Solder Terminal	.01 "
15	PA13A235	Spring	.03 "
17	W140	Washer	.01 "
18	W3	Washer	.01 "
19	S4A10	Screw	.01 "

Ref: Form No. 1655; July 15, 1955

SWITCH
Model Nos. 720, 720A

#720 SWITCHES

PA9936	R or L Color Shutters	.25 ea.
PA9951	Shutter spacer	.10 "
XA9933	Left Hand Frog Assembly	.38 "
XA9932	Right Hand Frog Assembly	.38 "
PA10492	Stud for Frog Assembly	.04 "
XA10698	Control Box	4.50 "

XA9932	Right Hand Frog Assembly	.38 "
XA9933	Left Hand Frog Assembly	.38 "
PA9936-R	Right Color Shutter	.25 "
PA9936-L	Left Color Shutter	.25 "
PA9951	Shutter Spacer	.10 "
PA10492	Stud for Frog Assembly	.04 "
XA10698	Control Box	4.50 "

#720-A SWITCHES

PA10905	Left Frog	.22 ea.
PA10904	Right Frog	.22 "
PA10925	Switch Pilot Stud	.04 "
PA9935	Lens	.05 "
PA10928	Right or left Lamp housing	.28 "
XA10698	Control Box	4.50 "

PA9935	Lens	.05 ea.
PA10037	Binding Posts Nuts	.02 "
XA10698	Control Box	4.50 "
PA10904	Right Frog	.22 "
PA10905	Left Frog	.22 "
PA10922	Plunger	.05 "
PA10925	Switch Pilot Stud	.04 "
PA10928	Lamp Housing	.28 "
PA10929	Switch Screw	
PA10930	Coil	1.10 "
PA11414	Spring	

 Ref: Sept. 22, 1950; Nov. 13, 1952

LOG LOADER
Model No. 751

INSTRUCTIONS FOR NO. 751 LOG LOADER

Place the log loader in front of a section of straight track.

Connect the **BLACK** wire of the **RAINBOW CABLE** to the **BASE POST** on the transformer.

Connect the **YELLOW** wire from the control box to the **15V POST** on the transformer.

If You Are Using a No. 14 Electronic Rectiformer

Hook the **BLACK** and **YELLOW** wires to the two **ALTERNATING CURRENT** posts.

Place the three logs on the Log Loader platform.

Your log Loader is now ready to operate.

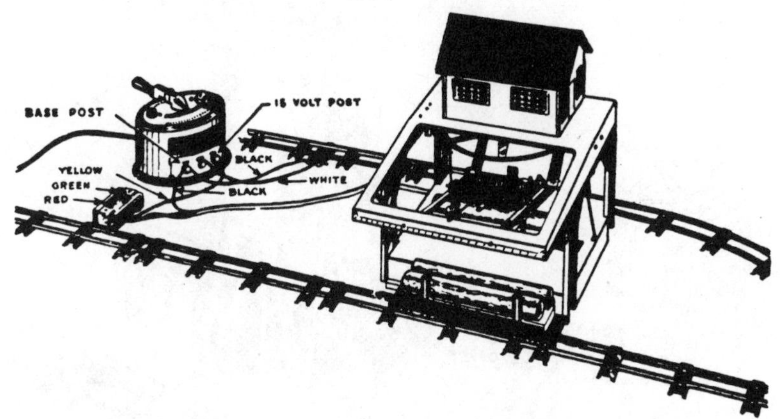

Press the **GREEN** button on the control box and one of the logs will be elevated to the carriage.

Press the **RED** button on the control box and the carriage will convey the log to the end of the arms and deposit it automatically into the empty car below, then return for a repeat operation.

Due to atmospheric conditions or use, the string which is used to elevate the carriage may stretch and become too long, thereby not allowing the log to release. If this happens, adjustment can be made by turning the nickel plated adjusting nut on the end of the carriage release rod, or by shortening the string a little.

If you have our No. 717 AUTOMATIC LOG DUMP CAR you can run a spur track to the back of the Log Loader, dump the logs automatically, then bring the train around to the front and have it loaded again.

(Hook up the No. 717 AUTOMATIC LOG CAR as shown in the instructions received with it.)

X2176-D	Stator Assembly	2.40	ea.
XA9917-A	Bearing Brkt. assembly	.28	"
XA9918	Rotor Assembly	1.05	"
PA9910	Roof	.75	"
PA9911	Log	.06	"
XA9219	Block and Pulley assembly	.25	"
PA9913	Base	1.60	"
P4553	12" Braided Twine	per ft. .01	
PA9889	Carriage Adjusting nut	.07	ea.

Ref: Form No. M2538; Sept. 22, 1950

AUTOMATIC SEABOARD COALER

Model Nos. 752, 752A, 23785

INSTRUCTIONS FOR SETTING UP AND OPERATING

After unpacking the No. 752 Seaboard Coaler, untie the string which holds the chute and track in place for shipment, then lift the track and truck assembly forward and insert the ends of the formed wire brace into the holes in the side of the upright. See that the cord is running through the various pulleys.

Now place the Coal Loader in the desired position in your track layout so the chute is over the track and coal will fall into the car below.

See diagram and hook-up as follows:

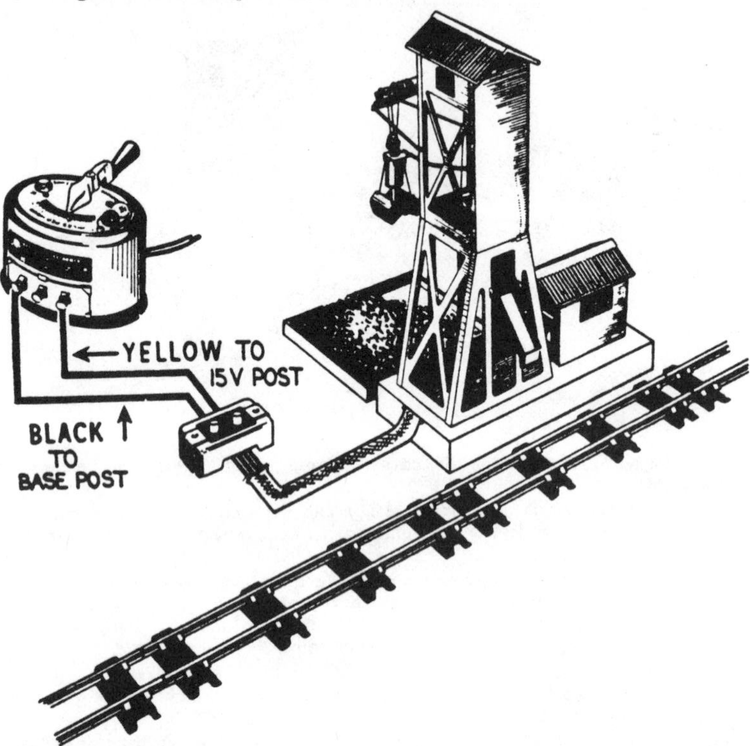

If you are using a transformer:—

Connect the **BLACK** wire to the **BASE POST** on the transformer.

Connect the **YELLOW** wire to the **15 VOLT POST** on the transformer.

If you are using a No. 14 Rectiformer:—

Connect the **YELLOW** and **BLACK** wires to the two **ALTERNATING CURRENT TAPS.**

Now press the **GREEN** button, on the Control Box, and the bucket will be lowered to the coal pile.

Press the **RED** button partially down and the jaws will clamp together. Press it all the way down, and the bucket will be elevated to the tower. Release the button and the coal will fall down the chute to the car.

OILING — Bearings and gears on the motor located in the engine house can be oiled by removing the roof and through the door. A few drops of light oil is all that is necessary.

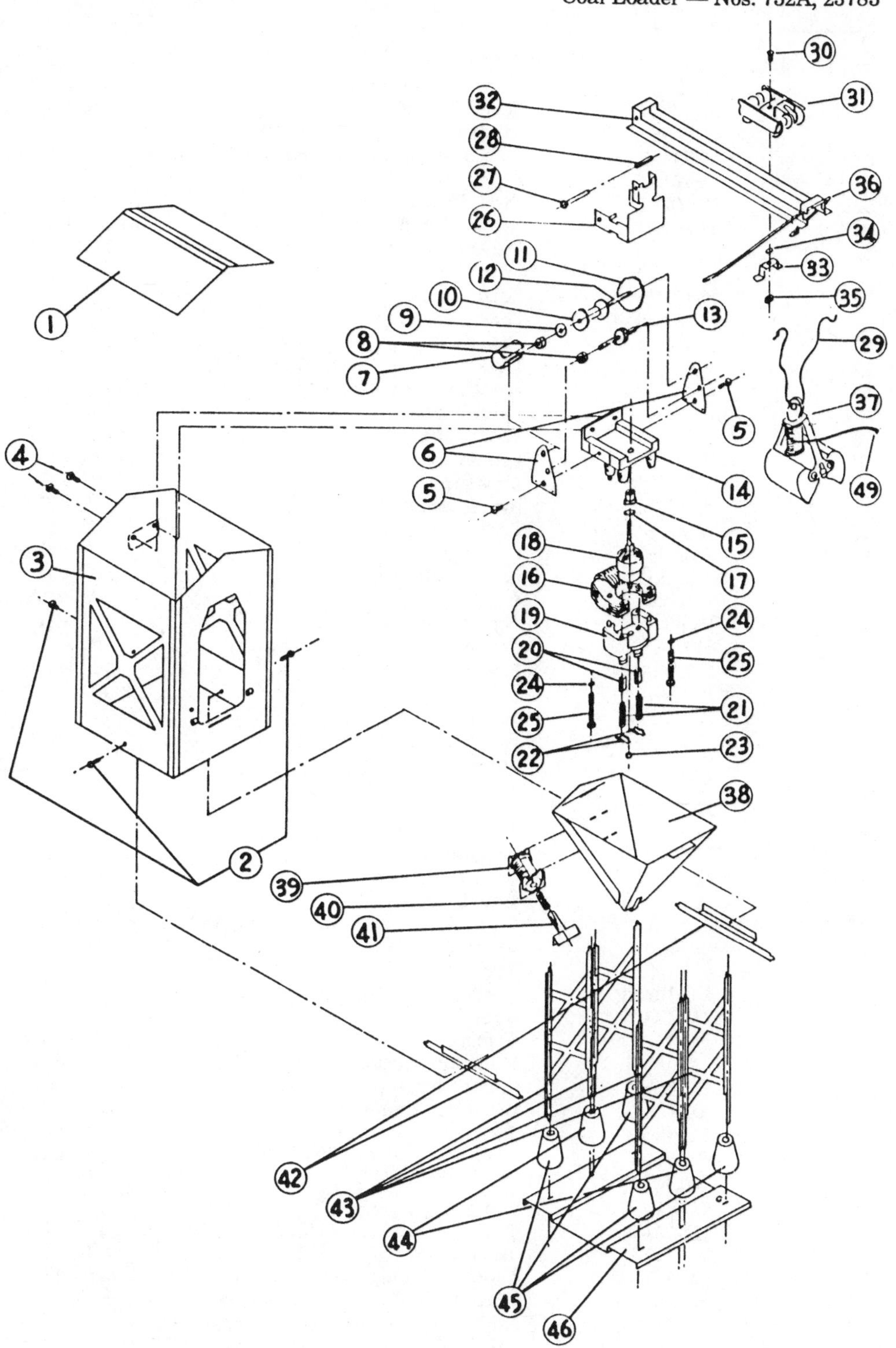
30
31
32
28
27
36
26
34
11
33
12
35
10
9
13
29
8
7
5
37
6
14
49
4
5
15
18
17
3
16
19
24
20
25
24
21
25
22
23
38
2
39
40
41
42
43
44
45
46

Coal Loader — Nos. 752A, 23785

DIA. NO.	PART NO.	DESCRIPTION		PRICE
1	PA13B392	Roof		.63 ea.
2	S171	#2 x 3/16 Type Z BH Screw		.01 ea.
3	XA13B388RP	Tower Assembly		5.64 ea.
	PA9039	Window		.03 ea.
4	S293	#6 x $\frac{1}{4}$ Type FPK Screw		.12 doz.
5	S242	Screw		.01 ea.
6	PA10221	Side Plate		.04 ea.
7	PA10826-A	Winch Guard		.10 ea.
8	X53-B	Collar Assembly		.17 ea.
9	PA10267	Friction Spring		.05 ea.
10	PA10225	Hoist Drum		.11 ea.
11	X2491-BRP	Gear Assembly. 66 T.		.59 ea.
12	PA10222	Shaft		.07 ea.
13	XA10223	Pinion & Worm gear Assembly		.79 ea.
14	XA10220RP	Motor Bracket & Bearing Assembly		.97 ea.
15	PA9575	Worm Bushing		.13 ea.
16	XA10266	Field Assembly		1.03 ea.
17	W83	Washer		.04 ea.
18	XA13C375	Armature Assembly		2.07 ea.
19	XA9565A	Brush Bracket Assembly		.55 ea.
20	PA9603	Brush		.13 ea.
21	PA10757A	Spring		.02 ea.
22	PA10754	Brush Tube Cap		.02 ea.
23	PA9522	Oil Wick		.01 ea.
24	PA3769	Lockwasher		.01 ea.
25	S33	Screw		.01 ea.
26	PA13A403	Bracket		.19 ea.
27	PA13A401	Idler Axle		.01 ea.
28	PA13A400	Idler		.15 ea.
29	PA11295B	Braided Nylon		.10 ea.
30	S1	Screw		.01 ea.
31	XA10230	Truck Assembly		1.46 ea.
32	XA13B399RP	Track		.58 ea.
33	PA10231	Truck Guide Strip		.10 ea.
34	W46	Lockwasher		.01 ea.
35	N1	#4-40 Hex Nut		.01 ea.
36	PA13A398	Track Brace		.10 ea.
37	XA10313RP	Clam Shell & Bucket Assembly		3.48 ea.
	P168	Sheave Pulley		.03 ea.
	P3965	Rivet		.02 ea.
38	XA13B384	Hopper Assembly		.48 ea.
39	XA13B381	Coil Assembly		.96 ea.
40	PA13A402	Spring		.02 ea.
41	XA13A394	Plunger Assembly		.16 ea.
42	PA13A411	Tower Brace		.17 ea.
43	PA9545A	Upright Girder		.45 ea.
44	PA9546B	Pier		.63 ea.
45	PA9546A	Pier		.07 ea.
46	PA13B397	Base		.74 ea.
47	XA14A966-3A	Control Box	NOT SHOWN	1.44 ea.
48	PA402-C	Tray	NOT SHOWN	.42 ea.
49	PA9267C	Tinsel Cord	NOT SHOWN	.30 ea.
50	PA13A208A	4 Cond. Cable	NOT SHOWN	.04 ft.
51	LW-1B2	Wire Yellow	NOT SHOWN	.02 ft.

Prices subject to change without notice

 Ref: Form No. M5237; June 1, 1960

PART NO.	DESCRIPTION	PRICE
XA9565-A	Brush Bracket Assembly	.50 ea.
XA9569	Armature Assembly	2.50 "
PA9603-A	Brush	.15 "
XA10223	Pinion and Worm Gear Assembly	.65 "
XA10230	Truck Assembly	1.20 "
XA10266	Field Assembly	.85 "
XA10313-RP	Clam Shell and Bucket Assembly	2.85 "
PA10754	Brush Cap	.02 "
PA10757	Brush Spring	.05 "

#752 SEABOARD COALER

PA9267-A	Bucket Cable	.15 ea.
XA10230	Truck Assembly	1.20 "
XA10223	Pinion and worm gear assembly	.65 "
XA9569	Armature	2.50 "
XA10266	Field assembly	.85 "
XA9565A	Brush Bracket Assembly	.50 "
PA9603A	Motor Brush	.15 "
PA10757	Brush Spring	.05 "
PA10754	Brush cap	.02 "
XA10313RP	Clam Shell and Bucket Assembly	2.85 "

TALKING STATION
Model Nos. 755, 755A

INSTRUCTIONS FOR SETTING UP AND OPERATING

This Talking Station is designed to operate on 60 cycle current only. It will operate from a transformer running the train on ALTERNATING CURRENT or from a transformer and rectifier running the train on DIRECT CURRENT.

First determine the approximate position in your layout where you want the station located, then remove a steel pin from the outside rail and replace with a fiber track pin, then several sections away repeat this operation. This will give you 2 or 3 sections of rail which is completely insulated from the rest of the track.

Next clip the #707 Track Terminal on the track so the BASE POST CLIP is connected to the insulated rail.

If you are using a TRANSFORMER only to operate the train on ALTERNATING CURRENT follow the wiring diagram in Figure #1.

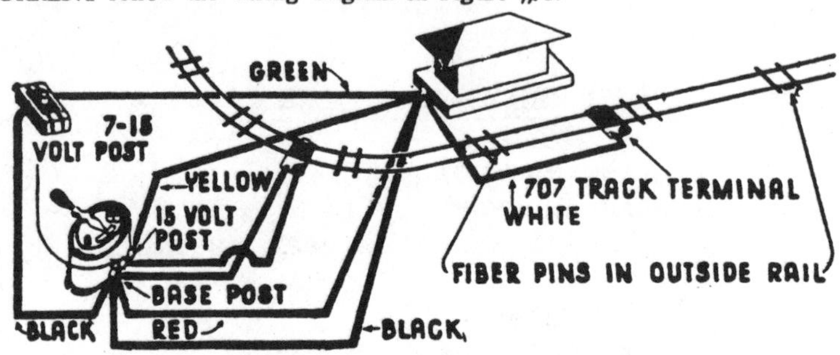

FIGURE 1

If you are using a TRANSFORMER and #15 DIRECTRONIC RECTIFIER to operate the train on DIRECT CURRENT follow the wiring diagram in Figure #2.

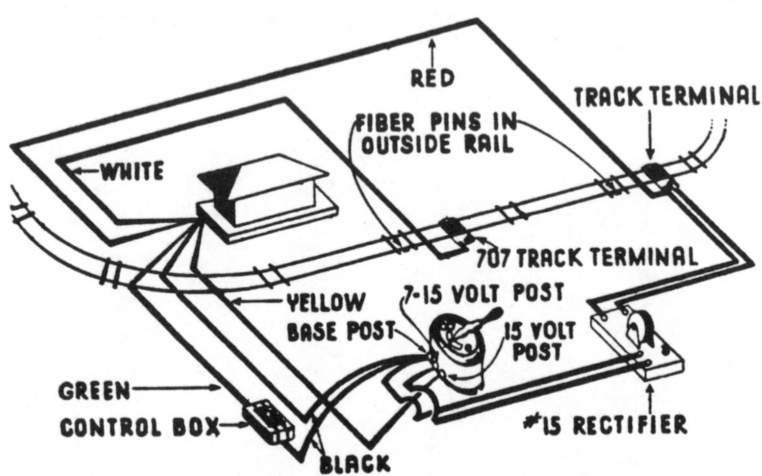

FIGURE 2

Next remove the cork from the needle in the reproducer and attach the horn to the reproducer neck — then insert the reproducer into the unit (See Figure 3) so the horn faces away from the motor and the two pins fit into the slots on the upright brackets and the needle is resting on the record.

 Ref: Form No. M2600

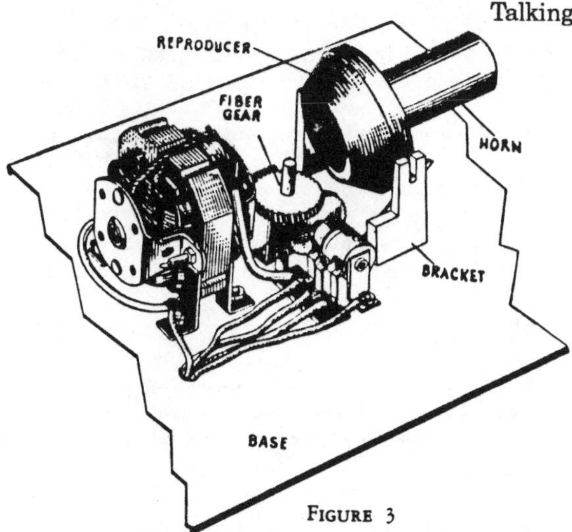

FIGURE 3

Now start the train, if it has a regular sequence reverse be sure the reversing unit is locked in a forward position, and as it approaches the station and the insulated portion of the track, press the control box button, and the train will stop at the station while the train announcer makes his announcement, then with a series of train noises the train will automatically start and run until you again press the button for a repeat performance. NOTE: on a small oval of track do not press the button a second time until the train has made several revolutions and the motor in the station has come to a stop.

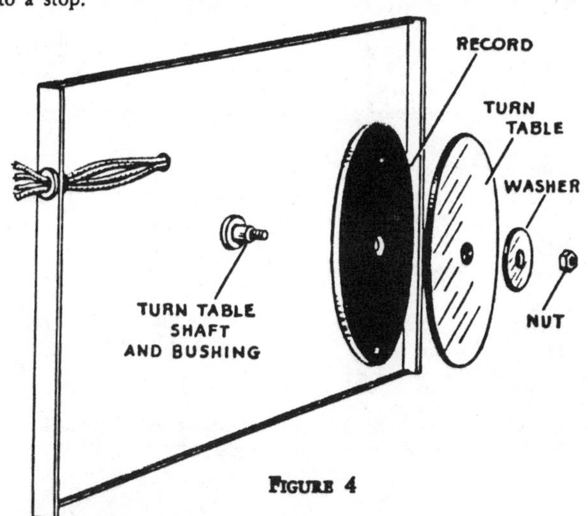

FIGURE 4

CHANGING THE RECORD

To change the record remove the nut at the end of the turntable shaft. (See Figure 4) Slide the turntable and the record off the shaft, turn the record over and replace on the shaft with the turntable and washer. Tighten up on the nut.

Replace the needle with any chrome plated needle every fifty times.

OILING

Keep all bearings well oiled, lubricate the gears with a small amount of vasoline or thin grease.

If the lamps should burn out replace it with either a 14 or 18 volt lamp.

For a maximum amount of sound open the station doors.

INSTRUCTIONS FOR SETTING UP AND OPERATING #755 TALKING STATION WITH 3 RAIL TRACK AND AN AMERICAN FLYER TRANSFORMER

First determine the approximate location in your layout where you want the station located. Then remove the steel pin from the center rail and replace with a fibre pin: several sections of track away repeat this operation. This will give you two or three sections of track with the center rail completely insulated from the rest of the track. Next fasten a track terminal in this section of track and follow the diagram below.

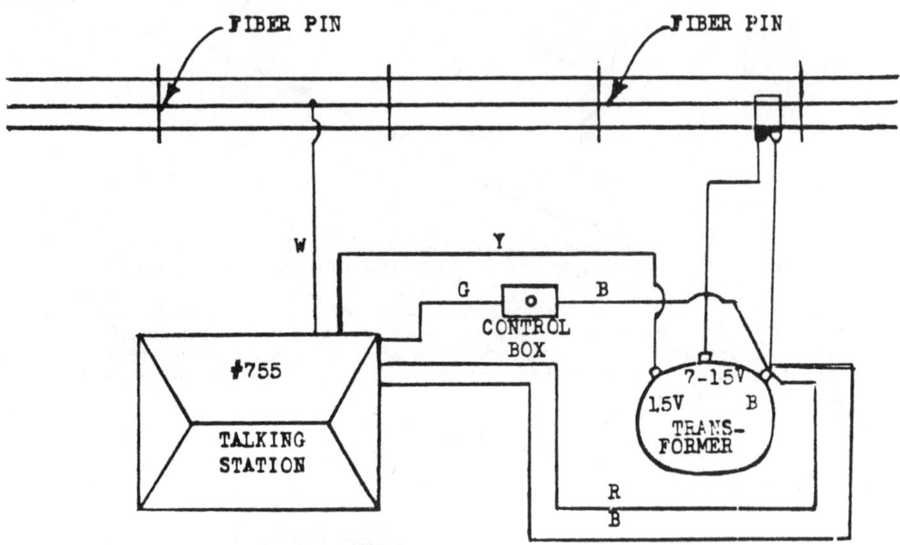

Connect the WHITE wire from the station to the track terminal clip which connects to the center rail in the special insulated section.

Connect the GREEN wire to clip under control box.
Connect the separate BLACK wire from other control box clip to BASE POST on transformer.
Connect the BLACK wire from station to BASE POST on transformer.
Connect the RED wire from station to BASE POST on transformer.
Connect the YELLOW wire from station to 15 VOLT POST on transformer.

Be sure wires from track to transformer are hooked as in the diagram. BASE POST to center rail and 7 TO 15 VOLT POST to outside rail.

IN HOOKING UP #755 TALKING STATION TO LIONEL TRANSFORMERS FOLLOW THE ABOVE DIAGRAM AND HOOK WIRES AS FOLLOWS.

Type "S" and "S220" Transformers:
"B" Post on transformer to center rail
"U" Post on transformer to outside rail.
Two black and one red wire from station to "B" Post on transformer.
Yellow wire from station to "C" Post on transformer.

Type "R" and "R220" Transformers:
"B" Post on transformer to center rail.

"F" Post on transformer to outside rail.
Two black and one red wire from station to "B" Post on transformer.
Yellow wire from station to "E" Post on transformer.

Type "RW" Transformers:
"U" Post on transformer to outside rail
"B" Post on transformer to center rail.
Two black and one red wire from station to "B" Post on transformer.
Yellow wire from station to "D" Post on transformer.

Type "RWM" Transformer:
"A" Post on transformer to center rail
"U" Post on transformer to outside rail
Two black and one red wire from station to "A" Post on transformer.
Yellow wire on station to "D" Post on transformer.

HOOKUP OF NO. 755A TALKING STATION
to
"KW" AND "ZW" LIONEL TRANSFORMERS

"KW" - 190 WATT

1. Connect wire from "U" Post to Center Rail.

2. Connect wire from "A" Post to Outside Rail.

3. Connect white wire from station to insulated center rail.

4. Connect black and red wire from station to "U" Post on Transformer.

5. Connect yellow wire from station to "D" Post on Transformer.

6. Connect green wire from station to control box clip.

7. Connect other wire from control box clip to "U" Post on transformer.

"ZW" - 300 WATT

1. Connect wire from "U" Post on transformer to center rail.

2. Connect wire from "A" Post on transformer to outside rail.

3. Connect white wire from station to insulated center rail.

4. Connect black and red wire from station to any "U" Post on transformer.

5. Connect yellow wire from station to "B" Post on transformer.

6. Connect green wire from station to clip under control box.

7. Connect short wire from other clip under control box to any "U" Post on transformer.

8. Connect set "BU" control lever on transformer at 16 volts.

N-1	Nut	.01 ea.
PA8554-A	Turntable only	.40 "
XA9163	Reproducing Assembly	3.50 "
XA10091	Track Terminal #707	.20 "
PA10721	Turntable Bushing	.20 "
XA10739	Turntable Shaft Assembly	.50 "
XA10740	Cam Shaft Assembly	.70 "
XA10744	Contact Base Assembly	.25 "
PA10746	Record	.85 "
PA10748	Needle	.10 "
PA11073	10 Ohm 10 Watt Resistor	1.04 "

#755 TALKING STATION

PART NO.	DESCRIPTION	PRICE
XA10739	Turntable Shaft assembly	.50 ea.
PA10721	Turntable Bushing	.20 "
PA8554A	Turntable only	.40 "
PA10748	Needle	.10 "
XA9163	Reproducing assembly	3.50 "
PA9176	Contact Springs	.10 "
XA10744	Contact Base Assembly	.25 "
XA10740	Cam Shaft Assembly	.70 "
XA10091	Track Terminal	.20 "
PA10746	Record	.85 "
PA11073	10 Ohm 10 watt resistor	1.04 "
W85	Washer	.15dz.
X4451-A	Brg. Brkt Assembly	.18 ea.
XA9917-B	Brg. & Motor Brkt Assembly	.28 "
X2177-F	Rotor assembly	1.00 "
X2176-D	Stator	2.40 "

 Ref: Nov. 13, 1952; Sept. 22, 1950

"SAM" THE SEMAPHORE MAN
Model Nos. 758, 758A

INSTRUCTIONS FOR SETTING UP AND OPERATING

First determine the approximate location in your layout where you wish the semaphore to be stationed.

Then remove a steel pin from the outside rail and replace with a fiber pin. Now several sections of track from this fiber pin repeat this operation. This will give you two or three sections of rail which are completely insulated from the rest of the track.

Next clip the 707 Track Terminal on the track so the **BASE POST** clip is connected to the insulated rail.

If you are using a Transformer and operating your train on an **ALTERNATING CURRENT** follow the wiring diagram in FIGURE 1.

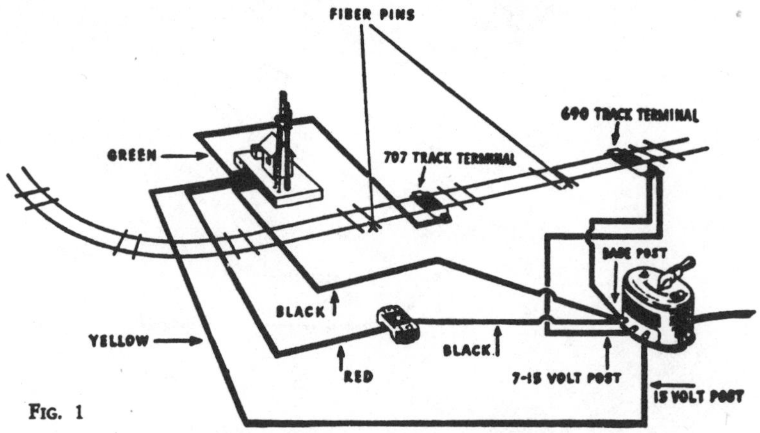

FIG. 1

If you are using a Transformer and #15 Directronic Rectifier to operate the train on **DIRECT CURRENT** follow the wiring in FIGURE 2.

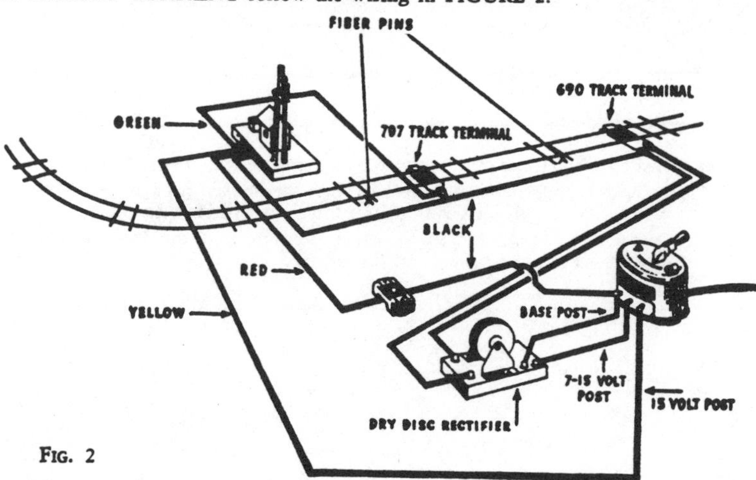

FIG. 2

When the current is turned on the semaphore arm will be in an upright position and the green light will show.

Allow the train to run around the track, press down the control box button, the door will open and "SAM", The Semaphore Man, will come out of the house. At the same time the semaphore arm will go to a down position and the red light will show. When the train enters the insulated section the train will stop.

By releasing the button the train will start again.

Ref: Form No. M2593

IF YOU ARE USING A NO. 15 DIRECTRONIC RECTIFIER AND TRANSFORMER AND OPERATING YOUR TRAIN ON D.C.

Study Figure 3, and proceed as follows.

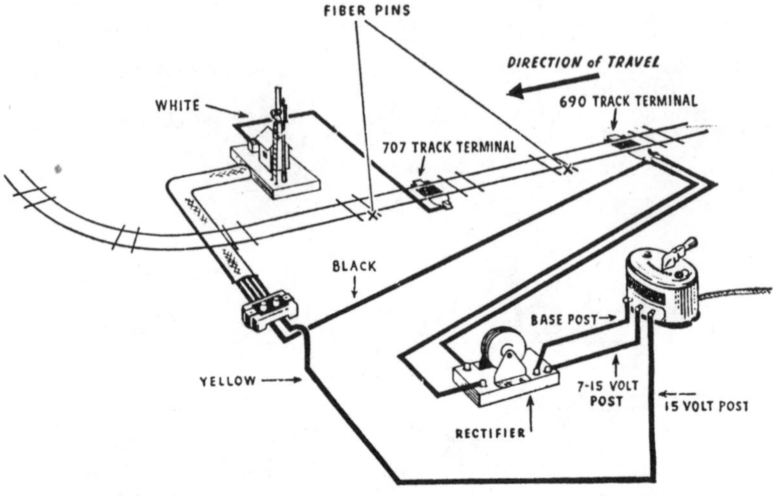

FIGURE 3.

Connect the **BLACK** wire from the Control Box to the **BASE POST CLIP** on the **No. 690 TRACK TERMINAL** which supplies current to the track.

Connect the **YELLOW** wire to the **15 VOLT POST** on the transformer.

If the unit should fail to function, switch the two wires on the D.C. terminals on the Rectifier base.

The Semaphore should now be ready to operate. Turn on the current and allow the train to run around the track.

Press the red button on the Control Box; the door will open and "Sam" will come out of the house, at the same time the Semaphore arm will go to a down position and the red light will show. When the train enters the insulated section, the train will stop.

Press the green button and "Sam" will go back into the house, the door will close, the signal arm will go to an upright position, and the train will start again.

NOTE: To change the lamp, loosen the small set screw in the lamp housing which will allow the socket to be pulled out to remove the lamp.

#758A SAM

S171	Screw	.01 ea.
PA8887	Spring	.05 "
PA10689	Man	.43 "
XA11073	Resistor	1.04 "

BELL DANGER SIGNAL
Model No. 759

INSTRUCTIONS FOR SETTING UP AND OPERATING

To hook up the No. 759 Bell Danger Signal, first determine the approximate location in your layout where you wish it to operate; then attach the two No. 696 Track Trips to the track one on each side of the highway which is to be protected, and have the trips about 2 feet apart. To do this, first place the trips under the track so that lower flange on one rail nests under the raised portion of the metal strip with the "U" shaped cutout and the locking lever locks on the same rail as that to which the **BASE POST** wire connects. Note Diagram.

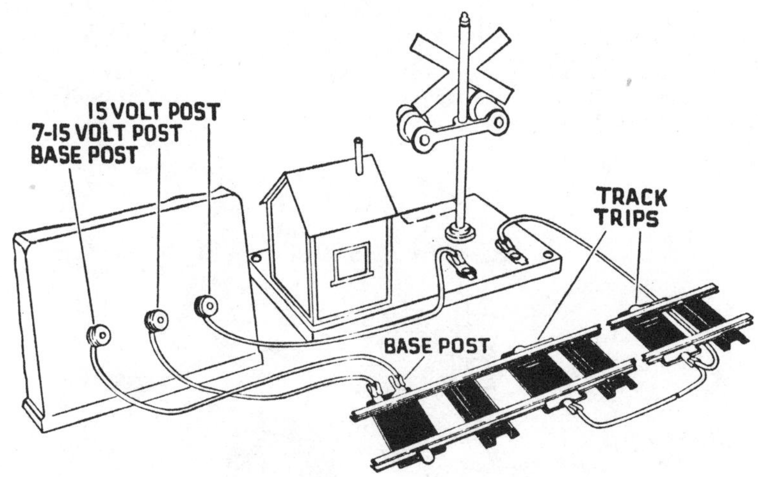

When Using A Transformer

Attach the **SHORT BLACK WIRE** from one terminal post on the signal to the terminal clip on the track trip.

Attach the **YELLOW WIRE** from the other terminal post on the signal to the **15 VOLT POST** on the transformer.

Next attach the **LONG BLACK WIRE** between the two clips on the No. 696 Track Trips.

The signal is now ready to operate. When the train passes over the track trip the red lamps will flash on and off, and bell will ring to warn any motorist of the approaching train.

PART NO.	DESCRIPTION		PRICE
XA9371-A	Roof & Chimney Assembly -	759 & 23759	.50 ea.
PA9353-C	House	759 & 23759	1.01 ea.
XA12A600	Coil Assembly	759 & 23759	.81 ea.
XA12A601RP	Plunger Assembly	759 & 23759	.06 ea.
XA12A592	Bell & Bracket Assembly	759 & 23759	.20 ea.
PA8999-R	Bulb		.30 ea.
#696	Track Trip		.40 ea.
PA4362	Rivet		.01 ea.
PA4364	Rivet		.01 ea.
PA4365	Rivet		.01 ea.

Ref: Form No. M3202

HIGHWAY FLASHER
Model No. 760

INSTRUCTIONS FOR SETTING UP AND OPERATING No. 760 HIGHWAY FLASHER

To hook up the No. 760 Highway Flasher, first determine the approximate location in your layout where you want it, then attach the No. 696 Track Trip to the Track. To do this, first place the trip under the track so that lower flange on one rail nests under the raised portion of the metal strip with the "U" shaped cutout and the locking lever locks on the same rail as that to which the **BASE POST** wire connects. **NOTE DIAGRAM.**

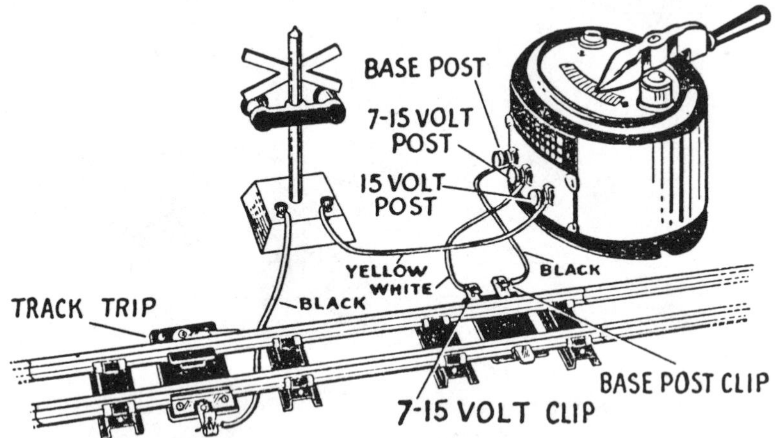

Next attach the **BLACK** wire from one terminal post on the signal to the terminal clip on the track trip.

Then attach the **YELLOW** wire from the other terminal post on the signal to the 15 **VOLT POST** on the transformer.

The signal is now ready to operate when the train passes over the track trip the red lamp will flash on and off to warn any motorist of the approaching train.

PART NO.	DESCRIPTION		PRICE
XA9371-A	Roof & Chimney Assembly -	759 & 23759	.50 ea.
PA9353-C	House	759 & 23759	1.01 ea.
XA12A600	Coil Assembly	759 & 23759	.81 ea.
XA12A601RP	Plunger Assembly	759 & 23759	.06 ea.
XA12A592	Bell & Bracket Assembly	759 & 23759	.20 ea.
PA8999-R	Bulb		.30 ea.
#696	Track Trip		.40 ea.
PA4362	Rivet		.01 ea.
PA4364	Rivet		.01 ea.
PA4365	Rivet		.01 ea.

 Ref: Form No. M2648

SEMAPHORE
Model Nos. 761, 23761

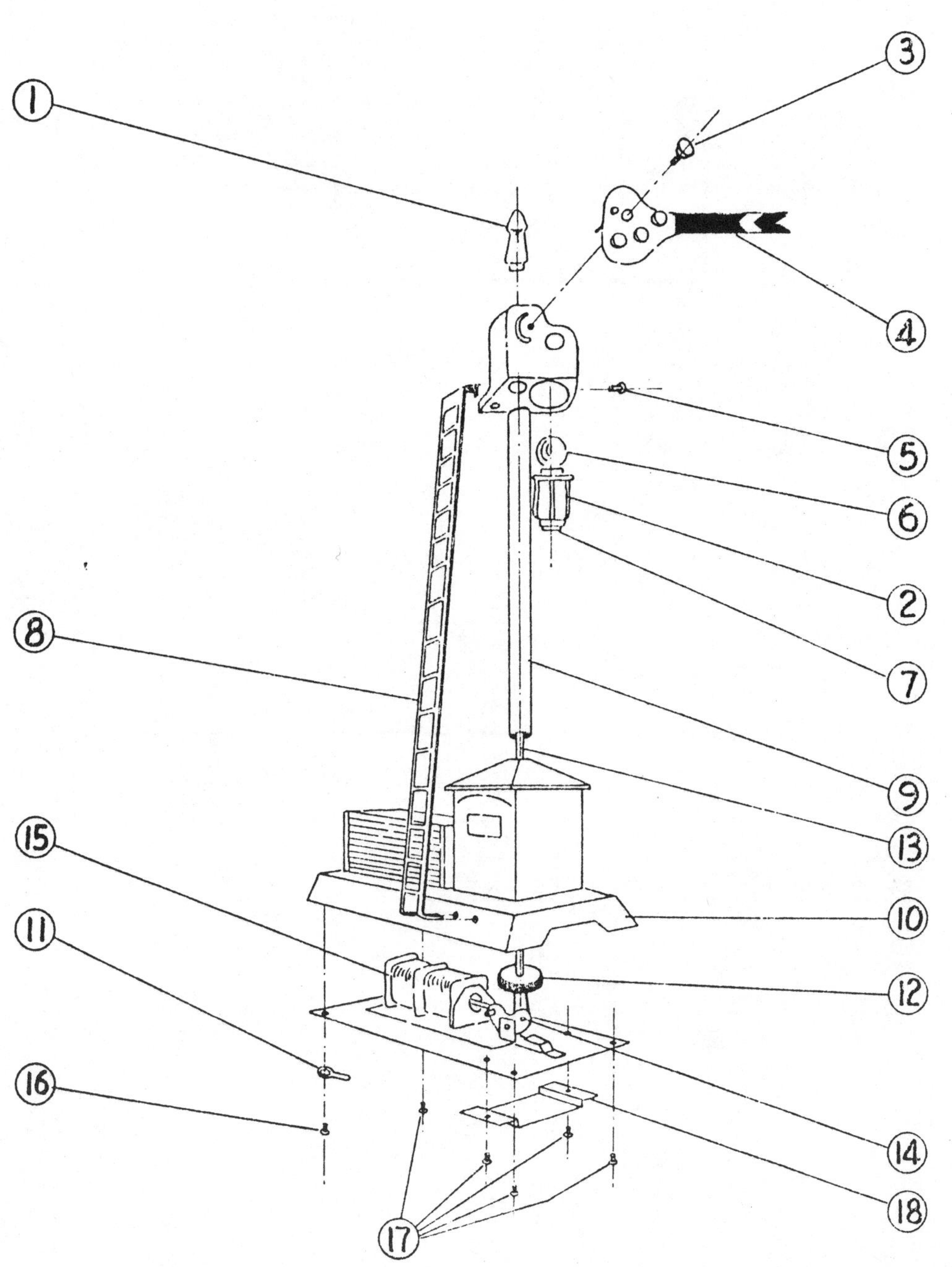

Ref: Form No. M5228; June 1, 1960

HOOK UP OF No. 761 SEMAPHORE TO A NO. 14 ELECTRONIC RECTIFORMER.

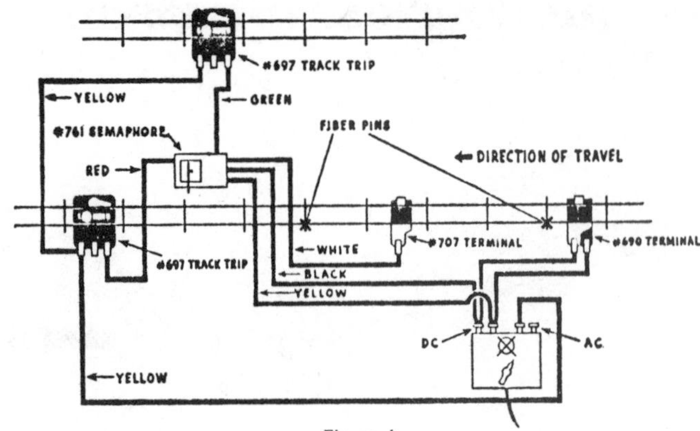

Figure 4.

Connect the **YELLOW** wire to the **INSIDE DC POST** on the rectiformer.
Connect the **BLACK** wire to the **OUTSIDE DC POST** on the rectiformer.
Connect the **WHITE** wire to the **No. 707 TRACK TERMINAL.**
Connect the **RED** wire to the #3 **CLIP ON No. 697 TRACK TRIP** which is in front of the controlled section.
Connect the **GREEN** wire to the #3 **CLIP** on the other track trip.
Connect the two No. 1 clips together on the track trips with a wire.
Connect a wire from the #1 Clip on one track trip to the **INSIDE AC POST** on the Rectiformer.
Be sure the wire from the **OUTSIDE DC POST** is connected to the **BASE POST CLIP** on the **No. 690 TRACK TERMINAL.**

HOOK UP OF No. 761 SEMAPHORE TO A #15 DIRECTRONIC RECTIFIER AND TRANSFORMER.

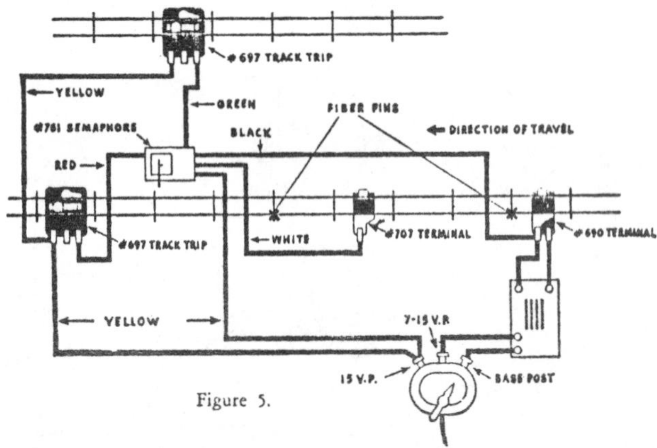

Figure 5.

Connect the **YELLOW** wire to the **15 VOLT POST** on the transformer.
Connect the **BLACK** wire to the **BASE POST CLIP** on the **No. 690 TRACK TERMINAL.**
Connect the **WHITE** wire to the No. 707 track terminal.
Connect the **RED** wire to the #3 clip on No. 697 track trip which is in front of the controlled section.
Connect the **GREEN** wire to the #3 clip on the other track trip.
Connect the two No. 1 clips on the track trips together with a wire.
Connect a wire from the #1 **CLIP** on one track trip to the **15 VOLT POST ON THE TRANSFORMER.**

When the train crosses the trip with the green wire attached the semaphore arm will go up, the green light will show and the controlled section will be alive.

When the train crosses the trip with the red wire attached the semaphore arm will go down, the red light will show and the controlled section will be dead.

If you are operating 2 trains on the track the one train will stand in the controlled section until the other train throws the arm up, thus forming a controlled block system to protect the train.

NO.	PART NO.	DESCRIPTION	PRICE
1	PA10938	Post Cap	.14 ea.
2	PA10939	Light Housing	.66 ea.
3	S-283	Shouldered Screw	.03 ea.
4	XA10941-RP	Signal Arm and Lens Assembly	.71 ea.
5	S185	#00 x 1/8 P.K. Screw	.01 ea.
6	PA9723	Clear Lamp	.30 ea.
7	XA10940-RP	Socket Cup Assembly	.67 ea.
8	PA10943	Ladder	.31 ea.
9	PA10937	Post	1.02 ea.
10	PA10936	Base	1.69 ea.
11	PA10059	Solder Terminal	.01 ea.
12	PA10958	Weight	.11 ea.
13	PA11144	Operating Rod	.54 ea.
14	PA10954	Rod Stud	.01 ea.
15	XA10946	Operating Mechanism Assembly	3.27 ea.
	PA10947	Operating Link	.03 ea.
	PA10953	Link Stud	.04 ea.
	XA10952	Plunger & Rod Assembly	.10 ea.
	XA10955	Coil Assembly	1.65 ea.
	PA10948	Contact	.11 ea.
	PA10946	Magnetic Shield	.08 ea.
	PA10945	Bottom Plate	.23 ea.
16	S171	2 x 3/16 P.K. Screw	.01 ea.
17	S183	2 x ¼ P.K. Screw	.01 ea.
18	PA11109	Contact Guard	.01 ea.

Prices subject to change without notice.

TWO-IN-ONE WHISTLE
Model No. 762

HOOK UP AND OPERATION OF

This Whistle is equipped with a high speed universal motor and can be blown with two distinct tones, one to simulate a train near at hand and one in the distance.

To hook up note diagram below and wire as follows.

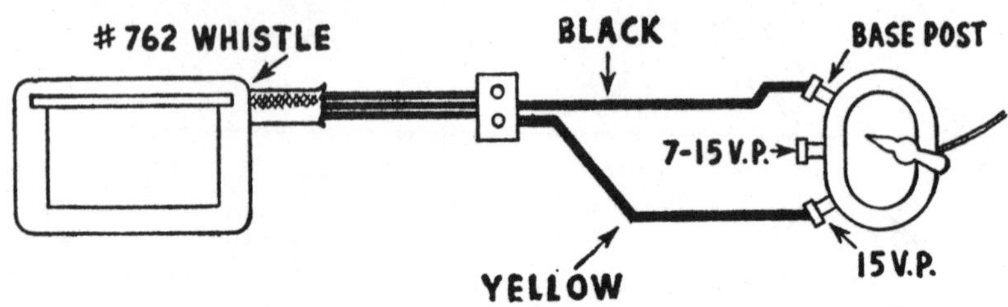

WHEN USING A TRANSFORMER OR TRANSFORMER AND RECTIFIER

Connect the YELLOW wire from the Control Box to the 15 VOLT POST on the transformer.

Connect the BLACK wire from the Control Box to the BASE POST on the transformer.

WHEN USING A NO. 14 ELECTRONIC RECTIFORMER

Connect the YELLOW wire to one ALTERNATING CURRENT POST.

Connect the BLACK wire to the other ALTERNATING CURRENT POST.

Press the GREEN BUTTON and the whistle will blow one tone.

Press the RED BUTTON and a different whistle tone will be blown.

OILING

To lubricate the motor, place a few drops of oil on the shaft bearing. Top bearing can be reached through a hole in top of the housing and bottom bearing is covered with a felt wick which can be saturated with oil. Do not get oil on the motor brushes as this will cause the commutator to get dirty and gummed up and slow down motor.

XA9431-A	Armature Assembly	1.75 ea.
XA9434	Field Assembly	.75 "
XA9565-B	Brush Bracket Assembly	.50 "
PA10757	Brush Spring	.05 "
PA10754	Brush Cap	.02 "
PA9603	Brush	.15 "
PA10989	Whistle Housing	.80 "
PA10992	Bottom Cover gasket	.04 "
PA10993	Top Cover gasket	.04 "
PA9432	Blower Fan	.25 "
XA11064	Billboard Label & Sign Assembly	.42 "

 Ref: Form No. M2688; Sept. 22, 1950

ANIMATED STATION PLATFORM AND CAR

Model No. 766

HOOK UP AND OPERATING INSTRUCTIONS

The No. 766 Animated Station Platform and Car unit consists of the following.

1 – No. 766 Animated Station Platform
1 – No. 735 Operating Coach
1 – Control Box Unit
2 – Wood Screws for Mounting the Control Box
4 – Miniature People

To install this unit, place it in a portion of the layout so there are at least 2 straight tracks to mount on the platform base. Nest the straight track between the tie holders as shown in the diagram.

NOTE . . . If only two sections of straight track are used, the station is to be placed on the inside of the oval. If more than two sections of straight track are used the station can be placed on either side of the track.

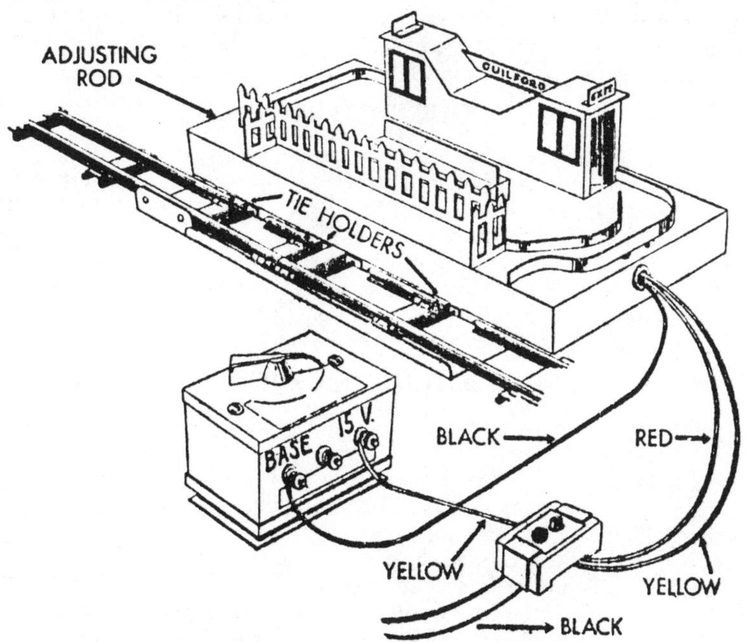

HOOK UP OF NO. 766 TO A TRANSFORMER

Connect **BLACK WIRE** from platform to **BASE POST** on transformer.

Connect **RED WIRE** from platform to wire clip under the red button on Control Box.

Connect **YELLOW WIRE** from platform to remaining spring clip on Control Box.

Connect **YELLOW WIRE** from Control Box to **15 VOLT POST** on transformer.

Ref: Form No. M2890

If this unit is used on a layout powered with a transformer do not use the **TWO BLACK WIRES** on the control box. They can be clipped off and discarded.

If unit is used on a layout run by direct current and powered by a transformer and rectifier connect one **BLACK WIRE** to the **BASE POST** on the transformer and the other **BLACK WIRE** to the **BASE POST** clip on the track terminal.

If the unit is used on a layout powered by a No. 16 Rectiformer connect one **BLACK WIRE** to the inside **A C POST** and the other **BLACK WIRE** to the **BASE POST** clip on the track terminal.

OPERATING INSTRUCTIONS

Place the people on the platform near the swinging gate, have the gate closed, then turn on the rotary switch on the Control Box. This will cause the floor mat to vibrate and the people will start walking around the platform. They will go down one ramp and up the other and continue to walk around.

The car should be placed on the track so the side with the two movable doors faces the platform, and the metal wheels on the one truck are to ride on the rail which has the Base Post current If your layout is wired so the Base Post current is in the other rail than that which the metal wheels are on, just spread the truck slightly, remove the wheel and axle assemblies and reverse the position of the wheels.

ADJUSTING INSTRUCTIONS

Due to variations in the line voltage it may be necessary to adjust the unit to get the correct amount of vibration for good operation. This can be done very easily by turning the adjusting rod, which is located on the opposite side of the platform from the wires.

If the unit is vibrating too fast or too slow, by turning the adjusting lever rod slowly the unit can be brought into correct adjustment. Start by turning in a clockwise direction for several revolutions; if the unit does not respond, turn rod in a counter clockwise direction.

CAR OPERATING INSTRUCTIONS

Run the train around the track and stop it so the operating coach is positioned in front of the platform. See that the outside of the movable doors are located at the edge of the floor mat. When the car is in this position the contact finger from the car truck should be resting on the contact strip which is attached to the platform.

Now open the gate fence and the one car door in front of it. As the people approach the car, press the red button on the Control Box which energizes the mat in the car and the people will walk from the platform into the car. Be sure door at opposite end of car is closed or people will continue through the car and back onto the platform. Run train arousd the track and stop it so car is again in position. Open the door at opposite end of car, press red button and people will walk out of car and onto the platform.

 Ref: Form No. M2890

REVOLVING AIRCRAFT BEACON
Model Nos. 769, 769A, 23769

INSTRUCTIONS FOR INSTALLING

No. 769A Revolving Beacon consists of a metal lattice work tower, a special lamp and a rotating lens housing. The lamp and lens housing are packed in their own containers. Install the Beacon as follows:

1. Connect one of the wires to the base post on the transformer. Connect the other wire to the 15 Volt post on the transformer.
2. Take lamp No. 461 from its package and screw it firmly into the socket on the top of the tower. Note that the top of the lamp has a small cup-like depression.
3. Unpack the rotary lens housing carefully and gently lower it over the lamp so that the steel pivot inside the housing rests in the cup on top of the lamp. **Handle the housing carefully. It is very delicate.**

After a minute or two the lamp will heat the air inside the housing and this warm air streaming through the vanes in the top of the housing will cause it to turn slowly. If you wish you can start it off by spinning it gently in clockwise direction.

IMPORTANT: If you wish the beacon to operate at its normal slow speed keep it out of drafts. The rotating housing is so light that a slight breeze will speed up its motion considerably, or stop it completely.

XA12A437-RP	Beacon Assembly	1.33 ea.
PA11383	Bulb	.30 ea.
XA12426-RP	Lamp Housing Assembly	36 ea.
P14C544-A	House - New Style	1.24 ea.
PA14A017	Vent - New Style	.03 ea.
PA9353	House - Old Style	1.00 ea.
XA9371-A	Roof & Chimney Assembly (old style)	.50 ea.
PA12B439	Platform	.23 ea.
PA12C689	Ladder	.11 ea.
PA12C389-B	Base	.58 ea.

Ref: Form No. M3213

LOADING PLATFORM
Model No. 770

INSTRUCTIONS FOR INSTALLING AND OPERATING

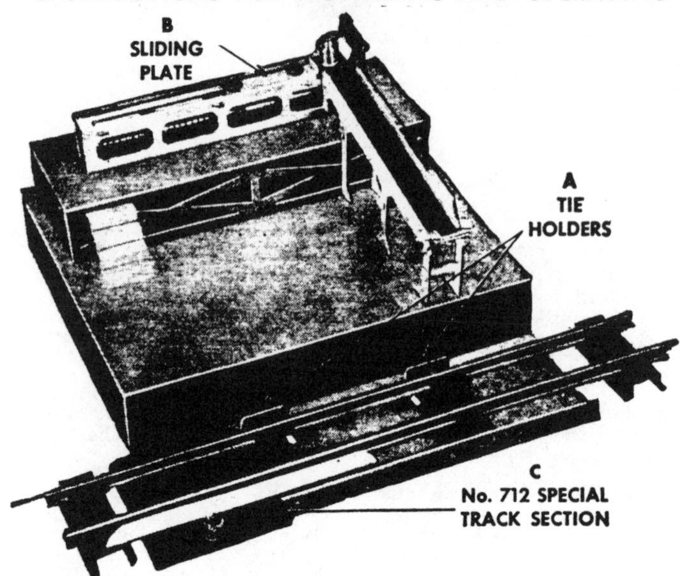

To install this unit place it in the layout so it is along a straight portion of the track. Then nest the track between the tie holders, "A" as shown.

HOOK UP TO A TRANSFORMER

Connect the **YELLOW wire** to the **15 VOLT POST** on the transformer.

Connect the **BLACK wire** from the platform to one of the clips underneath the control box.

Connect the **SHORT BLACK wire** from the other control box clip to the **BASE POST** on the transformer.

HOOK UP TO A TRANSFORMER AND NO. 15 RECTIFIER

Follow same procedure as described above.

HOOK UP TO A NO. 14 OR 16 RECTIFORMER

Connect the **YELLOW wire** to one of the **ALTERNATING CURRENT Posts** on the Rectiformer.

Connect the **BLACK wire** from the platform to one of the clips underneath the Control Box.

Connect the **SHORT BLACK wire** from the other **Control Box Clip** to the other **ALTERNATING CURRENT Post** on the Rectiformer.

The unit is now ready to operate and you will find by pushing the button on the Control Box that the man on the platform will go forward, when button is released the man will return to his original position and be waiting for work.

Next pull back the sliding Plate *"B"* in Figure 1 and place the four boxes or milk cans on the runway. They will be fed automatically to the man by spring pressure. Each time the button is pushed he will shove one of the units down the chute and onto or into a car which is waiting to receive the merchandise — when the man shoves the unit down the chute he automatically lowers the chute end. When the man goes back to his original position he raises the chute end so it will not interfere with any passing rolling stock.

To get the maximum amount of play value from this Loading Platform it should be used with the No. 732 or No. 734 operating cars — when doing so be sure that the No. 712 special track section is positioned on the track as shown at "C".

Ref: Form No. M2870A

PA11180	Box	.10 ea.
PA11257	Man	.38 "
PA11295	String (5½" Length)	.12 yd.
XA11520	Milk Can Assembly	.10 ea.

OPERATING STOCKYARD AND CAR
Model Nos. 771, 23771

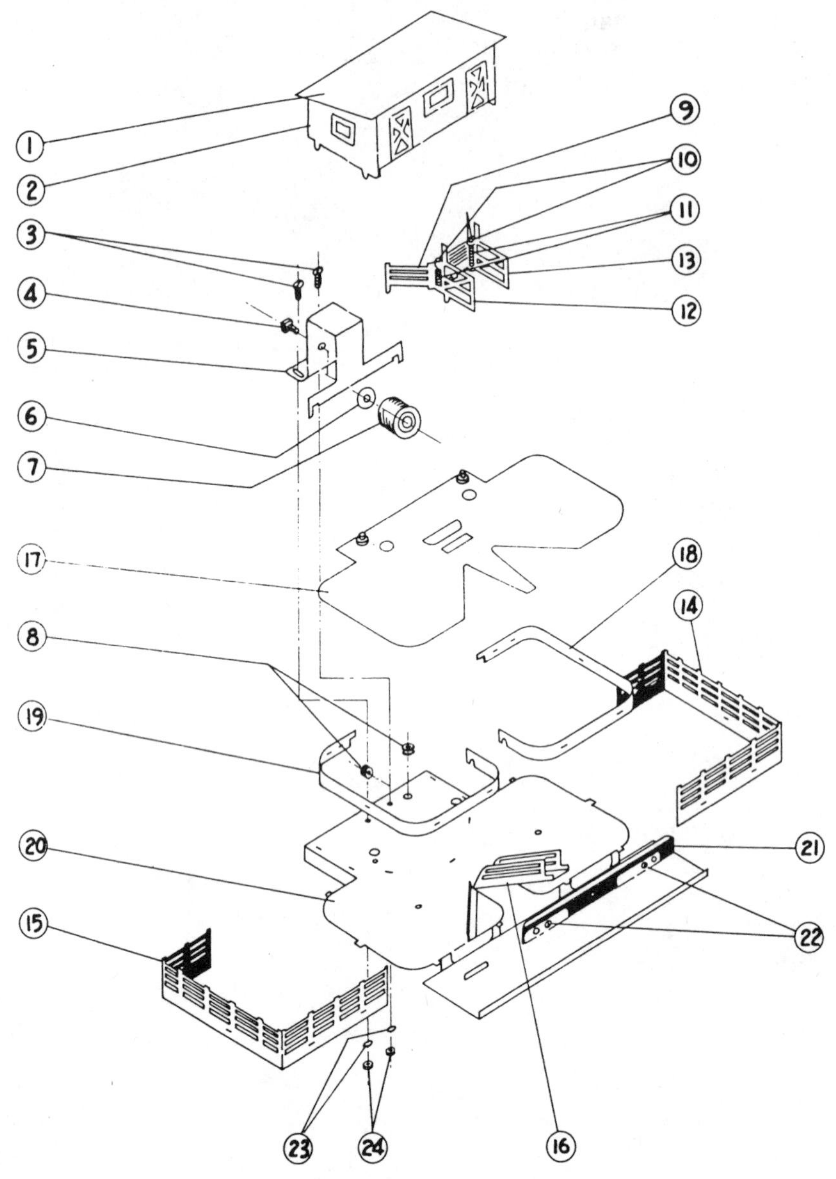

 Ref: Form No. M5235, June 1, 1960

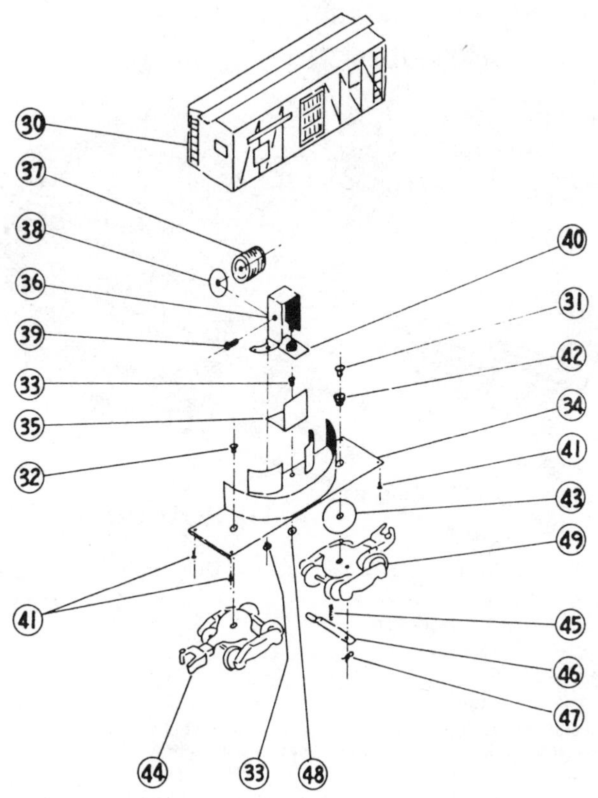
30
37
38
36
39
33
35
32
41
40
31
42
34
41
43
49
45
46
47
44
33
48

HOOK UP AND OPERATING INSTRUCTIONS FOR

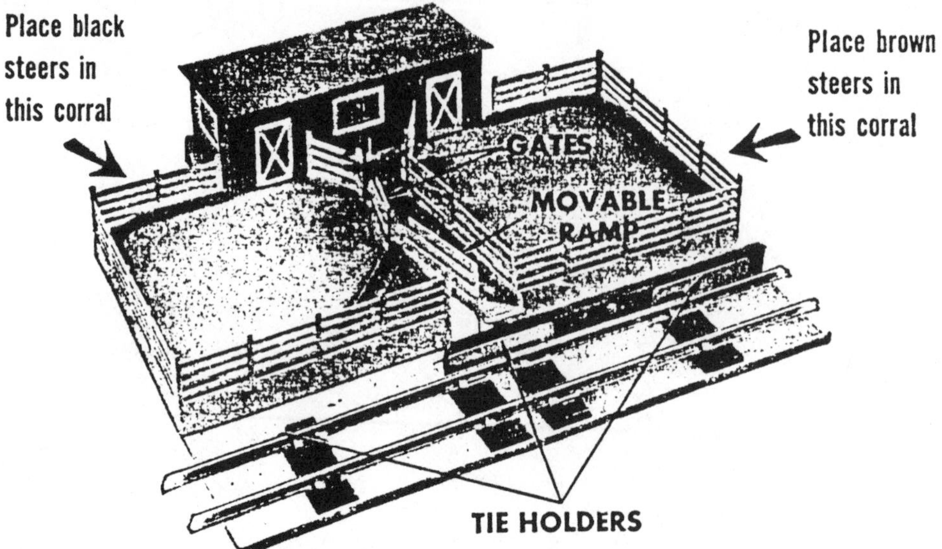

The No. 771 Operating Stock Yard and Car Unit consists of the following:

1 — No. 771 Stock Yard
1 — No. 736 Stock Car
1 — Control Box Unit
2 — Wood screws for mounting the control box
8 — Miniature steers

To install this unit, place it in a portion of the layout so there is at least 2 straight tracks to mount on the stock yard base — nest the straight track between the tie holders as shown in Fig. 1.

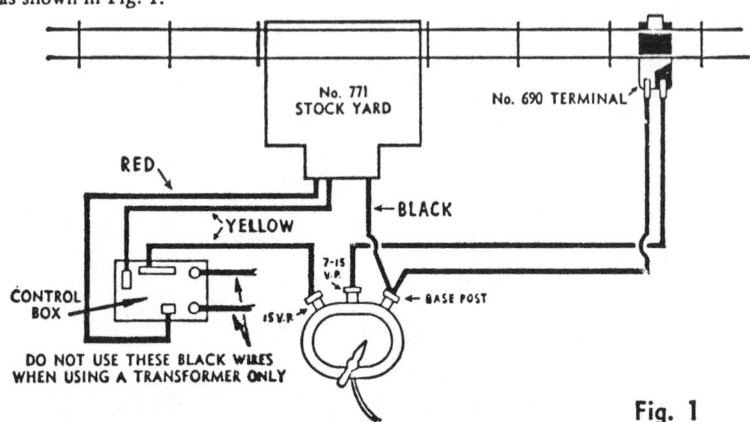

Fig. 1

HOOK UP OF NO. 771 TO A TRANSFORMER

Connect **BLACK WIRE** from Stock Yard to **BASE POST** on transformer.

Connect **RED WIRE** from Stock Yard to wire clip under the red button on Control Box.

Connect **YELLOW WIRE** from Stock Yard to remaining spring clip on Control Box.

Connect **YELLOW WIRE** from Control Box to **15 VOLT POST** on Transformer.

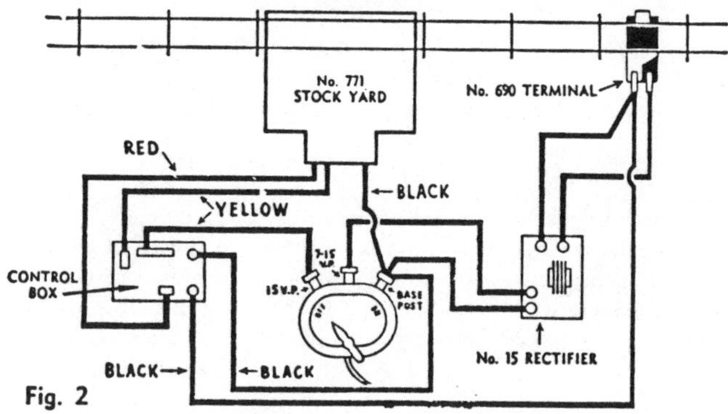

Fig. 2

HOOK UP OF NO. 771 WHEN USING A RECTIFIER AND TRANSFORMER

Connect **BLACK WIRE** from Stock Yard to **BASE POST** on transformer.

Connect **RED WIRE** from Stock Yard to wire clip under red button on Control Box.

Connect **YELLOW WIRE** from Stock Yard to remaining wire clip on Control Box.

Connect **YELLOW WIRE** from Control Box to the **15 VOLT POST** on the transformer.

Connect **ONE BLACK WIRE** from the Control Box to the **BASE POST** on the transformer.

Connect the **OTHER BLACK WIRE** from the Control Box to the **BASE POST CLIP** on the track terminal.

When car is to be operated Transformer Control handle must be turned off.

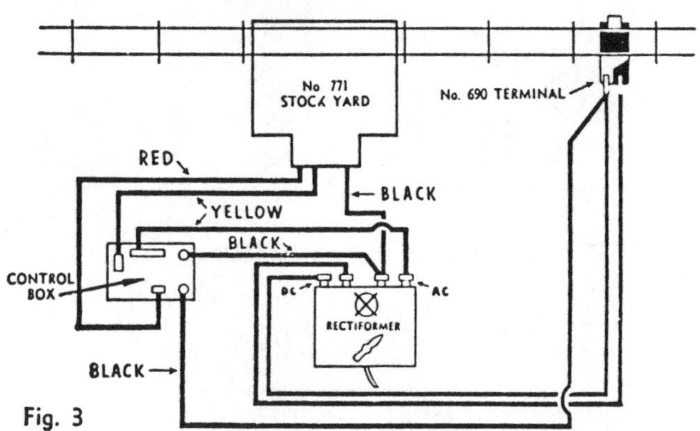

Fig. 3

HOOK UP OF NO. 771 WHEN USING A NO. 14 OR 16 RECTIFORMER

Connect **BLACK WIRE** from Stock yard to the **INSIDE AC POST** on Rectiformer.

Connect **RED WIRE** from Stock Yard to wire clip under red button on Control Box.

Connect **YELLOW WIRE** from Stock yard to remaining wire clip on Control Box.

Connect **YELLOW WIRE** from Control Box to **OUTSIDE AC POST** on Rectiformer.

Connect **ONE BLACK WIRE** from Control Box to **INSIDE AC POST** on Rectiformer.

Connect **OTHER BLACK WIRE** from Control Box to **BASE POST CLIP** on track terminal.

When car is to be operated Rectiformer control handle must be turned off.

OPERATING INSTRUCTIONS

Place the steers in the corral — 4 on each side, then turn on the rotary switch on the Control Box. This will cause the floor mat to vibrate and the steers will then mill around the corral and they can be left to mill continuously.

RAMP INSTRUCTIONS

The ramp on which the cattle travel to go into the car is movable up and down. It should always be raised into the up position when not being used. If left down the cars will strike it as they pass, — therefore, to load or unload the car, stop the train at the stock yard and position the stock car so one of the doors line up with the ramp, then lower the ramp to the door entrance. After car is loaded, raise the ramp before starting the train.

LOADING INSTRUCTIONS

When car is in position for loading, open one of the corral gates by pushing it toward the other gate and allow the cattle to go up the ramp. Press the red button on the Control Box — this will energize the vibrating mechanism in the car and allow the cattle to proceed into the car. At times you may find these little critters will get just as stubborn as real cattle in a stock yard and will need a helping hand — just prod them a little and they will continue to move.

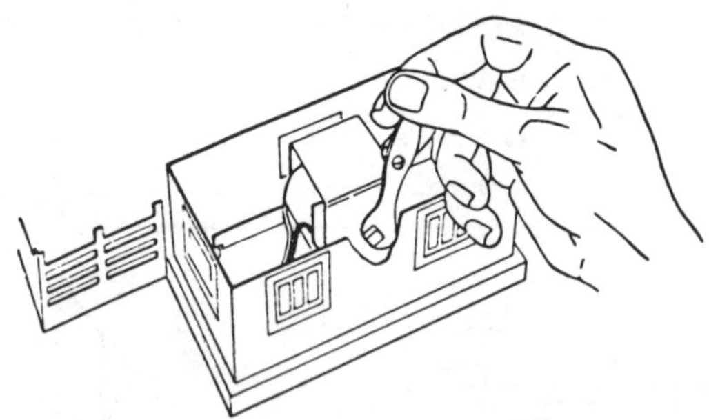

ADJUSTING INSTRUCTIONS

Due to variations in the line voltage it may be necessary to adjust the unit to get the correct amount of vibration for good operation. This can be done very easily by turning the adjusting screw, which is located on the back end of the vibrating bracket inside the house.

If the unit is vibrating too fast you can slow it down by turning the adjusting nut with the wrench counterclockwise till you get the desired amount of vibration.

If the unit is vibrating too slow you can speed it up by turning the adjusting nut with the wrench in a clockwise direction until you get the desired amount of vibration.

CAR INSTRUCTIONS

The car should be placed on the track so the side with the two doors faces the stock yard, and the metal wheels on the one truck are to ride on the rail which has the Base post current. If for some reason your layout is wired so the base post current is in the other rail than that which the metal wheels are on, just spread the truck slightly, remove the wheel and axle assembly, and reverse the position of the wheels. The cattle can enter either door but must leave the car from the opposite door from which they entered.

When loading the cattle into the car be sure the second door is closed or the animals will travel right through the car and out the door.

NO.	PART NO.	DESCRIPTION	PRICE
1	XA11290	Roof Assembly	.39 ea.
2	XA11273	House Front & Back Assembly	2.45 ea.
3	S36	#6-32 x 3/16 Screw	.04 dz.
4	W153	Adjusting Screw	.08 ea.
5	PA11271	Coil Bracket	.44 ea.
6	S153	Spring Washer	.04 ea.
7	XA11283	Magnet Coil Assembly	1.64 ea.
8	PA4356	Grommet	.02 ea.
9	PA11276	Gate Fence	.25 ea.
10	PA11277	Gate Pin	.02 ea.
11	P5970	Spring	.01 ea.
12	PA11275-L	Gate	.19 ea.
13	PA11275-R	Gate	.19 ea.
14	PA11268-R	Fence	.74 ea.
15	PA11268-L	Fence	.74 ea.
16	XA11278	Ramp & Hinge Assembly	.50 ea.
17	XA11270	Mat & Buttons Assembly	.61 ea.
18	PA11267-R	Guide Strip	.59 ea.
19	PA11267-L	Guide Strip	.59 ea.
20	XA11272	Track Plate, Platform & Trough Assy.	3.39 ea.
21	XA11287	Lever Strip Assembly	.18 ea.
22	S242	Screw	.01 ea.
23	W57	Lockwasher	.01 ea.
24	N11	Nut	.01 ea.
25	XA14A965-AE	Control Box	1.19 ea.
26	PM491	Wrench	.04 ea.
27	LW-1B2	Yellow Wire	.02 ft.
28	XA11285	Steer Assembly (Brown)	.40 ea.
29	XA11285-A	Steer Assembly (Black)	.40 ea.
30	PA10053-A	Body Old Style (Not Available)	
		Sub. w/ New Style	
	XA10053-BRP	Body, Door & Trim Assy. New Style	2.51 ea.
	PA10054-A	Door	.13 ea.
	PA15A471	Door Guide (new Style)	.01 ea.
	PA9969	Door Guide (old Style)	.02 ea.
	S185	Screw	.01 ea.
	PA9968	Door Lever	.06 ea.
	PA12B666	Break Handle	.01 ea.
31	PA10235	Truck Rivet	.03 ea.
32	PA9381	Truck Rivet	.02 ea.
33	PA4361	Rivet	.01 ea.
34	XA11204	Chassis & Stock Guide Assembly	1.81 ea.

cont'd

NO.	PART NO.	DESCRIPTION	PRICE
35	PA11203	Sidewall	.05 ea.
36	PA11202	Coil Bracket	.09 ea.
37	XA11206	Assembly Magnet Coil	1.19 ea.
38	W153	Washer	.04 ea.
39	S50-A	Screw	.01 ea.
40	XA11205-RP	Stock Mat & Button Assembly	.30 ea.
41	PA10456	Chassis Pin	.26 dz.
42	PA10209	Insulating Bushing	.02 ea.
43	PA8715-BX	Fibre Washer	.01 ea.
44	XA12A057	Truck Assembly	.98 ea.
	XA12A047	Knuckle Coupler	.29 ea.
	XA10238-A	Wheel & Axle	.08 ea.
	PA9990	Plastic Wheel	.03 ea.
	PA10238	Axle	.01 ea.
45	P9275	Spring	.02 ea.
46	PA11A980	Contact Arm	.03 ea.
47	PA11A944	Hair Pin Cotter	.01 ea.
48	PA1405	Washer	.01 ea.
49	XA12A050	Truck Assembly	1.65 pr.
	XA10238-B	Wheel & Axle Assembly	.07 ea.
	P10238	Axle	.01 ea.
	PA9991	Metal Wheel	.12 ea.
	PA9990	Plastic Wheel	.03 ea.

Prices subject to change without notice.

WATER TOWER

Model Nos. 772, 23772

P14C544-A	House	1.24 ea.
PA14A017	Vent	.03 ea.
PA9353	House - (old style)	1.00 ea.
XA9371-A	Roof & Chimney Assembly (old style)	.50 ea.
PA12C389	Base	.70 ea.
PA12A384	Tube	.83 ea.
PA10665	Bulb	.30 ea.

FLOODLIGHT TOWER
Model Nos. 774, 23774

INSTRUCTIONS FOR INSTALLING AMERICAN FLYER

No. 774 Floodlight Tower

American Flyer Floodlight Tower can be installed anywhere in the layout. After selecting the location. connect the Floodlight Tower to the transformer as follows:

Connect one of the wires to the base post on the transformer Connect the other wire to the 15 Volt post on the transformer.

If lamps fail to light, tighten bulbs, as they may have been loosened in transit.

PA10665	Bulb	.30 ea.
PA12B439-A	Platform	.22 ea.
PA12A689	Ladder	.11 ea.
PA12C389	Base	.70 ea.
P14C544-A	House	1.24 ea.
PA14A017	Vent	.03 ea.
PA9353	House - (old style)	1.00 ea.
XA9371-A	Roof & Chimney Assembly (old style)	.50 ea.

OIL DRUM LOADER

Model Nos. 779, 23779

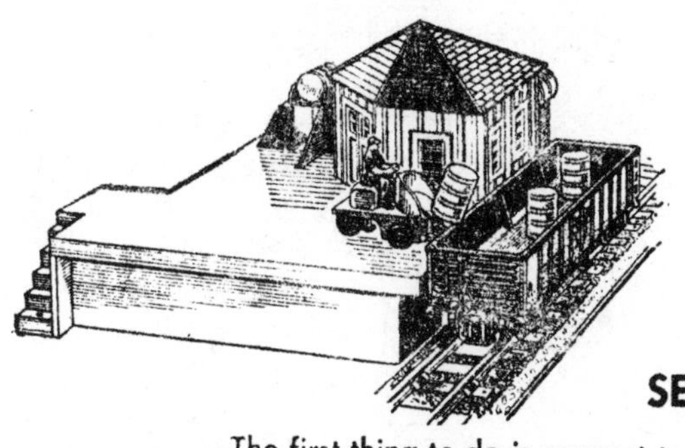

SERVICE INSTRUCTIONS

The first thing to do is connect to transformer and test for operation. If unit does not function, remove Oil Drums (#22) from ramp on Platform (#21) along with Truck Driver (#24) and Truck Assembly (#25). Turn unit upside down and take off two Screws (#18 and 19) to remove House (#9). Slip back Gearhousing Cover (#7). You can now check to see if the Connecting Link Assy (#26) or other parts in the Gearhousing assembly (#8) are binding.

1. To replace Connecting Link Assy (#26).

a. Take off Retaining Ring (#23) from post on Mounting Plate (#29).

b. Take off Retaining Ring (#1) and Washer (#2) and Spring (#3).

c. Pull out Connecting Link Assy from Gearhousing Assy (#8).

2. To replace Platform (#21).

a. Take off two Screws (#18) holding Motor Assy to platform.

b. Take off Screw (#28) and Nut (#12).

c. Unsolder two lead wires going to terminals on platform.

3. To Replace Motor parts.

a. Follow steps 1a, 2a and b.

b. Remove two Screws (#31) and Nuts (#12) holding motor assy together.

c. Take off Bearing Bracket (#20) by removing two Screws (#15), Washers (#16) and Nuts (#17).

d. Pull out Rotor (#10) with Sleeve (#13) and Washer (#14) from rest of assembly.

e. Take off Stator (#11) and unsolder lead wires to terminals.

f. Separate Gearhousing Assy (#8) from Mounting Plate (#29).

Ref: Form No. 1654; July 15, 1955

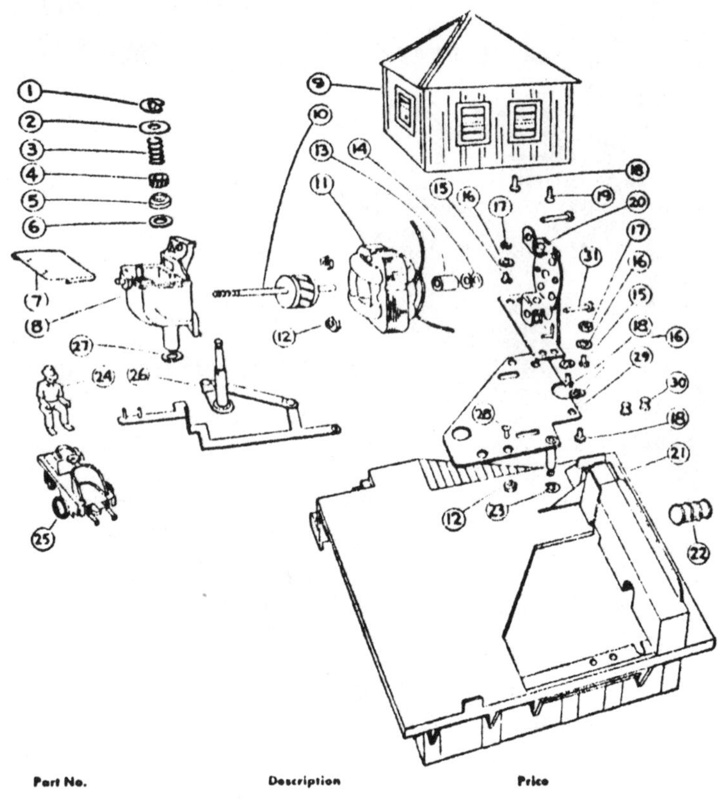

Diagram Number	Part No.	Description	Price
1	P10227	Retaining Ring	$ .03 ea.
2	W126	Washer	.05 dz.
3	PA13A027	Spring	.01 ea.
4	P12B406	Low Speed Worm Gear	.02 "
5	P12B450	Clutch	.06 "
6	W111	Felt Washer	.10 dz.
7	P11A281	Gear Housing Cover	.02 ea.
8	XA13A009-RP	Gear Housing Assy.	2.01 "
9	PA13D003	House	.94 "
10	XA13A032	Rotor	.90 "
11	X2C176-E	Stator	2.89 "
12	N11	Nut	.10 dz.
13	PA13A033	Paper Sleeve	.08 ea.
14	W113	Steel Washer	.02 "
15	S51	Screw	.03 dz.
16	P4654	Shake Proof Washer	.05 "
17	N26-O	Nut	.10 "
18	S91	Screw	.10 "
19	S245	Screw	.01 ea.
20	XA9917-A	Bearing Bracket	.28 "
21	XA13D004-RP	Platform	2.00 "
22	PA13A021	Oil Drum	.05 "
23	P10434	Retaining Ring	.01 "
24	PA13A022	Truck Driver	.35 "
25	XA13A029	Truck Assembly	.81 "
26	XA13A012-RP	Connecting Link Assy.	.54 "
27	W7	Steel Washer	.03 dz.
28	S46	Screw	.05 "
29	XA13B006-RP	Mounting Plate	.16 ea.
30	PA10037	Nut	.02 "
31	S24	Screw	.02 "

NOTE
ALL PARTS PRICES PRIOR TO FEB. 27, 1958 ARE SUBJECT TO 10% INCREASE FROM PRICES SHOWN ON SHEET.

 Ref: Form No. 1654; July 15, 1955

NO.	PART NO.	DESCRIPTION	PRICE
1		NOT USED	
2		NOT USED	
3		NOT USED	
4		NOT USED	
5		NOT USED	
6		NOT USED	
7		NOT USED	
8	X13B452ARP	GEAR HOUSING ASSEMBLY	2.41 EA.
9	PA13D003	HOUSE	1.03 EA.
10	XA13A032	ROTOR	.99 EA.
11	X2C176-E	STATOR	3.18 EA.
12	N11	NUT	.01 EA.
13	PA13A033	PAPER SLEEVE	.09 EA.
14	W113	STEEL WASHER	.02 EA.
15	S51	SCREW	.03 DZ.
16	P4654	SHAKE PROOF WASHER	.01 EA.
17	N26-0	NUT	.11 DZ.
18	S91	SCREW	.02 EA.
19	S245	SCREW	.01 EA.
20	XA9917-A	BEARING BRACKET	.46 EA.
21	XA13D004-RP	PLATFORM	2.20 EA.
22	PA13A021	OIL DRUM	.06 EA.
23	P10434	RETAINING RING	.01 EA.
24	PA13A022	TRUCK DRIVER	.39 EA.
25	XA13A029	TRUCK ASSEMBLY	.89 EA.
26	XA13A012-RP	CONNECTING LINK ASSEMBLY w/o SHAFT. SHAFT NOW IN DIA. # 8	.59 EA.
27	W7	STEEL WASHER	.01 EA.
28	S46	SCREW	.01 EA.
29	XA13B006-RP	MOUNTING PLATE	.18 EA.
30	PA10037-B	NUT	.02 EA.
31	S24	SCREW	.01 EA.

PRICES SUBJECT TO CHANGE WITHOUT NOTICE.

LOG LOADER
Model Nos. 787, 23787

SERVICE INSTRUCTIONS

The first thing to do is connect to transformer and test for operation. If unit does not function, remove logs from base along wih Roof (28) and proceed to locate trouble.

TO CHECK OR REPLACE THE FOLLOWING:

1. **Log Lifter (#21):**
   a. Turn log loader upside down and turn or take off speed Nuts (#22) to release Axle (#23) which can be slipped out of place. The log lifter (#21) is free and can be replaced.

2. **Base (#17):**
   a. Follow step #1.
   b. Unsolder two lead wires to terminals.
   c. Loosen screw and remove Cam (#20).
   d. Straighten out lugs of Ladder (#19) and top Assembly (#18).

3. **Cab (#1):**
   a. Insert screw driver or similar instrument, space between Cab (#1) and runway of top Assembly (#18) and pry up until Cab (#1) is released.

4. **House (#27):**
   a. Remove two screws (#29) which will be found underneath Top Assembly (#18).

5. **Separate Motor Assembly From Top Assembly (#18):**
   a. Follow step #4.
   b. Unsolder two lead wires to terminals.
   c. Loosen screw and take off cam (#20).
   d. Loosen Nut (#26) and remove Screw (#24) from gearhousing (#13).
   e. Remove two screws (#7), Nuts (#8), and Washers (#10).
   f. Take off two Truarc Rings (#15 & 16).

6. **To Disassemble and Replace Motor Parts:**
   a. Follow steps (#4 & 5).
   b. Remove two Nuts (#14).
   c. Take off Gearhousing (#13).
   d. Pull out Rotor (#11).
   e. Remove two Screws (#5) separating Bearing Bracket (#6) from Stator (#9).

PRICES--VOID

Diagram Number	Part No.	Description	Price
1	XA13B753RP	Cab	1.05 ea.
2	PA13A757	Hook	.16 ea.
3	PA13A022	Truck Driver	.35 ea.
4	PA13A758	Car Lift Support	.03 ea.
5	S24	Screw	.02 ea.
6	XA9917-A	Bearing Bracket	.28 ea.
7	S51	Screw	.03 dz.
8	N26-0	Nut	.10 dz.
9	X2C176-J	Stator	3.85 ea.
10	P4654	Lockwasher	.05 dz.
11	XA13A032	Rotor	.90 ea.
11a	PA13A033	Paper Sleeve	.08 ea.
11b	PA13A033-A	Paper Sleeve	.09 ea.
11c	W113	Steel Washer	.02 ea.
12	PA13A765	Car Lift Lever	.03 ea.
13	XA13B452RP	Gear Housing	2.19 ea.
14	N11	Nut	.10 dz.
15	P10226	Truarc Ring	.02 ea.
16	P10434	Truarc Ring	.01 ea.
17	XA13D751RP	Base	1.02 ea.
18	XA13B779RP	Top Assembly	3.17 ea.
19	PA13A772	Ladder	.06 ea.
20	XA13A761RP	Cam	.50 ea.
21	PA13A759	Log Lifter	.21 ea.
22	P10A951	Speed Nut	.01 ea.
23	PA13A768	Axle	.06 dz.
24	S20	Screw	.10 dz.
25	W57	Lockwasher	.04 dz.
26	N11	Nut	.10 dz.
27	PA13D979	House	.71 ea.
28	PA10219	Roof	.75 ea.
29	S183	Screw	.10 dz.
	PA13A777	Logs (not shown)	.03 ea.

OPERATING INSTRUCTIONS

INSTALLING

After the loader is removed from the box, remove small piece of tape which holds carriage and hook to the front of the elevated track. Place loader in the desired location in your layout. This can be along a mainline or between two lines of track as logs can be dumped on to either side of the platform if you are using a log dump car.

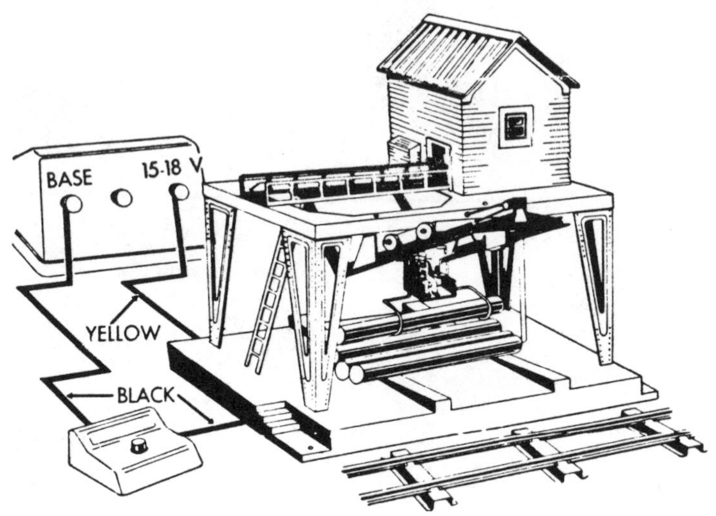

WIRING

Next, fasten the YELLOW wire from one of the TERMINAL POSTS on the log loader to the 15 or 18 VOLT POST on the transformer.

Connect the long BLACK wire from the other TERMINAL on the loader to one of the CLIPS underneath the control box.

Connect the short BLACK wire from the other control box clip to the BASE POST on the transformer.

Place or dump the logs on the platform of the loader.

OPERATION

Now press the control box button and hold it down. The carriage will descend and the hook will pick up one log which has been raised for it. The log will then be transported up over the car and dropped so it lands on to the car below. Any gondola or flat car with stakes can be used but much more play value will result if a log dump car is used.

LUBRICATING

The gears and rotor shaft can be lubricated by removing the roof. Use a light grease or vaseline on the gears and a light oil on the shafts and bearings.

 Ref: Form No. M3438; Dec. 1955

NO.	PART NO.	DESCRIPTION	PRICE
1	XA13B753-RP	Cab	1.15 ea.
2	PA13A757	Hook	.18 ea.
3	PA13A022	Truck Driver	.39 ea.
4	PA13A758	Car Lift Support	.03 ea.
5	S24	Screw	.01 ea.
6	XA9917-A	Bearing Bracket	.46 ea.
7	S51	Screw	.03 dz.
8	N26-0	Nut	.11 dz.
9	X2C176-J	Stator	4.24 ea.
10	P4654	Lockwasher	.01 ea.
11	XA13A032	Rotor	.99 ea.
11A	PA13A033	Paper Sleeve	.09 ea.
11B	PA13A033-A	Paper Sleeve	.10 ea.
11C	W113	Steel Washer	.02 ea.
12	PA13A765	Car Lift Lever	.03 ea.
13	XA13B452-RP	Gear Housing	2.41 ea.
14	N11	Nut	.01 ea.
15	P10226	Truarc Ring	.02 ea.
	PA14N359	Retaining Ring (Not Shown)	.02 ea.
16	P10434	Truarc Ring	.01 ea.
17	XA13D751RP	Base	1.12 ea.
18	XA13B779 RP	Top Assembly	3.49 ea.
19	PA13A772	Ladder	.07 ea.
20	XA13A761RP	Cam	.55 ea.
	S36	Screw	.04 dz.
21	PA13A759	Log Lifter	.23 ea.
22	P10A951	Speed Nut - Not Used - See Note	.01 ea.
23	PA13A768	Axle	.07 dz.
24		NOT USED	
25		NOT USED	
26		NOT USED	
27	PA13D979	House	.78 ea.
28	PA10219	Roof	1.09 ea.
29	S284	2 x 3/8 Type Z P.K. Screw	.01 ea.
	PA13A777	Logs (NOT SHOWN)	.03 ea.
	XA14A964-R	Control Box (NOT SHOWN)	.64 ea.

NOTE: For Retaining position of axle, dia. 23, plastic base is fused with a hot iron instead of using speed nut.

Prices subject to change without notice

NO.	PART NO.	DESCRIPTION	PRICE
1		Cab Not Available	
2	PA13A757	Hook	.19 ea.
3	PA13A022	Truck Driver	.41 ea.
4	PA13A758	Car Lift Support	.03 ea.
5	S24	Screw	.01 ea.
6	XA9917-A	Bearing Bracket	.48 ea.
7	S51	Screw	.03 dz.
8	N26-0	Nut	.01 ea.
9	X2C176-J	Stator	4.45 ea.
10	P4654	Lockwasher	.01 ea.
11	XA13A032	Rotor	1.04 ea.
11A		Paper Sleeve Not Available	
11B		Paper Sleeve Not Available	
11C	W113	Steel Washer	.02 ea.
12	PA13A765	Car Lift Lever	.03 ea.
13	XA13B452RP	Gear Housing	2.53 ea.
14	N11	Nut	.01 ea.
15		Truarc Ring Not Available	
16		Truarc Ring Not Available	
17		Base Not Available	
18		Top Assembly Not Available	
19		Ladder Not Available	
20	XA13A761RP	Cam	.58 ea.
21		Log Lifter Not Available	
22		Speed Nut - Not Used - See Note	
23	PA13A768	Axle	.07 dz.
24		NOT USED	
25		NOT USED	
26		NOT USED	
27	PA13D979	House	.82 ea.
28	PA10219	Roof	1.14 ea.
29		2 x 3/8 Type Z P.K. Screw Not Available	
	PA13A777	Logs (NOT SHOWN)	.03 ea.
	XA14A964R	Control Box (NOT SHOWN)	.67 ea.

NOTE: For Retaining position of axle, dia. 23, plastic base is fused with a hot iron instead of using speed nut.

Prices subject to change without notice.

 Ref: Form No. 1770; Oct. 1, 1962

UNION STATION AND TERMINAL

Model No. 792

INSTRUCTIONS

The Union Station and Terminal were made to be used as a combination unit or as two separate items. The Station is made so it can be used in a number of ways. The tower entrance can be placed at the center or one end of the long side or placed on the short side. Each location makes an entirely different appearing item.

NOTE DRAWINGS BELOW:

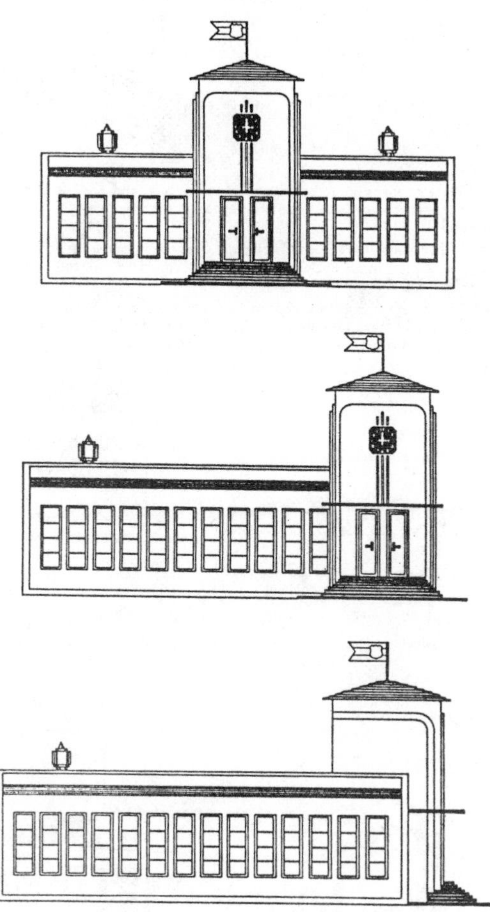

Ref: Form No. M3274

TO ASSEMBLE: Locate station in the layout; place roof on with ventilators up; place tower entrance at desired location; nest it over the edge of the building; place the step against the entrance and the tower ledge into the slots in the tower; then place the roof on the tower.

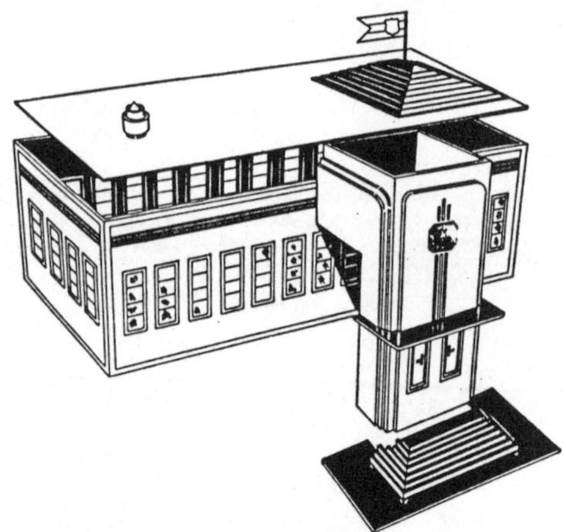

The two wires are to be connected to the base and 15 volt terminals on the transformer or can be connected to the track with a No. 690 track terminal.

When using the Terminal with the Station, it can be placed either along side the station to make a through Terminal or placed so it will be a dead end Terminal.

The 5 ramps can be arranged in various ways to permit one, two, or three track operations through the Terminal. More of the Terminals can be used if a longer Terminal or train shed is desired.

NOTE DRAWINGS BELOW.

TALKING STATION

Model No. 799

N-1	Nut	.01 "
PA8554-A	Turntable only	.40 "
XA9163	Reproducing Assembly	3.50 "
XA10091	Track terminal #707	.20 "
PA10721	Turntable Bushing	.20 "
XA10739	Turntable Shaft Assembly	.50 "
XA10740	Cam Shaft Assembly	.70 "
XA10744	Contact Base Assembly	.25 "
PA10746	Record	.85 "
PA13A269	Needle	.01 "
PA11073	10 ohm 10 Watt Resistor	1.04 "

Ref: Sept. 22, 1950

BILLBOARD WHISTLE

Model No. 23568

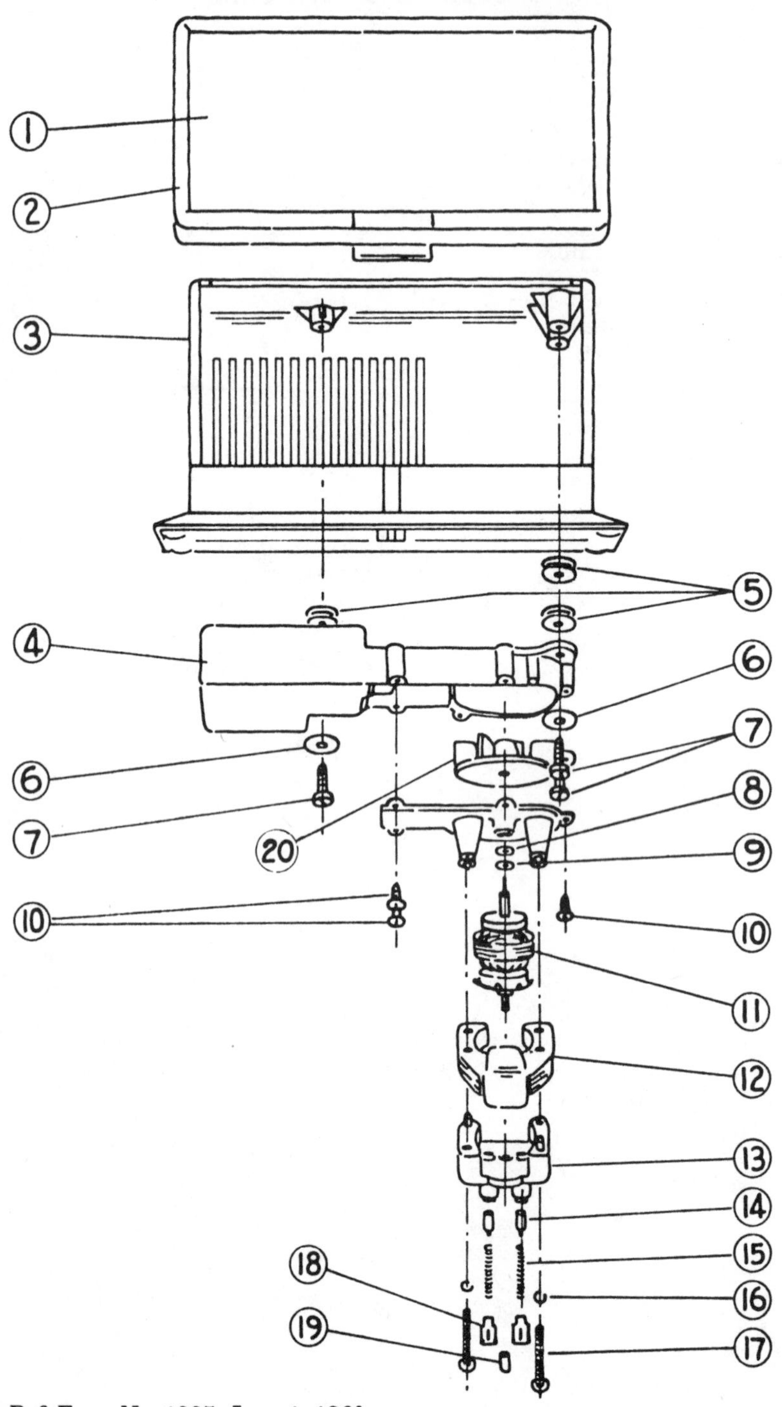

 Ref: Form No. 1995; June 1, 1960

NO.	PART NO.	DESCRIPTION	PRICE
1	PA13A420	Sign	.25 ea.
2	PA13C410	Sign Panel	.36 ea.
3	PA13D407	Housing	1.58 ea.
4	XA13A419	Whistle Body Assy.	.63 ea.
5	PA4356	Rubber Grommet	.02 ea.
6	W80	Steel Washer	.03 dz.
7	S306	#6 X 7/16" Type"Z"P. K. Screw	.02 ea.
8	P325D	Fibre Washer	.01 ea.
9	W83	Washer	.04 ea.
10	S230B	#4 X 1/4 Type "Z" P.K. Screw	.01 ea.
11	XA13C414A	Armature Assy.	2.43 Ea.
12	XA9434-A	Field Assy.	1.04 ea.
13	XA12B137	Brush Bracket Assy.	.55 ea.
14	PA9603	Motor Brush	.13 ea.
15	PA10757A	Brush Spring	.02 ea.
16	W57	Lockwasher	.01 ea.
17	S22A	6-32 X 1 1/8" Screw	.01 ea.
18	PA10754	Brush Cap	.02 ea.
19	PA9522	Oil Wick	.01 ea.
20	PA13A415	Fan Blade	.10 ea.
	XA14A964-B	Control Box NOT SHOWN	.64 ea.

NO.	PART NO.	DESCRIPTION	PRICE
1	PA13A420	Sign	.26 ea.
2	PA13C410	Sign Panel	.38 ea.
3	PA13D407	Housing	1.66 ea.
4	XA13A419	Whistle Body Assembly	.66 ea.
5	PA4356	Rubber Grommet	.02 ea.
6	W80	Steel Washer	.03 dz.
7	S306	#6 x 7/16" Type "Z" P.K. Screw	.02 ea.
8	P325D	Fibre Washer	.01 ea.
9	W83	Washer	.04 ea.
10	S230B	#4 x 1/4 Type "Z" P.K. Screw	.01 ea.
11	XA13C414A	Armature Assembly	2.55 ea.
12	XA9434-A	Field Assembly	1.09 ea.
13	XA12B137	Brush Bracket Assembly	.58 ea.
14	PA9603	Motor Brush	.14 ea.
15	PA10757A	Brush Spring	.02 ea.
16	W57	Lockwasher	.01 ea.
17	S22A	6-32 x 1 1/8" Screw	.01 ea.
18	PA10754	Brush Cap	.02 ea.
19	PA9522	Oil Wick	.01 ea.
20	PA13A415	Fan Blade	.11 ea.
	XA14A964-B	Control Box NOT SHOWN	.67 ea.

Ref: Form No. 1995; June 1, 1960; Rev. Oct. 1, 1962

CROSSING GATE
Model No. 23601, 23602

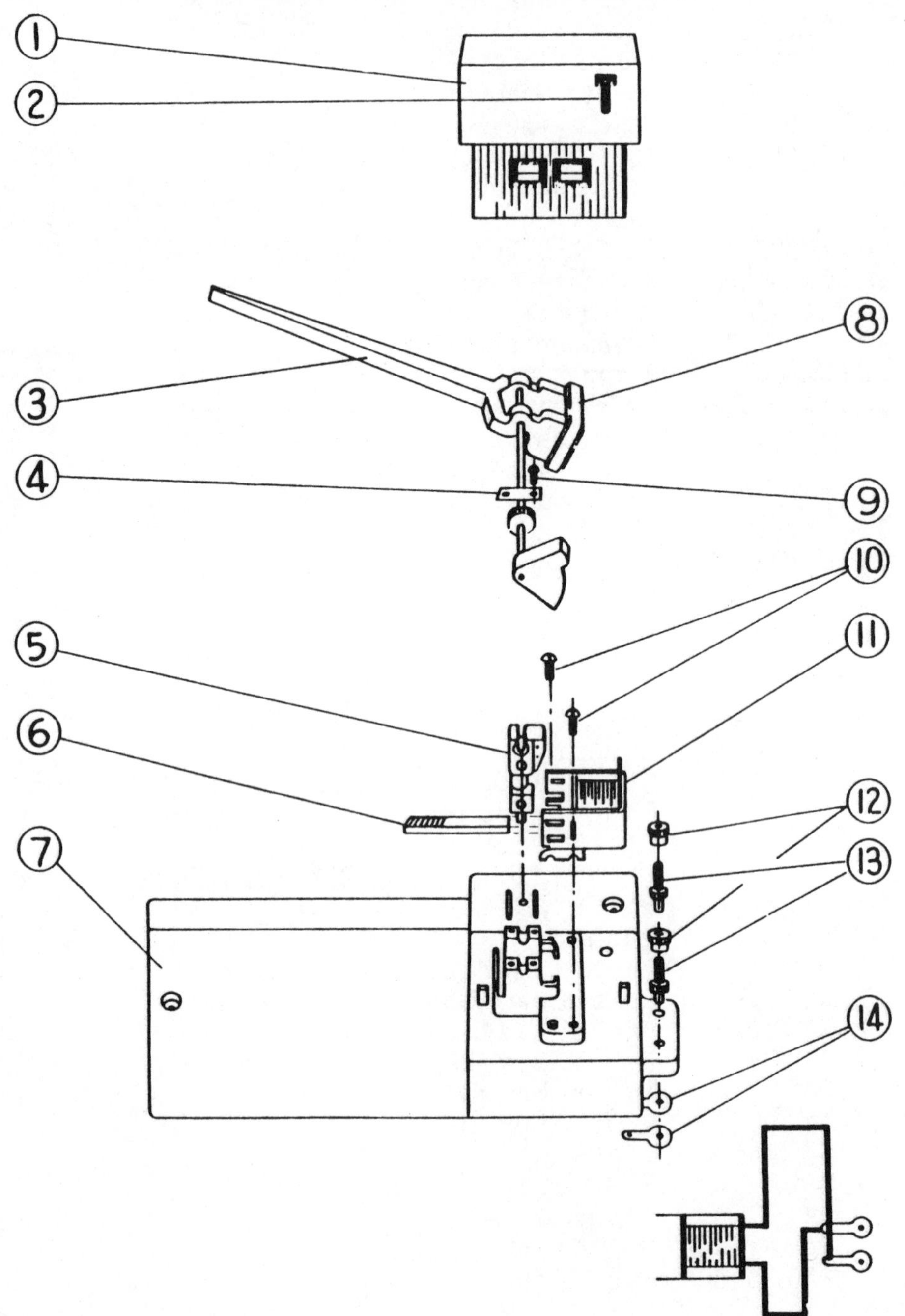

 Ref: Form No. M5231; June 1, 1960

NO.	PART NO.	DESCRIPTION	PRICE
1	P14C544-A	House	1.24 ea.
2	PA14A017	Vent	.03 ea.
3	XA15A454	Gate Axle Assembly	.61 ea.
	PA15B283	Gate Arm	.45 ea.
	P13A844A	12 Tooth Gear	.06 ea.
	PA15A509	Gate Axle	.06 ea.
	P14A539	Counter Weight	.04 ea.
4	P14A542	Axle Retainer	.02 ea.
5	PA15B284	Gate Support	.25 ea.
6	P14A528	Solenoid Core	.05 ea.
7	PA16D036	Base - 23602	.43 ea.
	PA15D282	Base - 23601	.61 ea.
8	PA15A511	Weight	.07 ea.
9	S171	#2 x 3/16" Type Z B.H. P.K. Screw	.01 ea.
10	S86	#4 x ¼ Type Z R.H. P.K. Screw	.09 dz.
11	XA15B510	Coil Assembly	.69 ea.
12	PA10037-B	Nut	.02 ea.
13	PA13A183	Binding Post	.03 ea.
14	PA6173	Solder Terminal	.01 ea.
	XA14A964-T	Control Box (not shown)	.64 ea.

1	P14C544-A	House	1.30 ea.
2	PA14A017	Vent	.03 ea.
3	XA15A454	Gate Axle Assembly	.64 ea.
	PA15B283	Gate Arm	.47 ea.
	P13A844A	12 Tooth Gear	.06 ea.
	PA15A509	Gate Axle	.06 ea.
	P14A539	Counter Weight	.04 ea.
4	P14A542	Axle Retainer	.02 ea.
5	PA15B284	Gate Support	.26 ea.
6	P14A528	Solenoid Core	.05 ea.
7	PA16D036	Base - 23602	.45 ea.
	PA15D282	Base - 23601	.64 ea.
8	PA15A511	Weight	.07 ea.
9	S171	#2 x 3/16" Type Z Screw	.01 ea.
10	S86	#4 x ¼ Type Z Screw	.01 ea.
11	XA15B510	Coil Assembly	.72 ea.
12	PA10037-B	Nut	.02 ea.
13	PA13A183	Binding Post	.03 ea.
14	PA6173	Solder Terminal	.01 ea.
	XA14A964-T	Control Box (Not Shown)	.67 ea.

Prices subject to change without notice.

BELL DANGER SIGNAL
Model No. 23763

PA8999-R	Red Bulb	.32 ea.
XA10268-A	(#696) Track Trip "S Gauge Standard T Track	.46 ea.
XA16A593	Signal Oper. Assembly Pike Master Track	.63 ea.

Prices subject to change without notice.

FLASHER
Model No. 23764

PA8999-R	Red Bulb	.32 ea.
XA10268-A	(#696) Track Trip "S Gauge Standard T Track	.46 ea.
XA16A593	Signal Oper. Assembly Pike Master Track	.63 ea.

STATION AND BAGGAGE SMASHER
Model No. 23789

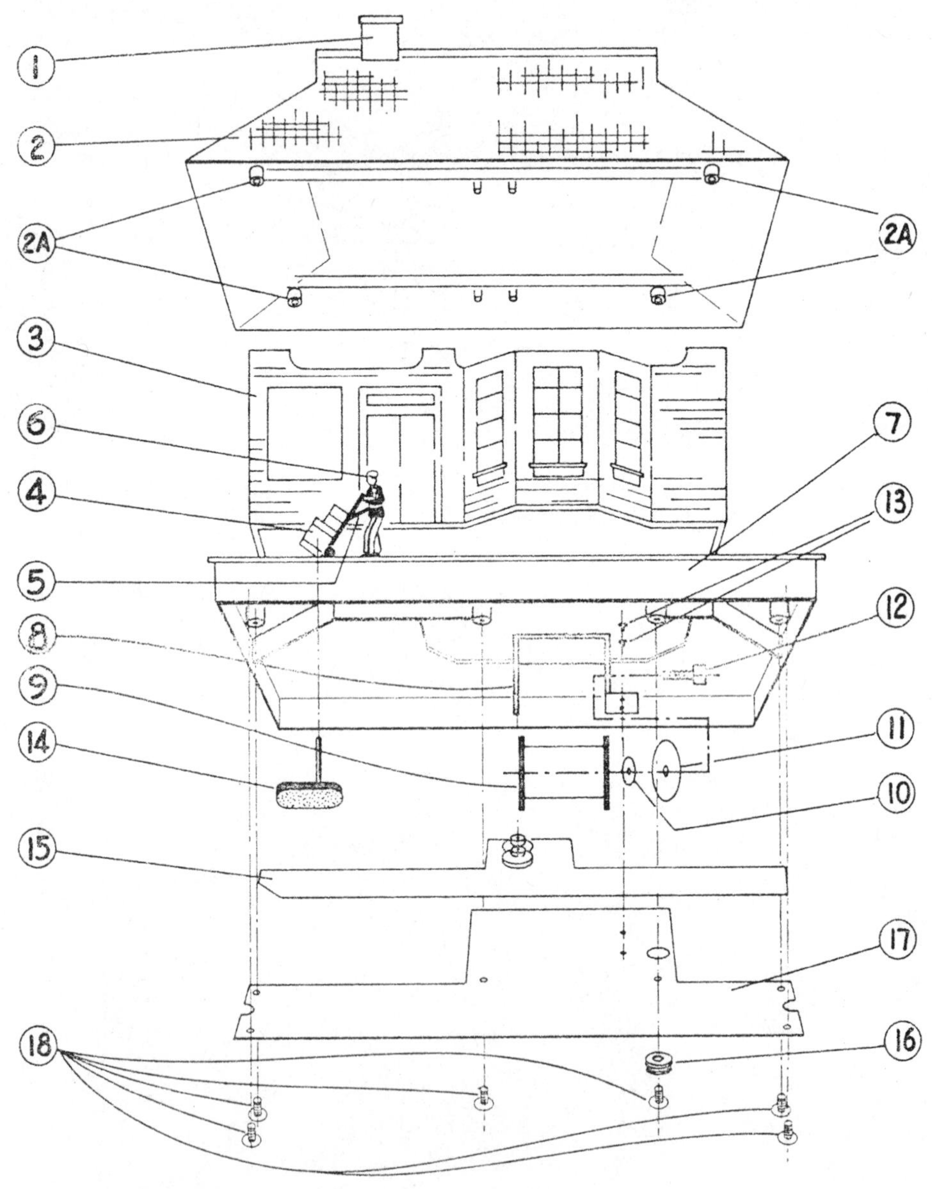

 Ref: Form No. M5227; June 1, 1960

NO.	PART NO.	DESCRIPTION	PRICE
1	PA14B201	Chimney	.09 ea.
2	PA14N044-ABB	Roof	1.56 ea.
2A	PA14A670	Sleeve	.01 ea.
3	XA14N043-RP	Station House Assembly	4.07 ea.
4	PA14A273	Hand Truck	.95 ea.
5	PA14A274	Pin	.03 ea.
6	PA14A272	Baggage Smasher	.50 ea.
7	PA14N042-BBA	Platform	2.12 ea.
8	PA14A271	Coil Bracket	.14 ea.
9	XA13A436-A	Magnet Coil Assembly	1.86 ea.
10	W84	Washer	.01 ea.
11	W153	Spring Washer	.04 ea.
12	S359	Adj. Screw	.08 ea.
13	PA5601	Rivet	.01 ea.
14	XA13A446-RP	Nap Base	.28 ea.
15	XA14A268	Mat Assembly	.24 ea.
16	PA4356	Grommet	.02 ea.
17	PA14B270	Coil Platform	.50 ea.
18	S222	#4 x 5/16 [illegible] Screw	.01 ea.
19	XA14A964-U	Control Box	.65 ea.
20	PM491	Wrench	.04 ea.
21	LW-1B2	Yellow Wire	.02 ft.

Prices subject to change without notice.

COW ON TRACK
Model No. 23791

To hook up and operate the Cow on Track, study the diagram below and proceed as follows:—

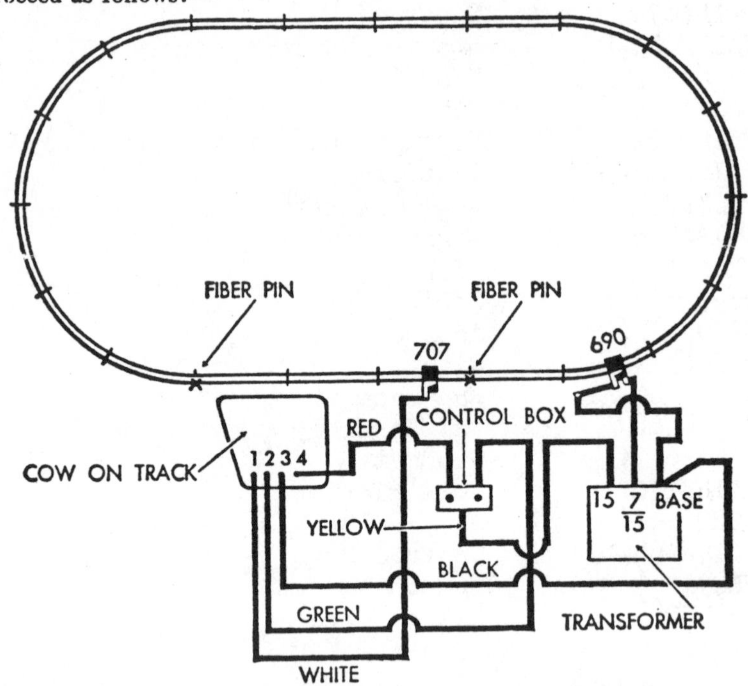

FIRST — determine the location in the layout where the item is to be operated, keeping in mind that while the cow is on the track the train will be stopped and when the cow leaves the track the train will proceed.

NEXT — at the desired location remove two metal track pins from the rails and replace them with the two fiber insulating pins. These pins should be about 3 track sections apart. Now connect the No. 707 Track Terminal to this insulated portion of the track.

Connect the WHITE WIRE from the No. 1 POST to the 707 TRACK TERMINAL.

Connect the GREEN WIRE from the control box to POST No. 2.

Connect the RED WIRE from the control box to POST No. 4.

Connect the YELLOW WIRE from the control box to the 15 or 18 VOLT POST on the transformer.

Connect the BLACK WIRE between POST No. 3 on the accessory and the BASE POST on the transformer.

The unit is now ready to operate. When the red button on the control box is pushed the cow will walk onto the track. This will kill the track voltage in the insulated section and stop the train. When the green button is pressed the cow will leave the track and the train will proceed.

 Ref: Form No. M3832

XA144A776	Solenoid Assembly	2.34 ea.
XA144A773	Plunger & Rod Assembly	.17 ea.
XA144A885	Lever & Contact Assembly	.08 ea.
XA10091	Track Terminal (707)	.22 ea.
PA144A785	Clamp	.01 ea.
PA144A781	14 Tooth Gear Seg.	.08 ea.
PA144A786	Cow	.64 ea.
PA11073	10 ohm. 10 W. Resistor	1.27 ea.
PA10037-B	Binding Post Nut	.02 ea.
XA144A965-AD	2 Button Control Box	.84 ea.

Prices subject to change without notice.

SAWMILL
Model No. 23796

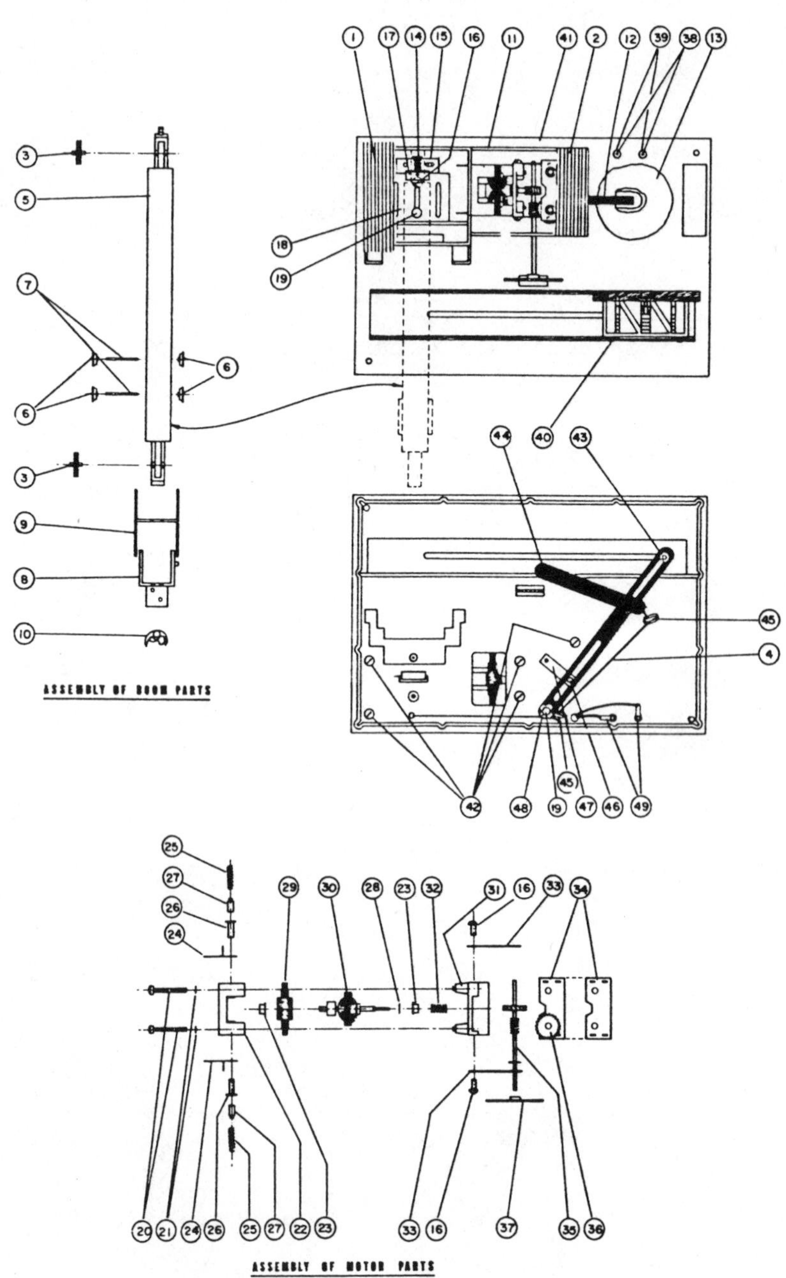

ASSEMBLY OF BOOM PARTS

ASSEMBLY OF MOTOR PARTS

 Ref: Form No. M5229; June 1, 1960

INSTRUCTIONS FOR ASSEMBLING & OPERATING

Assembling

Unpack loose pieces from box (except boom & cab assembly which is connected to saw mill with string). Remove saw mill from box and assemble boom and cab assembly to house, passing end of boom through cutout in front of house and hooking end of boom into slot in rear of house. See Fig. 1. Check to see if string is free and in pulleys, and also if hook swings freely in cab. (Remove piece of tape holding hook to cab during shipment.)

Position man in cab, inserting (2) projections on feet of man into holes in cab as shown in Fig. 1. Use a little household cement to fasten man to cab if necessary.

Place sawdust pile on base, matching locating pins on pile with holes in base as shown in Fig. 1.

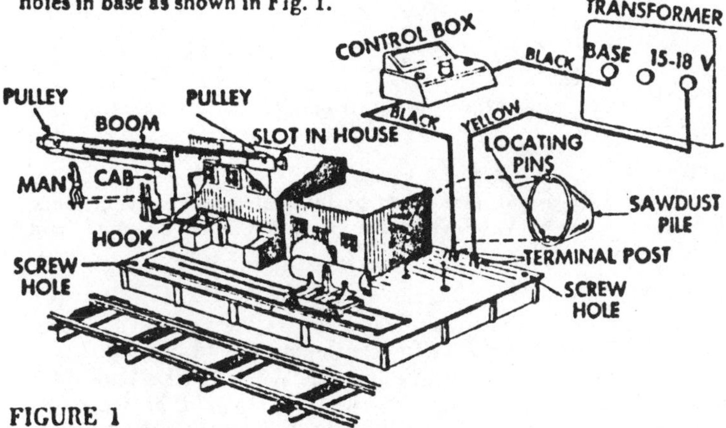

FIGURE 1

Place two roofs in position on building.

Place saw mill along section of straight track (either main or spur line.) After unit is in operation it may be necessary to move it a little so lumber drops properly into a gondola car. Unit may be then fastened down permanently with (2) suitable wood screws inserting screws through holes at opposite corners of base.

Wiring

Connect the YELLOW wire from one of the TERMINAL POSTS on the saw mill to the 15 or 18 volt POST on the transformer.

Connect the long BLACK wire from the other TERMINAL POST on the saw mill to one of the clips underneath the CONTROL BOX.

Connect the short BLACK wire from the other CONTROL BOX clip to the BASE POST on the transformer. See Fig. 1. The unit is now ready to operate.

Operation

Check operation of saw mill before loading lumber. Press the control box button and hold it down. Cab should move freely up and down boom and log car should travel back and forth across base.

Now insert pieces of lumber, ONE AT A TIME, into slot in side of house. Be sure to load each piece of lumber HORIZONTALLY, not vertically, as board may jam during operation if it is not lying flat. See Fig. 2. The vertical slot in side of house extending downward from loading slot is to be used for repositioning boards which have not been loaded properly.

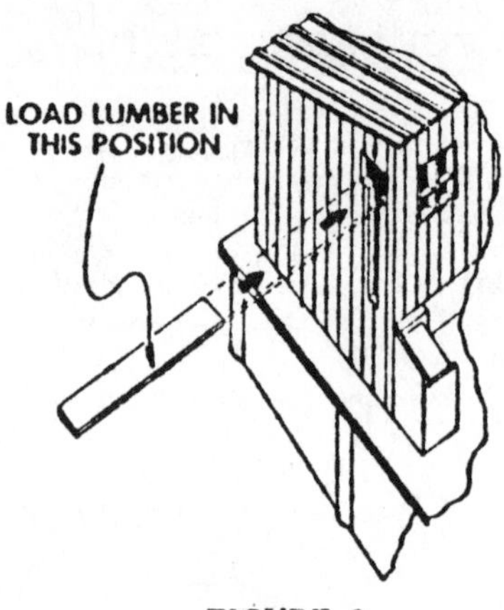

FIGURE 2

Use regular GONDOLA CAR to load lumber into.

Oiling

Bearings and gears on motor can be lubricated by removing roofs. Use a light grease or Vaseline on the gears and a few drops of light oil on the shafts and bearings.

Restringing

Should the string which raises and lowers the cab on the boom break, the following directions for restringing should be used.

Use a piece of good flexible line approximately 30 inches long (20# test hard braided nylon fish line is best). Run saw mill, by depressing button on control box, until lever in base is in extreme left position, looking at unit from the front. See Fig. 3. Tie a slip knot in one end of the string. Place over tab in front of cab and draw tight. Thread string up through front pulley, run along top of boom and down through rear pulley. Pass string through hole in base directly under rear end of boom and, turning saw mill over, thread string through (2) guides underneath base. Then thread string through hole in arm welded to lever. See Fig. 3.

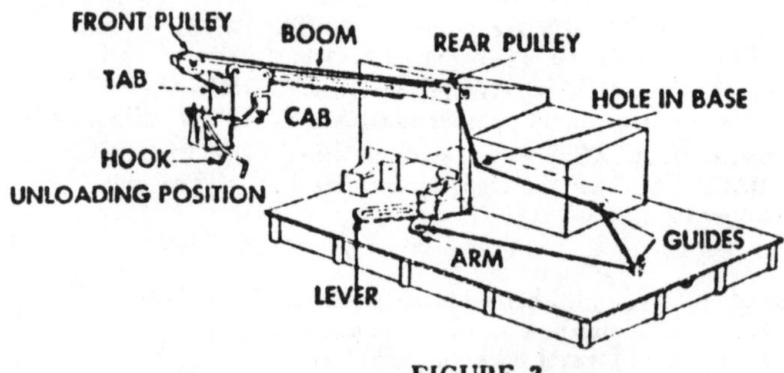

FIGURE 3

Now, with saw mill in upright position again, draw on string until cab and hook assembly is at upper end of boom (high enough to have hook in unload position but not out to extreme end of boom). Turn unit over again and tie string permanently to arm. Unit is now ready for operation again.

NO.	PART NO.	DESCRIPTION	PRICE
1	PA14A704	Roof	.19 ea.
2	PA14A700	Roof	.17 ea.
3	PA14A855	Pulley	.06 ea.
4	PA11295	20# Test Nylon Line	.14 yd.
5	PA14B674	Boom	.19 ea.
6	P13A916-T	Car Wheel	.08 ea.
7	PA14A696	Axle	.02 ea.
8	PA14A851	Cab	.14 ea.
9	PA14A697	Hook	.19 ea.
10	PA14A272-A	Baggage Smasher	.29 ea.
11	PA14C709	House	1.32 ea.
12	PA14A857	Sawdust Pipe	.06 ea.
13	PA14A856	Sawdust Pile	.25 ea.
14	PA14A858	Extension Spring	.11 ea.
15	PA14A677	Ejector Lever Bracket	.05 ea.
16	S319	#6 x 5/16 Type Z R.H. P.K. Screw	.02 ea.
17	PA14A676	Ejector Lever	.03 ea.
18	PA14A682	Ejector	.03 ea.
19	PA14A701	Stud	.05 ea.
20	S5N19	#6 x 32 x 1 Fillister Head Screw	.01 ea.
21	W57	Lockwasher	.01 ea.
22	PA14B859	Brush Bracket	.22 ea.
23	PA13A187	Rear Bearing	.04 ea.
24	PA14A852	Brush Holder	.08 ea.
25	PA13A130	Brush Spring	.03 ea.
26	PA10A984-14	Eyelet	.02 ea.
27	PA9603	Brush	.13 ea.
28	P325-D	Washer	.01 ea.
29	XA14A860	Field Assembly	.69 ea.
30	XA14B681	Armature	.72 ea.
31	PA14C853	Motor Bracket	.84 ea.
32	P10131-A	Worm	.15 ea.
33	PA14A850	Side Plate	.04 ea.
34	PA14A849	Top & Bottom Plate	.02 ea.
35	XA14A691	Drive Shaft Assembly	.42 ea.
36	XA14A694	Power Shaft Assembly	.20 ea.
37	PA14A687	Circular Saw	.12 ea.
38	PA13A183	Binding Post	.03 ea.
39	PA10037-B	Binding Post Nut	.02 ea.
40	XA14A683	Log Car Assembly	.37 ea.
	PA14A698	Log	.09 ea.
	A43	Escutcheon Pin	.07 dz.
41	PA14D711	Base	2.33 ea.
42	S91	#6 x 3/8 Type Z.R.H..P. K. Screw	.02 ea.
43	P10434	Tru Arc Ring	.01 ea.
44	XA14A684	Lever & Actuator Assembly	.31 ea.
45	PA14A708	Guide	.01 ea.
46	PA15A209	Drive Arm Stud	.03 ea.
47	PA14A689	Drive Arm	.08 ea.
48	PA10927	Spring Washer	.01 ea.
49	PA6173	Solder Terminal	.01 ea.
50	XA14A964-N	Single Control Box	.64 ea.

Ref: Form No. M5229; June 1, 1960

Sawmill — No. 23796

NO.	PART NO.	DESCRIPTION	PRICE
1	PA14A704	Roof	.20 ea.
2	PA14A700	Roof	.18 ea.
3	PA14A855	Pulley	.06 ea.
4	PA11295	20# Test Nylon Line	.15 yd.
5	PA14B674	Boom	.20 ea.
6	P13A916-T	Car Wheel	.08 ea.
7	PA14A696	Axle	.02 ea.
8	PA14A851	Cab	.15 ea.
9	PA14A697	Hook	.20 ea.
10	PA14A272-A	Baggage Smasher	.30 ea.
11	PA14C709	House	1.39 ea.
12	PA14A857	Sawdust Pipe	.06 ea.
13	PA14A856	Sawdust Pile	.26 ea.
14	PA14A858	Extension Spring	.12 ea.
15	PA14A677	Ejector Lever Bracket	.05 ea.
16	S319	#6 x 5/16 Type Z R.H. P.K. Screw	.02 ea.
17	PA14A676	Ejector Lever	.03 ea.
18	PA14A682	Ejector	.03 ea.
19	PA14A701	Stud	.05 ea.
20	S5N19	#6 x 32 x 1 Fillister Head Screw	.01 ea.
21	W57	Lockwasher	.01 ea.
22	PA14B859	Brush Bracket	.23 ea.
23	PA13A187	Rear Bearing	.04 ea.
24	PA14A852	Brush Holder	.08 ea.
25	PA13A130	Brush Spring	.03 ea.
26	PA10A984-14	Eyelet	.02 ea.
27	PA9603	Brush	.14 ea.
28	P325-D	Washer	.01 ea.
29	XA14A860	Field Assembly	.72 ea.
30	XA14B681	Armature	.76 ea.
31	PA14C853	Motor Bracket	.88 ea.
32	P10131-A	Worm	.16 ea.
33	PA14A850	Side Plate	.04 ea.
34	PA14A849	Top & Bottom Plate	.02 ea.
35	XA14A691	Drive Shaft Assembly	.44 ea.
36	XA14A694	Power Shaft Assembly	.21 ea.
37	PA14A687	Circular Saw	.13 ea.
38	PA13A183	Binding Post	.03 ea.
39	PA10037-B	Binding Post Nut	.02 ea.
40	XA14A683	Log Car Assembly	.39 ea.
	PA14A698	Log	.09 ea.
	A43	Escutcheon Pin	.07 dz.
41	PA14D711	Base	2.45 ea.
42	S91	#6 x 3/8 Type Z R.H. P.K. Screw	.02 ea.
43	P10434	Tru Arc Ring	.01 ea.
44	XA14A684	Lever & Actuator Assembly	.33 ea.
45	PA14A708	Guide	.01 ea.
46	PA15A209	Drive Arm Stud	.03 ea.
47	PA14A689	Drive Arm	.08 ea.
48	PA10927	Spring Washer	.01 ea.
49	PA6173	Solder Terminal	.01 ea.
50	XA14A964-N	Single Control Box	.67 ea.

 Ref: Form No. M5229; Oct. 1, 1962

HO CROSSING GATE
Model No. (659440)

INSTRUCTIONS FOR HO CROSSING GATE

The crossing gate should be positioned in your layout along a section of straight track. The item consists of a gate with gateman's shanty, two highway approaches, a center roadway section, control box, and necessary wires. First place the center roadway section between the rails so the two spacer projections nest between the ties. Next add the two highway approaches so they line up with the center roadway section. Cover the tie ends and come as close to the rail as possible. These three parts can be glued into position with any household cement.

Now position the gate at the desired side of the track alongside the highway approaches. The gate and shanty can be mounted with small flat head wood screws through the holes in the base. Study wiring diagram below.

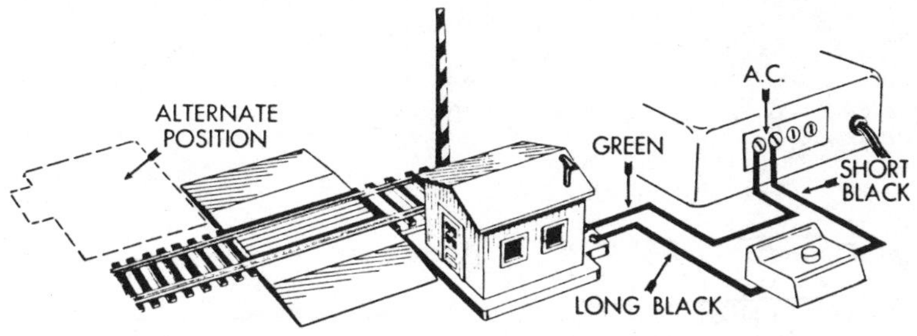

Connect the GREEN wire from one of the terminals on the gate base to one of the AC terminals on the Power Pack. Connect the long BLACK wire from the other terminal on the gate case to a clip underneath the control box. Connect the short BLACK wire from the other control box clip to the other AC terminal on the Power Pack.

The gate is now ready for operation. Start the train running and as it approaches the crossing press the control box button. The gate will lower. When the button is released the gate will again resume an upright position.

Ref: Form No. M3914

3/16 SCALE, TWO-RAIL ACTION CARS
Accessories

PART NO.	DESCRIPTION	PRICE
XA10528	Special Track Section (All action cars)	.41 ea.
XA10529	Special Track Section (Mail Pick-up Cars)	.78 "
#696	Track Trip (#760-759)	.40 "
PA8715-B	Washer (lighted and action cars)	.05 dz.
XA9219	Block & Pulley Assem. (644-944 cars, Mag.Crane & Log Loader)	.25 ea.
P9275	Spring (all action cars)	.04 "
XA9403-A	Lamp Bracket Assem. (all lighted cars except streamline)	.25 "
XA9403-B	Lamp Bracket Assem (streamline cars)	.25 "
PA9694	Automobile Stop (#715-915)	.06 "
PA9760	White Mail Bag (#718-918)	.15 "
PA9760G	Green Mail Bag (#718-918)	.15 "
PA9911-A	Log (#714-917)	.06 "
PA13405	Gas Truck (#915)	.23 "
XA11650	Man Assembly (#766)	.30 "
XA11651	Woman Assembly (#766)	.40 "
PA9968	Door Lever (box cars & cattle cars)	.05 "
PA9969	Door Guide (box cars & cattle cars)	.02 "
S185	P.K. Screw (" " " " ")	.10 dz.
PA9990	Plastic Car wheel	.10 ea.
PA9991	Metal Car Wheel	.10 "
PA10238	Axle	.02 "
XA10238-B	Wheel & Axle Assem. (1 metal & 1 plastic wheel--lighted and action cars)	.25 set
XA10238-A	Wheel & Axle Assem. (2 plastic wheels-all plain cars)	.25 "
PA10240	Insulated Bushing (lighted and action cars)	.02 ea.
PA10209	Insulated Bushing (lighted and action cars)	.02 "
PA10456	Chassis Pin (all cars)	.24 dz.
PA11192	Man (#732-734-974)	.15 ea.
PA11180	Box (#732-734-974)	.10 "
PA11198	Siding (#945)	.08 "
XA11205	Mat assem. (736 & 976)	.08 "
XA11306	Boom Assem. (#644-944)	1.00 "
XA11309	Pulley Block Assem. (#644-944)	.30 "
XA11313	Roof, Hinge, & Pulley Assem. (#644-944)	.64 "
PA11331	Truck Rivet	.07 "
PA11386	Generator (#946)	.30 "
PA11667	Door Pin (#734)	.15 dz.
PA12B666	Brake Handle (box cars)	.01 ea.
XA11437-B	Dump Car Body Assem. (919)	1.76 "
PA11432	Gear (919)	.02 "
PA11431	Gear Support (919)	.02 "
PA10066	Hand Wheel Rod (919)	.02 "
PA8963	Hand Wheel (919)	.04 "
XA11328	Crank Assem. (944-644)	.13 "
PA11327	Crank Spring (944-644)	.05 "
PA11308	Boom Pin (944-644)	.01 "
P4553	Twine (944-644)	.01 "
XA8862RP	Searchlight Assem. (946)	1.06 "
PA8863	Searchlight Lens (946)	.02 "
PA8864	Snap Ring (946)	.01 "
PA8861	Yoke (946)	.27 "
PA11572	Cleaner (948)	.03 "

cont'd

PART NO.	DESCRIPTION		PRICE
040-CC1	Reversing Switch	(#8B-12B)	.75 ea.
109-0045	Reset Button	(#8B Transformer)	2.00 "
109-0050	Reset Button/	(12B ")	2.00 "
PA10715	Selenium Plates	(#15 Rectifier)	4.50 "
XA10716	Double Pole Double Throw Switch (#15)		1.00 "
PA10830	Tube	(#14-#16 Rectiformer)	7.50 "
XA10383	Double Pole Double Throw Switch (#14-16)		.31 "
PA10037	Binding Post Nuts	(#760-592-A- 759)	.02 "
PA8999-R	Red Bulb	(#760-759)	.25 "
PA10665	Bulb	(946 and Lighted Cars)	.25 "
PA11383	Bulb only	(769A-753-754)	.25 "
XA11337-A	Rotary Top & Bulb	(769A-753-754)	.98 "
PA10249	Black Wire		.02 ft.
PA10210	Yellow Wire		.02 ft.
PA10260	Green Wire		.02 ft.
XA11582	Truck & Frame Assembly w/o wheels (all 4 wheel cars) Link Type		.22 ea.
XA9987-F	Truck & Frame Assembly w/o wheels (all 4 wheel cars) Link Type		.25 "
PA10467	Pins for coupler		.10 "
XA10469	Coupler & Weight Assembly		.15 "
PA10533	Contact Arm		.04 "
PA10692	Coupler Weight only		.05 "
XA10694	Truck & Frame assem. w/o wheels		.35 "
XA12A047	Knuckle Coupler		.22 "
XA12A051	4 Wheel Knuckle Coupler truck for Unlighted Cars		1.25 pr.
XA12A050	" " " " " " Lighted Cars		1.50 "
XA12A057 and XA12A050	(use one of each per car) 4 Wheel Knuckle Coupler Truck for Action Car		1.50 "
XA12N818	4 Wheel Knuckle Coupler Truck for Streamline Car		1.50 "
XA12N894	6 Wheel Knuckle Coupler Truck for Passenger Car		1.75 "
XA12N319	Knuckle Coupler Truck for Crane Car #944		1.75 "
XA12A053	Knuckle Coupler Truck for 6-Wheel Tender rear trucks for Hudson type Loco & Union Pacific		1.00 ea.
XA12N823	6-Wheel Knuckle Coupler Truck for #936 Depressed Center Car		1.75 pr.
PA9988	Rivets	(Freight Cars)	.03 ea.
PA9381	Rivets	(Freight & Passenger Cars)	.02 "
PA10235	Rivets	(Pullman and Express Cars)	.03 "
PA10235A	Rivets	(Tank Car)	.03 "
PA12A469	Rivets	(Hopper Car)	.045 "
PA11331	Rivets	(Crane Car)	.07 "
PA11305	Rivets	(Hopper and Gondola Cars w/ weights)	.06 "

CONTROL BOXES

PART NO.	DESCRIPTION	PRICE
XA10961-3	Control Box for #752-A Coaler	.53 "
XA10961-B	Control Box for #566-577 Whistle	.50 "
XA10961-D	Control Box for #596 Water Tank	.50 "
XA10961-E	Control Box for #706 Uncoupler	.50 "
XA10961-F	Control Box for #755 Talking Station & #799	.50 "
XA10961-H	Control Box for #718 and #918 Mail Pick Up Car	.50 "
XA10961-J	Control Box for #715 and #915	.80 "
XA10961-K	Control Box for #716 and #919	.80 "
XA10961-L	Control Box for #714,#717 and #914 Car	.80 "
XA10961-P	Control Box for #770 and K775 Platform	.50 "
XA10961-R	Control Box for #734, #974 Box Car	.50 "
XA10961-S	Control Box for #779 Oil Drum Loader	1.26 "
XA10961-T	Control Box for #561 Diesel Horn	.50 "

TRANSFORMER-RECTIFIER-RECTIFORMER

PART NO.	DESCRIPTION		PRICE
PA11A984	Bar Knob	(#2-4B)	.06 ea.
PA11A985	Post	(#2-4B)	.22 ea.
X9167-A	Contact Spring Ass'y.	(#2-4B)	.15 ea.
P1345	Adjusting Nut	(#2-4B)	.03 ea.
PA10483	Circuit Breaker	(#4B)	1.00 ea.
040-0001	Reversing Switch	(#8B-12B)	.75 ea.
109-0045	Reset Button	(#8B)	2.00 ea.
109-0050	Reset Button	(#12B)	2.00 ea.
13-834	Red Covers	(#8B-12B)	.10 ea.
13-835	Green Covers	(#8B-12B)	.10 ea.
PA11809-R	Red Bulb	(#17B-19B)	.35 ea.
PA11809-G	Green Bulb	(#17B-19B)	.35 ea.
PA11761	Switch	(#17B-19B)	1.05 ea.
PA11771	Volt Meter	(#17B-19B)	3.75 "
PA11763	Amp Meter	(#17B-19B)	3.75 "
XA11773	Handle	(#17B-19B)	.60 "
PA11826	Terminal Nuts	(#17B-19B)	.08 "
PA12A099	Circuit Breaker	(#17B-19B)	1.10 "
PA11749	Retaining Ring	(#17B-19B)	.02 "
PA11847	Retaining Ring	(#17B-19B)	.02 "
PA10715	Selenium Plates	(#15)	4.50 "
XA10716	Double Pole Double Throw Switch (#15)		1.00 "
PA10830	Tube	(#14-16)	7.50 "
XA10381	Tube Guard Ass'y.	(#14-16)	.18 "
XA10383	Double Pole Double Throw Switch (#14-16)		.31 "

MISCELLANEOUS PARTS

#696	Track Trip	(#760)	.40 ea.
PA8889-R	Red Bulb	(#760)	.25 "
XA9065	Magnet Coil	(#596)	.50 "
PA9542	Truck Man	(#586F)	.20 "
PA9557	Porter Casting	(#586F)	.25 "
XA9638	Minature Truck Platform & Chassis Ass'y. (586F)		.30 "
PA10037	Binding Post Nuts	(#760-592-A)	.02 "
PA10[illegible]65	Bulb (444)	(#767)	.25 "
XA11157	Antenna	(#767)	.35 "
XA11270	Assembly, Mat & Buttons	(#771)	.35 "
XA11283	Magnet Coil Ass'y.	(#771)	1.00 "
XA11285	Steer Ass'y.	(#771)	.20 "
XA11337-A	Rotary Top & Bulb	(#769A-753-754)	.98 "
PA11383	Bulb only	(#461) (#769A-753-754)	.25 "
XA11650	Man Ass'y.	(#766)	.30 "
XA11651	Woman Ass'y.	(#766)	.40 "
	Black Wire		.03 Ft.
	Yellow Wire		.03 "
	Green Wire		.03 "

AUTOMATIC TRAIN CONTROLLING SEMAPHORE
Model No. 2043

This unit includes one Automatic Semaphore, one Equipment Controlling Switch.

Instructions for Operating Automatic Train Controlling Semaphore.
(For Either Narrow or Wide Gauge)

This equipment is so designed that when the arm of the Semaphore is in a horizontal or "stop" position, a train will proceed along the track until it enters the insulated section of track, where it will stop. Upon the operator pushing a button on the Equipment Controlling Switch, the arm of the Semaphore will point straight up or in a "clear track" position, and the train will again proceed.

By pushing the opposite button on the Equipment Controlling Switch, the Semaphore arm will take a horizontal or "stop" position and the train will automatically come to a stop when it enters the sections of track controlled by the Semaphore.

TRACK TERMINAL OR CLIPS: You will note that the base of the Semaphore is equipped with two spring controlled clips. By hooking these clips over the center or "3rd rail" of the track sections and then adjusting the two stationary points on the base against the outside rail, the base will fit on either narrow or wide gauge tracks.

INSULATED TRACK UNIT: Connect four or more sections of straight track together. Remove the steel pin from the center rail at both ends of the track sections after they are joined together, being sure that the center rail of the insulated track unit does not come in contact with either end of the regular track. This is important and if this instruction is not carried out the Semaphore will not operate. These sections of straight track will be referred to as the INSULATED UNIT track. Any track layout may be constructed, but the INSULATED UNIT must be used as one section.

EQUIPMENT CONTROLLING SWITCH: This unit comes wired to the Automatic Semaphore and consists of a die cast housing covering two push button switches. By pressing the push buttons alternately, the Automatic Semaphore either stops or starts a train. This is an entirely new feature as the Semaphore is absolutely controlled by the train operator and not by the train.

AUTOMATIC SEMAPHORE: The Automatic Semaphore has a base equipped with two sliding clips. One clip painted green and the other clip painted red. At one end of the INSULATED UNIT hook the base clips to the track so that the RED clip is hooked to the center rail of the INSULATED UNIT and the GREEN clip is hooked to the center rail of a track section not in the insulated unit. It is understood that the Semaphore base is hooked to the track sections so as to cover the end sleeper of one uninsulated track section and one end sleeper of the INSULATED UNIT. The single wire from the Equipment Controlling Switch is connected to the single post on the Semaphore opposite the red and green posts. The Automatic Semaphore is now ready to operate. Push the RED button on the Equipment Controlling Switch and when the train enters the INSULATED UNIT the train will stop. To start the train simply push the GREEN button on the Equipment Controlling Switch and the Semaphore arm will move up to "clear" or "proceed" position and the train will start.

NOTE: If your train operates on less than 10 Volts, it will be necessary to attach the single wire from the Equipment Control Switch to a post on the transformer giving about 10 Volts, in place of attaching directly to the Semaphore.

METHOD FOR HOOKING UP AUTOMATIC TRAIN CONTROLLING SEMAPHORE TO A TRAIN SET.

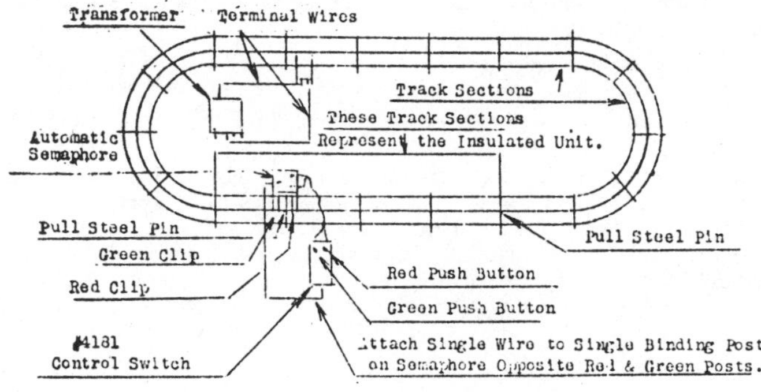

Ref: 1030-2M-36, I W O 4638

TRANSFORMERS

General Instructions

This transformer is designed specifically to operate electric trains and equipment and is not recommended for continuous or commercial use. It will operate on alternating current only of the voltage and frequency designated on its name plate. If you are not certain of the exact current in your home, call your electric light company before attaching transformer.

A 110 volt, 60 cycle transformer will operate successfully on voltages ranging from 100 to 120 volts, and from 50 to 133 cycles. A 25 cycle transformer will operate on frequencies from 25 cycles to 40 cycles. A transformer will not operate on direct current unless a #10 Inverter is used in series with the transformer.

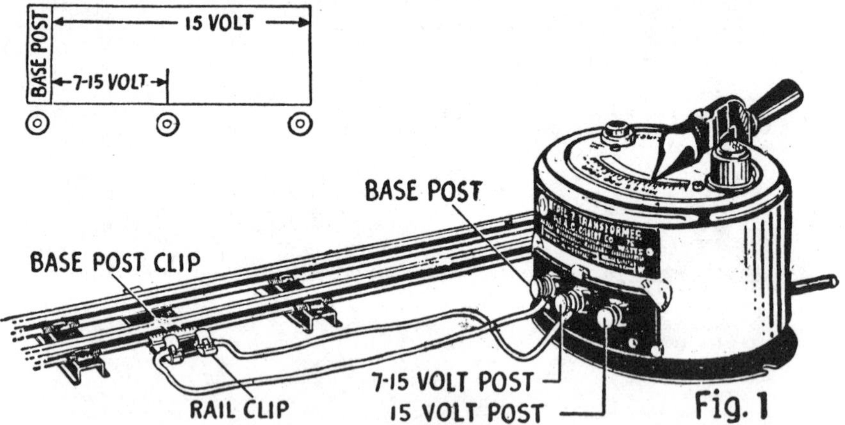

Fig. 1

Assuming that you have your track all properly set up and are now ready to wire the transformer, see Fig. 1 and proceed as follows:

Attach the track terminal to a straight section of track according to the directions furnished on the terminal envelope which is included with your train set.

Connect the BLACK wire between the Base Post of the transformer and the Base Post clip of the track terminal. Connect one end of the WHITE wire to the Remaining Clip of the track terminal and the other end to the 7 to 15 volt Post of the transformer.

Always start the train with a minimum amount of current and add more voltage by moving the control lever.

By connecting such accessories as No. 751 Log Loader, No. 583 Electromatic Crane, etc. to the 15 volt Post and the Base Post of the transformer the accessory is supplied with a constant 15 volts that is unaffected by the position of the regulating lever.

All AMERICAN FLYER TRANSFORMERS except the #2 are equipped with an Automatic Circuit Breaker. When a short circuit or overload occurs the red jewel lights and the breaker opens the circuit to prevent damage to the transformer. When the short or overload has been cleared the breaker is reset by simply pushing the "Reset Button" located on the top of the transformer. The Circuit Breaker protects both the 7 to 15 volt circuit and the 15 volt constant circuit against short circuit or overload.

 Ref: Form No. M2567

The #2B Transformer does not have the red jewel light or the Reset Button, but has a built in Thermostatic Circuit Breaker which resets itself when the short circuit is corrected.

The #8B and #12B Transformers are equipped with a green "Power On" indicating jewel.

The #12B Transformer has a line switch which can be used instead of pulling the plug to shut off the power supplied to the transformer when it is not in use.

The #12B Transformer is a Dual Transformer. It has two control levers which are marked "A" and "B", and two corresponding sets of three terminals as shown in Fig. 2.

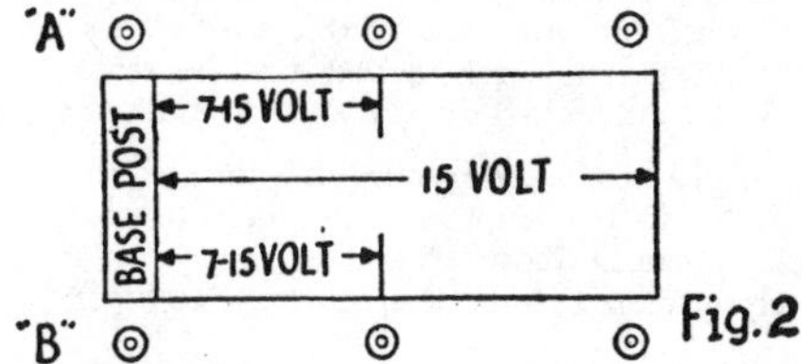

Fig. 2

Each throttle operates separately, thus permitting the operation of two or more trains simultaneously on two layouts as shown in Fig. 3, or two trains simultaneously on two sections of the same layout as shown in Fig. 4.

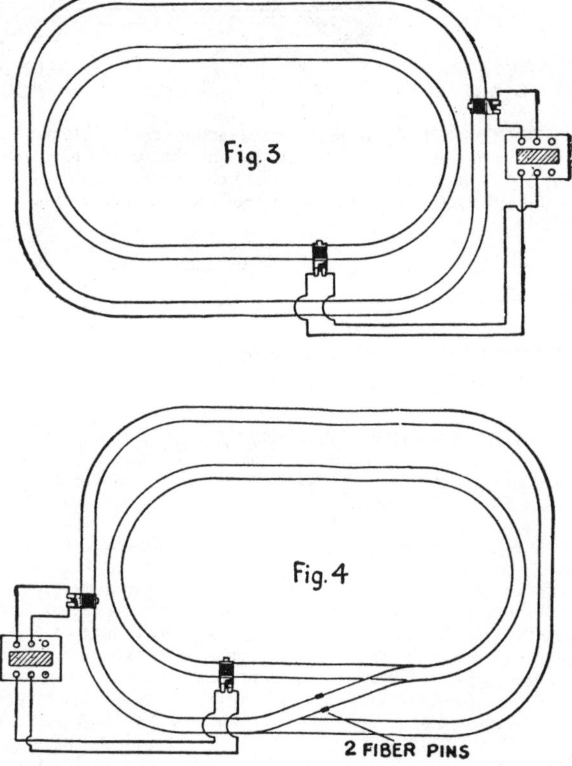

Fig. 3

Fig. 4

SPECIAL INSTRUCTIONS. During past years, transformers have been returned which owners claimed defective. In a large majority of cases we found, after investigating, that the transformer was all right and that the fault was with some other part of the train system. We give you, therefore, a few hints as to what to look for in case the train does not work when connections are made.

TO CHECK THE TRANSFORMER. Press Reset Button to be sure it is down. Turn the lever half on. Connect one end of a piece of wire to the Base Post and touch the 7 to 15 volt Post very lightly with the other end. (DO NOT HOLD THE WIRE ON THE 7-15 VOLT POST. JUST TOUCH IT LIGHTLY.) If a spark occurs the transformer is O.K. If no spark occurs the transformer is defective unless the fault is at the wall socket which can be checked by plugging in a bridge lamp.

Remove the train from the track and be sure there is no metal laying across the rails. Be sure all sections of track fit snugly together then . . .

TO TEST FOR A SHORT. Connect a wire from the Base Post of the transformer to the Base Post Clip of the track terminal. Connect another wire to the 7 to 15 volt Post of the transformer. Brush the other end of this wire across the other rail, if a spark occurs the system is shorted and each section must be removed and tested separately in the manner just described. Switches and crossovers can be tested in the same manner.

TO REPAIR A SHORT. By closely examining a shorted section of track you will discover that one or more of the clamps on a sleeper is touching the rail. With a sharp screw driver the clamp can be loosened and the fiber insulation piece shifted so that the rail is completely insulated from the sleepers. (See Fig. 5)

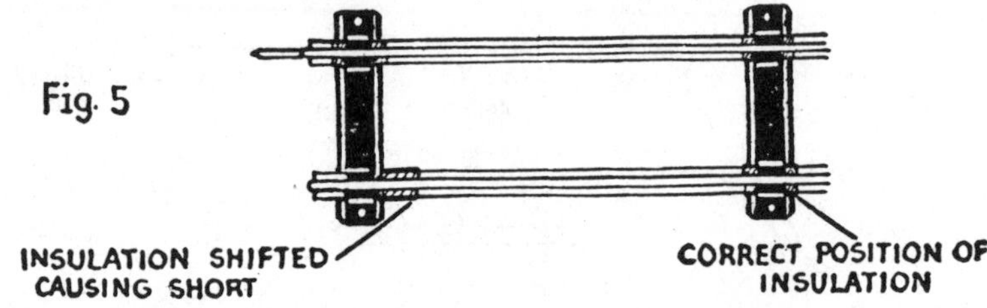

Fig. 5

TO TEST LOCOMOTIVE. Using the tested sections reassemble your layout and place your locomotive and tender on the track. Be sure the cut out lever on a Standard Remote Control Locomotive is not locked in a netural position. If it has been in neutral unlock it and move the transformer throttle to "Stop" and back to half on.

When placing the locomotive and tender on the track be sure the metal wheels on the front tender truck are on one rail and the metal wheels on the rear tender truck are on the other rail.

CAUTION: Ninety per cent of all transformer trouble is caused by permitting the train to lie across the rails and cause a short circuit when it jumps or is knocked off the track. If permitted to remain in this position the cars cause a short circuit and the transformer will burn out.

While AMERICAN FLYER TRANSFORMERS will easily stand 25 per cent overload without harm, we recommend disconnecting the transformer from the house current immediately when you are not going to use your train for even a short period or when the train jumps the track.

GUARANTEE: AMERICAN FLYER TRANSFORMERS are guaranteed to be mechanically and electrically perfect when they leave our factory. Any transformer which will not deliver its rated capacity indicated on the name plate, or has defective terminal posts or switch, will be reconditioned or replaced free of charge for a period of six months after the date of sale to the consumer. If used in accordance with the instructions which accompany it, the transformer will not burn out. These transformers are given four separate tests or inspections before packing, so therefore, we cannot assume the responsibility for burned out transformers. The Guarantee is void if any transformer is opened or tampered with or not used according to instructions.

DUAL CONTROL TRANSFORMER

General Instructions

Dual transformers are just what the name implies—two transformers in one. Each throttle can be operated independently from the other thus permitting the operation of two or more trains simultaneously on two layouts or two trains simultaneously on two sections of the same layout.

These transformers are designed specifically to operate electric trains and equipment and are not recommended for continuous or commercial use. They are to be operated on alternating current of 100 to 120 volts and will operate on frequencies of 50 to 133 Cycles.

Caution—These transformers should *NEVER* be plugged into 110 volt *DIRECT CURRENT*; if you are not certain of the exact type of current in your home, call your electric light or power company before attaching the transformer.

ASSEMBLY OF CONTROL LEVERS

The control levers for the transformer are packed in the box. To assemble the levers to the transformer, first loosen locking screw about three full turns; insert the cutout end of the lever rod, with the cutout section up, underneath the formed metal loop in the control section of the transformer (see Figure No. 1). Press lever down so it snaps into the spring lever holder. Next, fasten locking screw down so control lever will not come out when lifted.

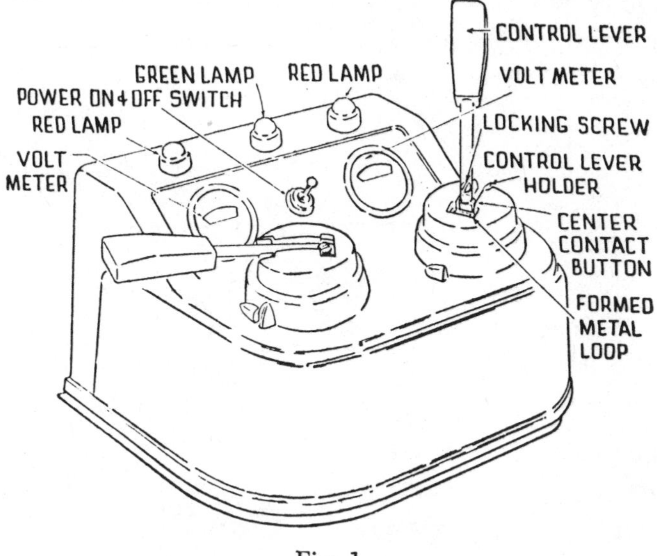

Fig. 1

Ref: Form No. M3177

VARIABLE VOLTAGE OPERATION

When the control levers are in position in the spring holders, they can be turned independently to vary the output voltage on either side which will be from 6 to 15 volts; when the control levers are all the way to the right, the voltage is on the low side at 6 volts and, as the control levers are moved to the left, the voltage gradually increases until the maximum of 15 volts is reached. This is clearly indicated by the voltmeters which are mounted on the transformer face directly underneath the red lights. To completely kill the track voltage, raise the control levers out of the spring control lever holders. This allows the center contact button to raise, breaking all current to the rails or if you so desire, you may shut off just one side by just raising the control lever on the side you wish to turn off.

DEAD MAN'S CONTROL

When these transformers were designed, a special feature—the American Flyer "Dead Man's Control"—was built into the mechanism. Just as in real railroading where "Dead Man's Control" is a fundamental safety feature on all trains, your American Flyer Transformer is now equipped to safeguard your passenger and freight train.

Here's how it works. When the transformer control lever is held down but not locked into the spring control lever holder, current flows through the transformer to the tracks and your trains and accessories will operate normally. Just as your control lever is released, however, the current is broken and power is cut off. Just like a real railroad engineer, you have to be "on the job" in order to run your trains!

TO REVERSE LOCOMOTIVES

For reversing trains, the control lever is to be at the desired speed. Then the control lever is to be raised and lowered twice, which will operate the sequence reverse switch in the locomotive making your loco go backwards. Repeat same to have loco go forward.

ATTACHING TO TRACK

Assuming that you have your track all properly set up and are now ready, connect whichever side of transformer you wish to the track (see Figure 2) and proceed as follows:

Attach the track terminal to the track according to the directions furnished on the track terminal envelope which is included in your train set.

Connect one wire from the base post on the transformer to the base post clip on the track terminal. Connect another wire from the 7-15 volt post on the transformer to the remaining clip on the track terminal.

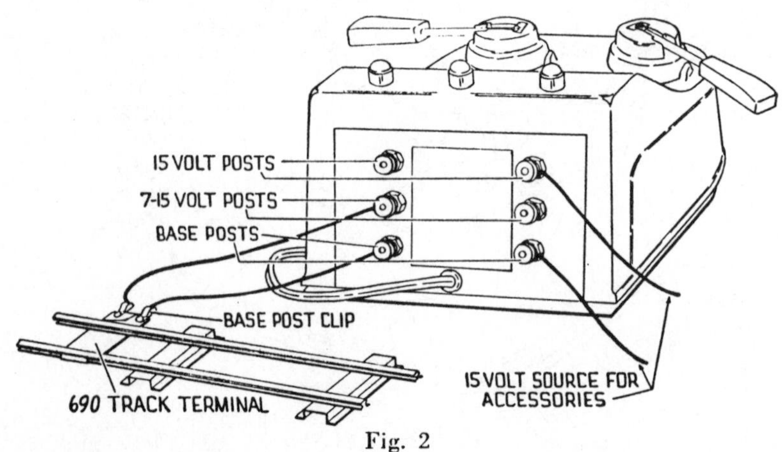

Fig. 2

ATTACHING TO TRACK FOR TWO TRAIN OPERATION ON SAME LAYOUT

As the base posts on your dual transformer are common, you can control either train independently from the other and have complete control of either one at all times. This means that you have to only insulate your inside rail with a fiber pin. You must however insulate your inside rail wherever you cross over from one loop to the other making sure your base post remains on the outside throughout the whole layout (see Figure No. 3).

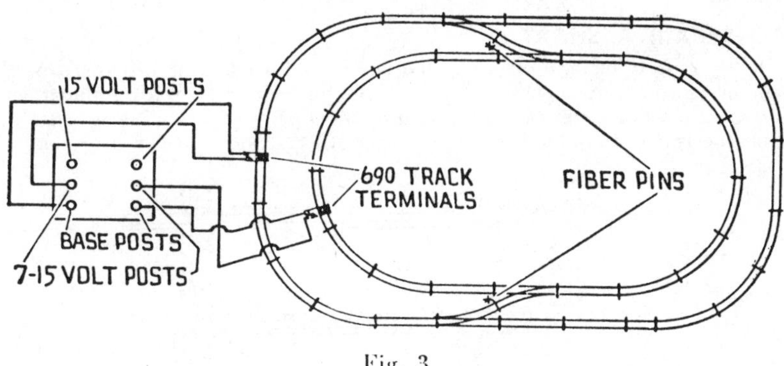

Fig. 3

ATTACHING EQUIPMENT

When connecting lighted and operating accessories, hook the wires to the base and the 15 volt post on either side of your transformer; this will allow them to work on a constant 15 volt current and will not be affected by the position of the control lever.

CIRCUIT BREAKERS

These transformers are equipped with (2) automatic self-setting type circuit breakers. In case of a short circuit or overload on either side of transformer, it will immediately break the circuit thus avoiding either side to burn out. As soon as the circuit breaks, the green light will dim and the red light will come on; when the over-load or short circuit is cleared up, the red light will go out and the green light will resume its brightness.

The 18B Dual Control Transformer has all the above features with the exception of your two volt meters shown on transformer face.

SPECIAL INSTRUCTIONS

During past years, transformers have been returned which owners claimed defective. In a large majority of cases we found, after investigating, that the transformer was all right and that the fault was with some other part of the train system. We give you, therefore, a few hints as to what to look for in case the train does not work when connections are made.

TO CHECK TRANSFORMER

Plug transformer cord in 110 volt A.C. outlet. Green light should now be on. Press control lever down so it is locked in the spring holder. Next fasten the bared end of a short piece of wire to the base post and lightly brush the other bared end across the 7-15 volt post. If a spark occurs, the transformer is putting out current, and you can read the amount of current delivered on the voltmeter. If the wire is held on the 7-15 volt post, the current breaker will open and the red light will light.

TO TEST TRACK LAYOUT FOR A SHORT CIRCUIT

Remove the train from the track and be sure there is no metal lying across the rails. Be sure all sections of track fit snugly; then connect a wire from the base post of the transformer to the base post clip of the track terminal. Connect another wire to the 7-15 volt post of the transformer. Brush the other end of this wire across the other rail; if a spark occurs, the system is shorted and each section must be removed and tested separately in the manner just described. Switches and crossovers can be tested in the same manner.

TO REPAIR A SHORT

By closely examining a shorted section of track, you will discover that one or more clamps on the sleeper is touching the rail. With a sharp screw driver, the clamp can be loosened and the fiber insulation piece shifted so that the rail is completely insulated from the sleepers (see Figure 4).

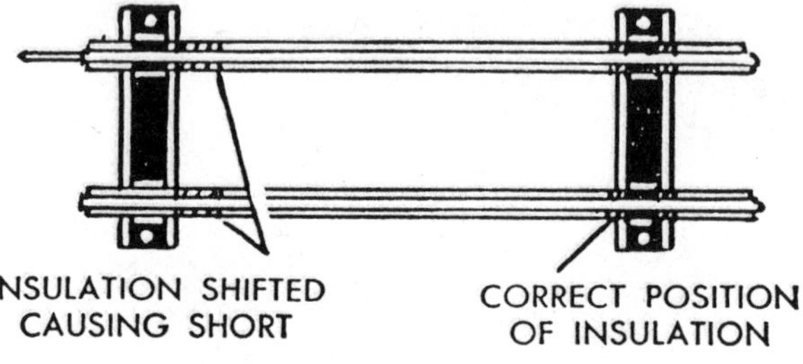

INSULATION SHIFTED CAUSING SHORT

CORRECT POSITION OF INSULATION

Fig. 4

TO TEST LOCOMOTIVE

Using the tested sections, reassemble your layout and place your locomotive and tender on the track. Be sure the cutout lever on a standard remote control locomotive is not locked in neutral position. If it has been in neutral, unlock it and move the transformer lever to full "on" position. Then raise and lower the handle several times. When placing the locomotive and tender on the track, be sure the metal wheels on the front tender truck are on one rail and the metal wheels on the rear tender truck are on the other rail.

CAUTION—Ninety percent of all transformer trouble is caused by permitting the train to lie across the rail and cause a short circuit when it jumps or is knocked off the track. If permitted to remain in this position, it will cause a short circuit and the circuit breaker will be making and breaking constantly until the short circuit is eliminated.

While American Flyer Transformers will easily stand 25 percent overload without harm, we recommend disconnecting the transformer from the house current immediately when you are not going to use your train for even a short period or when the train jumps the track.

TRANSFORMER IDENTIFICATION

The purpose of this identification sheet is to help you identify the transformer you have so that you may order the correct part. The left hand column gives the name of the part and you will note that the corresponding part number together with price is indicated below each of the different illustrations.

#1 — 25 Watt Capacity (2 post)
#1½ — 45 Watt Capacity (3 post)
Metal Case — No Circuit Breaker

#1½ — 50 Watt Capacity
Plastic Case — No Circuit Breaker

Description		*PART NO.*	*PRICE*	*PART NO.*	*PRICE*
Case				XA12C365RP	$ .98 ea.
Knob	**Old Style**	PA10352	$ .50 ea.		
	New Style	PA11A984	.06 ea.	PA12A375	.07 ea.
Screw (Case)				S3N72	.05 ea.
Nut (Case)					
Lockwasher (Case)					
Screw (Knob)		S342	.01 ea.	S3N77	.04 ea.
Terminal Post	**Old Style**	PA10849	.09 ea.		
	New Style	PA12A729	.07 ea.	PA12A729	.07 ea.
Adjusting Nut		P1345	.03 ea.	P1345	.03 ea.
Control Post	**Old Style**	PA10845	.03 ea.		
	New Style	PA11A988	.03 ea.		
Fibre Washer (Term.)		W55-B	.05 dz.		
Sleeving (Long)					
Sleeving (Short)					
Fibre Washer (Term.)		P325-A	.15 dz.		
Contact Spring		PA10850	.02 ea.	PA12A377	.03 ea.
Contact Washer		PA10851	.01 ea.	PA12A376	.01 ea.
Screw (Coil)					
Spring Washer (Contact)					
Circuit Breaker					
Insulating Strip (1½ Only)		PA12A096	.01 ea.		
Fibre Washer (Contact)		PA1310-B	.03 dz.		
Fibre Washer (Contact)		W1A56	.10 dz.	W1A63	.04 dz.
Washer (Support Cont.)		W131	.05 dz.	P2497	.04 dz.
Terminal Strip				PA12A452	.01 ea.
Contact Strip				PA12A450	.09 ea.

The purpose of this identification sheet is to help you identify the transformer you have so that you may order the correct part. The left hand column gives the name of the part and you will note that the corresponding part number together with price is indicated below each of the different illustrations.

#2 — 75 Watt Capacity Metal Case — No Circuit Breaker

#4B — 100 Watt Capacity Metal Case — Circuit Breaker

#4B — 100 Watt Capacity Plastic Case — Circuit Breaker

Description		#2 75 Watt Metal Case *PART NO.*	*PRICE*	#4B 100 Watt Metal Case *PART NO.*	*PRICE*	#4B 100 Watt Plastic Case *PART NO.*	*PRICE*
Case						XA12C476RP	$1.44 ea.
Knob	Old Style	PA10352	$ .50 ea.	PA10352	$ .50 ea.		
	New Style	PA11A984	.06 ea.	PA11A984	.06 ea.	PA12B572	.23 ea.
Screw (Case)		S208	.05 ea.	S208	.05 ea.	S3N80	.03 ea.
Nut (Case)		N32-0	.01 ea.	N32-0	.01 ea.		
Lockwasher (Case)		W33	.05 dz.	W33	.05 dz.		
Screw (Knob)		S342	.01 ea.	S342	.01 ea.	S3N77	.04 ea.
Terminal Post	Old Style						
	New Style						
Adjusting Nut		P1345	.03 ea.	P1345	.03 ea.	P1345	.03 ea.
Control Post	Old Style						
	New Style	PA11A985	.22 ea.	PA11A985	.22 ea.		
Fibre Washer (Term.)		W55	.05 dz.	W55	.05 dz.		
Sleeving (Long)		P532	.01 ea.	P532	.01 ea.		
Sleeving (Short)		P1039	.01 ea.	P1039	.01 ea.		
Fibre Washer (Term.)							
Contact Spring		X9367-A	.15 ea.	X9367-A	.15 ea.	PA12A377	.03 ea.
Contact Washer		P9137	.03 ea.	P9137	.03 ea.	PA12A376	.01 ea.
Screw (Coil)						S4N18	.07 ea.
Spring Washer (Contact)		W56	.01 ea.	W56	.01 ea.		
Circuit Breaker				PA10483	1.00 ea.	PA13A050	1.47 ea.
Insulating Strip (1½ Only)							
Fibre Washer (Contact)							
Fibre Washer (Contact)		P9366	.06 ea.	P9366	.06 ea.		
Washer (Support Cont.)						P2497	.04 dz.
Terminal Strip							
Contact Strip							

25 WATT TRANSFORMER
Model No. 1

INSTRUCTIONS

This transformer is designed specifically to operate the electric train with which it is packed, and is not recommended for continuous or commercial use. It will operate on 110-120 VOLT — 60 CYCLE ALTERNATING CURRENT.

TO HOOK UP. Assuming that you have your track all properly set up and are ready to wire the transformer.

First attach the track terminal to a section of track according to the directions furnished on the envelope in which the terminal is packed.

Connect a wire to each of the two terminal nuts on the top of your transformer and hook the other ends of the wires to the two clips on the track terminal.

Always start the train with a minimum amount of current and add more voltage by moving the control lever.

SPECIAL INSTRUCTIONS. During past years, transformers have been returned which owners claimed defective. In a large majority of cases we found, after investigating, that the transformer was all right and that the fault was with some other part of the train system. We give you, therefore, a few hints as to what to look for in case the train does not work when connections are made.

TO CHECK THE TRANSFORMER. Turn the lever half on. Connect one end of a piece of wire to one of the terminal posts and brush the other end of the wire over the other terminal post. (Do not hold wire on the terminal post, just brush it across.) If a spark occurs the transformer is alive and o.k. If no spark occurs the transformer is defective unless the fault is at the wall socket which can be checked by plugging in a bridge lamp.

Remove the train from the track and be sure there is no metal laying across the rails.

Be sure all sections of track fit snugly together then . . .

TO TEST FOR A SHORT. Connect a wire from one Terminal Post on the transformer to the Base Post Clip of the track terminal. Connect another wire to the other Terminal Post of the transformer. Brush the other end of this wire across the other rail, if a spark occurs the system is shorted and each section must be removed and tested separately in the manner described. Switches and crossovers can be tested in the same manner.

FIG. 1

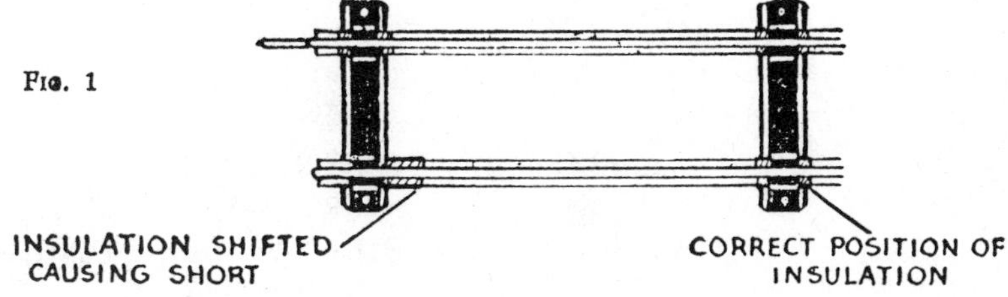

TO REPAIR A SHORT. By closely examining a shorted section of track you will discover that one or more of the clamps on a sleeper is touching the rail. With a sharp screwdriver the clamp can be loosened and the fiber insulation piece shifted so that the rail is completely insulated from the sleepers. (See Fig. 1)

TO TEST LOCOMOTIVE. Using the tested sections reassemble your layout and place your locomotive and tender on the track. Be sure the cut out lever on a Standard Remote Control Locomotive is not locked in a neutral position. If it has been in neutral unlock it and move the transformer throttle to "Stop" and back to half on.

Ref: Form No. M2668

When placing the locomotive and tender on the track be sure the metal wheels on the front tender truck are on one rail and the metal wheels on the rear tender truck are on the other rail.

CAUTION: Ninety per cent of all transformer trouble is caused by permitting the train to lie across the rails and cause a short circuit when it jumps or is knocked off the track. If permitted to remain in this position the cars cause a short circuit and the transformer will burn out.

While AMERICAN FLYER TRANSFORMERS will easily stand 25 per cent overload without harm, we recommend disconnecting the transformer from the current immediately when you are not going to use your train for even a short period or when the train jumps the track.

GUARANTEE: AMERICAN FLYER TRANSFORMERS are guaranteed to be mechanically and electrically perfect when they leave our factory. Any transformer which will not deliver its rated capacity indicated on the name plate, or has defective terminal posts or switch, will be reconditioned or replaced free of charge for a period of six months after the date of sale to the consumer. If used in accordance with the instructions which accompany it, the transformer will not burn out. These transformers are given four separate tests or inspections before packing, so therefore, we cannot assume the responsibility for burned out transformers. The Guarantee is void if any transformer is opened or tampered with or not used according to instructions.

(OLD STYLE)		CASE
	PA10352	KNOB
	S342	SCREW (KNOB)
	PA10849	TERMINAL POST
	P1345	ADJUSTING NUT
	PA10845	CONTROL POST
	W55-B	FIBRE WASHER (TERMINAL)
	P325-A	FIBRE WASHER (TERMINAL)
	PA10850	CONTACTP SPRING
	PA10851	CONTACT WASHER
	PA1310-B	FIBRE WASHER (CONTACT)
	W1A56	FIBRE WASHER (CONTACT)
	W131	WASHER (SUPPORT CONTACT)

(NEW STYLE)		CASE
	PA11A984	KNOB
	S342	SCREW (KNOB)
	PA12A729	TERMINAL POST
	P1345	ADJUSTING NUT
	PA11A988	CONTROL POST
	W55-B	FIBRE WASHER (TERMINAL)
	P325-A	FIBRE WASHER (TERMINAL)
	PA10850	CONTACT SPRING
	PA10851	CONTACT WASHER
	PA1310-B	FIBRE WASHER (CONTACT)
	W1A56	FIBRE WASHER (CONTACT)
	W131	WASHER (SUPPORT CONTACT)

NOTE 1: METAL CASE

NOTE 2: NO CIRCUIT BREAKER

45 WATT TRANSFORMER
Model No. 1-1/2

This transformer is designed specifically to operate electric trains and equipment and is not recommended for continuous or commercial use. It will operate on alternating current only of the voltage and frequency designated on its name plate. If you are not certain of the exact current in your home, call your electric light company before attaching transformer.

This 110 volt, 60 cycle transformer will operate successfully on voltage ranging from 100 to 120 volts, and from 50 to 133 cycles. A transformer will not operate on direct current.

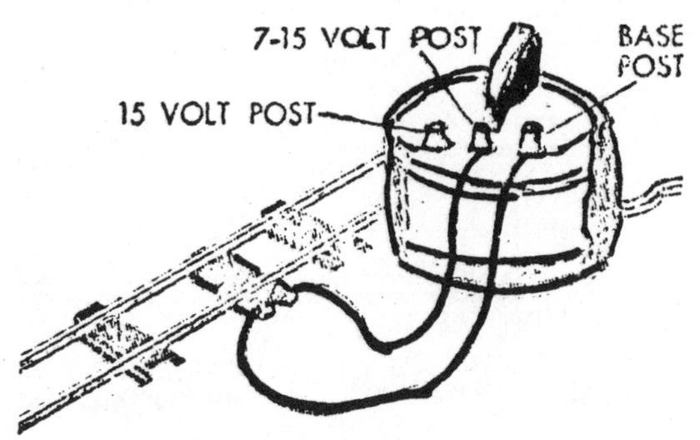

Fig. 1

Assuming that you have your track all properly set up and are now ready to wire the transformer, see Fig. 1 and proceed as follows:

Attach the track terminal to a straight section of track according to the directions furnished on the terminal envelope which is included with your train set.

Connect the **BLACK** wire between the Base Post of the transformer and the Base Post clip of the track terminal. Connect one end of the **WHITE** wire to the Remaining Clip of the track terminal and the other end to the 7 to 15 volt Post of the transformer.

Always start the train with a minimum amount of current and add more voltage by moving the control lever.

By connecting accessories to the 15 volt Post and the Base Post of the transformer the accessory is supplied with a constant 15 volts that is unaffected by the position of the regulating lever.

SPECIAL INSTRUCTIONS. During past years, transformers have been returned which owners claimed defective. In a large majority of cases we found, after investigating, that the transformer was all right and that the fault was with some other part of the train system. We give you, therefore, a few hints as to what to look for in case the train does not work when connections are made.

TO CHECK THE TRANSFORMER. Turn the lever half on. Connect one end of a piece of wire to the Base Post and touch the 7 to 15 volt Post very lightly with the other end. (DO NOT HOLD THE WIRE ON THE 7-15 VOLT POST. JUST TOUCH IT LIGHTLY.) If a spark occurs the transformer is O.K. If no spark occurs the transformer is defective unless the fault is at the wall socket which can be checked by plugging in a bridge lamp.

Remove the train from the track and be sure there is no metal laying across the rails. Be sure all sections of track fit snugly together then .

TO TEST FOR A SHORT. Connect a wire from the Base Post of the transformer to the Base Post Clip of the track terminal. Connect another wire to the 7 to 15 volt Post of the transformer. Brush the other end of this wire across the other rail; if a spark occurs the system is shorted and each section must be removed and tested separately in the manner just described. Switches and crossovers can be tested in the same manner.

TO REPAIR A SHORT. By closely examining a shorted section of track you will discover that one or more of the clamps on a sleeper is touching the rail. With a sharp screw driver the clamp can be loosened and the fiber insulation piece shifted so that the rail is completely insulated from the sleepers. (See Fig. 2.)

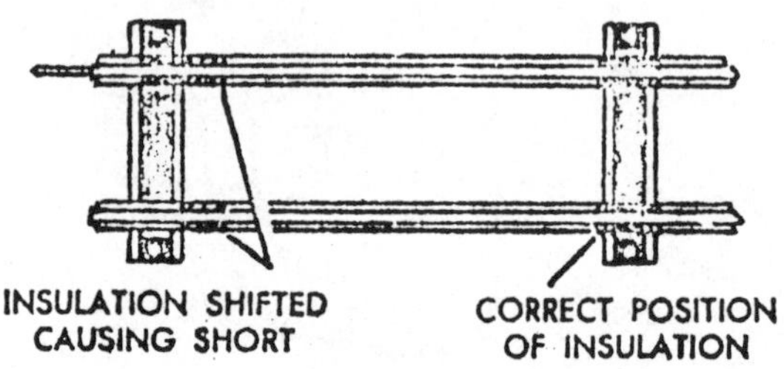

Fig. 2

TO TEST LOCOMOTIVE. Using the tested sections reassemble your layout and place your locomotive and tender on the track. Be sure the cut out lever on a Standard Remote Control Locomotive is not locked in a neutral position. If it has been in neutral unlock it and move the transformer throttle to "Stop" and back to half on.

When placing the locomotive and tender on the track be sure the metal wheels on the front tender truck are on one rail and the metal wheels on the rear tender truck are on the other rail.

CAUTION: Ninety percent of all transformer trouble is caused by permitting the train to lie across the rails and cause a short circuit when it jumps or is knocked off the track. If permitted to remain in this position the cars cause a short circuit and the transformer will burn out.

While American Flyer transformers will easily stand 25 percent overload without harm, we recommend disconnecting the transformer from the house current immediately when you are not going to use your train for even a short period or when the train jumps the track.

GUARANTEE: AMERICAN FLYER TRANSFORMERS are guaranteed to be mechanically and electrically perfect when they leave our factory. Any transformer which will not deliver its rated capacity indicated on the name plate, or has defective terminal posts or switch, will be reconditioned or replaced free of charge for a period of six months after the date of sale to the consumer. If used in accordance with the instructions which accompany it, the transformer will not burn out. These transformers are given four separate tests or inspections before packing, so therefore, we cannot assume the responsibility for burned out transformers. The Guarantee is void if any transformer is opened or tampered with or not used according to instructions.

50 WATT TRANSFORMER
Model No. 1-1/2

This transformer is designed specifically to operate electric trains and equipment and is not recommended for continuous or commercial use. It will operate on alternating current only of the voltage and frequency designated on its name plate. If you are not certain of the exact current in your home, call your electric light company before attaching transformer.

This 110 volt, 60 cycle transformer will operate successfully on voltages ranging from 100 to 120 volts, and from 50 to 133 cycles. A transformer will not operate on direct current.

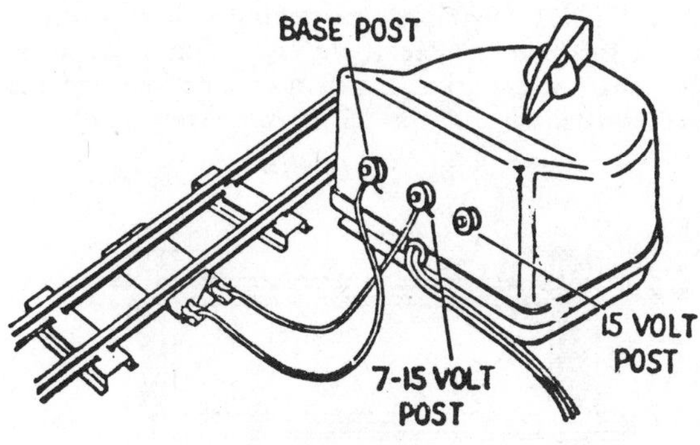

Fig. 1

Assuming that you have your track all properly set up and are now ready to wire the transformer, see Fig. 1 and proceed as follows:

Attach the track terminal to a straight section of track according to the directions furnished on the terminal envelope which is included with your train set.

Connect the **BLACK** wire between the Base Post of the transformer and the Base Post clip of the track terminal. Connect one end of the **WHITE** wire to the Remaining Clip of the track terminal and the other end to the 7 to 15 volt Post of the transformer.

Always start the train with a minimum amount of current and add more voltage by moving the control lever.

By connecting accessories to the 15 volt Post and the Base Post of the transformer the accessory is supplied with a constant 15 volts that is unaffected by the position of the regulating lever.

SPECIAL INSTRUCTIONS. During past years, transformers have been returned which owners claimed defective. In a large majority of cases we found, after investigating, that the transformer was all right and that the fault was with some other part of the train system. We give you, therefore, a few hints as to what to look for in case the train does not work when connections are made.

TO CHECK THE TRANSFORMER. Turn the lever half on. Connect one end of a piece of wire to the Base Post and touch the 7 to 15 volt Post very

Ref: Form No. M3158; Jan. 1955

lightly with the other end. (DO NOT HOLD THE WIRE ON THE 7-15 VOLT POST. JUST TOUCH IT LIGHTLY.) If a spark occurs the transformer is O.K. If no spark occurs the transformer is defective unless the fault is at the wall socket which can be checked by plugging in a bridge lamp. Remove the train from the track and be sure there is no metal laying across the rails. Be sure all sections of track fit snugly together then .

TO TEST FOR A SHORT. Connect a wire from the Base Post of the transformer to the Base Post Clip of the track terminal. Connect another wire to the 7 to 15 volt Post of the transformer. Brush the other end of this wire across the other rail; if a spark occurs the system is shorted and each section must be removed and tested separately in the manner just described. Switches and crossovers can be tested in the same manner.

TO REPAIR A SHORT. By closely examining a shorted section of track you will discover that one or more of the clamps on a sleeper is touching the rail. With a sharp screw driver the clamp can be loosened and the fiber insulation piece shifted so that the rail is completely insulated from the sleepers. (See Fig. 2.)

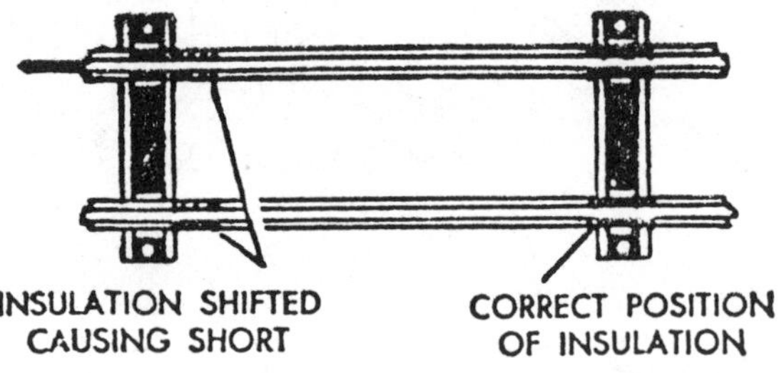

Fig. 2

TO TEST LOCOMOTIVE. Using the tested sections reassemble your layout and place your locomotive and tender on the track. Be sure the cut out lever on a Standard Remote Control Locomotive is not locked in a neutral position. If it has been in neutral unlock it and move the transformer throttle to "Stop" and back to half on.

When placing the locomotive and tender on the track be sure the metal wheels on the front tender truck are on one rail and the metal wheels on the rear tender truck are on the other rail.

CAUTION: Ninety percent of all transformer trouble is caused by permitting the train to lie across the rails and cause a short circuit when it jumps or is knocked off the track. If permitted to remain in this position the cars cause a short circuit and the transformer will burn out.

While American Flyer transformers will easily stand 25 percent overload without harm, we recommend disconnecting the transformer from the house current immediately when you are not going to use your train for even a short period or when the train jumps the track.

50 WATT TRANSFORMER
Model Nos. 1-1/2B, 22020

40 WATT TRANSFORMER
Model No. 22004

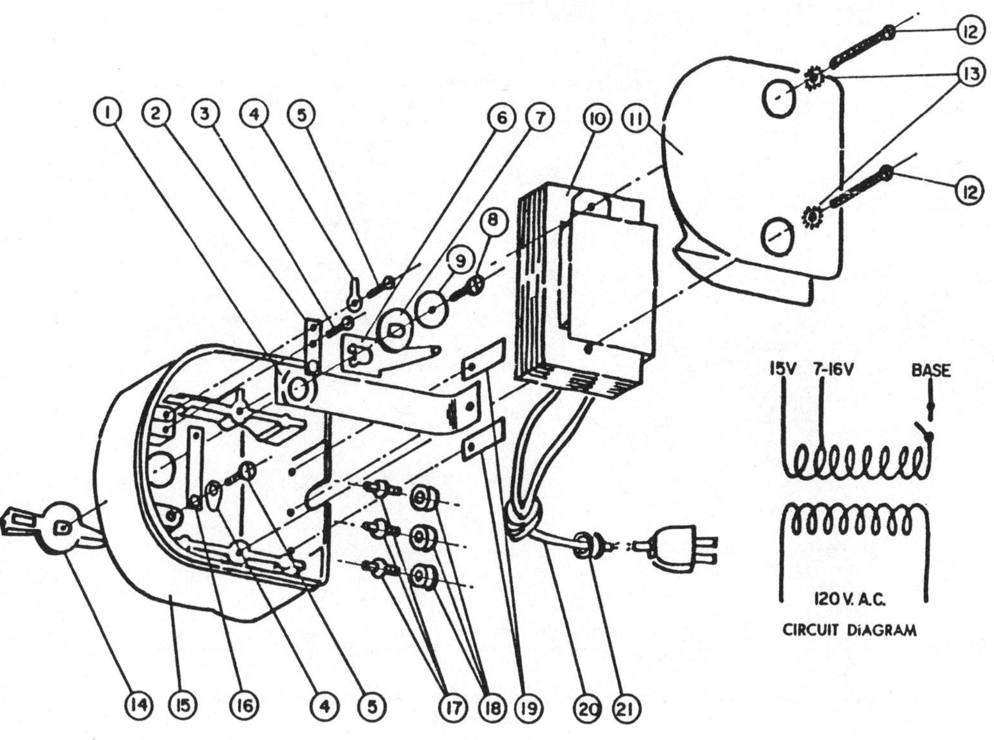

TEST SPECIFICATIONS

Tested at 120 Volts A. C.

(A) No lead Watts input to be no greater than 6 watts.
(B) Circuit breaker should break within 20 seconds when output terminals are shorted.
(C) Variable voltage should not be intermittent and should disconnect only at "off" position as control knob is operated.

DIA. NO.	PART NO.	DESCRIPTION	PRICE
1	PA12A450	Contact Strip	.10 ea.
2	XA13A786	Contact Arm Assembly	.13 ea.
3	S4N29	#4 x 3/8 Type F. R. H. P. K. Screw	.01 ea.
4	PA6173	Solder Terminal	.01 ea.
5	S5N57	#4 x 5/16 Type 25 R. H. P. K. Screw	.02 ea.
6	PA12A377	Contact Spring	.06 ea.
7	PA12A376	Washer	.01 ea.
8	S3N77	#4 x 3/8 Type 25 P. K. Screw	.04 ea.
9	P2497	Washer	.04 dz.
10	XA12B366	Coil Assembly (NOT SOLD AS SEPARATE PART)	
11	XA12A361	Mounting Plate Assembly	.47 ea.
12 & 13	S4N41	#6 x 1 3/16 Type 25 Shakeproof Screw	.05 ea.
14	PA12A375	Knob	.08 ea.
15	XA12C365ARP	Case Assembly	1.99 ea.
16	XA15A298	Bi Metal Contact Arm. Assembly	.23 ea.
17	P14A337	Terminal Post	.03 ea.
18	P14A342	Adjusting Nut	.04 ea.
19	PA12A452	Terminal Strip	.01 ea.
20		Cord & Plug (NOT SOLD SEPARATELY)	
21	PA12A451	Grommet	.11 ea.

* * * * * * * * * * * * *

TEST SPECIFICATIONS

Tested at 120 Volts A.C.

(A) No load Watts input to be no greater than 6 watts.
(B) Circuit breaker should break within 20 seconds when output terminals are shorted.
(C) Variable voltage should not be intermittent and should disconnect only at "off" position as control knob is operated.

DIA. NO.	PART NO.	DESCRIPTION	PRICE
1	PA12A450	Contact Strip	.11 ea.
2	XA13A786	Contact Arm Assembly	.14 ea.
3	S4N29	#4 x 3/8 Type F R.H. P.K. Screw	.01 ea.
4	PA6173	Solder Terminal	.01 ea.
5	S5N57	#4 x 5/16 Type 25 R.H. P.K. Screw	.02 ea.
6	PA12A377	Contact Spring	.06 ea.
7	PA12A376	Washer	.01 ea.
8	S3N77	#4 x 3/8 Type 25 P.K. Screw	.04 ea.
9	P2497	Washer	.04 dz.
10		Coil Assembly (NOT SOLD AS SEPARATE PART)	
11		Mounting Plate Assembly (NOT SOLD AS SEPARATE PART)	
12 & 13	S4N41	#6 x 1 3/16 Type 25 Shakeproof Screw	.05 ea.
14	PA12A375	Knob	.08 ea.
15	XA12C365ARP	Case Assembly (Marked 22020)	2.09 ea.
16	XA15A298	Bi Metal Contact Arm. Assembly	.24 ea.
17	P14A337	Terminal Post	.04 ea.
18	P14A342	Adjusting Nut	.04 ea.
19	PA12A452	Terminal Strip	.01 ea.
20		Cord & Plug (NOT SOLD SEPARATELY)	
21	PA12A451	Grommet	.12 ea.

 Ref: Form No. 1894; June 1, 1960; Rev. Oct. 1, 1962

Tested at 120 volts A.C.

(A) No load watts input to be no greater than 6 watts.
(B) Circuit breaker should break within 20 seconds when output terminals are shorted.
(C) Variable voltage should not be intermittent and should disconnect only at "off" position as control knob is operated.

DIA. NO.	PART NO.	DESCRIPTION	PRICE
1	PA12A450	Contact Strip	.10 ea.
2	XA13A786	Contact Arm Assembly	.13 ea.
3	S4N29	#4 x 3/8 Type F. R. H. P. K. Screw	.01 ea.
4	PA6173	Solder Terminal	.01 ea.
5	S5N57	#4 x 5/16" Type 25 R. H. P. K. Screw	.02 ea.
6	PA12A377	Contact Spring	.06 ea.
7	PA12A376	Washer	.01 ea.
8	S3N77	#4 x 3/8 Type 25 P. K. Screw	.04 ea.
9	P2497	Washer	.04 dz.
10	XA14B418	Coil Assembly (NOT SOLD SEPARATELY)	
11	XA14A506	Mounting Plate Assembly	.47 ea.
12 & 13	S5N09	#6 x 1" Type 25 Shakeproof Screw	.02 ea.
14	PA12A375	Knob	.08 ea.
15	XA12D365 CRP	Case Assembly (22004)	1.87 ea.
16	XA15A298	Bi Metal Contact Arm Assembly	.23 ea.
17	P14A337	Terminal Post	.03 ea.
18	P14A342	Adjusting Nut	.04 ea.
19	PA12A452	Terminal Strip	.01 ea.
20		Cord & Plug (NOT SOLD SEPARATELY)	
21	PA12A451	Grommet	.11 ea.

* * * * * * * *

1	PA12A450	Contact Strip	.11 ea.
2	XA13A786	Contact Arm Assembly	.14 ea.
3	S4N29	#4 x 3/8 Type F R.H. P.K. Screw	.01 ea.
4	PA6173	Solder Terminal	.01 ea.
5	S5N57	#4 x 5/16" Type 25 R.H. P.K. Screw	.02 ea.
6	PA12A377	Contact Spring	.06 ea.
7	PA12A376	Washer	.01 ea.
8	S3N77	#4 x 3/8 Type 25 P.K. Screw	.04 ea.
9	P2497	Washer	.04 dz.
10		Coil Assembly (NOT SOLD SEPARATELY)	
11		Mounting Plate Assembly (NOT SOLD SEPARATELY)	
12 & 13	S5N09	#6 x 1" Type 25 Shakeproof Screw	.02 ea.
14	PA12A375	Knob	.08 ea.
15	XA12D365 CRP	Case Assembly (22004)	1.96 ea.
16	XA15A298	Bi Metal Contact Arm Assembly	.24 ea.
17	P14A337	Terminal Post	.04 ea.
18	P14A342	Adjusting Nut	.04 ea.
19	PA12A452	Terminal Strip	.01 ea.
20		Cord & Plug (NOT SOLD SEPARATELY)	
21	PA12A451	Grommet	.12 ea.

* * * * * * * *

NOTE: DIA. NO. ITEMS 10, 11, AND 20 NOT AVAILABLE BY SEPARATE SALES.

50 WATT TRANSFORMER WITH CIRCUIT BREAKER Model No. 1-1/2B

This transformer is designed specifically to operate electric trains and equipment and is not recommended for continuous or commercial use. It will operate on alternating current only of the voltage and frequency designated on its name plate. If you are not certain of the exact current in your home, call your electric light company before attaching transformer.

This 110 volt, 60 cycle transformer will operate successfully on voltages ranging from 100 to 120 volts, and from 50 to 133 cycles. A transformer will not operate on direct current.

This transformer contains a thermostatic type circuit breaker to protect the transformer against overloads. The circuit breaker will open and disconnect the transformer from the layout, if the layout contains a short. When the temporary short is corrected the circuit breaker will reconnect the transformer to the layout. If the short is not remedied the circuit breaker will go on and off until the short is corrected.

It will also protect the transformer from continuous heavy current drain which will heat up the transformer to a point which may burn it out. In this case the circuit breaker will open regardless of whether or not current is drawn from the transformer.

Fig. 1

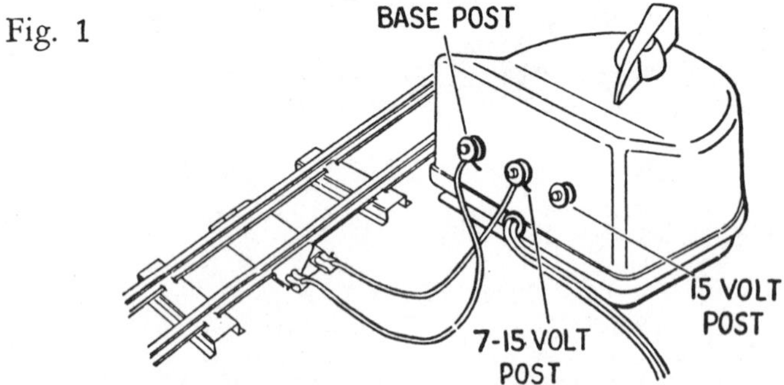

Assuming that you have your track all properly set up and are now ready to wire the transformer, see Fig. 1 and proceed as follows:

Attach the track terminal to a straight section of track according to the directions furnished on the terminal envelope which is included with your train set.

Connect the **BLACK** wire between the Base Post of the transformer and the Base Post clip of the track terminal. Connect one end of the **WHITE** wire to the Remaining Clip of the track terminal and the other end to the 7 to 15 volt Post of the transformer.

Always start the train with a minimum amount of current and add more voltage by moving the control lever.

By connecting accessories to the 15 volt Post and the Base Post of the transformer the accessory is supplied with a constant 15 volts that is unaffected by the position of the regulating lever.

 Ref: Form No. M3376

SPECIAL INSTRUCTIONS. During past years, transformers have been returned which owners claimed defective. In a large majority of cases we found, after investigating, that the transformer was all right and that the fault was with some other part of the train system. We give you, therefore, a few hints as to what to look for in case the train does not work when connections are made.

TO CHECK THE TRANSFORMER. Turn the lever half on. Connect one end of a piece of wire to the Base Post and touch the 7 to 15 volt Post very lightly with the other end. (DO NOT HOLD THE WIRE ON THE 7-15 VOLT POST. JUST TOUCH IT LIGHTLY.) If a spark occurs the transformer is O.K. If no spark occurs the transformer is defective unless the fault is at the wall socket which can be checked by plugging in a bridge lamp. Remove the train from the track and be sure there is no metal laying across the rails Be sure all sections of track fit snugly together then .

TO TEST FOR A SHORT. Connect a wire from the Base Post of the transformer to the Base Post Clip of the track terminal. Connect another wire to the 7 to 15 volt Post of the transformer. Brush the other end of this wire across the other rail; if a spark occurs the system is shorted and each section must be removed and tested separately in the manner just described. Switches and crossovers can be tested in the same manner.

TO REPAIR A SHORT. By closely examining a shorted section of track you will discover that one or more of the clamps on a sleeper is touching the rail. With a sharp screw driver the clamp can be loosened and the fiber insulation piece shifted so that the rail is completely insulated from the sleepers. (See Fig. 2.)

Fig. 2

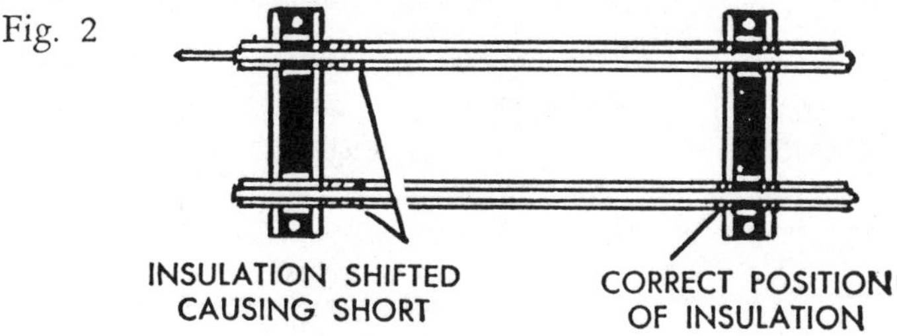

TO TEST LOCOMOTIVE. Using the tested sections reassemble your layout and place your locomotive and tender on the track. Be sure the cut out lever on a Standard Remote Control Locomotive is not locked in a neutral position. If it has been in neutral unlock it and move the transformer throttle to "Stop" and back to half on.

When placing the locomotive and tender on the track be sure the metal wheels on the front tender truck are on one rail and the metal wheels on the rear tender truck are on the other rail.

CAUTION: Ninety percent of all transformer trouble is caused by permitting the train to lie across the rails and cause a short circuit when it jumps or is knocked off the track. If permitted to remain in this position the cars cause a short circuit and the transformer will burn out.

While American Flyer transformers will easily stand 25 percent overload without harm, **we recommend disconnecting the transformer from the house current immediately when you are not going to use your train for even a short period or when the train jumps the track.**

Ref: Form No. M3376

75 WATT TRANSFORMER
Model No. 2

	PART NO.	DESCRIPTION
(OLD STYLE)		CASE
	PA10352	KNOB
	S208	SCREW (CASE)
	N32-0	NUT (CASE)
	W33	LOCK WASHER (CASE)
	S342	SCREW (KNOB)
	P1345	ADJUSTING NUT
	PA11A985	CONTROL POST
	P532	SLEEVING (LONG)
	P1039	SLEEVING (SHORT)
	W55	FIBRE WASHER (TERMINAL)
	X9367-A	CONTACT SPRING
	P9137	CONTACT WASHER
	W56	SPRING WASHER (CONTACT)
	P9366	FIBRE WASHER (CONTACT)

* * * * * *

	PART NO.	DESCRIPTION
(NEW STYLE)		CASE
	PA11A984	KNOB
	S208	SCREW (CASE)
	N32-0	NUT (CASE)
	W33	LOCK WASHER (CASE)
	S342	SCREW (KNOB)
	P1345	ADJUSTING NUT
	PA11A985	CONTROL POST
	P532	SLEEVING (LONG)
	P1039	SLEEVING (SHORT)
	W55	FIBRE WASHER (TERMINAL)
	X9367-A	CONTACT SPRING
	P9137	CONTACT WASHER
	W56	SPRING WASHER (CONTACT)
	P9366	FIBRE WASHER (CONTACT)

* *

NOTE 1: METAL CASE

NOTE 2: NO CIRCUIT BREAKER

100 WATT TRANSFORMER
Model No. 4B

DIA. NO.	PART NO.	DESCRIPTION
	XA12C476-RP	CASE
	PA12B572	KNOB
	S3N80	SCREW (CASE)
	S3N77	SCREW (KNOB)
	P1345	ADJUSTING NUT
	PA12A377	CONTACT SPRING
	PA12A376	CONTACT WASHER
	S4N18	SCREW (COIL)
	PA13A050	CIRCUIT BREAKER
	P2497	WASHER (SUPPORT CONTROL)

* *

NOTES

NOTE 1: PLASTIC CASE

NOTE 2: CIRCUIT BREAKER

	PART NO.	DESCRIPTION
(OLD STYLE)		CASE
	PA10352	KNOB
	S208	SCREW (CASE)
	N32-0	NUT (CASE)
	W33	LOCK WASHER (CASE)
	S342	SCREW (KNOB)
	P1345	ADJUSTING NUT
	PA11A985	CONTROL POST
	W55	FIBRE WASHER (TERMINAL)
	P532	SLEEVING (LONG)
	P1039	SLEEVING (SHORT)
	X9367-A	CONTACT SPRING
	P9137	CONTACT WASHER
	W56	SPRING WASHER (CONTACT)
	PA10483	CIRCUIT BREAKER
	P9366	FIBRE WASHER (CONTACT)

* * * * * *

	PART NO.	DESCRIPTION
(NEW STYLE)		CASE
	PA11A984	KNOB
	S208	SCREW (CASE)
	N32-0	NUT (CASE)
	W33	LOCK WASHER (CASE)
	S342	SCREW (KNOB)
	P1345	ADJUSTING NUT
	PA11A985	CONTROL POST
	W55	FIBRE WASHER (TERMINAL)
	P532	SLEEVING (LONG)
	P1039	SLEEVING (SHORT)
	X9367-A	CONTACT SPRING
	P9137	CONTACT WASHER
	W56	SPRING WASHER (CONTACT)
	PA10483	CIRCUIT BREAKER
	P9366	FIBRE WASHER (CONTACT)

* *

NOTE 1: METAL CASE

NOTE 2: CIRCUIT BREAKER

TRANSFORMER
Model Nos. 5, 6

INSTRUCTIONS

Assuming that you have your track all properly set-up and are now ready to hook up the transformer to the track layout proceed as follows:

Attach the track terminal to the track layout as per instructions on the terminal envelope, which is included with your train set. Fasten the two wires which are included with the track terminal to the terminal itself and to the transformer as shown in sketch below.

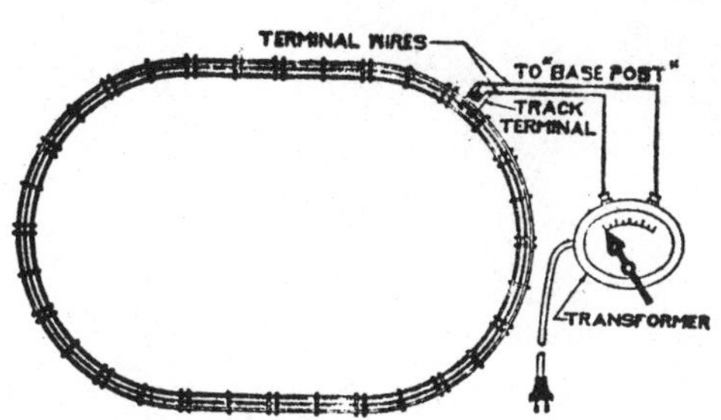

To start the train simply turn the control lever on the transformer to the right. After train has gained momentum, the speed may be regulated by turning the lever either to left or right.

Caution:

1—These transformers will not operate on Direct Current.

2—Be sure that the kind of power supplied by the Electric Light Company is alternating current and checks with voltage and cycle markings on transformer. If in doubt ask the Electric Company what kind of power they supply and obtain a transformer to meet their rating. Do not connect the transformer if the kind of power is not as listed on the transformer. If you do, you may burn out your transformer.

3—Do not connect the plug to the electric light circuit until you have your transformer completely hooked up with your track layout. Before plugging transformer into light socket or receptacle, make sure that it is properly connected as shown in above sketch.

4—Now go over your train layout carefully, see that all the wheels are on the track—push the train back and forth a few times to see that all the wheels turn properly—see that the sections of track are pushed tightly together and that all wires are tightly connected.

5—Before placing locomotive on track see that the current is turned off. Always start the train with a minimum amount of current and add more voltage by moving the regulating lever from left to right.

6—Be sure to turn off your electric current by pulling out the plug every time you leave your train. If the train jumps the track, turn off the current at the transformer, otherwise it will heat up and reduce its efficiency.

Short Circuits—Ninety per cent of all transformer trouble is caused by permitting the train to lie across the rails which causes a short circuit. Naturally, if there is a short circuit, the load on the transformer is much greater than it is designed to carry and it may burn out if the cause of the short circuit is not remedied. To avoid "burnouts" or short circuits in your layout, we recommend that you purchase circuit breaker No. 11. This circuit breaker is so designed that, in case of a "short circuit," it immediately shuts off the current to the train set.

TRANSFORMER
Model Nos. 8B, 12B

INSTRUCTIONS FOR REPAIRING CIRCUIT BREAKERS

ON 8B AND 12B TRANSFORMERS

1. The first step in the procedure would be to remove the 4 base screws near the bottom of the Transformer.
2. Remove the base.
3. Remove the two handle screws
4. Remove the handle
5. Remove the 4 screws in the corners of the nameplate
6. Lift off the case and free the cord.
7. Use either a small or an offset screw driver and tighten the adjustment screws on the bottom of the circuit breaker about 3/4 of a turn. This will tend to stiffen the bi-metal piece which will cause the circuit breaker to stand a little more load before throwing off.

 Ref: May 4, 1950

AUTOMATIC CIRCUIT BREAKER
Model No. 13

INSTRUCTIONS

The No. 13 Automatic Circuit Breaker is designed to give protection to any transformer which is not equipped with a Circuit Breaker.

To attach to a train layout — connect one wire from the circuit breaker to the **BASE POST** terminal on the transformer and connect the other wire to the **BASE POST CLIP** on the track terminal — which is supplying current to the track — Do not have any other wire running between these two positions. Note following diagram.

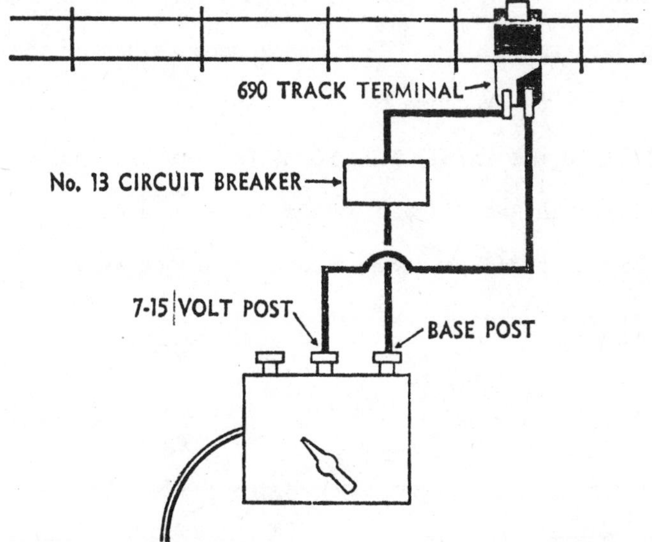

The wires from the Circuit Breaker then supply the current to the track and in case of a short circuit or overload on the layout the automatic thermostatic breaker in the box will open and not allow the transformer to burn out. As soon as the short circuit is corrected the circuit breaker will automatically reset itself.

ELECTRONIC RECTIFORMER
Model No. 14

Subject: Bridging #14 Rectiformer in special wiring hook-ups.

If you are using a No. 14 Electronic Rectiformer to operate your train set and encounter any difficulty in the hook-up of the No. 718 Mail Pickup Car, the No. 758 "Sam" the Semaphore Man or the No. 761 Semaphore, it can be overcome by connecting a short wire from the inside A.C. Post to the inside D.C. Post, (See drawing below).

If the No. 14 Rectiformer is stamped with a white letter "B" on the underneath side, this connection is unnecessary as the unit is bridged on the inside of the case.

 Ref: Feb. 26, 1957

DIRECTRONIC RECTIFIER AND TRANSFORMER

Model No. 15

HOOK-UP AND OPERATION OF AUTOMATIC UNLOADING CARS WHEN USING D.C. CURRENT SUPPLIED BY A NO. 15 DIRECTRONIC RECTIFIER AND TRANSFORMER.

To operate No. 715, No. 716 and No. 717 AUTOMATIC UNLOADING CARS.

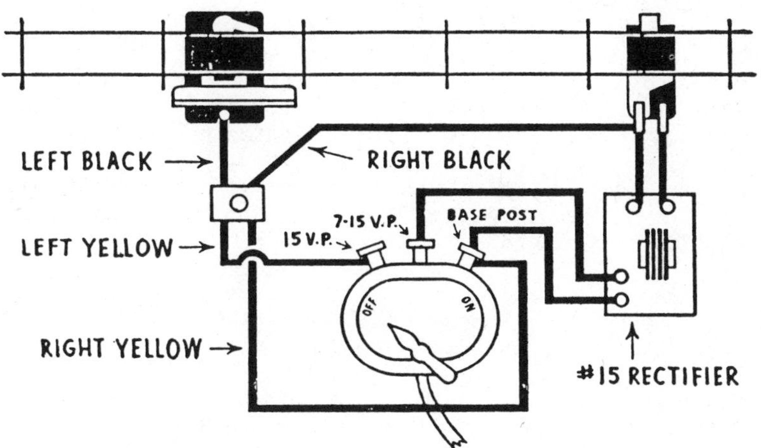

Study the above diagram and proceed as follows.

Be sure BASE POST clip on track terminal supplying current to the track is hooked on to the OUTSIDE rail.

Next fasten the No. 712 Special Pick-up Section to the rail at the desired location so the contact rail is running along side the same rail which has the BASE POST current.

IF YOUR LAYOUT REQUIRES THE NO. 712 SPECIAL TRACK PICKUP SECTION TO BE LOCATED ON THE OPPOSITE SIDE OF THE TRACK, BE SURE YOU CHANGE THE WHEEL AND AXLE ASSEMBLIES IN THE ONE TRUCK SO THAT THE METAL WHEELS ARE ON THE RAIL WHICH HAS THE BASE POST CURRENT.

Then fasten the **RIGHT HAND BLACK** wire from the control box to the **BASE POST** clip on the **TRACK TERMINAL.**

Fasten the **RIGHT HAND YELLOW** wire to the **BASE POST** on the transformer.

Fasten the **LEFT HAND BLACK** wire to the terminal post on the special pick-up track section.

Fasten the **LEFT HAND YELLOW** wire to the **15 VOLT POST** on the transformer.

When the train is operated and the automatic unloading car is to be used, stop the train so the small pick-up shoe protruding from one truck is resting on the metal strip on the special pick-up track section. Then by pushing the button on the control box the car will unload.

WHEN STOPPING THE TRAIN IT SHOULD BE DONE BY SHUTTING OFF THE CURRENT WITH THE TRANSFORMER HANDLE AND HANDLE SHOULD REMAIN TURNED OFF WHILE AUTOMATIC UNLOADING CAR IS DUMPING.

Ref: Form No. M2671

Subject: Testing #15 Directronic Rectifiers for Short Circuit

If you have a D. C. Layout and the circuit breaker on your transformer keeps cutting out causing the red light to keep lighting up, your rectifier may be shorted. The following directions can be followed to test the transformer and rectifier for a short.

1. Make sure that you have wired the rectifier and transformer according to instructions.

2. If the wiring is correct, then the next step is to check the transformer and to do this, it will be necessary to remove all wires on the three terminal posts and check same according to the transformer instructions on Page 17 of the instruction manual.

3. In the event that the transformer tests okay, put back the wires going to the base post and the 7-15 Volt post on the transformer so the rectifier can be checked.

4. The next step is to remove the two lead wires on the two front terminals on the rectifier marked "D.C. Connection to Track Terminal". This will disconnect the track from the circuit.

5. Now remove one lead wire entirely from one of the terminals on the rectifier marked "7-15 Volt Connection to Track Terminal". Take this lead wire and strike it a number of times on the terminal post, from which it was disconnected. If you get a spark and the selenium plates on the rectifier heat up, then it is shorted and should be returned to the factory in New Haven.

6. When you do not get a spark you will know the rectifier tests okay and that the trouble lies in some other part of your layout. We suggest that you check each individual accessory to remedy the trouble.

 Ref: May 4, 1950

TRANSFORMER
WITH CIRCUIT BREAKER
Model No. 15B

SPECIFICATIONS

Case is high impact molded material. Equipped with built-in circuit breaker which prevents burn-out due to over-load or shorts. Has three output terminals for simplified wiring. Exclusive "Dead Man's Control" to halt train when throttle is released.

Operates on 110-120 volts, 60 cycles A.C. with an output of 110 watts.

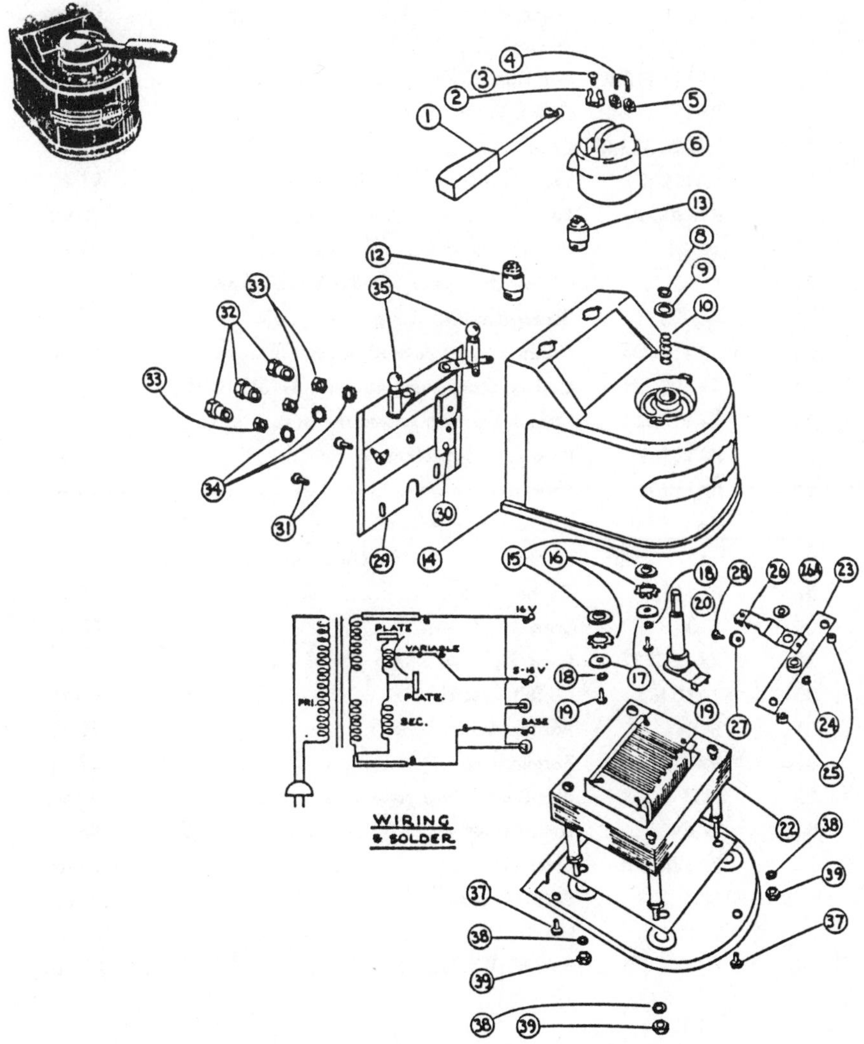

Diagram Number	Part No.	Description	Price
1	XA11773	Control Handle Assembly w/Screw	$ .60 ea.
2	PA11768	Clip	.02 ea.
3	S242	Screw	.01 ea.
4	PA11769	Retaining Pin	.08 ea.
5	N1	Nut	.01 ea.
6	PA13B092	Control Knob	.58 ea.
8	PA11847	Retaining Ring (Large)	.02 ea.
9	W140	Washer (Control Knob)	.01 ea.
10	PA11770	Spring	.05 ea.
12	PA12A112-R	Red Light Cover	.10 ea.
13	PA12A112-G	Green Light Cover	.10 ea.
14	XA12D323-RP	Case	1.60 ea.
15	PA11282	Washer (Control Knob)	.01 ea.
16	P10406-A	Retaining Spring (Control Knob)	.02 ea.
17	W141	Steel Washer Control Knob	.01 ea.
18		Lockwasher (NO LONGER NECESSARY)	
19	S4N02	Screw (Control Knob)	.04 ea.
20	XA11A934	Contact Lever & Stud Assembly	.56 ea.
22	XA12C325-RP	Coil & Stack Assembly (NOT SUPPLIED)	
23	XA11752-RP	Strip & Bearing Assembly	.10 ea.
24	PA11749	Retaining Ring (Small)	.02 ea.
25	PA11808	Short Sleeve	.04 ea.
26	XA11754	Contact Arm Assembly	.68 ea.
26A	XA11754-RP	Contact Arm & Strip & Bearing Assembly	.76 ea.
27	PA11757	Carbon Roller	.25 ea.
28	A43	Brad	.05 dz.
29	XA12C327	Back Plate Assembly (NOT SUPPLIED)	
30	PA10483	Circuit Breaker	1.00 ea.
31	S184	Parker Kalon Screw	.10 dz.
32	PA11826	Terminal Nut	.08 ea.
33	N57	Nut (Back Plate Assembly)	.05 ea.
34	W89	Lockwasher	.05 dz.
35	PA12A125	Lamp 18 Volt	.35 ea.
37	S4N03	Screw f/Base	.01 ea.
38	W33	Lockwasher	.05 dz.
39	N25	Nut (Coil & Stack)	.01 ea.

SERVICE INSTRUCTIONS

When a transformer is not functioning properly, the first thing to do would be to test for operation. Use a voltmeter and ammeter in checking the output. If transformer has to be taken apart, the plug must be removed from wall socket.

STEPS TO CHANGE PARTS:

1. BULB

(a). Remove light covers (#12 & 13).

(b). Replace burned out Bulb (#35) by pushing down, turning and lift up.

(c). Place cover back in place, by lining up the nibs on the cover (#12) with the slots on the Case (#14). Insert and twist until locked in place.

2. CASE

(a). Take off Handle (#1) by loosening screw. Remove two P.K. screws & nameplate.

(b). Remove Screws (#37) and lift Case (#14) from base.

(c). Remove Screws (#31) to free Case (#14) from Back Plate Assembly (#29).

(d). Take off Control Knob (#6) by removing two Screws (#19), and parts 15 to 18 from the underneath side of case. The knob is free and can be taken out of the case.

(e). Take off contact lever & stud assembly (#20) by removing parts 8 to 10, and pull part out of case.

(f). You can now replace Case (#14).

3. CONTROL KNOB

(a). Follow instructions on replacing case from A to D.

(b). Remove Screw (#3) and Clip (#2).

(c). Take off bead of solder and remove Nuts (#5) and Retaining Pin (#4).

(d). Replace broken or defective part.

(e). When re-assembling, make sure you have enough clearance to insert handle.

4. CLIP (#2) by removing Screw (#3).

5. RETAINING PIN

(a). Following instructions for removing case from A to D.

(b). Take off bead of solder and remove Nuts (#5) and Retaining Pin (#4).

(c). Replace broken or defective part.

(d). When re-assembling, make sure you have enough clearance to insert handle.

6. CONTACT LEVER AND STUD ASSEMBLY.

(a). Follow instructions on replacing case from A to E.

(b). Replace broken or defective part.

7. CONTACT ARM AND STRIP AND BEARING ASSEMBLY

(a). Follow instructions on replacing case from A to C.

(b). Remove two nuts and two screws along with the two short sleeves (#25), holding the strip and bearing to the coil.

8. CARBON ROLLER AND CONTACT ARM

(a). To change Contact Arm (#26), remove Retaining Ring (#24), and lift out broken or defective part.

(b). To change Carbon Roller (#27), take out Brad (#28) by clipping pointed end with cutting pliers. Pull brad out and replace part. Insert new brad and pinch the pointed end to keep roller from dropping out.

9. CIRCUIT BREAKER

(a). Remove two Screws (#31) and pull out Back Plate Assembly (#29).

(b). Remove parts 32 to 34 and pull out Circuit Breaker (#30) and Screw.

(c). Remove Screw from Circuit Breaker.

(d). Unsolder lead wires and resolder to new part.

SPECIAL INFORMATION

If the transformer operates properly, but the reading on the Voltmeter is erratic, then we suggest you check the tension of Contact Arm (#26) on coil or there may be specks of dirt on roller or coil surface.

When a transformer hums, it generally indicates that the wood wedges have become loose allowing the coil to vibrate. This can be overcome by adding an additional wood wedge.

If a circuit breaker does not function properly, we recommend a replacement instead of an adjustment. Also make sure the terminal screw in the circuit breaker is tight before assembling unit to case.

INSTRUCTIONS FOR CONVERSION OF CONTACT LEVER & STUD ASSEMBLY AND CONTACT ARM & STUD ASSY ON 15B-16B-19B-18B & 30B TRANSFORMERS

We have had a change of manufacture relative to the above parts and they are now obsolete and will no longer be supplied, but will be substituted with a complete Spring Stud Assembly.

On Parts Price Lists for 15B-16B-19B Transformers, cross out diagram 20-23-24-26 and 26A marking them obsolete. These parts will be replaced by XA12A933-RP Spring Stud Assy., priced at $1.31 each. At the same time, you will need a PA13A174 Terminal at $.03 each, along with an S300-PK screw at $.01 each.

On Parts Price Lists for the 18B and 30B Transformers cross out diagrams 20-21-23-24-26 and 26A, marking them obsolete. These parts will be replaced by XA12A944-RP (right) and XA12A945-RP (left) Spring Stud Assy., priced at $1.51 each. At the same time, you will need a PA13A174 Terminal at $.03 each along with a S300-PK screw at $.01 each.

Refer to Parts Price Sheet for the particular Transformer that you are converting and use the following method:

1.) Follow the service instructions on the last page of Parts List under step #2 to remove case.

2.) Unsolder lead wire from contact assembly (#26)

3.) Draw wire from underneath Coil Assembly (#22) to free wire and solder on PA13A174 Terminal, making sure the rear clamp on terminal is holding the insulation on the wire.

4.) If the Transformer is a 15B-16B or 19B model, the next move is to follow step #3 under Control Knob and remove contact lever and stud assy (#20). You can take off Contact Arm, strip and bearing assembly (#26A) by slipping off Lock Ring (#24).

If the Transformer is an 18B or 30B Model, you can follow the same procedure, only refer to step #5 under control knob to remove Contact Lever and Stud Assy. (#20).

5.) Install new XA12A933-RP Spring and Stud Assy for 15B-16B-19B Models and XA12A944-RP and XA12A945-RP Spring and Stud Assy for 18B and 30B Models and reassemble the parts back in the control knob (#6).

6.) The PA13A174 Terminal can be attached to the bottom of the new spring and Stud Assy., using the S300PK Screw.

7.) Slide the wire to one side, placing it underneath the fibre plate of the Coil Assy (#22), so that it will not interfere with the operation of the Control Knobs.

8.) Reassemble case.

ELECTRONIC RECTIFORMER
Model No. 16

INSTRUCTIONS

This Rectiformer is designed specifically to operate American Flyer Electronic Propulsion Trains, and will operate any Electric Trains which use 7 to 15 volts, but is not recommended for continuous or commercial use. It will operate only on 110-120 volt Alternating Current from 50 to 133 Cycles, and cannot be plugged into Direct Current without the use of an inverter.

There are two sets of terminals on the front of the Rectiformer. One set is marked "Direct Current for Trains," and this set is used to supply a variable voltage of from 7 to 15 volts to the track; the other set is marked "Alternating Current for Accessories," and supplies a constant 15 volt alternating current for accessory operation. See Fig. 1.

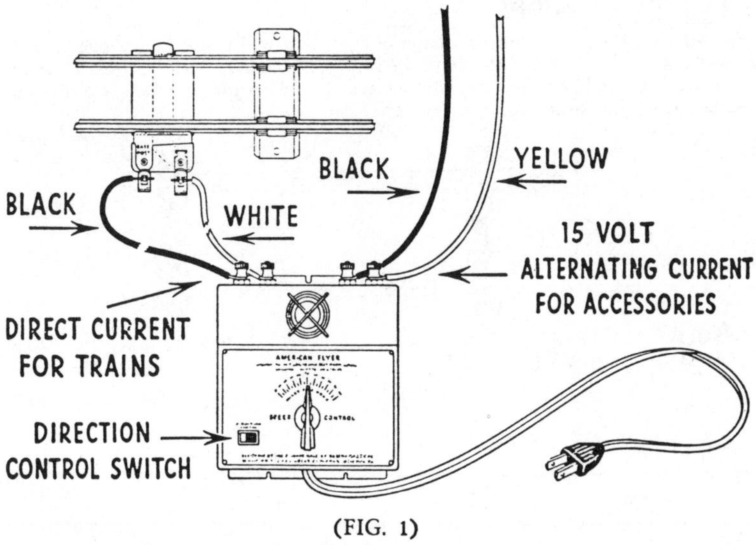

(FIG. 1)

Assuming that you have your track all properly set up and are now ready to wire the Rectiformer, see Fig. 1 and proceed as follows.

Attach the track terminal to a straight section of track according to the directions furnished on the terminal envelope which is included with your train set.

Connect one end of the Black wire to the Base Post Clip on the track terminal and the other end to one of the two terminals marked "Direct Current for Trains."

Connect one end of the White wire to the other rail clip on the track terminal and the other end to the other terminal marked "Direct Current for Trains."

Always start the train with a minimum amount of current and add more voltage by moving the speed control lever.

To reverse an Electronic Propulsion train, simply throw the red switch marked "Direction Control" which is mounted on the top of the rectiformer and it automatically changes the polarity of the current in the track, causing the locomotive to proceed in the opposite direction from which it has been going.

To reverse a regular sequence reversing locomotive, use the speed control handle to actuate the reversing unit, by turning it off and on.

All accessories such as the No. 751 Log Loader, No. 583 Electromatic Crane, etc., should be connected direct to the two terminals marked "Alternating Current for

Ref: Form No. M2826

Accessories." This will supply them with a constant 15 volts and will not be affected by the position of the regulating lever.

The #16 Electronic Rectiformer is equipped with a double automatic thermostatic circuit breaker which protects both the A.C. and D.C.

A short circuit anywhere in the train, track or equipment is indicated by a steady blinking of the blue light in the tube.

- **TO TEST FOR A SHORT**

Remove the train from the track and be sure there is no metal laying across the rails. Connect a wire to each of the terminals marked "Direct Current for Trains." and hold the bared end of one wire on one rail and lightly brush the bared end of the other wire across the other rail. If a bright blue light appears in the tube, there is a short somewhere in the track. The track must be taken apart and each piece tested separately in the manner just described. Switches and crossovers can be tested in the same manner.

- **TO REPAIR A SHORT**

By closely examining a shorted section of track you will discover that one or more of the clamps on a sleeper is touching the rail. With a sharp screw driver the clamp can be loosened and the fiber insulation piece shifted so that the rail is completely insulated from the sleepers. (See Fig. 2)

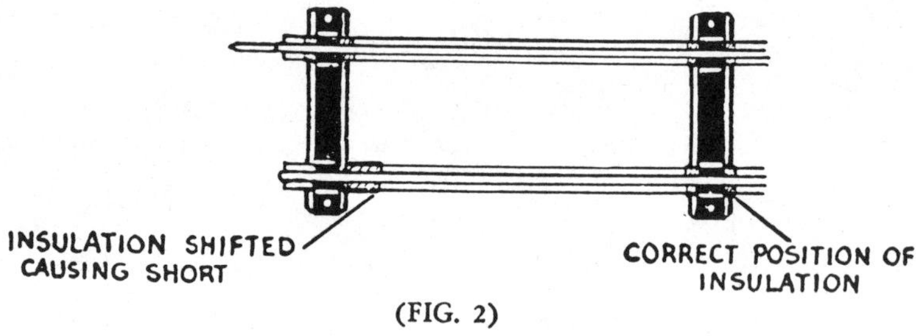

(FIG. 2)

- **TO CHECK RECTIFORMER**

Should your accessories continue to function and the train refuse to operate, it is an indication that the tube may be at fault. If an American Flyer Service Station is available in your locality, take the tube there and have it checked. In case you cannot locate a service man, the following suggestion will help you to determine if the tube is the cause of your trouble. Remove all locomotives and cars from the track, turn the speed lever to 100 M.P.H., check to see if the tube shows a dull red glow, if not, tube should be replaced; if the red glow is observed, short circuit the track with a piece of metal or screw-driver, touching it across both rails, and if the tube is functioning properly, it will immediately show a bright blue light and will start blinking. If this bright blue light does not show up, the tube should be replaced. They are available at your local American Flyer train dealer.

- **TO TEST LOCOMOTIVE**

Using the tested sections reassemble your layout and place your locomotive and tender on the track. Be sure the cut out lever on a Standard Remote Control Locomotive is not locked in a neutral position. If it has been in neutral unlock it and move the Rectiformer throttle to "Stop" and back to half on.

When placing the locomotive and tender on the track be sure the metal wheels on the front tender truck are on one rail and the metal wheels on the rear tender truck are on the other rail.

While AMERICAN FLYER RECTIFORMERS will easily stand 25 per cent overload without harm, we recommend disconnecting the rectiformer from the house current immediately when you are not going to use your train for even a short period or when the train jumps the track.

TRANSFORMER WITH CIRCUIT BREAKER Model No. 16B

SPECIFICATIONS

Case is high impact molded material. Equipped with built-in circuit breaker which prevents burn-out due to over-load or shorts. Has three output terminals for simplified wiring. Exclusive "Dead Man's Control" to halt train when throttle is released.

Operates on 110-120 volts, 60 cycles A.C. with an output of 190 watts.

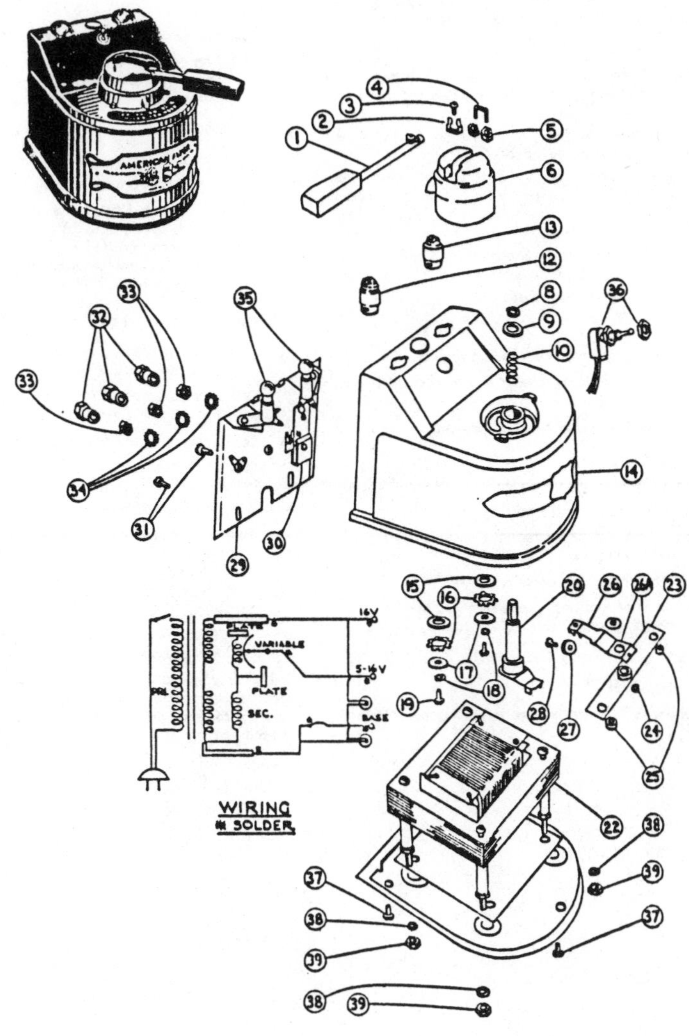

SERVICE INSTRUCTIONS

When a transformer is not functioning properly, the first thing to do would be to test for operation. Use a voltmeter and ammeter in checking the output. If transformer has to be taken apart, the plug must be removed from wall socket.

STEPS TO CHANGE PARTS:

1. BULB

(a). Remove light covers (#12 & 13).

(b). Replace burned out Bulb (#35) by pushing down, turning and lift up.

(c). Place cover back in place, by lining up the nibs on the Cover (#12) with the slots on the Case (#14). Insert and twist until locked in place.

2. CASE

(a). Take off Handle (#1) by loosening screw.

(b). Remove Screws (#37) and lift Case (#14) from base.

(c). Remove Screws (#31) to free Case (#14) from Back Plate Assembly (#29).

(d). Take off Control Knob (#6) by removing two Screws (#19) and parts 15 to 18 from the underneath side of case. The knob is free and can be taken out of the case.

(e). Take off Contact lever & stud assembly (#20) by removing parts 8 to 10, and pull part out of case.

(f). You can now replace Case (#14).

3. SWITCH

(a). Follow instructions on replacing case from A to C.

(b). Remove nut holding switch in the case and take out Switch (#36).

(c). Unsolder lead wires and replace part.

4. CONTROL KNOB

(a). Follow instructions on replacing case from A to D.

(b). Remove Screw (#3) and Clip (#2).

(c). Take off bead of solder and remove Nuts (#5) and Retaining Pin (#4).

(d). Replace broken or defective part.

(e). When re-assembling, make sure you have enough clearance to insert handle.

5. CLIP (#2) by removing Screw (#3).

6. RETAINING PIN

(a). Following instructions for removing case from A to D.

(b). Take off bead of solder and remove Nuts (#5) and Retaining Pin (#4).

(c). Replace broken or defective part.

(d). When re-assembling, make sure you have enough clearance to insert handle.

7. CONTACT LEVER AND STUD ASSEMBLY

(a). Follow instructions on replacing case from A to E.

(b). Replace broken or defective part.

8. CONTACT ARM AND STRIP AND BEARING ASSEMBLY

(a). Follow instructions on replacing case from A to C.

(b). Remove two nuts and two screws along with the two short sleeves (#25), holding the strip and bearing to the coil.

9. CARBON ROLLER AND CONTACT ARM

(a). To change Contact Arm (#26), remove Retaining Ring (#24), and lift out broken or defective part.

(b). To change Carbon Roller (#27), take out Brad (#28) by clipping pointed end with cutting pliers. Pull brad out and replace part. Insert new brad and pinch the pointed end to keep roller from dropping out.

10. CIRCUIT BREAKER

(a). Remove two Screws (#31) and pull out Back Plate Assembly (#29).

(b). Remove parts 32 to 34 and pull out Circuit Breaker (#30) and Screw.

(c). Remove Screw from Circuit Breaker.

(d). Unsolder lead wires and resolder to new part.

SPECIAL INFORMATION

If the transformer operates properly, but the reading on the Voltmeter is erratic, then we suggest you check the tension of Contact Arm (#26) on coil or there may be specks of dirt on roller or coil surface.

When a transformer hums, it generally indicates that the wood wedges have become loose allowing the coil to vibrate. This can be overcome by adding an additional wood wedge.

If a circuit breaker does not function properly, we recommend a replacement instead of an adjustment. Also make sure the terminal screw in the circuit breaker is tight before assembling unit to case.

Diagram Number	Part No.	Description	Price
1	XA11773	Control Handle Assembly w/Screw	$ .60 ea.
2	PA11768	Clip	.02 ea.
3	S242	Screw	.01 ea.
4	PA11769	Retaining Pin	.08 ea.
5	N1	Nut	.01 ea.
6	PA13B092	Control Knob	.58 ea.
8	PA11847	Retaining Ring (Large)	.02 ea.
9	W140	Washer (Control Knob)	.01 ea.
10	PA11770	Spring	.05 ea.
12	PA12A112-R	Red Light Cover	.10 ea.
13	PA12A112-G	Green Light Cover	.10 ea.
14	XA12D489-RP	Case and Nameplate Assembly	3.65 ea.
15	PA11282	Washer (Control Knob)	.01 ea.
16	P10406-A	Retaining Spring (Control Knob)	.02 ea.
17	W141	Steel Washer Control Knob	.01 ea.
18		Lockwasher (NO LONGER NECESSARY)	
19	S4N02	Screw (Control Knob)	.04 ea.
20	XA11A934	Contact Lever & Stud Assembly	.56 ea.
22	XA12C105-RP	Coil & Stack Assembly (NOT SUPPLIED)	
23	XA11752-RP	Strip & Bearing Assembly	.10 ea.
24	PA11749	Retaining Ring (Small)	.02 ea.
25	PA11808	Short Sleeve	.04 ea.
26	XA11754	Contact Arm Assembly	.68 ea.
26A	XA11754-RP	Contact Arm & Strip & Bearing Assembly	.76 ea.
27	PA11757	Carbon Roller	.25 ea.
28	A43	Brad	.05 dz.
29	XA12B493	Back Plate Assembly (NOT SUPPLIED)	
30	PA10483	Circuit Breaker	1.00 ea.
31	S184	Parker Kalon Screw	.10 dz.
32	PA11826	Terminal Nut	.08 ea.
33	N57	Nut (Back Plate Assembly)	.05 ea.
34	W89	Lockwasher	.05 dz.
35	PA12A125	Lamp 18 Volt	.35 ea.
36	PA11761	Switch	1.05 ea.
37	S4N03	Screw f/Base	.01 ea.
38	W33	Lockwasher	.05 dz.
39	N25	Nut (Coil & Stack)	.01 ea.

TRANSFORMER

Model No. 17B

This transformer is designed specifically to operate electric trains and equipment and is not recommended for continuous or commercial use. It has a rating of 190 Watts and is to be operated on alternating current of 100 to 120 Volts and will operate on frequencies of 50 to 133 cycles.

CAUTION. This transformer should never be plugged into 110 Volt DIRECT CURRENT; if you are not certain of the exact type of current in your home, call your electric light or power company before attaching the transformer.

ASSEMBLY OF HANDLE

The control handle for the transformer is packed separately in the box. To assemble the handle to the transformer, first loosen locking screw about three full turns; insert the cutout end of the handle rod, with the cutout section up, underneath the formed metal loop in the control section of the transformer (see Fig. No. 1). Press handle down so it snaps into the spring handle holder. Next, fasten locking screw down so handle will not come out when lifted.

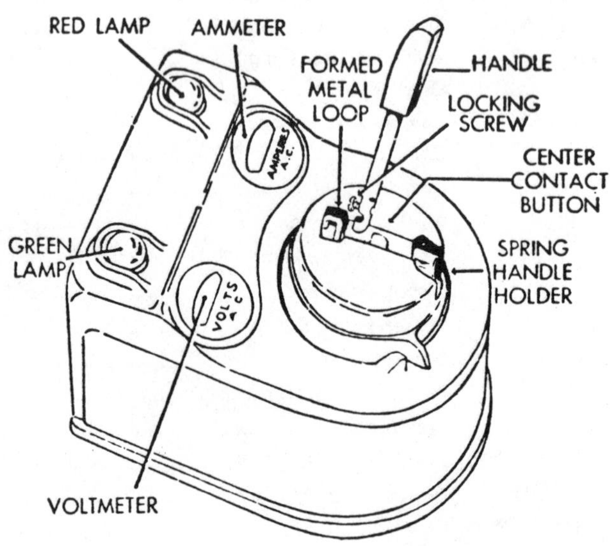

Fig. 1

VARIABLE VOLTAGE OPERATION

When the handle is in position in the spring holder, it can then be turned to vary the output voltage which will be from 6 to 15 Volts; when the handle is all the way to the right, the voltage is on the low side at 6 volts and, as the handle is moved to the left, the voltage gradually increases until the maximum of 15 volts is reached. This is clearly indicated by the voltmeter which is mounted on the transformer face directly underneath the green "power on" light. To completely kill the track voltage, raise the handle out of the spring handle holder which will allow the center contact button to raise, breaking all current to the rails.

DEAD MAN'S CONTROL

When this transformer was designed, a special feature — the American Flyer "Dead Man's Control" — was built into the mechanism. Just as in real railroading, where "Dead Man's Control" is a fundamental safety feature on all trains, your American Flyer Transformer is now equipped to safeguard your passenger and freight trains.

Here's how it works: when the transformer handle is held down, but not locked into the spring handle holder, current flows through the transformer to the tracks and your trains and accessories will operate normally. Just as soon as the handle is released, however, the current is broken and power is cut off. Just like a real railroad engineer, you have to be "on the job" in order to run your trains!

TO REVERSE LOCOMOTIVES

For reversing trains, the handle is to be raised and lowered twice, which will operate the sequence reverse switch in the locomotive.

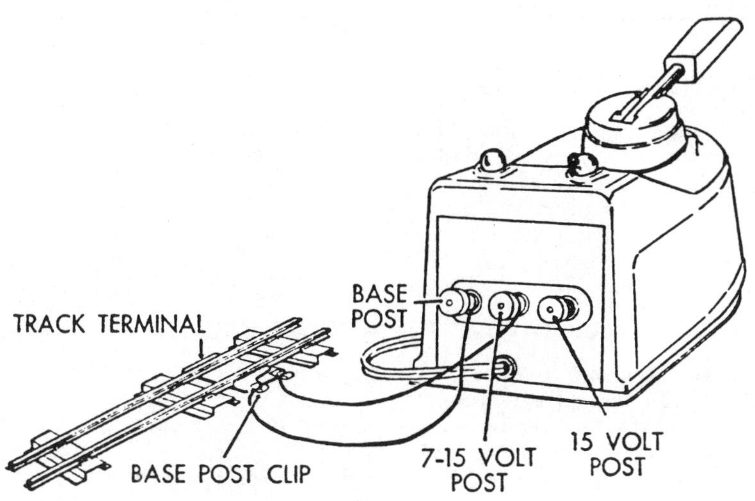

Fig. 2

ATTACHING TO TRACK

Assuming that you have your track all properly set up and are now ready, connect the transformer to the track. Note Figure No. 2 and proceed as follows:

Attach the track terminal to the track according to the directions furnished on the track terminal envelope, which is included in your train set.

Connect one wire from the base post on the transformer to the base post clip on the track terminal. Connect another wire from the 7-15 Volt Post on the transformer to the remaining clip on the track terminal.

CIRCUIT BREAKER

This transformer is equipped with an automatic self-setting type circuit breaker and, in case of a short circuit or overload, it will immediately break the circuit, thus avoiding transformer burnouts. As soon as the circuit breaks, the green light will dim and the red light will come on; when the circuit breaker resets itself, the red light will go out and the green light will resume its brightness.

AMMETER

This transformer is equipped with a 0-6 amp. Ammeter, which will register the load drawn from it by the equipment being operated.

ATTACHING EQUIPMENT

When connecting lighted and operating accessories, hook the wires to the base and the 15 volt post on the transformer; this will allow them to work on a constant 15V current and will not be affected by the position of the control lever.

SPECIAL INSTRUCTIONS

During past years, transformers have been returned which owners claimed defective. In a large majority of cases we found, after investigating, that the transformer was all right and that the fault was with some other part of the train system. We give you, therefore, a few hints as to what to look for in case the train does not work when connections are made.

TO CHECK TRANSFORMER

Plug transformer cord in 110V A.C. outlet. Green light should now be on. Press control lever down so it is locked in the spring holder. Next fasten the bared end of a short piece of wire to the base post and lightly brush the other bared end across the 7-15 volt post. If a spark occurs, the transformer is putting out current, and you can read the amount of current delivered on the voltmeter. If the wire is held on the 7-15 volt post, the current breaker will open and the red light will light.

TO TEST TRACK LAYOUT FOR A SHORT CIRCUIT

Remove the train from the track and be sure there is no metal lying across the rails. Be sure all sections of track fit snugly, then connect a wire from the base post of the transformer to the base post clip of the track terminal. Connect another wire to the 7-15 volt post of the transformer. Brush the other end of this wire across the other rail; if a spark occurs, the system is shorted and each section must be removed and tested separately in the manner just described. Switches and crossovers can be tested in the same manner.

TO REPAIR A SHORT

By closely examining a shorted section of track, you will discover that one or more clamps on the sleeper is touching the rail. With a sharp screw driver, the clamp can be loosened and the fiber insulation piece shifted so that the rail is completely insulated from the sleepers (See Fig. 3).

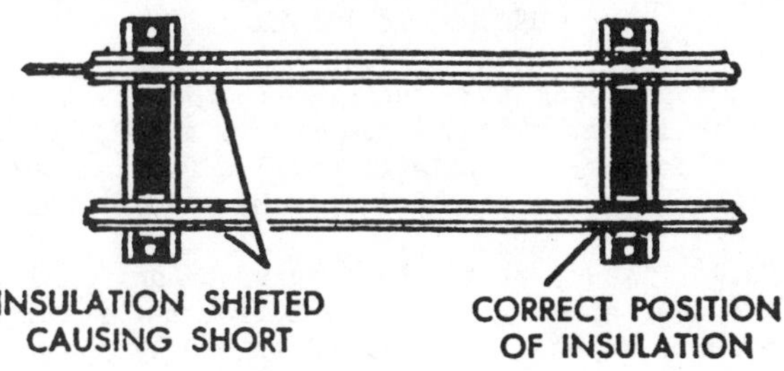

Fig. 3

TO TEST LOCOMOTIVE

Using the tested sections, reassemble your layout and place your locomotive and tender on the track. Be sure the cut out lever on a Standard Remote Control Locomotive is not locked in neutral position. If it has been in neutral, unlock it and move the transformer lever to full on position then raise and lower the handle several times. When placing the locomotive and tender on the track, be sure the metal wheels on the front tender truck are on one rail and the metal wheels on the rear tender truck are on the other rail.

CAUTION: Ninety percent of all transformer trouble is caused by permitting the train to lie across the rail and cause a short circuit when it jumps or is knocked off the track. If permitted to remain in this position, the cars cause a short circuit and the circuit breaker will be making and breaking constantly until the short circuit is eliminated.

While AMERICAN FLYER TRANSFORMERS will easily stand 25 percent overload without harm, we recommend disconnecting the transformer from the house current immediately when you are not going to use your train for even a short period or when the train jumps the track.

GUARANTEE: American Flyer Transformers are guaranteed to be mechanically perfect when they leave our factory. Any transformer which will not deliver its rated capacity indicated on the name plate, or has defective terminal posts or switch, will be reconditioned or replaced free of charge for a period of six months after the date of sale to the consumer. If used in accordance with the instructions which accompany it, the transformer will not burn out. These transformers are given four separate tests or inspections before packing, so therefore, we cannot assume the responsibility for burned out transformers. The Guarantee is void if any transformer is opened or tampered with or not used according to instructions.

FILTER
Model No. 18

INSTRUCTIONS FOR THE HOOK UP AND
USE OF #18 FILTER

When using an A.C. type locomotive such as the #324 A.C. Hudson or the #362 Santa Fe Diesel on a layout which is powered by a D.C. power supply such as a rectifier or rectiformer, the whistle unit in the locomotive may cause a noticeable hum. This hum can be eliminated by use of this No.18 Filter.

To hook up the No.18 Filter, study the diagram below. All that is necessary is to hook the two lead wires which project from the filter, to the two D.C. Terminals on the power supply; the ones which supply power to the track.

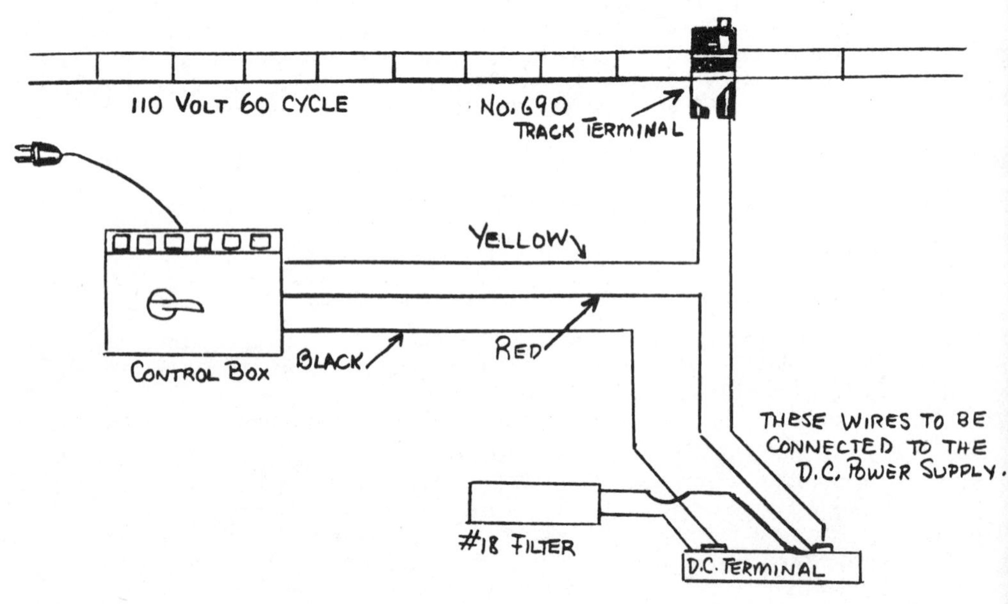

 Ref: Form No. M2868A; Apr. 24, 1956

TRANSFORMER WITH DOUBLE CIRCUIT BREAKER
Model Nos. 18B, 30B

No. 18B

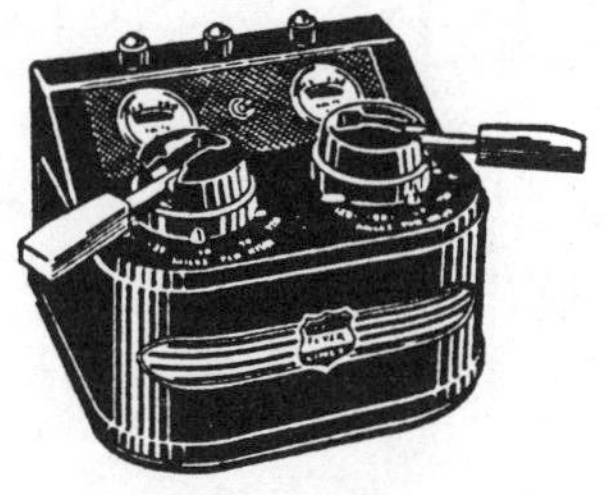

No. 30B

SPECIFICATIONS

Case is high impact molded material. Equipped with two built-in circuit breakers which prevent burn-out due to over-load or shorts. Has three output terminals for simplified wiring. Exclusive "Dead Man's Control" to halt train when throttle is released.

The #18B operates on 110-120 volts, 60 cycles A.C. with an output of 190 watts.

The #30B operates on 110-120 volts, 60 cycles A.C. with an output of 300 watts.

Ref: Form No. 1568; July 23, 1954

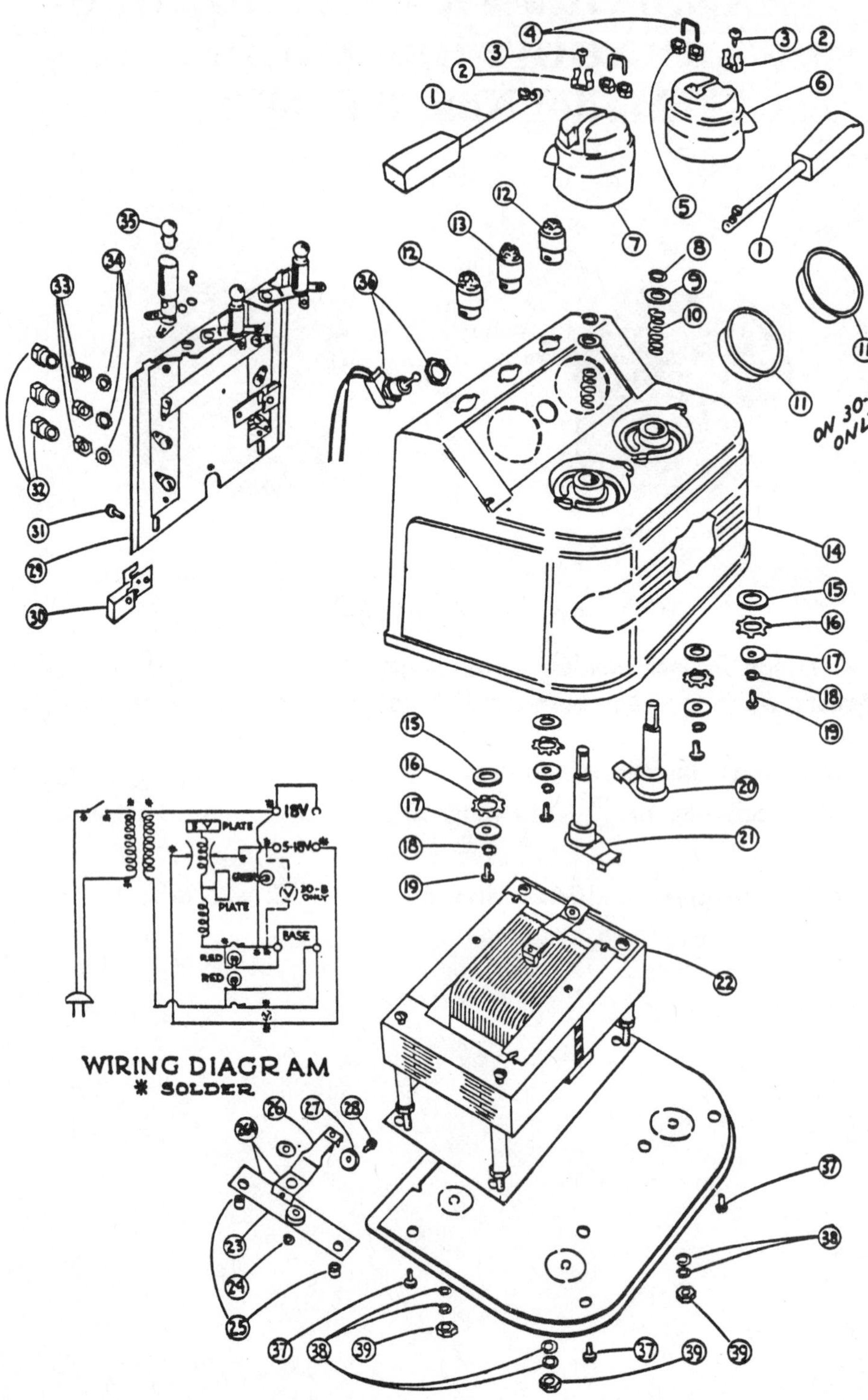
1
2
3
4
5
6
7
8
9
10
11
12
13
14
15
16
17
18
19
20
21
22
23
24
25
26
26A
27
28
29
30
31
32
33
34
35
36
37
38
39
ON 30-B ONLY
18V
PLATE
5-18V
30-B ONLY
BASE
RED
RED
WIRING DIAGRAM
✱ SOLDER

SERVICE INSTRUCTIONS

When a transformer is not functioning properly, the first thing to do would be to test for operation. Use a voltmeter and ammeter in checking the output. If transformer has to be taken apart, the plug must be removed from wall socket.

STEPS TO CHANGE PARTS:

1. **BULB**
   (a). Remove light covers (#12 & 13).
   (b). Replace burned out Bulb (#35) by pushing down, turning and lift up.
   (c). Place cover back in place, by lining up the nibs on the cover (#12) with the slots on the Case (#14). Insert and twist until locked in place.

2. **CASE**
   (a). Take off Handle (#1) by loosening screw.
   (b). Remove Screws (#37) and lift case (#14) from base.
   (c). Remove Screws (#31) to free Case (#14) from Back Plate Assembly (#29).
   (d). Take off Control Knob (#6) by removing two Screws (#19) and parts 15 to 18 from the underneath side of case. The knob is free and can be taken out of the case.
   (e). Take off Contact lever & stud assembly (#20) by removing parts 8 to 10, and pull part out of case.
   (f). You can now replace Case (#14).

3. **SWITCH**
   (a). Follow instructions on replacing case from A to C.
   (b). Remove nut holding switch in the case and take out Switch (#36).
   (c). Unsolder lead wires and replace part.

4. **VOLTMETER**
   (a). Follow instructions on replacing case from A to C.
   (b). Loosen nuts on meters (#11) and take off lead wires.
   (c). From the inside of case, push meter out by using thumbs.
   (d). Replace broken or defective part.

5. **CONTROL KNOB**
   (a). Follow instructions on replacing case from A to D.
   (b). Remove Screw (#3) and Clip (#2).
   (c). Take off bead of solder and remove Nuts (#5) and Retaining Pin (#4).
   (d). Replace broken or defective part.
   (e). When re-assembling, make sure you have enough clearance to insert handle.

6. **CLIP** (#2) by removing Screw (#3).

7. **RETAINING PIN**
   (a). Following instructions for removing case from A to D.
   (b). Take off bead of solder and remove Nuts (#5) and Retaining Pin (#4).
   (c). Replace broken or defective part.
   (d). When re-assembling, make sure you have enough clearance to insert handle.

8. **CONTACT LEVER AND STUD ASSEMBLY**
   (a). Follow instructions on replacing case from A to E.
   (b). Replace broken or defective part.

9. **CONTACT ARM AND STRIP AND BEARING ASSEMBLY**
   (a). Follow instructions on replacing case from A to C.
   (b). Remove two nuts and two screws along with the two short sleeves (#25), holding the strip and bearing to the coil.

10. **CARBON ROLLER AND CONTACT ARM**
    (a). To change Contact Arm (#26), remove Retaining Ring (#24), and lift out broken or defective part.
    (b). To change Carbon Roller (#27), take out Brad (#28) by clipping pointed end with cutting pliers. Pull brad out and replace part. Insert new brad and pinch the pointed end to keep roller from dropping out.

11. **CIRCUIT BREAKER**
    (a). Remove two Screws (#31) and pull out Back Plate Assembly (#29).
    (b). Remove parts 32 to 34 and pull out Circuit Breaker (#30) and Screw.
    (c). Remove Screw from Circuit Breaker.
    (d). Unsolder lead wires and resolder to new part.

SPECIAL INFORMATION

If the transformer operates properly, but the reading on the Voltmeter is erratic, then we suggest you check the tension of Contact Arm (#26) on coil or there may be specks of dirt on roller or coil surface.

When a transformer hums, it generally indicates that the wood wedges have become loose allowing the coil to vibrate. This can be overcome by adding an additional wood wedge.

If a circuit breaker does not function properly, we recommend a replacement instead of an adjustment. Also make sure the terminal screw in the circuit breaker is tight before assembling unit to case.

On the above transformers there are left and right control knobs and the above instructions can be followed to remove either one.

Diagram Number	Part No.	Description	Price
1	XA11773	Control Handle Assembly	$ .60 ea.
2	PA11768	Clip	.02 ea.
3	S-242	#6 x ¼" P.K. Screw	.01 ea.
4	PA11769	Retaining Pin	.08 ea.
5	N-1	#4-40 Hex Nut	.01 ea.
6	PA12B311	Control Knob, Right	.64 ea.
7	PA12B270	Control Knob, Left	.64 ea.
8	PA11847	Retainer Ring	.03 ea.
9	W-140	Washer	.01 ea.
10	PA11770	Spring	.08 ea.
11	PA11771	Volt Meter (for 30B only)	3.75 ea.
12	PA12A112-R	Red Light Cover	.10 ea.
13	PA12A112-G	Green Light Cover	.10 ea.
14	XA12D269-ARP	Case Assembly (for 30B only)	5.88 ea.
14	XA12D584-ARP	Case Assembly (for 18B only) (includes — PA12N271 Nameplate & 2-S218 "U" #2 x ¼" P.K. Screws)	5.83 ea.
15	PA11282	Washer	.01 ea.
16	P-10406-A	Retaining Spring	.02 ea.
17	W141	Steel Washer	.01 ea.
18		Lockwasher (NO LONGER NECESSARY)	
19	S4A02	#6-32 Screw	.10 dz.
20	XA12A266	Contact Lever & Stud Assembly, Right	1.00 ea.
21	XA12A267	Contact Lever & Stud Assembly, Left	1.00 ea.
22	XA12C642-RP	Coil & Stack Assembly (for 18B only) (NOT SUPPLIED)	
22	XA12C272-RP	Coil & Stack Assembly (for 30B only) (NOT SUPPLIED)	
23	XA12A294	Strip & Bearing Assembly	.22 ea.
24	PA11749	Retainer Ring	.02 ea.
25	PA11808	Short Sleeve	.04 ea.
26	XA11754	Contact Arm Assembly	.68 ea.
26A	XA11754-RP	Contact Arm & Strip Assembly	.40 ea.
27	PA11757	Carbon Roller	.25 ea.
28	A-43	Brad	.05 dz.
29	XA12C629	Back Plate & Wiring Assembly (NOT SUPPLIED)	
30	PA12A099	Circuit Breaker	1.10 ea.
31	S-184	#7 x ¼" P.K. Screw	.10 dz.
32	PA11826	Terminal Nut	.08 ea.
33	N-57	Nut	.05 ea.
34	W89	Lock Washer	.05 dz.
35	PA12A125	Lamp, Clear-24V	.35 ea.
36	PA11761	Switch	1.05 ea.
37	S4N03	#10-16 x ½ Th'd. Cut SC Type 25 PH STL.	.01 ea.
38	W-33	Lockwasher	.05 dz.
39	N-32-C	#10-32 Hex Nut	.10 dz.

TRANSFORMER
WITH CIRCUIT BREAKER
Model No. 19B

SPECIFICATIONS

Case is high impact molded material. Equipped with built-in circuit breaker which prevents burn-out due to over-load or shorts. Has three output terminals for simplified wiring. Exclusive "Dead Man's Control" to halt train when throttle is released.

Operates on 110-120 volts, 60 cycles A.C. with an output of 300 watts.

Ref: Form No. 1567; July 23, 1954

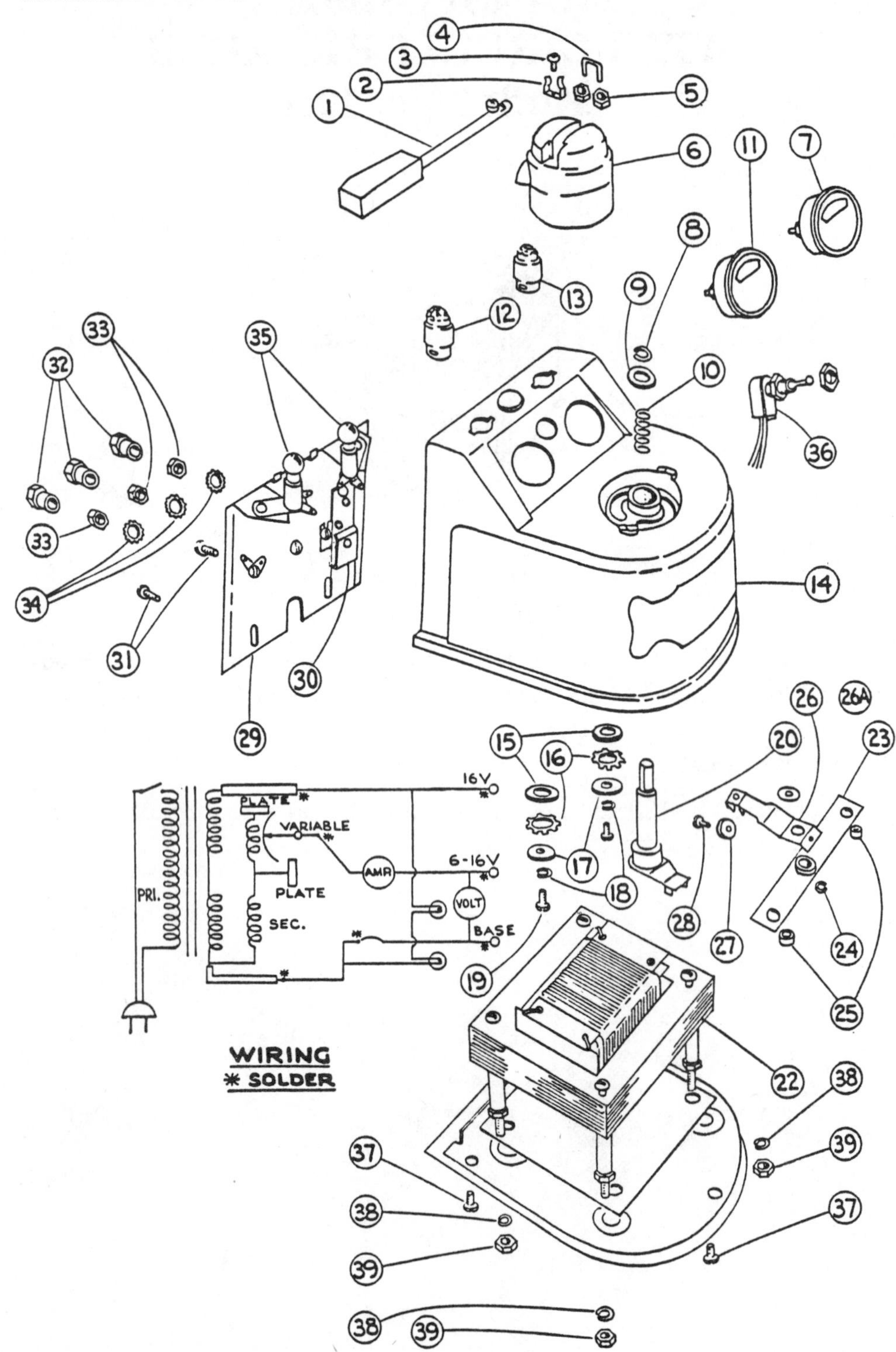
1
2
3
4
5
6
7
8
9
10
11
12
13
14
15
16
17
18
19
20
22
23
24
25
26
26A
27
28
29
30
31
32
33
34
35
36
37
38
39
16V
PLATE
VARIABLE
6-16V
AMR
PLATE
VOLT
PRI.
SEC.
BASE
WIRING
* SOLDER

SERVICE INSTRUCTIONS

When a transformer is not functioning properly, the first thing to do would be to test for operation. Use a voltmeter and ammeter in checking the output. If transformer has to be taken apart, the plug must be removed from wall socket.

STEPS TO CHANGE PARTS:

1. **BULB**
   (a). Remove light covers (#12 & 13).
   (b). Replace burned out Bulb (#35) by pushing down, turning and lift up.
   (c). Place cover back in place, by lining up the nibs on the Cover (#12) with the slots on the Case (#14). Insert and twist until locked in place.

2. **CASE**
   (a). Take off Handle (#1) by loosening screw.
   (b). Remove Screws (#37) and lift Case (#14) from base.
   (c). Remove Screws (#31) to free Case (#14) from Back Plate Assembly (#29).
   (d). Take off Control Knob (#6) by removing two Screws (#19) and parts 15 to 18 from the underneath side of case. The knob is free and can be taken out of the case.
   (e). Take off Contact lever & stud assembly (#20) by removing parts 8 to 10, and pull part out of case.
   (f). You can now replace Case (#14).

3. **SWITCH**
   (a). Follow instructions on replacing case from A to C.
   (b). Remove nut holding switch in the case and take out Switch (#36).
   (c). Unsolder lead wires and replace part.

4. **VOLTMETER AND AMMETER**
   (a). Follow instructions on replacing case from A to C.
   (b). Loosen nuts on meters (#7 & #11) and take off lead wires.
   (c). From the inside of case, push meter out by using thumbs.
   (d). Replace broken or defective part.

5. **CONTROL KNOB**
   (a). Follow instructions on replacing case from A to D.
   (b). Remove Screw (#3) and Clip (#2).
   (c). Take off bead of solder and remove Nuts (#5) and Retaining Pin (#4).
   (d). Replace broken or defective part.
   (e). When re-assembling, make sure you have enough clearance to insert handle.

6. **CLIP** (#2) by removing Screw (#3).

7. **RETAINING PIN**
   (a). Following instructions for removing case from A to D.
   (b). Take off bead of solder and remove Nuts (#5) and Retaining Pin (#4).
   (c). Replace broken or defective part.
   (d). When re-assembling, make sure you have enough clearance to insert handle.

8. **CONTACT LEVER AND STUD ASSEMBLY**
   (a). Follow instructions on replacing case from A to E.
   (b). Replace broken or defective part.

9. **CONTACT ARM AND STRIP AND BEARING ASSEMBLY**
   (a). Follow instructions on replacing case from A to C.
   (b). Remove two nuts and two screws along with the two short sleeves (#25), holding the strip and bearing to the coil.

10. **CARBON ROLLER AND CONTACT ARM**
    (a). To change Contact Arm (#26), remove Retaining Ring (#24), and lift out broken or defective part.
    (b). To change Carbon Roller (#27), take out Brad (#28) by clipping pointed end with cutting pliers. Pull brad out and replace part. Insert new brad and pinch the pointed end to keep roller from dropping out.

11. **CIRCUIT BREAKER**
    (a). Remove two Screws (#31) and pull out Back Plate Assembly (#29).
    (b). Remove parts 32 to 34 and pull out Circuit Breaker (#30) and Screw.
    (c). Remove Screw from Circuit Breaker.
    (d). Unsolder lead wires and resolder to new part.

SPECIAL INFORMATION

If the transformer operates properly, but the reading on the Voltmeter is erratic, then we suggest you check the tension of Contact Arm (#26) on coil or there may be specks of dirt on roller or coil surface.

When a transformer hums, it generally indicates that the wood wedges have become loose allowing the coil to vibrate. This can be overcome by adding an additional wood wedge.

If a circuit breaker does not function properly, we recommend a replacement instead of an adjustment. Also make sure the terminal screw in the circuit breaker is tight before assembling unit to case.

Diagram Number	Part No.	Description	Price
1	XA11773	Control Handle Assembly w/Screw	$ .60 ea.
2	PA11768	Clip	.02 ea.
3	S242	Screw	.01 ea.
4	PA11769	Retaining Pin	.08 ea.
5	N1	Nut	.01 ea.
6	PA13B092	Control Knob	.58 ea.
7	PA11763	Ammeter	3.75 ea.
8	PA11847	Retaining Ring (Large)	.02 ea.
9	W140	Washer (Control Knob)	.01 ea.
10	PA11770	Spring	.05 ea.
11	PA11771	Voltmeter	3.75 ea.
12	PA12A112R	Red Light Cover	.10 ea.
13	PA12A112G	Green Light Cover	.10 ea.
14	XA11765-RP	Case	5.48 ea.
15	PA11282	Washer (Control Knob)	.01 ea.
16	P10406-A	Retaining Spring (Control Knob)	.02 ea.
17	W141	Steel Washer (Control Knob)	.01 ea.
18		Lockwasher (NO LONGER NECESSARY)	
19	S4N02	Screw (Control Knob)	.04 ea.
20	XA11A934	Contact Lever & Stud Assembly	.56 ea.
22	XA11740-RP	Coil & Stack Assembly (NOT SUPPLIED)	
23	XA11752-RP	Strip & Bearing Assembly	.10 ea.
24	PA11749	Retaining Ring (Small)	.02 ea.
25	PA11808	Short Sleeve	.04 ea.
26	XA11754	Contact Arm Assembly	.68 ea.
26A	XA11754-RP	Contact Arm & Strip & Bearing Assembly	.76 ea.
27	PA11757	Carbon Roller	.25 ea.
28	A43	Brad	.05 dz.
29	XA11726-A	Back Plate Assembly (NOT SUPPLIED)	
30	PA12A099	Circuit Breaker	1.10 ea.
31	S184	Parker Kalon Screw	.10 dz.
32	PA11826	Terminal Nut	.08 ea.
33	N57	Nut (Back Plate Assembly)	.05 ea.
34	W89	Lockwasher	.05 dz.
35	PA12A125	Clear Lamp	.35 ea.
36	PA11761	Switch	1.05 ea.
37	S4N03	Screw for Base	.01 ea.
38	W33	Lockwasher	.05 dz.
39	N25	Nut (Coil & Stack)	.01 ea.

This transformer is designed specifically to operate electric trains and equipment and is not recommended for continuous or commercial use. It has a rating of 300 Watts and is to be operated on alternating current of 100 to 120 Volts and will operate on frequencies of 50 to 133 cycles.

CAUTION This transformer should never be plugged into 110 Volt DIRECT CURRENT; if you are not certain of the exact type of current in your home, call your electric light or power company before attaching the transformer.

ASSEMBLY OF HANDLE

The control handle for the transformer is packed separately in the box, to assemble the handle to the transformer insert the cutout end of the handle rod, with the cutout section up, underneath the formed metal loop in the control section of the transformer (see Fig. No. 1) and press handle down so it snaps into the spring handle holder.

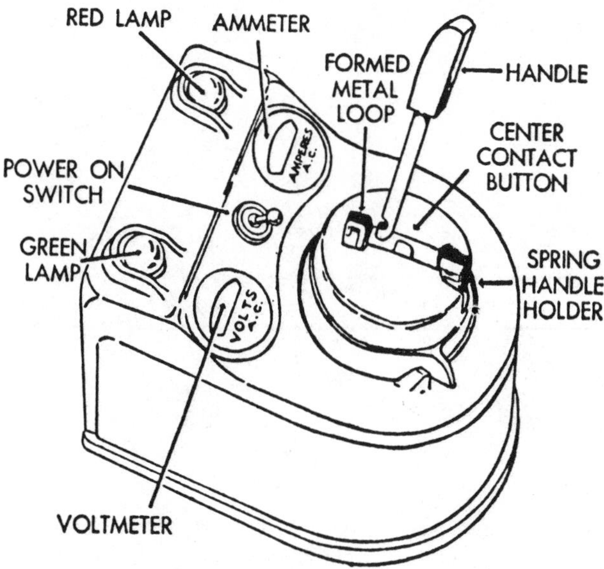

FIG. 1

VARIABLE VOLTAGE OPERATION

When the handle is in position in the spring holder, it can then be turned to vary the output voltage which will be from 6 to 15 Volts; when the handle is all the way to the right, the voltage is on the low side at 6 volts and, as the handle is moved to the left, the voltage gradually increases until the maximum of 15 volts is reached. This is clearly indicated by the voltmeter which is mounted on the transformer face directly underneath the green "power on" light. To completely kill the track voltage, raise the handle out of the spring handle holder which will allow the center contact button to raise, breaking all current to the rails.

DEAD MAN'S CONTROL

When this transformer was designed, a special feature — the American Flyer "Dead Man's Control" — was built into the mechanism. Just as in real railroading, where "Dead Man's Control" is a fundamental safety feature on all trains, your American Flyer Transformer is now equipped to safeguard your passenger and freight trains.

Here's how it works: when the transformer handle is held down, but not locked into the spring handle holder, current flows through the transformer to the tracks and your trains and accessories will operate normally. Just as soon as the handle is released, however, the current is broken and power is cut off. Just like a real railroad engineer, you have to be "on the job" in order to run your trains!

TO REVERSE LOCOMOTIVES

For reversing trains, the handle is to be raised and lowered twice, which will operate the sequence reverse switch in the locomotive.

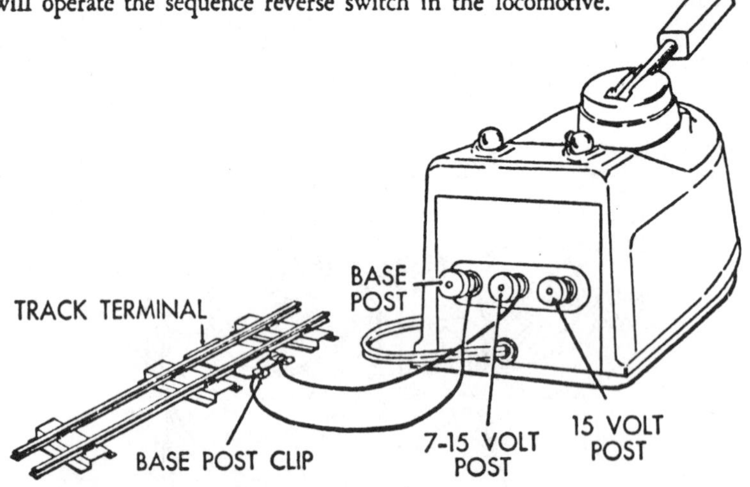

FIG. 2

ATTACHING TO TRACK

Assuming that you have your track all properly set up and are now ready, connect the transformer to the track. Note Figure No. 2 and proceed as follows:

Attach the track terminal to the track according to the directions furnished on the track terminal envelope, which is included in your train set.

Connect one wire from the base post on the transformer to the base post clip on the track terminal. Connect another wire from the 7-15 Volt Post on the transformer to the remaining clip on the track terminal.

CIRCUIT BREAKER

This transformer is equipped with an automatic self-setting type circuit breaker and, in case of a short circuit or overload, it will immediately break the circuit, thus avoiding transformer burnouts. As soon as the circuit breaks, the green light will dim and the red light will come on; when the circuit breaker resets itself, the red light will go out and the green light will resume its brightness.

AMMETER

This transformer is equipped with a 0-6 amp. Ammeter, which will register the load drawn from it by the equipment being operated.

POWER SWITCH

This transformer is equipped with an off-on power switch. This switch breaks the line voltage and eliminates the necessity of pulling the plug from the wall socket when the train is not being used. Be sure the switch is thrown to the "off" position and the green "Power on" light is out when the train is not in use.

ATTACHING EQUIPMENT

When connecting lighted and operating accessories, hook the wires to the base and 15 volt post of the transformer; this will allow them to work on a constant 15V current and will not be affected by the position of the control lever.

SPECIAL INSTRUCTIONS

During past years, transformers have been returned which owners claimed defective. In a large majority of cases we found, after investigating, that the transformer was all right and that the fault was with some other part of the train system. We give you, therefore, a few hints as to what to look for in case the train does not work when connections are made.

TO CHECK TRANSFORMER

Plug transformer cord in 110V A.C. outlet. Be sure power on switch is on (green light should now be on). Press control lever down so it is locked in the spring holder. Next fasten the bared end of a short piece of wire to the base post and lightly brush the other bared end across the 7-15 volt post. If a spark occurs, the transformer is putting out current, and you can read the amount of current delivered on the voltmeter. If the wire is held on the 7-15 volt post, the current breaker will open and the red light will light.

TO TEST TRACK LAYOUT FOR A SHORT CIRCUIT

Remove the train from the track and be sure there is no metal lying across the rails. Be sure all sections of track fit snugly, then connect a wire from the base post of the transformer to the base post clip of the track terminal. Connect another wire to the 7-15 volt post of the transformer. Brush the other end of this wire across the other rail; if a spark occurs, the system is shorted and each section must be removed and tested separately in the manner just described. Switches and crossovers can be tested in the same manner.

TO REPAIR A SHORT

By closely examining a shorted section of track, you will discover that one or more clamps on the sleeper is touching the rail. With a sharp screw driver, the clamp can be loosened and the fiber insulation piece shifted so that the rail is completely insulated from the sleepers (See Fig. 3).

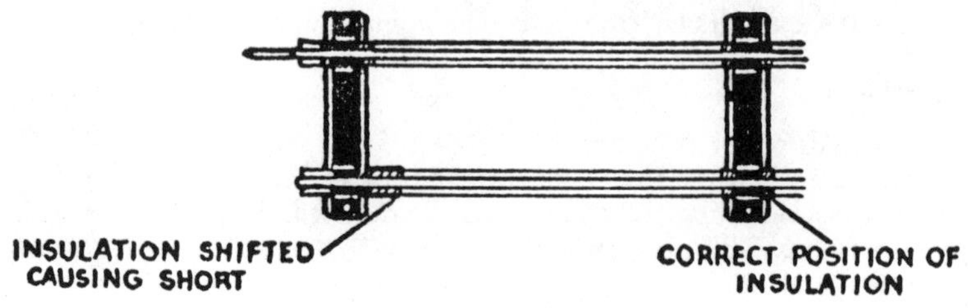

Fig. 3

TO TEST LOCOMOTIVE

Using the tested sections, reassemble your layout and place your locomotive and tender on the track. Be sure the cut out lever on a Standard Remote Control Locomotive is not locked in neutral position. If it has been in neutral, unlock it and move the transformer lever to full on position then raise and lower the handle several times. When placing the locomotive and tender on the track, be sure the metal wheels on the front tender truck are on one rail and the metal wheels on the rear tender truck are on the other rail.

CAUTION: Ninety percent of all transformer trouble is caused by permitting the train to lie across the rails and cause a short circuit when it jumps or is knocked off the track. If permitted to remain in this position, the cars cause a short circuit and the circuit breaker will be making and breaking constantly until the short circuit is eliminated.

While AMERICAN FLYER TRANSFORMERS will easily stand 25 percent overload without harm, we recommend disconnecting the transformer from the house current or shutting off the power on switch immediately when you are not going to use your train for even a short period or when the train jumps the track.

GUARANTEE: American Flyer Transformers are guaranteed to be mechanically perfect when they leave our factory. Any transformer which will not deliver its rated capacity indicated on the name plate, or has defective terminal posts or switch, will be reconditioned or replaced free of charge for a period of six months after the date of sale to the consumer. If used in accordance with the instructions which accompany it, the transformer will not burn out. These transformers are given four separate tests or inspections before packing, so therefore, we cannot assume the responsibility for burned out transformers. The Guarantee is void if any transformer is opened or tampered with or not used according to instructions.

100 WATT TRANSFORMER
Model No. 22030

DIA. NO.	PART NO.	DESCRIPTION	PRICE
1	PA12A571	Contact Strip	.11 ea.
2	PA14A083	Circuit Breaker	1.56 ea.
3	S4N70	#8 x 1 5/8" R.D. H.D. Screw	.07 ea.
4		NOT USED	
5		NOT USED	
6	PA12A377	Contact Spring	.06 ea.
7	PA12A376	Washer	.01 ea.
8	S3N77	#4 x 3/8 Type 25 P.K. Screw	.01 ea.
9	P2497	Washer	.04 dz.
10		Coil Assembly (NOT SOLD SEPARATELY)	
11		Base Assembly (NOT SOLD SEPARATELY)	
12 & 13	S3N80	#6 x 3/8 Rd. Hd. Screw	.03 ea.
14	PA12B572-C	Knob	.88 ea.
15	XA12N476RP	Case	1.85 ea.
16		NOT USED	
17		Terminal Post (NOT SOLD SEPARATELY)	
18	P14A342	Adjusting Nut	.04 ea.
19	P10817	Soldering Lugs	.02 ea.
20		Cord & Plug (NOT SOLD SEPARATELY)	
21	PA12A451	Grommet	.12 ea.

Prices subject to change without notice.

175 WATT TRANSFORMER
Model No. 22035

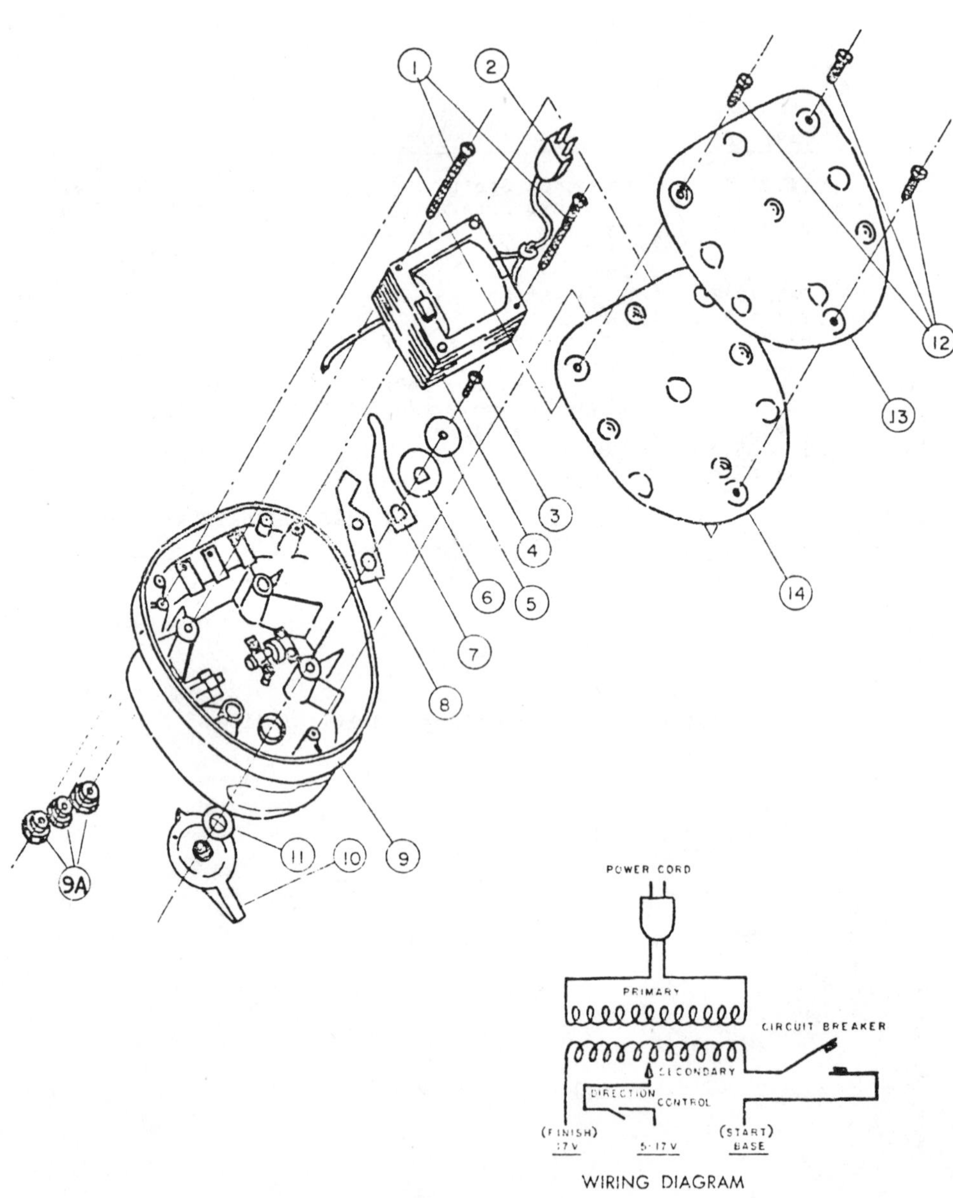

 Ref: Form No. 1997, June 1, 1960

NO.	PART NO.	DESCRIPTION	PRICE
1	S-4N70	#8 x 1 5/8 Type 25 R.H. Screw	.07 ea.
2	X-11A980-A	Cord & Plug Assembly(NOT SOLD SEPARATELY)	
3	S-3N77	#4 x 3/8 Type 25 P Hd. Shakeproof Screw	.04 ea.
4	XA-15B194-A	Coil & Stack Assembly (NOT SUPPLIED)	
5	P2497	Washer	.04 dz.
6	PA12A376	Washer	.01 ea.
7	PA15A189	Contact Spring	.09 ea.
8	PA15A190	Contact Plate	.11 ea.
9	XA15D197-ARP	Case & Contact Brkt. Assembly	7.55 ea.
	PA12A452	Terminal Strip	.01 ea.
	PA15D197-A	Case	5.20 ea.
	PA15A186-A	Contact Strip	.05 ea.
	P14A337	Terminal Post	.03 ea.
	PA15A193-A	Button	.44 ea.
	XA15A842 RP	Circuit Breaker Assembly	1.43 ea.
	PA15A188	Control Lever	.47 ea.
	S242	#6 x ¼ Type Z R.H. Screw	.01 ea.
	S5N61	#6 x 7/16 Type 25 Truss Hd. P.K. Screw	.02 ea.
	PA15A187-A	Bracket	.04 ea.
	LW - 1B6 - A8	Lead Wire	.03 ea.
9A	PA11826-A	Terminal Nut	.07 ea.
10	PA12B572-C	Control Knob	.84 ea.
11	W-2A29	Washer	.03 ea.
12	S4N03	#10-16 x ½ Type 25 Screw	.01 ea.
13	PA15C196-A	Mounting Plate	.64 ea.
14	PA15C196	Mounting Plate	.64 ea.
	PA12A451	Grommet (NOT SHOWN)	.11 ea.

1	S-4N70	#8 x 1 5/8 Type 25 R.H. Screw	.07 ea.
2		Cord & Plug Assembly (NOT SOLD SEPARATELY)	
3	S3N77	#4 x 3/8 Type 25 P Hd. Shakeproof Screw	.04 ea.
4		Coil & Stack Assembly (NOT SUPPLIED)	
5	P2497	Washer	.04 dz.
6	PA12A376	Washer	.01 ea.
7	PA15A189	Contact Spring	.09 ea.
8	PA15A190	Contact Plate	.12 ea.
9	XA15D197ARP	Case & Contact Brkt. Assembly	7.93 ea.
	PA12A452	Terminal Strip	.01 ea.
		Case Not Available	
	PA15A186A	Contact Strip	.05 ea.
	P14A337	Terminal Post	.0[illegible] ea.
	PA15A193A	Button	.46 ea.
	XA15A842RP	Circuit Breaker Assembly	1.82 ea.
	PA15A188	Control Lever	.49 ea.
	S242	#6 x ¼ Type Z R.H. Screw	.01 ea.
	S5N61	#6 x 7/16 Type 25 Truss Hd. P.K. Screw	.02 ea.
	PA15A187A	Bracket	.04 ea.
	LW-1B6-A8	Lead Wire	.03 ea.
9A	PA11826A	Terminal Nut	.07 ea.
10	PA12B572C	Control Knob	.88 ea.
11	W-2A29	Washer	.03 ea.
12	S4N03	#10-16 x ½ Type 25 Screw	.01 ea.
13		Mounting Plate (NOT SUPPLIED)	
14		Mounting Plate (NOT SUPPLIED)	
	PA12A451	Grommet (NOT SHOWN)	.12 ea.

350 WATT TRANSFORMER
Model No. 22090

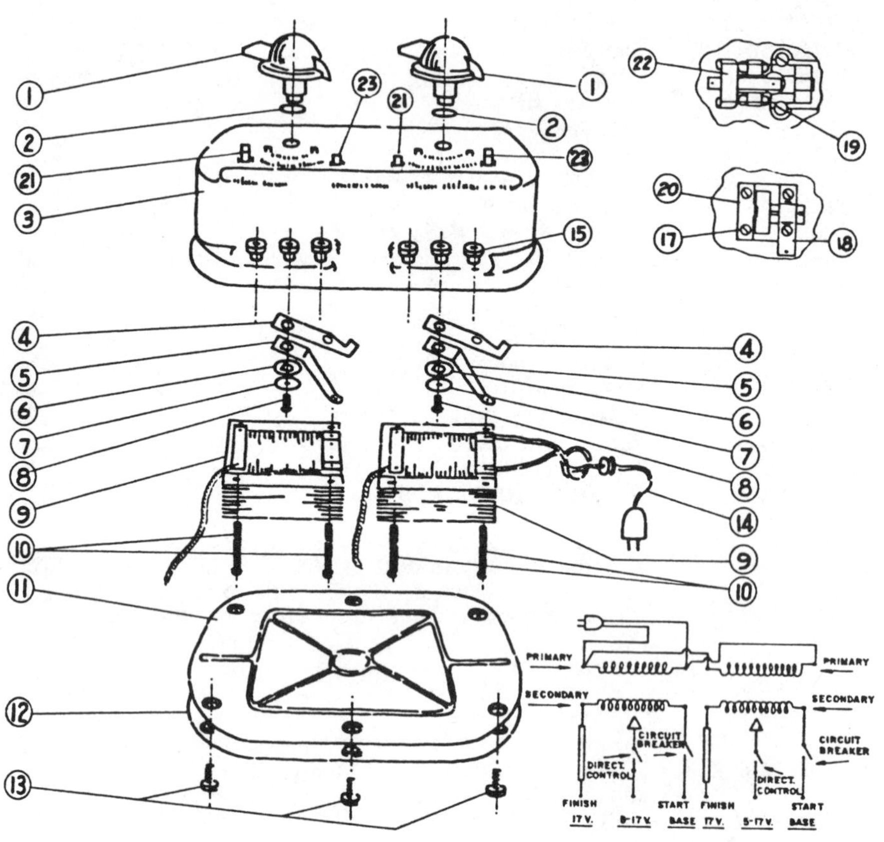

 Ref: Form No. 1998; June 1, 1960

NO.	PART NO.	DESCRIPTION	PRICE
1	PA12B572C	Knob	.88 ea.
2	W-2A29	Washer	.03 ea.
3	XA15N572ARP	Case	11.06 ea.
	P14A337	Terminal Post	.04 ea.
	PA12A452	Terminal Strip	.01 ea.
4	PA15A190	Contact Plate	.12 ea.
5	PA15A189	Contact Spring	.09 ea.
6	PA12A376	Washer	.01 ea.
7	P2497	Washer	.04 dz.
8	S-3N77	4 x 3/8 Type 25 P.H. Screw	.04 ea.
9		Coil and Stack Assembly	NOT SUPPLIED
10	S-4N70	8 x 1 5/8 Type 25 R.H. Screw	.0[illegible] ea.
11	PA15C569	Mounting Plate	1.19 ea.
12	PA15C569-A	Mounting Plate	1.19 ea.
13	S-4N03	#10-16 x 1/2 Type 25 Screw	.01 ea.
14		Cord and Plug Assembly	NOT SUPPLIED
	PA12A451	Grommet	.12 ea.
15	PA11826 - A	Terminal Nut	.07 ea.
16		NOT LISTED	
17	S242	6 x ¼ Type Z R.H. P.K. Screw	.01 ea.
18	PA15A186A	Contact Strip	.05 ea.
19	S5N61	6 x 7/16 Type 25 Truss H.D. P.K. Screw	.02 ea.
20	PA15A187A	Bracket	.04 ea.
21	PA15A193-A	Button	.46 ea.
22	XA15A842RP	Circuit Breaker	1.82 ea.
23	PA15A188	Control Lever	.49 ea.

Prices subject to change without notice.

TRACK ASSEMBLY

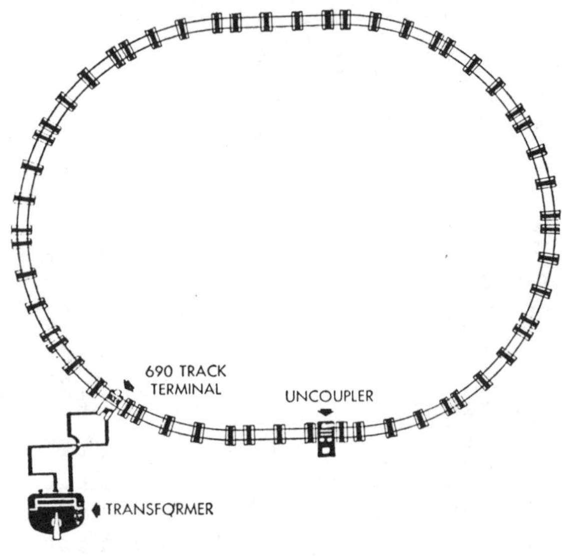

Every American Flyer train is packed with enough track to form either a circle or oval. 12 pieces of curve track form a circle 40″ in diameter; with the addition of straight track, the circle becomes an oval, and can be enlarged to any size you desire. Care must be taken when the track is put together, as a layout with poorly laid track will never operate properly.

Lay the track sections on an even surface and push together so the pins on each rail enter the hole in the end of the mating rail, until the gaps between the rails are completely closed. DO NOT TWIST, BEND OR SQUEEZE THE TRACK, causing distortion, or poor operation will result.

It is essential that all track joints fit together tightly, insuring a good electrical circuit and less chance of a voltage drop in the track.

If two sections of track fit together loosely, this can be remedied by bending both pins outward about 1/16″, as shown below. This will make a good connection both mechanically and electrically.

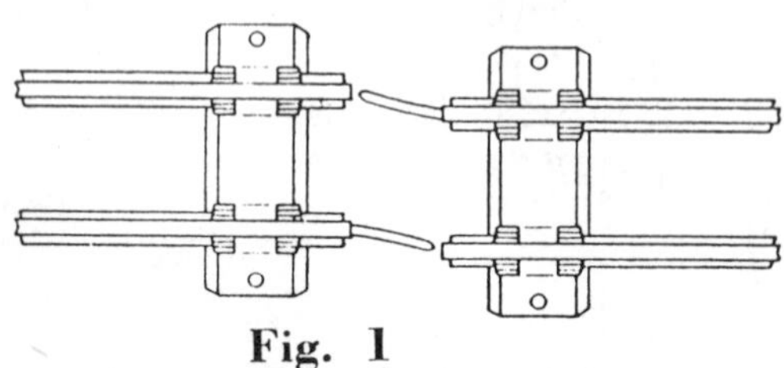

Fig. 1

ATTACHING THE TRACK TERMINAL

The track terminal serves as the connector plate to supply the current from the transformer to the rails. Clamp the terminal on the track as shown below.

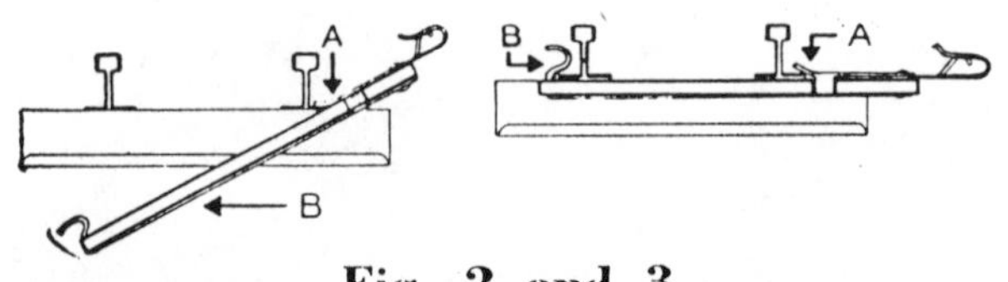

Fig. 2 and 3

Put shoulder "A" against bottom of outside rail, press spring "B" up and around bottom of other rail. Next, attach the wires to the clips on the terminal by pressing down and inserting the bared end of the wire into the exposed loops. Make sure no loose strands of wire are sticking out and contacting the other clip.

Fig. 4

CONNECTING THE TRANSFORMER

You are now ready to connect the wires to the transformer. Never attach wires direct to a household outlet as the train runs on the low voltage supplied by the transformer. The 110-120V household current is reduced to 7 to 16 volts.

The wires from the track terminal are now fastened to the transformer — one wire to the Base Post and one wire to the Center Post which gives you a variable voltage when the transformer handle is turned.

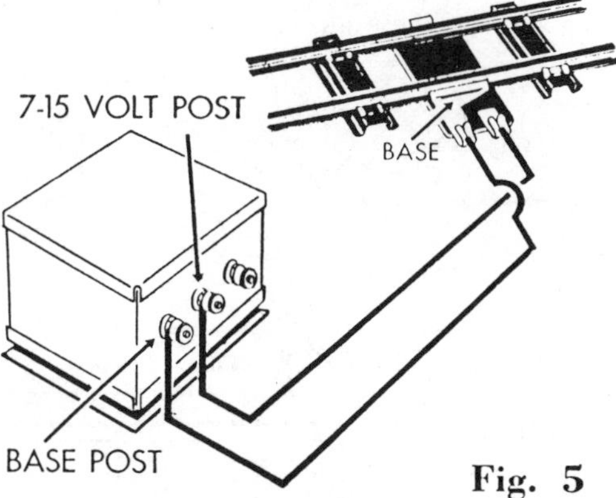

Fig. 5

The third post is for the operation of accessories and lights as the current between the two outside (Base and 16 Volt) Posts is constant and not affected when the transformer handle is operated.

Wrap the bared end of the wires around the transformer posts in a clockwise direction so the wire will not slip out when the thumb nut is tightened.

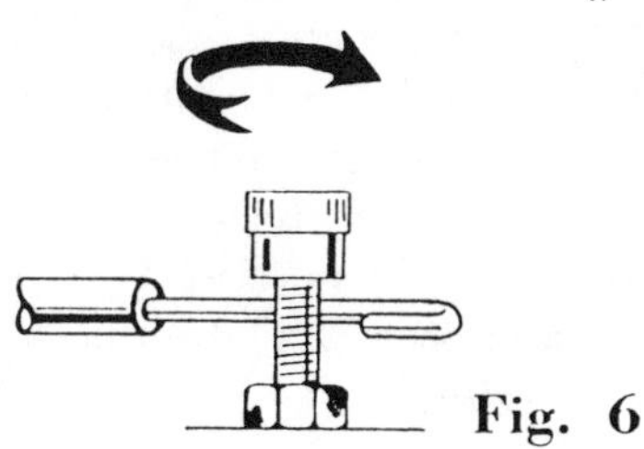

Fig. 6

OPERATING THE TRAIN

Now that the track is assembled and transformer connections are made, place the train on the track. Make sure all the wheels are on properly and the couplers are connected. Couplers can be opened by pressing up on the small coupler weight. Then when the coupler on one car bumps the coupler on the next car, the knuckle closes and couplers are locked together.

Plug the transformer cord in any convenient 110-120V AC household outlet, making sure handle is turned to the off position. Next. start moving the transformer handle to give current to the train.

The locomotive is equipped with a 4 step sequence reversing relay. When the locomotive is going forward, moving the lever to off and on again causes the locomotive to stop in neutral. Moving the lever off and on again will cause the train to reverse direction.

The reversing unit works automatically every time the current is interrupted. Therefore, if current is interrupted by dirty pick-up wheels on the loco or tender or dirt on the track. the loco will automatically go into neutral or reverse.

Underneath the tender of the steam type locos or underneath the diesel locos is a lever used to cut out the reversing operation. To allow the loco to move in one direction only, move lever while train is running. Have train on track and hold loco with one hand while shifting the reversing lever with the other.

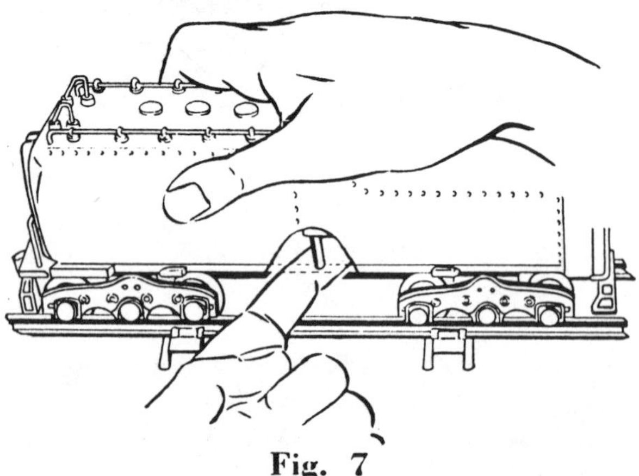

Fig. 7

UNCOUPLING THE CARS

The cars and locomotive of this train are equipped with real railroad knuckle couplers and can be uncoupled by remote control by using either the electrical or manual uncouplers or by raising the coupler weights with a pencil point.

The correct position for the weight, when the car is on the track, is shown on page 4. In some instances, due to rough handling in shipment or in playing with the train. the coupler may have been bent up or down. If it is too low. it may cause uncoupling when going over switches or a crossover; if it is too high, it may not uncouple when the ramp of the uncoupler is raised.

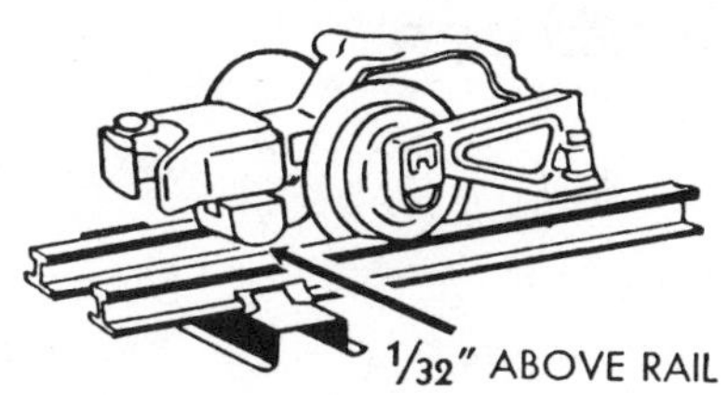

Fig. 8

The couplers on the cars should be adjusted so the bottom of the weight is slightly above the rail when the knuckle is closed. See Figure 8.

This will allow the ramp to raise the weight enough so the knuckle will be disengaged and the cars will separate.

TRAIN LUBRICATION

Your American Flyer train, like your auto or other fine mechanical devices, needs and deserves good care to give the fine service it was designed for. Therefore, a regular system of maintenance should be worked out. Be sure the car axles and locomotive is lubricated before operation, after it has been run for several days or after it has been in storage for a while.

Don't over-oil. A drop of fine oil at each axle bearing on the car and loco trucks — a little good thin grease on the gears and a drop of oil on the armature shafts is all that is necessary. Proper oil and grease can be obtained in American Flyer's No. 26 Service Kit.

TRANSFORMER AND TRACK MAINTENANCE

Take care of your transformer. Make sure the wall plug is pulled out when the train is not in use. Avoid all short circuits which might damage the transformer. Shorts can be caused in many ways. Note the drawing below. Keep the track free of dirt and grit. Clean it regularly with a rag and American Flyer's No. 27 Track Cleaning Fluid. If very dirty, use a light sandpaper on it first.

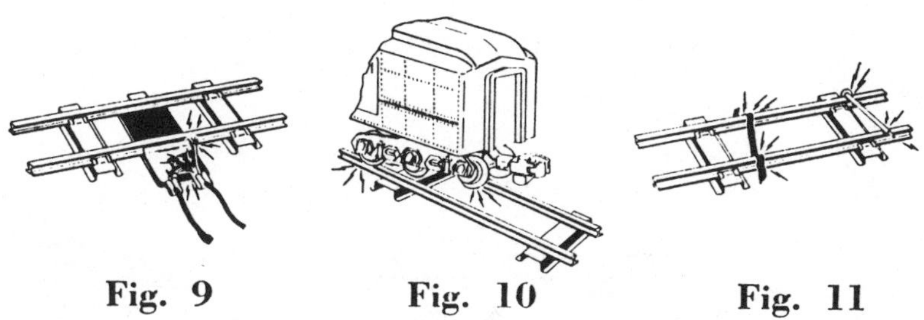

Fig. 9 Fig. 10 Fig. 11

WIRING DIAGRAM
Test Locomotives

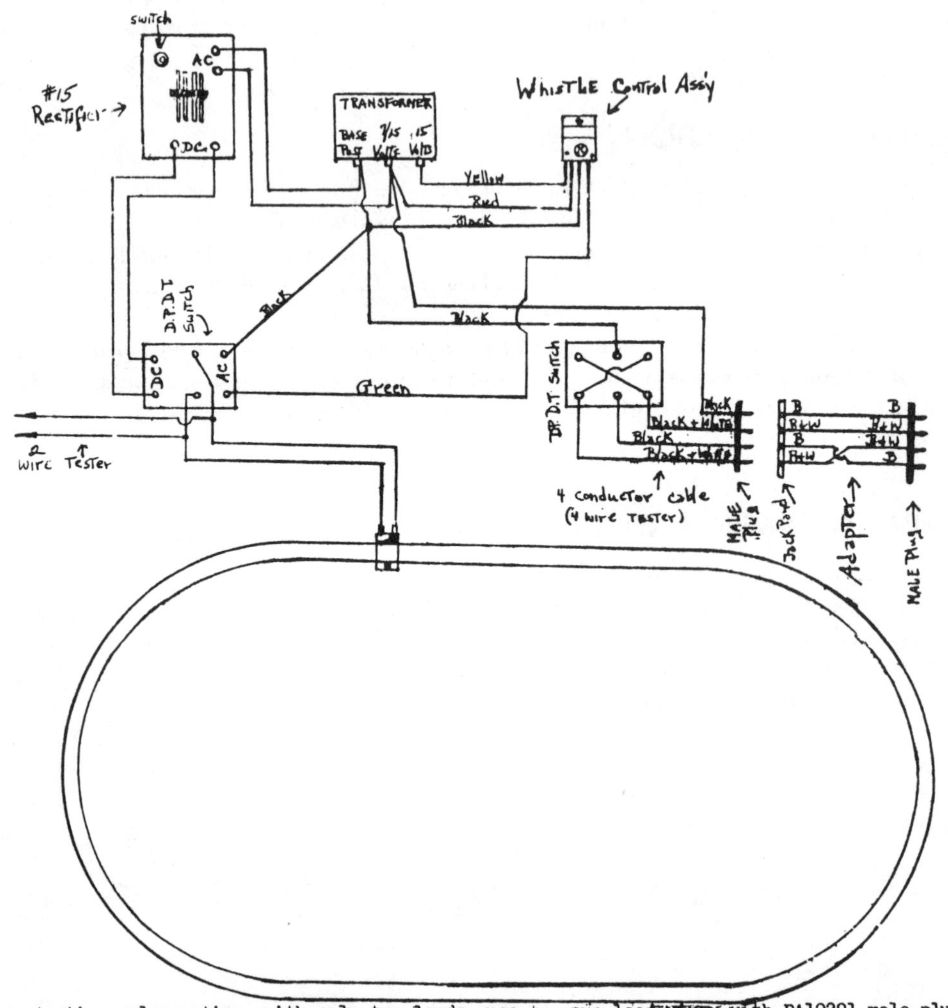

When testing a locomotive, with only two leads, use the two lead wires with PA10291 male plugs soldered on the end, which fit into the jack panel on the locomotive. If the locomotive has a 4 wire outlet, use 4 wire tester, consisting of a 4 conductor cable with a male plug on the end which can be inserted in the jack panel of locomotive.

Locomotive and Tenders having instant smoke, using 5 wire connectors, use the adapter which to be attached to the 4 wire tester with the male plug inserted in jack panel of locomotive When using this adapter, you will not be able to check the smoke unit, unless at the same time you use one lead from the 2 wire tester and touch it to the contact on the jack panel where th extra single wire is normally soldered.

 Ref: Nov. 29, 1955

TRACK LAYOUT

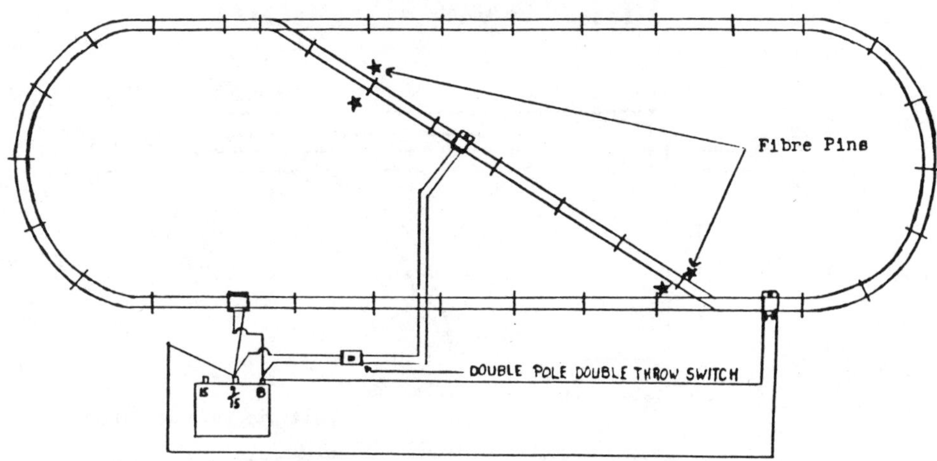

By insulating as shown in the above diagram, and throwing the double pole, double throw switch when train is in the insulated section, elimination of short circuits should be accoumplished.

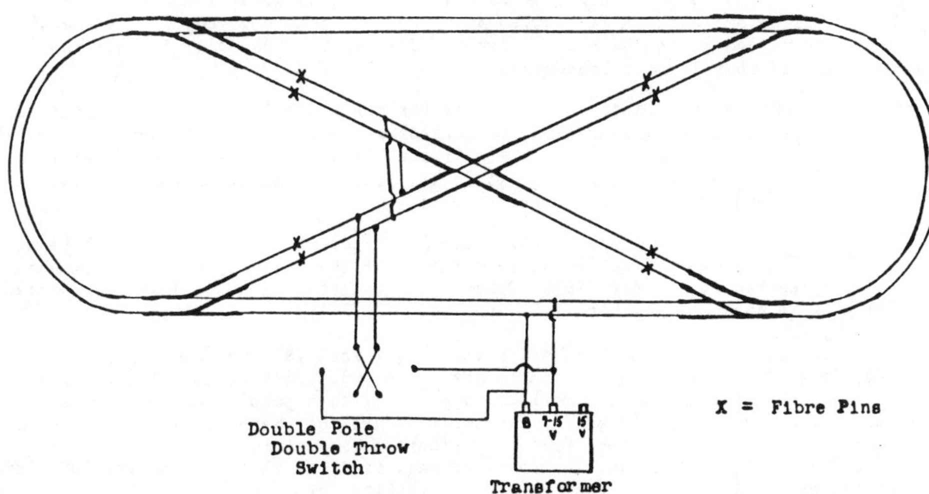

To operate a layout like this with D.C. it requires four (4) reverse loop sections and four (4) D.P.D.T. switches. Without the incorporation of indicator lights on each point in the reverse loop, it would be impossible to determine the polarity of the track. We strongly advise against a layout such as this using direct current unless you are thoroughly familiar with electrical circuits.

TRACK LAYOUT

The "Wye" Turnout

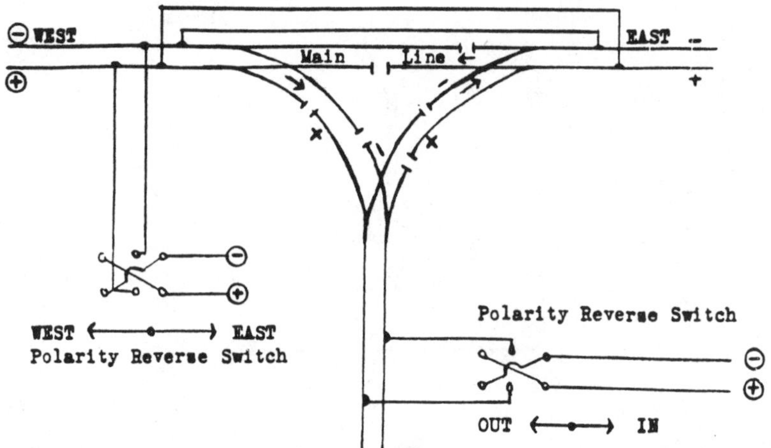

The "Wye" Turnout is very commonly used by the "Big" railroads and model railroaders alike. As well as being a convenient means of turning motive-power about, it saves maintenance costs, and space. A corner, or otherwise unused spot, offers an ideal location for the "Wye".

In the "Wye" Turnout, we have three turnouts or switches arranged frog-to-frog, and both rails between each frog, must have a "Gap". The "Gaps" should be placed as in the above diagram. Stagger the "Gaps" to include the wheelbase of your longest locomotive.

Current is fed to the points of the "Main Line" switches by installing jumper wires as shown above. The "Main Line" switches are controlled "in tandem" from one switchpoint controller. The "Branch" switch is operated by a separate controller. A polarity reversing switch fed from the "Main Line" circuit is installed ahead of the "Branch" switch-points.

In the above diagram, the "Main Line" polarity reversing switch is set for "EAST", the "Main Line" switches are set for the turnout, and the "Branch" polarity switch is set for "IN". Tracing the polarities, we notice the positive (+) rail is on the right hand rail into the "WEST" leg of the "Wye".

With the "Branch" polarity switch set for "IN", the outer rail in the "WEST" leg of the "Branch" switch is also plus (+). Both rails being positive on the right side of the locomotive, it proceeds to a point ahead of the "BRANCH" switch and stops. The "Branch" switch-points are then set-over to line up a route through the EAST leg of the "Wye". In order to produce movement into the EAST leg of the "Wye" we must change the positive rail from the WEST rail of the "BRANCH" switch to the EAST Rail. This is done by setting the "Branch" reversing switch to "OUT". We now have plus (+) in the right hand rail of the "Branch" switch and plus (+) in the right hand rail appruching the "Main Line" switch at EAST. We turn up the power and the locomotive moves through the EAST leg of the "Wye" past the points of the "Main Line" switch at EAST--IN REVERSE. The two "Main Line" switches are simultaneously set over and the "Main Line" polarity control is set for WEST. The positive (+) rail is now on the right side of the locomotive and it proceeds in the new direction--WEST.

 Ref: May 4, 1950

TRACK LAYOUT
Reversing Loops

The reverse loop is a convenient method of reversing the direction of travel of your train.

To do this it is necessary to have several insulated blocks - some additional wiring and a double pole double throw switch - without this a direct short circuit is encountered when the tracks are joined.

To install and wire a reverse loop first study the following diagram and proceed as follows:

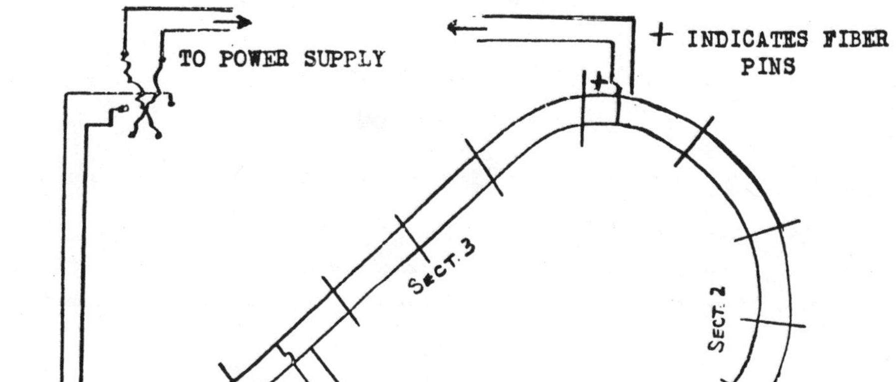

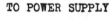

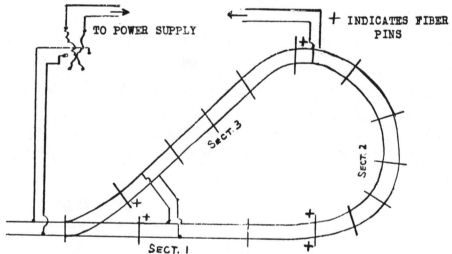

Pull out the steel pins and replace with #692 Fiber Pins at the six locations marked in the diagram.

Next connect the two wires in Sections 1 and 3 as shown.

Next connect wires from Section 2 to the power supply.

Next connect the double pole double throw switch to the track and power supply as shown in the diagram.

Let us now assume the train is running forward on the straight track which is Section 1, as it passes through this Section and into Section 2, the double pole double throw switch is thrown, which changes the polarity of both Section 1 and 3 and the track switch is then thrown to receive the train from Section 3. When the double pole double throw switch is thrown it does not affect the current in Section 2 on which the train is operating at the time changes in polarity are made.

TRACK LAYOUTS
Reverse Loop #2

The reverse loop is a convenient method of reversing the direction of travel of your train. To do this, it is necessary to have insulated blocks, and a double-pole double throw switch, plus additional wiring or a direct short circuit, will be encountered when the inside tracks are joined with the outside rail.

This particular reverse loop is recommended for A.C. operation only, and the diagram and wiring instructions are as follows:

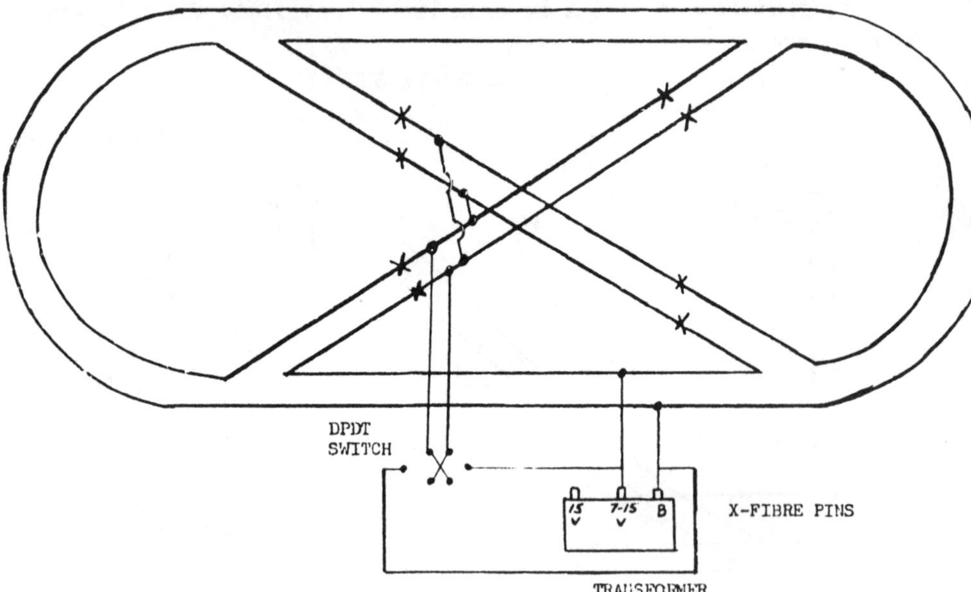

1.) Pull out the steel pins and replace with #692 Fibre-pins at eight locations marked "X" in the diagram.
2.) Connect two Jumper wires shown in the insulated section.
3.) Next, install the double-pole double throw switch and connect wires to insulated section and to the transformer.

Now you are ready to operate the reverse loop. Let us assume that the train is running forward clockwise on the outside circle, and as it passes the switch, and enters the insulated block, the double-pole double throw switch is thrown.

NOTE: We do not advocate the operating of a layout like this on D.C., as it requires extra special parts, and wiring, and unless a person is thoroughly familiar with electrical circuits, it would be impossible to determine the polarity of the track.

TRACK LAYOUT

Figure 8 with 90° Crossing

The diagram below shows how the track should be positioned to make a figure 8 type layout when using a 90° railroad crossing.

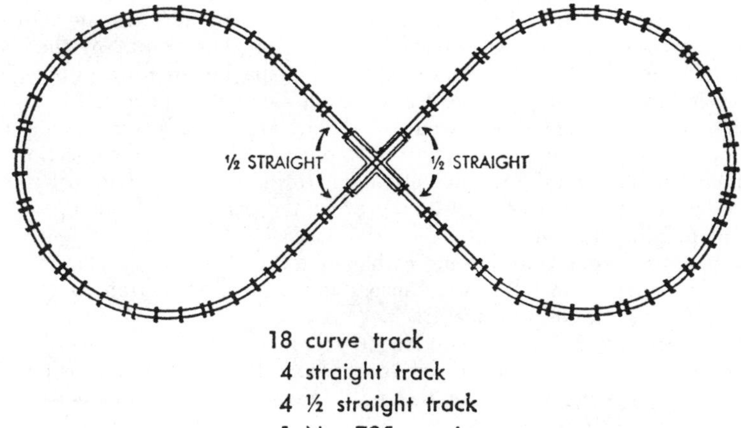

ELECTRIC TRACK TRIP
Model No. 670

INSTRUCTIONS FOR THE USE AND HOOK-UP OF No. 670 ELECTRIC TRACK TRIP

The No. 670 Electric Track Trip is designed to operate various types of American Flyer equipment. It is used to operate the No. 671 Semaphore and the No. 600 Crossing Gate with Bell. It can be used to blow whistles, control block signals, operate track switches automatically, or build a controlled block system in your layout.

The electric current that the locomotive draws passes through the coil in the track trip and closes a pair of contacts which are connected to the two terminals. There is no electrical connection between the controlled terminals and the track.

With the No. 670 Track Trip, it is possible to have as short or as long a controlled section of track as desired. The length of the controlled section is simply determined by the spacing of fibre pins which replace the steel pins in the track. In all cases the entire track layout should be fastened down securely. There are no adjustments on the No. 670 Track Trip. If the train is stopped in the controlled section of track by cutting off the current to the train, the track trip will open the circuit to the accessory and prevent the accessory from operating and possibly burning out.

If your layout contains more than one No. 670 Track Trip, it will be necessary to install a wire across the controlled section to provide current for the rest of the track.

If your layout contains one No. 670 Track Trip, the wire will not be necessary. For example: if in your whole layout you are using the No. 600 Crossing Gate with Bell only, no wire is necessary across the controlled section.

Now, if you use the No. 761 Semaphore, two No. 670 Track Trips are required. It will be necessary to install the wire across the section which has the green wire connected.

ATTACHING THE No. 670 TRACK TRIP TO TRACK

Catch bottom edge of rail in grooved pins and push track trip down until track trip snaps into position.

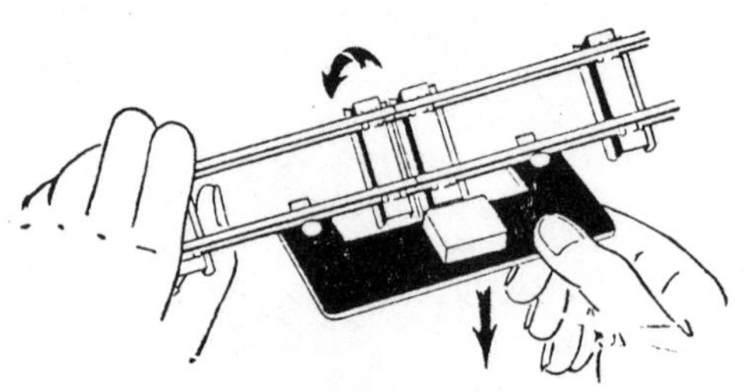

Fig. 1

To attach a wire to the track trip, wrap the wire *once* around the correct (see diagram of accessory used) grooved pin and proceed to attach to track.

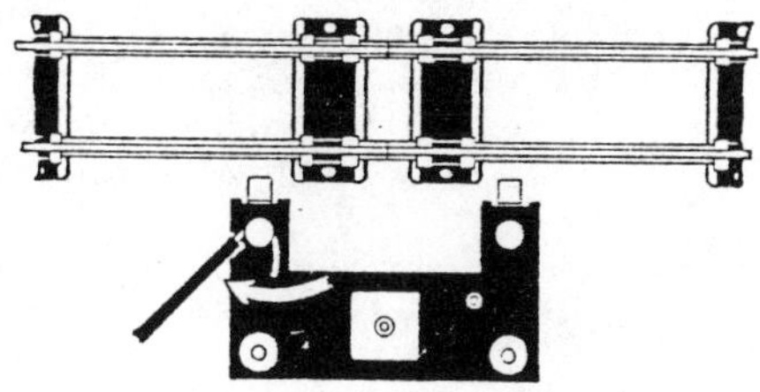

Fig. 2

HOOK-UP OF THE No. 761 SEMAPHORE

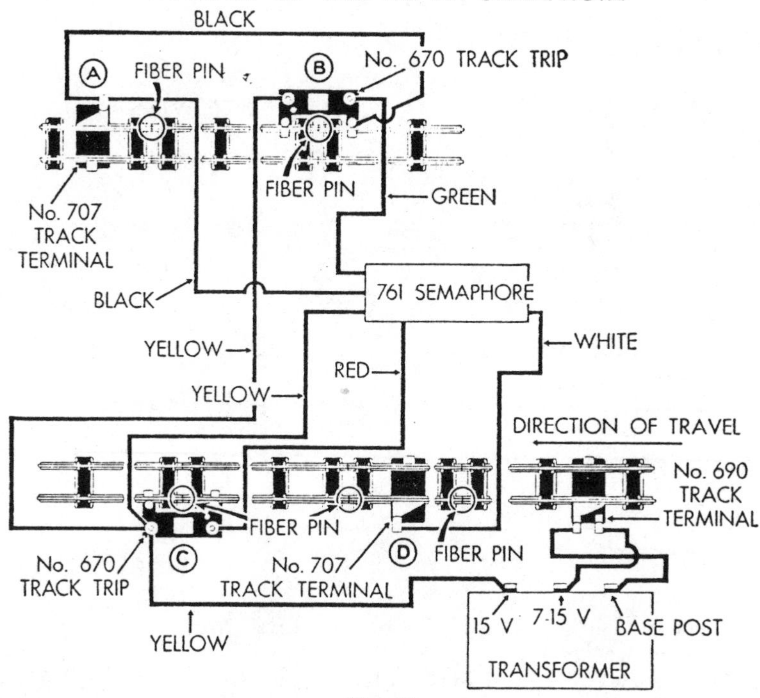

Fig. 3

Connect BLACK WIRE to TRACK TRIP (B) when installing the track trip to the track.

Connect other end of BLACK WIRE to the No. 707 TERMINAL (A).

Connect one end of a YELLOW WIRE to 15 VOLT POST on transformer.

Connect one end of another YELLOW WIRE to TERMINAL of track trip (B).

Connect YELLOW WIRE from semaphore and the ends of the above two yellow wires to TRACK TRIP (C).

Connect BLACK WIRE from semaphore to TERMINAL (A).

Connect GREEN WIRE of semaphore to TRACK TRIP (B).

Connect RED WIRE of semaphore to TRACK TRIP (C).

Connect WHITE WIRE of semaphore to TERMINAL (D).

When the train crosses the trip with the green wire attached, the semaphore arm will go up, the green light will show and the controlled section will be alive.

When the train crosses the trip with the red wire attached, the semaphore arm will go down, the red light will show and the controlled section will be dead.

If you are operating two trains on the track, the one train will stand in the controlled section until the other train throws the arm up, thus forming a controlled block system to protect the trains.

If, after you have the signal set up and operating, you find that the locomotive coasts through the block, increase the distance between the fiber pins in the section which has the white wire connected to the No. 707 Terminal.

HOOK-UP OF THE No. 600 CROSSING GATE WITH BELL

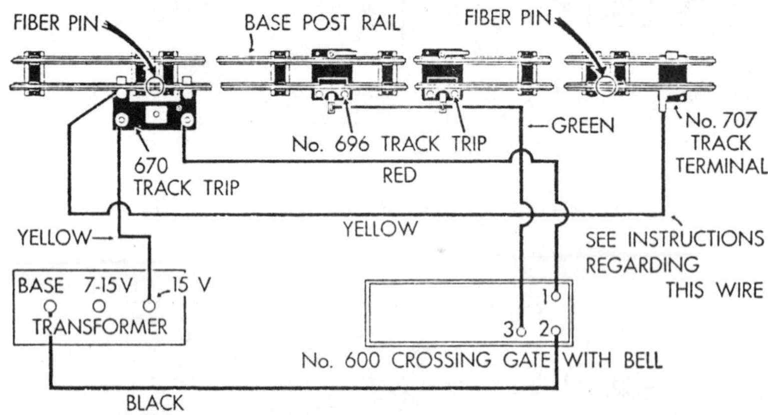

Fig. 4

Connect YELLOW WIRE to TRACK TRIP when installing the track trip to track.

Connect other end of YELLOW WIRE to the No. 707 TERMINAL. (This yellow wire is necessary only if another No. 670 Track Trip is installed on track.)

Connect BLACK WIRE from base post of transformer to CONNECTION No. 2 on the crossing gate.

Connect YELLOW WIRE from the 15 VOLT POST of transformer to a TERMINAL of the track trip.

Connect RED WIRE from TRACK TRIP to TERMINAL No. 1 on crossing gate.

Connect GREEN WIRE from one No. 696 TRACK TRIP to the other and to TERMINAL No. 3 of the crossing gate.

USE OF No. 670 TRACK TRIP FOR THROWING TRACK SWITCHES AUTOMATICALLY

Switches can be thrown automatically by the locomotive so that there is no chance of running into a switch which has been thrown against the oncoming train and causing a derailment.

This is accomplished by wiring the trips as shown in the following diagram.

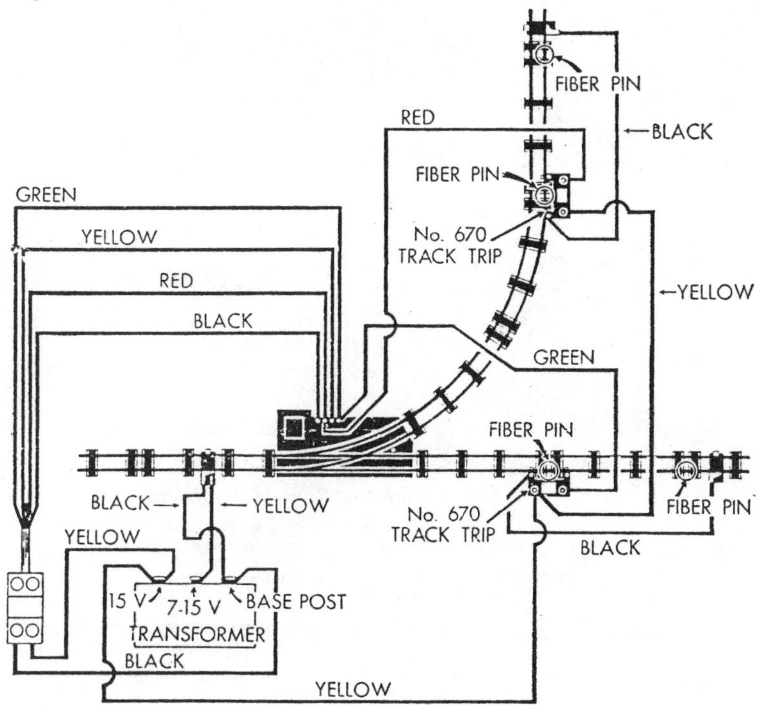

Fig. 5

TRACK TERMINAL
Model No. 690

INSTRUCTIONS FOR ATTACHING 3/16 SCALE TRACK TERMINAL No. 690

REG. U. S. PAT. OFF.

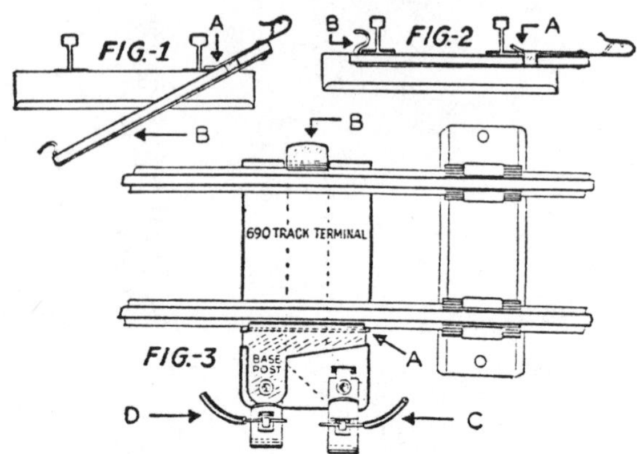

A.—Preferably use straight section of track and fasten as close to cross tie or sleeper as possible.

1.—See Fig. 1. Put shoulder shown as "A" against bottom of the outside rail.

2.—See Fig. 2. Press spring shown at "B" up and around bottom of other rail.

3.—See Fig. 3. Take wires shown as "C" and "D", cut off about one-half inch of insulation from each end of wire, and connect clip "D" marked "Base Post" to the Base Post Terminal on your transformer. Connect the other wire to clip "C" and then to your transformer terminal marked "7-15 volts."

If the terminal is used to supply track current to a piece of equipment, the wires "C" and "D" are connected to the two terminals on the equipment unless equipment instructions read otherwise.

TRACK LOCK
Model No. 693

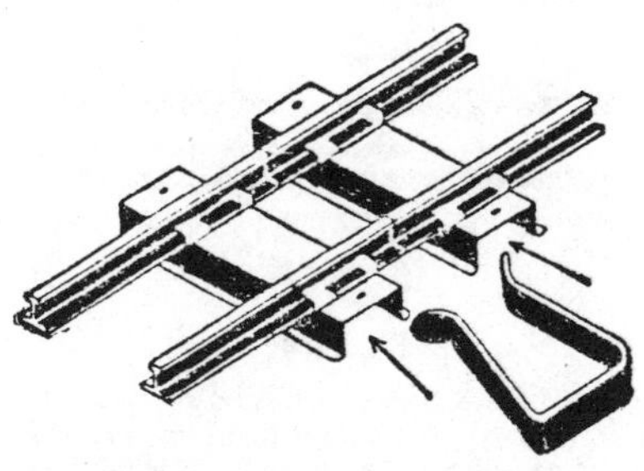

This lock is designed to keep tracks from separating when trains are being operated, and the track is not fastened down permanently.

To install, insert one leg of the lock into each sleeper or tie where the rails join, and push all the way in.

When taking track apart, first remove track lock.

PRESSURE-TYPE TRACK TRIP

Model No. 697

INSTRUCTIONS FOR THE USE AND HOOK UP OF NO. 697 PRESSURE TYPE TRACK TRIP

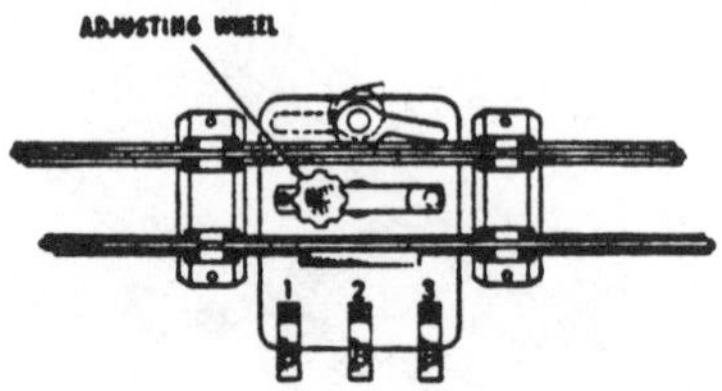

Figure 1.

The No. 697 Pressure type track trip is designed to operate various types of American Flyer Equipment. It is used to operate the No. 592 CROSSING GATE, and No. 761 SEMAPHORE. It can be used to BLOW WHISTLES, CONTROL BLOCK SIGNALS, OPERATE TRACK SWITCHES AUTOMATICALLY, or build a controlled block system in your layout.

It can be adjusted to be operated by the Locomotive only or by the entire train.

It has no electrical connection to the track and is wired direct to the power source and to the accessory it is to operate, then the weight of the passing train closes the circuit just as if you were to push a button on a control box, in the case of a whistle or crossing gate where you want the entire train to keep the circuit closed the trip would be adjusted so the lightest car would close the circuit. In the case of a semaphore it would be adjusted so only the locomotive would actuate the trip and the following cars would not affect it.

The trip can be attached to any section of track and THE TRACK ON EACH SIDE OF THE TRIP SHOULD NOT BE FASTENED DOWN SOLID FOR SEVERAL SECTIONS as the track must be free to move up and down to allow the contact to make and break.

The trip has three terminal clips marked 1, 2 and 3. Number 1 and 2 are a normally closed circuit when the train is off the trip. As the pressure is applied by the weight of the train it breaks the contact between 1 and 2 and closes the circuit between 1 and 3.

Therefore you would hook up the various pieces of American Flyer Equipment as follows.

ATTACHING No. 697 TRACK TRIP TO TRACK.

Insert the track trip under the track between two ties so that the bottom of one rail nests under the raised flange on the trip base, then close the locking lever so it clamps over the bottom of the other rail.

ADJUSTING No. 697 TRACK TRIP.

In Figure 1 you will note the adjusting wheel. If trip is to be set lighter so every car will actuate it, turn wheel COUNTER CLOCKWISE until desired results are obtained. If the pressure is to be increased so only the locomotive will cause it to function turn the wheel CLOCKWISE until the cars do not affect it as they pass.

See Following Pages for Hook-ups on

592 CROSSING GATE

761 SEMAPHORE

720 TRACK SWITCHES

577 WHISTLE

 Ref: Form No. M2667

CONNECTIONS FOR No. 592 CROSSING GATE TO TRANSFORMER

Study diagram #2 and connect as follows.

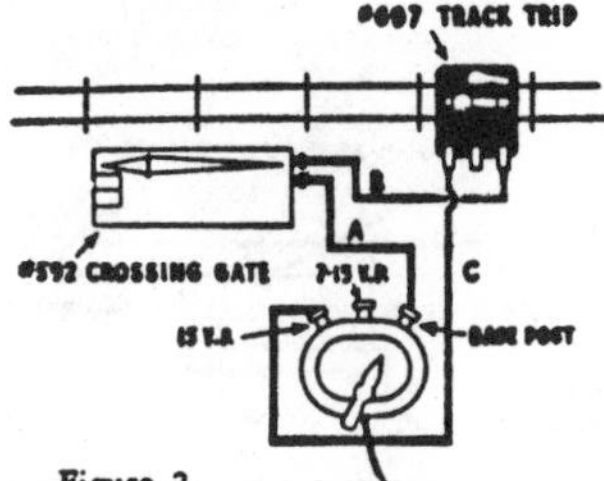

Figure 2.

Connect wire "A" from one of the terminal posts on the crossing gate to the **BASE POST** terminal on the transformer.

Connect wire "B" from the crossing gate to the No. 3 terminal clip on the track trip.

Connect wire "C" from the No. 1 terminal clip on the track trip to the **15 VOLT POST** on the transformer.

Then adjust the tension adjusting wheel so weight of the lightest car will cause contact and gate arms will go down.

HOOKING No. 592 GATE TO #14 ELECTRONIC RECTIFORMER.

Follow above directions but hook wire "A" to one ALTERNATING CURRENT POST and hook wire "C" to the other ALTERNATING CURRENT POST on the #14 RECTIFORMER.

HOOKING UP No. 592 GATE WHEN USING TRANSFORMER AND #15 DIRECTRONIC RECTIFIER. Use same hook up as to transformer.

CONNECTING THE No. 761 SEMAPHORE

At the desired location in your layout remove a section of track, with a pair of pliers remove the metal pin on the outside rail and replace it with one of the fiber pins which you receive with your semaphore. Replace the track in your layout. Two sections away, remove another section and replace the metal pin in the outside rail with the other fiber pin. You should now have two fiber pins separated by 2 sections of track. This is called the controlled section, because the signal controls whether or not this section has current supplied to it. If, after you have the signal set up and operating you find that the locomotive coasts through the block, increase the distance between the fiber pins.

Next snap the No. 707 track terminal into the controlled section. Be sure that the BASE POST clip is connected to the insulated outside rail. Then snap the regular No. 690 Track Terminal in a section of track anywhere outside the controlled section, WITH THE BASE POST CLIP CONTACTING THE OUTSIDE RAIL. Next attach the two No. 697 track trips to the track at approximately the location shown in Figure 3. In every case when using the No. 761 Semaphore it is necessary that the Base Post of the transformer be connected to the Base Post clip of the No. 960 track terminal.

HOOK UP THE NO. 761 SEMAPHORE TO A TRANSFORMER.

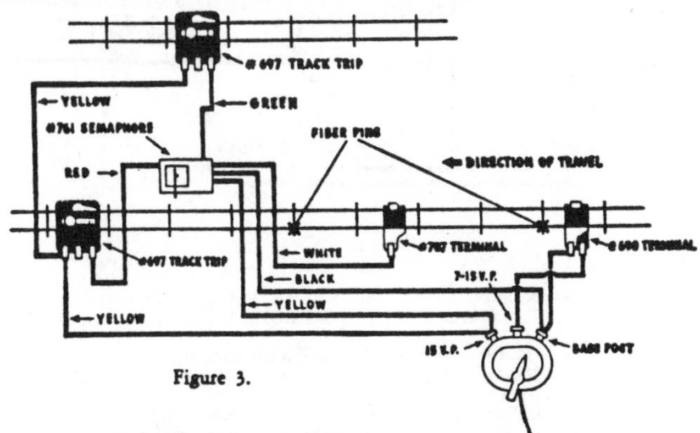

Figure 3.

Connect **YELLOW** wire to 15 **VOLT POST** on transformer.
Connect **BLACK** wire to **BASE POST** on transformer.
Connect **WHITE** wire to No. 707 **TRACK TERMINAL.**
Connect **RED** wire to **#3 CLIP ON NO. 697 TRACK TRIP WHICH IS ABOUT** 2 ft. in front of Controlled section.
Connect **GREEN** wire to **#3 CLIP ON THE OTHER TRACK TRIP.**
Connect the two No. 1 clips together on the track trip with a wire.
Connect a wire from the **#1 CLIP** on one track trip to the **15 VOLT POST** on the transformer.

HOOK UP OF No. 761 SEMAPHORE TO A NO. 14 ELECTRONIC RECTIFORMER.

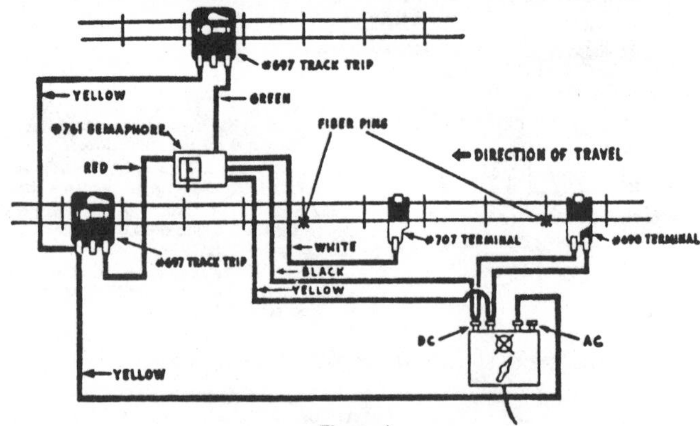

Figure 4.

Connect the **YELLOW** wire to the **INSIDE DC POST** on the rectiformer.
Connect the **BLACK** wire to the **OUTSIDE DC POST** on the rectiformer.
Connect the **WHITE** wire to the **No. 707 TRACK TERMINAL.**
Connect the **RED** wire to the **#3 CLIP ON No. 697 TRACK TRIP** which is in front of the controlled section.
Connect the **GREEN** wire to the **#3 CLIP** on the other track trip.
Connect the two No. 1 clips together on the track trips with a wire.
Connect a wire from the #1 Clip on one track trip to the **INSIDE AC POST** on the Rectiformer.
Be sure the wire from the **OUTSIDE DC POST** is connected to the **BASE POST CLIP** on the **No. 690 TRACK TERMINAL.**

HOOK UP OF No. 761 SEMAPHORE TO A #15 DIRECTRONIC RECTIFIER AND TRANSFORMER.

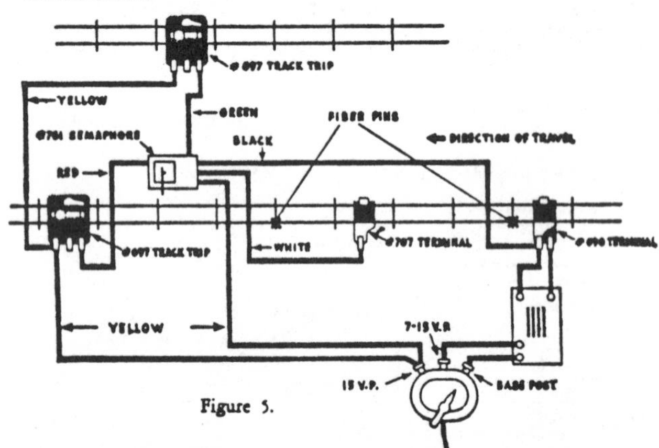

Figure 5.

Connect the **YELLOW** wire to the **15 VOLT POST** on the transformer.
Connect the **BLACK** wire to the **BASE POST CLIP** on the **No. 690 TRACK TERMINAL.**
Connect the **WHITE** wire to the No. 707 track terminal.
Connect the **RED** wire to the #3 clip on No. 697 track trip which is in front of the controlled section.
Connect the **GREEN** wire to the #3 clip on the other track trip.
Connect the two No. 1 clips on the track trips together with a wire.
Connect a wire from the #1 **CLIP** on one track trip to the **15 VOLT POST ON THE TRANSFORMER.**

When the train crosses the trip with the green wire attached the semaphore arm will go up, the green light will show and the controlled section will be alive.
When the train crosses the trip with the red wire attached the semaphore arm will go down, the red light will show and the controlled section will be dead.
If you are operating 2 trains on the track the one train will stand in the controlled section until the other train throws the arm up, thus forming a controlled block system to protect the train.

Connect RED wire to No. 1 CLIP on No. 697 Track Trip which is about 2 ft. in front of controlled section.

Connect GREEN wire to No. 1 CLIP on the other track trip.

Connect the two No. 1 clips together on the track trip with a wire.

Connect a wire from the No. 1 CLIP on one track trip to the 15 VOLT POST on the transformer.

When the train crosses the trip with the green wire attached the semaphore arm will go up, the green light will show and the controlled section will be alive.

When the train crosses the trip with the red wire attached the semaphore arm will go down, the red light will show and the controlled section will be dead.

If you are operating two trains on the track the one train will stand in the controlled section until the other train throws the arm up, thus forming a controlled block system to protect the train.

OPERATION AND HOOK-UP OF No. 600 CROSSING GATE WITH BELL

To hook up the No. 600 Crossing Gate with bell in your layout first determine the position where you wish it to operate. The bell will ring when the wheels of your locomotive and cars contact the No. 696 Track Trips. The crossing gate is lowered by pressure applied to the No. 697 Track Trip by the train.

It is important that the track is not fastened down for several sections on either side of the No. 697 trip. To hook up, study the following diagram and proceed as follows.

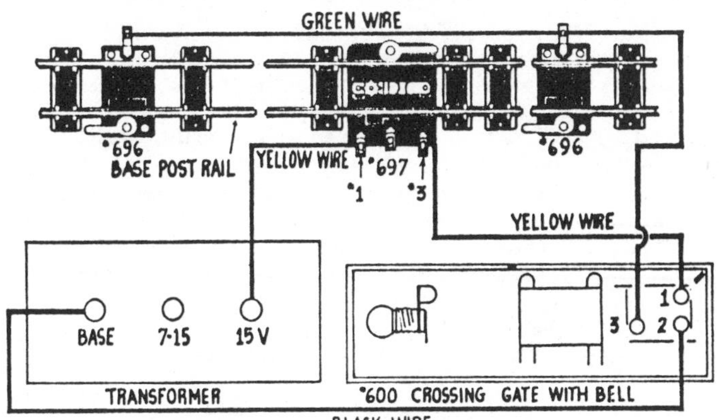

1. Clamp the two No. 696 Track Trips to the rail so that the locking lever locks on the rail having the base post current. These two trips should be several feet apart and connected together by the GREEN WIRE.
2. Connect a wire from the clip on one of the No. 696 trips to the No. 3 TERMINAL, underneath the gate.
3. Fasten the No. 697 Track Trip to the rail, between the two No. 696 trips, as shown in the drawing. Connect a YELLOW WIRE from the No. 3 CLIP on the No. 697 trip to the No. 1 TERMINAL underneath the gate.
4. Connect the other YELLOW WIRE from the No. 1 CLIP on the No. 697 trip to the 15 VOLT POST on the transformer.
5. Connect the BLACK WIRE from the No. 2 TERMINAL underneath the gate to the BASE POST on the transformer.

USE OF No. 697 TRACK TRIP FOR THROWING TRACK SWITCHES AUTOMATICALLY

Switches can be thrown automatically by the locomotive so that there is no chance of running into a switch which has been thrown against the oncoming train and causing a derailment.

This is accomplished by hooking the trip as shown in Figure 5.

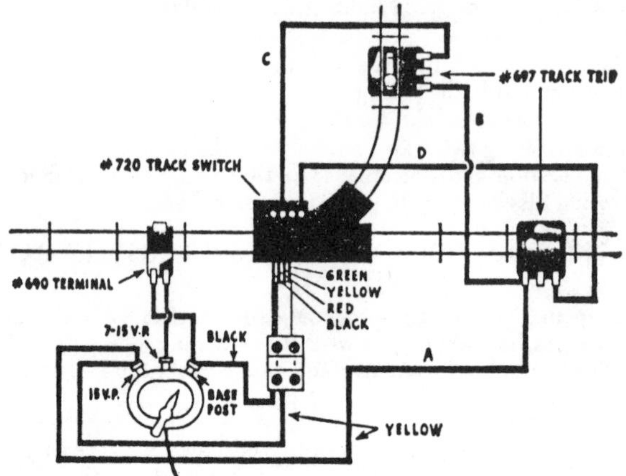

Figure 5.

Place a No. 697 trip ahead of the switch on both the curved and straight sections. Keep the trip about two sections of track from the switch. Hook the control box to the switches as instructed. Adjust trip so only the locomotive will actuate it, then, when the train approaches the switch and the switch is set against it, the trip will automatically cause the frog to throw open so the train could pass thru without derailing.

Next hook wire "A" from the No. 1 CLIP on the one track trip to the 15 VOLT POST on the transformer.

Connect the TWO No. 1 CLIPS on track trips with wire "B".

Connect wire "C" from No. 3 CLIP on track trip which is on the curved rail to the RED POST on the track switch.

Connect wire "D" from the No. 3 CLIP on track trip which is on the straight rail to the GREEN POST on the track switch.

HOOK UP No. 577 WHISTLES TO BLOW AUTOMATICALLY

Connect the green wire from the whistle to the No. 3 CLIP on a No. 697 track trip.

Connect a wire from the No. 1 CLIP on the trip to the BASE POST on the transformer.

In other words the No. 697 track trip acts the same as the control button and should be wired the same.

In addition to operating the above mentioned accessories the No. 697 track trip can be used in many ways to actuate lights, circuits, etc., which your ingenuity may suggest.

BUMPER FOR 3/16" SCALE TRACK

Model No. 730

INSTRUCTIONS FOR ATTACHING AND USING NO. 730 BUMPER FOR 3/16" SCALE TRACK

The No. 730 Bumper is designed to snap onto the end of a spur line of track and keep cars from running off the end.

The Bumper is very easily installed: —

Just place it at the end of the track so the flat part which projects down from the slanted surface rests against the end tie on the track and the two contact springs go down between the rails and lock on the bottom of them.

When the Bumper is snapped in place and the transformer is turned on, the red lamp will light.

MOUNTAIN PASS AND TRESTLE LAYOUT

Assembly Instructions

NOTE: Disregard any layouts found on other Instruction Sheets – Use only the layout diagram on this Sheet.

First take the track found in the Train Set and the extra track included and place them in the positions that they will occupy, as per the illustration. The straight sections of track are designated by an "S" alongside them; all other track sections are curved.

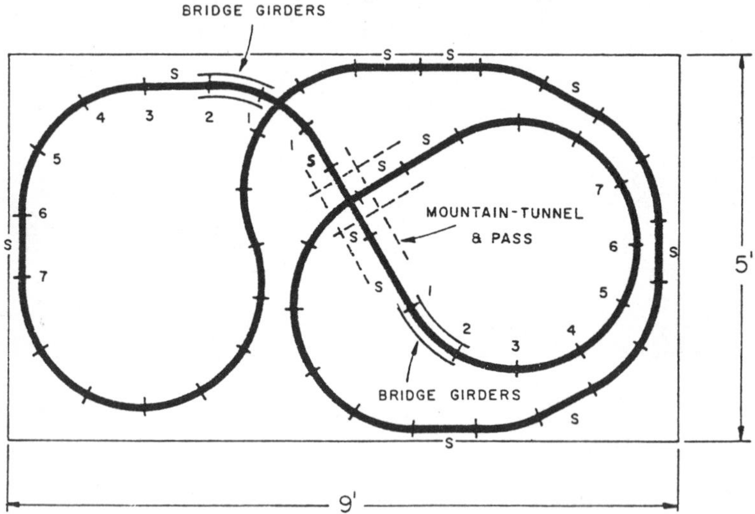

Now join your sections of track together. Remove the trestle and bridge sections from your #770 Set and fit togther as illustrated by the Instruction Sheet included. Place them alongside the track in the position noted on the sketch. Number one is the highest trestle, Number two the next highest and so on down to Number seven. Set them into position at the track joints as shown on the Instruction Sheet that is in your #770 Trestle Set. Set up the mountain pass as per the Instruction Sheet included with that set and place it into position in the spot designated in the illustration. Hook your transformer into position as per the instructions found in your Train Set. Put the locomotive and cars on the track, plug in your transformer and you are now ready to operate. The other equipment furnished with this layout can be placed in any position you desire. You now have a real running railroad with all the twists, turns, grades, tunnels and mountain cuts of a real live railroad. With this amount of track and equipment you can make any number of layouts that you can imagine.

 Ref: Form No. M5256

FIGURE 8 TRESTLE SET

Model No. 747

This overhead Figure 8 Trestle system was designed to greatly increase the play value of your train set.

The set consists of 52 upright pieces and 54 cross pieces. Only 52 cross pieces are needed and two spares are packed in case any should be broken or lost. The uprights start with 4 pieces 1" high and rise in groups of 4 every ⅓" to 5" high.

HOW TO ASSEMBLE

To start the trestle set-up, remove the printed trestle sheets from the box and separate the scrap sections of cardboard from the uprights and cross sections. Next, arrange the upright sections so you have 4 pieces all the same height in separate piles. This will eliminate the possibility of error in assembly.

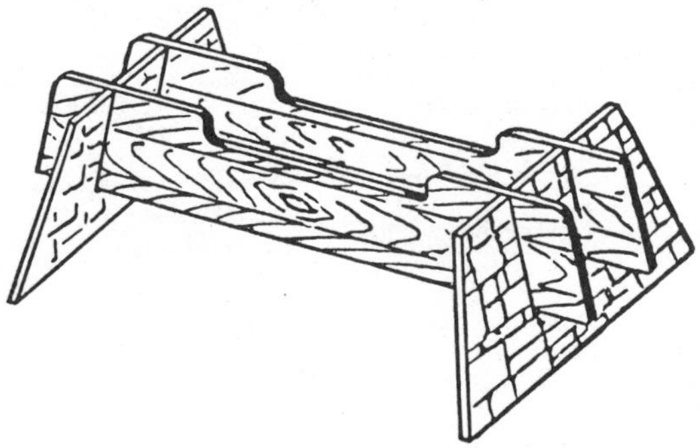

Now assemble two cross pieces to two upright of the same height until all parts have been put together. Be sure the slots on the cross pieces are pushed all the way into the slots of the uprights so the parts are locked together firmly and are even on top. Then put the track together as shown in the following diagram. You will need 20 curved and 6 straight pieces to form the figure 8.

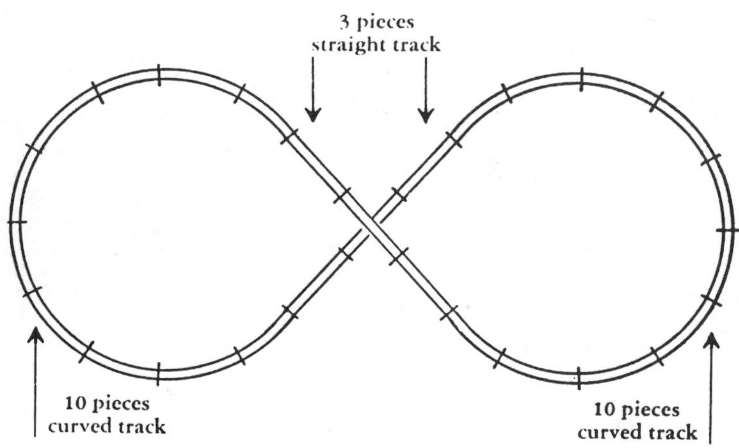

Ref: Form No. M3079B

You are now ready to assemble the uprights to the track. Start by placing the two smallest upright sections underneath the double cross ties of the center track of the lower straight portion of track.

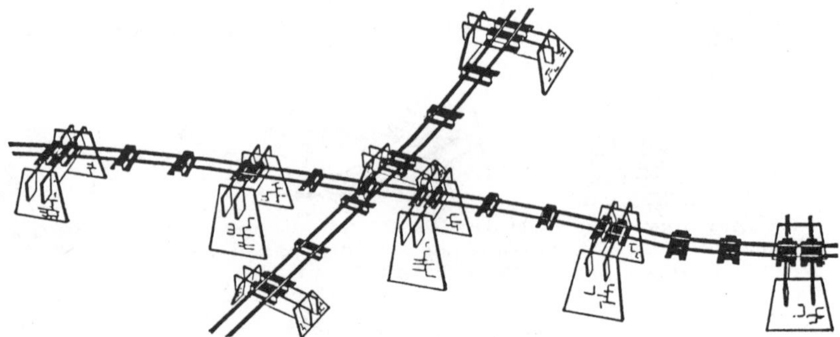

Next start adding a trestle section to each track joint. Be very careful to add the sections according to their height so that the rise is 1/3" to each section of track. When the highest section is reached, use both of them, then begin the down grade.

When finished you will have a complete over and under figure 8 layout. Connect the track terminal at any point around the track: Follow directions in the train manual for the hook-up and operation of the train.

The trestle parts of this set will also build a large oval track with a grade up and down. The following diagram shows one half of an oval track using the trestle set.

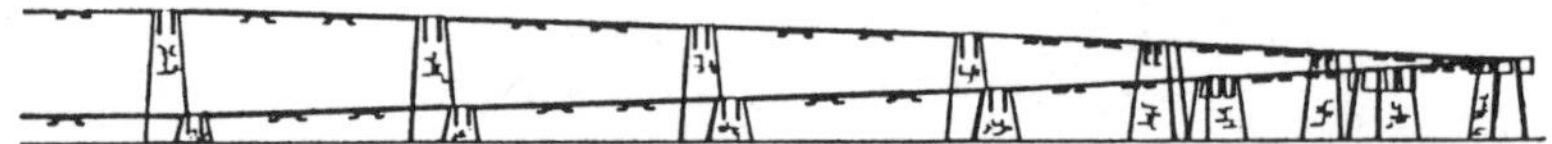

To build the oval, it is necessary to use 12 curve and 14 straight track and follow the same procedure of assembly and construction as explained in the figure 8 layout. The trestle pieces can also be used to build the up and down portions of a ramp in re ..lar layouts.

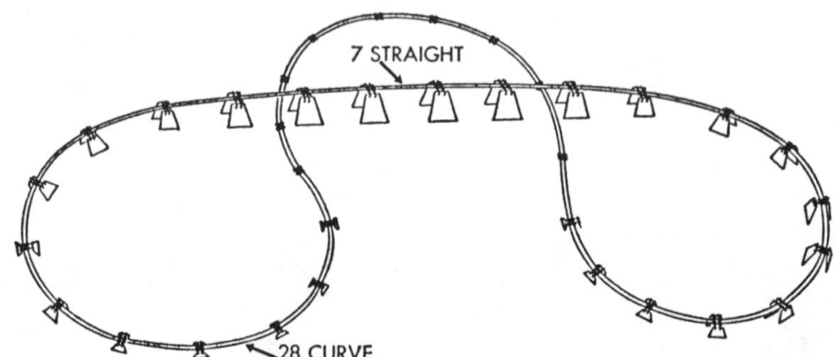

To build the above over and under layout, 28 curve track and 7 straight track are required. Lay the track as shown in the diagram and start inserting the two highest uprights under the center section of the straight track. Next insert the remaining 24 uprights so you have a gradual rise from the floor to the top level of 1/3" to each section of track.

TRESTLE

Model No. 780

The No. 780 Railroad Trestle set was designed to make good looking, sturdy overhead grades in miniature railroads. They are graduated so that the rise of the grade is 1/3" to the foot and the 24 pieces supplied will run the track from floor level, to a 4 inch height which will allow the building of nice over and under passes. Below are shown the smallest & largest piece.

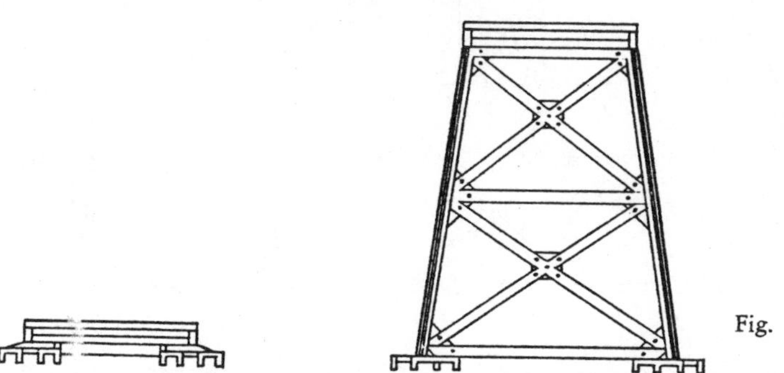

Fig. 1

The trestles are designed to be placed between two sections of track, with the bottom edge of the ties resting into the slots of the top of the trestle, the track is then held together with the No. 693 track lock. (Note drawing below.)

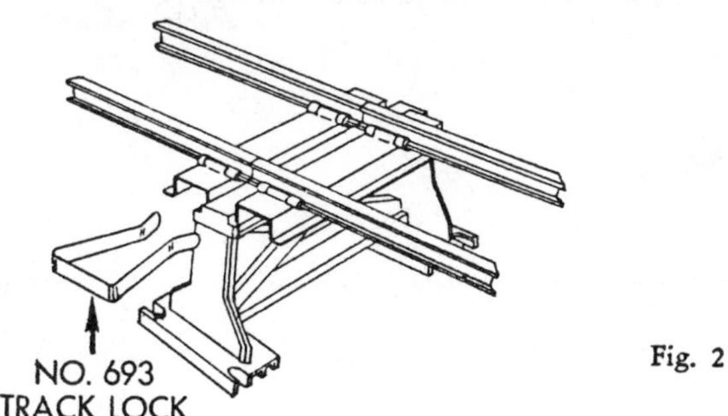

Fig. 2

ASSEMBLING TRACK

It is advisable to lay out the track first, leaving the track slightly apart at the joints where the trestles are to be inserted. Then insert the trestle piece and push the track together and insert the track lock.

Start adding the trestles using the smallest and gradually working up the grade, using the next height until the tallest piece is used. Then use the other tall piece and start down the grade.

FASTENING THE TRESTLES TO THE TABLE

Each trestle is equipped with 4 slots on the base which can be used for permanent mounting. This can be done by using No. 5 or 6 wood screws of whatever length may be necessary, depending on the type of material used to fasten to.

Ref: Form No. M3247

THE OVERHEAD FIGURE 8

To make the overhead figure 8 design, it is necessary to use 20 curve and 6 straight pieces of track and layout as shown below.

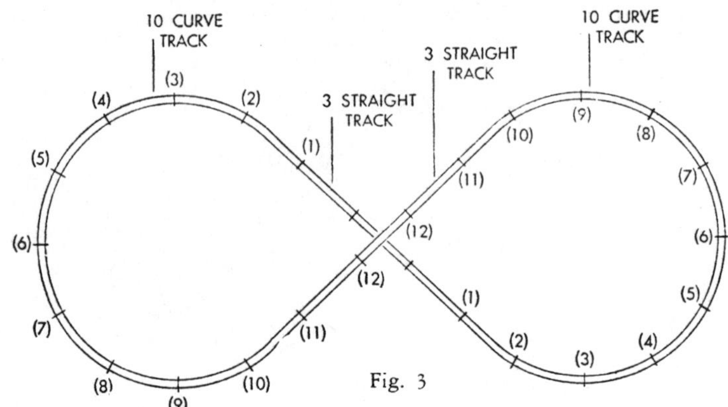

Fig. 3

The lower section of track is at the ground level and smallest trestle piece is to be used at joint marked No. 1. The trestles are then inserted in order of size so when No. 12 is reached, it is the tallest piece in the set.

Besides the Figure 8 set, the trestles can be used to make many different designs, and can be used to make a regular up and down grade in any oval track or large layout.

Always make sure the same basic rules of assembly as described above are followed.

TRESTLE
Model No. 26782

The No. 26782 Railroad Trestle set was designed to make good looking, sturdy overhead grades in miniature railroads. They are graduated so that the rise of the grade is ⅓″ to the foot and the 26 pieces supplied will raise the track to approximately a 5″ height which will allow the building of nice over and under passes. Below are shown the smallest & largest piece.

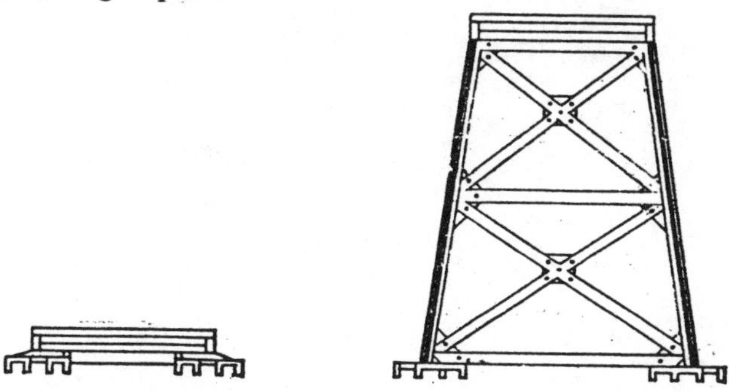

Fig. 1

The trestles are designed to be placed between two sections of track, with the bottom edge of the ties resting into the slots of the top of the trestle, the track is then held together with the track lock. (Note drawing below.)

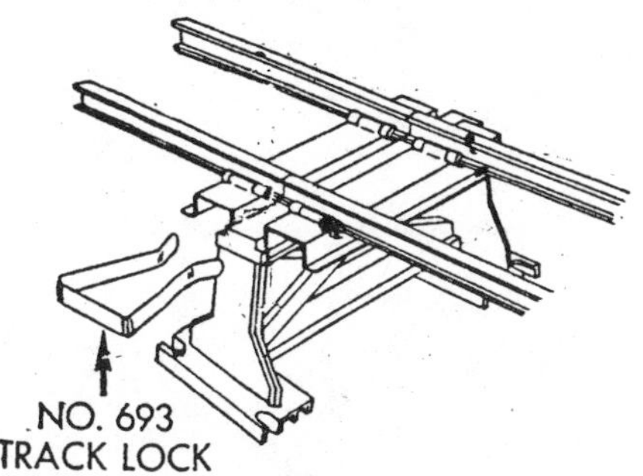

ASSEMBLING TRACK

It is advisable to lay out the track first, leaving the track slightly apart at the joints where the trestles are to be inserted. Then insert the trestle piece and push the track together and insert the track lock.

Start adding the trestles using the smallest and gradually working up the grade, using the next height until the tallest piece is used. Then use the other tall piece and start down the grade.

FASTENING THE TRESTLES TO THE TABLE

Each trestle is equipped with 4 slots on the base which can be used for permanent mounting. This can be done by using No. 5 or 6 wood screws of whatever length may be necessary, depending on the type of material used to fasten to.

THE OVERHEAD FIGURE 8

To make the overhead figure 8 design, it is necessary to use 20 curv and 6 straight pieces of track and layout as shown below.

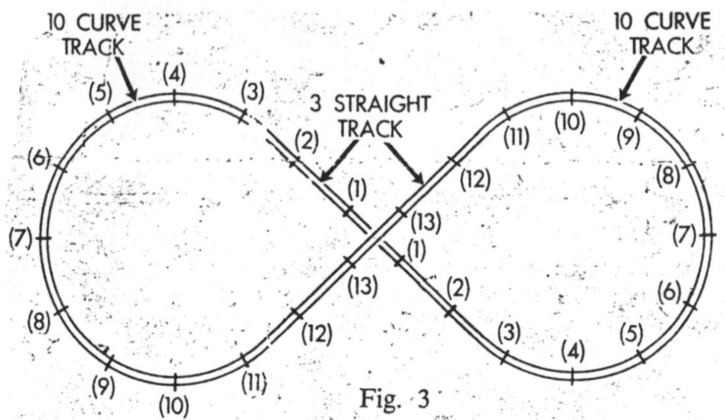

Fig. 3

S GAUGE POW-R-KLIP

Model No. 26810

INSTRUCTIONS FOR ATTACHING S GAUGE NO. 26810 POW-R-KLIP

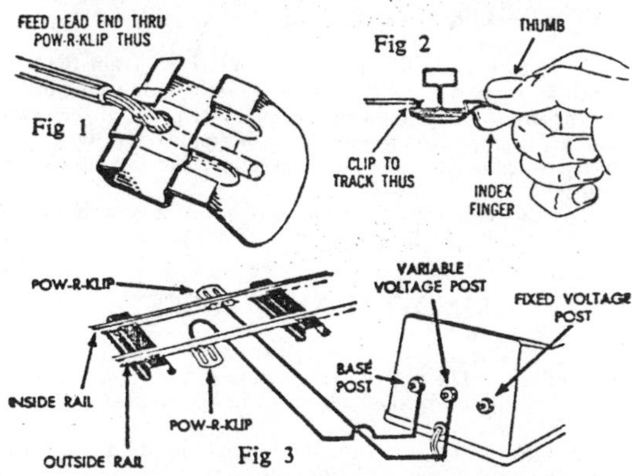

Using the lead wire included in this envelope, remove approximately ½" of insulation from end of wire. Twist strands together and feed bare end only into the POW-R-KLIP as shown in Fig. 1. Holding bared end of wire and POW-R-KLIP between index finger and thumb as shown in Fig. 2, force POW-R-KLIP onto underside of rail.

Attach two POW-R-KLIPS to track as shown in Fig. 3. Attach wire from outside rail to base post of transformer and attach wire from inside rail to variable voltage post. Wrap the bared end of wires around the transformer posts in a clockwise direction so that the wire will not slip out when the thumb nut is tightened.

NOTE: Use only STRANDED wire furnished. For best results do not snap POW-R-KLIPS and wire on and off the rail. POW-R-KLIPS can be used an indefinite number of times, but with each use, the best connections will be the first.

Ref: Form No. M4835 (PA 15N 915)

KNUCKLE COUPLERS
General Instructions

HOW TO EQUIP YOUR AMERICAN FLYER CARS AND TENDERS WITH KNUCKLE COUPLER TRUCKS

Complete sets of trucks are packaged along with the necessary rivets so that any car can be changed over to the more modern heavy duty trucks with knuckle couplers.

REMOVING THE CHASSIS

The first step is to remove the old trucks and rivets from the cars. If it is a two-piece car, such as a box car, the chassis must first be removed from the car body. This can be done by inserting a thin-bladed screwdriver between the chassis and body at the corners and gently prying up to loosen the drive pins. On some cars and tenders it will be necessary to remove the screws, or straighten out the tabs holding the body and chassis together.

After removing the body from the chassis, remove the wheels from the truck by slightly spreading the truck side.

REMOVING THE TRUCKS

To remove the truck it will be necessary to take out the truck rivet. This can be done in a number of ways. The turned-over portion of the rivet can be drilled off by drill press or hand drill, it may be filed off, or it can be driven our if a thin punch and hollow post is used.

In the case of lighted or action cars, the wire soldered to the head of the rivet should first be unsoldered and removed from the rivet.

NOTE: It is advisable to change only one truck at a time. Remove old truck and install new truck in its place so you do not get confused or use wrong rivets or parts in the assembly.

Each pair of trucks is packaged with the necessary rivets for mounting. Due to various types of chassis used, some trucks are packaged with several types of rivets. Be sure the correct rivet is used. Compare the body length with the rivet you have removed to make sure of using the right size.

RIVETS

Pictured below are various lengths and numbers of rivets.

PA9381 rivets are used on most freight cars using a pressed steel chassis.

PA10235 rivets are used on lighted and action cars, and on tenders where the truck is insulated from the chassis with a fiber bushing and washer.

PA9388 rivet is used on all cars using thick moulded chassis.

PA11331 rivet is used only on 644 crane cars.

PA 9381

PA 10235

PA 9988

PA 11331

ASSEMBLING NEW TRUCK AND COUPLER

After determining the correct rivet, place it through the hole in the chassis. (If it is a lighted or action car, be sure and use the insulating brushing and washer.) Next, place head of rivet on a solid surface. Then put the truck over the rivet shoulder and pien over the hollow end of the rivet. If no starting punch is available, a large nail can be used to start the turn over. Then finish turning rivet end over with a small hammer.

Care should be exercised in turning over the rivet so you don't hit the wheels or axles.

 Ref: Form No. M3244

ACTION CARS

Action cars require two different trucks. One has a pick-up finger to supply current to the coil. The pick-up finger, spring and locking ring are packaged with these trucks and must be assembled after the truck is mounted to the chassis. The cut-away diagram below shows the method of assembly.

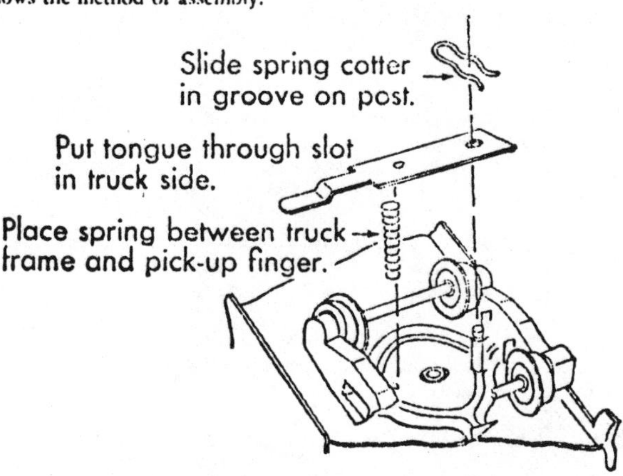
Slide spring cotter in groove on post.
Put tongue through slot in truck side.
Place spring between truck frame and pick-up finger.

STREAMLINE CARS

The aluminum streamline cars have a slide-in chassis. The cast ends must first be removed. The chassis is to be slid out (it rests between two runners). After installing the new trucks the metal end panels must be cut off at the bottom so they are at the same height as the chassis. This means removing 1/8" from the bottom.

COACHES AND PULLMAN CARS

If coaches are equipped with die cast chassis with steps, the inside corner surfaces may have to be filed away to give necessary clearance for the swing of the coupler.

FREIGHT CARS

The ends of the cars and chassis have a 1/4" wide cut-away opening which may have to be cut away at an angle as shown below. This cut-away is also necessary for coupler clearance.

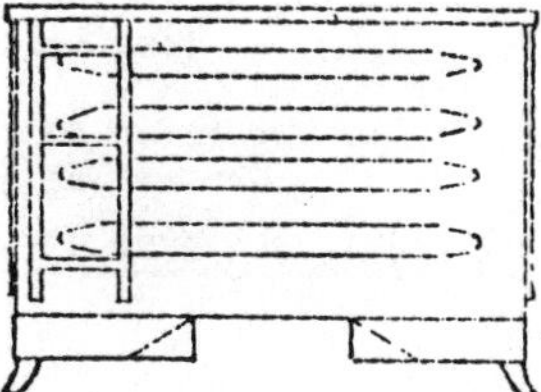

Cut away at dotted line.

COUPLER ADJUSTMENT

After new trucks have been installed on the car the coupler height should be adjusted so that when the coupler is closed the bottom of the weight is slightly above the top of the rail when car is placed on the tracks.

We now have a larger assortment of trucks for conversion purposes and we have reduced the price on most trucks previously listed. You may continue to charge $.50 per car plus price of trucks for conversion.

Hudson and Union Pacific Tenders can be converted. Diesel locomotives still cannot be converted.

The Atlantic,Pacific,Penn.,Royal Blue, and Nickel Plate Switcher can be converted, but in order to do so, the wheels and axles on the old truck will have to be switched to the knuckle coupler trucks.
PLEASE NOTE: The new truck frame will not exactly match the truck frame on the front of the tender. Use XA12A051 truck.

We are now supplying sets of Knuckle Coupler trucks (two trucks to a set) complete with the necessary rivets and instructions and each set packed in a separate box. It is possible for you to purchase these box sets from your distributor for resale.

You will probably, in most cases, wish to continue to purchase the car trucks and the rivets separately at the Authorized Service Station discount of 50% which is allowed you for repair parts.

Following is a list of the trucks now being supplied showing the part number of each.

PART NO	DESCRIPTION	RETAIL PRICE
XA12A051	4-wheel Knuckle Coupler truck for Unlighted Cars	$1.38 pr.
XA12A050	4-wheel Knuckle Coupler truck for Lighted Cars	1.65 "
XA12A057 and XA12A050 (use one of each per car)	4-wheel Knuckle Coupler truck for Action Car	1.81 "
XA12N818	4-wheel Knuckle Coupler truck for Streamline Cars	1.65 "
XA12N894	6-wheel Knuckle Coupler truck for Passenger Cars	1.93 "
XA12N319	Knuckle Coupler Truck for Crane Car #644	1.93 "
XA12A053	Knuckle Coupler Truck for 6-wheel Tender Rear Trucks for Hudson type Locomotive and Union Pacific (one truck only supplied)	1.30 ea.
XA12N823	6-Wheel Knuckle Coupler Truck for #636 Depressed Center Car	1.93 pr.

RIVETS REQUIRED FOR CONVERSION

NO.		PRICE
PA9988 Rivets	For cars #628,647,631,648, etc.	$.04ea. (packed 25 per box)
PA9381 Rivets	For cars #629,630,637,633R,649,651,650, etc.	.02ea. (packed 100 per box)
PA10235 Rivets	For cars #649,651,650, etc.	.03ea. (packed 100 per box)

cont'd

PA10235 A Rivets For #625 Tank Car — .07ea. (packed 100 per box)

PA12A469 Rivets For #632 Hopper Car — .045ea.

PA11331 Rivets For #644 Crane Car — .07ea. (packed 25 per box)

PA11305 Rivets For Hopper and Gondola Cars with weights — .07ea. (packed 50 per box)

INSTRUCTIONS FOR INSTALLING KNUCKLE COUPLER TRUCKS

On most Freight and Passenger cars, the first step is to remove the body of the car from the chassis so that the rivet holding the truck can be removed. On some cars a small pin holds the body to the chassis whereas other cars use self-tapping screws.

To remove body,use a thin bladed screw driver and pry gently between the chassis and body until the pins loosen. Where a self-tapping screw is used,these can be removed with a small screw driver.Do same on opposite side.

When removing the Caboose body from the chassis,use a thin bladed screw driver and pry underneath truck using steps on the body for leverage,and lift up lightly until the pins loosen. Then follow the general instructions for replacing trucks.

The rivets are now exposed and can be removed by drilling or punching out and new Knuckle Coupler truck installed using new truck rivets. On lighted cars, the wires have to be unsoldered before removing rivets.

After this has been completed,reassemble body to chassis using pin or screw as required. On some of the cars manufactured earlier having a plastic chassis,the same steps are followed,but the chassis and body have to be glued together.

If you do not have riveting equipment, the R-I Tool Kit will be very helpful to you when making conversions and for other purposes.

It consists of a rectangular base with two holders or anvils and one rivet punch.

To remove rivets,turn the car over and place the head of the rivet on the anvil with the knurled top and drill it out or file it off.

To rivet the new truck onto the chassis,place the head of the new rivet on the anvil with the smooth top,and peen the rivet with Rivet Punch.

INSTRUCTIONS FOR REPLACING KNUCKLE COUPLER

Take a small pair of needle nosed pliers and pry up the straps that hold the coupler to the end of the truck frame. Replace the coupler and bend down the strap with the pliers.

A few of the first Knuckle Couplers manufactured were screwed or riveted onto the truck frame. These cannot be replaced, but instead the complete truck will have to be replaced.

KNUCKLE COUPLER KIT

Model No. 520

The No. 520 Knuckle Coupler Kit is designed to allow the knuckle couplers to be installed on Freight and Passenger Cars and the rear of the tenders using 4 wheel steel formed trucks.

To install the coupler, first remove the front wheels and axle, place the head of the present coupler pin in the steel tube and tap the pin with a hammer to drive it out. See Fig. #1.

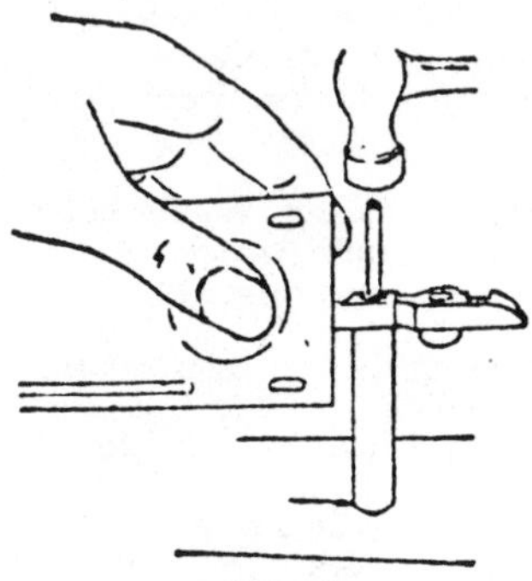

FIG. 1

Next place coupler on truck tongue, so it is all the way into the slot at back end of coupler.

Now insert split rivet through the hole in the tongue and the groove on the underneath side of the coupler. See Fig. #2. Then spread the ends of the split rivet with a screw driver or thin nosed pliers.

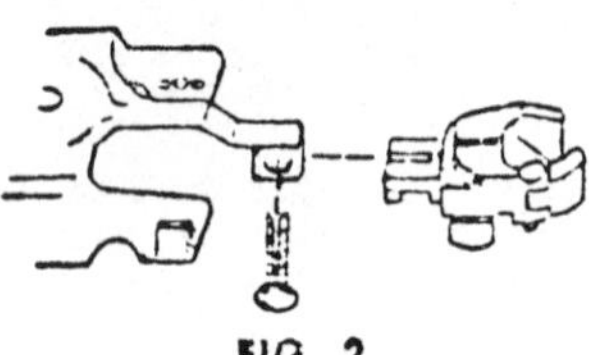

FIG. 2

When replacing wheels and axle on lighted and action cars or on tenders, be sure metal wheel is on correct side.

Adjust the coupler height so the weight is slightly above the rail when the car is on the track and the knuckle is closed. Be sure new coupler is square with rest of car.

 Ref: Form No. M3267

AUTOMATIC COUPLER

Model No. 694

In order to convert cars with old style couplers to the new automatic uncoupler type, it is necessary to:

1. Drill a .196 diameter hole (No. 9 drill). 1-5/32″ from each end of the chassis on the center line.

2. The lip at the end of the chassis is cut away for clearance as shown in the sketch.

3. The rivet is placed through the hole so that the head is on the upper side of the chassis.

4. Place truck over rivet and peen over end with a punch or peening hammer.

5. Wheels and axles can now be assembled to the trucks.

6. Place the car on the track and see that the rounded portion of the coupler is adjusted even with the top of the rail. Whatever adjustment is necessary can be made by a slight bending of the coupler strap.

In order to equip "0" gauge cars which already have our automatic couplers with new trucks to operate on our "3/16" scale track, just remove the old truck, rivet the new one in its place, following above instructions and using the same holes that the rivets were removed from.

Cars equipped with these couplers can be automatically uncoupled by the use of American Flyer's No. 706 Remote Control Uncoupler.

Ref: Form No. M2422

AUTOMATIC COUPLERS

● AUTOMATIC COUPLING

In addition to the Remote Control, your train is also equipped with the new Automatic Couplers. It is possible for you to couple the cars together without having to handle them in any way. Place the cars on the track, back the Locomotive and Tender slowly up to the first car. When they hit, reverse the Locomotive and you will find the car is coupled to the Tender. Repeat the operation to pick up the rest of the cars. To uncouple the cars, raise the couplers apart with the point of a pencil or use the American Flyer Uncouplers No. 705 or 706.

● LUBRICATION OF MOTOR

This train, like its prototype, must be kept well lubricated at all times to insure perfect performance and long life. For most satisfactory performance we suggest a lubrication of at least once to every four hours of actual operation. Also BEFORE OPERATING when you first get the train and after it has been put away for any length of time.

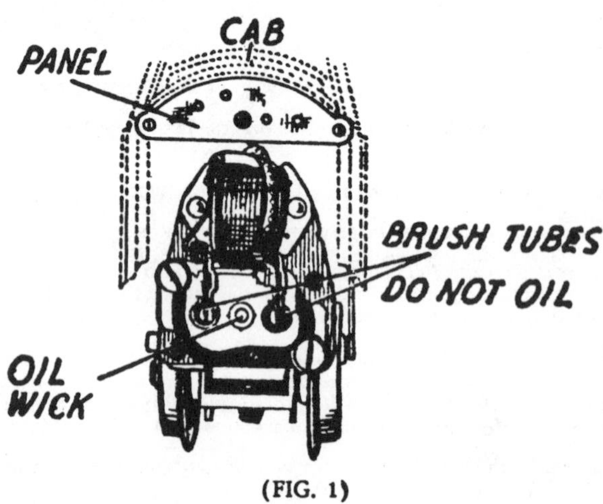

(FIG. 1)

Oil the car axles and the Locomotive at the following points:

1. The rear motor bearing wick reached through the rear of the locomotive cab. See Fig. 1. (Be careful not to get oil in the brush tubes.)

2. Turn the locomotive on its back. Back of the rear axel is a steel cover plate that can be removed by unfastening one screw. This exposes a drive gear which should be lubricated with a small amount of vaseline. The cover plate should be replaced to keep dust and dirt out of gears.

3. Oil the wheel bearings, the side rod bearings and the valve rod linkages. See Fig. 2.

A small drop of oil is all that is necessary. Apply oil with a toothpick or needle. After oiling run train around track a few times and then wipe the rails to remove any oil that might have run down on them. This not only keeps the rails bright and shiny but provides a good electrical contact and prevents the drive wheels from skidding.

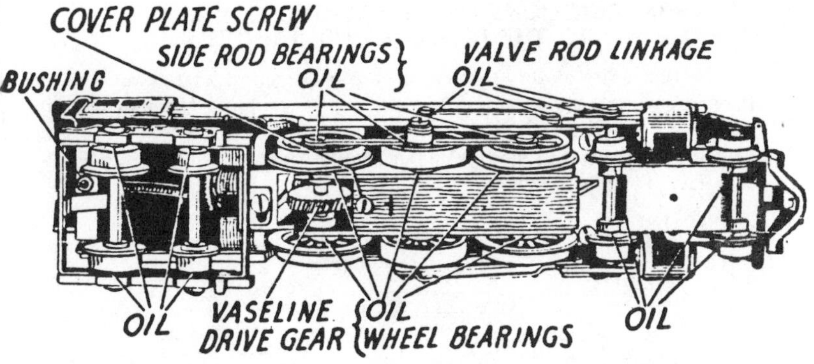

(FIG. 2)

● LUBRICATION OF SMOKE UNIT

Fig. 3 shows the lubrication points on the smoke and choo-choo unit. These can be reached from the left side of the locomotive and a little oil applied with a toothpick, small applicator or brush.

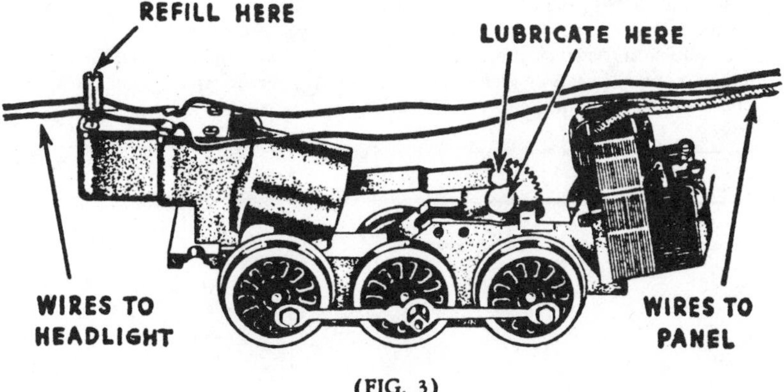

(FIG. 3)

COUPLINGS

INSTRUCTIONS FOR ATTACHING COUPLINGS TO THE DIESEL A AND B UNITS

The two units of this locomotive are packaged separately and in the attached envelope are the necessary screws and coupling for attaching the two units together.

The two screws and the black fiber coupler strap are used to connect the "A" and "B" units together.

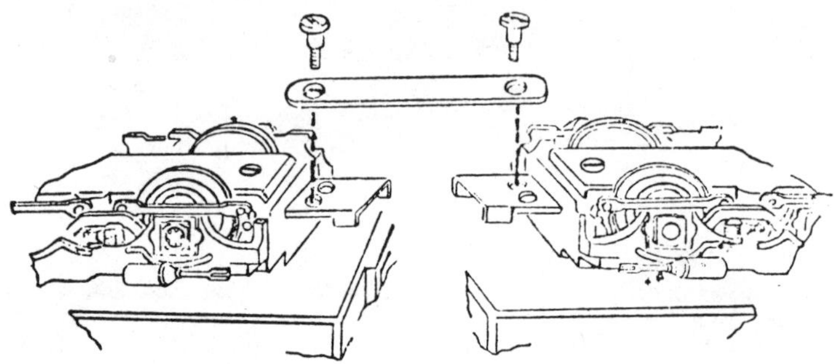

To attach the fiber coupler strap, place the "B" unit on its back, place one of the screws in one of the holes in the strap and insert the screw in the left hand hole on the truck bracket. Next attach the two units together with the other screw — fastening the screw into the corresponding hole on the rear truck of the "A Unit" — Note Diagram —

REMOTE AND MANUAL CONTROL AUTOMATIC UNCOUPLER

INSTRUCTIONS FOR OPERATING REMOTE AND MANUAL CONTROL AUTOMATIC UNCOUPLER

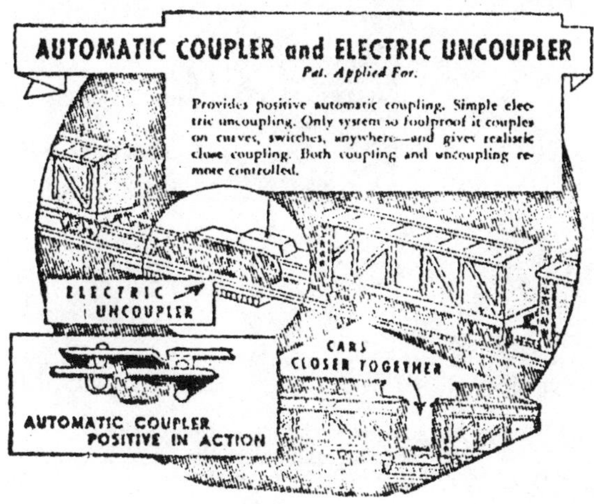

The operation of the uncoupler is very simple. Remove a section of straight track from your layout and replace it with the uncoupling unit. Connect one end of the long wire to the clip on the uncoupler. Connect the other end to one of the clips on the button switch. Connect one end of the short wire to the remaining clip on the button switch. Connect the other end of the wire to the center rail connection of the track clip.

The uncoupler is now ready to operate. As the cars pass the red marker press the button, the center part of the uncoupler will snap up and uncouple the cars.

The manual uncoupler operates in the same manner except a hand lever is used instead of the button.

Ref: Form No. M2057

REMOTE CONTROL UNCOUPLER
Model No. 706

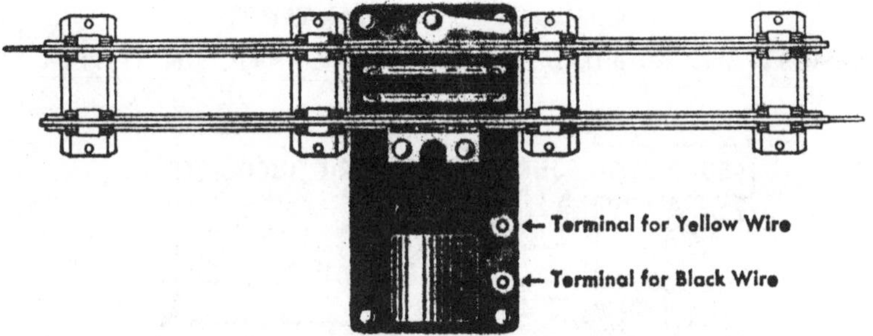

INSTRUCTIONS FOR OPERATING
REMOTE CONTROL AUTOMATIC UNCOUPLER No. 706

This uncoupler can be attached anywhere along the tracks and will uncouple on a curve as well as on straight track.

To attach, place it underneath the track, between two ties, so that lower edge of one rail rests under the raised portion of the metal strip with the "U" shaped cutout.

Turn locking lever so it clamps over the lower part of the other rail.

Connect YELLOW wire from one terminal to the 15 Volt Post on transformer.

Connect LONG BLACK wire from the other terminal to a clip underneath the Control Box.

Connect SHORT BLACK wire from the other Control Box clip to BASE POST on transformer.

The uncoupler is now ready to operate. As the cars pass over the uncoupler ramp, press the button, the ramp will snap up and uncouple the cars.

 Ref: Form No. M2594

LOCKOUT ELIMINATOR
Model No. 709

This unit is designed to supply a very low voltage to a normally dead block in the track, which enables the locomotive to stop at the desired location and start in the same direction without locking the remote control unit in an inoperative position.

This unit is to be used with the No. 761 Semaphore, and the No. 755 Talking Stations or No. 758 "Sam" the Semaphore Man, which were built without a resistor unit in them.

Since each of the above items use a dead block system to stop a train, the hook up in each case is the same.

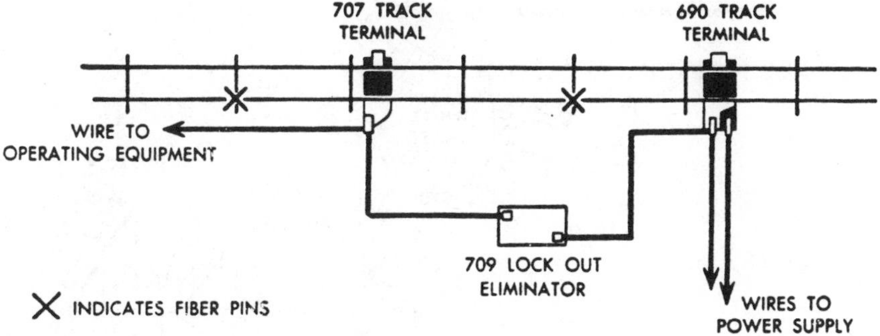

Connect the two wires which are included to the clips underneath the Lockout Eliminator Box, then hook the other end of one of the wires to the clip on the No. 707 Track Terminal which is located in the dead block.

Connect the other wire to the Base Post Clip on the No. 690 Track Terminal which is supplying current to your track.

This will now allow about 3 or 4 volts to filter into the dead block, which is not enough to run the train but will be just enough to keep the Remote Control unit from becoming disengaged, thus allowing the train to start up in its original direction when the equipment causes the block to become alive.

3/16" SCALE REMOTE CONTROL TRACK SWITCHES

Model No. 720

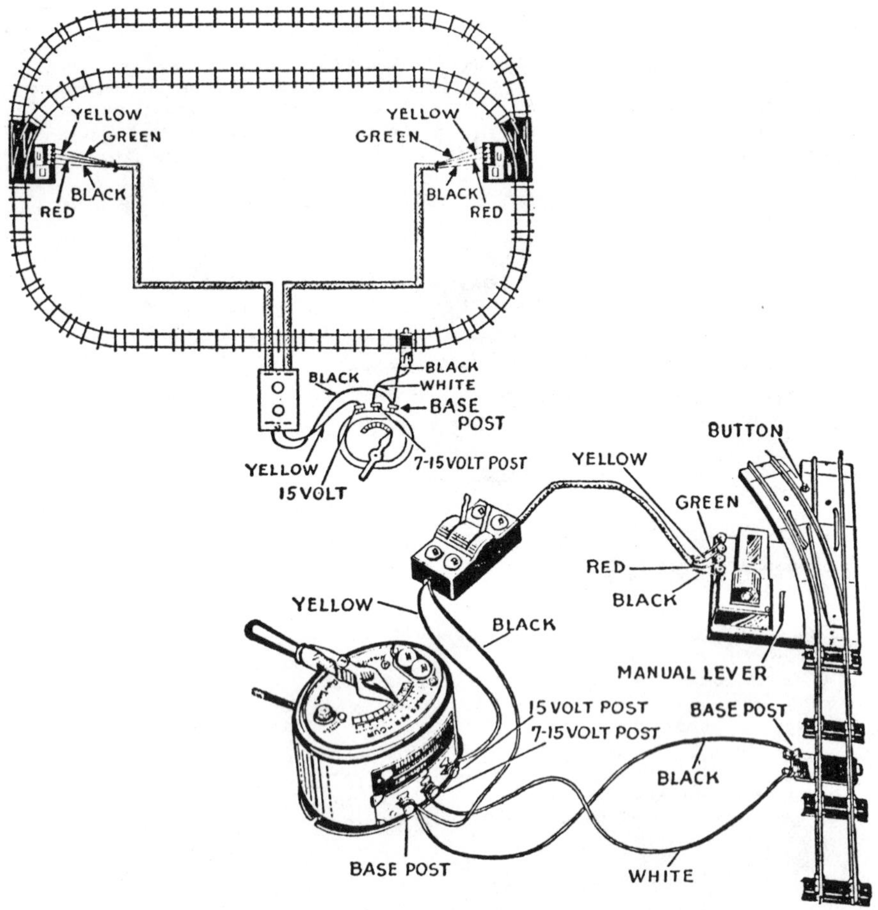

First set the switches in your layout and hook up the wires as shown in the diagram. The track terminal may be attached anywhere in the SINGLE line of track between the two switches.

These new AMERICAN FLYER switches are really two kinds of switches in one, that is, they can be used in the conventional manner or by simply moving a button, two or more trains can be operated at the same time without the use of special control buttons or block signals.

To use the switches in the regular manner, move the button toward the lights as far as it will go.

To operate two or more trains on the same layout at the same time, move the button away from the lights. With the button in this position trains will operate only on the loop the switch is set for. If the switch is set for the inside loop, any train which happens to be on the outside loop will stop. When the switch is reset for the outside loop, the train in this loop will start and the train in the inside loop will stop.

 Ref: Form No. M2442

When the switches are used for two train operation they MUST be operated in pairs, that is, they must both be set for the same loop, except in the case of spur lines where the end of the track is not connected to any part of the layout.

Use the Control Box levers to throw the switch frogs, do not throw them with the manual lever unless frog should stop in a center position or not close properly, then use the manual lever to throw frog all the way over.

To change lamp bulb, remove the two screws on lamp housing and replace lamp with a 3½ G-18 Volt lamp.

DIA. NO.	PART NO.	DESCRIPTION
1	S279	SCREW
2	PA10928-A	LAMP HOUSING
3	PA9935	LENS
4	PA10925	SWITCH PILOT STUD
5	PA10927	SPRING WASHER
6	PA10904	FROG (RIGHT)
	PA10905	FROG (LEFT)
7	PA10037	BINDING POST NUT
8	PA9723	LIGHT BULB
9	XA10906-RP	RIGHT ROAD BED ASSEMBLY
	XA10906-RP	LEFT ROAD BED ASSEMBLY
10	XA10916-R	MECHANISM ASSEMBLY (RIGHT)
	XA10916-L	MECHANISM ASSEMBLY (LEFT)
11	S240	SCREW
12	PA11414	SPRING
13	PA10922	PLUNGER
14	XA10930-A	COIL ASSEMBLY
15	PA10924	PLATE
16	S243	SCREW
17	XA10917-R	RIGHT LINK ASSEMBLY
	XA10917-L	LEFT LINK ASSEMBLY
18	PA10929	SWITCH SCREW
19	PA10926	BOTTOM COVER
20	PA10987-R	LONG BOTTOM COVER (RIGHT)
	PA10987-L	LONG BOTTOM COVER (LEFT)
21	XA10698	CONTROL BOX
21A	XA12B183	SINGLE CONTROL BOX
22	PA3395	BULB (GREEN)
23	PA2990	BULB (RED)

REMOTE CONTROL SWITCHES
Model Nos. 720A, 26760

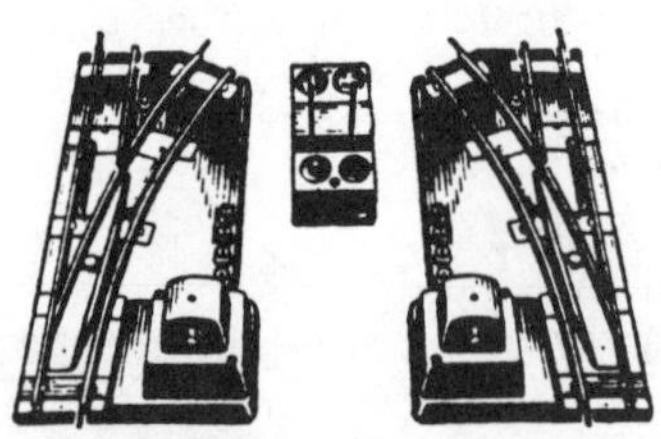

SERVICE INSTRUCTIONS

The first thing to do is connect unit to control box and transformer and check for operation.

1. **To replace Lamp Housing (#2) or Bulb (#8).**
   a. Remove two Screws (#1) to take off Lamp Housing (#2).
   b. Push out two Lens (#3).
   c. Unscrew Bulb (#8) from lamp bracket.

2. **To replace Frog (#6).**
   a. Remove five Screws (#1) holding Long Bottom Cover (#20) to Roadbed Assy (#9).
   b. Drive out Switch Pilot Stud (#4) along with Spring Washer (#5) and Frog (#6) will come right out.

3. **To replace Link Assy (#17) or Mechanism Assy (#10).**
   a. Follow steps 2a.
   b. Remove three Screws (#1) holding Bottom Cover (#19) to Roadbed Assy (#9).
   c. Take out Switch Screw (#18) and Plunger (#13) and Spring (#12) will come out.
   d. Remove four Screws (#11) and pull out Mechanism Assy (#10) and Link Assy (#17) from housing.
   e. Lift up shutter assy on Mechanism Assy (#10) slightly to free Link Assy (#17) which can be pulled out separating both parts.
   f. Unsolder lead wires from coil on the Mechanism Assy (#10) to the terminals on the roadbed.

4. **To replace Coil Assy (#14) on Mechanism Assy (#10).**
   a. Follow steps 3a to e.
   b. Bend back lugs and remove Coil Assy (#14) from Mechanism Assy (#10).

 Ref: Form No. 1657; July 15, 1955

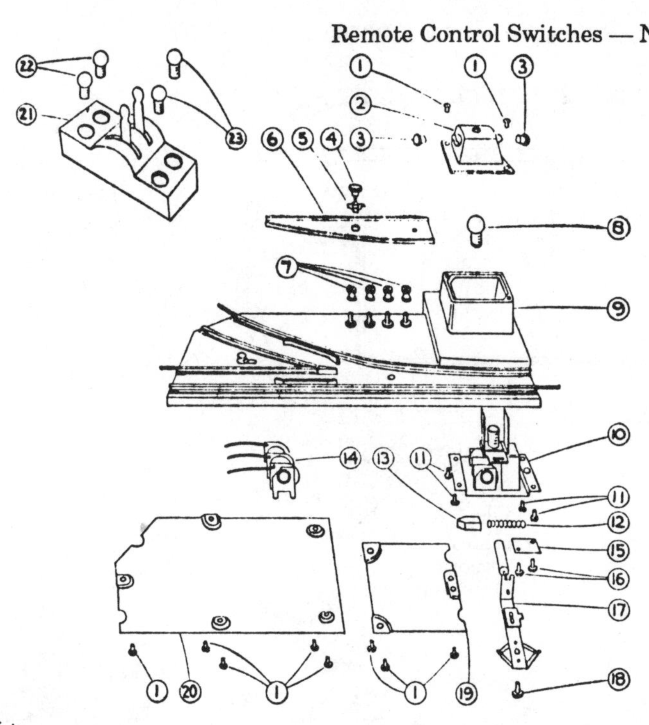

Diagram Number	Part No.	Description	Price
* 1	S279	Screw	$ .01 ea.
* 2	PA10928	Lamp Housing	.28 "
* 3	PA9935	Lens	.05 "
* 4	PA10925	Switch Pilot Stud	.04 "
* 5	PA10927	Spring Washer	.01 "
6	PA10904	Frog (Right)	.22 "
	PA10905	Frog (Left)	.22 "
* 7	PA10037-B	Binding Post Nut	.02 "
* 8	PA9723	Light Bulb	.30 "
9	XA10906-RP	Right Road Bed Assy.	2.25 "
	XA10906-RP	Left Road Bed Assy.	2.25 "
10	XA10916-R	Mechanism Assy. (Right)	2.25 "
	XA10916-L	Mechanism Assy. (Left)	2.25 "
*11	S240	Screw	.01 "
*12	PA11414	Spring	.02 "
*13	PA10922	Plunger	.05 "
*14	XA10930	Coil Assy.	1.10 "
*15	PA10924	Plate	.10 dz.
*16	S243	Screw	.10 "
17	XA10917-R	Right Link Assy.	.21 ea.
	XA10917-L	Left Link Assy.	.21 "
*18	PA10929	Switch Screw	.02 "
*19	PA10926	Bottom Cover	.10 "
20	PA10987-R	Long Bottom Cover	.22 "
	PA10987-L	Long Bottom Cover	.22 "
21	XA10698	Control Box	4.50 "
21-A	XA12B183	Single Control Box	3.50 "
22	PA3395	Bulb (green)	.30 "
23	PA2990	Bulb (Red)	.30 "

Note: Parts marked with an asterisk are used on both Right and Left Hand Switches.

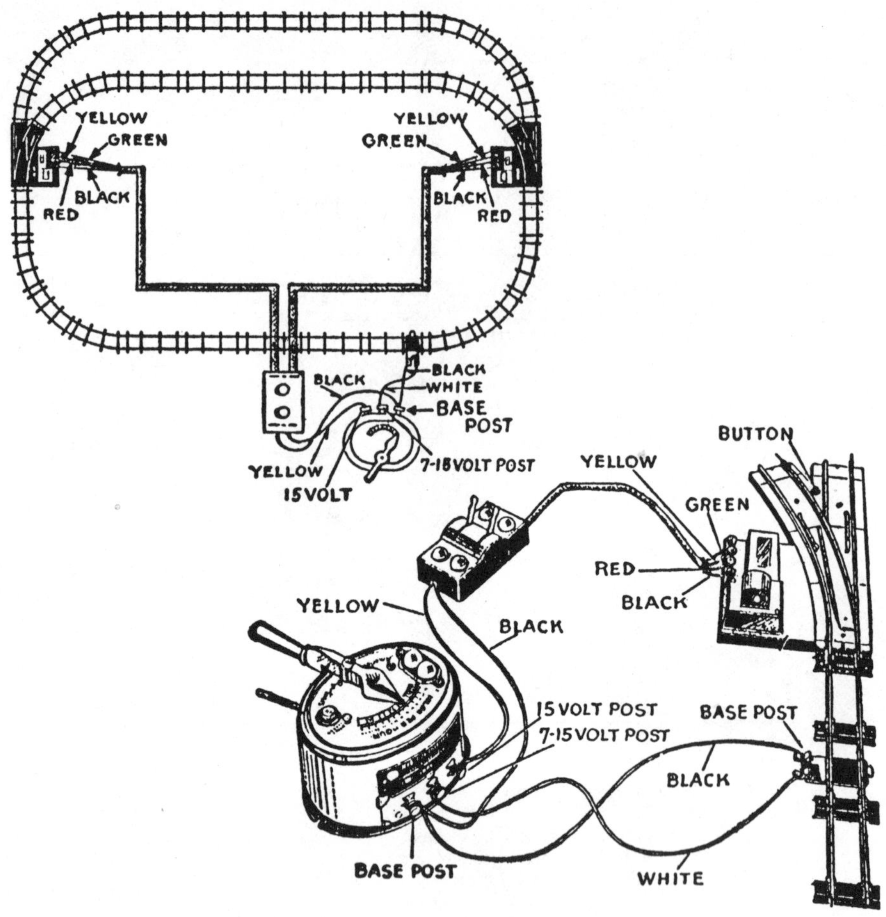

First set the switches in your layout and hook up the wires as shown in the diagram. The track terminal may be attached anywhere in the SINGLE line of track between the two switches.

These new AMERICAN FLYER switches are really two kinds of switches in one, that is, they can be used in the conventional manner or by simply moving a button, two or more trains can be operated at the same time without the use of special control buttons or block signals.

To use the switches in the regular manner, move the button toward the lights as far as it will go.

To operate two or more trains on the same layout at the same time, move the button away from the lights. With the button in this position trains will operate only on the loop the switch is set for. If the switch is set for the inside loop, any train which happens to be on the outside loop will stop. When the switch is reset for the outside loop, the train in this loop will start and the train in the inside loop will stop.

When the switches are used for two train operation they MUST be operated in pairs, that is, they must both be set for the same loop, except in the case of spur lines where the end of the track is not connected to any part of the layout.

Use the Control Box levers to throw the switch frogs.

To change lamp bulb, remove the two screws on lamp housing and replace lamp with a 3½ G-18 Volt lamp.

NO.	PART NO.	DESCRIPTION	PRICE
1		NOT USED	
2	PA10928	Lamp Housing	.31 ea.
3	PA9935	Lens	.06 ea.
4	PA15A296	Switch Pilot Stud	.04 ea.
5	PA10927	Spring Washer	.01 ea.
6	PA10904	Frog (Right)	.24 ea.
	PA10905	Frog (Left)	.24 ea.
7	PA10037-B	Binding Post Nut	.02 ea.
8	PA9723	Light Bulb	.30 ea.
9	XA15C341-RP	Road Bed Assembly (Right)	3.22 ea.
	XA15C342-LRP	Road Bed Assembly (Left)	3.22 ea.
10	XA10916 RRP	Mechanism Assembly (Right)	1.99 ea.
	XA10916 LRP	Mechanism Assembly (Left)	1.99 ea.
11	S86	4 x $\frac{1}{4}$ Type Z R. H. P. K. Screw	.09 dz.
12	PA14A088	Spring	.02 ea.
13	PA10922-A	Plunger	.06 ea.
14	XA10930	Coil	1.21 ea.
15	PA10924	Plate	.11 dz.
16	S183	2 x $\frac{1}{4}$ Type Z B. H. P. K. Screw	.01 ea.
17	XA10917-RA	Link Assembly (Right)	.23 ea.
	XA10917-LA	Link Assembly (Left)	.23 ea.
18	PA10929	Switch Screw	.02 ea.
19	PA15B328-L	Bottom Cover (Left)	.29 ea.
	PA15B328-R	Bottom Cover (Right)	.29 ea.
	S4N79	#4 x 1/8 Type Z B.H. P.K. Screw (Bottom Cover) NOT SHOWN	.01 ea.
20		NOT USED	
21	XA14B492	Control Box (used with pair)	5.45 ea.
21A	XA14B498	Single Switch Control Box (NOT SHOWN)	3.30 ea.
22		NOT USED	
23		NOT USED	

All parts unless marked Right or Left, commonly used on both switches.

Prices subject to change without notice

NO.	PART NO.	DESCRIPTION	PRICE
1		NOT USED	
2	PA10928	Lamp Housing	.33 ea.
3	PA9935	Lens	.06 ea.
4	PA15A296	Switch Pilot Stud	.04 ea.
5	PA10927	Spring Washer	.01 ea.
6	PA10904	Frog (Right)	.25 ea.
	PA10905	Frog (Left)	.25 ea.
7	PA10037-B	Binding Post Nut	.02 ea.
8	PA9723	Light Bulb	.32 ea.
9		Road Bed Assembly (right) Not Available	
		Road Bed Assembly (left) Not Available	
10	XA10916-RRP	Mechanism Assembly (Right)	2.09 ea.
	XA10916-LRP	Mechanism Assembly (Left)	2.09 ea.
11	S86	4 x 1/4 type Z R.H. P.K. Screw	.01 ea.
12	PA14A088	Spring	.02 ea.
13	PA10922-A	Plunger	.06 ea.
14	XA10930	Coil	1.27 ea.
15	PA10924	Plate	.01 ea.
16	S183	2 x 1/4 Type Z B.H. P.K. Screw	.01 ea.
17	XA10917-RA	Link Assembly (Right)	.24 ea.
	XA10917-LA	Link Assembly (Left)	.24 ea.
18	PA10929	Switch Screw	.02 ea.
19		Bottom Cover (left) Not Available	
		Bottom Cover (right) Not Available	
	S4N79	#4 x 1/8 Type Z B.H. P.K. Screw (Bottom Cover) NOT SHOWN	.01 ea.
20		NOT USED	
21	XA14B492	Control Box (Used with pair) No Lights	5.72 ea.
21A	XA14B498	Single Switch Control (NOT SHOWN) No Lights	3.47 ea.
22		NOT USED	
23		NOT USED	
		PARTS FOR CONTROL BOX (NOT SHOWN)	
	PA14495	Bus Bar	.02 ea.
	PA14497	Contact	.05 ea.
	P13737	Lever	.06 ea.
	PA4366	Rivet	.01 ea.

All parts unless marked Right or Left, commonly used on both switches.

Prices subject to change without notice.

REMOTE CONTROL SWITCHES

INSTRUCTIONS FOR INSTALLING
AMERICAN FLYER REMOTE CONTROL SWITCHES
IN A TRACK LAYOUT

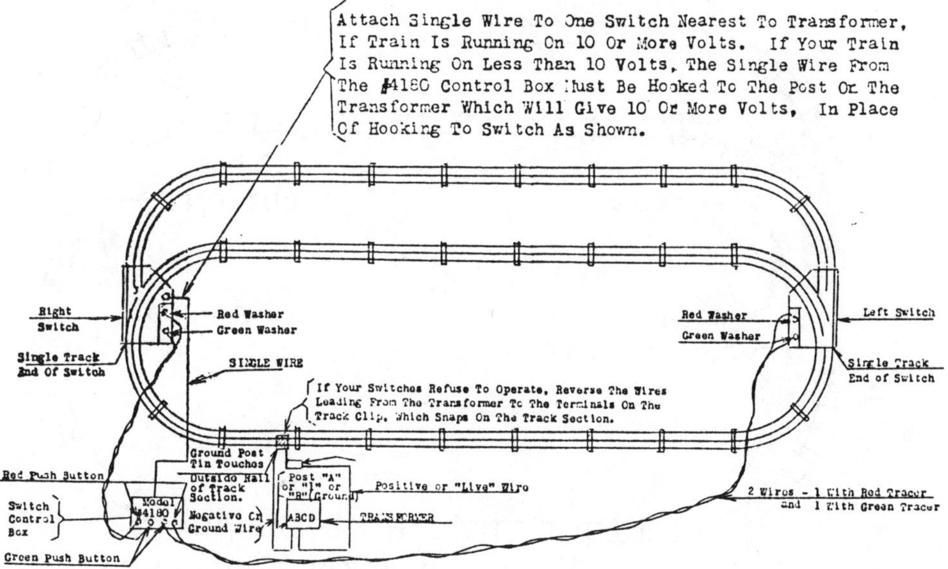

Attach Single Wire To One Switch Nearest To Transformer, If Train Is Running On 10 Or More Volts. If Your Train Is Running On Less Than 10 Volts, The Single Wire From The #4180 Control Box Must Be Hooked To The Post On The Transformer Which Will Give 10 Or More Volts, In Place Of Hooking To Switch As Shown.
Right Switch
Red Washer
Green Washer
Single Track End Of Switch
SINGLE WIRE
Red Washer
Green Washer
Left Switch
Single Track End of Switch
If Your Switches Refuse To Operate, Reverse The Wires Leading From The Transformer To The Terminals On The Track Clip, Which Snaps On The Track Section.
Ground Post Tin Touches Outside Rail of Track Section.
Red Push Button
Switch Control Box
Model #4180
Negative Or Ground Wire
Post "A" or "1" or "B" (Ground)
Positive or "Live" Wire
ABCD
TRANSFORMER
2 Wires - 1 With Red Tracer and 1 With Green Tracer
Green Push Button

Ref: W. O. 4890

MANUAL CONTROL TRACK SWITCHES

Model No. 722

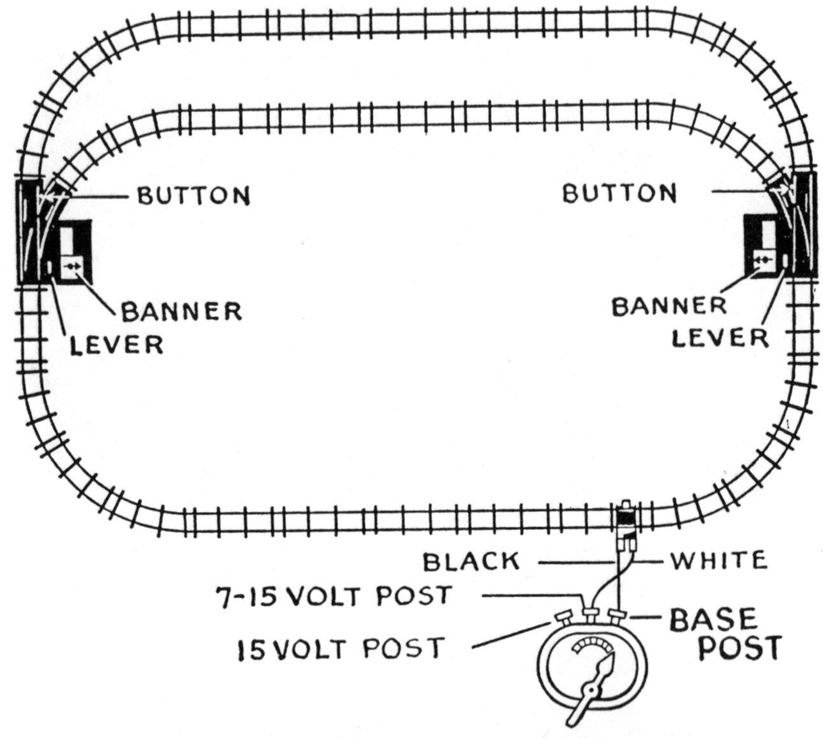

These switches are designed to be operated by hand and there are no wires to be connected, just place the switches in your layout at the desired location and be sure and hook the track terminal from the transformer to a spot in the single line of track between the two switches. The signal banner or target indicates the setting of the switch frog.

The switch frog is thrown by moving the manual lever to the opposite end of the slot. To avoid derailment be sure lever is thrown all the way.

These new AMERICAN FLYER switches are really two kinds of switches in one, that is, they can be used in the conventional manner or by simply moving a button, two or more trains can be operated at the same time without the use of special control buttons or block signals.

To use the switches in the regular manner move the button toward the banner as far as it will go.

To operate two or more trains on the same layout at the same time move the button away from the banner. With the button in this position trains will operate only on the loop the switch is set for. If the switch is set for the inside loop any train which happens to be on the outside loop will stop. When the switch is reset for the outside loop the train in this loop will start and the train in the inside loop will stop.

When the switches are used for two train operation they MUST be operated in pairs, that is, they must both be set for the same loop, except in the case of spur lines where the end of the track is not connected to any part of the layout.

MANUAL CONTROL TRACK SWITCHES

Model No. 722A

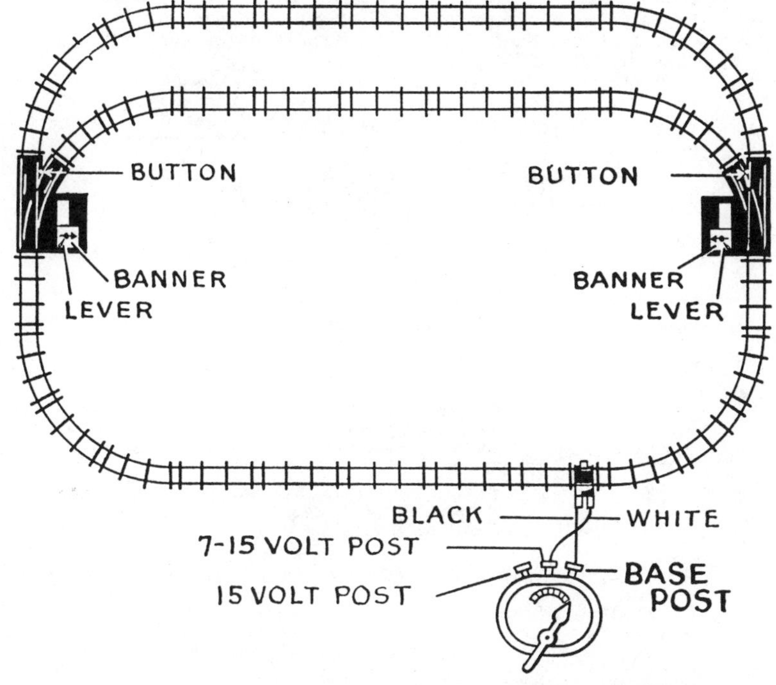

These switches are designed to be operated by hand and there are no wires to be connected, just place the switches in your layout at the desired location and be sure and hook the track terminal from the transformer to a spot in the single line of track between the two switches. The signal banner or target indicates the setting of the switch frog.

The switch frog is thrown by moving the manual lever located on top of housing. To avoid derailment be sure frog is thrown all the way.

These new American Flyer switches are really two kinds of switches in one, that is, they can be used in the conventional manner or by simply moving a button, two or more trains can be operated at the same time without the use of special control buttons or block signals.

To use the switches in the regular manner move the button toward the banner as far as it will go.

To operate two or more trains on the same layout at the same time move the button away from the banner. With the button in this position trains will operate only on the loop the switch is set for. If the switch is set for the inside loop any train which happens to be on the outside loop will stop. When the switch is reset for the outside loop the train in this loop will start and the train in the inside loop will stop.

When the switches are used for two train operation they must be operated in pairs, that is, they must both be set for the same loop, except in the case of spur lines where the end of the track is not connected to any part of the layout.

Ref: Form No. M2962

PIKE MASTER REMOTE CONTROL SWITCHES FOR S GAUGE TRAINS

KNOW YOUR SWITCHES

Switches are known as either Right Hand or Left Hand. This is determined by the direction they turn out as viewed by looking along the main line toward the point of the frog. A Right Hand Switch will curve out toward the right and a Left Hand Switch will curve out toward the left. See Fig. #1.

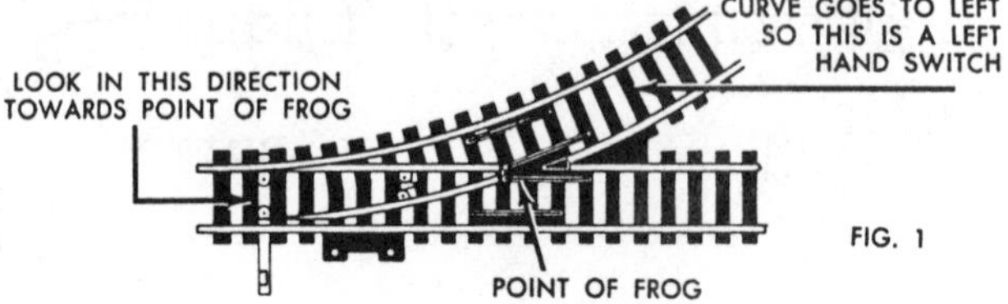

FIG. 1

INSTALLING YOUR SWITCHES IN THE LAYOUT

Place the switches into the desired position in your layout and make all mechanical connections (see Fig. #2) before wiring them for operation.

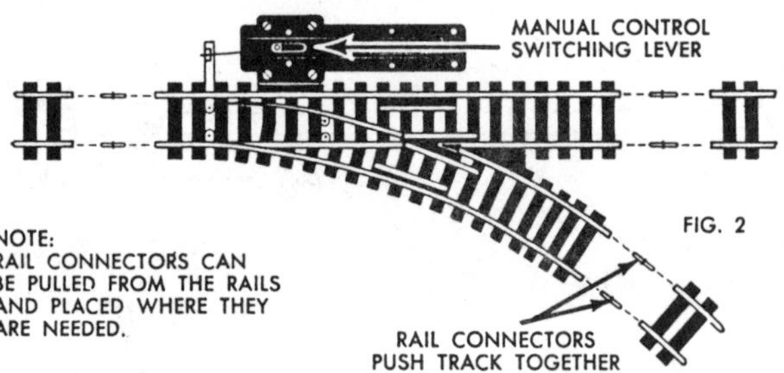

FIG. 2

WIRING THE SWITCHES

Now that you have your switch placed into the layout you are now ready to connect the controls for remote control operation. There is included with your switch a three stranded wire colored red, black and green. There is also a two stranded wire colored yellow and black. A switch control is included which has a red and green button and

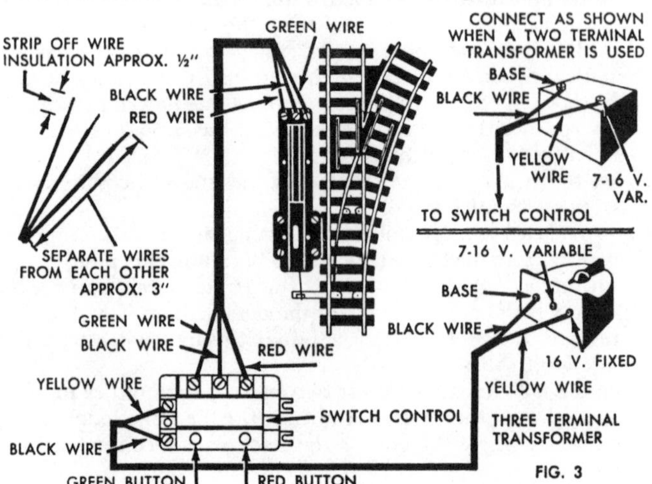

FIG. 3

also a plastic plate on which is marked for either a Right Hand Switch or Left Hand Switch. The numbers printed on the envelope can be glued onto this plastic plate and thus will indicate the switch that is controlled by that particular switch button. Follow the wiring scheme as pictured in the illustration below. See Fig. #3 & 4.

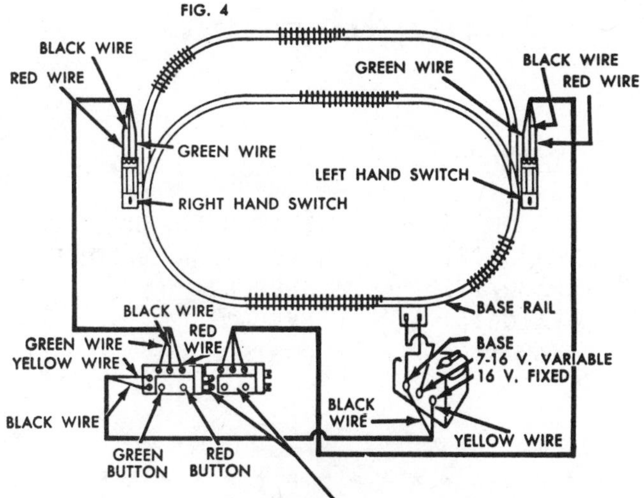

ATTACH THIS SWITCH CONTROL TO OTHER SWITCH CONTROL WITH TWO (2) SCREWS

OPERATION

When you press the green button the switch should always move so that you can run your train through on the main line (the straight section of the switch). When you press the red button the switch should always move in the position to let your train go on the curve section of the switch. NOTE: If for some reason the opposite occurs (that is when the red button is pushed it puts the switch in the direction of the straight track) and you have again checked your wiring to be sure that it agrees with the illustration; take the red and green wires at the switch itself and interchange them.

CAUTION: Never hold either button of the control box down longer than two seconds for this is more than ample to change the direction of the switch. By failing to follow this instruction you may damage the coil system.

REMOTE CONTROL PIKE MASTER SWITCH

Model No. 26320 (Right-Hand)

PART NO.	DESCRIPTION
XA30N141	SWITCH POWER UNIT
XA30A128	FROG LINK ASSEMBLY
PA30A171	SUPPORT
PA10115	EYELET
XA30N142	CONTROL BOX

* * * * * * * * * * * * * * * * * * *

Model No. 26321 (Left-Hand)

PART NO.	DESCRIPTION
XA30N141	SWITCH POWER UNIT
XA30A128	FROG LINK ASSEMBLY
PA30A171	SUPPORT
PA10115	EYELET
XA30N142	CONTROL BOX